Roger Jennings
Database Developer's Guide
with Visual Basic® 6

Roger Jennings

SAMS

201 West 103rd St., Indianapolis, Indiana, 46290 USA

Roger Jennings' Database Developer's Guide with Visual Basic® 6

Copyright © 1999 by Sams Publishing

International Standard Book Number: 0-672-31063-5

Library of Congress Catalog Card Number: 98-85091

Printed in the United States of America

First Printing: December 1998

00 99 98   4   3   2   1

Trademarks

Warning and Disclaimer

EXECUTIVE EDITOR
Chris Denny

ACQUISITIONS EDITOR
Chris Denny

DEVELOPMENT EDITOR
Anthony Amico

MANAGING EDITOR
Jodi Jensen

SENIOR EDITOR
Susan Ross Moore

COPY EDITOR
June Waldman

INDEXER
Johnna Van Hoose

PROOFREADER
Eddie Lushbaugh

TECHNICAL EDITOR
Jim Ferguson

SOFTWARE DEVELOPMENT SPECIALIST
John Warriner

TEAM COORDINATOR
Carol Ackerman

INTERIOR DESIGN
Ann Jones

COVER DESIGN
Ann Jones

LAYOUT TECHNICIANS
Tim Osborn
Staci Somers
Mark Walchle

CONTENTS AT A GLANCE

CONTENTS

DEDICATION

This book is dedicated to Maxwell Keith, attorney extraordinaire,
and Terry Keith—firm friends through bad times and good.

ACKNOWLEDGMENTS

Thanks to Microsoft's David Sceppa for clarification of ADO-related technical issues during the Visual Studio 6.0 beta testing phase. David's advice and examples posted in the data-related beta newsgroups played a major role in the development of this book. The contributions of all of the members of the OLE DB, ADO, and Visual Basic beta newsgroups were very valuable. Bill Storage of Nerve-Net and Instep Technology Inc.'s Deborah Kurata, author of *Doing Objects in Visual Basic 6*, were especially helpful in overcoming the obstacles encountered when implementing the WebClass, DHTML Page, and data-bound class examples.

Special thanks are due to Jim Ferguson of FMS, Inc., the technical editor for this book. Finally, special notes of appreciation to Chris Denny, Sams Publishing's executive editor, for handling the administrative chores associated with producing the third edition of this book, to Tony Amico, development editor, to Susan Moore, project editor, and to June Waldman, copy editor.

ABOUT THE AUTHOR

Roger Jennings is a consultant specializing in Windows client/server database systems. He was a member of the Microsoft technical beta testing team for every release of Visual Basic since version 2.0; all versions of Microsoft Access; Windows 3.1; Windows for Workgroups 3.1 and 3.11; Windows 95 and 98; Windows NT 3.5, 4.0, and 5.0 Server; the Microsoft ODBC 2.0 and 2.5 drivers; and Microsoft SQL Server 6.0, 6.5, and 7.0. Roger is the author of Sams Publishing's *Access 2 Developer's Guide* and three other books on Microsoft Access, plus books devoted to Windows 95, Windows NT Server 4.0, and Windows multimedia techniques. He is the co-author with Peter Hipson of Sams' *Database Developer's Guide with Visual C++ 4.0.* Roger is a contributing editor for Fawcette Technical Publication's *Visual Basic Programmer's Journal* (`http://www.devx.com/`) and co-authored with Microsoft's Greg Nelson "A Client/server Application: From Concept to Reality," which appeared on the *Microsoft Developer's Network* CD-ROM.

Roger has more than 25 years of computer-related experience, beginning with his work on the Wang 700 desktop calculator/computer, and he has presented technical papers on computer hardware and software to the Academy of Sciences of the former USSR, the Society of Automotive Engineers, the American Chemical Society, and a wide range of other scientific and technical organizations. Roger's full biography is at `http://www.mcp.com/publishers/sams/authors/roger_jennings/`. He's a principal of OakLeaf Systems, a Northern California software consulting firm and the Webmaster for Chump Change Records, `http://www.chumpchange.com/`. You can contact Roger at 70233.2161@compuserve.com.

TELL US WHAT YOU THINK!

As the reader of this book, *you* are our most important critic and commentator. We value your opinion and want to know what we're doing right, what we could do better, what areas you'd like to see us publish in, and any other words of wisdom you're willing to pass our way.

As the Executive Editor for the Visual Basic Programming team at Macmillan Computer Publishing, I welcome your comments. You can fax, email, or write me directly to let me know what you did or didn't like about this book—as well as what we can do to make our books stronger.

Please note that I cannot help you with technical problems related to the topic of this book, and that due to the high volume of mail I receive, I might not be able to reply to every message.

When you write, please be sure to include this book's title and author as well as your name and phone or fax number. I will carefully review your comments and share them with the author and editors who worked on the book.

Fax: 317-817-7070

Email: vb@mcp.com

Mail: Chris Denny
        Executive Editor
        Visual Basic Programming Team
        Macmillan Computer Publishing
        201 West 103rd Street
        Indianapolis, IN 46290 USA

INTRODUCTION

Microsoft Visual Basic, with more than one million developers worldwide, is the premier development platform for building Windows front ends to desktop and client/server databases. According to Microsoft data, more than 85% of all Visual Basic applications now access databases. Unquestionably, this percentage will increase with Visual Basic 6.0 and beyond.

The prior five releases of Visual Basic have eclipsed all other rapid application development (RAD) tools for database applications, such as Imprise (formerly Borland) Delphi and Sybase PowerBuilder. Visual Basic 6.0 is certain to account for a substantial increase in Microsoft's RAD tool market share. For a purportedly independent comparison of Visual Basic 6.0 and the current versions of Delphi and PowerBuilder, read "Benchmark: Rapid Application Development Tools" at `http://msdn.microsoft.com/vbasic/prodinfo/benchmarks/bench1.asp`. This NSTL, Inc. (formerly National Software Testing Laboratories) report was commissioned by Microsoft, so determine for yourself whether the report is biased or not.

Virtually all the major additions and improvements in Visual Basic 6.0 are data related, as demonstrated by the What's New in Visual Basic 6.0 page at `http://msdn.microsoft.com/vbasic/prodinfo/new.asp`. Eight of the nine "key features" of Visual Basic 6.0 on this page involve database connectivity.

OLE DB and ActiveX Data Objects (ADO), an Automation wrapper around OLE DB, represent the most significant upgrade to version 6.0. Chapter 1, "Staking Visual Basic's Claim to Enterprise Development," delivers an introduction to these new features. The remaining chapters of this third edition of *Database Developer's Guide with Visual Basic* provide full-depth coverage of all data-related components of version 6.0. This edition covers only OLE DB, ADO, ADO Multidimensional (ADO MD), and related database connectivity subjects; there is no Data Access Object (DAO) content in the book.

WHO SHOULD USE THIS BOOK?

This book is intended primarily, but not exclusively, for the following categories of readers:

- Visual Basic developers who want to take maximum advantage of Visual Basic 6.0's database connectivity to create production-grade front ends for a variety of desktop and client/server databases.

- Experienced Visual Basic developers who want to leverage their VBA skills for data-driven Internet and intranet development. WebClasses (IIS Applications for the Internet and intranets) and Dynamic HTML pages (DHTML Applications for intranets) substitute VBA for less-rich scripting languages and expedite the adoption of Web pages whose content is delivered by querying databases.

- Microsoft Access developers who need more control over their data display and editing forms than is afforded by the present versions of Microsoft Access. Visual Basic 6.0 database front ends also consume fewer Windows resources than equivalent Access 97 applications.

- Developers of character-based DOS database applications whose clients or organizational superiors finally have decided to migrate from DOS to Windows applications. (A remarkable number of commercial DOS database applications remain in widespread use.)

- Users of other database development platforms who need to create industrial-strength 32-bit database front ends running under Windows 9x or Windows NT 4+. Windows NT is rapidly gaining ground in the corporate marketplace in both the Server and Workstation versions.

- Programmers who would like to develop database applications by expending less than 25% of the time and effort required to create equivalent applications with C and C++. Those addicted to C++ can quickly create prototype database front ends with Visual Basic 6.0. (It is amazing how many Visual Basic prototypes become production database front ends.)

- Victims of the corporate downsizing who need to acquire Windows database development skills to remain gainfully employed.

- Users of proprietary GUI front-end development tools for client/server databases who are tired of forking over substantial per seat licensing fees for each client workstation that is attached to the server.

- Chief information officers (CIOs) or management information services (MIS) executives who need to make an informed decision as to which Windows front-end generator their organization will adopt as the standard.

- Others who are interested in seeing examples of commercially useful Visual Basic 6.0 database front ends that earn developers a comfortable or better-than-comfortable living.

Database Developer's Guide with Visual Basic 6 assumes that you have at least some experience with Visual Basic for Applications or one of the traditional PC programming languages for Windows, such as C++, Delphi, or PowerBuilder. This book doesn't contain an introduction to Visual Basic programming techniques; many excellent tutorial and reference books are available to fill this need. (The bibliography that appears later in this introduction lists some of the better books and other sources of information for beginning-to-intermediate-level Visual Basic Programmers.) Instead, *Database Developer's Guide with Visual Basic 6* begins with an overview of how Visual Basic fits in the desktop and client/server database market and proceeds directly to dealing with ActiveX Data Objects in Visual Basic. The entire content of this book is devoted to creating useful Visual Basic 6.0 database front ends with ADO, and every example of the Visual Basic code in this book involves one or more `ADODB.Connections` to database(s). With the exception of introductory projects, the application examples of this book are nontrivial, and many of the projects range between 2,000 and 7,500 lines of VBA code.

All the code examples in this book, except for minor code fragments, are included on the accompanying CD-ROM, along with Jet 3.51 sample databases and SQL scripts that generate the SQL Server stored procedures required by Chapters 21, "Using Transact-SQL Stored Procedures," and higher. The total size of the example project files is about 80MB. Some of the sample databases, such as that for Chapter 14, "Scheduling and Device Control with VBA and Jet," are quite large so you can use their tables for performance comparisons. Tips and notes are based on the experience of database developers with the beta and commercial releases of Visual Basic 6.0.

WHAT YOU NEED TO USE THIS BOOK EFFECTIVELY

You need the Professional Edition of Visual Basic 6.0 to use this book. The Learning Edition doesn't support ADO, which is the central theme of this book. You need at least the Developer Edition of SQL Server 6.5, which is included in the Enterprise Edition, to run the application examples of Chapters 18, "Working with Client/Server Databases," through 27, "Creating and Deploying MTS Components." Although the Beta 3 version of SQL Server 7.0 is used as the client/server RDBMS of this book, the examples work with version 6.5. Chapter 28, "Analyzing Multidimensional Data with OLAP and MDX," doesn't require SQL Server, but you must download the Microsoft Data Access Components (MDAC) 2.0 and the Data Access SDK 2.0 from `http://www.microsoft.com/data/mdac2.htm` to obtain the sample data cube (Bobsvid.cub), PivotTable Service support files, and the ADO MD data provider.

> **NOTE**
>
> If you haven't upgraded to Visual Studio 6.0 or Visual Basic 6.0, check Microsoft's Features by Edition page at `http://msdn.microsoft.com/vbasic/prodinfo/datasheet/feature.asp` for a list of what's included in the Learning, Professional, and Enterprise Editions.

Acquiring a license for Microsoft Access 97 is strongly recommended for those of you who intend to use Access .mdb database files in commercial front ends. Creating new databases and adding tables is easier and faster when you use Access 97 instead of Visual Basic 6.0's Visual Data Manager add-in. You can use Access 97's Query Design window to create a query graphically, test the result, and then copy the Access SQL statement underlying the query to your Visual Basic code. Using Access 97's Relationships window to establish rules for enforcing referential integrity and creating business rules that maintain domain integrity is much simpler than following Visual Basic 6.0's code-centric approach. Unfortunately, ADO 2.0 doesn't support Access-specific objects, such as Users and Groups, nor does ADO 2.0 let you create Access workgroup (.mdw) files to secure multiuser applications. An additional benefit of acquiring Access 97 is the availability of database design and documentation tools for Access that are not yet available to Visual Basic database developers. If you develop Visual Basic 6.0 database applications for a living, you'll save many times your investment in a copy of Access 97.

If you use Access 97 .mdb files for multiuser database front ends and want to scale up to a client/server database, the Microsoft Access Upsizing Toolkit (AUT) is the answer. The Upsizing Toolkit, a free add-in for Access 97, available from `http://www.microsoft.com/AccessDev/`, automatically exports tables from your .mdb files to a Microsoft SQL Server 6.x database. Unfortunately, the current version of AUT doesn't work with SQL Server 7.0. The Upsizing Wizard included in the AUT writes Transact-SQL (SQL Server's dialect of SQL) DDL statements that create Server tables, updates the tables with data from your .mdb file, and then adds indexes and default values for table fields. The Wizard also writes the Transact-SQL `CREATE TRIGGER` code necessary to maintain domain and referential integrity of SQL Server databases. If you're running SQL Server 6+, which offers declarative referential integrity (DRI), the Upsizing Wizard writes ANSI SQL-92 SQL statements for declarative referential integrity (DRI) during the table generation process.

THE COMPUTERS USED TO WRITE THIS BOOK

The chapters in Part V, "Multiuser And Client/Server Database Front Ends," use a variety of server and workstation configurations to demonstrate workgroup and client/server database networking techniques. All computers are networked with 10Mb/s network interface cards (NICs) using thin Ethernet (10Base-2) cabling. Two of the servers (OAKLEAF1 and OAKLEAF3) are multihomed with 100Base-T NICs. Following are the identifiers and IP addresses for each of the computers used to write this book, together with a brief description of each computer's configuration:

- OAKLEAF0 (131.254.7.1), the primary domain controller (PDC) for a six-computer network, runs Windows NT Server 4.0 on a 133MHz Pentium PC with 64MB of RAM. OAKLEAF0 is the primary database server and runs both SQL Server 6.5 and 7.0 in switched mode. OAKLEAF0 also runs Internet Information Server 4.0, Proxy Server 2.0, Transaction Server 2.0, and a beta version of Microsoft OLAP Server (code-named "Plato"). OAKLEAF0 uses an Adaptec AHA-2940UW SCSI adapter card to connect to a single Seagate ST15150W 4.3GB Barracuda disk drive formatted with two New Technology File System (NFTS) partitions, a Tandberg 1GB tape backup drive, and a SCSI CD-ROM drive.

NOTE

SQL Server 6.5 and 7.0 can coexist on a single server, but cannot run simultaneously. A Microsoft SQL Server - Switch (Common) choice of the Start, Programs menu enables you to select the version to run. Switching between servers is necessary for same-machine conversion of SQL Server 6.5 device (.dat) files to SQL Server 7.0 database (.mdf) and log (.ldf) files. Unlike prior iterations of SQL Server, the file structure of version 7.0 has changed dramatically. Switching between server versions on the same server permits comparing the performance of the two products without introducing hardware-related variables.

- OAKLEAF1 (131.254.7.2) is a 266MHz Pentium II PC server with 128MB of RAM dual-booting Windows 98 and Windows NT 4.0 Server with Service Pack 4 and the Windows NT 4.0 Option Pack. The Desktop version of SQL Server 7.0 runs under Windows 98 and the full version runs under Windows NT 4.0 Server with a late beta version of Service Pack 4. OAKLEAF 1 also runs Oracle 8.0.3 for Windows NT. OAKLEAF1 has two 4.3GB Quantum Fireball ST Ultra-DMA IDE drives, one formatted with FAT32 and the other with NTFS, and a 12X CD-ROM drive. Two 4.3GB Seagate Barracuda 4XL Ultra-SCSI drives formatted with NTFS in a RAID 0 striped set are connected to an Adaptec AHA-8945 SCSI/IEEE-1394 adapter. OAKLEAF1 is used for Digital Video (DV) editing and testing beta software. All Visual Basic 6.0 examples of this book were written and tested on OAKLEAF1.

- OAKLEAF2 (131.254.7.4) is a 200MHz Pentium MMX PC workstation with 32MB of RAM dual-booting Windows 95 and Windows NT 4.0 Workstation. The Desktop version of SQL Server 7.0 runs under Windows 95 and Windows NT 4.0. OAKLEAF2 has two 4.3GB Quantum Fireball ST Ultra-DMA IDE drives, both formatted with FAT16, an Iomega Zip drive, and a 12X CD-ROM drive. OAKLEAF2 was used to write this edition; no beta software is allowed on this machine.

- OAKLEAF3 (131.254.7.3) is a 233MHz Pentium II server with 96MB of RAM dual-booting Windows 95 and Windows NT 4.0 Server, which serves as a backup domain controller (BDC) for the OAKLEAF domain. OAKLEAF3 has two 4.3GB Quantum Fireball ST IDE drives formatted with FAT16, an 8X CD-ROM drive, an Iomega Jaz drive and uses an Adaptec AHA-2940UW SCSI adapter card to connect to two Seagate ST15150W 4.3GB Barracuda disk drives in a RAID 1 configuration formatted with NTFS. OAKLEAF3 runs SQL Server 7.0 as a secondary database server, Exchange Server, SMS Server, Internet Information Server 4.0, and Transaction Server 2.0. When running Windows 95, OAKLEAF3 is used for video and audio capture, editing, special effects, and still-graphics production.

- OAKLEAF4 (131.254.7.5) is a 120MHz Pentium notebook computer with 32MB of RAM running Windows 95. OAKLEAF4 connects to the network occasionally to update files.

- OAKLEAF5 (131.254.7.6) is a 200MHz Pentium MMX PC workstation with 96MB of RAM running Windows 98 and the Desktop version of SQL Server 7.0. OAKLEAF5 has a 4.3GB Quantum Fireball ST IDE drive formatted with FAT32 and a 12X CD-ROM drive. OAKLEAF5 is used for MIDI music composition, digital audio capture and editing, and beta-testing software that's incompatible with the beta software installed on OAKLEAF2.

HOW THIS BOOK IS ORGANIZED

Database Developer's Guide with Visual Basic 6 is divided into seven parts containing 28 chapters and a glossary. Each part deals with related database-application-design subjects. The parts are ordered in a way that parallels a typical database front-end development program. The content of each part and chapter of this book is described briefly in the sections that follow.

Part I, "Visual Basic 6.0 Data Access Objects and Bound Controls"

Part I introduces Visual Basic 6.0's capabilities as a Windows database front-end development environment.

- Chapter 1, "Staking Visual Basic's Claim to Enterprise Development," analyzes the new features that Visual Basic 6.0 offers database developers and how the language fits into Microsoft Corp.'s strategy to dominate the desktop and client/server database development markets.

- Chapter 2, "Understanding OLE DB and Universal Data Access," provides a detailed description of OLE DB 1.0 and ADO 2.0, together with examples of how to program ADO Connection, Command, Parameter, and Recordset objects using Jet 3.51 .mdb databases in the examples.

- Chapter 3, "Migrating from DAO to ADO," explains how to ease the transition from the now-obsolescent Data Access Object to ActiveX Data Objects, the foundation of Universal Data Access for Visual Basic programmers.

- Chapter 4, "Using the ADO Data Control with Bound Controls," introduces simple database front ends using the ADO Data control (ADODB) and other ADO-compliant data-aware controls that are bound to database tables with the native OLE DB provider for Access.

Part II, "Database and Query Design Concepts"

Part II deals with relational database design and using SQL to create SELECT and action (UPDATE, INSERT, and DELETE) queries that employ ADO and the Jet 3.51 database engine.

- Chapter 5, "Optimizing the Design of Relational Databases," shows you how to normalize data to eliminate data redundancy in your front end.
- Chapter 6, "Learning Structured Query Language," discusses ANSI SQL-89 and SQL-92 and how Jet SQL differs from the "standard" SQL used by client/server and mainframe databases.
- Chapter 7, "Running Crosstab and Action Queries," advances beyond simple SQL SELECT queries and shows you how to write queries that include TRANSFORM, PIVOT, INTO, and other less commonly used SQL reserved words that modify the data in your tables.
- Chapter 8, "Connecting to Desktop Data Sources with ODBC," shows you how to use MSDASQL, the Microsoft OLE DB Data Provider for ODBC, to connect to databases that don't yet have native OLE DB providers.

Part III, "An Introduction to Database Front-End Design"

Part III is devoted to creating commercial-quality, decision-support front ends for databases.

- Chapter 9, "Designing a Decision-Support Front End," describes the principals of converting raw data into easily comprehensible information that can be displayed on Visual Basic forms.
- Chapter 10, "Taking Full Advantage of Data-Bound ActiveX Controls," shows you how to combine each of Visual Basic's new data-bound controls and VBA code to customize control operation. Chapter 10 also introduces SHAPE syntax for generating hierarchical Recordsets.
- Chapter 11, "Graphing Summary Data from Crosstab Queries," demystifies version 2.0 of the Microsoft Chart control (Mschrt20.ocx) to create the broad-brush summary data presentations favored by top management.
- Chapter 12, "Printing with the Report Designer and VBA Code," shows you how to design printed reports and how to seamlessly integrate report generation with your database front ends through ADO data binding.

Part IV, "Advanced Programming for Data Access and Automation"

Part IV takes you deeper into the realm of commercial database front-end development.

- Chapter 13, "Drilling Down into Data from Graphs and Charts," goes into the details on graphical drill-down applications that let users obtained detailed data by clicking hot spots on summary graphs, charts, and grids.

- Chapter 14, "Scheduling and Device Control with VBA and Jet," examines a very complex database-driven Visual Basic 6.0 application that incorporates real-time infrared control of consumer electronics devices. This chapter's project has more than 7,500 lines of VBA code and queries a 19,000-record Jet 3.51 database derived from Windows 98's WebTV application.

- Chapter 15, "Writing Local Automation Components and ActiveX DLLs," describes how to create database-oriented Automation mini-servers and in-process ActiveX DLLS that you can use with Visual Basic 6.0 and other VBA-enabled clients.

- Chapter 16, "Creating User Controls for Database Applications," illustrates how to write your own ActiveX controls for inclusion in Visual Basic 6.0 database front ends.

Part V, "Multiuser and Client/Server Database Front Ends"

Until you reach Part V, *Database Developer's Guide with Visual Basic 6* is devoted to self-contained applications designed primarily for a single user. Part V provides the background and examples you need to add networking and client/server database capabilities to your Visual Basic 6.0 database front ends. Examples employ Windows 9*x*, Windows NT Server 4.0, Jet 3.51, and SQL Server 6.5 and 7.0.

- Chapter 17, "Networking Secure Multiuser Jet Databases," describes how to use peer-to-peer and network servers to share Jet 3.51 databases among members of a workgroup or throughout an entire organization.

- Chapter 18, "Working with Client/Server Databases," introduces SQL Server 7.0, explains how to use the AUT with SQL Server 6.x, shows you how to import Jet 3.51 tables to SQL Server 7.0, and explains the process of making ADO Connections to SQL Server with the Microsoft OLE DB Provider for SQL Server (SQLOLEDB).

- Chapter 19, "Processing Transactions and Bulk Operations," explains the basic principles of managing database consistency with transactions, using two-phase commit with the Microsoft Distributed Transaction Coordinator, database replication, and processing bulk updates with disconnected Recordsets.

- Chapter 20, "Porting Access OLTP Applications to Visual Basic 6.0," illustrates the process of converting a production-grade Access 97 client/server OLTP application to its Visual Basic 6.0 counterpart that uses ADO 2.0 to connect to SQL Server.

- Chapter 21, "Using Transact-SQL Stored Procedures," adapts the Visual Basic 6.0 OLTP application of Chapter 20 to take advantage of the dramatically improved performance offered by SQL Server 6.*x* or 7.0 stored procedures. Chapter 21 also illustrates how to minimize the VBA code required to pass parameter values to stored procedures by using the `Parameters` collection of the `DataEnvironment`'s `Command` object.

Part VI, "Databases, Intranets, and the Internet"

Part VI covers the new Internet features of Visual Basic 6.0—WebClasses (IIS Applications) and Dynamic HTML Pages (DHTML Applications)—with emphasis on database connectivity for intranet and Internet applications.

- Chapter 22, "Integrating Databases with Intranets and the Internet," starts out by cutting through the Microsoft's hype for its new Digital Nervous System (DNS) slogan and explains how Visual Basic 6.0 fits into the Windows Distributed interNet Applications Architecture (Windows DNA). You create simple data-enabled WebClass and DHTML projects for Internet and intranet deployment, respectively.

- Chapter 23, "Using ActiveX Document Objects with Intranets," shows you how to convert the OLTP application of Chapters 20 and 21 to an ActiveX document and then deploy it on your Web server with the Package and Deployment Wizard.

- Chapter 24, "Working with Remote Data Services," introduces lightweight, disconnected `ADOR.Recordset` objects that you can transport to and from browser clients with DCOM and HTTP protocols.

- Chapter 25, "Developing Data-Enabled Internet Applications," leads you through the design and modification of a production-quality IIS Application (`WebClass` project) written by Microsoft for its Visual Basic 6.0 Web site.

Part VII, "Enterprise-Level Development Techniques"

The Enterprise Edition of Visual Basic 6.0 is designed primarily for developers of advanced 32-bit client/server database front ends and complex applications that involve a group programming environment. You run Windows NT Server 4.0 with Service Pack 3+, install the Windows NT 4.0 Option pack, and have system administrator privileges for SQL Server 6.5+ to run the examples of Chapters 26 and 27.

- Chapter 26, "Taking Advantage of Microsoft Transaction Server 2.0," explains how MTS 2.0 and DTC combine to provide the middle tier for scalable three-tier client/server applications. This shows you how to install and test MTS 2.0 with the Sample Bank application that MTS 2.0 setup installs.

- Chapter 27, "Creating and Deploying MTS Components," guides you through the three-step process of converting the OLAP application of Chapter 21 from a monolithic client to a scalable three-tier application having data access managed by an MTS-hosted middle-tier ActiveX DLL.

- Chapter 28, "Analyzing Multidimensional Data with OLAP and MDX," introduces you to data mart and data warehouse concepts; multidimensional database schema; and using OLE DB for OLAP, ADO MD, and MDX to extract and display multidimensional data from a PivotTable data cube. You don't need SQL Server for the examples of this chapter, but you must download a copy of MDAC 2.0 and the Data Access SDK from `http://www.microsoft.com/data/` to obtain BobsVid.cub, OLE DB for OLAP, and ADO MD. The OLAP extensions aren't included with Visual Basic 6.0.

Glossary

The book concludes with a glossary of terms that might be unfamiliar to those new to Windows database programming, relational database front ends, and/or Windows NT. Emphasis is placed on defining the special terms, abbreviations, and acronyms used in this book, especially new terms relating to OLE DB, ADO, data warehouses and marts, OLAP, MDX, and ADO MD.

TYPOGRAPHIC CONVENTIONS USED IN THIS BOOK

This book uses a variety of typesetting styles to distinguish between explanatory material, the entries you type in Windows dialogs, and the code you enter in Visual Basic's code-editing window. The sections that follow describe the typographic conventions used in this book.

Key Combinations, Menu Choices, and Dialog Entries

Accelerator (Alt+*key*) and shortcut (Ctrl+*key*) combinations that you use to substitute for mouse operations are designated by joining the keys with a plus sign (+). Ctrl+C, for example, is the shortcut key for copying a selection to the Windows Clipboard. Alt+H is a common accelerator key combination that takes the place of clicking the Help button in dialogs. Some applications, such as Microsoft Word, use multiple-key shortcuts, such as Ctrl+Shift+*key*, to activate macros.

Accelerator keys for menu choices are indicated by underlining the accelerator key, as in <u>F</u>ile. Sequences of menu choices often are shown in the order needed to accomplish the action, such as <u>F</u>ile, <u>O</u>pen. Ellipses after menu choices that lead to dialogs do not appear in this book.

Entries that you make in dialogs or at the Windows caret (the name used in this book for the insertion point in documents) are set in boldface type. Where menu choices require an entry such as a filename in a dialog, the filename complies with 32-bit Windows conventions—for example, <u>F</u>ile, <u>O</u>pen **Vb3demo.vbp**. Completion of the entry by pressing the Tab key to move to another dialog control or by pressing the Enter key is assumed.

In the unlikely event that you need to press a succession of keystrokes, rather than a combination of keys, to accomplish an action, the necessary keys are separated by commas without intervening spaces, as in Alt,X,Y.

Filenames and Extensions

Filenames use uppercase and lowercase characters, as in PerSel32.exe. To comply with Windows 95 and Windows NT 4.0 filename display conventions, file extensions appear in all lowercase.

VBA Code, SQL Statements, and Source Code in Other Languages

Examples of VBA code, SQL statements, and source code fragments in other programming languages are set in monospace type. Reserved words in VBA are set in `bold monospace` type. Keywords, such as the names of objects, object data types, and collections, are set in `regular-weight monospace` type. Reserved words and keywords in Jet, Transact-SQL, and ANSI SQL dialects are set in `UPPERCASE MONOSPACE` type. Here's an example of the formatting of SQL statements:

```
SELECT Name, Address, City, Zip_Code
 FROM Customers
 WHERE Zip_Code >= 90000
```

For consistency, the Visual Basic line continuation character pair (_) is used when the length of an SQL statement exceeds the printing width of the page, despite the fact that this separator pair is not valid when embedded in a SQL statement `String` variable.

Special implementations of SQL that do not conform to ANSI SQL-92 standards, such as the `{ts DateVariable}` syntax that Microsoft Query uses to indicate the timestamp data type, appear as in the SQL dialog of the application. The `PIVOT` and `TRANSFORM` statements of Jet SQL that (unfortunately) were not included in SQL-92 or version 7.0 of Transact-SQL, however, retain uppercase status.

VBA Code Examples and Code Fragments

As mentioned earlier, all examples of VBA code, as well as code examples in other Basic dialects, such as Access (2.0) Basic and Word Basic, are set in a monospace typeface. Monospace type also is used for code fragments that are mixed with proportionally spaced explanatory text. Styles and weights are applied to code examples and fragments according to the following rules:

- VBA reserved words, operators, and symbols are set bold. All other syntactic elements of VBA, including keywords that are not reserved words, names of properties and methods, names of collections, and names of members of collections, are set in normal weight. An example is **Dim** cboFindName **As** Control.

- Names of symbolic constants appear in mixed case and no longer include underscores, as in strConnection. The VBA intrinsic constants, **True**, **False**, and **Null**, are reserved words and are set bold.

- Replaceable variable names, arguments, and parameters are set *monospace italic*. Data type identification tag prefixes that identify the data type of variables of Visual Basic's fundamental data types and the type of object for variables of object data types are not set italic, as in **Public WithEvents** envNwind **As Object**. (The **Object** data type is a VBA reserved word.)

- Although none of the application examples in this book use DAO, declarations of all ADO objects are preceded by ADODB (ADO 2.0) or ADOR (RDS Recordsets), as in **Dim** cnnPubs **As** ADODB.Connection or **Private** rstRowset **As** ADOR.Recordset.

- Replaceable reserved-word data types are set bold italic, as in **Dim** *anyVariable* **As** ***DataType***.

- Where square brackets (**[ ]**) are set bold, the brackets enclose the name of an object, property, or method that otherwise would be legal in VBA syntax only if surrounded by double quotation marks. Examples are names of fields in Jet databases that contain spaces or punctuation other than an underscore, and names of objects or members of collections that conflict with VBA reserved words. Square brackets set in normal weight type ([ ]) indicate an optional element, such as an optional argument of a function.

- French braces ({}) indicate that you must select one of the optional elements, separated by the pipe character (¦) and enclosed within the braces, as in **Do {While¦Until}...Loop**. The foregoing does not apply to the unusual employment of French braces by Microsoft Query in SQL statements.

- An ellipsis (. . .) indicates that the remaining or intervening code required to complete a statement or code structure is assumed and does not appear in the example.

- The code continuation character pair, a space followed by an underscore (_), is used when publishing limitations require that a statement be continued on another line of a code example.

Prefixed Tags for Data or Object Type Identification

The code examples in this book use two- or three-letter prefixed tags to identify the data type of variables and symbolic constants of the fundamental data types of Visual Basic and other Object Basic dialects, as well as object variables. The prefix tags used in this book are based on the Leszynski Naming Conventions for Microsoft Visual Basic (LNC). LNC is derived from a proposed standard for naming Access Basic objects and variables created by Stan Leszynski and Greg Reddick, which was originally published in Pinnacle Publishing Inc.'s *Smart Access* newsletter.

All the code examples in this book and on the accompanying CD-ROM use **Option** Explicit to specify that variables must be declared with **Public**, **Private**, **Const**, and/or **Dim** statements prior to assigning the variable a value in procedures. This book uses explicit data type assignment; variables of the **Variant** data type are declared **As Variant**, despite Visual Basic's assignment of **Variant** as the default data type. You won't find data type symbols, such as %, @, and ! used in this book, except for occasional appearance of the **$** symbol following the names of functions that explicitly return values of the **String** data type. The bang (!) symbol is reserved as a separator in statements that specify objects within container objects. Prefixed tags, related to those of Hungarian notation for C code, maintain consistency in data type identification for both conventional and object variables.

Examples of tagged variable names of the fundamental data types are str*StringVar*, int*IntegerVar*, lng*LongVar*, dat*DateTimeVar*, cur*CurrencyVar*, and var*VariantVar*. It is arguable whether the **Variant** data type is appropriately classified fundamental data type. Microsoft Corp. and this book use the term *fundamental data type* to distinguish conventional variables, including variables of the **Variant** data type, whose names are VBA reserved words, from variables of object data types, which may have names that are either reserved or keywords.

Prefix tags also are used to identify the type of object when you declare variables of the various object data types supported by Visual Basic. The most common object prefix tags in this book are env*DataEnvironment*, cnn*Connection*, cmm*Command*, rst*Recordset*, frm*Form*, and qdf*QueryDef*. Prefix tags for variables of the **Object** data type use the obj prefix.

A VISUAL BASIC AND DATABASE BIBLIOGRAPHY

As mentioned earlier in this introduction, *Database Developer's Guide with Visual Basic 6* is intended for readers who are familiar with writing VBA code and have experience designing simple Visual Basic forms. If your first Visual Basic application is a full-fledged database front end, you may want to acquire one or more tutorial or reference books on introductory or intermediate-level VBA programming. Access programmers who are porting Access 2.0+ applications to Visual Basic 6.0 will benefit from developer-level Visual Basic guides. You also may want more details on the 1992 version of ANSI SQL and SQL-92. The following sections provide recommendations of up-to-date books that fulfill these needs.

Introductions to Visual Basic Programming

The following books are designed to introduce database programmers to Visual Basic 4.0's event-driven graphical programming environment:

> *Teach Yourself Visual Basic 6 in 21 Days* by Greg Perry (Sams Publishing, ISBN 0-672-31310-3)
>
> *Visual Basic 6 Unleashed* by Rob Thayer (Sams Publishing, ISBN 0-672-31309-X)

The Primary Guide to SQL-92

If you want to fully understand the history and implementation of the American National Standards Institute's X3.135.1-1992 standard for SQL-92, you need a copy of Jim Melton and Alan R. Simpson's *Understanding the New SQL: A Complete Guide*, ISBN 1-55860-245-3 (San Mateo, CA, Morgan Kaufmann Publishers, 1993.) Jim Melton of Digital Equipment Corp. was the editor of the ANSI SQL-92 standard, which comprises more than 500 pages of fine print.

Publishers of Database Standards

The syntax of SQL is the subject of a standard that is published by the American National Standards Institute (ANSI). As of this writing, the current standard, X3.135.1-1992 or SQL-92, was available from

> American National Standards Institute
> 11 West 42nd Street
> New York, NY 10036
> (212) 642-4900 (Sales Department)

The SQL Access Group (SAG) consists of users and vendors of SQL database management systems. SAG publishes standards that supplement ANSI X3.135.1-1989, such as the Call-Level Interface (CLI) standard used by Microsoft's ODBC API. You can obtain SAG documents from

SQL Access Group
1010 El Camino Real, Suite 380
Menlo Park, CA 94025
(415) 323-7992 x221

KEEPING UP TO DATE ON VISUAL BASIC

Various sources of up-to-date information are available to Visual Basic developers in print and electronic formats. Both print periodicals and online sources address management and development issues that are applicable to database development as a whole. Several forums on CompuServe Information Services offer product support services for Access and Windows. The sections that follow describe some of the sources you can use to expand your Visual Basic horizons.

Periodicals

The following are a few of the magazines and newsletters that cover Access exclusively or in which articles on Microsoft Access appear on a regular basis:

- *Visual Basic Programmer's Journal* (*VBPJ*) is a monthly magazine from Fawcette Technical Publications that covers Visual Basic and VBA. *VBPJ* has a monthly column devoted to database topics, and at least one of the magazine's monthly feature stories covers advanced database programming or system architecture. Fawcette Technical Publications produces the Visual Basic Insider's Technical Summit (VBITS) conferences at multiple locations in North America, Europe, and Asia.

- *Web Builder* is a Fawcette publication devoted to Internet-related topics. Now that Visual Basic 6.0 offers a full-fledged Active Server Pages (ASP) and DHTML development environment, you can expect to see a substantial amount of *Web Builder*'s editorial space devoted to Visual Basic 6.0 WebClasses and DHTML Applications.

- *Access-Office-VB Advisor,* published by Advisor Communications International, Inc., is a full-color, bimonthly magazine originally intended for Access users and developers. Because of the similarities between developing Visual Basic and Access database applications, the magazine now covers both products. You can supplement your subscription with an accompanying diskette that includes sample databases, utilities, and other software tools for Access and Visual Basic.

- *DBMS* magazine, published by M&T, a Miller-Freeman company, is devoted to database technology as a whole, but DBMS concentrates on the growing field of client/server RDBMSs. *DBMS* covers subjects, such as SQL and relational database design, that are of interest to all developers, not just those who use Visual Basic.

- *Visual Basic Developer* and *Smart Access* are monthly newsletters from Pinnacle Publishing, Inc., which publishes other database-related newsletters and monographs. *Smart Access* is directed primarily to developers and Access power users. Both newsletters tend toward advanced topics, such as creating libraries and using the Windows API with Access and Visual Basic. A diskette is included with each issue.

The majority of these magazines are available from newsstands and bookstores.

Visual Basic Internet Links

The Internet is the primary source of information and peer-to-peer support for Visual Basic database developers. The following sections describe some of the most important sources of current information about Visual Basic 6.0.

Microsoft Developer Network

The Microsoft Developer Network (MSDN) is the primary source of official information about Visual Basic 6.0 and the other members of Visual Studio 6.0 The `http://msdn.microsoft.com/vbasic/` page provides links to news about Visual Basic 6.0, downloadable samples, and white papers. You complete free registration for MSDN Online to gain many of the benefits of the MSDN site, and you must register your copy of Visual Basic 6.0 or Visual Studio 6.0 before you can download the majority of the code samples available.

Macmillan Computer Reference

Macmillan Computer Reference (`http://www.mcp.com`) is an award-winning Web site that provides a complete online catalog of all computer-related books published by Macmillan Computer Publishing. The site also includes an online newsletter, press releases, and online bookstore. A wide variety of source code from MCP books, shareware, freeware, and demo software is available for downloading. The Visual Basic Resources page at `http://www.mcp.com/resources/prog/ms_developer/visual_basic/` has sample chapters from books about Visual Basic 6.0 from all Macmillan Computer Reference imprints.

VBPJ Development Exchange

Fawcette Technical Publication's Development Exchange (`http://www.devx.com`) includes the following zones devoted to programming topics: Visual Basic, Java, C++, Enterprise, and Web. You'll also find sites for *VBPJ*, *Java Pro*, and *Web Builder* magazine content, where you can read selected feature stories from current issues, plus a Product Guide, Book Guide, VBA Objects section, and Event Calendar. Free registration is required to take advantage of many of the DevX services, and Fawcette offers a Premier paid subscription service that provides access to the archives of past issues, including full source code, for each of its three magazines. DevX is by far the most popular third-party Web site for Visual Basic programmers.

Internet Usenet News Groups

The primary newsgroup feed for Visual Basic 6.0 discussions and peer support are the subgroups of the `microsoft.public.vstudio.vb` newsgroup. The independent `comp.lang.basic.visual.databases` and `comp.databases.ms-access` newsgroups are two of the most active Usenet areas devoted to Microsoft Visual Basic database and Access programming issues.

ACTIVEX DATA OBJECTS AND BOUND CONTROLS

PART

I

IN THIS PART

STAKING VISUAL BASIC'S CLAIM TO ENTERPRISE DEVELOPMENT

IN THIS CHAPTER

Visual Basic 6.0, together with the other members of Visual Studio 6.0, represents a major turning point in Microsoft's approach to database front-end development. ActiveX Data Objects (ADO) and OLE DB replace the Open Database Connectivity (ODBC) Application Programming Interface (API) as the preferred method for accessing shared-file and client/server databases. Internet technologies, such as Dynamic HTML (DHTML), Extensible Markup Language (XML), Active Server Pages (ASP), and ActiveX documents offer browser-based alternatives for displaying and updating data. Extensions to Visual Basic Class modules assist in writing middle-tier dynamic link libraries (DLLs) for Microsoft Transaction Server (MTS) 2.0. Improvements to Visual SourceSafe and the Microsoft Repository enhance coordination of multideveloper, enterprise-scale programming activities. A multitude of wizards and other graphical development tools aid developers new to Visual Basic.

Visual Basic plays a key role in the data access strategy of large and small organizations alike. Microsoft reports that more than 90% of all Visual Basic applications involve connections to relational database management systems (RDBMSs), up from 80% 2 years ago. Most of these programs currently involve Jet (Access) and Microsoft SQL Server RDBMSs, but Microsoft says that more than 50% of front ends for Oracle databases now are written in Visual Basic. Microsoft's inclusion of its own native OLE DB data provider and ODBC driver for Oracle 7.3 and 8.0 RDBMSs in Visual Studio 6.0 is certain to increase Visual Basic's penetration as a development tool in "Oracle shops."

This chapter provides an overview of the new and upgraded data-related features of Visual Basic 6.0. The emphasis here is on development strategies; the remainder of the book is devoted to implementation methods. Much of the content of this chapter assumes familiarity with the data-related capabilities of Visual Basic 5.0 and earlier. If you're a beginning database developer, you might want to skim this chapter and then skip to Chapter 4, "Using the ADO Data Control with Bound Controls," for a hands-on introduction to Visual Basic 6.0's new and improved data-related features.

SUMMARIZING VISUAL BASIC 6.0'S NEW DATA-RELATED FEATURES

Most of the new and improved features of Visual Basic 6.0 involve access to data, ranging from simple text files to complex data cubes created by Microsoft Decision Support Services (formerly code-named "Plato"). Many of the newly added objects, such as the Data Environment designer (DED), are intended to reduce the amount of VBA code required to implement ADO-based projects.

> **NOTE**
>
> Visual Basic developers disagree about the value of substituting graphical data design environments for ADO code in forms and/or modules. Creating ADO objects with code offers the advantage of self-documenting projects. Designers, such as DED, provide the benefits of object reusability and database connectivity standardization and minimize the number of lines of code to get a database front-end project running, but don't support conventional text-based `Connection` and `Command` documentation. The examples in the early chapters of this book use DED, wizards, and other graphical tools for `ADODB` object creation; advanced chapters rely primarily on VBA code to create `ADODB.Connection`, `Command,` and `Recordset` objects.

Following is a list of the most important new data-related features of Visual Basic 6.0 with cross-references to the chapters that initiate coverage of each topic:

▶**See** "Interfacing with Data," **p. 52**

* *OLE DB and ADO.* OLE DB data providers return COM-based Rowsets from tabular (text files, database tables, and messages) and hierarchical (file and directory systems) data sources. ADO is an automation wrapper for OLE DB that converts Rowsets to `ADODB.Recordsets.` ADO replaces the hierarchy of Data Access Objects (DAO), ODBCDirect, and Remote Data Objects (RDO) with a greatly simplified object model. This book is devoted exclusively to ADO; the few DAO, ODBCDirect, and RDO examples in the chapters that follow appear for comparison purposes only.

> **NOTE**
>
> `ADODB` is the class identifier for the ADO 2.0 type library. DAO, ODBCDirect, and ADO share common object names, such as `Recordset`. Thus it's a good programming practice to distinguish ADO from DAO objects by preceding the object with its class, as in `ADODB.Recordset` and `DAO.Recordset`. All code examples in this book use the `ADODB` prefix. ADO 2.0 is backward compatible with Visual Basic 5.0, so you don't need version 6.0 to write code-based projects using OLE DB and ADO. You can download the Microsoft Data Access Software Developer Kit (SDK) and the Microsoft Data Access Components (MDAC) version 2.0 from `http://www.microsoft.com/data/mdac2.htm`.

- *Data Environment designer (DED).* DED is an upgrade to Visual Basic 5.0 Enterprise Edition's User Connection designer for RDO. DED minimizes the amount of code required to establish connections to databases through OLE DB data providers and to return Recordset objects bound to ADO-compliant data-bound controls. DED is especially effective in generating parameters for stored procedures and creating hierarchical Recordsets. Data Links, a synonym for ADODB.Connection objects, provide the equivalent of ODBC data sources (DSNs) and DSN-less connections. Persistent Data Links, stored as .udl files, substitute for ODBC's file DSNs. Creating a new Data Project automatically adds a DED instance (DataEnvironment1).

- *Drag-and-drop form generation.* DED lets you drag a Command object to a form, which automatically adds the controls for data display and update, based on the stored procedure, view, table, or SQL query you specify. If you create a Command object with a parent-child (one-to-many) relationship between two tables, DED adds TextBoxes for the parent record fields and a DataGrid to display the child Recordset.

▶**See** "Opening the Data View Window," **p. 173** and "Using Visual Data Tools with Visual Basic 6.0, **p. 730**

- *Data View window.* Working with DED, the Data View window lets you explore the structure of databases and tables to which you have established a DED Connection object. The Data View window is the gateway to the Enterprise Edition's Visual Database Tools (VDTs).

> **NOTE**
>
> The Data View window supports modification and addition of client/server RDBMS (SQL Server and Oracle) objects. The Data View window is read-only for Jet and other shared-file databases.

▶**See** " Adding an ADODC to a Data Environment Designer Form," **p. 178**

- *ADO Data Control (ADODC).* ADODC replaces the intrinsic Data control of Visual Basic 5.0 and earlier, and the Remote Data Control (RDC) of Visual Basic 4.0 and 5.0 Enterprise Editions. Visual Basic 6.0 retains the DAO-based intrinsic Data control, and the Enterprise Edition includes RDO and RDC for "downlevel" (a Microsoft term for "backward") compatibility. You need ADODCs only for applications requiring a simple Recordset navigation control; ADO-compliant data-bound controls can connect directly to Recordset objects.

> **NOTE**
>
> Version 5.0 doesn't include ADO-compliant data-bound controls, but you can bind version 5.0 of the DBGrid, MSFlexGrid, DBCombo, DBList, TextBox, and CheckBox controls to International Software Group's ISGData control. The ISGData control is available for download at no charge from `http://www.isgsoft.com`.

▶**See** "Binding Controls to the ADO Data Control," **p. 189**

- *ADO-compliant data-bound controls.* The DataGrid control replaces DBGrid, and DataCombo and DataList controls replace DBList and DBCombo. The intrinsic TextBox, CheckBox, Image, and PictureBox controls are ADO compliant.

> **NOTE**
>
> ADO uses a new method of binding to OLE DB Rowset objects, so all data-bound ActiveX controls (OCXs), including third-party data-bound OCXs, must be modified to accommodate the IRowset interface of OLE DB data providers and service providers. You can expect ActiveX control vendors to make updated versions of their data-bound controls available on or shortly after the retail release of Visual Basic 6.0.

▶**See** "Creating and Displaying Hierarchical Recordsets," **p. 390**

- *Hierarchical Recordsets and the FlexGrid control.* A hierarchical `Recordset`, created by the MSDataShape OLE DB service provider, lets you include a child `Recordset` within a row of a conventional `Recordset` object. You can create a hierarchical `Recordset` with VBA code, but it's much easier to use DED to generate the required query. The read-only Hierarchical FlexGrid control (MSHFlexGrid) provides an expandable grid to display the contents of parent and child `Recordsets`.

- *Data Report designer.* The Data Report designer supplies a subset of the reporting capabilities of Microsoft Access, replacing the Crystal Reports add-in. Creating a new Data Project automatically adds a Data Report instance (`DataReport1`), which you should remove if your project doesn't require printed reports.

▶**See** "Using the Data Form Wizard to Create a Data Entry Form," **p. 173**

- *Data Form Wizard.* The new ADO-based Data Form Wizard is integrated with the Application, Chart, and FlexGrid Wizards. You also can launch the Wizard from the

<u>A</u>dd-Ins menu. This Wizard lets you select from the Jet 3.51 native OLE DB data provider (code-named "Jolt") for Jet tables or the OLE DB data provider for ODBC (code-named "Kagera") for client/server (remote) databases. Unlike DED's drag-and-drop addition of bound controls, the Data Form Wizard provides a standard set of command buttons for Recordset navigation and data updates.

▶**See** "Setting the DataFormat Property Value," **p. 190**

- *DataFormat object.* The DataFormat object (StdFormat) sits between an ADO data source and data consumer, providing custom formatting of Recordsets for display and editing.

- *Data Repeater control.* The Data Repeater control provides a framework for replicating a data-bound ActiveX control to emulate an Access continuous subform. The downside of the Data Repeater control is that you must compile a data-bound user control to an OCX before you can repeat it in a Visual Basic form.

- *Data source classes and data binding.* Programmers can write object-oriented Class modules that serve as the equivalent of OLE DB data providers, services, and consumers. The BindingsCollection object lets you create the functional equivalent of an ADODC with VBA code.

▶**See** "Designing Efficient MTS Components," **p. 1005**

- *MTSTransactionMode property of Class modules.* Class modules now offer a property to set the mode of transactions under the control of MTS 2.0. The MTSTransactionMode property value is ignored if MTS doesn't create the class instance.

▶**See** "Using Visual Data Tools with Visual Basic 6.0," **p. 730**

- *Visual Data Tools (VDTs).* Consisting of the Query Designer and Database Designer, VDTs (commonly called the *da Vinci* toolset) let you create views, modify data structures, and add tables to SQL Server and Oracle databases. Visual Basic 6.0 VDTs are a substantial improvement over those in version 5.0.

▶**See** "Troubleshooting Stored Procedures with the T-SQL Debugger," **p. 863** (Ch21)

- *SQL Editor.* The Enterprise Edition's SQL Editor provides an environment in which to write stored procedures for SQL Server and Oracle databases, as well as SQL Server triggers. The Enterprise Edition also provides stored procedure debugging capability for SQL Server 6.x and 7.0.

> **NOTE**
>
> With the exception of the VDTs, SQL Editor, and Transact-SQL (T-SQL) debugger, all of the preceding features are included in the Professional Edition of Visual Basic 6.0. To gain the most from this book, you need the Professional or Enterprise Edition of Visual Basic or Visual Studio 6.0.

The sections that follow provide detailed descriptions of the most important new features of the preceding list. Most of the examples use the Oracle for Windows NT Enterprise Edition 8.0.3 DEMO database. If you elect to duplicate the examples in this chapter, you'll find that SQL Server 6.x and 7.0 or Jet 3.5x data sources give equivalent results.

MIGRATING TO OLE DB AND ADO

Microsoft promotes the Component Object Model (COM) as the basic underpinning for all Windows application development, especially client/server projects. The COM specification defines a set of interfaces for creating reusable objects (components) that you combine into projects of ever-increasing scope and complexity. Although COM has been ported to several flavors of UNIX, COM today is primarily a Windows technology. UNIX vendors tout the Common Object Request Broker Architecture (CORBA), COM's primary competitor, as an "open" specification. In reality, both COM and CORBA are proprietary implementations of an open specification. COM's advantage is that Microsoft is the proprietor of more than 90% of the world's PC desktops and, with Windows NT 4+, a rapidly growing share of the network operating system market. Microsoft currently sells more Windows NT 4.0 Server licenses than licenses for all flavors of UNIX combined.

> **NOTE**
>
> You can keep up-to-date on new COM developments at `http://www.microsoft.com/com/`.

▶See "Positioning MTS in the Middleware Market," **p. 976**

Distributed COM (DCOM) provides the mechanism for connecting COM objects that reside on multiple networked computers. DCOM finally has replaced Network OLE for 32-bit applications, so only 16-bit applications continue to require Automation Manager and other Network OLE baggage. Windows 9x and Windows NT 4+ now include full support for DCOM, which provides connectivity to components hosted by MTS to implement three- and higher-tier architecture. Windows NT 4.0 Option Pack, a no-charge add-on that is included on CD-2 of Visual

Studio 6.0, installs MTS 2.0 and Microsoft Messaging Queue (MSMQ) 1.0, along with a variety of other server-based products. CORBA-based transaction managers, such as IBM's Component Broker, BEA's IceBerg, and IONA's OrbixOTM (all of which are in varying stages of development and carry substantial licensing fees), compete with MTS. Sun's Enterprise JavaBeans (EJB) is a proposed specification for a Java-based alternative to MTS. When this edition was written, EJB was a specification without a commercial implementation.

> **NOTE**
>
> Microsoft's continuing practice of bundling no-charge products that add important functionality to Windows NT 4+ has attracted the ire of the Software Publishers Association (SPA). The SPA, of which Microsoft was a member at the time this edition was written, traditionally has concentrated on fighting software piracy. In June 1998, SPA management, consisting primarily of UNIX vendors and other Microsoft competitors, issued a white paper titled "Competition in the Network Market: The Microsoft Challenge." Among the white paper's litany of complaints about Microsoft's aggressive marketing of Windows NT is a section titled "Setting the Rules: Controlling the Platform to Control Competition," which explains the relationship of COM, DCOM, and MTS to CORBA and UNIX transaction managers. You can download the complete white paper in Adobe Acrobat format from
> `http://www.spa.org/gvmnt/comp/servcomp.pdf`.

COM+ 1.0, which was in the beta-testing process when this edition was written, is Microsoft's answer to a future competitive threat from EJB. Microsoft's goals for COM+ include absorbing MTS, making COM components easier to deploy and manage, improving system performance, and increasing server scalability from hundreds to thousands of clients. COM+ adds event services, load balancing, asynchronous queuing services with MSMQ, and an in-memory database for the MTS catalog. Some features proposed for COM+ in late 1997, such as inheritance and improved garbage collection, no longer are scheduled to appear in COM+ 1.0.

OLE DB

▶**See** "Redesigning from the Bottom up with OLE DB," **p. 54**

OLE DB is Microsoft's strategic COM-based data access technology for desktop and client/server databases, as well as nontraditional data residing in message stores (Exchange Server) and directory systems (Windows NT 5.0's Active Directory Service). Despite the overwhelming success of ODBC, a C/C++ API, Microsoft has elected to replace ODBC with a collection of COM-based components classified as OLE DB data providers, service providers, and data consumers. OLE DB serves as the foundation of yet another Microsoft initiative, Universal Data Access, a subcomponent of the still vaguely defined Distributed interNet Architecture (DNA).

NOTE

The primary Microsoft site for OLE DB and other related technologies is http://www.microsoft.com/data/oledb/. You can read the OLE DB 2.0 specification at http://www.microsoft.com/data/oledb/oledb20.

Visual Basic 6.0 comes with a multitude of OLE DB data providers, and Distributed Transaction Services (DTS, required for MTS) adds a few more. The following six OLE DB data providers are of most importance for Visual Basic developers:

- *Microsoft Jet 3.51 OLE DB Provider,* a native OLE DB provider for Jet 3.51 and earlier databases.
- *Microsoft Jet 4.0 OLE DB Provider,* a native OLE DB provider for Jet 4.0 and earlier databases. Jet 4.0 is the format used by Microsoft Access 9.0 and other members of the Office 2000 family. Installing SQL Server 7.0 adds the Jet 4.0 provider to your \Windows\System[32] folder.
- *Microsoft OLE Provider for SQL Server,* a native OLE DB provider for SQL Server 6.x and later.
- *Microsoft OLE Provider for Oracle,* a native OLE DB provider for Oracle 7.3 and 8.0.3 and later.
- *Microsoft OLE Provider for DSS,* a native OLE DB provider for Microsoft Decision Support Service's cube, virtual cube, and the Microsoft PivotTable Service.
- *Microsoft OLE DB Provider for ODBC Drivers.* This provider replaces the ODBC driver manager and enables OLE DB connectivity to databases that don't yet have native OLE DB providers.

Native OLE DB providers deliver equal or better performance than ODBC drivers with direct C++ access to the OLE DB COM interfaces or ODBC API function calls. Despite the fact that Kagera is Visual Basic 6.0's default OLE DB provider, it's a good programming practice to use a native OLE DB provider when possible.

NOTE

Several additional OLE DB data providers are installed by Visual Basic 6.0. The Microsoft OLE DB Simple and Sample Providers are of interest primarily to developers of OLE DB data providers. The Simple Provider is a set of Internet Explorer APIs that work with in-memory arrays of `String` and `Variant` data types. The OLE DB Provider for Microsoft Directory Services lets you read and update the Active Directory of Windows NT 5.0.

ActiveX Data Objects

Visual Basic programmers can't make a direct connection to COM interfaces, so Microsoft provides Automation wrappers to give VBA and VBScript authors late-bound access to COM components through the `CreateObject` method. Project references to Automation type libraries permit early binding of Automation objects via `{Dim¦Private¦Public}` obj*Name* `As` *AutomationClass* declarations. The Automation wrapper for OLE DB is Microsoft ActiveX Data Objects 2.0 Library (Msado15.dll), which contains the `ADODB` type library. The type library defines the mapping of `ADODB` objects, such as `Connection`, `Command`, and `Recordset`, to corresponding OLE DB interfaces, ISessionObject, ICommand, and IRowset.

> **NOTE**
>
> Many ADO 2.0 DLLs, such as Msado15.dll, carry a 15 suffix, despite being version 2.0. The 15 suffix, which has caused considerable developer confusion, is required for downlevel compatibility with code that uses ADO version 1.5.

Creating a new Data Project automatically adds a core set of project references to data-related Automation DLLs and type libraries. Following is a list of the added references with their Automation class and file names:

- Microsoft ActiveX Data Objects 2.0 Library (`ADODB`, Msado15.dll)
- Microsoft Data Binding Collection (`MSBind`, Msbind.dll)
- Microsoft Data Report Designer v6.0 (`MSDataReportLib`, Msdbrptr.dll)
- Microsoft Data Formatting Object Library (`StdFormat`, Msstdfmt.dll)
- Microsoft Data Environment Instance 1.0 (`DERuntimeObjects`, Msderun.dll)
- Microsoft Data Source Interfaces (`MSDATASRC`, Msdatsrc.tlb)

▶**See** "Exploring Top-Level ADO Properties, Methods, and Events," **p. 67**

Figure 1.1 shows Object Browser displaying the first few members of the `Connection` class of the `ADODB` library. ADO's object model is based on RDO, a relatively thin wrapper over the ODBC API. Most Visual Basic 5.0 developers used the Enterprise Edition's RDO to connect front ends to client/server RDBMSs. ADO, however, doesn't have RDO's ODBC-to-server connectivity restriction. Like RDO, ADO objects fire events, but ADO offers finer event granularity than RDO offers. DAO and ODBCDirect don't trigger events. ADO gives developers who use any version of Visual Basic 6.0 access to a rich event model for each primary ADO object: `Connection`, `Command`, and `Recordset`.

FIGURE 1.1

Object Browser displaying a few members of the Connection *class of the* ADODB *type library.*

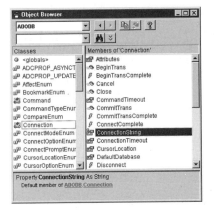

▶**See** "Opening an ADODB.Recordset Object on an ADODB.Connection with Code," **p. 58**

DAO programmers are accustomed to referencing a hierarchy of objects, DBEngine, Workspace, and Database, just to open a DAO.Recordset. ADO has a flat object model; you can open an ADODB.Recordset simply by setting property values and calling the Open method. It's a more common practice, however, to open a ADODB.Connection object and then set the ActiveConnection property value to the Connection object. This approach lets you open multiple ADODB.Recordset objects against a single Connection.

ADO is the clear choice for virtually all new database development with Visual Studio 6.0 tools, as well as the next version of Microsoft Office (9.0, also called Office 2000.) It's unlikely, however, that developers will be called on to upgrade existing Visual Basic 5.0 applications, especially front ends employing RDO 2.0. "If it ain't broke, don't fix it."

EXPLORING THE DATA ENVIRONMENT DESIGNER AND THE DATA VIEW WINDOW

DED is an upgraded version of Visual Basic 5.0 Enterprise Edition's User Connection designer for RDO. DED lets you connect to any database having a native OLE DB data provider or, using the OLE DB for ODBC provider (Kagera), an up-to-date ODBC driver. When you open a new Data Project, a DED instance (DataEnvironment1) automatically appears in the Project window. Double-clicking the DataEnvironment1 item opens the Data Project-DataEnvironent1 window.

A single DED instance can support a multitude of independent database connections. To make the first connection, you right-click Connection1 and choose <u>P</u>roperties to open the Provider page of the Data Link Properties sheet in which you select the OLE DB data provider (see Figure 1.2). Clicking Next displays the Connection page in which you specify the location of the database or server, the name of the database (if necessary), login ID, and password. The data provider you choose determines the set of controls on the Connection page; Figure 1.3 shows the

Connection page for the Microsoft OLE DB Provider for Oracle. Clicking Test Connection creates a temporary connection to the database and returns a `Test connection succeeded` message; if the connection doesn't work, you receive an error message from the provider.

FIGURE 1.2

Selecting an OLE DB data provider in the Provider page of the Data Link Properties sheet.

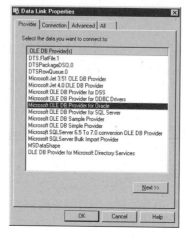

FIGURE 1.3

Setting `Connection` *properties for an Oracle 8.0.3 database.*

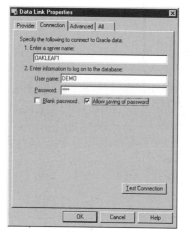

NOTE

A Data Link is a persistent `ADODB.Connection` object. You persist a `Connection` object by saving its properties in a pair of Data Environment (env*Name*.dsr/env*Name*.dca) files or in a Data Link (cnn*Name*.udl) file. An ADO Data Link file corresponds to an ODBC File Data Source (dsn*Name*.dsn) except that no default location is defined for .udl files. To create a Data Link file, right-click Explorer's Contents pane and choose New, Microsoft Data Link to add to the current folder a New Microsoft Data Link.udl file. Double-clicking the new file item opens the Data Link Properties sheet in which you set the properties of the Connection.

Figure 1.4 illustrates a DED instance with simultaneous connections to Oracle 8.0, SQL Server 7.0, and Jet 3.51 databases. Once you've specified at least one ADODB.Connection, choose View, Data View Window, which displays the members of the Data Environment Connections collection. Expanding a Connections node displays the database objects for the Connection that you can access through the Data View window. Expanding the Tables node displays a list of tables (see Figure 1.5), and expanding a *TableName* node lists the fields of the table. Double-clicking a field item displays a *FieldName* Properties sheet (see Figure 1.6).

FIGURE 1.4

The Data Environment designer with Connection *objects for Oracle, SQL Server, and Jet databases.*

FIGURE 1.5

The Data View window displaying the standard sets of database objects and table lists for Oracle, SQL Server, and Jet.

NOTE

Right-clicking the Tables node and choosing Filter by Owner lets you limit the Tables list to a particular owner. As an example, filtering the Oracle DEMO tables by the DEMO owner eliminates display of the MD$DICTVER table owned by MDSYS. You can elect to show system tables in the list by toggling the Show System Objects pop-up menu choice.

FIGURE 1.6

Properties of the CUSTOMER_ID field of the Oracle DEMO table.

Right-clicking a *TableName* node in the Data View window and choosing Open displays the table's data in a simple grid in the Run Table - *TableName* window. If you log in with sufficient privileges, you can add or edit table records. Choosing New Table lets you specify a table name and then set the properties of the fields in the New Table: *TableName* window. When you close the window, a message box lets you save or discard your changes.

NOTE

You can't modify properties of existing Jet tables nor add new tables to a Jet database from the Data View window. ADO 2.0 doesn't support Jet SQL Data Definition Language. You can only read Jet table and field property values and open existing tables to read, edit, or add records. Row-returning Jet `QueryDef` objects are classified as Views in the Data View window.

DED enforces a hierarchy of `ADODB.Connection`, `ADODB.Command`, and, for row-returning queries, `ADODB.Recordset` objects. To add a `Command` object to a selected `Connection`, click the `DataEnvironment1` Add Command button (second from the left) or choose Add Command from the pop-up menu to open the Command1 Properties sheet. Select the class of database object (Stored Procedure, Table, View or Synonym for Oracle) in the Database Object list and then select an object from the Object Name list (see Figure 1.7). Alternatively, select the SQL option and type an SQL statement in the text box. Clicking the SQL Builder button opens the VDT's query Design window. The da Vinci toolset is the subject of the "Using the Visual Data Tools" section later in the chapter.

FIGURE 1.7

Setting basic properties of a Command *object for a* Connection *to the DEMO tables of an Oracle 8 database.*

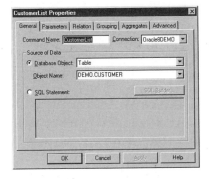

The Advanced page of the *CommandName* Properties sheet lets you choose between client- or server-side cursors, set the lock type, and specify other property values for Command execution (see Figure 1.8). The cursor location defaults to client side in DED but defaults to server side when creating Command or Recordset objects with VBA code. Unless you must take advantage of live server-side cursors, specify static client-side cursors, which use ADO's cursor engine, for client/server databases. ADO's client-side cursors are static by definition, so the Cursor Type list is disabled in Figure 1.8.

▶**See** "Comparing the Performance of DAO and ADO with Large Recordsets," **p. 544**

> **NOTE**
>
> Tests with large Jet tables and queries having more than 1,000 records indicate that using Jet's server-side cursor engine delivers better performance than ADO's client-side cursor engine delivers. With complex queries that deliver more than 10,000 records, Jet 3.51's cursor engine is 30% to 50% faster than ADO's.

FIGURE 1.8

Setting CursorLocation, LockType, *and other properties of a row-returning* Command *object.*

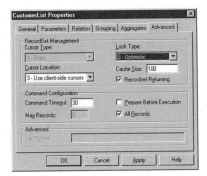

DED's achieves its objective of minimizing the amount of code needed to establish database connections and execute queries, especially parameterized queries. The Data View window depends totally on DED `Connections`. DED also provides the data source for Visual Basic 6.0's new report generator and leads you through the process of writing `SHAPE` statements to create hierarchical `Recordsets`. Multiple applications that require access to the same database(s) and have a common set of queries benefit from sharing a single designer file. It's a good programming practice, however, to use code to create `Connection`, `Command`, and `Recordset` objects in Class modules, especially when writing middle-tier DLLs for MTS. ADO code is self-documenting, an important consideration in multiprogrammer projects, and lets you fine-tune performance by setting `ADODB.Object` property values that aren't directly accessible from DED.

ADOPTING ADO-COMPLIANT CONTROLS

DED's ability to generate `Recordsets` from `Command` objects enables drag-and-drop generation of simple data entry forms. DED automatically names `ADODB.Recordset` objects by prepending `rs` to the `Connection` name and binds TextBoxes to each field of the `Recordset`. Bound TextBoxes, in OLE DB terminology, are *simple-bound data consumers*. Figure 1.9 illustrates the result of dragging the CustomerList `Command` to the default `frmDataEnv` form of a Data Project. A glaring defect of this simple process is the lack of controls to navigate the `Recordset`.

FIGURE 1.9

Dragging a row-returning DED Command *object to an empty form for viewing and editing the first record.*

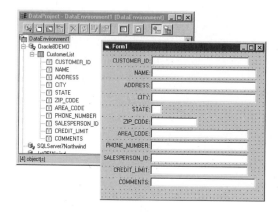

Fortunately, it's easy to add an ADODC to provide `Recordset` navigation. The following line of code in the `Form_Activate` event connects the ADODC to the `rsCustomerList` Recordset:

```
Set adcCustList.Recordset = DataEnvironment1.rsCustomerList
```

Figure 1.10 shows the form with the added ADODC control, `adcCustList`, and the `txtCOMMENTS` TextBox's `Multiline` property value changed to `True`.

FIGURE 1.10

*The form of
Figure 1.9 with an
added ADODC in
run mode.*

DED lets you define parent-child Command relationships to approximate Access's form-subform combinations. Selecting a Command and clicking the Add Child Command button (fourth from the left) adds another level to the Command hierarchy. You specify a related data source in the General page of the *ChildCommand* Properties sheet (see Figure 1.11), and then set the relationship between the parent and child data sources in the Relation page (see Figure 1.12).

FIGURE 1.11

*Setting data
source properties
for a child com-
mand.*

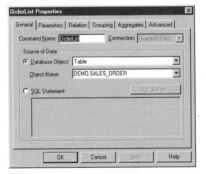

FIGURE 1.12

*Establishing the
relationship
between parent
and child data
sources.*

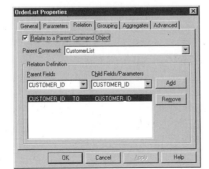

Dragging the parent Command node to a form adds a DataGrid control bound to the child Recordset (see Figure 1.13). OLE DB classifies DataGrids as *complex-bound data consumers.* As you navigate the parent Recordset with an ADODC, the child Recordset updates the DataGrid with related records (see Figure 1.14). Hierarchical parent-child Commands also are the data source for Hierarchical FlexGrid controls, the subject of the next section.

FIGURE 1.13

Generating a form-subform combination from a hierarchical Command object.

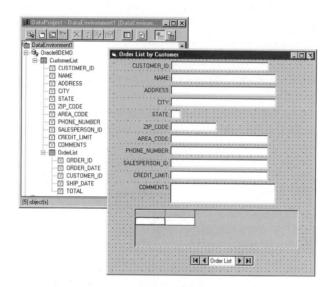

FIGURE 1.14

The form of Figure 1.13 with an added ADODC in run mode.

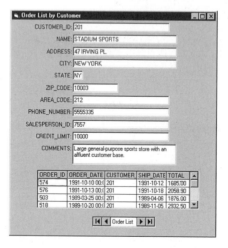

The DataGrid control emulates the DBGrid control of earlier versions of Visual Basic; the DataCombo and DataList controls substitute for Data Bound List controls. The updated FlexGrid control also binds to ADODB.Recordsets. ADO-compliant controls have additional data-related properties, such as DataMember, to accommodate binding to DED Command objects. Like prior versions, you also can assign the record source of ADO-compliant controls with VBA code.

BINDING HIERARCHICAL FLEXGRIDS TO RECORDSETS

The Hierarchical FlexGrid control (MSHFlexGrid) is an enhanced version of the FlexGrid control that selectively displays parent-child data in a single grid. Dragging the parent Command icon from DED with the right mouse button opens a context menu that lets you choose between a Data Grid, Hierarchical FlexGrid, or Bound Controls. The Hierarchical FlexGrid choice adds a bound MSHFlexGrid to the form. MSHFlexGrid defines the parent-child hierarchy as a set of bands (Band0 and Band1). You specify fields that appear in the Bands property page for the control (see Figure 1.15). When you run the project, the grid opens with the child band expanded; clicking the +/- symbol in the first column of the grid toggles expansion of the child band (see Figure 1.16).

FIGURE 1.15

Setting the properties of the parent band of an MSHFlexGrid control.

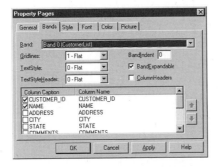

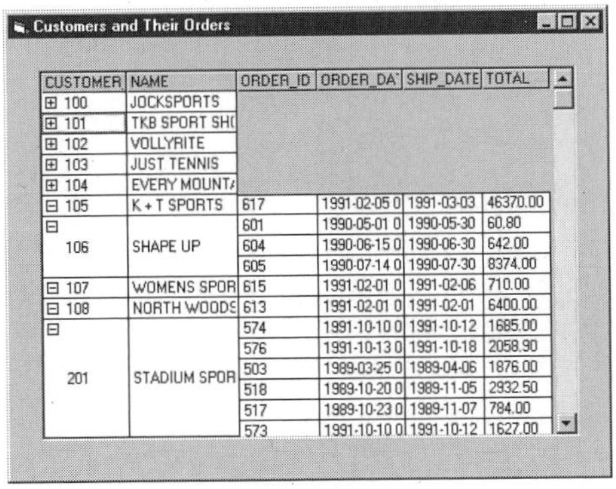

FIGURE 1.16

A partly expanded MSHFlexGrid control in run mode with unneeded columns removed.

Under the covers, ADO uses SHAPE statements, supported by the MSDataShape OLE DB provider, to generate the hierarchical Recordsets that populate the MSHFlexGrid control. Right-clicking the parent Command object and choosing <u>H</u>ierarchy Info opens the Hierarchy Information dialog that displays the Command's SHAPE statement (see Figure 1.17). Following is the statement that generates the Recordset for the CustomerList (parent) and OrderList (child) Commands:

```
SHAPE {SELECT * FROM "DEMO"."CUSTOMER"} AS CustomerList
    APPEND ({SELECT * FROM "DEMO"."SALES_ORDER"} AS OrderList
    RELATE CUSTOMER_ID TO CUSTOMER_ID) AS OrderList
```

FIGURE 1.17

The SHAPE statement that creates the hierarchical Recordset to populate the MSHFlexGrid of Figure 1.16.

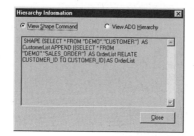

NOTE

Quoted identifiers ("...") in SQL and SHAPE statements for ADODB objects replace the traditional square bracket pair ([...])of Jet SQL. Technically, only object names with illegal SQL syntax (spaces or nonalphanumeric characters) require double-quote pairs.

PRINTING REPORTS WITH THE DATA REPORT DESIGNER

Visual Basic 6.0's fully integrated Data Report designer (DRD) finally replaces the Crystal Reports add-in of prior Visual Basic releases. You design Data Reports on a variant of a conventional Visual Basic form, which is similar to the UI for Access reports. The report designer adapts a small subset of Visual Basic native bound controls to the DataReport page of the ToolBox: RptLabel, RptTextBox, RptImage, RptLine, and RptShape. A unique RptFunction control lets you add calculated fields to the report.

DED's Command objects also serve as the DataSource for drag-and-drop generation of reports. You can create a simple DataReport with group headers and footers by specifying the name of a parent-child Command, such as CustomerList, as the value of the report's DataMember property. Drag the base table (parent) fields to print from the parent Command to the Group Header section, drag the related table fields from the child Command to the Detail section, and then delete the caption labels (see Figure 1.18). When you apply the Show method to the form, the report appears in print preview mode (see Figure 1.19). Clicking the Print button opens the common Print dialog.

FIGURE 1.18

Designing a report with detail records grouped by the parent Recordset of a hierarchical Command.

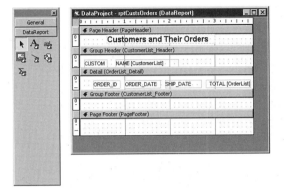

FIGURE 1.19

The report of Figure 1.18 in print preview (run) mode.

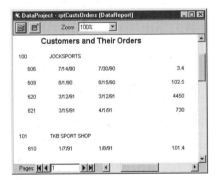

▶**See** "Using Command Aggregates for Subtotals and Totals," **p. 460**

The *CommandName* Properties sheet includes an Aggregates page that lets you generate group subtotals for detail records or grand totals for entire reports. Figure 1.20 shows the properties settings for an aggregate on the TOTAL field of the OrderList child Recordset. The SHAPE syntax to add the SUM aggregate is

```
SHAPE {SELECT * FROM "DEMO"."CUSTOMER"} AS CustomerList
    APPEND ({SELECT * FROM "DEMO"."SALES_ORDER"} AS OrderList
    RELATE CUSTOMER_ID TO CUSTOMER_ID) AS OrderList,
        SUM(OrderList.TOTAL) AS aggOrdersByCust
```

Aggregates are identified in DED's window by an icon with a +/- symbol. You drag the aggregate icon from DED's window to the Group Footer section of the report to print group subtotals (see Figure 1.21). The rptFunction control offers an alternative approach to printing subtotals and other aggregations (see Figure 1.22).

FIGURE 1.20

Specifying a SUM *aggregate on the* TOTAL *order amount for each customer.*

FIGURE 1.21

Adding the SUM *aggregate to the Group Footer section of the report.*

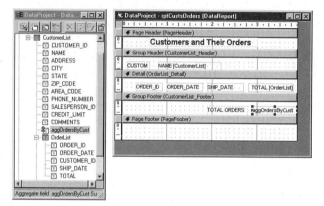

FIGURE 1.22

The report with a customer order subtotal in print preview (run) mode.

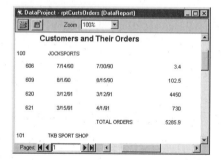

DRD doesn't offer the entire feature set of Access reports. DRD reports trigger relatively few events and offer no built-in subreport capability. You can't add ActiveX controls to DRD's DataReport objects. Full integration of DRD with other Visual Basic components, event trapping, and the simplicity of its design-mode UI make DRD a more-than-adequate replacement for Crystal Reports. DRD is likely to satisfy 90% or more of the printing needs of conventional database front ends.

AUTOMATING DESIGN WITH THE DATA FORM WIZARD

Visual Basic 6.0's Data Form Wizard, like its predecessors, generates standardized data entry and editing forms with command buttons and VBA code for Recordset navigation. The primary change to version 6.0 is substitution of ADO for DAO. The Data Form Wizard offers the choice of Access or Remote (ODBC) data sources. Access uses Jolt and Jet 3.51; Remote (ODBC) uses Kagera and requires an existing ODBC DSN or entries for a DSN-less ODBC connection. Unfortunately, the Wizard doesn't offer choices for the native OLE DB providers for SQL Server and Oracle.

The Wizard offers a variety of form layout choices: single-record, grid, master/detail, Hierarchical FlexGrid, and chart. Binding options include the ADODC, VBA code, and Class module. Figure 1.23 shows a single-record form generated from the CUSTOMERS table of the Oracle 8.0.3 DEMO database. The Recordset navigation control isn't an ADODC; it's a combination of four command buttons and a TextBox contained in a PictureBox control. The Click event of a Command button calls the MoveFirst, MovePrevious, MoveNext, or MoveLast method of the ADODB.Recordset object to which the TextBoxes are bound.

FIGURE 1.23

A single-record data entry and editing form generated by the Data Form Wizard.

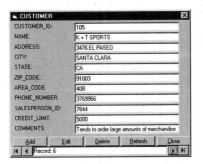

If your application requires a simple data entry or display form, the standard designs generated by the Wizard are likely to suffice. The primary value of the Data Form Wizard, however, is as a tool to aid beginning database developers in learning ADO programming techniques.

BINDING DATA SOURCES AND CONSUMERS

Visual Basic 5.0 and earlier required data binding definitions for data consumers to be implemented in design mode. As an example, the DataSource and other binding property values of bound TextBox, FlexGrid, DBGrids, and DBList controls are read-only in run mode. The intrinsic Data control and the Remote Data Control were the universal data providers for bound data consumers.

Visual Basic 6.0 and ADO 2.0 introduce a new set of binding capabilities for data consumers. You now can bind TextBox, CheckBox, Label, FlexGrid, Hierarchical FlexGrid, DataGrid, DataCombo, DataList, Image, and PictureBox controls directly to `ADODB.Recordset` objects with VBA **Set** `Control.DataSource` = `rstRecordset` statements. The ability to bind controls to Recordsets in run mode eliminates the need to include a hidden ADODC for each Recordset.

The `BindingsCollection` object adds data-aware features to Class modules, which enables objects you define to act as data sources for bound data consumers. You can roll your own ActiveX components, user controls, and ActiveX controls to contribute a standardized set of custom data sources, similar in function to DataEnvironment objects, to multiple projects.

The DataRepeater control takes advantage of the data consumer binding capabilities of user controls to create analogs of Access continuous subforms. For example, you can create a user control with TextBox, CheckBox (for Boolean fields), and Image (for LongBinary fields) controls. After compiling the user control to an .ocx file, you bind an invisible DataRepeater control to a Recordset and then specify the name of your ActiveX control as the `RepeatedControlName` property value of the DataRepeater. When you run the form, multiple instances of the repeated control display successive records of the bound Recordset (see Figure 1.24). You can interpose the `DataFormat` object between the DataRepeater and the ActiveX control to format the display of TextBoxes or Labels.

FIGURE 1.24

Emulating an Access subform with a compiled user control and the Data Repeater control.

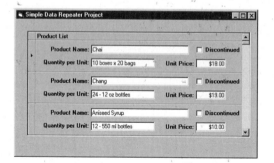

USING THE VISUAL DATA TOOLS

Visual Studio 6.0 Enterprise Edition's VDTs)—Query Designer and Database Designer—are upgraded versions of the da Vinci VDTs included with the Enterprise Edition of Visual Basic 5.0. The primary change is access to the VDTs from the new Data View window. Like the earlier version, the new VDTs currently work only with client/server databases; Jet's Data Definition Language isn't supported.

The Query Designer creates VIEWs, which are similar to Jet's persistent, row-returning QueryDef objects. Right-clicking the Views node for a database in the Data View window opens an empty New View window. You add tables to the VIEW by dragging Table items from the Data View window to the New View's upper pane. If declarative referential integrity (DRI) is in use, relationships between primary and foreign keys appear as a line between the related fields. A key icon indicates the primary key and the infinity symbol (∞) represents the foreign key of a one-to-many relationship.

Dragging field names to the column definition pane adds fields to the VIEW and simultaneously generates the required ANSI SQL statements for a CREATE VIEW statement. At any point in the process, right-clicking any pane (except the SQL statement pane) and choosing Run executes the query and displays the result set in the bottom pane's grid (see Figure 1.25). When you close the Query Designer window, a message box gives you the option to save the view with a descriptive name. If you're new to writing SQL SELECT queries, you can copy and paste statements from the SQL pane to your VBA code.

FIGURE 1.25

Creating a VIEW *in the Visual Data Tools' Query Design Window.*

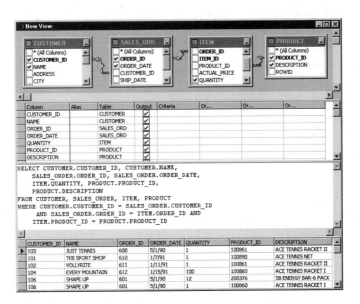

The Database Design tool creates database diagrams of existing databases and lets you add tables and establish relationships between tables. VDT's database diagrams resemble Access's Relationships window and offer a similar feature set. Like the Query Designer, relationships appear as lines between primary and foreign key fields. Figure 1.26 shows the relationships between four tables of the Oracle DEMO table set. Right-clicking a relationship line and choosing Properties displays a Properties sheet with pages that define table properties, including CONSTRAINTs, relationships (see Figure 1.27), and indexes and keys. Right-clicking an empty area of the window and choosing New Table opens a *TableName* window with a grid in which you define the field properties for the new table.

FIGURE 1.26

*Creating a new
Database
Diagram for an
Oracle database
with the da Vinci
Database Design
tool.*

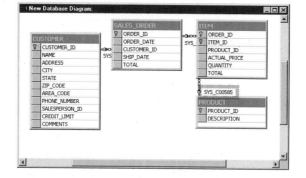

FIGURE 1.27

*The Relationships
page of the
Properties sheet
for the relation-
ship between the
CUSTOMER and
SALES_ORDER
tables.*

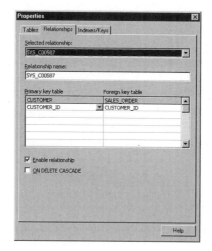

> **NOTE**
>
> Database Diagrams create *metadata* (data about the structure of the database
> and the properties of its objects) that's compatible with Microsoft Repository
> 2.0, included with Visual Basic 6.0.

Although technically not a VDT, the Stored Procedure editor expedites writing stored procedures for SQL Server and Oracle 7.3/8 databases. Right-clicking the Stored Procedures node in
the Data View window and selecting <u>N</u>ew Stored Procedure opens the New Stored Procedure
window. The window includes color-coded skeleton statements for SQL Server's Transact-SQL
or Oracle's P/SQL dialects (see Figure 1.28). You overwrite the placeholders for parameter definition and the body of the stored procedure with the appropriate SQL statements.

FIGURE 1.28

The Stored Procedure Editor with the default skeleton structure for an Oracle 7.3 or 8.0.3+ stored procedure.

NOTE

SQL Server 7.0 Enterprise Manager includes the da Vinci toolset. There are minor differences, however, in the launching and use of the SQL Server version of the VDTs.

WORKING WITH MICROSOFT SQL SERVER

Visual Studio 6.0 Enterprise Edition includes BackOffice 4.5 Developer Edition, which includes the Developer Edition of Microsoft SQL Server 6.5. SQL Server 7.0 (formerly code-named "Sphinx") didn't meet the release date of Visual Studio 6.0, and was in the beta-test stage when this edition was written. All of the client/server examples of this book use version 7.0 and, with minor exceptions where a feature isn't supported, also run against version 6.5. Beta 3 of SQL Server 7.0 is included with Microsoft Developer Network (MSDN) Enterprise Subscription. It's likely that an upgrade license for the Desktop Edition of SQL Server 7.0 will be included in the retail release of Visual Basic and Visual Studio 6.0 Enterprise Editions. The Desktop Edition has limitations on database size and simultaneous connections but runs on both Windows 9x and Windows NT 4.0+.

▶See "SQL Server 7.0 (Sphinx)," **p. 688**

SQL Server 7.0 is a major upgrade to prior versions. The most important change is that database devices (.dat files) have given way to individual database (.mdf) and log (.ldf) files that rely on the file system in use. To minimize administrative chores, the .mdf and .ldf files automatically expand and contract with their contents. The downside of the new file system is that all 6.x databases must be upgraded. Fortunately, the Version Upgrade Wizard expedites the upgrade process. Version 7.0 has many new scalability- and performance-related features aimed at removing the department-level stigmata carried by prior versions.

Another major change with version 7.0 is Enterprise Manager, which becomes an ODBC-based snap-in for Microsoft Management Console (MMC). The snap-in replaces SQL Server's 6.x's Enterprise Manager, which uses DB-Lib to connect to servers. Figure 1.29 shows the new Enterprise Manager displaying a list of the stored procedures for the sample application of Chapter 21, "Using Transact-SQL Stored Procedures." A new graphical Query Analyzer replaces version 6.x's aging, text-based ISQL/w application for executing SQL statements and writing stored procedures.

FIGURE 1.29

SQL Server 7.0's Enterprise Manager, a snap-in for Microsoft Management Console.

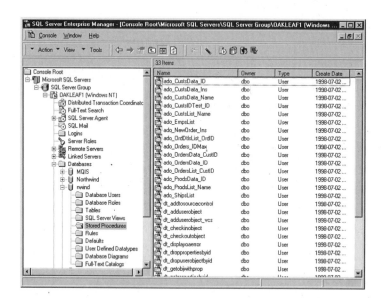

> **NOTE**
>
> Visual Studio 6.0 Enterprise Edition includes MTS 2.0, the subject of Chapter 26, "Taking Advantage of Microsoft Transaction Server 2.0," and Chapter 27, "Creating and Deploying MTS Components." MTS 2.0 and Microsoft Message Queue Server (MSMQ) 1.0 also are available when you install the no-charge Windows NT 4.0 Option Pack.

The Standard and Enterprise Editions of SQL Server 7.0 also include Microsoft SQL Support OLAP Services (MSSOS; formerly code-named "Plato"). MSSOS is an independent server designed for multidimensional, online analytical processing of the content of data warehouses. Chapter 28, "Analyzing Multidimensional Data with OLAP and MDX," introduces the MSOSS and the multidimensional expressions you must learn to obtain maximum benefit from MSSOS's data cubes.

SQL Server 7.0 and Visual Basic 6.0 Professional or Enterprise Edition are the logical combination to establish enterprise-level client/server database systems. SQL Server 7.0 and MSOSS offer unmatched price/performance benefits. Oracle, however, currently has the largest market share (at least by the measure of license fees) on Windows NT Server and remains the undisputed leader of the UNIX database market. Thus the client/server chapters of this book provide insights into the modifications required to adapt the Visual Basic procedures and code to accommodate Oracle 8.0.3+ databases.

UNDERSTANDING OLE DB AND UNIVERSAL DATA ACCESS

IN THIS CHAPTER

Visual Basic 6.0 marks a sea change in Microsoft's strategy for data access. Under the umbrella of "Universal Data Access," Microsoft wants all developers, not just Visual Basic programmers, to abandon Data Access Objects (DAO), ODBCDirect, Remote Data Objects (RDO), and the Open Database Connectivity (ODBC) API. Microsoft proposes to substitute a completely new approach to designing and writing database front ends based on a newly specified collection of Component Object Model (COM) interfaces called OLE DB. To encourage developers to adopt OLE DB–based programming, all the newly abandoned database technologies (referred to as *downlevel,* a synonym for "obsolete") are destined for maintenance mode. *Maintenance mode* is a technological purgatory in which only the most egregious bugs are fixed and upgrades occur infrequently, if ever. From 1998 on, OLE DB and its derivatives are Microsoft's mainstream data access technologies.

Microsoft's primary goals for Universal Data Access are to

- Extend the influence of COM in competition with other object models, primarily the UNIX Common Object Request Broker Architecture (CORBA)

- Provide the capability to accommodate less common data types, such as spreadsheets, e-mail messages, and file/directory systems

- Reduce development and support costs for the multiplicity of Windows-based data access architectures in common use today

This chapter introduces you to the fundamentals of Universal Data Access and Microsoft Data Access Components (MDAC), which make the use of OLE DB practical for Visual Basic programmers.

INTERFACING WITH DATA

Today's most popular method of connecting with sources of data are the ODBC API, and DAO. Thirty-two-bit ODBC drivers now are available for virtually every client/server relational database management system (RDBMS); most popular Indexed Sequential Access Method (ISAM) databases (Jet, xBase, FoxPro, and Paradox); spreadsheets (Excel); and delimited text files. Microsoft Office relies on ODBC drivers for most of its database connectivity features. Although other software publishers attempted to introduce alternatives to ODBC, such as Borland International's IDAPI, ODBC quickly became the de facto standard of the database industry. ODBC is a C/C++ Application Programming Interface (API); making direct use of the ODBC API in Visual Basic applications requires a large number of function prototype declarations (DECLAREs) and heavy-duty, low-level coding. Relatively few Visual Basic programmers access the ODBC API directly.

> **NOTE**
>
> The Java Database Connectivity (JDBC) API is a low-level API that defines for Java programmers a class hierarchy of objects and interfaces to SQL-based RDBMSs. JDBC is modeled closely on the ODBC API but offers the promise of cross-platform compatibility. Because of the lack of native ("pure") JDBC drivers, the most common approach is to use the JDBC API with a JDBC-ODBC bridge driver that connects to existing 32-bit ODBC drivers. Many Java enthusiasts contend that Microsoft is moving from ODBC to OLE DB to establish a COM hegemony in the Java world.

In 1994, Microsoft Access 2.0 introduced 16-bit DAO in conjunction with version 2.0 of the Jet database engine. Like ODBC, the Jet database engine is a C/C++ API. DAO provided what was then called an OLE Automation wrapper over the Jet API; up to that time OLE had been used primarily for creating and manipulating compound documents. DAO exposed a complex hierarchy of programmable data-related objects with the DBEngine object at the top. Lower objects in the hierarchy, Workspaces, Databases, TableDefs, QueryDefs, and Recordsets, were object layers under DBEngine. Jet databases permitted attaching other databases via ODBC, eliminating the need for low-level ODBC API programming. 32-bit Jet and DAO 3.0 appeared with the release of Access 95; when this book was written, Jet and DAO were in version 3.51. Microsoft has sold tens of millions of Access licenses, making Jet the most widely used desktop database in the world and DAO the default database object model for Windows programmers.

> **NOTE**
>
> Although DAO now is in maintenance mode, Jet is not. Microsoft intends to make continuing improvements to the Jet database engine for future versions of Access and the multitude of other Microsoft products that use Jet as their underlying data source. You can expect updates to ADO 2.0 and the native Jet OLE DB provider to accommodate Jet features that currently are either unsupported or have limited support.

The DAO/Jet combination is a heavyweight. Dao350.dll weighs in at 569KB and Msjet35.dll tips the scales at 1,022KB. Neither DAO or Jet is required for Visual Basic database front ends that communicate only with client/server databases, which represent an increasingly large percentage of Visual Basic applications. To eliminate the DAO/Jet footprint, Microsoft developed the lightweight (368KB) 32-bit RDO and its companion Remote Data Control (RDC) for the Enterprise Edition of Visual Basic 4.0. Microsoft designed RDO for maximum performance in the client/server environment and added enhancements for executing server stored procedures. RDO's object model differed considerably from that of DAO. To make RDO accessible to DAO programmers, Visual Basic 5.0 and Access 97 introduced yet another object model, ODBCDirect. Thirty-two–bit ODBCDirect provides a DAO wrapper for RDO to enable client/server front ends to communicate with back-end SQL RDBMSs without incurring the Jet overhead.

At this point, Microsoft found it had constructed a tower of database Babel. Teams of programmers were required to add new features to and remove at least the worst bugs from three significantly different database object models, one of which (DAO) was growing long in the tooth. Marketing managers wrote a multitude of white papers advising programmers which object model to adopt. Product support groups were deluged with calls from developers encountering difficulties moving from DAO to RDO or ODBCDirect.

Redesigning from the Bottom Up with OLE DB

The easiest and quickest approach to designing a new, unified data access model would involve ODBC as the intermediary for all data sources. The problem with this strategy is that ODBC relies on SQL to retrieve and modify data. SQL is quite satisfactory for client/server and Jet databases, which include their own SQL compiler or interpreter. However, many other sources of data, such as spreadsheets, email messages, and file and directory systems, aren't amenable to SQL's set-oriented command approach. ODBC drivers for Excel worksheets and text files, as an example, must include a custom SQL interpreter. SQL queries are poorly suited for hierarchical data structures, such as file and directory systems. The capability to deal with queries against directory systems is especially important for Microsoft's Active Directory Services, one of the major new features of Windows NT 5.0.

To accommodate the widest variety of data sources, as well as to spread the gospel of COM, Microsoft's data architects came up with an entirely new approach to data connectivity—OLE DB. OLE DB consists of three basic elements:

- *Data providers* that abstract information contained in data sources into a tabular (row-column) format called a *rowset*. Microsoft currently offers native OLE DB data providers for Jet, SQL Server, and Oracle databases, plus ODBC data sources. Other Microsoft OLE DB providers include an OLE DB Simple Provider for delimited text files and the MSDataShape provider for creating hierarchical data sets.

- *Data consumers* that display and/or manipulate rowsets, such as Visual Basic database front ends or OLE DB service providers.

- *Data services* (usually called OLE DB *service providers*) that consume data from providers and, in turn, provide data to consumers. Examples of data services are SQL query processors and cursor engines, which can create scrollable rowsets from forward-only rowsets. The query engine in Microsoft SQL Server 7.0 is an example of an OLE DB service provider.

2

UNDERSTANDING
OLE DB AND
DATA ACCESS

> **NOTE**
>
> Version 1.5 of the OLE DB specification was current when this book was written. You can download the latest version of the OLE DB Software Development Kit (SDK), which contains the current OLE DB specification, a set of native OLE DB data providers, and C++ sample applications, from `http://www.microsoft.com/data/oledb/download.htm`.

Figure 2.1 illustrates the relationship between OLE DB data providers, data consumers, and data services within Microsoft's Universal Data Access architecture. Database front ends written in C++ can connect directly to the OLE DB interfaces, which require function pointers and other low-level operations. High-level languages, such as Visual Basic and Java, use ActiveX Data Objects (ADO, an Automation wrapper over OLE DB) as an intermediary to connect to OLE DB's COM interfaces. Msado15.dll, which implements ADO 2.0, has a memory footprint of about 342K, slightly smaller than RDO's Msrdo20.dll and about 60 percent of the DAO 3.5 Dao350.dll.

FIGURE 2.1

Microsoft's Universal Data Access architecture and typical OLE DB data providers, services, and consumers.

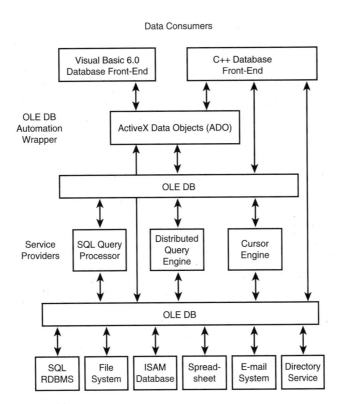

MDAC presently consists of OLE DB, ADO, and Remote Data Services (RDS, formerly Advanced Database Connector, or ADC), plus an ex officio member, ODBC. RDS, which is applicable only to browser-based applications, is the subject of Chapter 24, "Working with Remote Data Services." ODBC is only a temporary component of MDAC; ODBC ultimately will disappear as Microsoft and other independent software vendors (ISVs) create native OLE DB data providers for all common data sources. The remainder of this chapter is devoted to an overview of ADO, which is the primary means of database connectivity for the Visual Basic applications and code examples of this book.

Mapping OLE DB Interfaces to ADO

The OLE DB specification defines a set of interfaces to the following hierarchy of data objects:

- *DataSource* objects provide a set of functions to identify a particular OLE DB data provider, such as the Jet or SQL Server provider, and determine whether the caller has the required security permissions for the provider. If the provider is found and authentication succeeds, a connection to the data source results.

- *Session* objects provide an environment for creating rowsets and isolating transactions, especially with Microsoft Transaction Server (MTS). MTS is the subject of Chapter 26, "Taking Advantage of Microsoft Transaction Server 2.0," and Chapter 27, "Creating and Deploying MTS Components."

- *Command* objects include sets of functions to handle queries, usually (but not necessarily) in the form of SQL statements or names of stored procedures.

- *Rowset* objects, which may be created directly from Session objects or as the result of execution of Command objects. Rowset objects deliver data to the consumer through the IRowset interface.

ADO maps the four OLE DB objects to three top-level Automation objects that are more familiar to Visual Basic programmers, especially those who are experienced with RDO or ODBCDirect:

- Connection objects, which combine OLE DB's DataSource and Session objects to specify the OLE DB data provider, establish a connection to the data source and isolate transactions to a specific connection. The Execute method of the Connection object can return a forward-only ADODB.Recordset object.

- Command objects, which are directly analogous to OLE DB's Command object. ADODB.Command objects accept an SQL statement, the name of a table or the name of a stored procedure. Command objects are used primarily for executing SQL UPDATE, INSERT, DELETE, and SQL Data Definition Language (DDL) queries that don't return records. As demonstrated in the section "Opening an ADODB.Recordset Object from a DataEnvironment Object" later in this chapter, you also can return rows by executing an ADODB.Command object.

- Recordset objects, which correspond to OLE DB's Rowset objects and have properties and methods similar to a combination of DAO's Recordset and RDO's rdoResultset objects.

Figure 2.2 illustrates the relationships between OLE DB and ADO objects and their primary functions and methods, respectively. Unlike DAO objects, you can use the **New** reserved word to create and the Close method or the **Set** *ObjectName* = **Nothing** statement to destroy instances of ADODB.Connection, ADODB.Command, and ADODB.Recordset objects independently. The ADODB prefix, the name of the ADO type library, explicitly identifies ADO objects that share object names with DAO (Recordset) and ODBCDirect (Connection and Recordset).

> **NOTE**
>
> You don't need to use the ADODB prefix if you add to your project a reference only to the Microsoft ActiveX Data Objects 2.0 Library. If you also have a reference to the Microsoft DAO 3.5 Object Library, however, you must use the ADODB prefix to specify ADO objects and the DAO prefix for DAO Connection and Recordset objects. All ADO code examples in this book, except the lightweight ADOR, apply the ADODB prefix. Recordset objects are discussed in Chapter 24.

FIGURE 2.2

A comparison of OLE DB and ADO objects, OLE DB functions, and ADO methods.

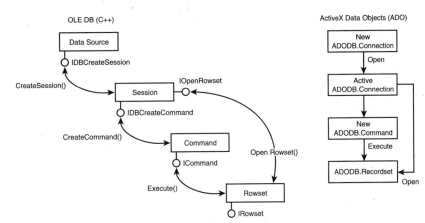

CREATING *ADODB.Recordset*S

The concept of database object independence is new to Visual Basic. The best way of demonstrating this feature is to compare DAO and ADO code to create a Recordset object from an SQL statement. DAO requires successive instantiation of each object in the DAO hierarchy: DBEngine, Workspace, Database, and Recordset, as in the following example:

```
Dim wsName As DAO.Workspace
Dim dbName As DAO.Database
```

```
Dim rsName As DAO.Recordset

Set wsName = DBEngine.Workspaces(0)
Set dbName = wsName.OpenDatabase ("DatabaseName.mdb")
Set rsName = dbName.OpenRecordset ("SQL Statement")
```

The most common approach with ADO is to create one or more independent instances of each object in the Declarations section of a form or module:

```
Private cnnName As New ADODB.Connection
Private cmmName As New ADODB.Command
Private rstName As New ADODB.Recordset
```

> **NOTE**
>
> This book uses cnn as the object type prefix for Connection, cmm for Command, and rst for Recordset. The cmm prefix is used because the cmd prefix traditionally identifies a command button control and the com prefix identifies the MSComm ActiveX control (Microsoft Comm Control 6.0). Prior editions of this book used rsd, rss, and rst to identify Recordset objects of the dynaset, snapshot, and table type, respectively. Although you're likely to find references to DAO.Recordset dynasets and snapshots in the Visual Basic 6.0 documentation, these terms don't apply to ADODB.Recordset objects. See the CursorType property of the ADODB.Recordset object in the "Recordset Properties" section later in this chapter for the CursorType equivalents of dynasets and snapshots.

After the initial declarations, you set the properties of the new object instances and apply methods—Open for Connections and Recordsets, or Execute for Commands—to activate the object. The examples that follow illustrate the independence of top-level ADO members.

> **NOTE**
>
> This chapter assumes familiarity with elementary DAO programming methods and the use of the simple data-bound controls, such as the Data control and the DBGrid control, included with prior versions of Visual Basic.

Opening an ADODB.Recordset Object on an ADODB.Connection with Code

To create a simple project that uses VBA code to open an ADODB.Recordset on an active ADODB.Connection object to the Nwind.mdb sample database, follow these steps:

1. Launch Visual Basic 6.0, if necessary, and open a new Data Project in the default (. . . \VB98) folder.

The Data Project is a new class of Visual Basic applications that automatically adds the required project reference to the Microsoft ActiveX Data Objects 2.0 library and adds to the toolbox the most commonly used controls for ADO-based database front ends. Default `frmDataEnv`, `DataEnvironment1`, and `DataReport1` items appear in the Project window.

2. Add an ADO Data control (ADODC) to the bottom of frmDataEnv. Set the `Name` property of the control to `adcNwind`.

3. Add a DataGrid to the form, set its `Name` property to `dtgNwind` and set its `DataSource` property to `adcNwind`. Set the `AllowAddNew` and `AllowDelete` property values to **True** if you want to test the updatability of the `Recordset`.

4. Add the following code to the Declarations section of the `frmDataEnv` module:

```
Private cnnNwind As New ADODB.Connection
Private rstNwind As New ADODB.Recordset
Private blnHasRun As Boolean
```

5. Add the following code to the `Form_Load` event handler:

```
Private Sub Form_Activate()
    If blnHasRun Then
        Exit Sub
    End If
    Dim strSQL As String

    DoEvents   'Allow the controls to appear

    'Specify the OLE DB provider and open the connection
    cnnNwind.Provider = "Microsoft.Jet.OLEDB.3.51"
    cnnNwind.Open App.Path & "\Nwind.mdb", "Admin"

    strSQL = "SELECT * FROM Customers"
    With rstNwind
        Set .ActiveConnection = cnnNwind
        .CursorType = adOpenKeyset
        .LockType = adLockOptimistic
        .Open strSQL
    End With

    'Connect the ADO Data control and DataGrid to the Recordset
    Set adcNwind.Recordset = rstNwind
    blnHasRun = True
End Sub
```

6. Run the project. Your form appears as shown in Figure 2.3 (adding the form caption is optional).

FIGURE 2.3

A DataGrid
control populated
by an
`ADODB.Record-`
`set` *created with*
code.

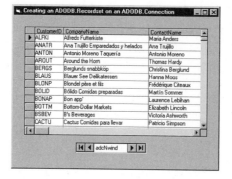

If you set the `AllowAddNew` and `AllowDelete` property values to **True** in preceding step 2, you can scroll to the bottom of the `Recordset`, add a new customer record, and then delete the record you just added. Setting the `CursorType` property value to `adOpenKeyset` and the `LockType` property value to `adLockOptimistic` creates an updatable (editable) `ADODB.Recordset` object. The Microsoft ActiveX Data Objects 2.0 Library defines all constants with the prefix `ad`.

Opening an `ADODB.Recordset` Object from a `DataEnvironment` Object

Visual Basic 6.0 extends the version 5.0 Enterprise Edition's `UserConnection` object for RDO to the `DataEnvironment` object for ADO. The `DataEnvironment` object, which you save as a designer (.dsr) file, lets you use drag-and-drop techniques to populate a form with text boxes bound to an `ADODB.Recordset` object created from an `ADODB.Command` object. To create a form with the Data Environment Designer (DED), follow these steps:

1. Close the preceding project, saving it as **ADONwind.vbp** in a work folder, if you want. (You must copy Nwind.mdb to the work folder to make ADONwind.vbp operational.)

2. Open a new DataProject and double-click the DataEvironment1 item in to open the DataEnvironment window. Right-click Connection1 and choose <u>P</u>roperties to open the Data Link Properties sheet.

> **NOTE**
>
> Data Link is a Microsoft synonym for a `Connection` object. You can store the properties of a `Connection` object in a .dsr file or in a DataLink file (.udl). 7

3. In the default Provider page, select the Microsoft Jet 3.51 OLE DB Provider item from the OLE DB Provider(s) list (see Figure 2.4). Click next to move to the Connection page.

FIGURE 2.4

Specifying a connection name and use of a connection string for a `DataEnvironment` *object.*

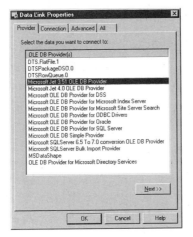

4. Click the builder button to open the Select Access Database dialog and double-click Nwind.mdb.

5. Click the Test button to check your connection (see Figure 2.5) and then click OK to close the Data Link Properties sheet.

FIGURE 2.5

Selecting the data provider, specifying the data source, and testing the connection.

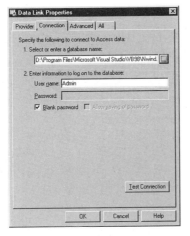

6. In the DataEnvironment1 Properties sheet, change the `Name` property to **envNwind**.

7. In the DataEnvironment window, right-click Connection1, select `Rename`, and change the name of Connection1 to cnnNwind.

8. Right-click the cnnNwind entry and choose Add Command from the pop-up menu to open the Command1 Properties sheet.

9. Change the Command Name to **Customers**, accept the default Database Object option, and select Table from the Database Object list.

   The `cmm` prefix isn't used for the Customers Command name because DED prepends `rs` to the Command Name to identify the `Recordset` generated by the `Command` object.

10. Select Customers from the Object Name list (see Figure 2.6)and then click OK to close the properties sheet.

FIGURE 2.6

Specifying the Command name, Command type, and the database table object name.

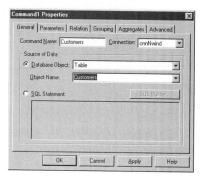

11. Click OK to close the properties sheet and expand the Customers item to display a list of fields of the Customers table (see Figure 2.7).

FIGURE 2.7

A Command *object of the table type added to the DataEnvironment's* Connection *object.*

12. Open `frmDataEnv`; then left-click and drag the Customers item to the form to add a control array of field name labels (`lblFieldLabel(n)`) and individual bound text boxes (`txtFieldName`) to the form.

   Select one of the text boxes and observe that the drag-and drop operation added the `DataField`, `DataMember`, and `DataSource` property values. `DataMember` is a new bound control property that points to the `Command` object. The `DataSource` property value, which ordinarily is the name of a Data control, points to the `DataEnvironment` object.

13. Rename your form to **frmCustomers**, specify frmCustomers as the start-up form and then run the project. The text boxes populate with the values of the first record of the Customers table (see Figure 2.8).

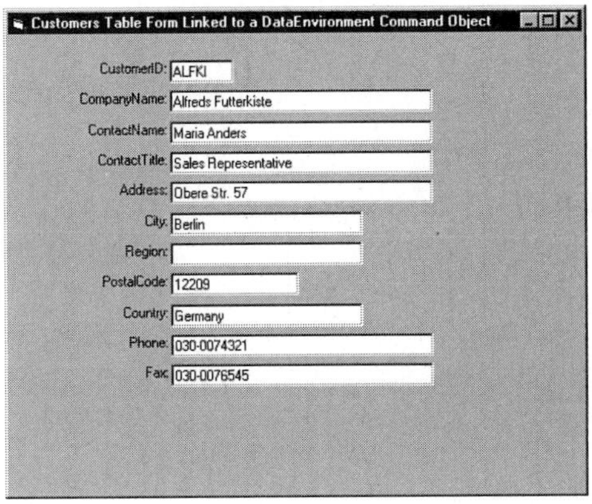

FIGURE 2.8

Field name labels and bound text boxes added by dragging a table-type Command *object from a DataEnvironment to a form.*

When you save the project, you are prompted to save envNwind as a designer (envNwind.dsr) file. The advantage of Data Environment Designer files is that you can reuse your Connection and Command objects in multiple Visual Basic projects. If you later decide to upgrade projects from Jet to a client/server RDBMS, you need only change the properties of the Connection object(s), assuming that you don't include Jet-specific code or use special Jet SQL syntax in the projects.

TIP

To add an existing DataEnvironment designer file to a new project, choose Project, Add File and select the env*Name*.dsr file in the Add File dialog.

The DataEnvironment's Command object is the functional equivalent of a hidden ADO Data control without the navigation features. When bound to form controls, the Command object generates a Recordset object identified as rs*CommandName*. To refer to the Recordset in form-level code, use the following syntax:

```
envDataEnvironmentName.rsCommandName.MethodName
varPropValue = envDataEnvironmentName.rsCommandName.PropertyName
```

As an example, add four record navigation buttons named cmdMoveFirst, cmdMoveNext, cmdMovePrevious, and cmdMoveLast to the form; add Caption property values Move First,

Move <u>N</u>ext, Move <u>P</u>revious, and Move <u>L</u>ast, respectively (see Figure 2.9). The code to position the Recordset's record pointer with the command buttons is

```
Private Sub cmdMoveFirst_Click()
    envNwind.rsCustomers.MoveFirst
End Sub

Private Sub cmdMoveNext_Click()
    If Not envNwind.rsCustomers.EOF Then
        envNwind.rsCustomers.MoveNext
    End If
End Sub

Private Sub cmdMovePrevious_Click()
    If Not envNwind.rsCustomers.BOF Then
        envNwind.rsCustomers.MovePrevious
    End If
End Sub

Private Sub cmdMoveLast_Click()
    envNwind.rsCustomers.MoveLast
End Sub
```

FIGURE 2.9

Adding record navigation buttons to a form bound to a DataEnvironment object.

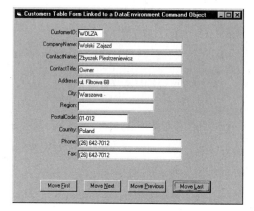

Adding a DataGrid Control Bound to a Command Object

You can choose between bound label/text box combinations and a DataGrid control bound to the DataEnvironment Command object. Follow these steps to add a DataGrid control to the form:

1. Select and delete all the labels and text boxes on the frmCustomers form.
2. Right-click and drag the Customers connection from the envNwind window to the form, which opens a context menu. (You must drag with the right mouse button to choose between bound labels/text boxes and a DataGrid control.)

3. Select <u>D</u>ata Grid to add a default-size bound DataGrid control to the form.

4. Resize the DataGrid control and rename it **dtgCustomers**.

   Observe that the values of the DataMember and DataSource properties are Customers and envNwind, respectively.

5. Run the project and test the effect of the record navigation buttons on the DataGrid control (see Figure 2.10).

FIGURE 2.10

A bound DataGrid control substituted for the label and text box controls of Figure 2.9.

Making Command-based Recordsets Updatable

The default Recordset generated by the DataEnvironment's Command object has client-side, read-only cursor. You can't edit, delete, or add new records to the Customers table in the dtgCustomers DataGrid control. To change the Customers Command object to provide an updatable Recordset for the DataGrid control, follow these steps:

1. Select the dtgCustomers DataGrid control and set the AllowAddNew and AllowDelete property values to **True**.

2. Right-click the Customers Command object in the envNwind window and choose <u>P</u>roperties to open the Customers Properties sheet.

3. Click the Advanced tab and accept the default Cursor Type and Cursor Location, the equivalent of specifying rstNwind.CursorType = adOpenStatic and rstNwind.CursorLocation = adUseClient in the code example earlier in the chapter.

NOTE

Visual Basic 6.0's controls bound to Jet databases are limited to client-side cursors, which use the OLE DB/ADO cursor engine. You can use server-side cursors, which use the Jet engine, to create Recordsets you manipulate with VBA code.

4. Select 3 - Optimistic from the Lock Type list, the equivalent of setting
   `rstNwind.LockType = adLockOptimistic` (see Figure 2.11).

FIGURE 2.11

Setting Command
*object properties to
provide an updata-
ble* Recordset
*object for the
DataGrid control.*

5. Click OK to close the Customer Properties sheet and then run the application.

6. Click the Move Last button to display the tentative append record, marked with an
   asterisk (*).

7. Type a few field values for a new fictitious record (see Figure 2.12) and then click the
   Move Previous button to add the new record to the table.

   Adding a new record requires moving the record pointer to make the addition to the
   table permanent. Until you move the record pointer, the changes you make to the table
   are temporary.

FIGURE 2.12

*Adding a new
record to the table
underlying an
updatable*
Recordset *of the
DataGrid control.*

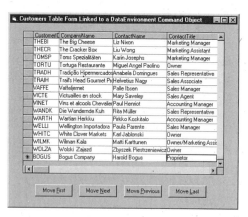

8. Select the record you just added by clicking the record selector button and press Delete to
   remove it from the table.

The preceding code and drag-and-drop examples are intended to familiarize you with the relationship between the high-level ADO members. The remainder of this chapter is devoted to a detailed description of the properties, methods, and events of ADO `Connection`, `Command`, and `Recordset` objects and the dependent ADODB collections, `Properties`, `Errors`, `Parameters`, and `Fields`.

EXPLORING TOP-LEVEL ADO PROPERTIES, METHODS, AND EVENTS

At this point in your ADO learning curve, a detailed list of properties, enumerations of constant values, methods, and events of ADO components might appear premature. However, understanding the capabilities and benefits of ADO requires at least basic familiarity with ADO programming techniques. Despite the power of Visual Basic 6.0's drag-and-drop data binding and database-related wizards, it's very unlikely that "codeless" Visual Basic database front ends will satisfy the requirements of production applications.

DAO objects don't fire events. With Visual Basic 4.0 and RDO 1.0, Microsoft added an event model for `rdoEnvironment`, `rdoConnection`, and `rdoResultset` objects. Visual Basic 5.0's RDO 2.0 increased the granularity of the data-related events, providing developers with much finer control over communication with SQL Server and other client/server RDBMSs. RDO was available only to purchasers of the Enterprise Edition; ADO offers a complete event model in all editions of Visual Basic 6.0.

The Object Browser and ADO

The Object Browser is the most useful tool for becoming acquainted with the properties, methods, and events of ADODB objects. To use the Object Browser with ADODB, follow these steps:

1. Open a new Data Project, which automatically adds a reference to the Microsoft ActiveX Data Objects 2.0 Library to the project.

2. Press F2 to open the Object Browser.

3. Select ADODB in the library (upper) list.

4. Select one of the top-level components, such as `Connection`, in the Classes (left) pane.

5. Select a property, event, or method, such as `Open`, in the Members of 'ObjectName' (right) pane. A short-form version of the syntax for the selected method or event appears in Object Browser's lower pane (see Figure 2.13).

FIGURE 2.13

*Object Browser
displaying the syn-
tax for the* Open
method of the
ADODB.Connec-
tion *object.*

ADO type libraries also include *enumerations* (lists) of numeric (usually **Long**) constant values
with an ad prefix. These constant enumerations are specific to one or more properties. Figure
2.14 shows Object Browser displaying the members of the ConnectModeEnum enumeration for
the **Mode** property of an ADODB.Connection object. The lower pane displays the **Long** value of
the constant.

FIGURE 2.14

*Object Browser
displaying the*
ConnectMod-
eEnum *list of con-
stants for the*
ADODB.Connec-
tion *object's* Mode
property.

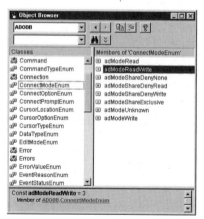

TIP

You can substitute the numeric value of enumerated constants for the constant name in Visual Basic code, but doing so isn't considered a good programming practice. Numeric values of the constants might change in subsequent
ADO versions, causing unexpected results when upgrading applications to a
new ADO release.

The `ADODB.Connection` Object

The `Connection` object is the primary top-level ADO component. You must successfully open a `Connection` object to a data source before you can use associated `Command` or `Recordset` objects.

Connection Properties

Table 2.1 lists the names and descriptions of the properties of the `ADODB.Connection` object. In addition to the properties listed in Table 2.1, the `Connection` object has a collection of provider-specific properties described in "The `Properties` collection of the `Connection` Object" section later in this chapter.

TABLE 2.1 PROPERTIES OF THE `ADODB.Connection` OBJECT

Property Name	Data Type and Purpose
Attributes	A **Long** read/write value that specifies use of retaining transactions by the sum of two constant values. The adXactCommitRetaining constant starts a new transaction when calling the CommitTrans method; adXactAbortRetaining starts a new transaction when calling the RollbackTrans method. The default value is 0, don't use retaining transactions.
CommandTimeout	A **Long** read/write value that determines the time in seconds before terminating an Execute call against an associated Command object. The default value is 30 seconds.
ConnectionString	A **String** read/write variable that supplies specific information required by a data or service provider to open a connection to the data source.
ConnectionTimeout	A **Long** read/write value that determines the number of seconds before terminating an unsuccessful Connection.Open method call. The default value is 15 seconds.
CursorLocation	A **Long** read/write value that determines whether the client-side (adUseClient) or the server-side (adUseServer) cursor engine is used. The default is adUseServer.
DefaultDatabase	A **String** read/write variable that specifies the name of the database to use if not specified in the ConnectionString. For SQL Server examples, the value often is pubs.

continues

TABLE 2.1   CONTINUED

Property Name	Data Type and Purpose
IsolationLevel	A **Long** read/write value that determines the behavior or transactions that interact with other simultaneous transactions (see Table 2.2).
Mode	A **Long** value that determines read and write permissions for the Connection (see Table 2.3).
Provider	A **String** read/write value that specifies the name of the OLE DB data or service provider if not specified in the ConnectionString. The default value is MSDASQL, the Microsoft OLE DB Provider for ODBC. The most common provider used in the early chapters of this book is Microsoft.Jet.OLEDB.3.51, more commonly known by its code name, Jolt.
State	A **Long** read-only value that specifies whether the connection is open, closed, or in an intermediate state (see Table 2.4).
Version	A **String** read-only value that returns the ADO version number.

NOTE

Most property values identified in Table 2.1 as being read/write are writable only when the connection is in the closed state.

The ability to specify the transaction isolation level applies only when you use the BeginTrans . . . CommitTrans . . . RollbackTrans methods (see Table 2.5) to define a transaction on a Connection object. If multiple database users simultaneously execute transactions, your application must specify how your application responds to other transactions in process. Table 2.2 lists the options for the degree of your application's isolation from other simultaneous transactions. Chapter 19, "Processing Transactions and Bulk Operations," Chapter 20, "Porting Access OLTP Applications to Visual Basic 6.0," and Chapter 26, "Taking Advantage of Microsoft Transaction Server 2.0," deal with ADO transactions.

> **NOTE**
>
> Using the `CreateWorkspace` method to run multiple transactions within individual `Workspace` objects provides transaction isolation in DAO. Similarly, RDO uses individual `rdoEnvironment` objects for transaction isolation. ADO doesn't provide the equivalent of `Workspace` or `rdoEnvironment` objects, so the degree of transaction isolation must be specified on the top-level `Connection` object.

TABLE 2.2 CONSTANT ENUMERATION FOR THE `IsolationLevel` PROPERTY

IsolationLevelEnum	*Description*
`adXactCursorStability`	Allows reading only of committed changes in other transactions (default value).
`adXactBrowse`	Allows reading of uncommitted changes in other transactions
`adXactChaos`	The transaction won't overwrite changes made to transaction(s) at a higher isolation level.
`adXactIsolated`	All transactions are independent of (isolated from) other transactions.
`adXactReadCommitted`	Same as `adXactCursorStability`.
`adXactReadUncommitted`	Same as `adXactBrowse`.
`adXactRepeatableRead`	Prohibits reading changes in other transactions.
`adXactSerializable`	Same as `adXactIsolated`.
`adXactUnspecified`	The transaction level of the provider can't be determined

> **NOTE**
>
> Enumeration tables in this book list the default value first, followed by the remaining constants in alphabetical order.

Unless you have a specific reason to specify a particular `ADODB.Connection.Mode` value, the default `adModeUnknown` is adequate. The Jet OLE DB provider defaults to `adModeShareDenyNone`. Table 2.3 lists all the constants for the `Mode` property. You often can improve performance of client/server decision-support applications by opening the connection as read only (`adModeRead`). Modifying the structure of a database with SQL's Data Definition Language (DDL) usually requires exclusive access to the database (`adModeShareExclusive`).

TABLE 2.3 CONSTANT ENUMERATION FOR THE Mode PROPERTY

ConnectModeEnum	*Description*
adModeUnknown	No connection permissions have been set on the data source (default value).
adModeRead	Connect with read-only permission.
adModeReadWrite	Connect with read/write permissions.
adModeShareDenyNone	Don't deny other users read or write access.
adModeShareDenyRead	Deny others permission to open a read connection to the data source.
adModeShareDenyWrite	Deny others permission to open a write connection to the data source.
adModeShareExclusive	Open the data source for exclusive use.
adModeWrite	Connect with write-only permission.

It's common to open and close Connections as needed to reduce the connection load on the database. (Each open connection to a client/server database consumes a block of memory.) In many cases, you must test whether the Connection object is open or closed before applying the Close or Open method, respectively, or changing Connection property values. Table 2.4 lists the constants that return the state of the Connection object. These constants also are applicable to the State property of the Command and Recordset objects.

TABLE 2.4 CONSTANT ENUMERATION FOR THE State PROPERTY

ObjectStateEnum	*Description*
adStateClosed	The Connection (or other object) is closed (default value).
adStateConnecting	A connection to the data source is in progress.
adStateExecuting	The Execute method of a Connection or Command object has been called.
adStateFetching	Rows are returning to a Recordset object.
adStateOpen	The Connection (or other object) is open (active).

Errors Collection and Error Objects

Figure 2.15 illustrates the relationship between top-level ADO components and their collections. The dependent Errors collection is a property of the Connection object and, if errors are encountered with any operation on the connection, contains one or more Error objects. The

`Errors` collection has one property, `Count`, which you test to determine whether an error has occurred after executing a method call on `Connection` objects as well as on `Command` and `Recordset` objects.

FIGURE 2.15

The `Connection`, `Command`, *and* `Recordset` *objects with their associated collections.*

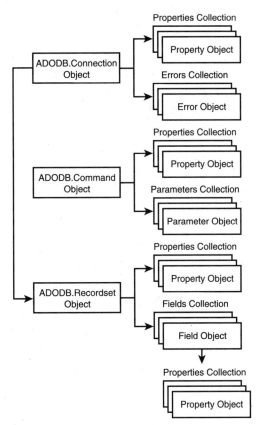

The `Errors` collection has two methods, `Clear` and `Item`. The `Clear` method deletes all current `Error` objects in the collection, resetting the value of `Count` to `0`. The `Item` method, which is the default method of the `Errors` and other collections, returns an object reference (pointer) to an `Error` object. The syntax for explicit and default use of the `Item` method is

```
Set errName = cnnName.Errors.Index({strName|intIndex})
Set errName = cnnName.Errors({strName|intIndex})
```

The `Error` object has the seven read-only properties listed in Table 2.5. `Error` objects have no methods or events. The `InfoMessage` event of the `Connection` object, described in the "Connection Events" section later in this chapter, fires when an `Error` object is added to the `Errors` collection and supplies a pointer to the newly added `Error` object.

TABLE 2.5 PROPERTY NAMES AND DESCRIPTIONS OF THE Error OBJECT

Property Name	Description
Description	A **String** value containing a brief text description of the error.
HelpContext	A **Long** value specifying the error's context ID in a Windows Help file.
HelpFile	A **String** value specifying the full path to and name of the Windows Help file, usually for the data provider.
NativeError	A **Long** value specifying a provider-specific error code.
Number	A **Long** value specifying the index of the Error in the Errors collection.
Source	A **String** value containing the name of the object that generated the error, ADODB.*ObjectName* for ADO errors.
SQLState	A **String** value (SQLSTATE) containing a five-letter code specified by the ANSI/ISO SQL-92 standard, consisting of two characters specifying Condition, followed by three characters for Subcondition.

> **NOTE**
>
> Unfortunately, not all RDBMS vendors implement SQLSTATE in the same way. If you test the SQLSTATE property value, make sure to follow the vendor-specific specifications for Condition and Subcondition values.

Listing 2.1 is an example of code to open a Connection (cnnNwind) and a Recordset (rstCusts) with conventional error handling; rstCusts supplies the Recordset property of an ADO Data control (adcCusts), which binds a DataGrid control (dtgCusts). The "Non-existent" table name generates a "Syntax error in FROM clause" error in the Debug window.

LISTING 2.1 VBA CODE TO WRITE Error PROPERTIES TO THE DEBUG WINDOW

```
Private Sub Form_Activate
    Dim cnnNwind As New ADODB.Connection
    Dim rstCusts As New ADODB.RecordSet

    On Error GoTo CatchErrors
    cnnNwind.Provider = "Microsoft.Jet.OLEDB.3.51"
    cnnNwind.Open App.Path & "\Nwind.mdb", "Admin"
    With rstCusts
        Set .ActiveConnection = cnnNwind
        .CursorType = adOpenKeyset
```

```
        .LockType = adLockBatchOptimistic
        .Open "SELECT * FROM Non-existent"
    End With
    Set adcCusts.Recordset = rstCusts
    Exit Sub

CatchErrors:
    Dim colErrors As Errors
    Dim errNwind As Error
    Set colErrors = cnnNwind.Errors
    For Each errNwind In colErrors
        Debug.Print "Description: " & errNwind.Description
        Debug.Print "Native Error: " & errNwind.NativeError; ""
        Debug.Print "SQL State:   " & errNwind.SQLState
        Debug.Print vbCrLf
    Next errNwind
    Set colErrors = Nothing
    Set errNwind = Nothing
    Set rstCusts = Nothing
    Set cnnNwind = Nothing
    Exit Sub
End Sub
```

Connection Methods

Table 2.6 lists the methods of the `ADODB.Connection` object. Only the `Execute`, `Open`, and `OpenSchema` methods accept argument values. The early chapters of this book primarily use the `Open` and `Close` methods. The `OpenSchema` method is of interest primarily for creating database diagrams, data transformation for data warehouses and marts, and online analytical processing (OLAP) applications.

TABLE 2.6   METHODS OF THE `ADODB.Connection` OBJECT

Method	*Description*
BeginTrans	Initiates a transaction; must be followed by `CommitTrans` and/or `RollbackTrans`.
Close	Closes the connection.
CommitTrans	Commits a transaction, making changes to the data source permanent. (Requires a prior call to the `BeginTrans` method.)
Execute	Returns a forward-only `Recordset` object from a SELECT SQL statement. Also used to execute statements that don't return `Recordsets`, such as INSERT, UPDATE, and DELETE queries or DDL statements.
Open	Opens a connection based on a connection string.

continues

TABLE 2.6 CONTINUED

Method	Description
OpenSchema	Returns a Recordset object that provides information on the structure of the data source (metadata).
RollbackTrans	Cancels a transaction, reversing any temporary changes made to the data source. (Requires a prior call to the BeginTrans method.)

The syntax of the Connection.Execute method, which returns a reference to an ADODB.Recordset object is

```
Set rstName = cnnName.Execute (strCommand, [lngRowsAffected[, lngOptions]])
```

Alternatively, you can use named arguments for all ADO methods. Named arguments, however, require considerably more typing than conventional comma-separated argument syntax. The named argument equivalent of the preceding **Set** statement is

```
Set rstName = cnnName.Execute (Command:=strCommand, _
    RowsAffected:=lngRowsAffected, Options:=lngOptions)
```

> **NOTE**
>
> This book prefixes argument names with a two- or three-character prefix denoting their data type, in accordance with "The Leszynski Naming Conventions for Microsoft Visual Basic," by Stan Leszynski. Use the argument name, without the lowercase prefix, to identify the named argument.

If strCommand doesn't return a Recordset, the syntax is

```
cnnName.Execute strCommand, [lngRowsAffected[, lngOptions]]
```

The value of strCommand can be an SQL statement, a table name, the name of a stored procedure, or an arbitrary text string acceptable to the data provider. For best performance, specify a value for the lngOptions argument (see Table 2.7) so the provider doesn't need to interpret the statement to determine its type. The optional lngRowsAffected argument returns the number of rows affected by an INSERT, UPDATE, or DELETE query; these types of queries return a closed Recordset object. A SELECT query returns 0 to lngRowsAffected and an open, forward-only Recordset with 0 or more rows.

> **NOTE**
>
> Forward-only `Recordset` objects, created by what Microsoft calls a "firehose cursor," provide the best performance and minimum network traffic in a client/server environment. However, forward-only `Recordsets` are limited to manipulation by VBA code. If you set the `Recordset` property of an ADO Data control to a forward-only `Recordset`, controls bound to the ADO Data control won't display field values.

TABLE 2.7 CONSTANT ENUMERATION FOR THE `lngOptions` ARGUMENT OF THE `Execute` METHOD

CommandTypeEnum	*Description*
`adCmdUnknown`	The type of command isn't specified (default). The data provider determines the syntax of the command.
`adCmdFile`	The command is the name of a file in a format appropriate to the object type.
`adCmdStoredProc`	The command is the name of a stored procedure.
`adCmdTable`	The command is a table name, generating an internal `SELECT * FROM` *TableName* query.
adCmdTableDirect	The command is a table name, retrieving rows directly from the table
`adCmdText`	The command is an SQL statement.

The syntax of the `Open` method is

```
cnnName.Open [strConnect[, strUID[, strPwd]]]
```

You can include the property values required to open a `Connection` in the `strConnect` argument, as in the following example for a DSN-less connection to the SQL Server pubs sample database using the MSDASQL OLE DB for ODBC provider:

```
strConnect = "provider=MSDASQL;driver={SQL Server};server=OAKLEAF0;" & _
    "uid=sa;pwd=;database=pubs"
```

> **NOTE**
>
> Technically, the `provider=MSDASQL` element of the preceding connection string isn't required, because MSDASQL is the default OLE DB provider for ADO. However, a good programming practice is to explicitly identify the provider, either within the connection string or as the value of the `Provider` property.

Alternatively, the connection string values may be preassigned to the `Connection`'s `Provider` and `ConnectionString` properties. The following example is for a connection to Visual Basic 6.0's unsecured Nwind.mdb sample database:

```
With cnnNwind
    .Provider = "Microsoft.Jet.OLEDB.3.51"
    .ConnectionString = App.Path & "\Nwind.mdb"
    .Open
End With
```

In this case, all the information required to open a connection to Nwind.mdb is provided as property values, so the `Open` method needs no argument values.

> **NOTE**
>
> ADO is relatively new, so developers use a variety of programming conventions for opening `Connection`, `Command`, and `Recordset` objects. Most of the examples in this book preset property values to minimize the length of the `strConnect` argument of the `Open` method. The use of property values, instead of long `strConnect` argument values, makes ADO code more readable.

If you're creating a data dictionary or designing a generic query processor, the `OpenSchema` method is likely to be of interest to you. Otherwise, you might wish to skip the details of the `OpenSchema` method, which is included here for completeness. Schema information is called *metadata*, data that describes the structure of data.

The `OpenSchema` method uses the following syntax to open a forward-only `Recordset` object over an active connection, `cnnName`:

```
Set rstName = cnnName.OpenSchema (lngQueryType[, lngCriteria[, guidSchemaID]])
```

The `lngQueryType` argument specifies the type of information delivered to the `Recordset`, which is likely to be more than you want to know about the schema. As an example, the forward-only `Recordset` returned by setting `lngQueryType` to the `adSchemaColumns` constant has 29 columns. Figure 2.16 shows a part of the schema `Recordset` for the Nwind.mdb database upsized to SQL Server 7.0. You can restrict the number of columns returned by providing a constant value for the optional `lngCriteria` argument. Table 2.8 lists the constants for the `lngQueryType` and `lngCriteria` arguments. The `lngCriteria` constant names are defined by OLE DB and use C/C++ naming convention; thus these constant names are upper case and don't use the ad prefix. You can combine criteria constants by addition to supply additional columns, as follows:

```
lngCriteria = TABLE_SCHEMA + TABLE_NAME + COLUMN_NAME
```

FIGURE 2.16

An MSFlexGrid control displaying column information for each table in the Nwind.mdb database upsized to SQL Server 7.0.

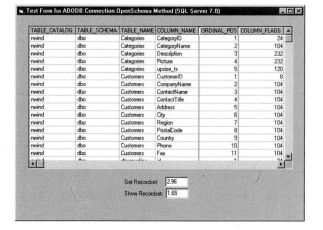

NOTE

The Access 97 Upsizing Wizard (Wzcs97.mda) doesn't work with SQL Server 7.0. To use the Upsizing Wizard, you must create an SQL Server 6.5 database for upsizing and then upgrade the version 6.5 database to SQL Server 7.0.

TABLE 2.8 CONSTANT ENUMERATION FOR THE lngQueryType AND CONSTANT VALUES FOR THE lngCriteria ARGUMENTS OF THE OpenSchema METHOD

SchemaEnum	*Criteria Constants*
adSchemaAsserts	CONSTRAINT_CATALOG
	CONSTRAINT_SCHEMA
	CONSTRAINT_NAME
adSchemaCatalogs	CATALOG_NAME
adSchemaCharacterSets	CHARACTER_SET_CATALOG
	CHARACTER_SET_SCHEMA
	CHARACTER_SET_NAME
adSchemaCheckConstraints	CONSTRAINT_CATALOG
	CONSTRAINT_SCHEMA
	CONSTRAINT_NAME
adSchemaCollations	COLLATION_CATALOG
	COLLATION_SCHEMA
	COLLATION_NAME

continues

TABLE 2.8 CONTINUED

SchemaEnum	Criteria Constants
adSchemaColumnDomainUsage	DOMAIN_CATALOG
	DOMAIN_SCHEMA
	DOMAIN_NAME
	COLUMN_NAME
adSchemaColumnPrivileges	TABLE_CATALOG
	TABLE_SCHEMA
	TABLE_NAME
	COLUMN_NAME
	GRANTOR
	GRANTEE
adSchemaColumns	TABLE_CATALOG
	TABLE_SCHEMA
	TABLE_NAME
	COLUMN_NAME
adSchemaConstraintColumnUsage	TABLE_CATALOG
	TABLE_SCHEMA
	TABLE_NAME
	COLUMN_NAME
adSchemaConstraintTableUsage	TABLE_CATALOG
	TABLE_SCHEMA
	TABLE_NAME
adSchemaForeignKeys	PK_TABLE_CATALOG
	PK_TABLE_SCHEMA
	PK_TABLE_NAME
	FK_TABLE_CATALOG
	FK_TABLE_SCHEMA
	FK_TABLE_NAME
adSchemaIndexes	TABLE_CATALOG
	TABLE_SCHEMA
	INDEX_NAME
	TYPE
	TABLE_NAME
adSchemaKeyColumnUsage	CONSTRAINT_CATALOG
	CONSTRAINT_SCHEMA
	CONSTRAINT_NAME
	TABLE_CATALOG
	TABLE_SCHEMA
	TABLE_NAME
	COLUMN_NAME

SchemaEnum	Criteria Constants
adSchemaPrimaryKeys	PK_TABLE_CATALOG
	PK_TABLE_SCHEMA
	PK_TABLE_NAME
adSchemaProcedureColumns	PROCEDURE_CATALOG
	PROCEDURE_SCHEMA
	PROCEDURE_NAME
	COLUMN_NAME
adSchemaProcedureParameters	PROCEDURE_CATALOG
	PROCEDURE_SCHEMA
	PROCEDURE_NAME
	PARAMTER_NAME
adSchemaProcedures	PROCEDURE_CATALOG
	PROCEDURE_SCHEMA
	PROCEDURE_NAME
	PARAMTER_TYPE
adSchemaProviderSpecific	See following note
adSchemaProviderTypes	DATA_TYPE
	BEST_MATCH
adSchemaReferentialConstraints	CONSTRAINT_CATALOG
	CONSTRAINT_SCHEMA
	CONSTRAINT_NAME
adSchemaSchemata	CATALOG_NAME
	SCHEMA_NAME
	SCHEMA_OWNER
adSchemaSQLLanguages	None
adSchemaStatistics	TABLE_CATALOG
	TABLE_SCHEMA
	TABLE_NAME
adSchemaTableConstraints	CONSTRAINT_CATALOG
	CONSTRAINT_SCHEMA
	CONSTRAINT_NAME
	TABLE_CATALOG
	TABLE_SCHEMA
	TABLE_NAME
	CONSTRAINT_TYPE
adSchemaTablePrivileges	TABLE_CATALOG
	TABLE_SCHEMA
	TABLE_NAME
	GRANTOR
	GRANTEE

2

UNDERSTANDING
OLE DB AND
DATA ACCESS

continues

TABLE 2.8 CONTINUED

SchemaEnum	Criteria Constants
adSchemaTables	TABLE_CATALOG
	TABLE_SCHEMA
	TABLE_NAME
	TABLE_TYPE
adSchemaTranslations	TRANSLATION_CATALOG
	TRANSLATION_SCHEMA
	TRANSLATION_NAME
adSchemaUsagePrivileges	OBJECT_CATALOG
	OBJECT_SCHEMA
	OBJECT_NAME
	OBJECT_TYPE
	GRANTOR
	GRANTEE
adSchemaViewColumnUsage	VIEW_CATALOG
	VIEW_SCHEMA
	VIEW_NAME
adSchemaViewTableUsage	VIEW_CATALOG
	VIEW_SCHEMA
	VIEW_NAME
adSchemaViews	TABLE_CATALOG
	TABLE_SCHEMA
	TABLE_NAME

NOTE

Third-party software developers can specify a provider-specific schema in lieu of conforming to the OLE DB 1.5+ specification. To use a provider-specific schema, assign adSchemaProviderSpecific as the lng*QueryType* argument value and supply the globally unique identifier (GUID) of the schema as the value of the guid*SchemaID* argument.

Connection Events

Events are useful for trapping errors, eliminating the need to poll the values of properties, such as State, and performing asynchronous database operations. Microsoft modeled ADO's Connection events on a combination of the event models for RDO 2.0's rdoEngine, rdoEnvironment, and rdoConnection objects. (The ADODB.Connection object combines the functionality of these three RDO objects.) To expose the ADODB.Connection events to your application, you must use the `WithEvents` reserved word (without **New**) to declare the `ADODB.Connection` object in the General Declarations section of a class or form module and then use a **Set** statement with **New** to create an instance of the object, as shown in following example:

```
Private WithEvents cnnName As ADODB.Connection

Private Sub Form_Load
   Set cnnName = New ADODB.Connection
   ...
   Code using the Connection object
   ...
   cnnName.Close
End Sub
```

The preceding syntax is required for most Automation objects that *source* (expose) events. Event-handling subprocedures for Automation events often are called *event sinks*. Source and sink terminology derives from the early days of transistors.

Table 2.9 lists the events that appear in the Procedures list of the code-editing window for the *cnnName* Connection object and a description of when the events fire.

TABLE 2.9   EVENTS FIRED BY THE ADODB.Connection OBJECT

Event Name	*When Fired*
BeginTransComplete	After the `BeginTrans` method executes
CommitTransComplete	After the `CommitTrans` method executes
ConnectComplete	After a `Connection` to the data source succeeds
Disconnect	After a `Connection` is closed
ExecuteComplete	On completion of the `Connection.Execute` or `Command.Execute` method call
InfoMessage	When an `Error` object is added to the `ADODB.Connection.Errors` collection
RollbackTransComplete	After the `RollbackTrans` method executes
WillConnect	On calling the `Connection.Open` method
WillExecute	On calling the `Connection.Execute` or `Command.Execute` method

2

UNDERSTANDING
OLE DB AND
DATA ACCESS

> **NOTE**
>
> The `Command` object doesn't fire events. If you attempt to declare **Private WithEvents** *cmmName* **As** `ADODB.Command`, you receive a compile error, "Object Does Not Source Automation Events." The `Connection` object sources events for `Command` objects.

With the exception of the `CommitTransComplete` and `RollbackTransComplete` events, each event of the `ADODB.Connection` object has a slightly different subprocedure headers:

```
Private Sub cnnName_BeginTransComplete _
  (ByVal TransactionLevel As Long, _
   ByVal pError As ADODB.Error, _
        adStatus As ADODB.EventStatusEnum, _
   ByVal pConnection As ADODB.Connection)

Private Sub cnnName_CommitTransComplete _
  (ByVal pError As ADODB.Error, _
        adStatus As ADODB.EventStatusEnum, _
   ByVal pConnection As ADODB.Connection)

Private Sub cnnName_ConnectComplete _
  (ByVal pError As ADODB.Error, _
        adStatus As ADODB.EventStatusEnum, _
   ByVal pConnection As ADODB.Connection)

Private Sub cnnName_Disconnect _
        (adStatus As ADODB.EventStatusEnum, _
   ByVal pConnection As ADODB.Connection)

Private Sub cnnName_ExecuteComplete _
  (ByVal RecordsAffected As Long, _
   ByVal pError As ADODB.Error, _
        adStatus As ADODB.EventStatusEnum, _
   ByVal pCommand As ADODB.Command, _
   ByVal pRecordset As ADODB.Recordset, _
   ByVal pConnection As ADODB.Connection)

Private Sub cnnName_InfoMessage _
  (ByVal pError As ADODB.Error, _
        adStatus As ADODB.EventStatusEnum, _
   ByVal pConnection As ADODB.Connection)

Private Sub cnnName_RollbackTransComplete _
  (ByVal pError As ADODB.Error, _
        adStatus As ADODB.EventStatusEnum, _
   ByVal pConnection As ADODB.Connection)

Private Sub cnnName_WillConnect _
        (ConnectionString As String, _
         UserID As String, _
         Password As String, _
         Options As Long, _
         adStatus As ADODB.EventStatusEnum, _
   ByVal pConnection As ADODB.Connection)

Private Sub cnnName_WillExecute _
        (Source As String, _
```

```
        CursorType As ADODB.CursorTypeEnum, _
        LockType As ADODB.LockTypeEnum, _
        Options As Long, _
        adStatus As ADODB.EventStatusEnum, _
ByVal pCommand As ADODB.Command, _
ByVal pRecordset As ADODB.Recordset, _
ByVal pConnection As ADODB.Connection)
```

In the preceding examples, the **ByVal** reserved word identifies read-only property values, such as TransactionLevel, or objects dependent on the Connection object, such as Command and Recordset objects. Arguments prefixed by p are pointers (references) to top-level objects (pConnection, pCommand, and pRecordset) or members of collections (pError).

Table 2.10 lists the names and descriptions of the constant values for the adStatus parameter. Use event-handling code to test the value of the parameter to determine the success or reason for failure of the operation that fires the event.

TABLE 2.10 CONSTANT VALUES FOR THE adStatus PARAMETER OF ADODB EVENT-HANDLING SUBPROCEDURES

EventStatusEnum	*Description*
adStatusCancel	The operation was canceled by the user.
adStatusCantDeny	The operation was unable to deny access by other users to the data source.
adStatusErrorsOccurred	The operation resulted in errors that appear as member(s) of the Errors collection.
adStatusOK	The operation succeeded.
asStatusUnwantedEvent	An unanticipated event fired during the operation.

NOTE

Relatively few developers currently use event-handling code in ordinary database front ends. DAO, which offers no event model, dominates today's spectrum of Windows data access techniques. ADO's event model initially will be of primary interest to developers migrating from RDO to ADO. Developers of data warehousing and OLAP applications, which often involve very long-running queries, are most likely to use events in conjunction with asynchronous query operations.

The ADODB.Command Object

The Command object is analogous to RDO's rdoQuery object. The primary purpose of the Command object is to execute parameterized stored procedures, either in the form of temporary prepared statements or persistent, precompiled SQL statements. Command objects also are useful when you want to persist (store) one or more queries for multiple execution on the same Connection. When creating Recordsets, an efficient approach is to bypass the Command object and use the Recordset.Open method, described in the "Recordset Methods" section later in this chapter.

▶ **See** "Hierarchical Recordsets," p. **167**

Command Properties

The Command object has relatively few properties, many of which duplicate those of the Connection object. Table 2.11 lists the names and descriptions of the Command object's properties. Like the Connection object, the Command object has its own provider-specific Properties collection, described in "Properties Collection of the Command Object" section later in this chapter.

TABLE 2.11   PROPERTIES OF THE Command OBJECT

Property Name	Description
ActiveConnection	A pointer to the Connection object associated with the Command. Use **Set** cmm*Name*.ActiveConnection = cnn*Name* for an existing open Connection. Alternatively, you can use a valid connection string to create a new connection without associating a named Connection object. The default value is **Null**.
CommandText	A **String** read/write value that specifies an SQL statement, table name, stored procedure name, or an arbitrary string acceptable to the provider for the ActiveConnection. The value of the CommandType property determines the format of the CommandText value. The default value is an empty string, " ".
CommandTimeout	A **Long** read/write value that determines the time in seconds before terminating an Command.Execute call. This value overrides the Connection.CommandTimeout setting. The default value is **30** seconds.
CommandType	A **Long** read/write value that specifies how the data provider interprets the value of the CommandText property. (CommandType is the equivalent of the optional lng*CommandType* argument of the Connection.Execute method, described earlier in the chapter (refer to Table 2.7). The default value is adCmdUnknown.

Property Name	Description
Name	A **String** read/write value specifying the name of the command, such as cmmNwind.
Prepared	A **Boolean** read/write value that determines whether the data source compiles the CommandText SQL statement as a *prepared statement* (a temporary stored procedure). The prepared statement exists only for the lifetime of the Command's ActiveConnection. Many client/server RDBMSs, including Microsoft SQL Server, support prepared statements. If the data source doesn't support prepared statements, setting Prepared to **True** results in a trappable error.
State	A **Long** read/write value specifying the status of the Command. Refer to Table 2.5 for ObjectStateEnum constant values.

2

UNDERSTANDING
OLE DB AND
DATA ACCESS

> **TIP**
>
> Always set the CommandType property to the appropriate adCmd... constant value. If you accept the default adCmdUnknown value, the data provider must test the value of CommandText to determine if it is the name of a stored procedure, a table, or an SQL statement before executing the query. If the targeted database contains a large number of objects, testing the CommandText value for each Command object you execute can significantly reduce performance.

> **TIP**
>
> The initial execution of a prepared statement often is slower than for a conventional SQL query because some data sources must compile, rather than interpret, the statement. Thus you should limit use of prepared statements to parameterized queries in which the query is executed multiple times with differing parameter values.

Parameters **Collection**

To supply and accept parameter values, the Command object uses the Parameters collection, which is analogous to the rdoParameters collection of the rdoQuery object and similar to the DAO and ODBCDirect Parameters collections. ADODB.Parameters is independent of its parent, ADODB.Command, but you must associate the Parameters collection with a Command object before defining or using Parameter objects.

> **NOTE**
>
> The ADODB.Command object greatly simplifies the arcane ODBC escape syntax used by ODBCDirect and RDO to call parameterized stored procedures. As an example, to call a stored procedure having two input parameters and a return value, the SQL property of an ODBCDirect QueryDef or RDO rdoQuery object is { ? = call sp_*Name* (?, ?) }, where the first ? is the return value and the remaining two ?s represent the two input parameters. You must predeclare an ODBCDirect Parameter or rdoParameter object to accept or supply each of the parameter values. ADO enables you to specify cmm*Name*.CommandText = sp_*Name* and automatically obtains the properties (except Value for input parameters) of each Parameter object for you.

The Parameters collection has a single read-only **Long** property, Count, and the methods listed in Table 2.12. The syntax for the Count property is

lng*NumParms* = cmm*Name*.Parameters.Count

TABLE 2.12 METHOD NAMES, DESCRIPTIONS, AND CALLING SYNTAX FOR THE Parameters COLLECTION

Method Name	*Description and VBA Calling Syntax*
Append	Appends a Parameter object created by the cmm*Name*.CreateParameter method, described in the next section, to the collection. The calling syntax is Parameters.Append prm*Name*.
Delete	Deletes a Parameter object from the collection. The calling syntax is cmm*Name*.Parameters.Delete {str*Name*¦int*Index*}, where str*Name* is the name of the Parameter or int*Index* is the 0-based ordinal position (index) of the Parameter in the collection.
Item	Returns an object reference to a Parameter. The calling syntax is **Set** prm*Name* = cmm*Name*.Parameters.Index({str*Name*¦int*Index*}).
Refresh	Retrieves the properties of the current set of parameters for the stored procedure or query specified as the value of the CommandText property. The calling syntax is cmm*Name*.Parameters.Refresh. If you don't specify your own members of the Parameters collection with the CreateParameter method, accessing any member of the Parameters collection automatically calls the Refresh method. If you apply the Refresh method to a data source that doesn't support stored procedures, prepared statements, or parameterized queries, the Parameters collection is empty (cmm*Name*.Parameters.Count = 0).

> **NOTE**
>
> You gain a performance improvement for the initial execution of your stored procedure or query if you use the `cmmName.CreateParameter` method to predefine the required `Parameter` objects. The `Refresh` method makes a round-trip to the server to retrieve the properties of each `Parameter`.

Parameter **Object**

One `Parameter` object must exist in the `Parameters` collection for each parameter of the stored procedure, prepared statement, or query. Table 2.13 lists the property names and descriptions of the `Parameter` object. The syntax for getting and setting `Parameter` property values is

typPropValue = cmm*Name*.Parameters({str*Name*¦lng*Index*}).*PropertyName*

cmm*Name*.Parameters({str*Name*¦lng*Index*}).*PropertyName* = *typPropValue*

You don't need to use the `Index` property of the `Parameters` collection; `Index` is the default property of `Parameters`.

TABLE 2.13 PROPERTY NAMES AND DESCRIPTIONS FOR Parameter OBJECTS

Property Name	Description
Attributes	A **Long** read/write value representing the sum of the adParam... constants listed in Table 2.14.
Direction	A **Long** read/write value representing one of the adParam... constants listed in Table 2.15.
Name	A **String** read/write value containing the name of the `Parameter` object, such as prm*StartDate*. The name of the `Parameter` object need not (and usually does not) correspond to the name of the corresponding parameter variable of the stored procedure. After the `Parameter` is appended to the `Parameters` collection, the `Name` property value is read-only.
NumericScale	A **Byte** read/write value specifying the number of decimal places for numeric values.
Precision	A **Byte** read/write value specifying the total number of digits (including decimal digits) for numeric values.
Size	A **Long** read/write value specifying the maximum length of variable-length data types supplied as the `Value` property. You must set the `Size` property value before setting the `Value` property to variable-length data.

continues

TABLE 2.13 CONTINUED

Property Name	Description
Type	A **Long** read/write value representing a valid OLE DB 1.5+ data type, as listed in Table 2.16.
Value	The value of the parameter having a data type corresponding to the value of the Type property.

TABLE 2.14 CONSTANT VALUES FOR THE Attributes PROPERTY OF THE Parameter OBJECT

ParameterAttributesEnum	Description
adParamSigned	The Parameter accepts signed values (default).
adParamNullable	The Parameter accepts **Null** values.
adParamLong	The Parameter accepts long binary data.

TABLE 2.15 CONSTANT VALUES FOR THE Direction PROPERTY OF THE Parameter OBJECT

ParameterDirectionEnum	Description
adParamInput	Specifies an input parameter (default).
adParamOutput	Specifies an output parameter.
adParamInputOutput	Specifies an input/output parameter.
adParamReturnValue	Specifies the return value of a stored procedure.

The Type property has the largest collection of constants of any ADO enumeration, as evidenced by the length of Table 2.16. Most of these data types aren't available to Visual Basic programmers; those that correspond to native VBA data types appear in a bold monospace font in the "Description of Data Type" column. (The remainder are data types for members of the Fields collection of the Recordset object or OLE DB data types accessible only to C/C++ programmers.) In most cases, you only need to choose among adChar (for **String** values), adInteger (for **Long** values), and adCurrency (for **Currency** values). You use the adDate data type to pass Date/Time parameter values to Jet databases, but not to most stored procedures. Stored procedures generally accept datetime parameter values as the adChar data type, with a format, such as mm/dd/yyyy, acceptable to the RDBMS.

TABLE 2.16 CONSTANT VALUES FOR THE Type PROPERTY OF THE Parameter AND Field OBJECTS

DataTypeEnum	Description of Data Type	OLE DB Data Type
adArray	**Or**'d with another data type specifying a safe-array of that data type	DBTYPE_ARRAY

DataTypeEnum	*Description of Data Type*	*OLE DB Data Type*
adBigInt	8-byte signed integer	DBTYPE_I8
adBinary	Binary value	DBTYPE_BYTES
adBoolean	**Boolean** value	DBTYPE_BOOL
adByRef	**Or**'d with another type specifying a pointer to data of the other type	DBTYPE_BYREF
adBSTR	**Null**-terminated Unicode character string	DBTYPE_BSTR
adChapter	Identifies a chaptered rowset, a field of a hierarchical **Recordset** that contains a child **Recordset**	DBTYPE_CHAPTER
adChar	**String** value	DBTYPE_STR
adCurrency	**Currency** values are fixed-point numbers with four decimal digits stored in an 8-byte, signed integer, which is scaled (divided) by 10,000	DBTYPE_CY
adDate	**Date** values are stored as a **Double** value, the integer part being the number of days since December 30, 1899, and the decimal part the fraction of a day	DBTYPE_DATE
adDBDate	Date value in *yyyymmdd* format	DBTYPE_DBDATE
adDBTime	Time value in *hhmmss*	DBTYPE_DBTIME
adDBTimeStamp	Date-time stamp in *yyyymmddhhmmss* format plus a fraction of a second in billionths (nanoseconds)	DBTYPE_DBTIMESTAMP
adDecimal	Exact numeric value with a specified precision and scale	DBTYPE_DECIMAL

2

UNDERSTANDING
OLE DB AND
DATA ACCESS

continues

TABLE 2.16 CONTINUED

DataTypeEnum	Description of Data Type	OLE DB Data Type
adDouble	**Double**-precision floating-point value	DBTYPE_R8
adEmpty	No value specified (not the same as **Null**)	DBTYPE_EMPTY
adError	32-bit error code	DBTYPE_ERROR
adGUID	Globally unique identifier (GUID)	DBTYPE_GUID
adIDispatch	Pointer to an IDispatch interface on an OLE object	DBTYPE_IDISPATCH
adInteger	4-byte signed **Long** integer	DBTYPE_I4
adIUnknown	Pointer to an IUnknown interface on an OLE object	DBTYPE_IUNKNOWN
adLongVarBinary	Long binary value (Parameter objects only)	Not applicable
adLongVarChar	**String** value greater than 225 characters (Parameter objects only)	Not applicable
adLongVarWChar	Long null-terminated string value (Parameter objects only)	Not applicable
adNumeric	Exact numeric value with a specified precision and scale	DBTYPE_NUMERIC
adSingle	**Single**-precision floating-point value	DBTYPE_R4
adSmallInt	2-byte signed **Integer**	DBTYPE_I2
adTinyInt	1-byte signed integer	DBTYPE_I1
adUnsignedBigInt	8-byte unsigned integer	DBTYPE_UI8
adUnsignedInt	4-byte unsigned integer	DBTYPE_UI4
adUnsignedSmallInt	2-byte unsigned integer	DBTYPE_UI2
adUnsignedTinyInt	1-byte unsigned integer (**Byte**)	DBTYPE_UI1

DataTypeEnum	Description of Data Type	OLE DB Data Type
adUserDefined	User-defined variable	DBTYPE_UDT
adVarBinary	Binary value (Parameter objects only)	Not applicable
adVarChar	**String** value (Parameter objects only)	Not applicable
adVariant	Automation (VBA) **Variant**	DBTYPE_VARIANT
adVector	**Or**'d with another type to specify that the data is a DBVECTOR structure	DBTYPE_VECTOR
adVarWChar	Null-terminated Unicode character string (Parameter objects only)	Not applicable
adWChar	Null-terminated Unicode character string	DBTYPE_WSTR

> **NOTE**
>
> The values for the Type property in the preceding table are valid for the Type property of the Field object, discussed later in the chapter, except for those data types in which "Parameter objects only" appears in the "Description of Data Type" column. The members of DataTypeEnum are designed to accommodate the widest possible range of desktop and client/server RDBMSs, but the ad constant names are closely related to those for the field data types of Microsoft SQL Server 7.0, which now supports Unicode strings.

The Parameter object has a single method, AppendChunk, which you use to append long text (adLongText) or long binary (adLongVarChar) **Variant** data as a parameter value. The syntax of the AppendChunk method call is

```
cmmName.Parameters({strName¦lngIndex}) = varChunk
```

The adParamLong flag of the Parameter.Attributes property must be set in order to apply the AppendChunk method. If you call AppendChunk more than once on a single Parameter, the second and later calls append the current value of varChunk to the parameter value.

Code to Pass Parameter Values to a Stored Procedure

Listing 2.2 is the code for an abbreviated version of an application that compares the performance of conventional SQL statements, parameterized stored procedures, and prepared statements. The code of Listing 2.2 is limited to executing a simple SQL Server 7.0 stored procedure with a Command object. The sp_orders stored procedure has two datetime input parameters, @BegDate and @EndDate, the values for which are supplied by the Text property of two text boxes, txtBegDate and txtEndDate, respectively. The sp_orders stored procedure, whose SQL statement follows, returns all columns of the Orders table of an upsized Nwind.mdb database; rows are returned for values of the OrderDate field between the values entered in txtBegDate and txtEndDate.

```
CREATE PROCEDURE sp_orders
    @BegDate datetime,
    @EndDate datetime
AS
    SELECT * FROM Orders
    WHERE OrderDate >= @BegDate AND
        OrderDate <= @EndDate
```

The code of Listing 2.2 populates a MSFlexGrid control. The value of the RecordCount property of forward-only Recordsets is either 0 (**False**, no records) or -1 (**True**, one or more records), so you must use the AddItem method to populate the MSFlexGrid control.

LISTING 2.2 CODE USING A Command OBJECT TO EXECUTE A PARAMETERIZED STORED PROCEDURE

```
Option Explicit
Private cnnOrders As New ADODB.Connection
Private cmmOrders As New ADODB.Command
Private strSQL As String

'Modify the constant values to suit your SQL Server installation
Private Const strConnect = "User ID=sa;Data Source=nwind;Location=OAKLEAF2"

Private Sub cmdExecute_Click()
    Dim rstOrders As New ADODB.Recordset
    Dim strMsg As String

    DoEvents   'Allow the form to paint

    Me.MousePointer = vbHourglass
    'Establish the connection
    cnnOrders.ConnectionTimeout = 15
    cnnOrders.Provider = "SQLOLEDB" 'Native SQL Server OLE DB Provider
    cnnOrders.Open strConnect

    'Call a simple SQL Server stored procedure on the
    'Orders table with two datetime parameters, @BegDate and @EndDate

    With cmmOrders
        Set .ActiveConnection = cnnOrders
        .CommandType = adCmdStoredProc
```

```vb
        .CommandText = "sp_orders"
        'Parameters(0) is pre-defined return value
        .Parameters(1).Type = adChar
        .Parameters(1).Size = Len(txtBegDate.Text)
        .Parameters(1).Direction = adParamInput
        .Parameters(1).Value = txtBegDate.Text
        .Parameters(2).Type = adChar
        .Parameters(2).Size = Len(txtEndDate.Text)
        .Parameters(2).Direction = adParamInput
        .Parameters(2).Value = txtEndDate.Text
        Set rstOrders = .Execute   'Recordset is ForwardOnly
    End With

    If rstOrders.RecordCount Then
        Call FillFlexGrid(rstOrders)
    Else
        MsgBox "Your input parameters returned no records.", _
            vbOKOnly + vbInformation, "ADO Stored Procedure"
    End If
    Set rstOrders = Nothing
End Sub

Private Sub FillFlexGrid(rstOrders As ADODB.Recordset)
    'Generic procedure for filling MSFlexGrid from a Recordset
    Dim intCol As Integer
    Dim strItem As String

    With flxGrid
        .ScrollBars = flexScrollBarNone 'Prevents flashing during load
        .FixedCols = 0
        .FixedRows = 1
        .Rows = 1 'Eliminates an empty top row
        .Cols = rstOrders.Fields.Count
        .Row = 0
        For intCol = 0 To .Cols - 1
            .Col = intCol
            .Text = rstOrders.Fields(intCol).Name
        Next intCol
        'AddItem method is required because RecordCount is unknown
        Do Until rstOrders.EOF
            strItem = ""
            For intCol = 0 To .Cols - 1
                strItem = strItem & rstOrders.Fields(intCol).Value & vbTab
            Next intCol
            .AddItem strItem
            rstOrders.MoveNext
        Loop
        .ScrollBars = flexScrollBarBoth
    End With
End Sub
```

ADO creates the `Parameters` collection automatically by querying the data source when the `cnnOrders.Parameters(1).Type = adChar` line executes. If you don't define your own `Parameters` collection, `cnnName.Parameters(0)` automatically is reserved for the return value of a stored procedure.

Command Methods

Command objects have only two methods, `CreateParameter` and `Execute`. You must declare a `ADODB.Parameter` object, `prmName`, prior to executing `CreateParameter`. The syntax of the `CreateParameter` method call is

```
Set prmName = cmmName.CreateParameter [strName[, lngType[, _
    lngDirection[, lngSize[, varValue]]]]]
cmmName.Parameters.Append prmName
```

The arguments of `CreateParameter` are optional only if you subsequently set the required `Parameter` property values before executing the `Command`. For example, if you supply only the `strName` argument, you must set the remaining properties, as in the following example:

```
Set prmName = cmmName.CreateParameter strName
cmmName.Parameters.Append prmName
prmName.Type = adChar
prmName.Direction = adParamInput
prmName.Size = Len(varValue)
prmName.Value = varValue
```

The syntax of the `Command.Execute` method is similar to that for the `Connection.Execute` method except for the argument list. The following syntax is for `Command` objects that return `Recordsets`:

```
Set rstName = cmmName.Execute ([lngRowsAffected[, _
    avarParameters[, lngOptions]]])
```

For `Commands` that don't return rows, use this form:

```
cmmName.Execute [lngRowsAffected[, avarParameters[, lngOptions]]]
```

All the arguments of the `Execute` method are optional if you set the required `Command` property values before applying the `Execute` method. Refer to Listing 2.2 for an example of the use of the `Command.Execute` method without arguments.

> **TIP**
>
> Presetting all property values of the `Command` object, rather than supplying argument values to the `Execute` method, makes your VBA code easier for others to comprehend.

Like the `Connection.Execute` method, the returned value of lng*RowsAffected* is 0 for SELECT and DDL queries and the number of rows modified by INSERT, UPDATE, and DELETE queries. The avar*Parameters* argument is an optional **Variant** array of parameter values. Using the `Parameters` collection is a better practice than using the avar*Parameters* argument, because output parameters don't return correct values to the array. For lng*Options* constant values, refer to Table 2.7.

The `ADODB.Recordset` Object

Creating and viewing `Recordsets` is the ultimate objective of most Visual Basic database front ends. Up to this point, all the `Recordsets` discussed in this chapter are forward-only and thus read-only. Opening an independent `ADODB.Recordset` object offers a myriad of cursor, locking, and other options. You must explicitly open a `Recordset` with a scrollable cursor if you want to use code to create the `Recordset` for an ADO Data control (ADODC) or other data-bound controls. Unlike Jet and ODBCDirect `Recordsets`, `ADODB.Recordset` objects expose a number of events that are especially useful for validating `Recordset` updates. Microsoft modeled `ADODB.Recordset` events on the event repertoire of the RDO 2.0 `rdoResultset` object.

`Recordset` Properties

Microsoft attempted to make `ADODB.Recordset` objects backward compatible with `DAO.Recordset` and `rdoResultset` objects to minimize the amount of code you must change to migrate existing applications from DAO or RDO to ADO. Unfortunately, the attempt at backward compatibility for code-intensive database applications didn't fully succeed. You must make substantial changes in DAO or RDO code to accommodate ADO's updated `Recordset` object. Thus most developers will probably use ADO for new Visual Basic database front-end applications and stick with DAO or RDO for existing projects.

Table 2.17 lists the names and descriptions of the standard property set of `ADODB.Recordset` objects. An asterisk (*) follows the property name of those properties that are identical to or substantially similar to properties of `DAO.Recordset` or `rdoResultset` objects. `ADODB.Recordset` objects have substantially fewer properties than `DAO.Recordset` objects have, and several added `ADODB.Recordset` objects don't have corresponding `DAO.Recordset` properties. The standard property set for `ADODB.Recordset` objects are those properties supported by the most common OLE DB data providers for relational databases.

TABLE 2.17   PROPERTY NAMES AND DESCRIPTIONS FOR `ADODB.Recordset` OBJECTS

Property Name	Description
AbsolutePage	A **Long** read/write value that sets or returns the number of the page in which the current record is located or one of the constant values of `PositionEnum` (see Table

continues

TABLE 2.17   CONTINUED

Property Name	Description
	2.18). You must set the PageSize property value before getting or setting the value of AbsolutePage. AbsolutePage is 1-based; if the current record is in the first page, AbsolutePage returns 1. Setting the value of AbsolutePage causes the current record to be set to the first record of the specified page.
AbsolutePosition*	A **Long** read/write value (1-based) that sets or returns the position of the current record. The maximum value of AbsolutePosition is the value of the RecordCount property.
ActiveCommand	A **String** read/write value specifying the name of a previously opened Command object with which the Recordset is associated.
ActiveConnection	A pointer to a previously opened Connection object with which the Recordset is associated or a fully-qualified ConnectionString value.
BOF*	A **Boolean** read-only value that, when **True**, indicates that the record pointer is positioned before the first row of the Recordset and there is no current record.
Bookmark*	A **Variant** read/write value that returns a reference to a specific record or uses a Bookmark value to set the record pointer to a specific record.
CacheSize*	A **Long** read/write value that specifies the number of records stored in local (cache) memory. The minimum (default) value is 1. Increasing the value of CacheSize minimizes round trips to the server to obtain additional rows when scrolling through Recordsets.
CursorLocation	A **Long** read/write value that specifies the location of a scrollable cursor, subject to the availability of the specified CursorType on the client or server (see Table 2.19). The default is to use a cursor provided by the OLE DB data source.
CursorType*	A **Long** read/write value that specifies the type of Recordset cursor (see Table 2.20). The default is a forward-only cursor.
DataMember	Returns a pointer to an associated *DataEnvironment*.Command object.
DataSource	Returns a pointer to an associated *DataEnvironment*.Connection object.

Property Name	Description
EditMode*	A **Long** read-only value that returns the status of editing of the Recordset (see Table 2.21).
EOF*	A **Boolean** read-only value that, when **True**, indicates that the record pointer is beyond the last row of the Recordset and there is no current record.
Filter*	A **Variant** read/write value that can be a criteria string (a valid SQL WHERE clause without the WHERE reserved word), an array of Bookmark values specifying a particular set of records, or a constant value from FilterGroupEnum (see Table 2.22).
LockType*	A **Long** read/write value that specifies the record-locking method employed when opening the Recordset (see Table 2.23). The default is read-only, corresponding to the read-only characteristic of a forward-only cursors
MarshalOptions	A **Long** read/write value that specifies which set of records is returned to the server after client-side modification. The MarshallOptions property applies only to the lightweight ADOR.Recordset object, a member of RDS. ADOR.Recordset objects are one of the subjects of Chapter 24, "Working with Remote Data Services."
MaxRecords*	A **Long** read/write value that specifies the maximum number of records to be returned by a SELECT query or stored procedure. The default value is 0, all records.
PageCount	A **Long** read-only value that returns the number of pages in a Recordset. You must set the PageSize value to cause PageCount to return a meaningful value. If the Recordset doesn't support the PageCount property, the value is -1.
PageSize	A **Long** read/write value that sets or returns the number of records in a logical page. You use logical pages to break large Recordsets into easily manageable groups. A common technique is to set the PageSize value to the number of records displayed in a DataGrid, MSFlexGrid, or hierarchical FlexGrid control. PageSize isn't related to the size of table pages used for locking in Jet (2K) or SQL Server (2K in version 6.5 and earlier, 8K in version 7.0) databases.
PersistFormat	A **Long** read/write value the sets or returns the format of Recordset files created by calling the Save method.

continues

TABLE 2.17   CONTINUED

Property Name	Description
	The only current constant value (PersistFormatEnum) is adPersistADTG (the default format, Advanced Data TableGram)
RecordCount*	A **Long** read-only value that returns the number of records in Recordsets with scrollable cursors if the Recordset supports approximate positioning or Bookmarks. (See the Recordset.Supports method later in this chapter.) If not, you must apply the MoveLast method to obtain an accurate RecordCount value, which retrieves and counts all records. If a forward-only Recordset has one or more records, RecordCount returns -1 (**True**). An empty Recordset of any type returns 0 (**False**).
Sort*	A **String** read/write value consisting of an SQL ORDER BY clause without the ORDER BY reserved words, that specifies the sort order of the Recordset.
Source*	A **String** read/write value that may be an SQL statement, a table name, a stored procedure name, or the name of an associated Command object. If you supply the name of a Command object, the Source property returns the value of the Command.CommandText text property. Use the lng*Options* argument of the Open method to specify the type of the value supplied to the Source property.
State	A **Long** read/write value representing one of the constant values of ObjectStateEnum (refer to Table 2.5).
Status*	A **Long** read-only value that indicates the status of batch operations or other multiple-record (bulk) operations on the Recordset (see Table 2.24).

The most obvious omission in the preceding table is the DAO.Recordset NoMatch property value used to test whether applying one of the DAO.Recordset.Find... methods or the DAO.Recordset.Seek method succeeds. The new ADODB.Recordset.Find method, listed in the "Recordset Methods" section later in this chapter, substitutes for DAO's FindFirst, FindNext, FindPrevious, and FindLast methods. The Find method uses the EOF property value for testing the existence of one or more records matching the Find criteria.

▶ See "Adopting ADODB.Recordset *Find* Methods," p. **152**

> **NOTE**
>
> Chapter 3, "Migrating from DAO to ADO," describes in detail the differences between the usage of the ADODB.Recordset.Find and DAO.Recordset.Find... methods, as well as other differences between the code you use to traverse and manipulate these two types of Recordset objects.

Another omission in the ADODB.Recordset object's preceding property list is the PercentPosition property. The workaround, however, is easy:

rst*Name*.AbsolutePostion = **Int**(int*PercentPosition* * rst*Name*.RecordCount / 100)

Tables 2.18 through 2.24 enumerate the valid constant values for the AbsolutePage, CursorLocation, CursorType, EditMode, Filter, LockType, and Status properties.

TABLE 2.18 CONSTANT VALUES FOR THE AbsolutePage PROPERTY

PositionEnum	Description
adPosUnknown	The data provider doesn't support pages, the Recordset is empty, or the data provider can't determine the page number.
adPosBOF	The record pointer is positioned at the beginning of the file. (The BOF property is **True**.)
adPosEOF	The record pointer is positioned at the end of the file. (The EOF property is **True**.)

TABLE 2.19 CONSTANT VALUES FOR THE CursorLocation PROPERTY

CursorLocationEnum	Description
adUseClient	Use cursor(s) provided by a cursor library located on the client. The ADOR.Recordset requires a client-side cursor.
adUseServer	Use cursor(s) supplied by the data source, usually (but not necessarily) located on a server (default value).

TABLE 2.20 CONSTANT VALUES FOR THE CursorType PROPERTY

CursorTypeEnum	Description
adOpenForwardOnly	Provides only unidirectional cursor movement and a read-only Recordset (default value).
adOpenDynamic	Provides a scrollable cursor that displays all changes, including new records, that other users make to the Recordset.

continues

TABLE 2.20   CONTINUED

CursorTypeEnum	Description
adOpenKeyset	Provides a scrollable cursor that hides only records added by other users, simlar to a `DAO.Recordset` of the dynaset type.
adOpenStatic	Provides a scrollable cursor over a static copy of the `Recordset`. Similar to a `DAO.Recordset` of the snapshot type, but updatable.

TABLE 2.21   CONSTANT VALUES FOR THE `EditMode` PROPERTY

EditModeEnum	Description
adEditNone	No editing operation is in progress (default value).
adEditAdd	A tentative append record has been added, but not saved to the database table(s).
adEditInProgress	Data in the current record has been modified, but not saved to the database table(s).

TABLE 2.22   CONSTANT VALUES FOR THE `Filter` PROPERTY

FilterGroupEnum	Description
adFilterNone	Removes an existing filter and exposes all records of the Recordset (equivalent to setting the `Filter` property to an empty string, the default value).
adFilterAffectedRecords	View only records affected by the last execution of the `CancelBatch`, `Delete`, `Resync`, or `UpdateBatch` method.
adFilterFetchedRecords	View only records in the current cache. The number of records is set by the `CacheSize` property.
adFilterPendingRecords	View only records that have been modified but not yet processed by the data source (for batch update mode only)

TABLE 2.23   CONSTANT VALUES FOR THE `LockType` PROPERTY

LockTypeEnum	Description
adLockReadOnly	Specifies read-only access (default value)
adLockBatchOptimistic	Use batch update mode instead of the default immediate update mode
adLockOptimistic	Use optimistic locking (lock the record or page only during the update process)
adLockPessimistic	Use pessimistic locking (lock the record or page during editing and the updated process)

TABLE 2.24 CONSTANT VALUES FOR THE Status PROPERTY (APPLIES TO BATCH OR BULK Recordset OPERATIONS ONLY.)

RecordStatusEnum	*Description of Record Status*
adRecOK	Updated successfully.
adRecNew	Added successfully.
adRecModified	Modified successfully.
adRecDeleted	Deleted successfully.
adRecUnmodified	Not modified.
adRecInvalid	Not saved; the Bookmark property is invalid.
adRecMultipleChanges	Not saved; saving would affect other records.
adRecPendingChanges	Not saved; the record refers to a pending insert operation).
adRecCanceled	Not saved; the operation was canceled.
adRecCantRelease	Not saved; existing record locks prevented saving.
adRecConcurrencyViolation	Not saved; an optimistic concurrency locking problem occurred.
adRecIntegrityViolation	Not saved; the operation would violate integrity constraints.
adRecMaxChangesExceeded	Not saved; an excessive number of pending changes exist.
adRecObjectOpen	Not saved; a conflict with an open storage object occurred.
adRecOutOfMemory	Not saved; the machine is out of memory.
adRecPermissionDenied	Not saved; the user doesn't have required permissions.
adRecSchemaViolation	Not saved; the record structure doesn't match the database schema.
adRecDBDeleted	Not saved or deleted; the record was previously deleted.

Fields Collection and Field Objects

Like DAO's Fields collection, ADO's dependent Fields collection is a property of the Recordset object, making the columns of the Recordset accessible to VBA code and bound controls. Like the Parameters collection described earlier in the chapter, the Fields collection has one property, Count, but only two methods, Item and Refresh. You can't append new Field objects to the Fields collection. Refer to the FillFlexGrid subprocedure in Listing 2.2 for an example of VBA code that accesses Field objects.

All but one (Value) of the property values of Field objects are read-only, because the values of the Field properties are derived from the database schema. The Value property is read-only in forward-only Recordsets and Recordsets opened with read-only locking. Table 2.25 lists the names and descriptions of the properties of the Field object.

TABLE 2.25 PROPERTY NAMES AND DESCRIPTIONS OF THE Field OBJECT

ActualSize	A **Long** read-only value representing the length of the Field's value by character count.
Attributes	A **Long** read-only value that represents the sum of the constants (flags) included in FieldAttributeEnum (see Table 2.26).
DefinedSize	A **Long** read-only value specifying the maximum length of the Field's value by character count. For example, a Jet text or SQL Server varchar field may have a maximum (defined) size of 25 characters, but the length of the data in the specified field of the current record.
Name	A **String** read-only value that returns the field (column) name.
NumericScale	A **Byte** read-only value specifying the number of decimal places for numeric values.
OriginalValue	A **Variant** read-only value that represents the Value property of the field before applying the Update method to the Recordset. (The CancelUpdate method uses OriginalValue to replace a changed Value property.)
Precision	A **Byte** read-only value specifying the total number of digits (including decimal digits) for numeric values.
Type	A **Long** read-only value specifying the data type of the field. Refer to Table 2.16 for Type constant values.
UnderlyingValue	A **Variant** read-only value representing the current value of the field in the database table(s). You can compare the values of OriginalValue and UnderlyingValue to determine whether a persistent change has been made to the database, perhaps by another user.
Value	A **Variant** read/write value of a subtype appropriate to the value of the Type property for the field. If the Recordset isn't updatable, the Value property is read-only.

TIP

Value is the default property of the Field object, but a good programming practice is to set and return field values by explicit use of the Value property name in VBA code. In most cases, using *varName* = rst*Name*.Fields(*n*).Value instead of *varName* = rst*Name*.Fields(*n*) results in a slight performance improvement.

TABLE 2.26 CONSTANT VALUES AND DESCRIPTIONS FOR THE Attributes PROPERTY OF THE Field OBJECT

FieldAttributeEnum	*Description*
adFldMayDefer	The field is deferred, meaning that Values are retrieved from the data source only when explicitly requested.
adFldUpdatable	The field is read/write (updatable).
adFldUnknownUpdatable	The data provider can't determine whether the field is updatable. Your only recourse is to attempt an update and trap the error that occurs if the field isn't updatable.
adFldFixed	The field contains fixed-length data with the length determined by the data type or field specification.
adFldIsNullable	The field accepts **Null** values.
adFldMayBeNull	The field can return **Null** values.
adFldLong	The field has a long binary data type, which permits the use of the AppendChunk and GetChunk methods.
adFldRowID	The field is a row identifier (typically an identity, AutoIncrement, or GUID data type).
adFldRowVersion	The field contains a timestamp or similar value for determining the time of the last update.
adFldCacheDeferred	The provider caches field values. Multiple reads are made on the cached value, not the database table.

The Field object has two methods, AppendChunk and GetChunk, which are applicable only to fields of various long binary data types, indicated by an adFldLong flag in the Attributes property of the field. The AppendChunk method is discussed in the "Parameter Object" section earlier in this chapter. The syntax for the AppendChunk method call, which writes **Variant** data to a long binary field (fldName), is

```
fldName.AppendChunk varData
```

NOTE

ADO 2.0 doesn't support the Access OLE Object field data type, which adds a proprietary object wrapper around the data (such as a bitmap) to identify the OLE server that created the object (for bitmaps, usually Windows Paint). If your application must handle OLE Object fields, use Data and DBGrid controls with DAO.Recordset objects.

The GetChunk method lets you read long binary data in blocks of the size you specify. Following is the syntax for the GetChunk method:

varName = *fldName*.GetChunk(*lngSize*)

A common practice is to place AppendChunk and GetChunk method calls within **Do Until...Loop** structures to break up the long binary value into chunks of manageable size. In the case of the GetChunk method, if you set the value of *lngSize* to less than the value of the field's ActualSize property, the first GetChunk call retrieves *lngSize* bytes. Successive GetChunk calls retrieve *lngSize* bytes beginning at the next byte after the end of the preceding call. If the remaining number of bytes is less than *lngSize*, only the remaining bytes appear in *varName*. After you retrieve the field's bytes, or if the field is empty, GetChunk returns **Null**.

> **NOTE**
>
> Changing the position of the record pointer of the field's Recordset resets GetChunk's byte pointer. Accessing a different Recordset and moving its record pointer doesn't affect the other Recordset's GetChunk record pointer.

Recordset **Methods**

ADODB.Recordset methods are an amalgam of the DAO.Recordset and rdoResultset methods. Supports is the only method that doesn't have an equivalent in DAO or RDO. Table 2.27 lists the names, descriptions, and calling syntax for Recordset methods. OLE DB data providers aren't required to support all of the methods of the Recordset object. If you don't know which methods the data provider supports, you must use the Supports method with the appropriate constant from CursorOptionEnum, listed in Table 2.30, to test for support of methods that are provider dependent. Provider-dependent methods are indicated by an asterisk after the method name in Table 2.27.

TABLE 2.27   NAMES AND DESCRIPTIONS OF METHODS OF THE Recordset OBJECT

Method Name	*Description and Calling Syntax*
AddNew*	Adds a new record to an updatable Recordset. The calling syntax is rst*Name*.AddNew [{var*Field*¦avar*Fields*}, {var*Value*¦avar*Values*}], where var*Field* is a single field name, avar*Fields* is an array of field names, var*Value* is single value, and avar*Values* is an array of values for the columns defined by the members of avar*Fields*. Calling the Update method adds the new record to the database table(s). If you add a new records to a Recordset having a primary key field that is not the first field of the Recordset, you must supply the name and value of the primary key field in the AddNew statement.

Method Name	Description and Calling Syntax
Cancel	Cancels execution of an asynchronous query and terminates creation of multiple Recordsets from stored procedures or compound SQL statements. The calling syntax is rstName.Cancel.
CancelBatch*	Cancels a pending batch update operation on a Recordset whose LockEdits property value is adBatchOptimistic. The calling syntax is rstName.CancelBatch [lngAffectRecords]. The optional lngAffectRecords argument is one of the constants of AffectEnum (see Table 2.28).
CancelUpdate*	Cancels a pending change to the table(s) underlying the Recordset before applying the Update method. The calling syntax is rstName.CancelUpdate.
Clone	Creates a duplicate Recordset object with an independent record pointer. The calling syntax is **Set** rstDupe = rstName.Clone().
Close	Closes a Recordset object, allowing reuse of the Recordset variable by setting new Recordset property values and applying the Open method. The calling syntax is rstName.Close.
Delete*	Deletes the current record immediately from the Recordset and the underlying tables, unless the LockEdits property value of the Recordset is set to adLockBatchOptimistic. The calling syntax is rstName.Delete.
Find	Searches for a record based on criteria you supply. The calling syntax is rstName.Find strCriteria[, lngSkipRecords, lngSearchDirection[, lngStart]], where strCriteria is a valid SQL WHERE clause without the WHERE keyword, the optional lngSkipRecords value is the number of records to skip before applying Find, lngSearchDirection specifies the search direction (adSearchForward, the default, or adSearchBackward), and the optional varStart value specifies the Bookmark value of the record at which to start the search or one of the members of BookmarkEnum (see Table 2.29). If Find succeeds, the EOF property returns **True**; otherwise, EOF returns **False**.
GetRows	Returns a two-dimensional (row, column) **Variant** array of records. The calling syntax is avarName = rstName.GetRows(lngRows[, varStart[, {strFieldName¦lngFieldIndex¦avarFieldNames¦avarFieldIndexes}]]), where lngRows is the number of rows to return, varStart specifies a Bookmark value of the record at which to

continues

2

UNDERSTANDING OLE DB AND DATA ACCESS

TABLE 2.27   CONTINUED

Method Name	Description and Calling Syntax
	start the search or one of the members of BookmarkEnum (see Table 2.29), and the third optional argument is the name or index of a single column, or a **Variant** array of column names or indexes. If you don't specify a value of the third argument, GetRows returns all columns of the Recordset.
GetString	By default, returns a tab-separated **String** value for a specified number of records, with records separated by return codes. The calling syntax is str*Clip* = rst*Name*.GetString (lng*Rows*[, str*ColumnDelimiter*[, str*RowDelimiter*, [str*NullExpr*]]]), where lng*Rows* is the number of rows to return, str*ColumnDelimiter* is an optional column-separation character (vbTab is the default), str*RowDelimiter* is an optional row-separation character (vbCR is the default), and str*NullExpr* is an optional value to substitute when encountering **Null** values (an empty string, "", is the default value.) The primary use of the GetString method is to populate MSFlexGrid or MSHFlxGrid controls by setting the Clip property value of the control to str*Clip*.
Move*	Moves the record pointer from the current record. The calling syntax is rst*Name*.Move lng*NumRecords*[, var*Start*], where lng*NumRecords* is the number of records by which to move the record pointer, and the optional var*Start* value specifies the Bookmark of the record at which to start the search or one of the members of BookmarkEnum (see Table 2.29).
MoveFirst*	Moves the record pointer to the first record. The calling syntax is rst*Name*.MoveFirst.
MoveLast*	Moves the record pointer to the last record. The calling syntax is rst*Name*.MoveLast.
MoveNext	Moves the record pointer to the next record. The calling syntax is rst*Name*.MoveNext. The MoveNext method is the only Move... method that you can apply to a forward-only Recordset.
MovePrevious*	Moves the record pointer to the previous record. The calling syntax is rst*Name*.MovePrevious.
NextRecordset	Returns additional Recordset objects generated by a compound SQL statement, such as SELECT * FROM Orders; SELECT * FROM Customers, or a stored procedure that returns multiple Recordsets. The calling syntax is rst*Next* = rst*Name*.NextRecordset[(lng*RecordsAffected*)], where lng*RecordsAffected* is an optional return value that specifies the number of records in rst*Next*. If no additional Recordset exists, rst*Next* is set to **Nothing**.

Method Name	Description and Calling Syntax
Open	Opens a `Recordset` on an active `Command` or `Connection` object. The calling syntax is `rstName.Open [varSource[,` `varActiveConnection[, lngCursorType[,` `lngLockType[, lngOptions]]]]]`. The Open arguments are optional if you set the equivalent `Recordset` property values, which is the practice recommended in this book. For valid values, refer to the `Source`, `ActiveConnection`, `CursorType`, and `LockType` properties in Table 2.17 and to the `CommandTypeEnum` values listed in Table 2.7 for the `lngOptions` property.
Requery	Refreshes the content of the `Recordset` from the underlying table(s), the equivalent of calling `Close` then `Open`. `Requery` is a very resource-intensive operation. The calling syntax is `rstName.Requery`.
Resync*	Refreshes a specified subset of the `Recordset` from the underlying table(s). The calling syntax is `rstName.Resync` `[lngAffectRecords]`, where `lngAffectRecords` is one of the members of `AffectEnum` (see Table 2.28). If you select `adAffectCurrent` or `adAffectGroup` as the value of `lngAffectRecords`, you reduce the required resources in comparison with `adAffectAll` (the default).
Save	Creates a file containing a persistent copy of the `Recordset`. The calling syntax is `rstName.Save strFileName`, where `strFileName` is the path to and the name of the file. You open a Recordset from a file with an `rstName.Open strFileName,` `Options:=adCmdFile` statement. This book uses .rst as the extension for persistent `Recordsets`.
Supports	Returns **True** if the `Recordset`'s data provider supports a specified cursor-dependent method; otherwise, `Supports` returns **False**. The calling syntax is `blnSupported =` `rstName.Supports(lngCursorOptions)`. Table 2.30 lists the names and descriptions of the `CursorOptionsEnum` values.
Update*	Applies the result of modifications to the `Recordset` to the underlying table(s) of the data source. For batch operations, `Update` applies the modifications only to the local (cached) `Recordset`. The calling syntax is `rstName.Update`.
UpdateBatch*	Applies the result of all modifications made to a batch-type `Recordset` (`LockType` property set to `adBatchOptimistic`, and `CursorType` property set to `adOpenKeyset` or `adOpenStatic`) to the underlying table(s) of the data source. The calling syntax is `rstName.UpdateBatch [lngAffectRecords]`, where `lngAffectRecords` is a member of `AffectEnum` (see Table 2.28).

2

UNDERSTANDING
OLE DB AND
DATA ACCESS

> **NOTE**
>
> The `Edit` method of `DAO.Recordset` and `rdoResultset` objects is missing from Table 2.27. To change the value of one or more fields of the current record of an `ADODB.Recordset` object, simply execute `rstName.Fields(n).Value = varValue` for each field whose value you want to change and then execute `rstName.Update`. `ADODB.Recordset` objects don't support the `Edit` method.

> **TIP**
>
> To improve the performance of `Recordset` objects opened on `Connection` objects, set the required property values of the `Recordset` object and then use a named argument to specify the `intOptions` value of the `Open` method, as in `rstName.Open Options:=adCmdText`. This syntax is easier to read and less prone to error than the alternative, `rstName.Open , , , , adCmdText`.

TABLE 2.28   NAMES AND DESCRIPTIONS OF CONSTANTS FOR THE `lngAffectRecords` ARGUMENT

AffectEnum	*Description*
`adAffectAll`	Include all records in the `Recordset` object, including any records hidden by the `Filter` property value (the default)
`adAffectCurrent`	Include only the current record
`adAffectGroup`	Include only those records that meet the current Filter criteria

TABLE 2.29   NAMES AND DESCRIPTIONS OF BOOKMARK CONSTANTS FOR THE `varStart` ARGUMENT

BookmarkEnum	*Description*
`adBookmarkCurrent`	Start at the current record (the default value)
`adBookmarkFirst`	Start at the first record
`adBookmarkLast`	Start at the last record

TABLE 2.30   NAMES AND DESCRIPTIONS OF CONSTANTS FOR THE `Supports` METHOD

CursorOptionEnum	*Permits*
`adAddNew`	Calling the `AddNew` method
`adApproxPosition`	Setting and getting `AbsolutePosition` and `AbsolutePage` property values
`adBookmark`	Setting and getting the `Bookmark` property value

CursorOptionEnum	Permits
adDelete	Calling the Delete method
adHoldRecords	Retrieving additional records or changing the retrieval record pointer position without committing pending changes
adMovePrevious	Calling the GetRows, Move, MoveFirst, and MovePrevious methods (indicates a bi-directional scrollable cursor)
adResync	Calling the Resync method
adUpdate	Calling the Update method
adUpdateBatch	Calling the UpdateBatch and CancelBatch methods

Disconnected Recordsets

If you set the value of the Recordset's LockEdits property to adBatchOptimistic and the CursorType property to adKeyset or adStatic, you create a batch-type Recordset that you can disconnect from the data source, modify, reopen the Connection object, and send the updates to the data source over the new connection. A Recordset without an active connection is called a *disconnected Recordset*. The advantage of a disconnected Recordset is that you eliminate a need for an active server connection during extended editing sessions.

Following is an example of VBA pseudocode that creates and operates on a disconnected Recordset and then uses the BatchUpdate method to persist the changes in the data source:

```
Set rstName = New ADODB.Recordset
With rstName
    .ActiveConnection = cnnName
    .CursorType = adStatic
    .LockEdits = adBatchOptimistic
    .Open "SELECT * FROM TableName WHERE Criteria", Options:=adCmdText
    Set .ActiveConnection = Nothing 'Disconnect the Recordset
    'Close the Connection, if desired
    'Modify the field values of multiple records here
    .Update  'Update the locally-cached Recordset
    'Reopen the connection, if closed
    Set .ActiveConnection = cnnName
    .UpdateBatch  'Send all changes to the data source
End With
rstName.Close
```

If calling the UpdateBatch method causes conflicts with other users' modifications to the underlying table(s), you receive a trappable error and the Errors collection contains Error object(s) that identify the conflict(s). Unlike transactions, which require all attempted modifications to succeed or all to be rolled back, Recordset batch modifications that don't cause conflicts are made permanent in the data source.

Recordset Events

The `ADODB.Recordset` event model differs greatly from that of the `rdoResultset` object of RDO 2.0. ADO offers substantially more granularity of events than RDO does. Table 2.31 lists the names of `Recordset` events and the condition under which the event fires.

TABLE 2.31 NAMES AND OCCURRENCE OF Recordset EVENTS

Event Name	When Fired
EndOfRecordset	When the record pointer attempts to move beyond the last record
FieldChangeComplete	After a change to the value of a field
MoveComplete	After execution of the Move or Move... methods
RecordChangeComplete	After an edit to a single record
RecordsetChangeComplete	After cached changes are applied to the underlying tables
WillChangeField	Before a change to a field value
WillChangeRecord	Before an edit to a single record
WillChangeRecordset	Before cached changes are applied to the underlying tables
WillMove	After execution of the Move or Move... methods

Following are the subprocedure headers for each of the `Recordset` event handlers:

```
Private Sub rstName_EndOfRecordset _
        (fMoreData As Boolean, _
         adStatus As ADODB.EventStatusEnum, _
    ByVal pRecordset As ADODB.Recordset)

Private Sub rstName_FieldChangeComplete _
    (ByVal cFields As Long, _
     ByVal Fields As Variant, _
     ByVal pError As ADODB.Error, _
         adStatus As ADODB.EventStatusEnum, _
     ByVal pRecordset As ADODB.Recordset)

Private Sub rstName_MoveComplete _
    (ByVal adReason As ADODB.EventReasonEnum, _
     ByVal pError As ADODB.Error, _
         adStatus As ADODB.EventStatusEnum, _
     ByVal pRecordset As ADODB.Recordset)

Private Sub rstName_RecordChangeComplete _
    (ByVal adReason As ADODB.EventReasonEnum, _
     ByVal cRecords As Long, _
```

```
    ByVal pError As ADODB.Error, _
        adStatus As ADODB.EventStatusEnum, _
    ByVal pRecordset As ADODB.Recordset)

Private Sub rstName_RecordsetChangeComplete _
    (ByVal adReason As ADODB.EventReasonEnum, _
    ByVal pError As ADODB.Error, _
        adStatus As ADODB.EventStatusEnum, _
    ByVal pRecordset As ADODB.Recordset)

Private Sub rstName_WillChangeField _
    (ByVal cFields As Long, _
    ByVal Fields As Variant, _
        adStatus As ADODB.EventStatusEnum, _
    ByVal pRecordset As ADODB.Recordset)

Private Sub rstName_WillChangeRecord _
    (ByVal adReason As ADODB.EventReasonEnum, _
    ByVal cRecords As Long, _
        adStatus As ADODB.EventStatusEnum, _
    ByVal pRecordset As ADODB.Recordset)

Private Sub rstName_WillChangeRecordset _
    (ByVal adReason As ADODB.EventReasonEnum, _
        adStatus As ADODB.EventStatusEnum, _
    ByVal pRecordset As ADODB.Recordset)

Private Sub rstName_WillMove _
    (ByVal adReason As ADODB.EventReasonEnum, _
        adStatus As ADODB.EventStatusEnum, _
    ByVal pRecordset As ADODB.Recordset)
```

Each event-handling subprocedure header returns a pointer (reference) to the Recordset object that fired the event (pRecordset). Events that fire after execution of a method include a pointer (pError) to an Error object in the Connection.Errors collection if an error occurs; otherwise, pError is **Null**.

Table 2.32 lists the constant names and descriptions for the adReason parameter, which specifies the method that caused the event to fire. The ability to test the event for its underlying reason adds greatly to the granularity of the Recordset events. Only a subset of the members of EventReasonEnum apply to each event handler. Refer to Table 2.10 for constant names and descriptions for the adStatus parameter.

TABLE 2.32 CONSTANT VALUES FOR THE adReason PARAMETER

EventReasonEnum	*Reason for Firing Event*
adRsnAddNew	Call to the AddNew method
adRsnClose	Call to the Close method
adRsnDelete	Call to the Delete method

TABLE 2.32   CONTINUED

EventReasonEnum	*Reason for Firing Event*
adRsnFirstChange	When the first change is made to a field value of a row
adRsnMove	Call to the Move method
adRsnMoveFirst	Call to the MoveFirst method
adRsnMoveLast	Call to the MoveLast method
adRsnMovePrevious	Call to the MovePrevious method
adRsnRequery	Call to the Requery method
adRsnResync	Call to the Resync method
adRsnUndoAddNew	AddNew operation was canceled by the user
adRsnUndoDelete	Delete operation was canceled by the user
adRsnUndoUpdate	Update operation was canceled by the user
adRsnUpdate	Call to the Update method

NOTE

Members of EventReasonEnum are closely related to the Row ... Notification and Rowset ... Notification properties of the Connection.Properties collection for the Jet native OLE DB provider listed in Table 2.33.

EXAMINING PROVIDER-SPECIFIC ADODB.PROPERTIES COLLECTIONS

The OLE DB specification requires data providers to expose a set of properties and values (DBPROPSET) that define the basic capabilities of the provider. The standard set of DB_PROPSET members are defined in the "OLE DB Properties" appendix of the OLE DB specification. Data provider developers are free to add custom properties to their data providers. The Properties collection has the usual single property, Count, and the Item and Refresh methods. The names and descriptions of properties of ADODB.Property objects appear in Table 2.33.

NOTE

The final pages of this very long chapter are devoted to what some might consider a "laundry list" of arcane property names and unfathomable values. The primary purpose of including this and the following sections in the

continues

Understanding OLE DB and Universal Data Access

CHAPTER 2

115

2

UNDERSTANDING
OLE DB AND
DATA ACCESS

"Understanding OLE DB and Data Access Components" chapter of this book is to illustrate the connection between ADO and OLE DB. In addition, a chapter on ADO components is not complete without a discussion of every ADODB object.

As mentioned earlier in this chapter, ADO is an Automation wrapper for the OLE DB COM interfaces. You probably won't need to read or write provider-specific property values for simple Visual Basic 6.0 database front ends. High-performance front ends that are designed to access a variety of client/server RDBMSs, however, are likely to require that you interrogate the provider to determine its capabilities. This requirement is especially true for the initial set of native OLE DB providers, which are likely to undergo many successive updates until reaching the level of stability of today's ODBC drivers.

TABLE 2.33 NAMES AND DESCRIPTIONS OF PROPERTIES OF THE ADODB.Property OBJECT

Property Name	Description
Attributes	Provider-specific flags, the sum of which determine characteristics of the Property object (see Table 2.34).
Name	A text description of the data object.
Type	The **Variant** subtype value for the Value, such as vbBoolean.
Value	A **Variant** value of the subtype specified by the Type value. The read/write status of the value is determined by Attributes flags.

TABLE 2.34 NAMES AND DESCRIPTIONS OF PROPERTIES OF THE ADODB.Property OBJECT

PropertyAttributesEnum	Description
adPropNotSupported	The provider doesn't support this Property.
adPropRequired	You must provide a value for Property.Value prior to initializing the data source by calling the Open method.
adPropOptional	Property.Value is optional (complement of adPropRequired).
adPropRead	You can read Property.Value.
adPropWrite	You can set Property.Value.

The information in the tables of the following sections was created using the following VBA pseudocode:

```
Dim adoObject As New ADODB.ObjectType
Dim prpObject As ADODB.Property

With adoObject
   ...Set object properties
```

```
    .Open [Arguments]
    For Each prpObject In ADODB.ObjectName
        Debug.Print prpObject.Name & vbTab & prpObject.Value
    Next prpObject
End With
```

The lists of the property names and values in the tables that follow are based on the index of the Property within the Properties collection, in top-to-bottom, then left-to-right sequence.

> **NOTE**
>
> Explanations of the values returned by ADODB.Property objects appear in Appendix C of the "OLE DB Programmer's Reference, Version 2.0" part of the OLE DB SDK 2.0. You can download the current version of the OLE DB SDK from http://www.microsoft.com/data/oledb/.

The Properties Collection of the Connection Object

Table 2.35 lists the name and values of the 72 properties of a Connection object opened on Nwind.mdb with the Microsoft.Jet.OLEDB.3.51 (Jolt) native OLE DB data provider. These properties derive from members of the Data Source (DBPROPSET_DATASOURCE) and Data Source Information (DBPROPSET_DATAINFO). For example, Current Catalog corresponds to DBPROP_CURRENTCATALOG (the sole property of DBPROPSET_DATASOURCE) and Active Sessions corresponds to DBPROP_ACTIVESESSIONS (the first property of DBPROPSET_DATAINFO).

TABLE 2.35   PROPERTY NAMES AND VALUES FOR A Connection OBJECT USING THE MICROSOFT.JET.OLEDB.3.51 PROVIDER TO CONNECT TO THE NWIND.MDB DATABASE

Property Name	Value	Property Name	Value
Current Catalog*		Table Term	Table
Active Sessions	128	User Name	Admin
Asynchable Commit	False	Pass By Ref Accessors	False
Catalog Location	1	Transaction DDL	8
Catalog Term	Database	Asynchable Abort	False
Column Definition	1	Data Source Object Threading Model	1
NULL Concatenation Behavior	2	Column Set Notification	3
Data Source Name	C:\... \Nwind.mdb	Row Delete Notification	3

Property Name	Value	Property Name	Value
Read-Only Data Source	False	Row First Change Notification	3
DBMS Name	MS Jet	Row Insert Notification	3
DBMS Version	03.51.0000	Row Resynchronization Notification	0
GROUP BY Support	4	Rowset Release Notification	3
Heterogenous Table Support	2	Rowset Fetch Position Change Notification	3
Identifier Case Sensitivity	8	Row Undo Change Notification	3
Maximum Index Size	255	Row Undo Delete Notification	3
Maximum Row Size	2012	Row Undo Insert Notification	3
Maximum Row Size Includes BLOB	False	Row Update Notification	3
Maximum Tables in SELECT	0	Output Parameter Availability	1
Multiple Storage Objects	True	Persistent ID Type	4
Multi-Table Update	True	Multiple Parameter Sets	True
NULL Collation Order	4	Rowset Conversions on Command	True
OLE Object Support	1	Multiple Results	0
ORDER BY Columns in Select List	False	Cache Authentication	True
Prepare Abort Behavior	1	Encrypt Password	False
Prepare Commit Behavior	2	Mask Password	False
Procedure Term	STORED QUERY	Password	
Provider Name	MSJTOR35.DLL	Persist Encrypted	False

continues

TABLE 2.35   CONTINUED

Property Name	Value	Property Name	Value
OLE DB Version	01.10	Persist Security Info	False
Provider Version	03.51.1014	User ID	Admin
Schema Term	Schema	Data Source	C:\...\ Nwind.mdb
Schema Usage	0	Window Handle	0
SQL Support	8	Mode	16
Structured Storage	9	Prompt	2
Subquery Support	31	Extended Properties	;COUNTRY=0 ;CP=1252 ;LANGID= 0x0409
Isolation Levels	4096	Locale Identifier	1033
Isolation Retention	9	Jet OLEDB: Registry Path	

Table 2.36 lists the 83 properties of a `Connection` object opened on an SQL Server 7.0 database using ADO's default OLE DB-Over-ODBC provider, MSDASQL. Not only does SQLOLEDB expose 11 more `Property` objects, the members of the `Properties` collection differ dramatically from those that appear when using the Jolt provider.

TABLE 2.36   PROPERTY NAMES AND VALUES FOR A `Connection` OBJECT USING THE MSDASQL OLE DB-OVER-ODBC PROVIDER TO CONNECT TO AN UPSIZED NWIND DATABASE ON SQL SERVER 7.0

Property Name	Value	Property Name	Value
Password		Prepare Abort Behavior	2
Persist Security Info		Prepare Commit Behavior	2
User ID		Procedure Term	stored procedure
Data Source		Provider Name MSDASQL.DLL	
Window Handle		OLE DB Version	01.50
Locale Identifier	1033	Provider Version 1.50.3506	.00

Property Name	Value	Property Name	Value
Location		Quoted Identifier Sensitivity	8
Mode		Rowset Conversions on Command	True
Prompt	4	Schema Term	owner
Extended Properties	DRIVER=SQL Server; SERVER= OAKLEAF0; UID=sa;PWD=; WSID= OAKLEAF1; DATABASE= nwind	Schema Usage	31
Connect Timeout	15	SQL Support	267
Active Sessions	0	Structured Storage	1
Asynchable Abort	False	Subquery Support	31
Asynchable Commit	False	Transaction DDL	8
Pass By Ref Accessors	True	Isolation Levels	1118464
Catalog Location	1	Isolation Retention	0
Catalog Term	database	Table Term	table
Catalog Usage	7	User Name	dbo
Column Definition	1	Current Catalog	nwind
NULL Concatenation Behavior	1	Accessible Procedures	True
Data Source Name		Accessible Tables	True
Read-Only Data Source	False	Driver Name SQLSRV32.DLL	
DBMS Name	Microsoft SQL Server	Driver Version 03.70.0390	
DBMS Version	07.00.0390	Driver ODBC Version	03.60
Data Source Object Threading Model	1	File Usage	0

continues

2

UNDERSTANDING
OLE DB AND
DATA ACCESS

TABLE 2.36   CONTINUED

Property Name	Value	Property Name	Value
GROUP BY Support	2	Like Escape Clause	Y
Heterogenous Table Support	0	Max Columns in Group By	0
Identifier Case Sensitivity	8	Max Columns in Index	16
Maximum Index Size	8062	Max Columns in Order By	0
Maximum Row Size	8062	Max Columns in Select	4096
Maximum Row Size Includes BLOB	False	Max Columns in Table	1024
Maximum Tables in SELECT	32	Numeric Functions	16777215
Multiple Parameter Sets	True	Integrity Enhancement Facility	True
Multiple Results	1	SQL Grammar Support	1
Multiple Storage Objects	False	Outer Join Capabilities	127
Multi-Table Update	False	Outer Joins	Y
NULL Collation Order	1	Stored Procedures	True
OLE Object Support	1	Special Characters	#$ÀÁÂÃÄÅÆ ÇÈÉÊËÌÍÎÏ ÐÑÒÓÔÕÖØ ????????? ????????? ?????????? öøÙÚÛÜÝÞÿ
ORDER BY Columns in Select List	False	String Functions	5242879
Output Parameter Availability	4	System Functions	7
Persistent ID Type	4	Time/Date Functions	2097151
		Active Statements	1

The `Properties` Collection of the `Command` Object

Table 2.37 lists the 71 properties for a `Command` object opened on a `Connection` to SQL Server 7.0 with the native OLE DB SQL Server provider, SQLOLEDB. Like the `Connection` object, the `Execute` method of the `Command` object can return a forward-only `Recordset` object, so properties for the `Recordset`, such as `Row ... Notification` and `Rowset ... Notification` must be included. Properties whose names begin with `I`, such as `IRowset`, return values that specify whether the `Recordset` object supports the particular OLE DB COM interface.

TABLE 2.37 PROPERTY NAMES AND VALUES FOR A Command OBJECT USING THE NATIVE SQLOLEDB PROVIDER TO CONNECT TO AN UPSIZED NWIND DATABASE ON SQL SERVER 7.0

Property Name	Value	Property Name	Value
IAccessor	True	Column Set Notification	3
IColumnsInfo	True	Row Delete Notification	3
IColumnsRowset	True	Row First Change Notification	3
IConnectionPointContainer	True	Row Insert Notification	3
IConvertType	True	Row Resynchronization Notification	3
IRowset	True	Rowset Release Notification	3
IRowsetChange	False	Rowset Fetch Position Change Notification	3
IRowsetIdentity	False	Row Undo Change Notification	3
IRowsetInfo	True	Row Undo Delete Notification	3
Bookmarkable	False	Row Undo Insert Notification	3
IRowsetResynch	False	Row Update Notification	3
IRowsetScroll	False	Others' Inserts Visible	False
IRowsetUpdate	False	Others' Changes Visible	False
ISupportErrorInfo	True	Own Inserts Visible	False
ISequentialStream	True	Own Changes Visible	False
Preserve on Abort	False	Quick Restart	False
Blocking Storage Objects	True	Reentrant Events	True
Include Bookmark Data	False	Remove Deleted Rows	False

continues

TABLE 2.37 CONTINUED

Property Name	Value	Property Name	Value
Skip Deleted Bookmarks	False	Report Multiple Changes	False
Bookmark Type	1	Return Pending Inserts	False
Fetch Backwards	False	Row Privileges	False
Hold Rows	False	Row Threading Model	1
Scroll Backwards	False	Server Cursor	False
Change Inserted Rows	True	Strong Row Identity	False
Column Privileges	False	Objects Transacted	False
Command Time Out	30	Updatability	0
Preserve on Commit	False	Concurrency Type	15
Defer Column	False	Position on the last row after insert	False
Delay Storage Object Updates	False	FOR BROWSE columns hidden	False
Immobile Rows	True	No FOR BROWSE table	False
Literal Bookmarks	False	Log text and image operations	True
Literal Row Identity	True	Maximum BLOB Length	0
Maximum Open Rows	0	Fastload Options	
Maximum Pending Rows	0	Keep Nulls	False
Maximum Rows	0	Keep Identity	False
Notification Phases	31		

The `Properties` Collection of the `Recordset` Object

Table 2.38 lists the names and values of the 64 properties of a `Recordset` object created by calling the `Open` method of the `Recordset` object with its `ActiveConnection` property set to a `Connection` object using the Microsoft.Jet.OLEDB.3.51 provider. Property names with a `JetOLEDB:` prefix are specific to Jet databases; a few of these properties aren't supported by Jet 3.5*x*.

TABLE 2.38 PROPERTY NAMES AND VALUES FOR A Recordset OBJECT USING THE NATIVE MICROSOFT.JET.OLEDB.3.51 PROVIDER TO CONNECT TO THE NWIND.MDB DATABASE

Property Name	Value	Property Name	Value
Preserve on Abort	False	Row Threading Model	1
Blocking Storage Objects	True	Objects Transacted	True

Property Name	Value	Property Name	Value
Include Bookmark Data	True	Updatability	7
Skip Deleted Bookmarks	False	Strong Row Identity	False
Bookmark Type	1	IAccessor	True
Cache Deferred Columns	False	IColumnsInfo	True
Fetch Backwards	True	IColumnsRowset	False
Hold Rows	True	IConnectionPointContainer	True
Scroll Backwards	True	IRowset	True
Column Privileges	True	IRowsetChange	True
Preserve on Commit	True	IRowsetIdentity	False
Defer Column	True	IRowsetInfo	True
Delay Storage Object Updates	True	Bookmarkable	True
Immobile Rows	True	IRowsetResynch	False
Literal Bookmarks	False	IRowsetScroll	True
Literal Row Identity	False	IRowsetUpdate	True
Maximum Open Rows	0	ISupportErrorInfo	False
Maximum Pending Rows	1	ILockBytes	True
Maximum Rows	0	ISequentialStream	True
Column Writable	True	IStorage	False
Memory Usage	0	IStream	False
Notification Phases	27	IRowsetIndex	False
Bookmarks Ordered	False	Append-Only Rowset	False
Others' Inserts Visible	False	Change Inserted Rows	True
Others' Changes Visible	True	Return Pending Inserts	False
Own Inserts Visible	True	IConvertType	True
Own Changes Visible	True	Jet OLEDB:Partial Bulk Ops	False
Quick Restart	True	Jet OLEDB:Optimistic Locking	True
Reentrant Events	False	Jet OLEDB:Pass Through Query Connect String	
Remove Deleted Rows	True	Jet OLEDB:ODBC Pass-Through Statement	False
Report Multiple Changes	True	Jet OLEDB:Grbit Value	0
Row Privileges	False	Jet OLEDB:Use Grbit	0

MIGRATING FROM DAO AND RDO TO ADO

IN THIS CHAPTER

Despite the success of the Jet database engine and Data Access Objects (DAO) in the desktop database market, and the expanding role of Remote Data Objects (RDO) in high-performance client/server front ends, Microsoft wants Visual Basic 6.0 and, ultimately, Access 9.0 developers to move to ActiveX Data Objects (ADO). To encourage Visual Basic developers to make the switch to ADO, Microsoft includes in Visual Basic 6.0 a multitude of new and improved data-related objects, many of which offer a wizard or a set of dialogs to specify property values. The most important of these new objects is the `DataEnvironment`, an expanded version of the RDO `UserConnection` object. The "Opening an `ADODB.Recordset` Object from a `DataEnvironment` Object" section of Chapter 2, "Understanding OLE DB and Universal Data Access," provides an introduction to the use of `DataEnvironment` objects.

All Access developers and most Visual Basic database programmers are well acquainted with DAO. The two prior editions of this book incorporated extensive and detailed coverage of DAO. This chapter is the only chapter of *Database Developer's Guide with Visual Basic 6* that discusses DAO and RDO; the remainder of the book deals exclusively with ADO. A minor exception is the "Programming Jet Security Features with DAO 3.5" section of Chapter 17, "Networking Secure Multiuser Jet Databases."

▶ See "The Practical Grammar of a Simple SQL SELECT Statement," **p. 255**

NOTE

Like Chapter 2, this chapter assumes familiarity with elementary Visual Basic database programming techniques using the Jet database engine. If you're a first-time Visual Basic database programmer, you might want to skip this chapter and proceed to Chapter 4, "Using the ADO Data Control with Bound Controls." SQL SELECT statements appear throughout this chapter. If you're not conversant with SQL syntax, read the first part of Chapter 6, "Learning Structured Query Language," which deals with basic SELECT queries.

COMPARING ADO, DAO, AND RDO OBJECT MODELS

The first step to migrating from the obsolescent DAO 3.5x and RDO 2.0 object models to ADO 2.0 is to understand the similarities and differences between the old and new object models. Microsoft designed ADO as "a superset of RDO." One of the objectives of ADO architecture is to support Microsoft's vision of "SQL Server Everywhere." The introduction of the desktop version of SQL Server 7.0, which runs under Windows 95 and 98, illustrates Microsoft's intention to move ultimately to the client/server model for all of its database development platforms. A single object model optimized for both Jet (ISAM) and client/server RDBMSs paves the way for a simple application upgrade path from Jet to SQL Server 7+.

NOTE

Microsoft's public announcement in early 1998 of the desktop version of SQL Server 7.0 resulted in several "Jet Is Dead" articles in the trade press. For example, the February 9, 1998, issue of *PC Week* magazine reported, "The end is in sight for Microsoft's Jet database engine. Database developers, take note." Like the ill-reported demise of Mark Twain, rumors of the death of Jet are greatly exaggerated. Jet currently is used by 25 Microsoft products, including Windows NT, Money, Internet Information Server, Index Server, and Project. A Jet variation serves as the message store for Exchange Server. Jet probably will survive well into the twenty-first century, despite the description of the desktop version of SQL Server 7.0 as an "alternative database engine" for Access 9.0. Don't confuse DAO with Jet; DAO is a data-oriented object model, not a database engine.

ADO 2.0 versus DAO 3.5x

DAO is an extraordinarily complex data model, comprising the 13 collections and 17 objects (including objects that are members of collections) illustrated in Figure 3.1. The complexity ensued from Microsoft's original design, which required DAO to accommodate Jet's array of Access-specific elements, such as the Groups, Users, and Containers collections.

FIGURE 3.1

The complete hierarchy of DAO 3.5x collections and objects for Jet 3.5x databases.

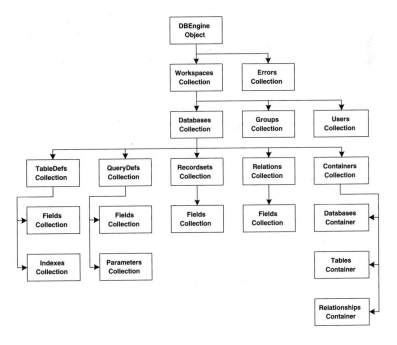

ADO takes OLE DB's least-common-denominator approach to database access by dispensing with DAO's hierarchical object model. Instead of an object hierarchy, ADO defines an independent and essentially flat set of top-level objects described at length in Chapter 2. Figure 3.2 illustrates the relationships between the most-used members of DAO and ADO. ADO's `Error(s)` object and collection, `Recordset` object, and `Field(s)` object and collection have direct DAO counterparts. ADO's `Connection` object corresponds, in general, to DAO's `Workspace` object, and the ADO `Command` object closely resembles the DAO `QueryDef` object. `Error`, `Recordset`, and `Field` objects serve identical purposes in ADO and DAO, and `Parameter` objects (not shown in Figure 3.2) perform similar functions. The properties and methods of ADO objects, however, differ markedly from those of the corresponding DAO objects. Thus as illustrated by the properties and methods tables of Chapter 2, you can't simply change the object declarations in your existing DAO code when migrating existing applications to ADO.

FIGURE 3.2

A comparison of the most-used objects of DAO 3.5 and ADO 2.0.

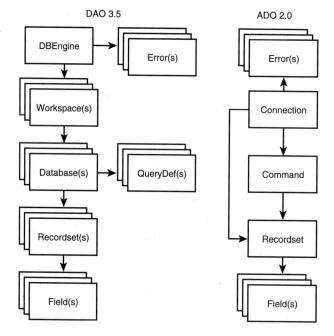

NOTE

The native OLE DB provider for Jet 3.5x databases, Microsoft.Jet.OLEDB.3.51 (more commonly known as *Jolt*) doesn't support Access-specific objects, such as `Groups`, `Users`, `Containers`, and `Documents` collections or objects, nor does it directly support `TableDef(s)` or `QueryDef(s)`. Version 4.0 of Jolt will accommodate all of these collections and objects.

In addition to making code changes to accommodate ADO, you also must upgrade most bound controls from DAO to ADO because ADO and DAO use different data binding COM interfaces, IRowset and ICursor, respectively. OLE DB's IRowset interface is much more versatile than ICursor, accommodating any class of data that can be delivered in a row-column format. The IRowset interface supports hierarchical data structures, described in the "Replacing Form/Subform Combinations with Hierarchical Grids" section later in this chapter. ICursor can't handle hierarchical Recordsets. Following are compatibility guidelines for data-related Visual Basic controls:

- The intrinsic (DAO) Data control and the DBGrid and RDO Data ActiveX controls don't work with ADO.

- The intrinsic bound controls (TextBox, PictureBox, Label, and so on) and the Masked Edit control work with both ADO and DAO data sources.

- You must use the ActiveX ADO Data control (ADODC), DataGrid, DataList, DataCombo, FlexGrid, and Hierarchical FlexGrid (MSHFlexGrid) controls with ADO data sources.

- None of the ADO-specific ActiveX controls support the ICursor interface, so they can't be used with DAO data sources.

- Data-bound ActiveX controls from third parties might not support the ICursor interface. You must test each third-party control to determine its compatibility with ADO 2.0.

> **NOTE**
>
> International Software Group, Inc. (ISG) offers an ISGData ActiveX control (Isgdata.ocx) that accommodates ADO data sources and binds the intrinsic Data controls and other ActiveX controls that support only the ICursor interface. The ISGData control enables Visual Basic 5.0 developers to take advantage of new ADO features. You also can use the ISGData control and the intrinsic bound controls of Visual Basic 6.0 to minimize changes to existing forms. You can download a royalty-free copy of the ISGData control from http://www.isg-soft.com. ISG, which publishes ISG Navigator, was one of the first independent software vendors (ISVs) to market third-party OLE DB data and service providers.

ADO 2.0 versus RDO 2.0

The ADO object model closely resembles that of RDO, which is not surprising when you consider Microsoft's emphasis on client/server RDBMSs (and especially SQL Server) as the preferred database engine for current and future database front-end development languages. RDO is dedicated to ODBC as its data source; ADO accommodates all native OLE DB data providers and the generic OLE DB-over-ODBC data source, MSDASQL. As noted in Chapter 1,

"Staking Visual Basic's Claim to Enterprise Development," one of the major advantages of ADO over RDO is that you don't need to purchase the Enterprise Edition of Visual Basic to gain the RDO-related benefits of ADO. Microsoft Access has never supported RDO; Access 9.0 support for ADO assures widespread adoption of ADO by database developers.

> **NOTE**
>
> The MSDASQL OLE DB provider (originally code-named Kagera) is a stop-gap product that is likely to disappear from general use as soon as native OLE DB providers are available for all popular ISAM and client/server RDBMSs, as well as for other commonly used ODBC data sources, such as Excel worksheets. Properly designed native OLE DB data providers hold the potential for better performance than MSDASQL with ODBC drivers. OLE DB offers a streamlined method for enumerating available providers that is considerably more sophisticated than ODBC's Driver Manager.

Figure 3.3 compares RDO 2.0 and ADO 2.0 objects. ADO doesn't include the equivalent of the `rdoEnvironment(s)` collection and object, because the `rdoEnvironment` object is associated with an individual ODBC `hEnv` handle. The `Properties` collections of ADO's `Connection`, `Command`, and `Recordset` objects aren't shown in Figure 3.3

FIGURE 3.3

A comparison of the object structure of RDO 2.0 and ADO 2.0.

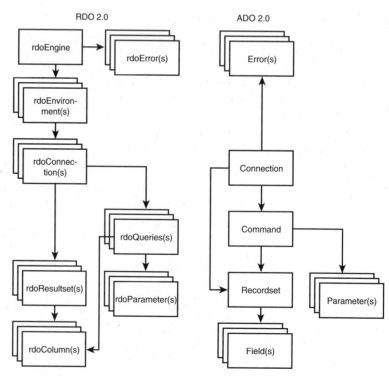

> **NOTE**
>
> Figure 3.3 illustrates `rdoParameter(s)` and `ADODB.Parameter(s)` collections and objects because parameters are important to the execution of stored procedures. One of the primary reasons Microsoft added RDO to the Enterprise Editions of Visual Basic 4.0 and 5.0 was to support input and output parameters and to return values of stored procedures. The `rdoTable(s)` collection and object are omitted because `ADODB.Recordset` objects supply the equivalent of `rdoTable` objects when you set the value of the `CommandType` property value of a `Connection` or `Command` object to `adCmdTable` and supply a table name as the initial argument of the `Open` method.

▶ **See** "Connection Events," **p. 82**

▶ **See** "Recordset Events," **p. 112**

Like RDO 2.0, ADO 2.0 offers a granular event model; the advantage of ADO 2.0 is that its event model applies to all data sources that offer event notification, not just client/server RDBMSs. Members of the `Properties` collections of `Connection`, `Command`, and `Recordset` objects specify the notifications issued by the object, which translate into events. Chapter 2's Table 2.35, which lists provider-specific properties of the `Command` object using the OLE DB provider for Jet, includes its collection of `Notification` properties.

ADO supports RDO 2.0's `BatchUpdate` method, which lets you make multiple changes to the locally cached `Recordset` object and apply all of the changes to the underlying data source tables in a single operation. Setting the `LockType` property of the `Recordset` object to `adLockBatchOptimistic` enables batch operations on the underlying tables. The "Migrating from `rdoResultsets` and ODBCDirect `Recordsets` to `ADODB.Recordsets`" section later in this chapter provides a detailed comparison of ADO 2.0 and RDO 2.0 properties, methods, and events.

You can't use the RDO Data control (MSRDC) with OLE DB data providers because, like the intrinsic Data control, MSRDC uses the ICursor interface. The Microsoft RemoteData Control 6.0 (Msrdc20.ocx) is included with Visual Basic 6.0 Enterprise Edition only for backward compatibility.

▶ **See** "Opening an `ADODB.Recordset` Object from a `DataEnvironment` Object," **p. 58**

3

MIGRATING FROM DAO AND RDO TO ADO

> **NOTE**
>
> The Data Environment Designer (DED) for ADO in Visual Basic 6.0 replaces the User Connection Designer for RDO in the Enterprise Edition of Visual Basic 5.0. UserConnection objects are restricted to ODBC data sources; DataEnvironment objects connect to any OLE DB data source.

MOVING FROM DAO.Recordset TO ADODB.Recordset OBJECTS

The differences between the standard property and method sets of DAO.Recordset and ADODB.Recordset objects alone are sufficient to make it impractical to convert database front ends with many data-related objects and substantial amounts of VBA code from DAO 3.5x to ADO 2.0. Chapter 14, "Scheduling and Device Control with Jet and VBA," exemplifies the amount of work required to change a complex DAO 3.51 project to ADO 2.0. Microsoft recommends that all new database front-end applications, regardless of the development platform or language, use ADO. The following comparisons between the properties and methods of the DAO.Recordset and ADODB.Recordset object are intended to smooth the way for your transition from DAO 3.5x to ADO 2.0.

> **NOTE**
>
> The importance of ADO and OLE DB to the future of Microsoft's data-related activities is such that if it were feasible to write a wizard to convert DAO and RDO applications to ADO 2.0, Visual Basic 6.0 would have a wizard to do so. It doesn't.

Comparing DAO.Recordset and ADODB.Recordset Properties

Table 3.1 lists the properties of DAO.Recordset objects and the corresponding ADODB.Recordset properties if ADO 2.0 provides a comparable property. The Comments and Workarounds column provides recommended substitutions of ADODB.Recordset properties or methods for unsupported DAO.Recordset properties.

> **NOTE**
>
> Table 3.1 doesn't include properties specific to DAO.Recordset objects opened on ODBCDirect Connections. ODBCDirect is a DAO "wrapper" for RDO. The "Comparing rdoResultset and ADODB.Recordset Properties" section later in the chapter covers ODBCDirect Recordset properties.

TABLE 3.1   A COMPARISON OF THE PROPERTIES OF DAO.`Recordset` AND ADODB.`Recordset` OBJECTS

DAO.Recordset	ADODB.Recordset	*Comments and Workarounds*
AbsolutePosition	AbsolutePosition	No difference.
BOF	BOF	No difference.
Bookmark	Bookmark	No difference.
Bookmarkable		Use the Supports method with the adBookmark flag.
CacheSize	CacheSize	No difference.
CacheStart		Not supported.
DateCreated		Jet specific.
EditMode	EditMode	Constant names changed from dbEdit... to adEdit....
EOF	EOF	
Filter	Filter	ADODB.Recordset adds adFilter... constants.
Index		For table-type Recordsets only, not supported.
LastModified		Jet specific, not supported.
LastUpdated		Jet specific, not supported.
LockEdits	LockEdits	adLock... constants provide addition options.
Name		ADODB.Recordsets aren't named members of collections.
NoMatch	EOF (forward Find) or BOF (backward Find)	NoMatch is the equivalent of the expression EOF **Or** BOF.
PercentPosition		Use AbsolutePosition and RecordCount to calculate.
RecordCount	RecordCount	No difference.
Restartable		All ADODB.Recordsets support Requery.
Sort	Sort	No difference.
Transactions		ADODB.Connection. IsolationLevel > 0 is similar, but not identical.

continues

3

MIRGRATING FROM DAO AND RDO TO ADO

TABLE 3.1 CONTINUED

DAO.Recordset	ADODB.Recordset	*Comments and Workarounds*
Type	CursorType	Constant names changed from dbOpen... to adOpen....
Updatable		Use the Supports method with the adUpdate flag.
ValidationRule		Jet specific, not supported.
ValidationText		Jet specific, not supported.

Comparing DAO.Recordset and ADODB.Recordset Methods

Table 3.2 lists the methods of DAO.Recordset objects and the corresponding ADODB.Recordset methods, where ADO 2.0 provides a comparable method. Correlation of methods between the two objects is better than that for properties.

> **NOTE**
>
> Like Table 3.1, Table 3.2 doesn't include ODBCDirect-related methods. The "Comparing rdoResultset and ADODB.Recordset Methods" section later in the chapter deals with ODBCDirect Recordset methods.

TABLE 3.2 A COMPARISON OF THE METHODS OF DAO.Recordset AND ADODB.Recordset OBJECTS

DAO.Recordset	ADODB.Recordset	*Comments*
AddNew	AddNew	ADODB.Recordset version supports Fields and Values arguments.
CancelUpdate	CancelUpdate	No difference.
Clone	Clone	No difference.
Close	Close	No difference.
CopyQueryDef		ADO doesn't support QueryDefs.
Delete	Delete	No difference.
Edit		Not supported (ADO doesn't require calling Edit before Update).

FillCache		Not supported.
Find...	Find	Multiple Find... methods are replaced by the single Find method with added arguments.
GetRows	GetRows	No difference.
Move	Move	No difference.
Move...	Move...	No difference.
OpenRecordset	Open	Open is a method of the ADODB.Recordset object; OpenRecordset is a method of DAO Database, QueryDef, and TableDef objects. (The Open method's argument list differs from OpenRecordset's.)
Requery	Requery	No difference.
Seek		Not supported (no Index property, because ADO doesn't support Table objects).
Update	Update	ADODB.Recordset version supports Fields and Values arguments to create Recordsets with code.

▶ **See** " Replacing Compound FindFirst and FindNext Methods with Find," **p. 552**

p. 552

NOTE

The ADODB.Recordset's Find method differs greatly from the DAO.Recordset's FindFirst, FindNext, FindPrevious, and FindLast (Find...) methods. The primary difference is that Find is limited to a single-field criterion, while Find... accepts any valid SQL WHERE clause (without WHERE). This restriction to the Find method requires inelegant workarounds when converting complex search criteria from DAO to ADO. The "Adopting ADODB.Recordset Find Methods" section, later in the chapter, provides code examples for converting single-field operations from Find... to Find.

MANIPULATING ADODB.Recordset OBJECTS WITH VBA CODE

Microsoft provides Visual Basic 6.0 developers with an arsenal of data-bound controls to minimize the amount of code needed to create simple database front ends. You add an ADO Data control to a form, set its data-related properties and then add a grid (or list, combo, or text box) bound to the ADO Data control. Data-bound controls are the easiest approach to displaying and editing data within a Visual Basic project.

Few, if any, production Visual Basic front-end applications make extensive use of bound controls. Each ADO Data control requires at least one and sometime several active connections to its associated database. Multiple database connections aren't a significant issue with single-user database front ends where the database resides on the client PC. Minimizing the number of active connections, however, is critical for networked multiuser and client/server front ends. Client connections consume server memory resources, and active connections generate substantial network traffic. To maximize overall performance and minimize resource consumption, the vast majority of Visual Basic database developers create and manage Recordset objects with code. Thus the examples of this chapter concentrate on VBA code for manipulating ADO components.

> **NOTE**
>
> Another benefit of the use of code to manipulate ADO components is application maintainability and self-documentation. It's much easier for others to grasp the design and execution pattern of your application by reading VBA code. The alternative requires reading in the Properties window numerous property values of a myriad of data-bound controls. The Data Environment Designer minimizes lines of code to open Connection, Command, and Recordset objects but doesn't self-document your project. Making changes to property values, such as the name or location of a database, is much easier using the search-and-replace feature of the Visual Basic code editor than typing the required changes in the Properties window for the controls.

Creating a Recordset Directly

▶ See "Recordset Methods," p. 107

The best demonstration of ADO object independence is the ability to open directly an ADODB.Recordset object without specifying an ADODB.Connection or ADODB.Command object. Opening a Recordset directly requires a complete ConnectionString for the ActiveConnection argument of the ADODB.Recordset.Open method.

The following VBA code illustrates direct opening of a `Recordset` for an ADO Data control (adcNwind), using the native OLE DB data provider for Jet, Microsoft.Jet.OLEDB.3.51:

```
Private Sub Form_Load()
    Dim rstNwind As New ADODB.Recordset
    Dim strConnect As String
    Dim strSQL As String

    strConnect = "User ID=Admin;Password=;Data Source=" & App.Path & _
        "\Nwind.mdb;Provider=Microsoft.Jet.OLEDB.3.51"
    strSQL = "SELECT * FROM Orders WHERE OrderDate " & _
        "BETWEEN #1/1/95# AND #12/31/95#"
    rstNwind.Open strSQL, strConnect, adOpenKeyset, _
        adLockOptimistic, adCmdText
    Set adcNwind.Recordset = rstNwind
End Sub
```

> **NOTE**
>
> The ADOOpen.vbp project, described in the "Recycling `Connection` and `Recordset` Objects with the `Close` and `Open` Methods" section later in this chapter, demonstrates all the `Recordset` creation methods in this and the succeeding sections.

In the preceding example, the third and fourth arguments of the `Open` method specify the values of the `CursorType` and `LockType` properties of the resulting `Recordset` object. The `Provider=Microsoft.Jet.OLEDB.3.51` element of the connection string supplies the value for the `Provider` property. `Recordsets` created with VBA code default to a server-side `CursorLocation` (adUseServer), which provides better performance with Jet databases. The default `CursorLocation` for `Recordsets` you create with the Data Environment Designer is adUseClient.

> **NOTE**
>
> The complete `ConnectionString` for the native OLE DB provider for SQL Server, SQLOLEDB, with the default sa user and no password is strConnect = "User ID=sa;Password=;Data Source=nwind;Location=OAKLEAF0;Provider=SQLOLEDB". To use the default OLE DB-Over-ODBC driver, MSDASQL (formerly known as Kagera), with a DSN-less ODBC connection, specify strConnect = "driver={SQL Server};server=OAK-LEAF0;uid=sa;pwd=;database=nwind". MSDASQL is the default OLE DB service provider for ADO, so you don't need to add ;Provider=MSDASQL to the string. When using SQL Server or another client/server RDBMS, replace the Jet-specific # date delimiters in the SQL statement with single quotes (').

Compare the simplicity of the preceding code with that commonly used to open a similar
DAO.Recordset object over the Orders table of Nwind.mdb using DAO 3.5:

```
Private Sub Form_Load()
    Dim wsNwind As DAO.Workspace
    Dim dbNwind As DAO.Database
    Dim rsNwind As DAO.Recordset
    Dim strConnect As String
    Dim strSQL As String

    strConnect = App.Path & "\Nwind.mdb"
    strSQL = "SELECT * FROM Orders WHERE OrderDate BETWEEN #1/1/95# AND #12/31/95#"

    Set wsNwind = DBEngine.Workspaces(0) 'The default workspace
    Set dbNwind = wsNwind.OpenDatabase(strConnect)
    Set rsNwind = dbNwind.OpenRecordset(strSQL, dbOpenDynaset)
    Set dtcNwind.Recordset = rsNwind
    dtcNwind.Refresh
End Sub
```

DAO must instantiate three database objects, whereas ADO requires only one. There isn't a
perceptible difference in the execution time of the two preceding event handlers on Pentium
client PCs. Minimizing the number of concurrently open objects, however, is a good programming practice because it conserves resources. Resource conservation through minimizing object
instances is especially important when writing Visual Basic database components that run on
servers.

> **NOTE**
>
> Most of the code examples of this chapter create a Recordset object that's
> assigned to the Recordset property of an ADODC. Binding a DataGrid to the
> ADODC expedites testing the execution of the code examples. If you decide to
> use the ADODC and data-bound controls in production applications, setting the
> Recordset property in code is preferable to setting the DataSource, DataMember,
> and other data-related properties of the control in design mode, either directly
> or by using the Data Environment Designer.

Opening a Recordset on a Connection Object

▶ **See** "Connection Properties," **p. 69**

▶ **See** "Connection Methods," **p. 75**

The preferred method of opening a Recordset object is to open a Connection object and pass
a reference to the Connection object as the value of the ActiveConnection property of the
Recordset. The advantage of this approach is the ability to independently manage the database

connection. The primary change to the preceding example is the shortened Jet connection string, which specifies only the name and location of the database. The ADO `Connection.Open` method is related closely to the DAO `Workspace.OpenDatabase` method.

The following code opens an updatable `Recordset` on an active `Connection` object:

```
Private Sub Form_Load()
    Dim cnnNwind As New ADODB.Connection
    Dim rstNwind As New ADODB.Recordset
    Dim strConnect As String
    Dim strSQL As String

    strConnect = App.Path & "\Nwind.mdb"
    cnnNwind.Provider = "Microsoft.Jet.OLEDB.3.51"
    cnnNwind.Open strConnect, "Admin" ', "Password", if secured
    strSQL = "SELECT * FROM Orders WHERE OrderDate " & _
        "BETWEEN #1/1/95# AND #12/31/95#"
    rstNwind.Open strSQL, cnnNwind, adOpenKeyset, _
        adLockOptimistic, adCmdText
    Set adcNwind.Recordset = rstNwind
End Sub
```

Alternatively, you can use the `Execute` method of the `Connection` object to open a default forward-only `Recordset`, regardless of values you preassign to the `CursorType` property. Forward-only `Recordsets` are fast and efficient for applications that manipulate `Recordsets` only with code. You can assign a forward-only `Recordset` to the `ADODC.Recordset` property without generating an error, but controls bound to the ADO Data control won't display the records.

The following VBA code example uses the `Execute` method to open the `Recordset`:

```
Private Sub Form_Load()
    Dim cnnNwind As New ADODB.Connection
    Dim rstNwind As New ADODB.Recordset
    Dim strConnect As String
    Dim strSQL As String

    strConnect = App.Path & "\Nwind.mdb"
    cnnNwind.Provider = "Microsoft.Jet.OLEDB.3.51"
    cnnNwind.Open strConnect, "Admin" ', "Password", if secure
    strSQL = "SELECT * FROM Orders WHERE OrderDate " & _
        "BETWEEN #1/1/95# AND #12/31/95#"
    Set rstNwind = cnnNwind.Execute(strSQL)
    '...Code to manipulate the Recordset goes here
End Sub
```

Opening a Recordset on a `Command` Object

The `ADODB.Command` object is similar in function to the `DAO.QueryDef` object but can be independent of any other ADO component. The full connection string of the `Command` object is the same as that for the `Connection` object. You use the `Execute` method to execute SQL `INSERT`,

UPDATE, and DELETE statements, none of which returns rows. Calling the Execute method with a stored procedure or a row-returning SQL statement as its argument returns a forward-only Recordset. To return an updatable Recordset, you call the Recordset.Open method and pass a reference to the Command object as the first (Source) argument; there is no active connection, so the second Recordset.Open argument is empty.

The following VBA code example illustrates opening an updatable Recordset on a Command object:

```
Private Sub Form_Load()
    Dim cmmNwind As New ADODB.Command
    Dim rstNwind As New ADODB.Recordset
    Dim strConnect As String
    Dim strSQL As String

    strConnect = "User ID=Admin;Password=;Data Source=" & App.Path & _
        "\Nwind.mdb;Provider=Microsoft.Jet.OLEDB.3.51"
    strSQL = "SELECT * FROM Orders WHERE OrderDate " & _
        "BETWEEN #1/1/95# AND #12/31/95#"
    With cmmNwind
        .ActiveConnection = strConnect
        .CommandType = adCmdText
        .CommandText = strSQL
    End With
    rstNwind.Open cmmNwind, , adOpenKeyset, adLockOptimistic, adCmdText
    Set adcNwind.Recordset = rstNwind
End Sub
```

▶ **See** "Opening an ADODB.Recordset Object from a DataEnvironment Object," **p. 60**

Using code to open a Recordset directly on a Command object is uncommon because this method has no advantage over creating a Recordset directly or on a Connection object. The purpose of the preceding example is to illustrate with code the technique employed by the DataEnvironment object to automatically generate an updatable Recordset object (rsCommandName) from a persistent Command object you create with the Data Environment Designer.

Specifying a Jet Workgroup File for Secure Databases

▶ **See** "Assigning User Accounts and Securing Jet Databases," **p. 668**

The preceding code examples assume use of the unsecured Jet 3.0 Nwind.mdb sample database included with Visual Basic 6.0. The User ID=Admin;Password=; elements of the connection string and the "Admin" argument value aren't required to connect to an unsecured Jet database.

Microsoft Access 7+ *workgroup files*, called *system databases* by Access 1.*x* and 2.0, store User names, group names, and passwords for secure Jet databases. The default workgroup file for 32-bit Jet databases isSystem.mdw; 16-bit versions use SYSTEM.MDA. Secure Jet databases are most commonly used in networked multiuser applications. You must provide the location and name of the workgroup file to open a connection to multiuser Jet database(s) with an active workgroup file.

> **NOTE**
>
> Jet 3.5x doesn't support the security-related SQL reserved words GRANT and REVOKE and version 3.51 of the native OLE DB Jet data provider isn't able to alter database permissions or the workgroup file. You must use the appropriate version of Access to add, delete, or modify groups, users, and passwords, as well as to grant or revoke database object permissions for groups and users.

The method of specifying the workgroup file depends on the OLE DB data provider. For the default MSDASQL ODBC provider, the DSN-less ODBC connection string for a secure Jet database is

```
strConnect = "driver=Microsoft Access Driver (*.mdb);" & _
             "dbq=\\ServerName\ShareName\Database.mdb;" & _
             "systemdb=\\ServerName\ShareName\System.mdw;" & _
             "uid=UserName;pwd=Password"
```

> **NOTE**
>
> DSN-less connections, introduced with Visual Basic 5.0, eliminate the need to create individual user, system, or file ODBC data sources on client PCs. With few exceptions, the ODBC examples in this book use DSN-less connections. Chapter 8, "Connecting to Desktop Data Sources with ODBC," describes the syntax of DSN-less connections and how to use the ODBC Administrator application to create user, system, and file data sources for secure Jet databases.

▶ **See** "The Properties collection of the Connection Object," **p. 116**

ADO 2.0 components don't have native UserID or Password properties, although you can (and often must) pass these values as arguments of the Connection.Open method. The connection string for the native OLE DB Jet data provider doesn't include a SystemDB=System.mdw element. To specify the location and name of the workgroup file using the Jet provider, you must pass the value to the provider-specific Connection property Jet OLEDB:System database, as in the following example:

```
Private Sub Form_Load()
    Dim cnnNwind As New ADODB.Connection
    Dim rstNwind As New ADODB.Recordset
    Dim strConnect As String
    Dim strSQL As String
```

```
    strConnect = App.Path & "\Nwind.mdb"
    With cnnNwind
        .Provider = "Microsoft.Jet.OLEDB.3.51"
        .Properties("Jet OLEDB:System database") = _
            "\\Carioca\Secure\System.mdw"
        .Open strConnect, "badenp", "iemanja"
    End With
    strSQL = "SELECT * FROM Orders WHERE OrderDate " & _
        "BETWEEN #1/1/95# AND #12/31/95#"
    rstNwind.Open strSQL, cnnNwind, adOpenKeyset, _
        adLockOptimistic, adCmdText
    Set adcNwind.Recordset = rstNwind
End Sub
```

TIP

It's faster to specify the ordinal value (`Index`) rather than the `Name` of the member of a collection having a large number of values. However, using `.Properties(34)` instead of `.Properties("Jet OLEDB:System database")` in the preceding example isn't safe. Successive revisions of an OLE DB data provider might involve adding or deleting members of its `Properties` collection. Such modifications are likely to affect the ordinal value of the `Property` object whose value you want to get or set.

Alternatively, you can specify the user name, password, and the location and name of the workgroup file in the value of the `ConnectionString` property, as follows:

```
strConn = "User ID=Name;Password=Pwd;" & _
    "Data Source=\\servername\sharename\database.mdb;" & _
    "Provider=Microsoft.Jet.OLEDB.3.51;" & _
    "Jet OLEDB:System database=\\servername\sharename\wrkgrp.mdw;"
```

Batching Table Updates

RDO 2.0 introduced batch operations on client/server table(s) underlying an `rdoResultset` object. ADO offers the same capability for any OLE DB data provider that supports batch operations. To set up `ADODB.Recordset` batch operations, follow these basic steps:

1. Set the value of the `Recordset`'s `LockType` property to `adLockBatchOptimistic`.
2. Set the value of the `CursorType` property to `adOpenKeyset` or `adOpenStatic`.
3. Set the value of the `CursorLocation` property to `adUseClient`.
4. Call the `Open` method to create the locally cached `Recordset`.
5. Alter the content of the `Recordset` by changing cell values, adding new rows, or deleting rows, as desired.

6. Call the `UpdateBatch` method to apply the changes to the underlying table(s) or call `CancelBatch` to retain the original table values.

The following VBA code opens a Jet `Recordset` object for batch-optimistic updating by editing records in a `DataGrid` control bound to the `adcNwind` ADO Data control:

```
Option Explicit
Private cnnNwind As New ADODB.Connection
Private rstNwind As New ADODB.Recordset

Private Sub Form_Activate()
   Dim strConnect As String
   Dim strSQL As String

   strConnect = App.Path & "\Nwind.mdb"
   cnnNwind.Provider = "Microsoft.Jet.OLEDB.3.51"
   cnnNwind.Open strConnect, "Admin" ', "Password", if the database is secure
   strSQL = "SELECT * FROM Orders WHERE OrderDate " & _
      "BETWEEN #1/1/95# AND #12/31/95#"
   rstNwind.CursorLocation = adUseClient
   rstNwind.Open strSQL, cnnNwind, adOpenKeyset, adLockBatchOptimistic, adCmdText
   Set adcNwind.Recordset = rstNwind
End Sub
```

Assuming two command buttons, `cmdUpdate` and `cmdCancel`, the following `Click` event handlers update the tables or cancel the batch operation and restore the original record values to the DataGrid control:

```
Private Sub cmdUpdate_Click()
   rstNwind.UpdateBatch
End Sub

Private Sub cmdCancel_Click()
   rstNwind.CancelBatch
   rstNwind.Requery
End Sub
```

Batch operations are an alternative to transactions or may be executed within a transaction. The primary advantage of batch operations is the ability to use members of the `Errors` collection to determine the outcome of the operation and to resolve problems with updating individual table records. Chapter 19, "Processing Transactions and Bulk Operations," covers use of the `UpdateBatch` method in detail.

TAKING ADVANTAGE OF NEW `ADODB.Recordset` FEATURES

`ADODB.Recordsets` offer several new, important features not found in `DAO.Recordset` and `rdoResultset` objects. The most important of these features enables you to save the content of a `Recordset` to a local file, called a *persistent `Recordset`*. The sections that follow describe the VBA code required to utilize the new `ADODB.Recordset` features.

Saving and Opening File-Type Recordsets

You can save an `ADODB.Recordset` to a specially formatted file by calling the `Save` method and then opening a new `Recordset` from the content of the saved file. The following code example saves the `rstNwind` Recordset to a Orders.rst file:

```
Private Sub cmdSaveAsFile_Click()
    Dim rstNwind As New ADODB.Recordset
    Dim strConnect As String
    Dim strSQL As String
    Dim strFile As String

    strConnect = "User ID=Admin;Password=;Data Source=" & App.Path & _
        "\Nwind.mdb;Provider=Microsoft.Jet.OLEDB.3.51"
    strSQL = "SELECT * FROM Orders WHERE OrderDate " & _
        "BETWEEN #1/1/95# AND #12/31/95#"
    strFile = App.Path & "\Orders.rst"
    rstNwind.Open strSQL, strConnect, adOpenStatic, _
        adLockOptimistic, adCmdText
    rstNwind.Save strFile
```

Figure 3.4 shows Notepad (with WordWrap turned on) displaying the first few hundred bytes of the ADTG file created by the preceding example, most of which is readable. *ADTG* is an acronym for *Advanced Data TableGram*, the format used to transmit the content of `ADOR.Recordset` objects over TCP/IP connections, including the Internet. The file header is a list of column names. Record data follows the header. Microsoft doesn't make public the file specification for default ADTG format of persistent `Recordset`s.

FIGURE 3.4

Notepad displaying part of the content of a file saved from a Recordset object in ATDG.

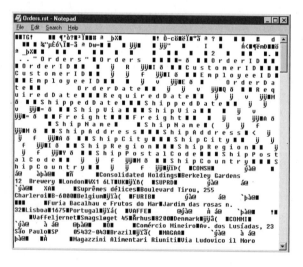

To open a Recordset from a saved file, supply the location and name of the file as the value of the first (Source) argument of the Recordset.Open method and set the value of the Options argument to adCmdFile, as in the following example:

```
Private Sub cmdLoadFromFile_Click()
    Dim rstNwind As New ADODB.Recordset
    Dim strFile As String

    strFile = App.Path & "\Nwind.rst"
    rstNwind.Open strFile,, adOpenStatic, adLockPessimistic, adCmdFile
Set adcNwind.Recordset = rstNwind
End Sub
```

You don't need to specify a provider, because the storage format of persistent Recordsets is determined by the OLE DB specification and is provider independent.

▶ **See** "Reviewing the Code of the Ado2oltp Project," **p. 796**

> **TIP**
>
> Persistent Recordsets are particularly useful in client/server front ends for storing local tables. Using local tables conserves connections to the server RDBMS and reduces network traffic. Most Visual Basic developers use a Jet database to hold lookup tables for state or province names and their abbreviations or for storing user application preferences. Using a Recordset file as a storage mechanism saves the substantial resource overhead of the Jet database engine.

Editing and Adding Rows with Variant Values and Arrays

ADODB.Recordset objects also enable you to edit row values of or add rows to a Recordset from a matching pair of **Variant** values or arrays. The Update and AddNew methods each have an optional argument pair, Fields and Values, that accepts a single **Variant** field name and its value, respectively, or a pair of **Variant** arrays of field names and corresponding column values.

The field name(s) must exactly match the values of the Recordset.Field(s) object(s) and the **Variant** subtype of the corresponding field values must match the data type of the field. Assuming an open Recordset, rstOrders, you can add a new row to the Orders table with the following code:

```
rstOrders.AddNew Array("CustomerID", "EmployeeID", _
    "OrderDate", "RequiredDate"), _
    Array("VINET", 5, #6/6/98#, #6/20/98#)
rstOrders.Update
```

NOTE

You don't include the `OrderID` field name or value, because the `OrderID` field of the Nwind.mdb Orders table is an AutoNumber (automatically incrementing) field.

To modify specific field values of the current record, use the following code:

```
rstOrders.Update Array("OrderDate", "RequiredDate"), _
    Array(#6/10/98#, #6/30/98#)
```

▶ See "Recordset Methods," **p. 106**

NOTE

Don't precede the `Update` method call with the `Edit` method. As noted in Chapter 2, the `ADODB.Recordset` object doesn't support an `Edit` method. An edit operation is implied by calling the `Update` method.

Variant arrays are a shorthand version of the traditional approach to adding to or editing Recordsets. ADO supports the following equivalents to the preceding examples:

```
With rstOrders
    .AddNew
    .Fields("CustomerID").Value = "VINET"
    .Fields("EmployeeID").Value = "5"
    .Fields("OrderDate").Value = #6/6/98#
    .Fields("RequiredDate").Value = #6/20/98#
    .Update
End With

With rstOrders
    .Fields("OrderDate").Value = #6/10/98#
    .Fields("RequiredDate").Value = #6/30/98#
    .Update
End With
```

TIP

`Value` is the default property of the `Field` object, so you can set cell values with `.Fields("`*FieldName*`") =` var*Value* or `.Fields(int`*Index*`) =` var*Value* statements. A good programming practice, however, is to explicitly add the `Value` property name when setting or getting a cell value. Using the `Value` property often delivers a slight performance improvement. Under some circumstances, failure to use the `Value` property name will cause your code to fail or produce an unexpected result.

Recycling `Connection` and `Recordset` Objects with the `Close` and `Open` Methods

▶ **See** Table 2.4, "Constant Enumeration for the `State` Property," **p. 72**

The `Connection` and `Recordset` object instances you declare as form level or module level are reusable. While open (in use), most of the properties of `Connection` and `Recordset` objects are read-only. Applying the `Close` method makes the object ready to accept a new set of property values and another call to the `Open` method. You must use the value of the `State` property of the object to determine whether to apply the `Close` method before preparing for another `Open` method call. The default `State` of an object is `adStateClosed` until opened. If you apply the `Close` method to an object you haven't previously opened, an error occurs.

Use the following code to perform the `State` test:

```
If {Connection¦Recordset}.State = adStateOpen Then
    {Connection¦Recordset}.Close
End If
```

> **NOTE**
>
> The `Command` object doesn't have `Open` and `Close` methods, so you seldom need to be concerned with its state. Once the `Command` has executed, you can change its property values and apply the `Execute` method. If the `Command` object executes long-running queries, you can test the `cmmName.State` property to determine whether execution has completed (`cmmName.State <> adStateExecuting`).

The ADOOpen.vbp project, in the \Ddg_vb6\Chaptr03 folder of the accompanying CD-ROM, demonstrates reuse of `Connection` and `Recordset` objects. In addition, the project demonstrates the five methods described earlier in the chapter for creating `Recordset` objects (see Figure 3.5). Rather than set `Connection` and `Recordset` property values with argument values for the `Open` method, as in the VBA code examples earlier in the chapter, the code of the `frmRecordsets` form sets the necessary property values directly. This style, used throughout the remainder of this book, makes ADO code more readable.

FIGURE 3.5

*The single form of
the ADOOpen pro-
ject for testing the
five methods of
creating a
Recordset object.*

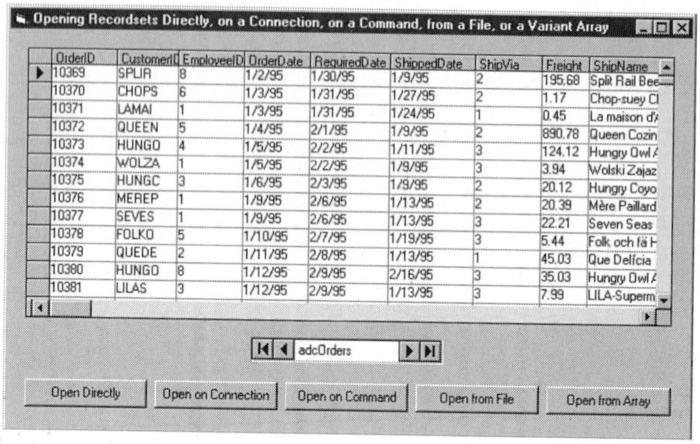

▶ See "ANSI SQL Reserved Words and Jet SQL Keywords," **p. 281**

NOTE

The TOP 100 predicate of the SQL statement used to create the Recordset
objects returns only the first 100 rows of the query result set. Maintaining a
constant Recordset size enables you to compare the performance of the different methods.

LISTING 3.1   VBA CODE FOR THE ADOOPEN PROJECT

```
Option Explicit
Private cnnOrders As New ADODB.Connection
Private cmmOrders As New ADODB.Command
Private rstOrders As New ADODB.RecordSet
Private strConnect As String
Private strSQL As String
Private avarData As Variant
Private avarValues() As Variant
Private avarFields() As Variant
Private Const strSQL1 = "SELECT TOP 100 * FROM Orders WHERE OrderDate BETWEEN #"
Private Const strSQL2 = "# AND #12/31/95#"

Private Sub cmdDirect_Click()
    'Create a Recordset directly
    strSQL = strSQL1 & "1/1/95" & strSQL2
    Call DirectRecordset(strSQL)
    Set adcOrders.Recordset = rstOrders
    adcOrders.Refresh
End Sub

Private Sub DirectRecordset(strSQL As String)
    'Create the Recordset
    'Called by Open Directly, Open from File, and Open from Array
```

```
    strConnect = "User ID=Admin;Password=;Data Source=" & App.Path & _
        "\Orders.mdb;Provider=Microsoft.Jet.OLEDB.3.51"
    With rstOrders
        If .State = adStateOpen Then
            .Close
        End If
        .LockType = adLockOptimistic
        .CursorLocation = adUseClient
        .CursorType = adOpenKeyset
        .ActiveConnection = strConnect
        .Open strSQL, Options:=adCmdText
    End With
End Sub

Private Sub cmdConnection_Click()
    'Create a Recordset on a Connection object
    'Change the start date to create an unique Recordset
    strSQL = strSQL1 & "2/1/95" & strSQL2
    strConnect = App.Path & "\Orders.mdb"
    With cnnOrders
        If .State = adStateOpen Then
            .Close
        End If
        .Provider = "Microsoft.Jet.OLEDB.3.51"
        .Open strConnect, "Admin"
    End With
    With rstOrders
        If .State = adStateOpen Then
            .Close
        End If
        .LockType = adLockOptimistic
        .CursorLocation = adUseClient
        .CursorType = adOpenKeySet
        .ActiveConnection = cnnOrders
        .Open strSQL, Options:=adCmdText
    End With
    Set adcOrders.Recordset = rstOrders
    adcOrders.Refresh
End Sub

Private Sub cmdCommand_Click()
    'Create a Recordset on a Command object
    'Change the start date to create an unique Recordset
    strSQL = strSQL1 & "3/1/95" & strSQL2
    strConnect = "User ID=Admin;Password=;Data Source=" & App.Path & _
        "\Orders.mdb;Provider=Microsoft.Jet.OLEDB.3.51"
    With cmmOrders
        .ActiveConnection = strConnect
        .CommandType = adCmdText
        .CommandText = strSQL
    End With
```

3

**MIRGRATING
FROM DAO AND
RDO TO ADO**

continues

LISTING 3.1 CONTINUED

```
    With rstOrders
        If .State = adStateOpen Then
            .Close
        End If
        .LockType = adLockOptimistic
        .CursorLocation = adUseClient
        .CursorType = adOpenKeySet
        Set .Source = cmmOrders
        .Open
    End With
    Set adcOrders.Recordset = rstOrders
    adcOrders.Refresh
End Sub

Private Sub cmdFromFile_Click()
    'Create a Recordset from a file
    Dim strFile As String

    'Change the start date to create an unique Recordset
    strSQL = strSQL1 & "4/1/95" & strSQL2
    strFile = App.Path & "\Orders.rst"
    On Error GoTo CreateFile
    If FileLen(strFile) Then
        On Error GoTo 0
        With rstOrders
            If .State = adStateOpen Then
                .Close
            End If
            .LockType = adLockOptimistic
            .CursorLocation = adUseClient
            .CursorType = adOpenKeyset
            .Open strFile, Options:=adCmdFile
        End With
Set adcOrders.Recordset = rstOrders
        Set dtgOrders.DataSource = adcOrders
End If
    Exit Sub

CreateFile:
    Call DirectRecordset(strSQL)
    rstOrders.Save strFile
    MsgBox "Created missing Orders.rst file. Click Open from File again.", _
        vbOKOnly, "Orders.rst File Needed"
    Exit Sub
End Sub

Private Sub cmdFromArray_Click()
    'Fill a Recordset from a matched pair of Variant arrays
    Dim fldOrders As ADODB.Field
```

```
Dim intCol As Integer
Dim intRow As Long

'Change the start date to create an unique Recordset
strSQL = strSQL1 & "5/1/95" & strSQL2
strConnect = "User ID=Admin;Password=;Data Source=" & App.Path & _
    "\Orders.mdb;Provider=Microsoft.Jet.OLEDB.3.51"

With cmmOrders
    'Delete existing records in the Test table, if any
    .ActiveConnection = strConnect
    .CommandType = adCmdText
    .CommandText = "DELETE * FROM Test"
    .Execute
End With
If rstOrders.State = adStateClosed Then
    'Create the Recordset
    Call DirectRecordset(strSQL)
End If

'Use GetRows to create the data array
avarData = rstOrders.GetRows(adGetRowsRest)
'Specify the size of the Values and Fields arrays
ReDim avarValues(rstOrders.Fields.Count - 1)
ReDim avarFields(rstOrders.Fields.Count - 1)
intCol = 0
For Each fldOrders In rstOrders.Fields
    'Set the Fields array values
    avarFields(intCol) = fldOrders.Name
    intCol = intCol + 1
Next fldOrders
With rstOrders
    .Close
.LockType = adLockBatchOptimistic
.CursorLocation = adUseClient
    .CursorType = adOpenStatic
    .ActiveConnection = strConnect
    'Test has no records at this point
    .Open "SELECT * FROM Test", Options:=adCmdText
    For intRow = 0 To UBound(avarData, 2) - 1
        'Move through the rows
        For intCol = 0 To UBound(avarData, 1) - 1
            'Set the Values array values
            avarValues(intCol) = avarData(intCol, intRow)
        Next intCol
        'Add the row to the Recordset
        .AddNew avarFields, avarValues
        .Update
    Next intRow
    'Update the Temp table
    .UpdateBatch
```

continues

LISTING 3.1   CONTINUED

```
    End With
    Set adcOrders.Recordset = rstOrders,
    adcOrders.Refresh
End Sub
```

The `cmdFromArray_Click()` event handler of the preceding listing uses the Test table to avoid making permanent changes to the Orders table of the Orders.mdb database. (Orders.mdb is derived from the Orders table of Nwind.mdb.) The Jet data type of OrderID primary key field of the Test table is `Long Integer`, not `AutoNumber`, permitting adding rows with `OrderID` values. The code does the following:

1. Deletes existing records in the Test table, if any
2. Generates a two-dimensional **Variant** array of `Recordset` columns and rows (`avarData`) by calling the `GetRows` method
3. Creates a **Variant** array of the field names of the Temp table (`avarFields`)
4. Moves data row by row from the `avarData` to the `avarValues` array
5. Adds each row to the `Recordset` by calling the `Update` method

▶ **See** "Disconnected Recordsets," **p. 111**

When all rows are added to the locally cached `Recordset`, the `UpdateBatch` method adds the 100 rows to the Temp table. If you open a `Recordset` on a `Connection` object, you can suspend the connection by disconnecting the `Recordset` (**Set** `rstName`.ActiveConnection = **Nothing**) after calling the `GetRows` method and reconnecting immediately prior to calling `BatchUpdate` (**Set** `rstName`.ActiveConnection = `cnnName`).

ADOPTING ADODB.Recordset Find METHODS

▶ **See** "Recordset Methods," **p. 106**

The single `Find` method of `ADODB.Recordset` objects replaces `DAO.Recordset`'s familiar `FindFirst`, `FindLast`, `FindNext` and `FindPrevious` methods. The `Find` method will probably be a stumbling block for both experienced and beginning Visual Basic database programmers, especially with the disappearance of the `NoMatch` property.

The syntax of the `Find` method is

`rstName`.Find str*Criteria*[, lng*SkipRecords*, lng*SearchDirection*[, var*Start*]]

where str*Criteria* is the definition of the record(s) for which you're searching. There is a major difference in str*Criteria* argument values between the `Find` and `Find...` methods: str*Criteria* no longer accepts any valid SQL WHERE clause. Comparison operators are limited

to =, >, >=, <, <=, or LIKE 'str*Like*'. As mentioned in a note in the "Comparing
DAO.Recordset and ADODB.Recordset Methods," earlier in the chapter, comparisons are limited
to a single field of the table. The examples of this chapter use simple single-field comparisons.
Chapter 14's Vb6pg.vbp project illustrates the ungainly workarounds required for multi-field
Find operations.

Table 3.3 lists the lng*SkipRecords*, lng*SearchDirection*, and var*Start* argument values to
emulate the DAO.Recordset and rdoResultset Find... methods.

TABLE 3.3 EMULATING THE TRADITIONAL Find... METHODS WITH ARGUMENT VALUES OF THE
Find METHOD

Find... *Method*	*Skip Records*	*SearchDirection*	*Start*
FindFirst	0	adSearchForward	adBookmarkFirst
FindLast	0	adSearchBackward	adBookmarkLast
FindNext	1	adSearchForward	adBookmarkCurrent
FindPrevious	1	adSearchBackward	adBookmarkCurrent

The ADOFind.vbp project in the \Ddg_vb6\Chaptr03 folder of the accompanying CD-ROM
demonstrates use of the Find method's arguments to locate records in the Orders table with a
specific CustomerID value. Figure 3.6 shows the frmFindMethod form of ADOFind.vbp. To test
the Find method, select a CustomerID value from the combo box and then click one of the
enabled Find... buttons. If found, the record pointer of the DataGrid control moves to the newly
selected record. The text box indicates the status of the Find operation. Listing 3.2 contains the
VBA code behind frmFindMethod.

3

MIRGRATING FROM DAO AND RDO TO ADO

FIGURE 3.6

*The ADOFind pro-
ject for testing the*
Find *and* Move
methods.

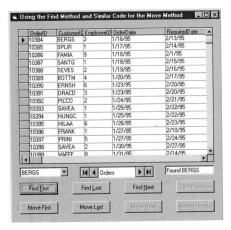

> **NOTE**
>
> Why Microsoft didn't conform both the DAO.Recordset Find... and Move...
> methods to the single Find and Move methods, respectively, is unclear. A possible answer is added code complexity when substituting Move for the MoveNext method; almost all Recordset navigation code uses MoveNext. The cmdMove_Click event handler of Listing 3.2 illustrates the use of the Move method to emulate MoveFirst, MoveLast, MoveNext, and MovePrevious operations.

LISTING 3.2 VBA CODE DEMONSTRATING THE Find METHOD AND SIMILAR CODE FOR THE Move METHOD

```
Option Explicit
Private cnnOrders As New ADODB.Connection
Private rstOrders As New ADODB.Recordset
Private strConnect As String
Private strSQL As String

Private Sub Form_Load()
    'Open the connection
    strConnect = App.Path & "\Orders.mdb"
    cnnOrders.Provider = "Microsoft.Jet.OLEDB.3.51"
    cnnOrders.Open strConnect, "Admin" ', "Password", if the database is secure
    'Load the combo list
    strSQL = "SELECT DISTINCT CustomerID FROM Orders ORDER BY CustomerID"
    Set rstOrders = cnnOrders.Execute(strSQL)
    Do Until rstOrders.EOF
        cboCustomerID.AddItem rstOrders.Fields(0).Value
        rstOrders.MoveNext
    Loop
    cboCustomerID.ListIndex = 0
    rstOrders.Close
End Sub

Private Sub Form_Activate()
    'Populate the DataGrid
    strSQL = "SELECT * FROM Orders WHERE OrderDate BETWEEN #1/1/95# AND #12/31/95#"
    rstOrders.Open strSQL, cnnOrders, adOpenKeyset, adLockOptimistic, adCmdText
    Set adcOrders.Recordset = rstOrders
End Sub

Private Sub cmdFind_Click(intIndex As Integer)
    'Find records for the customer selected in cboCustomerID
    Dim strCriteria As String
    Dim lngSkipRecords As Long
    Dim lngDirection As Long
    Dim varBookmark As Variant
```

```
    strCriteria = "CustomerID = '" & _
        cboCustomerID.List(cboCustomerID.ListIndex) & "'"
    With rstOrders
        Select Case intIndex
            Case 0
                'Find First
                .MoveFirst
                lngSkipRecords = 0
                lngDirection = adSearchForward
                cmdFind(2).Enabled = True
                cmdFind(3).Enabled = False
            Case 1
                'Find Last
                .MoveLast
                lngSkipRecords = 0
                lngDirection = adSearchBackward
                cmdFind(2).Enabled = False
                cmdFind(3).Enabled = True
            Case 2
                'Find Next
                lngSkipRecords = 1
                lngDirection = adSearchForward
                cmdFind(3).Enabled = True
            Case 3
                'Find Previous
                lngSkipRecords = 1
                lngDirection = adSearchBackward
                cmdFind(2).Enabled = True
        End Select
        varBookmark = .Bookmark
        .Find strCriteria, lngSkipRecords, lngDirection
        If .EOF Then
            txtStatus.Text = "Not Found (EOF)"
            .Bookmark = varBookmark
            Beep
        ElseIf .BOF Then
            txtStatus.Text = "Not Found (BOF)"
            .Bookmark = varBookmark
            Beep
        Else
            txtStatus.Text = "Found " & _
                cboCustomerID.List(cboCustomerID.ListIndex)
        End If
    End With
End Sub

Private Sub cmdMove_Click(intIndex As Integer)
    'Use Move with code similar to that for the Find method
    Dim lngSkipRecords As Long
    Dim varStart As Variant
    Dim varBookmark As Variant
```

continues

3

```
With rstOrders
    Select Case intIndex
        Case 0
            'Move First
            lngSkipRecords = 0
            varStart = adBookmarkFirst
            cmdMove(2).Enabled = True
            cmdMove(3).Enabled = False
        Case 1
            'Move Last
            lngSkipRecords = 0
            varStart = adBookmarkLast
            cmdMove(2).Enabled = False
            cmdMove(3).Enabled = True
        Case 2
            'Move Next
            lngSkipRecords = 1
            varStart = adBookmarkCurrent
            cmdMove(3).Enabled = True
        Case 3
            'Move Previous
            lngSkipRecords = -1
            varStart = adBookmarkCurrent
            cmdMove(2).Enabled = True
    End Select
    varBookmark = .Bookmark
    .Move lngSkipRecords, varStart
    If .EOF Then
        txtStatus.Text = "At EOF"
        .Bookmark = varBookmark
        Beep
    ElseIf .BOF Then
        txtStatus.Text = "At BOF"
        .Bookmark = varBookmark
        Beep
    Else
        txtStatus.Text = "Valid Row"
    End If
End With
End Sub
```

> **NOTE**
>
> As noted earlier in Table 3.2, `ADODB.Recordset` objects don't support the `Seek` method of `DAO.Recordset` objects opened on indexed ISAM tables (using the `adOpenTable` value for the `OpenRecordset` method's `Options` argument). Few developers use the `Seek` method because of `Seek`'s somewhat obscure syntax and the lack of support for `Seek` by indexed client/server tables connected by ODBC. The Jet database engine and most client/server RDBMSs have built-in query optimizers that automatically use the appropriate index, if such an index exists, to speed execution of the `Find` method with server-side cursors. It's not a good practice, however, to use `Find` with shared Jet or client/server databases. Instead, use a `SELECT` statement with `WHERE` criteria to return the record(s) you want.

MIGRATING FROM `rdoResultsets` AND ODBCDIRECT `Recordsets` TO `ADODB.Recordsets`

The architecture of ADO is based on RDO, but RDO-specific properties, methods, and events differ substantially from ADO. Microsoft designed RDO specifically for ODBC connections to client/server RDBMSs. ADO, on the other hand, is designed for connections to any source of tabular data, ranging from email messages to hierarchical data structures typical of early mainframe databases and online analytical processing (OLAP) servers. Thus ADO properties, methods, and events are more generic than their RDO counterparts.

> **NOTE**
>
> OLE DB data providers aren't required to support all the properties, methods, and events described in this and the preceding chapter. Testing the return value of the `Supports` method with `CursorOptionEnum` flags is the only reliable method of determining whether the data provider supports a particular method and any properties associated with the method.

Comparing `rdoResultset` and `ADODB.Recordset` Properties

Table 3.4 lists `rdoResultset`- and ODBCDirect-specific properties and their ADO counterparts if present in ADO 2.0. An asterisk in the `rdoResultset` column indicates the properties that also are supported by ODBCDirect, some of which use different names for the ODBCDirect variant. Table 3.4 doesn't include the properties of Table 3.1 that are common to all `DAO.Recordset` (Jet and ODBCDirect) and `rdoResultset` objects.

TABLE 3.4 A COMPARISON OF THE PROPERTIES OF rdoResultset AND ADODB.Recordset OBJECTS

rdoResultset	ADODB.Recordset	Comments and Workarounds
ActiveConnection*	ActiveConnection	No difference (Connection for ODBCDirect).
BatchCollisionCount*	Errors collection	No direct equivalent.
BatchCollisionRows*	Errors collection	No direct equivalent.
BatchSize*		Not supported (client/server-specific).
hStmt		Not supported (handle to a statement, ODBC API only).
RowCount*	RecordCount	No difference other than the property name; ODBCDirect uses RecordCount.
Status	Status	RecordStatusEnum offers more granular Status constants.
StillExecuting*	State	Tests the adStateExecuting or adStateFetching flags.
UpdateCriteria*	UpdateBatch method	Specifies a member of AffectEnum as the value of the lngAffectRecords argument; UpdateOptions for ODBCDirect.
UpdateOperation		Not supported.

Comparing rdoResultset and ADODB.Recordset Methods

Table 3.5 lists rdoResultset methods, two of which are supported by ODBCDirect Recordsets (indicated by asterisks), and the corresponding ADODB.Recordset methods. Name changes are the primary difference between the two sets of methods.

TABLE 3.5 A COMPARISON OF THE METHODS OF rdoResultset AND ADODB.Recordset OBJECTS

rdoResultset	ADODB.Recordset	Comments
BatchUpdate	UpdateBatch	Arguments differ.
Cancel*	Cancel	No difference.

rdoResultset	ADODB.Recordset	Comments
CancelBatch	CancelBatch	No difference.
	Find	Added by ADO
GetClipString	GetString	Name change only.
MoreResults*	NextRecordset	Has an optional lngRecordsAffected argument; ODBCDirect has a NextRecordset method.
OpenResultset	Open	Open is a method of the ADODB.Recordset object; OpenResultset is a method of rdoConnection, rdoQuery, and rdoTable objects. (The Open method's argument list is similar to that of OpenResultset.)

Comparing `rdoResultset` and `ADODB.Recordset` Events

The event model of ADODB.Recordset objects differs significantly from that of rdoResultsets, as illustrated by Table 3.6. ADODB.Recordset objects have a much richer set of events than do those of rdoResultsets. ODBCDirect DAO.Recordsets don't fire events.

TABLE 3.6 A COMPARISON OF rdoResultset AND ADODB.Recordset EVENTS

rdoResultset	ADODB.Recordset	Comments
Associate		Not supported.
Dissociate		Not supported.
ResultsChanged	RecordsetChangeComplete	Arguments differ.
RowCurrencyChange	MoveComplete	Arguments differ.
RowStatusChanged	RecordChangeComplete	Arguments differ.
WillAssociate		Not supported.
WillDissociate		Not supported.
WillUpdateRows	WillChangeRecordset	Arguments differ.

UNDERSTANDING HIERARCHICAL Recordsets

▶ **See** "The Relational Database Model," **p. 215**

Visual Basic 6.0 and ADO 2.0 support *relational hierarchical* Recordsets, which are based on relation(s) between corresponding columns of compatible data sources. Each relation is similar to the many-to-one relation expressed in an SQL WHERE `Table2.ForeignKeyField =` `Table1.PrimaryKeyField` statement to create an INNER JOIN between the related and base tables, respectively. You create a hierarchical Recordset by defining a parent Command object to return all or specified fields of *Table1* and a child Command object to return all or specified fields of *Table2*. You then specify in the child command the *PrimaryKeyField* and *ForeignKeyField* of the INNER JOIN between parent and child to define the relation between the two tables.

A hierarchical Recordset contains columns for each of the fields specified in the SELECT statement, but the Recordset.RecordCount property returns only the number of rows of the base (parent) table (*Table1*). The column values for the fields of the related (child) table (*Table2*) return multiple rows—one row for each record of the related table whose foreign key field matches the primary key field of the base table. MSDataShape, an OLE DB service provider (Msadds.dll), is responsible for creating hierarchical ADODB.Resultsets at runtime.

▶ **See** "First Normal Form," **p. 228**

> **NOTE**
>
> Hierarchical Recordsets violate the first rule of relational database design: First normal form requires tables to be flat and not to contain any repeating groups. Each column value of a related-table field has a repeating group if the query returns more than one record from the related table.

Figure 3.7 shows a Hierarchical FlexGrid control (MSHFlexGrid) displaying part of a hierarchical Recordset created from the Order and Order Details tables of Nwind.mdb. The advantage of an MSHFlexGrid displaying a hierarchical Recordset is its ability to emulate a TreeView control (one of the Windows Common Controls), in row-column format. The record selector buttons of the MSHFlexGrid control include a square symbol containing a + or - symbol; clicking the square alternates between collapsed (+) and expanded (-, the default) display of a record. When collapsed, the fields of the related table are hidden, as illustrated in Figure 3.7 by the row for OrderID 10334.

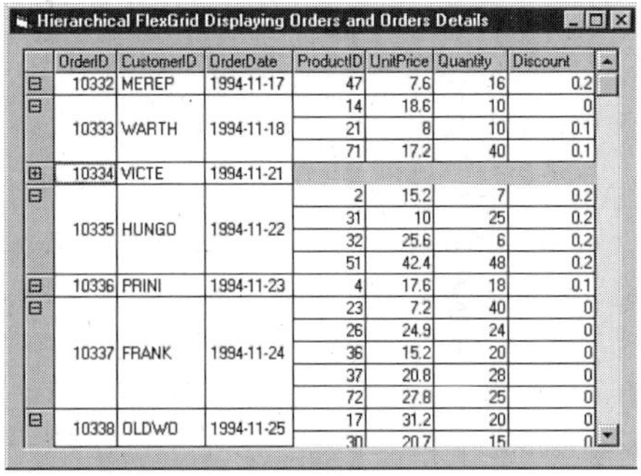

FIGURE 3.7

The Hierarchical FlexGrid control bound to a two-level hierarchical Recordset.

If your database contains deeply nested relationships, you can extend the number of levels in the hierarchy to reach the lowest member in the chain of relationships. From a practical standpoint, the maximum number of levels for display in an MSHFlexGrid control is four or five. Figure 3.8 shows a three-level hierarchy created from the Customers, Orders, and Order Details tables of Nwind.mdb. Each field that represents the primary key in a relationship with the next lower member of the hierarchy has its own square expand/collapse symbol.

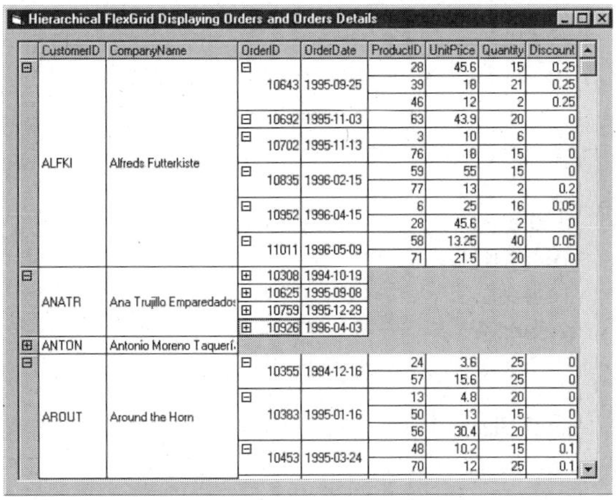

FIGURE 3.8

A three-level Hierarchical FlexGrid control displaying a Recordset *created from the Customers, Orders, and Order Details tables of Nwind.mdb.*

NOTE

The MSHFlexGrid control refers to levels as *bands*. The Customers Command is Band 0, Orders is Band 1, and OrderDetails is Band 2. The properties sheet for the MSHFlexGrid control enables you to specify the Recordset fields that appear as columns in each of the bands.

▶ See "SQL Aggregate Functions and the GROUP BY and HAVING Clauses," **p. 279**

In addition to the parent-child relationships illustrated by Figures 3.7 and 3.8, hierarchical Recordsets offer the following two alternatives:

- *Grouping*, in which you specify in the SQL statement for the Command object the field on which to group the data, the equivalent of *FieldName* in an SQL GROUP BY *FieldName* clause. Figure 3.9 shows an MSFlexGrid control displaying the Recordset of a group-based command on the Country field of Nwind.mdb's Customers table.

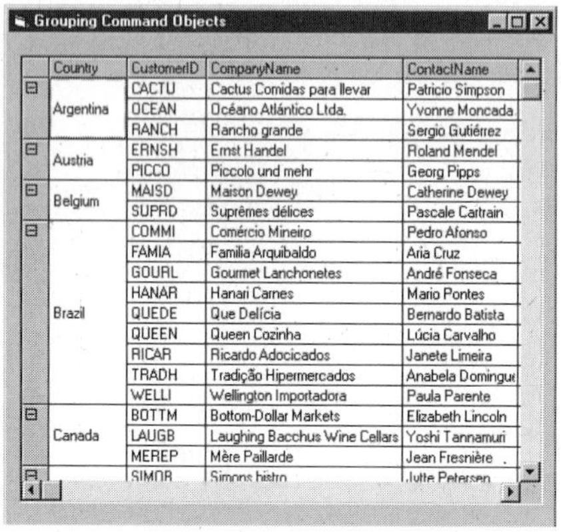

FIGURE 3.9

The Recordset *of a group-based* Command *object displayed in the MSHFlexGrid control.*

▶ **See** "Using Crosstab Queries to Present Summary Data," **p. 288**

- *Aggregation*, in which you specify an SQL aggregate function (AVG, COUNT, MAX, MIN, STDDEV, and SUM) of one or more fields. With the exception of COUNT, the field(s) must be of a numeric data type. It's possible, but very uncommon, to use MAX and MIN aggregtes on character fields. You can define aggregates on any relation- or group-based hierarchical Recordset. The parent Command object also offers a grand total aggregate. Figure 3.10 shows an MSFlexGrid control with grouping on the Orders table's ShipCountry field and the SUM aggregate applied to the Freight field. Grouping with aggregation is related to Jet's crosstab queries.

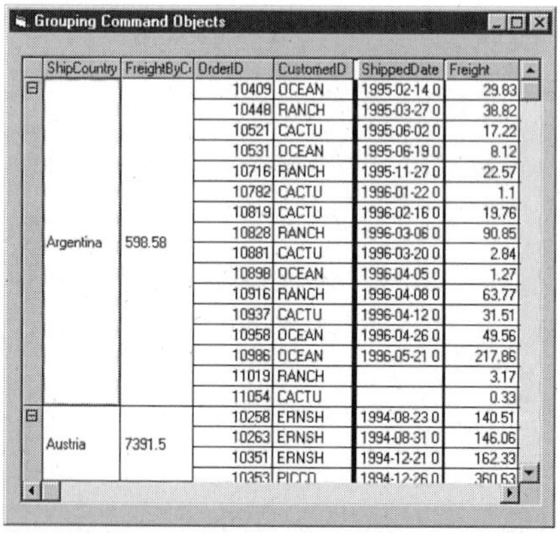

FIGURE 3.10

The MSHFlexGrid control displaying the Recordset of a group-based Command object with a SUM aggregate.

> **NOTE**
>
> Chapter 10, "Taking Full Advantage of Data-Bound ActiveX Controls," covers the MSHFlexGrid control in detail and shows you how to display group-based and aggregate hierarchical Recordsets.

Creating a Relational Hierarchical Recordset with the Data Environment Designer

You can write VBA code to create and manipulate hierarchical Recordsets, but using the Data Environment Designer is a much simpler and quicker approach. The following steps create a simple, two-level relational hierarchy from the Orders and Order Details tables of Nwind.mdb:

1. Open a new Data Project and double-click the DataEnvironment1 object to open the Data Environment window.

2. Rename Connection1 to **cnnNwind**, right-click cnnNwind, and choose Properties to open the Data Link Properties sheet.

3. Select the Microsoft Jet 3.51 OLE DB Provider in the OLE DB Provider(s) list and click Next. In the Connection page, click the builder button, select Nwind.mdb, and click OK to close the Select Access Database dialog. Accept the remaining defaults and click Test Connection to verify your choices, and click OK to close the Data Link Properties sheet.

4. With cnnNwind selected in the DataEnvironment1 window, click the Add Command button to add Command1. Right-click Command1 and choose Properties to open the Command1 Properties sheet, and change the Command Name to **Orders**.

5. Select the Database Object option, open the associated list, and select Table; then open the Object Name list and select Orders.

6. Click the Advanced tab and select 2 - Use Server-Side Cursors in the Cursor Location list, 1 - Keyset in the Cursor Type list, and 3 - Optimistic in the Lock Type list.

7. Click OK to save the Orders connection.

8. With the Orders connection selected in the DataEnvironment1 window, click the Add Child Command button to add Command1. Open the Command1 Properties sheet, and change the name to **OrderDetails**.

9. Select Table as the Database Object and Order Details as the Object Name.

10. Click the Relation tab to establish the parent-child relation.

    The Relation page proposes the relation if the two tables or queries have columns with identical names. The Relate to a Parent Command Object check box is marked, the Parent Fields list contains OrderID, and the Child Fields list contains OrderID.

11. Click Add to add the relation to the list box (see Figure 3.11).

FIGURE 3.11

Adding a relation on the OrderID *fields of the Orders and Order Details tables of Nwind.mdb to create a hierarchical* Recordset.

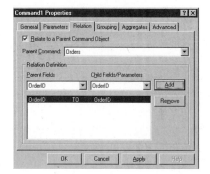

12. Click OK to save the OrderDetails child command and close the properties sheet.

13. Select the DataEnvironment1 item, open the Properties window, and change the Name property value to **envNwind**.

14. Right-click the envNwind item and choose Expand All to display the fields of the parent and child commands (see Figure 3.12).

FIGURE 3.12

The fields of the parent Orders *and child* OrderDetails *commands of the* cnnNwind *connection.*

15. Right-click the Orders item and choose Hierarchy Info to open the Hierarchy Information dialog. The default View Shape Command option shows the statement required by MSDataShape to create the hierarchical Recordset (see Figure 3.13, top). Choosing the View ADO Hierarchy option displays the relationship between the rsOrders Recordset and the OrderDetails child command (see Figure 3.13, bottom).

16. Click OK to close the Hierarchy Info dialog.

FIGURE 3.13

The VBA code for the View Shape Command option (top) and a hierarchy diagram for the rsOrders *hierarchical* Recordset *(bottom).*

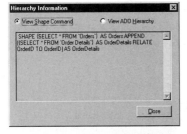

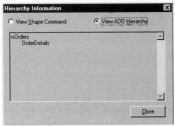

Following is the statement passed to the MSShape object to create the rsOrders relation-based hierarchical Recordset:

```
SHAPE {SELECT * FROM `Orders`} AS Orders
     APPEND ({SELECT * FROM `Order_Details`} AS OrderDetails
     RELATE OrderID TO OrderID) AS OrderDetails
```

NOTE

DED uses as field delimiters the opening single quote (`, under the ~ key) instead of the traditional square brace pairs ([ ]) of Jet SQL. Field delimiters are required only when the field name contains characters, such as spaces, which are incompatible with SQL naming conventions. The DED surrounds all field names within SELECT statements with delimiters.

The SHAPE, APPEND, and RELATE keywords, and the French braces surrounding SELECT statements are specific to the MSShape service provider. Execution of the preceding statement follows these steps:

1. The SHAPE statement calls the MSShape service provider, which passes the {SELECT ...} statement to the data provider, in this case Jolt. The Orders alias is the name of the parent command, which creates the rsOrders Recordset.

2. The APPEND verb indicates that the following parenthetical statement is a child command. The columns of the child result set returned by the command are appended to the columns of the parent Recordset.

3

MIRGRATING FROM DAO AND RDO TO ADO

3. The RELATE *PrimaryKeyField* TO *ForeignKeyField* expression specifies the field names that establish the relationship between the parent and child result sets.

> **NOTE**
>
> SHAPE, APPEND, and RELATE are Microsoft-specific keywords, not ANSI SQL-92 reserved words. The SELECT statement's syntax must conform to the language of the data provider, such as Jet SQL for Jolt or Transact-SQL for SQLOLEDB, the Microsoft SQL Server provider.

Displaying a Hierarchical Recordset in a Hierarchical FlexGrid Control

The process of adding an MSFlexGrid control bound to a hierarchical Recordset is similar to that for a DataGrid control bound to a conventional Recordset. To bind an MSFlexGrid control to the Orders Command object, do the following:

1. Open the default frmDataEnv form and expand its size to about 6,000 by 9,000 twips.
2. In the envNwind window, right-click the Orders command, drag the field symbol to the form, and then release the right mouse button.
3. Select Hierarchical FlexGrid from the pop-up menu to add the control, bound to the Orders command, to the form.
4. Size the MSHFlexGrid control to a height of about 5,500 twips and a width of 8,400 twips and change its name to **hfgOrders**.
5. Right-click hfgOrders and choose Properties from the pop-up menu to open the MSHFlexGrid Property Pages; then click the Bands tab.
6. With the default Band 0 selected in the Bands list, clear the check boxes for the fields of the parent command (Orders) that you don't want to appear in hfgOrders. For this example, clear all but OrderID, CustomerID, and OrderDate check boxes (see Figure 3.14).

FIGURE 3.14

Specifying the parent columns to appear in Band 0 of a MSHFlexGrid control.

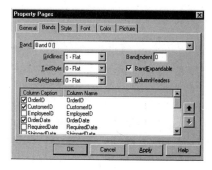

7. Select Band 1 (OrderDetails) in the Bands list and clear the OrderID check box. (The OrderID value is provided by Band 0.)

8. Click OK to close the Property Pages sheet and run the project. Your form appears as shown earlier in Figure 3.7.

> **NOTE**
>
> Alternatively, you can bind a manually added hfgOrders control to the rsOrders Recordset by setting the value of the hfgOrder DataSource property to envNwind and its DataMembers property to Orders.

Replacing Access's Form/Subform Combinations with Hierarchical Recordsets

Microsoft Access's ease of creating linked form/subform combinations is one of its primary features. Access uses the term *master-child* to define the relationship between the table bound to the form and the table underlying the subform. The properties that specify the linked fields of the tables for the master-child relationship are LinkMasterFields and LinkChildFields, respectively. Figure 3.15 shows the Orders form of the Access 97 Northwind.mdb sample database. The Orders table is the underlying record source for the form (master), populating the Ship To information and other order-related data displayed by labels, combo boxes, text boxes, and check boxes. The Order Details table is the record source for the Orders Subform (child), which populates the datasheet (Access's equivalent to a bound DBGrid control) to display order line items.

FIGURE 3.15

The Orders form and Orders Subform of the Northwind.mdb sample database in Access 97.

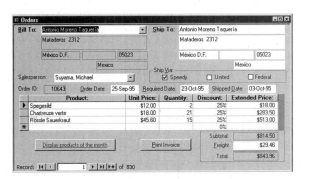

Before Visual Basic 6.0, emulating Access's form/subform features required a substantial amount of VBA code to synchronize the content of a DBGrid or MSFlexGrid control with the current record of the Recordset populating the form's text boxes. Binding form text boxes to the parent command and an MHSFlexGrid or a DataGrid control to the child command of a hierarchical `Recordset` emulates the Access form/subform combination. The contents of the grid are synchronized automatically to the active parent record; like Access, no VBA code is required for synchronization.

▶ **See** "Generating Continuous Subforms with the DataRepeater Control," **p. ???** (Ch16)

NOTE

Visual Basic 6.0 doesn't limit you to grids for displaying multiple records generated by the child command. The Microsoft DataRepeater control 6.0 enables you to emulate Access's continuous subforms. The DataRepeater control is a scrollable container for Visual Basic data-bound controls. Each record creates an image of user control and its controls. Generating a continuous subform requires that you compile the user control to an ActiveX control (.ocx). Chapter 16, "Creating User Controls for Database Applications," shows you how to design user controls and compile them to ActiveX controls.

To create a synchronized form/subform grid from the `envNwind DataEnvironment` object, follow these steps:

1. Add a new form to your Data Project named **frmParentChild**.

2. From the envNwind window, left-click and drag the `Orders` (parent) command to the form to create a bound text box for each field of the Orders table.

3. Create two columns of text boxes by selecting and dragging the last seven text boxes to the right of the first seven. Position the MSHFlexGrid1 control immediately below the text boxes.

4. Add an ADODC control from the toolbox between the bottom text boxes and the DataGrid. Name the control **adcOrders**.

5. Add the following line of code to the `Form_Activate` event handler to bind `adcOrders` to the `rsOrders Recordset`:

   Set adcOrders.Recordset = envNwind.rsOrders

6. Choose Project|DataProject Properties and select frmParentChild from the StartUp Form list. Click OK to close the Data Project - Properties sheet.

7. Run your project and verify that the content of the MSHFlexGrid corresponds to the order selected with the ADO Data control (see Figure 3.16).

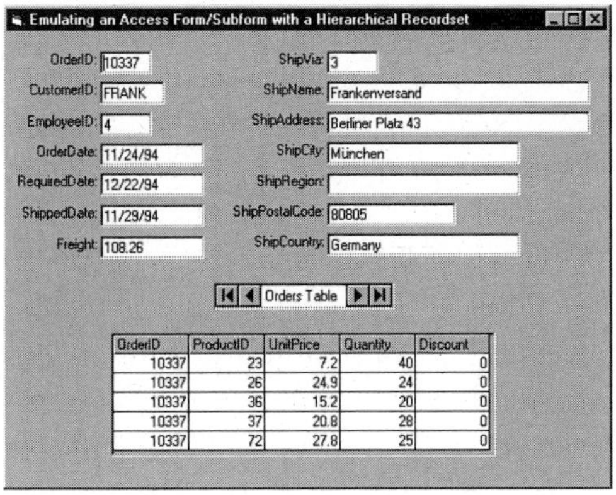

FIGURE 3.16

Emulating an Access form/sub-form with text boxes bound to a parent command and a Hierarchical FlexGrid control bound to a child command.

NOTE

Alternatively, you can manually add the MSHFlexGrid or a DataGrid control to the form; then set the value of its DataSource property to envNwind and the DataMember property to the OrderDetails command. The next chapter, "Using the ADO Data Control with Bound Controls," details the properties, methods, and events of ADODC, DataGrid, and other ADO-enabled bound controls.

USING THE ADO DATA
CONTROL WITH BOUND
CONTROLS

IN THIS CHAPTER

The ADO Data Control (ADODC) is an ActiveX control (Msadodc.ocx) that replaces the native Data control of Visual Basic 5.0 and earlier. ADODC serves as an OLE DB data provider for OLE DB[en]compliant bound data consumer controls, which are called *data-bound controls* in this book. ADODC supplies VCR-style graphic Recordset navigation capability and can be bound to row-returning DataEnvironment (DE) Command objects. Navigating a Recordset means moving the record pointer, which specifies the current record, to the desired position. With the ADODC and TextBoxes or a DataGrid, you can create a simple data display and editing application without writing a single line of VBA code.

The new Visual Basic 6.0 data-bound controls let you assign as their data provider a DE Command object's rs*Command* Recordset in design mode or ADODB.Recordsets in VBA code. Unlike prior versions of Visual Basic, you can change the control's data provider in run mode. For the majority of front-end designs, most developers omit the ADODC to minimize application resource consumption. Database developers new to Visual Basic, however, usually begin the learning process by creating relatively simple front-end applications with ADODCs. Thus this chapter begins with examples of ADODC's use with TextBox, CheckBox, Image, and DataGrid controls and then provides a detailed description of the properties and methods of the ADODC. Topics later in the chapter cover alternative methods of binding complex data consumer controls, such as the DataGrid, DataCombo, Hierarchical FlexGrid, and DataList to Commands and Recordsets.

> **NOTE**
>
> The examples of this chapter assume familiarity with programming techniques for native Visual Basic controls, such as TextBoxes, ComboBoxes, ListBoxes, and the like, as well as using the project References dialog and the Object Browser. If you're not up to speed on these topics, a Visual Basic tutorial, such as Sams Publishing's *Teach Yourself Visual Basic 6 in 21 Days* by Greg Perry (ISBN 0672-31310-3) provides the foundation you need to complete this chapter's examples.

CREATING SIMPLE TEXT BOX DATA DISPLAY AND EDITING FORMS

Classic data display and editing forms consist of a collection of TextBoxes bound to fields of a table or query. The layout of these forms dates from the early days of data terminals attached to mainframe computers. If the underlying table or query is updatable, the data entry operator can edit existing data or add new records. Unlike forms using DataGrids, which display multiple records and navigate tables or query result sets via built-in scroll bars, TextBox-based forms require control(s) for record navigation. The ADODC is the code-free approach to traversing an ADODB.Recordset object.

Using the Data Form Wizard to Create a Data Entry Form

The fastest method to create a conventional data entry form is to use the Data Form Wizard. Follow these steps to design a data entry form for the Employees table of the Nwind.mdb sample database:

1. Open a new Data Project.

2. The Data Form Wizard doesn't appear as a default Add-Ins menu choice, so choose Add-Ins, Add-In Manager to open the Add-In Manager dialog. Select VB 6 Data Form Wizard from the Available Add-Ins list, mark the Loaded/Unloaded and Load on Startup check boxes, and click OK to load the Wizard and close the dialog.

3. Choose Add-Ins, Data Form Wizard to open the first Wizard dialog. Click Next to bypass the profile selection process.

4. In the Database Type dialog, select Access in the list and click Next.

5. In the Database Name dialog, click Browse to open the Access Database dialog, double-click Nwind.mdb to select the file and close the dialog, and then click Next.

6. In the Form dialog, type **frmEmployees** in the name text box, accept the Single Record and ADO Data Control defaults (see Figure 4.1), and click Next.

FIGURE 4.1

Selecting the type of form and binding type in the Data Form Wizard - Form dialog.

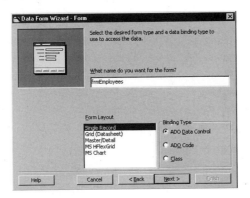

7. In the Record Source dialog, select Employees from the Record Source list and click the right-pointing double-arrow button to move all the fields from the Available Fields to the Selected Fields list. Select each field and use the up-down arrow buttons to rearrange the fields into a logical order. Select EmployeeID as the column to sort by (see Figure 4.2) and click Next.

> **NOTE**
>
> Unfortunately, the wizard displays the field list in alphabetical order by field name, rather than by the sequence (ordinal) of fields in the table.

FIGURE 4.2

Specifying the table name and columns to display in the Form Wizard - Form dialog.

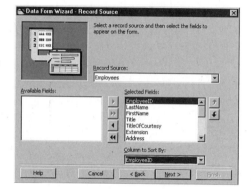

8. In the Control Selection dialog, click Clear All and then click Next.

9. In the Finished! dialog, click the builder button to open the Save Profile dialog and save the profile as **EmployeesForm.rwp**. Click Finish to display frmEmployees in design mode (see Figure 4.3, left).

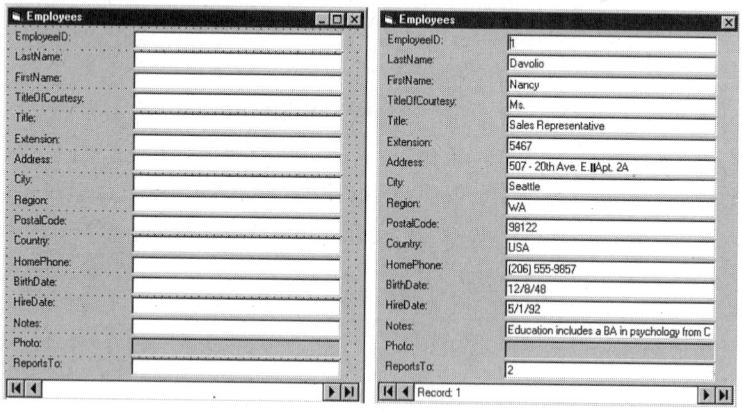

FIGURE 4.3

The data entry form created by the Data Form Wizard in design mode (left) and run mode (right).

> **NOTE**
>
> The wizard's profile file doesn't save the Record Source or field order information, making a profile of limited usefulness for regenerating a form by loading a saved .rwp file.

10. Choose Project, Project1 Properties to open the Project1 - Project Properties dialog. Select frmEmployees from the Startup Object list and click OK.

11. Press F5 to open frmEmployees. Click OK to dismiss the message that a control can't bind to the Photo field, and the form appears in run mode (refer to Figure 4.3, right).

> **NOTE**
>
> The Photo field of the Nwind.mdb database uses Access's OLE Object field data type, which stores employee photos in OLE compound document format. Visual Basic Image and Picture Box controls support only bitmap, icon, metafile, enhanced metafile, Joint Photographic Expert Group (JPEG), and Graphic Interchange Format (GIF) files stored in fields of the Long Binary (adLongBinary) data type. The wizard selects for Long Binary fields a PictureBox control, which can't display a field containing image data with an Access OLE Object wrapper.

Clicking the VCR buttons of the ADODC, from left to right, applies the MoveFirst, MovePrevious, MoveNext, or Move Last method to the underlying ADODC.Recordset object, named datPrimaryRS for wizard-generated forms.

Exploring ADODC and Data Link Properties Sheets

To examine some of the data-related properties of the ADODC, right-click the ADODC and select ADODC Properties to open the Property Pages (properties sheet) for the control. The General page displays part of the ADODC's ConnectionString property (see Figure 4.4). The complete ConnectionString property value is

```
Provider=Microsoft.Jet.OLEDB.3.51;
Persist Security Info=False;
Data Source=C:\Program Files\Microsoft Visual Studio\VB98\Nwind.mdb
```

4

USING THE ADO
DATA CONTROL

FIGURE 4.4

*The General page
of the Property
Pages for the
ADODC.*

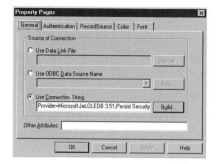

Clicking Build opens the Data Link Properties sheet for the ADODB.Connection object, which generates the ConnectionString property value, as follows:

- The default Connection page specifies the location and name of the .mdb file, Data Source = ...;, set in the wizard's Database Name dialog (see Figure 4.5).

FIGURE 4.5

*The Connection
page of the Data
Link Properties
sheet for the
ADODC's
ConnectionStri
ng property value.*

- The Persist Security Info = False; component (the default) disables the Password text box and associated check boxes.

- The Provider page sets the Provider=Microsoft.Jet.OLEDB.3.51; component of the ConnectionString.

- The Advanced page determines database access privileges. The default for Jet databases is Share Deny None (read/write privileges on a shared .mdb file).

▶ **See** "Specifying a Jet Workgroup File for Secure Databases," **p. 140** and "Supplementing Workgroup Security with Jet's Security Features," **p. 681**

- The All page summarizes the `ConnectionString` settings and lets you enter values for Jet-specific (`Jet OLEDB:`) properties, such as `Jet OLEDB: Database Password` for password-protected databases or `Jet OLEDB: System Database` to specify the location and name of the workgroup file (.mdw) for secure Jet databases (see Figure 4.6).

FIGURE 4.6

Adding a Jet-specific property value that points to the workgroup file of a secure Jet database.

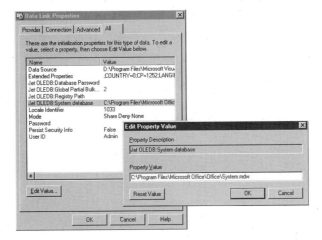

The `RecordSource` page of the ADODC's Property Pages sheet specifies the `CommandType` and `CommandText` property values required to create the `ADODB.Command` object that returns the ADODC's `Recordset` (see Figure 4.7). The full text of the SQL statement for the `Recordset` of the form of Figure 4.3 is

```
SELECT EmployeeID, LastName, FirstName, TitleOfCourtesy, Title,
    Extension, Address, City, Region, PostalCode, Country,
    HomePhone, BirthDate, HireDate, Notes, Photo, ReportsTo
FROM Employees
```

FIGURE 4.7

The Connection page of the Data Link Properties sheet for the ADODC's `ConnectionStri ng` *property value.*

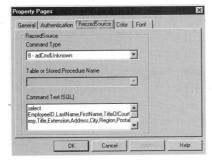

4

USING THE ADO DATA CONTROL

> **NOTE**
>
> The wizard sets the `CommandType` property of the `Command` object to `adCmdUnknown`. The correct `CommandType` property value for an SQL statement as the value of the `CommandText` property is `adCmdText`. Use the `adCmdTable` value when assigning a table name as the value of `adCmdText`.

Enabling Addition of New Records

The ADODC of the wizard's form provides data navigation, display, and editing capabilities, but doesn't let you add a new record. To enable the addition of records, select the ADODC on the form in design view, click the Properties button of the toolbar, and change the value of the EOFAction to 2 - adDoAddNew. To add a new record, click the last record button and then the next record button. You must complete all required fields, which have constraints stored within the Employees table, to append the new record; otherwise, you receive an error when you attempt to move the record pointer with the ADODC.

> **NOTE**
>
> The process of adding a new record with the ADODC isn't intuitive, so a better approach is to use a New Employee command button to add an empty (tentative append) record and a Cancel button with event-handling code to eliminate error messages resulting from constraint violations. Another advantage of employing command buttons for updates is the option of using `BatchOptimistic` locking and the `UpdateBatch` method to send all changes to the database or cancel the changes in a single operation. The "Introducing Batch Optimistic Updates" section later in the chapter illustrates the advantages of this feature.

Adding an ADODC to a Data Environment Designer Form

Dragging a row-returning `Command` from the Data Environment Designer (DED) to a form generates a set of TextBoxes similar to those added by the Data Form Wizard. Unlike the wizard, DED doesn't add an ADODC or navigation command buttons. Creating the equivalent of the preceding single-record form involves this process:

1. In the DataEnvironment window of a Data Project, add a `Connection` to the database.
2. Add to the `Connection` a row-returning `Command` object based on a table or query.
3. Drag the `Connection` object to a form to generate TextBox controls bound to the Connection's `Recordset`.
4. Add an ADODC to the form and bind it to the `Command` object.

The advantage of using DED to generate a form is that you create a persistent designer file (.dsr), which can be reused in other applications. Object reuse is the primary benefit of object-based programming techniques. A designer file, the contents of which closely resemble a Visual Basic .frm file, stores only the properties of the objects you add. The Data Environment designer is capable of storing multiple `Connection` and `Command` objects, so you can create a single .dsr file with all of the data sources you need for a very large-scale project or multiple projects.

Creating the `Connection` Object

The following procedure creates a `DataEnvironment Connection` object to the Nwind.mdb sample database:

1. Open a new Data Project, which automatically adds default `DataEnvironment1` and `DataReport1` instances.

2. In the Project Explorer, remove `DataReport1` from the project and double-click the DataEnvironment1 item to open the DataProject - DataEnvironment1 window.

3. In the Project Explorer, rename `DataEnvironment1` to **envData**. (You can't rename a DataEnvironment object until you open the DataEnvironment window.)

4. Rename `Connection1` to **cnnNwind**. Right-click the `cnnNwind` node and choose Properties to open the Data Link Properties sheet for the `Connection`.

5. On the Provider page, select Microsoft Jet 3.51 OLE DB Provider in the OLE DB Provider(s) list and click Next.

6. On the Connection page, click the Builder button and double-click Nwind.mdb in the Select Access Database dialog. Accept the default Admin user name and blank password and then click Test Connection to verify your entries.

7. On the Advanced page, verify the Access Permissions are Share Deny None.

8. Click OK to close the Data Link Properties sheet.

Adding a Command Object for the Employees Table

The next step is to create a row-returning `Command` object with `cnnNwind` as the value of the `ActiveConnection` property:

1. With cnnNwind selected in the DataProject - envData window, click the toolbar's Add Command button (second button from the left) to open the Command1 Properties sheet.

2. In the Command Name text box, rename Command1 to **Employees**. (No object type prefix is used for the `Command` name because DED prefixes `rs` to the `Command` name to designate the resulting `Recordset`.)

3. Accept the default Connection, `cnnNwind`, select Table from the Database Object list, and select Employees from Object Name list (see Figure 4.8).

FIGURE 4.8

Setting Command
property values to
return a
Recordset *from*
the Employees
table.

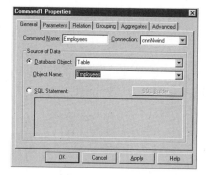

> **NOTE**
>
> Alternatively, select the SQL Statement option, and type the SQL statement created by the Data Form Wizard as it appears in the earlier "Exploring ADODC and Data Link Properties Sheets" section. The form can't display the Photo field, so delete Photo from the SQL statement's field list.

4. In the Advanced page, select 3 - Optimistic from the Lock Type list and accept the remaining default values (see Figure 4.9).

FIGURE 4.9

Specifying opti-
mistic locking to
permit updates to
the Employees
table.

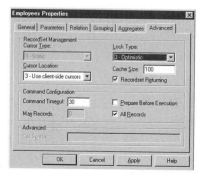

5. Click OK to close the Command1 Properties sheet. (The next time you open it, the title appears as Employees Properties.) DED's window displays the Employees node under the cnnNwind node.

6. Expand the Employees node to display the table's field list. Right-click a field and choose Properties to display the Field Properties sheet for the field (see Figure 4.10).

FIGURE **4.10**

Displaying the entire field list and field properties for one field of the Recordset *generated by a row-returning command.*

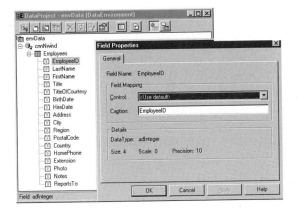

The Field Properties sheet's Control list lets you attempt to bind the field to any registered ActiveX object; the list is not limited to bindable components. If you want to inspect or alter the default control/field data type relationships, do the following:

1. Right-click the envData node and choose Options to open the Options properties sheet for the DataEnvironment object.

2. In the Field Mapping page, mark the Show All Data Types check box to expand the Category/DataType list to include field data subtypes.

3. Select the data type for which you want to change the default control and select an appropriate bindable ActiveX control from the Control list. As an example, if a Long Varbinary (image) field contains a digital video (.avi or .asf) file, choose the ActiveMovie Control Object (see Figure 4.11).

FIGURE **4.11**

Changing the default control for Long Varbinary fields to the ActiveMovie Control.

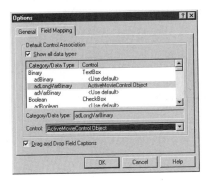

4. Click OK to change the default control/field data type relationships.

The new default relationships you set remain in effect for all subsequent row-returning Commands you specify.

4

USING THE ADO
DATA CONTROL

Field names appear as labels on DED-generated forms. If you don't want to include captions to the left of text boxes, clear the Drag and Drop Field Captions check box on the Field Mapping page. You can customize field captions in the Field Properties sheet's Caption text box.

Generating the Data Entry Form

Drag-and drop form generation by DED is a simple and fast process. The following steps create a form ready for the addition of an ADODC:

1. Open the default `frmDataEnv` form, expand its size to approximately 6,000 by 7,000 twips, and position it to the right of DED's window.

2. Right-click and drag the Employees Command node near the top of `frmDataEnv`, dropping it at about one-third of the width of the form. DED adds caption Labels and field TextBoxes to the form (see Figure 4.12).

FIGURE 4.12

Labels and TextBoxes for the Employees table added to the default `frmDataEnv` form of a Data Project.

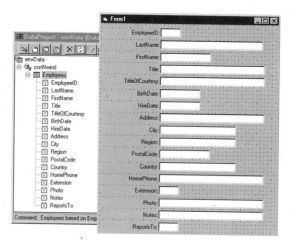

NOTE

Unlike the Data Form Wizard, DED attempts to size the width of the TextBoxes in accordance with the field data type.

---

3. Press F5 to display the form in run mode.

NOTE

Unlike the Employees form created by the Data Form Wizard, you don't receive an error if you include the Photo field in your form design. The text box displays ?/l, not the bitmap.

4. Return to design mode and delete the Label and TextBox for the Photo field. Expand the Notes TextBox to occupy the Photo field's former position and set the Notes TextBox's `Multiline` property to **True** and the `Scrollbars` property to 2 - Vertical. Drag the bottom of the form down to make room for an ADODC control.

5. Change the name of the form to **frmEmployees** and change the Caption property to **Employee Data Entry Form**.

6. Click F5 to check the design of the form in run mode (see Figure 4.13).

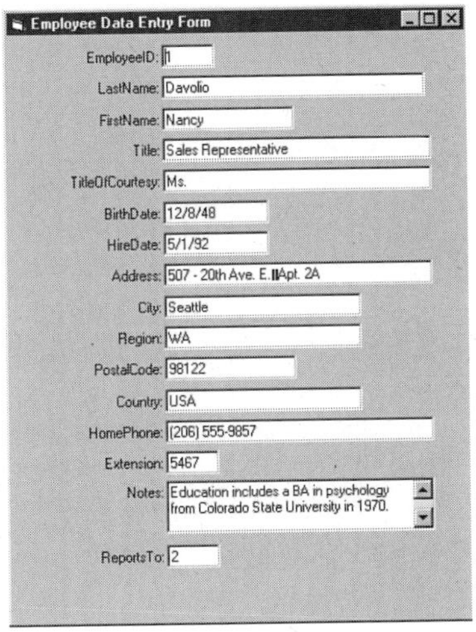

FIGURE 4.13

The modified DED-generated Employee Data Entry Form ready for addition of an ADODC for navigation.

NOTE

The default U.S. English date format for bound text boxes is M/d/yy (month, day, and two-digit year). This format violates the basic rules of Year 2000 (Y2K) compliance, which require display and entry of four-digit year values. Sections later in the chapter describe how to format date/time fields to comply with accepted Y2K standards.

The two vertical bars in the Address field represent return and linefeed characters embedded in the text. Use of formatting characters within text (varchar) fields isn't a good database programming (or data entry) practice. Formatting characters in memo (long varchar) fields is commonplace and doesn't violate database programming standards.

4

USING THE ADO DATA CONTROL

Adding and Binding the ADODC to the Recordset

The final operation is adding an ADODC to the form and binding the ADODC to the rsEmployees Recordset generated by the Employees Command. In this case, the data provider is rsEmployees, not the ADODC. To provide Recordset navigation with an ADODC, do the following:

1. Add an ADODC to the bottom of frmEmployees.

2. Rename ADODC1 to **adcEmployees** and add **Employees** as the value of its Caption property.

3. Add the following line of VBA code to the Form_Activate event handler:

   Set adcEmployees.Recordset = envData.rsEmployees

   rsEmployees appears in the Auto List Members list for the Employees Command. The preceding statement binds adcEmployees to rsEmployees.

4. Press F5 and test the navigation capabilities of adcEmployees (see Figure 4.14).

FIGURE 4.14

The DED-generated form with an ADODC added for Recordset *navigation.*

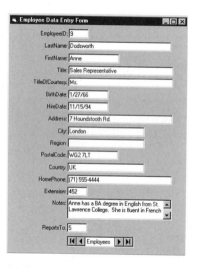

If you want to try adding records to the Employees table, set the EOFAction property of adcEmployees to 2 - adDoAddNew. EmployeeID is an autonumber field, so don't enter a value. All other required entries must meet the field constraints stored with the Employees table in Nwind.mdb. Error messages warn you of constraint violations.

NOTE

The completed project described in the preceding sections, DedEntry.vbp, is located in the \Ddg_vb6\Chaptr04 folder of the accompanying CD-ROM.

EXPLORING ADODC'S DATA-RELATED PROPERTIES AND EVENTS

The preceding sections demonstrate the use of the ADODC as a data provider and a `Recordset` navigation aid. The following sections provide detailed descriptions of the ADODC's data-related properties and events.

ADODC Properties

Like almost all ActiveX controls, the ADODC has a properties sheet that lets you set a limited number of property values. To access all data-related ADODC properties, use Visual Basic's Properties window. Figure 4.15 shows the default Data category properties for an ADODC, many of which correspond to the `ADODB.Object` properties discussed in Chapter 2, "Understanding OLE DB and Universal Data Access." Table 4.1 lists ADODC properties of the Data category and their purpose.

FIGURE 4.15

Default Data category property values for the ADODC.

TABLE 4.1 PROPERTIES OF THE ADODC AND THEIR PURPOSE

Property	Purpose
.BOFAction	The `MovePrevious` behavior with the record pointer at the first record. An `adDoMoveFirst` value causes the current record to remain the first record; `adStayBOF` moves the record pointer to `BOF`, where there is no current record.
CacheSize	The number of records stored by the data provider in local (cache) memory. The default value is 1. It's a common practice to set the number of records to the number of visible rows in a DataGrid or MSFlexGrid.

continues

TABLE 4.1 CONTINUED

Property	Purpose
CommandTimeout	The number of seconds allowed a Command object to execute before abandoning the attempt and returning an error message.
CommandType	The type of Command that provides the RecordSource property value. Valid values are adCmdUnknown (default), adCmdText (SQL statement), adCmdTable (table name), and adCmdStoredProc (stored procedure). Selecting adCmdStoredProc permits the creation of Recordsets from Jet row-returning QueryDef objects. The adCmdTableDirect (table name) and adCmdFile (opens a persistent Recordset file) values aren't available from the CommandType property options list.
ConnectionString	The string the defines the parameters required to connect to a specified data source through an OLE DB data provider, usually set with the Property Pages of the ADODC. (See the "Exploring ADODC and Data Link Properties Sheets" section earlier in the chapter for ADODC connection strings.)
ConnectionTimeout	The number of seconds allowed a Connection object to establish a connection to the data source before abandoning the attempt and returning an error message.
CursorLocation	The cursor engine used by the ADODC. Choices are adUseClient (the default, which uses the ADO cursor engine) or adUseServer (uses the server's engine).
CursorType	The type of cursor. For server-side cursors, the choices are adOpenStatic (similar to a DAO snapshot), adKeyset (similar to a DAO dynaset), or adOpenDyanmic (similar to an ODBCDirect Dynamic cursor). Client-side cursors (adUseClient) are always static, regardless of the CursorType value you specify.
EOFAction	The MoveNext behavior with the record pointer at the end of the Recordset. The adDoMoveLast (default) value causes the current record to remain the last record; adStayEOF positions the record pointer to EOF (no current record); and adDoAddNew positions the record pointer on an empty (tentative append) record.
LockType	The locking behavior of the ADODC's Recordset. Choices are adLockOptimistic (default, locks only during the update process), adLockReadOnly, adLockPessimistic (locks during the editing and update process), and adLockBatchOptimistic (permits multiple updates in a single operation). The adLockUnspecified value (-1, True) uses the data provider's default locking method.

Property	Purpose
MaxRecords	The maximum number of records to be returned from a row-returning Command. The default value is 0, which returns all records.
Mode	The access permissions to the data source. The default is adModeShareDenyNone for Jet databases. Other choices for Jet databases are adModeRead, adModeWrite, adModeReadWrite, adModeShareDenyRead, adModeShareDenyWrite, adModeShareExclusive. adModeUnknown accepts the server's default permissions for the current user.
Password	The password for the user specified by the UserName property value. Passwords appear in clear text, so they are not secure. An empty (**Null**) password is the default for Jet's Admin user.
RecordSource	The table name, SQL statement, or stored procedure name that defines the ADODC's Recordset.
UserName	The login name for the current user. Jet's default UserName is Admin.

ADODC Events

▶ **See** "Recordset Events," **p. 57**

The native Data control for DAO doesn't trigger events; the replacement ADODC offers nine data-related events that you can intercept with VBA event-handling code. All ADODC data-related events apply to the underlying Recordset and correspond to the Recordset events described in Chapter 2. Table 4.2, which duplicates Table 2.31, lists ADODC's events and when they occur. You validate data entry with code in WillChange... event handlers.

TABLE 4.2   NAMES AND OCCURRENCE OF RECORDSET EVENTS

Event Name	When Fired
EndOfRecordset	When the record pointer moves beyond the last record
FieldChangeComplete	After a change to the value of a field
MoveComplete	After execution of the Move or Move... methods applied to the ADODC.Recordset object
RecordChangeComplete	After an edit to a single record
RecordsetChangeComplete	After edits to multiple records
WillChangeField	Before applying a change to a field value

continues

TABLE 4.2   CONTINUED

Event Name	When Fired
WillChangeRecord	Before applying an edit to a single record
WillChangeRecordset	Before applying edits to multiple records
WillMove	After execution of the Move or Move... methods but before the position of the record pointer changes

▶ **See** "Recordset Methods," **p. 107**

NOTE

The ADODC and other data-related ActiveX controls expose properties and events, but don't expose methods. All the Recordset methods, described in Chapter 2, apply to the ADODC.Recordset property, which is a pointer to the underlying Recordset.

INTRODUCING BATCH OPTIMISTIC UPDATES

Most experienced Visual Basic developers eschew bound controls for updating data in multi-user and client/server applications. Multiple (also called batch) updates to Recordsets with conventional DAO bound controls are quite inefficient because each change to a record requires a round-trip over the network to the server. Making changes to or adding multiple records in bound data grids, called *browse editing*, is particularly troublesome in client/server environments. Remote Data Objects (RDO), introduced with Visual Basic 4.0 Enterprise Edition, overcame the multiple round-trip problem with batch optimistic updates. ADO includes batch optimistic updates in all Visual Basic 6.0 editions.

▶ **See** "Working with Bulk Updates and Disconnected Recordsets," **p. 764**

Batch optimistic updates store all changes to the Recordset in local (cache or buffer) memory. When the changes are complete, executing the UpdateBatch method applies all changes to the underlying tables. Unless you specifically need immediate changes to tables, using batch optimistic updates for all data editing operations is a good database programming practice.

To substitute batch optimistic for default optimistic updates with an ADODC control, do the following:

1. Change the ADODC.LockType property to 3 - adLockBatchOptimistic.
2. If you've specified a server-side cursor, change the CursorLocation property to 3 - adUseClient. BatchOptimistic updates require a client-side cursor.

3. Add an Update All command button to the form with the following line in the
   `cmdUpdate_Click` event handler:

   `adcName.Recordset.UpdateBatch`

▶ **See** "Working with Bulk Updates and Disconnected Recordsets," **p. 764**

Batch optimistic updates also enable *disconnected Recordsets*, which can be edited without an active connection to the data provider. When you're ready to apply the updates, you reestablish the connection to the data provider, then persist the changes to the underlying tables. Disconnected Recordsets minimize the number of active database connections, which is important in multiuser and client/server applications.

SIMPLE-BINDING DATA CONSUMER CONTROLS

TextBoxes, CheckBoxes, and other intrinsic controls capable of binding to a single field of a Recordset and displaying field data from a single row are classified as *simple-bound*. The most important change to ADO-compliant bound controls is the ability to bind directly to a Command or Recordset object without requiring an ADODC as the data provider. Prior to Visual Basic 6.0, all bound data consumer controls required as their data source a visible or hidden Data control.

NOTE
You can bind Visual Basic 6.0's native simple-bound controls to ADODCs, DataEnvironment objects, and ADODB.Recordsets, as well as to the native Data control for DAO and the Remote Data Control (RDC) of RDO 2.0. You can't bind ADO-compliant complex-bound controls (DataGrid, DataList, DataRepeater, and MSHFlexGrid) to the Data control.

Figure 4.16 shows the Properties window displaying the data-related properties of the txtHireDate bound TextBox of the Data Project described in the "Adding an ADODC to a Data Environment Designer Form" section earlier in the chapter. The default value of the DataFormat property, discussed later in this section, is **Null**.

FIGURE 4.16

Data category properties for the HireDate field of the rsEmployees *Recordset.*

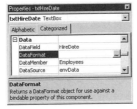

4

USING THE ADO
DATA CONTROL

Simple-bound controls have the data-related properties listed in Table 4.3.

TABLE 4.3 DATA-RELATED PROPERTIES OF SIMPLE-BOUND CONTROLS

Property	Purpose
DataField	The name of the Recordset field to display
DataFormat	A StdDataFormat object specified in the Property Pages for the DataFormat property
DataMember	The name of a row-returning DataEnvironment Command object or DataMember of a Class module or user control specified by the value of the DataSource property
DataSource	The name of an ADODC, DataEnvironment object, Recordset, or Class module or user control acting as a data provider

Setting the **DataFormat** Property Value

The formatting of bound TextBox values defaults to a set of standard, locale-specific formats for general numbers, currency, dates, and text. To alter the default format for a TextBox control, do the following:

1. Display the Properties window for the TextBox to format.

2. Click the builder button of the DataFormat property text box to open the Format page of the Properties Pages sheet. The Format Item list is disabled for simple-bound controls.

3. Select the format you want from the Format Type list. If the format offers options, a Format list appears.

4. Select the specific format for the TextBox in the Format list (see Figure 4.17).

FIGURE 4.17

Specifying a four-digit year format for a DataField *of the DateTime data type for Y2K conformance.*

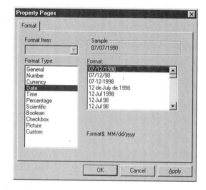

5. Click OK to apply the selected format.

> **TIP**
>
> Again, the U.S. English default `StdFormatObject` for Jet DateTime fields is `M/d/yy`, which violates generally accepted Y2K compliance requirements. Make sure to format all dates to four-digit years (`M/d/yyyy` or `MM/dd/yyyy`) to conform to Y2K rules.

The `StdDataFormat` object, which performs formatting operations, is an OLE DB service provider in an ADO automation wrapper. The `StdFormat` service provider greatly simplifies formatting of many simple- and complex-bound controls. When you open a new Data Project, a reference to the Microsoft Data Formatting Object Library, included in Msstdfmt.dll, is added to the project. Figure 4.18 shows Object Browser displaying members of the `StdFormat` library.

FIGURE 4.18

Member objects and collections of the `StdFormat` *library.*

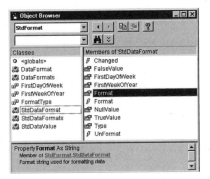

Each `StdDataFormat` is a member of the `StdDataFormats` collection, the names of which members appear in the Format Type list of the Property Pages. The `StdDataFormat.Format` property value is a string that corresponds to the format argument of Visual Basic's `Format` function. As an example, the value of the Format property for a four-year date with leading zeros for month and day is `"MM/dd/yyyy"`.

`StdDataFormat` objects fire events when applying (`Format`), modifying (`Changed`), or removing (`UnFormat`) formats. Few projects are likely to require intercepting these events, but the events are available if needed.

Using Code to Simple-Bind a Control

Unlike earlier Visual Basic versions, you can simple-bind ADO-compliant controls to a data provider at runtime with VBA code. If the `DataSource` is a `DataEnvironment` object, there's

4

USING THE ADO
DATA CONTROL

little or no benefit to using code to bind TextBoxes and other simple-bound controls to a field of a `Recordset` created by a row-returning `Command` object unless you want to reuse the controls with a different `DataSource` or `DataMember`.

The most common scenario in which you use code to bind controls is when you've created the `Recordset` with code. Listing 4.1 illustrates the code required to create a `Recordset` directly (without a `Connection` or `Command` object), bind fields of the `Recordset` to a set of nine TextBoxes, and bind the `Recordset`'s record pointer to an ADODC for navigation. The code of Listing 4.1 depends on TextBoxes being named txt*FieldName*, the recommended practice for naming bound text boxes.

LISTING 4.1 BINDING TEXTBOXES AND AN ADODC TO A CODE-CREATED *RECORDSET*

```
Private rsEmployees As New ADODB.Recordset

Private Sub Form_Activate()
    Dim ctlTextBox As Control
    'Open Recordset directly
    With rsEmployees
        .ActiveConnection = "Provider=Microsoft.Jet.OLEDB.3.51;" & _
            "Persist Security Info=False; Data Source=C:\Program Files" & _
            "\Microsoft Visual Studio\VB98\Nwind.mdb"
        .Source = "SELECT EmployeeID, LastName, FirstName, Title, " & _
            "Address, City, Region, PostalCode, Country FROM Employees"
        .CursorLocation = adUseClient
        .CursorType = adOpenStatic
        .LockType = adLockOptimistic
        .Open
    End With

    'Iterate the Controls collection
    For Each ctlTextBox In Me.Controls
        If TypeOf ctlTextBox Is TextBox Then
            With ctlTextBox
                'Pointer to rsEmployees
                Set .DataSource = rsEmployees
                'Extract the field name
                .DataField = Mid(.Name, 4)
            End With
        End If
    Next ctlTextBox

    'Bind the ADODC for navigation
    Set adcEmployees.Recordset = rsEmployees
End Sub
```

> **NOTE**
>
> It's important to set the `Recordset.CursorLocation` property to `adUseClient` when binding a `Recordset` to ADODCs and bound controls. The default `CursorLocation` with VBA code is `adUseServer`, which has a default CursorType of `adOpenForward` only. A forward-only (firehose) cursor causes an error (`The rowset does not support fetching backwards`) when you click the last, previous, or first record button of an ADODC control. (Clicking the last record button isn't a backward fetch, but `Recordsets` with firehouse cursors support only the `MoveNext` method.) You can demonstrate the error by commenting the `CursorLocation`, `CursorType`, and `LockType` lines in the preceding example.

Figure 4.19 shows the abbreviated version of DedEntry.vbp's `frmEmployees` form in design mode with empty Data category property values. The VbaEntry.vbp project, in the \Ddg_vb6\Chaptr04 folder demonstrates execution of the code of Listing 4.1.

FIG 4.19

A simple data entry form with controls bound to a Recordset in run mode.

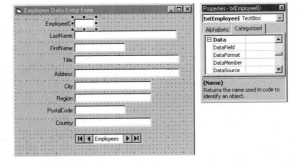

COMPLEX-BINDING DATA CONSUMER CONTROLS

Controls that display multiple fields, multiple records, or both are complex-bound to the OLE DB data provider's IRowset interface. Visual Basic 6.0's complex-bound visible controls are the DataGrid, Hierarchical FlexGrid, and DataList controls. Only the DataGrid permits updates to `Recordsets`; the remaining controls are read-only.

> **NOTE**
>
> The MSFlexGrid control, introduced with Visual Basic 4.0, binds only to the Data control. MSFlexGrid lacks the DataBindings, DataField, and DataMember properties required to bind to the ADODC. You can, however, bind MSFlexGrids to `ADODB.Recordsets` with code. The ADO2OLTP.vbp example of Chapter 20, "Porting Access OLTP Applications to Visual Basic 6.0," has two MSFlexGrids populated by `Recordsets`.

Binding a DataGrid to a `DataEnvironment` Object

The DataGrid is beginning Visual Basic developers' most commonly used complex-bound data consumer control. The DataGrid is an enhanced, ADO-enabled version of Visual Basic 5.0's DAO-based DBGrid control. Do the following to bind an updatable DataGrid to the `Employees` Command of the `envData DataEnvironment` object:

1. Open a new Data Project and remove `DataEnvironment1` and `DataReport1`.

2. Choose <u>P</u>roject, <u>A</u>dd File and add the envData.dsr designer file, created earlier in the chapter, to the project.

3. Open envData's Designer window, right-click and drag the Employees `Connection` node to `frmDataEnv`, and select <u>D</u>ataGrid from the context menu.

4. Expand the form and DataGrid to a reasonable size, change the name of the form to **frmDataGrid**, and add a descriptive caption.

5. Right-click the DataGrid, choose Retrieve Fields, and click OK in the message box that warns you that the layout of the DataGrid is about to be replaced. Field names appear in the fixed column headers.

6. Press F5 to display the DataGrid in run mode (see Figure 4.20). The default property values prevent adding new records to or deleting records from the `rsEmployees Recordset`.

FIGURE 4.20

Displaying the contents of the Employees table in a DataGrid bound to the `DataEnviron-` *ment's Employees Command.*

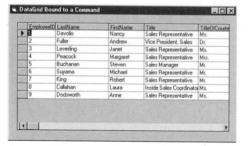

7. To enable adding and deleting records, return to design mode, right-click the DataGrid and choose Properties to open the Property Pages for the control. On the default General page, mark the `AllowAddNew` and `AllowDelete` check boxes, add a caption to the DataGrid, and click Apply (see Figure 4.21).

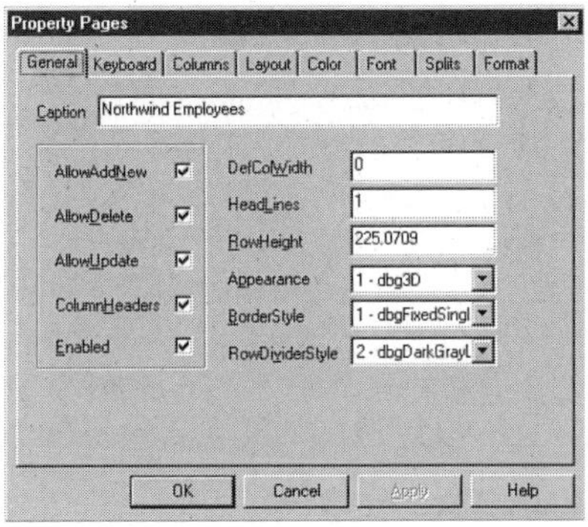

FIGURE **4.21**

*Enabling record
addition and dele-
tion, and adding a
caption to the
DataGrid.*

8. To permit use of the tab key to navigate columns and records, on the Keyboard page, select 2 - dbgGridNavigation from the `TabAction` list and mark the `WrapCellPointer` check box. Click Apply.

9. On the Columns page, select each column in the Columns list box and edit the captions for readability and appropriate column width.

10. TitleOfCourtesy isn't of great importance to Northwind, so on the Layout page, select Column 4 (TitleOfCourtesy) from the Columns list and clear the Visible check box to hide the column (see Figure 4.22).

FIGURE **4.22**

*Hiding the
TitleOfCourtesy
column of the
DataGrid.*

4

NOTE

The Layout page also lets you set the width of the columns in twips. You can either estimate the required width of each column at this point or wait until after checking your modifications in run mode to fix the column widths.

11. Each record of the OLE Object Photo field contains ¦/¦ characters, which differ from the ?\¦ characters shown in the Photo field's text box, so hide the Photo column.

12. On the Format page, which has an enabled Format Item list for complex-bound controls, select the BirthDate, change the format to Y2K-compliant MM/dd/yyyy format, and click Apply. Do the same for the HireDate column. Click OK to close the Property Pages.

13. In the Properties window, change the Name of the DataGrid to **dtgEmployees**.

14. Press F5 again to display the modified grid in run mode (see Figure 4.23).

FIGURE 4.23

The Northwind Employees DataGrid after modifying its default properties in the Property Pages.

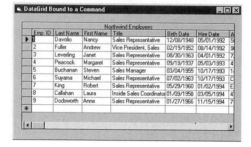

The data-related properties of the DataGrid that appear in the Properties window are AllowAddNew, AllowDelete, AllowUpdate, DataMember, and DataSource, all of which can be set in run mode with code. The DataGrid's DataMember and DataSource properties correspond to those of the ADODC.

You also can set the column-dependent properties of the DataGrid with code. The Columns collection provides access to each Column object of the control. The generalized VBA syntax for setting Column properties in code is

dtg*Name*.Columns(lng*Index*).*Property* = *typValue*.

Figure 4.24 illustrates setting column widths with code in the Form_Activate event handler. DataGrid.Column objects have 18 properties and two methods. Figure 4.25 shows Object Browser displaying the member functions of the Column object of the MSDataGridLib library.

FIGURE 4.24

Setting DataGrid column widths in the Form_Activate event handler.

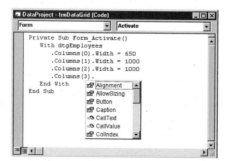

FIGURE 4.25

Object Browser displaying the member functions of the MSDataGridLib's Column *member object.*

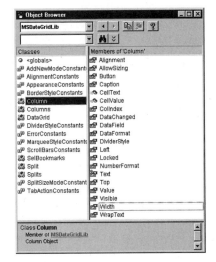

Picking Items from Bound DataList Controls

The two DataList controls, DataCombo and DataList, primarily are used as pick lists for displaying related records. The following sections describe how to populate a DataCombo control with a Command object and use the DataCombo's selection to populate a Hierarchical FlexGrid control.

Using a DataCombo as a Pick List for a Hierarchical Flex Grid

The most common form of pick list uses the Text property value of a DataCombo whose list contains the primary key fields to create an SQL SELECT statement with a WHERE clause constraint on the foreign key of a related table. In this example, selecting an OrderID value from a DataCombo populated from the Nwind.mdb Orders table displays in a Hierarchical FlexGrid related records from the Order Details table.

To bind a DataCombo to the Orders table and an MSHFlexGrid to Order Details records selected from the DataCombo, follow these steps:

1. Open a new Data Project and remove DataEnvironment1 and DataReport1.
2. Choose Project, Add File and add the envData.dsr designer file, created earlier in the chapter, to the project.
3. Open envData's designer window and click the Add Command button to open the Command1 Properties sheet.
4. In the General page, type **Orders** as the name of the Command, select cnnNwind from the Connection list, if necessary, and select the SQL Statement option.

4

USING THE ADO
DATA CONTROL

5. Type the following SQL SELECT statement in the text box to populate the DataCombo's list:

   SELECT OrderID FROM Orders ORDER BY OrderID DESC

   (see Figure 4.26).

6. Click OK to accept the other default properties of the Command.

7. DED doesn't offer a drag-and-drop choice for DataList controls, so add a DataCombo from the Toolbox to frmDataEnv and rename frmDataEnv to **frmDataCombo**.

8. In the DataCombo's Properties window, change the name to **dcbOrders**, set the RowSource to envData, the RowMember to Orders, and the ListField and BoundColumn properties to OrderID. Leave the other data-related properties of the DataCombo empty.

9. Add another Command in envData named **OrderDetails** to cnnNwind, select Table in the Database Object list, and select Order Details in the Object Name list. Click OK to close the OrderDetails Properties sheet.

10. Right click and drag the OrderDetails Command below dcbOrders on frmDataCombo, and select Hierarchical FlexGrid from the context menu.

11. Right-click the MSHFlexGrid and choose Retrieve Structure to populate the column headers with the field names of the OrderDetails table.

12. Change the name of the MSHFlexGrid to **hfgOrderDetails**. Orders

13. Add the code of Listing 4.2 to frmDataCombo.

14. Press F5 to run and test the project (see Figure 4.27).

LISTING 4.2 USING AN ORDERS COMBOLIST AS A PICK LIST FOR THE ORDER DETAILS TABLE

```
Private strSQL As String
Private rstOrderDetails As New ADODB.Recordset

Private Sub Form_Activate()
    'Open the Order Details Recordset directly
    With rstOrderDetails
```

```
            .ActiveConnection = "Provider=Microsoft.Jet.OLEDB.3.51;" & _
                "Persist Security Info=False;Data Source=C:\Program Files\" & _
                "Microsoft Visual Studio\VB98\Nwind.mdb"
            .Source = "SELECT * FROM [Order Details] ORDER BY OrderID DESC"
            .CursorLocation = adUseClient
            .CursorType = adOpenStatic
            .Open
            dcbOrders.Text = .Fields(0)
        End With
        'Clear the DataMember property
        hfgOrderDetails.DataMember = ""
        'Populate hfgOrderDetails
        Call dcbOrders_Click(2)
End Sub

Private Sub dcbOrders_Click(Area As Integer)
    If Area = 2 And Len(dcbOrders.Text) > 0 Then
        'Click on List element
        strSQL = "SELECT * FROM [Order Details] " & _
            "WHERE OrderID = " & dcbOrders.Text
        With rstOrderDetails
            If .State = adStateOpen Then
                .Close
            End If
            .Source = strSQL
            .Open
        End With
        Set hfgOrderDetails.DataSource = rstOrderDetails
    End If
End Sub
```

> **NOTE**
>
> An alternative to recreating the Recordset for each OrderID selection is to
> apply the Filter property with an rstOrderDetails.Filter = "OrderID = " &
> dcbOrderDetails.Text statement. It's usually faster, especially in multiuser and
> client/server applications, to re-create Recordsets having only a few records
> with a new SELECT statement. The "Populating an MSHFlexGrid from an
> Employee List Selection" section at the end of the chapter shows how to use
> the Filter property in lieu of a WHERE constraint.

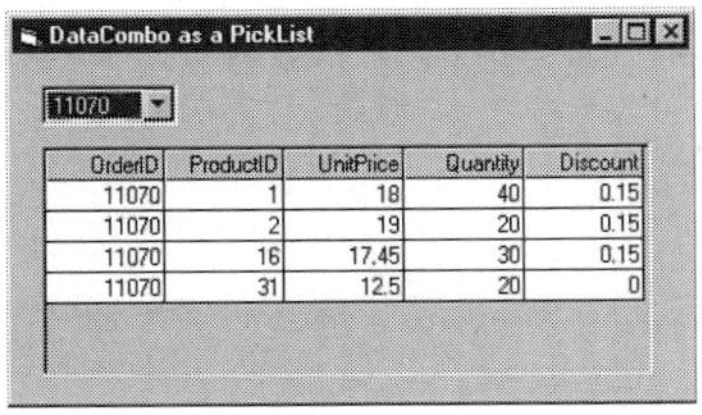

4

USING THE ADO
DATA CONTROL

FIGURE 4.27

*The DataCombo
pick list for the
Hierarchical
FlexGrid control in
run mode.*

Formatting Hierarchical FlexGrid Columns

Unlike the DataGrid, the MSHFlexGrid control doesn't have a Format page in its Properties sheet, nor does it directly support `StdDataFormat` objects. Instead, you format the text in the grid with the VBA `Format` function. The following example, which replaces the `Set hfgOrderDetails.DataSource = rstOrderDetails` statement of the dcbOrder_Click event handler, formats the currency and percent columns by replacing the General-formatted cell text with Currency- and Percent-formatted text.

```
With hfgOrderDetails
    Set .DataSource = rstOrderDetails
    For intCtr = 0 To .Rows - 1
        .Row = intCtr
        .Col = 2
        .Text = Format(.Text, "$0.00")
        .Col = 4
        .Text = Format(.Text, "00.0%")
    Next intCtr
End With
```

NOTE

Bound MSHFlexGrid controls are read-only, so altering the content of the grid doesn't attempt to update the underlying `Recordset` object with data of the incorrect data type. (Formatted numbers change from numeric to character data in the MSHFlexGrid control.)

Figure 4.28 illustrates the formatting applied to the MSHFlexGrid by adding the preceding code. The DataCbo.vbp project in the \Ddg_vb6\Chaptr04 folder includes the formatting code.

FIGURE 4.28

Formatting applied to the UnitPrice and Discount columns of the MSHFlexGrid control.

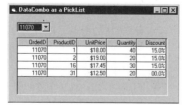

TIP

As a rule, it's a good programming practice to avoid using a combo list to pick from a drop-down list of more than 100 or so items. For very long lists, change the `Style` property value to 0 - dbcDropDownCombo, which lets the user type the first few characters of the list item sought in the text box element of the control to position the list near the desired item.

Binding DataList Controls

The DataList control has data-related properties almost identical to the DataCombo control, but isn't as well suited as the DataCombo for picking items from longer lists. Typically, you use a DataList for relatively short lists of items of significant length, for example, a list of first and last names.

▶ **See** "Creating Required Visual Basic Objects," **p. 782**

> **NOTE**
>
> Visual Basic 6.0 doesn't offer a direct equivalent of Access's multicolumn list box. If you need a multicolumn list box, substitute a MSHFlexGrid control. Alternatively, you can bind a MSFlexGrid control to an ADODB.Recordset object with code or use a ListView control populated by code. For new projects, the MSHFlexGrid is the preferred ADO-compliant control.

Binding a DataList to a Command Object

Follow these steps to populate a DataList with last and first names from Nwind.mdb's Employees table:

1. Open a new Data Project and remove DataEnvironment1 and DataReport1.

2. Choose Project, Add File and add the envData.dsr designer file, created earlier in the chapter, to the project.

3. Open envData's designer window, and click the Add Command button to open the Command1 Properties sheet.

4. In the General page, type **EmpsList** as the name of the Command, select cnnNwind from the Connection list, and select the SQL Statement option.

5. Type the following SQL SELECT statement in the text box to populate the DataList with formatted *LastName, FirstName* items and provide a primary key value (EmployeeID) for a WHERE clause criterion:

```
SELECT EmployeeID, LastName & ", " & FirstName AS EmpName
    FROM Employees
    ORDER BY LastName, FirstName
```

6. From the Toolbox, add a DataList control to frmDataEnv. Change the name of the control to **dltEmpsList** and change the name of the form to **frmDataList**.

7. Set the value of the RowSource property to envData, RowMember to EmpsList, ListField to EmpName, and BoundColumn to EmployeeID.

8. Press F5 to check the operation of the DataList (see Figure 4.29).

FIGURE 4.29

A DataList control bound to a DED-generated Recordset.

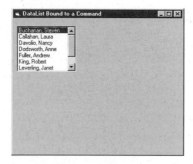

Populating an MSHFlexGrid from an Employee List Selection

An alternative to replacing the Recordset that serves as the DataSource of an MSHFlexGrid control is to create a Recordset containing all records in the related table or query result set and then apply a filter having the pick list choice. In this example, the dltEmpsList.BoundText property provides the foreign key (EmployeeID) value to filter the Orders table Recordset with an rstOrders.Filter = "EmployeeID = " & dltEmpsList.BoundText statement. After applying a filter to the Recordset, you must apply the Refresh method to the bound MSHFlexGrid control to assure consistent execution.

Do the following to bind an MSHFlexGrid control to the Orders table and apply a filter based on Employee selection in the DataList:

1. Add an MSHFlexGrid to frmDataList and rename the control to **hfgOrders**.
2. Set the FixedCols property value of hfgOrders to 0, the AllowUserResizing property to 1 - flexResizeColumns, and the Visible property to **False**.

> **NOTE**
>
> Setting the Visible property of the MSHFlexGrid to **False** prevents the appearance of the grid with unselected records on form activation. The Visible property is set to **True** after making a selection in the DataList.

3. Add the code of Listing 4.3 to frmDataList to create the rstOrders Recordset to populate hfgOrders and apply a selected employee filter to rstOrders.
4. Press F5 to run the project, and click items in dltEmpsList to test the use of the Filter property (see Figure 4.30).

The DataList.vbp project is included in the \Ddg_vb6\Chaptr04 folder of the accompanying CD-ROM.

LISTING 4.3 USING AN EMPLOYEES DATALIST TO FILTER THE ORDERS TABLE

```
Private rstOrders As New ADODB.Recordset
Private strSQL As String

Private Sub Form_Activate()
    strSQL = "SELECT EmployeeID, OrderID, OrderDate, ShipName, " & _
        "ShipCity, ShipCountry FROM Orders ORDER by OrderDate DESC"
    'Open the Orders Recordset directly
    With rstOrders
        .ActiveConnection = "Provider=Microsoft.Jet.OLEDB.3.51;" & _
            "Persist Security Info=False;Data Source=C:\Program Files\" & _
            "Microsoft Visual Studio\VB98\Nwind.mdb"
        .Source = strSQL
        .CursorLocation = adUseClient
        .CursorType = adOpenStatic
        .LockType = adLockReadOnly
        .Open
    End With
    Set hfgOrders.Recordset = rstOrders
End Sub

Private Sub dltEmpsList_Click()
    Dim intCtr As Integer

    'Filter the selected employee records
    rstOrders.Filter = "EmployeeID = " & dltEmpsList.BoundText
    With hfgOrders
        .Refresh
        'Reformat the date for Y2K compliance
        DoEvents
        .Visible = True
        For intCtr = 0 To .Rows - 1
            .Row = intCtr
            .Col = 2
            .Text = Format(.Text, "MM/dd/yyyy")
        Next intCtr
    End With
End Sub
```

TIP

The **DoEvents** instruction in the preceding listing is critical to proper execution of the Y2K formatting code. If you don't add **DoEvents**, formatting is applied to the contents of the MSHFlexGrid prior to completion of the Refresh method's execution. Comment DoEvents and run the project to verify this behavior.

DATABASE AND QUERY DESIGN CONCEPTS

PART II

IN THIS PART

OPTIMIZING THE DESIGN OF RELATIONAL DATABASES

IN THIS CHAPTER

This chapter describes the theoretical and practical sides of relational database management systems (RDBMSs), including how to design a relational database system or a set of relational tables to achieve optimum performance with Visual Basic 6.0 database applications. This book distinguishes between a client/server RDBMS such as Microsoft SQL Server, a desktop RDBMS such as Microsoft Access, and a set of relational tables such as a database created from a collection of dBASE table and index files. The database design principles you learn in this chapter apply equally to each of these database systems. This chapter also covers indexing methods that improve the speed of searching for a specific record in a table and increase the performance when two or more related tables are joined. A brief description of data warehousing technology and online analytical processing (OLAP) concludes the chapter.

Visual Basic 6.0 is an ideal tool for use with client/server RDBMSs (also called SQL databases), so a substantial part of this book is devoted to creating front ends for displaying and updating data in networked client/server environments. This chapter is intended for readers with limited database design experience. If you're an accomplished relational database developer, you might want to skim this chapter now and proceed to Chapter 6, "Learning Structured Query Language."

CLASSIFYING DATABASE SYSTEMS

The history of digital computers is inexorably tied to the concurrent development of database methodology. It is probably a safe estimate that at least 80 percent of worldwide computer resources and programming activities are devoted to database applications.

The first military and commercial applications for tabulating machines and digital computers were devoted to retrieving, calculating, and reporting on data stored in the form of punched cards. For example, a deck of cards containing the names and addresses of customers constituted a database table. Another deck of punched cards, containing information on the invoices issued to customers for a given period, represented another table. Using a collating device, you could shuffle the two decks so that a new deck was created wherein each customer card was followed by the cards detailing the orders for that customer. You could then use the cards to print a report in which the customer's card provided a report subheading and all of the orders for the customer were printed under the subheading. Cards from other decks could be collated into the two-level deck to create more detailed reports. Early tabulating machines included the capability to create customer subtotals and order grand totals. Figure 5.1 shows the effect of collating two decks of cards to print a report of invoices.

FIGURE 5.1

Collating punched cards for customers and invoices to print a report.

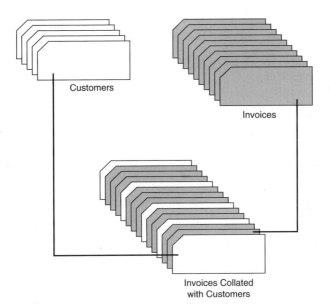

Customers

Invoices

Invoices Collated
with Customers

The obvious problem with the punched-card collation technique was that every time you wanted a different report, you had to separate (decollate) the cards back into their original decks and then manually run a different set of collation processes. Replacing tabulating machines with computers equipped with nine-track magnetic tape drives solved many of the problems associated with moving decks of cards back and forth between collators. You transferred the data from a sorted deck of cards to a magnetic tape, mounted the tapes you needed on tape drives, and then let the computer combine (merge) the data on the "table" tapes onto a new tape whose data was identical to that of a collated deck of punched cards. Then you could print a report from the data on the newly recorded tape.

Punched-card decks and magnetic tapes are sequential devices. Finding a particular record requires that you search from the first card of the deck or first record of a tape and read each card or record until you find a match (or determine that no matching record exists.) When high-capacity random-access data storage devices (such as disk drives) became available, searching for a particular record became much faster, even if you had to read each record in the table. To speed the process, sorting and indexing methods were developed to minimize the number of records the computer had to read until matching data was found. The seminal work in this field is volume 3 of Stanford University Professor Donald E. Knuth's *Art of Computer Programming* series, *Sorting and Searching,* originally published in 1973. Addison-Wesley published the second edition of *Sorting and Searching* (ISBN 0-201-89685-0) in early 1998.

Advances in computer technology after the advent of the random-access disk drive have occurred primarily in the form of architectural, rather than conceptual, changes to both

5

OPTIMIZING
RELATIONAL
DATABASES

hardware and software. The pace of improvement in the operating speed and the rate of cost reduction of computer hardware has far outdistanced the rate of progress in software engineering, especially in database design and programming methodology. You can make substantial improvement in the performance of an ill-conceived and poorly implemented database design simply by acquiring a faster computer. The price of a new computer is usually much less than the cost of reengineering the organization's legacy database structure. Ultimately, however, poor database designs and implementations result in a severe case of organizational inefficiency. One purpose of this chapter is to provide a sufficient background in database design to make sure that the database structures you create don't fall into this category.

The sections that follow discuss elementary database terminology in the object-oriented language to which you were introduced in Chapter 2, "Understanding OLE DB and Universal Data Access." Also, the different types of computer database structures most commonly used today are described and compared.

Database Terminology

Whatever the data storage and retrieval mechanism used, a *database* is a collection of one or more table objects. A *table* (also called a *relation* or *tuple*) is a database object that consists of a collection of *rows* (*records*) that share a collection of properties. The values associated with the properties of a table appear in *columns* (*fields*). Row-column (spreadsheet) terminology is most commonly used in databases that employ SQL statements to manipulate table data, whereas desktop databases commonly use record-field. This book uses the terms *record* and *field* when referring to persistent database objects (RDBMS tables and saved `Recordset` objects), and *row* and *column* when referring to virtual tables (`Recordset` objects) created from tables by queries. The distinction between the two forms of terminology, however, is not very significant. Figure 5.2 illustrates the generalized structure of a database table.

FIGURE 5.2

The generalized structure of a database table.

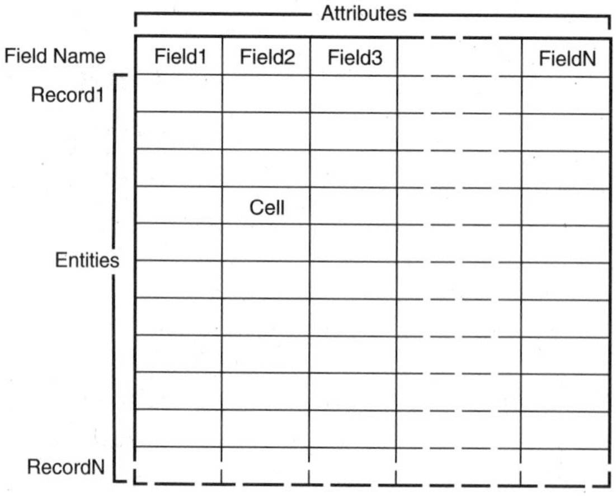

The following list describes the most important properties of database table objects. These property descriptions and rules apply to tables of conventional databases that use only fundamental data types—character strings and numerical values.

- A *record* is a representation of a real-world object such as a person, a firm, an invoice, or one side of a transaction involving money. A record of a table is the equivalent of one punched card in a deck. In formal database terminology, a row or record is an *entity*. Synonyms for entities include *data entities*, *data objects*, *data instances*, or *instances*. Tables are the *collection* (set) of all entities of a single entity class. Statisticians call a table a *homogeneous universe*.

- A *field* describes one of the characteristics of the objects represented by records. A field corresponds to a column of a spreadsheet or `Recordset`.

- The intersection between a row and a column is called an *attribute*, which represents the value of a significant property of a real-world object. Attributes also are called *cells* and *data cells*—terms derived from spreadsheet applications. All the attributes contained in a single column of a table are called an *attribute class*.

- The fundamental rule of all table objects is that each field is devoted to one and only one property. (This rule is implied by the terms *attribute* and *attribute class*.) Attribute values are said to be *atomic*, used here as a synonym for *indivisible*. Each field is assigned a field name that is unique within the table. A `Name` field that contains entries such as "Dr. John R. Jones Jr." is not atomic; the field actually consists of five attributes: title, first name, middle initial, last name, and suffix. You can sacrifice the atomicity of fields to a limited degree without incurring serious problems. A common practice is to combine first name and middle initial, and sometimes the suffix, in a single field.

- It's desirable, but not essential, for each record in a table to have a set of attributes by which you can uniquely distinguish one record in the table from any other record. This set is called the *entity identifier* or *identifier*. In some cases, such as tables that contain the line items of invoices, records don't have a unique identifier. A good database-design practice, however, is to provide such an identifier, even if you must add an item or line number attribute class to establish the uniqueness.

- The field(s) that include the identifier attributes are called the *primary key* or *primary key field(s)* of the table. By definition, the attribute value or set of attribute values that make up the primary key must be unique for each record. Records in related tables are joined by values of the primary key in one table and by equal values in the primary key or the foreign key(s) of the other table. A *foreign key* is one or more attributes of a joined table that do not constitute the primary key of the table.

- Tables that contain records identifying objects that are inherently unique, such as human beings, are called *primary* or *base* tables. Each record of a primary table must have one or more attributes that uniquely identify the entity. Theoretically, all U.S. citizens have a unique Social Security number used for identification purposes. Thus an employee table in the U.S. should be able to use a single attribute—a Social Security number—to serve as an entity identifier. A duplicate Social Security number indicates either a data entry error, a counterfeit Social Security card, or an error on the part of the Social Security Administration.

- Tables are logical constructs—that is, tables need not be stored on a disk drive in a tabular format. Desktop database managers that originated as DOS versions, such as dBASE and Paradox, have a file structure that duplicates the appearance of the table. However, most mainframe and client/server database management systems store many tables (and even more than one database) within a single physical file. Microsoft Access 1.0 was the first widely used desktop RDBMS to store all the tables that constitute a single database in one Jet .mdb file. Thus Jet .mdb files are called *containers* of tables. No easily discernible relationship exists between the physical and logical structures of tables of mainframe, client/server, and Jet database types.

NOTE

Files that contain one or more databases commonly are called *devices*. Versions 6.5 and earlier of Microsoft SQL Server use fixed-size device (.dat) files. SQL Server 7.0 uses a pair of conventional operating system files (*DBname*_data.mdf) and *DBname*_log.ldf) for each database. Unlike device files, .mdf and .ldf files grow and shrink automatically as data is added to or deleted from the database. The move from device to database files is one of the major changes in SQL Server 7.0.

- The concept of a *record number* was introduced to the world of PC databases by dBASE II. The record number, returned by xBase's RECNO() function, is an artificial construct that refers to the relative physical position (called the *offset*) of a record in a table file. The record numbers change when you physically reorder (sort) the table file. Record number is not an attribute of a table, unless you create a field and add record number values (often called a *record ID* field). Jet's AutoIncrement field data type and SQL Server's IDENTITY property differ from xBase's record number because the AutoIncrement and IDENTITY values don't change when you reorder the set.

NOTE

The AbsolutePosition property of an ADODB.Recordset or DAO.Recordset object emulates xBase's RECNO() function with one important exception: AbsolutePosition returns the relative position of the record within the Recordset, not in the order of addition to the table.

A database consists of one or more tables; if more than one table is included in a relational database, the entities described in the tables should be related by at least one attribute class (field) that is common to two of the tables. The formal statistical name for a database is a *heterogeneous universe*. This book adheres to the term *database*. Object-oriented databases (OODBs) do not conform strictly to the atomicity rules for attributes. Similarly, Access's OLE `Object` field data type (`Long Binary`, `dbLongBinary` in Jet terminology) is not atomic because the data in the fields of the OLE Object field data type contains both the object's data (or only the presentation for a linked object) and a reference to the application that created the object. The object type of the content of Access OLE `Object` fields may vary from record to record.

A *query* is a method by which you obtain access to a subset of records from one or more tables that have attribute values satisfying some criteria. A variety of ways are available to process queries against databases. Processing queries against databases with the Jet database engine is the subject of the next chapter, "Learning Structured Query Language." You also can use queries to modify the data in tables; this type of query is described in Chapter 7, "Running Crosstab and Action Queries."

Flat-File Databases

The simplest database form consists of one table with records having enough columns to contain all the data you need to describe the entity class. The term *flat-file* is derived from the fact that the database itself is two-dimensional—the number of table fields determine the database's width, and the quantity of table records specify its height. There are no related tables in the database, so the concept of data depth, the third dimension, does not apply. Any database that contains only one table is, by definition, a flat-file database.

Flat-file databases are suitable for simple telephone and mailing lists. The Windows 3.*x* Cardfile is an example of a simple flat-file database. Ranges of cells, which are designated as "databases" by spreadsheet applications, also are flat-files. A mailing-list database, as an example, has designated fields for names, addresses, and multiple telephone numbers. Data files used in Microsoft Word's print merge operations are flat-file databases.

You run into problems with flat-file databases when you attempt to expand the use of a mailing-list database to include sales contacts, for example. If you develop more than one sales contact at a firm, you must add the data for the new contact in one of two ways:

- Add a new record with duplicate data in all fields except the contact and, perhaps, the telephone number field.
- Add new fields so that you can have more than one contact name and telephone number field per record. In this case, you must add enough contact field pairs to accommodate the maximum number of contacts you expect to add for a single firm. The added fields are called *repeating groups*.

Both choices are inefficient and can waste a considerable amount of disk space, depending on the database file structure you use. Adding extra records duplicates data, and adding new fields results in many records that have no values (nulls or, worse yet, spaces) for multiple contact and telephone number fields. Adding new fields causes trouble when you want to print reports. It is especially difficult to format printed reports that have repeating groups.

Regardless of the deficiencies of flat-file databases, many of the early mainframe computers offered only flat-file database structures. All spreadsheet applications offer "database" cell ranges that you can sort by a variety of methods. Although spreadsheet "databases" appear to be flat, this is seldom truly the case. One of the particular problems with spreadsheet databases is that the spreadsheet data model naturally leads to inconsistencies in attribute values and repeating groups. Time-series data contained in worksheets is a classic example of a repeating group. The section "Organizing Entity Classes" later in this chapter shows you how to deal with inconsistent entity classes that occur in worksheet databases, and the "Normalizing Table Data" section describes how to eliminate repeating groups.

The Network and Hierarchical Database Models

The inability of flat-file databases to efficiently deal with data that involved repeating groups of data led to the development of a variety of different database structures (called *models*) for mainframe computers. The first standardized and widely accepted model for mainframe databases was the *network model* developed by the Committee for Data System Languages (CODASYL), which also developed Common Business Oriented Language (COBOL) to write applications that manipulate the data in CODASYL network databases. Although the CODASYL database model has its drawbacks, an extraordinary number of mainframe CODASYL databases remain in use today. Billions of lines of COBOL code are in use every-day in North America.

CODASYL databases substitute the term *record type* for table, but the characteristics of a CODASYL record type are fundamentally the same as the properties of a table. CODASYL record types contain pointers to records of other record types. A *pointer* is a value that specifies the location of a record in a file or in memory. For example, a customer record contains a pointer to an invoice for the customer, which in turn contains a pointer to another invoice record for the customer, and so on. The general term used to describe pointer-based record types is *linked list*; the pointers link the records into an organized structure called a *network*. Network databases offer excellent performance when you are seeking a set of records that pertain to a specific object because the relations between records (pointers) are a permanent part of the database. However, the speed of network databases degrades when you want to browse the database for records that match specific criteria, such as all customers in California who purchased more than $5,000 worth of product "A" in September 1998.

Note

The problem with CODASYL databases is that database applications (primarily COBOL programs) need to update the data values and the pointers of records that have been added, deleted, or edited. The need to sequentially update both data and pointers adds a great deal of complexity to transaction-processing applications for CODASYL databases.

IBM developed the *hierarchical model* for its IMS mainframe database product line, which uses the DL/1 language. The hierarchical model deals with repeating groups by using a data structure that resembles an upside-down tree: Data in primary records constitute the branches, and data in repeating groups are the leaves. The advantage of the hierarchical model is that the methods required to find related records are simpler than the techniques needed by the network model. As with the CODASYL model, a large number of hierarchical databases are running on mainframe computers today.

The Relational Database Model

The *relational database model* revolutionized the database world and enabled PCs to replace expensive minicomputers and mainframes for many database applications. The relational database model was developed in 1970 by Dr. E. F. Codd of IBM's San Jose Research Laboratories. The primary advantage of the relational model is that it eliminates the need to mix pointers and data in tables. Instead, records are linked by *relations* between attribute values. A *relation* consists of a linkage between records in two tables that have identical attribute values. Figure 5.3 illustrates relations between attribute values of relational tables that constitute part of a sales database.

Figure 5.3

Relationships between tables in a sales database.

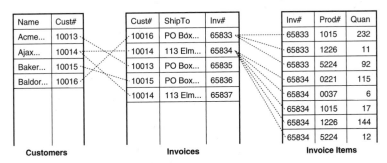

Name	Cust#
Acme...	10013
Ajax...	10014
Baker...	10015
Baldor...	10016

Customers

Cust#	ShipTo	Inv#
10016	PO Box...	65833
10014	113 Elm...	65834
10013	PO Box...	65835
10015	PO Box...	65836
10014	113 Elm...	65837

Invoices

Inv#	Prod#	Quan
65833	1015	232
65833	1226	11
65833	5224	92
65834	0221	115
65834	0037	6
65834	1015	17
65834	1226	144
65834	5224	12

Invoice Items

Because relational tables don't contain pointers, the data in relational tables is independent of the methods used by the database management system to manipulate the records. A RDBMS is an executable application that can store data in and retrieve data from sets of related tables in a database. The RDBMS creates transitory *virtual pointers* to records of relational tables in memory. Virtual pointers appear as they are needed to relate (*join*) tables and are disposed of when a database application no longer requires the relation. The "joins" between tables are shown as dashed lines in Figure 5.3. Joins are created between primary key fields and foreign key fields of relational tables. The primary and foreign key fields of the tables of Figure 5.3 are listed in Table 5.1.

TABLE 5.1 THE PRIMARY AND FOREIGN KEYS OF THE TABLES DEPICTED IN FIGURE 5.3

Table	Primary Key	Foreign Key
Customers	Cust#	None
Invoices	Inv#	Cust#
Invoice Items	Inv# and Prod#	Inv#

Relational databases require duplicate data among tables but don't permit duplication of data within tables. You must duplicate the values of the primary key of one table as the foreign key of dependent tables. A *dependent table* is a table that requires a relationship with another table to identify its entities fully. Dependent tables often are called *secondary* or *related tables*. Thus the Invoices table is dependent on the Customers table to supply the real-world name and address of the customer represented by values in the Cust# field. Similarly, the Invoice Items table is dependent on the Invoices table to identify the real-world object (in this case an invoice) to which records are related.

The three types of relations defined by the relational database models are described in the following list:

- One-to-one relations require that one and only one record in a dependent table can relate to a record in a primary table. One-to-one relations are relatively uncommon in relational databases.

- One-to-many relations enable more than one dependent table to relate to a record in a primary table. The term *many-to-one* also is used to describe one-to-many relations. One-to-many relations constitute the relational database model's answer to the repeating-groups problem. Repeating groups are converted to individual records in the table on the "many" side of the relation. One-to-many relations are the most commonly found relations.

- Many-to-many relations are not true relations because many-to-many relations between two tables require an intervening table, called a *relation* table, to hold the values of the foreign keys. (Relational database theory defines relations between two tables only.) If Figure 5.3 had included a Products table to describe the products represented by the Prod# field of the Invoice Items table, then the Invoice Items table would serve as a relation table between the Invoices and Products tables. Some relation tables include only foreign key fields.

The proper definition of the relations between entity classes and the correct designation of primary and foreign keys constitute the foundation of effective relational database design methods. The relational database model is built on formal mathematical concepts embedded in relational algebra. Fortunately, you don't need to be a mathematician to design a relational database structure. A set of five rules, discussed in the "Rules for Relational Database Design" section later in this chapter, defines the process of creating tables that conform to the relational model.

Types of Relational Database Managers

The preceding description of the relational database model made the important point that the properties of (such as the data in) a relational table object are independent of the methods used to manipulate the data. Consequently, you can use any RDBMS application to process the data contained in a set of relational tables. For example, you can export the data in the tables of an IBM DB2 mainframe database as a set of text files that preserve the tables' structure. You can then import the text files into tables created by another database management system. Alternatively, you can use an ODBC driver for DB2 and a network gateway to the DB2 database to access the data directly in a Visual Basic application. The independence of data and implementation in relational databases also enables you to attach tables from one database type to another. Joins between tables in more than one RDBMS type are called *heterogeneous joins*. You can join an attached DB2 table to the native tables in a Jet database without going through the export-import exercise. SQL Server 7.0 enables you to create heterogeneous joins between SQL Server tables and any type of tabular data for which an OLE DB data provider is available.

TIP

Relational database managers differ in the types of data you can store in tables and in how you name the fields of tables. Many RDBMSs, such as SQL Server, include the long varbinary or image field data type, which enables you to store image data in tables; others, including the most commonly used early versions of IBM's DB2, do not support long varbinary fields or their equivalent. You can embed spaces and other punctuation symbols in Jet table and field names, but you can't in most other RDBMS tables. If you are designing a database that may be ported from the original RDMBS to another relational database implementation, make sure you use only the fundamental field data types and conform to the table- and field-naming conventions of the least versatile of the RDBMSs.

Substantial differences do occur in how various RDBMSs are implemented. Someone new to database management or someone converting from a mainframe database system to a desktop database manager often overlooks these differences. The following sections discuss how mainframe, minicomputer, and client/server databases differ from traditional desktop database managers.

Relational SQL Database Management Systems

Full-featured client/server RDBMSs separate the database management application (server or *back end*) from the individual (client) applications that display, print, and update the information in the database. Client/server RDBMSs, such as Microsoft SQL Server, run as a service on the server computer, although Microsoft offers a desktop version of SQL Server 7.0 that runs on any 32-bit Windows platform. Most client/server RDBMSs historically have run under one or more flavors of the UNIX operating system, but Windows NT 4.0+ rapidly is gaining ground on UNIX as an application server operating system. The client/server RDBMS is responsible for the following activities:

- Creating new databases and one or more files to contain the databases. (Several databases may reside in a single fixed disk file, which SQL Server 6.5 and earlier calls a *device*.)

- Implementing database security to prevent unauthorized persons from gaining access to the database and the information it contains.

- Maintaining a catalog of the objects in the database, including information on the owner (creator) of the database and the tables it contains. Catalogs that describe database objects are called *metadata* (data about data).

- Generating a log of all modifications made to the database so that the database can be reconstructed from a prior backup copy combined with the information contained in the log (in the event of a hardware failure). Such files are called *transaction logs*.

- Managing concurrency issues so that multiple users can access the data without encountering significant delays in displaying or updating data. Concurrency issues are handled by temporary locks placed on individual records, pages of a table, or the entire table.

- Interpreting queries transmitted to the database by user applications and returning or updating records that correspond to the criteria embedded in the query statement. Virtually all client/server RDBMSs use statements written in SQL to process queries— thus the generic name SQL RDBMS.

- Executing *stored procedures*, which are precompiled queries that you execute by name in an SQL statement. Stored procedures speed the execution of commonly used queries by eliminating the necessity for the server to optimize and compile the query each time it runs. The Visual Basic 6.0 ADODB.Command object is designed expressly for executing server stored procedures. The Visual Basic 5.0 ODBCDirect and Remote Data Object (RDO) 2.0 also have stored-procedure execution capabilities.

- Preserving referential integrity, maintaining consistency, and enforcing domain integrity rules to prevent corruption of the data contained in the tables. Client/server RDBMSs commonly use preprogrammed *triggers*, a special type of stored procedure, that generate an error when an application attempts to execute a query that violates the rules.

Separate database applications (front ends) are responsible for creating the query statements sent to the database management system and for processing the rows of data returned by the query. Front ends handle all data formatting, display, and report-printing chores. A primary advantage of using an SQL RDBMS is that the RDBMS itself implements the features in the preceding list, such as security and integrity. Therefore, the code to implement these features doesn't need be added to each different front-end application. Chapter 18, "Working with Client/Server Databases," describes the features of client/server RDBMSs in greater detail.

Three-Tier Client/Server Architecture and Business Rules

The stored procedures of client/server databases used to execute predefined queries and maintain database integrity use SQL plus proprietary SQL language extensions such as Transact-SQL, used by Microsoft and Sybase SQL Server products. SQL is a set-oriented, not a procedural, programming language; therefore, dialects of SQL are not well suited to writing programs for validating data in accordance with complex business rules. An example of a complex business rule is this:

> The current credit limit of a customer is equal to the customer's maximum credit limit, less uncontested open invoices and orders in process, unless the customer has outstanding, uncontested invoices beyond terms plus 10 days, or if the total amount of contested invoices exceeds 50 percent of the total amount of open invoices. If a pending order exceeds the customer's calculated credit limit, or any customer payment is behind terms plus 10 days, approval must be obtained from the credit manager prior to accepting the order.

Such a test is impossible to program as a conventional, linear SQL stored procedure, because the last condition requires the credit manager to intervene in the process.

Three-tier client/server architecture adds a *business services* processing layer between the front-end client, which provides *user services*, and the back-end server, which supplies *data services*. The intermediate processing layer, sometimes called a *line-of-business object* (LOBject) or *business object*, processes requests from client applications, tests the requests for conformance with programmed business rules, and sends conforming requests to the back-end RDBMS, which updates the affected tables. Visual Basic 6.0 lets you create *Remote Automation Components* (RACs) that reside on an application server, which need not be the server that runs the RDBMS. Each client usually creates its own instance of the RAC, but clients also may share a pool of pre-created objects or wait their turn to use a single business object instance. Figure 5.4 illustrates the architecture of basic three-tier client/server applications that communicate by distributed COM (DCOM).

FIGURE 5.4

Basic three-tier client/server database architecture with multiple RAC instances.

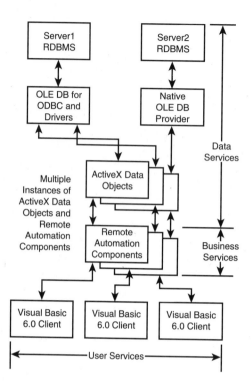

NOTE

Microsoft Transaction Server (MTS) is a combination transaction manager (TM) and object request broker (ORB) that simplifies deployment and management of RACs created with Visual Basic 6.0. MTS is the subject of Chapter 26, "Taking Advantage of Microsoft Transaction Server 2.0." Chapter 27, "Creating and Deploying MTS Components," describes how to write ActiveX DLLs for inclusion in MTS packages.

Microsoft Access: A Hybrid RDBMS

Microsoft Access is a cross between a conventional one-table-per-file desktop database manager and a complete, full-featured SQL RDBMS. Access uses a single database file that includes all the tables native to the database. The Jet database engine enforces referential integrity for native tables at the database level, so you don't need VBA code. Jet 2+ enforces domain integrity at the field and table levels when you alter the value of a constrained field. Jet databases include system tables that catalog the objects in the database, and multiuser concurrency issues are handled by the database drivers.

Access enables you to break the back-end/front-end barrier that separates RDBMSs from desktop DBMSs. Application code; objects, such as forms and reports; and tables can be included in the same database file. Microsoft used Access's capability to include both front-end and back-end components in a single .mdb file as strong selling point. It soon became apparent to Access developers that separating application and database objects into individual .mdb files was a better design. You create a Jet database that contains only tables and attach these tables to an Access .mdb file that provides the front-end functionality. The dual-file approach enables you to substitute Visual Basic 6.0 and ADO or DAO for Access and DAO as the front-end development tool for single-user or multiuser Jet databases.

> **NOTE**
>
> Microsoft announced in early January 1998 that Access 9.0 will offer the desktop version of SQL Server 7.0 as an "alternative database engine." The extent to which Access developers abandon Jet in favor of SQL Server for single-user applications remains to be seen.

Usernames and passwords are stored in a separate .mdw workgroup (formerly .mda) library file, because a Jet .mdb file can contain only one database. You can put sets of unrelated tables in a single .mdb file, but this practice is not generally recommended. Jet's proprietary flavor of SQL is the native method of manipulating data in tables—it's not an afterthought. The Jet DLLs that implement the database functionality are independent from the Msaccess.exe file that includes the code you use to create forms and reports. Jet databases are about as close as you're likely to get to a RDBMS in a low-cost, mass-distributed software product that offers multiuser databases without payment of per seat client-licensing fees.

Using Jet .mdb database files with Visual Basic front ends approximates the capabilities and performance of workstation-class client/server RDBMSs at a substantially lower cost for both hardware and software. If you're currently using one-file-per-table DBMSs, consider attaching the tables to a Jet database during the transition stage while your new 32-bit Windows front ends and your existing applications need to simultaneously access the tables. When the transition to Visual Basic front ends is completed, you can import the data to a Jet database and take full advantage of the additional features .mdb files offer. When you outgrow the Jet database structure, you can use the Access Upsizing tools to perform a quick and easy port to SQL Server 6.5. You connect to a client/server database with the Microsoft OLE DB Provider for ODBC Drivers (MSDASQL) and SQL Server ODBC driver, or the native OLE DB Provider for SQL Server (SQLOLEDB).

NOTE

The Access 97 Upsizing Tool library (Wzcs97.mda) works with SQL Server versions 4.21a, 6.0, and 6.5, but not with SQL Server 7.0.

MODELING DATA

The first step in designing a relational (or any other) database is to determine what objects need to be represented by database entities and what properties of each of these objects require inclusion as attribute classes. The process of identifying the tables required in the database and the fields that each table needs is called *data modeling*. You can take two approaches during the process of data modeling:

- Application-oriented design techniques start with a description of the type of application(s) required by the potential users of the database. From the description of the application, you design a database that provides the necessary data. This approach is called the *bottom-up* approach because applications are ordinarily at the bottom of the database hierarchy.

- Subject-oriented design methodology begins by defining the objects that relate to the subject matter of the database as a whole. This approach is called *top-down* database design. The content of the database determines what information front-end applications can present to the user.

Although application-oriented design can enable you to quickly create an ad hoc database structure and the applications to accomplish a specific goal, bottom-up design is seldom a satisfactory long-term solution to an organization's information needs. It is common to find several application-oriented databases within an organization that have duplicate data, such as independent customer lists. When the firm acquires a new customer, each of the customer tables needs to be updated. This process is inefficient and error prone.

Subject-oriented database design is a far more satisfactory method. You might want to divide the design process into department-level or workgroup-related databases, such as those in the following list:

- A *sales* database that has tables based on customer, order and line item, invoice and line item, and product entity classes.

- A *production* database with tables for parts, suppliers, bills of material, and cost accounting information. The product and invoice tables of the sales department's database would be attached to the production database.

- A *personnel* database with tables for employees, payroll data, benefits, training, and other subjects relating to human resources management. The production and sales databases would attach to the employees table—production for the purposes of cost accounting purposes, and sales for commissions.

- An *accounting* database, with tables comprising the general ledger and subsidiary ledgers, would attach to most tables in the other databases to obtain access to current finance-related information. Accounting databases often are broken down into individual orders, accounts receivable, accounts payable, and general ledger databases.

There is no fixed set of rules to determine which shared tables should be located in what database. Often these decisions are arbitrary or are based on political, rather than logical, reasoning. Department-level databases are especially suited for multiuser Jet databases running on peer-to-peer networks with 30 or fewer users. Each department can have its own part-time database administrator (DBA) who backs up the database, grants and revokes the rights of users to share individual tables in the database, and periodically compacts the database to regain the space occupied by deleted records.

Database Diagrams

Diagramming relations between tables can aid in visualizing database design. *Entity-relation* (E-R) diagrams, also called *entity-attribute-relation* (EAR) diagrams, are one of the most widely used methods for depicting the relations between database tables. The E-R diagramming method was introduced by Peter Chen in 1976. An E-R diagram consists of rectangles that represent the entity classes (tables). Ellipses above the table rectangles show the attribute class (field) involved in the relation. Parallelograms connect pairs of table rectangles and field ellipses to represent the relation between the fields. Figure 5.5 illustrates an E-R diagram for the Customers and Invoices tables of the database described in Figure 5.3 and Table 5.1. The *1* and *m* adjacent to the table rectangles indicate a one-to-many relationship between the two tables.

FIGURE 5.5

An entity-relationship diagram showing the relationship between the Customers and Invoices tables.

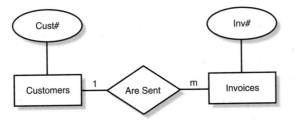

E-R diagrams describe relations by predicates. One of the definitions of *predicate* is "a term designating a property or relation." If you remember parsing sentences in grammar school

English classes, you'll observe that *Customers* is the subject, *are sent* is the predicate, and *invoices* is the predicate object of a complete sentence. E-R diagrams can describe virtually any type of allowable relation between two tables by adding additional symbols to the basic diagram shown in Figure 5.5. Many E-R diagrams are required to define relationships between the numerous entities in enterprisewide databases.

 ▶ **See** "Specifying Primary Keys and Relationships in Database Diagrams," **p. 718**

> **NOTE**
>
> Visual Basic 6.0's DataEnvironment object and the enables you to create simple graphic SQL Server database diagrams, which are stored in the database as SQL Server 6.5+ DatabaseDiagram objects. The diagrams are similar to those of the Access Relationships window but lack some of the Access version's subtle design features, such as automatic alignment of relationship links with primary and foreign key text boxes.

Using Modeling Tools for Database Design

Designing databases to accommodate the information requirements of an entire firm is a major undertaking. Therefore, computer-aided software engineering (CASE) tools often are used for the design of complex database systems. CASE tools for database design usually include the following capabilities:

- Business model generation—The first step in the use of a high-end CASE tool is to create an operational model of an enterprise, which consists of defining virtually every activity involved in operating the organization. Accurately modeling the operations of a large firm as it relates to information requirements is an extraordinarily difficult and time-consuming process.

- Schema development—A database schema is a diagram that describes the entire information system pictorially, usually with less detail than that offered by E-R diagrams. The schema for a large information system with a multiplicity of databases can cover an entire wall of a large office or conference room.

- Relation diagramming—Some CASE tools support several methods of diagramming relations between tables. Most, but not all, CASE tools support E-R diagrams, as well as other pictorial methods, such as Bachman diagrams or SQL Server 6.5+'s DatabaseDiagram objects.

- Data dictionary development—A data dictionary is a full description of each table in the database and each field of every table. The dictionary also includes other properties of tables and fields, such as primary keys, foreign keys, indexes, field data types, and constraints on field values.

- Repository creation—A repository is a database that is part of the CASE tool. The repository contains all the details of the structure and composition of the database. Data in the repository is used to create schema, relation diagrams, and data dictionaries. The repository is also responsible for maintaining version control when you change the database's design. Microsoft and Texas Instruments have joined forces to develop an object-oriented repository for 32-bit Windows application and database development.

- Database generation—After you've designed the database, the CASE tool creates the SQL Data Definition Language (DDL) statements necessary to create the database and its tables. You then send the statements to the RDBMS, which builds the database for you.

- Data flow diagramming—Some database CASE tools include the capability to create data flow diagrams that describe how data is added to tables and how tables are updated. Data flow diagrams, however, are application related, not database design related. Therefore, data flow diagramming capability is a prerequisite for qualification as a CASE database tool.

Mainframe database developers have various CASE tools from which to choose. Several CASE tools serve the client/server market, for example, System Architect from Popkin Software & Systems and ER*win* from Logic Works.

RULES FOR RELATIONAL DATABASE DESIGN

If you use a modeling tool to create your database structure, the modeling tool automatically creates tables that comply with the basic rules of relational database design. Database developers, however, often are faced with the task of importing or using existing data that is not in a suitable format for a relational database. It's quite common for database developers to face the task of transforming data contained in spreadsheet "databases" into tables of a relational database. Another scenario is the conversion of a poorly designed, dysfunctional database, or a CODASYL network database that contains repeating groups, into a proper relational structure. (COBOL permits the use of the `GroupName OCCURS Several TIMES` statement to create repeating groups in network databases.)

The sections that follow describe the methods you use to transform nonrelational data to fully relational form.

Organizing Entity Classes

The "Flat-File Databases" section of this chapter noted that the worksheet data model often contains inconsistent entities in rows. The stock prices example, shown in Figure 5.6, is an Excel worksheet whose structure violates every rule applicable to relational database tables except attribute atomicity. STOCKS is a worksheet that lists the New York Stock Exchange's (NYSE) closing, high, and low prices for shares and the sales volume of 25 stocks for a five-day period. Rows contain different entities, and columns B through F are repeating groups. The following examples use the Stocks5.xls workbook in Excel 5.0/7.0 format, which is included on the accompanying CD-ROM. You'll find Stocks5.xls in the \Ddg_vb6\Chaptr05 folder.

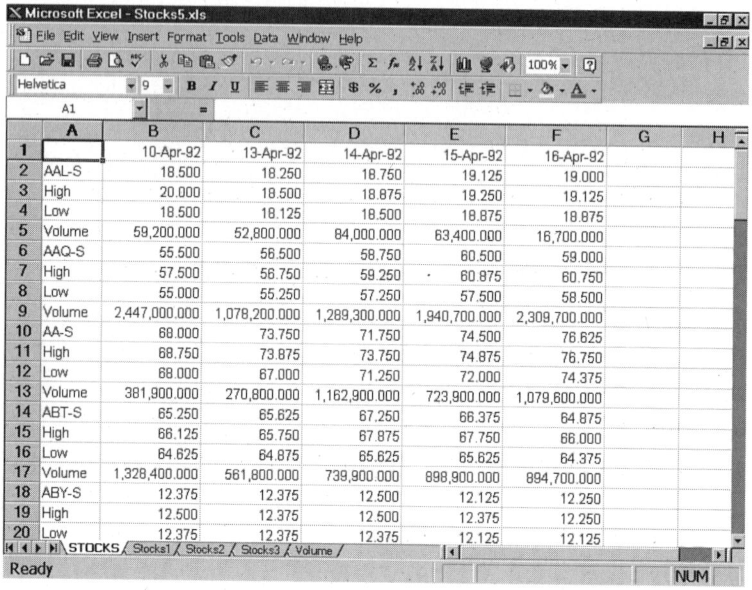

	A	B	C	D	E	F	G	H
1		10-Apr-92	13-Apr-92	14-Apr-92	15-Apr-92	16-Apr-92		
2	AAL-S	18.500	18.250	18.750	19.125	19.000		
3	High	20.000	18.500	18.875	19.250	19.125		
4	Low	18.500	18.125	18.500	18.875	18.875		
5	Volume	59,200.000	52,800.000	84,000.000	63,400.000	16,700.000		
6	AAQ-S	55.500	56.500	58.750	60.500	59.000		
7	High	57.500	56.750	59.250	60.875	60.750		
8	Low	55.000	55.250	57.250	57.500	58.500		
9	Volume	2,447,000.000	1,078,200.000	1,289,300.000	1,940,700.000	2,309,700.000		
10	AA-S	68.000	73.750	71.750	74.500	76.625		
11	High	68.750	73.875	73.750	74.875	76.750		
12	Low	68.000	67.000	71.250	72.000	74.375		
13	Volume	381,900.000	270,800.000	1,162,900.000	723,900.000	1,079,600.000		
14	ABT-S	65.250	65.625	67.250	66.375	64.875		
15	High	66.125	65.750	67.875	67.750	66.000		
16	Low	64.625	64.875	65.625	65.625	64.375		
17	Volume	1,328,400.000	561,800.000	739,900.000	898,900.000	894,700.000		
18	ABY-S	12.375	12.375	12.500	12.125	12.250		
19	High	12.500	12.375	12.500	12.375	12.250		
20	Low	12.375	12.375	12.375	12.125	12.125		

FIGURE 5.6
A worksheet whose structure is the antithesis of proper database table design.

You need to separate the entity classes according to the object each entity class represents. The four entity classes of the STOCKS worksheet of the Stocks5.xls workbook are the closing price, the highest transaction price, the lowest transaction price, and the trading volume of a particular stock on a given day. To separate the entity classes you need to add a column so that the stock is identified by its abbreviation in each row. You can identify the data entities by their classes—Close, High, Low, and Volume—plus the abbreviation for the stock, which is added to the new column with a simple recorded Excel VBA macro. Then you sort the data with the Entity and Key columns. The result of this process appears, as shown for the Stocks1 worksheet, in Figure 5.7.

NOTE

The dates column represents a mixed entity type (three prices in dollars and the volume in shares), but each entity is now identified by its type. Therefore, you can divide the entities into separate tables at any point in the transformation process.

FIGURE 5.7
The STOCKS worksheet with entities sorted by entity class.

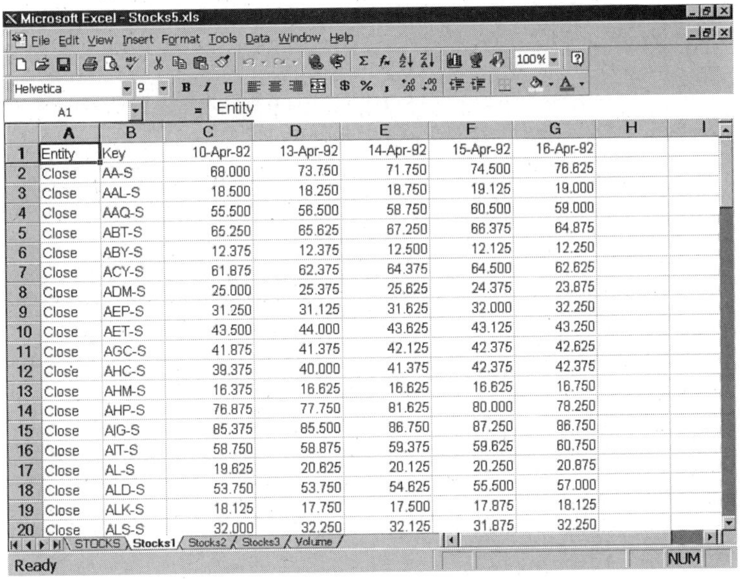

	A	B	C	D	E	F	G
1	Entity	Key	10-Apr-92	13-Apr-92	14-Apr-92	15-Apr-92	16-Apr-92
2	Close	AA-S	68.000	73.750	71.750	74.500	76.625
3	Close	AAL-S	18.500	18.250	18.750	19.125	19.000
4	Close	AAQ-S	55.500	56.500	58.750	60.500	59.000
5	Close	ABT-S	65.250	65.625	67.250	66.375	64.875
6	Close	ABY-S	12.375	12.375	12.500	12.125	12.250
7	Close	ACY-S	61.875	62.375	64.375	64.500	62.625
8	Close	ADM-S	25.000	25.375	25.625	24.375	23.875
9	Close	AEP-S	31.250	31.125	31.625	32.000	32.250
10	Close	AET-S	43.500	44.000	43.625	43.125	43.250
11	Close	AGC-S	41.875	41.375	42.125	42.375	42.625
12	Close	AHC-S	39.375	40.000	41.375	42.375	42.375
13	Close	AHM-S	16.375	16.625	16.625	16.625	16.750
14	Close	AHP-S	76.875	77.750	81.625	80.000	78.250
15	Close	AIG-S	85.375	85.500	86.750	87.250	86.750
16	Close	AIT-S	58.750	58.875	59.375	59.625	60.750
17	Close	AL-S	19.625	20.625	20.125	20.250	20.875
18	Close	ALD-S	53.750	53.750	54.625	55.500	57.000
19	Close	ALK-S	18.125	17.750	17.500	17.875	18.125
20	Close	ALS-S	32.000	32.250	32.125	31.875	32.250

Now you have a table that contains entities with consistent attribute values because you moved the inconsistent stock name abbreviation to its own attribute class, Key, and replaced the stock abbreviation in the Entity column A to a value consistent with the Entity attribute class, Close. However, the repeating-groups problem remains.

NOTE

This chapter uses manual worksheet methods of manipulating tabular data because worksheet techniques, such as selecting, cutting, and pasting groups of cells, represent the easiest and fastest way to change the structure of tabular data. If you need to transform a large amount of worksheet data into relational tables, you should use VBA `Automation` methods or create general-purpose VBA macros in the worksheet application to automate the transformation process.

Normalizing Table Data

The process of transforming existing data into relational form is called *normalization*. Normalization of data is based on the assumption that you have organized your data into a tabular structure wherein the tables contain only a single entity class. Here are the objectives of data normalization:

- To eliminate duplicated information contained in tables
- To accommodate future changes to the structure of tables

- To minimize the impact of changes to database structure on the front-end applications that process the data

The sections that follow describe the five steps that constitute full normalization of relational tables. In most cases, you can halt the normalization process at the third normal form. Many developers bypass the fourth and fifth normal forms because these normalization rules appear arcane and inapplicable to everyday database design.

First Normal Form

The first normal form requires that tables be flat and contain no repeating groups. A data cell of a flat table may contain only one atomic (indivisible) data value. If your imported data contains multiple data items in a single field, you need to add one or more new fields to contain each data item; then move the multiple data items into the new field.

The Nwind.mdb sample database of Visual Basic 6.0 and Access 97's Northwind.mdb includes a table, Customers, whose `Address` field contains data that violates the first normal form because some cells contain a two-line address. Figure 5.8 shows the Customers table of Northwind.mdb in Access datasheet mode. The multiple-line addresses for Hungry Coyote Import Store and Island Trading, shown with gridlines emphasized, violate the atomicity rule. Therefore, you need another field, such as `Location`, to contain the second line of two-line entries in the `Address` field. For parcel delivery services, such as Federal Express, you need the physical address in the `Location` field for firms that use postal boxes to receive their mail.

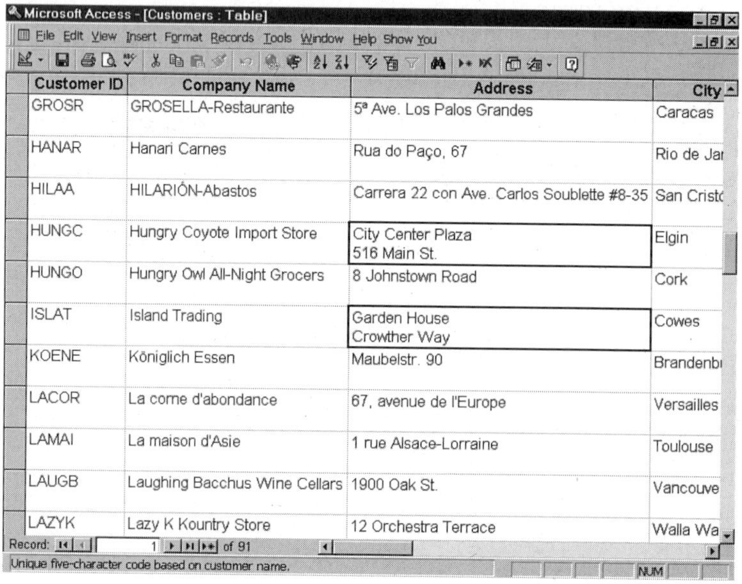
Microsoft Access - [Customers : Table]
File Edit View Insert Format Records Tools Window Help Show You
Customer ID | Company Name | Address | City
GROSR | GROSELLA-Restaurante | 5ª Ave. Los Palos Grandes | Caracas
HANAR | Hanari Carnes | Rua do Paço, 67 | Rio de Jai
HILAA | HILARIÓN-Abastos | Carrera 22 con Ave. Carlos Soublette #8-35 | San Cristc
HUNGC | Hungry Coyote Import Store | City Center Plaza 516 Main St. | Elgin
HUNGO | Hungry Owl All-Night Grocers | 8 Johnstown Road | Cork
ISLAT | Island Trading | Garden House Crowther Way | Cowes
KOENE | Königlich Essen | Maubelstr. 90 | Brandenbı
LACOR | La corne d'abondance | 67, avenue de l'Europe | Versailles
LAMAI | La maison d'Asie | 1 rue Alsace-Lorraine | Toulouse
LAUGB | Laughing Bacchus Wine Cellars | 1900 Oak St. | Vancouve
LAZYK | Lazy K Kountry Store | 12 Orchestra Terrace | Walla Wa
Record: 1 of 91
Unique five-character code based on customer name.
NUM

FIGURE 5.8
First normal form violations in the Customers table of Access 97's Northwind.mdb sample database.

NOTE

If you're an xBase or Paradox developer, you might think that adding a field to contain the physical location portion of the address causes unwarranted expansion of the size of the Customers table. This is not the case with Jet tables, because Jet databases use variable-length fields for the Text field data type. If an entry is missing in the `Location` field for a customer, the field contains only the **`Null`** value in databases that support **`Null`** values. The size is an issue applicable to fixed-width xBase and Paradox table fields because you must provide enough width to accommodate both lines of the address, whether you use one or two fields to contain the address data. Jet tables use variable-length fields for Text entries. An alternative to adding a `Location` field is to create a separate table for location data that has an optional one-to-one relation with the Customers table. This process is less efficient than accepting **`Null`** or blank values in records that do not have `Location` values.

Eliminating repeating groups is often a tougher process when you're transforming worksheet data. Four of the five columns of stock price data shown earlier in Figure 5.7 are repeating groups. The quick-and-dirty method of eliminating repeating groups is a series of copy, cut, paste, and fill operations. You add another column to specify the date for each entry. Then you cut and paste the cells for the four repeating groups into the column renamed from the beginning date of the series to `PriceVolume`. The final step is to sort the data on the `Entity`, `Key`, and `Date` fields. A portion of the resulting worksheet (Stocks2) appears in Figure 5.9. Instead of 101 rows for the 25 stocks, you now have 501 rows and what appears to be a large amount of duplicated data. However, your data is now in first normal form.

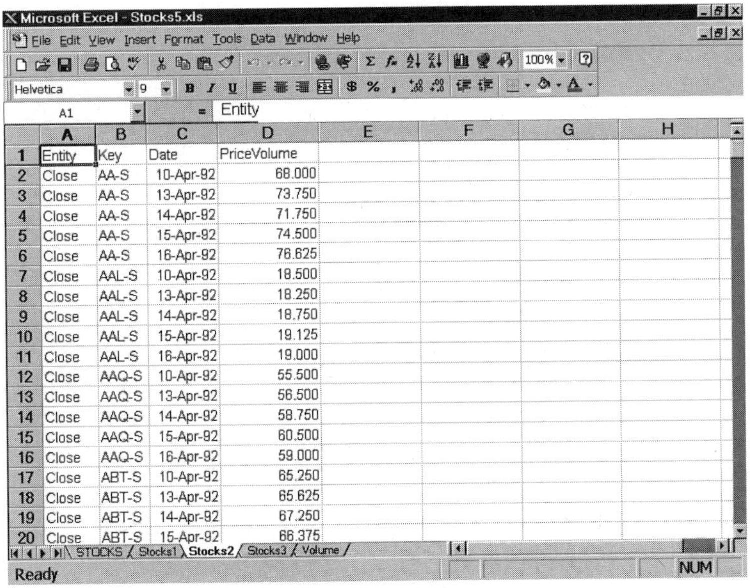

	A	B	C	D
1	Entity	Key	Date	PriceVolume
2	Close	AA-S	10-Apr-92	68.000
3	Close	AA-S	13-Apr-92	73.750
4	Close	AA-S	14-Apr-92	71.750
5	Close	AA-S	15-Apr-92	74.500
6	Close	AA-S	16-Apr-92	76.625
7	Close	AAL-S	10-Apr-92	18.500
8	Close	AAL-S	13-Apr-92	18.250
9	Close	AAL-S	14-Apr-92	18.750
10	Close	AAL-S	15-Apr-92	19.125
11	Close	AAL-S	16-Apr-92	19.000
12	Close	AAQ-S	10-Apr-92	55.500
13	Close	AAQ-S	13-Apr-92	56.500
14	Close	AAQ-S	14-Apr-92	58.750
15	Close	AAQ-S	15-Apr-92	60.500
16	Close	AAQ-S	16-Apr-92	59.000
17	Close	ABT-S	10-Apr-92	65.250
18	Close	ABT-S	13-Apr-92	65.625
19	Close	ABT-S	14-Apr-92	67.250
20	Close	ABT-S	15-Apr-92	66.375

FIGURE 5.9
The STOCKS worksheet transformed to first normal form in the Stocks2 worksheet.

Second Normal Form

Second normal form requires that all data in nonkey fields of a table be fully dependent on the primary key and on each element (field) of the primary key when the primary key is a composite primary key. *Fully dependent on* is a synonym for "uniquely identified by." The data shown in Figure 5.9 clearly shows that the only nonkey column of Stocks2 is `PriceVolume`. The `Entity`, `Key`, and `Date` fields are members of the composite primary key. The sorting process used in the preceding section proves this point.

Database designers don't agree on whether or not objects that have a common attribute class, such as price, should be combined into a single table with an identifier to indicate the type of price, such as `List`, `Distributor`, or `OEM` for products, or in this case, `Close`, `High`, and `Low` transaction price for the day. This process is called *subclassing* an entity. There's no argument, however, that the volume data deserves its own worksheet, at least for now, so you cut the volume data from Stocks2 and paste it to a new worksheet called Volume. You can delete the `Entity` column from the Volume sheet because the name of the sheet now specifies the entity class.

The data in the Volume sheet, with field names added, is shown in Figure 5.10. Each entity now is uniquely identified by the two-part composite primary key comprising the `Key` and `Date` fields. You can import the data from the Volume sheet into a table from any application that supports importing Excel 5.0/7.0 tables contained in a workbook—Access 97, for example. Both the Stocks2 and Volume worksheets contain data in second normal form.

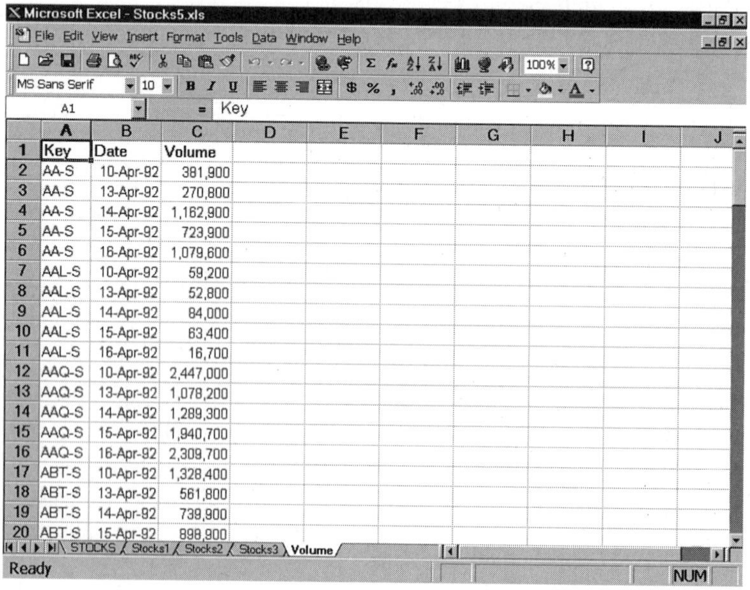

	A	B	C
1	Key	Date	Volume
2	AA-S	10-Apr-92	381,900
3	AA-S	13-Apr-92	270,800
4	AA-S	14-Apr-92	1,162,900
5	AA-S	15-Apr-92	723,900
6	AA-S	16-Apr-92	1,079,600
7	AAL-S	10-Apr-92	59,200
8	AAL-S	13-Apr-92	52,800
9	AAL-S	14-Apr-92	84,000
10	AAL-S	15-Apr-92	63,400
11	AAL-S	16-Apr-92	16,700
12	AAQ-S	10-Apr-92	2,447,000
13	AAQ-S	13-Apr-92	1,078,200
14	AAQ-S	14-Apr-92	1,289,300
15	AAQ-S	15-Apr-92	1,940,700
16	AAQ-S	16-Apr-92	2,309,700
17	ABT-S	10-Apr-92	1,328,400
18	ABT-S	13-Apr-92	561,800
19	ABT-S	14-Apr-92	739,900
20	ABT-S	15-Apr-92	898,900

FIGURE 5.10
The Volume worksheet in second normal form.

Third Normal Form

Third normal form requires that all nonkey fields of a table be dependent on the table's primary key and independent of one another. Thus the data in a table must be normalized to second normal form to ensure dependency on the primary key. The issue here is the dependencies of nonkey fields. A field is dependent on another field if a change in the value of one nonkey field forces a change in the value of another nonkey field.

At this point in the normalization process, you have the following three choices for how to design the table(s) to hold the stock price data:

- Leave the data remaining in the Stocks2 worksheet as is and create one Prices table, using the Entity column to subclass the price entity. This method requires a three-field composite key.
- Create a Prices table with three columns, High, Low, and Close, using `Key` and `Date` as the composite primary key. You could even add the volume data to the Volume field and then have only one record per stock per day.
- Create three separate prices tables, High, Low, and Close, and use Key and Date as the composite primary key. In this case, you don't subclass the entities.

The decision on your available choices for a table structure that meets the third normal form is a judgment call based on the meaning of the term *independent*. Are stock prices and trading volumes truly independent of one another? Are the opening, high, and low prices dependent upon the vagaries of the stock market and the whims of traders, and thus independent of one another? These questions mix the concepts of dependence and causality. Although a higher opening price is likely to result in a higher closing price, the causality is exogenous to the data itself. *Exogenous data* is data that is determined by factors beyond the control of any of the users of the database. The values of the data in the table are determined by data published by the NYSE after the exchange closes for the day. Therefore, the values of each of the attribute classes are independent of one another, and you can choose any of the three methods to structure your stock prices table(s).

Overnormalizing Data and Performance Considerations

After you have determined that your data structure meets the third normal form, the most important consideration is to avoid overnormalization of your data. *Overnormalization* is the result of applying too strict an interpretation of dependency at the third normal stage. Creating separate tables for High, Low, and Close prices, as well as share-trading Volume, is overkill. You need to join three tables in a one-to-one relationship to display the four data values for a stock. This process will be very slow unless you create indexes on the primary key of each table. You have four tables, so you need four indexes. Even after indexing, the performance of your stock prices database will not be as fast as a table that contains all the values. In addition, the four indexes will be larger than a single index on a table that contains fields for all four attributes.

The rule for third normal form should have two corollary rules:

- Combine all entities of an object class that can be uniquely identified by the primary (composite) key and whose nonkey values either are independent of one another or are exogenous to the database and all related databases into a single table, unless the combination violates the fourth normal form. Combining entities into a single table is called *integrating data*.

- Decompose data into tables that require one-to-one relationships only when the relationship is optional or when you need to apply security measures to nonkey values, and your RDBMS does support column-level permissions. *Decomposing data* means breaking a table into two or more tables without destroying the meaningfulness of the data.

Therefore, the suggested corollary rules for the third normal form answer the question of which structure is the best (which was posed in the preceding section). Create a new Stocks3 worksheet with fields for the High, Low, and Close prices, as well as for the trading Volume. Then paste the appropriate cells to Stocks3 and add field names. Figure 5.11 shows the result of this process.

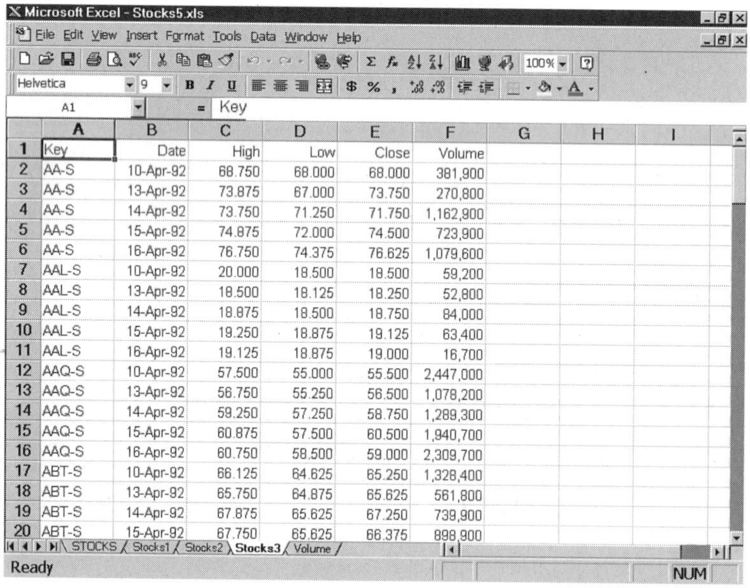

FIGURE 5.11

The stock prices data in third normal form.

	A	B	C	D	E	F
1	Key	Date	High	Low	Close	Volume
2	AA-S	10-Apr-92	68.750	68.000	68.000	381,900
3	AA-S	13-Apr-92	73.875	87.000	73.750	270,800
4	AA-S	14-Apr-92	73.750	71.250	71.750	1,162,900
5	AA-S	15-Apr-92	74.875	72.000	74.500	723,900
6	AA-S	16-Apr-92	76.750	74.375	76.625	1,079,600
7	AAL-S	10-Apr-92	20.000	18.500	18.500	59,200
8	AAL-S	13-Apr-92	18.500	18.125	18.250	52,800
9	AAL-S	14-Apr-92	18.875	18.500	18.750	84,000
10	AAL-S	15-Apr-92	19.250	18.875	19.125	63,400
11	AAL-S	16-Apr-92	19.125	18.875	19.000	16,700
12	AAQ-S	10-Apr-92	57.500	55.000	55.500	2,447,000
13	AAQ-S	13-Apr-92	56.750	55.250	56.500	1,078,200
14	AAQ-S	14-Apr-92	59.250	57.250	58.750	1,289,300
15	AAQ-S	15-Apr-92	60.875	57.500	60.500	1,940,700
16	AAQ-S	16-Apr-92	60.750	58.500	59.000	2,309,700
17	ABT-S	10-Apr-92	66.125	64.625	65.250	1,328,400
18	ABT-S	13-Apr-92	65.750	64.875	65.625	561,800
19	ABT-S	14-Apr-92	67.875	65.625	67.250	739,900
20	ABT-S	15-Apr-92	67.750	65.625	66.375	898,900

Fourth Normal Form

Fourth normal form requires that independent data entities not be stored in the same table when many-to-many relations exist between these entities. If many-to-many relations exist between data entities, the entities are not truly independent; therefore, such tables usually fail the third normal form test. The fourth normal form requires you to create a relation table that contains any data entities that have many-to-many relations with other tables. The stock prices data does not contain data in a many-to-many relation, so this data cannot be used to demonstrate decomposition of tables to the fourth normal form.

Fifth Normal Form

Fifth normal form requires you to be able to exactly reconstruct the original table from the new table(s) into which the original table was decomposed or transformed. Applying the fifth normal form to your resulting table is a good test to make sure you did not lose data in the process of decomposition or transformation. The Stocks3 worksheet contains every piece of data contained in the original STOCKS worksheet; therefore, with enough cutting, pasting, and sorting, you could restore it. Proving compliance with fifth normal form is often a tedious process. Fortunately, it does not require you to be able to use ANSI SQL statements to reconstruct the original table.

INDEXING TABLES FOR PERFORMANCE AND DOMAIN INTEGRITY

The primary purpose of adding indexes to tables is to increase the speed of searches for specific data values. If you want to display all persons named Smith in the LastName field of a table, creating an index on the LastName field results in a substantial improvement in the search performance. Without an index, the database manager must start at the beginning of the table and then test every record for the occurrence of "Smith" in the LastName field. If you create an index on the LastName field of the table, the searching operation uses the index, not the table itself, to find the first record where LastName = 'Smith'.

Joining two tables by the primary key field(s) of one table and the foreign key field(s) of another table is a special case of searching for records. When you join two tables, the search criterion becomes *Table2.ForeignKey* = *Table1.PrimaryKey*. The index must match every foreign key value with a primary key value. Without an index on both the primary key field(s) and the foreign key field(s), joining large tables can take a very long time.

The sections that follow describe the indexing methods in common use with today's desktop data managers and client/server RDBMSs, the structure of database tables and indexes, and how to choose the fields of tables to index so that you achieve optimum application performance.

Table Indexing Methods

An *index,* in simplified terms, consists of a table of pointers to records or groups of records. The records that contain pointer values, usually with an unsigned long integer data type, are organized in a binary hierarchy to reduce the number of tests required to find a record that matches the search criteria. Indexes traditionally refer to the three levels of the hierarchy as the root, branch, and leaf level. (Here again, the analogy to an inverted tree is used.) However, the number of levels in the branch hierarchy actually depends on the number of records in the indexed table. The root leads to one of two branches, and each branch leads to another branch until you reach the leaf level, which is indivisible. The leaf level of the index contains the pointers to the individual records or, in the case of Jet and most client/server databases, the pages that contain the records. The branches contain pointers to other branches in the index or to the leaves.

The exact method of indexing field values varies with the database manager you use; dBASE (.NDX and .MDX files), FoxPro (.IDX and .CDX), Clipper (.NTX), Paradox (.PX), Btrieve, and Jet indexes vary in structure. (Btrieve and Jet don't store indexes in separate files, so no file classifications are given for these two databases.) Regardless of the indexing method, indexing techniques reduce the number of records that must be searched to find the first record matching the search criteria. The most efficient indexes are those that find the first matching record with the fewest number of tests (passes) of the value of the indexed field.

Records and Data Pages

Traditional desktop data managers store fixed-width records in individual files and store indexes on the fields of the file in one or more index files. FoxPro 2+ and dBASE IV enable you to store multiple indexes for a single table in a single .CDX and .MDX file, respectively. The table files used by these database managers have fixed-length records, so you can identify a record by its offset (its distance in bytes) from the beginning of the data in the file, immediately after the header portion of the file. Therefore, pointers to records in these files consist of offset values.

Jet and most client/server databases store indexes as special structures (not tables) within the database file. These database types support variable-length fields for Text (varchar), Memo (text, long varchar), OLE Object (long varbinary) and Binary field data types (varbinary and long varbinary). To prevent the tables from becoming full of holes when you delete records or extend the length of a variable-length field, Jet and SQL Server databases use pages, rather than records, to store data. Jet and SQL Server 6.5 and earlier pages are 2K long, corresponding to the standard size of a cluster on a fixed disk of moderate size formatted by Windows 95 or DOS. (As the size of fixed disk partitions grows, so does the size of the clusters. As an example, the cluster size of a 1G file using the DOS and Windows 95 standard FAT file system is 32K.) Therefore, if you increase the number of characters in a text field, the worst case condition is that the RDBMS must move 2K of data to make room for the data. If the page doesn't have enough empty space (called *slack*) to hold the lengthened data, the RDBMS creates a new page and moves the data in the record to the new page. Figure 5.12 illustrates the structure of the 2K data pages employed by Jet and SQL Server 6.*x* databases with about 1.7K of variable-length records and roughly 350 bytes of slack.

FIGURE 5.12

A page in a Jet or SQL Server database with variable-length records.

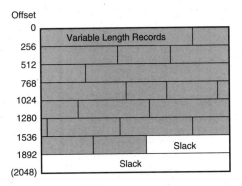

> **NOTE**
>
> The drawback to the page-locking methodology is that you lock an entire page when updating a record in the page. If the record you are updating is very small, the lock can affect a number of records that you are not editing. If you use the optimistic locking technique offered by Jet and SQL Server, the lock is likely to be transparent to other database users, especially if your front-end application is very fast. dBASE and Paradox tables use record locking, which affects only the single record being edited. SQL Server 6.5 introduced optional record locking for INSERT operations, and SQL Server 7.0 provides record locking for INSERT and UPDATE operations. SQL Server 7.0 uses larger 8KB pages for better performance. Jet continues to use 2KB page locking for all update operations.

Balanced B-Tree Indexes

The most common method of indexing tables is the balanced binary tree (B-tree) method originally proposed by Russian mathematicians G. M. Adleson-Velski and E. M. Landis in 1963. Prior to the B-tree method, editing, inserting, and deleting indexed fields of records caused the index trees to become lopsided, increasing the number of passes required to find the record or page with a matching value. The balanced B-tree method reorganizes the tree to ensure that each branch connects either to two other branches or to a leaf. Therefore, the B-tree index needs to be reorganized each time you add or delete a record. B-tree indexes speed decision-support queries at the expense of transaction-processing performance. In a B-tree index structure, the length of a search path to a leaf is never more than 145 percent of the optimum path.

Choosing Fields to Index

According to a truism in the database industry regarding the indexing of the fields of tables: Index only the fields you need to index to enhance the performance of your database front ends, and don't index any other fields. The more indexes you add to a table, the longer it takes to update entries that affect the value(s) of indexed field(s) and to add a new record, which requires updating all indexes. The problem here is knowing which fields improve application performance. The first step is to identify your options. The following list discusses how the database types, supported by the Jet database engine, handle the indexing of primary key fields:

- Jet tables, for which you specify primary key field(s) in a `TableDef` object, have no-duplicates indexes that are automatically created by the Jet database engine on these field(s). Most client/server databases that you connect with the ODBC API also have no-duplicates indexes on primary key field(s), although the indexes usually aren't created automatically. A no-duplicates index prevents the addition of a record with duplicate values in the primary key field(s). You cannot remove the primary key index or specify "duplicates OK" without deleting the primary key designation.

- Clustered indexes reorganize the pages of the database in the order of the clustered index. Microsoft and Sybase SQL Server offer clustered indexes, which need not be of the no-duplicates type.

- Paradox tables require no-duplicates indexes on the primary key field(s). If FILENAME.PX index file is not in the same directory as the corresponding FILENAME.DB file, your application can read the file but not update it. (If FILENAME.PX is missing, the Jet database engine creates a non-updatable `Recordset` object from the table data.)

- dBASE tables created by xBase applications do not support designating field(s) as primary key field(s), and you cannot create the equivalent of a no-duplicates index on dBASE tables. Even after you execute the xBase `SET UNIQUE ON` statement, xBase applications enable you to append as many records as you want with duplicate values in the indexed fields you use in lieu of primary key fields. (The index ignores records with duplicate indexed field values.) Your application needs to test for duplicate values and prevent the addition of records that would cause duplicated indexed field values. (You need the index so you can quickly find whether a duplicate value exists.) You can update data in dBASE table files with the Jet database engine because no primary key can be specified.

After you've determined whether you need to create a (primary) key field(s) index, you need to consider what other fields to index. The following list provides some suggestions that apply to all database types:

▶ **See** "Reducing Fact Table Storage Requirements," p. **1049**

- Use short codes to identify entities that don't have properties designed to identify the entity, such as part numbers for products. Creating indexes on long text fields, such as product names, unnecessarily increases the size of the index table, slows performance, and wastes disk space. Short codes are especially important when designing fact tables for online analaytical processing (OLAP) applications.

- Indexes based on numeric values usually have better performance than indexes on character fields. Using autoincrementing fields—Jet 3.*x*'s AutoIncrement (formerly Counter) field data type, for example—as a primary key field sometimes is feasible when you import existing data

- Index the foreign key field(s) that participate in joins with other tables.

- Index the foreign key fields that your client will search most often.

- Don't create a separate index for the indexed fields of the composite primary key. Almost all database management systems enable searches on partial key matches, so such an index would duplicate the existing primary key index.

- Avoid using the Like "*Criteria" statements in Jet SQL and LIKE '%Criteria' statements in ANSI SQL. Queries that contain these statements cannot use indexes.

- Don't try to create indexes on fields of the long data types—long varchar (Jet Memo fields) or long varbinary (Access OLE Object fields). Neither the Jet database engine nor the client/server RDBMSs can create indexes on these field data types.

If you follow the rules in the preceding list, you aren't likely to go too far wrong in choosing the fields of your tables to index. If you're using Jet tables and have a copy of Microsoft Access, comparing the performance of queries with and without foreign key indexes is a simple process. The Jet database engine and all client/server RDBMSs use query optimization techniques to choose the appropriate index(es) when your front-end application processes an SQL query.

> **NOTE**
>
> You need at least several hundred (preferably several thousand) records to test the effect of indexing foreign key fields on your application's performance. The more records, the better the test. If you or your client observe that the performance of your Visual Basic 6.0 front end deteriorates as the number of records in the database increases, you may have failed to add an index on an important foreign key. Use Access or SQL Server Enterprise Manager to add the new index. (SQL Server 7.0's Enterprise Manager has a Create Index Wizard to simplify the process.) The query optimizer in both the Jet database engine and SQL Server automatically uses the new index when the new index aids a query's performance.

WAREHOUSING AND ANALYZING OLTP DATA

Data warehouses and their smaller siblings, data marts, are hot topics in the trade press and on the database conference circuit. The rush to build corporate data warehouses and marts has caused periodic shortages of the large, high-speed Ultrawide SCSI disk drives needed to hold tens or hundreds of gigabytes (G), or multiple terabytes (T; 1,000G) of summary data gathered from companywide and external databases. The most common objective of a data warehouse or mart is to make data from disparate sources easily available to those who need it most: executives, managers, and analysts. The most common source data is from online transaction processing (OLTP) databases for order and invoice processing, manufacturing, and purchasing. One of the objectives of establishing data warehouses and marts is to prevent execution of decision-support queries from interfering with critical OLTP operations, such as entering new orders or sending invoices to customers.

Data warehouses and data marts differ in scope as follows:

- A *data warehouse* aggregates data from all sources within an enterprise and often from outside services, such as online market research organizations. Many data warehouses use specialized RDBMSs designed specifically for analyzing vast amounts of stored data; Red Brick Warehouse from Red Brick Systems, Inc.; Ann Arbor Software Corp.'s Essbase; and Praxis International, Inc.'s OmniWarehouse typify these specialized products. Conventional RDBMSs, such as Oracle, Informix, Sybase, Teradata, and DB2 also can be used. Most data warehouses run on large, highly scalable minicomputers running UNIX, often called UNIX boxes. Capacities range from 100GB to 10TB or more. Budgets to establish large, centralized data warehouses can exceed $10 million.

- A *data mart* stores a subset of an organization's data, often for a particular department (sales or manufacturing) or business function (inventory or production control). Data marts range in size from about 10GB to 100GB or so and usually involve implementation budgets in the $100,000 to $1 million range. Microsoft SQL Server is well suited to data mart applications because of SQL Server's ease of administration and excellent performance/cost ratio. Microsoft claims that "[h]alf of SQL Server users use data warehousing," but the customer examples cited by Microsoft in late 1996 range in size from about 7GB to 60GB. Multiple data marts can be combined into a hierarchical structure to create a distributed data warehouse.

Creating a data warehouse or mart involves the following basic steps:

1. Identifying the source data. Most large organizations have a variety of database types (hierarchical, network, and relational) running on mainframes, minicomputers, and microcomputer-based servers. These databases are likely to be geographically dispersed, requiring connection via a wide-area network (WAN).

2. Specifying the design of the target database(s). Data modeling tools create the metadata that defines the structure of the source and target (mart or warehouse) database(s), including specification of source and target tables, relationships, and fields. In most cases, a separate repository database stores the metadata, which defines the transformation between source and target databases.

3. Extracting, transforming, and cleansing the source data. The extraction and transformation process is similar to the traditional methods used for creating periodic database summary tables (called *rolling up the data*). Jet SQL's crosstab queries, created with PIVOT and TRANSFORM statements, and SQL Server's ROLLUP and CUBE operators, are useful for rollups. Data cleansing, which consists primarily of correcting data entry errors, is essential to assure data consistency. This entire process is repeated at fixed intervals, the frequency of which determines the currency of the target data. Weekly rollups, run on weekends or other periods of relatively low OLTP activity, are common. If the source data is stable, only incremental data need be added. Unfortunately, source data seldom is stable, at least in the short term, so a common practice is to reroll all data subject to retroactive changes, such as canceled orders or invoice adjustments.

4. Providing and supporting data analysis tools for users. One of the objectives of data warehouses and marts is to enable users to generate their own decision-support queries. Enabling users to design their own queries, rather than depend on information services (IS) personnel to write the necessary SQL statements, provides users with ad hoc and exploratory reporting capability. Several vendors offer graphical online analytical processing (OLAP) tools for multidimensional data analysis. *Data-mining* tools let users seek unforeseen relationships between data using sophisticated statistical methods.

Microsoft Decision Support Services (MSDSS) 1.0, an OLAP server code-named *Plato* when this book was written, is a system for providing multidimensional access to data in existing RDBMSs, including data warehouses and marts. MSDSS, the subject of Chapter 28,

"Analyzing Multidimensional Data with OLAP and MDX," is included with the Standard and Enterprise versions of SQL Server 7.0. Although MSDSS can work with any RDBMS that has an ODBC driver, it's especially well suited to OLE DB integration with SQL Server 7.0. MSDSS, which runs only on Microsoft NT Server 4+, comes with a set of tools to create hierarchical *data cubes*. *Drilling down* is a common term used to describe moving to a lower (more detailed) level in a hierarchy.

Data cubes are defined by a set of dimensions (axes), such as those in the following list:

- Geographical location. A typical geographical hierarchy is continent, country, region, and sales territory.

- Product category. A large consumer products manufacturer might have an extensive "product tree," with paper products, toiletries, and foodstuffs at the root, and tens of thousands of individual SKUs (stock-keeping units) as leaves.

- Time series. Most analyses use year, quarter, and month hierarchies, but many retail merchants need weekly or even daily sales breakdowns.

- Scenarios. The most common scenario headings are plan (budget), actual, variance, and percent variance.

Measures, also called *facts*, represent the numeric data in the cells at the intersection of the axes. Using the preceding dimensions, the most common measures are unit sales, dollar sales, percent of total sales, cost of sales, and gross margin.

The number of cells required to populate a data cube (called a *facts table*) easily attains astronomical proportions. For instance, if a firm has 100 sales territories, 10,000 products, 52 weeks of data, five measures, and four scenarios, the theoretical number of populated cells at the lowest level of the hierarchies is $100 * 10,000 * 52 * 5 * 4 = 1,040,000,000$. This number doesn't include aggregated values computed for every level higher in the hierarchy, easily another billion or two. A database holding every cell of such a facts table would be extremely large and almost impossibly cumbersome to manipulate. OLAP servers work with a *dynamic sparse matrix*, which minimizes the size of the facts table by generating a large percentage of the cell values on-the-fly.

OLAP tools come in a variety of flavors:

- Multidimensional OLAP (MOLAP) requires its own multidimensional database (called a *persistent store*) and query language, which is optimized for analytical operations. MOLAP tools are expensive to license, require data to be loaded from the data warehouse or mart, and have high administrative overhead.

- Relational OLAP (ROLAP) directly accesses data in the warehouse or mart using extensions to conventional ANSI SQL. ROLAP eliminates the need for a separate multidimensional database but must generate (abstract) each data cube needed by an analyst. Performance issues make ROLAP tools better suited for marts than for warehouses.

- Hybrid OLAP (HOLAP) combines MOLAP and ROLAP features to effect a compromise of storage size, administrative chores, and operational speed.

MSDSS accommodates all three of the preceding OLAP flavors and is closely integrated with SQL Server 7.0 as the back-end warehouse/mart database and Excel as the front end to display data cubes stored by MSDSS. Because of its inclusion with SQL Server 7.0, MSDSS is substantially less costly to license than current OLAP offerings from Arbor Software, Oracle, and Red Brick Systems, some of the major players in the OLAP market. Microsoft also announced in January 1998 that Excel 9.0 will include PivotTable services, a client-side cache that enables mobile users to use PivotTables to "slice and dice" data cubes while disconnected from the MSDSS server.

> **NOTE**
>
> MSDSS uses OLE DB for OLAP, which was in the final specification development stage when this book was written. OLE DB for OLAP defines *Dataset* objects, which may have any number of axes (dimensions). Datasets are specified by Multidimensional Expressions (MDX), which are derived from conventional SQL. The current OLE DB for OLAP specification is available at
> `http://www.microsoft.com/data/oledb/olap/`.

LEARNING STRUCTURED QUERY LANGUAGE

IN THIS CHAPTER

Structured Query Language, or SQL as it has come to be called, is the lingua franca of relational database management systems (RDBMSs). Visual Basic and Microsoft Access both use SQL exclusively to process queries against desktop, client/server, and even mainframe databases. Access includes a graphical query by example (QBE) tool—the Query Design window—to write Jet (Access) SQL statements for you. With Access you can develop fairly sophisticated applications without even looking at an SQL statement in Access's SQL window. Visual Studio 6.0 includes a set of Visual Data Tools (VDTs), which provide database diagramming and graphical SQL query-building capabilities for SQL Server 6.*x* and 7.0, and Oracle 7.3 and 8.0.3+ databases. These tools aren't as graphically sophisticated or as easy to use as their Access relatives, but they are quite useful for creating and modifying client/server database schema.

> **NOTE**
>
> Microsoft Access, without a version number, refers to Access 2.0 and Access for Windows 95 versions 7.0 (Access 95) and 8.0 (Access 97). There are no major differences between Jet SQL in these three versions of Access. Access 2.0 added a substantial number of reserved words to the SQL vocabulary of Access 1.*x*. The TOP *n* and TOP *n* PERCENT Jet SQL reserved words, introduced in Jet 3.0, are discussed in the "Comparing the Jet SQL Dialect with ANSI SQL-92" section, and subqueries are covered by the "Using Nested Queries and Subqueries" section of this chapter. SQL statements for adding tables to Jet databases, plus adding fields and indexes to Jet tables are two of the subjects of Chapter 7, "Running Crosstab and Action Queries." Microsoft calls the Access dialect of SQL *Microsoft Jet Database Engine SQL*; this book uses the term *Jet SQL*. You'll find significant differences between Jet SQL and Microsoft SQL Server's Transact-SQL. The differences are described in the appropriate sections of this chapter.

The first part of this chapter introduces the standardized version of SQL specified by the American National Standards Institute (ANSI), a standard known as X.3.135-1992 and called *SQL-92* in this book. (When you see SQL-89 or SQL-92, the reference is to ANSI SQL, not the Access variety.) ANSI SQL-92 has been accepted by the International Standards Organization (ISO), a branch of the United Nations headquartered in Geneva, and the International Electrotechnical Commission (IEC) as ISO/IEC 9075:1992, or *Database Language SQL*. A separate ANSI standard, X.3.168-1989, defines *Database Language Embedded SQL*. Thus SQL-92 is a thoroughly standardized language—much more so than xBase, for which no independent standards yet exist.

Today's client/server RDBMSs support SQL-89 and many of SQL-92's new SQL reserved words. Most RDBMSs also add their own reserved words to create proprietary SQL dialects, such as SQL Server's Transact-SQL. A knowledge of ANSI SQL is required to use SQL passthrough techniques with the Jet 3.5 database engine and to employ Visual Basic 6.0's new ActiveX Data Object (ADO), ODBCDirect, or the Remote Data Object (RDO) and Remote Data Control (RDC) of the Enterprise Edition. The RDO/RDC combination is replaced in Visual Basic 6.0 by ADO and the new DataGrid control.

The "Comparing the Jet SQL Dialect with ANSI SQL-92" section of this chapter discusses the differences between SQL-92 and Jet SQL. If you're fluent in the ANSI versions of SQL, either SQL-89 or SQL-92, you'll probably want to skip to this section, which deals with the specific flavor of SQL used by the Jet 3.5*x* database engine. Although this chapter describes the general SQL syntax for queries that modify data (called *action queries* by Access and in this book) and the crosstab queries of Jet SQL, examples of the use of these types of queries are described in Chapters 7 and 9, "Designing a Decision-Support Front End".

NOTE

The ANSI-ISO SQL committee has prepared a working draft of the next version of SQL, tentatively called *SQL3*. At a January 1996 meeting in Madrid, the committee officials estimated that the final standard for SQL3 won't arrive until 1999. SQL-89 and SQL-92 address only character-based information; SQL3 addresses the issue of storing and retrieving objects in relational databases. The 1996 working draft lists the following "significant new features" of SQL3:

- Support for active "rules," called *triggers*
- Support for abstract data types (objects)
- Support for multiple `null` states
- Support for `PENDANT` referential integrity
- A recursive `UNION` operation for query expressions
- Support for enumerated and Boolean data types
- Support for `SENSITIVE` cursors

Most RDBMSs, including SQL Server, currently support triggers. Triggers most commonly are used to enforce referential integrity and data consistency. Supporting abstract data types (object extensions) for object-relational databases is the feature delaying the normally three-year standard update cycle for SQL. RDBMS vendors are adding their own proprietary object extensions to SQL. Because of the delay in releasing the SQL3 specification, standards-based object extensions will probably not prevail. You can view the 600+ pages of the latest official ANSI-IEC SQL3 working draft at

`http://epoch.cs.berkeley.edu:8000/sequoia/schema/STANDARDS/SQL3/sql3part2.txt`.

REVIEWING THE FOUNDATIONS OF SQL

Dr. E. F. Codd's relational database model of 1970, discussed in Chapter 5, "Optimizing the Design of Relational Databases," was a theoretical description of how relational databases are designed, not how they are used. You need a database application language to create tables and specify the fields the tables contain, to establish relations between tables, and to manipulate the data in the database. The first language that Dr. Codd and his associates at the IBM San Jose laboratory defined was Structured English Query Language (SEQUEL), which was designed for use with a prototype relational database that IBM called System R. The second version of SEQUEL, called SEQUEL/2, was later renamed SQL. Technically, SQL is the name of an IBM data manipulation language, not an abbreviation for *structured query language*.

The sections that follow describe the differences between SQL and the procedural languages commonly used for computer programming, as well as how applications use SQL with desktop, client/server, and mainframe databases.

Elements of SQL Statements

This book has made extensive use of the term *query* without defining it. Because Visual Basic 6.0 uses SQL to process all queries, this book defines *query* as an expression in any dialect of SQL that defines an operation to be performed by a database management system. A query usually contains at least the following three elements:

- A *verb* (such as SELECT) that determines the type of operation
- A *predicate object* that specifies one or more field names of one or more table object(s), such as * to specify all of the fields of a table
- A *prepositional clause* that determines the object(s) in the database on which the verb acts (such as FROM *TableName*)

The simplest SQL query that you can construct is SELECT * FROM *TableName*, which returns the entire content of *TableName* as the query result set. Queries are classified in this book as *select queries*, which return data (query result sets), or *action queries*, which modify the data contained in a database without returning any data.

IBM's original version of SQL, implemented as SEQUEL, had relatively few reserved words and simple syntax. Over the years, publishers of database management software have added new reserved words to the language. Many of the reserved words in proprietary versions of SQL have found their way into the ANSI SQL standards. Vendors of SQL RDBMSs that claim adherence to the ANSI standards have the option of adding their own reserved words to the language, as long as the added reserved words don't conflict with the usage of the ANSI-specified reserved words. Transact-SQL, the language used by the Microsoft and Sybase versions of SQL Server, has many more reserved words than conventional ANSI SQL. Transact-SQL even

Learning Structured Query Language

CHAPTER 6

247

6

LEARNING
STRUCTURED
QUERY LANGUAGE

includes reserved words that enable conditional execution and loops within SQL statements. (The CASE, NULLIF, and COALESCE reserved words of SQL-92 are rather primitive for conditional execution purposes.) Jet SQL includes the TRANSFORM and PIVOT statements needed to create crosstab queries that, although missing from ANSI SQL, are a very useful construct. You can write ANSI SQL statements that create crosstab queries, but such statements have a very complex syntax.

A further discussion of the details of the syntax of SQL statements appears after the following sections, which describe the basic characteristics of the SQL language and how you combine SQL and conventional Visual Basic source code statements.

Differences Between SQL and Procedural Computer Languages

All dialects of SQL are fourth-generation languages (4GLs). The term *fourth-generation* derives from the following descriptions of the generations in the development of languages to control the operation of computers:

- *First-generation* languages (1GLs) required you to program in the binary language of the computer's hardware, called object or machine code. (In this case, the computer is the object.) As an example, in the early days of mini- and microcomputers, you started (booted) the computer by setting a series of switches that sent instructions directly to the computer's CPU. After you booted the computer, you could load binary-coded instructions with a paper tape reader. 1GLs represent programming the hard way. The first computer operating systems (OS) were written directly in machine code and loaded from paper tape or punched cards.

- *Second-generation* languages (2GLs) greatly improved the programming process by using assembly language to eliminate the necessity of setting individual bits of CPU instructions. Assembly language enables you to use simple alphabetic codes—called mnemonic codes because they are easier to remember than binary instructions—and octal or hexadecimal values to substitute for one or more CPU instructions in the more arcane object code. After you write an assembly language program, you compile the assembly code into object code instructions that the CPU can execute. Microsoft's MASM is a popular assembly language compiler for Intel 80x86 CPUs. Assembly language remains widely used today when speed or direct access to the computer hardware is needed.

- *Third-generation* languages (3GLs), typified by the early versions of FORTRAN (FORmula TRANslator) and BASIC (Beginners' All-Purpose Symbolic Instruction Code), allowed programmers to substitute simple statements, usually in a structured version of English, for assembly code. 3GLs are called *procedural languages* because the statements you write in a 3GL are procedures that the computer executes in the sequence you specify in your program's source code. Theoretically, procedural languages should be independent of the type of CPU for which you compile your source code. Few 3GL languages actually achieve the goal of being fully platform independent; most, like Microsoft Visual Basic and Visual C++, are designed for 80x86 CPUs. The Java language promises platform independence, but Java's database access using JDBC (Java Database Connector) currently is more primitive than Windows-based applications using Jet or ODBC.

- *Fourth-generation* languages are often called nonprocedural languages. The source code you write in 4GLs tells the computer the ultimate result you want, not how to achieve the result. SQL is generally considered to be a 4GL language because, for example, your SQL query statements specify the data you want the database manager (DBM) to send you, rather than instructions that tell the DBM how to accomplish this feat.

NOTE

Whether SQL is a true 4GL is subject to controversy because the SQL statements you write are actually executed by a 3GL or, in some cases, a 2GL language that deals directly with the data stored in the database file(s) and is responsible for sending your application the data in a format the application can understand.

Regardless of the controversy over whether or not generic SQL is a 4GL, you need to be aware of some other differences between SQL and conventional 3GLs. The most important of these differences are as follows:

- SQL is a *set-oriented* language, whereas most 3GLs can be called *array-oriented* languages. SQL returns sets of data in a logical tabular format. The query return sets are dependent on the data in the database, and you are not likely to be able to predict the number of rows (data set members) that a query will return. The number of members of the data set may vary each time you execute a query and may vary almost instantaneously in a multiuser environment. 3GLs can handle only a fixed number of tabular data elements at a time, specified by the dimensions that you assign to a two-dimensional array variable. Therefore, the application needs to know how many columns and rows are contained in the result set of an SQL query so the application can handle the data with row-by-row, column-by-column methods. The Recordset object of Visual Basic 6.0 handles this transformation for you automatically.

- SQL is a *weakly typed* language, whereas most 3GLs are *strongly typed*. You do not need to specify field data types in SQL statements; SQL queries return whatever data types have been assigned to the fields that constitute the columns of the query return set. Most compiled 3GL languages are strongly typed. COBOL, C, C++, Pascal, Modula-2, and

Learning Structured Query Language

CHAPTER 6

249

6

LEARNING
STRUCTURED
QUERY LANGUAGE

ADA are examples of strongly typed, compiled programming languages. Strongly typed languages require that you declare the names and data types of all your variables before you assign values to the variables. If the data type of a query column does not correspond to the data type you defined for the receiving variable, an error (sometimes called an impedance mismatch error) occurs. Visual Basic began as an interpreted language and traditionally has been weakly typed. Version 6.0 of VBA used by Visual Basic 6.0 is strongly typed, which may require developers to rewrite parts of their existing code. To overcome the necessity of knowing the data type of the table fields in advance of a query, Visual Basic provides the **Variant** data type, which accepts any variable type commonly found in the tables of databases.

Consider yourself fortunate that you're using Visual Basic 6.0 to process SQL statements. In most cases, you don't need to worry about how many rows a query will return or what data types occur in the query result set's columns. The Recordset object receiving the data handles these details for you. You don't need to recompile and link your Visual Basic application each time you change a query statement; just change the statement and run your application again. Visual Basic automatically "compiles" the changes to pseudo-code for you.

Types of ANSI SQL

The current ANSI SQL standards recognize four methods of executing SQL statements. The methods you use depend on your application programming environment, as described in the following list:

- Interactive SQL enables you to enter SQL statements at a command line prompt, similar to dBASE's dot prompt. As mentioned in Chapter 1, "Staking Visual Basic's Claim to Enterprise Development," the use of the interactive dBASE command LIST is quite similar to interactive SQL's SELECT statement. Mainframe and client/server RDBMSs also provide interactive SQL capability; Microsoft SQL Server provides the isql and Isql_w applications for this purpose. Using interactive SQL is also called *direct invocation*. Interactive SQL is called a *bulk process;* if you enter a query at the SQL prompt, the result of your query appears on your computer's display. RDBMSs offer a variety of methods of providing a scrollable display of interactive query result sets.

- Embedded SQL enables you to execute SQL statements by preceding the SQL statement with a keyword, such as EXEC SQL in C. Typically, you declare variables that you intend to use to receive data from an SQL query between EXEC SQL BEGIN DECLARE SECTION and EXEC SQL END DECLARE SECTION statements. You need a precompiler that is specific to the RDBMS being used and the programming language. The advantage to embedded SQL is that you assign attribute classes to a single variable in a one-step process; the disadvantage is that you have to deal with query return sets on a row-by-row basis, rather than the bulk process of interactive SQL.

- Module SQL enables you to compile SQL statements separately from your 3GL source code and then link the compiled object modules into your executable program. SQL modules are similar to Visual Basic 6.0 code modules: The modules include declarations of variables and temporary tables to contain query result sets, and you can pass argument values from your 3GL to parameters of procedures declared in SQL modules. The stored procedures that execute precompiled queries on database servers share many characteristics with module SQL.

- Dynamic SQL enables you to create SQL statements whose content you cannot predict when you write the statement. (The preceding SQL types are classified as *static SQL*.) As an example of dynamic SQL, you may want to design a Visual Basic application that can process queries against a variety of databases. Dynamic SQL enables you to send queries to the database in the form of strings. You can, for example, send a query to the database and obtain detailed information from the database catalog that describes the tables and fields of tables in the database. Once you know the structure of the database, you or the user of your application can construct a custom query that adds the correct field names to the query. Visual Basic's implementation of Jet SQL resembles a combination of dynamic and static SQL, although the Jet database engine handles the details of reading the catalog information for you automatically when your application creates a `Recordset` object from the database.

Technically, static SQL and dynamic SQL are methods of binding SQL statements to database application programs. *Binding* refers to how you combine or attach SQL statements to your source or object code, how you pass values to SQL statements, and how you process query result sets. A third method of binding SQL statements is the call-level interface (CLI). The Microsoft Open Database Connectivity (ODBC) API uses the CLI developed by the SQL Access Group (SAG), a consortium of RDBMS publishers and users. A CLI accepts SQL statements from your application in the form of strings and then passes the statements directly to the server for execution. The server notifies the CLI when the data is available and then returns the data to your application. Details of the ODBC CLI are given in Chapter 18, "Working with Client/Server Databases."

If you are a COBOL coder or a C/C++ programmer who is accustomed to writing embedded SQL statements, you'll need to adjust to Visual Basic's automatic creation of virtual tables when you execute a `SELECT` query, rather than executing `CURSOR`-related `FETCH` statements to obtain the query result rows one by one.

WRITING ANSI SQL STATEMENTS

ANSI SQL statements have a very flexible format. Unlike all dialects of BASIC, which separate statements with newline pairs (carriage return and line feed), and Java, C, C++, and Pascal, which use semicolons as statement terminators, SQL does not require you to separate the

Learning Structured Query Language

CHAPTER 6

251

6

LEARNING
STRUCTURED
QUERY LANGUAGE

elements that constitute a complete SQL statement with newline pairs, semicolons, or even a space in most cases. (SQL ignores most white space, which comprises newline pairs, tabs, and extra spaces.) Therefore, you can use white space to format your SQL statements to make them more readable. The examples of SQL statements in this book place groups of related identifiers and SQL reserved words on separate lines and use indentation to identify continued lines. Here's an example of a Jet SQL crosstab query statement that uses this formatting convention:

```
TRANSFORM Sum(CLng([Order Details].UnitPrice*Quantity*
    (1 - Discount)*100)/100) AS ProductAmount
  SELECT Products.ProductName, Orders.CustomerID
  FROM Orders, Products, [Order Details],
    Orders INNER JOIN [Order Details] ON Orders.OrderID =
      [Order Details].OrderID,
    Products INNER JOIN [Order Details] ON Products.ProductID =
      [Order Details].ProductID
  WHERE Year(OrderDate)=1995
  GROUP BY Products.ProductName, Orders.CustomerID
  ORDER BY Products.ProductName
  PIVOT "Qtr " & DatePart("q",OrderDate) In("Qtr 1",
    "Qtr 2","Qtr 3","Qtr 4")
```

> **NOTE**
>
> The square brackets surrounding the [Order Details] table name are specific to Jet SQL and group table or field names (literals) that contain spaces or other punctuation that is illegal in the naming rules for tables and fields of SQL RDBMSs. SQL Server 7.0's Transact-SQL also accepts square brackets or double quotes to specify literals. Jet SQL commonly uses a double quotation mark (") to replace the single quote mark or apostrophe ('), which acts as the string-identifier character in most implementations of SQL. (A single quote works just as well in Jet SQL.) The preceding example of the SQL statement for a crosstab query is based on the tables in the Jet 3.0 Nwind.mdb sample database included with Visual Basic 6.0.

The sections that follow describe the formal grammar of SQL and explain how you categorize SQL statements. Also, they provide examples of writing a variety of select queries in ANSI SQL.

Categories of SQL Statements

ANSI SQL is divided into the following six basic categories of statements, presented here in the order of most frequent use:

- *Data query language* (DQL) statements, also called *data retrieval statements*, obtain data from tables and determine how the data is presented to your application. The SELECT reserved word is the most commonly used verb in DQL (and in all of SQL). Other commonly used DQL reserved words are WHERE, ORDER BY, GROUP BY, and HAVING; these DQL reserved words often are used in conjunction with other categories of SQL statements.

- *Data manipulation language* (DML) statements include the INSERT, UPDATE, and DELETE verbs, which append, modify, and delete rows in tables, respectively. You use DML verbs to construct action queries. Some texts combine DQL statements into the DML category.

- *Transaction processing language* (TPL) statements enable you to make sure that all the rows of tables affected by a DML statement are updated at once. TPL statements include BEGIN TRANSACTION, COMMIT, and ROLLBACK.

- *Data control language* (DCL) statements determine access of individual users and groups of users to objects in the database through permissions that you GRANT or REVOKE. Some RDBMSs enable you to GRANT or REVOKE permissions to individual columns of tables.

- *Data definition language* (DDL) statements enable you to create new tables in a database (CREATE TABLE); add indexes to tables (CREATE INDEX); establish constraints on field values (NOT NULL, CHECK, and CONSTRAINT); define relations between tables (PRIMARY KEY, FOREIGN KEY, and REFERENCES); and delete tables and indexes (DROP TABLE and DROP INDEX). DDL also includes many reserved words that relate to obtaining data from the database catalog. This book classifies DDL queries as action queries because DDL queries do not return records.

- *Cursor control language* (CCL) statements, such as DECLARE CURSOR, FETCH INTO, and UPDATE WHERE CURRENT, operate on individual rows of one or more tables.

A publisher of a DBM who claims to conform to ANSI SQL isn't obligated to support all the reserved words in the SQL-92 standard. In fact, it is probably safe to state that there is no commercial RDBMS (at this book's writing) that implements all the SQL-92 keywords for interactive SQL. The Jet 3.5 database engine, for example, does not support any DCL reserved words. You use the Data Access Object's programmatic security objects with Visual Basic reserved words and keywords instead. The Jet 3.5 engine does not need to support CCL statements, because Jet doesn't manipulate cursors with SQL statements. ADO, ODBCDirect, and RDO support Microsoft SQL Server 6+'s scrollable cursors.

NOTE

A *cursor* is a pointer to a particular row of a query result set, equivalent to the record pointer of an ADODB.Recordset object. Early versions of client/server RDBMSs didn't offer cursors; front-end applications had to manipulate the query result set with low-level code. The first client/server RDBMS cursors were forward-only and not updatable; bidirectional (scrollable), updatable cursors are a relatively recent development. Forward-only cursors, which Microsoft calls *firehose cursors*, offer better performance than scrollable (static, keyset, or dynamic) server-side cursors.

Learning Structured Query Language

CHAPTER 6

253

6

LEARNING
STRUCTURED
QUERY LANGUAGE

This book uses the terminology defined by Appendix C of the *Programmer's Reference for the Microsoft ODBC Software Development Kit* (SDK) to define the following levels of SQL grammatical compliance:

- Minimum—The statements (grammar) that barely qualify a DBM as an SQL DBM, but not an RDBMS. A DBM that provides only the minimum grammar is not salable in today's market.

- Core—Comprising minimum grammar plus basic DDL and DCL commands, additional DML functions, data types other than CHAR, SQL aggregate functions, such as SUM( ) and AVG( ), and a wider variety of allowable expressions to select records. Most desktop DBMs, to which SQL has been added, support core SQL grammar and little more.

- Extended—Comprising minimum and core grammar plus DML outer joins, more complex expressions in DML statements, all ANSI SQL data types (as well as long varchar and long varbinary), batch SQL statements, and procedure calls. There are two levels of conformance (1 and 2) of the extended SQL grammar. Conformance of ODBC drivers to extended grammar levels is discussed in Chapter 18.

NOTE

SQL-92 includes a leveling specification that defines Entry SQL, Intermediate SQL, and Full SQL. SQL Server 7.0's Transact-SQL complies with Entry SQL requirements and incorporates a few Intermediate SQL and Full SQL features. The SQL-92 conformance levels don't correspond to the ODBC conformance levels. Jet supports cascading deletions and updates on related tables to automatically preserve referential integrity, but doesn't use Intermediate SQL's ON CASCADE DELETE or Full SQL's ON CASCADE UPDATE predicates for this purpose. Transact-SQL doesn't support the CASCADE keyword, so you must write Transact-SQL triggers to perform cascading operations. SQL Server 7.0 supports multiple triggers on a single event (INSERT, UPDATE, or DELETE) and optional recursive triggers, which can call themselves either directly or through other triggers.

The Formal Grammar of SQL

The formal grammar of SQL is represented in the Backus Naur form (BNF), which is used to specify the formal grammar of many computer programming languages. Here is the full BNF of the verb that specifies the operation a query is to perform on a database:

```
<action> ::=
SELECT
¦DELETE
¦INSERT [ <left paren> <privilege column list> <right paren>]
```

```
¦UPDATE [ <left paren> <privilege column list> <right paren>]
¦REFERENCES [ <left paren> <privilege column list> <right paren>]
¦USAGE
...
<privilege column list> ::= <column name list>
...
<column name list> ::= <column name> [{<comma>, <column name>} ...]
```

To use BNF representation, you locate the class (<action> in the preceding example) where the reserved word is included. Members of the class are separated with the vertical bar (¦) character. Optional parameters of reserved words and elements are enclosed with square brackets ([ ]). Literal values, such as <privilege column list>, are enclosed within angle braces (<>), and elements that must be grouped, such as a comma preceding a second <column name>, are enclosed within French (curly) braces ({ }). You then search the list of elements to find the allowable composition of an element. In the previous example, the <privilege column list> is composed of the <column name list>. Then check to see whether <column name list> has a composition (in this case, one or more <column name> elements). This process is tedious, especially when the elements are not arranged in alphabetical order.

Microsoft uses a simplified form of BNF to describe the grammar supported by the present version of the ODBC API. The Jet SQL syntax rules eliminate the use of the ::= characters to indicate the allowable substitution of values for an element and instead substitute a tabular format, as illustrated in Table 6.1. Ellipses (...) in the table indicate that you have to search for the element; the element is not contiguous with the preceding element of the table.

TABLE 6.1   THE PARTIAL SYNTAX OF THE JET SQL SELECT STATEMENT

Element	*Syntax*
select-statement	SELECT[ALL¦DISTINCT¦DISTINCTROW] select-list table-expression
	...
select-list	*¦select-sublist[{, select-sublist}...]
select-sublist	table-name.*¦expression [AS column-alias]¦column-name
	...
table-expression	from-clause¦[where-clause]¦[group-by-clause]¦[having-clause]¦[order-by-clause]
	...
from-clause	FROM table-reference-list
table-reference-list	table-reference [{, table-reference}...]
table-reference	table-name [AS correlation-name¦joined-table]

Element	Syntax
	...
table-name	base-table-name¦querydef-name¦attached-table-name¦correlation-name

▶ **See** "Abandoning Jet *QueryDef* Objects," p. **339**

> **NOTE**
>
> The DISTINCTROW qualifier and the querydef-name element are specific to Jet SQL. DISTINCTROW is discussed in the section "Theta Joins and the DISTINCTROW Keyword" of this chapter, and Chapter 3, "Migrating from DAO to ADO," discusses the Jet QueryDef object. ADO provides very limited support for QueryDef objects.

After you've looked up all the allowable forms of the elements in the table, you may have forgotten the keyword whose syntax you set out to determine. The modified BNF form used by Microsoft is unquestionably easier to use than full BNF, which is used in the ANSI-ISO SQL standards.

The Practical Grammar of a Simple SQL SELECT Statement

Here's a more practical representation of the syntax of a typical ANSI SQL statement, which substitutes underscores for hyphens:

```
SELECT [ALL¦DISTINCT] select_list
  FROM table_names
   [WHERE {search_criteria¦join_criteria}
     [{AND¦OR search_criteria}]
  [ORDER BY {field_list} [ASC¦DESC]]
```

The following list explains the use of each SQL reserved word in the preceding statement:

- SELECT specifies that the query is to return data from the database rather than modify the data in the database. The *select_list* element contains the name of the field(s) of the table that are to appear in the query. Multiple fields appear in a comma-separated list. The asterisk (*) specifies that data from all fields of a table is returned. If more than one table is involved (joined) in the query, you use the *table_name.field_name* syntax, where the period (.) separates the name of the table from the name of the field.

- The ALL qualifier specifies that you want the query to return all rows, regardless of duplicate values; DISTINCT returns only nonduplicate rows but takes longer to execute.

- FROM begins a clause that specifies the name of the table(s) that contain the fields that you include in your *select_list*. If more than one table is involved in *select_list*, *table_list* consists of comma-separated table names.

- WHERE begins a clause that serves two purposes in ANSI SQL: specifying the fields on which tables are joined and limiting the records returned to those records with field values that meet a particular criterion or set of criteria. The WHERE clause must include an operator and two operands, the first of which must be a field name. (The field name need not appear in the *select_list*, but the *table_name* that includes *field_name* must be included in the *table_names* list.)

- SQL operators include LIKE, IS {NULL¦NOT NULL}, and IN, as well as the arithmetic operators <, <=, =, =>, >, and <>. If you use the arithmetic equal operator (=) and specify *table_name.field_name* values for both operands, you create an equi-join (also called an INNER JOIN) between the two tables on the specified fields. You can create left and right joins by using the special operators *= and =*, respectively, if your DBM supports outer joins. (Both left and right joins are called OUTER JOINs.) Types of joins are discussed in the "Joining Tables" section later in the chapter.

NOTE

If you use more than one table in your query, make sure to create a join between the tables with a WHERE Table1.*field_name* = Table2.*field_name* clause. If you omit the statement that creates the join, your query will return the Cartesian product of the two tables. A *Cartesian product* is all the combinations of fields and rows in the two tables. It results in an extremely large query return set and, if the tables have a large number of records, can cause your computer to run out of memory. (The term *Cartesian* is derived from the name of a famous French mathematician, René Déscartes.) A Cartesian product is the ultimate "query from hell."

- ORDER BY defines a clause that determines the sort order of the records returned by the SELECT statement. You specify the field(s) on which you want to sort the query result set by the *table_names* list. You can specify a descending sort with the DESC qualifier; ascending (ASC) is the default. As in other lists, if you have more than one *table_name*, you use a comma-separated list. You use the *table_name.field_name* specifier if you have joined tables.

Depending on the dialect of SQL your database uses and the method of transmitting the SQL statement to the DBM, you may need to terminate the SQL statement with a semicolon. (Jet

Learning Structured Query Language

CHAPTER 6

257

6

LEARNING
STRUCTURED
QUERY LANGUAGE

SQL no longer requires the semicolon; statements you send directly to the server through the ODBC driver do not use terminating semicolons.)

Using the Visual Data Sample Application to Explore Queries

In Visual Basic 6.0, the Visual Data Manager add-in and VisData sample application (...\MSDN98\98VS\1033\Samples\VB98\Visdata\Visdata.vbp) are improved versions of the Visual Data Manager application that originated with Visual Basic 2.0. VisData falls into the category of ad hoc query generators. You can use VisData to test some simple SQL statements by following these steps:

1. Choose <u>A</u>dd-Ins, <u>V</u>isual Data Manager to launch VisData.

2. In VisData, choose <u>F</u>ile, Open <u>D</u>ataBase; then choose Microsoft Access to display the Open Microsoft Access Databases dialog.

3. Choose Biblio.mdb from your ...*VB98* folder and click the Open button. Biblio.mdb is a Jet 3.0 database. If a message box asks whether you want to use a System.md? file, click No. The properties, TableDef, and QueryDef objects of Biblio.mdb appear in the TreeView control of the Database window.

4. If the SQL Statement window doesn't appear, choose <u>W</u>indow, <u>S</u>QL; then choose <u>W</u>indow, <u>T</u>ile to display both MDI child windows.

5. Click the Use DBGrid Control on New Form button to display the query result set in a bound grid control and click the Dynaset-type Recordset button.

6. Type **SELECT * FROM Authors** in the SQL Statement window as a simple query to check whether VisData works (see Figure 6.1.)

FIGURE 6.1

The Visual Data Manager add-in with an SQL test query.

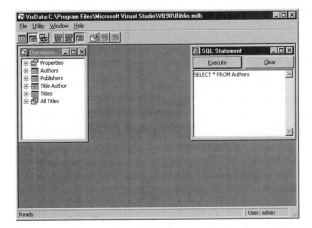

7. Click the Execute button of the SQL Statement window and click No when the Is This a SQL PassThrough Query? message appears. The query result set appears in the grid control of the SELECT * FROM Authors window. Figure 6.2 displays part of the query result set.

FIGURE 6.2

The Query Result window of the VisData add-in using the DBGrid control option.

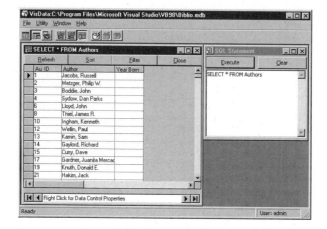

8. Close the Query Result Set window and click the Clear button of the SQL Statement window. Type **SELECT * FROM Publishers WHERE State = 'NY'** in the SQL Statement window; then click the Execute button. (Single and double quotes are interchangeable in Jet SQL.) Click No when the Is This a SQL PassThrough Query? message appears. The SELECT * FROM Publishers WHERE State = 'NY' window appears, as shown in Figure 6.3. By default, Jet sorts the Recordset by the primary key (PubID) value.

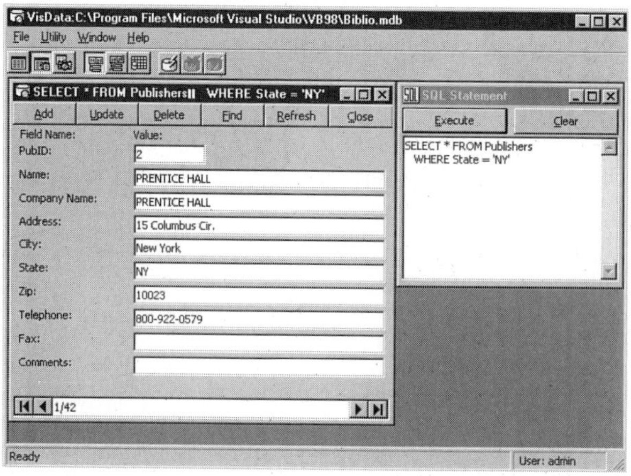

FIGURE 6.3

A query that returns records for publishers located in New York.

Learning Structured Query Language

CHAPTER 6

259

6

LEARNING
STRUCTURED
QUERY LANGUAGE

9. Close the SELECT * FROM Publishers WHERE State = 'NY' window again and add **ORDER BY Zip** to the end of your SQL statement. Execute the query, and the result appears as shown in Figure 6.4.

FIGURE 6.4

The records for publishers in New York sorted by Zip code.

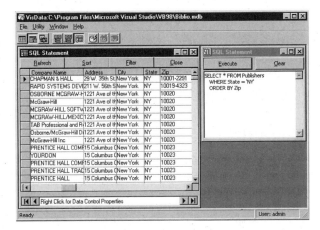

10. Replace the * in the SELECT statement that returns all fields with **PubID, [Company Name], City** so that only three of the fields appear in the DBGrid window. The result, shown in Figure 6.5, demonstrates that you do not have to include the fields you use for the WHERE and ORDER BY clauses in the *field_names* list of your SELECT statement.

NOTE

The square brackets ([ ]) surrounding Company Name are necessary when a field name or a table name contains a space. Only Jet databases permit spaces and punctuation other than the underscore (_) in field names. Using spaces in field and table names, or to name any other database object, is not considered a good database-programming practice. Spaces in database field and table names appear in this book only when such names are included in sample databases created by others.

FIGURE 6.5

The query return set displaying only three fields of the Publishers table.

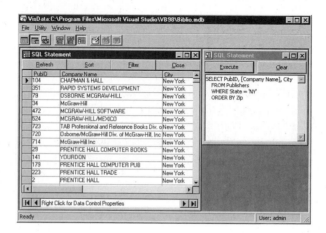

> **NOTE**
>
> The DBGrid window of VisData contains buttons that enable you to filter the records so that only selected records appear and to sort the records on selected fields. A filter is the equivalent of adding a WHERE `field_name where_expression` clause to your SQL statement. The sort button adds an ORDER BY `field_names` clause. You also can sort in field order by clicking the field name header of the DBGrid control.

Microsoft designed the VisData sample application to demonstrate the features of Visual Basic 6.0 that pertain to manipulating and displaying data contained in the tables of databases. VisData is a rich source of Visual Basic code examples. VisData includes a class module, `VisDataClass`, that enables you to use VisData as a Visual Basic 6.0 add-in or run VisData as an OLE Automation server. VisData also contains useful examples of code to create and control the appearance of MDI child forms.

SQL Operators and Expressions

As mentioned previously in this chapter, SQL provides the basic arithmetic operators: <, <=, =, =>, > and <>. SQL adds a set of operators that are used in conjunction with values of fields of the text data type (LIKE and IN) and to deal with NULL values in fields (IS NULL and IS NOT NULL). The Jet 3.5 database engine also supports the use of many of the native string and numeric functions of VBA in SQL statements to calculate column values of query return sets. (Few of these VBA functions are included in ANSI SQL.)

> **NOTE**
>
> Access supports the use of user-defined functions (UDFs) in SQL statements to calculate column values in queries. Visual Basic only supports native VBA functions that are reserved words, such as **Val()**. Functions other than SQL aggregate functions are called implementation specific in ANSI SQL. *Implementation specific* means that the supplier of the RDBMS is free to add functions to the supplier's implementation of ANSI SQL, unless the names of such functions conflict with SQL-92 reserved words.

Most operators in SQL statements are dyadic. Dyadic functions require two operands. (All arithmetic functions and BETWEEN are dyadic.) Operators such as LIKE, IN, IS NULL, and IS NOT NULL are monadic. Monadic operators require only one operand. All expressions that you create with comparison operators return **True** or **False**, not a value. The sections that follow describe the use of the common dyadic and monadic operators of ANSI SQL.

Dyadic Arithmetic Operators and Functions

The use of arithmetic operators with SQL does not differ greatly from their use in Visual Basic or other computer languages. The following is a list of the points you need to remember about arithmetic operators and functions used in SQL statements (especially in WHERE clauses):

- The = and <> comparison operators are used for both text and numeric field data types. The angle bracket pair "not equal" symbol (<>) is equivalent to the != combination used to represent not equal in ANSI SQL. (SQL does not use the equal sign as an assignment operator.)

- The arithmetic comparison operators <, <=, =>, and > are primarily intended for use with operands having numeric field data types. If you use the preceding comparison operators with values of the text field data type, the numeric ANSI values of each character of the two fields are compared in left-to-right sequence.

> **NOTE**
>
> To compare the values of text fields that represent numbers, such as the Zip field of the Publishers table of Biblio.mdb, you enclose the numeric value in single or double quotes. An example of this usage is SELECT * FROM Publishers WHERE Zip > '12000'.

- The remaining arithmetic operators—+, -, *, /, and ^ or ** (exponentiation operator, implementation-specific)—are not comparison operators. These operators apply only to calculated columns of query result sets, the subject of the next section.

- Avoid the use of any Visual Basic native function to define a calculated column when you use the SQL Passthrough method, ADO, ODBCDirect, or RDO to process queries directly on the RDBMS server. Few client/server databases presently support the Val() function or its SQL-92 counterpart, the CAST predicate.

- The BETWEEN predicate in ANSI SQL and the Between operator in Jet SQL are used with numeric or date-time field data types. The syntax is *field_name* BETWEEN *Value1* AND *Value2*. This syntax is equivalent to the expression *field_name* => *Value1* OR *field_name* <= *Value2*. Jet SQL requires you to surround date-time values with number signs (#) as in DateField Between #1-1-97# And #12-31-97#. Dates in most SQL RDBMSs are treated as strings. NOT BETWEEN negates the BETWEEN predicate.

> **NOTE**
>
> Where Jet SQL uses syntax that is not specified by ANSI SQL, such as the use of number signs (#) to indicate date-time field data types, or where examples of complete statements are given in Jet SQL, the SQL reserved words that are also VBA keywords or reserved words appear in the uppercase and lowercase conventions of VBA.

Calculated Query Columns

You can create calculated columns in query return sets by defining fields that use SQL arithmetic operators. You also can use functions that are supported by the Jet 3.0 database engine or your client/server RDBMS. Ordinarily, calculated columns are derived from fields of numeric field data types. Biblio.mdb uses a numeric data type (the autoincrementing long integer Counter field) for ID fields; therefore, you can use the PubID field or Val(Zip) expression as the basis for the calculated field. Type **SELECT PubID, Name, Zip, (3 * Val(Zip)) AS Zip_Times_3 FROM Publishers** in the SQL Statement window of VisData. The query result set appears in Figure 6.6.

FIGURE 6.6

A calculated column added to the query against the Publishers table.

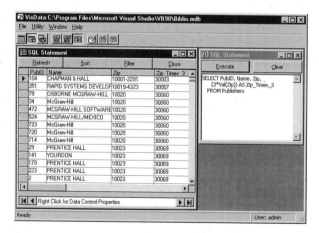

The AS qualifier designates an alias for the column name, *column_alias*. With Jet 3.0, the AS qualifier is optional; you can substitute a space for the AS qualifier, as in SELECT PubID, Name, Zip, 3*Val(Zip) Zip_Times_3 FROM Publishers. If you don't supply the [AS] *column_alias* qualifier, the column name is Expr1003 when you use the Jet database engine. Jet 1.*x* provided a default AS Expr1 column alias for calculated columns; the *column_alias* that appears when you use ODBC to connect to databases is implementation specific. IBM's DB2, for example, doesn't support aliasing of column names with the AS qualifier. ODBC drivers for DB2 and DB2/2 may assign the field name from which the calculated column value is derived or apply an arbitrary name, such as Col_1.

NOTE

If you must include spaces in the *column_alias*, make sure that you enclose the *column_alias* within square brackets for the Jet database engine and in single quote marks for RDBMSs that support spaces in *column_alias* fields. Although you may see column names such as Col 1 when you execute queries against DB2 or other mainframe databases in an emulated 3270 terminal session, these *column_alias* values are generated by the local query tool running on your PC, not by DB2.

Monadic Text Operators, NULL Value Predicates, and Functions

One of the most useful operators for the WHERE criterion of fields of the text field data type is ANSI SQL's LIKE predicate, called the Like operator in Jet SQL. (The terms *predicate* and *operator* are used interchangeably in this context.) The LIKE predicate enables you to search for one or more characters you specify at any location in the text. Table 6.2 shows the syntax of the ANSI SQL LIKE predicate and the Jet SQL Like operator used in the WHERE clause of an SQL statement.

TABLE 6.2 FORMS OF THE ANSI SQL Like AND JET SQL Like PREDICATES

Purpose	*ANSI SQL*	*Jet SQL*	*Returns*
Match any text that contains the characters	LIKE '%am%'	Like "*am*"	ram, rams, damsel, amnesty
Match any text beginning with the characters	LIKE 'John%'	Like "John*"	Johnson, Johnsson

continues

TABLE 6.2 CONTINUED

Purpose	ANSI SQL	Jet SQL	Returns
Match any text ending with the characters	LIKE '%son'	Like "*son"	Johnson, Anderson
Match the text and any single trailing character	LIKE 'Glen_'	Like "Glen?"	Glenn, Glens
Match the text and any single preceding character	LIKE '_am'	Like "?am"	dam, Pam, ram
Match the text with one preceding character and any trailing characters	LIKE '_am%'	Like "_am*"	dams, Pam, Ramses

The IS NULL and IS NOT NULL predicates test whether a value has been entered in a field. IS NULL returns False and IS NOT NULL returns **True** if a value, including an empty string "" or 0, is present in the field. The VBA **IsNull**(*field_name*) function and the SQL *field_name* IS NULL expressions are equivalent.

NOTE

For consistency with ANSI SQL-92, the native OLE DB data provider (Microsoft.JET.OLEDB.3.51, commonly called by its code name, *Jolt*) uses the % and _ wildcards, not Jet's ? and *. This inconsistency requires you to alter existing DAO code to accommodate ADO's use of the SQL wildcards.

You determine the case sensitivity (whether uppercase characters match lowercase characters) of Visual Basic database applications that use the Jet 3+ database engine with the Option Compare Binary (case sensitive) or Option Compare Text (not case sensitive) keywords. The case sensitivity of the LIKE predicate for client/server RDBMSs to which you send queries with the SQL passthrough option is installation specific. The DBA sets the case sensitivity of searches upon installing the RDBMS or creating a new database. You can use the SQL-92 UPPER() and LOWER() functions with SQL passthrough queries or the equivalent VBA functions, **UCase**() and **LCase**(), to remove case sensitivity from matches. (Jet 3.0 does not support ANSI SQL UPPER() and LOWER() functions.)

Learning Structured Query Language

CHAPTER 6

265

6

LEARNING
STRUCTURED
QUERY LANGUAGE

The SQL-92 `POSITION()` function returns the position of characters in a test field using the syntax `POSITION(`*`characters`* `IN` *`field_name`*`)`. The equivalent Jet SQL function is `InStr(`*`field_name, characters`*`)`, which is also a VBA function. If *characters* are not found in *field_name*, both functions return 0.

The SQL-92 `SUBSTRING()` function returns a set of characters with `SUBSTRING(`*`field_name`* `FROM` *`start_postion`* `FOR` *`number_of_characters`*`)`. The Jet SQL equivalent is VBA's `Mid(`*`field_name, start_position`*`[,` *`number_of_characters`*`])`. Both functions are quite useful for selecting and parsing text fields.

SQL Server's Transact-SQL provides the `IF...ELSE` and `SELECT...CASE...WHEN...THEN` structures for conditional execution. Jet SQL's VBA inline-if function, `IIf(`*`LogicalExpression, ReturnValueIfTrue, ReturnValueIfFalse`*`)` is a less versatile substitute for `IF...ELSE`.

Joining Tables

As mentioned earlier in this chapter, you can join two tables by using *`table_name.field_name`* operands with a comparison operator in the `WHERE` clause of an SQL statement. Additional tables can be joined by combining two sets of join statements with the `AND` operator. SQL-86 and SQL-89 supported only `WHERE` joins. You can create equi-joins, natural equi-joins, left and right equi-joins, not-equal joins, and self-joins with the `WHERE` clause. Joins that are created with the equal (=) operator use *equi-* as the prefix.

SQL-92 added the `JOIN` reserved words plus the `CROSS`, `NATURAL`, `INNER`, `OUTER`, `FULL`, `LEFT`, and `RIGHT` qualifiers to describe a variety of `JOIN`s. At the time this book was written, few RDBMSs supported the `JOIN` statement. (Microsoft SQL Server, for example, did not include the `JOIN` statement in versions of Transact-SQL earlier than 6.5.) Jet SQL supports `INNER`, `LEFT`, and `RIGHT` `JOIN`s with SQL-92 syntax using the `ON` predicate. Jet SQL supports neither the `USING` clause nor the `CROSS`, `NATURAL`, or `FULL` qualifiers for `JOIN`s.

A `CROSS JOIN` returns the Cartesian product of two tables. The term `CROSS` is derived from *cross-product*, a synonym for *Cartesian product*. You can emulate a `CROSS JOIN` by leaving out the join components of the `WHERE` clause of a `SELECT` statement that includes a table name from more than one table. Figure 6.7 shows VisData's DBGrid window displaying the first 10 rows of the 4,540,842-row Cartesian product created by entering `SELECT Publishers.Name, Authors.Author FROM Publishers, Authors` in the SQL Statement window. There are 727 Publishers records and 6,246 Authors records, thus the query returns 4,540,842 rows (727 * 6,246 = 4,540,842). It is highly unlikely that you would want to create a `CROSS JOIN` in any database application, unless you apply a very specific `WHERE` clause constraint to the statement.

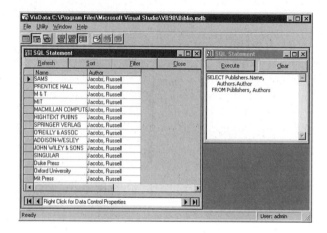

FIGURE 6.7

Fourteen rows of the 4,540,842-row Cartesian product from the Publishers and Authors table.

CAUTION

If you try the preceding CROSS JOIN example, make sure you specify a Recordset of the DAO dynaset type and don't attempt to sort the table. Creating a snapshot-type DAO.Recordset or sorting the table is likely to take an hour or more, depending on the speed of your PC and disk drive. A dynaset-type Recordset only returns a sufficient number of rows to populate the visible rows in the DBGrid control.

The common types of joins that you can create with SQL-89, SQL-92, and Jet SQL are described in the sections that follow.

NOTE

All joins, except the CROSS JOIN or Cartesian product, require you to use either identical field data types for the two fields or a function, where supported by the RDBMS, to convert dissimilar field data types to a common type.

Conventional Inner or Equi-Joins

The most common type of join is the equi-join or INNER JOIN. You create an equi-join with a WHERE clause using the following generalized statement:

```
SELECT Table1.field_name, ... Table2.field_name ...
    FROM Table1, Table2
    WHERE Table1.field_name = Table2.field_name
```

The SQL-92 JOIN syntax to achieve the same result is as follows:

```
SELECT Table1.field_name, ... Table2.field_name ...
    FROM Table1 INNER JOIN Table2
        ON Table1.field_name = Table2.field_name
```

A single-column equi-join between the PubID field of the Publishers table and the PubID field of the Titles table of the Biblio.mdb database appears as follows:

```
SELECT Publishers.Name, Titles.ISBN, Titles.Title
    FROM Publishers INNER JOIN Titles
        ON Publishers.PubID = Titles.PubID
```

When you execute this query with the VisData application, the Publishers and Titles tables are joined by the PubID columns of both fields. The result of the join appears in Figure 6.8.

> **NOTE**
>
> The INNER qualifier is optional in SQL-92 but is required in Jet SQL. If you omit the INNER qualifier when you use the Jet database engine, you receive the message Syntax Error in FROM Clause when you attempt to execute the query.

FIGURE 6.8
VisData displaying an equi-join on the PubID *fields of the Publishers and Titles tables.*

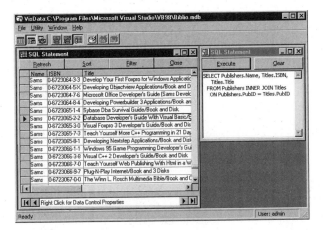

> **NOTE**
>
> Natural equi-joins create joins automatically between identically named fields of two tables and don't require the ON predicate in the JOIN statement. Jet SQL does not support the NATURAL JOIN statement, and no commercial client/server RDBMS had implemented NATURAL JOIN at the time this book was written.

The Jet SQL statements that you create in the graphical QBE design mode of Access generate an expanded JOIN syntax. Access separates the JOIN statement from a complete FROM clause with a comma and then repeats the table names in a separate, fully defined JOIN statement. The Jet SQL syntax shown in the following example gives the same result as the preceding ANSI SQL-92 example:

```
SELECT DISTINCTROW Publishers.Name, Titles.ISBN, Titles.Title
    FROM Publishers, Titles,
    Publishers INNER JOIN Titles
        ON Publishers.PubID = Titles.PubID
```

The purpose of the optional DISTINCTROW statement in Jet SQL is discussed in the section "Comparing the Jet SQL Dialect with ANSI SQL-92" later in the chapter.

The equivalent of the two preceding syntax examples, using the WHERE clause to create the join, is as follows:

```
SELECT Publishers.Name, Titles.ISBN, Titles.Title
    FROM Publishers, Titles
    WHERE Publishers.PubID = Titles.PubID
```

The result of using INNER JOIN and the WHERE clause to create an equi-join is the same. The SQL WHERE clause is simpler, so few developers use the JOIN syntax.

NOTE

Equi-joins return only rows in which the values of the joined fields match. Field values of records of either table that do not have matching values in the other table do not appear in the query result set returned by an equi-join. If no match occurs between any of the records, no rows are returned. A query result set without rows is called a *null set*; a No Current Record error results when you attempt to navigate with a Data control bound to a null set.

Multiple Equi-Joins

You can create multiple equi-joins to link several tables by pairs of fields with common data values. For example, you can link the Publishers, Titles, Title Author, and Authors tables of Biblio.mdb with the following Jet SQL statement:

```
SELECT DISTINCTROW Titles.Title, Publishers.Name,
        Titles.ISBN, Authors.Author
    FROM Publishers INNER JOIN
      (Authors INNER JOIN
      (Titles INNER JOIN [Title Author]
          ON Titles.ISBN = [Title Author].ISBN)
          ON Authors.Au_ID = [Title Author].Au_ID)
          ON Publishers.PubID = Titles.PubID
```

Learning Structured Query Language

CHAPTER 6

269

6

LEARNING
STRUCTURED
QUERY LANGUAGE

The preceding SQL statement uses *nested* joins to create the required relationships to display title, publisher, and author data for each book. Using JOIN syntax becomes quite complex when it involves multiple joins. Access's graphical QBE window enables you to create such SQL statements much faster than you can write and test them yourself. The query result set from the preceding Jet SQL query appears in Figure 6.9.

FIGURE 6.9

The query result set with four tables joined.

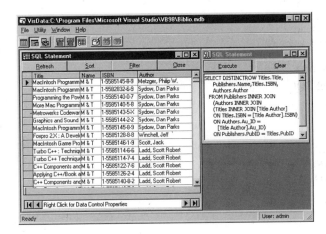

The equivalent of the preceding example using the ANSI SQL WHERE clause is as follows:

```
SELECT Titles.Title, Publishers.Name,
     Titles.ISBN, Authors.Author
   FROM Publishers, Titles, Authors, [Title Author]
   WHERE Titles.ISBN = [Title Author].ISBN AND
        Authors.Au_ID = [Title Author].Au_ID AND
        Publishers.PubID = Titles.PubID
```

> **NOTE**
>
> As a rule, using the WHERE clause to specify equi-joins results in simpler query statements than specifying INNER JOINs. When you need to create OUTER JOINs, the subject of the next section, you might want to use INNER JOIN statements to maintain consistency in Jet SQL statements.

Outer Joins

INNER JOINs (equi-joins) return only rows with matching field values. OUTER JOINs return all the rows of one table and only those rows in the other table that have matching values. There are two types of OUTER JOIN:

- A LEFT OUTER JOIN returns all rows of the table or result set to the left of the LEFT OUTER JOIN statement and only those rows of the table to the right of the statement with matching field values. In WHERE clauses, the *= operator specifies a LEFT OUTER JOIN.

- A RIGHT OUTER JOIN returns all rows of the table or result set to the right of the RIGHT OUTER JOIN statement and only those rows of the table to the left of the statement with matching field values. In WHERE clauses, the =* operator specifies a RIGHT OUTER JOIN.

By convention, joins are created in one-to-many form; that is, the primary table that represents the "one" side of the relation appears to the left of the JOIN expression, or the operator of the WHERE clause, and the related table of the "many" side appears to the right of the expression or operator. You use LEFT OUTER JOINs to display all records of the primary table, regardless of matching records in the related table. RIGHT OUTER JOINs are useful for finding orphan records. *Orphan records* are records in related tables that have no related records in the primary tables; orphan records are a result of violated referential integrity rules.

The SQL-92 syntax for a statement that returns all Titles records, regardless of matching values in the Authors table is as follows:

```
SELECT Titles.Title, [Title Author].ISBN, [Title Author].Au_ID
    FROM Titles LEFT OUTER JOIN [Title Author]
        ON Titles.ISBN = [Title Author].ISBN
```

The equivalent join using the WHERE clause is created by the following query:

```
SELECT Titles.Title, [Title Author].ISBN, [Title Author].Au_ID
    FROM Titles
        WHERE Titles.ISBN *= [Title Author].ISBN
```

Jet SQL requires you to use the special syntax described in the preceding section does not permit you to add the OUTER reserved word in the JOIN statement; Access 97 permits adding the OUTER reserved word, but disregards it during execution. The Jet SQL equivalent of the previous query example is as follows:

```
SELECT DISTINCTROW Titles.Title, [Title Author].ISBN,
    [Title Author].Au_ID
    FROM Titles LEFT JOIN [Title Author]
        ON Titles.ISBN = [Title Author].ISBN
```

The result of running the preceding query against the Biblio.mdb database appears in Figure 6.10. You get 279 rows, instead of 241 rows, when you execute the LEFT JOIN because 38 Title records don't have corresponding records in the Title Author table.

FIGURE 6.10

The result of substituting LEFT JOIN *for* INNER JOIN *in a query against the Biblio.mdb database.*

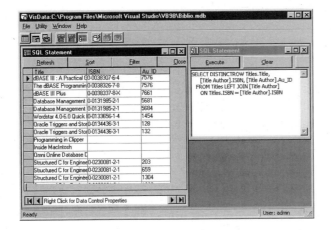

NOTE

Jet SQL doesn't support the `*=` and `=*` operators in WHERE clauses. You need to use the LEFT JOIN or RIGHT JOIN reserved words to create outer joins when you use the Jet database engine. This restriction does not apply to SQL passthrough queries that you execute on servers that support `*=` and `=*` operators, such as Microsoft SQL Server.

NOTE

If you attempt to add the Authors table to the preceding SQL statement, you receive the following message: Error 3296: Join Expression Not Supported. The Jet 3.5x database engine cannot process the following SQL statement with a single query:

```
SELECT DISTINCTROW Titles.Title, Titles.ISBN,
    [Title Author].Au_ID
  FROM Authors INNER JOIN
    (Titles LEFT JOIN [Title Author]
    ON Titles.ISBN = [Title Author].ISBN)
    ON Authors.Au_ID = [Title Author].Au_ID
```

You must use two nested queries: The first query creates the LEFT JOIN query result set, and the second query INNER JOINs the Authors table to the Title Author table. Nested queries are one of the subjects of the "Using Nested Queries and Subqueries" section, later in this chapter.

Theta Joins and the DISTINCTROW Keyword

You can create joins using comparison operators other than =, *=, and =*. Joins that are not equi-joins are called *theta joins*. The most common form of theta joins is the not-equal (theta) join that uses the WHERE `table_name.field_name <> table_name.field_name` syntax. The Biblio.mdb database does not contain tables with fields that lend themselves to demonstrating not-equal joins. Open the Nwind.mdb database to execute a Jet SQL query to find records in the Orders table whose ShipAddress value differs from the Address value in the Customers field by employing the following query:

```
SELECT DISTINCTROW Customers.CompanyName, Customers.Address,
     Orders.ShipAddress
  FROM Customers, Orders,
  Customers INNER JOIN Orders
     ON Customers.CustomerID = Orders.CustomerID
  WHERE Orders.ShipAddress<>Customers.Address
```

The preceding query, which uses the field names from Nwind.mdb, results in the query return set that is shown in Figure 6.11.

FIGURE 6.11

A not-equal theta join to display customers whose shipping and billing addresses are not the same.

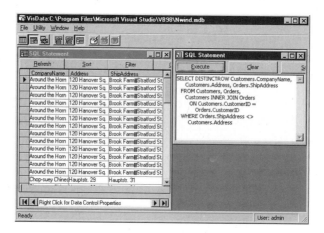

If you execute the same query without Jet SQL's DISTINCTROW qualifier, you get the same result. However, if you substitute the ANSI SQL DISTINCT qualifier for Jet SQL's DISTINCTROW, the result is distinctly different, as illustrated by Figure 6.12.

The five-row query result set in Figure 6.12 is created by the following statement, which is the same in Jet SQL and ANSI SQL:

```
SELECT DISTINCT Customers.CompanyName, Customers.Address,
     Orders.ShipAddress
  FROM Customers, Orders
WHERE Customers.CustomerID = Orders.CustomerID
  AND Orders.ShipAddress <> Customers.Address
```

Learning Structured Query Language

CHAPTER 6

273

6

LEARNING
STRUCTURED
QUERY LANGUAGE

FIGURE 6.12

The effect of applying the DISTINCT *qualifier to the query in Figure 6.11.*

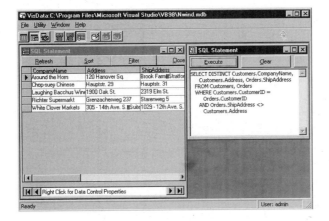

The DISTINCT qualifier tells the query to return only rows that have differing values in the fields specified in the SELECT statement. Jet SQL's DISTINCTROW qualifier causes the return set to include each row in which a discrepancy occurs in any value in any field in the two tables (not just the fields specified to be displayed by the SELECT statement).

Self-Joins and Composite Columns

A *self-join* is a join created between two fields of the same table having similar field data types. The first field is usually the primary key field and the second field of the join is ordinarily a foreign key field that relates to the primary key field, although this structure is not a requirement for a self-join. (The preceding may be a requirement to make the result of the self-join meaningful, however.)

When you create a self-join, the RDBMS creates a copy of the original table and then joins the copy to the original table. No tables in Biblio.mdb offer fields on which you can create a meaningful self-join. The Employees table of Nwind.mdb, however, includes the ReportsTo field that specifies the EmployeeID of an employee's supervisor. The Jet SQL statement to create a self-join on the Employees table to display the name of an employee's supervisor follows.:

```
SELECT Employees.EmployeeID] AS EmpID,
     Employees.LastName] & ", " & Employees.FirstName AS Employee,
     Employees.ReportsTo AS SupID,
     EmpCopy.LastName & ", " & EmpCopy.First Name AS Supervisor
  FROM Employees, Employees AS EmpCopy,
     Employees INNER JOIN EmpCopy
     ON Employees.ReportsTo = EmpCopy.Employee ID
```

You create a temporary copy of the table, named EmpCopy, with the FROM... Employees AS EmpCopy clause. Each field name of the query is aliased with an AS qualifier. The Employee and Supervisor columns are composite columns whose values are created by combining last names and comma-spaces with the first names. The query result set from the preceding SQL statement appears in Figure 6.13.

FIGURE 6.13

The query result set of a self-join on the Employees table of Nwind.mdb.

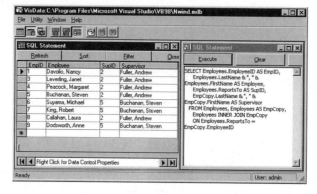

ANSI SQL does not provide a SELF INNER JOIN, but you can create the equivalent by using the ANSI version of the preceding statement. You can substitute a WHERE Employees.ReportsTo = EmpCopy.EmployeeID clause for the INNER JOIN...ON statement.

> **NOTE**
>
> Self-joins are relatively uncommon, because a table in fourth normal form would not include an equivalent of the ReportsTo field. A separate table would relate the EmployeeID values of employees and supervisors. However, creating a separate table to contain information that can be held in a single table without ambiguity is generally considered overnormalization. Fear of overnormalization is the primary reason that most developers stop normalizing tables at the third normal form.

Using Nested Queries and Subqueries

The Jet database engine enables you to create persistent QueryDef objects that you can substitute for tables in SQL statements. A QueryDef is said to be *persistent* because the QueryDef is stored as a named Document object in a Jet database. A QueryDef is similar to an SQL VIEW created from an SQL statement. Basing a query on a QueryDef object instead of on a table is called *nesting* queries. The Jet database engine treats TableDef and QueryDef objects as one object class for naming purposes; thus you can't have a QueryDef and a table with the same name in a single database. When you execute a query based on a QueryDef, Jet first executes the query defined by the QueryDef object (sometimes called an *inner query*) to return its result set as a Recordset object. Then Jet executes the primary query (also called an *outer query*) against the Recordset.

Learning Structured Query Language

CHAPTER 6

275

6

LEARNING
STRUCTURED
QUERY LANGUAGE

A nested query is the only convenient method of eliminating the Error 3296: Join Expression Not Supported Message when combining `INNER` and `OUTER JOIN`s, as described in the "Outer Joins" section earlier in this chapter. To use VisData to create a persistent `QueryDef` and join the `QueryDef`'s `Recordset` with the Authors table, follow these steps:

1. Clear the SQL window and type the following SQL statement for the `QueryDef` in the SQL Window's text box:

```
SELECT DISTINCTROW Titles.Title, [Title Author].ISBN,
    [Title Author].Au_ID
  FROM Titles LEFT JOIN [Title Author]
    ON Titles.ISBN = [Title Author].ISBN
```

2. Execute the query to check your syntax. Click the Save button to open the VisData input box and type **qdfAllTitles** in the text box (see Figure 6.14). Click OK to save your query in Biblio.mdb and to close the input box. Click No when asked whether this is an SQL passthrough query.

FIGURE 6.14

Saving an inner query as a `QueryDef` *object.*

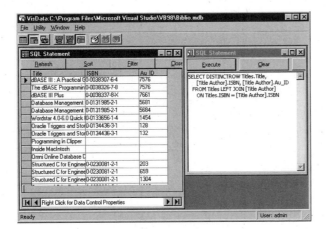

3. Clear the SQL window and type the following SQL statement:

```
SELECT DISTINCTROW qdfAllTitles.Title, qdfAllTitles.ISBN,
    Authors.Author
  FROM qdfAllTitles LEFT JOIN Authors
    ON qdfAllTitles.Au_ID = Authors.Au_ID
```

4. Click the Execute button to run the inner and outer queries. The query result set appears in Figure 6.15.

FIGURE **6.15**

Executing the outer query runs the inner query first.

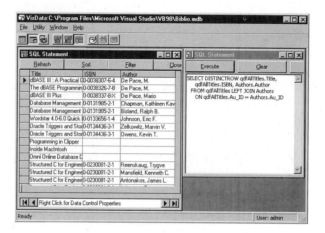

Nested queries and subqueries are closely related. Access 2.0 added the subquery capability to Jet 2.0. In the preceding example, the `QueryDef` takes the place of an SQL subquery. You can use subqueries in the *field_list* of a SELECT statement or as criteria in WHERE and HAVING clauses of queries. Subqueries are limited to returning a single column and come in the following two flavors:

- Subset subqueries define a SELECT query result set to limit the set of records on which the outer (primary) query operates. The typical syntax for an outer query with a subset inner subquery is this:

```
SELECT field_list
   FROM table_list
   WHERE field_name [NOT] IN
      (SELECT field_name
          FROM table_name
          WHERE search_criteria)
```

The IN predicate, in this case, is the equivalent of the = operator, which creates an equi-join in conventional SQL syntax; using the NOT operator is the equivalent of the <> theta join operator. Subqueries do not have an equivalent for the *= operator, so you can't create the equivalent of the preceding `QueryDef` with a subquery.

- Comparison subqueries evaluate numeric values to limit the records on which the outer query operates. The syntax of an outer query with a comparison subquery is this:

```
SELECT field_list
   FROM table_list
   WHERE field_name {<¦<=¦=¦=>¦>} {ANY¦SOME¦ALL}
      (SELECT field_name
          FROM table_name
          WHERE search_criteria)
```

Learning Structured Query Language

CHAPTER 6

277

6

LEARNING
STRUCTURED
QUERY LANGUAGE

The ANY or SOME predicate returns records for which a comparison with any of the records in the subquery returns **True**. The ALL predicate returns records for which a comparison with all records in the subquery returns **True**.

The following SQL statement returns records for any product in the Products table of Nwind.mdb that has a unit price equal to or greater than any item in the Order Details table carrying a discount of 25 percent or more:

```
SELECT ProductID, ProductName, CategoryID
   FROM Products
   WHERE UnitPrice > ANY
      (SELECT UnitPrice FROM [Order Details]
         WHERE Discount >= .25)
```

The preceding query returns 76 of the 77 records in the Products table; only ProductID 33, Geitost, does not meet the search criterion (see Figure 6.16). If you substitute ALL for ANY, the query returns only one record—Product ID 38, Côte de Blaye—undoubtedly a French wine of exceptional vintage. The price of Côte de Blaye is equal to or greater than all the products for which a discount of 25 percent or greater was applicable.

FIGURE 6.16

The result set of a nested query using the ANY operator.

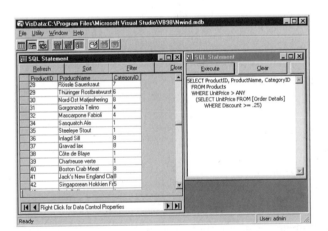

Subqueries can be used in conjunction with the INSERT, UPDATE, and DELETE action queries described in Chapter 7, "Running Crosstab and Action Queries." For additional examples of the use of subqueries, search Visual Basic 6.0's online Help for *subqueries*. Subqueries are useful, but they are not easy to write correctly. In most cases, a nested query can be used in place of a subquery. The advantage of a nested query is that the Jet engine precompiles the inner QueryDef, so you're likely to obtain a performance benefit. SQL Server VIEWs, which are closely related to QueryDefs that return rows, usually offer performance benefits compared to running subqueries.

UNION Queries

UNION queries, which were introduced with Jet 2.0, enable you to combine the query result set of two independent queries. The general syntax of the UNION query follows.

```
{TABLE table_name1|SELECT field_list1 FROM table_list1}
    UNION [ALL]
        {TABLE table_name2|SELECT field_list2 FROM table_list2}
```

The number of fields of *table_name1* must equal the number of fields of *table_name2* or *field_list2*, but the fields need not be of the same data type. Duplicate rows are not returned unless you add the ALL predicate. Following is an example of an SQL statement, derived from an example included in the "UNION Operation" Help topic, that returns records for Brazilian customers and suppliers:

```
SELECT CompanyName, City, SupplierID AS ID
    FROM Suppliers
    WHERE Country = "Brazil"
    UNION SELECT CompanyName, City, CustomerID
        FROM Customers
        WHERE Country = "Brazil"
    ORDER BY City
```

SupplierID is of the Long data type and CustomerID is of the Text data type, as shown in Figure 6.17. The field names of the query result set, including aliases, are based on the field names of the first query. You can add an ORDER BY clause at the end of the UNION query to specify the sort order of the entire query result set.

FIGURE 6.17

The result set of a UNION query having values of two different data types in the ID field.

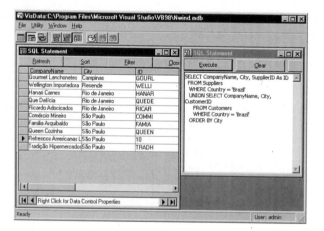

SQL Aggregate Functions and the GROUP BY and HAVING Clauses

ANSI SQL includes set functions (called *SQL aggregate functions* in this book) that act on sets of records. The standard SQL-92 aggregate functions are described in the following list. The `field_name` argument of the functions can be the name of a field (with a `table_name.` specifier if required) or the all-fields specifier, an asterisk (*). Here's the list:

- COUNT(*field_name*) returns the number of rows that contain NOT NULL values of *field_name*. COUNT(*) returns the number of rows in the table or query, without regard for NULL values in fields.
- MAX(*field_name*) returns the largest value of *field_name* in the set.
- MIN(*field_name*) returns the smallest value of *field_name* in the set.
- SUM(*field_name*) returns the total value of *field_name* in the set.
- AVG(*field_name*) returns the arithmetic average (mean) value of *field_name* in the set.

The SQL aggregate functions can act on persistent tables or virtual tables, such as query result sets. The basic syntax of queries that use the SQL aggregate functions is this:

```
SELECT FUNCTION(field_name¦*) [AS column_alias]
```

The preceding example returns a single record with the value of the SQL aggregate function you choose. You can test the SQL aggregate functions with Biblio.mdb using the following query:

```
SELECT COUNT(*) AS Count,
       SUM(PubID) AS Total,
       AVG(PubID) AS Average,
       MIN(PubID) AS Minimum,
       MAX(PubID) AS Maximum
    FROM Publishers
```

The result of the preceding aggregate query appears in Figure 6.18.

FIGURE 6.18

A simple aggregate query that returns the sum, average, minimum, and maximum values of a numeric set.

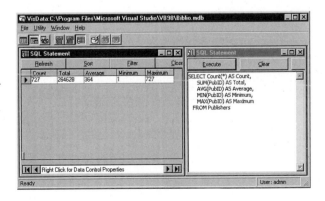

Databases with significant content usually have tables that contain fields representing classification of objects. The Biblio.mdb database does not have such a classification, but the Products tables of Nwind.mdb classifies an eclectic assortment of exotic foodstuffs into eight categories. You use the GROUP BY clause when you want to obtain values of the SQL aggregate functions for each class of an object. The GROUP BY clause creates a virtual table called, not surprisingly, a *grouped table*.

The following Jet SQL query counts the number of items in each food category included in the CategoryID field of the Products table of Nwind.mdb and then calculates three total and average values for each category:

```
SELECT CategoryID AS Category,
     COUNT(ProductID) AS Items,
     Format(AVG(UnitPrice), "$#,##0.00") AS Avg_UP,
     SUM(UnitsInStock) AS Sum_Stock,
     SUM(UnitsOnOrder) AS Sum_Ordered
   FROM Products
   GROUP BY CategoryID
```

> **NOTE**
>
> The preceding query uses the VBA **Format**() function to format the values returned for average unit price (Avg_UP) in conventional monetary format. This feature is not found in ANSI SQL.

The result of the preceding query appears in Figure 6.19.

FIGURE 6.19

Using GROUP BY with the SQL aggregate functions.

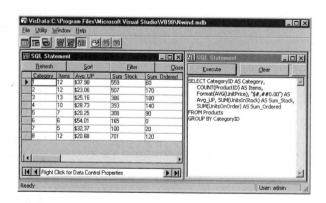

If you wanted to restrict group (category) membership by a particular criteria, you might think that you could use a WHERE clause to establish the criteria. However, WHERE clauses apply to the entire table. The HAVING clause acts like the WHERE clause for groups. Therefore, to limit the applicability of the SQL aggregate functions to a particular set of a group, you would add the HAVING clause with the IN() operator. The following Jet SQL example returns only rows for the 1 (Beverages) and 2 (Condiments) categories:

```
SELECT CategoryID AS Category,
       COUNT(ProductID) AS Items,
       Format(AVG(UnitPrice), "$#,##0.00") AS Avg_UP,
       SUM(UnitsInStock) AS Sum_Stock,
       SUM(UnitsOnOrder) AS Sum_Ordered
   FROM Products
   GROUP BY CategoryID
   HAVING CategoryID IN(1, 2)
```

COMPARING THE JET SQL DIALECT WITH ANSI SQL-92

The preceding sections of this chapter outlined many of the syntactical differences between Jet SQL and ANSI SQL-92 (plus earlier versions of ANSI SQL such as SQL-86 and SQL-89). Jet SQL does not support ANSI SQL Data Control Language(DCL) for granting and revoking user permissions for database objects. Both Access 97 and Visual Basic 6.0 enable you to modify permissions for users and groups by altering the value of the Permission property of a Container or Document object with VBA code. Access 97 establishes permissions through the user interface and includes a Security Wizard; Visual Basic 6.0 requires you to create your own user interface for security administration. Jet SQL does not support Cursor Control Language (CCL). The Jet 3.5 database engine handles all cursor-related activities.

The sections that follow summarize the differences between the keywords of Jet SQL and the reserved words of ANSI SQL, as well as how Jet SQL deals with the data types defined by ANSI SQL.

ANSI SQL Reserved Words and Jet SQL Keywords

ANSI SQL reserved words, by tradition, are set in uppercase type. Reserved words in ANSI SQL may not be used as names of objects, such as tables or fields, or as names of parameters or variables used in SQL statements. This book refers to elements of Jet SQL syntax as *keywords* because, with the exception of some Jet SQL functions, Jet SQL keywords are not reserved words in VBA. Although you could use Jet SQL keywords as names of objects, such use is not a generally accepted programming practice (GAPP).

The commonly used ANSI SQL reserved words (including functions) and symbols that do not have a direct equivalent Jet SQL reserved word or symbol are listed in Table 6.3. This table does not include many of the new reserved words added to SQL-89 by SQL-92, because these reserved words have not yet been implemented in the versions of client/server RDBMS that had been released as commercial products at the time this book was written.

TABLE 6.3   COMMON ANSI SQL RESERVED WORDS THAT DO NOT HAVE A DIRECT EQUIVALENT IN JET SQL

Reserved Word	Category	Substitute
AUTHORIZATION	DCL	Not supported in Jet SQL
BEGIN	TPL	Visual Basic `BeginTrans` method
CHECK	DDL	Not supported in Jet DDL
CLOSE	DCL	Jet SQL does not support DCL
COMMIT	TPL	Visual Basic `CommitTrans` method
CREATE VIEW	DDL	Not supported in Access DDL
CURRENT	CCL	Jet 3.5 handles cursor control
CURSOR	CCL	(See preceding)
DECLARE	CCL	(See preceding)
DROP VIEW	DDL	Not supported in Access DDL
FETCH	CCL	Field name of a `Recordset` object
GRANT	DCL	Not supported in Jet SQL
IN subquery	DQL	Use a query against a query `Dynaset` instead of a subquery
POSITION()	DQL	Use `InStr()`
PRIVILEGES	DCL	Not Supported in Jet SQL
REVOKE	DCL	(See preceding)
ROLLBACK	TPL	Use `Rollback` method
SUBSTRING()	DQL	Use `Mid()` functions
WORK	TPL	Not required by the `BeginTrans` method
*=	DQL	Use LEFT JOIN
=*	DQL	Use RIGHT JOIN
!= (not equal)	DQL	Use the <> for not equal
: (variable prefix)	DQL	Use PARAMETERS statement (if needed)

Table 6.4 lists Jet SQL keywords that are not reserved words in ANSI SQL. Many of the Jet SQL keywords describe data types that you specify by using the `db...` constants described in Chapter 2, "Understanding OLE DB and Universal Data Access." Data type conversion to and from ANSI SQL is discussed shortly.

TABLE 6.4 JET SQL KEYWORDS AND SYMBOLS THAT ARE NOT RESERVED WORDS OR SYMBOLS IN ANSI SQL

Jet SQL	ANSI SQL	Category	Purpose
BINARY	No equivalent	DDL	Not an official Jet data type (used for SID field in System.mdw)
BOOLEAN	No equivalent	DDL	Logical field data type (0 or -1 values only)
BYTE	No equivalent	DDL	**Asc**()/**Chr**() data type, 1-byte integer (tinyint of SQL Server)
CURRENCY	No equivalent	DDL	Currency data type
DATETIME	No equivalent	DDL	Date/Time field data type (Variant subtype 7)
DISTINCTROW	No equivalent	DQL	Creates an updatable Recordset object
DOUBLE number	REAL	DDL	**Double**-precision floating point
IN predicate with crosstab queries	No equivalent	DQL	Defines fixed-column headers for crosstab queries
LONG	INT[EGER]	DDL	**Long** integer data type
LONGBINARY	No equivalent	DDL	OLE Object field data type
LONGTEXT	No equivalent	DDL	Memo field data type
(WITH) OWNERACCESS (OPTION)	No equivalent	DQL	Runs queries with object owner's permissions
PARAMETERS	No equivalent	DQL	User- or program-entered query parameters (should be avoided in Visual Basic code)
PERCENT	No equivalent	DQL	Used with TOP
PIVOT	No equivalent	DQL	Used in crosstab queries
SHORT	SMALLINT	DDL	**Integer** data type, 2 bytes
SINGLE	FLOAT	DDL	**Single**-precision real number
TEXT	VARCHAR[ACTER]	DDL	Text data type
TOP	No equivalent	DQL	TOP n or TOP n PERCENT

continues

TABLE 6.4   CONTINUED

Jet SQL	ANSI SQL	Category	Purpose
TRANSFORM	No equivalent	DQL	Specifies a crosstab query
? (LIKE wild card)	_ (wild card)	DQL	Single character with Like
* (LIKE wild card)	% (wild card)	DQL	Zero or more characters
# (LIKE wild card)	No equivalent	DQL	Single digit, 0 through 9
# (date specifier)	No equivalent	DQL	Enclose date/time values
<> (not equal)	!=	DQL	Visual Basic uses ! as a separator

> **NOTE**
>
> The T-SQL bit data type corresponds to Jet SQL's BOOLEAN data type. SQL Server 7.0's Transact-SQL now supports the TOP and TOP *nn* PERCENT reserved words.

Jet SQL provides the four SQL statistical aggregate functions listed in Table 6.5 that are not included in ANSI SQL. These Jet SQL statistical aggregate functions are set in uppercase and lowercase type in the Microsoft Visual Basic documentation but are set in uppercase type in this book.

TABLE 6.5   JET SQL STATISTICAL AGGREGATE FUNCTIONS

Access Function	Purpose
STDDEV()	Standard deviation of a population sample
STDDEVP()	Standard deviation of a population
VAR()	Statistical variation of a population sample
VARP()	Statistical variation of a population

Table 6.6 lists the Jet SQL keywords that often appear in uppercase and lowercase, rather than the all-uppercase SQL format in the Microsoft documentation and Visual Basic code examples supplied with Visual Basic 6.0. Jet SQL keywords that also are Visual Basic reserved words appear in bold type.

TABLE 6.6   TYPESETTING CONVENTIONS FOR JET SQL KEYWORDS AND VISUAL BASIC 6.0 RESERVED WORDS

Jet SQL and Visual Basic	ANSI SQL and This Book	Jet SQL and Visual Basic	ANSI SQL and This Book
And	AND	Max()	MAX()
Avg()	AVG()	Min()	MIN()

Learning Structured Query Language

Chapter 6

285

6

LEARNING
STRUCTURED
QUERY LANGUAGE

Jet SQL and Visual Basic	ANSI SQL and This Book	Jet SQL and Visual Basic	ANSI SQL and This Book
Between	BETWEEN	**Not**	NOT
Count()	COUNT()	**Null**	NULL
Is	IS	**Or**	OR
Like	LIKE	Sum()	SUM()

Data Type Conversion Between ANSI SQL and Jet SQL

Table 6.7 lists the data types specified by ANSI SQL-92 and the equivalent data types of Jet SQL, when equivalent data types exist. Categories of ANSI SQL data types precede the SQL-92 data type identifier.

TABLE 6.7 DATA TYPE CONVERSION TO AND FROM ANSI SQL AND JET SQL

ANSI SQL-92	Jet SQL	Variant Subtype	Comments
Exact Numeric	Number		
INTEGER	Long (Integer)	3	2 bytes
SMALLINT	Integer	2	4 bytes
NUMERIC[(p[, s])]	Not supported		p = precision, s = scale
DECIMAL[(p[, s])]	Not supported		p = precision, s = scale
Approximate Numeric	Number		
REAL	Double (Precision)	5	8 bytes
DOUBLE PRECISION	Not supported		16 bytes
FLOAT	Single (Precision)	4	4 bytes
Character (Text)	Text		
CHARACTER[(n)]	String	8	(Text fields are variable length)
CHARACTER VARYING	String8		
Bit Strings	None supported		

continues

TABLE 6.7 CONTINUED

ANSI SQL-92	Jet SQL	Variant Subtype	Comments
BIT[(n)]	Not supported		(Binary fields are variable length)
BIT VARYING	Not supported		(Used by Microsoft)
Datetimes			
DATE	Not supported		10 bytes
TIME	Not supported		8 bytes (plus fraction)
TIMESTAMP	Date/Time	7	19 bytes
TIME WITH TIME ZONE	Not supported		14 bytes
TIMESTAMP WITH TIME ZONE	Not supported	25 bytes	
Intervals (Datetimes)	None supported		

Many of the data types listed in the Jet SQL column of Table 6.7 as "not supported" are converted by OLE DB data providers or ODBC drivers to standard ODBC data types that are compatible Jet SQL data types. When you use attached database files, data types are converted by the Jet database engine's ISAM driver for dBASE, FoxPro, Paradox, and Btrieve files. Data type conversion by ODBC and ISAM drivers is one of the subjects of Chapter 8, "Connecting to Desktop Data Sources with ODBC."

RUNNING CROSSTAB AND ACTION QUERIES

IN THIS CHAPTER

Up to this point in *Database Developer's Guide with Visual Basic 6*, you've only been introduced to the most basic SQL queries: SELECT queries. This chapter describes the five additional types of queries—crosstab, append, update, delete, and make-table—you can execute with Jet SQL's Data Manipulation Language (DML). The crosstab query is a special form of SELECT query that summarizes data in spreadsheet style, most often in time-series format. You're likely to find that 75% or more of the decision-support applications you create for your firm or clients include crosstab queries. In many cases, the crosstab query result set serves as the data source for graphs and charts.

The remaining four types of queries described in this chapter are called *action* queries. Microsoft Access introduced the action query terminology for manipulative (DML) queries that update the data in existing tables and create new tables. Action queries substitute for lengthy blocks of VBA code when you need to modify the content of tables in your database or you want to create a new database table.

USING CROSSTAB QUERIES TO PRESENT SUMMARY DATA

Even before the early days of the personal computer and the historic VisiCalc spreadsheet application, management was accustomed to viewing summary data in the row/column format of accountant worksheets. Worksheets that are used for comparative performance analysis fall into two basic categories:

Time-series format	This format implies that column titles contain date intervals, such as months, quarters, or years, and that row titles designate the category of data being compared. The underlying detail data is grouped by both data category and time period. Time-series summary data often is used to prepare line graphs or bar charts with sales as the y-axis (*vertical axis* or *abscissa*) and time as the x-axis (*horizontal axis* or *ordinate*).
Classification format	This format uses column titles with the names of individuals, regions, divisions, or other organizational categories, and data categories for the row titles. This format is restricted to a single, predetermined time period. (Multiple time periods can be represented by "stacking" worksheets with an identical format that can be consolidated by adding the values of corresponding cells.) The most common graphical representation of data from classification worksheets is the pie chart.

Today's spreadsheet applications, such as Lotus 1-2-3 and Microsoft Excel, replace the drudgery of preparing handwritten worksheets with automated computer-based procedures. However, most of the detail information needed to prepare summary data for management is available only in the fields of tables of relational accounting databases. Chapter 5, "Optimizing the Design of Relational Databases," demonstrates that most spreadsheet data formats violate the "no repeating groups" rule of relational tables. Conventional ANSI SQL statements return data in relational form, not in spreadsheet format. Therefore, a substantial amount of data manipulation is ordinarily required to create a time-series or classification spreadsheet from relational data. In fact, the *denormalization* process is almost as complex as the process described in Chapter 5 for normalizing spreadsheet data to relational form.

> **NOTE**
>
> Denormalized data structures are a primary characteristic of the star and snowflake schemas of the multidimensional databases designed for data warehouses. When designing multidimensional data structures, you must disregard conventional relational design theory and follow the new rules for online analytical processing (OLAP) databases.

The sections that follow describe how summary data is returned by ANSI SQL and how you use Jet SQL's TRANSFORM and PIVOT statements to automate the denormalization of relational data to spreadsheet format.

> **NOTE**
>
> The crosstab query syntax in this chapter is specific to Jet databases; client/server databases, such as Oracle8 and SQL Server, don't support the TRANSFORM and PIVOT keywords required to automate the generation of crosstab result sets. In the client/server world, data warehousing and multidimensional analysis—commonly referred to as OLAP[md]handle data aggregation and display of more sophisticated crosstab equivalents. Chapter 28, "Analyzing Multidimensional Data with OLAP and MDX," describes the use of Microsoft SQL Server OLAP Services (MSSOS, formerly code-named "Plato") to display crosstab-like time-series and classification summarizations.

Summary Data Created with the GROUP BY Clause

▶ **See** "Using the Visual Data Sample Application to Explore Queries," **p. 257**

Figure 7.1 illustrates the format of data returned by conventional SELECT queries that use the SQL aggregate function SUM to prepare data from which you can create a time-series worksheet.

The tables used to create the query result set shown in the left SQL window of Figure 7.1 are the Categories, Products, Orders, and Order Details tables; their values are derived from Visual Basic 6.0's Nwind.mdb sample database. The query result set totals the orders received for each of the eight categories of products for the four calendar quarters of 1995, the last full year of data in Nwind.mdb. Thus the grid contains 8×4 (or 32) records.

FIGURE 7.1

Using two GROUP BY criteria to aggregate the values of orders by category and date.

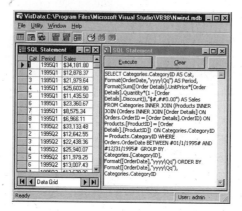

The query used to create the ADODB.Recordset shown in the right window of Figure 7.1 is rather lengthy and deserves further explanation. Following is the complete Jet SQL statement to generate the aggregation shown in the left window of Figure 7.1:

```
SELECT Categories.CategoryID AS Cat,
    Format(OrderDate,"yyyy\Qq") AS Period,
    Format(SUM([Order Details].UnitPrice*
      [Order Details].Quantity*(1 - [Order Details].Discount)),
      "$#,##0.00") AS Sales
  FROM Categories
  INNER JOIN (Products
    INNER JOIN (Orders
      INNER JOIN [Order Details]
      ON Orders.OrderID = [Order Details].OrderID)
    ON Products.[ProductID] = [Order Details].[ProductID])
  ON Categories.CategoryID = Products.CategoryID
  WHERE Orders.OrderDate BETWEEN #01/1/95# AND #12/31/95#
  GROUP BY Categories.[CategoryID], Format([OrderDate],"yyyy\Qq")
  ORDER BY Format([OrderDate],"yyyy\Qq"), Categories.CategoryID
```

> **NOTE**
>
> The word Format in the preceding table isn't in all capital letters because Format isn't an ANSI-92 or Jet SQL reserved word.

The following list describes each element of the preceding Jet SQL statement:

- The three AS predicates of the following statement alias the CategoryID field as Cat and the two formatted fields as Period and Sales, respectively:

```
SELECT Categories.CategoryID AS Cat,
Format(OrderDate,"yyyy\Qq") AS Period,
Format(Sum([Order Details].UnitPrice*(1 - [Order Details].Discount)
    [Order Details].Quantity),"$#,##0.00") AS Sales
```

- The first **Format**() function causes the order date to appear as the four-digit year (yyyy, for Y2K compliance), followed by a literal *Q* (\Q) and the number of the quarter (q) that corresponds to the order date. A backslash preceding a character in a format string designates the character that follows as a literal character rather than as a format identifier character.

▶ See "SQL Aggregate Functions and the GROUP BY and HAVING Clauses," **p. 279**

- The SUM SQL aggregate function totals the product of the discounted (1 - [Order Details].Discount) UnitPrice and Quantity fields of the Order Details table; these fields are needed to compute the extended amount of each invoice line item.

- The **Format** function embedded within the SUM function adds the dollar sign ($), comma thousands separator (#,##0), and trailing cents columns (.00) to the values in the Sales column. This function wouldn't be required in Access applications because U.S. and Canadian **Currency** values are automatically formatted with #,##0.00. Visual Basic bound controls don't automatically format the **Currency** data type.

▶ See "Conventional Inner or Equi-Joins," **p. 266**

- The following clause identifies the tables from which data is selected:

```
FROM Categories INNER JOIN (Products INNER JOIN (Orders
INNER JOIN [Order Details] ON Orders.OrderID = [Order Details].OrderID)
ON Products.ProductID = [Order Details].ProductID)
ON Categories.CategoryID = Products.CategoryID
```

The FROM statement lists the first table, Categories, and then specifies how the remaining tables in the query are joined to it. Notice that the INNER JOIN clauses are nested so that they include a total of four different tables: The Categories table is joined to the Products table, the Products table is in turn joined to the Orders table, and the Orders table is joined to the Order Details table.

- The innermost join (the INNER JOIN enclosed in the deepest level of parentheses in the following statement) creates an equi-join between the Orders table and the Order Details table so that you can use a WHERE clause to limit the records from Order Details that are totaled for each category to a range of dates. Here's the join:

```
Orders INNER JOIN [Order Details]
ON Orders.OrderID = [Order Details].OrderID
```

- The next innermost level of join creates the needed equi-join between the Order Details table and the Products table so that the values in the Order Details table for each product category are associated with the CategoryID value. Here's the join:

```
Products INNER JOIN (Orders INNER JOIN [Order Details]
ON Orders.OrderID = [Order Details].OrderID)
ON Products.ProductID = [Order Details].ProductID
```

- The outermost join creates an equi-join between the Categories table and the result of the two nested INNER JOIN clauses. This join is needed to identify products by Category because the Order Details table contains a ProductID field, but not a CategoryID field. (This join could be eliminated by substituting Products.[CategoryID] for Categories.[CategoryID] in the SELECT statement. The join is included in the example because you might want to use the CategoryName field, rather than the CategoryID field, for the row titles.)

```
Categories INNER JOIN (Products INNER JOIN (Orders INNER JOIN [Order Details]
ON Orders.OrderID = [Order Details].OrderID)
ON Products.ProductID = [Order Details].ProductID)
ON Categories.CategoryID = Products.CategoryID
```

- The WHERE Orders.[OrderDate] Between #01/1/95# And #12/31/95# criterion limits the aggregation to records for the year 1995.

- The GROUP BY Categories.[CategoryID], Format([OrderDate],"yyyy\Qq") clause results in data being grouped by product category and by the quarter of the year. The sequence of the grouping is not significant in this query. It is customary to use the same Format function in the GROUP BY clause as is used in the SELECT statement that displays the grouping value. The literal "\Q", however, isn't necessary to achieve the proper grouping.

- The ORDER BY Format([OrderDate],"yyyy\Qq"), Categories.CategoryID clause sorts the result set by quarter and then by category.

It's clear from the rows returned by the preceding query and illustrated in Figure 7.1 that a substantial rearrangement of worksheet cells is required when you import this data into a worksheet intended for displaying data in time-series format.

▶ See "Understanding Measures and Dimensions," **p. 1045**

> **NOTE**
>
> SQL statements with the complexity of those described in this section common-
> ly are used to generate aggregated fact tables for OLAP. The fact table created
> here provides the quarterly level of a time-dimension hierarchy, which might
> consist of year, quarter, month, and week, and the category level of a product-
> dimension hierarchy, typically division, category, product, and package. If you
> plan to implement data warehouses and design Visual Basic OLAP front ends,
> you need a firm foundation in writing aggregation queries of this type.

USING TRANSFORM AND PIVOT TO CREATE CROSSTAB QUERIES

Jet SQL's crosstab query feature solves the data cell rearrangement problem. Two Jet SQL keywords, TRANSFORM and PIVOT, handle the denormalization of the data. The elements of a Jet
SQL crosstab query are as follows:

- The object of the TRANSFORM predicate specifies the values for the data cells and must
  contain one of the SQL aggregate functions, such as SUM() or AVG(). You use the
  Format() function to determine the appearance of the data.

- The SELECT statement designates the row titles. The field you specify with the SELECT
  statement must be the same as the GROUP BY field.

- The FROM statement specifies each of the tables involved in the query. The tables may be
  identified by the INNER JOIN statements, without the conventional comma-separated
  table_names list.

- The GROUP BY clause aggregates row data. Only one field is permitted in the GROUP BY
  clause of a conventional crosstab query.

- The optional ORDER BY clause sorts the rows by the value of the single field specified in
  the SELECT and GROUP BY statements. You need not add the ORDER BY clause if the field
  specified by the SELECT statement is a primary key field and you want the rows ordered
  by the primary key.

- The PIVOT statement determines the column grouping and supplies the column titles.
  Column titles consist of the value of the grouping criterion. The object of the PIVOT predicate takes the place of the second GROUP BY field of the SQL statements in the two preceding examples.

Figure 7.2 shows the initial syntax of the Jet SQL statement that creates the crosstab query return set illustrated in Figure 7.3. The statement in the SQL window of Figure 7.2 consists of the SQL statement illustrated in Figure 7.1, plus the necessary modifications to make the statement conform to the rules of crosstab queries given in the preceding list.

FIGURE 7.2

Executing a crosstab query with the VisData application.

Following is the SQL statement of Figure 7.2, formatted for clarity:

```
TRANSFORM Format(SUM([Order Details].UnitPrice*
    [Order Details].Quantity*(1 - [Order Details].Discount)),"$#,##0")
    AS Sales
    SELECT Categories.CategoryName FROM (Categories
        INNER JOIN Products ON Categories.CategoryID = Products.CategoryID)
            INNER JOIN (Orders INNER JOIN [Order Details]
            ON Orders.OrderID = [Order Details].OrderID)
        ON Products.ProductID = [Order Details].ProductID
    WHERE Orders.OrderDate Between #1/1/95# And #12/31/95#
    GROUP BY Categories.CategoryName
    ORDER BY Categories.CategoryName
PIVOT Format([OrderDate],"yyyy\Qq")
```

FIGURE 7.3

The crosstab query result set from the SQL statement in Figure 7.2.

CategoryName	1995Q1	1995Q2	1995Q3	1995Q4
Beverages	$34,182	$33,133	$17,212	$17,953
Condiments	$12,878	$12,643	$11,595	$13,926
Confections	$21,980	$22,438	$15,743	$19,591
Dairy Products	$25,604	$25,940	$27,670	$37,282
Grains/Cereals	$11,435	$11,979	$16,219	$14,190
Meat/Poultry	$23,361	$13,007	$14,618	$26,179
Produce	$8,575	$12,670	$11,758	$12,970
Seafood	$6,966	$13,550	$19,857	$23,822

Nested INNER JOIN statements, like the ones shown in Figure 7.1 and Figure 7.2, are quite difficult to interpret correctly and are even more difficult to write. A simpler approach to specifying inner joins uses a compound WHERE clause. The following SQL-89 WHERE clause syntax achieves the same result as the INNER JOIN syntax of the preceding example:

```
TRANSFORM Format(SUM([Order Details].UnitPrice *
    [Order Details].Quantity*(1 - [Order Details].Discount)),
    "$#,##0") AS Sales
  SELECT Categories.CategoryName
    FROM Categories, [Order Details], Orders, Products
    WHERE Products.CategoryID = Categories.CategoryID
      AND [Order Details].OrderID = Orders.OrderID
      AND [Order Details].ProductID = Products.ProductID
      AND Orders.OrderDate BETWEEN #01/1/95# AND #12/31/95#
    GROUP BY Categories.CategoryName
    ORDER BY Categories.CategoryName
PIVOT Format(Orders.OrderDate,"yyyy\Qq")
```

Text versions of the two preceding SQL statements are Crosstab.sql and Ct_where.sql in \Ddg_vb6\Chaptr07.

7

RUNNING CROSSTAB AND ACTION QUERIES

> **TIP**
>
> If you use Microsoft Access to create and test the text for SQL statements to generate crosstab queries, you'll find that Visual Basic applications execute Access crosstab query syntax without generating an error. However, your code is simpler and more readable if you use the WHERE *Table1.Field* = *Table2.Field* clause instead of INNER JOIN syntax to create equi-joins.

Creating Fixed Column Headers with the IN Predicate

If you change the PIVOT statement in the preceding example from PIVOT Format([OrderDate],"yyyy\Qq") to PIVOT Format([OrderDate],"MMM yy") to create a monthly rather than a quarterly crosstab query, the column titles appear in a strange sequence, illustrated by Figure 7.4. The PIVOT statement automatically orders the columns alphabetically.

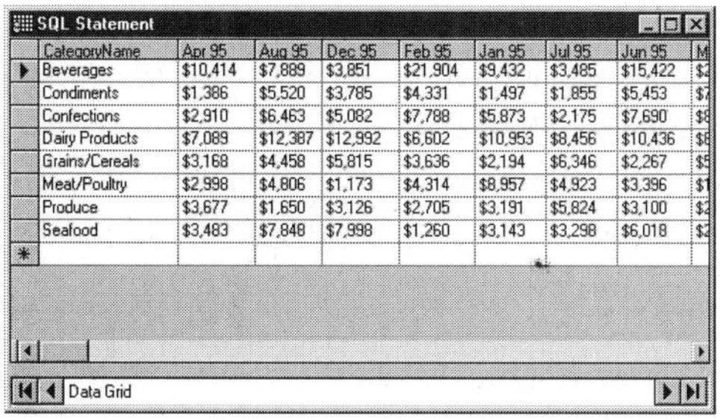

FIGURE 7.4

Monthly column headings sorted alphabetically.

CategoryName	Apr 95	Aug 95	Dec 95	Feb 95	Jan 95	Jul 95	Jun 95	M
Beverages	$10,414	$7,889	$3,851	$21,904	$9,432	$3,485	$15,422	$
Condiments	$1,386	$5,520	$3,785	$4,331	$1,497	$1,855	$5,453	$
Confections	$2,910	$6,463	$5,082	$7,788	$5,873	$2,175	$7,690	$
Dairy Products	$7,089	$12,387	$12,992	$6,602	$10,953	$8,456	$10,436	$
Grains/Cereals	$3,168	$4,458	$5,815	$3,636	$2,194	$6,346	$2,267	$
Meat/Poultry	$2,998	$4,806	$1,173	$4,314	$8,957	$4,923	$3,396	$
Produce	$3,677	$1,650	$3,126	$2,705	$3,191	$5,824	$3,100	$
Seafood	$3,483	$7,848	$7,998	$1,260	$3,143	$3,298	$6,018	$

You could solve the column sequence problem by changing the `PIVOT` statement to `PIVOT Format([OrderDate],"mm/yy")` to provide column titles 01/95 . . . 12/95, but many people prefer the three-letter abbreviations for months. Jet SQL enables you to use the `IN` predicate to create fixed column names that appear in any sequence you specify. The example that follows demonstrates the `PIVOT . . . IN` statement to create monthly column titles for any year:

```
PIVOT Format([OrderDate],"MMM")
   IN ("Jan", "Feb", "Mar", "Apr", "May", "Jun", "Jul", "Aug",
      "Sep", "Oct", "Nov", "Dec")
```

The preceding `PIVOT` statement, saved as \Ddg_vb6\Chaptr07\In_pred.sql, gives the more satisfactory result shown in Figure 7.5.

FIGURE 7.5

The query of Figure 7.4 with corrected column heads.

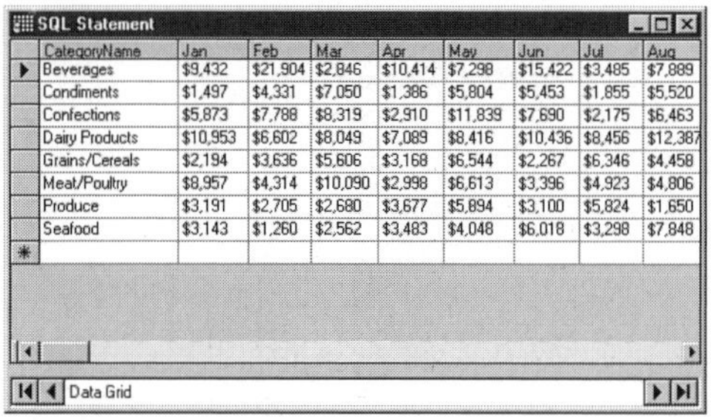

NOTE

Make sure the WHERE clause of your query limits aggregation to a single year or less when using fixed column headers with month names or abbreviations. If the query spans more than a year, the monthly column totals will be overstated.

The only restriction on the values of the arguments of the `IN()` predicate is that each value must exactly match, except for case, the values returned by the formatted `PIVOT` statement. If you misspell one of the argument values, the data rows of the column with the mistaken header are empty.

Creating a Classification Crosstab Query

With a few simple changes and additions to the preceding query, you can create a crosstab query in classification format to compare sales of product categories, by employee, during a specific time period. The following SQL statement adds the Employees table to the query and displays the last name of each employee of Northwind Traders as column headings, with sales by category for 1995 as the data cell values:

```
TRANSFORM Format(SUM([Order Details].UnitPrice *
      [Order Details].Quantity*(1 - [Order Details].Discount)),
      "$#,##0") AS Sales
   SELECT Categories.CategoryName AS Category
```

```
       FROM Categories, [Order Details], Orders, Products,
          Employees
       WHERE Products.CategoryID = Categories.CategoryID
          AND [Order Details].OrderID = Orders.OrderID
          AND [Order Details].ProductID = Products.ProductID
          AND Orders.EmployeeID = Employees.EmployeeID
          AND Orders.OrderDate BETWEEN #01/1/95# AND #12/31/95#
       GROUP BY Categories.CategoryName
       ORDER BY Categories.CategoryName
PIVOT Employees.LastName
```

Figure 7.6 shows the crosstab query result set returned by the preceding SQL statement that is executed in the VisData application. The SQL statement text file is \Ddg_vb6\Chaptr07\Ct_class.sql.

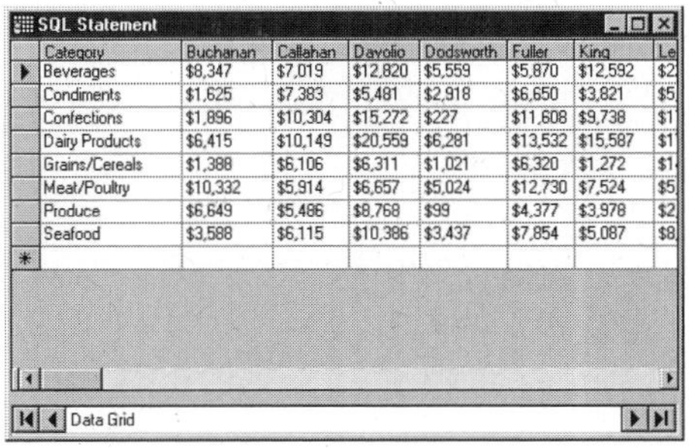

SQL Statement

Category	Buchanan	Callahan	Davolio	Dodsworth	Fuller	King	Le
Beverages	$8,347	$7,019	$12,820	$5,559	$5,870	$12,592	$2
Condiments	$1,625	$7,383	$5,481	$2,918	$6,650	$3,821	$5
Confections	$1,896	$10,304	$15,272	$227	$11,608	$9,738	$1
Dairy Products	$6,415	$10,149	$20,559	$6,281	$13,532	$15,587	$1
Grains/Cereals	$1,388	$6,106	$6,311	$1,021	$6,320	$1,272	$1
Meat/Poultry	$10,332	$5,914	$6,657	$5,024	$12,730	$7,524	$5
Produce	$6,649	$5,486	$8,768	$99	$4,377	$3,978	$2
Seafood	$3,588	$6,115	$10,386	$3,437	$7,854	$5,087	$8

Data Grid

FIGURE 7.6
A classification crosstab query executed in the VisData application.

> **NOTE**
>
> Applications that display crosstab query result sets commonly use ComboBox controls to substitute variables, such as ranges of dates and time-series granularity (year, quarter, month), for the fixed values used in the preceding examples.

EXECUTING CROSSTAB QUERIES AS DATAENVIRONMENT *COMMANDS*

Visual Basic 6.0's Data Environment window lets you quickly prototype decision-support applications that use crosstab queries. Simple application prototypes offer the opportunity for users to validate your query designs prior to investing a substantial amount of time in writing a complete Visual Basic front end.

To create a simple crosstab prototype project that displays query result sets from the preceding examples, do the following:

1. Open a new Data Project, remove `DataReport1`, and change the name of `DataEnvironment1` to **envData**.

▶ **See** "Creating the Connection **Object," p. 179**

2. Change the name of Connection1 to **cnnNwind** and specify Nwind.mdb as the data source.

3. Add a new **Sales1995Q** Command to cnnNwind. Select the SQL Statement option and copy into the text box the contents of Ct_where.sql from \Ddg_vb6\Chaptr07 (see Figure 7.7). Click OK to add the Command.

FIGURE 7.7

Creating a
Command *to exe-*
cute a crosstab
query.

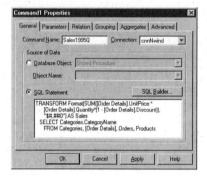

4. Select cnnNwind and add a second **Sales1995M** Command. Select the SQL Statement option and copy In_pred.sql from \Ddg_vb6\Chaptr07 into the text box. Click OK.

NOTE

Accept all remaining default values for the Command, including read-only lock-ing, because crosstab queries don't produce updatable Recordsets and the MSHFlexGrid control is read-only.

5. Add a second **Sales1995M** Command to cnnNwind. Select the SQL Statement option, and copy In_pred.sql from \Ddg_vb6\Chaptr07 into the text box. Click OK.

6. Add a third **Sales1995Emp** Command to cnnNwind. Select the SQL Statement option and copy Ct_class.sql from \Ddg_vb6\Chaptr07 into the text box. Click OK.

7. Expand the Command nodes in the DataEnvironment window to verify that the column names for your queries are correct (see Figure 7.8). Expanding a Command node exe-cutes the query to obtain the column names, simultaneously testing your query syntax.

FIGURE 7.8

Three crosstab Commands *added to the* cnnNwind Connection.

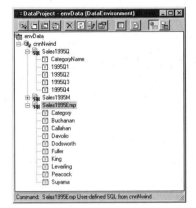

8. Open the default frmDataEnv form, rename it to **frmCrosstab**, and type a descriptive Caption property.

9. Right-click the Sales1995Q Command, drag the Command to the form result set, and choose Hierarchical FlexGrid. Rename the MSHFlexGrid **hfgCrosstab**.

10. Press F5 to execute the query and display the Sales1995Q result set (see Figure 7.9).

FIGURE 7.9

Displaying a crosstab query result set in an MSHFlexGrid control.

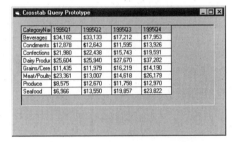

11. Add three command buttons named **cmd1995Q**, **cmd1995M**, and **cmd1995Emp** to frmCrosstab and set the Caption property to **1995 Quarterly Sales**, **1995 <u>M</u>onthly Sales**, and **1995 Sales by <u>E</u>mployee**, respectively.

12. Add the following event-handling code for the command buttons:

```
Private Sub cmd1995Q_Click()
    With hfgCrosstab
        .DataMember = "Sales1995Q"
        .Refresh
    End With
End Sub
```

```
Private Sub cmd1995M_Click()
    With hfgCrosstab
        .DataMember = "Sales1995M"
        .Refresh
    End With
End Sub

Private Sub cmd1995Emp_Click()
    With hfgCrosstab
        .DataMember = "Sales1995Emp"
        .Refresh
    End With
End Sub
```

13. Press F5 to run the project and test each execution of each query (see Figure 7.10).

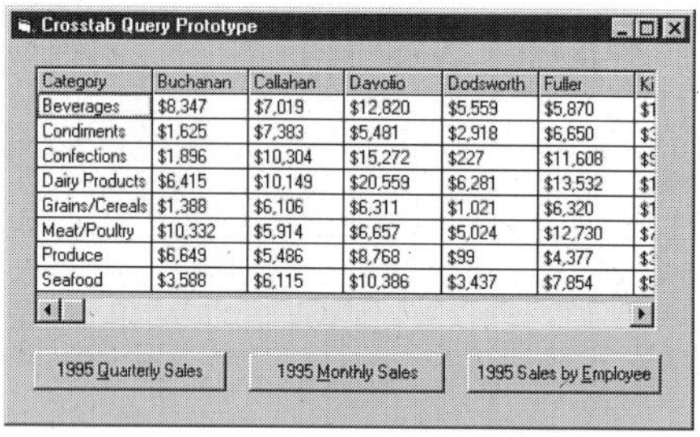

FIGURE 7.10

Displaying a series of crosstab query result sets in the same MSHFlexGrid control.

NOTE

The preceding sample project, Crosstab.vbp, is included in the \Ddg_vb6\Chaptr07 folder of the accompanying CD-ROM.

DEFINING ACTION QUERIES

Action queries provide a method of creating or modifying persistent database objects without the necessity of writing low-level VBA code to manipulate table or query record pointers. Action queries are especially effective when you want to use a single operation to add, delete, or modify many records in a database. (An operation that makes changes to multiple sets of records is called a *bulk update*.) The following list briefly describes the four types of action queries:

- *Append queries* use the INSERT INTO `table_name` predicate followed by a conventional SELECT statement to specify the fields and criteria used to determine the data to be appended to `table_name`.

- *Delete queries* use the DELETE FROM `table_name` WHERE `criteria` syntax to delete records whose data meets the `criteria`.

- *Update queries* use the UPDATE `table_name` SET `field_name` = `expression` statement with a WHERE clause to establish which records are updated.

- *Make-table queries* use SELECT `field_names` INTO `dest_table` FROM `source_table` statements to create a new table, `dest_table`, with fields specified by the `field_names` list.

Examples of the use of these four SQL statements are presented in separate sections later in this chapter.

Executing Action Queries with VBA Code

Action queries don't select a group of records; as a result, action queries don't return Recordset objects. You use the Execute method to carry out action queries. The differences between the two methods of executing action queries are described in the following two sections.

▶ **See** "Connection Methods," **p. 75**

You execute action queries by applying the Execute method to an ADODB.Connection or ADODB.Command object. The syntax for execution on a Connection object is

```
cnnName.Execute strSQL, [lngRecordsAffected,
    [adCmdText [+ adExecuteAsync]]]
```

▶ **See** "Command Methods," **p. 96**

Using the Command object requires you to specify the CommandText property and then execute the Command:

```
cmmName.CommandText = strSQL
cmmName.Execute[lngRecordsAffected, [avarParameters,
    [adCmdText [+ adExecuteAsync]]]]
```

Following is a description of the arguments for the preceding syntax examples:

- strSQL is the SQL statement for the action query.

- lngRecordsAffected is an optional buffer argument that returns the number of records added, deleted, or updated by the query.

- avarParameters is an optional argument for the Command object only that contains a single-dimension **Variant** array of parameter values created by an **Array**(varParam1, varParam2, . . . varParamN) function.

- adCmdText is an optional argument that instructs the query processor to treat strSQL as an SQL statement.

- adExecuteAsync is an optional argument (flag) arithmetically added to adCmdText, if present, to execute the query asynchronously.

The `ExecuteComplete` event fires when the action query finishes executing, either synchronously (program execution waits for completion) or asynchronously (program execution continues while the query executes).

Equivalents of Action Queries in VBA Code

Each of the preceding types of action SQL statements (except the make-table type) has corresponding `ADODB.Recordset` methods. ADO 2.0 doesn't support Jet's `TableDefs` collection or `TableDef` object. Table 7.1 lists the action query type, SQL statement, and the equivalent `ADODB.Recordset` code. The `rsName` object in Table 7.1 must be an updatable `Recordset` object having a static, dynamic, or keyset cursor.

TABLE 7.1   COMPARING ACTION QUERY SQL STATEMENTS AND VISUAL BASIC METHODS

Action Query	SQL Syntax	Visual Basic Method(s)

Append	`INSERT INTO`	`rsName.AddNew`
		 `rsName("Field") =`
		 `Value . . . rsName.Update`

Delete	`DELETE . . . FROM`	`rsName.Delete`
Update	`UPDATE . . . SET`	`rsName("Field") =` `Value . . .rsName.Update`

Maintaining Referential Integrity When Executing Action Queries

When you use append, delete, and update queries, you need to observe the referential integrity rules described in Chapter 5. If you're using a Jet database created in Microsoft Access with default relations you established with the Relationships dialog box, the Jet database engine enforces referential integrity rules for you. (This approach assumes that you marked the Enforce Referential Integrity check box when you established the default relations.)

▶ See "Defining Transactions and the ACID Test," **p. 739**

The Jet database engine enforces referential integrity by applying transaction-processing methods with append, delete, and update operations. The Jet engine adds the equivalent of a `BEGIN TRANS[ACTION]` command before your SQL statement and terminates the statement with a `COMMIT TRANS[ACTION]` command. If, for example, your delete or append SQL statement would create orphaned records, the Jet database engine detects this violation of referential integrity and issues the equivalent of a `ROLLBACK TRANS[ACTION]` command, instead of executing `COMMIT TRANS[ACTION]`. The transaction commands are based on SQL Server's SQL implementation; equivalent methods of the `ADODB.Connection` object are `BeginTrans`, `CommitTrans`, and `RollbackTrans`, respectively.

If you use a database type other than a Jet or a client/server database, it's up to you to enforce referential integrity with VBA code.

USING THE SQL ACTION QUERIES

The following examples use the four types of action queries supported by Jet SQL. All four examples use the Crosstab.mdb database opened in the VisData application.

Creating New Tables with Make-Table Queries

To avoid modifying the existing tables in the Crosstab.mdb database, the first action query example creates a new table from the Orders table, tblOrders, which includes all orders that have order dates earlier than December 31, 1994. To test make-table action query syntax, type the following in VisData's SQL Statement window:

```
SELECT *, OrderDate
    INTO tblOrders
    FROM Orders
    WHERE OrderDate<#1/1/95#
```

You must include the `OrderDate` entry in the `SELECT` list because Jet SQL does not enable you to specify a `WHERE` criterion on a field that is not explicitly declared in the `SELECT` list. Figure 7.11 shows the new tblOrders node expanded to display the field list.

7

RUNNING
CROSSTAB AND
ACTION QUERIES

FIGURE 7.11

Creating in VisData a new table from obsolete sales orders.

NOTE

The tblOrders table doesn't appear in the Tables/Queries window of the VisData application until you right-click any table name in the list and then choose Refresh List from the pop-up shortcut menu. This menu choice applies the `Refresh` method to the collections of the Crosstab.mdb database. (The Tables viewing option must also be selected in the Tables/Queries window of the VisData application.)

Use a make-table query to create a backup of a table prior to testing other SQL action statements on the table. If your append, update, or delete query gives an unexpected result, you can start fresh by deleting all records in the original table and appending all records from the backup table.

You can add an IN clause to your make-table query to create a table in another database. The full syntax of an SQL make-table clause is this:

```
SELECT [ALL¦DISTINCT¦DISTINCTROW] select_list
    INTO dest_table [IN database_name[ connect_string]]
    FROM source_table
    WHERE criteria
```

Thus you can create a tblOrders table in the C:\Program Files\Microsoft Office\Office\Samples\Northwind.mdb database (if you have the Northwind Traders database installed in the default directory) with the following statement:

```
SELECT *, OrderDate
    INTO tblOrders
        IN "C:\Program Files\Microsoft Office\Office\Samples\Northwind.mdb "
    FROM Orders
    WHERE OrderDate<#1/1/95#
```

Appending Records to Existing Tables

You can append records for dates earlier than 1994 to the tblOrders table with the following append query statement:

```
INSERT INTO tblOrders (OrderID, CustomerID, EmployeeID,
     OrderDate], ShippedDate)
    SELECT OrderID, CustomerID, EmployeeID, OrderDate,
        ShippedDate
    FROM Orders
    WHERE OrderDate <#1/1/94#
```

You need to explicitly declare the field list of both the destination table (tblOrders) and the source table (Orders) if you use a WHERE criterion. The preceding field list adds only the important field values of the Orders table. The field list of the destination table must be enclosed within parentheses. If you attempt to use the asterisk (*) to add all fields and then add the [OrderDate] field to the SELECT statement as in the make-table example, you receive a syntax-error message.

Updating Data Values in Tables

To change values in data fields, you use the UPDATE predicate. The SET clause specifies the expression used to update one or more fields. The following update action query SQL statement changes the ShippedDate field in the tblOrders table for every order shipped in April 1994 to a date two days later by adding two to the existing value of the ShippedDate field:

```
UPDATE tblOrders
    SET ShippedDate = ShippedDate + 2
    WHERE OrderDate BETWEEN #4/1/94# AND #4/30/94#;
```

If you want to update the values of more than one field, add the field name, the equal sign (=), and an expression separated from the preceding SET expression with a comma (,).

Deleting Records from Tables

The simplest and most potentially destructive of the action queries is the delete query. If you execute a delete query and forget to add a WHERE criterion, all the records in your table can disappear in an instant. To delete the records for the last half of 1994 from the tblOrders table, use the following statement:

```
DELETE FROM tblOrders
    WHERE [OrderDate] Between #7/1/94# And #12/31/94#;
```

You now can safely verify that the DELETE FROM tblOrders statement without the WHERE clause does indeed delete all records in the table.

CONNECTING TO DESKTOP DATA SOURCES WITH ODBC

IN THIS CHAPTER

Microsoft's Open Database Connectivity (ODBC) Application Programming Interface (API) was one of the first members of the Windows Open Services API (WOSA) to be released as a commercial product. WOSA is a suite of application programming interfaces for Windows applications intended to simplify and standardize the programming of a variety of classes of Windows-based procedures. Other widely used components of WOSA include the Messaging API (MAPI) employed by Microsoft Mail and Microsoft Exchange and the Telephony API (TAPI) for modem control, call routing, and voice mail. The License Service API (LSAPI), Windows SNA API, Windows Sockets, Microsoft Remote Procedure Call (RPC), Extensions for Real-Time Market Data (WOSA/XRT), and Extensions for Financial Services (WOSA/XFS) were the most commonly used WOSA components when this edition was written.

> **NOTE**
>
> WOSA rapidly is approaching obsolescence. Microsoft intends ultimately to replace the WOSA C/C++ APIs with COM components under the Windows Distributed interNet Architecture (DNA) banner. OLE DB and OLE DB for online analytical processing (OLAP) are the first two DNA members; OLE DB is a direct substitute for ODBC. DNA Financial Services (DNA FS) is destined to replace WOSA/XRT for the securities industry and WOSA/XFS for banking. A white paper describing DNA FS is available for download at
> `http://www.microsoft.com/industry/finserv/dna/windna_banking.stm`. A general white paper describing Windows DNA technology is available at `http://www.microsoft.com/dna/overview/dnawp.asp`. COM+, which was in the beta-testing stage when this edition was written, is a key ingredient in automating the integration of Windows DNA components.

This chapter explains the structure of the ODBC API and how ADO uses the ODBC API with the Microsoft OLE DB Provider for ODBC (commonly called by its code name, "Kagera"). Kagera takes the place of the ODBC Driver Manager, so performance is about the same as using ODBC with DAO 3.5. You need only use the ODBC API and Kagera if you want to connect to desktop database tables, such as those of dBASE, FoxPro, Visual FoxPro, or Paradox 4.x. The native OLE DB data provider for Jet 3.5x (code-named "Jolt") and ADO 2.0 don't support desktop database tables, other than Jet tables, attached to Jet databases. Thus you must use the ODBC drivers for non-Jet desktop database tables until Microsoft or third parties release native OLE DB data providers for these products. You must also use Kagera to connect ADO to client/server relational database management systems (RDBMSs) that don't have native OLE DB data providers. This chapter briefly explains how to use the ODBC API and ODBC drivers with client/server RDBMSs such as Microsoft SQL Server, Sybase, Oracle, and Informix.

8

CONNECTING TO
DESKTOP DATA
SOURCES

> **NOTE**
>
> Visual Studio 6.0 installs version 3.51 of the ODBC Administrator, ODBC Driver Manager, and ODBC support files, plus ODBC drivers you select during the Visual Studio installation process. Desktop database drivers, with the exception of that for Visual FoxPro 6.0, also are version 3.51. Client/server RDBMS drivers, such as those for Microsoft SQL Server and Oracle don't follow the ODBC component version numbering system.

UNDERSTANDING THE STRUCTURE OF THE ODBC API

The ODBC API consists of Windows dynamic link libraries (DLLs) that include sets of functions to provide the following two fundamental database services for all database types for which ODBC drivers are available:

- Installing, setting up, and removing ODBC data sources. A *data source* is a named connection to a database, commonly called a data source name (DSN). You need an ODBC driver for each different type of database to which your applications connect through Kagera. ODBC uses the Odbcinst.dll library to set up and remove data sources. Odbcad32.exe is a 32-bit standalone, executable application (ODBC Administrator) for setting up ODBC data sources; Odbcad32.exe's icon appears in Control Panel's window.

- Managing the communication of queries and other SQL statements from client front ends to database server back ends and the transfer of query result sets or confirmations of the execution of action queries in the reverse direction. Kagera, the ODBC driver for the data source, passes SQL statements to the driver. After the Jet query engine or a client/server RDBMS processes a SELECT query, Kagera returns the rows through to your application. ODBC drivers for other desktop databases process the query with their own engine. When processing an INSERT, UPDATE, or DELETE query, the driver returns the number of rows affected by the query.

The ODBC API implements SQL as a call-level interface (CLI). A call-level interface employs a set of standard functions to perform specific duties, such as translating SQL queries from ANSI SQL to the dialect of SQL used by the desktop database or RDBMS, representing the products' field data types by an extended set of SQL-92 field data types, and handling error conditions. The ODBC API conforms to the CLI standard (SQL CAE specification—1992) developed by the SQL Access Group (SAG), a consortium of client/server RDBMS software publishers and users who have a large stake in the success of client/server database technology.

Visual Basic database applications that use the ODBC API have a multitiered structure, similar to the structure for the desktop databases supported by the ISAM DLLs for the Jet database engine. The full structure of a Visual Basic database application that uses the features of the ODBC API appears in Figure 8.1.

FIGURE 8.1

The architecture of the ODBC API as it is employed by Visual Basic 6.0 database applications using ADO.

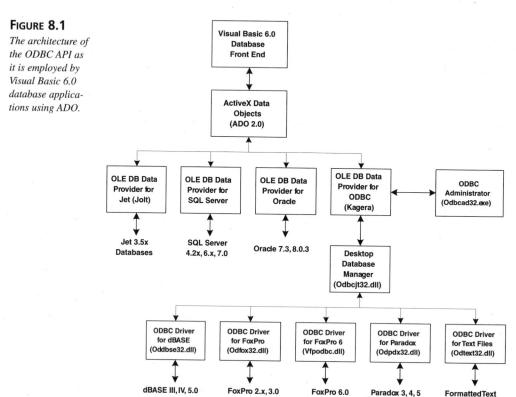

Microsoft supplies an ODBC driver for its versions of SQL Server 4.21 through 7.0; the Sqlsvr32.dll driver (version 3.70 for Visual Studio 6) also can be used with Sybase SQL Server through version 4.9.2. (Sqlsvr32.dll also is compatible with Sybase System 10, but does not provide for advanced features of the newer Sybase RDBMS.) Visual Studio 6.0 installs a single-tier driver (shown in Figure 8.1), which accommodates the most common database and text file formats. Independent software vendors (ISVs), such as Intersolv, supply suites of ODBC drivers for a variety of desktop DBMs and client/server RDBMSs.

The following sections describe the basic features of the ODBC API and how to use the ODBC API with desktop database managers and unconventional data sources, such as worksheets and text files.

Single-Tier and Multiple-Tier ODBC Drivers

ODBC drivers are classified as members of one of the following categories:

- *Single-tier* ODBC drivers are designed for use with DBMs that do not have the capability of processing ANSI SQL statements. Single-tier drivers translate ANSI SQL statements into a long series of low-level instructions that operate directly on the file(s) that constitute the database. At present, Microsoft single-tier ODBC drivers connect to dBASE, FoxPro, Visual FoxPro, Paradox, Excel, and text files. You must obtain a third-party ODBC driver for Btrieve databases.

- *Multiple-tier* ODBC drivers rely on the client/server RDBMS to process SQL statements. Using the back-end server to process queries is a more efficient process than the single-tier approach in a multiuser environment. Network traffic is minimized because the server returns only the rows specified by the criteria of your SQL statement. Visual Basic 6.0 includes Sqlsvr32.dll, the 32-bit ODBC version 3.70 driver for Microsoft SQL Server 4.2x, 6.x, and 7.0. Visual Studio 6.0 also includes a Microsoft 32-bit ODBC driver for Oracle 7.3 and 8.x databases. To use the Oracle driver, you must have the Oracle client DLLs installed on the computer.

This chapter concentrates on the use of single-tier ODBC drivers because it's likely that native OLE DB data providers for all popular client/server RDBMSs will be available by the time you read this book.

ODBC API Conformance Levels

Three levels of conformance to the ODBC API are defined: core level, level1, and level2. to the ODBC API are defined: core level, level 1, and level 2. The general definitions of each of the three levels are as follows:

- *Core-level* conformance provides for connecting to the database, preparing and executing SQL statements, receiving query-result data sets, committing or rolling back transactions, and retrieving error information.

- *Level 1* conformance is similar to core-level conformance and adds connectivity to data sources with dialogs designed specifically for the ODBC driver, get- and set-connection options, and obtain-catalog and driver/data source capabilities.

- *Level 2* conformance is similar to level 1 conformance and adds the ability to list and browse the connections to data sources available to the client, retrieve query results sets in array format, use scrollable cursors, and obtain additional catalog information (such as privileges, keys, and lists of stored procedures).

Core-level conformance meets the requirements of the SAG CLI specification. Most early commercial ODBC drivers provide level 1 conformance, plus the scrollable cursor feature of

ODBC SQL Conformance Levels

The ODBC API specifies three levels of conformance to SQL grammar: minimum, core, and extended. The SQL conformance levels define the ANSI SQL reserved words that ODBC drivers and data sources must be able to process. Table 8.1 lists the data manipulation language (DML), data definition language (DDL), and data control language (DCL) SQL reserved words required for each level of conformance. SQL data types and expressions also are listed. Successively higher levels of grammar include the grammar of the lower levels. The core SQL grammar conforms to the requirements of the SQL Access Group CAE SQL draft specification—1991; almost all commercial ODBC drivers conform at least to the core-level SQL grammar.

TABLE 8.1 SQL GRAMMAR, DATA TYPE, AND EXPRESSION SUPPORT OF ODBC GRAMMAR CONFORMANCE LEVELS

Level	DML Statements	DDL/DCL Statements	Data Types	Expressions
Minimum	SELECT, INSERT, UPDATED SEARCHED, DELETE SEARCHED, COMMIT TRANSACTION, ROLLBACK TRANSACTION	CREATE TABLE, DROP TABLE	CHAR	Simple arithmetic
Core	Full SELECT, positioned UPDATE, and positioned DELETE	ALTER TABLE, CREATE INDEX, DROP INDEX, CREATE VIEW, DROP VIEW, GRANT, REVOKE	VARCHAR, DECIMAL, NUMERIC, SMALLINT, INTEGER, REAL, FLOAT, DOUBLE PRECISION	Subqueries and aggregate functions
Extended	LEFT OUTER JOIN, RIGHT	Batch SQL statements,	LONG VARCHAR,	SUB-STRING,

Level	DML Statements	DDL/DCL Statements	Data Types	Expressions
	OUTER JOIN	stored procedures	BIT, TINYINT, BIGINT, BINARY, VARBINARY, LONG VARBINARY, DATE, TIME, TIMESTAMP	ABS

The extended-level SQL grammar category is a catchall for extensions to ANSI SQL that were standardized in SQL-92, such as reserved words to enforce referential integrity and nonstandard reserved words that are found in many RDBMS implementations of SQL.

> **NOTE**
>
> At the time this book was written, there were no commercial ODBC drivers that fully supported the equivalent of Access SQL's PIVOT and TRANSFORM keywords used to create crosstab queries. The crosstab query, a subject of the previous chapter, is one of the most useful forms of summary queries. In most cases, the Access database engine sends GROUP BY statements to the server and then transforms the results into crosstab form.

Built-in ODBC Scalar Functions

The ODBC API contains various built-in functions you can use to make the ANSI SQL code you send to the RDBMS's ODBC driver independent of the RDBMS in use. To implement the ODBC scalar functions, you use the ODBC escape shorthand syntax. Escape shorthand syntax, called simply *escape syntax* in this book, encloses the shorthand syntax within French braces ({}). The escape syntax for all ODBC functions is

```
{fn ODBCFunction([Argument(s)])}
```

Thus to return the first name and last name of a person from values in the first_name and last_name fields of a table, you use the following statement:

```
{fn CONCAT(first_name, CONCAT(' ', last_name))}
```

You need an embedded CONCAT() function because CONCAT() only supports concatenation of two strings. (This function is unlike concatenation with Visual Basic's & symbol, which enables you to concatenate numeric data types with strings.) Note that the standard literal string identifier character is the single quote (', an apostrophe) in ANSI SQL.

The sections that follow provide lists that compare the ODBC scalar functions for string, numeric, and date/time values with the equivalent functions of Visual Basic 6.0 (where equivalents exist). This information is derived from the *Programmer's Reference for the Microsoft Open Database Connectivity Software Development Kit* version 2.0 and the ODBC SDK version 2.10, which is included on the MSDN CD-ROMs.

> **NOTE**
>
> In most cases, you can use the built-in functions of Visual Basic 6.0 in your application code to perform the same operations offered by the ODBC scalar functions. However, you may need to use the ODBC scalar functions to create joins between table fields of different data types.

String Manipulation Functions

Table 8.2 lists the ODBC 3.x string functions and their equivalent functions, where available, in VBA.

TABLE 8.2   THE SCALAR STRING FUNCTIONS OF ODBC VERSION 3.*x*

ODBC String Function	*VBA*	*Purpose*
ASCII(*string_exp*)	**Asc**(*string_exp*)	Returns the ASCII code value of the leftmost character of a string function>
CHAR(*integer_exp*)	**Chr**(*integer_exp*)	Returns the ASCII character whose code is *integer_exp*
CONCAT(*string1*, *string2*)	**&**	Concatenates *string1* and *string2*
INSERT(*string1*, *start*, *length*, *string2*)	None	Replaces the length characters of *string1* beginning at *string2*
LEFT(*string_exp*, *count*)	**Left**(*string_exp*, *count*)	Returns the leftmost count characters

ODBC String Function	VBA	Purpose
LENGTH(*string_exp*)	**Len**(*string_exp*)	Returns an integer representing the length of the string
LOCATE(*string1*, *string2*[, *start*])	**InStr**(*string1*, *string2*[, *start*])	Returns an integer representing the position of *string2* in *string1*
LCASE(string_exp)	**LCase**(*string_exp*)	Returns an all-lowercase string
REPEAT(*string_exp*, consisting *count*)	**String**(*string_ exp*, *count*)	Returns a string of *string_exp* repeated *count* times
RIGHT(*string_exp*, *count*)	**Right**(*string_exp*, *count*)	Returns the rightmost *count* characters
RTRIM(*string_exp*)	**RTrim**(*string_exp*)	Removes trailing blanks
SUBSTRING(*string_exp*, *start*, *length*)	**Mid**(*string_exp*, *start*, *length*)	Returns *length* characters beginning at *start*
UCASE(*string_exp*)	**UCase**(*string_exp*)	Returns an all-uppercase string

8

CONNECTING TO
DESKTOP DATA
SOURCES

Numeric Scalar Functions

Table 8.3 lists the ODBC numeric functions (except for trigonometric functions) and their equivalent functions, where available, in VBA.

TABLE 8.3   THE NUMERIC SCALAR FUNCTIONS AVAILABLE IN ODBC VERSION 3.*x*

ODBC Numeric Function	VBA	Purpose
ABS(*numeric_exp*)	**Abs**(*numeric_exp*)	Returns the absolute value of the expression
CEILING(*numeric_exp*)	**Int**(*numeric_exp*)	Returns the smallest integer greater than the expression

continues

TABLE 8.3   CONTINUED

ODBC Numeric Function	VBA	Purpose
EXP(*numeric_exp*)	**Exp**(*numeric_exp*)	Returns the exponential value of the expressionexponential value function
FLOOR(*numeric_exp*)	**Fix**(*numeric_exp*)	Returns the largest integer less than or equal to the expression
LOG(*float_exp*)	**Log**(*float_exp*)	Returns the natural (Naperian) logarithm of the expression
MOD(*integer_exp*)	**Mod**(*integer_exp*)	Returns the remainder of integer division as an integer
PI()	None	Returns the value of π as a floating-point number
RAND([*integer_exp*])	**Rnd**([*integer_exp*])	Returns a random floating-point number with an optional seed value
SIGN(*numeric_exp*)	**Sgn**(*numeric_exp*)	Returns -1 for values less than 0, 0 for 0 values, and 1 for values greater than 0
SQRT(*float_exp*)	**Sqr**(*float_exp*)	Returns the square root of a floating point value

Date, Time, and Timestamp Functions

Table 8.4 lists the ODBC date, time, and timestamp functions and their equivalent functions, where available, in VBA.

TABLE 8.4   THE DATE/TIME SCALAR FUNCTIONS OF ODBC VERSION 3.X

ODBC Date/ Time Function	VBA	Purpose
NOW()	**Now**	Returns the date and time in TIMESTAMP format
CURDATE()	**Date**	Returns the current date
CURTIME()	**Time**	Returns the current time
DAYOFMONTH(*date_exp*)	**DatePart** ("d", *date_exp*)	Returns the day of the month

ODBC Date/ Time Function	VBA	Purpose
DAYOFWEEK(*date_exp*)	**DatePart**("w", *date_exp*)	Returns the day of the week (Sunday = 1)
DAYOFYEAR(*date_exp*)	**DatePart**("y", *date_exp*)	Returns the Julian date
HOUR(*time_exp*)	None	Returns the hour (0 to 23)
MINUTE(*time_exp*)	None	Returns the minute (0 to 59)
MONTH(*date_exp*)	**DatePart**("m", *date_exp*)	Returns the number of the month
QUARTER(*date_exp*)	**DatePart**("q", *date_exp*)	Returns the number of the calendar quarter
SECOND(*time_exp*)	None	Returns the second (0 to 60)
WEEK(*date_exp*)	**DatePart**("ww", *date_exp*)	Returns the week number (1 to 52—used primarily by European firms)
YEAR(*date_exp*)	**DatePart**("yyyy", *date_exp*)	Returns the four-digit year

EXPLORING ODBC INITIALIZATION FILES AND REGISTRY ENTRIES

Thirty-two-bit Odbcad32.exe creates or deletes entries in the two ODBC initialization files in your \Windows or \Winnt folder and the Windows 9x or Windows NT Registry. The purpose of these two initialization files, the Registry entries, and the relevance of the entries they contain are explained in the sections that follow.

The Three DSN Types

ODBC 3.5+ offers the three following types of DSNs:

- *User DSNs* are specific to the individual logged on to the server or workstation. DSN information is located in the HKEY_CURRENT_USER Registry hive.
- *System DSNs* are available to all workstation users and, when installed on the server, are accessible by all server-side applications. DSN data appears in the HKEY_LOCAL_MACHINE hive.

- *File DSNs* (*Filename*.dsn) are text files defining a DSN. File DSNs may be stored locally or on a network share. File DSNs don't use Registry entries. File DSNs are ODBC's equivalent to ADO's Data Link files (*Filename*.udl).

▶ **See** "Designing Efficient MTS Components," p. **1005**

> **TIP**
>
> If you must use ODBC to connect Microsoft Transaction Server (MTS) components to databases, don't use a File DSN. File DSNs cause a serious performance hit. Use a System DSN on the MTS server to provide database connectivity to components.

The most common DSN type for workstations is a User DSN; servers always use System DSN. Figure 8.2 shows a System DSN (FoodMart) installed by Visual Studio 6.0 and a DSN added to test the Microsoft Oracle ODBC driver. Sections later in the chapter describe how to create DSNs.

FIGURE 8.2

The System DSN page of the ODBC Data Source Administrator with Jet and Oracle8 data sources.

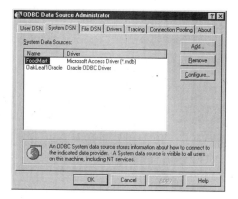

Odbcinst.ini

After installing the ODBC driver manager and administrator files, the first step in providing SQL connectivity is to install ODBC drivers for the types of databases to which your applications connect. By default, Visual Studio 6.0 installs 10 ODBC drivers. Entries for available 32-bit ODBC drivers appear in the [ODBC 32 bit Drivers] section of Odbcinst.ini. The content of the \Window6 s\Odbcinst.ini file of the OAKLEAF1 workstation computer used to write this edition appears as follows:

```
[ODBC 32 bit Drivers]
SQL Server (32 bit)=Installed
Microsoft ODBC for Oracle (32 bit)=Installed
Microsoft Visual FoxPro Driver (32 bit)=Installed
Microsoft Access Driver (*.mdb) (32 bit)=Installed
```

```
Microsoft Excel Driver (*.xls) (32 bit)=Installed
Microsoft Text Driver (*.txt; *.csv) (32 bit)=Installed
Microsoft dBase Driver (*.dbf) (32 bit)=Installed
Microsoft Paradox Driver (*.db ) (32 bit)=Installed
Microsoft FoxPro Driver (*.dbf) (32 bit)=Installed
Oracle ODBC Driver (32 bit)=Installed

[SQL Server (32 bit)]
Driver=C:\WINNT\System32\sqlsrv32.dll
Setup=C:\WINNT\System32\sqlsrv32.dll
32Bit=1

[Microsoft ODBC for Oracle (32 bit)]
Driver=C:\WINNT\System32\MSORCL32.DLL
Setup=C:\WINNT\System32\MSORCL32.DLL
32Bit=1

[Microsoft Visual FoxPro Driver (32 bit)]
Driver=C:\WINNT\System32\vfpodbc.dll
Setup=C:\WINNT\System32\vfpodbc.dll
32Bit=1

[Microsoft Access Driver (*.mdb) (32 bit)]
Driver=C:\WINNT\System32\odbcjt32.dll
Setup=C:\WINNT\System32\odbcjt32.dll
32Bit=1

[Microsoft Excel Driver (*.xls) (32 bit)]
Driver=C:\WINNT\System32\odbcjt32.dll
Setup=C:\WINNT\System32\odexl32.dll
32Bit=1

[Microsoft Text Driver (*.txt; *.csv) (32 bit)]
Driver=C:\WINNT\System32\odbcjt32.dll
Setup=C:\WINNT\System32\odtext32.dll
32Bit=1

[Microsoft dBase Driver (*.dbf) (32 bit)]
Driver=C:\WINNT\System32\odbcjt32.dll
Setup=C:\WINNT\System32\oddbse32.dll
32Bit=1

[Microsoft Paradox Driver (*.db ) (32 bit)]
Driver=C:\WINNT\System32\odbcjt32.dll
Setup=C:\WINNT\System32\odpdx32.dll
32Bit=1

[Microsoft FoxPro Driver (*.dbf) (32 bit)]
Driver=C:\WINNT\System32\odbcjt32.dll
Setup=C:\WINNT\System32\odfox32.dll
32Bit=1
```

8

CONNECTING TO DESKTOP DATA SOURCES

```
[Oracle ODBC Driver (32 bit)]
Driver=C:\WINNT\System32\SQORA32.DLL
Setup=C:\WINNT\System32\SQORAS32.DLL
32Bit=1
```

Only 32-bit data sources appear in the Drivers page when you launch the 32-bit ODBC Administrator application from Windows 9x or Windows NT's Control Panel and then click the Drivers tab of the ODBC Data Source Administrator properties sheet. Figure 8.3 shows ODBC Administrator displaying the drivers listed in the [ODBC 32 bit Drivers] section of the preceding Odbdinst.ini file. You can create a DSN for any of the listed drivers.

FIGURE 8.3

The Drivers page of the 32-bit ODBC Data Source Administrator application.

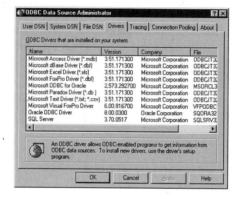

Odbc.ini

Entries in the Odbc.ini initialization file designate the ODBC data sources that appear in the User DSN and System DSN pages of the ODBC Administrator application. File DSNs aren't listed in Odbc.ini. As is the case for Odbcinst.ini, Odbc.ini has a two-tiered structure. A list of data sources appears in the Odbc.ini [ODBC Data Sources] section, followed by a section (MQIS, for example) that provides the location of the ODBC driver for the data source.

> **NOTE**
>
> Earlier versions of ODBC stored detailed information about the ODBC connection in Odbc.ini. Detailed settings for individual 32-bit drivers now are stored in the Registry.

The content of the Odbc.ini file that is used in conjunction with the Odbcinst.ini file (described in the preceding section) appears as follows:

```
[ODBC 32 bit Data Sources]
MQIS=SQL Server (32 bit)
MS Access 97 Database=Microsoft Access Driver (*.mdb) (32 bit)
Visual FoxPro Database=Microsoft Visual FoxPro Driver (32 bit)
Visual FoxPro Tables=Microsoft Visual FoxPro Driver (32 bit)
FoodMart=Microsoft Access Driver (*.mdb) (32 bit)
OakLeaf1Oracle=Oracle ODBC Driver (32 bit)

[MQIS]
Driver32=D:\WINNT\System32\sqlsrv32.dll

[MS Access 97 Database]
Driver32=D:\WINNT\System32\odbcjt32.dll

[Visual FoxPro Database]
Driver32=D:\WINNT\System32\vfpodbc.dll

[Visual FoxPro Tables]
Driver32=D:\WINNT\System32\vfpodbc.dll

[FoodMart]
Driver32=D:\WINNT\System32\odbcjt32.dll

[OakLeaf1Oracle]
Driver32=D:\WINNT\System32\SQORA32.DLL
```

The first four entries in Odbc.ini are User DSNs (see Figure 8.4). MQIS is the data source for Microsoft Message Queue Server installed from the Windows NT 4.0 Option Pack; the Access and FoxPro data sources are installed by Microsoft Office 97. The FoodMart and OakLeaf1Oracle entries are System DSNs (refer to Figure 8.2).

8

CONNECTING TO
DESKTOP DATA
SOURCES

FIGURE 8.4

ODBC user data sources for SQL Server and desktop databases shown on the User DSN page of ODBC Administrator.

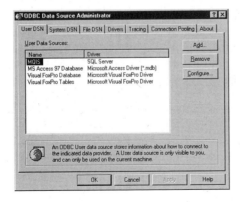

ODBCINST.INI and ODBC.INI Registry Keys

Information on 32-bit ODBC drivers and data sources that use 32-bit ODBC drivers contained in Odbcinst.ini and Odbc.ini is duplicated in the Registry. The HKEY_LOCAL_MACHINE\SOFT-WARE\ODBC\ODBCINST.INI key includes a set of subkeys that duplicate the sections of Odbcinst.ini (see Figure 8.5). The subkeys of HKEY_CURRENT_USER\Software\ODBC\ODBC.INI are the same as the sections of Odbc.ini, as illustrated by Figure 8.6. Data sources might vary for multiple users of the same computer, which explains the location of data source information in the HKEY_CURRENT_USER subkey. Information on 16-bit drivers and data sources that rely only on 16-bit drivers does not appear in the Windows 9x or the Windows NT Registry.

FIGURE 8.5

Entries in the ODBCINST.INI *Registry subkey for installed 32-bit ODBC 3.51 drivers.*

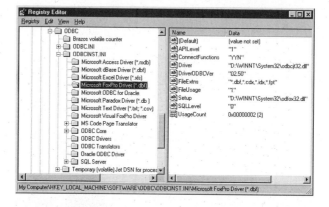

FIGURE 8.6

Entries in the ODBC.INI *Registry subkey for ODBC data sources based on 32-bit ODBC 3.51 drivers.*

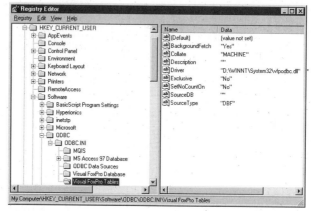

Duplication of 32-bit entries in the Odbcinst.ini, Odbc.ini, and the Registry appears to be intended for backward compatibility when upgrading Windows 3.1x to Windows 9x. Many developers directly edit the Windows 3.x ODBCINST.INI and ODBC.INI files either manually or in code (using the Windows API's WritePrivateProfileString function). Use the 32-bit ODBC Administrator to edit these entries so as to create the required Registry entries. The SaveSettings function of Visual Basic 6.0 is only capable of adding entries to the HKEY_CURRENT_USER\Software\VB and VBA Program Settings\AppName\SectionName subkeys.

Connection Pooling and Tracing

ODBC 3.51, like ADO 2.0, offers connection pooling to minimize repeated opening and closing of connections to databases as a result of short periods of front-end inactivity. Connection pooling is available for Microsoft's Access, SQL Server, and Oracle drivers, and many third-party ODBC drivers. Connection pooling is more important for client/server RDBMSs than for desktop databases. Figure 8.7 shows the Connection Pooling page of the ODBC Administrator.

FIGURE 8.7

Setting the ConnectionTime out *and* RetryWaitInter val *properties for Microsoft's Oracle ODBC driver.*

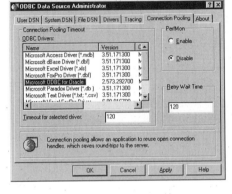

ODBC maintains a cached connection for a period determined by the value (seconds) in the Timeout for Selected Driver text box. The Retry Wait Time entry (seconds) determines the time to wait to retry a failed connection to a server or a remote desktop database file. Enabling PerfMon (Performance Monitor) logs connection statistics.

You can trace ODBC API calls for troubleshooting by clicking the Start Tracing Now button of the Tracing page (see Figure 8.8). Alternatively, you can trace ODBC API calls from within Visual Studio Analyzer. Tracing causes a severe performance hit to database access, and trace logs (Sql.log) can become very large if you forget to stop the tracing process.

FIGURE 8.8

The Tracing page of the ODBC Administrator.

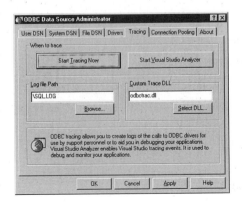

8

CONNECTING TO
DESKTOP DATA
SOURCES

> **NOTE**
>
> Verify that you have the latest versions of Microsoft's ODBC Administrator, Driver Manager, and support files in the About page of the ODBC Administrator. Unless noted in accompanying Readme.txt files for new ODBC components, all files listed in the About page should have the same version number.

CREATING AND USING A DSN FOR DBASE TABLES

The continuing requirement for ODBC DSNs in an ADO development environment is to support desktop database formats for which native OLE DB data providers aren't available. It's likely that Microsoft will supply OLE DB data providers for Visual FoxPro tables and databases, as well as Excel worksheets and formatted text files. Availability of OLE DB data providers for dBASE and Paradox tables depends on the priorities of Inprise Corp. (formerly Borland International) and Corel Systems Corp., respectively.

Creating a New System DSN

To create an ODBC System DSN for a set of dBASE 5 tables and indexes created from Nwind.mdb's Orders and Order Details tables, do the following:

1. Launch ODBC Data Source Administrator from Control Panel and click the System DSN tab.

2. Click Add to open the New Data Source dialog; then select the Microsoft dBase Driver (*.dbf) from the list (see Figure 8.9).

FIGURE 8.9

Selecting the dBASE driver for a System DSN.

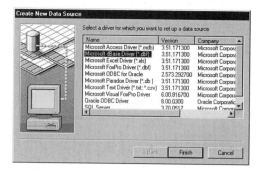

3. Click Finish to open the ODBC dBASE Setup dialog, click Options, and clear the Current Directory check box.

4. Type the name of the DSN in the Data Source Name text box and a description in the Description Text box.

5. Click Select Directory to open the Select Directory dialog and navigate to the folder in which the dBASE *.dbf and *.mdx files are located (see Figure 8.10). Click OK to close the dialog.

FIGURE 8.10

*Selecting the folder containing dBASE *.dbf files.*

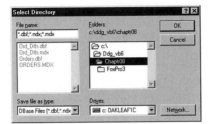

> **NOTE**
>
> A set of test dBASE files—Orders.dbf, Orders.mdx, Ord_Dtls.dbf, and Ord_Dtls.mdx—is included in the \Ddg_vb6\Chaptr08 folder of the accompanying CD-ROM.

6. Click Select Indexes to open the Select Indexes dialog to verify the presence of *.mdx or *.ndx indexes in the folder. Click OK to close the dialog.

> **NOTE**
>
> dBASE indexes are specified in a *Tablename*.inf file for each table in the database.

7. Unless you have a specific reason to change the default settings in the Driver frame of the Setup dialog, click OK to add your new System DSN to Odbc.ini and the Registry.

   The new System DSN appears in the System Data Sources list (see Figure 8.12). You can edit the properties of the DSN by clicking Configure to reopen the ODBC dBASE Setup Dialog.

Figure 8.12 shows the Registry entries for the dBASE System DSN.

Connecting to the dBASE Data Source Through Kagera

To test the Microsoft OLE DB Provider for ODBC with the new dBASE System DSN, do this:

1. Open a new test Data Project and double-click the DataEnvironment1 entry to open the DataEnvironment window.

FIGURE 8.11

The new dBASE System DSN added to ODBC Administrator's System Data Sources list.

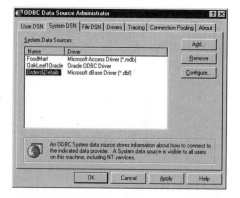

FIGURE 8.12

Registry entries for a dBASE system DSN.

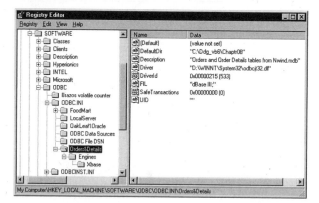

2. Right-click the Connection1 item and choose Properties to open the Connection1 Properties sheet.

3. Accept the default Microsoft OLE DB Provider for ODBC in the OLE DB providers list and click Next to display the Connection page.

4. In the Connection page, select the name of the dBASE System DSN (Orders&Details for this example) in the Use Data Source Name list and click Test Connection.

5. In the Advanced page, mark the Share Deny None check box in the Access Permissions list. Click OK to close the Connection1 Properties sheet.

6. Choose View, Data View Window to open the Data View window. Expand the Connection1 nodes to display the field lists for the two sample tables (see Figure 8.13).

7. Double-click one of the table nodes to open the Run Table window and display the table's contents (see Figure 8.14).

FIGURE 8.13

Connections, tables, and fields of a pair of dBASE tables displayed in the Data View window.

NOTE

dBASE has a table name length limitation of 10 characters, so some of the table names are truncated.

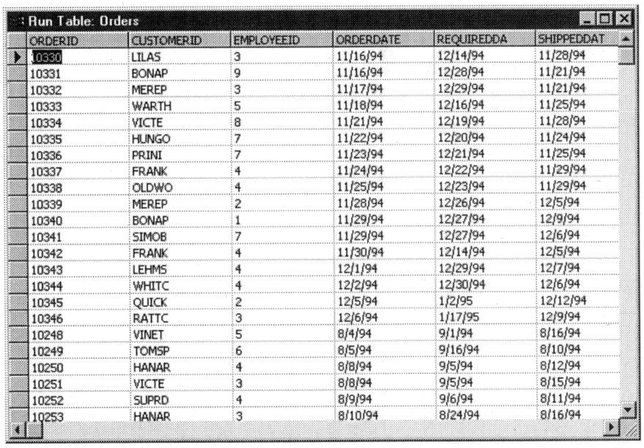

FIGURE 8.14

The first few records of the dBASE Orders.dbf table displayed in Data View's Run Table window.

ORDERID	CUSTOMERID	EMPLOYEEID	ORDERDATE	REQUIREDDA	SHIPPEDDAT
10330	LILAS	3	11/16/94	12/14/94	11/28/94
10331	BONAP	9	11/16/94	12/28/94	11/21/94
10332	MEREP	3	11/17/94	12/29/94	11/21/94
10333	WARTH	5	11/18/94	12/16/94	11/25/94
10334	VICTE	8	11/21/94	12/19/94	11/28/94
10335	HUNGO	7	11/22/94	12/20/94	11/24/94
10336	PRINI	7	11/23/94	12/21/94	11/25/94
10337	FRANK	4	11/24/94	12/22/94	11/29/94
10338	OLDWO	4	11/25/94	12/23/94	11/29/94
10339	MEREP	2	11/28/94	12/26/94	12/5/94
10340	BONAP	1	11/29/94	12/27/94	12/9/94
10341	SIMOB	7	11/29/94	12/27/94	12/6/94
10342	FRANK	4	11/30/94	12/14/94	12/5/94
10343	LEHMS	4	12/1/94	12/29/94	12/7/94
10344	WHITC	4	12/2/94	12/30/94	12/6/94
10345	QUICK	2	12/5/94	1/2/95	12/12/94
10346	RATTC	3	12/6/94	1/17/95	12/9/94
10248	VINET	5	8/4/94	9/1/94	8/16/94
10249	TOMSP	6	8/5/94	9/16/94	8/10/94
10250	HANAR	4	8/8/94	9/5/94	8/12/94
10251	VICTE	3	8/8/94	9/5/94	8/15/94
10252	SUPRD	4	8/9/94	9/6/94	8/11/94
10253	HANAR	3	8/10/94	8/24/94	8/16/94

At this point, you can use the dBASE Order.dbf and Ord_Dtls.dbf files with all supported `ADODB.Object` methods and properties. Neither ADO or DAO support transactions on dBASE `Connections` and `Workspaces`, respectively.

> **NOTE**
>
> A Jet 3.51 database file, Attached.mdb, is included in the \Ddg_vb6\Chaptr08 folder of the accompanying CD-ROM. Attached.mdb has attached dBASE, FoxPro, and Paradox tables. The purpose of Attached.mdb is to demonstrate the error (`Unspecified Error 3055`) you receive when attempting to use an `ADODB.Connection` object with the Jet provider (Jolt) to open attached tables (other than attached Jet tables).

AN INTRODUCTION TO
DATABASE FRONT-END DESIGN

PART

III

IN THIS PART

Designing a
Decision-Support
Front End

IN THIS CHAPTER

Your first production-database application that uses Visual Basic 6.0 is likely to be used for decision-support purposes. Industry sources estimate that decision-support applications constitute 75% or more of all of the database applications in use today. When you create a decision-support application for use with an existing relational database, you don't need to be concerned with database design, maintaining referential and domain integrity, or concurrency problems. (You do, however, need to take consistency issues into account if you're summarizing data.)

The purpose of a decision-support application is to transform raw data into useful information. Your primary task is to provide the users of your application with a simple, straightforward method of obtaining the data they need. This chapter begins by discussing how to organize that data. The chapter also discusses designing the user interface to make your application easy to understand and gives examples of forms that display information in graphical and tabular format. Finally, the chapter presents examples of the Visual Basic 6.0 code needed to create the graph, chart, and grid objects that display the selected information to the user.

NOTE

Browser-based decision-support applications have increased greatly in popularity as corporations add TCP/IP-based intranets and telecommuting and mobile employees gain Internet connectivity to intranets from home or on the road. The chapters in the first five sections of this book concentrate on conventional Visual Basic front-end designs that use standard forms for data input and display. Many of these forms can be deployed on an intranet as ActiveX Document objects, the subject of Chapter 23, "Using ActiveX Document Objects with Intranets." The principles of data organization and information presentation in the first few sections of this chapter apply to conventional and browser-based decision-support applications.

ORGANIZING THE DATA BEHIND A DECISION-SUPPORT FRONT END

The objective of most of today's decision-support applications is to replace printed reports with onscreen presentations of information. A successful decision-support application supplies "Information at Your Fingertips" (a Microsoft-trademarked corporate slogan). For midlevel managers and below, the video display unit (VDU) of a PC is the most common presentation platform. At the vice-presidential level and higher rungs in the corporate ladder, the information often is displayed on large-screen or projection video systems acting as a VDU for one PC in a conference setting.

Specifying the Data Sources

Typical relationships of data sources and information systems for a typical manufacturing company appear in the hierarchical structure shown in Figure 9.1. Data entry and online transaction processing (OLTP) activities primarily are confined to the lowest level of the hierarchy: operational databases. (The operational database level of the hierarchy often is called "the trenches.") The levels above the operational databases involve little or no data entry; these upper levels in the hierarchy are referred to as information systems (IS) or management information systems (MIS). The diagram shown in Figure 9.1 divides the information systems category into functional information systems at the directorate and vice-presidential level, and planning and forecasting information systems that are used by top management and corporate staff.

FIGURE 9.1

The hierarchy of information systems and databases for a manufacturing firm.

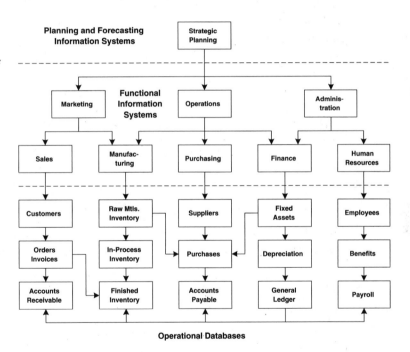

Depending on the size of the company and the type of computer hardware the firm uses, the operational databases may be located in a centralized mainframe system or distributed across several database servers in a client/server RDBMS environment. Combinations of mainframe and client/server environments are common for firms that are in the process of downsizing and distributing their operational databases. A small manufacturing firm might have all its operational databases in the form of multiple .DBF files that reside on a single file server.

If you're developing database applications for a firm with $10 million or more in annual sales, be prepared to deal with the connectivity issues raised by a wide variety of network operating systems and database management systems, including legacy (a synonym for *obsolete* among proponents of client/server RDBMSs) network and hierarchical DBMs. It's not uncommon for developers of database front ends to spend more time solving connectivity problems, both DBM and network related, than they spend designing, coding, and testing the entire front-end application.

You also might need to integrate data from online data sources into your database front-end application. Credit information from Dun & Bradstreet and TRW, stock prices from the Dow Jones News Service, and syndicated real estate transaction data from commercial providers are just a few of the uses for the data communication features of Visual Basic 6.0's aging Mscomm32.ocx control or third-party File Transfer Protocol (FTP) controls. Another data source that you may need to incorporate in your applications is the CD-ROM. Virtually all the 1990 census data is now available from the U.S. Bureau of the Census in .DBF format on CD-ROMs, and many companies publish phone, business, and other directories in .DBF and other desktop database formats on CD-ROMs.

> **NOTE**
>
> Although the World Wide Web provides access to a remarkable number of commercial databases, such as *Billboard* magazine's database of gold and platinum records, most syndicated (pay-per-view or pay-per-item) data currently is accessible only through terminal emulation. For example, access to SoundScan data, which tracks weekly retail sales of albums, requires terminal emulation software. Similarly, the Pacer system, which provides access to Federal District Court and Bankruptcy Court dockets, uses VT52/VT100 terminal emulation, a relic of the early days of electronic bulletin board services. Thus Mscomm32.ocx and more-sophisticated third-party communication controls aren't yet obsolete.

Determining the Level of Detail Required

Before the advent of the RDBMS and client/server computing technology, the principal source of functional information, as well as planning and forecasting information, was a multitude of printed reports. Each report was the product of a batch operation that required a program, usually written in COBOL, to execute the embedded SQL or other instructions that create a formatted report. In many cases, reports were created with more than the optimal level of detail because of a lack of programming resources to write, test, and deploy production programs to summarize the data. The capability for users of client applications to create their own ad hoc queries with whatever degree of detail they desire is the driving force behind the front-end application generator market.

Unless you're dealing with data that has been rolled up (the subject of the next section), your decision-support, front-end application accesses tables in operational databases. The level of detail you provide in a decision-support application usually varies inversely with the position of the users in the organizational hierarchy. As you progress upward in the corporate "food chain," tabular data gives way to graphs and charts for trend analysis, and the frequency of reporting often slows from daily to weekly or monthly. Top management usually is interested in longer-term trends, while mid-level managers and supervisors must act immediately to prevent short-term problems from turning into long-term disasters. The list that follows describes the three basic categories of decision-support applications:

- *Executive summaries* and planning information consist of graphs and charts that depict financial performance versus internal projections, prior fiscal periods, and often the results reported by competitors. This category of report is the most likely to require integration of data from online sources operated by data utilities, such as Dialog Information Services, or from firms that specialize in providing online econometric data.

- *Functional summaries*, such as reports of orders for the director of sales or daily cash-flow reports from the director of finance, most often are run weekly. At the directorate level, tabular data is the rule. The data from the directors' reports usually is consolidated into monthly reports issued at the vice-presidential level. Graphs compare current operating results with recent historical data, usually for a 1-year period or less.

- *Operational data summaries* are required by supervisory personnel to evaluate day-to-day performance at the departmental or regional level. Credit managers need real-time access to the payment histories of customers placing new orders. Exception-reporting applications, which are used on the shop floor (for example, applications that identify parts shortages or quality control problems), may need to run on an hourly or shift basis. Tabular formats, rather than graphic presentations, are most common at the operational level.

Figure 9.2 is a diagram that shows the layers of information that constitute typical marketing decision-support applications corresponding to the three categories in the preceding list. The executive summary for the vice president of marketing consolidates sales of all products in all regions. The functional summary for the director of sales includes sales of a particular product line in all regions. The operational data viewed by the regional sales manager reports sales in one region for all products.

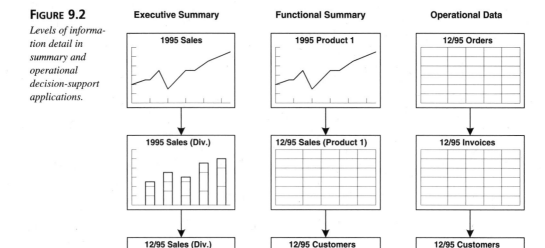

FIGURE 9.2

Levels of information detail in summary and operational decision-support applications.

One of the principal objections of management personnel to MIS reports, whether displayed online or in the form of computer printouts, is excessive detail. If you use a 9-point MS Sans Serif font with a tightly spaced Visual Basic grid, you can display several times as much data on a VDU as is possible with a character-based DOS application. You have similar potential with today's laser printers. For management, it is the aggregated data that is important, together with exception highlighting. If you need to provide one or two levels of detail behind the summary data, first offer the detail behind the exceptions and then make additional detail information an option.

Maintaining Performance and Data Consistency with Rollups

Impatience is another personal trait that increases with the level of authority and responsibility in an organization. Operatives in the trenches may be satisfied with an application that takes a minute or more to present a screen of data—a 3270 terminal on an overtaxed mainframe may take several minutes to update a session. If your summary queries (especially crosstab queries) need to traverse tens of thousands of records containing line items for a year's collection of invoices, you are certain to face an unsatisfied client when you deliver your production front end.

The traditional (and still the best) approach to maintaining adequate performance for time-series, decision-support applications is to consolidate time-based detail data into new tables. This process is called *rolling up data*, which should be familiar to all mainframe COBOL programmers. Consolidating data, other than creating monthly and yearly rollups for accounting purposes, has been relatively uncommon in PC-based database applications. The advent of data warehouse and data mart deployment on Intel-based servers running Windows NT 4+ makes online analytical processing (OLAP) a reality for medium-sized firms and even small companies. OLAP relies on aggregated fact tables produced from operational data by a rollup process. Microsoft SQL Server OLAP Services server (code-named "Plato" during its development phase) is included with SQL Server 7.0, dramatically lowering the entry barrier for establishing data marts. Chapter 28, "Analyzing Multidimensional Data with OLAP and MDX," introduces techniques for data warehousing and creating front ends for MSDSS databases.

▶ **See** "Reducing Fact Table Storage Requirements," **p. 1049**

TIP
When designing rollups, take into account the likelihood of ultimately converting your relational rollups to the highly denormalized star or snowflake schema of warehouse databases. Use numeric product, geographical, employee, and customer codes for primary key values if possible; if not, keep character-based keys short. Minimizing the size of primary keys leads to data storage efficiency for the very large (millions of rows) fact tables associated with data warehousing schemas.

Intel Pentium II and multiple Pentium Pro PCs running Windows NT 4+ at clock speeds of 200MHz or greater are now the most popular CPUs for database servers, and the cost of fixed-disk storage broke the $100-per-gigabyte barrier in late 1997. By the end of 1998, high-performance ultrawide SCSI drives are likely to be priced at about $50/GB. Therefore, the economic disincentive of replicating data is minimal.

Although rolling up data violates the no-duplicated-data rule for relational databases (because rolled up data is derived from existing tables), you'll probably want to aggregate data when your summary queries need to process more than a few thousand records. Following are the guidelines for how and when to roll up data:

- Avoid cascading rollups when possible. A *cascading rollup* is a rollup operation that summarizes data that has been rolled up at a greater detail level. If a retroactive change to the underlying detail occurs, you need to reaggregate each level in the process.

- Roll up data at intervals that are likely to be the least subject to retroactive changes. An example is 3-month rollups for corporations whose quarterly financial reports are subject to independent audit. Monthly rollups may be necessary to achieve acceptable application performance, but monthly rollups should not be cascaded into quarterly aggregations because retroactive changes may be made in the underlying operational databases. Quarterly rollups are based on records in the operational databases.

- Never roll up data at the operational-database record level; roll up data only into nonoperational databases. An example of rolling up data at the operational level is the Order Amount field of the Orders table of the Northwind Traders database that was provided with Microsoft Access version 2.0 (this design abnormality is no longer present in the Northwind.mdb provided with Access 95 or Access 97). The value in the Order Amount field was the sum of the product of the Order Quantity and Unit Price fields of the line item records in the Order Details table for a single order. Changes that occur in the Order Details table, including partial shipments, must be immediately rolled into records in the Orders table to maintain data consistency. Rollups should be executed on a real-time basis.

- Roll up data during periods of transaction-processing inactivity, such as nights or weekends. One of the advantages of rolling up data is the elimination of consistency errors that can occur when you aggregate detail information that is being updated simultaneously. You can write a stored procedure that runs unattended on the server to roll up data at predetermined intervals if your application uses Microsoft SQL Server or another client/server RDBMS that supports stored procedures and offers a scheduling agent.

In the typical information-system hierarchy illustrated earlier in Figure 9.1, rollups of sales, manufacturing, purchasing, finance, and human resources operational databases occur at the director level. Another rollup further consolidates data for the vice presidents of marketing, operations, and administration.

The performance improvement you can achieve by rolling up data lets you design Visual Basic decision-support applications that replace slide shows created with Microsoft PowerPoint or similar Windows presentation applications. Using a presentation application to export and re-create graphs and tables in the form of slides is an inefficient, time-consuming process. Many firms now prepare monthly or weekly presentations by transferring summary data to presentation slides. A well-designed Visual Basic decision-support application can return its development cost many times by eliminating the data import and conversion steps. Your Visual Basic presentation application needs to be totally bulletproof, and you'll probably want to store the rolled up data on a local fixed disk to avoid the embarrassment that attends the appearance of blank screens or messages that read `Unable to connect to server` during the presentation.

DEVELOPING QUERY STRATEGIES

After you identify your data sources, you need to implement a query strategy. The sections that follow discuss some of the issues you need to resolve before you commit to a particular strategy to obtain the `Recordset` objects on which to base your decision-support applications.

Abandoning Jet `QueryDef` Objects

▶ See "Gaining a Performance Boost with Stored Procedures," **p. 819**

DAO-based decision-support applications that have a fixed feature set traditionally have used Jet's persistent, row-returning `QueryDef` objects. `QueryDefs` are Jet's analog of stored procedures implemented by client/server RDBMSs. ADO calls row-returning `QueryDefs` *views*; an SQL `VIEW` is a stored, precompiled query. You can store `QueryDef` objects only in Jet databases, but `QueryDefs` can operate against client/server tables attached by ODBC to the Jet database. Thus `QueryDefs` aren't limited to execution against Jet tables. The Jet query processor compiles the `QueryDef` on initial execution to create a query execution plan; subsequent executions don't require compilation process.

Unfortunately, ADO 2.0, the Microsoft OLE DB Provider for Jet 3.51 (Jolt), Data Environment Designer (DED), and the Data View window provide only limited support for Jet `QueryDefs`. As examples, the `Command` properties sheet doesn't include action `QueryDef` objects in its list of Stored Procedures or Views, and the Data View window doesn't display action `QueryDefs`. If you attempt to execute in VBA code a make-table or other action `QueryDef` on a `Connection` or `Command` object specifying `adCmdTable` as the `CommandType`, you receive the following error message: `An action query can't be used as a row source`. Specifying `adCmdText`, `adCmdStoredProc`, `adCmdTableDirect`, or `adCmdUnknown` results in an `Invalid SQL statement; expected 'DELETE', 'INSERT', 'PROCEDURE', 'SELECT,' or 'UPDATE'.`

The Data View window for a Jet Connection doesn't support parameterized QueryDefs; if you attempt to execute the Invoices Filter QueryDef of Nwind.mdb, a No value given for one or more required parameters error message appears, instead of an input box for the parameter value. Further, the Parameters page of the Command Properties sheet is disabled for Jet QueryDefs. Future versions of ADO and Jolt are likely to provide more complete QueryDef support.

NOTE

The loss of QueryDef functionality when migrating from DAO to ADO 2.0 requires developers to embed the QueryDef's SQL code in Visual Basic applications. The benefit to using embedded SQL statements is twofold—the code is self-documenting and complete in itself, and upsizing applications from Jet to SQL Server or other client/server RDBMSs usually requires only minor changes to the SQL statements. Major alterations, however, are required to process the equivalent of Jet crosstab queries with ANSI SQL statements.

Designing SQL Rollup Queries

▶ See "Creating New Tables with Make-Table Queries," **p. 303**

Rollup queries are make-table queries that you execute from within a Visual Basic application. Rollup queries use the SQL aggregate SUM function to total numeric values contained in tables of operational databases. Typically, a rollup query creates a new table with the following fields:

- Period—One or more fields that identify the range of dates for which the operational data is summed. You can use separate fields for the year and subperiod (quarter, month, or week). You also can combine these two fields with a coding system, such as 1998Q4 (fourth quarter of 1998), 199812 (December 1998), or 1998W52 (last week of 1998). As a rule, you'll find that using separate fields for the year and subperiod makes subsequent record selection simpler.

- Attribute—One or more optional fields that describe an object class or object. Attributes include categories of products, individual products, geographic regions, or persons (individual salespeople, for instance).

- Value—One or more numeric fields that contain the result of the summation of the values of operational database records for the period. If you use more than one value field in the rollup table, the operational database table must contain each field. For example, you can sum both the Quantity and [Unit Price]*Quantity values of a table containing invoice line items to obtain total units sold and total sales and then divide total sales by total units sold to obtain average unit price.

The easiest way to develop rollup queries is to create a group of summary make-table QueryDef objects in a Jet database with Microsoft Access. After testing the queries in Access, you copy the SQL statements for the queries to your project. Writing and debugging complex SQL statements directly in Visual Basic is a time-consuming and often *very* frustrating activity.

The Dec_supt.mdb sample database, which is included on the accompanying CD-ROM, contains several make-table QueryDef objects. The Jet SQL statement of the qryMonthlySalesRollup QueryDef object that creates the data for the graph of the Button Bar form of Figure 9.5 (later in this chapter) is as follows:

```
SELECT Format(Orders.[ShippedDate],"yyyy") AS Year,
     Format(Orders.[ShippedDate],"mm") AS Month,
   SUM([Order Details].[UnitPrice]*[Order Details].Quantity*
     (1-[Order Details].Discount)) AS Sales
   INTO tblSalesRollupMonth
   FROM Orders, [Order Details]
   WHERE Orders.[OrderID]=[Order Details].[OrderID]
   GROUP BY Format(Orders.[ShippedDate],"yyyy"),
     Format(Orders.[ShippedDate],"mm")
HAVING Format([Orders].[ShippedDate],"yyyy"))="1995";
```

> **NOTE**
>
> Dec_supt.mdb links source data tables from Visual Basic 6.0's Nwind.mdb, which Dec_supt.mdb expects to find in its default location, C:\Program Files\Microsoft Visual Studio\VB98. If you installed Visual Basic 6.0 in another location, use Access's Linked Table Manager add-in to refresh the links to the proper folder.

The Jet SQL statement differs from ANSI SQL syntax in the use of the VBA Format function to return parts of dates (in the Year and Month fields) and in the GROUP BY and HAVING clauses. If this query were executed against a client/server RDBMS, such as Microsoft SQL Server, you would replace the Format function with the appropriate ANSI SQL scalar function, YEAR and MONTH. The GROUP BY aggregations you use must correspond exactly to the corresponding SELECT descriptors in your SQL statement.

The SUM SQL aggregate function totals the net sale amount, taking into account the discount, if any, offered to the customer on a particular product. The INTO statement identifies the name of the table that is created by the query. The initial GROUP BY criterion that groups orders by the year in which the order was shipped is included in the GROUP BY clause because you might want to specify more than 1 year in the HAVING clause with an AND operator. This example uses 1995, the latest year for which a full 12 months of data exists in the version Nwind.mdb included with Visual Basic 6.0.

9

DESIGNING A FRONT END

If the tblSalesRollupMonth table doesn't exist, the query creates the table. If the tblSalesRollupMonth table exists, Access deletes the existing table before the new table is created. When you execute a make-table query from an `ADODB.Connection` or `ADODB.Command` object, you must drop the existing table before generating the new table.

NOTE

You might encounter a special problem with some rollup queries in Jet databases that use AutoNumber or Counter field types. The Jet database engine does not permit you to create tables that have more than one AutoNumber field. If your rollup queries try to combine data from two or more tables and you include more than one AutoNumber field in the rollup table, the query will fail. For example, you can't use a rollup query like qryMonthlySalesRollup (included in the Dec_supt.mdb sample table for this chapter) directly on the Categories and Products tables in the Nwind.mdb sample database, because the query attempts to create a new table containing the `ProductID` (from Products) and `CategoryID` (from Categories) fields, both of which are AutoNumber fields.

To get around this problem, use the `Format` function with no formatting template, as in this expression: `Format(Products.[ProductID], "") AS ProductID`. The `Format` function interprets an empty format string as "General Number." By using the `Format` function in this way, you cause the AutoNumber field to appear in the `Recordset` resulting from your query as an unformatted Number field. You can use this technique to avoid the multiple AutoNumber field error in the qryMonthlySalesRollupProduct and the qryQuarterlySalesRollupProduct queries of the Dec_supt.mdb database.

Importing `QueryDef` SQL Statements from Access

If you take the proceeding chapter's advice to use Access 97+ to create and test your make-table queries, follow these steps to import multiple SQL statements into your VBA code:

1. Declare variables, such as `strSQL1`, `strSQL2`, and so forth, for each SQL statement you intend to import. Alternatively, create a subprocedure with a `Case` structure to assign multiple SQL statements to a single variable, such as `strSQL`.

2. Open the `QueryDef`'s SQL window. Figure 9.3 shows Access 8.0's SQL window for the qryMonthlySalesRollup `QueryDef`.

FIGURE 9.3

A typical make-table QueryDef *displayed in Access 8.0's SQL window.*

```
qryMonthlySalesRollup : Make Table Query
SELECT Format(Orders.[ShippedDate],"yyyy") AS Year,
Format(Orders.[ShippedDate],"mm") AS Month,
Sum([Order Details].[UnitPrice]*[Order Details].Quantity*
(1-[Order Details].Discount)) AS Sales INTO tblSalesRollupMonth
FROM Orders, [Order Details]
WHERE (([Orders.OrderID]=[Order Details].[OrderID]))
GROUP BY Format(Orders.[ShippedDate],"yyyy"),
Format(Orders.[ShippedDate],"mm")
HAVING (((Format([Orders].[ShippedDate],"yyyy"))="1995"));
```

3. Copy the SQL statement to the Clipboard and then paste the statement into your Visual Basic subprocedure.

4. Insert strSQL[#] = at the beginning of the statement.

5. Break the statement into shorter lines and a more readable format by inserting quotes and line continuation characters (" & _ ... ").

6. Replace double quotes surrounding string arguments ("1995") with single quotes ('1995').

7. Replace double quotes for Format strings ("yyyy") with a pair of double quotes (""yyyy""). The Visual Basic interpreter treats "" as a character, rather than as a **String** variable terminator.

8. Indent complex statements to improve readability.

The following example illustrates changes made to the qryMonthlySalesRollup SQL statement to conform to VBA standards:

```
strSQL = "SELECT Format(Orders.ShippedDate,""yyyy"") AS Year, " & _
    "Format(Orders.ShippedDate,""mm"") AS Month, " & _
  "SUM([Order Details].UnitPrice*[Order Details].Quantity*" & _
    "(1-[Order Details].Discount)) AS Sales " & _
  "INTO tblSalesRollupMonth " & _
  "FROM Orders, [Order Details] " & _
  "WHERE Orders.OrderID = [Order Details].OrderID " & _
  "GROUP BY Format(Orders.[ShippedDate],""yyyy""), " & _
    "Format(Orders.[ShippedDate],""mm"") " & _
  "HAVING Format([Orders].[ShippedDate], ""yyyy"") = '1995'"
```

Creating a test application to check execution of your VBA make-table queries against a Jet database is a relatively simple process. Figure 9.4 shows the single form of the Rollups.vbp project, which is included in the \Ddg_vb6\Chaptr09 folder of the accompanying CD-ROM. frmRollups executes the VBA equivalents of the six QueryDefs in Dec_supt.mdb. Listing 9.1 contains the VBA code behind frmRollups.

9

DESIGNING A FRONT END

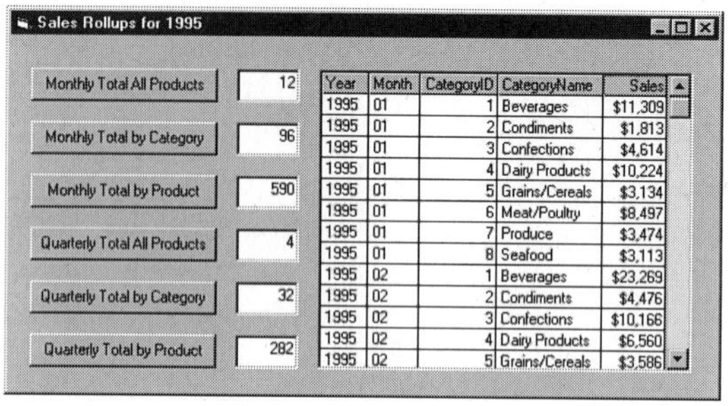

FIGURE 9.4

The Rollups.vbp test project displaying the query result set from the VBA equivalent of the qryMonthlySalesRollupCategory QueryDef.

> **NOTE**
>
> The rollup queries of `frmRollups` create tables similar to fact tables of star schemas but have description fields that don't usually appear in fact tables. The table shown in Figure 9.4, as an example, includes the CategoryName field, which is larger (contains more bytes) than the total of all the other fields of the table. For a star schema, the CategoryName value would be provided by a dimension table with a Categories level above a Products level joined by the CategoryID keys. All the tables created by the Rollups.vbp project are missing the geographic dimension common to star schemas for sales distribution analysis.

LISTING 9.1 CODE TO EXECUTE AND DISPLAY THE RESULTS OF MAKE-TABLE QUERIES

```
Option Explicit
Private strSQL As String
Private strTable As String
Private lngRecords As Long

Private Sub cmdRollup_Click(intIndex As Integer)
    'Generate the SQL statements and specify the resulting tables
    Select Case intIndex
        Case 0
            strTable = "tblSalesRollupMonth"
            strSQL = "SELECT Format(Orders.ShippedDate,""yyyy"") AS Year, " & _
                "Format(Orders.ShippedDate,""mm"") AS Month, " & _
                "SUM([Order Details].UnitPrice*[Order Details].Quantity*" & _
                "(1-[Order Details].Discount)) AS Sales " & _
                "INTO tblSalesRollupMonth " & _
                "FROM Orders, [Order Details] " & _
                "WHERE Orders.OrderID = [Order Details].OrderID " & _
                "GROUP BY Format(Orders.[ShippedDate],""yyyy""), " & _
                "Format(Orders.[ShippedDate],""mm"") " & _
                "HAVING Format([Orders].[ShippedDate], ""yyyy"") = '1995'"
        Case 1
            strTable = "tblCategoryRollupMonth"
            strSQL = "SELECT Format(Orders.ShippedDate,""yyyy"") AS Year, " & _
```

```
            "Format(Orders.ShippedDate,""mm""") AS Month, " & _
            "Categories.CategoryID, Categories.CategoryName, " & _
        "SUM([Order Details].UnitPrice*[Order Details].Quantity*" & _
            "(1-[Order Details].Discount)) AS Sales " & _
        "INTO tblCategoryRollupMonth " & _
        "FROM Orders, [Order Details], Products, Categories " & _
        "WHERE Orders.OrderID = [Order Details].OrderID " & _
            "AND [Order Details].ProductID = Products.ProductID " & _
            "AND Products.CategoryID = Categories.CategoryID " & _
        "GROUP BY Format(Orders.ShippedDate,""yyyy""), " & _
            "Format(Orders.ShippedDate,""mm""), " & _
            "Categories.CategoryID, Categories.CategoryName " & _
        "HAVING Format(Orders.ShippedDate,""yyyy"")='1995'"
Case 2
    strTable = "tblProductRollupMonth"
    strSQL = "SELECT Format(Orders.ShippedDate,""yyyy""") AS Year, " & _
        "Format(Orders.ShippedDate,""mm""") AS Month, " & _
        "Format(Categories.CategoryID,""""") AS CategoryID, " & _
        "Format(Products.ProductID,""""") AS ProductID, " & _
        "Products.ProductName, " & _
        "SUM([Order Details].UnitPrice*[Order Details].Quantity*" & _
            "(1-[Order Details].Discount)) AS Sales " & _
        "INTO tblProductRollupMonth " & _
        "FROM Orders, [Order Details], Products, Categories " & _
        "WHERE Orders.OrderID = [Order Details].OrderID " & _
            "AND [Order Details].ProductID = Products.ProductID " & _
            "AND Products.CategoryID = Categories.CategoryID " & _
        "GROUP BY Format(Orders.ShippedDate,""mm""), " & _
            "Categories.CategoryID, Products.ProductID, " & _
            "Products.ProductName, Format(ShippedDate,""yyyy""") " & _
        "HAVING Format(ShippedDate,""yyyy"")='1995'"
Case 3
    strTable = "tblSalesRollupQuarter"
    strSQL = "SELECT Format(Orders.ShippedDate,""yyyy""") AS Year, " & _
            "Format(Orders.ShippedDate,""q""") AS Quarter, " & _
        "SUM([Order Details].UnitPrice*[Order Details].Quantity*" & _
            "(1-[Order Details].Discount)) AS Sales " & _
        "INTO tblSalesRollupQuarter " & _
        "FROM Orders, [Order Details] " & _
        "WHERE Orders.OrderID = [Order Details].OrderID " & _
        "GROUP BY Format(Orders.[ShippedDate],""yyyy""), " & _
            "Format(Orders.[ShippedDate],""q""") " & _
        "HAVING Format([Orders].[ShippedDate], ""yyyy"") = '1995'"
Case 4
    strTable = "tblCategoryRollupQuarter"
    strSQL = "SELECT Format(Orders.ShippedDate,""yyyy""") AS Year, " & _
            "Format(Orders.ShippedDate,""q""") AS Quarter, " & _
            "Categories.CategoryID, Categories.CategoryName, " & _
        "SUM([Order Details].UnitPrice*[Order Details].Quantity*" & _
            "(1-[Order Details].Discount)) AS Sales " & _
        "INTO tblCategoryRollupQuarter " & _
```

continues

LISTING 9.1   CONTINUED

```
                "FROM Orders, [Order Details], Products, Categories " & _
                "WHERE Orders.OrderID = [Order Details].OrderID " & _
                    "AND [Order Details].ProductID = Products.ProductID " & _
                    "AND Products.CategoryID = Categories.CategoryID " & _
                "GROUP BY Format(Orders.ShippedDate,""yyyy""), " & _
                    "Format(Orders.ShippedDate,""q""), " & _
                    "Categories.CategoryID, Categories.CategoryName " & _
                "HAVING Format(Orders.ShippedDate,""yyyy"")='1995'"
        Case 5
            strTable = "tblProductRollupQuarter"
            strSQL = "SELECT Format(Orders.ShippedDate,""yyyy"") AS Year, " & _
                "Format(Orders.ShippedDate,""q"") AS Quarter, " & _
                "Format(Categories.CategoryID,"""") AS CategoryID, " & _
                "Format(Products.ProductID,"""") AS ProductID, " & _
                "Products.ProductName, " & _
                "SUM([Order Details].UnitPrice*[Order Details].Quantity*" & _
                    "(1-[Order Details].Discount)) AS Sales " & _
                "INTO tblProductRollupQuarter " & _
                "FROM Orders, [Order Details], Products, Categories " & _
                "WHERE Orders.OrderID = [Order Details].OrderID " & _
                    "AND [Order Details].ProductID = Products.ProductID " & _
                    "AND Products.CategoryID = Categories.CategoryID " & _
                "GROUP BY Format(Orders.ShippedDate,""q""), " & _
                    "Categories.CategoryID, Products.ProductID, " & _
                    "Products.ProductName, Format(ShippedDate,""yyyy"") " & _
                "HAVING Format(ShippedDate,""yyyy"")='1995'"
    End Select
    Call MakeTables
    txtRecords(intIndex).Text = lngRecords
End Sub

Private Sub MakeTables()
    'Execute the queries against a Connection
    Dim cnnDecSupt As New ADODB.Connection
    Dim rstDecSupt As New ADODB.Recordset
    Dim intRow As Integer

    Me.MousePointer = vbHourglass
    With cnnDecSupt
        'Define and open the Connection
        .Provider = "Microsoft.Jet.OLEDB.3.51"
        .ConnectionString = App.Path & "\Dec_supt.mdb"
        .Mode = adModeShareDenyNone
        .Open
        'Delete the table to be overwritten
        On Error Resume Next
        .Execute "DROP TABLE " & strTable, , adCmdText
        On Error GoTo 0
        'Create the new table
```

```
      .Execute strSQL, lngRecords, adCmdText
      'Populate the grid to check results
      With rstDecSupt
         If .State = adStateOpen Then
            .Close
         End If
         Set .ActiveConnection = cnnDecSupt
         .CursorType = adOpenStatic
         .Source = strTable
         .MaxRecords = 25
         .Open
      End With
      With hfgRollups
         Set .Recordset = rstDecSupt
         .Refresh
         .Col = .Cols - 1
         For intRow = 0 To .Rows - 1
            .Row = intRow
            If Len(.Text) > 0 Then
               .Text = Format(.Text, "$#,###0")
            End If
         Next intRow
         .Row = 0
      End With
      Me.MousePointer = vbDefault
   End With
   Set cnnDecSupt = Nothing
End Sub
```

The MakeTables subprocedure demonstrates the simplicity of executing multiple make-table queries against an ADODB.Connection and displaying test Recordsets in a MSHFlexGrid control. A production application would reuse a module-level or form-level Connection object, but creating a new Connection for each execution takes an insignificant period of time compared to that for generating the tables.

TIP

Don't succumb to the temptation to reduce the amount of code by eliminating duplicate or near-duplicate clauses in multiple, complex SQL statements. Although many of the clauses or parts of clauses in the SQL statements are identical or similar to one another, breaking up the statements and substituting values with case statements usually makes the code almost impossible to read and very difficult to troubleshoot.

9

DESIGNING A
FRONT END

Implementing Ad Hoc Queries

One of the incentives for purchasing database front-end application generators is that their users can generate their own ad hoc queries against large databases. The intensity of the desire to create ad hoc queries usually is inversely proportional to the individual's position in the corporate hierarchy. In the upper corporate echelons, executives want the click of a single button to deliver the summary information they need. At the operational level, managers and supervisors want the opportunity to choose from various record-selection options (on-demand reporting) or construct their own queries (ad hoc reporting).

When an unhindered user executes a SELECT * query against large mainframe or client/server databases, it can bring even the highest performance RDBMS to its knees. Accidentally or intentionally returning all of the records in a monster table, called a "query from hell," can cause severe network congestion, at least until the user's RAM and disk swap file space is exhausted. The worst-case scenario is the accidental creation of a Cartesian product by the omission of a join condition when more than one table is involved in a query. Some RDBMSs detect this condition and refuse to execute the query. Others, such as applications that use the Jet database engine, attempt to return every combination of records in the tables.

CAUTION

Don't create decision-support applications that enable users to enter their own SQL SELECT statements against production databases. Use command buttons, combo boxes, or list boxes to restrict the fields to be displayed and to add required WHERE clause record-selection criteria.

DESIGNING THE USER INTERFACE

Microsoft Windows achieved its commercial success because Windows 3.*x* provided a graphic interface that most users preferred to the DOS command-line prompt. Windows 9*x* and Windows NT 4+ have increased the commercial success of Windows with their enhanced ease of use and better integration of the graphical user interface with the underlying operating system. Windows applications dominate the PC software market because they use design elements that, at least in most cases, conform to the common user access (CUA) architecture developed by IBM Corp. in the 1980s. The CUA specification describes the design and operation of menus and other common control objects, such as check boxes, radio (now option) buttons, and message dialog boxes. The sample applications in this book employ the principles embodied in Microsoft's interface guidelines.

The primary objective of the CUA specification is to create uniformity in the overall appearance and basic operational characteristics of computer applications. CUA principles apply to character-based DOS applications executed on PCs and to mainframe sessions running on 3270 terminals. The user interface of Microsoft Windows 3.*x*, Windows 9*x*, Windows NT, and IBM OS/2 for PCs, XWindows and Motif for UNIX systems, and System 7.*x* for Macintosh computers conform in most respects to IBM's basic CUA specification. Therefore, if you're accustomed to Microsoft Word for the Macintosh, you can quickly adapt to using Microsoft Word for the PC.

The sections that follow describe some of the basic requirements of the user interface for database decision-support applications designed for use at the upper-management level. Subsequent chapters in this book provide similar guidance for more flexible decision-support applications and data-entry (online transaction-processing) applications.

Optimizing Application Usability

The usability of mainstream Windows applications ultimately determines their success in the software market. Feature-list comparisons in product advertising and magazine reviews may influence the purchasing decisions of individual users, but the primary purchasers of Windows applications are large corporations. The objective of these corporate purchasers is to minimize the time and training expenses that are required for their personnel to learn and use the applications effectively. Thus applications are rated by their usability, a wholly subjective attribute. An application that one user finds intuitive and easy to use may be totally incomprehensible to another user.

Testing applications for usability is an art, not a science, and it is a primitive art at best. Commercial firms that conduct usability tests on major software products charge $100,000 or more for testing relatively simple Windows applications. Microsoft Corp. has invested hundreds of millions of dollars in usability testing of Windows 9x, Windows NT, and Microsoft 32-bit Windows applications. The applications that you create are unlikely to undergo commercial usability tests. Instead, your client may simply inform you that he or she does not understand how to use your application without reading the manual. When that happens, your application has just failed the ultimate usability test.

The following sections describe characteristics of applications that achieve high usability ratings and show you how to implement these characteristics in the forms that constitute a simple executive-level, decision-support application.

Striving for Simplicity

When you design decision-support applications, your watchword is *simplicity*. Application simplicity is achieved by applying the following rules to your application design:

- Don't add features to an application that are not needed to accomplish the client's fundamental objective. When in doubt, don't implement a feature that is not in the minimum capabilities list. Wait for the client to request additional features. If you need special features to test the application, hide these features from other users.

- Don't attempt to display more than one type of information on a single form. For example, do not combine graphs and tabular information on the same form. Instead, hide the graph window and show the window with the tabular data.

The preceding two rules are especially important for executive-summary, decision-support applications because top executives are unlikely to be PC power users. A simple, intuitive user interface and a limited feature list are the two primary characteristics of professional-quality, executive-summary applications.

Figure 9.5 illustrates the first form of a hypothetical executive-summary, decision-support application that displays sales information for a 1-year period. A button bar is the primary navigation device for the application. The button bar enables the user to make the following choices:

- Display total corporate sales by month, using a line graph that also includes lines representing the statistical arithmetic mean and the best-fit slope for the period.

- Display monthly sales by division with a stacked vertical bar chart or an area chart.

- Display sales by product for the year to date or for a particular quarter or month in pie chart format.

- Attach the current object or parts of the object displayed by the form to an email message that requests additional data about a particular element of an object. The graph, chart, or selected cells of a grid control in the window are copied to the Clipboard and then pasted into an email message.

- Create an email message that requests information about, or that makes comments on, the object pasted into the message.

- Save the current data, messages, and annotations in a file for future reference.

- Exit the application when finished with the review of the current data.

FIGURE 9.5

The opening form of an executive-summary, decision-support application.

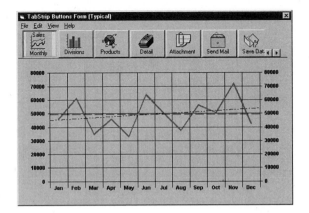

The project and data source for the forms for Figures 9.5 through 9.8 are Ui_examp.mdb and Dec_supt.mdb, respectively, which are installed from the accompanying CD-ROM into your C:\Ddg_vb6\Chaptr09 folder. Dec_supt.mdb contains the rolled up tables generated by the six make-table queries of the Rollups.vbp project. Ui_examp.mdb is an upgraded, ADO 2.0 version of a Visual Basic 5.0 DAO-based application of the same name, which is included in the \Ddg_vb6\Chaptr09\DAO_Ver folder for comparison.

The following list describes the design principles embodied in the decision-support form shown in Figure 9.5.

- The form uses Windows 9*x*'s standard neutral gray background to present a conservative appearance and to avoid strong contrast with colored objects. Large areas of white or vivid colors are distracting to the user of an application.

- There is no opening form or splash screen. A *splash screen* is a form or design element that identifies the application. (An example of a splash screen is the copyright message that appears when you first launch Visual Basic 6, Microsoft Word, Excel, or other main-stream Windows applications.) You might need an initial login window to obtain the password required to start the application and to log the user into a secure database.

- The buttons present large targets for the mouse. Each button has an icon and a caption to explain the purpose of the button. Button bars and toolbars that provide one-click equivalents for common menu choices are common features of today's Windows applications. (The button bar in the form shown in Figure 9.5 was constructed by using a TabStrip control with its `Style` property set to 1 so that its tabs are displayed as buttons. The size of the graphic image displayed in the tab button dictates the size of the buttons; the images used on this form are 56 pixels wide and 56 pixels high.) Button bars enable you to create a simple and attractive user interface. Alternatively, you can use Visual Basic 6.0's Toolbar control to provide a toolbar that matches those of other Windows applications.

- Three-dimensional push buttons, provided by a TabStrip control (with Style set to 1) or by a Toolbar control indicate the user's current display choice or other operation. The TabStrip and Toolbar controls are provided by the Microsoft Windows Common Controls 6.0 component library (Mscomctl.ocx). To use the TabStrip or Toolbar controls in your project, choose Project, Components to add a reference to the Microsoft Windows Common Controls 6.0 library to your project.

- A menu lets the user make choices that aren't implemented by buttons. In production applications, a menu choice duplicates the action of each button. (Ui_examp uses the view menu to choose the type of form displayed.)

- The form is designed to occupy almost the entire display area in normal mode. The form does not have sizable borders (BorderStyle = 1, Fixed Single), and no maximize button is provided (MaxButton = **False**) so that the width of the form is forced to correspond to the total width of the button set. If you are designing the application for presentation, set the size of the form to the entire display area.

- The preferred user interface for decision-support applications is multiple document interface (MDI) child forms that display documents (graphs, charts, and tables) with common menus and button bars. (Ui_examp.vbp does not use MDI forms.) Although Microsoft claims the single document interface (SDI) is the preferred UI for Windows 9x applications, all members of the Office 97 software suite continue to use MDI windows. Showing and hiding objects on a single form is an alternative approach for simple applications.

The form shown in Figure 9.5 (and the forms of Figures 9.6 through 9.8, which follow) serves as the foundation of the form designs for most of the decision-support sample applications presented in this book.

NOTE

To display graphic images on the tabs or buttons of a TabStrip, SSTab, or Toolbar control, first create an Image control on your form to store the images for your tabs and buttons. The ultimate size of tabs and buttons in TabStrip, SSTab, and Toolbar controls is dictated by the size of the largest graphic image you display on the control. If the images are different sizes, the control zooms smaller images to match the size of the largest image. In all cases, the control attempts to display the image as a square, stretching the image's height or width as needed. For best results, use images that are already (or within a pixel or two) square. The examples shown in this chapter use images that are 56 pixels, 48 pixels, and 16 pixels square.

The VBA code that supplies the values on which the graphs shown in this chapter are based is described in the section, "Creating Graphs from Rolled-Up Data," later in this chapter.

Maintaining Consistency

Ralph Waldo Emerson's adage from *Self-Reliance*, "A foolish consistency is the hobgoblin of little minds," doesn't apply to computer applications. Both internal consistency and external consistency of the user interface are principal requirements of a properly designed Windows application. The following list describes these two types of consistencies:

- Internal (endogenous) consistency implies that the appearance of all forms and the behavior of all controls on the forms that constitute your application are similar. If the behavior of a button or menu choice needs to differ under certain conditions, change the appearance of the icon (change a color, for example) or alter the Caption property value for the menu choice.

- External (exogenous) consistency means that the appearance and behavior of your application are similar to other mainstream Windows applications. If, for example, your client primarily uses Microsoft applications, the appearance and operational characteristics of your application should be modeled on the current version of Excel, Microsoft Mail, or Microsoft Query.

You need to meet the following criteria to maintain internal consistency:

- All the forms that constitute the application should have a similar appearance. Background colors, typeface families, and the size of display elements should remain constant throughout the application. It is easier to read sans serif fonts, such as Arial and MS Sans Serif, than to read fonts with serifs, such as Times New Roman or MS Serif. Use the bold attribute for label captions, graph and chart labels and legends, and numerical values in grid controls. Use standard bitmapped and TrueType fonts that are supplied with Windows 95; let users change the fonts to their own favorites but only if absolutely necessary.

- The location and sequence of navigation devices should remain constant for all forms. Buttons and menu choices that appear on more than one form always appear in the same sequence and in the same position (where feasible).

- Icons that are used to identify objects or operations should have the same appearance in all forms. If the images you use for the icons adequately represent and distinguish the objects or operations, you can eliminate captions in second-level forms where you need more buttons than will fit in a single row if the buttons have captions.

Figure 9.6 is an example of a form that uses a row of buttons created with a Toolbar control, rather than with a TabStrip control. The toolbar form is internally consistent with the TabStrip button bar form shown in Figure 9.5. The difference between a Toolbar and a TabStrip button bar is that a toolbar can be placed only at the top (the typical location), bottom, or sides of a form; a TabStrip control (whether it displays tabs or buttons) can be placed anywhere on a form. Using smaller buttons without captions often is necessary when your forms have more buttons than the width of the display can accommodate.

To display the toolbar form that is shown in Figure 9.6, click the Divisions button of the TabStrip Buttons form (with the bar chart bitmap) or choose the View, Large Toolbar Form menu command of the Ui_examp application.

FIGURE 9.6

A bar chart decision-support form with large toolbar buttons.

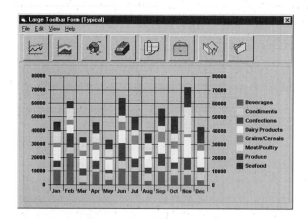

Figure 9.7 shows the bar chart display of Figure 9.6 presented as an area chart. You change the Image property of the division toolbar button to select a different bitmap from the Image control associated with Toolbar control when you display an area chart. Changing to a button bitmap representing an area chart preserves internal consistency between the button and the look of the form that appears when you click the button.

In Figure 9.6, notice that the displayed chart is a bar chart. The second button has an area chart icon. Clicking this button changes to the area chart shown in Figure 9.7. Notice, in Figure 9.7, that the button's icon is now changed to a bar chart icon. The button icon always indicates the type of chart that will be displayed as a result of clicking the button—not the type of chart currently being displayed.

FIGURE 9.7

Replacing a bar chart with an area chart and changing the button bitmap to correspond to the new action resulting from future button clicks.

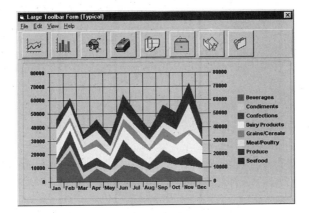

Here are the rules for maintaining external application consistency:

- Choose a mainstream Windows application as the model for your application's button bar or toolbar. Microsoft Exchange or Outlook is a good choice as a model for button bar forms, and Excel 8.0's standard toolbar represents a good starting point for forms that need more than eight buttons.

- Buttons with icons that are identical to or similar to icons found in other mainstream applications should perform the same or similar functions in your application.

- Use a consistent font for button captions. Microsoft uses the 8.25-point MS Sans Serif Roman font for most button captions and as the default typeface for numeric values; your application should follow suit. Roman is the term for a font with no attributes—for example, not bold, not italic, and not underlined. MS Sans Serif is a bitmapped font that closely resembles Linotype Corp.'s Helvetica typeface family.

- Use a common menu and button bar on an MDI parent form and employ MDI child forms to present graphs, charts, and grid controls based on your application's queries. (The Ui_examp application does not use MDI forms because the button bars and toolbars differ from form to form.)

- Windows 9x common dialogs (used for opening and saving files, as well as for other common operations) and message boxes usually have a sculpted appearance and a light gray background.

Identifying Toolbar Button Functions

It's difficult to create a collection of small icons that unambiguously represents a variety of operations (typical toolbar icons are 16×16, 32×32, and 48×48 pixels). Figure 9.8 illustrates the use of a Toolbar control with ToolTips (pop-up labels built into the toolbar button object) that appear when the mouse pointer is positioned on the surface of the button. The Toolbar control was a new feature in Visual Basic 4; the toolbar in Figures 9.6 through 9.8 is a single object, which contains a collection of button objects. The ToolTips that appear are a property of the button. To make these ToolTip labels appear, you set the `ToolTipText` property of the particular button. All the code needed to display and hide the ToolTips is intrinsic to the Toolbar control.

By using the Toolbar control, you can easily create a "look and feel" for your applications that is similar to that found in recent releases of major Microsoft productivity applications and programming tools—Excel, Access, and Word. By changing the `Visible` property of a Toolbar control, you can provide your application with multiple toolbars; the Toolbar control even has an `AllowCustomize` property, which, if **True**, permits users to customize the toolbars in your application.

Using ToolTips for the buttons in a Toolbar control is a better method of identifying the purpose of a button than displaying the same information in a status bar at the bottom of a form. No eye movement is necessary to read the adjacent label caption, whereas a substantial eye movement is required to traverse the VDU from the top toolbar to the bottom status bar. Minimizing the eye movement required to accomplish each of the application's tasks is one of the principles of good user interface design.

FIGURE 9.8

Using ToolTips and a Toolbar control for buttons on a form.

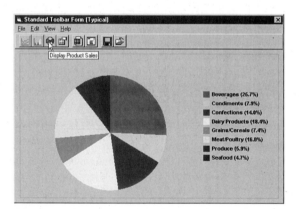

CREATING AND USING BUTTON BARS AND TOOLBARS

The documentation that accompanies Visual Basic 6.0 describes how to use the graphics capabilities of Visual Basic but provides little or no practical advice for adding images to command buttons, TabStrip and SSTab tabs, and toolbar button controls. The sections that follow describe how to obtain the bitmapped images you need for your toolbar buttons, how to create

Windows bitmap (.bmp) files with Windows Paint, and how to add the image contained in a .bmp file to the `Picture` property of a command button or to an Image control for subsequent use in a Toolbar, TabStrip, or SSTab control.

Obtaining and Modifying Button Bitmaps

Visual Basic includes a plethora of icons and bitmaps that you can use to decorate conventional command buttons, tabs, or faces of toolbar buttons. The buttons used in the TabStrip Buttons and Toolbar forms in Figures 9.5 through 9.7 are based on icons that Visual Basic installs in your \Program Files\Microsoft Visual Studio\Common\Graphics\Bitmaps and ...\Icons folders.. Figure 9.9 displays a large icon view of the icons provided in the ...\Icons\Office folder. (Because these are .ico files, Windows 9x can display the actual icon image in the directory listing; you must use the QuickView command or Paint to view the appearance of the sample bitmaps supplied with Visual Basic 6.0).

FIGURE 9.9

The content of the ... \Graphics\ Icons\Office folder.

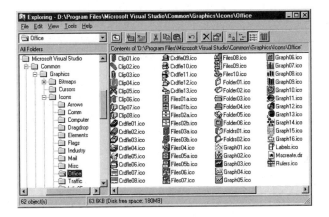

You can use .gif, .jpg, .ico, or .bmp files to provide the `Picture`, `DownPicture`, and `DisabledPicture` properties of buttons.

Adding Code to Show and Hide Forms

The event handler for the `Click` event of TabStrip or toolbar buttons (except the button that represents the currently selected form) uses the `Show` method to open the new form and then executes the `Hide` method to make the current form temporarily disappear. If the form you select has not been opened, the `Show` method automatically executes the `Load` method. (Using the `Load` method by itself does not create an instance of a form's window.) You can force a form's `Load` method to execute by using the Visual Basic `Unload` statement immediately before invoking the `Show` method (as is done in the Ui_examp sample application).

The generalized code structure for showing and hiding forms is this:

```
Sub ShowNewForm
    frmNewFormName.Show
    [DoEvents]
    frmCurrentFormName.Hide
End Sub
```

To prevent your application from disappearing from the display, apply the Show method to the new form before you Hide the currently open form. The optional DoEvents statement enables Windows to process the messages necessary to display the frmNewFormName form before hiding the window that displays the current form. DoEvents is necessary only when you load a form that has a substantial amount of code that needs to be executed when the Form_Load event of the new form is triggered.

CREATING GRAPHS FROM ROLLED-UP DATA

The Microsoft Chart Control 6.0 (OLE DB) lets you create a variety of graphs and charts from data supplied by your application's queries. This book distinguishes between the terms *graph* and *chart*. A graph consists of data points, usually connected by lines. A chart uses two-dimensional objects, such as bars or other filled-screen areas, to represent the data. Graphs and charts usually employ display colors or print patterns to distinguish sets of data. All the graphs and charts in the sample forms discussed in this chapter use rolled-up data created by the set of make-table queries discussed earlier in this chapter.

> **NOTE**
>
> Version 6.0 of MSChart (Mschrt20.ocx) is ADO enabled and can be bound to ADODB.Recordsets. The Visual Basic Chart Wizard provides a shortcut to adding data-bound graphs and charts to forms. In many cases, the Chart Wizard doesn't deliver a usable graph or chart; you must tweak the Wizard's design to produce a readable result. Thus the examples in this chapter use VBA code to define and populate graphs and charts.

The sections that follow give examples of the code you use to create the graphs shown in the preceding Figures 9.5 through 9.8 with the MSChart control.

Generating Line Graphs

The graph showing Monthly Sales for 1995, as shown in Figure 9.5 earlier in this chapter, uses Dec_supt.mdb's tblSalesRollupMonth table created from data contained in Nwind.mdb. Most of the properties of the graph are set in design mode. When you view the Monthly Sales for

1995 graph in design mode, the data points that create the sales line are created by a random number generator. In run mode, your code supplies dynamic properties and the values of each data point.

Listing 9.2 contains the code for the Declarations section and the Main subprocedure of the Ui_examp.vbp. All but the most trivial examples in this book initiate their execution with the Main subprocedure, which initializes the values of **Public** (global) and procedure-level variables. As a rule, you declare ADODB.Connection objects with **Public** scope to avoid the necessity of opening the Database objects each time you open a new form. You also might want to declare general-purpose Command and Recordset object variables as **Public** variables to eliminate the need to declare these objects in the code behind your forms.

The two arrays, strMonths and strQuarters, contain month names (three-letter abbreviations, the full month name, and string month numbers, 01…12), and the ordinal names of quarters (First…Fourth), respectively. Declare these two arrays as **Public** variables and add the code to initialize these arrays to the Main procedure of most of your decision-support applications.

This book doesn't use the tag prefix a to designate array variables. The trailing parenthesis of array variables that are prefixed with one of Visual Basic's fundamental data type abbreviations, such as str or var, is adequate to indicate that the variable is an array. Indexes to array variables don't employ the standard ai prefix, as in aint*VarName*. Instead, the code uses a general-purpose (intCtr) counter variable or a variable that includes an abbreviated description of the source of the index (intCol or intRow).

LISTING 9.2 THE DECLARATIONS SECTION AND Main SUBPROCEDURE OF UI_EXAMP.BAS

```
'Arrays for month names (short and long form), and quarters
Public strMonths(12, 3) As String
Public strQuarters(4) As String
'Read-only connection to Dec_Supt.mdb
Public cnnDecSupt As New ADODB.Connection

Sub Main()
    'Purpose:   Open example database, initialize arrays, etc.
    Dim intCtr As Integer

    With cnnDecSupt
        'Define and open the Connection
        .Provider = "Microsoft.Jet.OLEDB.3.51"
        .ConnectionString = App.Path & "\Dec_supt.mdb"
        .Mode = adModeShareDenyWrite
        .Open
    End With
    'initialize the strMonths array
    For intCtr = 1 To 12
        strMonths(intCtr, 1) = Format(DateSerial(1995, intCtr, 1), "mmm")
```

9

continues

LISTING 9.2 CONTINUED

```
        strMonths(intCtr, 2) = Format(DateSerial(1995, intCtr, 1), "mmmm")
        If intCtr < 10 Then
            strMonths(intCtr, 3) = "0" & Trim(Str(intCtr))
        Else
            strMonths(intCtr, 3) = Trim(Str(intCtr))
        End If
    Next intCtr

    'initialize the strQuarters array
    strQuarters(1) = "First"
    strQuarters(2) = "Second"
    strQuarters(3) = "Third"
    strQuarters(4) = "Fourth"

    'Open the initial form
    frmTabButtons.Show
End Sub
```

Unless you want to create an animated graph, in which displaying the individual data points is delayed by a timer control, you send the data to the MSChart control in the Form_Load subprocedure or by performing an action in the Form_Load procedure that results in a call to the procedure that draws the chart. Listing 9.3 is the code that draws the simple line graph that is illustrated in Figure 9.5. Form_Load in TabStrip.frm ensures that the first button of the TabStrip control (whose Key property is "tabMonthlySales") is selected. Whenever you select a tab (whether displayed as a tab or as a button) of a TabStrip control, the TabStrip control's Click event is generated. The Click event-handling procedure for the TabStrip control (not shown in Listing 9.3) calls the DrawMonthlySalesGraph subprocedure, which supplies data and properties to the MSChart control.

LISTING 9.3 THE CODE TO CREATE AND DISPLAY A LINE GRAPH WITH THE MSCHART CONTROL

```
Private Sub Form_Load()
    'Ensure that first tab button is selected,
    'which also draws the first chart
    tabButtons.Tabs("tabMonthlySales").Selected = True
End Sub

Private Sub DrawMonthlySalesGraph()
    'Purpose:   Draw the monthly sales graph using the data in
    '               tblSalesRollupMonth

    Dim rstMonthlySales As New ADODB.Recordset
    Dim objGrid As MSChart20Lib.DataGrid
```

```
Dim intCtr As Integer


'Open the rollup table, and position record pointer to first record
With rstMonthlySales
    Set .ActiveConnection = cnnDecSupt
    .Source = "SELECT * FROM tblSalesRollupMonth"
    .LockType = adLockReadOnly
    .CursorLocation = adUseClient
    .Open
    .MoveFirst
End With
'Get a handle to the chart's underlying data grid
Set objGrid = chtMonthlySales.DataGrid

'Set the chart's data grid size: one level of row labels, no column
'labels, 12 rows of data (one for each month), and one data column
objGrid.SetSize RowLabelCount:=1, _
                ColumnLabelCount:=0, _
                DataRowCount:=12, _
                DataColumnCount:=1


'Set chart runtime properties
With chtMonthlySales
    'Set the chart type - a two-dimensional line chart
    .chartType = VtChChartType2dLine
    'Set chart statistics lines - show mean and regression (best fit)
    .Plot.SeriesCollection(1).StatLine.Flag = _
        VtChStatsRegression + VtChStatsMean
End With

'Load the data points explicitly
intCtr = 1
With rstMonthlySales
    Do Until .EOF Or intCtr > 12
        objGrid.SetData Row:=intCtr, Column:=1, _
                    DataPoint:=.Fields("Sales"), _
                    nullflag:=False
        objGrid.RowLabel(intCtr, 1) = strMonths(intCtr, 1)
        .MoveNext
        intCtr = intCtr + 1
    Loop
End With
DoEvents 'Ensure that system events are processed after loop

'Setting objects to Nothing is a good programming practices
End Sub
```

> **NOTE**
>
> The MSChart control doesn't provide intrinsic methods for printing or saving the graph or chart image. To print the graph's image, use the `EditCopy` method of the MSChart control to copy both the graphical display of the chart (as a Windows Metafile image) and the chart's underlying data to the Windows Clipboard. Then print the graph's image by using the `Clipboard.GetData` method to retrieve the image data and use the `Printer.PaintPicture` method to paint the image on the printer device. (Use the `Printer.EndDoc` method to cause the image to be printed.)
>
> There is no way to save the MSChart control's image to a disk file. Instead, use Visual Basic's file statements to write the chart's underlying data to a text file, which later can be used to recreate the graph in Word, Access, Excel, MSGraph8, and any other applications that can import comma-delimited data files.

Only the TabStrip Buttons form includes a full implementation of menu choices and button operations for the graph object. The remainder of the forms in Ui_examp.vbp primarily are intended to demonstrate differences in user interface features rather than to exemplify a fully developed application.

Presenting Bar and Area Charts

You create the bar and area charts shown in Figures 9.6 and 9.7 with the VBA code shown in Listing 9.4. The code in Listing 9.4 is more complex than that for the simple line chart of the previous listing because eight sets (categories) of 12 data points (months) are plotted. You also must create a legend that identifies the data sets by color for the display and by different patterns for printing.

LISTING 9.4   THE CODE TO CREATE AND DISPLAY A BAR OR AREA CHART WITH THE MSCHART CONTROL

```
Private Sub Form_Load()
    'Set the tag for the Divisions toolbar button to select an Area Chart
    tlbButtons.Buttons("btnDivision").Tag = "AreaChart"

    'Draw the chart; due to a quirk in the MSChart object, the chart
    'must initially be drawn twice to accurately display the stacked
    'area chart - subsequent chart changes need only be drawn once.
    Call DrawMonthlyDivisionsChart
    Call DrawMonthlyDivisionsChart
End Sub

Private Sub DrawMonthlyDivisionsChart()
    'Purpose:   Draw either an area chart or a vertical stacked bar chart
    '           by division (Category ID) from the monthly sales rollup
```

```
'           by category.

Dim rstMonthlyDivs As New ADODB.Recordset
Dim objGrid As MSChart20Lib.DataGrid
Dim intMonth As Integer
Dim intDivision As Integer

With chtAreaBar
    If tlbButtons.Buttons("btnDivision").Tag = "AreaChart" Then
        'change the button face
        tlbButtons.Buttons("btnDivision").Image = 2
        'Set the graph type to area chart
        .chartType = VtChChartType2dArea
    Else
        'change the button face
        tlbButtons.Buttons("btnDivision").Image = 3
        'Set the graph type to vertical bar chart
        .chartType = VtChChartType2dBar
    End If

    'Set additional chart properties
    .Stacking = True
    .ShowLegend = True
    Set objGrid = .DataGrid
End With

'Set the table object and move to first record
With rstMonthlyDivs
    Set .ActiveConnection = cnnDecSupt
    .Source = "SELECT * FROM tblCategoryRollupMonth"
    .LockType = adLockReadOnly
    .CursorLocation = adUseClient
    .Open
    .MoveLast
End With

With objGrid
    'Set data grid size: one level of row labels, one level of column
    'labels, as many rows of data as there are records in the recordset,
    'and eight data columns
    .SetSize RowLabelCount:=1, _
            ColumnLabelCount:=1, _
            DataRowCount:=(rstMonthlyDivs.RecordCount \ 8), _
            DataColumnCount:=8

    'Create legends for each column from the first 8 records
    rstMonthlyDivs.MoveFirst
    For intDivision = 1 To 8
        .ColumnLabel(intDivision, 1) = rstMonthlyDivs![CategoryName]
        rstMonthlyDivs.MoveNext
    Next intDivision
```

continues

LISTING 9.4 CONTINUED

```
    'Get the 12 data points (months) in each of 8 data sets (categories)
    intDivision = 1
    intMonth = 1
    rstMonthlyDivs.MoveFirst
    Do Until rstMonthlyDivs.EOF
        'Add the new data point
        .SetData Row:=intMonth, Column:=intDivision, _
                DataPoint:=rstMonthlyDivs.Fields("Sales"), _
                nullflag:=False
        If intDivision = 1 Then
            'Add the label text to the x-axis
            .RowLabel(intMonth, 1) = strMonths(intMonth, 1)
        End If

        rstMonthlyDivs.MoveNext
        intDivision = intDivision + 1
        If intDivision = 9 Then
            'The divisions cycle is complete
            intDivision = 1
            intMonth = intMonth + 1
        End If
    Loop
    DoEvents
End With

'Refresh the chart
chtAreaBar.Layout
Set rstMonthlyDivs = Nothing
End Sub
```

Displaying Pie Charts

The code to draw the pie chart shown in Figure 9.8, which displays sales distribution by product for the first quarter of 1995, appears in Listing 9.5. If you want to display the numerical percentage for each product category, you must sum the total sales for the period before you create the pie chart. Calculate the percentage of total sales and add the value in parentheses to the label that appears in the chart's legend.

LISTING 9.5 THE CODE TO CREATE AND DISPLAY A PIE CHART WITH THE MSCHART CONTROL

```
Private Sub Form_Load()
  'Generate the graph
  Call DrawQuarterlyProductsPieChart
End Sub

Private Sub DrawQuarterlyProductsPieChart()
    'Purpose:   Draw the category pie chart from
```

```
'               data in tblCategoryRollupQuarter.

Dim rstCatSales As New ADODB.Recordset
Dim objGrid As MSChart20Lib.DataGrid
Dim varTotalSales As Variant
Dim intCtr As Integer
Dim strLabel As String

'Open the rollup Recordset
With rstCatSales
    Set .ActiveConnection = cnnDecSupt
    .Source = "SELECT * FROM tblCategoryRollupQuarter"
    .LockType = adLockReadOnly
    .CursorLocation = adUseClient
    .Open
    .MoveFirst
End With

'Set chart characteristics
With chtPie
    .chartType = VtChChartType2dPie
    .ShowLegend = True
    .AllowSelections = False
End With

'get a handle to the chart's underlying data grid
Set objGrid = chtPie.DataGrid

'Set the chart's data grid size: one level of row labels, one level
'of column labels, 1 row of data, and 8 columns of data (one for
'each product category)
objGrid.SetSize RowLabelCount:=0, _
                ColumnLabelCount:=1, _
                DataRowCount:=1, _
                DataColumnCount:=8

'Sum the data to get total sales for the quarter
intCtr = 1
Do Until rstCatSales.EOF Or intCtr > 8
    If Not IsNull(rstCatSales!Sales) Then
        varTotalSales = varTotalSales + rstCatSales!Sales
    End If
    intCtr = intCtr + 1
    rstCatSales.MoveNext
    DoEvents
Loop

'Load the data points explicitly
intCtr = 1
rstCatSales.MoveFirst
Do Until rstCatSales.EOF Or intCtr > 8
```

continues

LISTING 9.5 CONTINUED

```
        strLabel = rstCatSales!CategoryName & " (" & _
                Format((rstCatSales!Sales / varTotalSales), "#0.0%") & ")   "
        With objGrid
            .SetData Row:=1, Column:=intCtr, _
                    DataPoint:=rstCatSales!Sales, _
                    nullflag:=False
            .ColumnLabel(intCtr, 1) = strLabel
        End With
        rstCatSales.MoveNext
        intCtr = intCtr + 1
    Loop
    DoEvents
    Set rstCatSales = Nothing
End Sub
```

DISPLAYING DETAIL DATA WITH THE MSFLEXGRID CONTROL

Visual Basic 6 provides four types of grid controls you can use to display tabular data such as the details behind the charts and graphs shown in Figures 9.3 through 9.6—MSFlexGrid, MSHFlexGrid, DBGrid, and DataGrid. The MSFlexGrid control replaces the Grid control of Visual Basic 3.x and 4.0, and MSHFlexGrid is the ADO-enabled version of MSFlexGrid introduced in Visual Basic 6.0. DataGrid is the ADO-enabled version of DBGrid. MSFlexGrid and DBGrid bind to DAO.Recordsets; MSHFlexGrid and DataGrid bind to ADODB.Recordsets.

There are many cases where you prefer to populate a grid manually, creating an unbound grid control. In some cases, the tabular data you want to display might not come from a Recordset, or you might not want to display the entire Recordset in the grid. In other cases, you might want to display column headings that differ from the column headings that are part of the Recordset you're displaying, or to add row labels and display the data in row-major order (essentially, turning the table of data on its side, called *pivoting*).

The MSFlexGrid control is Visual Basic's primary method of displaying unbound tabular data, such as the tabular detail behind a graph or chart presentation. Unlike the DBGrid and DataGrid controls, which are designed primarily for the purpose of displaying bound data, the MSFlexGrid control provides properties and methods that make it easy to control the number of rows and columns in the grid, add or change column headings, and to manually populate the grid with data. The Ui_examp.vbp project therefore uses the MSFlexGrid control to display the tabular data behind its charts and graphs.

▶ **See** "Using Crosstab Queries to Present Summary Data," **p. 288**

The Ui_examp.vbp project uses an MSFlexGrid control and a simple Visual Basic routine to display data created by the tblMonthlyProductSales rollup and a crosstab query derived from the qryMonthlyProductSalesCrosstab query of Dec_supt.mdb. The SQL statement to create the Recordset object (which you manipulate to supply data to the MSFlexGrid control) is as follows:

```
TRANSFORM Sum(Sales) AS SumOfSales
    SELECT ProductID, ProductName
      FROM tblProductRollupMonth
      WHERE CategoryID = '1'
      GROUP BY ProductID, ProductName
PIVOT Month
    In('01','02','03','04','05','06','07','08','09','10','11','12')
```

The Detail Grid form containing the data generated by the preceding SQL statement appears in Figure 9.10. The first row (row 0) and the first two columns (0 and 1) of the grid are fixed (by default, the first row and column of an MSFlexGrid control are always fixed). The ID and Product Name columns remain in position regardless of the location of the slider of the horizontal scrollbar. The first row, which contains the column headers, remains fixed despite the movement of a vertical scrollbar. A vertical scrollbar appears only if the number of rows exceeds that which can be displayed within the Height property value of the grid.

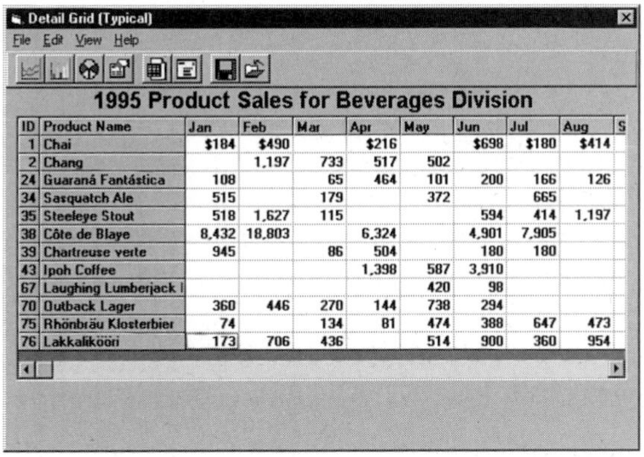

FIGURE 9.10

An MSFlexGrid control with data from the crosstab query for monthly sales by product category.

ID	Product Name	Jan	Feb	Mar	Apr	May	Jun	Jul	Aug	S
1	Chai	$184	$490		$216		$698	$180	$414	
2	Chang		1,197	733	517	502				
24	Guaraná Fantástica	108		65	464	101	200	166	126	
34	Sasquatch Ale	515		179		372		665		
35	Steeleye Stout	518	1,627	115			594	414	1,197	
38	Côte de Blaye	8,432	18,803		6,324		4,901	7,905		
39	Chartreuse verte	945		86	504		180	180		
43	Ipoh Coffee				1,398	587	3,910			
67	Laughing Lumberjack I					420	98			
70	Outback Lager	360	446	270	144	738	294			
75	Rhönbräu Klosterbier	74		134	81	474	388	647	473	
76	Lakkalikööri	173	706	436		514	900	360	954	

The code that loads the grid with the data from the crosstab query is similar to that used to create graphs with multiple data sets. Listing 9.6 sets the number of rows of the grid based on the number of records returned by the query. Then you add the column headings and use nested loops to add the data in column-by-row sequence. Populating the grid control is an example of using integer arguments (instead of field name strings) to specify members of the Fields collection.

LISTING 9.6 THE CODE TO DISPLAY CROSSTAB DATA IN AN MSFLEXGRID CONTROL

```
Private Sub Form_Load()
   Call CategoryProductsGrid
End Sub

Private Sub CategoryProductsGrid()
   'Purpose: Dimension and add data to a grid control

   'Declare the required object and conventional variables
   Dim rstMPS As New ADODB.Recordset
   Dim strSQL As String
   Dim intCol As Integer
   Dim intRow As Integer

   'Open the crosstab Recordset with Category 1 as the "Division"
   strSQL = "TRANSFORM Sum(Sales) AS SumOfSales " & _
            "SELECT ProductID, ProductName " & _
            "FROM tblProductRollupMonth " & _
            "WHERE CategoryID = '1' " & _
            "GROUP BY ProductID, ProductName " & _
            "PIVOT Month "In ('01','02','03','04','05','06'," & _
                 "'07','08','09','10','11','12')"
   With rstMPS
      .ActiveConnection = cnnDecSupt
      .Source = strSQL
      .LockType = adLockReadOnly
      .CursorLocation = adUseClient
      .Open
   End With

   With grdMPS
      'Set the vertical dimensions of the grid control
      .Rows = rstMPS.RecordCount + 1
      .Height = .RowHeight(0) * .Rows + 460

      'Don't exceed the space available on the form
      If .Height > 4095 Then
         .Height = 4095
      End If

      'Set horizontal dimension of the grid control
      .Cols = rstMPS.Fields.Count

      'Add column headers to the grid (Product ID, Product Name, and months)
      .Row = 0
      For intCol = 0 To 13
         .Col = intCol
         If intCol = 0 Then
            'Product ID column
            .Text = "ID"
```

```
                .ColWidth(intCol) = 300
                .FixedAlignment(intCol) = flexAlignCenterCenter
            ElseIf intCol = 1 Then
                'Product Name column
                .Text = "Product Name"
                .ColWidth(intCol) = 2000
                .FixedAlignment(intCol) = flexAlignLeftCenter
            Else
                '12 monthly data columns
                .Text = strMonths(intCol - 1, 1)
                .ColWidth(intCol) = 742
                .FixedAlignment(intCol) = 2
                .ColAlignment(intCol) = flexAlignRightCenter
            End If
        Next intCol

        'Add the data from the Recordset object to the grid
        intRow = 1
        rstMPS.MoveFirst
        Do Until rstMPS.EOF
            'Process one record at a time
            For intCol = 0 To 13
                'The table data is arranged in rows of columns
                .Row = intRow
                .Col = intCol
                If Not IsNull(rstMPS.Fields(intCol)) Then
                    'Attempting to insert Null values causes an error
                    If intCol > 1 Then
                        If intRow = 1 Then
                            .Text = Format(CCur(rstMPS.Fields(intCol)), "$#,##0")
                        Else
                            .Text = Format(CCur(rstMPS.Fields(intCol)), "#,##0")
                        End If
                    Else
                        .Text = rstMPS.Fields(intCol)
                    End If
                End If
            Next intCol
            rstMPS.MoveNext
            intRow = intRow + 1
            DoEvents
        Loop

        'Lock the first two columns of the control
        .FixedCols = 2
    End With
    DoEvents
    'Free the memory
    Set rstMPS = Nothing
End Sub
```

9

If your queries return relatively few (less than 100) rows to an MSFlexGrid control, the performance of your Visual Basic 6.0 application is likely to be slightly better than an identical application created with an MSHFlexGrid or a DataGrid control bound to a `ADODB.Recordset` with a server-side keyset or dynamic cursor. As the number of rows increases, the bound control gains the advantage because a Jet server-side keyset or dynamic cursor returns only 100 or so records to `Recordset` objects before painting the subform. If you manually fill the MSFlexGrid control in the `Form_Load` event handler with the data from a few hundred or more rows, your form takes a substantial period of time to open. It's a good application design practice, however, to limit the number of rows presented to the user to 25 or fewer in a single grid.

> **NOTE**
>
> Although bound MSHFlexGrid and DataGrid controls require much less VBA code to populate than using unbound techniques, the basic MSFlexGrid control consumes fewer client resources and offers excellent flexibility of data presentation. As an example, you can easily add row and column totals (called crossfooting) to an unbound MSFlexGrid control by adding a row to the grid. You sum the values of each column and row as you iterate the columns and rows in your `Do While…Loop` structure. Users of summary decision-support forms appreciate crossfooting grids that contain time-series data.

TAKING FULL ADVANTAGE OF DATA-BOUND ACTIVEX CONTROLS

IN THIS CHAPTER

A controversy exists among professional database developers and administrators regarding the use of bound controls for updating tables in production multiuser applications and especially in client/server front ends. The primary issue relates to users having a "live" connection to multiple database tables that causes excessive network traffic. User updates from DataGrids, called browse-mode editing, often result in concurrency problems when multiple users attempt to simultaneously update the same record(s). Lack of proper safeguards in the client front end or the database can lead to data inconsistency or *deadlock*, a condition in which two users place write locks on related records in joined tables. A deadlock freezes the records, preventing updates and, in some cases, the ability of other users to read the records.

▶ **See** "Defining Transactions and the ACID Test," **p. 739**

Jet 3.5x's intrinsic transaction processing of action queries, combined with internal enforcement of referential integrity by Jet and client/server RDBMSs, lessen the risks previously associated with Visual Basic's (and Access's) bound controls. The primary advantage of Visual Basic's complex-bound controls is rapid application development (RAD). Thus many developers use bound controls to create application prototypes and then convert the prototypes to production applications that substitute unbound for bound controls. Passing values from unbound controls through VBA code to `BeginTrans...CommitTrans` operations, or to Transact-SQL stored procedures having `BEGIN TRANS...COMMIT TRANS` statements, lets you "wrap" update operations within explicit transactions. Transactions assure that all members of a set of updates to the database tables proceed without conflict; if a conflict occurs, the updates are canceled to return the tables to their original, consistent status.

Regardless of your stand (or your clients' or employer's position) on the bound-versus-unbound issue, every Visual Basic developer should understand the workings of data-bound controls. Data-bound controls let you quickly create prototypes of database front ends to which you later can add VBA code to upgrade the front ends to production specifications. This chapter expands the introduction to simple- and complex-bound controls of Chapter 4, "Using the ADO Data Control with Bound Controls."

WORKING WITH DATAGRIDS AND HIERARCHICAL FLEXGRIDS

▶ **See** "Reviewing the Code of the Ado2oltp Project," **p. 796**

The DataGrid control, which replaces the DBGrid control of previous Visual Basic versions, is the most important complex-bound control of Visual Basic 6.0. The content of DataGrids is updatable, so the control can be used for browse-mode editing of updatable `Recordsets`. Another application for DataGrids is adding multiple records, such as sales order or invoice line items, to a table in a single operation. Chapter 20, "Porting Access OLTP Applications to Visual Basic 6.0," includes an example of the use of a DataGrid for entering sales order line items. One of the primary advantages of the DataGrid control is easy design-time formatting; you can set column width, alignment, and numeric format, such as currency, in the property pages of the DataGrid.

The Hierarchical FlexGrid (MSHFlexGrid) control, derived from Visual Basic 5.0's FlexGrid control, is a read-only grid commonly used to display multiple lines of data in decision-support applications. The MSHFlexGrid also serves as a substitute for Access's multicolumn list box, which isn't included in Visual Basic 6.0's control repertoire. With conventional Recordsets, FlexGrid and MSHFlexGrids are, for the most part, interchangeable. Chapter 20's Ado2oltp.vbp project substitutes FlexGrids for Access list boxes to display lists of customers, orders, and order line items. An MSHFlexGrid is required to display ADO 2.0's new hierarchical Recordsets, the subject of the "Creating and Displaying Hierarchical Recordsets" section later in the chapter. MSHFlexGrid and FlexGrid controls don't offer the simple design-time formatting features of DataGrids. You must add VBA code to the Form_Load event handler to specify column widths and other display formatting.

Formatting the DataGrid Control

The Properties window for the DataGrid control does not provide access to individual columns for formatting purposes. When you add a DataGrid control to a form, the default appearance of the control in design mode consists of an empty column header and an empty row (see Figure 10.1). To format the DataGrid control, right-click the surface of the control to display the context menu and then choose Retrieve Fields to populate the column headers in design mode. Figure 10.2 shows the headings retrieved for the first six columns of a DataGrid bound to the Products table of the Nwind.mdb sample database.

FIGURE 10.1
Choosing Retrieve Fields from the DataGrid's context menu.

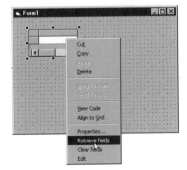

FIGURE **10.2**

*Column names
retrieved from
Nwind.mdb's
Products table.*

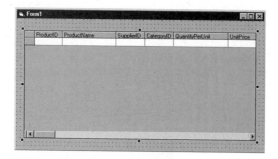

To add a caption to the DataGrid control, change the column headings; alternatively, set the font attributes for the column headings and/or the remainder of the grid and then right-click the DataGrid control to open the context menu and choose Properties. The Properties sheet for the grid provides the following eight pages to format the DataGrid control:

- The *General* page, shown in Figure 10.3, lets you add a caption bar to the control and set 11 property values that also appear in Visual Basic's Properties window for DataGrid controls. The most important of the General properties are `AllowAddNew`, `AllowDelete`, and `AllowUpdate`, whose check boxes must be marked to make the DataGrid fully updatable.

FIGURE **10.3**

*The General page
of the DataGrid's
Properties sheet.*

- The *Keyboard* page, illustrated by Figure 10.4, controls navigation features of the control. `AllowArrows` (default) enables the cursor keys for moving between columns and rows. Marking the `WrapCellPointer` check box enables the cursor and tab keys to move the selection from the last column of the current record to the first column of the next record. Setting `TabAction` to `2 - dbgGridNavigation` enables the tab key for record navigation. The settings shown in Figure 10.4 are recommended for updating `Recordsets` with DataGrids.

FIGURE 10.4

*Setting DataGrid
navigation proper-
ties in the Keyboard
page.*

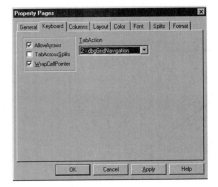

- The *Columns* page, shown in Figure 10.5, provides design-mode access to the `Columns` collection of the DataGrid control and lets you set `Caption` and `DataField` property values of each `Column` object in the collection. A common practice is to change the `Caption` property to make column headers more readable by adding spaces to field names or substituting a more common descriptor. You can change the sequence of the columns by selecting alternative `DataField` values.

FIGURE 10.5

Specifying the
`Caption` *and*
`DataField` *proper-
ties for a* `Column`
object.

- The *Layout* page, illustrated by Figure 10.6, lets you set additional `Column` properties. The most important features of the Columns page are the ability to set the `Alignment` and `Width` properties of each column. Right alignment is preferred for numeric values. You can prevent changing values by marking the Locked check box, prevent resizing the width of the column by clearing the AllowSizing check box, hide the column by clearing the Visible check box, allow multiline text entry by marking the WrapText check box, and add a drop-down list button by marking the Button check box.

> **NOTE**
>
> You can't set the `Alignment` property of the column header and the columnar data independently. Thus you can't emulate exactly the formatting of Access 97 datasheets, which center column headers regardless of the formatting of the data in the column.

FIGURE 10.6

Specifying additional `Column` *properties in the Layout page.*

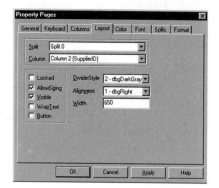

- The *Colors* page sets the `ForeColor` and `BackColor` properties of the column headings and the remainder of the control, duplicating the ForeColor and BackColor entries in Visual Basic 6.0's Properties window.

- The *Fonts* page lets you selectively set the typeface family (font), size, and attributes for the column headers and caption (if any), plus the body of the DataGrid control.

- The *Splits* page lets you divide the columns of the DataGrid to provide multiple, independently scrollable views of a common data source. Split DataGrid controls are difficult for the average user to navigate, so splits aren't used in the examples of this book.

- The *Format* page, shown in Figure 10.7, lets you apply specific formatting to individual columns, such as a Currency format for the UnitPrice column. Accept the default General format for text columns and apply the Number format, with the appropriate number of decimal places, to numeric fields. Apply the Checkbox format to columns of the Boolean (Yes/No) field data type, such as the Discontinued column, if you intend to bind a check box control to the column. With the exception of the Checkbox format, the `Format` property of a `Column` object uses format strings identical to those of VBA's **Format** function.

FIGURE 10.7

Applying the Currency format to a UnitPrice column.

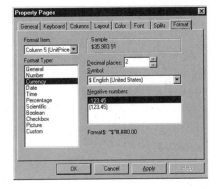

TIP

To maintain Y2K compliance, always format date fields with four-character years, as in `"MM/dd/yyyy"`.

Figure 10.8 shows the first seven columns and first 12 rows of the Products table of the Nwind.mdb database displayed by the `dtgProducts` control in run mode. The bold attribute is applied to the caption bar and the column headers font by setting the HeadFont's Bold attribute in the Fonts page.

FIGURE 10.8

The formatted DataGrid control in run mode.

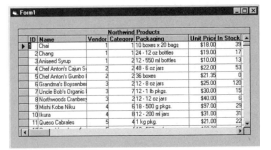

Special Properties, Methods, and Events of the DataGrid Control

The DataGrid control shares many properties, methods, and events with the DAO-bound DBGrid control. The DataGrid control offers a number of features that reduce the amount of VBA code necessary to alter the display of data or modify the displayed data. The following sections describe how to sort grid data by column values, hide individual columns, and validate edits to the underlying `Recordset`.

10

DATA-BOUND
ACTIVEX
CONTROLS

Using the `HeadClick` Event to Sort by Columns

Users of applications with DataGrid controls are likely to want to sort the underlying `Recordset` on fields other than the primary key field (if a primary key field exists). FlexGrids and MSHFlexGrids have a `Sort` property, but the DataGrid doesn't. However, you can sort the DataGrid's underlying `Recordset` object and then apply the `DataGrid.Refresh` method to redisplay the rows in sorted order.

The DataGrid.vbp project in the \Ddg_vb6\Chaptr10 folder of the accompanying CD-ROM illustrates sorting a DataGrid with the `DataGrid_HeadClick` event handler. The `DataSource` of the `dtgProducts` DataGrid on `frmProducts` is the `envData DataEnvironment`, and the `DataMember` is the `Products` command, which generates the `rsProducts Recordset`. The following code sorts the rows of `dtgProducts` by the column header you click.

```
Private Sub dtgProducts_HeadClick(ByVal intColIndex As Integer)
    'Sort by clicked column
    With envData.rsProducts
        .Sort = .Fields(intColIndex).Name & " ASC"
    End With
    dtgProducts.Refresh
End Sub
```

Figure 10.9 shows the result of clicking the column header of the ProductName (Name) column. Sorting by the In Stock column displays the out-of-stock or low-stock items at the top of the list. Clicking the ID column returns the row order to the original primary key sequence.

FIGURE 10.9

The result of using the HeadClick *event to sort the DataGrid's* Recordset *by clicking a column header.*

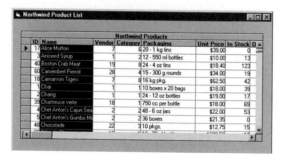

If the `Recordset` contains a Text (Memo, `Type = 11`) or LongBinary (OLE Object, `Type = 12`) field and you click the column header of one of these columns, you receive a `Can't sort on Memo or OLE object ([FieldName])` error message. You can disable sorting on Memo and OLE Object fields by checking the field data type with the following code:

```
Private Sub dtgProducts_HeadClick(ByVal intColIndex As Integer)
    'Sort by clicked column
    With envData.rsProducts
        If .Fields(intColIndex).Type < 11 Then
            .Sort = .Fields(intColIndex).Name & " ASC"
        [Else
            'Add optional "nocando" message box here]
        End If
    End With
    dtgProducts.Refresh
End Sub
```

Changing Columns Displayed in Run Mode

You can control the number of columns displayed in run mode by manipulating the Columns collection of the DataGrid control. The simplest method of hiding one or more columns is to set the value of the Visible property of the appropriate Column object to **False**. Hiding columns is useful when the display area is limited and users must scan specific columns to find a particular record. The following two event-handling subprocedures hide selected columns and display all columns in response to clicking the Some Columns and All Columns command buttons (see Figure 10.10).

```
Private Sub cmdSomeCols_Click()
    'Hide Vendor and Category columns
    With dtgProducts
        .Columns(2).Visible = False
        .Columns(3).Visible = False
        .Columns(5).Visible = False
    End With
    cmdAllCols.Enabled = True
    cmdSomeCols.Enabled = False
End Sub


Private Sub cmdAllCols_Click()
    'Show all columns
    Dim intCol As Integer
    With dtgProducts
        For intCol = 0 To .Columns.Count - 1
            .Columns(intCol).Visible = True
        Next intCol
    End With
    cmdSomeCols.Enabled = True
    cmdAllCols.Enabled = False
End Sub
```

FIGURE 10.10

Hiding columns of a DataGrid control with VBA code.

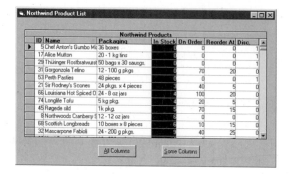

Using DataGrid Events to Validate Updates

The DataGrid control has a variety of events that are triggered when you edit the underlying `Recordset` object. Table 10.1 lists the events that are triggered when you update a column value or delete, insert, or update a row in a DataGrid control. You add validation code to the `Before...` events to ensure data consistency and to preserve referential integrity. The `Before...` events include a `Cancel` argument that, by setting `Cancel = True`, lets you abort the action in case the entry fails the validation test.

TABLE 10.1 `Before...` AND `After...` EVENTS OF THE DATAGRID CONTROL

Event	When Triggered
BeforeColEdit	After moving to a new cell but before typing the first character in a cell
ColEdit	After typing the first character in a cell
AfterColEdit	Immediately follows the `AfterColUpdate` event
BeforeColUpdate	After altering the value of a cell and moving to a new cell but before the content of the DataGrid buffer changes
AfterColUpdate	After changing the content of the DataGrid buffer for the updated column (same as `AfterColEdit` event)
BeforeDelete	After selecting a row and pressing the Delete key but before the row is deleted from the `Recordset`
AfterDelete	After deletion of the row from the `Recordset`
BeforeInsert	After entering at least one character in a column of the tentative append record but before the row is added to the `Recordset`

Event	When Triggered
AfterInsert	After the row is added to the Recordset
BeforeUpdate	After changing the value in any column and moving to a new record but before the Recordset is updated
AfterUpdate	After updating the row of the Recordset

The code in Listing 10.1 shows examples that display message boxes to identify the point at which each event listed in Table 10.1 is triggered.

LISTING 10.1   CODE TO CREATE MESSAGE BOXES IDENTIFYING THE OCCURRENCE OF *Before...* AND *After...* EVENTS OF THE DATAGRID CONTROL

```
Private Sub dtgProducts_BeforeColUpdate(ByVal intColIndex As Integer, _
     varOldValue As Variant, intCancel As Integer)
   Dim strWarn As String
   strWarn = strMsg & "update the column value from '" & _
      varOldValue & "' to '" & _
      dtgProducts.Columns(intColIndex).Value &  "'?"
   If MsgBox(strWarn, vbYesNo + vbQuestion, "Confirm Update") = _
        vbNo Then
      intCancel = True
   End If
End Sub


Private Sub dtgProducts_AfterColUpdate(ByVal intColIndex As Integer)
   MsgBox "Column " & intColIndex + 1 & " updated.", _
      vbInformation, "Update Confirmation"
End Sub


Private Sub dtgProducts_BeforeDelete(intCancel As Integer)
   Dim strWarn As String
   strWarn = strMsg & "delete this row?"
   If MsgBox(strWarn, vbYesNo + vbQuestion, "Confirm Delete") = _
        vbNo Then
      intCancel = True
   End If
End Sub


Private Sub dtgProducts_AfterDelete()
   MsgBox "Row deleted.", vbInformation, "Delete Confirmation"
End Sub


Private Sub dtgProducts_BeforeInsert(intCancel As Integer)
   Dim strWarn As String
   strWarn = strMsg & "add this new row?"
   If MsgBox(strWarn, vbYesNo + vbQuestion, "Confirm Insert") = _
```

continues

LISTING 10.1 CONTINUED

```
        vbNo Then
      intCancel = True
    End If
End Sub

Private Sub dtgProducts_AfterInsert()
    MsgBox "New row added.", vbInformation, "Insert Confirmation"
End Sub

Private Sub dtgProducts_BeforeUpdate(intCancel As Integer)
    Dim strWarn As String
    strWarn = strMsg & "update this row?"
    If MsgBox(strWarn, vbYesNo + vbQuestion, "Confirm Update") = _
        vbNo Then
      intCancel = True
    End If
End Sub

Private Sub dtgProducts_AfterUpdate()
    MsgBox "Row updated.", vbInformation, "Update Confirmation"
End Sub
```

> **NOTE**
>
> The preceding event handlers are incorporated in the DataGrid.vbp project in the \Ddg_vb6\Chaptr10 folder of the accompanying CD-ROM. Data type prefixes have been added to names of arguments of the event handlers in accordance with the variable naming conventions used in this book.

Formatting MSFlexGrid and MSHFlexGrid Controls

Selecting an MSHFlexGrid when you right-click and drag a Data Environment Command object to a form adds an empty MSHFlexGrid1 control with two empty column headers and a single empty row (see Figure 10.11). Right-clicking the control and choosing Retrieve Structure has an effect similar to that of the Retrieve Fields command for a DataGrid. Retrieve Structure, however, doesn't attempt to guess the correct width for a column based on the width of the column's Caption or the cell data; all column widths are identical in design and run modes (see Figure 10.12).

FIGURE 10.11

An `MSHFlexGrid1`
control bound to
the `rsProducts`
Recordset.

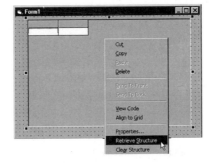

FIGURE 10.12

The unformatted
`MSHFlexGrid1` *con-*
trol in run mode.

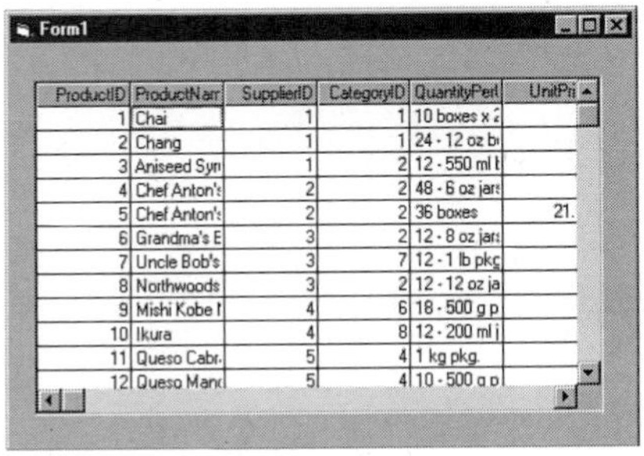

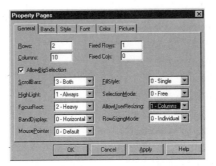

The MSHFlexGrid and the DataGrid are similar in that right-clicking either control and choosing <u>P</u>roperties opens the Properties sheet for the control. However, the similarity ends at this
point. The General page, shown in Figure 10.13, sets the basic navigation features and overall
appearance of the control.

FIGURE 10.13

The General prop-
erties page for
MSHFlexGrid
controls.

Some of the property settings, such as `Rows` and `Columns`, are self-evident. Following is an
explanation of those properties that aren't self-explanatory:

- `AllowBigSelection`, when marked, causes a click on a header to select an entire column
  and, if one or more fixed columns are specified, an entire row.

- `HighLight` determines when a selection is highlighted by a focus rectangle and reverse video (1 - Always [default], 0 - Never, and 2 - With Focus).

- `FocusRectangle` emphasizes or de-emphasizes identification of the cell with the focus (1 - Light [default], 0 - None, and 2 - Heavy).

- `BandDisplay` determines the banding orientation (0 - Horizontal [default] or 1 - Vertical). Bands are one of the subjects of the "Creating and Displaying Hierarchical `Recordsets`" section later in the chapter.

- `FillStyle` determines how formatting applied to a single text cell applies to other selected text cells (0 - Single or 1 - Repeat).

- `SelectionMode` specifies whether cell selection by the mouse is unconstrained (0 - Free [default]), row-wise (1 - ByRow), or column-wise (1 - ByCol).

- `AllowUserResizing` controls the ability of the user to resize columns and rows in run mode (0 - None [default], 1 - Columns, 2 - Rows, or 3 - Both). A better default choice for most applications is 1 - Columns.

- `RowSizingMode` specifies whether resizing a row (with `AllowUserResizing` set to 2 - Rows or 3 - Both) affects only the selected row (0 - Individual [default]) or all rows (1 - All).

The Bands page for the default Band 0 (see Figure 10.14) lets you specify Gridlines style, TextStyle, and TextStyleHeader. The default values cause the appearance of MSHFlexGrids to resemble DataGrids. Marking ColumnHeaders adds *another* fixed row of column headers to the control. Clearing the check box in the Column Caption - Column Name list hides the selected column. MSHFlexGrids bound to hierarchical `Recordsets` have a band for each level in the hierarchy.

FIGURE 10.14

The Bands page for MSHFlexGrid controls.

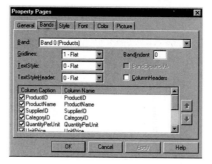

Taking Advantage of the MergeCells Feature

The most important property of the Style page (see Figure 10.15) is MergeCells. The MSHFlexGrid (and the MSFlexGrid) lets you specify whether the grid allows merging rows and/or columns with identical values into a single, expanded cell. You can specify allowable merge operations by selecting the appropriate `MergeCells` property value (0 - Never [default], 1 - Free, 2 - Restrict Rows, 3 - Restrict Cols, or 4 - Restrict All).

FIGURE 10.15
Enabling cell merging in the Style page.

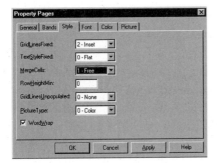

Merging cells is particularly effective when displaying a `Recordset` generated by a one-to-many join. As an example, the `CustomersOrders Command` of the DataGrid.dsr designer file is based on the following SQL statement:

```
SELECT Customers.CustomerID, Customers.CompanyName,
      Orders.OrderID, Orders.OrderDate, Orders.ShippedDate
   FROM Customers, Orders
   WHERE Customers.CustomerID = Orders.CustomerID
   ORDER BY Customers.CustomerID ASC, Orders.OrderID DESC
```

The `frmMerge` form's `hfgMerge` control is bound to the `rsCustomersOrders Recordset`. Conventional presentation of the `rsCustomersOrders` in an MSHFlexGrid appears in Figure 10.16. The CustomerID and CompanyName column values repeat for each order.

CustomerID	CompanyName	OrderID	OrderDate	ShippedD.
ALFKI	Alfreds Futterkiste	11011	5/9/96	5/13/96
ALFKI	Alfreds Futterkiste	10952	4/15/96	4/23/96
ALFKI	Alfreds Futterkiste	10835	2/15/96	2/21/96
ALFKI	Alfreds Futterkiste	10702	11/13/95	11/21/95
ALFKI	Alfreds Futterkiste	10692	11/3/95	11/13/95
ALFKI	Alfreds Futterkiste	10643	9/25/95	10/3/95
ANATR	Ana Trujillo	10926	4/3/96	4/10/96
ANATR	Ana Trujillo	10759	12/29/95	1/12/96
ANATR	Ana Trujillo	10625	9/8/95	9/14/95
ANATR	Ana Trujillo	10308	10/19/94	10/25/94
ANTON	Antonio Moreno	10856	2/28/96	3/12/96
ANTON	Antonio Moreno	10682	10/26/95	11/1/95
ANTON	Antonio Moreno	10677	10/23/95	10/27/95
ANTON	Antonio Moreno	10573	7/20/95	7/21/95
ANTON	Antonio Moreno	10535	6/13/95	6/21/95
ANTON	Antonio Moreno	10507	5/16/95	5/23/95

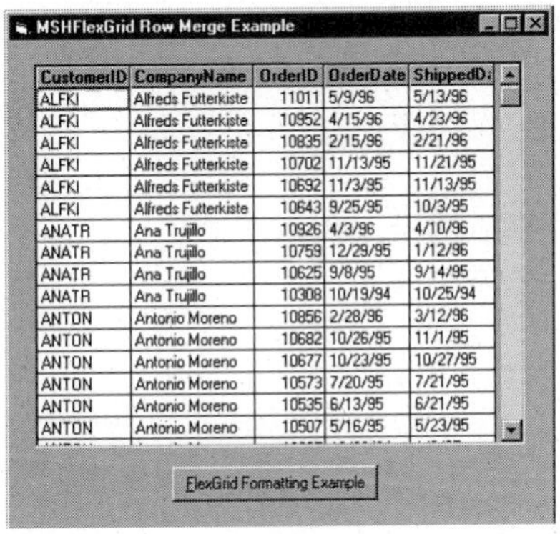

FIGURE 10.16
Conventional MSHFlexGrid display of a `Recordset` *with a one-to-many join.*

Setting the value of the MergeCells property doesn't automatically merge cells with identical values. You must add VBA code to set the MergeCols(intCol) and/or MergeRows(intRow) property values of the MSHFlexGrid to **True**, as in this example:

```
Private Sub Form_Load()
    'Merge the first two columns
    With hfgMerge
        .MergeCol(0) = True
        .MergeCol(1) = True
    End With
End Sub
```

When you open frmMerge with the preceding event handler, the merged rows appear as illustrated by Figure 10.17.

▶ **See** "Grids to Display Cellset Subobjects," **p. 1067**

FIGURE 10.17

An example of MSHFlexGrid cell merging.

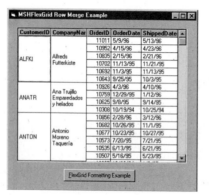

> **NOTE**
>
> Forms for the two MSHFlexGrid examples are included in the FlexGrid.vbp project in the \Ddg_vb6\Chaptr10 folder of the accompanying CD-ROM. Click the Merge Example button to display frmMerge and the FlexGrid Formatting Example button to return to frmFlexGrid. Chapter 28, "Analyzing Multidimensional Data with OLAP and MDX," includes another example of MSHFlexGrid cell merging.

Formatting MSHFlexGrid Cells with VBA Code

▶ **See** "Displaying Detail Data with the MSFlexGrid Control," **p. 366**

You can handle most formatting requirements of DataGrids with design-time Property Pages, but MSHFlexGrids (and MSFlexGrids) require you to write code to set property values because of their lack of `Columns` collections. You set the `ColAlignment` and `ColWidth` property values for each column, set the value of the `Col` property to a particular column, and then set the caption text in the `Form_Load` event handler. Finally, in the `Form_Activate` event handler, you apply special formats to the `Text` values of each cell with the **Format** function. Listing 10.2 illustrates the VBA code required to format the `hfgProducts` control for consistency the `dtgProduct` control of the DataGrid.vbp project.

LISTING 10.2   CODE TO FORMAT THE HFGPRODUCTS CONTROL

```
Private Sub Form_Load()
    'Format the MSHFlexGrid columns
    Dim intCtr As Integer

    With hfgProducts
        'Set default column alignment
        For intCtr = 0 To .Cols - 1
            .ColAlignment(intCtr) = flexAlignRightCenter
        Next intCtr
        'Handle text column exceptions
        .ColAlignment(1) = flexAlignLeftCenter
        .ColAlignment(4) = flexAlignLeftCenter

        'Set column widths in twips
        .ColWidth(0) = 300
        .ColWidth(1) = 1740
        .ColWidth(2) = 700
        .ColWidth(3) = 850
        .ColWidth(4) = 1740
        .ColWidth(5) = 800
        .ColWidth(6) = 950
        .ColWidth(7) = 900
        .ColWidth(8) = 1000
        .ColWidth(9) = 1000

        'Change the column header captions
        .Row = 0
        .Col = 0
        .Text = "ID"
        .Col = 1
        .Text = "Name"
        .Col = 2
        .Text = "Vendor"
```

continues

10

DATA-BOUND
ACTIVEX
CONTROLS

LISTING 10.2 CONTINUED

```
        .Col = 3
        .Text = "Category"
        .Col = 4
        .Text = "Package"
        .Col = 5
        .Text = "Price"
        .Col = 6
        .Text = "On Hand"
        .Col = 7
        .Text = "On Order"
        .Col = 8
        .Text = "Reorder At"
        .Col = 9
        .Text = "Disc."
    End With
End Sub

Private Sub Form_Activate()
    'Format the UnitPrice column
    Dim intCtr As Integer

    With hfgProducts
        .Col = 5
        For intCtr = 1 To .Rows - 1
            .Row = intCtr
            .Text = Format(.Text, "$#0.00")
        Next intCtr
    End With
End Sub
```

Figure 10.18 shows a few of the formatted columns of the `hfgProducts` control in run mode.

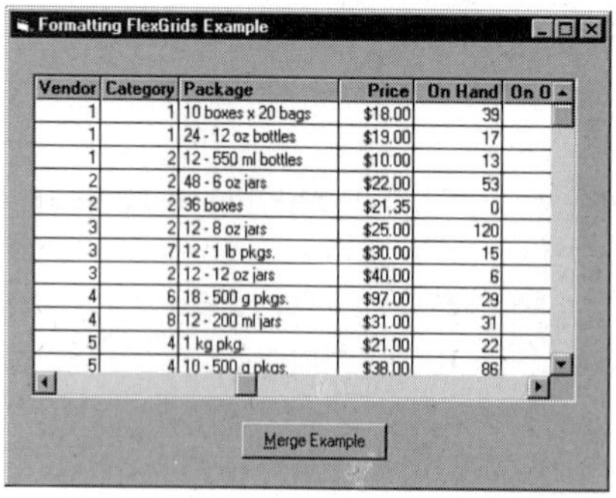

FIGURE 10.18

The formatted
hfgProducts
MSHFlexGrid
control in run
mode.

Microsoft Y2K police didn't catch up with the culprits who developed the DataGrid, FlexGrid, and MSFlexGrid controls. Date fields (for the U.S. English locale) default to `"M/d/yy"` format in all three grids. Thus you must reformat date fields of FlexGrid and MSHFlexGrid controls with code similar to the following:

```
Private Sub Form_Activate()
    'Format the dates for Y2K compliance
    Dim intRow As Integer
    Dim intCol As Integer

    With hfgMerge
        For intRow = 1 To .Rows - 1
            For intCol = 3 To 4
                .Col = intCol
                .Row = intRow
                .Text = Format(.Text, "MM/dd/yyyy")
            Next intCol
        Next intRow
    End With
End Sub
```

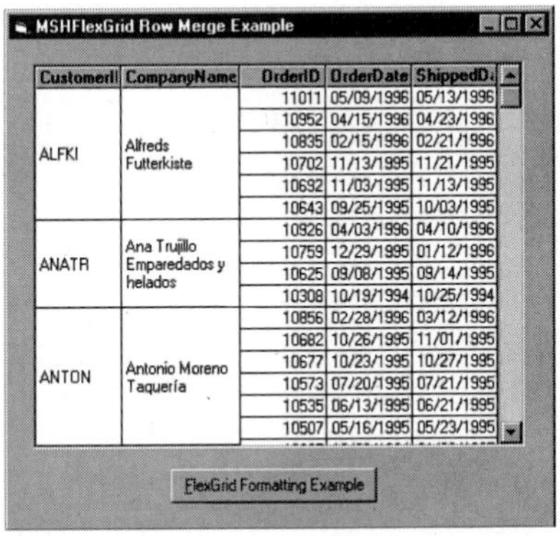

FIGURE 10.19

Date fields of the hfgMerge *control formatted for Y2K compliance.*

Sorting on MSHFlexGrid Columns

Unlike the DataGrid, which requires that you sort the underlying `Recordset`, the MSHFlexGrid has a built-in `Sort` property. To sort an MSHFlexGrid, you specify the column by an `MSHFlexGrid.Col = n` statement and then set the `MSHFlexGrid.Sort` property to one of the `flexSort...` constants listed in Table 10.2. It's not necessary to call the `Refresh` method after changing the `Sort` property value.

10

TABLE 10.2   ENUMERATION OF ALLOWABLE VALUES FOR THE MSHFLEXGRID'S Sort PROPERTY

Constant	Value	Sort Order
flexSortNone	0	No sorting (original order)
flexSortGenericAscending	1	Ascending sort on estimate of string or number values
flexSortGenericDescending	2	Descending sort on estimate of string or number values
flexSortNumericAscending	3	Converts strings to numbers and sorts ascending
flexSortNumericDescending	4	Converts strings to numbers and sorts descending
flexSortStringNoCaseAsending	5	Ascending case-insensitive string sort
flexSortNoCaseDescending	6	Descending case-insensitive string sort
flexSortStringAscending	7	Ascending case-sensitive string sort
flexSortStringDescending	8	Descending case-sensitive string sort
flexSortCustom	9	Lets you use the Compare event handler to perform a special sort

CREATING AND DISPLAYING HIERARCHICAL Recordsets

▶ **See** "The Network and Hierarchical Database Models," **p. 214**
and "Normalizing Table Data," **p. 227**

OLE DB and ADO 2.0 enable the creation of hierarchical Recordsets, which resemble Recordsets generated by one-to-many joins but have an internal structure more closely related to tables of hierarchical databases. A hierarchical Recordset, called a *chaptered rowset* by the OLE DB specification, substitutes a **Variant** array (*detail set*) for the usual atomic value of a Recordset cell. Hierarchical Recordsets violate the fundamental rule of relational databases: Tables shall be flat and contain no repeating groups (first normal form). The MSDataShape OLE DB service provider, interposed between the OLE DB data provider and consumer, generates the chaptered rowset in accordance with SHAPE statements. SHAPE statements are related to SQL, but SHAPE grammar has its own unique keywords, such as APPEND, COMPUTE, and RELATE.

Hierarchical Recordsets are more efficient than conventional Recordsets having one-to-many relationships. Hierarchical Recordsets minimize the number of repetitive column values from the one side of the relationship; only the primary and foreign key values on which the relationship is based are duplicated. The more INNER JOINs in the Recordset's Source SQL statement, the more efficient hierarchical Recordsets become. Consider using hierarchical Recordsets whenever you must pass a substantial amount of related data over a slow or heavily trafficked network connection, such as a WAN or the Internet.

Generating Hierarchical Commands with the Data Environment Designer

The first step in displaying a hierarchical Recordset in an MSHFlexGrid control is to generate the Recordset with a parent and one or more child commands. The easiest method of generating hierarchical Recordsets is to use the Data Environment Designer (DED) to create parent-child Command relationships. To create a three-level Customers-Orders-Order Details hierarchical Recordset and view its SHAPE command, do the following:

1. Open a new Data Project and create a cnnNwind Connection object for Nwind.mdb.

2. Add a Command object for the highest level of the hierarchy, in this case the Customers table. Only the CustomerID and CompanyName fields are required, so the SQL statement for the Customers Command is SELECT CustomerID, CompanyName FROM Customers.

3. Right-click the Customers command and choose Add Child Command from the context menu. Rename the command to Orders and choose Properties from its context menu to open the Orders Properties sheet.

4. Select the SQL Statement option and type **SELECT CustomerID, OrderID, OrderDate, ShippedDate FROM Orders ORDER BY OrderDate DESC** in the text box.

5. Click the Relation tab, accept the default entries, and click Add to specify CustomerID as the Parent and Child Fields for the relationship (see Figure 10.20). Click OK to close the Orders Properties sheet.

   Default Parent and Child Fields are selected correctly if the two Commands have a common field name.

FIGURE 10.20

Defining the relationship between fields of a parent and child Command object.

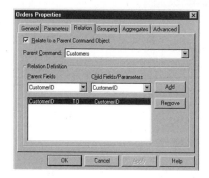

6. Right-click the Orders command and choose Add Child Command from the context menu. Rename the command to OrderDetails and choose Properties from its context menu to open the Orders Properties sheet.

7. Select the SQL Statement option and type **SELECT OrderID, Quantity, ProductID FROM [Order Details]** in the text box.

8. Click the Relation tab, accept the default entries, and click Add to specify OrderID as the Parent and Child Fields for the relationship. Click OK to close the OrderDetails Properties sheet.

9. In the DataEnvironment window, expand the Customers, Orders, and OrderDetails nodes to display the Command objects' fields (see Figure 10.21).

FIGURE 10.21

The Command hierarchy displayed in the DataEnvironment window.

10. Right-click the Customers node and choose Hierarchy Info from the context menu to open the Hierarchy Info dialog, which displays the SHAPE statement required to create the hierarchical Recordset (see Figure 10.22).

FIGURE 10.22

The SHAPE statement created by the Data Environment Designer for a three-level hierarchy.

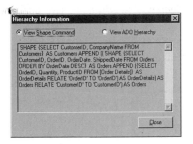

11. Select the View ADO Hierarchy option to display the hierarchy structure (see Figure 10.23). Click Close to close the Hierarchy Info dialog.

FIGURE 10.23

An alternative view of the rsCustomers hierarchy in the Hierarchy Info dialog.

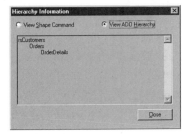

The full text of the SHAPE statement, which the MSDataShape OLE DB service provider parses, follows.

```
SHAPE {SELECT CustomerID, CompanyName FROM Customers} AS Customers
    APPEND ((SHAPE {SELECT CustomerID, OrderID, OrderDate, ShippedDate
        FROM Orders ORDER BY OrderDate DESC} AS Orders
            APPEND ({SELECT OrderID, Quantity, ProductID
                FROM [Order Details]} AS OrderDetails
            RELATE 'OrderID' TO 'OrderID') AS OrderDetails) AS Orders
    RELATE 'CustomerID' TO 'CustomerID') AS Orders
```

The elements of the preceding statement are as follows:

- SHAPE invokes the MSDataShape OLE DB service provider.
- {SELECT ...} is an ANSI SQL statement that defines the Recordset or its detail sets. French braces must surround SQL statements.
- AS specifies the alias that defines the *Command*.Name property.
- APPEND adds the detail set to the Recordset. One APPEND statement is required for each generation (child, grandchild, great-grandchild, and so on).

10

- RELATE establishes the fields on which the parent-child or child-grandchild relationship is based, similar to a join created by a WHERE *Field1* = *Field2* clause. RELATE clauses have a one-to-one correspondence with APPEND clauses.

A SHAPE statement serves as the Source property value of a Recordset object having "MSDataShape" as the Provider property value. The "Manipulating Hierarchical Recordsets with Code" section, later in the chapter, describes how to create and access detail sets with VBA code.

Displaying the rsCustomers Recordset in an MSHFlexGrid

As with conventional Recordsets, you use drag and drop to add to a form an MSHFlexGrid bound to a hierarchical Recordset. To add to frmDataEnv an MSHFlexGrid bound to the Customers command and eliminate duplicate columns, do the following:

1. Right-click and drag the Customers Command to frmDataEnv, selecting Hierarchical FlexGrid from the context menu.

2. Expand frmDataEnv and the MSHFlexGrid1 control and then run the project. MSHFlexGrid1 displays the contents of rsCustomers in a fully expanded format (see Figure 10.24). Click the minus symbol to collapse and plus sign to expand rows in the hierarchical columns.

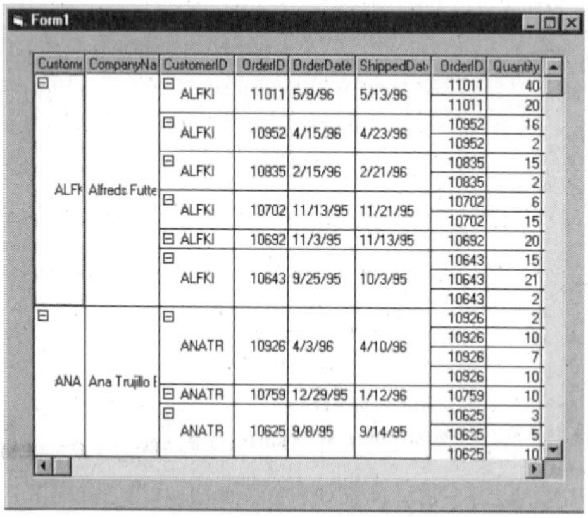

Figure 10.24

The rsCustomers Recordset displayed by an unformatted MSHFlexGrid control.

3. The second CustomerID and OrderID columns contain duplicate information, so return to design mode, right-click the MSHFlexGrid control, and choose Properties to open the Properties sheet.

4. Click the Bands tab and select Band 1 (Orders) in the Band list.

5. Clear the CustomerID check box and click Apply (see Figure 10.25).

FIGURE 10.25

Removing the extra CustomerID column of Band 1.

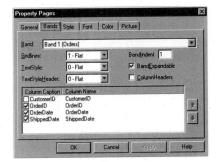

6. Select Band 2 (OrderDetails) in the Band list and clear the OrderID check box.

7. Click the Style tab and mark the WordWrap check box to permit the CompanyName column to display the entire field value.

8. Click OK to close the Properties sheet; then run the project. The MSHFlexGrid appears as illustrated in Figure 10.26.

FIGURE 10.26

The MSHFlexGrid with duplicate CustomerID and OrderID columns removed.

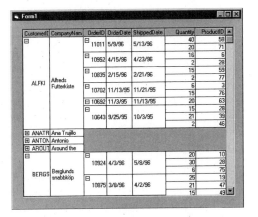

The presentation of hierarchical `Recordsets` in MSHFlexGrid controls is quite similar to that of conventional `Recordsets` generated from SQL statements with one or more `INNER JOINs` with column merging. The primary difference is that you can't expand and collapse the hierarchy of a conventional `Recordset`.

> **NOTE**
>
> The Hrst.vbp project in the \Ddg_vb6\Chaptr10 folder of the accompanying CD-ROM contains the sample hierarchical `Recordset` form (`frmHrstDED`, `Hrst_ded.frm`) created in the preceding two sections.

Manipulating Hierarchical Recordsets with Code

The MSHFlexGrid is the only Visual Basic 6.0 control that presents hierarchical Recordsets in a useful graphical format without adding VBA code. You can, however, substitute VBA code and a SHAPE statement for the three Commands used in the example of the two preceding sections. Listing 10.3 shows the code in the CreateShape **Public** subprocedure needed to open a Connection having MSDataShape as the (OLE DB service) Provider and Microsoft.Jet.OLEDB.3.51 (Jolt) as the Data Provider and opens a hierarchical Recordset from a SHAPE statement. The Form_Load event handler calls CreateShape and binds the MSHFlexGrid to the Recordset.

LISTING 10.3 VBA CODE TO CREATE AND BIND A HIERARCHICAL Recordset TO AN MSHFLEXGRID CONTROL

```
Option Explicit
Private cnnNwind As New ADODB.Connection
Public rstHCusts As New ADODB.Recordset
Public blnHasRun As Boolean

Public Sub CreateShape()
   Dim strFile As String
   Dim strShape As String

   If blnHasRun Then
      Exit Sub
   End If

   'Define Connection and Recordset Source properties
   strFile = "C:\Program Files\Microsoft Visual Studio\VB98\Nwind.mdb"
   strShape = _
   "SHAPE {SELECT CustomerID, CompanyName FROM Customers} AS Customers " & _
      "APPEND ((SHAPE {SELECT CustomerID, OrderID, OrderDate, ShippedDate " & _
         "FROM Orders ORDER BY OrderDate DESC} AS Orders " & _
            "APPEND ({SELECT OrderID, Quantity, ProductID " & _
               "FROM [Order Details]} AS OrderDetails " & _
            "RELATE 'OrderID' TO 'OrderID') AS OrderDetails) AS Orders " & _
         "RELATE 'CustomerID' TO 'CustomerID') AS Orders"

   'Open the Connection
   With cnnNwind
      .Provider = "MSDataShape.1"
      .Open "Data Source=" & strFile & ";Data Provider=Microsoft.Jet.OLEDB.3.51"
   End With

   'Open the hierarchical Recordset
   With rstHCusts
      Set .ActiveConnection = cnnNwind
      'The ADO 2.0 cursor engine handles hierarchical Recordsets
```

```
      .CursorLocation = adUseClient
      .CursorType = adOpenStatic
      .LockType = adLockReadOnly
      .Source = strShape
      .Open
   End With
   blnHasRun = True
End Sub

Private Sub Form_Load()
   Call CreateShape
   'Bind the MSHFlexGrid to the Recordset
   Set hfgHCusts.Recordset = rstHCusts
End Sub
```

After you've created and tested a hierarchical `Recordset` in an MSHFlexGrid control, you can write the VBA code to independently access the records in the `Recordset` and the rowset chapters (detail sets). Figure 10.27 shows a simple form (`frmHrstCode`) with a DataCombo bound to the parent Customers `Recordset`, an unbound list box to display the records of the `Orders` child `Recordset` for a selected customer, and an MSHFlexGrid that lists the line items of the `OrderDetails` grandchild `Recordset` for the selected order. Listing 10.4 shows the code behind `frmHrstCode`.

FIGURE 10.27

The `frmHrstCode` *form for testing the behavior of bound and unbound controls with hierarchical* `Recordset` *objects.*

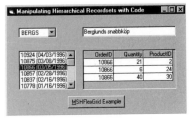

LISTING 10.4   VBA CODE TO DISPLAY THE `OrderDetails` GRANDCHILD Recordset BASED ON SELECTIONS FROM THE PARENT (*Customers*) AND CHILD (*Orders*) RecordsetS

```
Option Explicit
Private varOrders As Variant
Private varDetails As Variant

Private Sub Form_Load()
   Call CreateShape
   'Bind the DataCombo list to the Recordset
   With dcbCustID
      Set .RowSource = rstHCusts
      .ListField = "CustomerID"
      .Text = rstHCusts(0)
```

continues

LISTING 10.4   CONTINUED

```
    End With
    Call dcbCustID_Click(2)
    DoEvents
    Call lstOrders_Click
End Sub

Private Sub dcbCustID_Click(intArea As Integer)
    If intArea = 2 Then
        'Populate the unbound Orders list box
        With rstHCusts
            .MoveFirst
            .Find "CustomerID = '" & dcbCustID.Text & "'"
            txtCompanyName.Text = .Fields(1)
            'Define the child Recordset
            varOrders = .Fields("Orders")
        End With
        With lstOrders
            .Clear
            Do Until varOrders.EOF
                .AddItem varOrders(1) & " (" & Format(varOrders(2), "MM/dd/yyyy") & ")"
                varOrders.MoveNext
            Loop
        End With
    End If
End Sub

Private Sub lstOrders_Click()
    Dim strFind As String

    'Get the OrderID value
    With lstOrders
        If .ListIndex = -1 Then
            .ListIndex = 0
        End If
        strFind = "OrderID = " & Left(.List(.ListIndex), 5)
    End With

    'Search the child Recordset and create the grandchild
    With varOrders
        .MoveFirst
        .Find strFind
        'Define the grandchild Recordset
        varDetails = .Fields("OrderDetails")
        'Bind the MSHFlexGrid to the grandchild
        Set hfgDetails.Recordset = varDetails
    End With
End Sub
```

The varOrders and varDetails **Variant** arrays are type vbObject (9), not vbArray (8192) or vbDataObject (13). Both of these variables share most of the properties, methods, and events of conventional Recordsets. As an example, varOrders has five fields—CustomerID, OrderID, OrderData, ShippedDate, and OrderDetails. OrderDetails is the chapter field for the OrderDetails grandchild Recordset. If you specify optimistic or batch optimistic locking, you can update nonkey values in the parent, child, and grandchild Recordsets.

NOTE

The example in the MSDN online help topic, Accessing Rows in a Hierarchical Recordset, shipped with Visual Studio 6.0 contains an error in the following line:

Set rsChapter = rst("chapter")

The VBA **Set** reserved word isn't used when assigning a chapter to a **Variant** variable of the vbObject type.

SAVING AND DISPLAYING IMAGES WITH PICTUREBOX AND IMAGE CONTROLS

Visual Basic 6.0 includes simple-bound PictureBox and Image intrinsic controls that you can use to display bitmaps and metafiles. Both controls bind to data in fields of Jet's OLE Object field data type, called a LongBinary field by Visual Basic. PictureBox and Image controls accommodate bitmap (.bmp, .dib, and .ico) and vector image (.wmf and .emf) files. (A .wmf file also can include a bitmapped image.)

The Image control is a "lightweight" object; it consumes fewer resources than a PictureBox control consumes and paints faster, too. An Image control lets you scale the image to fit the confines of the control by setting the value of the Stretch property to **True**; the PictureBox control doesn't offer a Stretch property. Thus the sample video image database application discussed in the following two sections uses the Image control.

A Visual Basic Video Logging System for Sony VISCA Devices

Applications for image databases range from simple photographic cataloging systems to full-fledged imaging workflow applications. One of the more interesting applications for image controls is capturing and storing video *picons*, which are still images representing the beginning (and often the ending) frame of a live video image. Very small picons often are used in video-editing applications to identify video *clips* (an individual segment of recorded video content) on a timeline. Adobe Premiere, as an example, uses picons to identify clips added to either of the two video timelines of its Construction window. The ViscaLog.vbp project, whose sole form appears in Figure 10.28, is a simple Visual Basic 6.0 application that logs the beginning and ending times of Digital Video (DV) or Hi8 analog video clips to produce a batch (.pbl) file that automates the digital video capture process of Adobe Premiere 4.2+.

FIGURE 10.28

The ViscaLog form displaying a picon for a video clip (image courtesy of Chump Change Records).

ViscaLog is designed to control the operation of a Sony Hi8 videotape player called the Vdeck, which uses the Sony VISCA (Video Systems Control Architecture) protocol. Sony discontinued production of the all VISCA products in 1996, but tens of thousands of CVD-1000 Vdeck and VI-1000 Vbox devices remain in use today. If you have a Hi8 camcorder, you can purchase a used CVD-1000 for $750 or less to assemble-edit your tapes. VISCA lets you connect to a COM port up to seven Vdecks and/or Vboxes in a daisy-chain arrangement. The Vbox converts the VISCA command set to Sony's consumer LANC (Local Application Numeric Code, also called Control-L) protocol that's standard on most Sony and Canon camcorders, and high-end VCRs.

The Vdeck and the Sony EV-S5000 and EV-S7000 Hi8 VCRs can read and record RC timecode, which is necessary for accurate logging of videotapes. You need a Vbox to control LANC-compliant Hi8 camcorders, the Sony DCR-VX1000 and Canon XL-1 Digital Video (DV) camcorders, or Sony EV-S5000/EV-S7000 VCRs with VISCA. Videotape timecode is based on the Society of Motion Picture and Television Engineers (SMPTE) HH:MM:SS:FF format, where FF represents video or movie frames. RC timecode usually is based on 30 frames/s (fps), called SMPTE *nondrop* timecode; DV uses SMPTE *drop-frame* timecode based on broadcast color television's 29.97 fps frame rate.

Windows 9*x* and Windows NT 4.0 include a built-in VISCA driver (Mcivisca.drv) for the Media Control Interface (MCI). To set up the VISCA driver for one of your serial ports, do the following:

1. Attach the VISCA serial cable to an unused COM port and turn on the VDeck or Vbox power.

2. Open Control Panel's Multimedia tool, expand the Media Control Devices node, and double-click the VISCA VCR Driver item to open the General page of the VISCA VCR Device (Media Control) Properties sheet.

3. The VISCA driver is disabled by default, so select the Use This Media Control option.

4. Click the Settings button to open the MCI VISCA Configuration dialog and select in the Comm Port list the COM port to which you connected the VISCA cable.

5. Click Detect to test the VISCA connection and determine the number of devices in the VISCA chain (see Figure 10.29). The VISCA LED on your VDeck or VBox lights if the driver and cabling are working.

6. Reboot your computer to assure that the driver is fully operational.

FIGURE 10.29

Enabling and test-ing the VISCA VCR MCI driver in Control Panel's Multimedia tool.

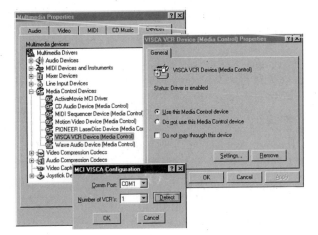

You can use the 32-bit mciSendStringA functions to issue simple English-language commands to VISCA devices, which MCI calls the vcr device type. A full description of the MCI com-mand string syntax for the vcr device type is included in the Media Control Interface section of the Win32 SDK. Before you can use either function, you must declare two function proto-types (mciSendString and mciGetErrorString) contained in 32-bit WINMM.DLL or 16-bit MMSYSTEM.DLL; both of these libraries are installed during Windows 95 setup. Listing 10.5 shows the prototype declarations for the two functions needed for 32-bit applications that use MCI command strings.

LISTING 10.5 FUNCTION PROTOTYPE DECLARATIONS REQUIRED TO USE MCI COMMAND STRINGS

```
Option Explicit
'Win32 MCI functions
Declare Function mciSendString Lib "winmm.dll" _
   Alias "mciSendStringA" _
  (ByVal lpstrCommand As String, _
   ByVal lpstrReturnString As String, _
   ByVal uReturnLength As Long, _
   ByVal hWndCallback As Long) As Long
Declare Function mciGetErrorString Lib "winmm.dll" _
   Alias "mciGetErrorStringA" _
  (ByVal dwError As Long, _
   ByVal lpstrBuffer As String, _
   ByVal uLength As Long) As Long

Public mciCommand   As String        'Command
Public mciReturn    As String * 256  'Return string
Public mciErrString As String * 256  'Error string
Public mciError     As Long          'Error number

Public mciReturnLen As Long   'Length of return string
Public mcihWnd      As Long   'Callback window handle
Public mciErrLen    As Long   'Length of error string
Public mciErrResult   As Long   'Return value of error
```

> **NOTE**
>
> The ViscaLog.vbp project is located in the \Ddg_vb6\Chaptr09 folder of the accompanying CD-ROM. ViscaLog.mdb, located in the same folder, includes samples of 320- by 240-pixel live video captures using the Play Inc.'s Snappy video capture device. The Snappy.ocx OLE Control (not an ActiveX control) is included on the software CD-ROM for version 3.0 of the Snappy. To use the ViscaLog application, you need at least one VISCA device connected to a COM port and a Snappy 3.0 connected to LPT1. If you run ViscaLog without a VISCA device, click OK when the `Please insert a tape in the drive` message appears.

You set up the *vcr* device (alias `Vdeck` in ViscaLog) in the `Form_Load` event handler of the main ViscaLog form, as shown in Listing 10.6.

LISTING 10.6 TYPICAL INITIALIZATION CODE FOR THE MCI *vcr* DEVICE TYPE

```
Private Sub Form_Load()
    'Set up initial conditions
    Me.Left = (Screen.Width - Me.Width) / 2
    Me.Top = (Screen.Height - Me.Height) / 2
    fMarkIn = True
    txtIn.Font.Bold = True
    fMarkOut = True
    txtOut.Font.Bold = True
    dtcLog.EOFAction = 0
    'Open the ViSCA device, vcr for a single device
    'If you have more than one ViSCA device, use vcr1, vcr2, etc.
    Call SendCommand("Open vcr alias Vdeck")
    'Check for presence of tape in drive
    Call SendCommand("Status Vdeck media present")
    If txtReturn.Text <> "true" Then
        'No tape in drive
        MsgBox "Please insert a tape in the drive.", 0, "Drive Not Ready"
    End If
    'Turn on VISCA RCTC detection
    Call SendCommand("Set Vdeck time mode detect")
    'Set the time code to SMPTE drop-frame (210.97 fps)
    Call SendCommand("Set Vdeck time format smpte 30 drop")
    'Set screen display to timecode
    Call SendCommand("Set Vdeck index timecode")
    'Turn on timecode display, if available
    Call SendCommand("Index Vdeck on")
    'Set the preroll time to 20 frames
    Call SendCommand("Set Vdeck preroll 00:00:00:20")
    'Clear the Clipboard
    Clipboard.Clear
End Sub
```

ViscaLog's behind-the-scenes data acquisition activity consists of a Timer control that interrogates the Vdeck device to determine the tape position. Every 100 milliseconds (about three video frames), the timSMPTE_Timer event handler interrogates the Vdeck, which returns the current tape position as an SMPTE HH:MM:SS:FF string to the txtReturn text box. If the in and/or out points of the video clip aren't set, the current tape position is continuously written to the bound txtIn and/or txtOut text boxes with the following code:

```
Private Sub timSMPTE_Timer()
    'Load timecode for in and out point text boxes
    'Timer interval is set at 100 ms (3+ frames)
    Call SendCommand("Status Vdeck Position")
    'Don't overwrite existing clip in and out points
    If Not fMarkIn Then
        txtIn.Text = txtReturn.Text
```

```
    End If
    If Not fMarkOut Then
        txtOut.Text = txtReturn.Text
    End If
End Sub
```

Marking the in and out points with the Mark In and Mark Out command buttons while the tape is moving can cause up to a four-frame offset. The tape position buttons at the bottom of the form are the primary means to obtain frame-accurate clips; you use the Pause, Forward, and Reverse buttons to move to a specific frame with the Step command, as shown in Listing 10.7. Alternatively, you can type the timecodes in the In and Out text boxes. Clicking the Test Clip button plays the clip so you can visually and aurally check your in and out points.

LISTING 10.7   EVENT HANDLERS FOR CONTROLLING OPERATION OF AN MCI vcr DEVICE

```
Private Sub cmdTest_Click()
    'Cue the deck to play from in point to out point
    Call SendCommand("Cue Vdeck from " & txtIn.Text & _
        " to " & txtOut.Text & " preroll wait")
    Call SendCommand("Play Vdeck")
End Sub

Private Sub cmdLoad_Click()
    'Rewind to 2 minute standard start position
    Call SendCommand("Set Vdeck time mode detect wait")
    Call SendCommand("Seek Vdeck to 00:02:00:00")
End Sub

Private Sub cmdReverse_Click()
    If fMarkIn And fMarkOut Then
        'Rewind in 10X mode
        Call SendCommand("Play Vdeck reverse scan")
    Else
        'Single step reverse
        Call SendCommand("Step Vdeck by 1 reverse")
    End If
End Sub

Private Sub cmdStop_Click()
    'Stop the drive
    Call SendCommand("Stop Vdeck")
End Sub

Private Sub cmdPause_Click()
    'Put the deck in pause mode
    Call SendCommand("Pause Vdeck")
End Sub
```

```vb
Private Sub cmdPlay_Click()
    'Put the deck in play mode
    Call SendCommand("Play Vdeck")
End Sub

Private Sub cmdForward_Click()
    If fMarkIn And fMarkOut Then
        'Play in 10X forward mode
        Call SendCommand("Play Vdeck scan")
    Else
        'Single step forward
        Call SendCommand("Step Vdeck by 1")
    End If
End Sub

Private Sub cmdEject_Click()
    'Stop the tape drive, if running
    Call SendCommand("Stop Vdeck wait")
    'Rewind to the beginning of the tape
    Call SendCommand("Seek Vdeck to start wait")
    'Eject the tape
    Call SendCommand("Set Vdeck door open")
End Sub
```

Using AVIT Research's LANC ActiveX Control

The LancLog.vbp project substitutes AVIT Research's Lanc32.ocx and a serial-to-LANC adapter box/cable for the Sony VISCA driver and serial-to-VISCA cable. AVIT's Contol-L Development Kit (http://www.york.ac.uk/~adv3/lanc/devkit.htm) currently is the least expensive means of controlling LANC-enabled camcorders and VCRs for linear video editing and frame selection for still image capture. The LANC protocol is an arcane sequence of bytes sent and received in a serial format related to RS-232-C. The LANC connector is a 2.5-mm stereo mini-plug; not the standard 3.5-mm stereo mini-plug used by sound cards. AVIT's Control-L Website (http://www.york.ac.uk/~adv3/lanc/lanc.htm) is the most complete and accessible source of information about the LANC protocol.

Lanc32.ocx comes with a simple Visual Basic demonstration application (VBExample.vbp), which includes a simple device control form (see Figure 10.30). A module (Lanc32.bas) supplies constant definitions for common LANC commands. Before running VBExample.vbp, you must specify in the Form_Initialize event handler the COM port to which the serial-to-LANC converter is connected (LancControl1.ComPort = {1¦2}).

10

DATA-BOUND
ACTIVEX
CONTROLS

FIGURE 10.30
AVIT Research's test form for the Control-L Development Kit.

The LancLog.vbp project in the \Ddg_vb6\Chaptr10 folder of the accompanying CD-ROM is a modification of the ViscaLog.vbp project. LancLog.vbp substitutes calls to Lanc32.ocx's LancCommand method for the MCI commands of ViscaLog.vbp. The published LANC protocol lacks some of VISCA's editing features, such as the Cue instruction, but Lanc32.ocx is adequate for frame capture positioning and simple assembly editing. You can view several Snappy frame captures from a Canon XL-1 DV camcorder at

http://www.chumpchange.com/parkplace/video/musicvideo.htm.

> **NOTE**
>
> The preferred device control and video/still-image capture interface for DV camcorders and VCRs is IEEE 1394, more commonly known as FireWire, an Apple Computer trademark. Sony calls it's implementation of IEEE 1394 i.LINK. Windows 98 and Windows NT 4.0 includes basic support for IEEE 1394. Intel promised IEEE 1394 on PC motherboards by late 1998, but reneged on their commitment at the behest of consumer PC manufacturers who objected to the $10 to $15 added cost for the connector and chip(s). Thus taking advantage of IEEE 1394 for non-linear digital video editing currently requires a $500 to $700 investment in an IEEE 1394 adapter card and video editing software, such as Adobe Premiere 5.0. For additional information on the DV format and DV-over-IEEE 1394, go to
>
> http://www.chumpchange.com/parkplace/video/technical.htm.

Capturing, Displaying, and Saving Video Picons

Play, Inc.'s Snappy video capture device and the Snappy.ocx OLE control constitute a simple and low-cost approach to video picon capture. The Snappy, which has a street price of under $100, plugs into your PC's printer port and has RCA connectors for composite analog video input from a VCR or camcorder and optional loop-through output to a TV monitor. Installation of the Snappy takes no more than 5 minutes and, unlike higher-priced video-overlay cards, you don't need an open expansion slot or a connection to your graphic card's feature connector.

> **NOTE**
>
> Jet tables that contain full-color (24-bit color depth) bitmap (.bmp or .dib) images become very large, especially if you add images of 320- by 240-pixel or larger size. As an example, a 320- by 240-pixel image with 24-bit color depth requires 320×240×3 or more than 230KB of storage space. Snappy can save files in compressed Joint Photographic Experts Group (JPEG) format, which saves a substantial amount of storage space without excessive loss of image quality. Using JPEG compression at a 75% image quality reduces the file size from 230KB (.bmp) to 11KB (.jpg).

Listing 10.8 shows the form's event-handling code for alternately displaying a preview image, which refreshes at about 1 frame/s, in an unbound `imgPreview` Image control, and capturing a 320- by 240-pixel image to the bound `imgPicon` control. The captured image initially appears as a device-independent bitmap (DIB) in `imgPicon`. To minimize storage size, the DIB is saved as a JPEG file (Image.jpg), the content of which replaces the DIB in `imgPicon`.

LISTING 10.8 EVENT HANDLERS FOR PREVIEWING VIDEO DATA AND SAVING A JPEG-COMPRESSED BITMAP TO THE PICON FIELD OF THE TAPELOG TABLE

```
Private Sub cmdSnap_Click()
    'Toggle between preview and capture mode
    If blnPreview Then
        'Place the deck in pause mode for capture
        Call SendCommand("Pause Vdeck wait")
        imgPreview.Visible = False
        imgPicon.Visible = True
        ocxSnappy.Snap
    Else
        Call SendCommand("Play Vdeck")
        imgPreview.Visible = True
        imgPicon.Visible = False
        ocxSnappy.Preview
    End If
End Sub

Private Sub ocxSnappy_PictureAvailable()
    'Copy the image to the bound Image control
    imgPicon.Picture = ocxSnappy.Picture
    'Save the image in compressed JPEG format
    ocxSnappy.SaveFileName = App.Path & "\Image.jpg"
    ocxSnappy.SavePicture
    DoEvents
    'Load the compressed image into the bound Image control
```

continues

10

DATA-BOUND ACTIVEX CONTROLS

LISTING 10.8 CONTINUED

```
    imgPicon.Picture = LoadPicture(App.Path & "\Image.jpg")
    adcLog.Recordset.Update
    cmdSnap.Caption = "Prev&iew"
    blnPreview = False
End Sub

Private Sub ocxSnappy_PreviewAvailable()
    'Update preview image at about 1 fps
    imgPreview.Picture = ocxSnappy.Picture
    cmdSnap.Caption = "Capt&ure"
    blnPreview = True
End Sub
```

Creating a Batch Capture Log for Use by Adobe Premiere

The objective of ViscaLog is to create an ASCII batch capture file for Adobe Premiere from the Log table of ViscaLog.mdb. Premiere's batch capture file import format requires a tab-separated text file with Reel Name (tape number), In, Out, and File Name, with optional Comment and Settings fields. Controls are bound to the Recordset object of the adcLog control, so a Recordset clone is used to create the required text file (see Listing 10.9.) A drive letter prefix, determined by the estimated accumulated size of the clip files, is added to the .avi filename.

LISTING 10.9 CODE TO CREATE A FORMATTED TEXT FILE FROM A RecordsetClone OBJECT

```
Private Sub cmdExport_Click()
    'Export the log in Adobe Premiere batch format
    Dim rsdLog As Recordset
    Dim strLog As String
    Dim strID As String

    Screen.MousePointer = 11
    'Create a recordset clone
    Set rsdLog = dtcLog.Recordset.Clone
    'Delete the existing file
    On Error Resume Next
    Kill "ViscaLog.txt"
    On Error GoTo 0
    'Open the batch file
    Open "ViscaLog.txt" For Append As #1
    rsdLog.MoveFirst
    Do Until rsdLog.EOF
        'Create padded four-character clip ID string
        Select Case rsdLog(0)
            Case Is > 999
```

```
                strID = CStr(rsdLog(0))
        Case Is > 99
                strID = "0" & CStr(rsdLog(0))
        Case Is > 9
                strID = "00" & CStr(rsdLog(0))
        Case Else
                strID = "000" & CStr(rsdLog(0))
    End Select
    'Reel name
    strLog = "Tape " & rsdLog(1) & Chr$(9)
    'In point
    strLog = strLog & rsdLog(2) & Chr$(9)
    'Out point
    strLog = strLog & rsdLog(3) & Chr$(9)
    '.AVI file name (no extension)
    strLog = strLog & "Clip" & strID & Chr$(9)
    'Scene
    strLog = strLog & rsdLog(7)
    'Append the record to the batch file
    Print #1, strLog
    rsdLog.MoveNext
Loop
'Close everything
Close #1
rsdLog.Close
Set rsdLog = Nothing
Screen.MousePointer = 0
End Sub
```

GRAPHING SUMMARY DATA CREATED FROM CROSSTAB QUERIES

IN THIS CHAPTER

It's a safe bet that most decision-support applications you create with Visual Basic will include at least one graph or chart. The decision-support applications you develop for upper management's review and for planning purposes are likely to consist of a standard repertoire of graphs plus various drilldown features to display the detailed data behind the graphs. Chapter 9, "Designing a Decision-Support Front End," introduces the use of MSChart ActiveX controls to create graphs based on data summarized by crosstab queries.

This chapter expands the examples of Chapter 9 by showing you how to organize a graph- and chart-based decision-support application, how to use the multiple document interface with graphs and charts, and how to provide the navigational tools your clients need for drilldown applications. Unlike Chapter 9's sample application, which uses VBA code to set the data points for graphs and grids, this chapter's Graphs.vbp sample project takes advantage of the data-binding capabilities of the new MSChart version 2.0 and MSHFlexGrid controls to populate charts, graphs, and grids. Chapter 13, "Drilling Down into Data from Graphs and Charts," builds on the examples created in this chapter.

ORGANIZING A CHART-BASED DECISION-SUPPORT APPLICATION

One major task that developers of decision-support applications for management face is organizing the hierarchical structure of the display. A typical decision-support application, designed for executive management, is likely to comprise at least the six sets of graphs shown in Figure 11.1. Regardless of the size of the firm for which you're developing the application, most decision-support applications use a similar collection of graphs and charts.

> **NOTE**
>
> The design techniques illustrated in this chapter also apply to front ends for online analytical processing (OLAP) systems, the subject of Chapter 28, "Analyzing Multidimensional Data with OLAP and MDX." OLAP systems, such as Microsoft Decision Support Services (MSDSS), deliver the equivalent of crosstab query result sets. Jet's crosstab queries offer a simple introduction to the process of summarizing numerical data.

In addition to the 21 graphs and charts shown in Figure 11.1, you usually must provide overlay graphs that compare the current year's performance with that of prior years. Performance comparisons are a vital component of all decision-support applications. The following list describes the graph and chart types for each of the elements depicted in Figure 11.1.

FIGURE 11.1

Organization of the charts and graphs that constitute a decision-support application for executive management.

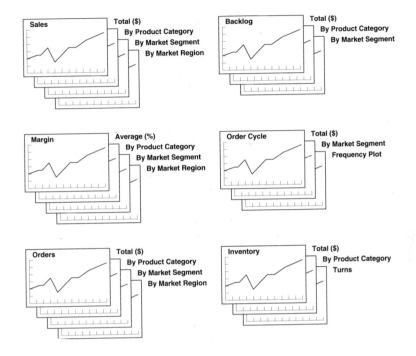

- *Single-line graphs* display total year-to-date sales, year-to-date orders, average margin percentage, monthly backlog, and monthly inventory levels. You can superimpose additional data, such as averages, standard deviations, and trend lines, as well as historical data, on these line graphs.

- *Area charts* display the second level of detail information that constitutes a cumulative value. These charts include sales, orders, and backlog, displayed by product category, market segment, or sales region, each identified by a standard color. Inventory is displayed by product category only. You need a method to select the particular category, segment, or region to display a line chart on which you can superimpose historical data for comparison purposes.

- *Multiple-line graphs* display detail information that is not cumulative in nature, such as averages. Thus average margins for all product categories, market segments, and sales regions are displayed on a single graph by multiple lines. You use the same selection method as you use for area charts to create multiple-line graphs to provide historical comparisons.

- *Histograms* are useful for displaying frequency distribution. Information such as order-cycle times (the number of days between the receipt of an order and shipment of the order) and inventory turns (the number of days in which the current inventory will be exhausted at the current sales rate) can be displayed by histograms.

The sections that follow describe additional issues that arise when you create a major decision-support application.

Combining Management Levels in a Single Application

Chapter 9 discusses how the level of information is stratified by management level. Creating separate applications to provide information at different management levels is an inefficient process. In such cases, you have two or three applications to support and maintain, instead of one master application. Many "hands-on" executives want to display data that is ordinarily the province of operational management. The better approach is to include summary data that is accessible by executives but not by operational management. You can determine who can display which graphs by requiring users to log in to the application with a user ID and password that matches entries in a users table. Permissions are incorporated in fields of the users table. Login methods are discussed later in this chapter.

Whereas executive management sees the summary data for the corporation as a whole, operational managers are limited to viewing graphs that are related to their particular regimes. As an example, regional sales managers can display sales, margins, orders, backlogs, and order cycle times for orders originating in their particular region. Similarly, product-line managers can view data that relates to the single product category they manage. Table 11.1 lists the typical sets of graphs and charts in a multilevel decision-support application.

TABLE 11.1 ACCESS TO DECISION-SUPPORT CHARTS AND GRAPHS BY MANAGEMENT LEVEL

Graph or Chart and Sequence	Executive Management	Regional Sales Management	Product-Line Management
Sales 1	Total	Regional totals	Category total
Sales 2	Category	Product in region	Product in category
Sales 3	Segment	Customer in region	Segment in category
Sales 4	Region	Employee in region	
Margin 1	Average	Regional average	Category average
Margin 2	Category	Product in region	Product in category
Margin 3	Segment	Customer in region	Segment in category
Margin 4	Region	Employee in region	
Orders 1	Total	Regional totals	Category total
Orders 2	Category	Product in region	Product in category
Orders 3	Segment	Customer in region	Segment in category
Orders 4	Region	Employee in region	
Backlog 1	Total	Regional totals	Category

Graph or Chart and Sequence	Executive Management	Regional Sales Management	Product-Line Management
Backlog 2	Segment	Customer in region	Product in category
Order Cycle 1	Average	Regional average	
Order Cycle 2	Segment	Customer averages	
Inventory 1 Category	Total		
Inventory 2 Product	Category		

It's clear from Table 11.1 that a decision-support application for a large firm easily can require 100 different graphs. When you add the capability to display historical data, the permutations and combinations of graphs range in the hundreds or even the thousands. Completing a table of the graphs and charts that constitutes the decision-support application, as well as completing the tables that display the numerical values behind the charts, is the first major milestone in the organization process. You obtain approval of your table of graphs and charts from the client and then begin to build the backbone of your application.

Developing a Graph-and-Chart Definitions Table

Clients who commission data-support applications are notorious for being fickle in the extreme. You're likely to find that your client will make ad hoc changes to your graph and chart table in the midst of the development process. If you hard-code table hierarchies and definitions, you are in *big* trouble. A more flexible approach is to create a graph-and-chart definitions table whose fields provide most or all of the parameters required to display a chart. You can add, delete, or change the access rights to charts simply by updating records in the table.

> **NOTE**
>
> The term *commission* is used in the first sentence of the preceding paragraph because designing decision-support applications is an art, not a science. A well-designed decision-support application paints a portrait of the corporation in graphs and charts.

Table 11.2 lists some of the fields that constitute the graph-and-chart definitions table, tblDefinitions, for the sample decision-support application of this chapter. With two exceptions, the fields listed in Table 11.2 are used in the code examples that follow; the exceptions are GraphQuery1 and GraphQuery2. Code is used to generate all the SQL statements required to create Recordset objects to supply data for the graphs.

TABLE 11.2   THE STRUCTURE OF THE TBLDEFINITIONS TABLE OF GRAPHS.MDB

Field	Data Type	Description
Code	Text	Two-character numeric code for the graph
Category	Text	Category of the graph (Sales, Margins, Orders, Backlog, and so on)
Level	Integer	Level of the graph in the hierarchy (1 = top, 2+ = drilldown)
GraphCaption	Text	Caption for the MDI form title bar
Units	Text	Units ($, %, Days, and so on)
Crossfoot	Text	Column and row headers for crosstab grids
Type	Text	Type of graph (line, multiline, and so on)
GraphType	Integer	GraphType value of the graph control
GraphStyle	Double	GraphStyle value of the graph control
Access	Text	Who can view the graph: (E)xecutives, (R)egional sales managers, (P)roduct managers, and so on
Periodicity	Text	(W)eekly, (M)onthly, (Q)uarterly, (Y)early
Periods	Double	Number of periods in graph
DataTable	Text	Name of the table supplying the data (for example, tblSalesTotalMonth)
DataField	Text	Name of the field that supplies the data for the graph
Legend	Yes/No	Is a legend required?
LegendTable	Text	Name of the table that contains the legend information
LegendField	Text	Name of the field containing the legend code
LegendTextField	Text	Name of the field containing the description of the legend
GridRowHeader	Text	Text for the grid-row header above the legend text
UseActivated	Yes/No	Test whether a category is active
TableQuery1	Text	Base query to roll up data for the graph
TableQuery2	Text	A rollup subquery (if needed)
GraphQuery1	Text	Name of a `QueryDef` object to create the graph query (if used)
GraphQuery2	Text	A subquery for the graph `QueryDef` object (if needed)

Figure 11.2 shows the left-most fields of the data in tblDefinitions that are used to create the graphs described in this chapter.

FIGURE 11.2

The first seven fields of tblDefinitions displayed in Access 97's table datasheet.

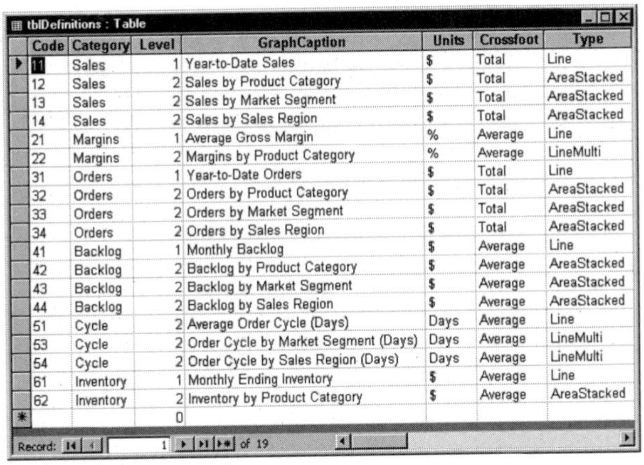

Code	Category	Level	GraphCaption	Units	Crossfoot	Type
11	Sales	1	Year-to-Date Sales	$	Total	Line
12	Sales	2	Sales by Product Category	$	Total	AreaStacked
13	Sales	2	Sales by Market Segment	$	Total	AreaStacked
14	Sales	2	Sales by Sales Region	$	Total	AreaStacked
21	Margins	1	Average Gross Margin	%	Average	Line
22	Margins	2	Margins by Product Category	%	Average	LineMulti
31	Orders	1	Year-to-Date Orders	$	Total	Line
32	Orders	2	Orders by Product Category	$	Total	AreaStacked
33	Orders	2	Orders by Market Segment	$	Total	AreaStacked
34	Orders	2	Orders by Sales Region	$	Total	AreaStacked
41	Backlog	1	Monthly Backlog	$	Average	Line
42	Backlog	2	Backlog by Product Category	$	Average	AreaStacked
43	Backlog	2	Backlog by Market Segment	$	Average	AreaStacked
44	Backlog	2	Backlog by Sales Region	$	Average	AreaStacked
51	Cycle	2	Average Order Cycle (Days)	Days	Average	Line
53	Cycle	2	Order Cycle by Market Segment (Days)	Days	Average	LineMulti
54	Cycle	2	Order Cycle by Sales Region (Days)	Days	Average	LineMulti
61	Inventory	1	Monthly Ending Inventory	$	Average	Line
62	Inventory	2	Inventory by Product Category	$	Average	AreaStacked

Creating Data to Test Your Application

You might find that you must create your decision-support application without having operational data or rolled up summary tables available to test the application. If you don't have the tables required to create the rolled up data, you can use a sample database, such as Nwind.mdb, to generate much of the test data you need with make-table queries. Access 97+ is the logical application in which to write and test the make-table queries, saving them in the form of QueryDefs. The Graphs.mdb database that supplies the data for the examples in this chapter uses a combination of tables attached from Nwind.mdb and make-table queries to generate the rolled up data needed to create the graphs and charts shown in the sections that follow.

Generating Backlog Rollups

Northwind Traders doesn't maintain separate tables for orders and invoices. Apparently, Northwind creates an invoice when the product is shipped, indicated by an entry in the Date Shipped field of the Orders table. Therefore, to determine monthly backlog data, you need to compare the date on which the order was booked with the shipping date. If the month of the ShippedDate field doesn't match the month of the OrderDate field, the order was pending at the end of the month and the record for the order is included in the backlog rollups.

NOTE

Combining order entry and invoicing data in a single table violates the rule that entities in a table represent only a single object. Orders and invoices are different real-world objects. Combining orders and invoices in a single table also precludes shipping partial orders and then processing backorders when the goods become available in inventory.

The qryMonthlyBacklogTotal QueryDef object of Graphs.mdb creates the tblBacklogTotalMonth table. The SQL statement that generates the total backlog data by year and month (from the date of the first entry in the Orders table through the end of the year 1995) is this:

```
SELECT Format(Orders.OrderDate,"yyyy") AS Year,
    Format(Orders.OrderDate,"mm") AS Month,
    Sum([Order Details].UnitPrice*[Order Details].Quantity*
        (1-[Order Details].Discount)) AS Backlog
    INTO tblBacklogTotalMonth
    FROM Orders, [Order Details]
    WHERE ((Orders.OrderID = Order Details].OrderID)
      AND ((Format(Orders.ShippedDate,"mmyy"))<>
          Format(Orders.OrderDate,"mmyy"))
      AND (Orders.OrderDate < #01/1/96#))
    GROUP BY Format(Orders.OrderDate,"yyyy"),
        Format(Orders.OrderDate,"mm")
```

The other QueryDef objects that create backlog by product category, market segment, and sales region tables add a GROUP BY criterion to the SQL statement.

Simulating Product Cost and Inventory Level Data

Although the Products table of Nwind.mdb includes a UnitPrice field, there is no field for unit cost. To generate margin data, you need to know the cost of the product on a monthly basis. To keep your margin graphs from appearing as straight lines, you add a random factor to the cost data. You also can factor in the effect of inflation and, because Northwind Traders deals internationally, you can add the effects of international currency value fluctuations relative to the dollar to make your simulated cost data appear more realistic. The Products table also has a UnitsInStock field that presumably indicates the current inventory level of each product. However, you need monthly inventory data, not just the current inventory. Therefore, you also need to generate fictitious inventory levels for each month.

Before you write an application to generate the unit cost and inventory level values for each product and period, you need to create the table to hold the values. The SQL statement that follows creates the tblInventory table that contains one record for each product in the Products table for every month of every year for which data exists in the tblSalesTotalMonth table:

```
SELECT tblSalesTotalMonth.Year,
    tblSalesTotalMonth.Month,
    Products.ProductID,
    Products.UnitPrice
    INTO tblInventory
    FROM Products, tblSalesTotalMonth
```

If you look closely at the preceding SQL statement (open the qryCartesianInventory QueryDef in Access or VisData), you see that the statement generates the Cartesian product of the tblSalesTotalMonth and Products tables. The Cartesian product is generated because no join is created between the two tables with either a WHERE or INNER JOIN statement. This situation is one of the few times when you purposely create a Cartesian product.

The next step is to modify the structure of tblInventory to provide the Sales (Number, Double), Units (Number, Long Integer), LandedCost (Currency), and Quantity (Number, Long Integer) fields for the table. Then you write an update query to add the Sales and Units data for each product for each month. For update queries with Access tables, you use the INNER JOIN syntax to create the required joins between the three fields of each table, as shown in the following SQL statement for qryCartesianJoin:

```
UPDATE tblInventory, tblSalesProductMonth,
    tblInventory INNER JOIN tblSalesProductMonth
        ON tblInventory.Year = tblSalesProductMonth.Year,
    tblInventory INNER JOIN tblSalesProductMonth
        ON tblInventory.Month = tblSalesProductMonth.Month,
    tblInventory INNER JOIN tblSalesProductMonth
        ON tblInventory.ProductID =
            tblSalesProductMonth.ProductID
    SET tblInventory.Sales = tblSalesProductMonth.Sales,
        tblInventory.Units = tblSalesProductsMonth.Units
```

The Randomize application (Randomiz.vbp and Randomiz.frm in the \Ddg_vb6\Chaptr10 folder of the accompanying CD-ROM adds the monthly unit cost data and inventory level data you need to tblInventory. The code that responds to a click of the Randomize button of frminventory appears in Listing 11.1.

> **NOTE**
>
> Randomiz.vbp and all the other sample applications in this chapter require that the Graphs.mdb sample database included on the accompanying CD-ROM be located in the default C:\Ddg_vb6\Chaptr10 folder. Graphs.mdb includes files that are attached from Microsoft's Nwind.mdb that Graphs.mdb expects to find in your C:\Program Files\Microsoft Visual Studio\VB98 folder. The use of the attached files from Nwind.mdb isn't necessary to execute the sample applications in this chapter.

LISTING 11.1 CODE TO CREATE RANDOMIZED VALUES FOR MONTHLY UNIT COST AND INVENTORY LEVELS FOR EACH PRODUCT

```
Private Sub cmdRandomize_Click()
    'Purpose:    Random number generator for the inventory table
    '            Creates inflation-weighted costs (weighted average) and
    '            randomized inventory quantities for each month
```

continues

LISTING 11.1 CONTINUED

```
Dim cnnInv As New ADODB.Connection
Dim rstInv As New ADODB.Recordset
Dim varCost As Variant
Dim intCtr As Integer
Dim intMonth As Integer
Dim lngQuantity As Long
Dim lngLastQuan As Long
Dim lngLastProd As Long

'Open Connection
With cnnInv
    .Provider = "Microsoft.Jet.OLEDB.3.51"
    .ConnectionString = "Data Source=" & App.Path & "\graphs.mdb"
    .Mode = adModeReadWrite
    .Open
End With

'Open Recordset
With rstInv
    Set .ActiveConnection = cnnInv
    'Jet is faster than ADO cursor engine
    .CursorLocation = adUseServer
    .CursorType = adOpenStatic
    .LockType = adLockPessimistic
    .Source = "SELECT * FROM tblInventory"
    .Open
End With

'Use the timer device to seed a new random number
Randomize

'Go to the first record (for safety)
intCtr = 1
rstInv.MoveFirst

'Define this procedure as a single transaction
cnnInv.BeginTrans

'Loop through all of the records
Do Until rstInv.EOF
    txtCounter.Text = intCtr
    txtCounter.Refresh          'increment record counter and update

    'Introduce random element varying initial gross margin from 40 to 50%
    varCost = (0.5 + 0.01 * (Int(9 * Rnd + 1))) * rstInv("UnitPrice")

    'Introduce inflationary factors totaling 10% from 1991 through 1996
    intMonth = 12 * (Val(rstInv("Year")) - 1991) + Val(rstInv("Month"))
```

```
    varCost = varCost * (1 + 0.1 * Val(rstInv("Month"))) / 32)

    'Create quantities on hand that are related, more or less, to cost
    Select Case varCost
    Case Is > 100
        lngQuantity = Int(40 - 10 + 1) * Rnd + 10
    Case Is > 50
        lngQuantity = Int(50 - 12 + 1) * Rnd + 12
    Case Is > 25
        lngQuantity = Int(60 - 16 + 1) * Rnd + 16
    Case Is > 10
        lngQuantity = Int(80 - 20 + 1) * Rnd + 20
    Case Else
        lngQuantity = Int(100 - 25 + 1) * Rnd + 25
    End Select

    With rstInv
        'If no sales were made during the month, use the last month's quantity
        If IsNull(.Fields("Sales")) And _
            .Fields("ProductID") = lngLastProd Then
            lngQuantity = lngLastQuan
        End If

        'Save the last Quantity and Product ID values
        lngLastQuan = lngQuantity
        lngLastProd = .Fields("ProductID")

        'Update the Landed Cost and Quantity Fields
        .Fields("LandedCost") = varCost
        .Fields("Quantity") = lngQuantity
        .Update

        'Go to the next record
        .MoveNext
        intCtr = intCtr + 1
    End With
Loop

'Commit the updates to all of the records
cnnInv.CommitTrans
End Sub
```

Figure 11.3 shows 22 of the 2,464 records of tblInventory with the randomized LandedCost
and Quantity entries filled by the code of the cmdRandomize_Click event handler. Only the
Year, Month, LandedCost, and Quantity fields are needed for the Inventory table of
Graphs.mdb, which simulates a real Northwind Traders Inventory table. The
tblInventoryProductMonth consists of a copy of the Inventory table for naming consistency
with tables that contain rolled up data.

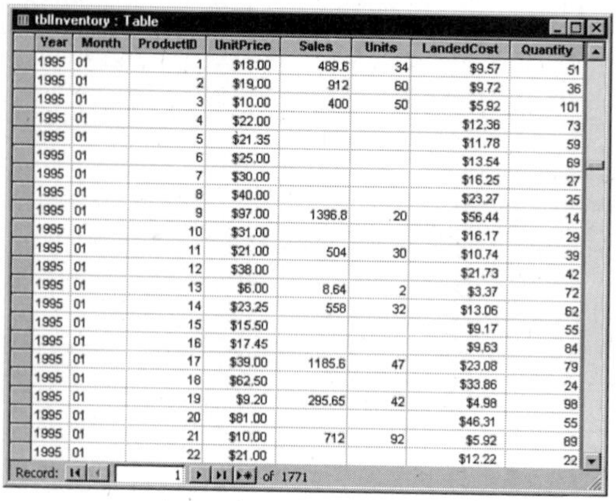

FIGURE **11.3**

Values added to tblInventory by the randomizing code of Listing 11.1.

Year	Month	ProductID	UnitPrice	Sales	Units	LandedCost	Quantity
1995	01	1	$18.00	489.6	34	$9.57	51
1995	01	2	$19.00	912	60	$9.72	36
1995	01	3	$10.00	400	50	$5.92	101
1995	01	4	$22.00			$12.36	73
1995	01	5	$21.35			$11.78	59
1995	01	6	$25.00			$13.54	69
1995	01	7	$30.00			$16.25	27
1995	01	8	$40.00			$23.27	25
1995	01	9	$97.00	1396.8	20	$56.44	14
1995	01	10	$31.00			$16.17	29
1995	01	11	$21.00	504	30	$10.74	39
1995	01	12	$38.00			$21.73	42
1995	01	13	$6.00	8.64	2	$3.37	72
1995	01	14	$23.25	558	32	$13.06	62
1995	01	15	$15.50			$9.17	55
1995	01	16	$17.45			$9.63	84
1995	01	17	$39.00	1185.6	47	$23.08	79
1995	01	18	$62.50			$33.86	24
1995	01	19	$9.20	295.65	42	$4.98	98
1995	01	20	$81.00			$46.31	55
1995	01	21	$10.00	712	92	$5.92	89
1995	01	22	$21.00			$12.22	22

Record: |◄| ◄ | 1 | ► |►I|►*| of 1771

DECIDING ON A NAVIGATION METHOD FOR COMPLEX DECISION-SUPPORT APPLICATIONS

The potential of displaying several hundred different forms in a variety of sequences requires you to provide a simple and intuitive method of navigating between the graphs and charts that are accessible to the user.

- Navigating the morass of charts and graphs is best accomplished by providing a set of buttons that let the user choose the class and type of graph to display. Toggle buttons are best suited for this purpose because the appearance of the button in the down state provides a visual clue to the class and chart being displayed. Menu choices duplicate the action of the button sets.

- Displaying the detail behind charts and graphs with Grid controls requires that you create and display a Grid control whose data is derived from the data that underlies the graph. You can save the user a step by providing historical data when he or she chooses to display detail information for totals graphs that have only a single line.

- Drilling down to display the detail behind a graphic element lets the user display detail data for a single month. When you double-click a line segment or a particular area of the chart, you can display summary data for the month or allow the user to view one of several sets of very detailed information for the chosen month.

- Drilling down from cells on FlexGrid controls is another method of displaying very detailed information for a particular period and category of data. Double-clicking a FlexGrid control leads to another grid or certain data set choices; this process is identical to the graphic "hot spot" drilldown process described previously.

Figure 11.4 shows the starting point of the Graphs sample application for this chapter— Graphs.vbp in the \Ddg_vb6\Chaptr10 folder of the accompanying CD-ROM. The button bar design and some of the code that displays the initial graph shown in Figure 11.4 are derived from the Ui_examp.vbp application in Chapter 9. The sections that follow describe the development of the Graphs applications and provide listings for the code that handles basic display capabilities.

FIGURE 11.4

The opening form of the Graphs application.

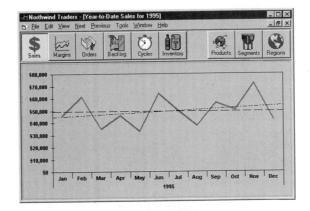

Using the Multiple Document Interface

Your decision-support applications will have at least two classes of windows: graphs and grids. Grids may have two or more classes: grids that show detail data by category and grids that compare historical data. Although you can use the Show and Hide methods to display separate forms for each class of window, using the Windows multiple document interface (MDI) is a better approach. If you use separate forms for each class of window, you must create a set of menus and menu event handlers for each form. Using MDI forms enables you to use a common set of menus for all your graphs and grids.

Creating MDI applications with Visual Basic 6.0 is a simple, straightforward process:

1. Add an MDI parent form to your application by choosing Project, Add MDI Form from the Visual Basic menu. Each application can have only one MDI parent form. MDI parent forms can contain only menus and PictureBox or Toolbar controls have a much more limited set of properties than conventional or MDI child forms have. You can add other controls within a picture box control on the MDI parent form.

> **NOTE**
>
> This chapter's example takes advantage of a PictureBox control's ability to contain two Toolbar controls, each with a set of grouped buttons. You can place only a single Toolbar control directly on a form. If you need more than one set of grouped buttons, you must use a PictureBox containing two or more toolbars.

2. Add MDI child forms to your application by choosing <u>P</u>roject, Add <u>F</u>orm and then setting the MDIChild property of the new form to True. You can have as many MDI children as you want in your application, but all the child windows are constrained to display within the surface of the parent window. When you apply the Show method to an MDI child form, both the parent and child forms are loaded and displayed automatically. All MDI child forms are modeless; you cannot create a modal MDI child form.

> **NOTE**
>
> You can display multiple MDI child forms in the parent form container and cascade or tile the multiple MDI child forms. The Graphs sample application uses this MDI feature only in a limited way, primarily for demonstration purposes. Inexperienced PC users tend to become confused by a multiplicity of forms on their display.

Table 11.3 lists the seven possible combinations of window states that are available to applications that use MDI parent and child windows.

TABLE 11.3 THE SEVEN COMBINATIONS OF WINDOW STATES FOR MDI PARENT AND CHILD FORMS

Parent State	Child State	Comment
Maximized	Maximized	This is the most likely combination you'll want to use as the default for decision-support applications. The title of the MDI child form appears in brackets in the title bar of the parent form. The menu bar appears as the menu bar of the child window. Only one MDI child window can appear when the child window is maximized.
Maximized	Normal	The title of the MDI child form appears in the child form's own menu bar. You can display multiple child forms in cascaded, horizontally tiled, and vertically tiled arrangements. A standard set of Windows menu choices controls the arrangement and a list of open MDI children.

Parent State	Child State	Comment
Maximized	Minimized	The MDI child form is minimized to an icon, and the surface of the parent form or the next open child form appears. Set the `BackColor` property value of the parent form to change from the standard dark gray (`&H8000000C&`).
Normal	Maximized	Similar to the maximized/maximized state except that the MDI parent form's window is sizeable. Normal/maximized is the state used to create most of the figures that appear in this chapter.
Normal	Normal	The MDI child form's title bar appears, and both the parent and child windows are sizeable. You use code in the `MDIForm_Resize` event-handling subprocedure to scale the MDI form to fit the resized parent window. Figure 11.5 (which follows) is an example of the appearance of the Graphs application in normal/normal windows mode.
Normal	Minimized	The active MDI child form is minimized to an icon. Any other open MDI child windows appear in their current window state.
Minimized	Not Applicable	The MDI parent window is minimized to an icon, and no MDI child windows are visible.

Designing the Navigation Toolbar

The Graphs application uses a button toolbar that is derived from the design of the button bar discussed in Chapter 9. Figure 11.5 illustrates the buttons used for the Graphs sample application in the normal/normal window state. The toolbar consists of two sets (groups) of buttons in two Toolbar controls contained in a PictureBox; the first six buttons (from left to right), shown in Figure 11.5, determine the class of the graph, and the last three buttons determine the type of the graph or chart displayed. Thus the user clicks the Sales, Margins, Orders, Backlog, Cycles, or Inventory button to display the monthly totals for the chosen graph class. To display the chosen class of data by product line, market segment, or sales region, the user clicks one of the second set of buttons. To redisplay the totals line chart, the user clicks another class button.

You place toolbars in the child window when the button complement changes in accordance with which child window is active. The toolbar buttons for the Graphs application are constant throughout the application for a single category of user. (You do need to disable or "disappear" specific graph-type buttons for graph classes to which the type does not apply, however.) Thus you can place the toolbar for the Graphs application on the MDI parent form.

Figure 11.5 shows the two toolbars for the Graphs application contained in the MDI parent form. The document control menu is open in Figure 11.5 to demonstrate that removing the minimize button from an MDI child form by setting the value of the `MinButton` property to **False** also removes the Minimize menu choice from the document control menu.

To add controls to the MDI parent form, you add a picture box to the form that is deep enough to contain the buttons of the two toolbars. When you add a picture box to an MDI parent form, the value of the `Align` property automatically is set to 1 (Align top) and the `Width` property is set to the `ScaleWidth` value of the form. The `ScaleWidth` property is the width of the client area of the MDI parent form. The client area is the area inside the borders of the parent form, below the menu, and below a picture box (when present). The `ScaleWidth` value of a parent form is 120 twips less than the value of the `Width` property, because sizable borders are 60 twips (3 points) wide.

Figure 11.5

The Graphs MDI parent and child forms with the toolbar contained in the parent window.

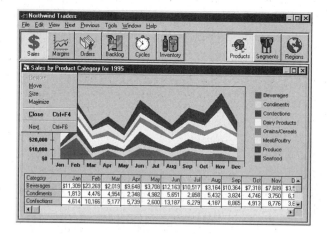

The Menu Structure of the MDI Parent Form

The menu bar choices shown in Figure 11.5 are, with two exceptions, common to a variety of Windows applications and appear in the established sequence for MDI applications. Menu choices with accelerator-key (Alt+*key*) combinations are provided for each action you can accomplish with a button, plus additional actions for which no toolbar buttons are provided. It is a good design practice to include menu choices that duplicate the action of every button of every toolbar in your application.

The two nonstandard menu bar choices, Next and Previous, take the place of Next and Previous buttons or a pair of arrow buttons on the MDI form. Substituting menu bar choices (Next and Previous have no pull-down menus) for command buttons is unconventional, but it provides display navigation similar to a browser. If your toolbar has enough space to accommodate Next and Previous buttons, you can add them to the toolbar and remove the two menu bar choices.

Figure 11.6 shows the Menu Editor dialog for the MDIToolbar form of the Graphs application that displays the choices for the Window menu. The choices shown—Cascade, Tile, and Arrange Icons—are provided only as examples. (The Graphs application does not enable the user to cascade windows, and when the tiling of child windows is necessary or practical, applying the Arrange method in the application's code controls the display of multiple windows.) Marking the Window List check box adds a list of the open MDI child windows to the Window menu in run mode. The window list automatically is separated by a horizontal line from the menu choices you add to the Window menu.

FIGURE 11.6

The standard menu choices of the Windows menu of MDI applications.

Code to Scale the Toolbar Buttons, MDI Child Forms, and Graphs

The chtMonthly graph control of the frmMDIGraph form and its associated code is similar to the Butn_bar.frm file of Chapter 8's Ui_examp.vbp application. However, you need to scale both the MDI child form and the graph contained in the MDI child form if (1) the user changes the window state of either the parent or the child form, or (2) the user resizes the parent form in the normal window state. It's also useful to maintain the position of the three graph type buttons to the right. You use the MDIForm_Resize event-handling subprocedure of the MDI parent form to change both the size of the MDI child forms and the graph control (or other scalable control objects, such as image boxes) contained in the MDI child form.

The code in Listing 11.2 resizes the MDI form, toolbar buttons, graph, and grid to occupy the largest available area within the constraints of each object's container. (The MSHFlexGrid control of the Graphs application is discussed later in this chapter.) In the Graphs application, the ResizeFormAndGraph subprocedure is executed by the MDIForm_Resize and the Form_Resize event handlers of the parent and child forms, respectively. If the user resizes a normal-state child window with the mouse (or with the Size choice of the document control menu and the arrow keys), the Resize event is triggered and the child window springs back to fill the client area of the parent form. Clicking any toolbar button calls `ResizeFormAndGraph` after the graph or chart is re-created.

LISTING 11.2   CODE TO RESIZE THE MDI CHILD FORM AND ITS GRAPH

```
Public Sub ResizeFormAndGraph()
    'Purpose:    Resize the form, graph and buttons
    'Note:       This function is recursive without the flag

    Dim intLeft As Integer   'Left distance from client edge

    If blnInhibitResize Or (frmMDIToolbar.WindowState = 1) Then
        'Prevent recursion and don't try changing size of an icon
        Exit Sub
    End If

    With frmMDIToolbar
        'Don't allow resizing smaller than 8400 twips
        If .Width < 8400 Then
            .Width = 8400
        End If
    End With

    With frmMDIGraph
        If .WindowState = 0 Then
            'Window is in normal mode so resizing is valid
            .Top = 0
            .Left = 0
            .Width = frmMDIToolbar.ScaleWidth
            .Height = frmMDIToolbar.ScaleHeight
        End If
    End With

    blnInhibitResize = True     'Prevent recursion

    DoEvents 'Give the window a chance to change size

    'Set the dimensions of the graph
    With frmMDIGraph.chtMonthly
        .Width = frmMDIGraph.ScaleWidth
        .Top = 0
        .Left = 0
    End With

    'Set the height of the graph, taking into account the grid size
    If frmMDIGraph.grdMonthly.Visible Then
        Call SetGridPosition
    Else
        With frmMDIGraph.chtMonthly
            If blnIsCrosstab Then
```

```
            .Height = frmMDIGraph.ScaleHeight - 300
        Else
            frmMDIGraph.chtMonthly.Height = frmMDIGraph.ScaleHeight
        End If
    End With
End If

'Set the widths of the grid columns
Call SetColWidths

'Set the position of the graph type buttons
With frmMDIToolbar.tlbGraphType
    .Left = frmMDIToolbar.Width - (.Width + 170)
End With

'Reset the recursion flag
blnInhibitResize = False
End Sub
```

SETTING GRAPH PROPERTIES IN DESIGN MODE

You establish the basic design parameters for your graphs and charts by setting the design-time properties of the Chart ActiveX control. MSChrt20.ocx shares the properties of Visual Basic 5.0's MSChart.ocx. Visual Basic 6.0's MSChrt20.ocx adds `DataSource` and `DataMember` properties for binding to `DataEnvironment` and `DataEnvironment.Command` or `ADODB.Recordset` objects, respectively. Graphs.vbp generates a `Recordset` object and binds it to the chtMontly object with a **Set** `chtMonthly.DataSource = rstGraph` statement.

The properties sheet of MSChrt20.ocx has the following eight pages:

- *Chart* sets the initial Chart Type property and offers a set of five display options for legends, markers, stacking series, and specifying series in `Recordset` rows (see Figure 11.7). Graphs.vbp either sets these values with VBA code or relies on data binding to provide automatic generation of legends.

FIGURE 11.7

The Chart page of the MSChrt20.ocx Properties sheet.

- *Axis* establishes the line and scaling properties for X, Y, and Second Y axes. The Second Y axis repeats the Y axis scale at the right of the graph. To eliminate the repeated scale, clear the Show Scale check box for the Second Y axis (see Figure 11.8).

FIGURE 11.8

Removing the scale for the Second Y axis.

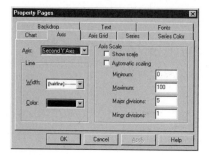

- *Axis Grid* adds scale gridlines on the X, Y, and Second Y axes. Gridlines unnecessarily clutter graphs and charts used to display trends, so the Style of each axis's gridlines is set to **Null** (see Figure 11.9).

FIGURE 11.9

Removing all gridlines from the chart.

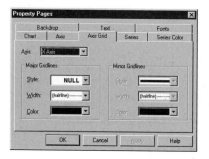

- *Series* lets you add a standard set of statistics to one or more series of your graph and provides a set of options that apply to the selected series. The six default single-line graphs of Graphs.vbp include Mean and Regression statistics, which are set in code (see Figure 11.10). Series are identified as R1...Rn for Series In Rows and C1...Cn for Series In Columns.

- *Series Color* lets you choose the color of the line or area for each series. The default colors are satisfactory for most applications.

- *Backdrop* specifies the `Interior` (background) and `Border` properties for the Chart, Title, Footnote, and Legend. Accept the default property values unless you want special formatting.

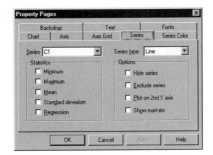

FIGURE 11.10

*Statistics and
Options selections
on the Series page
of the graph prop-
erties sheet.*

- *Text* lets you type the text for the chart Title, Footnote, X Axis Title, and Y Axis Title and specify the Alignment and Orientation of the text. No Text entries are required for Graphs.vbp.

- *Fonts* settings override the default values for the text of the Title, Footnote, Legend, and Axis Labels. Graphs.vbp uses the default font, 8-point MS Sans Serif bold.

IMPLEMENTING THE FIRST TWO CHART LEVELS

Up to this point, the examples have used the default Monthly Sales for 1995 data, which appears as the default graph when you launch the Graphs application. (The only year in Nwind.mdb for which there is a full year of data is 1995.) The sections that follow describe the primary functions and subprocedures of Graphs.vbp that, except as noted, are contained in the Graphs.bas module.

The Enhanced `DrawMonthlyGraph()` Function

After you establish your data sources, the next step is to rewrite the `DrawMonthlyGraph` proce-dure of Chapter 8 for bound data and to use the fields of records in the tblDefinitions table of Graphs.mdb to supply the following values for each graph:

- The caption for the `frmMDIGraph` form—the MDI child form that contains the Graph, Grid, and other controls related to the first chart level

- The name of the table that supplies the data for the graph or chart and the name of the field that has the numerical values

- The `tlbChartClass` and `tlbChartType` buttons' value (0 or 1) that corresponds to the graph or chart on display (incorporated in the Code field for level 1 forms)

Listing 11.3 shows the Visual Basic code used to create graphs from data contained in two dif-ferent levels of tables: (1) simple monthly-summary tables typical of those that store rolled up data from detail tables of mainframe and minicomputer databases and (2) crosstab tables you create from data in rollup tables using Jet SQL's TRANSFORM and PIVOT statements. Simple level 1 tables require processing the Recordset with series in rows, and crosstab level 2 tables (blnCrosstab = **True**) require series in columns. The number of series for a crosstab Recordset is equal to its RecordCount.

The code shown in Listing 11.3 re-creates the rstGraph Recordset for each new graph. Crosstab queries return **Null**s for cells with no data, but the Chart control doesn't handle **Null**s gracefully. After encountering a **Null** value in a series, no more data points appear; thus you must replace **Null** values in the Recordset with zeroes. Crosstab Recordsets aren't updatable, so you must save the Recordset as a file and then reopen it to replace **Null**s with zeroes. Fortunately, saving and reopening small Recordsets to and from files is very fast. The ChartData property returns a **Variant** array of all chart data, including x-axis labels. Code in DrawMonthlyGraph replaces the month numbers of the Recordset (01...12) with month abbreviations (Jan...Dec). It's much easier to change x-axis labels in the ChartData array than by operating on each Label object with VBA code.

CAUTION

Be sure to move the record pointer of the chart's Recordset before opening the graph. If you don't apply a Move..., GetRows, or similar method to the Recordset, the chart doesn't display the point for the first row or column of the data. Hopefully, this bug will be fixed in a future Visual Studio Service Pack.

NOTE

The modGraphs module contains the declarations of **Public** variables, including all the object variables required for the Graphs application. The MDIForm_Load and Form_Load procedures for the MDI parent (frmMDIToolbar) and child (frmMDIGraph) forms establish the initial size as well as other variable values that apply only to these two forms.

LISTING 11.3   THE CODE FOR THE DrawMonthlyGraph SUBPROCEDURE, WHICH CREATES THE DATA FOR THE GRAPH AND GRID CONTROLS

```
Public Sub DrawMonthlyGraph()
    'Draw the graph specified by the buttons

    Dim strSQL As String 'SQL statement for graph
    Dim varData() As Variant
    Dim blnNulls As Boolean
    Dim lblYAxis As MSChart20Lib.Label
```

```
frmMDIGraph.grdMonthly.Visible = False

With rstGraphDefs
    If .Fields("Legend") Then
        'Only crosstab queries have legends
        blnIsCrosstab = True
    Else
        blnIsCrosstab = False
    End If
    frmMDIGraph.Caption = .Fields("GraphCaption") & " for " & strYear
End With

'Get the SQL statement for the graph
strSQL = strCreateSQL()

With rstGraph
    If .State = adStateOpen Then
        .Close
    End If
    Set .ActiveConnection = cnnGraphs
    .CursorType = adOpenDynamic
    .CursorLocation = adUseClient
    .Source = strSQL
    .Open
    'If you don't move the record pointer, January is missing
    .MoveFirst
    'Check for null values
    Do Until .EOF
        blnNulls = False
        For intCtr = 0 To .Fields.Count - 1
            If IsNull(.Fields(intCtr).Value) Then
                blnNulls = True
                Exit Do
            End If
        Next intCtr
        .MoveNext
    Loop
    .MoveFirst

    If blnNulls Then
        'Crosstab Recordsets aren't updatable, so save the
        'Recordset as a file, then re-open it
        On Error Resume Next
        Kill App.Path & "\Crosstab.rst"
        On Error GoTo 0
        .Save App.Path & "\Crosstab.rst"
        .Close
        .Open App.Path & "\Crosstab.rst", , adOpenDynamic, _
            adLockOptimistic, adCmdFile
        .MoveFirst
```

continues

LISTING 11.3 CONTINUED

```
        Do Until .EOF
            For intCtr = 0 To .Fields.Count - 1
                blnNulls = False
                If IsNull(.Fields(intCtr).Value) Then
                    blnNulls = True
                    .Fields(intCtr).Value = 0
                End If
            Next intCtr
            If blnNulls Then
                .Update
            End If
            .MoveNext
        Loop
        .MoveFirst
    End If
End With

With frmMDIGraph.chtMonthly
    'Set the Recordset of the graph
    Set .DataSource = rstGraph
    'Determine the format
    If InStr(rstGraphDefs.Fields("DataTable"), "Margin") Then
        strFormat = "#0.0%"
    ElseIf InStr(rstGraphDefs.Fields("DataTable"), "Cycle") Then
        strFormat = "#0.00"
    Else
        strFormat = "$#,##0"
    End If
    'Apply the format to the Y-axis labels
    For intCtr = 1 To .Plot.Axis(VtChAxisIdY).Labels.Count
        Set lblYAxis = .Plot.Axis(VtChAxisIdY).Labels(intCtr)
        lblYAxis.Format = strFormat
    Next intCtr
    If blnIsCrosstab Then
        If Right(strFormat, 1) = "%" Then
            'Set up the multiline graph
            .chartType = VtChChartType2dLine
            .Stacking = False
        Else
            'Set up the stacked area chart
            .chartType = VtChChartType2dArea
            .Stacking = True
        End If
        'Use rows, not columns, for series
        .Plot.DataSeriesInRow = True
        'Turn off the statistics
```

```
        .Plot.SeriesCollection(1).StatLine.Flag = 0
        'Replace month number with month abbreviation
        varData = .ChartData
        For intCtr = 1 To UBound(varData, 2)
            varData(0, intCtr) = strMonths(intCtr, 1)
        Next intCtr
        .ChartData = varData
        'Display the legend
        .ShowLegend = True
    Else
        'Set up the line graph
        .chartType = VtChChartType2dLine
        .Stacking = False
        .Plot.DataSeriesInRow = False
        .Plot.SeriesCollection(1).StatLine.Flag = _
            VtChStatsRegression + VtChStatsMean
        .ShowLegend = False
        'Change the x-axis labels to month names
        varData = .ChartData
        For intCtr = 1 To UBound(varData)
            varData(intCtr, 1) = strMonths(intCtr, 1)
        Next intCtr
        .ChartData = varData
    End If

    DoEvents
    .Visible = True
End With
'Load the grid
Call LoadFlexGrid
End Sub
```

TIP

Use the `Clipboard.SetText strSQL` method when you're developing the code to write complex SQL statements. You can paste the SQL statement into the SQL Statement window of the VisData application or into the SQL text box of Access's query design window to check for syntax errors and view the query result table.

The code in Listing 11.3 calls the `LoadFlexGrid` subprocedure, which supplies data for the cells of the Grid control `grdMonthly` on the `frmMDIGraphs` form. The code used to populate the MSHFlexGrid control is described in the section titled "Adding a Detail Grid to the MDI Child Form," later in this chapter.

Creating the SQL Statements for SELECT and Crosstab Recordsets

The two SQL statements you need for creating the Recordset object to supply the data to the line graph and area chart that display monthly gross margins by category are as follows:

```
SELECT Year, Month, Margin AS SumOfData
   FROM tblMarginAverageMonth
   WHERE Year = "1995" ;

   TRANSFORM SUM(Margin) AS SumOfData
   SELECT [CategoryID]
      FROM tblMarginCategoryMonth
   WHERE Year = "1995"
   GROUP BY [CategoryID]
   PIVOT Month IN ("01", "02", "03", "04", "05", "06",
                   "07", "08", "09", "10", "11", "12");
```

> **TIP**
>
> Although the crosstab query statement uses the SUM() SQL aggregate function in the TRANSFORM clause, there is only one record for the margins of products in a given category for each year and month. Thus the crosstab query "sums" a single record and serves only to reformat the data from a tabular structure to spreadsheet style. If your crosstab query is based on a table with more than one record per query, you could use the AVG() function to determine the average margin. Using the AVG() function, however, does not return the sales-weighted average margin that your clients are likely to want. Therefore, you should use individual rollup tables to create each type of graph that displays percentages.

The code for the strCreateSQL() function shown in Listing 11.4 is typical of the functions needed to create crosstab queries for a variety of decision-support applications. The IN() predicate ensures that columns are created for 12 months even if some months do not have any data. Using a fixed number of months makes programming simpler and provides a constant abscissa for the graphs. The current record of tblDefinitions supplies the table and field names for each query.

LISTING 11.4   CODE TO CREATE REQUIRED SELECT AND CROSSTAB QUERY STATEMENTS

```
Public Function strCreateSQL() As String
   'Purpose:   Create the SQL statement for SELECT and crosstab queries
   'Called by: DrawMonthlyGraph

   Dim strSQLTransform As String  'TRANSFORM clause
   Dim strSQLSelect As String     'SELECT clause
   Dim strSQLFrom As String       'FROM clause
```

```
Dim strSQLWhere As String          'WHERE criterion
Dim strSQLGroupBy As String        'GROUP BY clause
Dim strSQLPivot As String          'PIVOT clause
Dim strSQLIn As String             'IN predicate
Dim strTemp As String              'Holder for legend data
Dim intDataSets As Integer         'Data sets in crosstab

'Create the basic FROM and WHERE clauses
strSQLFrom = "FROM " & rstGraphDefs("DataTable") & " "
strSQLWhere = "WHERE Year = '" & strYear & "' "

If blnIsCrosstab Then
    'Create the SELECT statement for the crosstab
    strSQLSelect = "SELECT [" & rstGraphDefs("LegendField") & "] "

    'Define Access SQL crosstab clauses
    strSQLTransform = "TRANSFORM Sum(" & rstGraphDefs("DataField") & _
        ") AS SumOfData "
    strSQLGroupBy = "GROUP BY [" & rstGraphDefs("LegendField") & "] "
    strSQLPivot = "PIVOT Month "

    'Create the legends from the appropriate table
    With rstLegend
        If .State = adStateOpen Then
            .Close
        End If
        Set .ActiveConnection = cnnGraphs
        .CursorLocation = adUseClient
        .CursorType = adOpenDynamic
        .Source = "SELECT * FROM " & rstGraphDefs("LegendTable")
        .Open
        .MoveFirst
        Do Until .EOF
            'Create a list of quoted, comma-separated strings
            If rstGraphDefs("UseActivated") Then
                'Test if category is presently active
                If .Fields("Activated") Then
                    'Add the category to the IN predicate
                    intDataSets = intDataSets + 1
                    'The following two lines work with DAO but not ADO
                    'strLegendText(intDataSets) = _
                        .Fields(rstGraphDefs.Fields("LegendTextField"))
                    'strLegend(intDataSets) = _
                        .Fields(rstGraphDefs.Fields("LegendField"))
                    'This is the workaround:
                    strTemp = rstGraphDefs.Fields("LegendTextField")
                    strLegendText(intDataSets) = .Fields(strTemp)
                    strTemp = rstGraphDefs.Fields("LegendField")
                    strLegend(intDataSets) = .Fields(strTemp)
                End If
```

continues

LISTING 11.4   CONTINUED

```
            Else
                'Add all categories to the IN predicate
                intDataSets = intDataSets + 1
                'Same workaround as above
                strTemp = rstGraphDefs.Fields("LegendTextField")
                strLegendText(intDataSets) = .Fields(strTemp)
                strTemp = rstGraphDefs.Fields("LegendField")
                strLegend(intDataSets) = .Fields(strTemp)
            End If
            .MoveNext
        Loop
    End With

    'Create the IN predicate from the strMonths() array
    strSQLIn = "IN ("
    For intCtr = 1 To 12
        strSQLIn = strSQLIn & Chr(34) & strMonths(intCtr, 3) & Chr(34) & ", "
    Next intCtr
    strSQLIn = Left(strSQLIn, Len(strSQLIn) - 2) & ")"

    'Concatenate the SQL clauses for the crosstab query
    strCreateSQL = strSQLTransform & strSQLSelect & strSQLFrom & _
        strSQLWhere & strSQLGroupBy & strSQLPivot & strSQLIn & ";"
Else
    'Create a conventional SELECT query statement
    strSQLSelect = "SELECT Year, Month, " & _
        rstGraphDefs("DataField") & " AS SumOfData "

    'Concatenate the SQL clauses for the SELECT query.
    strCreateSQL = strSQLSelect & strSQLFrom & strSQLWhere & ";"
End If
End Function
```

ADDING A DETAIL GRID TO THE MDI CHILD FORM

Graphs and charts are an excellent means of depicting trends, but (at least in the business world) numbers are what count. Therefore, you need to provide the user of a graphic-based application the capability to display the values that underlie the graph. The simplest method of displaying numerical data underlying the graph is to use the MSHFlexGrid control, as shown in the normal window state in Figure 11.11. To make the MSHFlexGrid control in Figure 11.11 appear when one of the area charts is displayed by the Graphs project, choose View, Detail from the Graphs application's menu.

FIGURE 11.11

An MSHFlexGrid control that displays the data underlying the regional sales stacked area chart.

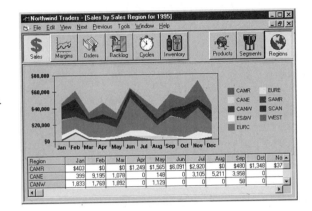

When the user chooses the normal window state, a grid with more than four rows squeezes the graph into an area with a small vertical dimension. Thus the `ResizeFormAndGraph` subprocedure changes the height of the grid to four rows when the window state is normal, as illustrated by Figure 11.11. If the user maximizes the window, the grid is changed to show all of the available columns, as shown in Figure 11.12.

The sections that follow describe the Visual Basic code used to define, populate, format, and size the Grid control, as well as to add crossfoot totals to the grid. Adding crossfoot totals to a Visual Basic MSHFlexGrid control is much simpler than adding row and column totals to an Access continuous form because Access requires you to place the column headers in the form header and the column totals in the form footer.

FIGURE 11.12

A level 2 multiline graph in the maximized window state with a full-table grid.

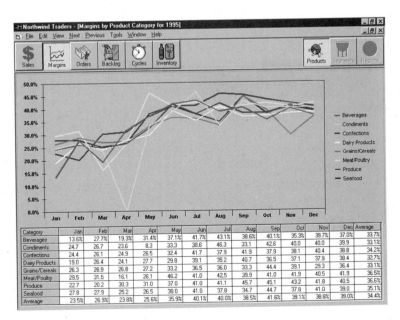

Adding the Code to Populate an MSHFlexGrid Control

The code to specify the dimensions of the grid, create the column and row headers, and add the values to the data cells of the grid shown in Figures 11.11 and 11.12 appears in Listing 11.5. The code adds an extra column at the right to the grid to accommodate row totals. Crosstab grids get an extra row to hold column totals. Creating row and column totals is the subject of the next section. The SetColWidths subprocedure determines the widths of the grid's columns. SetColWidths is a separate subprocedure because you also need to change the column widths when the user resizes the MDI parent window.

LISTING 11.5 THE TWO PROCEDURES REQUIRED TO CREATE AND SIZE AN MSHFLEXGRID CONTROL TO DISPLAY NUMERICAL GRAPH DATA

```
Public Sub LoadFlexGrid()
    'Purpose:    Set up the grid data
    'Called by: DrawMonthlyChart

    Dim intRow As Integer
    Dim intCol As Integer

    With frmMDIGraph.grdMonthly
        .ClearStructure
        .Clear
        .FixedCols = 0
        'Add a column for totals
        If blnIsCrosstab Then
            'Add a column and row for crossfooting
            Set .DataSource = rstGraph
        Else
            .Rows = 2
            .Row = 1
            intCol = 1
            rstGraph.MoveFirst
            Do Until rstGraph.EOF
                .Col = intCol
                If IsNull(rstGraph.Fields("SumOfData")) Then
                    .Text = 0
                Else
                    .Text = rstGraph.Fields("SumOfData")
                End If
                rstGraph.MoveNext
                intCol = intCol + 1
            Loop
        End If
        'Add the row total column
        .Cols = 14
```

```
.Col = 0
.Row = 0
.Text = rstGraphDefs.Fields("GridRowHeader")
.Col = 13
.Text = rstGraphDefs.Fields("Crossfoot")
.Col = 0
'Format the values
For intRow = 0 To .Rows - 1
    .Row = intRow
    For intCol = 1 To .Cols - 2
        .Col = intCol
        If intRow = 0 Then
            'Month names for column headers
            .Text = strMonths(intCol, 1)
        Else
            If intRow = 1 Then
                'If Right(strFormat, 1) = "%" Then
                '    .Text = Val(.Text) / 100
                'End If
                .Text = Format(.Text, strFormat)
            Else
                If Left(strFormat, 1) = "$" Then
                    'Drop the $
                    .Text = Format(.Text, Right(strFormat, 5))
                ElseIf Right(strFormat, 1) = "%" Then
                    .Text = Val(.Text) * 100
                    'Drop the %
                    .Text = Format(.Text, Left(strFormat, 4)) + "    "
                Else
                    .Text = Format(.Text, strFormat)
                End If
            End If
        End If
    Next intCol
Next intRow
DoEvents
.Visible = True
If blnIsCrosstab Then
    .Rows = .Rows + 1
End If
.Row = .Rows - 1
.Col = 0
.Text = rstGraphDefs.Fields("Crossfoot")
.Row = 0
.FixedCols = 1
For intCol = 1 To .Cols - 1
    .ColAlignmentHeader(intCol) = flexAlignCenterCenter
Next intCol
```

continues

LISTING 11.5   CONTINUED

```
    End With
    Call ResizeFormAndGraph
    Call SetColWidths
    Call CrossfootGrid
End Sub

Public Sub SetColWidths()
    'Set the column widths for numerical values

    With frmMDIGraph.grdMonthly
        For intCtr = 0 To .Cols - 1
            If blnIsCrosstab Then
                'Use fixed column widths for crosstabs
                If frmMDIToolbar.WindowState = vbMaximized Then
                    .ColWidth(intCtr) = 800
                Else
                    .ColWidth(intCtr) = 650
                End If
            Else
                'Use variable column widths for monthly data
                .ColWidth(intCtr) = Int(.Width / .Cols) - 8
            End If
        Next intCtr
        If blnIsCrosstab Then
            'Fix the first two column widths
            .ColWidth(0) = 1200
        End If
        'Fix the last column
        If blnIsCrosstab Then
            .ColWidth(.Cols - 1) = 900
        End If
        .ColAlignmentHeader(.Cols - 1) = flexAlignRightCenter
        .ColAlignment(.Cols - 1) = flexAlignRightCenter
    End With
End Sub
```

Adding Row, Column, and Crossfoot Totals to the Grid

Grid controls also can provide your client with crossfooted row and column totals, as shown in the MSHFlexGrid control of preceding Figure 11.12. Listing 11.6 is the code used to create totals for dollar values and averages for percentage and other values that require averaging, such as order-cycle time in days. A substantial part of the code for the CrossfootGrid subprocedure is needed to compute averages properly. The Margins by Product Category graph uses the averaging method.

LISTING 11.6   THE CODE TO CREATE ROW AND COLUMN TOTALS AND TO CROSSFOOT THE GRID
DATA

```
Public Sub CrossfootGrid()
    'Purpose:   Crossfoot the grid
    'Called by: LoadFlexGrid
    'Uses the Recordset, which is faster than using grid Text values

    Dim curColTotals(13) As Currency
    Dim curRowTotals() As Currency
    Dim curGrandTotalRow As Currency
    Dim curGrandTotalCol As Currency
    Dim intRow As Integer
    Dim intCol As Integer

    ReDim curRowTotals(rstGraph.RecordCount + 1)
    intRow = 1
    With rstGraph
        .MoveFirst
        If blnIsCrosstab Then
            Do Until .EOF
                For intCol = 1 To .Fields.Count - 1
                    'Aggregate the column and row totals
                    If Not IsNull(.Fields(intCol).Value) Then
                        curColTotals(intCol) = curColTotals(intCol) + _
                            .Fields(intCol).Value
                        curRowTotals(intRow) = curRowTotals(intRow) + _
                            .Fields(intCol).Value
                    End If
                Next intCol
                With frmMDIGraph.grdMonthly
                    'Current row
                    .Row = intRow
                    'Last (total) column
                    .Col = .Cols - 1
                    If rstGraphDefs.Fields("Crossfoot") = "Total" Then
                        'Total row values
                        If intRow = 1 Then
                            'Dollar signs for first total
                            .Text = Format(curRowTotals(intRow), strFormat)
                        Else
                            .Text = Format(curRowTotals(intRow), _
                                Right(strFormat, 6))
                        End If
                    Else
                        'Average the row values
                        If intRow = 1 Then
                            'Dollar signs for first total
```

continues

LISTING 11.6 CONTINUED

```
                .Text = Format(curRowTotals(intRow) / _
                    (rstGraph.Fields.Count - 1), strFormat)
            Else
                .Text = Format(curRowTotals(intRow) / _
                    (rstGraph.Fields.Count - 1), Right(strFormat, 6))
            End If
        End If
    End With
    curGrandTotalRow = curGrandTotalRow + curRowTotals(intRow)
    .MoveNext
    intRow = intRow + 1
Loop


'Add the column totals or averages to the last row
With frmMDIGraph.grdMonthly
    .Row = .Rows - 1
    For intCol = 1 To .Cols - 1
        .Col = intCol
        If rstGraphDefs.Fields("Crossfoot") = "Total" Then
            'Totals
            .Text = Format(curColTotals(intCol), strFormat)
        Else
            'Averages
            .Text = Format(curColTotals(intCol) / _
                rstGraph.RecordCount, strFormat)
        End If
    Next intCol
    .Col = .Cols - 1
    If rstGraphDefs.Fields("Crossfoot") = "Total" Then
        'Grand total
        .Text = Format(curGrandTotalRow, strFormat)
    Else
        'Grand average (not an average of averages)
        .Text = Format(curGrandTotalRow / (rstGraph.RecordCount _
            * (rstGraph.Fields.Count - 1)), strFormat)
    End If
End With
Else
    'Total a single row for line graphs
    Do Until .EOF
        curGrandTotalRow = curGrandTotalRow + .Fields("SumOfData")
        .MoveNext
    Loop
    With frmMDIGraph.grdMonthly
        .Row = 1
        .Col = .Cols - 1
        If rstGraphDefs.Fields("Crossfoot") = "Total" Then
            .Text = Format(curGrandTotalRow, strFormat)
        Else
```

```
            .Text = Format(curGrandTotalRow / _
                rstGraph.RecordCount, strFormat)
        End If
      End With
    End If
  End With
End Sub
```

NOTE

The format of the data for MSHFlexGrid controls that display dollar totals and averages for other values should comply with conventional accounting practices. The first row of values includes a dollar sign ($) or a percentage symbol (%). The symbol is omitted from the remaining rows of data. Dollar signs indicate totals, and percentage symbols can represent averages or totals of individual percentage values (usually 100 percent). The `Format()` statements in the `LoadFlexGrid` subprocedure of Listing 11.5 and the `CrossfootGrid` subprocedure of Listing 11.6 follow this formatting standard.

WRITING THE CODE TO NAVIGATE BETWEEN GRAPHS AND CHARTS

Each toolbar requires a procedure to display the corresponding graph. Listing 11.7 is an example of code to display a particular graph based on the index of the push button within the toolbar and the value of the button. Similar code is used in the `gpbGraphType_Click` subprocedure, which enables you to choose the type of level 2 area chart or multiline chart to display.

LISTING 11.7 THE EVENT HANDLERS AND SUBPROCEDURES TO DISPLAY GRAPHS BY CLASS AND TYPE

```
Private Sub tlbGraphClass_ButtonClick(ByVal Button As MSComctlLib.Button)
  'Purpose: Display first graph in class sequence

  Dim strCode As String
  Dim intCntr As Integer

  'Don't do any work if the button value is false
  If Button.Value = 0 Then
      Exit Sub
  End If

  'Prevent recursion on value change
```

continues

LISTING 11.7   CONTINUED

```
    If blnInhibit Then
        Exit Sub
    End If

    blnInhibit = True

    For intCtr = 1 To 3    'Reset the type buttons
        tlbGraphType.Buttons(intCtr).Value = tbrUnpressed
    Next intCtr

    strCode = LTrim(Str(Button.Index)) & "1" 'Set the graph code

    Call DisplayNewGraphClass(strCode)
    DoEvents

    'Show the form, in case another form is on top
    frmMDIGraph.Show
    DoEvents
    blnInhibit = False    'Reset the inhibit flag
End Sub

Private Sub tlbGraphType_ButtonClick(ByVal Button As MSComctlLib.Button)
    'Purpose: Display the graph type for the selected class

    Dim strCode As String
    Dim intCtr As Integer

    'Prevent response to class changes
    If blnInhibit Then
        Exit Sub
    End If

    blnInhibit = True

    'Determine which class button is selected
    For intCtr = 1 To 6
        If tlbGraphClass.Buttons(intCtr).Value = tbrPressed Then
            Exit For
        End If
    Next intCtr

    'Is the button being turned on or off?
    If Button.Value = tbrPressed Then
        strCode = LTrim(Str(intCtr)) & LTrim(Str(Button.Index + 1))
    Else
        strCode = LTrim(Str(intCtr)) & "1"
    End If
```

```
        Call DisplayNewGraphType(strCode)

        blnInhibit = False
        frmMDIGraph.Show
End Sub

Public Sub DisplayNewGraphClass(strCode As String)
    'Purpose:   Test to see if the graph is different

    'Don't reprocess the current graph
    With rstGraphDefs
        If .EOF Then
            .MoveFirst
        End If
        If .Fields("Code") <> strCode Then
            .MoveFirst
            .Find "Code = '" & strCode & "'"
            If Not .EOF Then
                'Disable the unused buttons for the class
                Call DisableTypeButtons

                'Get the graph data
                Call DrawMonthlyGraph
                DoEvents
            End If
        End If
    End With
End Sub

Public Sub DisplayNewGraphType(strCode As String)
    'Purpose: Display a different graph type

    With rstGraphDefs
        .MoveFirst
        .Find "Code = '" & strCode & "'"
        If .EOF Then
            'Should not occur; buttons for missing selections are disables
            MsgBox prompt:="Graph not available for this selection.", _
                Buttons:=vbCritical, Title:="Developer at Work"
        Else
            Call DrawMonthlyGraph
            DoEvents
        End If
    End With
End Sub
```

The event handlers for the navigational code, associated with push buttons and menu choices, appear in the frmMDIToolbar form.

PRINTING AND SAVING GRAPHS AND CHARTS

The Pinnacle/BPS Graph control included with Visual Basic 4.0 and earlier provided relatively simple means for printing graphs and saving graphs as Windows metafiles (*FileName*.wmf). MSChrt20.ocx lacks Print and Save methods, so you must copy the chart to the Clipboard object and then paste the Clipboard image to a hidden PictureBox control to print or save the chart. The two menu event handlers of Listing 11.8 illustrate the code required to print and save charts. Although the Clipboard format of the chart is a metafile, the format of the file saved from a PictureBox is a Windows bitmap.

LISTING 11.8   MENU EVENT HANDLERS TO PRINT AND SAVE A GRAPH OR CHART

```
Private Sub mnuFilePrint_Click()
    'Print the graph as a Windows metafile
    Dim intWinState As Integer
    Dim intCopies As Integer
    Dim intCopy As Integer

    On Error GoTo errPrint

    With frmMDIGraph.dlgPrintSetup
        .CancelError = True
        .ShowPrinter
        intCopies = .Copies
    End With

    'Expand to full screen to get large graph
    intWinState = frmMDIToolbar.WindowState
    frmMDIToolbar.WindowState = vbMaximized
    frmMDIGraph.chtMonthly.EditCopy

    'Return to prior mode
    frmMDIToolbar.WindowState = intWinState
    frmMDIGraph.picGraph.Picture = Clipboard.GetData
    For intCopy = 1 To intCopies
        Printer.Print ""
        Printer.PaintPicture frmMDIGraph.picGraph.Picture, 0, 0
        'Add a caption at mid page
        Printer.CurrentY = Printer.ScaleHeight / 2
        Printer.FontSize = 18
        Printer.CurrentX = 1500
        Printer.Print "Northwind Traders - " & frmMDIGraph.Caption
        'Finish the printing (not pretty, but readable)
        Printer.EndDoc
    Next intCopy
errPrint:
    Exit Sub
End Sub
```

```
Private Sub mnuFileSave_Click()
    'Create a bitmap from the graph
    'The clipboard image is a metafile, but saves only as a bitmap
    Dim intWinState As Integer
    Dim strFileName As String

    'Expand to full screen to get large graph
    intWinState = frmMDIToolbar.WindowState
    frmMDIToolbar.WindowState = vbMaximized
    frmMDIGraph.chtMonthly.EditCopy

    'Return to prior mode
    frmMDIToolbar.WindowState = intWinState
    frmMDIGraph.picGraph.Picture = Clipboard.GetData
    strFileName = App.Path & "\" & frmMDIGraph.Caption & ".bmp"

    'Save it as a bitmap
    SavePicture frmMDIGraph.picGraph, strFileName
    MsgBox "Graph saved to " & strFileName, _
        vbInformation, "Save Graph Bitmap"
End Sub
```

PRINTING WITH THE REPORT DESIGNER AND VBA CODE

IN THIS CHAPTER

Visual Basic 6.0's new Data Report Designer (DRD) is a lightweight replacement for Seagate Software's Crystal Reports ActiveX or VBX control included with prior Professional and Enterprise versions of Visual Basic. DRD is fully integrated with the Data Environment Designer (DED), and projects that include DataReport objects must have a .dsr file to supply DRD's DataSource and DataMember property values. Like version 1.0 of any new product or feature, DRD has a few shortcomings. In this case, the shortcomings are especially noticeable in the export of HTML and text files from DataReports. DRD lacks the design flexibility and event granularity of Access reports; DataReport objects have a very sparse collection of properties, methods, and events. If you need only relatively simple columnar reports, such as those described in the first half of this chapter, DED is likely to suffice. Otherwise, evaluate seasoned third-party ActiveX report designers from Seagate Software or Data Dynamics.

Reports for specialized applications, such as printing odd-shaped labels, defy graphic layout techniques. In this case, you must revert to VBA code and the Printer object. Writing report-printing code is a tedious process, but the satisfaction you experience when your printed page conforms exactly to your initial vision usually compensates for the coding drudgery. The last half of this chapter describes how to write VBA code for printing reports with very complex formats.

DESIGNING AND PRINTING A SIMPLE DataReport

Opening a new Data Project adds an empty DED and DRD instance to the Project Explorer. DataReport1 is removed from prior chapters' examples that start with a Data Project. This section and the following sections that cover DRD-based reports use the default DataReport1 as the starting point for report design. Like DataEnvironments, there's no limit to the number of DataReport objects you can add to a project. Each DataReport in your project requires its own DRD runtime instance.

Opening the empty DataReport1 instance disables the Toolbox's General form controls and adds a DataReport button at the bottom of the Toolbox. Clicking DataReport displays a set of DataReport-specific controls—RptLabel, RptTextBox, RptImage, RptLine, RptShape, and RptFunction. With the exception of RptFunction, each Rpt... control corresponds to the native (General) Visual Basic 6.0 toolset. Rpt... controls, however, have fewer properties than their General counterparts and trigger no events. The default DataReport1 in design mode consists of Page Header, Detail, and Page Footer sections (see Figure 12.1). Each section has its own set of common properties—Name, ForcePageBreak, Height, KeepTogether, and Visible, but no events. The DRD "form" acts as the report's print preview window and has a subset of the properties and methods of conventional Visual Basic forms. The event model of a DRD "form," however, differs markedly from ordinary forms. DRD's events are associated with asynchronous processing of an entire report and don't fire at page, section, or individual record levels.

FIGURE **12.1**

The default DataReport1 *instance in design mode.*

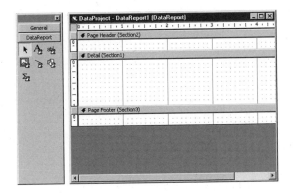

▶ See "Creating and Displaying Hierarchical Recordsets," **p. 390**

DRD obtains the overall structure of the report, including section headers and footers, if any, from the *DataEnvironment.*Command object that supplies the DataReport's DataMember property value. Simple reports have only Report Headers, Page Headers, Detail section, Page Footers, and Report Footers. A simple report is a list of rows from a Recordset defined by a single Command object. More complex reports, the subject of sections later in the chapter, use hierarchical Recordsets to group detail records and add aggregates, such as subtotals and totals, to the report.

TIP

Design the full *DataEnvironment.*Command structure and naming convention for a report before you begin the report design and formatting process. Making changes to Command names or other Command properties often requires that you re-retrieve the structure of the Command. Retrieving the Command structure removes all current DRD controls. The time you spent laying out and formatting controls is lost. You can recover some formatted RptLabel and RptTextBox controls by copying them to the Clipboard before retrieving a new structure, but you must alter the DataSource, DataMember, and/or DataField property values of bound RptTextBoxes if you change the names of any DataSource or DataMember objects.

Starting with a Semiformatted Simple Report

DRD makes generating simple columnar reports without row and column totals a relatively quick and easy process. The process for designing Visual Basic DataReports is quite similar to designing Access reports, but there's no Report Wizard to assist you, and the controls lack Access's automatic formatting features for specific field data types, such as **Currency**.

To generate your first report with DED and DRD, do the following:

1. Open a new Data Project, rename `DataEnvironment1` to **envRepts**, and rename `DataReport1` to **rptOrders**. You must open the `DataEnvironment1` and `DataReport1` window to gain access to the properties sheets for these objects.

2. In the `envNwind` window, rename `Connection1` to **cnnNwind**, open the Data Link Properties sheet, select Microsoft Jet 3.51 OLE DB Provider in the Provider page, and specify Visual Basic 6.0's Nwind.mdb database in the Connection page. Click OK to accept the remaining defaults for the `Connection`.

3. Add a new `Command` to `cnnNwind` named **Ords1995Prod**, select View from the Database Object list, and the Quarterly Orders by Product crosstab `QueryDef` from the Object Name list. Click OK to accept the remaining defaults for the `Command`; reports commonly use read-only `Recordsets` and client-side cursors.

4. Expand the Ords1995Prod node of the `envReports` window to display the crosstab query's column list and drag the Ords1995Prod node's icon to the Detail section of `rptOrders`.

   This step adds RptLabels for column names and RptTextBoxes for row values and automatically sets the `DataMember` and `DataFields` properties of the text boxes to the `Ords1995Prod Command` and to the columns of the `QueryDef`, respectively.

5. Select the `rptOrders` by clicking on an empty window region and set the `DataSource` and `DataMember` property values to cnnNwind and Ords1995Prod, respectively.

   Unlike form operations, dragging a `Command` from the Data Environment window doesn't automatically set the `DataSource` and `DataMember` properties of the `DataReport`.

6. Drag the ProductName:, CustomerID:, and Qtr1: through Qtr4: RptLabels to top of the Page Header section, leaving no horizontal space between the labels.

   Delete the Order Year: label and OrderYear text box. The report is for a single year, 1995.

7. Drag the six text boxes to the top of the detail form, shortening the width of each text box by 0.1 inch (one dot) so that the text boxes exactly align under the labels.

8. Drag the Page Footer bar to the bottom of the Detail text boxes to minimize the space between detail rows on the form.

9. Right-click one of the sections and choose Show Report Header/Footer to add two additional sections to the form.

10. Add an unbound RptLabel control from the toolbox to the Report Header and type **1995 Quarterly Sales by Product** as the label `Caption`. Format the `Font` appropriately for a report header.

11. Multiselect all labels in the Page Header section and all text boxes in the Detail section and change the Font Size to 9 points for improved readability.

12. Multiselect only the labels and set their Bold and Underlined Font properties to **True**. The DataReport in design mode appears as shown in Figure 12.2.

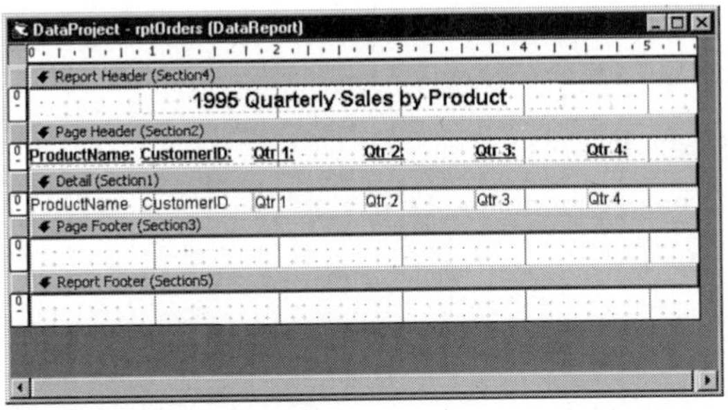

FIGURE 12.2

A simple DataReport *in design mode.*

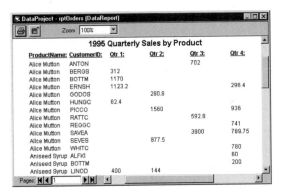

13. Choose Project, DataProject Properties; select rptOrders as the Startup Object; and rename DataProject to **OrdersReports**. Add a Project Description if you want.

14. Press F5 to run rptOrders. Figure 12.3 illustrates the simple report's window in run mode.

FIGURE 12.3

The simple DataReport *of Figure 12.2 in run mode.*

The preceding steps, with the exception of retrieving the command structure, are the foundation for designing reports of much greater complexity.

Sizing, Aligning, and Formatting Report Controls

The report shown in Figures 12.2 and 12.3 won't win any graphics design awards, but it demonstrates that you can create a report with minimal formatting in less than 5 minutes. To make the report more readable, do the following:

1. Increase the width of the ProductID column to 1.5 inches, decrease the width of the CustomerID column to 0.5 inch, and adjust the positions of the Qtr1...Qtr4 columns to align with the right edge of the CustomerID column.

2. Edit the `Caption` property of the labels to eliminate the colon and read **Product Name**, **Cust ID**, **1995Q1**, **1995Q2**, **1995Q3**, and **1995Q4**.

3. Multiselect the 1995Q1...1995Q4 labels and Qtr 1...Qtr4 text boxes and change the `Alignment` property value to 1 - rptJustifyRight. Always right justify columns of numeric data.

4. Select the Qtr 1 text box and change the `DataFormat` property value to Currency with 0 decimal places. Do the same for the Qtr 2, Qtr 3, and Qtr 4 text boxes.

> **NOTE**
>
> Multiselected text boxes don't let you set the `DataFormat` property value. However, the `DataField` property value, which isn't appropriate to a multiselect operation, *is* accessible. One of the inevitable Service Packs for Visual Basic 6.0 should fix this bug.

5. Run the form to verify the `Caption`, `Alignment`, and `DataFormat` property values (see Figure 12.4).

FIGURE 12.4

Improving report readability by formatting Page Header captions and Detail section rows.

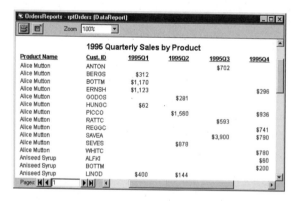

To print the form, click the Print button in run mode to display the standard Windows print dialog. Alternatively, you can call the `rptOrders.Print` method in VBA code.

Setting Printing Margins

The `DataReport` Properties window specifies dimensions in twips (1,440 twips/inch.) Developers in locales that use the metric system have it easier with millimeters as the standard scaling unit. The default printing margins are 1 inch (1,440 twips) for the TopMargin, LeftMargin, and BottomMargin properties of the form. The right printing margin is determined by the Width property of the DataReport, which can include whitespace to the right of the right-most object.

You can save report pages by adjusting the TopMargin and BottomMargin property values to 720 twips or fewer. As an example, with top and bottom printing margins of 500 twips, the report shown in Figure 12.4 shrinks from 18 to 16 pages.

GROUPING DETAIL RECORDS

▶ **See** "Taking Advantage of the MergeCells Feature," **p. 385**

The repeating ProductName column values in the form of Figure 14.4 detract from readability and consume extra toner or ink. The Command Properties sheet has a Grouping page that creates a hierarchical Recordset with duplicate column values removed. The action of the Grouping Command is similar to specifying the MergeCells property of an MSHFlexGrid or MSFlexGrid control.

Creating Child Commands for Grouping

1. Open the Ords1995Prod Properties sheet and click the Grouping tab.
2. Mark the Group Command Object check box, which creates a new hierarchical (child) Command with a _Grouping suffix.
3. Select ProductName in the Fields in Command list and click the right arrow button to move the column name to the Fields Used for Grouping list (see Figure 12.5).
4. Click OK to add the Grouping child Command, which creates the required hierarchical Recordset.

FIGURE 12.5

Grouping a report on a column of the Recordset *underlying a* DataReport.

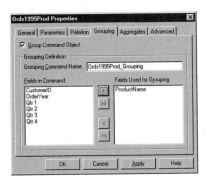

5. Expand the newly created Summary Fields in Ords1995Prod_Grouping and Details Fields in Ords1995Prod nodes to display the hierarchical `Recordsets`' columns.

6. Right-click the parent Command node and choose Hierarchy Info to open the dialog that displays the SHAPE statement for the grouping operation (see Figure 12.6).

FIGURE 12.6

A SHAPE *grouping statement for a hierarchical* DataReport Command.

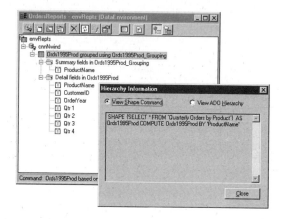

7. Press F5 to run rptOrders. Instead of a 16-page or 18-page report, the grouping operation results in a 1-page report showing only the records for the first ProductName value, Alice Mutton.

▶ **See** "Generating Hierarchical Commands with the Data Environment Designer," **p. 391**

Grouping Commands enable computation of group subtotals within reports with a COMPUTE...BY construct in the SHAPE statement. The following SHAPE statement for the Ords1995Prod_Grouping Command created in the preceding steps defines a grouping without calculated subtotals or totals:

```
SHAPE {SELECT * FROM `Quarterly Orders by Product`}
    AS Ords1995Prod
 COMPUTE Ords1995Prod BY 'ProductName'
```

The "Using Command Aggregates for Subtotals and Totals" section later in the chapter explains how to add subtotals and grand totals to DataReports with the COMPUTE instruction.

NOTE

SHAPE statements use the opening single quote pairs (` ... `) within SELECT statements, instead of conventional single quote (' ... '), double-quote (" ... "), or square bracket ([...]) pairs as object identifiers.

Adding Group Headers and Footers to the Report

At this point, logic dictates that simply adding a set of Group Headers and Group Footers by right-clicking a section and choosing Insert Group Header/Footer should accommodate the new Ords1995Prod_Grouping Command structure. Unfortunately, logic doesn't prevail in this case, and you must manually match the new hierarchical Command structure with your DataReport design. As noted in the tip in the "Designing and Printing a Simple DataReport" section earlier in the chapter, retrieving or re-retrieving the structure of the Command destroys the entire DataReport and your tediously formatted controls.

Follow these steps to add a Group Header/Footer pair and change the DataMember property to the highest member of the Command hierarchy:

1. Right-click a section and choose Insert Group Header/Footer to add the new section pair to the report.

2. Right-click an empty area of the DataReport and open its Properties sheet.

3. Change the DataMember property value from Ords1995Prod to Ords1995Prod_Grouping. The DataMember must be the top (parent) Command, which is renamed by adding the _Grouping suffix.

4. Run the report to verify that grouping on the ProductName column operates correctly, indicated by whitespace between successive groups of product names.

5. Return to design mode and delete the ProductName text box in the Detail section to eliminate the repeated field.

6. Drag the ProductName item from the Summary Fields in the Ords1995Prod_Grouping Command to the Group Header.

7. Delete the new ProductName caption label, resize the new ProductName text box to the same width as its predecessor, and set the Font.Size property to 9 points (see Figure 12.7).

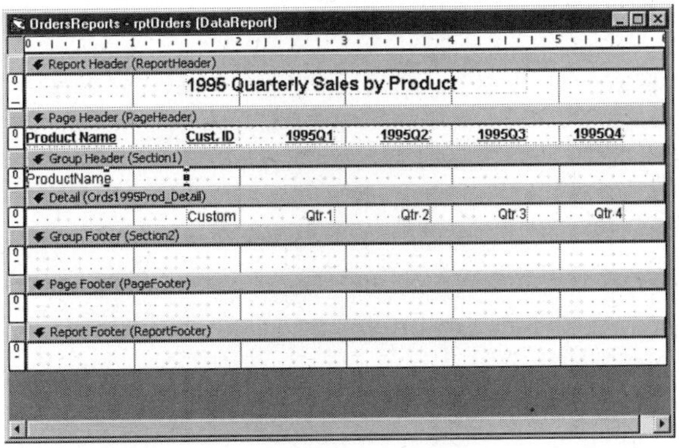

FIGURE 12.7
Nondestructively adding a Group Header/Footer pair to an existing DataReport.

8. Run the grouped report to verify your design changes (see Figure 12.8).

FIGURE 12.8

The grouped report with duplicate product names removed.

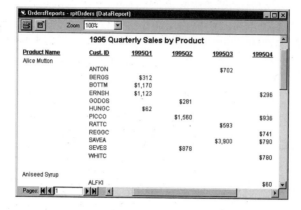

USING COMMAND AGGREGATES FOR SUBTOTALS AND GRAND TOTALS

Most readers of reports want subtotals and grand totals of columnar values. Once you've added a grouping `Command`, you can add a group subtotal for each numeric field of the `DataReport`. Providing a grand total aggregate requires adding another level to the `Command` hierarchy.

Adding a Group Subtotal to the `Command` Hierarchy

To add a ProductName group subtotal for each quarter to the `DataReport` command, do the following:

1. Open the Ords1995Prod Properties sheet from the DataEnvironment window and click the Aggregates tab.

2. In the Aggregates page, click Add to create an Aggregate1 item in the Aggregates list.

3. Type **Prod_Q1** as the Name of new aggregate and accept the default Sum Function and Aggregate On Grouping.

4. Select Qtr 1 as the Field to aggregate.

5. Click Apply to add the new aggregate to the Command structure.

6. Repeat steps 2 through 4 for each remaining quarter, naming the aggregates **Prod_Q2**, **Prod_Q3**, and **Prod_Q4** and selecting Field Qtr 2, Qtr 3, and Qtr 4, respectively (see Figure 12.9).

FIGURE 12.9

Adding Aggregates for DataReport *grouped subtotals.*

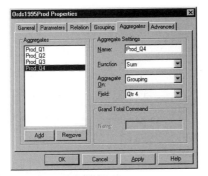

7. Click OK to return to the DataEnvironment window, which appears as illustrated in Figure 12.10.

FIGURE 12.10

Aggregates for grouped subtotals added to the Ords1995Prod_ Grouping Command.

Following is the reformatted SHAPE statement for the four quarterly subtotals on the grouped hierarchical Recordset:

```
SHAPE {SELECT * FROM `Quarterly Orders by Product`}
    AS Ords1995Prod
  COMPUTE Ords1995Prod,
    SUM(Ords1995Prod.'Qtr 1') AS Prod_Q1,
    SUM(Ords1995Prod.'Qtr 2') AS Prod_Q2,
    SUM(Ords1995Prod.'Qtr 3') AS Prod_Q3,
    SUM(Ords1995Prod.'Qtr 4') AS Prod_Q4
  BY 'ProductName'
```

Adding the Product Subtotal to the Group Footer

After you create the aggregate members of the Summary Fields in Ords1995Prod_Grouping `Command`, the final steps to add the subtotal text boxes to the `DataReport` are

1. Drag the Prod_Q1 aggregate to the Group Footer section of `rptOrders`.

2. Delete the aggregate name label and move the Prod_Q1 RptText box under the Qtr 1 text box of the Details section. Adjust the width of the Prod_Q1 text box to match the Qtr 1 text box above.

3. Repeat steps 1 and 2 for the Prod_Q2, Prod_Q3, and Prod_Q4 aggregates.

4. Multiselect all four of the Prod_Q# text boxes, set the `Font.Size` property to 9 points, and the `Alignment` property to 1 - rptJustifyRight.

5. Select each text box individually and apply the Currency with 0 Decimal Places `DataFormat`.

6. Copy the ProductName RptText box of the Group Header to the Clipboard, select the Group Footer section, and paste the text box at the upper left of the section.

7. Add an unbound RptLabel to the Group Footer under the CustomerID text box of the Detail section. Size the width of the label to that of the CustomerID text box.

8. Change the height of the text box from the default 288 twips to 240 twips to match the height of the other text boxes and then change the `Font.Size` property to 9 points. Change the `Caption` property to **Totals:** (see Figure 12.11).

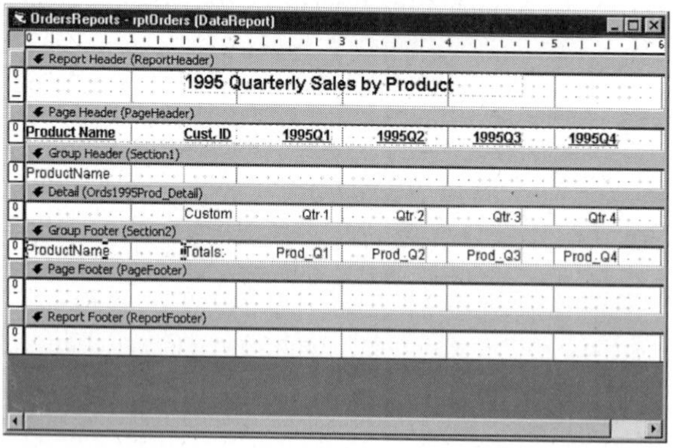

FIGURE 12.11

Adding formatted product order subtotals to the DataReport.

> **NOTE**
>
> Unlike conventional form controls, you can't use Ctrl+Shift to change the size of Rpt... controls independent of grid coordinates. This inconsistency is likely to be remedied by a Service Pack update or in the next version of Visual Basic.

9. Run the `DataReport` to check your progress (see Figure 12.12).

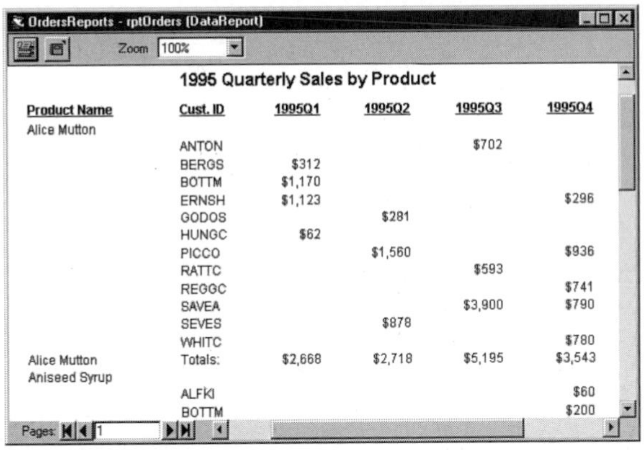

FIGURE 12.12
The design of Figure 12.11 in print preview mode.

> **NOTE**
>
> Online help states that setting the `KeepTogether` property value of a `DataReport` section determines whether page breaks occur within a section. Setting the `KeepTogether` property of the `ProductName` section in DRD version 6.0 appears to have no affect on the printed report.

Displaying Subtotal Aggregates in Hierarchical FlexGrids

The primary use for subtotal aggregates is in reports, but you also can display subtotals to MSHFlexGrid controls. To display in an MSHFlexGrid the hierarchical `Recordset` created in the preceding "Adding a Group Subtotal to the `Command` Hierarchy" section, do the following:

1. Open `frmDataEnv`, right-click the Ords1995Prod Grouped Using Ords1995Prod_Grouping `Command` in the DataEnvironment window, and drag the `Command` to `frmDataEnv`.
2. Choose Hierarchical FlexGrid from the menu and then enlarge the form and MSHFlexGrid control. Rename the control to **hfgOrders**.
3. Right-click `hfgOrders` and choose Retrieve Structure. The column layout, although not optimal, is suitable for a quick check of a hierarchical `Recordset` prior to restructuring a `DataReport` for a revised `Command` hierarchy.
4. Right-click `hfgOrders` again and choose Properties; then click the Bands tab. Select Band 1 (Ords1995Prod) and clear the Column Caption check box for ProductName and OrderYear to eliminate duplicate row values in these columns (see Figure 12.13).

FIGURE 12.13

Removing columns with duplicate row values from the MSHFlexGrid.

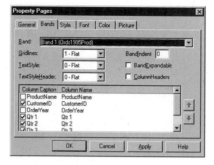

5. Change the Startup Object in the OrdersReports Properties sheet to `frmDataEnv` and run the form with the unformatted MSHFlexGrid (see Figure 12.14).

FIGURE 12.14

A hierarchical Command *for a* DataReport *displayed in an* MSHFlexGrid *control.*

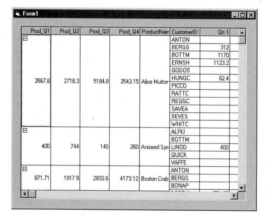

Formatting MSHFlexGrid Controls for Group Aggregates

Version 6.0 (actually 1.0) of the MSHFlexGrid control has an obscure bug that affects its ability to rearrange column formatting to optimize the layout of reports with multiple bands. Each member of the Command hierarchy is assigned to a band; Band 0 contains the columns of Ords1995Prod_Grouping, and Band 1 contains the columns of Ords1995Prod. In design mode, the structure (column layout) of the MSHFlexGrid appears as desired, with the ProductName column in Band 0, Column 0 (see Figure 12.15). Running the form, however, results in the ProductName column appearing in Band 0, Column 4 (refer to Figure 12.14).

Unfortunately, the DataField(int*Band*, int*Col*) property of MSHFlexGrids is read-only, so you can't reorganize the column order to move the ProductName column to the left-most position in code. However, if you alter the column sequence of the quarterly product subtotals in Band 0, the ProductName column returns to the correct location (see Figure 12.16).

Printing with the Report Designer and VBA Code

CHAPTER 12

465

12

PRINTING WITH
THE REPORT
DESIGNER

FIGURE 12.15

The design of the MSHFlexGrid control showing the ProductName field in Band 0, Column 0.

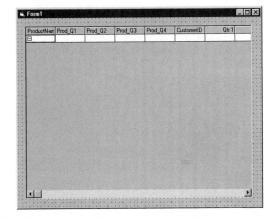

FIGURE 12.16

Changing the sequence of the quarterly subtotals to move the ProductName field to Band 0, Column 0.

NOTE

Microsoft might issue a Service Pack for Visual Basic 6.0 that corrects the column sequence bug in the MSHFlexGrid control. If so, skip the following workaround.

The workaround for the MSHFlexGrid column sequence problem, which requires rearranging the sequence of the group aggregates, is as follows:

1. In the Aggregates page of the Ords1995Prod Properties sheet, select Prod_Q1 and click Remove.

2. Click Add, change the name of Aggregate1 to **Prod_Q1**, and set the Field to Qtr 1; then click Apply (see Figure 12.17).

FIGURE 12.17

Changing the sequence of the quarterly subtotals to fix the MSHFlexGrid's column location bug.

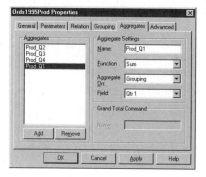

3. Close the Command Properties sheet, right-click the hfgOrders, and choose Retrieve Structure.

4. Open the hfgOrders' Properties sheet to the Bands page, select Prod_Q1 at the bottom of the Column Caption list, and click the up arrow to move Prod_Q1 below ProductName. Click Apply.

5. Select Band 1 and clear the ProductName and OrderYear check boxes. Click OK to return to frmDataEnv.

6. Run frmDataEnv. The column sequence for Band 0 now is correct.

Formatting the MSHFlexGrid to correspond as closely as possible to the report layout with the default 0 - Horizontal or 1 - Vertical band display requires the following code:

```
Private Sub Form_Load()
   Dim intBand As Integer
   Dim intCol As Integer

   With hfgOrders
      .ColWidth(0, 0) = 1500
      .ColHeaderCaption(0, 0) = "Product Name"
      'Above doesn't work for Band 0, workaround:
      .Col = 0
      .Row = 0
      .Text = "Product Name"
      .ColHeaderCaption(1, 0) = "Cust. ID"
      .ColWidth(0, 1) = 700
      For intBand = 0 To 1
         For intCol = 1 To 4
            .ColWidth(intCol, intBand) = 700
            .ColAlignmentBand(intBand, intCol) = flexAlignRightCenter
            .ColHeaderCaption(intBand, intCol) = "1995Q" & intCol
            'Above doesn't work for Band 0, workaround:
            .Col = intCol
            .Text = "1995Q" & intCol
         Next intCol
```

```
        Next intBand
    End With
End Sub
```

Figure 12.18 illustrates the result of applying the preceding formatting code to the MSHFlexGrid with horizontal banding. Formatting isn't applied to the Text property of each cell because version 6.0 of the MSHFlexGrid has problems formatting multiband cells having horizontal banding.

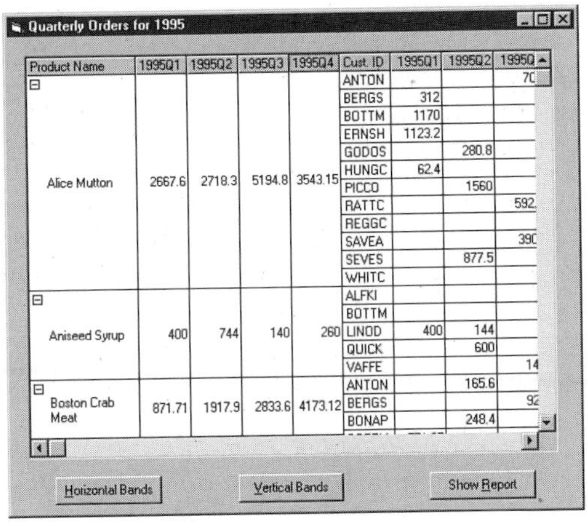

FIGURE 12.18

Changing column headers of an MSHFlexGrid control to correspond to report column headers.

NOTE

One of the problems with formatting *MSHFlexGrid*.Text values is that, contrary to the online help topic for the Rows property, Rows doesn't support a *lngBand* argument; expressions such as lngRows = *MSHFlexGrid*.Rows(0) result in a Wrong number of arguments or Invalid property assignment message. Workarounds in the preceding VBA code accommodate problems with the ColHeaderCaption property for Band 0.

Vertical banding more closely resembles the report layout, although subtotal aggregates appear above the detail rows in an MSHFlexGrid and below the detail rows in reports. It's relatively easy to format by replacing the Text values of vertically banded MSHFlexGrids, which have only five columns, as demonstrated by the following code:

```
Private Sub Form_Activate()
    Dim intCol As Integer
    Dim lngRow As Long

    With hfgOrders
```

```
If .BandDisplay = flexBandDisplayVertical Then
    'Format the text only if in vertical format
    .ExpandAll
    For intCol = 1 To 4
        .Col = intCol
        For lngRow = 1 To .Rows - 1
            .Row = lngRow
            If .BandLevel = 0 Then
                .Text = Format(.Text, "$#,##0")
            Else
                .Text = Format(.Text, "#,##0")
            End If
        Next lngRow
    Next intCol
    .CollapseAll
End If
End With
End Sub
```

The `Form_Activate` event handler contains the formatting code; traversing the entire grid requires at least a few seconds, so showing the grid before formatting improves perceived performance. After the cells are properly formatted in vertical format, changing to horizontal banding retains the currency (`"$#,##0"` or `"#,##0"`) format. You must set the `BandIndent` property of Band 1 to `0` in the Bands page of the MSHFlexGrid Properties sheet to stack the CustomerID values under the ProductName entry in Column 0. Figure 12.19 shows the vertically banded MSHFlexGrid with the Alice Mutton entry expanded. For consistency with accounting traditions, only the subtotals display a leading dollar sign.

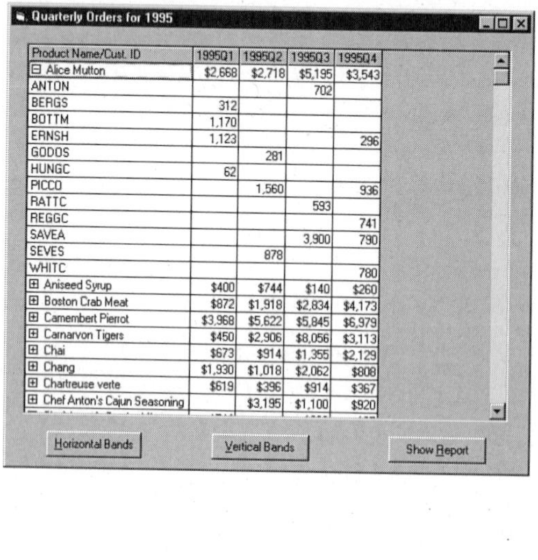

FIGURE 12.19

Displaying the hierarchical Recordset *in an MSHFlexGrid with the vertical banding option and U.S. currency text formatting applied.*

Adding a Report Grand Total

The logical location for report grand totals is the Report Footer section. Again, DataReports defy logic by requiring an additional Group Header and Footer pair to accommodate GrandTotal aggregates. In this case, the Group Header is empty. GrandTotal aggregates become the highest member of the Command hierarchy, so again you must change the DataMember property value of the DataReport to the name of the added Command.

To add yearly totals for each quarter to the report, do the following:

1. Open the Ords1995Prod Properties sheet to the Aggregates page.
2. Click Add to add Aggregate1 below the quarterly product subtotals; also, change the Name of the aggregate to **Total_Q1**.
3. Select GrandTotal in the Aggregate On list and type **ReptTotals** in the Grand Total Command Name text box.
4. Select Prod_Q1 as the Field to aggregate and then click Apply.
5. Repeat steps 2 through 4, except for naming the Grand Total Command, for Total_Q2, Total_Q3, and Total_Q4, based on the Prod_Q2, Prod_Q3, and Prod_Q4 subtotals, respectively (see Figure 12.20).

FIGURE 12.20

Adding GrandTotals for each of the year 1995's quarters.

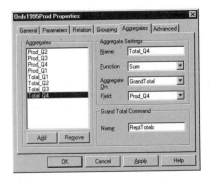

6. Close the Properties sheet to return to the DataEnvironment window, which appears as shown in Figure 12.21 after expanding the ReptTotals node.
7. Right-click a report section and choose Insert Group Header/Footer to open the Insert New Group Header/Footer dialog. Click the up arrow to move the position of the header and footer outside the existing ProductName group section (see Figure 12.22).
8. In the rptOrders Properties sheet, change the DataMember property value to ReptTotals.

FIGURE 12.21
The Ords1995Prod Command *with grand totals added.*

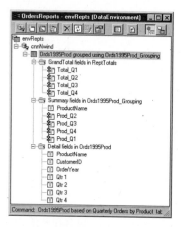

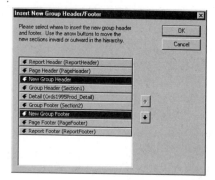

9. Drag the Total_Q1...Total_Q4 aggregate icons from the GrandTotal Fields in ReptTotals command in the DataEnviornment window to the new Group Footer. Remove the field caption labels, position the GrandTotal rptTextBoxes under those of the ProductName section, and adjust their width to match the text boxes above.

10. Multiselect Total_Q1...Total_Q4 text boxes and set the `Alignment` property value to 1 - rptJustifyRight. In the Font dialog, set the `Font.Size` property to 9 points and mark the Underline Effects check box.

NOTE

Accounting standards specify that grand totals be double-underlined, but that property isn't available for Visual Basic text boxes.

11. Individually select each GrandTotal text box and set the DataFormat property to Currency with 0 decimal places.

12. Add a RptLabel to the form under the ProductName text box, change its Caption to **Totals for 1995:**, and match its Height property and Font properties to the adjacent text boxes (see Figure 12.23).

FIGURE 12.23

Adding and formatting GrandTotal aggregate text boxes to the DataReport.

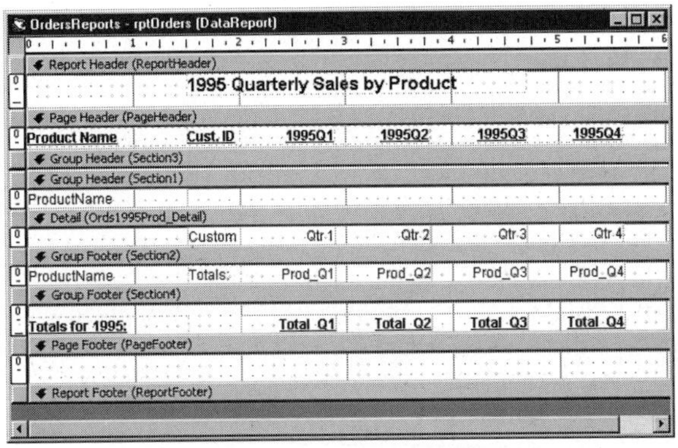

13. Change the startup form to the report, run the report, and move to the last page to check the validity and appearance of the GrandTotals text boxes (see Figure 12.24).

FIGURE 12.24

The DataReport with GrandTotal aggregates on the last page.

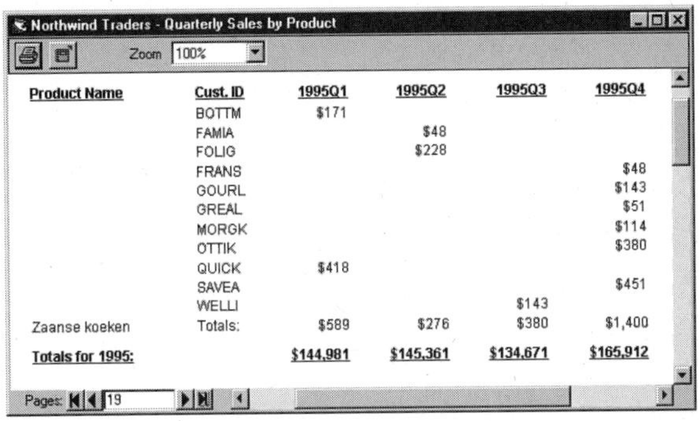

NOTE

If you start with a completed hierarchical Command structure and choose Retrieve Structure to set up the Group Headers/Footers, the name of the associated Command replaces the (Section#) group labels, as in Detail (Ords1995Prod_Detail).

Inserting Page Numbers and Dates in Page Footers

A common practice is to add page numbers, usually in Page # of # (total pages) format, and the date on which the report was printed to the bottom of each report page. DRD provides a number of predefined RptLabel controls, the content of which is defined by a `%Code` symbol, that you can add to the Page Footer section.

You gain access to these predefined controls by right-clicking the Page Footer section, choosing Insert Control, and selecting the control you want from a submenu.

To add page numbers and dates to the DataReport, do the following:

1. Right-click the Page Footer section, choose Insert Control, and choose Current Page Number to add a page number label (Caption = "%p").

2. Repeat step 1, but choose Label to add a RptLabel for the Page caption. Change the Caption property to **Page** and move the label to the extreme left of the section. Adjust the width of the Page label and move the Current Page Number label to the Page label's right.

3. Repeat step 2, but change the Caption property to **of** and position the label to the right of the Current Page Number label.

4. Repeat step 1, but choose Total Number of Pages (Caption = "%P").

5. Repeat step 3, but change the Caption property to **pages**.

6. Multiselect the four labels and change the Font.Size property to 9 points.

7. Select the %p and %P labels and set the Alignment property to 2 - rptJustifyCenter.

8. Insert a Current Date (Long Format) label (Caption = "%D"), position it under the Total_Q4 text box, change its Font.Size property to 9 points, and set its Alignment property to 1 - rptJustifyRight (see Figure 12.25).

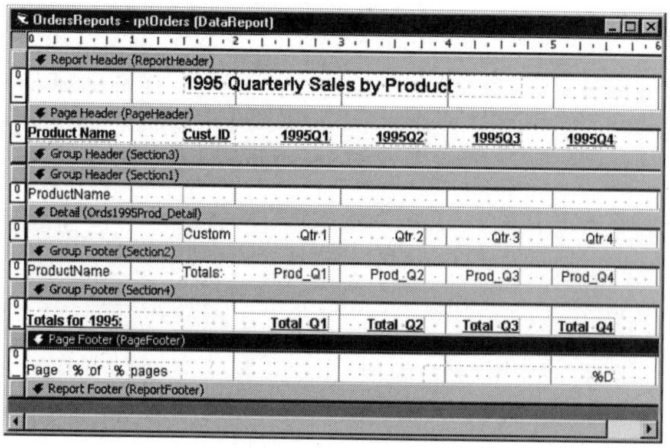

FIGURE 12.25

Page numbers and report printing date labels added to the Page Footer section.

9. Run the report to check the formatting of the Page Footer (see Figure 12.26).

FIGURE 12.26

The DataReport in run mode with footers at the bottom of each page.

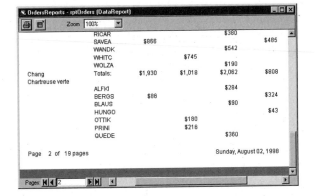

> **NOTE**
>
> `DataReport.Caption` property settings are ephemeral in version 6.0. Changes to the `Caption` property don't survive changes to report design. During the course of the preceding sections, the default caption (OrdersReports - rptOrders (DataReport)) was repeatedly changed to Northwind Traders - Quarterly Sales by Product (refer to Figure 12.24). Each design change, however, caused the default report caption to reappear (see Figure 12.26). Perhaps a Service Pack will fix this bug.

CROSSFOOTING REPORTS WITH ROW TOTALS

Marketing and product managers want year-to-date and yearly totals for detail rows, as well as grouping and GrandTotal aggregates. Accountants want *crossfooted* reports; crossfooting defines a set of row and column totals that add to the same number. Crossfooting a report proves that the report's arithmetic is correct, but, of course, doesn't attest to the accuracy of the detail content.

Crossfooting the rptOrders report requires adding a 1995Year caption to the Page Header and adding total columns to the Detail section, plus the ProductName and GrandTotal Group Footer sections. To generate the totals, you must replace the Ords1995Prod Command's `QueryDef` with a Jet SQL statement to add the four quarterly values to the crosstab query's result set.

Handling NULL Values of Crosstab Query Result Sets

Following is a conventional Jet SELECT query intended to sum to a computed column named Year the Qtr 1...Qtr 4 columns of the Quarterly Orders by Product crosstab query:

```
SELECT ProductName, CustomerID, [Qtr 1], [Qtr 2], [Qtr 3], [Qtr 4],
    ([Qtr 1]) + [Qtr 2] + [Qtr 3] + [Qtr 4]) AS Year
FROM [Quarterly Orders by Product]
```

Executing this query results in the Year column containing mostly NULL values. The Jet expression processor for summation returns a NULL value if any of the operands are NULL, which is the case for almost every row of the crosstab query result set. Thus you must use Jet's inline If function, IIf, whose syntax is identical to VBA's **IIf** function, and the Jet IsNull function to substitute 0 for NULL operands. The following Jet SQL statement handles the NULL problem:

```
SELECT ProductName, CustomerID, [Qtr 1], [Qtr 2], [Qtr 3], [Qtr 4],
    IIf(IsNull([Qtr 1]), 0, [Qtr 1]) + IIf(IsNull([Qtr 2]), 0, [Qtr 2]) +
    IIf(IsNull([Qtr 3]), 0, [Qtr 3]) + IIf(IsNull([Qtr 4]), 0, [Qtr 4])
    AS Year
FROM [Quarterly Orders by Product]
```

> **NOTE**
>
> The preceding SQL statement is valid only for the Jet OLE DB native data provider. ANSI SQL, used by client/server RDBMSs, doesn't support Jet's IIf and IsNull functions. ANSI SQL doesn't include the PIVOT and TRANSFORM statements required to quickly generate crosstab queries.

Fortunately, changing from a specified database object, such as a view, to an SQL SELECT statement that returns at least the same columns as the object doesn't affect the design or execution of the bound DataReport.

To change the data source of the Ords1995Prod Command from the Quarterly Orders by Product view to the preceding SQL statement, do the following:

1. Open the Ords1995Prod Properties sheet and select the SQL Statement option.

2. Type the preceding SELECT statement into the SQL Statement window (see Figure 12.27).

3. Click Apply to make the change and test the syntax of the statement you typed.

4. Display the Aggregates page, click Add, change the Name of Aggregate1 to **Prod_Year**, select Year in the Fields list, and click Apply.

5. Click Add, change the Name to **Total_Year**, select GrandTotal in the Aggregate On list, select Prod_Year in the Fields list, and click Apply (see Figure 12.28).

FIGURE 12.27

Changing the Source of Data from a Jet QueryDef *(View) to an SQL Statement that adds a computed Year total column.*

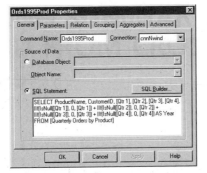

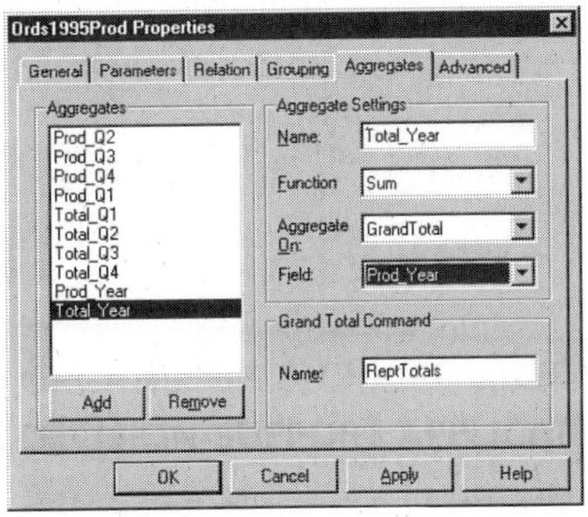

FIGURE 12.28

Adding new aggregates for the yearly grouping and grand totals.

5. Click OK to close the Properties sheet; then expand the Ords1995Prod Command nodes, if necessary, to display the added aggregates (see Figure 12.29).

FIGURE 12.29

The added row total aggregates displayed in the DataEnvironment window.

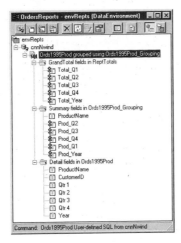

6. Run rptOrders to verify that changing the Command's data source and adding the new aggregates doesn't affect the existing printable report.

Adding Row Totals to a DataReport

Adding new columns to an existing DataReport is a relatively painless process. To add the row totals columns to your report design, follow these steps:

1. Expand the width of rptOrders to about 6.5 inches.

2. Copy the 1995Q4 label to the Clipboard and paste the copy to the right of the 1994Q4 label. Change the Caption property to **1995 Year**.

3. Copy and paste the Qtr 4 text box in the Details section and change the DataField property value to **Year**.

4. Copy and paste the Prod_Q4 text box in the ProductName Group Footer section and change its DataField property to **Prod_Year**.

5. Copy and paste the Total_Q4 text box in the GrandTotal Group Footer section and change its DataField property to **Total_Year** (see Figure 12.30).

FIGURE 12.30

One RptLabel and three RptTextBoxes added for the row total aggregates.

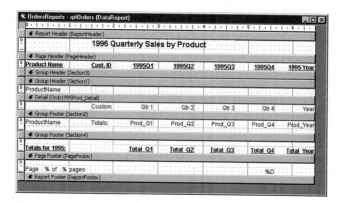

6. Change the LeftMargin and RightMargin property values to **720** twips to prevent a Report width is greater than paper width error message.

7. Run the report to verify addition and proper formatting of the row totals in each section of the report (see Figure 12.31).

FIGURE 12.31

The DataReport *in print preview mode with row totals added.*

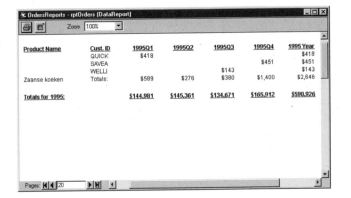

> **NOTE**
>
> The quarterly GrandTotal values don't sum to the yearly grand total in Figure 12.31 because of rounding errors. If you're creating crossfooted reports for accountants, set the DataFormat.DecimalPlaces property of text boxes using the currency format to 2. Whole dollars usually satisfy sales and marketing types, who seldom make the effort to verify crossfoot totals.

SUBSTITUTING RPTFUNCTION CONTROLS FOR AGGREGATE VALUES

The RptFunction control, which you can add only to a Group Footer of a DataReport, can take the place of aggregate fields created by grouped Command objects. Table 12.1 enumerates the allowable values of the *RptFunction*.FunctionType property, equivalent Command aggregate functions (where available), and the value displayed by the RptFunction control.

TABLE 12.1 VALUES OF THE RPTFUNCTION'S FunctionType PROPERTY AND CORRESPONDING Command AGGREGATES

Constant	Value	Aggregate	Displayed Value in RptFunction
rptFuncSum	0	Sum	Sum of numeric field values
rptFuncAvg	1	Average	Average of numeric field values
rptFuncMin	2	Minimum	Minimum value of a numeric field
rptFuncMax	3	Maximum	Maximum value of a numeric field

continues

TABLE 12.1   CONTINUED

Constant	Value	Aggregate	Displayed Value in RptFunction
rptFuncRCnt	4	Count	Number of rows in a report section
rptFuncVCnt	5	N/A	Number of fields with non-NULL values
rptFuncSDEV	6	Standard Deviation	Standard deviation for a column of numbers
rptFuncSERR	7	N/A	Standard error of estimate for a column of figures

To demonstrate the equivalency of bound RptFunction controls to Command aggregates, try the following:

1. Right-click the ProductName Group Footer, then choose Insert Control and Function to add an unbound RptFunction control with the default SUM(Unbound) Text property value to the section. Position the control under the Prod_Q1 text box.

2. In the Properties window for the RptFunction control, set the DataMember property to Ords1995Prod, the DataField property to Qtr 1, and the DataFormat to Currency with 0 Decimal Places.

3. Set the Alignment property to 1 - rptJustifyRight and the Font.Size property to 9 points.

4. Repeat steps 1 through 3 to add another RptFunction control to the GrandTotal Group Footer. Set its DataMember property to Ords1995Prod_Grouping and its DataField to Prod_Q1.

5. Match the Alignment and Font property values to those of the Total_Q1 text box (see Figure 12.32).

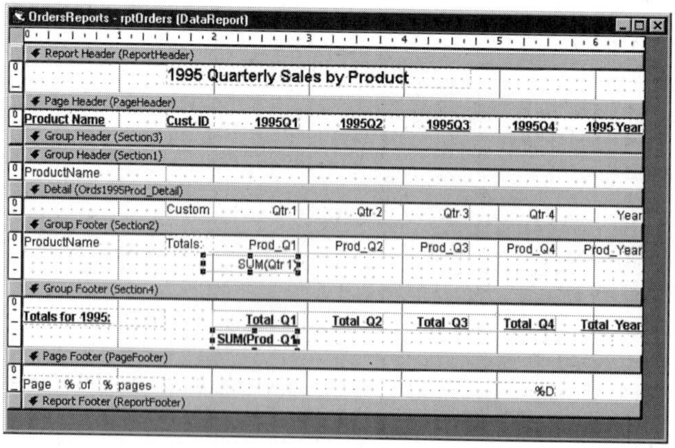

FIGURE 12.32

Adding RptFunction controls to emulate RptTextBoxes bound to aggregate Command fields.

6. Run the `DataReport` to verify that the values in the RptFunction controls are the same as those in the corresponding RptTextBoxes bound to the `Command` aggregate fields. Remove the two controls after testing.

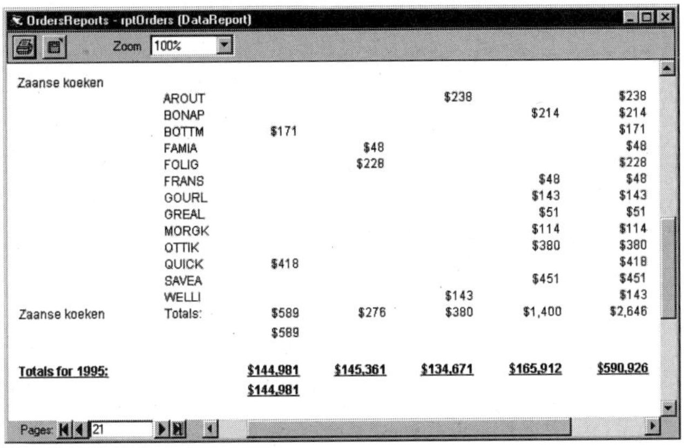

FIGURE 12.33

The `DataReport` in print preview mode with RptFunction controls duplicating RptTextBox controls bound to fields of Control aggregates.

> **NOTE**
>
> The completed `rptOrders` DataReport and `frmOrders` form, which includes the Hierarchical FlexGrid control that displays `Command` aggregate fields, is included in the OrdRepts.vbp project located in the \Ddg_vb6\Chaptr12 folder of the accompanying CD-ROM.

EXPORTING `DataReports` TO HTML AND TEXT FILES

The print preview (run) mode of `DataReports` offers an Export feature to save reports in HTML or text format. Clicking the Export button opens the Export dialog that lets you choose between 8-bit/DBCS code page or Unicode versions of HTML or text. Figure 12.34 illustrates Internet Explorer 4.01 displaying the last page of the OrdRept.htm file created from `rptOrders`.

Importing the HTML file into Microsoft Word 97 illustrates that the extraordinary complexity of the HTML table structure contributes to formatting problems (see Figure 12.35). Instead of the 7 table columns required for report fields, the HTML table structure has 21 columns, with cell merging used to accommodate wide text fields. Viewing the very complex HTML source for the table structures in Windows NT 4.0's Visual Notepad is sure to discourage any but the most fervent HTML hacker from attempting to alter the source to resolve formatting problems.

FIGURE 12.34

Table layout problems of DRD's report Export HTML feature evidenced by the staggered totals on the last page of rptOrders.

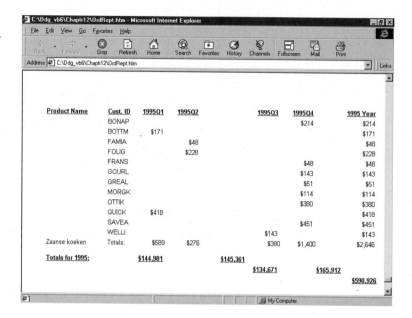

FIGURE 12.35

The HTML table of Figure 12.34 imported into Microsoft Word 97 (with the Office Service Pack applied).

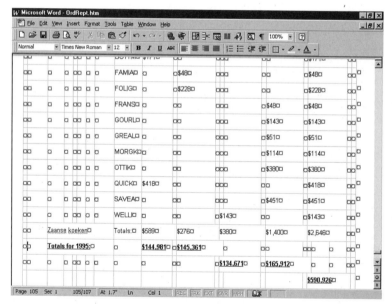

> **NOTE**
>
> Maintaining exact column alignment of RptLabels and RptTextBoxes in your
> DataReport design is critical to obtaining even a semblance of the desired for-
> mat in exported .htm and .txt files. Special care was taken in the design stages
> of rptOrders to assure that labels and text boxes were perfectly aligned on the
> grid. If you don't exactly align columns, formatting of exported files usually
> deteriorates to the point of total unusability.

Exporting rptOrders to a text file results in layout problems similar to that for HTML files
(see Figure 12.36), so at least part of the layout problems are due to unresolved problems with
column/row alignment detection in the main report parser.

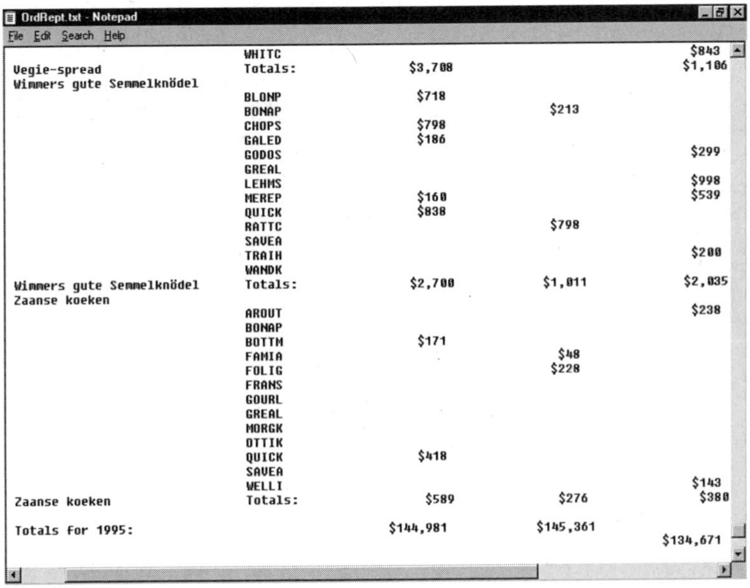

FIGURE 12.36

*Layout problems
similar to those of
Figures 12.34 and
12.35 exhibited by
exported text files.*

> **NOTE**
>
> The preceding examples clearly show that the HTML and text file export fea-
> ture of DRD version 6.0 isn't fully cooked. Hopefully, a Visual Basic 6.0 Service
> Pack will address these formatting problems. XML export, one of the features
>
> *continues*

> of Microsoft Office 2000, might solve some of the layout problems, but XML support isn't yet consistent between Netscape Navigator and Microsoft Explorer. Displaying files exported in XLM format is likely to be limited during the next few years to corporate intranets or owners of the Office 2000 suite. Until the export problems are resolved, and probably thereafter, using Active Server Pages (.asp files) to generate HTML content from Recordsets underlying reports is by far the better approach.

PRINTING WITH VBA CODE

Technically, using VBA code for printing isn't a database-specific topic; Printer properties, methods, and coding techniques have changed very little since the release of Visual Basic 2.0. DRD's inherent report formatting limitations, however, often require Visual Basic database developers to roll their own printing code. Thus coverage of printing from ADODB.Recordset objects warrants coverage in this book.

Chapter 14, "Scheduling and Device Control with Jet and VBA," describes a very complex single-user application (VBPG.vbp) that emulates with Visual Basic 6.0 the Program Guide feature of the Windows 98 WebTV for Windows add-in. VBPG.vbp uses WebTV's programming database (Tss.mdb) to display a program guide and to remotely control consumer electronic VCRs for recording preselected program episodes. Printing is a significant component of VBPG.vbp; the application prints individual pressure-sensitive labels for standard VCR cassettes and a catalog of recorded episodes. The data source for the cassette labels is the tblRecord table of VBPG.mdb; catalog data comes from VBPG.mdb's tblTapes.

The PrintVBA.vbp project, in the \Ddg_vb6\Chaptr12 folder of the accompanying CD-ROM, includes the following three printing forms from Chapter 14's VBPG.vbp:

- frmPrintSetup (PrtSetup.frm) determines the type of pressure-sensitive cassette labels to print—spine only or a spine/body combination. The form also sets the top and left printing margins, opens the Windows common Print Setup dialog, and prints a test label to check printer alignment (see Figure 12.37).

- frmPrintLabels (PrtLabel.frm) prints a single cassette spine label or spine/body combination. Only a single label from a multiple-label sheet is printed at one time, so provision is made to select the current label position (see Figure 12.38). Printing a label adds a record for the tape to tblTapes. Tapes are sequentially numbered, spine labels list the episode date and name, and body labels add the starting time of each episode (see Figure 12.39).

FIGURE 12.37

The Print Setup dialog for selecting the type of VCR cassette label to print.

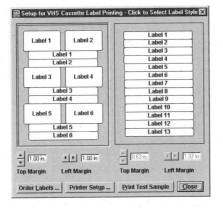

FIGURE 12.38

Specifying the printing margins for VCR cassette labels and the label number to print.

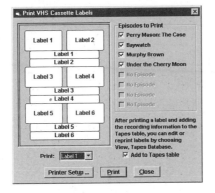

FIGURE 12.39

An example of a combination spine/body label printed as Label 1.

Printed by VBPG on 08/03/98 (LP)
00:00 10/01/97 Perry Mason: The Case of the
Fatal Framing
02:00 05/27/98 Baywatch
03:00 05/28/98 Murphy Brown
03:30 05/29/98 Under the Cherry Moon
(Partial)

Tape 10/01/97 Perry Mason: The Case of the Fatal Framing
6   05/27/98 Baywatch
05/28/98 Murphy Brown
(LP) 05/29/98 Under the Cherry Moon (Partial)

- `frmPrintTapes` (PrtTapes.frm) prints a catalog of tapes of recorded TV program episodes based on records in tblTapes. Like `frmPrintLabels`, `frmPrintTapes` also lets you set top and left printing margins (see Figure 12.40). Headings include the tape number, date of first recorded episode, and tape speed—Standard Play, Long Play, or Extended Play. An episode description column is optional (see Figure 12.41).

FIGURE 12.40

Specifying the printing margins and range of tape numbers for a tape catalog.

A simple selection form (`frmPrintSelect`, PrtMain.frm) opens the `ADODB.Connection` (`cnnUser`) and `ADODB.Recordset` (`rsUser`, `rsRecord`, and `rsTapes`) objects and provides command buttons to open the forms of the preceding list. The `modGlobals` module (PrtVars.bas) declares the **Public** variables shared by multiple forms.

Printing Cassette Labels

The `cmdPrint_Click` event handler of `frmPrintLabels` contains all the printing code for VCR cassette labels (see Listing 12.1). The subprocedure first checks for correct printer orientation (labels are designed for portrait mode), sets the top and left printing margins from the `frmPrintSetup`, determines whether the user is reprinting labels from the rsTapes table, and then creates from tblRecord or tblTapes an array of the episode lines to be printed on the body label. Like most VBA printing code, the majority of the lines involve setting the starting print position with `Printer.CurrentX` and `Printer.CurrentY` statements. The value of the **Public** `intTPI` variable is 1,440, which is the number of printer twips per inch. Check the `modGlobals` module to identify other variables not declared as **Private** or by **Dim** in `frmPrintLabels`.

NOTE

`Printer.`**Print** statements can't be abbreviated to `.`**Print** within **With** `Printer` `...` **End With** structures, because the **Print** method isn't defined by the `Printer` object's type library. **Print** is a VBA reserved word.

VHS Tape Catalog Printed by VBPG on Monday, August 03, 1998 - Page 1

Start	Date	Source	Program Title	Description
			Tape 21 09/06/97 (EP)	
00:00	09/06/97	KTOP	Feather River Camp Press Conference	
00:30	09/06/97	KRON	Hypertek (Partial)	A profile of young people who test games for a computer company; a visit to a convention with new toys and gadgets.
00:42	09/06/97	KPIX	49er Preview	
01:12	09/06/97	KQED	Collecting Across America	"Star Wars."
			Tape 22 09/06/97 to 09/07/97 (LP)	
00:00	09/06/97	KTVU	And Then There Was One	An entire family is diagnosed as HIV-positive. Amy Madigan, Dennis Boutsikaris, Jane Daly (1994, ***)
02:00	09/06/97	KRON	Pretender	Jarod Russell works as a firefighter while investigating a smoke-eater's murder.
			Tape 23 09/07/97 to 09/08/97 (EP)	
00:00	09/07/97	KRON	Dateline	With co-anchors Jane Pauley and Stone Phillips. Correspondents include Lea Thompson and Dennis Murphy. Segment information to be announced.
01:00	09/07/97	KPIX	Touched by an Angel	A judge suspends Monica when she misses her performance evaluation.
02:00	09/07/97	KGO	Men Are From Mars, Women Are From Venus	Six couples are profiled.
04:00	09/07/97	KOFY	Cops	
04:30	09/07/97	FNC	News Now	
04:40	09/08/97	AMC	The Out-of-Towners	A vacationing couple encounters countless urban disasters. Jack Lemmon, Sandy Dennis, Milt Kamen (1970, ***)
			Tape 24 09/08/97 to 09/09/97 (LP)	
00:00	09/08/97	A&E	Poirot	A rose is named after Poirot at a flower show; a gift of seeds makes Hastings ill.
01:00	09/08/97	A&E	Miss Marple	A home becomes a nightmare when the wife has visions of murder.
02:00	09/08/97	A&E	Law & Order	Stone discovers that a slain police officer was linked to a murder.
03:00	09/08/97	A&E	Biography	A profile of ruthless gangster Dutch Schultz.
			Tape 26 09/09/97 to 09/10/97 (LP)	
00:00	09/09/97	HBOW	Days of Thunder (Partial)	A cocky challenger enters the world of stock-car racing. Tom Cruise, Robert Duvall, Nicole Kidman (violence, adult situations, adult language, 1990, ***)
01:54	09/09/97	HBOW	First Time Felon	A convicted drug dealer attempts to rehabilitate himself. Omar Epps, Delroy Lindo, Rachel Ticotin (1997,)
			Tape 28 09/10/97 to 09/15/97 (EP)	
00:00	09/10/97	HBOW	Steal Big, Steal Little	An unscrupulous man forces his twin brother off his land. Andy Garcia, Alan Arkin, Rachel Ticotin (adult situations, 1995, **)
02:30	09/10/97	HBOW	First Knight	The evil Malagant threatens the peace of Camelot. Sean Connery, Richard Gere, Julia Ormond (violence, 1995, ***)
			Tape 29 09/15/97 to 10/01/97 (EP)	
00:00	09/15/97	KTVU	Seinfeld	Jerry gives Elaine Indian statue.
00:30	09/16/97	KTVU	Married... With Children	Al's a cartoon hit.
01:00	09/16/97	KTVU	Cheers	
01:30	09/16/97	KTVU	Baywatch	A murdering seductress uses Mitch in her latest scheme.
02:30	09/16/97	KTVU	First Business	Trend in the boating industry.
03:00	09/16/97	KTVU	Headline News	
03:30	09/16/97	KTVU	News	

12

PRINTING WITH THE REPORT DESIGNER

FIGURE 12.41 *An example of a catalog page with an optional description column.*

LISTING 12.1   CODE TO PRINT A SINGLE VCR CASSETTE SPINE OR COMBINATION SPINE/BODY LABEL FROM DATA IN THE TBLTAPES OR TBLRECORD TABLE

```
Private Sub cmdPrint_Click()
    'Print the label in one of 6 (combo) or 11 (spine) positions
    Dim sngTop As Single      'Top margin
    Dim sngLeft As Single     'Left margin
    Dim intLine As Integer    'Line number
    Dim intExtraLines As Integer
    Dim intTime As Integer
    Dim strTime As String
    Dim strMode As String     'Record mode (SP/LP/EP)
    Dim strPrint As String
    Dim strTest As String
    Dim strTape As String
    Dim strLines(8, 2) As String
    Dim strMsg As String
    Dim blnAddRecord As Boolean
    Dim intX As Integer       'Printer X
    Dim intY As Integer       'Printer Y
    Dim intAddRecord As Integer
    Dim intLabelCtr As Integer
    Dim sngPrintWidth As Single    'Width of label printing

    If Printer.ScaleWidth > Printer.ScaleHeight Then
        'Printer is in landscape orientation; abort
        strMsg = "Printer is in landscape mode. Click Printer "
        strMsg = strMsg & "Setup and change to portrait mode."
        MsgBox strMsg, vbCritical, "Wrong Printer Orientation"
        Unload Me
        Exit Sub
    End If

    'Basic printer setup
    Printer.Font.Name = "Ariel"
    Printer.Font.Size = 10
    sngComboTop = rsUser.Fields("ComboTopMargin").Value
    sngComboLeft = rsUser.Fields("ComboLeftMargin").Value
    sngSpineTop = rsUser.Fields("SpineTopMargin").Value
    sngSpineLeft = rsUser.Fields("SpineLeftMargin").Value

    intTime = 0
    If chkTapesTable.Value = 1 And Not blnFromTapes Then
        blnAddRecord = True
        If rsTapes.RecordCount = 0 Then
            'First use of table
            intTape = Val(InputBox("Enter starting tape number", _
                First Use of Tapes Table", 1))
        Else
            'Test for duplicate entry (retry of print)
            rsTapes.MoveFirst
```

```
        rsTapes.MoveLast
        rsTapes.MoveFirst
        Do Until rsRecord.EOF
            rsTapes.Find "EpisodeDate = #" & rsRecord(4) & "#"
            If Not rsTapes.EOF Then
                'It may be a duplicate, check with user
                strMsg = "The Tapes table shows that " & _
                    rsRecord(3) & " of " & Format(Date, "mm/dd/yy")
                strMsg = strMsg & " has been recorded on tape " & _
                    rsTapes(0) & ". "
                strMsg = strMsg & "Do you want to add the records for " & _
                    "this tape to the Tapes table?"
                intAddRecord = MsgBox(strMsg, vbQuestion + vbYesNoCancel, _
                    "Duplicate Record in Tapes Table")
                If intAddRecord = vbNo Then
                    intTape = rsTapes(0)
                    blnAddRecord = False
                ElseIf intAddRecord = vbCancel Then
                    Unload Me
                    Exit Sub
                End If
                Exit Do
            End If
            rsRecord.MoveNext
        Loop
        If blnAddRecord Then
            rsTapes.MoveLast
            intTape = rsTapes(0) + 1
        End If
    End If
End If
If blnFromTapes Then
    intTape = intTapeNum
End If
strTape = LTrim(CStr(intTape))

'Specify the record mode
If blnFromTapes Then
    rsRecord.MoveFirst
    Select Case rsRecord(10)
        Case 1
            strMode = " (SP)"
        Case 2
            strMode = " (LP)"
        Case 3
            strMode = " (EP)"
    End Select
    chkTapesTable.Value = 1
Else
    Select Case rsUser.Fields("RecordMode").Value
```

continues

12

PRINTING WITH
THE REPORT
DESIGNER

LISTING 12.1 CONTINUED

```
        Case 1
            strMode = " (SP)"
        Case 2
            strMode = " (LP)"
        Case 3
            strMode = " (EP)"
    End Select
End If

'Initialize the Lines array (safety)
For intLine = 0 To 7
    strLines(intLine, 0) = ""
    strLines(intLine, 1) = ""
Next intLine

'Maximum number of extra lines
intExtraLines = 10
For intEpisode = 0 To 7
    If chkEpisode(intEpisode).Value = 1 Then
        intExtraLines = intExtraLines - 1
    End If
Next intEpisode
'Adjust the margins for the printer's margin (first label)
sngTop = sngComboTop - (11 - Printer.ScaleHeight / 1440) / 2
sngLeft = sngComboLeft - (8.5 - Printer.ScaleWidth / 1440) / 2
intY = intTPI * (sngTop + 0.1)
intX = intTPI * (sngLeft + 0.1)
If blnCombo Then
    sngPrintWidth = 3.125 - 0.2 '0.1-inch right and left
    'First combo label is at top and left margins
    'Combo face lables are 3.125 by 1.8125
    'First spine label starts at 1.8125 down from top margin
    'Second combo label starts 3.375 from left margin
    If intLabel > 2 Then
        'Second set of labels
        intY = intY + intTPI * 3.156
    End If
    If intLabel > 4 Then
        'Third set of lables
        intY = intY + intTPI * 3.156
    End If
    If intLabel Mod 2 = 0 Then
        'Even numbered face labels print right by 3.375"
        intX = intX + intTPI * 3.375
    End If
    With Printer
        .CurrentY = intY
        .CurrentX = intX
        .FontBold = True
```

```
        If chkTapesTable.Value = 1 Then
            Printer.Print "Tape " & intTape & " created by VBPG on " & _
                Format(Date, "mm/dd/yy") & strMode
        Else
            Printer.Print "Printed by VBPG on " & _
                Format(Date, "mm/dd/yy") & strMode
        End If
        .FontBold = True
    End With
    intY = intY + (intTPI * 0.2)
Else
    'First spine label is at top and left margins
    'Spine lables are 5.75 by 0.75
    sngPrintWidth = 3.125
End If
With Printer
    .CurrentY = intY
    .CurrentX = intX
    rsRecord.MoveFirst
    For intLine = 0 To 7
        'Print the lines
        If intTime < 60 Then
            strTime = "00:" & Format(intTime, "00") & " "
        Else
            strTime = Format(intTime \ 60, "00") & ":" & _
                Format(intTime Mod 60, "00") & " "
        End If
        If chkEpisode(intLine).Value = 1 Then
            strPrint = strTime & Format(rsRecord(4), "mm/dd/yy") & _
                " " & rsRecord(3)
            strTest = strPrint
            If .TextWidth(strPrint) > sngPrintWidth * 1440 Then
                'TextWidth is too wide
                If InStr(strPrint, " (Partial)") Then
                    'Remove (Partial)
                    strPrint = Left(strPrint, InStr(strPrint, " (Partial)") - 1)
                End If
                If .TextWidth(strPrint) > sngPrintWidth * 1440 Then
                    'Work from the back and find spaces until it fits
                    intPos = Len(strPrint)
                    Do While .TextWidth(strPrint) > sngPrintWidth * 1440 _
                            And intPos > 20
                        If Mid(strPrint, intPos, 1) = " " Then
                            strPrint = Left(strPrint, intPos - 1)
                        End If
                        intPos = intPos - 1
                    Loop
                End If
                strLines(intLine, 1) = Mid(strTest, Len(strPrint) + 1)
            End If
```

continues

LISTING 12.1 CONTINUED

```
                        'Add the line to the array
                        strLines(intLine, 0) = strPrint
                        If blnCombo Then
                            'Applies only to combo labels
                            Printer.Print strPrint
                            If Len(strLines(intLine, 1)) > 0 And intExtraLines > 0 Then
                                intY = intY + (intTPI * 0.13)
                                .CurrentY = intY
                                'Indent the added info
                                .CurrentX = intX + Printer.TextWidth("00:00 00/00/00")
                                Printer.Print strLines(intLine, 1)
                                intExtraLines = intExtraLines - 1
                            End If
                            'Reposition the print point
                            .CurrentX = intX
                            intY = intY + (intTPI * 0.15)
                            .CurrentY = intY
                        End If
                        'Increment the starting time
                        intTime = intTime + rsRecord(6)
                        If chkTapesTable.Value = 1 And blnAddRecord Then
                            rsTapes.AddNew
                            rsTapes(0) = intTape        'Tape number
                            rsTapes(1) = strTime        'Time into tape
                            rsTapes(2) = rsRecord(4)    'Date of episode
                            If InStr(rsRecord(2), Chr(13)) Then
                                'Remove CR from satellite entries
                                rsTapes(3) = Left(rsRecord(2), _
                                    InStr(rsRecord(2), Chr(13)) - 1)
                            Else
                                rsTapes(3) = rsRecord(2) 'Station
                            End If
                            rsTapes(4) = rsRecord(3)    'Episode name
                            rsTapes(5) = rsRecord(7)    'Episode description
                            'Record mode (SP/LP/EP)
                            rsTapes(6) = rsUser.Fields("RecordMode").Value
                            rsTapes.Update
                        End If
                    End If
                    If Not rsRecord.EOF Then
                        rsRecord.MoveNext
                    End If
                Next intLine
            End With
            If blnCombo Then
                'Print the spine label, 0.438 to the right of face label edge
                intX = intTPI * (sngLeft + 0.438 + 0.1)
                'First is down 1.813 from top of face label
                intY = intTPI * (sngTop + 1.813 + 0.05)
```

```
    If intLabel > 2 Then
        'Second set of labels
        intY = intY + intTPI * 3.156
    End If
    If intLabel > 4 Then
        'Third set of lables
        intY = intY + intTPI * 3.156
    End If
    If intLabel Mod 2 = 0 Then
        'Even-numbered spine lables are down 0.656
        intY = intY + intTPI * 0.656
    End If
Else
    'Position printer for first spine-only label
    intY = intTPI * (sngTop + 0.04)
    intX = intTPI * (sngLeft + 0.1)
    If intLabel > 1 Then
        For intLabelCtr = 2 To intLabel
            'Label pitch
            intY = intY + intTPI * 0.75
        Next intLabelCtr
    End If
End If
With Printer
    For intLine = 0 To 3
        .CurrentY = intY
        .CurrentX = intX
        'Print tape number
        .Font.Bold = True
        Select Case intLine
            Case 0
                If intTape < 100 Then
                    Printer.Print "Tape"
                Else
                    Printer.Print "    " & Left(strTape, 1)
                End If
            Case 1
                If intTape < 100 Then
                    Printer.Print "    " & Left(strTape, 1)
                Else
                    Printer.Print "    " & Mid(strTape, 2, 1)
                End If
            Case 2
                If intTape < 100 Then
                    Printer.Print "    " & Mid(strTape, 2, 1)
                Else
                    Printer.Print "    " & Mid(strTape, 3, 1)
                End If
            Case 3
                Printer.Print strMode
```

continues

LISTING 12.1   CONTINUED

```
        End Select
        .CurrentY = intY
        .CurrentX = intX + Printer.TextWidth("Tape ")
        .Font.Bold = False
        If Len(strLines(intLine, 0)) > 0 Then
            If Len(strLines(intLine + 4, 0)) > 0 Then
                'Print two short lines
                If blnCombo Then
                    'Combo labels don't print the starting time
                    Printer.Print Mid(strLines(intLine, 0), 6)
                Else
                    Printer.Print strLines(intLine, 0)
                End If
                .CurrentY = intY
                If blnCombo Then
                    .CurrentX = intX + (intTPI * 5.688 / 2)
                    Printer.Print Mid(strLines(intLine + 4, 0), 6)
                Else
                    .CurrentX = intX + intTPI * ((5.75 / 2) + 0.25)
                    Printer.Print strLines(intLine + 4, 0)
                End If
            Else
                'Print a single wide line
                If blnCombo Then
                    Printer.Print Mid(strLines(intLine, 0), 6) & _
                        strLines(intLine, 1)
                Else
                    Printer.Print strLines(intLine, 0) & strLines(intLine, 1)
                End If
            End If
        End If
        intY = intY + intTPI * 0.15
    Next intLine
    .EndDoc  'Print the page
End With
If blnCombo Then
    'Increment the last combo label data
    If intLabel < 6 Then
        rsUser.Fields("NextComboLabel").Value = intLabel + 1
    Else
        Beep
        MsgBox "New sheet of combo cassette labels required.", _
            vbExclamation, "Last Label Printed"
        rsUser.Fields("NextComboLabel").Value = 1
    End If
Else
    'Increment the last spine label data
    If intLabel < 13 Then
        rsUser.Fields("NextSpineLabel").Value = intLabel + 1
```

```
        Else
            Beep
            MsgBox "New sheet of spine cassette labels required.", _
                vbExclamation, "Last Label Printed"
            rsUser.Fields("NextSpineLabel").Value = 1
        End If
    End If
    rsUser.Update
    'Update the combo box
    If blnCombo Then
        cboPrintLabel.ListIndex = rsUser.Fields("NextComboLabel").Value - 1
    Else
        cboPrintLabel.ListIndex = rsUser.Fields("NextSpineLabel").Value - 1
    End If
    If blnFromTapes Then
        'Dump the sample Record records
        cnnUser.Execute ("DELETE * FROM tblRecord")
        rsRecord.Requery
    End If
End Sub
```

If you duplicate a large number of tapes, either commercially or for family and friends, you can easily modify the preceding code to print multiple copies of the same label on a single sheet. Write a loop subprocedure that calls the cmdPrint_Click subprocedure 6 times for combo labels or 13 times for spine labels and increments the value of intLabel by one for each execution of the loop.

Printing the Tape Catalog

The tape catalog obtains its data from tblTapes via the rsTapes Recordset. The loop structure of frmPrintTapes' cmdPrint_Click event handler is typical of that for multipage reports (see Listing 12.2). The outer loop is for pages, and the inner loop is for rsTapes rows that fit a single page. Look-ahead code, which emulates the *Section*.KeepTogether property of Visual Basic and Access reports, prevents individual tape entries from being split between two pages. Most of the printing code appears in the PrintPageHeader subprocedure, called once for each page, and in the PrintTapeLines subprocedure, called once for each tape in the catalog. The optional episode description text is obtained from Starsight's description of the program stored in Tss.mdb.

LISTING 12.2 CODE TO PRINT A TAPE CATALOG WITH STARTING AND ENDING TAPE, INCLUDING AN OPTIONAL DESCRIPTION COLUMN

```
Private Sub cmdPrint_Click()
    'Print the catalog
    Dim datFirst As Date
```

continues

LISTING 12.2   CONTINUED

```
Dim datLast As Date
Dim strReset As String        'Standard tapes reset string
strReset = "SELECT * FROM tblTapes ORDER BY TapeID, EpisodeStart"
With Printer
    If .ScaleWidth > .ScaleHeight Then
        'Printer is in landscape mode
        sngTop = sngTapesTop - (8.5 - .ScaleHeight / 1440) / 2
        sngLeft = sngTapesLeft - (11 - .ScaleWidth / 1440) / 2
        sngTitleWidth = 3.1
        sngDescrWidth = 5
        blnLandscape = True
    Else
        sngTop = sngTapesTop - (11 - .ScaleHeight / 1440) / 2
        sngLeft = sngTapesLeft - (8.5 - .ScaleWidth / 1440) / 2
        sngTitleWidth = 2.6
        sngDescrWidth = 3
        blnLandscape = False
    End If
    .Font.Name = "Ariel"
End With
'Test for valid tape numbers
With rsTapes
    .MoveFirst
    .Find "TapeID = " & Val(txtTapeEnd.Text)
    If .EOF Then
        strMsg = "First tape " & txtTapeEnd.Text & " not found."
        MsgBox strMsg, vbExclamation, "Wrong Ending Tape Number"
        Exit Sub
    End If
    .MoveFirst
    .Find "TapeID = " & Val(txtTapeStart.Text)
    If .EOF Then
        strMsg = "Last tape " & txtTapeStart.Text & " not found."
        MsgBox strMsg, vbExclamation, "Wrong Starting Tape Number"
        Exit Sub
    End If
    intTape = -1
    intPage = 1
    cmdPrint.Enabled = False
    If optStyle(0).Value = True Then
        'Print in tape number sequence
        If .State = adStateOpen Then
            .Close
        End If
        Set .ActiveConnection = cnnUser
        .Source = strReset
        .CursorType = adOpenStatic
        .CursorLocation = adUseServer
        .LockType = adLockOptimistic
```

```
.Open
.MoveFirst
Do Until .EOF
    'Page loop
    If rsTapes(0) > Val(txtTapeEnd.Text) Then
        'Last tape is printed
        Exit Do
    End If
    Call PrintPageHeader(intPage)
    Do Until .EOF
        If rsTapes(0) > Val(txtTapeEnd.Text) Then
            Exit Do
        End If
        If rsTapes(0) <> intTape Then
            'New tape number
            intLines = 0
            datFirst = Format(rsTapes(2), "mm/dd/yy")
            intTape = rsTapes(0)
            varMark = .Bookmark
            'Lookahead for orphan blocks
            Do While rsTapes(0) = intTape
                'Check the number of lines required for a tape
                If chkDescription.Value And _
                        Printer.TextWidth(rsTapes(5)) > sngDescrWidth _
                        * intTPI Then
                    'Description requires more than one line
                    intLines = intLines + Printer.TextWidth(rsTapes(5)) _
                        \ (sngDescrWidth * intTPI)
                    If Printer.TextWidth(rsTapes(5)) Mod (sngDescrWidth _
                            * intTPI) > 0 Then
                        'Characters are left over
                        intLines = intLines + 1
                    End If
                Else
                    'Line for title
                    intLines = intLines + 1
                    If Printer.TextWidth(rsTapes(4)) > sngTitleWidth * _
                            intTPI Then
                        'Title requires two lines
                        intLines = intLines + 1
                    End If
                End If
                .MoveNext
                If .EOF Then
                    Exit Do
                End If
            Loop
            If Printer.CurrentY > Printer.ScaleHeight - _
                    ((intLines + 1) * 0.15 * intTPI) Then
                'Last tape won't fit on the page
```

continues

LISTING 12.2   CONTINUED

```
                intTape = intTape - 1
                '.Bookmark = strMark
                .Bookmark = varMark
                Exit Do
            End If
            If .EOF Then
                .MoveLast
            End If
            datLast = Format(rsTapes(2), "mm/dd/yy")
            .Bookmark = varMark
            'Print tape header line
            Printer.Font.Bold = True
            strPrint = "Tape " & intTape & " " & _
                Format(datFirst, "mm/dd/yy")
            If datFirst <> datLast Then
                strPrint = strPrint + " to " & Format(datLast, "mm/dd/yy")
            End If
            'Add the record mode (SP/LP/EP)
            If chkDescription Then
                Select Case rsTapes(6)
                    Case 1
                        strPrint = strPrint & " (SP)"
                    Case 2
                        strPrint = strPrint & " (LP)"
                    Case 3
                        strPrint = strPrint & " (EP)"
                End Select
            Else
                Select Case rsTapes(6)
                    Case 1
                        strPrint = strPrint & " (Standard Play)"
                    Case 2
                        strPrint = strPrint & " (Long Play)"
                    Case 3
                        strPrint = strPrint & " (Extended Play)"
                End Select
            End If
            intX = (sngLeft + 1.8) * intTPI
            Printer.CurrentX = intX
            intY = intY + (0.2 * intTPI)
            Printer.CurrentY = intY
            Printer.Print strPrint
        End If
        Call PrintTapeLines
        .MoveNext
        'Prevent overrun in case of lookahead failure
        If Printer.CurrentY > Printer.ScaleHeight Then
            Exit Do
        End If
```

```
            Loop
            Printer.EndDoc
            intPage = intPage + 1
        Loop
    End If
    If optStyle(0).Value = True Then
        'Print by source

    End If
    End With
    cmdPrint.Enabled = True
End Sub

Private Sub PrintPageHeader(intPage As Integer)
    'Print page title and column headers
    intY = sngTop * intTPI
    intX = sngLeft * intTPI
    With Printer
        'Print method is missing from type library
        'because Print is a VBA reserved word
        Printer.Print
        .Font.Size = 12
        .CurrentY = intY
        .CurrentX = intX
        .Font.Bold = True
        'Page title
        Printer.Print "VHS Tape Catalog Printed by VBPG on " & _
            Format(Date, "Long Date") & " - Page " & intPage
        .Font.Size = 11
        intY = intY + (0.25 * intTPI)
        .CurrentY = intY
        .CurrentX = intX
        .Font.Underline = True
        If optStyle(0).Value = False Then
            'Tape header required
            Printer.Print "Tape"
            intX = intX + (0.5 * intTPI)
            .CurrentY = intY
            .CurrentX = intX
        End If
        Printer.Print "Start"
        intX = intX + (0.5 * intTPI)
        .CurrentY = intY
        .CurrentX = intX
        Printer.Print "Date"
        intX = intX + (0.65 * intTPI)
        .CurrentY = intY
        .CurrentX = intX
        If optStyle(1).Value = False Then
            'Source header required
```

continues

LISTING 12.2 CONTINUED

```
        Printer.Print "Source"
        intX = intX + (0.65 * intTPI)
        .CurrentY = intY
        .CurrentX = intX
    End If
    If blnLandscape Then
        Printer.Print "Program Title" & Space(42)
    Else
        Printer.Print "Program Title" & Space(32)
    End If
    intX = intX + (sngTitleWidth * intTPI)
    .CurrentY = intY
    .CurrentX = intX
    If chkDescription.Value = 1 Then
        'Description required
        If blnLandscape Then
            Printer.Print "Description" & Space(80)
        Else
            Printer.Print "Description" & Space(50)
        End If
    End If
    intY = intY + (0.05 * intTPI)
    .CurrentY = intY
    .Font.Underline = False
    .Font.Bold = False
    .Font.Size = 10
    End With
End Sub


Private Sub PrintTapeLines()
    'Print the tape line items
    Dim strTitle As String
    Dim strExtraLine As String
    Dim intPos As Integer
    Dim intLines As Integer 'Lines of description
    Dim intLine As Integer  'Current description line
    Dim strDescr As String  'Description string
    Dim astrDescr(6) As String 'Array of description

    'For safety
    For intPos = 0 To 5
        astrDescr(intPos) = ""
    Next intPos

    With Printer
        .Font.Bold = False
        intY = intY + (0.15 * intTPI)
        .CurrentY = intY
        intX = sngLeft * intTPI
```

```
.CurrentX = intX
'Print the Recordset columns
Printer.Print rsTapes(1)
intX = intX + (0.5 * intTPI)
.CurrentY = intY
.CurrentX = intX
Printer.Print Format(rsTapes(2), "mm/dd/yy")
intX = intX + (0.65 * intTPI)
.CurrentY = intY
.CurrentX = intX
Printer.Print rsTapes(3)
intX = intX + (0.65 * intTPI)
.CurrentY = intY
.CurrentX = intX
strTitle = rsTapes(4)
If chkDescription Then
    'Description column requires shortened title
    strTest = strTitle
    If .TextWidth(strTitle) > sngTitleWidth * intTPI Then
        'Maximum title length is 2.6 or 3.1 inches
        'Work from the back and find spaces until it fits
        intPos = Len(strTitle)
        Do While .TextWidth(strTitle) > sngTitleWidth * intTPI _
            And intPos > 20
            If Mid(strTitle, intPos, 1) = " " Then
                strTitle = Left(strTitle, intPos - 1)
            End If
            intPos = intPos - 1
        Loop
        strExtraLine = LTrim(Mid(strTest, Len(strTitle) + 1))
    Else
        strExtraLine = ""
    End If
    If .TextWidth(rsTapes(5)) > sngDescrWidth * intTPI Then
        'Create the description array
        intLines = .TextWidth(rsTapes(5)) \ (sngDescrWidth * intTPI)
        If .TextWidth(rsTapes(5)) Mod (sngDescrWidth * intTPI) > 0 Then
            'Characters are left over
            intLines = intLines + 1
        End If
        strDescr = rsTapes(5)
        strTest = strDescr
        For intLine = 0 To (intLines - 1)
            If InStr(strDescr, " ") Then
                intPos = Len(strDescr)
                Do While .TextWidth(strDescr) > sngDescrWidth * intTPI _
                    And intPos > 0
                    If Mid(strDescr, intPos, 1) = " " Then
                        strDescr = Left(strDescr, intPos - 1)
                    End If
```

continues

LISTING 12.2   CONTINUED

```
                      intPos = intPos - 1
                  Loop
              End If
              astrDescr(intLine) = strDescr
              'Get the next block of text
              strDescr = LTrim(Mid(strTest, Len(strDescr) + 1))
              strTest = strDescr
          Next intLine
        Else
          astrDescr(0) = rsTapes(5)
          intLines = 1
        End If
    End If
    Printer.Print strTitle
    If Len(astrDescr(0)) > 0 Then
        .CurrentY = intY
        .CurrentX = intX + (sngTitleWidth * intTPI)
        Printer.Print astrDescr(0)
    End If
    If Len(strExtraLine) > 0 Then
        intY = intY + (0.15 * intTPI)
        .CurrentY = intY
        .CurrentX = intX
        Printer.Print strExtraLine
        If Len(astrDescr(1)) > 0 Then
            .CurrentY = intY
            .CurrentX = intX + (sngTitleWidth * intTPI)
            Printer.Print astrDescr(1)
        End If
    Else
        If Len(astrDescr(1)) > 0 Then
            intY = intY + (0.15 * intTPI)
            .CurrentY = intY
            .CurrentX = intX + (sngTitleWidth * intTPI)
            Printer.Print astrDescr(1)
        End If
    End If
    'Print any remaining description lines
    intX = intX + (sngTitleWidth * intTPI)
    For intLine = 3 To intLines
        If Len(astrDescr(intLine - 1)) > 0 Then
            intY = intY + (0.15 * intTPI)
            .CurrentY = intY
            .CurrentX = intX
            Printer.Print astrDescr(intLine - 1)
        End If
    Next intLine
  End With
End Sub
```

The `PrintTapeLines` subprocedure uses extensively the `Printer.TextWidth` property value to determine whether an episode name or description requires more than one printed line. The `TextWidth` value ordinarily is accurate to within a few twips.

Writing and testing VBA printing code is tedious, but after you become accustomed to working with twips and `CurrentX`, `CurrentY`, `TextWidth`, and `TextHeight` properties, you can create custom-designed reports quite quickly. As a rule, writing single-purpose printing code is more efficient than attempting to devise a general-purpose printing procedure that accommodates a wide range of report formats.

ADVANCED PROGRAMMING FOR DATA ACCESS AND AUTOMATION

PART IV

IN THIS PART

DRILLING DOWN INTO DATA FROM GRAPHS AND CHARTS

IN THIS CHAPTER

Drilldown applications that employ graphs require a variety of methods for choosing the detail data that your application displays in the form of a grid or spreadsheet. This chapter extends your use of ActiveX data objects to include unbound MSFlexGrid controls that are populated with data from ADODB.Recordset objects generated by SQL statements you create with Visual Basic code. The content of the SQL statement that serves as the Source property of an ADODB.Recordset object is determined by the graph that is currently displayed plus the graphs that were chosen at higher levels in the drilldown hierarchy.

The first sample application in this chapter shows you how to use the DoubleClick event with the MouseDown event to establish an SQL WHERE clause criteria for the Snapshot-type Recordset object. You compare the X and Y mouse coordinates returned by the MouseDown event with the coordinates of the labels of an area chart to determine the month for which detail data is desired. You can use this MouseDown_DoubleClick technique for drilldown navigation purposes with any type of graph or chart.

TAKING ADVANTAGE OF Chart EVENTS

Visual Basic 6.0's MSChrt20.ocx offers various events that you can trap to activate drilldown operations. Each visible chart object —Axis, Chart, Footnote, Legend, Plot, Point, PointLabel, and Series—has the following three categories of events:

- *Selected* fires when the user single-clicks the object. Single-clicking an object adds selection point(s) to the object. Selection points are small rectangles that display the complementary color of their background. Clicking a series line or area selects the entire series; if a legend is present, the legend item for the series also is selected (see Figure 13.1). You can use a SeriesSelected event handler to highlight the corresponding row of data in a grid.

  Clicking one of the series selection points deselects the series and selects a single data point. Clicking the location of other (now invisible) series selection points selects another single data point. You must click the background of the chart, another chart object, or another series to return to series selection mode.

FIGURE **13.1**

An area chart with a series (Seafood) and its corresponding legend item selected.

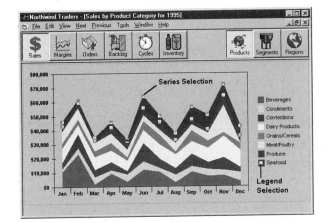

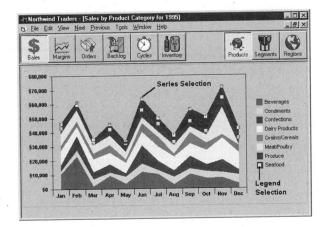

- *Activated* fires when the user double-clicks a visible chart object. Double-clicking a single data point, however, doesn't cause a change from series to single-point activation mode. In most cases, you use the chart object's Activated event to launch a drilldown operation.

- *Updated* fires when the value of an object, such as a data point, changes. The DataGrid object triggers only DataUpdated events.

Arguments of the event handler depend on the selected or activated object. Following is a list of arguments and their values:

- AxisId (**Integer**) indicates the selected or activated chart Axis object. Values are VtChAxisIdX, VtChAxisIdY, VtChAxisIdY2, and, if a three-dimensional chart, VtChAxisIdZ. AxisIndex always returns 1 because AxisIndex isn't implemented.

- LabelSetIndex (**Integer**) identifies the level of the selected or activated AxisLabel object, beginning with 1 for the first level of labels. Unfortunately, Microsoft still hasn't implemented the LabelIndex argument to return the index of the individual label selected.

- Series (**Integer**) identifies the line or area selected or activated, beginning with 1 for the first series.

- DataPoint (**Integer**) identifies a single data point within a series.

- MouseFlags (**Integer**) applies to all objects. MouseFlags returns a value that indicates whether the Shift key (VtChMouseFlagShiftKeyDown) and/or the Control key (VtChMouseFlagControlKeyDown) is depressed when selecting or activating the object.

- Cancel (**Integer**) applies to all objects, but isn't implemented by the current version of MSChrt20.ocx.

NOTE

Event-handling arguments that Microsoft hasn't implemented in MSChrt20.ocx, the second version of MSChart.ocx, probably never will be implemented. Apparently, determining the currently selected or activated label was too difficult for the developer(s) of the Chart control. The workaround for lack of a correct LabelIndex value is especially clumsy.

The following two sections provide examples of the use of the SeriesSelected and PointSelected events.

NOTE

The sample project for this chapter, Drilldn.vbp (located in the \Ddg_vb6\Chaptr13 folder of the accompanying CD-ROM), is an extension of the Graphs.vbp project of Chapter 11, "Graphing Summary Data Created from Crosstab Queries."

Selecting an MSHFlexGrid Row with the SeriesSelected Event

Listing 13.1 shows the code required to select a row in the multiline MSHFlexGrid control based on the user's series selection. The subprocedures of Listing 13.1 are included in the frmMDIGraph form. Clicking anywhere within the chtMonthly object (Axis, Plot, or Legend) or changing a DataGrid value clears the MSHFlexGrid selection. Figure 13.2 illustrates selection of the Seafood series.

LISTING 13.1 CODE TO SELECT AND CLEAR A ROW OF AN MSHFLEXGRID CONTROL BASED ON A SERIES SELECTION

```
Private Sub chtMonthly_SeriesSelected(intSeries As Integer, _
                              MouseFlags As Integer, _
                              Cancel As Integer)
    If blnIsCrosstab Then
       'Select the corresponding grid row (crosstabs only)
       With hfgMonthly
          .Col = 0
          .Row = intSeries
          .ColSel = .Cols - 1
       End With
    End If
End Sub

Private Sub chtMonthly_ChartSelected(intMouseFlags As Integer, intCancel As Integer)
    Call ClearGridSelection
End Sub

Private Sub chtMonthly_AxisSelected(axisID As Integer, AxisIndex As Integer, _
                               MouseFlags As Integer, Cancel As Integer)
    Call ClearGridSelection
End Sub

Private Sub chtMonthly_LegendSelected(MouseFlags As Integer, Cancel As Integer)
    Call ClearGridSelection
End Sub

Private Sub chtMonthly_PlotSelected(MouseFlags As Integer, Cancel As Integer)
    Call ClearGridSelection
End Sub

Private Sub ClearGridSelection()
    'Clear the current grid selection
    With hfgMonthly
       .Col = 0
       .Row = 0
    End With
End Sub
```

13

DRILLING DOWN INTO DATA

FIGURE 13.2

Selecting a row in a MSHFlexGrid corresponding to the selected series of a crosstab chart.

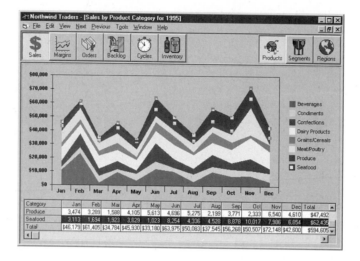

Selecting an Individual Cell with the `PointSelected` Event

Adding the following event-handling code to `frmMDIGraph` selects a single cell corresponding to the month (single-line graphs) or month and series (crosstab charts), as illustrated in Figure 13.3.

```
Private Sub chtMonthly_PointSelected(intSeries As Integer, _
                                     intDataPoint As Integer, _
                                     MouseFlags As Integer, _
                                     Cancel As Integer)
    'Select the corresponding cell (crosstab chart or single-line graph)
    With hfgMonthly
        .Row = 0
        .Col = 0
        .Row = intSeries
        .Col = intDataPoint - 1
        .ColSel = intDataPoint
    End With
End Sub
```

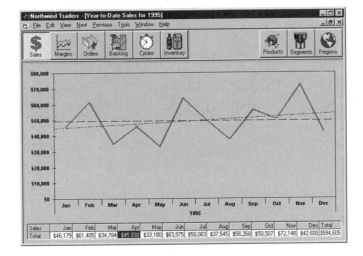

FIGURE 13.3

*Selecting a cell in
a MSHFlexGrid
corresponding to
the selected data
point of a single-
line graph.*

DISPLAYING A SINGLE SERIES FROM A STACKED AREA CHART

Stacked area charts are useful for displaying aggregated information, but stacking makes it difficult for users to determine trends or values for data points of individual series. You can use a Shift+click on the area of a series to display a single-line graph of the data points. You reset the line graph to the area chart by clicking any area of the graph except the line. Because detail level increases, this procedure qualifies as a drilldown operation.

You would need many lines of code to re-create the line graph from scratch; temporarily altering the ChartData array is a far simpler approach. The ChartData array for the typical area chart Recordset of Drilldn.vbp has 9 by 13 members, representing rows and columns, respectively. The 0 member of each dimension holds the x-axis labels and legend labels, respectively. To display a single series member, you must replace ChartData with a 2- by 13-member array containing the first (0) row (for x-axis labels) and the row corresponding to the data points of the selected series.

The Chart control automatically sets the color of each series member's line or area. The first eight members of the standard color sequence are red, green, blue, yellow, magenta, cyan, dark gray, and brown. Without code to set the proper line color, every single-line graph would display a red line. Fortunately, the Chart control offers a method of overriding the automatic pen (line) or brush (area) color with the *Chart*.Plot.SeriesCollection(*n*).DataPoints(-1).Brush.FillColor.Set method. The Set method takes three **Integer** arguments that represent the RGB values of the desired color. Thus you must specify an array of RGB values that match those of the automatic color sequence. Alternatively, you can specify your own color set and pass the values to Set during generation of the original area chart.

Listing 13.2 shows the additions to the code of Listing 13.1 required to implement the Shift+click display of a single-line graph from a selection in the area chart. The intColors array values appear in the chtMonthly_SeriesSelected event handler for completeness. In a production application, set these values in a Form_Load or **Sub** Main subprocedure.

LISTING 13.2 CODE TO DISPLAY A SSINGLE-LINE GRAPH FROM A SHIFT+CLICK SELECTION OF AN AREA CHART SERIES

```
Option Explicit

Private blnOneSeries As Boolean
Private intSeriesNum As Integer
Private intColors(8, 2) As Integer

Private Sub chtMonthly_SeriesSelected(intSeries As Integer, _
                               intMouseFlags As Integer, _
                               Cancel As Integer)
    'Select corresponding row in the MSHFlexGrid
    'With Shift+click on a crosstab chart, display a single line chart

    Dim varChart As Variant
    Dim varSeries(1, 12) As Variant
    Dim intCol As Integer
    Dim intRed As Integer
    Dim intGreen As Integer
    Dim intBlue As Integer

    'RGB arrays for the first eight series
    'Red
    intColors(1, 0) = 255
    intColors(1, 1) = 0
    intColors(1, 2) = 0
    'Green
    intColors(2, 0) = 0
    intColors(2, 1) = 255
    intColors(2, 2) = 0
    'Blue
    intColors(3, 0) = 0
    intColors(3, 1) = 0
    intColors(3, 2) = 255
    'Yellow
    intColors(4, 0) = 255
    intColors(4, 1) = 255
    intColors(4, 2) = 0
    'Magenta
    intColors(5, 0) = 255
    intColors(5, 1) = 0
    intColors(5, 2) = 255
    'Cyan
    intColors(6, 0) = 0
    intColors(6, 1) = 255
```

```
    intColors(6, 2) = 255
    'DarkGray
    intColors(7, 0) = 63
    intColors(7, 1) = 63
intColors(7, 2) = 63
    'Brown
    intColors(8, 0) = 128
    intColors(8, 1) = 27
    intColors(8, 2) = 21


If blnIsCrosstab Then
    If intMouseFlags = 5 Then
        'Shift key held down to select line chart
        intSeriesNum = intSeries
        With chtMonthly
            'Create an 2x13 array for the single series
            varChart = chtMonthly.ChartData
            For intCol = 0 To 12
                varSeries(0, intCol) = varChart(0, intCol)
                varSeries(1, intCol) = varChart(intSeries, intCol)
            Next intCol
            'Change the chart type
            .chartType = VtChChartType2dLine
            .ChartData = varSeries
            .Stacking = False
            'Set the appropriate color
            If intSeries < 9 Then
                .Plot.SeriesCollection(1).DataPoints(-1).Brush. _
                    FillColor.Set intColors(intSeries, 0), _
                    intColors(intSeries, 1), intColors(intSeries, 2)
            End If
            DoEvents
            blnOneSeries = True
        End With
    End If
    'Select the corresponding grid row (crosstabs only)
    With hfgMonthly
        .Col = 0
        If blnOneSeries Then
            .Row = intSeriesNum
        Else
            .Row = intSeries
        End If
        .ColSel = .Cols - 1
    End With
End If
End Sub

Private Sub ClearGridSelection()
    'Clear the current grid selection
    'Reset the line graph to the area chart
```

continues

13

LISTING 13.2 CONTINUED

```
    Dim intSeries As Integer

    With hfgMonthly
        .Col = 0
        .Row = 0
    End With
    If blnOneSeries Then
        'Return the graph to the original condition and color
        With chtMonthly
            'varData is global, set by DrawMonthlyGraph
            .ChartData = varData
            'Reset to the area chart
            If InStr(frmMDIToolbar.Caption, "Margin") Then
                .Stacking = False
                .chartType = VtChChartType2dLine
            Else
                .Stacking = True
                .chartType = VtChChartType2dArea
            End If
            'Reset the series color
            For intSeries = 1 To 8
                .Plot.SeriesCollection(intSeries).DataPoints(-1) _
                    .Brush.FillColor.Set intColors(intSeries, 0), _
                    intColors(intSeries, 1), intColors(intSeries, 2)
            Next intSeries
        End With
        blnOneSeries = False
        'Fix up the tool tip
        Call SetToolTipText
    End If
End Sub

Private Sub chtMonthly_DataUpdated(Row As Integer, _
                                  Column As Integer, _
                                  labelRow As Integer, _
                                  labelColumn As Integer, _
                                  labelSetIndex As Integer, _
                                  updateFlags As Integer)
    'Fix up the tool tip
    Call SetToolTipText
End Sub

Private Sub SetToolTipText()
    'Set the appropriate tool tip text for the control
    With chtMonthly
        If blnIsCrosstab Then
            If blnOneSeries Then
                .ToolTipText = "Click an empty area of the chart, " & _
                    "an axis, or legend to restore all series."
```

```
      Else
          .ToolTipText = "Press shift and click a series to " & _
              "display a single-series line chart."
      End If
   Else
       .ToolTipText = "Click the line, then a data point to " & _
          "highlight data in the grid."
   End If
  End With
End Sub
```

Figure 13.4 illustrates execution of the `chtMonthly_SeriesSelected` event handler Shift+click selection of the Confections category from the Sales by Product Category for 1995 area chart.

FIGURE 13.4

A single-line graph of a year's sales of products in the Confections category.

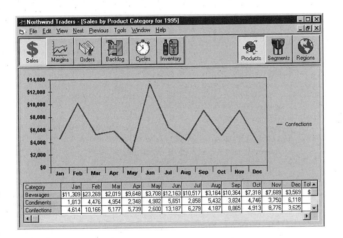

ADDING A DRILLDOWN PIE CHART TO THE Drilldn.vbp PROJECT

Pie charts are useful for displaying the relative contribution of members to aggregates, such as percentage of sales by product category. SQL statements to generate `Recordsets` for pie charts are relatively simple, and creating a simple data-bound pie chart with a legend is a relatively straightforward process. Adding to Drilldn.vbp a new MDI child form containing only a Chart control takes advantage of the original MDI project design discussed in Chapter 11.

Attempts to add or modify elements of the pie chart, however, demonstrate that MSChrt20.ocx is either a work in process or, more likely, an orphaned control suffering from a severe set of permanent disabilities and abandoned by its developers.

Choosing a Drilldown Launch Strategy

Pie charts are best suited to displaying data from only a few records—8 to 10 at most. A logical use for a pie chart is to display contribution by product category to monthly sales, orders, backlog, and inventory totals. Double-clicking (object activation) is the most common method of launching a drilldown form, so the following code in the `PointActivated` event handler of `frmMDIGraph` displays the `frmMDIPieChart` form and calls its `LoadPieChart` subprocedure to generate the data for the pie chart:

```
Private Sub chtMonthly_PointActivated(intSeries As Integer, _
                                  intDataPoint As Integer, _
                                  MouseFlags As Integer, _
                                  Cancel As Integer)
    If Not IsNull(rstGraphDefs.Fields("Drilldown1Table")) Then
        intPieSeries = intSeries
        intPiePoint = intDataPoint
        Call frmMDIPieChart.LoadPieChart
        Me.Hide
        With frmMDIPieChart
            .Show
            .WindowState = vbMaximized
        End With
    End If
End Sub
```

Double-clicking an inactive area of the pie chart is the most intuitive method of returning to the original graph. Thus the ...`Activated` event handlers for the `Chart`, `Title`, `Plot`, `Axis`, and `Legend` objects contain the following code:

```
Private Sub chtPieChart_ChartActivated(MouseFlags As Integer, _
                                   Cancel As Integer)
    'Return to graphs/charts form
    Me.Hide
    frmMDIGraph.Show
End Sub
```

Adding a new MDI child form to the project requires minor additions to the `ResizeFormAndGraph` subprocedure of the `modGraphs` module to handle user resizing of the MDI parent form. Resizing the `chtPieChart` control is simplified by the lack of a grid on the pie chart form.

Setting Pie Chart Properties in Design Mode

Unlike most third-party chart controls, MSChrt20.ocx provides only a 2D pie chart and doesn't offer niceties, such as exploding wedges. Many of the properties advertised by Object Browser as read-write, such as `Chart.Font.Bold` and `Chart.Font.Size`, return a `Property is write-only` error message when you attempt to set their values with code. Following are the design mode property values for `chtPieChart`:

- On the Chart page, Chart Type is 2D Pie, and the Show Legend Series in Rows check boxes are marked.
- On the Text page, Title Alignment is centered.
- On the Fonts page, Title font is set to 12-point Arial bold, and Legend font is set to 9-point Arial bold.

It's desirable to change the Font.Size property for both the Title and Legend objects when resizing the form, but the write-only problem precludes doing so.

Generating the Pie Chart Data

The tblDefinitions table of Graphs.mdb requires additional fields—Drilldown1Table, Drilldown1Field1, Drilldown1Field2, and Drilldown1Title—to provide the field definitions for the SQL statement that generates the pie chart's Recordset and to supply a title for the chart. Following is a typical SQL statement to generate a pie chart displaying the distribution of orders by product category:

```
SELECT CategoryName, Orders
    FROM tblOrdersCategoryMonth
    WHERE Year = '1995' AND Val(Month) = 5
```

Listing 13.3 shows the code for the LoadPieChart subprocedure, which includes a workaround for failure of pie charts to accept varData = Chart.ChartData...Chart.ChartData = varData constructs used elsewhere in the project with line graphs and area charts. The workaround saves the read-only Recordset to a file and then reopens a read-write Recordset from the file. The loop adds dollar amounts and percentages to the CategoryName field of the Recordset that displays in the chart's legend.

LISTING 13.3 CODE TO BIND A PIE CHART TO A SAVED AND MODIFIED Recordset

```
Public Sub LoadPieChart()
    Dim strSQL As String
    Dim rstPieChart As New ADODB.Recordset
    Dim intCtr As Integer
    Dim curTotal As Currency

    Me.Caption = rstGraphDefs.Fields("Drilldown1Title") & _
        " " & strMonths(intPiePoint, 2) & ", " & strYear
    With rstGraphDefs
        strSQL = "SELECT " & .Fields("Drilldown1Field1") & _
            ", " & .Fields("Drilldown1Field2") & _
            " FROM " & .Fields("Drilldown1Table") & _
            " WHERE Year = '" & strYear & "' AND Val(Month) = " & intPiePoint
    End With
    With rstPieChart
```

continues

13

LISTING 13.3 CONTINUED

```
         If .State = adStateOpen Then
             .Close
         End If
         Set .ActiveConnection = cnnGraphs
         .CursorLocation = adUseClient
         .CursorType = adOpenDynamic
         .LockType = adLockReadOnly
         .Source = strSQL
         .Open
         If .RecordCount Then
             .MoveFirst
             'Get the total for percent calculations
             curTotal = 0
             Do Until .EOF
                 curTotal = curTotal + .Fields(1).Value
                 .MoveNext
             Loop
             'Using the ChartData array doesn't work for pie charts
             'Thus a local copy of the Recordset must be modified
             On Error Resume Next
             Kill App.Path & "\PieChart.rst"
             On Error GoTo 0
             .Save App.Path & "\PieChart.rst"
             .Close
             .Open App.Path & "\PieChart.rst", , adOpenDynamic, _
                 adLockOptimistic, adCmdFile
             'Move the record pointer to get the first value
             .MoveFirst
             Do Until .EOF
                 .Fields(0).Value = .Fields(0).Value & ", " & _
                     Format(.Fields(1), "$#,##0") & ", " & _
                     Format(.Fields(1) / curTotal, "#0.0%")
                 .Update
                 .MoveNext
             Loop
             .MoveFirst
         Else
             'Error
             Exit Sub
         End If
     End With
     With chtPieChart
         Set .DataSource = rstPieChart
         .Title.Text = Me.Caption & " - " & _
             Format(curTotal, "$#,##0") & " Total"
         'Following results in "Property is write-only" error, despite the
         'attempted write operation; values must be set in design mode
         '.Title.Font.Size = 12
         '.Title.Font.Bold = True
     End With
End Sub
```

Figure 13.5 shows a typical pie chart created by the preceding code.

FIGURE 13.5

A pie chart displaying the distribution of orders by product category for the selected month.

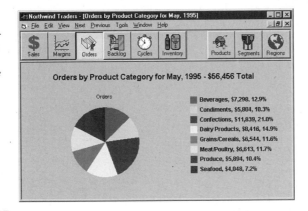

NOTE

A more logical approach to displaying dollar amounts and percentages is to pass the values to the DataPointLabels of the pie chart. Like the LabelIndex property, however, the Chart control still doesn't provide access to individual DataPointLabels, despite the elapse of more than 18 months between the release of MSChart.ocx with Visual Basic 5.0 and MSChrt20.ocx with version 6.0. The help topic for the DataPoints collection for version 5.0's MSChart.ocx states the following:

"Identifies a specific data point within the current series. For this version of the chart, −1 is the only valid value for this argument. This allows you [sic] two make changes to the default settings for all data points in the series. Settings cannot be changed for individual data points within the series."

The help file for MSchrt20.ocx contains the identical statement, the first sentence of which is clearly in error, and the third sentence of which contains the same error in grammar. Contrary to the help topic for and Object Browser description of the Text property of the DataPointLabel object ("Returns/sets the point label text"), the DataPointLabel.Text property is read-only. Thus you can't add labels to show percentages or dollar values to the pie chart.

USING MouseDown AND Double-Click EVENTS TO ACTIVATE DRILLDOWN

Graphic decision-support applications should give the user easy access to detail data underlying the information that appears on the current form. For example, you might want to display the pie chart for sales by product (frmMDIPieChart) for the month when the user double-clicks one of the labels of the total sales graph, instead of the three steps required to activate a data point. As mentioned in the earlier "Taking Advantage of Chart Events" section, Microsoft didn't implement the LabelIndex argument of the AxisLabelSelected event handler. You could use command buttons with month abbreviations to choose a month. The 12 command buttons, however, would occupy a substantial amount of display real estate and would detract from the appearance of the form. Detecting the mouse position when DblClick events occur and taking action based on the mouse coordinates is the most appropriate method to activate drilldown code in this case.

Figure 13.6 shows the Year-to-Date Sales graph with a small test form that you can use to develop the code that detects the mouse position when the user double-clicks an x-axis label. Adding a test form that displays the mouse coordinates and the dimensions of the chart saves a great deal of time when you need to determine the values of constants that convert mouse coordinates into a specific drilldown action. You need to use the relative location of the mouse, expressed as the ratio of mouse position to the dimensions of the control, because the user can resize the form and the control at will.

Listing 13.4 shows the code in frmMDIChart required to detect a double-click on the label of a chart and return the number of the month when the user double-clicks a month name abbreviation. The chtMonthly_MouseDown subprocedure detects the mouse position prior to triggering the chtMonthly_AxisLabelActivated event. The small Test Month Mouse Position (frmTestMonth) form, shown in Figure 13.6, appears only if the blnTest flag is set to **True**.

FIGURE 13.6

A test form to determine the mouse position when double-clicking a month label.

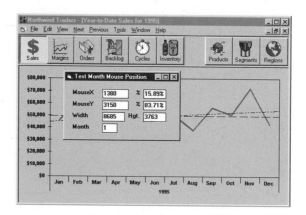

The chtMonthly_AxisLabelActivated event fires only when you double-click the text of the label, not the surrounding area. Thus it isn't necessary to check the y-axis position of the mouse. The offset of the y-axis from the left edge of the chart is 1,000 twips for all charts of dollar amounts and between 850 and 900 twips for charts having other y-axis units, such as percentage and days. Subtracting 1,000 twips from the total width of the plot, determined by the difference between the values of chtMonthly.Plot.LocationRect.Max.X and chtMonthly.Plot.LocationRect.Max.X, supplies the net width. Applying the offset to the mouse X position and integer-dividing by (net width/12) returns the month number, which is equal to the DataPoint number.

LISTING 13.4 CODE TO DETECT THE DOUBLE-CLICKING OF A MONTH LABEL ON A LINE GRAPH AND DISPLAY THE PIE CHART

```
Private Sub chtMonthly_AxisLabelActivated(intAxisID As Integer, _
                                    AxisIndex As Integer, _
                                    labelSetIndex As Integer, _
                                    LabelIndex As Integer, _
                                    MouseFlags As Integer, _
                                    Cancel As Integer)
    'Purpose: Determine the month from the mouse position

    Dim intMonth As Integer
    Dim intMinX As Integer
    Dim intMaxX As Integer
    Dim intPlotX As Integer
    Dim intOffsetX As Integer

    If intAxisID <> 0 Then
        'Not the x-axis
        Exit Sub
    End If

    'Set blnTest True to display the mouse position test form
    blnTest = False

    'The position of the y-axis is at a constant 1,000 twips
    'for $ graphs, about 850-900 for others
    intOffsetX = 1000
    intMonth = 0
    With chtMonthly
        'Calculate the month number
        intMinX = .Plot.LocationRect.Min.X
        intMaxX = .Plot.LocationRect.Max.X
        intPlotX = intMaxX - intMinX - intOffsetX
        'Integer divide the mouse X position by the width of x-axis divisions
        intMonth = 1 + (sngMouseX - intMinX - intOffsetX) \ (intPlotX / 12)
        If blnTest Then
            'Global constant blnTest determines appearance of form
            With frmTestMonth
                'Show the mouse position test form
                .Show
                .txtMouseX = sngMouseX
                .txtMouseY = sngMouseY
                .txtMouseXPct = Format(sngMouseX / _
```

continues

13

DRILLING DOWN
INTO DATA

LISTING 13.4   CONTINUED

```
                              frmMDIGraph.chtMonthly.Width, "##0.00%")
            .txtMouseYPct = Format(sngMouseY / _
                              frmMDIGraph.chtMonthly.Height, "##0.00%")
            .txtWidth = frmMDIGraph.chtMonthly.Width
            .txtHeight = frmMDIGraph.chtMonthly.Height
            .txtMonthNum = intMonth
            blnTestForm = True
        End With
      End If
   End With
   blnInhibitResize = False
   If intMonth > 0 Then
      Call chtMonthly_PointActivated(1, intMonth, 0, 0)
   End If
End Sub

Private Sub chtMonthly_MouseDown(Button As Integer, _
                                 Shift As Integer, _
                                 sngX As Single, _
                                 sngY As Single)
   sngMouseX = sngX
   sngMouseY = sngY
End Sub

Private Sub chtMonthly_MouseMove(Button As Integer, _
                                 Shift As Integer, _
                                 sngX As Single, _
                                 sngY As Single)

   If blnTestForm Then
      sngMouseX = sngX
      sngMouseY = sngY
      With frmTestMonth
        .txtMouseX = sngMouseX
        .txtMouseY = sngMouseY
        .txtMouseXPct = Format(sngMouseX / _
                    frmMDIGraph.chtMonthly.Width, "##0.00%")
        .txtMouseYPct = Format(sngMouseY / _
                    frmMDIGraph.chtMonthly.Height, "##0.00%")
      End With
   End If
End Sub
```

CHOOSING THE DRILLDOWN PATH WITH A PIE CHART

A common programming practice is to provide users with a choice of the detail data to display at levels that are lower in the hierarchy than the user can access with toolbar buttons. You can add another set of buttons if you have sufficient display area available. Alternatively, you can use option buttons within a frame that also contains OK and Cancel command buttons to process or cancel the user's choice. The sections that follow describe how to add a drilldown level to the pie chart.

> **NOTE**
>
> The GUI guidelines for Windows applications don't allow an option button choice to execute an action. Only object activation, command buttons, and menu choices execute actions.

Figure 13.7 illustrates one approach to providing the user a choice of the detail information to display after selecting or activating a wedge of the pie chart. The normally hidden frame control (fraOptions) is contained in frmMDIPieChart. Double-clicking (activating) a pie chart wedge makes fraOptions visible.

FIGURE 13.7

Adding an option frame to the pie chart.

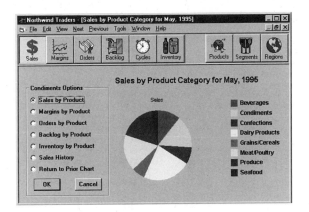

The code in Listing 13.5 performs the following functions, which result in the display shown in Figure 13.7:

- Moves the pie chart to the right to make room for the fraOptions frame and reduces chart's width. If frmMDIPieChart isn't maximized, the chart title is truncated.

- Sets the initial size of the hidden MSHFlexGrid control to display the default option (Sales by Product).

- Replaces the Recordset to which the pie chart is bound with the original version. This step reduces the width of the Legend object to increase the space available for the Plot object.

- Adds the name of the selected Series to the frame caption. Pie chart wedges are Series, not DataPoint objects.

- Shows the frame to the left the pie chart.

Clicking Cancel restores the pie chart to its original appearance. Selecting the {Sales|Margins|Orders|Backlog|Inventory} by Product option and clicking OK executes the drilldown operation. Selecting the Sales History option displays a single-line graph of year-to-date sales for the selected product. Return to Prior Chart takes you back to the originating year-to-date line graph.

LISTING 13.5 CODE TO DISPLAY ON THE PIE CHART A FRAME CONTROL TO SELECT DRILLDOWN OPTIONS AND RESTORE THE PIE CHART TO ITS ORIGINAL APPEARANCE

```
Private Sub ShowOptionFrame()
    Dim rstPieChart As New ADODB.Recordset

    strChartTitle = chtPieChart.Title
    strTitle = strChartTitle

    'Center frame vertically and show it
    With fraOptions
        .Top = (Me.Height - .Height) / 2
        .Visible = True
    End With
    optDrill(1).SetFocus
    With hfgDrillDown
        'Set position and size of grid
        .Top = fraOptions.Top + 80
        .Height = fraOptions.Height - 80
        .Left = fraOptions.Left + fraOptions.Width + 500
        .ColWidth(0) = 400
        .ColWidth(1) = 2600
        .ColWidth(2) = 1000
        .Width = 4870
    End With
    'Move the pie chart to the right and reduce its width
    With chtPieChart
        .Left = .Left + (0.8 * fraOptions.Width)
        .Width = Me.ScaleWidth - .Left
        If frmMDIToolbar.WindowState <> vbMaximized Then
            'Reduce the width of the title
            If InStr(strTitle, " - ") Then
                strTitle = Left(strTitle, InStr(strTitle, " - ") - 1)
            End If
            .Title = strTitle
        End If
        rstPieChart.Open App.Path & "\PieChart.rst", , _
            adOpenDynamic, adLockOptimistic, adCmdFile
        'If you don't move the record pointer, Beverages is missing
        rstPieChart.MoveLast
        Set .DataSource = rstPieChart
```

```
        'Set the caption (note the multiplier when using the DataGrid)
        fraOptions.Caption = .DataGrid.ColumnLabel((intActiveSeries * 2), _
            1) & " Options"
    End With
    With lblDrillDown
        'Center over the frame and grid
        .Top = hfgDrillDown.Top - 500
        .Left = fraOptions.Left
        .Width = fraOptions.Width + hfgDrillDown.Width + 500
        .Caption = Me.Caption & " - " & _
            chtPieChart.DataGrid.ColumnLabel((intActiveSeries * 2), 1)
    End With
    Set rstPieChart = Nothing
End Sub


Private Sub RestorePieChart()
    'Purpose:  Hide the frame and grid
    '          Restore the pie chart to its original state

    Dim rstPieEnhan As New ADODB.Recordset

    'Hide the MSHFlexGrid and make the chart visible
    hfgDrillDown.Visible = False
    lblDrillDown.Visible = False
    chtPieChart.Visible = True

    'Get the original data
    rstPieEnhan.Open App.Path & "\PieEnhan.rst", , _
        adOpenDynamic, adLockOptimistic, adCmdFile
    'If you don't move the record pointer, Beverages is missing
    rstPieEnhan.MoveLast
    With chtPieChart
        .Title = strChartTitle
        .Left = 0
        .Width = Me.ScaleWidth
        Set .DataSource = rstPieEnhan
    End With
    Set rstPieEnhan = Nothing
    DoEvents 'Let it happen
End Sub
```

13

NOTE

The two subprocedures of Listing 13.5 illustrate the use of persistent
`Recordset`s to save and restore chart data. Most `Recordset` (.rst) files are very
small and usually are cached in RAM. Thus, saving and opening persistent
`Recordset` files has little or no impact on the performance of the application.

POPULATING AN MSHFLEXGRID WITH THE SELECTED DRILLDOWN DATA

Clicking the OK button on the `frmDrillOptions` form makes visible an MSHFlexGrid control that displays the data you chose with the option buttons in the *Category* Options frame. The Sales History option displays a single-line graph from the appropriate crosstab query, {Sales|Margins|Orders|Backlog|Inventory} by Product Category.

You must translate the choices made in lower levels of the drilldown application into an SQL statement to create the `Recordset` that populates the MSHFlexGrid control. You need the following three data to translate option selections into appropriate Jet SQL syntax:

- The name of the table from which the data is derived, constructed from `"tbl"` & `rstGraphDefs.Fields("Drilldown1Field2")` & `strOption` & `"Month"`, where `strOption` is {Product|CustomerCategory|RegionCategory}.

> **NOTE**
>
> The Graphs.mdb file in the \Ddg_vb6\Chaptr13 folder of the accompanying CD-ROM differs slightly from the Graphs.mdb file of Chapter 11. Minor modifications to the make-table QueryDef objects and the resulting tables are made to provide consistent field naming conventions across all source tables.

- The name of the field that supplies the data, provided by the `strOptions` value.
- The month and year selected at level 1 (line graphs) or 2 (area charts) if a month was double-clicked. The current year is available from the `strYear` global variable. The month and year serve as criteria for the WHERE clause of the SQL statement.

The ANSI SQL statement that you need to display the product ID, product name, and sales volume data for a typical selection is as follows:

```
SELECT Products.ProductID, Products.ProductName,
    tblSalesProductMonth.Sales
FROM Products, tblSalesProductMonth
WHERE tblSalesProductMonth.ProductID = Products.ProductID
    AND tblSalesProductMonth.CategoryID = 1
    AND tblSalesProductMonth.Year = '1995'
    AND tblSalesProductMonth.Month = '01'
ORDER BY Products.ProductID;
```

Figure 13.8 shows the result of executing the preceding SQL statement in the VisData application. The MSHFlexGrid control that you use to display the data on the pie chart form resembles the data grid window of VisData.

FIGURE 13.8

The query result for a typical drilldown grid.

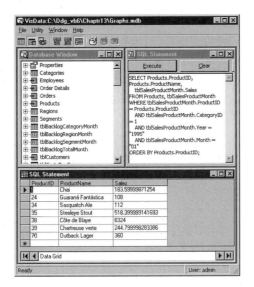

NOTE

This version of the `Drilldn.vbp` project supports only third-level drilldown by product. The tblSalesProductMonth, tblMarginProductMonth, tblOrdersProductMonth, tblBacklogProductMonth, and tblInventoryProductMonth tables provide the source data for the five drilldown options. You can extend the application to support other drilldown categories, such as sales of products by regions and customers. You must write the required make-table queries in Access by using the existing QueryDefs as models. Then add appropriate code to Drilldn.vbp's `frmMDIPieChart` to support the new categories.

Listing 13.6 illustrates VBA code to create the required SQL statement for the `ADODB.Recordset` to which the MSHFlexGrid, `hfgDrillDown`, is then bound. For options except Margins by Product, an additional column displays the percentage contribution of each product to sales, orders, backlog, and inventory. An added row displays the average margin for the category or the total for all other options.

```
Private Sub cmdOK_Click()
    'Determine the option selected and act accordingly
    Dim intCtr As Integer
    Dim strCode As String
    Dim strTableName As String
    Dim strSQL As String
    Dim rstDrillDown As New ADODB.Recordset
    Dim curTotal As Currency
    Dim curItem As Currency

    For intCtr = 1 To 7
        If optDrill(intCtr) Then
            Select Case intCtr
                Case 1
                    strOption = "Sales"
                Case 2
                    strOption = "Margin"
                Case 3
                    strOption = "Orders"
                Case 4
                    strOption = "Backlog"
                Case 5
                    strOption = "Inventory"
                Case 6
                    'Display the single-line graph from the Category crosstab
                    Call RestorePieChart
                    strCode = Left(rstGraphDefs.Fields("Code"), 1) & "2"
                    Call DisplayNewGraphType(strCode)
                    blnIsCrosstab = True
                    Call ResizeFormAndGraph
                    Call frmMDIGraph.chtMonthly_SeriesSelected(intActiveSeries, _
                        5, 0)
                    frmMDIGraph.Show
                    Exit Sub
                Case 7
                    'Return to the original line graph
                    Call RestorePieChart
                    frmMDIGraph.Show
                    Exit Sub
            End Select
        End If
    Next intCtr

    'Define the source table
    strTableName = "tbl" & strOption & "ProductMonth"
    'Generate the SQL statement
    strSQL = "SELECT Products.ProductID, Products.ProductName, " & _
    strTableName & "." & strOption & _
    " FROM Products, " & strTableName & _
```

```
" WHERE " & strTableName & ".ProductID = Products.ProductID" & _
" AND " & strTableName & ".CategoryID = " & intActiveSeries & _
" AND " & strTableName & ".Year = '" & strYear & "'" & _
" AND Val(" & strTableName & ".Month) = " & intPiePoint & _
" ORDER BY Products.ProductID;"

'Create the Recordset
With rstDrillDown
    Set .ActiveConnection = cnnGraphs
    .CursorLocation = adUseClient
    .CursorType = adOpenDynamic
    .LockType = adLockReadOnly
    .Source = strSQL
    .Open
End With
chtPieChart.Visible = False

'Change the title to reflect content
strTitle = strOption & Mid(strTitle, InStr(strTitle, " "))
lblDrillDown.Caption = strTitle

'Load the grid
With hfgDrillDown
    curTotal = 0
    Set .DataSource = rstDrillDown
    .FixedRows = 0
    .Col = 0
    .Row = 0
    .Text = "ID"
    If strOption <> "Margin" Then
        'Add a column for percentage contribution
        .Cols = .Cols + 1
        .Col = .Cols - 1
        .ColWidth(.Col) = 800
        .Text = "Percent"
    End If
    .FixedRows = 1
    For intCtr = 1 To .Rows - 1
        .Col = 2
        .Row = intCtr
        curTotal = curTotal + .Text
        If strOption = "Margin" Then
            'Format percentage (% automatically scales values)
            .Text = Format(.Text, "#0.0%")
        Else
            'Format dollars
            If intCtr = 1 Then
                .Text = Format(.Text, "$#,##0")
            Else
                .Text = Format(.Text, "#,##0")
            End If
```

continues

LISTING 13.6   CONTINUED

```
            End If
        Next intCtr

        'Add a total or average row
        .Rows = .Rows + 1
        .Row = .Rows - 1
        If strOption = "Margin" Then
            'Average Margin
            .Text = Format(curTotal / rstDrillDown.RecordCount, "#0.0%")
        Else
            .Text = Format(curTotal, "$#,##0")
        End If
        .Col = 1
        If strOption = "Margin" Then
            .Text = "Average Margin"
        Else
            .Text = "Total " & strOption
            'Display percent contribution
            .Col = .Cols - 1
            intCtr = 1
            With rstDrillDown
                .MoveFirst
                Do Until .EOF
                    hfgDrillDown.Row = intCtr
                    hfgDrillDown.Text = Format(.Fields(strOption) / _
                        curTotal, "#0.0%")
                    .MoveNext
                    intCtr = intCtr + 1
                Loop
            End With
            .Row = .Rows - 1
            .Text = "100.0%"
        End If
        If .Rows > 14 Then
            'Make room for scrollbar
            .Width = 4870 + 275
        Else
            .Width = 4870
        End If
        .Visible = True
    End With
    lblDrillDown.Visible = True
    Set rstDrillDown = Nothing
End Sub
```

Figure 13.9 illustrates a typical drilldown grid displaying inventory of products in the Condiments category for May 1995. To display this set of data, do the following:

- Launch `Drilldn.vbp`, which opens with the Year-to-Date Sales for 1995 line graph. If Drilldn.vbp is running, click the Sales button to display the line graph.

- Double-click (activate) the May chart label to open `frmMDIPieChart` displaying Sales by Product Category for May 1995 - $33,180 Total.

- Double-click the green Condiments pie wedge to make `fraOptions` visible.

- Select Inventory by Product and click OK to populate and make the `hfgDrillDown` grid visible.

FIGURE 13.9

The bound MSHFlexGrid control displaying May 1995 inventory data for products in the Condiments category.

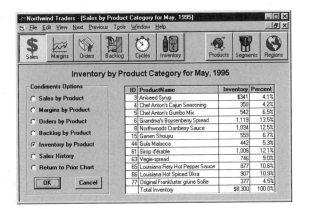

NOTE

Limitations of the current version of the Mschrt20.ocx control cause it to have little usefulness in production database front ends. For commercial projects, a third-party ActiveX chart control is a better choice. If you decide to license a third-party chart control, make sure that the control fully supports ADO data binding with `DataSource` and `DataMember` properties. Data binding saves at least 50% of the lines of code, compared to manual loading of the control's DataGrid equivalent. Although the examples of this chapter don't use `DataEnvironment` objects, a commercial ADO-compliant control should support binding to a row-returning *DataEnvironment*.`Command` object.

SCHEDULING AND DEVICE CONTROL WITH JET AND VBA

IN THIS CHAPTER

Databases often are used for time-based scheduling applications, but integrating databases with real-time control of external devices is much less common. Windows 98's WebTV feature, also called TV Viewer, combines Jet 3.51 databases and components of Microsoft Broadcast Architecture to create the WebTV program guide. Whether many PC owners want to watch TV on a computer monitor is open to question, but there's no doubt that home PCs ultimately will become a central control component for audio/visual entertainment centers.

Unlike GemStar's VCR+ and other consumer electronics program guides for videocassette recorders, WebTV currently lacks the ability to record selected programs automatically. This omission isn't surprising, because very complex code is required to accommodate the wide variety of device control techniques for VCRs, TV sets, Digital Broadcast System (DBS) set-top boxes, and C-band satellite integrated receiver-decoders (IRDs). Future versions of WebTV or third-party products are likely to add remote-control features, but only if the consumer-electronics industry gravitates to a single device-interconnect standard.

This chapter describes the process of integrating a complex scheduling database with commercially available infrared (IR) transmitters that connect to a PC serial port and control a variety of consumer video devices. When this edition was written, these microprocessor-controlled devices were rather expensive ($200 and up) and were available only from home-automation distributors or manufacturers. Lower-cost Universal Serial Bus (USB) IR transmitters are likely to appear in 1999. By 2000 the IEEE-1394 High-Performance Serial Bus (more commonly known by Apple Computer's trademark, FireWire) will control consumer electronics devices and deliver digital audio/video data streams in high-end home entertainment systems.

The Vb6pg.vbp project in the \Ddg_vb6\Chaptr14 folder of the accompanying CD-ROM has 25 forms and contains more than 7,500 lines of VBA code. VB6PG demonstrates the following database-related techniques:

- Working with non-traditional databases. WebTV's Tss.mdb is an extraordinarily complex Jet 3.51 database with 30 tables and 33 QueryDefs. Eight tables are linked to Epg.mdb, which stores user preferences. Tss.mdb is updated periodically, usually every day, either by automatically connecting to the Microsoft Web site or from data embedded in the vertical blanking interval (VBI) of TV broadcast signals.

- Generating complex SQL statements with code. The Recordset that supplies data to the grid requires a complex join of four tables. Removing stations from the display and differentiating broadcast and satellite channels involves lengthy IN and NOT IN predicates, which you generate by double-clicking grid labels.

- Displaying time-based information from a Recordset. Like WebTV's program guide, VB6PG displays program information in a navigable grid. The VB6PG grid consists of Label control arrays that emulate the behavior of WebTV's grid, with event handlers added to control TV viewing and recording. Control objects are native Visual Basic controls, with the exception of the Common Dialog and Comm controls.

- Date/time arithmetic. VB6PG makes extensive use of the **DateAdd** and **DatePart** functions for time shifting and day/hour/minute testing.

- `Recordset` navigation with `Bookmarks`. VB6PG makes extensive use of individual `Bookmarks` and `Bookmark` arrays to position the `Recordset` for grid population.

- Real-time COM port programming. Current IR devices connected to one of the PC's COM port requires use of the Microsoft Comm ActiveX control, which hasn't changed significantly from its Visual Basic 2.0 VBX counterpart. COM port programming with Visual Basic is more an art than a science.

- Printing lists and labels from database content. VB6PG maintains a database of recorded episodes. You can print a complete list of all recordings by tape number, plus spine and cover labels for VHS cassettes on standard, die-cut laser printer label stock. No commercial program guides currently are capable of printing labels for VHS cassettes.

- Converting Visual Basic DAO applications to ADO 2.0. VB6PG originated as a Visual Basic 5.0 project using DAO 3.5. Some features of DAO, such as the capability to compact Jet databases, aren't available in ADO 2.0 with the native Jet OLE DB data provider (Jolt). VB6PG also demonstrates workarounds for the criterion limitations of the `ADODB.Recordet`'s `Find` method.

VB6PG isn't a commercial-quality program, but any proficient Visual Basic developer can use it as the foundation for grid-based scheduling applications. The primary purpose of VB6PG is to illustrate real-time display and device control programming techniques with relational tables as the data source.

NOTE

VB6PG is based on a Visual Basic 5.0 project, Vb5pg.vbp, in the \Ddg_vb6\Chaptr14\Vb5pg folder of the accompanying CD-ROM. The only difference between VB6PG and VB5PG is the replacement of DAO 3.51 with ADO 2.0. If you install a project to local drive folders other than C:\Ddg_vb6\Chaptr 14 and C:\Ddg_vb6\Chaptr 14\Vb5pg, you may receive error messages regarding incorrect ConnectString property values of ADODCs. You can safely disregard these errors unless you have one of the IR devices installed. Proper operation of the two supported IR serial control devices with VB5PG and VB6PG has been verified for Windows 9x, but not Windows NT 4.0.

NAVIGATING THE VISUAL BASIC PROGRAM GUIDE

Running Vb6pg.vbp without copying Tss.mdb to the project folder uses a sample database, Samptss.mdb, to populate the grid of VB6PG's `frmGuide` form. Samptss.mdb contains composite listings of San Francisco Bay Area broadcast stations and cable channels from an early version of TV Viewer. When you start Vb6pg.vbp for the first time on a given day, the dates of the Samptss.mdb records are changed to start on the preceding day. Figure 14.1 shows VB6PG's grid displaying off-air broadcast and C-band satellite programming for a 2-hour period. The grid is sized to enable display within a TV set's normal viewable area in 640×480 mode. A video card or scan converter with a composite or S-video output is necessary to view the grid on a TV set.

FIGURE 14.1

VB6PG's program guide form displaying broadcast and satellite programming for the first 10 channels.

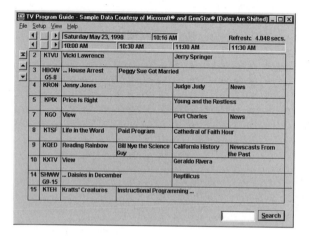

Following are the methods to navigate the grid; event handlers of the `frmGuide` form appear in parenthesis:

- Click the two sets of command buttons at the top of the grid to change the date and starting time of the grid (`cmdDay_Click` and `cmdTime_Click`). The center buttons change the date to the system date and the current time to system time.

- Click the first time header (10:00 AM in Figure 14.1) to display a combo list in which you can select the grid starting time quickly (`lblBlock_Click`).

- Click the three command buttons at the left of the grid to display the first 10 channels (top) or move to the preceding (middle) or succeeding (bottom) 10-channel group (`cmdChannel_Click`).

- Click an episode title to display its starting and ending times and description at the bottom left (`lblBlock1_Click`, `lblBlock2_Click`, `lblBlock3_Click`, and `lblBlock4_Click`).

- Type a keyword in the text box at the lower right and then click Search to search for a particular program (cmdSearch_Click). If found, the grid repopulates to place the episode at the upper right of the grid; the time and description of the program appear at the bottom left. If more than one episode matches, the Search button caption changes to Next (see Figure 14.2).

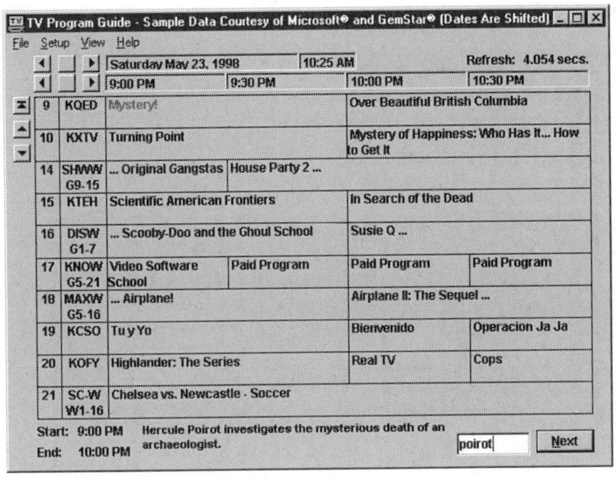

FIGURE 14.2

The program search feature displaying the first of multiple records for the search term "poirot."

- Double-click the channel number to remove a channel from the grid (lblChannel_Click). This feature provides parental channel blocking or conflicting channel designations.
- Double-click the station call letters to identify channels as over-the-air broadcast stations (lblStation_Click). This feature currently is useful for users of antennas for receiving broadcast stations and C-band or DBS satellite dishes for other programming. Identifying over-the-air versus cable channels will become a requirement when Digital TV (DTV, formerly High-Definition TV [HDTV] and ATV) becomes a reality. Cable operators aren't likely to deliver HDTV programming during the early years of DTV.

The tblUserData table of Vbpg.mdb stores lists of blocked and broadcast channels. When you launch VB6PG with data from Tss.mdb the first record contains user data. The second record stores user data for Samptss.mdb.

Using the Keyboard Navigation Feature

The program guide displayed on a TV set isn't amenable to use of a mouse, so VB6PG includes code to implement keystroke navigation, preferably with a cordless (IR) keyboard. All keyboard operations use the numeric keypad and the four arrow keys; press NumLock to activate the numeric keypad. The Form_KeyDown event handler of frmGuide processes all keyboard operations. Following are VB6PG's keyboard navigation methods for the grid:

- Press 5 to toggle keyboard navigation on and off. Alternatively, you can use the Home key to toggle keyboard navigation and the End key to turn off keyboard navigation.

- Press 8 (up arrow) for later or 2 (down arrow) for earlier grid starting time.

- Press 6 (right arrow) to move to the next day or 2 (left arrow) to move the prior day.

- Press 3 (PgDn) to move to higher channels or 9 (PgUp) for lower channels. Press 7 (Home) to move to the lowest channel.

- Press the right and left arrow keys for horizontal grid navigation. A highlighted label indicates the current selection. Selection wraps to the next or preceding line.

- Press the down and up arrow keys for vertical grid navigation. Vertical navigation doesn't wrap.

- Press Page Down to record the episode.

- Press Page Up to switch the TV set to the selected channel.

- Press Delete to turn on TV set power.

- Press the numeric keypad's + or - keys to increase or decrease the TV audio volume.

If you don't have one of the two supported IR control devices in operation, recording is simulated and the TV set controls are inoperative.

Opening Forms for Recording and Device Control

Recording episodes requires setting up the remote control device for the VCR and other optional devices, such as a TV set, DSS set-top box, and C-band IRD. To set up a remote control device for recording, do the following:

1. Double-click the episode title to open the Record Selected Episodes form (frmRecord), which displays each program recorded on the current tape (see Figure 14.3). If the episode has already started, you are warned. If the tape has insufficient recording time remaining, a similar warning appears.

FIGURE 14.3

Setting up to add an episode to the recording schedule.

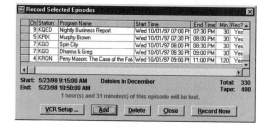

2. Click the VCR Setup button of the Record Selected Episodes form to open the setup form for the recording VCR. If you haven't specified the VCR model, set the type of device controller in use and skip to step 4. Only two IR controller models are enabled in the current version of VB6PG.

3. Specify the tape length, recording speed, control device in use, source of the VCR's analog line input(s), the maximum time required to reposition a C-band satellite dish, and use of the VCR's channel 3 or 4 input for the RF output of a DSS or C-band IRD (see Figure 14.4).

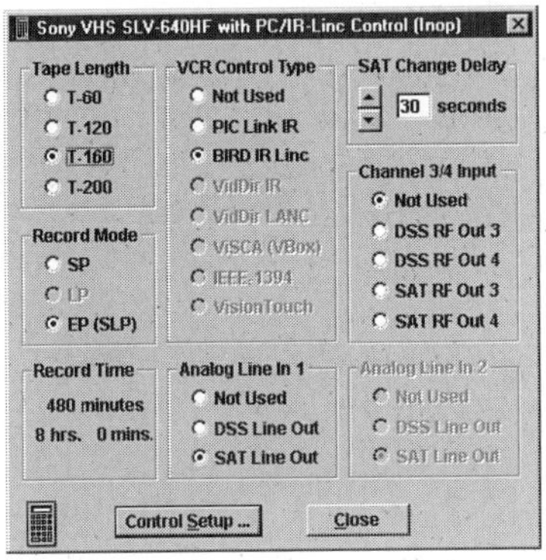

FIGURE 14.4

Setting up a Sony VHS VCR with the BIRD PC/IR-Linc infrared controller.

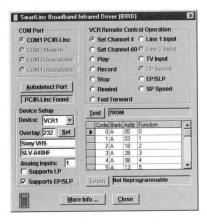

4. Click Control Setup to open the form for the selected device controller and test available COM ports for presence of the selected device. The COM port test also detects internal and external modems. If the device is found, it is assigned to the COM port.

5. Select the VCR recording device from the combo list. If you have installed the IR controller, you can test remote control of the VCR by selecting one of the VCR Remote Control Operation options and clicking Test. Codes sent to the controller appear in the text box adjacent to the Test button (see Figure 14.5). ASCII codes W03B, W005, and W01D correspond to 6, 0, and Enter, which sets the VCR to channel 60. Testing Record sends codes W011 (Stop) and W009 (Record). Each tape transport operation precedes the command string with W011.

FIGURE 14.5

Testing the BIRD SmartLinc (PC/IR-Linc) infrared driver on COM1.

The BIRD PC/IR Linc controller has a preprogrammed ROM with the IR control codes for a wide variety of consumer-electronics devices, similar to "all in one" handheld IR remote controls. The tblBIRDBankKey table of Vbpg.mdb stores the controller's operation codes. The controller also has nonvolatile RAM to store custom code sets for devices not included in ROM banks, similar to "learning" IR remote controls. The Celadon PIC Link Serial Interface and PIC-200 IR Remote Control combination doesn't have a ROM table, so the PIC-200 requires a teaching process for each device.

Specifying C-Band Satellite Mapping and IRD Control

VB6PG maps the Samptss.mdb or Tss.mdb nonbroadcast cable channel listings to C-band satellite names and transponder numbers stored in the tblSatellite table of the VBPG.mdb. Choose Setup, C-Band Channels to open the C-Band Satellite Channel Assignment form (frmSatellite). Channel numbers in the DataGrid control are for reference only (see Figure 14.6). When you close the form, additions and changes are saved in the Station Name field of the Station table. Clearing the Enable C-Band Data check box removes the satellite channel assignments.

FIGURE 14.6

Mapping program-
mer codes
(Network) to call
letters (Station
Name) with satel-
lite codes and
transponder num-
bers.

Once you set up the VCR for remote control, you can program the device controller for your C-band IRD. Choose Setup, C-Band IR Control to open SmartLink form with satellite test options. The PC/IR Linc controller doesn't have a ROM table for the NextLevel 4DTV digital satellite IRD, so you must manually program the required commands using the PC/IR Linc's learning mode. The Test button sends positioning and transponder number codes to the IRD (see Figure 14.7). Selecting A&E and clicking Test sends W102 (View), W11A (Satellite Menu), W113 (G), W113 (5), W11D (Enter), W11B (2), W12B (3), and W11D (Enter). The Satellite Change Delay setting on the VCR setup form determines the delay between the W11D and W11B commands, which allows the dish time to reach its assigned position prior to changing transponders.

FIGURE 14.7

Setting up and testing the PC/IR Linc's satellite IRD commands.

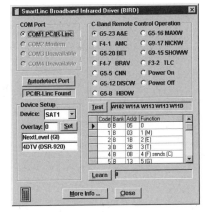

> **NOTE**
>
> VB6PG makes provision for IR control of high-power DSS/DBS set-top boxes in anticipation of the availability of Adaptec's PCI add-in cards for DirecTV and EchoStar dishes. When this edition was written neither DirecTV or EchoStar had announced their intention to use the Windows 98 Broadcast Architecture to add DSS/DBS programming data to the WebTV program guide.

WORKING WITH WEBTV'S SCHEDULING DATABASE

Installing Windows 98's WebTV application adds Epg.mdb, Tss.mdb, and Tss.mdw to the \Program Files\TV Viewer folder. After downloading program guide data from the Microsoft Web site, you can examine the structure of Tss.mdw with Access 97. Tss.mdw is unsecured by default, so you don't need to specify Tss.mdw as the workgroup file unless you implement WebTV's parental control features. Figure 14.8 shows the relationships between 16 of the 22 tables of Tss.mdb.

FIGURE 14.8

Displaying the relationships between Tss.mdb tables with Access 97.

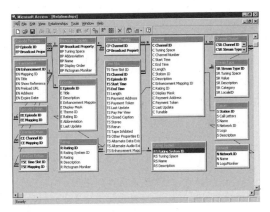

> **NOTE**
>
> Most of Tss.mdw's table and field names contain spaces, which is not a recommended database design practice. The reason that Microsoft's developers decided to use spaces, instead of underscores, in table and field names is not clear. For consistency with Microsoft's database naming conventions, VB6PG's query column aliases use spaces. Tss.mdb's table names don't use plural nouns, which also is a departure from the standard database naming practices used in this book.

The basic program guide uses only four Tss.mdb tables: Time Slot, Channel, Episode, and Station. The grid `Recordset` needs to display channel number, broadcast station or cable programmer code, program or episode name, and a description of the episode (if available). Starting and ending times determine the left-right location of the episode title in the grid. The basic query to generate the `rstPG Recordset` for the program guide is

```
SELECT [Time Slot].[TS Time Slot ID],
     Channel.[C Channel Number],
     Station.[S Name] AS [Call Letters],
     DateAdd("h",-7,[TS Start Time]) AS [Start Time],
     [Time Slot].[TS Length], DateAdd("h",-7,[TS End Time]) AS [End Time],
     Episode.[E Title], Episode.[E Description]
  FROM (Station
     INNER JOIN Channel
         ON Station.[S Station ID] = Channel.[C Station ID])
        INNER JOIN (Episode
           INNER JOIN [Time Slot]
              ON Episode.[E Episode ID] = [Time Slot].[TS Episode ID])
           ON Channel.[C Channel ID] = [Time Slot].[TS Channel ID]
  ORDER BY Channel.[C Channel Number],
     Station.[S Name],
     DateAdd("h",-7,[TS Start Time])
```

> **NOTE**
>
> The `DateAdd("h",-7,[TS Start Time])` expressions in the preceding query convert Tss.mdb's Greenwich mean time (GMT) values to Pacific daylight time (PDT), a 7-hour time difference.

Figure 14.9 shows the qryPG `QueryDef`, included in Samptss.mdb, in Access 97's Query Design view. Figure 14.10 is a screen capture of the first 19 of the 19,708 rows of the query result set.

FIGURE 14.9
Access 97's Query Design view displaying the query to generate the `rstPG` `Recordset` *used to populate the program guide grid.*

qryPG : Select Query

TS Time	C Channel	Call Letter	Start Time	TS Len	End Time	E Title	E Description
183	2	KTVU	5/28/98 1:00:00 AM	60	5/28/98 2:00:00 AM	In Person With Maure	Forgiveness.
184	2	KTVU	5/28/98 2:00:00 AM	60	5/28/98 3:00:00 AM	Jerry Springer	Secret love affairs reveale
185	2	KTVU	5/28/98 3:00:00 AM	120	5/28/98 5:00:00 AM	Far Out Man	A burned-out hippie pursue
186	2	KTVU	5/28/98 5:00:00 AM	30	5/28/98 5:30:00 AM	First Business	
187	2	KTVU	5/28/98 5:30:00 AM	30	5/28/98 6:00:00 AM	Headline News	
189	2	KTVU	5/28/98 7:00:00 AM	120	5/28/98 9:00:00 AM	Mornings on Two	
190	2	KTVU	5/28/98 9:00:00 AM	60	5/28/98 10:00:00 AM	In Person With Maure	Kids "divorcing" parents.
191	2	KTVU	5/28/98 10:00:00 AM	60	5/28/98 11:00:00 AM	Vicki Lawrence	
192	2	KTVU	5/28/98 11:00:00 AM	60	5/28/98 12:00:00 PM	Jerry Springer	Stole her sister's husband.
194	2	KTVU	5/28/98 12:30:00 PM	30	5/28/98 1:00:00 PM	Murphy Brown	Murphy goes to a men-only
195	2	KTVU	5/28/98 1:00:00 PM	60	5/28/98 2:00:00 PM	Crook & Chase	TV time machine.
196	2	KTVU	5/28/98 2:00:00 PM	30	5/28/98 2:30:00 PM	Bobby's World	
197	2	KTVU	5/28/98 2:30:00 PM	30	5/28/98 3:00:00 PM	Bobby's World	
198	2	KTVU	5/28/98 3:00:00 PM	30	5/28/98 3:30:00 PM	Adventures of Batm	
199	2	KTVU	5/28/98 3:30:00 PM	30	5/28/98 4:00:00 PM	Eeklstravaganza	
200	2	KTVU	5/28/98 4:00:00 PM	30	5/28/98 4:30:00 PM	Big Bad Beetleborgs	
201	2	KTVU	5/28/98 4:30:00 PM	30	5/28/98 5:00:00 PM	Goosebumps	
7694	2	KTVU	5/28/98 5:00:00 PM	60	5/28/98 6:00:00 PM	Baywatch	Shauni decides that she an
7695	2	KTVU	5/28/98 6:00:00 PM	30	5/28/98 6:30:00 PM	Home Improvement	Al may propose to Ilene.

Record: 1 of 19078

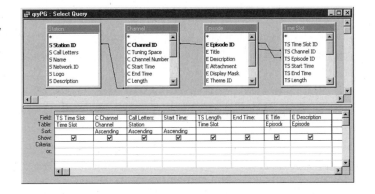

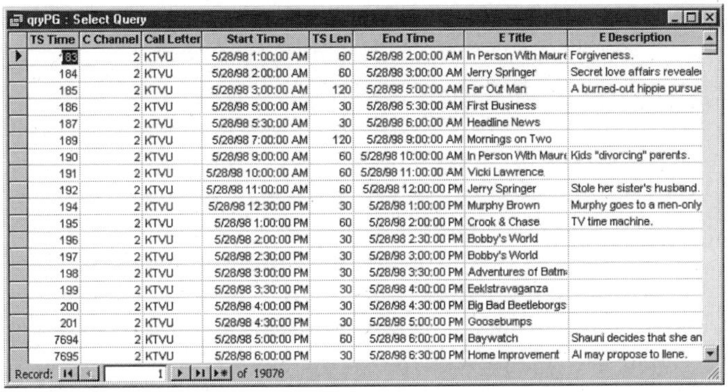

FIGURE 14.10
The first 19 rows of the query result set created by the SQL statement for the `rsPG Recordset`.

Specifying a particular set of channels requires use of the `IN` predicate and a comma-separated values list, as in the following example to display only off-air broadcast stations:

```
SELECT [Time Slot].[TS Time Slot ID],
       Channel.[C Channel Number],
       Station.[S Name] AS [Call Letters],
       DateAdd("h",-7,[TS Start Time]) AS [Start Time],
       [Time Slot].[TS Length], DateAdd("h",-7,[TS End Time]) AS [End Time],
       Episode.[E Title], Episode.[E Description]
   FROM (Station
       INNER JOIN Channel
             ON Station.[S Station ID] = Channel.[C Station ID])
          INNER JOIN (Episode
             INNER JOIN [Time Slot]
                ON Episode.[E Episode ID] = [Time Slot].[TS Episode ID])
             ON Channel.[C Channel ID] = [Time Slot].[TS Channel ID]
   WHERE [Channel].[C Channel Number] & [Station].[S Call Letters]
      IN('2KTVU', '4KRON', '5KPIX', '7KGO', '8KTSF', '9KQED',
         '10KXTV', '15KTEH', '19KCSO', '20KOFY', '24KSTS', '25KTNC',
         '26KTSF', '28KLXV', '44KBHK', '60KCSM', '64KFTL', '65KLXV',
         '66KPST')
```

```
ORDER BY Channel.[C Channel Number],
    Station.[S Name],
    DateAdd("h",-7,[TS Start Time])
```

VB6PG eliminates blocked channels by negating the IN predicate and its value set, as in NOT
IN('3KCRA', ...'53BOX').

COMPARING THE PERFORMANCE OF DAO AND ADO WITH LARGE RECORDSETS

Before embarking on upgrading a large Visual Basic database application from DAO 3.51 and
its predecessors to ADO 2.0, it's a good practice to verify that the upgrade won't cause a serious performance hit. Performance comparisons are especially important for client applications,
such as VB6PG, that create and manipulate large Recordsets. It's equally important to run tests
on PC configurations with varying amounts of RAM, such as Windows 9x with 16M and 32M,
and Windows NT Workstation 4+ with 32M and 64M. Paging Recordsets to disk can result in
a major-scale performance hit.

The Tsstest.vbp project, in the \Ddg_vb6\Chaptr14 folder of the accompanying CD-ROM, compares the time to create ADODB.Recordset and DAO.Recordset objects from the two SQL statements of the preceding section and the Samptss.mdb database. The frmTssTest form uses
ADODC/DataGrid and Data/DBGrid pairs with text boxes that display the time (in seconds) to
generate the keyset/Dynaset Recordset, respectively, plus the time to populate the DataGrid or
DBGrid control by assigning the Recordset to the ADODC or Data control. Only the time to
open the Recordset is germane to VB6PG; real-world applications don't populate grids with
thousands of records.

Figure 14.11 shows Tsstest.exe displaying typical times to create the entire 19,078-record
ADODB.Recordset and to populate the entire DataGrid. Mark the Use DAO check box to compare times for the default ADO and the DAO Recordsets. To compare the performance of
client-side (adUseClient) and server-side (adUseServer) cursors, mark the Client Cursor check

box. Marking the Read-Only Recordset check box generates read-only `ADODB.Recordsets` and `DAO.Recordsets` of the Snapshot type. The data shown in Figure 14.11's text boxes is for a client with a 266-MHz Pentium II, 128M of RAM, and a 4.3G Ultra-DMA/33 fixed disk running Windows NT 4.0 (SP4). Task Manager reports that Tsstest.exe's process consumes about 13M of RAM.

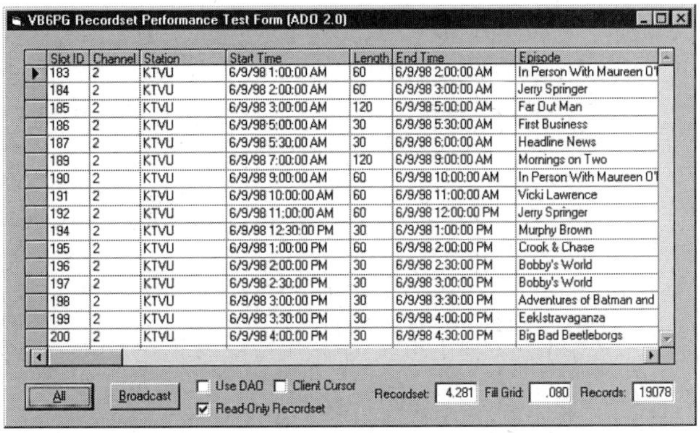

FIGURE 14.11

Tsstest.exe displaying times to create a 19,078-row ADO keyset Recordset *and populate a DataGrid control*

Listing 14.1 shows the code behind `frmTssTest`. To avoid a lengthy startup delay, the form opens without creating a `Recordset`. The ADODC control has empty `CommandString` and `RecordSource` property values; the `DataSource` and `DataMember` properties of the DataGrid control also are empty. Similarly, the Data control's `DatabaseName` and `RecordSource` properties values are empty; the DBGrid control's `DataSource` property is set to the Data control. Unlike the DataGrid, the Data control's `DataSource` property is read-only at run time.

LISTING 14.1 CODE TO COMPARE THE TIMES TO OPEN LARGE ADO 2.0 AND DAO 3.51 Recordset OBJECTS AND TO POPULATE GRIDS

```
Option Explicit
Private cnnTss As New ADODB.Connection
Private rstADO As New ADODB.Recordset
Private dbTss As DAO.Database
Private rstDAO As DAO.Recordset
Private strSQLAll As String
Private strSQLBcst As String
Private sngTimer As Single

Private Sub Form_Load()
    'Position grids
    dtgTssTest.Height = 4335
    dbgTssTest.Height = 4335
    dbgTssTest.Top = dtgTssTest.Top
```

continues

LISTING 14.1 CONTINUED

```
'Open Connection and Database objects
cnnTss.Open "Provider=Microsoft.Jet.OLEDB.3.51;Data Source=" & _
   App.Path & "\samptss.mdb"
Set dbTss = DBEngine.OpenDatabase(App.Path & "\samptss.mdb")

'Set up SQL statements
strSQLAll = "SELECT [Time Slot].[TS Time Slot ID], " & _
   "Channel.[C Channel Number], Station.[S Name] AS [Call Letters], " & _
   "DateAdd(""h"",-7,[TS Start Time]) AS [Start Time], " & _
   "[Time Slot].[TS Length], DateAdd(""h"",-7,[TS End Time]) " & _
   "AS [End Time], Episode.[E Title], Episode.[E Description] " & _
   "FROM (Station INNER JOIN Channel ON Station.[S Station ID] = " & _
   "Channel.[C Station ID]) INNER JOIN (Episode INNER JOIN [Time Slot] " & _
   "ON Episode.[E Episode ID] = [Time Slot].[TS Episode ID]) " & _
   "ON Channel.[C Channel ID] = [Time Slot].[TS Channel ID] " & _
   "ORDER BY Channel.[C Channel Number], Station.[S Name], " & _
   "DateAdd(""h"",-7,[TS Start Time]);"

strSQLBcst = "SELECT [Time Slot].[TS Time Slot ID], " & _
   "Channel.[C Channel Number], Station.[S Name] AS [Call Letters], " & _
   "DateAdd(""h"",-7,[TS Start Time]) AS [Start Time], " & _
   "[Time Slot].[TS Length], DateAdd(""h"",-7,[TS End Time]) " & _
   "AS [End Time], Episode.[E Title], Episode.[E Description] " & _
   "FROM (Station INNER JOIN Channel ON Station.[S Station ID] = " & _
   "Channel.[C Station ID]) INNER JOIN (Episode INNER JOIN [Time Slot] " & _
   "ON Episode.[E Episode ID] = [Time Slot].[TS Episode ID]) " & _
   "ON Channel.[C Channel ID] = [Time Slot].[TS Channel ID] " & _
   "WHERE [Channel].[C Channel Number] & [Station].[S Call Letters] " & _
   "IN('2KTVU', '4KRON', '5KPIX', '7KGO', '8KTSF', '9KQED', '10KXTV', " & _
   "'15KTEH', '19KCSO', '20KOFY', '24KSTS', '25KTNC', '26KTSF', " & _
   "'28KLXV', '44KBHK', '60KCSM', '64KFTL', '65KLXV', '66KPST') " & _
   "ORDER BY Channel.[C Channel Number], Station.[S Name], " & _
   "DateAdd(""h"",-7,[TS Start Time]);"
End Sub

Private Sub chkUseDAO_Click()
   If chkUseDAO.Value = 0 Then
      dtgTssTest.Visible = True
      dbgTssTest.Visible = False
      chkUseClient.Visible = True
   Else
      dtgTssTest.Visible = False
      dbgTssTest.Visible = True
      chkUseClient.Visible = False
   End If
End Sub

Private Sub cmdPGAll_Click()
   If chkUseDAO.Value = 0 Then
```

```
        Call ADORecordset(strSQLAll)
    Else
        Call DAORecordset(strSQLAll)
    End If
End Sub

Private Sub cmdPGBcst_Click()
    If chkUseDAO.Value = 0 Then
        Call ADORecordset(strSQLBcst)
    Else
        Call DAORecordset(strSQLBcst)
    End If
End Sub

Private Sub ADORecordset(strSQL As String)
    'Create the ADODB.Recordset
    Me.Caption = "VB6PG Recordset Performance Test Form (ADO 2.0)"
    Me.MousePointer = vbHourglass
    txtTimer1.Text = ""
    txtTimer2.Text = ""
    txtCount.Text = ""
    DoEvents
    sngTimer = Timer
    With rstADO
        If .State = adStateOpen Then
            .Close
        End If
        Set .ActiveConnection = cnnTss
        .Source = strSQL
        If chkUseClient.Value = 0 Then
            .CursorLocation = adUseServer
        Else
            .CursorLocation = adUseClient
        End If
        If chkReadOnly.Value = 0 Then
            .CursorType = adOpenKeyset
        Else
            .CursorType = adOpenReadOnly   'Default
        End If
        .LockType = adLockOptimistic
        .Open
        .MoveLast
        .MoveFirst
        txtCount.Text = .RecordCount
    End With
    txtTimer1.Text = Format(Timer - sngTimer, "#.000")
    DoEvents
    sngTimer = Timer
    With adcTssTest
        Set .Recordset = rstADO
        Set dtgTssTest.DataSource = adcTssTest
```

continues

LISTING 14.1 CONTINUED

```
      .Refresh
   End With
   txtTimer2.Text = Format(Timer - sngTimer, "#.000")
   Me.MousePointer = vbDefault
End Sub

Private Sub DAORecordset(strSQL As String)
   'Create the DAO.Recordset
   Me.Caption = "VB6PG Recordset Performance Test Form (DAO 3.51)"
   Me.MousePointer = vbHourglass
   txtTimer1.Text = ""
   txtTimer2.Text = ""
   txtCount.Text = ""
   DoEvents
   sngTimer = Timer
   If chkReadOnly.Value = 0 Then
      Set rstDAO = dbTss.OpenRecordset(strSQL, dbOpenDynaset)
   Else
      Set rstDAO = dbTss.OpenRecordset(strSQL, dbOpenShapshot)
   End If
   'For the RecordCount
   rstDAO.MoveLast
   rstDAO.MoveFirst
   txtCount.Text = rstDAO.RecordCount
   txtTimer1.Text = Format(Timer - sngTimer, "#.000")
   DoEvents
   sngTimer = Timer
   On Error Resume Next 'SQL string length problem
   With dtcTssTest
      Set .Recordset = rstDAO
      .Refresh
   End With
   txtTimer2.Text = Format(Timer - sngTimer, "#.000")
   Me.MousePointer = vbDefault
End Sub
```

Table 14.1 lists timing data for opening ADO 2.0 server-side and DAO 3.51 Recordsets and populating grids for a 266-MHz Pentium II client with 128M of RAM running Windows 98. Tsstest.exe is the sole running application. Based on the results achieved, no substantial performance benefit occurs when upgrading the original VB5PG application to ADO 2.0. The only justification for expending the time to upgrade a project as large as VB5PG is faith that future versions of ADO will offer improved performance with large Recordsets.

TABLE 14.1 TIME IN SECONDS TO OPEN DAO 3.51 AND ADO Recordset OBJECTS AND TO POPULATE GRIDS

Operation	DAO 3.51 Recordset	DAO 3.51 DBGrid	ADO 2.0 Recordset	ADO 2.0 Open DataGrid
All (19,078 records)	4.688	0.648	5.160	0.168
All (after five repeats)	4.581	0.051	4.449	0.021
Broadcast (3,961 records)	0.941	0.101	0.988	0.010
Broadcast (five repeats)	0.930	0.031	0.980	0.008

UPGRADING PROJECTS FROM DAO TO ADO

Listing 14.1 illustrates several of the steps required to convert DAO-based applications to ADO. Following is a more complete list of the programming changes needed to upgrade VBA code and data-bound control objects to ADO:

- Add a project reference to the Microsoft ActiveX Data Objects 2.0 Library.

- Replace DAO.Database and DAO.Recordset object variable declarations with {Dim¦Private¦Public} cnn*Name* **As New** ADODB.Connection and **As New** ADODB.Recordset statements, respectively.

- Delete DAO.Workspace variable declarations for transactions. ADO transactions use the BeginTrans, CommitTrans, and RollbackTrans methods of the Connection object.

- Replace **Set** db*Name* = DBEngine(0).OpenDatabase("db*Name*.mdb") statements with cnn*Name*.Open "Provider=Microsoft.Jet.OLEDB.3.51;Data Source=dbName.mdb".

- Replace **Set** rsName = db*Name*.OpenRecordset(str*Source*[, int*Type*]) statements with the following typical structure:

```
With rsName
  [If .State = adStateOpen Then
      .Close
    End If]
    Set .ActiveConnection = cnnName
    .Source = strSource
  [.CursorLocation = adUseClient]
  [.CursorType = adOpenStatic]
  [.LockType = adLockOptimistic]
    .Open
End With
```

Specifying property values makes your code more readable. The alternative is to supply argument values to the Open method. You need only test the State property value if your code reuses the *rsName* Recordset. The "Opening New ADODB.Recordset Objects" section later in the chapter discusses CursorLocation and CursorType values. The LockType property setting is needed only for Recordsets that your code updates.

- Replace the LIKE predicate's Jet-specific wildcards (* and ?) with their ANSI SQL equivalents (% and _, respectively) in SQL statements. Retain the Jet-specific wildcards in the LIKE clause of Find operations.

- Add .Value, .Text, and other property names to objects for which the default value is used. Adding the explicit Value property to Field object interrogation improves performance dramatically.

> **NOTE**
>
> The original VB5PG code uses the ordinal to specify fields as in intCOMPort = rsUser(23), which results in defaulting the Fields and Value properties. VB6PG eliminates the use of default properties and substitutes the field name for the ordinal to improve code readability, as in intCOMPort = rsUser.Fields("ComPortIR").Value. For slightly better performance, specify the two property names but substitute the ordinal for the field name.

- Remove *rsName*.Edit statements, which ADO omits when updating Recordset rows.

- Change *wsName*.{BeginTrans|CommitTrans|Rollback} to *cnnName*.{BeginTrans|CommitTrans|RollbackTrans} statements.

▶ See "Adopting ADODB.Recordset Find Methods," p. 152

- Replace Recordset FindFirst, FindNext, and FindPrevious method calls with the Find method and the appropriate SearchDirectionEnum constant. The default direction constant is adSearchForward for replacing DAO's FindFirst and FindNext methods; use adSearchBackward for FindPrevious. Apply the MoveFirst method to assure that Find starts at the beginning of the Recordset when replacing FindFirst, and apply the MoveNext method prior to replacements for FindNext. ADO offers no equivalent of FindLast, so you must loop the Find method, saving Bookmark values, and then position the cursor with the last valid Bookmark value.

- Replace compound Find criteria strings with criterion strings that reference only a single Recordset column. The next section provides examples of the changes necessary to upgrade VB6PG's frmGuide form to ADO 2.0.

- Replace If [Not] *rsName*.NoMatch Then statements with If [Not] *rsName*.EOF Then for forward and If [Not] *rsName*.BOF Then for backward searches. ADO doesn't support the NoMatch property.

- Change Bookmark **String** variables to **Variant**s. ADO uses **Variant** type 3 (vbLong, **Long** integer), not type 8 (vbString).

- Replace Data controls with ADODC controls, DBGrids with DataGrids, and Data Bound Lists with DataLists. It isn't necessary to replace MSFlexGrid controls, because version 6.0 of MSFlexGrid works with either the Data or ADODC control.

- Remove the reference to the Microsoft DAO 3.51 Object Library and remove DAO-based controls from the Toolbox.

NOTE

The preceding list isn't numbered, because most of the intermediate changes can be done in any sequence. The upgrade of VB5PG to VB6PG followed the sequence listed on a form-by-form basis, starting with frmGuide. The DAO 3.51 reference and DBGrid control were removed at the end of the coversion process.

Opening New `ADODB.Recordset` Objects

ADO provides more flexibility than DAO when opening `Recordset`s, but a variety of properties can cause a choice crisis when moving from DAO to ADO. Following are recommendations for setting `ADODB.Recordset` properties for Jet databases:

- ADO code defaults to server-side cursors (adUseServer); tests with Tsstest.exe demonstrate server-side cursors are much faster than client-side cursors (adUseClient). The reverse is true for most client/server applications that use ADO.

- `ADODB.Recordset`s created by the Data Environment Designer (DED) `Command` objects default to adUseClient. If you use DED with Jet databases, make sure to select 2 - Use server-side cursor in the Cursor Location list of the *ConnectionName* Properties sheet's Advanced page.

- A forward-only cursor results if you don't assign a CursorType value of adOpenKeyset, adOpenDynamic, or adOpenStatic in code. You can't assign a Recordset with a forward-only cursor to an ADODC control.

- If you specify adUseClient, your only CursorType choices are adOpenForwardOnly or adOpenStatic. Selecting a client-side cursor overrides CursorType choices that aren't valid for adUseClient.

- A read-only Recordset results unless you specify a LockType value of adLockOptimistic, adLockPessimistic, or adLockBatchOptimistic. The default LockType is adLockReadOnly. For large ADODB.Recordsets from Jet tables, adLockOptimistic provides slightly improved performance compared with adLockRead only.

- For multiuser applications, substitute `adOpenKeyset` or `adOpenDynamic` and `adUseServer` for dbOpenDynaset and `adOpenStatic` for dbOpenSnapshot. Always specify `adLockOptimistic` to reduce concurrency issues.

The most expeditious method of replacing DAO db*Name*.`OpenRecordset(`str*SQL*, dbOpenDynaset`)` method calls against Jet databases is to write a generic Recordset block, such as the following:

```
With rsName
    If .State = adStateOpen Then
        .Close
    End If
    .ActiveConnection = cnnName
    .Source = strSource
    .CursorLocation = adUseServer
    .CursorType = adOpenStatic
    .LockType = adLockOptimistic
    .Open
End With
```

Search for all instances of `OpenRecordset`, add the **With ... End With** block below the method call, and then comment the `OpenRecordset` line. Change `rsName` to the name of the `Recordset` and `strSource` to the appropriate variable name or SQL statement from the `OpenRecordset` statement. When you get the application to compile and run without errors, optimize the property values of each `Recordset` for its intended use and delete the commented line. This approach is particularly effective for large projects such as VB6PG, which has 36 `OpenRecordset` method calls.

Replacing Compound `FindFirst` and `FindNext` Methods with `Find`

`Find` creates the most vexing problems when upgrading client applications. You must replace all instances of `NoMatch` with `EOF` or `BOF` and eliminate compound criteria. Compound criteria or use of other unsupported `WHERE` clause predicates results in runtime error 3001 (`The application is using arguments that are of the wrong type, are out of acceptable range or are in conflict with one another`). Compound criteria is defined here as a search string that references two or more fields of a `Recordset` with `AND` or `OR` clauses. In many cases, you can replace the compound search string with a succession of searches. In `frmGuide`'s `cmdChannel_Click` event handler, as an example, the original compound search criteria is

```
rsPG.FindFirst "[C Channel Number] = " & intLastChannel & _
    " AND [Call Letters] = '" & strLastStation & "'"
```

The preceding statement returns an ambiguous result when the same channel number is assigned to a broadcast station and a cable or satellite programmer. The replacement is `MoveFirst` and two successive `Find` operations:

```
rsPG.MoveFirst
```

```
...
rsPG.Find "[C Channel Number] = " & intLastChannel
rsPG.Find "[Call Letters] = '" & strLastStation & "'"
```

The second `rsPG.Find` operation locates the next record with the specified name. In this example, which uses values from an existing record for `intLastChannel` and `intLastStation`, error trapping isn't necessary, and two `Find` method calls are sufficient. For the general case, however, you must validate the second `Find` result, moving to `EOF` if validation fails. You also can avoid a `Find` operation if the first criterion isn't satisfied, as in the following example:

```
With rsPG
   .MoveFirst
   ...
   .Find "[C Channel Number] = " & intLastChannel
   If Not .EOF Then
      .Find "[Call Letters] = '" & strLastStation & "'"
      If .Fields("C Channel Number").Value <> intLastChannel Then
         .Find "[Call Letters] = 'X'" 'Move to EOF
      End If
   End If
End With
```

A more complex situation occurs with the search string to find a particular record by a keyword search, as in `frmGuide`'s `cmdSearch_Click` event handler:

```
strSearch = "([E Title] LIKE '*" & txtSearch.Text & "*' " & _
            "OR [E Description] LIKE '*" & txtSearch.Text & "*') " & _
            "AND [Start Time] >= #" & DateAdd("n", -fldLength, Now) & "#"
...
rsPG.FindFirst strSearch
```

The `strSearch` criteria finds the first record with a keyword match either in the title or the description of episodes that haven't ended when conducting the search. In this case, you start the search at the first record that meets the date/time criterion and then perform two sequential searches, if necessary, to find the episode. Following is replacement code that stores a temporary `Bookmark` value to return to an intermediate starting position in the `Recordset`:

```
With rsPG
   .MoveFirst 'Start from beginning
   .Find "[Start Time] >= #" & DateAdd("n", -fldLength, Now) & "#"
   If Not .EOF Then
      varTestBM = .Bookmark
      .Find "[E Title] LIKE '*" & txtSearch.Text & "*'"
      If .EOF Then
         .Bookmark = varTestBM
         .Find "[E Description] LIKE '*" & txtSearch.Text & "*'"
      End If
   End If
End With
```

Listing 14.2 shows the code for the updated `cmdSearch_Click` event handler. The original `FindFirst`, `FindNext`, and `FindPrevious` method calls and other DAO-specific statements are commented for comparison. Listing 14.2 demonstrates that Microsoft's decision to constrain the ADO 2.0 `Find` method to single-field operations requires cumbersome workarounds for sophisticated search operations.

> **NOTE**
>
> The `Find` method's limitations derive from the current OLE DB 2.0 specification, which requires only single-field search capability. Adding multifield search capability requires an update to or an optional extension of the OLE DB leveling specifications.

LISTING 14.2   REPLACING COMPOUND `Find` METHOD CALLS IN THE `cmdSearch_Click` EVENT HANDLER

```
Private Sub cmdSearch_Click()
    'Search for matching program title or description on now or later
    'Note: Search order is in channel then time sequence
    Dim strSearch As String
    Dim varTestBM As Variant

    If Len(txtSearch.Text) = 0 Then
        lblDescription.Caption = "No search string specified."
        Exit Sub
    End If


    lblDescription.Visible = False
    DoEvents
    txtSearch.Enabled = False
    cmdSearch.Enabled = False
    'strSearch = "([E Title] LIKE '*" & txtSearch & "*'" & _
    '  " OR [E Description] LIKE '*" & txtSearch & _
    '  "*') AND [Start Time] >= #" & DateAdd("n", -fldLength, Now) & "#"
    'rsPG.FindFirst strSearch
    If cmdSearch.Caption = "&Search" Then
        With rsPG
            .MoveFirst 'Start from beginning
            .Find "[Start Time] >= #" & DateAdd("n", -fldLength, Now) & "#"
            If Not .EOF Then
                varTestBM = .Bookmark
                .Find "[E Title] LIKE '*" & txtSearch.Text & "*'"
                If .EOF Then
                    .Bookmark = varTestBM
                    .Find "[E Description] LIKE '*" & txtSearch.Text & "*'"
                End If
            End If
        End With
```

```
Else
    'Search is continuing
    With rsPG
        .Bookmark = varSearchBM
        .MoveNext 'Move off the current record
        If Not .EOF Then
            varTestBM = .Bookmark
            .Find "[E Title] LIKE '*" & txtSearch.Text & "*'"
            If .EOF Then
                .Bookmark = varTestBM
                .Find "[E Description] LIKE '*" & txtSearch.Text & "*'"
            End If
        End If
    End With
End If
lblDescription.Visible = True
DoEvents
If rsPG.EOF Then
    lblDescription.Caption = "No match found for '" & txtSearch.Text & "'."
    timDescription.Enabled = True
    cmdSearch.Caption = "&Search"
Else
    varSearchBM = rsPG.Bookmark
    If InStr(strBlocked, (fldChannel & fldStation)) = 0 Then
        'Found and not blocked
        datCurrent = CDate(Format(fldStart, "mm/dd/yy"))
        lblDay.Caption = " " & Format(datCurrent, "dddd mmmm d, yyyy")
        datTime = CDate(Format(fldStart, "h:mm AMPM"))
        Call LoadBlockTimes
        Call FillGrid
        lblBlock1(0).ForeColor = &HFF&
        Call lblBlock1_Click(0)
    Else
        lblDescription.Caption = "Match is for a blocked channel"
    End If
    'Are there more matching records?
    'rsPG.FindNext strSearch
    With rsPG
        rsPG.Bookmark = varSearchBM
        .MoveNext
        If Not .EOF Then
            varTestBM = .Bookmark
            .Find "[E Title] LIKE '*" & txtSearch.Text & "*'"
            If .EOF Then
                .Bookmark = varTestBM
                .Find "[E Description] LIKE '*" & txtSearch.Text & "*'"
            End If
        End If
    End With
    'If rsPG.NoMatch Then
    If rsPG.EOF Then
```

continues

LISTING 14.2 CONTINUED

```
            cmdSearch.Caption = "&Search"
            lblDescription.Caption = "No more records for " & txtSearch.Text
        Else
            'rsPG.FindPrevious strSearch
            cmdSearch.Caption = "&Next"
        End If
        rsPG.Bookmark = varSearchBM
    End If
    txtSearch.Enabled = True
    cmdSearch.Enabled = True
End Sub
```

NOTE

An alternative method for positioning a Recordset to a particular record is to apply the Filter property, which accepts compound criteria strings. After setting the Filter property value, you must save the Recordset.Bookmark value of the selected record, set the Filter property value to an empty string, and then set Recordset.Bookmark to the saved value. Using the Filter property is discussed at the end of the next section.

TRAVERSING A RECORDSET TO FILL A CUSTOM GRID

FillGrid, which executes for each date/time or channel change, is the most complex subprocedure of VB6PG. One of the objectives of the design of FillGrid was to provide a means for testing techniques to speed Recordset operations based on date/time values. Date/time arithmetic, including comparison, generally is slower than operations on other numeric data types.

FillGrid performs the following basic operations:

- Makes the 40 labels of the grid visible, resets the label widths, clears captions, and resets foreground and background colors to default values. Labels are 10-member control arrays (lblBlock1, lblBlock2, lblBlock3, and lblBlock4).

- Adds captions for programs selected by the times specified in the column headers (lblBlock array). The code aligns programs that start at other than on the hour or half-hour to the closest grid position. Programs with lengths shorter than 15 minutes are ignored.

- Wraps labels for programs that extend through midnight to the next day.

- Assigns the unique Time Slot (primary key) value to the Tag property of the label, which provides access to the program description text by a simple Find operation on the Recordset.

- Expands the width of the label for programs having a duration greater than 30 minutes and hides overlaid labels.

- Detects whether the program begins earlier than the first time block (lblBlock(0)). If so, a leading ellipsis is added to the program title.

- Detects whether the program ends after the last time block (lblBlock(3)). If so, a trailing ellipsis is added to the program title.

> **NOTE**
>
> Two-dimensional label control arrays, if offered by Visual Basic, would have greatly simplified the FillGrid code.

Because of its usage frequency, the speed of FillGrid operations determines the perceived performance of the entire project. The initial FillGrid code included no performance optimization. Traversing the entire Recordset to populate the grid from Samptss.mdb required approximately 2.5 seconds. Subsequent optimizations reduced FillGrid's execution time by half or more, depending on the number of individual programs appearing in the current grid.

- Assign Field objects (fldChannel, fldStation, fldStart, and so on) to Recordset fields, instead of using rs*Name*.Fields(str*FieldName*) or rs*Name*.Fields(int*Ordinal*). Use of Field objects speeds performance by about 30%.

- Use MoveNext to skip records for expired programs on a given channel/station combination with a datTest comparison. The datTest value is set three hours prior to the first block time to accommodate long programs.

- Use MoveNext to skip records for a given channel/station combination that begins more than 15 minutes after the last block time. The combination of this and the preceding MoveNext operations gives about a 50% performance boost with Recordsets having several days of data.

- Substitute **Single** for **Date** data types for multiple date/time comparisons on the same record. Operations on **Single** values are significantly faster, improving overall performance by about 10%.

- Add the explicit .Value property when retrieving (or setting) the value of ADODB Field objects. Doing so results in a 10% speedup.

Listing 14.3 is the code for the FillGrid subprocedure with comments preceding the code added to optimize performance. The optimization techniques for the FillGrid subprocedure are applicable to a variety of situations in which you must test values of large numbers of records, only a few of which meet a set of complex criteria.

LISTING 14.3 OPTIMIZED CODE FOR THE FillGrid SUBPROCEDURE

```
Public Sub FillGrid()
   'Fill the EPG grid with program data
   'This procedure is optimized for speed
   Dim intRow As Integer      'Grid rows (0 to 9)
   Dim sngBlock(6) As Single  'Block start times
   Dim sngTimer As Single     'Timer for refresh rate
   Dim sngStart As Single     'Episode start time
   Dim sngEnd As Single       'Episode end time
   Dim blnExtends As Boolean  'Extends beyond time range
   Dim datTest As Date        'Used to skip records
   Dim strMins As String      'Minutes for trimming
   Dim strHour As String      'Hour for trimming
   Dim datStart As Date       'Temporary start date/time
   Dim datEnd As Date         'Temporary end date/time

   blnFilling = True
   sngTimer = Timer
   'Clear and prior block style changes
   For intCtr = 0 To 9
      With lblBlock1(intCtr)
         .Tag = ""
         .Caption = ""
         .Width = intWidth
         .Visible = True
         .ForeColor = lngFore
         .BackColor = lngBack
      End With
      With lblBlock2(intCtr)
         .Tag = ""
         .Caption = ""
         .Width = intWidth
         .Visible = True
         .ForeColor = lngFore
         .BackColor = lngBack
      End With
      With lblBlock3(intCtr)
         .Tag = ""
         .Caption = ""
         .Width = intWidth
         .Visible = True
         .ForeColor = lngFore
         .BackColor = lngBack
      End With
      With lblBlock4(intCtr)
         .Tag = ""
         .Caption = ""
         .Width = intWidth
         .Visible = True
         .ForeColor = lngFore
```

```
            .BackColor = lngBack
        End With
    Next intCtr

    'Beginning and ending times (Single) for four 30-minute blocks
    'Used in date/time comparisons
    For intCtr = 0 To 3
        sngBlock(intCtr) = CSng(CDate(lblBlock(intCtr).Caption))
    Next intCtr
    'Dummy block to test for time beyond range
    sngBlock(4) = CSng(DateAdd("n", 30, CDate(lblBlock(3).Caption)))

    'Set the test date for loop speedup (three hour block, maximum)
    datTest = datCurrent + DateAdd("h", -3, CDate(lblBlock(0).Caption))

    'Fill the program guide
    strStation = ""
    intChannel = 0
    intRow = 0
    intBlock = 1

    'Solves No Current Record problem at 11:00 pm. wakeup
    If rsPG.EOF Then
        rsPG.MoveFirst
    End If

    'Bypass any blocked channels
    If Len(strBlocked) > 4 Then
        Do Until InStr(strBlocked, (fldChannel.Value & fldStation.Value)) = 0
            rsPG.MoveNext
            If rsPG.EOF Then
                'This condition occurs only if the last
                'channel is blocked
                Exit Do
            End If
        Loop
        If rsPG.EOF Then
            'Added in conjunction with above
            If intRow < 9 Then
                'Clear the remaining rows of grid
                Call ClearRows(intRow)
            End If
            Exit Sub
        End If
    End If

    'Add first channel number and call letters
    lblChannel(intRow).Caption = fldChannel.Value
    lblStation(intRow).Caption = fldStation.Value
    intChannel = fldChannel.Value
    strStation = fldStation.Value
```

continues

LISTING 14.3   CONTINUED

```
'Loop through Recordset (about 19,000 records for Samptss.mdb)
Do Until rsPG.EOF
    'Used with change to next day for strange ending times
    datStart = fldStart.Value
    datEnd = fldEnd.Value
    DoEvents
    If blnAbort Then
        'Provide for quick change of time or date
        blnFilling = False
        blnAbort = False
        Exit Do
    End If
    If intBlock < 5 Then
        'Use today's records only (handles invalid early datCurrent values)
        Do While fldChannel.Value = intChannel And _
            fldStation.Value = strStation _
            And DatePart("y", datCurrent) <> DatePart("y", fldStart.Value)
        rsPG.MoveNext
        If rsPG.EOF Then
            Exit Do
        End If
        Loop
        If Not rsPG.EOF Then
            'Channel, station and date/time test (speeds up processing)
            Do While fldChannel.Value = intChannel _
                And fldStation.Value = strStation _
                And fldStart.Value < datTest
            rsPG.MoveNext
            If rsPG.EOF Then
                Exit Do
            End If
            Loop
        End If
        If rsPG.EOF Then
            If intRow < 9 Then
                'Clear the remaining rows of grid
                Call ClearRows(intRow)
            End If
            Exit Do
        End If
    End If
    'Takes care of more than one station on a channel
    'for broadcast/cable
    If fldChannel.Value = intChannel _
        And fldStation.Value = strStation Then
        'Use Single, not Date data type for tests (speed increase)
        'Round start and end times up to 7 minutes to :00 or :30
        'TBS, for example, starts programs at :05 and :35
        strMins = Format(fldStart.Value, "nn")
        If InStr("0030", strMins) Then
            sngStart = fldStart.Value - Int(fldStart.Value)
```

```
        Else
            strHour = Format(fldStart.Value, "hh")
        If Val(strMins) < 16 Then
            sngStart = CSng(CDate(strHour & ":00"))
        ElseIf Val(strMins) > 15 And Val(strMins) < 46 Then
            sngStart = CSng(CDate(strHour & ":30"))
        ElseIf Val(strMins) > 45 Then
            If strHour = "23" Then
                'Move to 00:00 the next day
                sngStart = 0
                datStart = datStart + 1
                datStart = CDate(Int(CSng(datStart)))
            Else
                'Increment the hour by 1
                strHour = CStr(Val(strHour) + 1)
                If Val(strHour) < 10 Then
                    strHour = "0" & strHour
                End If
                sngStart = CSng(CDate(strHour & ":00"))
            End If
        Else
            'Can't handle the strange time
            sngStart = fldStart.Value - Int(fldStart.Value)
        End If
    End If
    'End time trimming
    strMins = Format(fldEnd.Value, "nn")
    If InStr("0030", strMins) Then
        sngEnd = fldEnd.Value - Int(fldEnd.Value)
    Else
        strHour = Format(fldEnd.Value, "hh")
        If Val(strMins) < 16 Then
            sngEnd = CSng(CDate(strHour & ":00"))
        ElseIf Val(strMins) > 15 And Val(strMins) < 46 Then
            sngEnd = CSng(CDate(strHour & ":30"))
        ElseIf Val(strMins) > 45 Then
            'Handles programs that end at, for instance :45
            'Move the end time to the next even hour, except at midnight
            If strHour = "23" Then
                'Move to 00:00 the next day
                sngEnd = 0
                datEnd = datEnd + 1
                datEnd = CDate(Int(CSng(datEnd)))
            Else
                'Increment the hour by 1
                strHour = CStr(Val(strHour) + 1)
                If Val(strHour) < 10 Then
                    strHour = "0" & strHour
                End If
                sngEnd = CSng(CDate(strHour & ":00"))
            End If
```

continues

LISTING 14.3 CONTINUED

```
        Else
            'Can't handle the strange time
            sngEnd = fldStart.Value - Int(fldStart.Value)
        End If
    End If
    '/ 25 takes care of slightly short programs
    intLength = Int(fldLength.Value / 25)
    If intLength = 0 Then
        intLength = 1
    End If
    If sngEnd > sngBlock(4) Or (Day(datStart) <> Day(datEnd) _
            And intLength > 1) Then
        'Program extends beyond grid time range
        blnExtends = True
    Else
        blnExtends = False
    End If
    'Earlier program extends into the time range
    If sngEnd > sngBlock(intBlock - 1) _
            And sngStart < sngBlock(intBlock - 1) Then
        If blnExtends Then
            'Earlier program extends beyond the time range
            Select Case intBlock
                Case 1
                    lblBlock1(intRow).Caption = " ... " _& _
                        fldTitle.Value & " ..."
                    lblBlock1(intRow).Width = (intWidth * 4) - 36
                    lblBlock2(intRow).Visible = False
                    lblBlock3(intRow).Visible = False
                    lblBlock4(intRow).Visible = False
                Case 2
                    lblBlock2(intRow).Caption = " ... " & _
                        fldTitle.Value & " ..."
                    lblBlock2(intRow).Width = (intWidth * 3) - 24
                    lblBlock3(intRow).Visible = False
                    lblBlock4(intRow).Visible = False
                Case 3
                    lblBlock3(intRow).Caption = " ... " & _
                        fldTitle.Value & " ..."
                    lblBlock3(intRow).Width = (intWidth * 2) - 12
                    lblBlock4(intRow).Visible = False
                Case 4
                    lblBlock4(intRow).Caption = " ... " & _
                        fldTitle.Value & " ..."
            End Select
            intBlock = 5
        Else
            'Case structures take care of programs that start
            'at odd times (usually cable/satellite)
```

```
            'Typically, such programs start at :15 or :45
            Select Case intBlock
                Case 1
                    lblBlock1(intRow).Caption = " ... " & fldTitle.Value
                    lblBlock1(intRow).Tag = CStr(fldTimeSlot)
                Case 2
                    lblBlock2(intRow).Caption = " ... " & fldTitle.Value
                    lblBlock2(intRow).Tag = CStr(fldTimeSlot.Value)
                Case 3
                    lblBlock3(intRow).Caption = " ... " & fldTitle.Value
                    lblBlock3(intRow).Tag = CStr(fldTimeSlot.Value)
                Case 4
                    lblBlock4(intRow).Caption = " ... " & fldTitle.Value
                    lblBlock4(intRow).Tag = CStr(fldTimeSlot.Value)
            End Select
            'Earlier program occupies the appropriate blocks
            If sngEnd > sngBlock(3) Then
                lblBlock2(intRow).Visible = False
                lblBlock3(intRow).Visible = False
                lblBlock4(intRow).Visible = False
                lblBlock1(intRow).Width = (intWidth * 4) - 36
                intBlock = 5
            ElseIf sngEnd > sngBlock(2) Then
                lblBlock2(intRow).Visible = False
                lblBlock3(intRow).Visible = False
                lblBlock1(intRow).Width = (intWidth * 3) - 24
                intBlock = 4
            ElseIf sngEnd > sngBlock(1) Then
                lblBlock2(intRow).Visible = False
                lblBlock1(intRow).Width = (intWidth * 2) - 12
                intBlock = 3
            Else
                intBlock = 2
            End If
        End If
    Else
        'Conventional time blocks start here
        '(allowance for midnight ending)
        If sngStart >= sngBlock(intBlock - 1) And _
                sngStart <= sngBlock(intBlock) Then
            'Time slot corresponds to block time
            Select Case intBlock
                'Case for each time block
                Case 1
                    'Add Episode ID tag for description search
                    lblBlock1(intRow).Tag = CStr(fldTimeSlot.Value)
                    If blnExtends Then
                        'Episode extends beyond last block time
                        lblBlock1(intRow).Caption = " " & _
                            fldTitle.Value & " ..."
                        lblBlock1(intRow).Width = (intWidth * 4) - 36
```

continues

14

LISTING 14.3 CONTINUED

```
         Else
             lblBlock1(intRow).Caption = " " & fldTitle.Value
             lblBlock1(intRow).Width = (intWidth * intLength) _
                - (12 * (intLength - 1))
         End If
         intBlock = intBlock + 1
         If fldLength.Value > 30 Then
             'Block is longer than standard 30 minutes
             lblBlock2(intRow).Visible = False
             intBlock = intBlock + 1
             If fldLength.Value > 60 Then
                 lblBlock3(intRow).Visible = False
                 intBlock = intBlock + 1
                 If fldLength.Value > 90 Then
                     lblBlock4(intRow).Visible = False
                     intBlock = intBlock + 1
                 End If
             End If
         End If
      Case 2
         lblBlock2(intRow).Tag = CStr(fldTimeSlot.Value)
         If blnExtends Then
             lblBlock2(intRow).Caption = " " & _
                 fldTitle.Value & " ..."
             lblBlock2(intRow).Width = (intWidth * 3) - 24
         Else
             lblBlock2(intRow).Caption = " " & fldTitle.Value
             lblBlock2(intRow).Width = (intWidth * intLength) _
                - (12 * (intLength - 1))
         End If
         intBlock = intBlock + 1
         If fldLength.Value > 30 Then
             lblBlock3(intRow).Visible = False
             intBlock = intBlock + 1
             If fldLength.Value > 60 Then
                 lblBlock4(intRow).Visible = False
                 intBlock = intBlock + 1
             End If
         End If
      Case 3
         lblBlock3(intRow).Tag = CStr(fldTimeSlot.Value)
         If blnExtends Then
             lblBlock3(intRow).Caption = " " & _
                 fldTitle.Value & " ..."
             lblBlock3(intRow).Width = (intWidth * 2) - 12
         Else
             lblBlock3(intRow).Caption = " " & fldTitle.Value
             lblBlock3(intRow).Width = (intWidth * intLength) _
                - (12 * (intLength - 1))
```

```
                End If
                intBlock = intBlock + 1
                If fldLength.Value > 30 Then
                    lblBlock4(intRow).Visible = False
                    intBlock = intBlock + intLength
                End If
            Case 4
                intBlock = intBlock + 1
                lblBlock4(intRow).Tag = CStr(fldTimeSlot.Value)
                If blnExtends Then
                    lblBlock4(intRow).Caption = " " & _
                        fldTitle.Value & " ..."
                Else
                    lblBlock4(intRow).Caption = " " & fldTitle.Value
                End If
            End Select
        End If
    End If
End If
'Trim oversize labels
Select Case intBlock
    Case 1
        If lblBlock1(intRow).Width > (intWidth * 4) - 36 Then
            lblBlock1(intRow).Width = (intWidth * 4) - 36
        End If
    Case 2
        If lblBlock2(intRow).Width > (intWidth * 3) - 24 Then
            lblBlock2(intRow).Width = (intWidth * 3) - 24
        End If
    Case 3
        If lblBlock3(intRow).Width > (intWidth * 2) - 12 Then
            lblBlock3(intRow).Width = (intWidth * 2) - 12
        End If
End Select
If intBlock = 5 Then
    'Bypass the remainder of the records for the station
    Do While fldChannel.Value = intChannel And _
            fldStation.Value = strStation
        rsPG.MoveNext
        If rsPG.EOF Then
            Exit Do
        End If
    Loop
    If rsPG.EOF Then
        If intRow < 9 Then
            'Clear the remaining rows of grid
            Call ClearRows(intRow)
        End If
        Exit Do
    End If
```

continues

LISTING 14.3 CONTINUED

```
        End If
        'To solve no current record problem if nav keys held down
        If rsPG.EOF Then
            rsPG.MoveLast
            Exit Sub
        End If
        'Test status of loop
        If fldChannel.Value <> intChannel Or _
            fldStation.Value <> strStation Then
            'New station, start over (stay on current record)
            intRow = intRow + 1
            '10 station rows
            If intRow > 9 Then
                intLastChannel = fldChannel.Value
                strLastStation = fldStation.Value
                Exit Do
            End If
            If Len(strBlocked) > 4 Then
                'Bypass any blocked channels
                Do Until InStr(strBlocked, (fldChannel.Value & _
                    fldStation.Value)) = 0
                    rsPG.MoveNext
                    If rsPG.EOF Then
                        If intRow < 9 Then
                            'Clear the remaining rows of grid
                            Call ClearRows(intRow)
                        End If
                        Exit Do
                    End If
                Loop
            End If
            If rsPG.EOF Then
                Exit Do
            Else
                'Add channel number and call letters
                lblChannel(intRow).Caption = fldChannel.Value
                lblStation(intRow).Caption = fldStation.Value
                strStation = fldStation.Value
                intChannel = fldChannel.Value
                intBlock = 1
            End If
        Else
            rsPG.MoveNext
            If rsPG.EOF Then
                If intRow < 9 Then
                    'Clear the remaining rows of grid
                    Call ClearRows(intRow)
                End If
                Exit Do
            End If
        End If
```

```
    Loop

    'Reset the key navigation values
    intGridX = 0
    intGridY = 0
    intLastX = 0

    'Display the refresh time
    lblStatus.Visible = False
    sngTimer = Timer - sngTimer
    lblRefreshTime.Caption = Format(sngTimer, "0.000")
    blnFilling = False
    Call ShowToRecord
End Sub
```

Many approaches to speed populating the grid were tested during development of the original VB5PG project. Ordering the `Recordset` by the Start Time field (to reduce the number of records traversed) made the code much more complex and didn't significantly improve performance. The following `Filter` criteria was tested to restrict the active records in `rsPG` to a 6-hour group:

```
datTest = datCurrent + DateAdd("h", -3, CDate(lblBlock(0).Caption))
datLast = datCurrent + DateAdd("h", 1, CDate(lblBlock(3).Caption))
rsPG.Filter = ""
rsPG.Filter = "[Start Time] >= #" & datTest & _
    "# AND [Start Time] <= #" & datLast & "#"
```

Filtering the `Recordset`, which minimizes the number of `MoveNext` operations, resulted in an unexpected 5% loss of performance, apparently because of the time required to apply the filter to the `Recordset`. When considering applying a `Filter` to a `Recordset`, be sure to test alternatives, such as the `MoveNext` methods described in this chapter. Another approach is to recreate the `Recordset` with an SQL statement that includes the `Filter` criteria in a `WHERE` clause.

> **NOTE**
>
> Unlike the `Find` method, the `Filter` property allows compound criteria and multiple fields in the `Filter` expression.

EXPLORING THE REMAINDER OF THE VB6PG PROJECT

VB6PG uses the Vbpg.mdb database to store user- and device-specific information in the following tables:

- *tblUserData* (`rsUser`) stores user-related information, primarily for printing and device control, in 41 fields. The first record is used with Tss.mdb; the second record is standard setup data for use with Samptss.mdb.

- *tblC-Band* (rsSAT) stores C-band satellite names, transponder numbers, and channel identifiers.

- *tblDevices* (rsDevices) stores consumer electronics device descriptions and current settings. Test records support one TV set, two DSS receivers, five VCRs, and two satellite IRDs.

- *tblRecord* (rsRecord) holds temporary records for each recording operation specified for a single tape. When the tape is full, the records move to *tblTapes*, which stores the tape catalog.

- *tblBIRDBankKey* and *tblPICPageKey* (rsIRCodes) store function settings and IR key values for the BIRD SmartLinc and the PIC-200 IR Remote Control, respectively. *tblIRCodes* (rsTSCodes) is a temporary (troubleshooting) table that stores the history of codes sent to the IR controller during the preceding 24 hours.

- *tblTestCaptions* (rsTest) supplies the Caption value for the 12 option buttons used to test operation of the IR controller with VCRs, TV sets, and satellite IRDs.

- *tblPrintTest* (rsRecord) stores typical recording data for printing test VCR labels.

The subprocedures and event handlers described in the sections that follow use read-write ADODB.Recordsets created over these tables with SELECT * FROM tbl*Name* statements.

Real-Time Operations

VB6PG is a time-based application, so Timer controls play an important role in its operations. Following are the timers used by VB6PG:

- One-second (timSeconds_Timer) and synchronized one-minute (timMinutes_Timer) event handlers in frmGuide automatically advance the grid on the hour and half-hour.

- The timSeconds_Timer event handler calls frmGuide's CheckRecordStatus subprocedure to determine whether a program to be recorded has already started. If so, CheckRecordStatus sets the VCR tuner channel, DBS channel, or satellite code/transponder combination and starts the recording process. If the end of the program is detected, CheckRecordStatus stops the VCR.

- frmBIRDLinc and frmPICLink use timers (timTimeOut) to enable command buttons after sending a series of instructions to the IR device controller.

The frmBIRDLinc and frmPICLink forms have procedures to set up the COM port and detect the presence of the controller (OpenPort), create an array of IR codes for the specified device (DeviceInit), and send a standard set of commands (VCRChannel, VCRStop, VCRRecord, and so on) to the device. The structure of the code for these forms is designed for easy conversion to Automation components or ActiveX DLLs.

Printing Cassette Labels and Tape Lists

▶ **See** "Printing with VBA Code," p. **482**

One of the features of VB6PG is the capability to print with laser or ink-jet printers spine-only or combination spine-cover (combo) labels on standard die-cut sheets with pressure-sensitive adhesive. Choose <u>F</u>ile, Print Set<u>u</u>p to open the form in which to select the label style (see Figure 14.12). Click the Print Test Sample button to open the Test Combo Cassette Label form (see Figure 14.13). Labels can accommodate up to eight episodes. Clicking the Print button prints a single set of spine and face labels in the position selected from the Print list.

FIGURE 14.12

*Selecting the label style in the Setup for VHS Cassette Label Printing form (*frmPrintSetup*).*

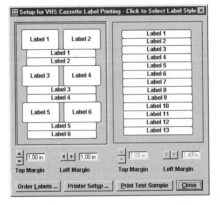

FIGURE 14.13

*Printing a pair of test spine/face labels with the Printing Test Combo Cassette Label form (*frmPrintLabels*).*

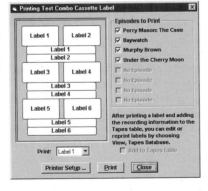

14

Conventional printer code is used to print cassette labels and tape catalogs in VB6PG, because Visual Basic 6.0's DataReports don't provide the formatting capabilities required by VB6PG. The frmPrintLabels form's cmdPrint_Click event handler executes the very complex code required to print the labels in a specific position. It's unlikely that the Report Writer can be programmed to deliver the same result as that of cmdPrint_Click. If you have a videotape collection, you can easily adapt frmPrintSetup and frmPrintLabels to print VHS cassette labels from an existing tape database.

WRITING LOCAL AUTOMATION COMPONENTS AND ACTIVEX DLLS

IN THIS CHAPTER

Creating Windows applications from reusable components is the first step toward a truly object-oriented development environment. Building database applications from a collection of standardized objects can save a substantial amount of programming and testing time. Another advantage of the component approach to application design is that you can structure your object architecture to model business or other organizational practices. In database applications, the major role of reusable components, often called business objects, is to implement business rules. The basic definition of a business rule is a set of constraints that applies to the data entry elements of a specific business activity, such as entering orders or issuing invoices.

One of Visual Basic's most important features is that it can create Automation components, also called ActiveX EXEs and ActiveX DLLs. ActiveX is a Microsoft trademark. You can use Visual Basic 6.0's Automation capabilities to encapsulate code that is common to multiple applications in a single object and then access the object from any client application that supports Automation. Thus an Automation component you create with Visual Basic 6.0 can be used not only with other Visual Basic applications but also by Microsoft Excel, Access, PowerPoint, Project, Internet Explorer, and Internet Information Server. This chapter describes how to create 32-bit database-related local Automation components that reside on the same computer as the client application. Chapter 27, "Creating and Deploying MTS Components," is devoted to shared, three-tier Automation DLLs that reside on a remote application server and communicate with clients via Distributed COM (DCOM).

NOTE

It isn't necessary to use Microsoft Transaction Server (MTS) to host remote ActiveX EXEs, but MTS is required to supply the process in which to run remote ActiveX DLLs. MTS is a combination transaction processor (TP) and object request broker (ORB), but you don't need to use MTS's TP features when hosting ActiveX DLLs. Remote ActiveX EXEs and DLLs can't contain visible components, such as forms or message boxes. Running stateless DLLs under MTS provides much better performance than executing stateful components, such as those described in this chapter.

DEFINING THE ROLE OF AUTOMATION COMPONENTS

The traditional structure of a Visual Basic application consists of a collection of forms with embedded event-handling subprocedures. Modules incorporate declarations of **Public** variables, plus independent subprocedures and functions that are called by one or more event subprocedures or, in the case of **Sub** Main, by instantiation of the application. If you apply modular application design methodology to the initial design of your programs, you can take advantage of the reuse of standard forms and modules in multiple applications. Substituting Visual Basic 6.0 hierarchical class modules for conventional module code is a first step toward creating reusable objects that don't require forms.

Creating a standalone Automation component to contain common forms and related code simplifies project management by providing an independent object that provides a predefined service or set of services. After you create an Automation component with Visual Basic 6.0, you can add a reference to the component in any client application that supports Automation. Then you can use the client application's Object Browser to examine the **Public** properties and methods exposed by the component. Your client also can read and write the values of **Private** properties with Property Get and Property Let procedures, respectively.

In database applications, Automation components often isolate *data services* and *user services*. Data services are provided by a RDBMS, such as the Jet database engine or Microsoft SQL Server. In the case of SQL Server, data services are implemented by OLE DB with ADO-compliant applications or ODBC in conjunction with Jet's Data Access Object (DAO) or the Remote Data Object (RDO). User services represent the visual interface to the data incorporated in a client application. Interposing an Automation server (*business services*) between data services and user services results in a three-tiered structure, as shown in Figure 15.1. The isolation of data-specific elements, such as database, table, and field names and data types, from the user services layer makes the applications that provide user services independent of the underlying data structures. If you change the schema of the underlying database, you need only alter the Automation server. Without the middle-tier Automation server, altering the schema would require rewriting every front end that accesses the database.

FIGURE **15.1**

Contrasting two-tier and three-tier database application structures.

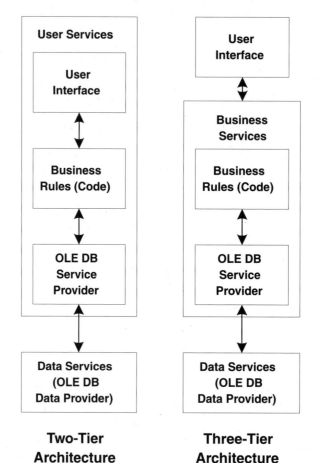

Two-Tier Architecture

Three-Tier Architecture

> **NOTE**
>
> Various naming conventions exist for each of the three tiers of the database application architecture shown in Figure 15.1. This book's use of the term *data services* includes functions performed by the RDBMS, implemented by client/server RDBMS stored procedures and triggers, or by Jet's built-in data validation and referential integrity maintenance features for .mdb files. *User services* represent the visual front end to the RDBMS. In migrating from a conventional two-tier architecture to a three-tier system, much of the code that would ordinarily be included in the user services tier, such as logging in to the database, is moved to the business services layer. Three-tier database application design usually implies a client/server RDBMS back end; this book does not distinguish between client/server and Jet databases when discussing the partitioning of database applications. In three-tier architecture, all client applications use the business services layer to gain access to the underlying data services, which might be provided by more than one RDBMS.

Another advantage of using an Automation component is a built-in version control system for Visual Basic clients. This rudimentary version control system is implemented by establishing a version number for the component's type library. Type library version numbers aren't the same as the file version number you specify in Visual Basic 6.0's EXE Options dialog. The Visual Basic client's .exe file includes the type library version number for each Automation component for which a reference is included in your project. If the type library version number of your Automation component doesn't correspond to the embedded version number, the client displays error 429, `Automation component cannot create object`, when the component is instantiated by a client's reference to one of its methods or properties. You implement version control by maintaining a reference to the prior version by entering the path to the compiled prior version in the Compatible Server text box of the Project page of the Options dialog. Visual Basic defines the following three degrees of compatibility:

- Version identical. No changes to the exposed properties and methods (interfaces) between the prior and the new version.

- Version compatible. New interfaces have been added, but prior interfaces are the same; the component supports existing and upgraded clients.

- Version incompatible. New interfaces replace prior interfaces; the component supports only upgraded clients. (Attempts to use the component with prior clients fail.)

15

WRITING ACTIVE
DLLs

DECIDING BETWEEN IN-PROCESS AND OUT-OF-PROCESS COMPONENTS

Visual Basic 6.0 lets you create either in-process components (DLLs) that run in the same process space as the client application or out-of-process (.exe) components that run in their own process space. References to Automation components declared as {**Private**¦**Public**} **WithEvents** and ActiveX controls, a special type of in-process component, are capable of firing events.

> **NOTE**
>
> Except for a common login dialog for all database user services, most business services implemented by Automation components lack forms or other visual elements, such as message boxes. This condition is especially true for local out-of-process components that are candidates for conversion to remote Automation components. A remote component would display its visual elements on the server, not the client. Therefore, any Automation component should include complete runtime error-trapping and error-reporting code. Generic error handlers for the client can be implemented as in-process DLLs.

The following two sections describe the advantages and limitations of in-process and out-of-process components for three-tier database applications.

In-Process Automation Components

In-process Automation components are analogous to conventional Windows DLLs. Instead of exporting functions to client applications, in-process components expose one or more objects created by class modules, plus the properties and methods applicable to each object. ActiveX controls are an extension of the in-process Automation component concept. ActiveX controls expose to the client only a single object, but also expose events associated with the control's user interface. ActiveX controls are the subject of the next chapter, "Creating User Controls for Database Applications."

Following is a list of the salient features offered by in-process components:

- Faster execution. Out-of-process components use lightweight remote procedure calls (LRPCs) across process boundaries. LRPCs are much slower than in-process function calls. In-process components share their address space with the client application so pointers, rather than variable values, can be passed ByRef.

- No modeless forms. All visual elements of an in-process component must be modal, which requires that in-process components include a **Sub** Main subprocedure, to assure that all Automation clients can use the component. (A Visual Basic startup form must be modeless.) This requirement isn't a significant limitation in database applications, because the user services layer supplies the forms with which users interact.

- Clients handle error processing. All errors must be trapped to prevent shutting down the client application when an error occurs in the in-process component. Errors should be returned as values of methods to the client for processing; therefore, methods are better implemented as functions than as subprocedures.

- Can be remoted only when running under MTS. By definition, an object on a remote computer cannot run in the local computer's process space. However, a remote out-of-process component can call one or more in-process components stored on the same remote computer. MTS provides a process in which to run *packages*, which contain one or more in-process DLLs.

If your primary goal is to maximize performance, in-process components are the logical choice for 32-bit clients. Executing in-process component code is almost as fast as executing the same code contained in a conventional Visual Basic 6.0 form or module.

Out-of-Process Automation Components

Out-of-process Automation components, compiled as .exe files, offer greater versatility at the expense of somewhat slower operation. Out-of-process components offer the following features:

- Can include modeless forms. You can create the equivalent of a complete Visual Basic application that can be manipulated by any client application that supports Automation, such as Microsoft Excel or Access. As noted earlier in the chapter, most Automation components used in database applications don't include visual elements. The sample applications of this chapter, however, include forms.

- Can be run independently. You can design an out-of-process component with a user interface to run in standalone or component mode. The read-only App.StartMode property returns 0 (vbSModeStandalone) when started directly from Windows or 1 (vbSModeAutomation) when started by an Automation client. In standalone mode, the component displays the user interface; in automation mode, you can choose to display the user interface on loading or by applying a class method, such as Show.

In most cases, you first compile and test new components as in-process .exe files. You then can compile a second version as an in-process .dll, which allows you to compare the performance of the two versions.

BUILDING A SIMPLE AUTOMATION COMPONENT

One of the most common development scenarios for Automation components is extracting common code and, in many cases, form(s) from existing Visual Basic 3.0+ applications and converting these Visual Basic objects to in-process or out-of-process Automation components. Converting existing code to complex Automation components also is more instructive than creating components to perform trivial functions, such as database login dialogs.

The example described in the following sections is derived from components of a production Visual Basic 3.0 database application called CycleTime. CycleTime is a client/server front-end application designed for reporting production metrics of a variety of semiconductor products and product groups over a wide range of time periods. The metrics, in this case, are the elapsed times in days and fractions of days between the occurrence of two specific events, such as testing and packaging.

The 16-bit Visual Basic 3.0 production version of CycleTime has 24 forms and six modules. Two of the CycleTime forms, PER_SEL.FRM for date manipulation and PROD_GRP.FRM for product grouping, together with their module files, are particularly useful for creating a variety of related 32-bit Visual Basic, Access, and Excel applications for analyzing sales and production metrics, as well as for financial reporting. The sections that follow describe the process used to convert the original Visual Basic 3.0 PER_SEL.FRM and PER_SEL.BAS components to an Automation component. Conversion of PROD_GRP.FRM and PROD_GRP.BAS, which includes database operations, to a three-tier Automation component is described later in this chapter.

Upgrading the Period Selection Components to 32 Bits

A surprisingly large number of Visual Basic 3.0 database front-ends remain in use today. Despite the success of Windows 9x in the consumer market, many firms continue to use 16-bit Windows 3.11 or Windows for Workgroups as their primary desktop and laptop operating system. Even after upgrading to Windows 9x or Windows NT 4.0, it's a common practice to continue using production 16-bit Visual Basic front ends. The "If it ain't broke, don't fix it" adage has strong adherents in corporate information technology departments faced with massive Year 2000 (Y2K) projects. Ultimately, however, most Visual Basic 3.0 front ends will be converted to Visual Basic 6+.

The process for upgrading components of a 16-bit Visual Basic 3.0 application to 32-bit Visual Basic 6.0 in preparation for conversion of the components to an Automation component is similar to that involved in upgrading complete applications from 16 to 32 bits. Assuming that you have 32-bit controls to replace all the VBXs in the forms you plan to convert, follow these steps:

1. Copy the production source files for the Visual Basic 3.0 version of the project to a new folder. Save all forms as ASCII text files. You cannot convert forms from Visual Basic 3.0 binary format in Visual Basic 6.0.

   Alternatively, load the project in 16-bit Visual Basic 4.0 to convert forms stored in Visual Basic 3.0 binary format to Visual Basic 4.0 format and substitute OLE controls for .VBXs. (This method was used to convert both the Period Selection and Product Grouping forms to Visual Basic 6.0-compatible versions.)

2. Create a new project and add the forms and modules to it.

3. Add references to required libraries, such as Microsoft DAO 3.51 Object Library, to the project.

4. Add the required ActiveX controls to the project. If your forms use .VBXs that don't have corresponding Visual Basic 6.0 .ocxs, copy the corresponding 32-bit Visual Basic 4.0 .ocxs from the \Common\Tools\VB\Controls folder of disk 3 of the Visual Studio 6.0 distribution CD-ROMs. Double-click Vbctrls.reg to register the design mode licenses for the controls.

> **NOTE**
>
> The \Common\Tools\VB\Controls\Readme.txt file has full instructions for installing Visual Basic 4.0 .ocxs required for conversion of Visual Basic 3.0 applications. The Prod_sel.vbp project uses Visual Basic 4.0's Msoutl32.ocx, which has been replaced by the TreeView control of the Windows Common Controls 6.0. More than 200 lines of VBA code changes are required to replace the Outline control with the TreeView control. Thus Prod_sel.frm continues to use Msoutl32.ocx.

5. Open the project in Visual Basic 6.0 to substitute 32-bit OCXs for 16-bit OCXs and VBXs.

6. When you verify that your component(s) behave correctly, save and compile the project to test its performance.

7. Change all two-digit year references to four-digit years for Y2K compliance.

8. If forms are included, make cosmetic changes for conformance to 32-bit form design standards, such as the regular (not bold) font attribute for control captions.

The preceding steps were used to convert the components of the original 16-bit CycleTime (CYCLTIME.MAK) to the 32-bit version. Figure 15.2 shows the Period Selection form run from a simple demonstration form. Open and run Per_sel.vbp and then click the Period Selection button to display the Period Selection form. You select from various date formats with the option buttons and choose a time period with one of the five enabled option buttons. (Quarterly periods aren't implemented in this version.) You can choose arbitrary starting and ending dates with the UpDown buttons in the From Date and To Date frames. When you click the OK button of the Period Selection form, values of the global `gvarDateFrom`, `gvarDateTo`, and `gstrDateRange` variables appear in the text boxes of StdDemo.frm. The output of Per_Sel.frm is used to create a `WHERE Date BETWEEN 'From Date' AND 'To Date'` constraint for queries against an SQL database. Forms of this type are common in applications created for large organizations that use a variety of date formats and calendars.

FIGURE 15.2

*Running the Period
Selection form from the
`frmDemo` form.*

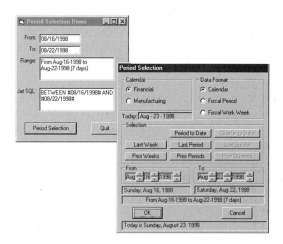

> **NOTE**
>
> The source code files for the Per_sel.vbp project and the other sample applications of this chapter are located in the \Ddg_vb6 \Chaptr15 folder of the accompanying CD-ROM. The code for the Period Selection form (Per_Sel.frm and Per_Sel.bas) includes a complex series of calendar algorithms written by the firm that uses the application. The calendar algorithms, which aren't optimized, use the **Variant** data type exclusively and don't employ the variable naming conventions used elsewhere in this book. "Wrapper" code added to adapt the calendar algorithms, in most cases, uses standard naming conventions. Per_sel.frm is updated to Y2K standards by changing two-digit calendar year displays to four-digit representations.

Converting the 32-Bit Period Selection Form to an Automation Component

Automation components consist of at least one class module (.cls), plus other optional modules and, for local components, forms. The class module is necessary to cause Visual Basic 6.0 to create a type library for the component. The following sections describe starting a new ActiveX EXE project, naming conventions for components, adding a **Sub** Main procedure to a code module, adding a typical class module for a single-purpose component, testing, and debugging the component.

Starting an ActiveX EXE Project

Starting a new project for an Automation component is similar to the process of beginning a conventional EXE project. Instead of the default Form1, a new ActiveX EXE project creates a default Class1 module. To start conversion of Per_sel.vbp to the new Per_svr.vbp project, do the following:

1. Choose File, New Project to open the New Project dialog.

2. Double-click ActiveX EXE to add the Class1.cls module to the project. Save the class module with an appropriate name, Per_svr.cls for this example.

3. Add the required form(s) and module(s) to the project, Per_sel.frm and Per_sel.bas for this example.

4. Save the form(s) and module(s) to new files so that code changes don't affect the standard EXE versions. Save Per_sel.frm as Per_svr.frm and Per_sel.bas as Per_svr.bas.

5. Save the project. Name the project file Per_svr.vbp for this example.

Specifying the Properties of Automation Components

Visual Basic automatically creates an entry for the component in the Windows 95 or Windows NT Registry when you run or compile a Visual Basic 6.0 Automation component. Before you create an Automation component, you should define the names that the component registers. The most important names are those of the type library for the component and for the classes (objects) exposed by the component, as described in the following list:

- The name of your project establishes the name of the type library (TypeLib) and must be unique. An attempt to register a new component with the same TypeLib name as an existing component either fails or overwrites the TypeLib information for the existing component. The TypeLib for the Per_svr.vbp project is `PeriodServer`. You set the project name in the General page of the Project1 Properties sheet, as shown in Figure 15.3. The entry you make in the Project Description text box appears in the Available References list of the References dialog when the component is running in Visual Basic or after the

15

WRITING ACTIVE
DLLS

component is compiled. The default property values set in the Component page of the Project1 Properties sheet (ActiveX Component and Project Compatibility) are satisfactory for the project.

- The name(s) of the class module(s) determine the name(s) of the class(es) exported. If your class name is unique, client applications can create an instance of the class by reference to its name only, as in **Dim svrClassVar As New ClassName**. It is safer to use a *fully qualified class name* (the entire programmatic ID or ProgID), as in **Dim svrClassVar As New TypeName.ClassName**. The class name for the Per_Svr.vbp project, which has only one class, is PeriodSelection, as shown in Figure 15.4.

FIGURE 15.3

Establishing the name of the component's TypeLib in the Project Name text box of the General page of the Project1 Properties sheet.

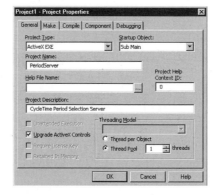

FIGURE 15.4

Specifying the object class name in the Name text box of the Properties window for the class module.

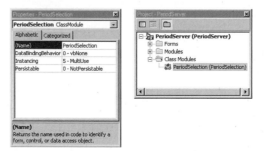

In addition to specifying the class name, you also must set the type of instantiation allowed for your class module in the Instancing text box of the class module's Properties sheet. Following are the six types of component instancing, in descending order of their most common usage:

- *MultiUse* (the default) allows one running instance of the Automation component to supply objects to multiple client applications. Each open client application can create one or more new instances of a particular object. The limitation of MultiUse components is *method blocking*; if one client is executing a method, other clients must wait to execute any method of the object class until the first method completes execution. (OLE 2+

automatically serializes requests from clients.) MultiUse is most commonly used for local components.

- *SingleUse* opens an instance of the component for each client application that calls the component. SingleUse uses more resources but prevents method blocking from interfering with simultaneous execution of methods of objects of the same class. This feature is especially important when the component method takes a significant amount of time to execute. Most Remote Automation components are SingleUse. You can't specify SingleUse for in-process DLLs.

- *Private* is a special class of components that you don't want client applications to instantiate. Private components can be useful for exposing collections to which clients can add members.

- *PublicNotCreatable* requires that the component create the objects for clients to access. Clients can't use the `CreateObject` function or the **New** operator to instantiate the component.

- *GlobalMultiUse* and *GlobalSingleUse* let clients invoke methods and access properties as global functions and variables, respectively. Clients don't need to create an instance of the class explicitly. GlobalSingleUse isn't permitted for in-process DLLs.

Visual Basic 6.0 class modules have two new properties, *DataBindingBehavior* and *Persistable*, which offer the following features:

- *DataBindingBehavior* lets you create Automation components that act as data consumers by emulating ADO-compliant bound controls. You can select `vbSimpleBound` (binds to a single cell of a `Recordset`, like bound TextBox and Label controls) or `vbComplexBound` (binds to an entire `Recordset`, similar to the DataGrid and MSHFlexGrid controls). Data binding of user controls is one of the subjects of the next chapter.

- *Persistable* lets you persist the state of property values across multiple instances of the object. `InitProperties`, `ReadProperties`, and `WriteProperties` events, plus a `PropertiesChanged` method are added to the class. The class Instancing property value must be MultiUse, SingleUse, GlobalMultiUse, or GlobalSingleUse to be persistable.

NOTE

The preceding discussion might appear to be out of order. Ordinarily, you might write code and then set the project name and class name properties of an Automation component when you first run the component. The importance of correctly setting the properties of the component is such that you should set these values *before* adding code to the class module.

15

WRITING ACTIVE
DLLs

Adding a Sub Main to a Module

All Automation components should have a **Sub** Main procedure in a .bas module (not the class module) even if the **Sub** Main has no code. (ActiveX DLLs *require* a **Sub** Main procedure.) You can use the **Sub** Main procedure to test the value of the App.StartMode property to determine whether the component is started in standalone or component mode, as in the following example:

```
Sub Main()
    'The following code lets you use standalone mode
    'with out-of-process components
    If App.StartMode = vbSModeStandalone Then
        frmPeriodSelect.Show vbModal
    End If
End Sub
```

Adding a test of the App.StartMode property lets you demonstrate out-of-process components having user-interface components without running a test application.

Adding a Method to the Class Module

When creating an Automation component from elements of an existing project, such as Per_sel.vbp, you add a class module to a project that exposes method(s) and, optionally, properties of objects of the class. Using arguments of methods to set and return property values is faster than setting and reading the values of individual properties exposed by Property Let and Property Get procedures, respectively, for out-of-process components. (Property procedures are useful, however, for access to property values that you set only occasionally.)

If your Automation component contains only a single exposed object, it's likely to require only one method, which you create with either a **Public Sub** or **Public Function** procedure. Using a **Function** procedure lets you return a value that indicates application of the method succeeded (**True**), was canceled by the component (**False**), or encountered an execution error (Err.Number value, **Long**). If your component includes a visual element, such as a modal form, a Show method is the logical name for a function to display the dialog. You can pass **Variant** values to and from the arguments of the Show method. Listing 15.1 shows the code for the Show method of the PeriodServer.PeriodSelection class created by the PerSvr.cls module of the Per_svr.vbp project. The Show method returns three user-chosen values, DateFrom, DateTo, and DateRange, to the client application.

LISTING 15.1 CODE TO IMPLEMENT THE Show METHOD OF THE
PeriodServer.PeriodSelection CLASS

```
Option Explicit

Public Function Show(DateFrom As Variant, _
                     DateTo As Variant, _
                     DateRange As Variant) As Long
    'Declare the class instance
    Dim frmPerSel As New frmPeriodSelect
    Show = True
    'Show the frmPerSel form modally
    frmPerSel.Show vbModal
    'fCancel is set True by the cmdCancel_Click procedure
    'fCancel also can be set by error-handling routines
    If fCancel Then
        Show = False
    Else
        'Assign values to the function arguments
        DateFrom = gvarDateFrom
        DateTo = gvarDateTo
        DateRange = CVar(gstrDateRange)
    End If
    'Unload the modal form
    Unload frmPerSel
End Function
```

> **NOTE**
>
> The source code for the Per_svr.vbp project, Per_svr.frm, Per_svr.cls, and
> Per_svr.mod, appears in the \Ddg_vb6\Chaptr15 folder of the accompanying
> CD-ROM. You can run PerSel32.exe as a standalone application.

After you add the class module(s) needed by your component, do the following:

1. Verify that the property settings for your project and the class module are in accordance with those specified in the preceding "Specifying the Properties of Automation Components" section.

2. Temporarily set the Start Mode property to Standalone in the Component page of the PeriodServer Properties sheet.

3. Choose Run, Start with Full Compile to perform a preliminary test of your component code.

4. Click OK to close the Debugging page of the Product Server Properties sheet that appears when you run the project for the first time.

> **NOTE**
>
> You must add a global `Boolean` variable, `fCancel`, to the Declarations section of Per_svr.bas and an `fCancel` = **True** line to the `cmdCancel_Click` subprocedure of Per_svr.frm for the project to compile.

Testing the Period Selection Component

You should create an independent Visual Basic 6.0 project to test your component before you compile the component to a .exe or .dll file. The test project needs only a single form with a command button to activate the Automation component with **Dim** obj*Name* **As New** *ClassName* and typ*RetValue* = obj*Name*.*MethodName*[(*Arguments*)] statements. Text boxes are useful for displaying return values of arguments; alternatively, you can use the **Debug**.Print *ArgName* statement to check argument values in the debug window. Listing 15.2 shows the code required to create an instance of the `PeriodSelect` class and display the return values of the arguments of the `Show` method in three text boxes. The code of Listing 15.2 is included in the Test_ps.frm of the Test_ps.vbp project.

LISTING 15.2   VBA CODE TO INSTANTIATE A MEMBER OF THE PeriodSelection CLASS AND TEST THE PERIOD SELECTION COMPONENT

```
Option Explicit

Private Sub cmdTestPerSel_Click()
    'Test procedure for PeriodSelection class
    Dim fSuccess As Long
    Dim varDateFrom As Variant
    Dim varDateTo As Variant
    Dim varDateRange As Variant

    'Full object syntax:
    Dim svrPerSel As New PeriodServer.PeriodSelection
    'Alternative shorthand object syntax if class
    'name is not duplicated in Registry:
    'Dim svrPerSel As New PeriodSelection

    'Apply the Show method
    fSuccess = svrPerSel.Show(varDateFrom, _
                            varDateTo, _
                            varDateRange)

    If fSuccess Then
        'Populate the text boxes with return values
        txtDateFrom.Text = Format(varDateFrom, "mmm-dd-yy")
        txtDateTo.Text = Format(varDateTo, "mmm-dd-yy")
```

```
        txtDateRange.Text = varDateRange
    Else
        'User canceled or error occurred
        txtDateFrom.Text = "Error"
        txtDateTo.Text = "Error"
        txtDateRange.Text = "Error"
    End If
End Sub
```

To test the new component, follow these generic steps:

1. Run the component project in Visual Basic 6.0 to create a temporary Registry entry for the component. Make sure the component continues to run by choosing Run and verifying that the Break, End, and Restart menu choices are enabled. (Alternatively, you can check the task list to verify that the component is running.) Minimize this instance of Visual Basic to reduce screen clutter.

2. Launch another instance of Visual Basic 6.0 and open your test project.

3. Choose Project, References to open the References dialog and find the reference for your component, which usually appears in alphabetical order in the Available References list (see Figure 15.5). Mark the check box for your component. (If you have compiled your component, you see two entries with the same description; enable only the reference for the component with the .vbp file extension running from Visual Basic.)

4. Run the test application to check the performance of the component. You can test .exe and .dll versions of your MultiUse component by these steps.

5. If testing indicates problems, you can set breakpoints in the component code to isolate bugs. In some cases, you might need to add temporary **Debug**.Print *VarName* statements to your component code for troubleshooting.

NOTE

If you followed the preceding steps, the Period Selection form appears when you click Test PeriodSelect Object, but many of the labels are missing values. Clicking OK causes the Date Range text box to display Date Label. The cause of this problem is the subject of the next section, "Debugging Automation Components."

---

6. After eliminating component bugs, choose File, Make EXE File or File, Make DLL File to compile your component.

7. Close the instance of Visual Basic that's running the component.

8. In the instance of Visual Basic running the test application, open the References dialog. The Available References entry for the previously referenced component will be prefixed with MISSING: because Visual Basic has removed the temporary Registry entry.

9. Locate the new reference to the .exe or .dll file (again, at the bottom of the Available References list) and mark the check box for the component reference.

10. Run the test project to verify that the compiled version of the component behaves as expected.

FIGURE 15.5

Creating a reference to the temporary Registry entry for the Automation component running in Visual Basic.

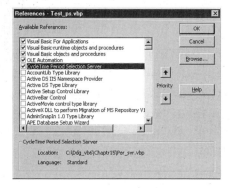

Figure 15.6 shows the Test_PS.frm of the Test_PS.vbp project with the Period Selection form open after previously launching and closing the Period Selection component. Follow the preceding steps to run Per_svr.vbp and Test_PS.vbp to demonstrate the component test, compile Per_svr.exe, and test the final version. Figure 15.7 shows a similar test form created with Access 97.

FIGURE 15.6

Testing the PerSel32.vbp Period Selection component with the Test_PS.vbp project.

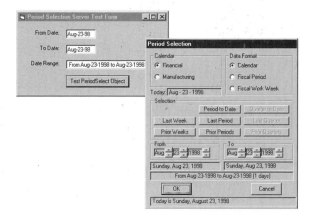

FIGURE 15.7

Testing the Per_svr.exe Period Selection component with an Access 97 test form.

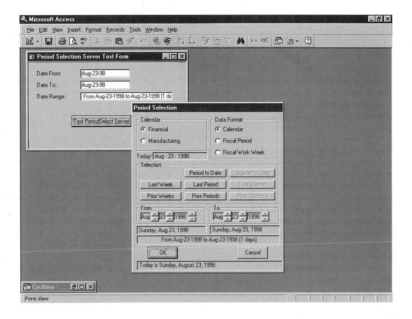

If you have problems with Automation server registration, the first step is to determine whether the server is registered and the Registry entries point to the location of your server's .exe file. Figure 15.8 shows the Windows NT 4.0 Registry Editor displaying the Registry entries for the `PeriodServer.PeriodSelection` component.

FIGURE 15.8

Windows NT 4.0's RegEdit tool displaying the value of the LocalServer32 key for Per_svr.exe.

Debugging Automation Components

Component applications that compile without errors may not behave as expected. As an example, code in modules that refer to specific forms by their `Name` property is virtually guaranteed to fail. The reason for this problem is the instancing of form objects by the **Dim**

frm*InstanceName* **As New** frm*OriginalName* statement. Code that explicitly refers to
frm*OriginalName* does not execute correctly (or at all) because the active instance of the form
is frm*InstanceName*, not frm*OriginalName*. Using code in PerSel.bas imported without modification from the original Visual Basic 3.0 PER_SEL.BAS module results in failure to update
label and 3D panel captions in several locations of the 32-bit Visual Basic 6.0 PerSel.frm form.

The most expedient remedy is to move procedures that contain explicit references to the
instanced form from the .bas module to the .frm module and then remove the
frm*OriginalName* prefixes of references to control properties. Listing 15.3 shows the before
and after versions of the SetCalDates subprocedure. The first version of the SetCalDates subprocedure was contained in PER_SEL.BAS. The second version of SetCalDates is the revised
version relocated to Per_svr.frm. Similar treatment is applied to the GetPeriodToDate and
GetDates subprocedures. Moving the procedures to the form module is feasible because the
F_DATE and T_DATE variables in the subprocedures are declared **Public** in Per_sel.bas and
Per_svr.bas.

LISTING 15.3 THE ORIGINAL SetCalDates SUBPROCEDURE FROM PER_SEL.BAS AND THE
REVISED VERSION OF SetCalDates MOVED TO PER_SVR.FRM

```
Sub SetCalDates()
    'Purpose:   Use date format functions to display dates (faster)
    'Note: Moved to frmPeriodSelect and "frmPeriodSelect." removed
    frmPeriodSelect.lblDateFrom(1).Caption = Format(F_Date, "mmm")
    frmPeriodSelect.lblDateFrom(2).Caption = Format(F_Date, "dd")
    frmPeriodSelect.lblDateFrom(3).Caption = Format(F_Date, "yy")
    frmPeriodSelect.tdpDateFrom.Caption = _
       Format(F_Date, "dddd, mmm d, yyyy")

    frmPeriodSelect.lblDateTo(1).Caption = Format(T_Date, "mmm")
    frmPeriodSelect.lblDateTo(2).Caption = Format(T_Date, "dd")
    frmPeriodSelect.lblDateTo(3).Caption = Format(T_Date, "yy")
    frmPeriodSelect.tdpDateTo.Caption = _
       Format(T_Date, "dddd, mmm d, yyyy")
    frmPeriodSelect.Date_Label = "From " & _
       Format(F_Date, "mmm-dd-yy") & " to " & _
       Format(T_Date, "mmm-dd-yy") & " (" & _
       (DateDiff("d", F_Date, T_Date) + 1) & " days)"
End Sub

Sub SetCalDates()
    'Purpose:   Use date format functions to display dates (faster)
    'Note: Moved from modPeriodSelect and "frmPeriodSelect." removed
    lblDateFrom(1).Caption = Format(F_Date, "mmm")
    lblDateFrom(2).Caption = Format(F_Date, "dd")
    lblDateFrom(3).Caption = Format(F_Date, "yy")
    tdpDateFrom.Caption = Format(F_Date, "dddd, mmm d, yyyy")

    lblDateTo(1).Caption = Format(T_Date, "mmm")
```

```
    lblDateTo(2).Caption = Format(T_Date, "dd")
    lblDateTo(3).Caption = Format(T_Date, "yy")
    tdpDateTo.Caption = Format(T_Date, "dddd, mmm d, yyyy")
    Date_Label = "From " & Format(F_Date, "mmm-dd-yy") & _
        " to " & Format(T_Date, "mmm-dd-yy") & _
        " (" & (DateDiff("d", F_Date, T_Date) + 1) & " days)"
End Sub
```

Declaring **Public** variables used by multiple instances of a class in an Automation component is not considered a generally accepted automation component programming practice (GAACPP). The problem with **Public** variables is that instances of other classes created by multiple client applications that refer to the **Public** variables might obtain values inappropriate to a particular class instance. If your component is SingleUse, the **Public** variable problem doesn't occur. Similarly, a MultiUse component having a single object doesn't suffer from **Public** variable problems because OLE 2+ serializes the application of methods to successive instances of classes. Diligent testing with multiple client applications (Access 97 and Visual Basic 6.0) of the MultiUse Per_svr.exe component created from Per_svr.vbp doesn't reveal a problem with the use of **Public** date variables.

Error Handling for the Period Selection Component

Other than generating an internal error message if the user attempts to set an invalid date with the spin button controls of Per_Svr.frm, the code for the Per_svr.vbp project doesn't include error trapping. Extensive testing and large-scale commercial deployment of the CycleTime front end indicates that error trapping is not necessary for the relatively simple event-handling code and the date-manipulation algorithms of the original source code.

If error handling is necessary, **On Error GoTo** *ProcName*Error statements can be added to suspect procedures. The error-handling code can pass the value of **Err.**Number to a generic error-processing procedure in PerSel.frm that returns the **Long** value of **Err.**Number to the Show method's return value prior to execution of an Unload frmPerSel statement.

CREATING A COMPLEX THREE-TIER AUTOMATION COMPONENT

Automation components that require multiple forms present a more formidable programming challenge than do invisible components or components that display only a single modal form. The Prod_svr.vbp project is an example of an Automation component that requires several forms and message boxes to provide the equivalent functionality of the original Product Grouping components. Prod_svr.vbp qualifies for three-tier status because it employs ADO 2.0 and the Jet 3.51 database engine as lower-level Automation components.

15

WRITING ACTIVE DLLs

> **NOTE**
>
> Three-tier architecture purists would argue that applications employing Prod_svr.exe don't qualify for three-tier status, because Prod_svr.exe cannot be run remotely on a networked application component. (As noted earlier in this chapter, Remote Automation components created with Visual Basic 6.0 cannot incorporate user-interface components.)

Prod_svr.vbp demonstrates an alternative to Per_svr.vbp's technique, described in the preceding sections, for dealing with explicit references to form names. Prod_svr.vbp includes three forms, Prod_svr.frm, Load_svr.frm, and Save_svr.frm. Load_svr.frm, a simple message form that advises users to wait while the Prod_svr.frm opens, cannot be modal; thus Load_svr.frm appears only when running Prod_svr.exe in standalone mode. (In standalone mode, Prod_svr.frm is opened as a modeless form.) Save_svr.frm, which lets users name custom product grouping selections for saving in their local CyclTime.mdb database, must reference a variety of controls on Prod_svr.frm.

The sections that follow describe the overall design of the CycleTime Product Grouping component and the changes to the original code that are necessary to transform these elements into an Automation component.

The Design of the Product Grouping Component

The Product Grouping component provides users with a means to specify multiple categories of semiconductor products for collective analysis. Products are classified in a six-level hierarchy in which the lowest (leaf) level is called AFM. AFMs use an arbitrary two-character alphanumeric code to specify a group of closely related products. The overall design of the Product Grouping component is applicable to a wide variety of database front ends that deal with hierarchical list selections.

The output of the Product Grouping component creates an SQL IN clause that consists of the field name followed by IN(, a comma-separated list of leaf-level AFMs enclosed in single quotes, and closing parenthesis. The IN clause text can be used as a criterion for an SQL statement created by any application capable of querying the component RDBMS. Following is an example of the IN criterion clause for the All Corporate (Test) grouping selection:

```
i_afm_c IN('M9', '0F', '17', '1H', '25', '2A', '2G',
'2X', '3N', '6X', '95', '99', '9A', '9D', '9N', '9X',
'E1', 'M1', 'TR', '10', '11', '3A', '3B', '3C', '7A')
```

Standard and user-specified grouping selections are stored in the tblGroupSelections table of the user's local CyclTime.mdb database. Each record includes the selection name (SelName), hierarchy structure name (StructName), item data to populate the list box (SelData), a list of selected AFMs (SelAFMs), a list of leaf-level AFMs corresponding to the selected AFMs (LeafAFMs), and the text of the SQL IN clause (LeafSQLIn). Items in the SelData, SelAFMs, and LeafAFMs fields are separated with backslashes (\). The FreqQueryTime and DetailQueryTime fields store the time in seconds for execution of the user's most recent summary and detail query against the client/server RDBMS.

> **NOTE**
>
> CyclTime.mdb and the source code for the Prod_svr.vbp project are included in the \DDV_VB4\32_bit\Chaptr15 folder of the accompanying CD-ROM. You can run Prod_svr.vbp as a standalone application. Alternatively, you can open and run Prod_svr.vbp as an ActiveX component and then open and run Test_PG.vbp in a separate instance of Visual Basic 6.0 to test Prod_svr.vbp as an Automation component. Make sure that the reference to the CycleTime Product Grouping component in Test_PG.vbp points to the location of Prod_svr.vbp on your computer.

Upon opening Prod_svr.frm, the left-hand Outline control (Available product groupings) displays a collapsed version of the entire product hierarchy of the firm. The items in the Outline control are derived from one or more lists of product structures contained in table(s) that periodically are updated by downloads from the server RDBMS. The tblNSORG0 table contains the data for the standard product structure in a nonrelational format containing repeating rows. This table is generated by a COBOL program from the firm's mainframe database as a flat (ASCII) file. The flat file is imported into Excel for review and then imported into a Jet table, which is subsequently exported to the server for distribution to users. The LoadAvailList subprocedure of frmProdGroup adds the items from the records of tblNSORG0 into the appropriate hierarchical level of the Outline control. (Most of the code included in the LoadAvailList subprocedure is based on a routine developed by an employee of the semiconductor firm and does not use conventional variable naming conventions.)

Double-clicking a folder in the Outline control expands or collapses the list hierarchy. Clicking the Level 1…Level 5 command buttons in the Available list shows an increasingly detailed view of the product hierarchy. Clicking the AFM button expands the list to display the entire product hierarchy. Right-clicking an item in the Available list (or selecting an item and clicking the Add -> button) copies the item(s) from the Available to the Selected Outline control. Selecting an item in the Selected list and clicking the Delete button removes the item and any subordinate items. Changes to the Selected list mark the grouping "dirty." The user saves the revised product grouping by clicking the Save Selection button or clicking the OK button. In either case, the Save Current Selection form (SaveSel.frm) appears, as shown in Figure 15.9. Save_svr.frm contains the code necessary to update an existing grouping record and to create a new record in tblGroupSelections.

FIGURE 15.9

The Save_svr.frm for saving a new or modified product grouping to the tblGroupSelections table of CyclTime.mdb.

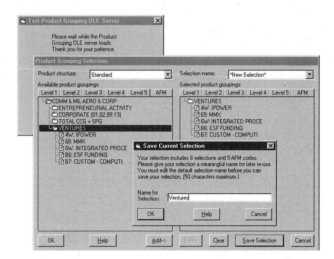

Adding the **Show** Method to the **ProductGrouping** Class

The original code of SAVE_SEL.FRM contains many references to frmProdGroup, the main form of the component. To minimize the amount of code rewriting and testing time in the conversion of the product grouping function to an Automation component, the instance of the form class is made accessible to all form and module code by adding a **Public** gfrmGrouping **As New** frmProdGroup statement in the declarations section of the Prod_svr.bas module, instead of using the conventional **Dim** frmGrouping **As New** frmProdGroup statement in the class module. Declaring the main form variable as **Public** allows replacement of Save_svr.frm's frmProdGroup references with gfrmGrouping. Declaring as **Public** object variables referenced by class modules isn't recommended as a standard practice when creating new Automation components. The ability to use this technique, however, makes the conversion of existing, complex Visual Basic application components to Automation components a relatively easy process.

All the data created or updated by an instance of frmProdGroup is contained in the current record of the tblGroupSelections of CyclTime.mdb, so it's not necessary to provide arguments for the Show method or to expose other properties of the ProductGrouping class. Following is the simplified code for the function in Prod_svr.cls to create the Show method, which appears as follows:

```
Public Function Show() As Long
    gfOK = False
    'Show frmProdGroup modally
    gfrmGrouping.Show vbModal
    'Set True by OK button
    Show = gfOK
    Unload gfrmGrouping
End Function
```

Tests that compare the speed of launching the Product Grouping form in its original implementation (from the CycTim32.vbp project) and the MultiUse version (from Test_PG.vbp) show that it takes about 20% longer to open the first instance of the component version. (Running on a 128MB 266-MHz Pentium II PC, the opening time is about 1 second for the original version and 1.2 seconds for the component version.) Although performance is one of the major criteria in database application design, the benefits of using component architecture in building complex database applications usually outweigh their somewhat slower response time.

Creating User Controls for Database Applications

IN THIS APPENDIX

Visual Basic 5.0 introduced user controls, which emulate conventional ActiveX controls written in C++. User controls are ActiveX DLLs that expose events, in addition to the properties and methods of conventional in-process Automation components discussed in the preceding chapter, "Writing Local Automation Components and ActiveX DLLs." Visual Basic user controls, compiled as .ocx files, differ from their C++ counterparts by requiring the presence of the Visual Basic runtime engine (Msvbvm60.dll) on the user's computer. Like in-process Automation servers, ActiveX controls can be used with any 32-bit Windows application that supports Automation. Although it's possible to employ user controls in Internet applications, the download time for Msvbvm60.dll—about 8 minutes for 1.4MB at 28.8kbps—and lack of native support by Netscape Navigator makes user controls more appropriate for intranet applications.

 The new DataRepeater ActiveX control requires you to design and compile a user control to use with the DataRepeater, and the DataRepeater depends on the `BindingCollection` object to make the connection to the repeated control. Thus this chapter begins with examples of simple user controls designed to emulate Access continuous forms and subforms. The remainder of this chapter describes the `BindingCollection` object in the context of ActiveX controls and how to take full advantage of the improved data-binding features in Visual Basic 6.0.

EMULATING AN ACCESS CONTINUOUS FORM WITH THE DATAREPEATER CONTROL

Two of Microsoft Access's most used features are the continuous form and subform. Continuous forms display multiple rows of a `Recordset` with fields bound to successive instances of individual controls. Typically, text field values appear in text box controls, Yes/No (**Boolean**) fields in check boxes, and OLE Object fields in Access's Bound Object Frames. Continuous forms also let you substitute combo boxes for text boxes to provide a pick list of valid foreign key values. Continuous forms provide a fully formatted substitute for datasheets, the Access counterpart of Visual Basic's DataGrid control.

Access 97's Northwind.mdb sample database includes two examples of continuous forms. The Product List form has three text boxes and a check box, which bind to the ProductName, QuantityPerUnit, and UnitPrice fields of the Products table, respectively. A check box binds to the Discontinued field. Figure 16.1 shows the Product List form in run and design modes. You navigate through the 77 records of the Products table by moving the vertical scrollbar of the form. As you reposition the scrollbar, values from successive sets of rows appear in each visible instance of the form. As you increase the depth of the form, additional instances of the form become visible. Increasing the width of the form automatically expands the width of the Detail section of the form that contains the repeating control instances.

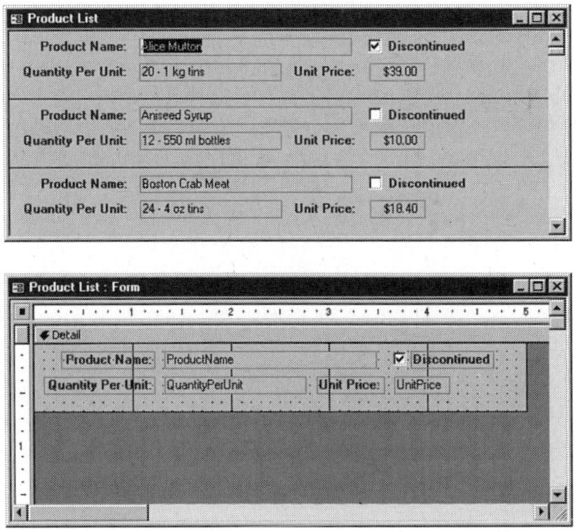

FIGURE 16.1

*Access 97's
Product List con-
tinuous form in
run mode (top)
and design mode
(bottom).*

Access offers form headers and footers in which you add single-instance controls, such as labels for column headings in form headers and total text boxes and/or form navigation controls in form footers. Figure 16.2 shows the Customer Phone List form in run and design modes. This form has Form and Page Headers, a Detail section, and Page and Form Footers. The Page Header and Footer don't appear in run mode; these elements are visible only on printed versions of the form. The buttons at the bottom of the form apply an alphabetic filter to the Recordset. The Form Footer includes Access's standard record navigation buttons, which are superfluous in this design; the buttons and scrollbar provide full navigation capability.

FIGURE 16.2

*Access 97's
Customer Phone
List form in run
mode (top) and
design mode (bot-
tom).*

Visual Basic's DataRepeater control provides a container for hosting multiple instances of a compiled user control to create the equivalent of the Detail section of an Access continuous form or subform. You must add controls to the form to emulate a Form Header and Footer. Visual Basic doesn't provide equivalents of Page Headers and Footers, nor does Visual Basic offer Access's built-in continuous-form printing capabilities.

> **NOTE**
>
> The following two sections are derived from Visual Basic 6.0's online help topic Using the DataRepeater Control. The version of the help topic used to write the book (the commercial release of Visual Studio 6.0) has a critical omission (marking the This Property Binds to Data Field check box for one property), which causes the data-bound user control to fail when not used with the DataRepeater control. This omission is corrected in the "Adding a DataRepeater Control to Host the ActiveX Control" section.

Designing and Compiling a Simple User Control

The first step in the process of creating a continuous data-bound form is to design a user control to display and, optionally, update fields of a single record. The ProductList user control requires three text boxes and a check box to display the ProductName, QuantityPerUnit, UnitPrice, and Discontinued fields of the Products table. Each control requires a **Public Property Let** property procedure to read the field value and optional **Public Property Get** property procedure to update the field value. ControlName_*Changed* event handlers trap user updates to field values.

> **NOTE**
>
> The stateless Automation components described in the preceding chapter use method arguments to transfer data to and from the host application. User controls, which are stateful, require property procedures to pass data values to and from the control.

Write a simple user control for the DataRepeater by following these steps:

1. Open a new ActiveX Control project and rename the default UserControl1 to **ProductList**. Size the control to approximate the dimensions of the Access Product List form of Figure 16.1 (7,125 by 960 twips).

2. Add three text boxes (txtData) and labels (lblCaption) as control arrays to the form with indexes 0, 1, and 2.

3. Add a single check box (chkData) as a single-member control array with an index of 0.

> **NOTE**
>
> Control arrays speed addition of controls and contribute to reusability of the design of the user control.

4. Align the controls to correspond with those of the Access Product list (see Figure 16.3).

FIGURE 16.3

The ProductList user control in design mode.

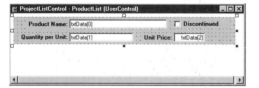

5. Add **Property Let** and **Property Get** property procedures for each field, plus txtData(*n*)_Changed and chkData(0)_Changed event handlers to the control (see Listing 16.1). The property names—Name, Package, Price, and Disc—need not match the field names.

6. Choose <u>T</u>ools, Procedure <u>A</u>ttributes to open the Procedure Attributes dialog and then click Advanced to expand the dialog.

7. Select Name in the Name list and then mark the Property Is Data Bound, This Property Binds to Data Field, and Show in Bindings Collection at Design Time check boxes (see Figure 16.4). Optionally, add a brief description of the property. Click Apply to set the property values.

FIGURE 16.4

Adding a property to the user control's BindingCollection *object.*

NOTE

You don't need to mark the This Property Binds to Data Field check box to make the compiled control operable with the DataRepeater control. However, you *must* mark This Property Binds to Data Field for one (and only one) property to make the control operable as a single-instance user control or compiled ActiveX control. Designating a property with This Property Binds to Data Field connects the DataSource to the control. Failure to mark This Property Binds to Data Field for one property results in a user control that won't display data.

---

8. Repeat step 7 for the Package, Price, and Disc subprocedures, but don't mark the This Property Binds to Data Field check box. Click OK to close the Procedure Attributes dialog.

9. In the User Control property sheet, change the Public property value to **True**.

10. Press Ctr+F5 to compile and run your control. Click OK when the Debugging page of the Project Properties sheet appears. The compiled control appears by default in Internet Explorer (see Figure 16.5).

FIGURE 16.5
*The ProductList
control displayed
in Internet
Explorer 4.01.*

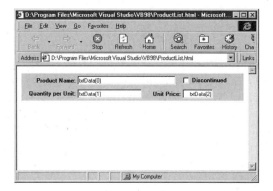

11. In the Project1 Properties sheet, name the project **ProdListCtl** and accept the default values for compiling ActiveX controls. ActiveX controls don't require a Startup Object. The name of the type library for the control becomes ProdListCtl.ProductList.

12. Save the user control as **ProdList.ctl** and the project as **ProdList.vbp** in a folder other than \Ddg_vb6\Chaptr16.

13. Choose File, Make ProdList.ocx to compile ProdList.ctl to an ActiveX control and then close ProdList.vbp.

LISTING 16.1 INITIAL VBA CODE FOR THE PRODUCTLIST USER CONTROL

```
Public Property Get Name() As String
   'ProductName field (string, for update)
   Name = txtData(0).Text
End Property


Public Property Let Name(ByVal newName As String)
   'ProductName field
   txtData(0).Text = newName
End Property


Public Property Get Package() As String
   'QuantityPerUnit field (string, for update)
   Package = txtData(1).Text
End Property


Public Property Let Package(ByVal newPackage As String)
   'QuantityPerUnit field
   txtData(1).Text = newPackage
End Property


Public Property Get Price() As String
   'UnitPrice field (string for update)
   Price = txtData(2).Text
```

continues

LISTING 16.1 CONTNUED

```
End Property

Public Property Let Price(ByVal newPrice As String)
    'UnitPrice field (update)
    txtData(2).Text = newPrice
End Property

Public Property Get Disc() As Integer
    'Discontinued field (Yes/No, update)
    '1/0 conversion to Boolean True/False is handled by the Format object
    Disc = chkData(0).Value
End Property

Public Property Let Disc(ByVal newDisc As Integer)
    'Discontinued field
    '1/0 conversion to Boolean True/False is handled by the Format object
    chkData(0).Value = newDisc
End Property

Private Sub txtData_Change(intIndex As Integer)
    'Trap text box change for update
    Select Case intIndex
        Case 0
            PropertyChanged "Name"
        Case 1
            PropertyChanged "Package"
        Case 2
            PropertyChanged "Price"
    End Select
End Sub

Private Sub chkData_Change(intIndex As Integer)
    'Trap check box change for update
    Select Case intIndex
        Case 0
            PropertyChanged "Disc"
    End Select
End Sub
```

NOTE

ProdList.vbp, ProdList.ctl, and ProdList.ocx are included in the
\Ddg_vb6\Chaptr16 folder of the accompanying CD-ROM. You must recompile
ProdList.ocx from ProdList.vbp or run **RegSvr32 ProdList.ocx** from the folder
containing the control to register ProdList.ocx.

Adding a DataRepeater Control to Host the ActiveX Control

An invisible DataRepeater control hosts multiple instances of the ActiveX control and binds the fields of the Recordset to the appropriate **Public** property through a BindingCollection object.

1. Open a new Data Project, remove DataReport1, and rename frmDataEnv to **frmDataRepeater**. Type **Simple DataRepeater Project** as the Caption for the form.

2. In the DataEnvironment1 window, change the name of the DataEnvironment object to **envJet** and create a Connection named cnnNwind to the Nwind.mdb sample database. Use the Jet 3.51 OLE DB provider for the Connection.

3. Add a Command named **Products** to cnnNwind having the following SQL statement:
   ```
   SELECT ProductName, QuantityPerUnit, UnitPrice, Discontinued
       FROM Products
   ```

4. In the Advanced page of the Products Properties sheet for the Command, set the Lock Type value to 3 - Optimistic. Make sure the Cursor Location property is set to the default 3 - Use Client-Side Cursors. (Server-side cursors don't work properly with the DataRepeater control.)

5. Add a DataRepeater control from the Toolbox to the form. Size the form and control to contain approximately three instances of ProdList.ocx.

6. In the Properties window for DataRepeater1, change the Name property value to **drpProdList**, set DataSource to envJet and DataMember to Products to bind the DataRepeater control to the DataEnvironment object.

7. Open the RepeatedControl list and select ProdListCtl.ProductList as the ActiveX control to be repeated. The RepeatedControl list uses the ProgrammaticID (ProgID), not the name, of the control for identification.

8. Open the Properties sheet for drpProdList. In the General page, type **Northwind Product List** as the Caption and set CaptionStyle to 3 - drpCentered. In the Font page, the settings of which apply only to the caption, mark the Bold check box.

9. Click the RepeaterBindings tab, select Name in the PropertyName list, select ProductName in the DataField list, and click Add to bind the ProductName field to the Name property.

10. Repeat step 9 for Package and QuantityPerUnit, Price and UnitPrice, and Disc and Discontinued (see Figure 16.6). Click OK to set the bindings.

FIGURE 16.6

Binding properties to fields in the DataRepeater control's RepeaterBindings page.

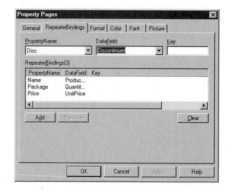

11. Click the Format tab, select `Price` in the Format Item list, select Currency in the Format Type list, and click Apply. The data type of `Price` must be **String** to apply the Currency format.

12. Select `Disc` in Format Item, select Checkbox in Format Type, and click Apply. Specifying the Checkbox format handles the discrepancy between check box values (marked = 1, cleared = 0) and **Boolean** values (**True** = -1, and **False** = 0) of the Discontinued field. Click OK to close the Properties sheet.

13. Press Ctrl+F5 to compile and run the project. The form with the DataRepeater control appears as shown in Figure 16.7.

FIGURE 16.7

The DataRepeater control in run mode containing three instances of the ProdList.ocx control.

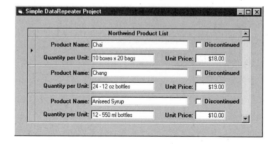

14. Save your project in a folder other than \Ddg_vb6\Chaptr16, naming `frmDataRepeater` as **DataRptr.frm**, envJet as **DataRptr.env**, and the project as **DataRptr.vbp**.

Overcoming Recordset Update Failures

The version of the DataBindings collection used to write this book doesn't persist Recordset updates in underlying tables. Although instances of changes to individual values of the ProductList control persist during scrolling and *Recordset_RecordChangeComplete* events reflect the changed values, changes don't propagate through the DataBinding object to the table underlying the Recordset. The workaround for this problem is inelegant, at best.

Listing 16.2 shows the code necessary in the `DataEnvironment` to compare property and field values in the Immediate window and a workaround to persist changes. Attempting to change values in the `WillChangeRecord` event handler causes reentrancy, and you can't call the `Recordset.Update` method in `RecordChangeComplete`. Thus the only `Recordset` event handler that fires before changing the current record and permits forced `Recordset` updates is the `WillMove` event. The `WillMove` event fires repeatedly during initialization of the DataRepeater control bound to the `Recordset`, so you must detect completion of the DataRepeater's initialization process within the *DataRepeater*_`RepeatedControlLoaded` event handler, as illustrated by the following code in `frmDataRepeater`:

```
Private Sub drpProdList_RepeatedControlLoaded()
   'blnLoaded is declared Public is the modDataRepeater module
   blnLoaded = True
End Sub
```

LISTING 16.2   CODE IN envJet TO COMPARE Recordset AND PROPERTY VALUES AND TO FORCE UPDATES TO THE TABLE UNDERLYING THE Recordset

```
Private Sub rsProducts_RecordChangeComplete _
   (ByVal adReason As ADODB.EventReasonEnum, _
   ByVal cRecords As Long, _
   ByVal pError As ADODB.Error, _
        adStatus As ADODB.EventStatusEnum, _
   ByVal pRecordset As ADODB.Recordset)

   'Activate the line below to compare field values
   'Call DebugChanges(True)
End Sub

Private Sub rsProducts_WillChangeRecord _
   (ByVal adReason As ADODB.EventReasonEnum, _
   ByVal cRecords As Long, _
        adStatus As ADODB.EventStatusEnum, _
   ByVal pRecordset As ADODB.Recordset)

   'Activate the line below to compare field values
   'Call DebugChanges(False)
End Sub

Private Sub DebugChanges(blnComplete As Boolean)
   With frmDataRepeater.drpProdList.RepeatedControl
      Debug.Print ""
      If blnComplete Then
         Debug.Print "RecordChangeComplete Event"
      Else
         Debug.Print "WillChangeRecord Event"
      End If
      Debug.Print .Name, rsProducts.Fields(0)
```

continues

LISTING 16.2 CONTINUED

```
        Debug.Print .Package, rsProducts.Fields(1)
        Debug.Print .Price, rsProducts.Fields(2)
        Debug.Print .Disc, rsProducts.Fields(3)
    End With
End Sub

Private Sub rsProducts_WillMove _
  (ByVal adReason As ADODB.EventReasonEnum, _
        adStatus As ADODB.EventStatusEnum, _
    ByVal pRecordset As ADODB.Recordset)

    If blnLoaded Then
        'Test for changes and update field accordingly
        With frmDataRepeater.drpProdList.RepeatedControl
            If .Name <> rsProducts.Fields(0).Value Then
                rsProducts.Fields(0).Value = .Name
                rsProducts.Update
            End If
            If .Package <> rsProducts.Fields(1).Value Then
                rsProducts.Fields(1).Value = .Package
                rsProducts.Update
            End If
            'Handle the String to Currency conversion
            If CCur(Mid(.Price, 2)) <> rsProducts.Fields(2).Value Then
                rsProducts.Fields(2).Value = CCur(Mid(.Price, 2))
                rsProducts.Update
            End If
            'Handle the CheckBox.Value to Boolean issue
            If .Disc = 1 Then
                If rsProducts.Fields(2).Value = False Then
                    rsProducts.Fields(2).VALUE = True
                    rsProducts.Update
                End If
            Else
                If rsProducts.Fields(2).Value = True Then
                    rsProducts.Fields(2).Value = False
                    rsProducts.Update
                End If
            End If
        End With
    End If
End Sub
```

The code of the rsProducts_WillMove event handler is complicated by the differences between the property and field data types of the Price/UnitPrice and Disc/Discontinued pairs. The Format object of the DataBindings collection ordinarily conforms property to field data types, and vice versa. The "Debugging Data-Bound ActiveX Controls" section later in the chapter also requires code to conform the property and field data types.

> **NOTE**
>
> The workaround of Listing 16.2 won't be necessary after Microsoft releases an up-dated version of the `BindingCollection` object or defines the object property values necessary to persist `Recordset` changes. The sample code in online help's Using the DataRepeater Control topic currently doesn't persist changes.

AUTOMATING CONTROL GENERATION WITH WIZARDS

The Access Phone List form, illustrated by Figure 16.2, is an example of a continuous form whose content varies as a result of user action. Clicking one of the A...Z buttons applies the `Filter` method to the underlying `Recordset`, displaying only those records whose CompanyName value begins the with selected letter. Clicking the All button removes the filter. Field values are updatable in the Access Phone List form, but conventional phone lists are read-only. The sections that follow describe how to design a read-only, data-bound list control; automatically add code to support standard and control-specific properties with the ActiveX Control Interface Wizard; and add a properties sheet for the control.

Designing Repeated Controls to Save Form Real Estate

Each instance of the ProductList control repeats field captions, which occupy excessive space on the form and reduce the number of visible instances of the control. You minimize the amount of scrolling required to display a specific instance by arranging the fields in a single row and using the caption of the DataRepeater control to show individual captions for each field. Figure 16.8 shows the design of the PhoneList user control, which has a control array of four labels—`lblField(0)`...`lblField(3)`— to display the CompanyName, ContactName, Phone, and Fax fields of Nwind.mdb's Customers table. Set the `Caption` property to the name of the control. The form's `BackColor` property is light gray in the figure to illustrate the spacing of the labels. Set the `BackColor` property of the form and the labels to `&H80000005&` prior to compiling PhnList.ocx.

FIGURE 16.8

The PhoneList user control in design mode.

> **NOTE**
>
> A more logical approach would be to set the `BackStyle` property value of the form and labels to 0 - Transparent to let the background color of the DataRepeater control appear. Using a transparent form and labels, however, results in the DataRepeater control obscuring the selected instance with a gray bar. Thus the `BackStyle` property of all user control objects is set to 1 - Opaque.

Table 16.1 lists the locations and dimensions in twips of the form and labels for the PhoneList user control. After setting property values of the user control and its label controls, name the control **PhoneList** and the project **PhnListCtl** and then save the control as **PhnList.ctl** and the project as **PhnList.vbp** in a folder other than \Ddg_vb6\Chaptr16.

TABLE 16.1   LEFT, TOP, WIDTH, AND HEIGHT PROPERTY VALUES FOR THE PHONELIST USER CONTROL

Object	Left	Top	Width	Height
User Control	N/A	N/A	8,100	255
lblField(0)	120	0	2,535	255
lblField(1)	2,760	0	1,815	255
lblField(2)	4,680	0	1,575	255
lblField(3)	6,360	0	1,575	255

Using the ActiveX Control Interface Wizard

The ActiveX Control Interface Wizard writes all the VBA code required to specify a set of **Property Let** and **Property Get** procedures for standard and custom properties of a user control. You must add all required native and other ActiveX controls to the user control before running the Wizard.

To add a set of standard property procedures for ActiveX controls, add custom properties for the label controls, persist standard property values with `PropertyBag` objects, and specify data binding for the labels, do the following:

1. Install the ActiveX Control Interface Wizard, if necessary, by choosing Add-Ins, Add-In Manager; double-clicking the VB6 ActiveX Ctrl Interface Wizard item in the Available Add-Ins list; and clicking OK to add the Wizard to the Add-Ins menu.

2. With the PhoneList control active, choose Add-Ins, ActiveX Control Interface Wizard to open the Introduction dialog. Click Next to open the Select Interface Members dialog.

3. The Wizard provides a default set of Selected Names from the Available Names list (see Figure 16.9). Unless you have a particular reason to change the list, accept the default set and click Next to open the Create Custom Interface Members dialog with an empty My Custom Members list.

FIGURE 16.9

Part of the default set of properties specified by the ActiveX Control Interface Wizard.

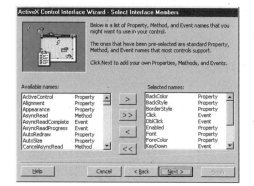

4. Click New to open the Add Custom Member dialog, type **Field0** as the name of the member for the `lblField(0).Caption` property, and click OK to close the dialog.

5. Repeat step 4 for the three remaining labels, naming the members **Field1**, **Field2**, and **Field3** (see Figure 16.10).

FIGURE 16.10

Adding the Field0...Field3 custom members to the control.

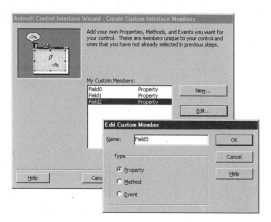

6. If you want to expose the `BackColor` property of each label, add `Field0BackColor...Field3BackColor` custom members to the control. Click Next to open the Set Mapping dialog.

7. Select each of the standard members in sequence from the Public Name list, select User Control from the Control list, and accept the default corresponding property in the Member list.

8. Select `Field0...Field3` in sequence from the Public Name list, select `lblField(0)...lblField(3)` from the Control list, and select `Caption` as the Member (see Figure 16.11).

FIGURE 16.11

Mapping the
`Field0...Field3`
custom members
to the `Caption`
property of the
`lblField(0)...`
`lblField(3)`
controls.

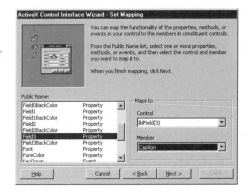

9. If you added the `Field(n)BackColor` members in step 6, select `Field0BackColor...Field3BackColro` in sequence from the Public Name list, select `lblField(0)...lblField(3)` from the Control list, and select `BackColor` as the Member. Click Next.

10. If you mapped all of the standard and custom members in steps 7, 8, and 9, the Finished dialog appears.

    If you missed any members, the Set Attributes dialog appears. If you see the Set Attributes dialog, click Back and map the member(s) whose Control value is (None).

11. Click Finish with the View Summary Report check box marked to open the ActiveX Control Interface Wizard Summary dialog, which contains a laundry list of to-do items. You can save the file to Ctlwiz.txt file for later review. Click OK to dismiss the Wizard.

12. Open the code editing window for PhoneList and review the **Event** declarations, **Property Get** and **Property Let** procedures the Wizard added, and the `UserControl_ReadProperties` and `UserControl_WriteProperties` event handlers, which persist default property values in `PropertyBag` objects.

13. The Wizard has a problem with property values of control arrays, so change the multiple `lblField(0)` (Caption) properties to `lblField(0)...lblField(3)` in the `UserControl_ReadProperties` and `UserControl_WriteProperties` event handlers (see the three highlighted lines in Figure 16.12).

Creating User Controls for Database Applications

CHAPTER 16

613

16

CREATING USER
CONTROLS FOR
DATABASE APPS

FIGURE 16.12

Fixing the
`Property Bag`'s
*Caption property
values for the*
`lblField(n)`
control array

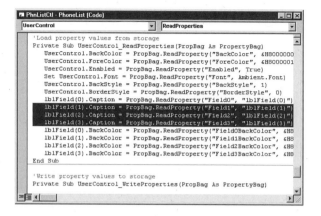

14. Choose <u>T</u>ools, Procedure <u>A</u>ttributes to open the Procedure Attributes dialog.

15. Select `Field0` in the Name list, mark the Property Is Data Bound, This Property Binds to DataField, and Show in DataBindings Collection at Design Time check boxes. The description added by the Wizard isn't appropriate to data-bound members, so change the description, if you want.

16. Repeat step 15 for `Field1`...`Field3`, but don't mark the This Property Binds to DataField check box.

17. Press Ctrl+F5 to compile and run the user control in Internet Explorer. If you made the corrections to the code in step 13, you see only the three default caption values against IE's white background.

18. Choose <u>R</u>un, <u>E</u>nd; then choose <u>F</u>ile, Ma<u>k</u>e PhnList.ocx and save the project.

Creating a Production Form for the Customer Phone List

Emulating the Access Customer Phone List form requires, in addition to a DataRepeater control, adding 26 command buttons labeled <u>A</u>...<u>Z</u> to apply an alphabetic filter to the `Recordset`, plus an All <u>2</u>6 button to display all records.

1. Open a new Data Project, remove `DataReport1`, rename `frmDataEnv` to **frmPhoneList**, and rename `DataEnvironment1` to **envPhoneList**.

2. Change the name of `Connection1` to **cnnNwind**, open cnnNwind's Properties sheet. Select the Jet OLE DB provider and specify Nwind.mdb as the database.

3. Add a `Command` named **PhoneList** to cnnNwind and type the following as its SQL statement:

```
SELECT CompanyName, ContactName, Phone, Fax
    FROM Customers
```

4. Accept the remaining default `Command` properties, 3 - Use Client-Side Cursors as the Cursor Location and 1 - Read-Only as the Lock Type, and click OK.

5. Size `frmPhoneList` to about 8,655 by 5,775 twips and change its `Caption` to **Northwind Traders Customer Phone List**.

6. Add a DataRepeater control to the form, set its `Name` property to **drpPhoneList**, size the control to about 8,055 by 4,560 twips, and open its Properties window.

7. Set the `DataSource` property to `envPhoneList` and the `DataMember` property to `PhoneList`. Open the `RepeatedControlName` list and select PhnListCtl.PhoneList.

8. Open the `drpPhoneList` Properties sheet. On the General page, set Appearance to 0 - drpFlat and clear the RowIndicator check box. Row indicators aren't required for read-only forms.

9. On the Font page, mark the Bold check box attribute for the caption and then return to the General page. Type the following as value of the `Caption` property:

   ```
   Company Name    Contact Name    Telephone    Fax
   ```

   Adjust the number of spaces between the individual field captions to align the first character with that of the label names below. (Click Apply after you add spaces to check the alignment.) Run the project to check your work so far.

10. At the bottom of the form, add 26 small buttons as a control array (`cmdFilter(0)`...`cmdFilter(25)`) with `Caption` property values of `?`, and a single `cmdNoFilter` button with an `All 26` Caption. The design of your form should resemble that shown in Figure 16.13.

FIGURE 16.13

The Northwind Customer Telephone List form in design mode.

11. Add the code of Listing 16.3 to the form to resize, relocate, and add A...Z captions to the command buttons, apply the appropriate filter, and remove the filter to display all records.

LISTING 16.3 CODE TO MANIPULATE COMMAND BUTTONS AND APPLY OR REMOVE THE
Recordset Filter IN frmPhoneList

```
Private strFilter As String

Private Sub Form_Load()
    'Set up the filter buttons
    Dim intCtr As Integer
    Dim intLeft As Integer
    intLeft = cmdFilter(0).Left
    For intCtr = 0 To 25
        With cmdFilter(intCtr)
            .Caption = "&" & Chr(intCtr + 65)
            .Width = 220
            .Left = intLeft + 285 * intCtr
        End With
    Next intCtr
End Sub

Private Sub cmdFilter_Click(intIndex As Integer)
    'Apply the alphabetic filter
    strFilter = "CompanyName Like '" & Chr(intIndex + 65) & "*'"
    With envPhoneList.rsPhoneList
        .Filter = ""
        .Filter = strFilter
    End With
End Sub

Private Sub cmdNoFilter_Click()
    'Remove the filter
    With envPhoneList.rsPhoneList
        .Filter = adFilterNone
        .Requery
    End With
    'If you don't reconnect the DataSource, either
    'the first record or no records appear, even if
    'you apply the .Refresh method
    With drpPhoneList
        'Make the DataRepeater display all records
        Set .DataSource = Nothing
        Set .DataSource = envPhoneList
        .Refresh
    End With
End Sub
```

> **NOTE**
>
> You must disconnect and then reconnect the DataSource of the DataRepeater control when removing the filter. Setting the *Recordset*.Filter property to adFilterNone, with or without calling the *Recordset*.Requery method, results in either one or no records appearing in the DataRepeater control, regardless of a call to the *DataRepeater*.Refresh method.

12. Press Ctrl+F5 to compile and run the project. The frmPhoneList form appears as shown in Figure 16.14.

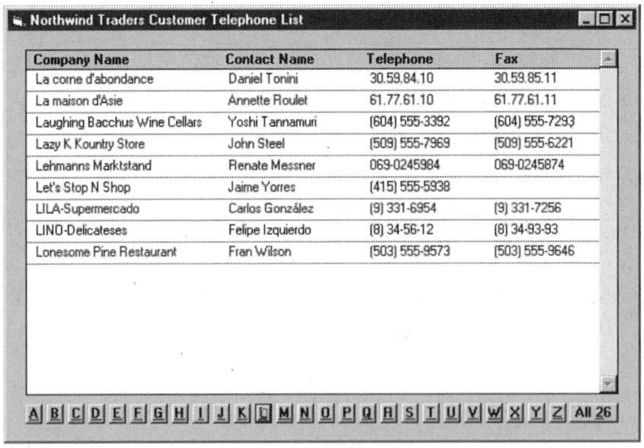

FIGURE 16.14

The Northwind Customer Telephone List form in design mode.

> **NOTE**
>
> PhnList.vbp, PhnList.ctl, PhnList.ocx, PhnRptr.vbp, PhnRptr.frm, and PhnRptr.dsr are included in the \Ddg_vb6\Chaptr16 folder of the accompanying CD-ROM. You must recompile PhnList.ocx from PhnList.vbp or run **RegSvr32 PhnList.ocx** from the folder containing the control to register PhnList.ocx.

Adding Property Pages with the Property Page Wizard

Commercial ActiveX controls offer one or more property pages to set static property values in design mode. To add standard and custom property pages to PhnList.ctl, follow these steps:

1. If necessary, use the Add-In Manager to add the Property Page Wizard to the <u>A</u>dd-Ins menu.

2. Open the PhnList.vbp project and then open PhnList.ctl.

3. Launch the Property Page Wizard and click Next to open the Select the Property Pages dialog.

4. Accept the two default standard pages, StandardColor and StandardFont and click Add to open the Property Page Name dialog.

5. Type PhnList in the text box and click OK to add PhnList to the list box.

6. Select PhnList and click the up arrow twice to move PhnList to the top of the list box (see Figure 16.15). Click next to open the Add Properties dialog.

FIGURE 16.15

Specifying a custom and two standard property pages for the PhoneList control.

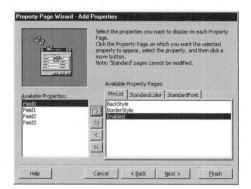

7. In the PhnList page, select `BackStyle` and click the > button to add the `BackStyle` property to the PhnList list.

8. Repeat step 7 for the `BorderStyle` and `Enabled` properties (see Figure 16.16).

FIGURE 16.16

Adding custom properties to the PhnList page.

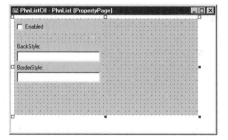

9. Click the StandardColor tab to verify that the StandardColor page includes all the properties for which you want the ability to change the color.

10. Click Next to open the Finished! dialog. You have the option of displaying the Wizard's Summary Report. Click Finish to add the pages to your control and to save the Summary Report if you want.

Clicking Finish also adds a Property Pages node and PhnList item to the Project Explorer window.

11. Double-click the PhnList Property Page item to open the custom property page form, which displays a check box for the `Enabled` property and two text boxes for entering `BackStyle` and `BorderStyle` property values (see Figure 16.17).

FIGURE 16.17

The Property Page Wizard's hack at creating a custom property page for setting Boolean and Integer values.

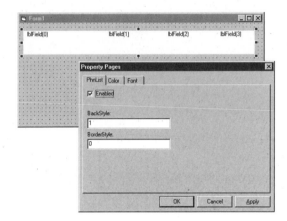

12. Save the project and accept the default filename to save the custom properties page, PhnList.pag.

13. Compile PhnList.ctl to PhnList.ocx and then open a new Standard EXE project.

14. Add the Phone List control to the project's Components, add an instance of the control to Form1, and then right-click the control to open the properties page.

NOTE

Properties set in the Properties page also appear in the Properties window for the control.

---

15. To test the Property Pages, click the PhnList tab and change the value of the `BorderStyle` property from 0 to 1. Click the Color tab and change the color of each item in the Properties list to light gray (Scroll Bars with Windows System Colors), the default background color of Visual Basic forms. The control now appears as illustrated by Figure 16.18.

16. Run the project to verify that the new properties settings work in run mode.

FIGURE 16.18
*Testing operation
of the properties
page of
PhnList.ocx.*

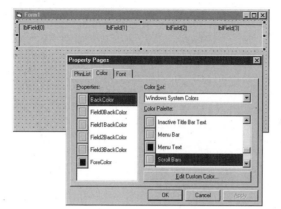

NOTE

The PhnList.pag properties page is rudimentary at best. A complete properties sheet would include the ability to set the ForeColor and Font properties of each label of the control, as well as the Width, Height, and Left values. Increasing the Height value of a label requires a corresponding increase in the Height of the user control. To make the control generic for any type of list, you can add a few more labels and set the Visible property of each label in the properties sheet.

EXPLORING THE BindingCollection OBJECT

Visual Basic 6.0's BindingCollection object enhances the data-binding features introduced in Visual Basic 5.0. Visual Basic 5.0 required all data-bound controls to use a Data or Remote Data control as their data source. Visual Basic 6.0's BindingCollection lets you bind any OLE DB data source to any OLE DB data consumer, including ActiveX controls. You must use ADO 2+ to take full advantage of the new BindingCollection. The preceding sections of this chapter provide examples of practical uses for the BindingCollection with ActiveX controls. The frmDataRepeater and frmPhoneList forms enable you to examine the properties of each BindingCollection in run mode.

> **NOTE**
>
> The name `BindingCollection` departs from Microsoft's recommended naming convention for collections—the plural of the member object (`Binding` in this case). The `BindingCollection` object differs from most other collections because it has additional properties and methods specific to ADO data binding.

Properties, Methods, and Events of the `BindingCollection`, `Binding`, and `StdDataFormat` Objects

The `BindingCollection` is a data consumer (from the `DataSource`) and a data provider (to a native control, ActiveX control, or Automation component). Table 16.2 lists the members of the `BindingCollection` object in alphabetical order. Axll properties are read/write in run mode unless otherwise indicated in the Description column. Like other ADO data consumers, you can change the `DataMember` and `DataSource` properties in run mode.

TABLE 16.2   PROPERTIES, METHODS, AND EVENTS OF THE `BindingCollection` OBJECT

Member	Type	Description
Add	Method	Adds a new `Binding` object to the collection
Clear	Method	Removes all `Binding` objects from the collection
Count	Property	Returns the number of `Binding` objects in the collection
DataMember	Property (Object)	Points to a `Command` object of a `DataEnvironment` object when a `DataEnvironment` object serves as the `DataSource` (requires **Set**)
DataSource	Property (Object)	Points to the `DataEnvironment` or `Recordset` data provider (requires **Set**)
Error	Event	Returns the error number, description, and `Binding` object when a runtime error occurs
Item	Property (Object)	Returns a `Binding` object based on a numeric or an optional **String** Index argument (Key) set in the properties page for the `Binding`. Item is the default property and is read-only in run mode.
Remove	Method	Removes the `Binding` object specified by the Index argument
UpdateControls	Method	Refetches data from the `DataSource` and updates the control(s) of the data consumer

Member	Type	Description
UpdateMode	Property	Determines the condition under which the bound Recordset object is updated. Values are members of the UpdateMode enumeration (vbUpdateWhenPropertyChanges, vbUpdateWhenRowChanges, or vbUsePropertyAttributes).

NOTE

All Binding members of a BindingCollection must share the same DataMember and DataSource objects.

Binding objects connect a particular DataField object of the data provider to a data consumer, such as a bound TextBox or a property of an ActiveX control or Automation component. Table 16.3 lists the properties of the Binding object, which are read-write in run mode unless otherwise noted in the Description column.

TABLE 16.3 PROPERTIES OF THE Binding OBJECT

Property	Description
DataChanged	Returns **True** if the data has changed as a result of editing or other operation (not changing the current record)
DataField	Sets or returns the name of the field to which the consumer is bound
DataFormat	Sets or returns a StdDataFormat object
Key	Sets or returns a **String** description of the Binding, which must be unique within a BindingCollection
Object	Returns a pointer to the bound object (read-only)
PropertyName	Returns the Name of the property to which the object is bound

---

NOTE

A simple-bound ActiveX control or automation component binds only to a single data field. Complex-bound controls and objects bind to multiple fields and, optionally, multiple rows. The user controls described in this chapter are complex bound to support multiple fields but display data from a single row only.

▶ **See** "Simple-Binding Data Consumer Controls," **p. 189**

The `StdDataFormat` object is a member of the `StdDataFormats` collection, which in turn is a member of the `StdFormat` class. Adding a `BindingsCollection` automatically adds a corresponding `StdDataFormats` collection with a `StdDataFormat` member for each `Binding`. The `StdDataFormat` object handles transformation of `Recordset` field data types to the data type required by the bound control or property. Table 16.4 lists the properties and events of the `StdDataFormat` object.

TABLE 16.4   PROPERTIES AND EVENTS OF THE `StdDataFormat` OBJECT

Member	Type	Description
Changed	Event	Fires after a change to the `Format` property
FalseValue	Property	Value to use if source data value is **False** (ordinarily 0)
FirstDayOfWeek	Property	A member of the `FirstDayOfWeek` enumeration (defaults to `fmtDayUseSystem`)
FirstDayOfYear	Property	A member of the `FirstDayOfYear` enumeration (defaults to `fmtWeekUseSystem`)
Format	Property	A format string or standard format name acceptable to the Visual Basic **Format** function.
Format	Event	Fires before applying the format to a property
NullValue	Property	Value to use if source data value is **Null**
TrueValue	Property	Value to use if source data value is **True** (1 for check boxes)
Type	Property	A member of the `FormatType` enumeration for standard formatting (as an example, `fmtCheckBox` for check boxes)
Unformat	Event	Fires before removing the format when updating `Recordsets`

Adding a `BindingCollection` to a User Control with the `DataBindings` Property

User controls and compiled ActiveX controls having data-binding options set in the Procedure Attributes dialog add a `DataBindings` property to their Properties window. Visual Basic automatically adds an empty `Binding` object to the `BindingCollection` for each property you mark the Property Is Data Bound and Show in DataBindings Collection (sic) at Design Time. In design mode, you specify the properties of each `Binding` object in the Data Bindings dialog.

> **NOTE**
>
> There is no "DataBindings" collection in Visual Basic 6.0. `DataBindings` is an extender property of a control that points to the `BindingCollection` object for each `DataSource` of the control.

To create a `BindingCollection` and `StdDataFormat` test form with a data-bound user control, do the following:

1. Open a new Data Project, remove `DataReport1` and `DataEnvironment1`, save frmDataEnv as BindTest.frm, and save the project as **BindTest.prj** in the same folder as your other projects in this chapter. (Don't use \Ddg_vb6\Chaptr16.)

2. Choose Project, Add User Control and select ProdList.ctl from the list of existing controls to add the ProductList control to the toolbox.

3. Add an ADODC control under the ProductList control for `Recordset` navigation.

4. In the Properties sheet for the ADODC, build a `ConnectionString` with the Jet 3.51 OLE DB provider to the Nwind.mdb database.

5. In the adcProdList Properties window, rename the control to **adcProdList** and set the `CursorType` to 1 - adOpenKeyset. Accept the remainder of the default properties for the control.

6. Select the `RecordSource` property and click the builder (ellipsis) button to open the RecordSource property page.

7. Select 1 - adCommandText in the Command Type list and type the following SQL statement in the Command Text (SQL) text box:

```
SELECT ProductName, QuantityPerUnit, UnitPrice, Discontinued
    FROM Products
```

8. Open the Properties window for `ProductList1`, rename the control to **ctlProdList**, select `DataBindings`, and verify that the `DataBindingBehavior` property value is set to 2 - vbComplexBound to accommodate multiple fields. Click the builder button to open the Data Bindings dialog for the control.

9. With the `Name` property selected in the Data Bindings dialog, open the Data Source list and select adcProdList. In the Data Field list, select ProductName to bind `ProductName` to the `Name` property of the user control. Accept the default General `StdDataFormat` in the Data Format list.

10. Repeat step 9 for the `Package`, `Price`, and `Disc` properties, binding these properties to QuantityPerUnit, UnitPrice, and Discontinued fields, respectively. Select Currency from the Data Format Properties page as the Data Format for `Price` and Checkbox as the Data Format for `Disc` (see Figure 16.19).

FIGURE **16.19**

Setting Binding *object properties in the Data Bindings property sheet.*

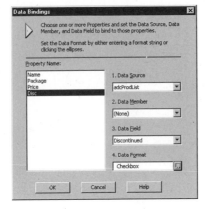

11. Press Ctrl+F5 to compile and run the project. You encounter a Run-time error '380' Invalid property value message. The error occurs at the chkData(0).Value = newDisc line of the **Public Property Let** Disc property procedure.

NOTE

The error you receive is the result of a bug in the operation of the Data Bindings properties sheet, discussed in the "Debugging Data-bound ActiveX Controls" section that follows. The problem doesn't occur when setting data formats in the DataRepeater control's Format page. This bug is present in the released version of Visual Studio 6.0. If Microsoft releases a Service Pack for Visual Studio 6.0 and you install the Service Pack, you won't encounter this error.

---

12. End the project. You receive an Unable to bind to field or DataMember 'Discontinued' message.

13. Open the Data Bindings properties sheet and select the Disc property. The Data Format has returned to its default value, General. Select the Price property; like the Disc property, the Data Format has reverted to General.

14. Temporarily comment out the chkData(0).Value = newDisc line and rerun the project. The runtime error no longer occurs, but the Price text box (txtData(2)) doesn't display Currency formatting (see Figure 16.20).

Creating User Controls for Database Applications

CHAPTER 16

625

16

CREATING USER
CONTROLS FOR
DATABASE APPS

FIGURE 16.20

The
frmBindingTest
*form with the mod-
ified ProductList
user control in run
mode.*

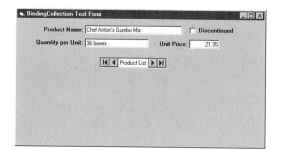

The chkDisc(0) check box requires an **Integer** value, but the Discontinued field is of the Boolean (Access Yes/No) field data type. Failure to apply the correct StdDataFormat conversion (Checkbox) causes the runtime error. The StdDataFormat properties applied in design mode don't persist in run mode.

DEBUGGING DATA-BOUND ACTIVEX CONTROLS

Complex data-bound ActiveX controls almost always require debugging in user control mode. Simple controls, such as ProductList, also require debugging when you encounter a problem such as that described in the preceding section. Technically, failure to persist the StdDataFormat objects for the BindingCollection object is a container, not a control problem. Regardless of the source of the problem, you must write a workaround if you want to use the same compiled ProductList control with a DataRepeater control, which doesn't exhibit the formatting problem, and with single-instance containers (forms) that use the Data Bindings dialog to specify the BindingCollection members in design mode.

The workaround for the impersistent StdDataFormats collection offers the opportunity to explore run mode programming of the BindingCollection object, whose run mode surrogate is the DataBindings collection of the control. Listing 16.4 shows the code required to set the format for the Price property to Currency and that of the Disc property to Checkbox. Figure 16.21 shows frmBindingTest in run mode displaying the proper formatting.

LISTING 16.4 CODE TO DISPLAY BINDINGS AND WORK AROUND THE PROBLEM WITH IMPERSISTENT StdDataFormat OBJECTS

```
Private Sub Form_Load()
    'Display and fix the format problem
    lstMembers.Clear
    lstFields.Clear
    lstFormats.Clear
    Dim dtbBinding As DataBinding
    Dim sdfFormat As StdDataFormat
    For Each dtbBinding In ctlProdList.DataBindings
```

continues

LISTING 16.4 CONTINUED

```
    With dtbBinding
        Set .DataSource = adcProdList
        Set sdfFormat = .DataFormat
        lstMembers.AddItem .PropertyName
        lstFields.AddItem .DataField
        If .PropertyName = "Price" Then
            sdfFormat.Format = "Currency"
        ElseIf .PropertyName = "Disc" Then
            'Following doesn't work
            'sdfFormat.Format = "Checkbox"
            sdfFormat.Type = fmtCheckbox
        End If
        lstFormats.AddItem sdfFormat.Format
    End With
Next dtbBinding
With adcProdList.Recordset
    'Refresh the first record for formatting
    If .RecordCount > 1 Then
        .MoveNext
        .MoveFirst
    End If
End With
End Sub
```

NOTE

The sdfFormat.Format = "Checkbox" line of Listing 16.4 doesn't work, because "Checkbox" isn't a "named format" acceptable to the **Format** function. Thus you must specify fmtCheckBox as the value of the Format.Type property to coerce **True/False** to 1/0 and vice versa for check boxes.

FIGURE 16.21

The frmBindingTest *form with three added list boxes illustrating format fixes for the original (unmodified) version of the ProductList user control.*

Creating User Controls for Database Applications

CHAPTER 16

627

16

CREATING USER
CONTROLS FOR
DATABASE APPS

While testing the code of Listing 16.4, all `DataSource` and `DataField` properties for the control repeatedly vanished, indicating additional (but less repeatable) persistence problems with `DataBindings` set in design mode. Listing 16.5 illustrates the changes to the code of Listing 16.4 to bullet proof the application by assuring that `DataBindings` are set properly in run mode.

NOTE

The code for BindTest.vbp is included in the \Ddg_vb6\Chaptr16 folder of the accompanying CD-ROM.

LISTING 16.5 CHANGES TO THE CODE OF LISTING 16.4 TO BIND IN RUN MODE FIELDS OF A Recordset TO CONTROL PROPERTIES

```
Private Sub Form_Load()
    'Display and fix the format problem
    lstMembers.Clear
    lstFields.Clear
    lstFormats.Clear
    Dim dtbBinding As DataBinding
    Dim sdfFormat As StdDataFormat
    For Each dtbBinding In ctlProdList.DataBindings
        With dtbBinding
            Set .DataSource = adcProdList
            Set sdfFormat = .DataFormat
            'Fix the occasional loss of field bindings problem
            Select Case .PropertyName
                Case "Name"
                    .DataField = "ProductName"
                Case "Package"
                    .DataField = "QuantityPerUnit"
                Case "Price"
                    .DataField = "UnitPrice"
                    sdfFormat.Format = "Currency"
                Case "Disc"
                    .DataField = "Discontinued"
                    sdfFormat.Type = fmtCheckbox
            End Select
            DoEvents
            lstMembers.AddItem .PropertyName
            lstFields.AddItem .DataField
            lstFormats.AddItem sdfFormat.Format
        End With
    Next dtbBinding
    With adcProdList.Recordset
        'Refresh the first record for formatting
```

continues

LISTING 16.5   CONTINUED

```
        If .RecordCount > 1 Then
            .MoveNext
            .MoveFirst
        End If
    End With
End Sub
```

NOTE

Single instances of the properly formatted ProductList user control update the underlying table without resorting to the added code shown in Listing 16.2.

MULTIUSER AND CLIENT/SERVER DATABASE FRONT ENDS

PART

V

IN THIS PART

NETWORKING SECURE MULTIUSER JET DATABASES

IN THIS CHAPTER

Most production Visual Basic 6.0 database applications you create are likely to be used in a multiuser environment. By definition, a multiuser environment requires all users of a database application to be connected by a network to share one or more common database files. Surveys of database users in late-1997 indicate that more than 90 percent of all database applications are networked. Your first multiuser front end is likely to use Transmission Control Protocol/Internet Protocol (TCP/IP) as the network protocol running on Ethernet to connect to a Jet database running on a Windows NT or NetWare server. TCP/IP has replaced NetWare's IPX/SPX and the Windows NetBEUI protocols primarily because of the widespread adoption of Internet-related networking standards. Ethernet, which is now reaching one gigabyte in speed, remains the standard networking medium. Jet databases offer flexibility, simplicity, and freedom from the per-seat client-licensing fees of client/server relational database management systems (RDBMSs). Windows NT Server 4.0 is outpacing new installations of NetWare 4.1+, but NetWare still has the lion's share of the file server business.

Visual Basic developers whose database applications have been limited to single-user products need a grasp of networking methods and terminology. Therefore, this chapter begins with a general discussion of network structures, network operating systems and applications, communication protocols, adapter cards, cabling, and other issues that face developers who need to get database applications up and running on a variety of networks. If you're a networking pro, you can skip these sections. The remainder of this chapter is devoted to network security issues for shared (multiuser) Jet 2.5 (16-bit) and 3.5 (32-bit) .mdb files. The remaining chapters of Part V, "Multiuser and Client/Server Database Front Ends," deal primarily with client/server RDBMSs.

UNDERSTANDING NETWORK TOPOLOGY AND OPERATIONS

Topology in the computer world is a description of how computers are connected in a network. Users can be connected to the network by a variety of network adapter cards, network operating protocols, and cables. A local area network (LAN) consists of computers in a single facility that are connected with some form of cabling. You're not restricted to a copper (wire) or glass (fiber optic) connection to the network; you also can connect with remote dial-up access through a conventional or cellular telephone equipped with a modem, a leased telephone line, a low-power wireless (radio frequency or RF) connection, or even a satellite link. LANs in different locations can be connected into wide area networks (WANs) by high-speed telephone lines using T1, T3, frame relay, ISDN, CATV cable modems, or ATM hardware and data communication protocols. The concentrators, routers, bridges, gateways, and protocols that are used to create WANs are discussed later in this chapter.

The Scope of PC Networks

The primary classification of networks is by scope. The scope of a network is determined by the number and proximity of the computers connected to the network. The basic network scope classifications—workgroup, departmental, and enterprisewide—are described in the three sections that follow.

Workgroup Networks

Workgroup networks connect a limited number of users (usually 25 or less) who share files, printers, and other computer resources. Microsoft's Windows Network is the most common workgroup network operating system (NOS). Workgroup networks usually are self-administered; that is, the members of the workgroup control permissions (also called authority) to share workgroup resources.

Workgroup computers usually are connected by peer-to-peer networks and use a single network protocol. Any computer in a peer-to-peer network may share its resources, such as files and printers, with other computers in the workgroup. Access is designed specifically for workgroup computing. Figure 17.1 shows a five-member workgroup network using Ethernet adapter cards and cabling. One of the workgroup computers shares a fax modem and a printer with other members of the workgroup. A coaxial cable (10BASE-2, thin Ethernet, or ThinNet) is shown as the Ethernet transport medium in the network diagrams of this chapter for simplicity. 10BASE-2 has been deployed much more extensively in Europe than in North America. Today, 10BASE-T is the most common network transport medium; 10BASE-T and its faster counterpart, 100BASE-T, require a hub or switch to connect more than two computers. Hubs are discussed in the section titled, "Hubs, Switches, Bridges, Routers, and Gateways," which follows shortly.

FIGURE 17.1

A five-member workgroup network with a shared fax modem and laser printer.

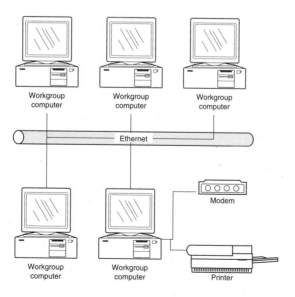

> **TIP**
>
> A common rule of thumb among developers is that Jet 3.5x databases are capable of reliably handling a maximum of about 25 users updating a single database simultaneously. Jet can support at least 100 simultaneous read-only users. Consider upsizing Jet applications to SQL Server or another client/server RDBMS when the number of simultaneous updating users approaches 20. If your database application is critical to a firm's operation or must run 24 hours per day, 7 days per week (24×]7), start with a client/server RDBMS.

Departmental Networks

Departmental networks use dedicated server computers that provide resources to client workstations, usually within a single facility. Novell NetWare, Microsoft Windows NT Server, IBM's Warp (formerly LAN) Server for OS/2, and Banyan VINES are examples of client/server NOSs. Departmental networks often include remote access services (RAS) that enable users, such as field salespersons, to connect to the server with a modem-equipped computer. Servers fall into the following three classes:

- File servers enable multiple users to share files that contain data required by a common application. Typically, these files contain word processing documents, worksheets, or desktop database tables. The applications that access the files are responsible, in conjunction with the NOS, for page or record locking to prevent two users from modifying the same record in a database. Word processing and spreadsheet applications usually lock the entire file while a user has the file open for editing. File servers also share networked peripherals, such as printers. Novell NetWare is classified as a file server NOS, although NetWare Loadable Modules (NLMs) allow NetWare servers to act as application servers.

- Application servers are designed to optimize application execution from the server instead of a local fixed disk drive. Running .exe files and loading DDLs of today's Windows mega apps from the network can cause severe network congestion problems. The advantage of using an application server is that all users work with the same version of the application, and updates and upgrades to applications are much easier to administer. A single server can provide both file- and application-sharing services. Windows NT is classified as an application server because it offers application-specific features, such as symmetric multiprocessing (SMP) and the capability to run client/server applications as services that load on server startup. The capability to run back-end applications such as Microsoft Exchange Server, System Management Server, and SNA Server as services has become the most important distinguishing feature of application servers.

- Database servers are application servers that usually are devoted to running the back end of a client/server RDBMS as a service. The performance of the RDBMS or other server-resident applications is degraded if the server computer also is used for file or application sharing. The database administrator (DBA) usually handles administration of the RDBMS from a workstation. Microsoft SQL Server 6.5+ runs under Windows NT Server 4.0+, which is considered a NOS (as well as a general-purpose operating system) in this book.

A variety of computer types (PCs, Macs, and UNIX workstations, for example), each of which uses a different network protocol (such as NetBEUI, IPX/SPX, and TCP/IP), may be connected as clients in a departmental network. Windows 95/98 and Windows NT support simultaneous use of NetBEUI, IPX, and TCP/IP protocols. Departmental networks use gateways to connect to mainframe computers. One or more full-time network administrators (NAs or NWAs) usually are assigned to manage departmental networks. Independent, self-administered workgroups may exist within the departmental network, although most NWAs discourage ad hoc peer-to-peer networking. Figure 17.2 shows a simple departmental network with a single file and/or application server. The server is equipped with a single- or multiple-line modem to provide remote access service to mobile users and telecommuters.

FIGURE 17.2

A simple departmental network with a shared printer and a RAS modem.

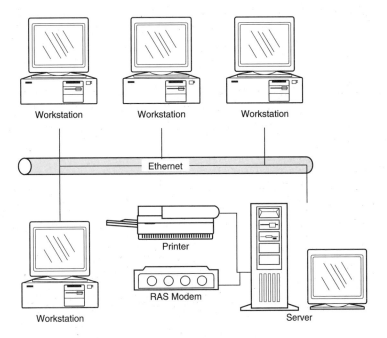

Enterprisewide Networks

Enterprisewide networks connect departmental LANs, often across large distances. Figure 17.3 depicts one of the departmental or *headquarters* LANs that make up an enterprisewide network. Most enterprisewide networks use a variety of communication methods to link LANs into a WAN; the type of interconnection depends on the distance between the individual LANs. Concentrators, bridges, and routers are hardware devices that transfer packets of data between the LANs.

The LAN in Figure 17.3 uses Ethernet running the TCP/IP protocol and includes a connection to a mainframe computer through a gateway, as well as a bridge to a fiber-optic (FDDI) and a copper token-ring network. Connections to North American LANs in the WAN are made through a T1 switch that provides access to high-speed telephone lines. T1 lines also are used to create dedicated links to the Internet. Overseas subsidiaries communicate through a satellite link. Because of the complexity of WANs, most firms that operate enterprisewide networks have a staff that manages the communications aspects of the WAN.

FIGURE 17.3

A headquarters LAN that acts as the hub of a wide area network.

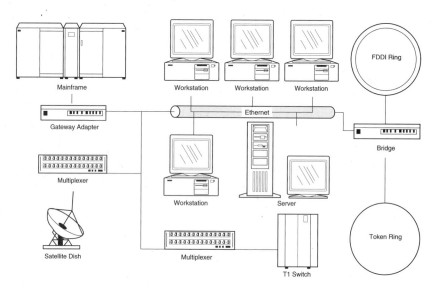

Domains, Workgroups, Servers, and Workstations

Early in the history of PC-based networks, the most common configuration was the departmental LAN illustrated by Figure 17.2—a single file server running NetWare and sharing its resources with a group of workstations. As the number of users in a LAN grows, additional servers are added to accommodate more shared files and applications, as well as expanding database files. When users number in the thousands and WANs span continents, the simple client/server model no longer suffices for network administration. Therefore, an additional tier, the domain, was added to the client/server hierarchy. The concept of domains originated with TCP/IP and the Internet; when you access Microsoft's Web site, `http://www.microsoft.com`, you are connected to the Microsoft domain, `microsoft.com`. The `microsoft.com` domain comprises tens of thousands of computers scattered over the globe, but most of the domain members are in Redmond.

Figure 17.4 shows the relationships between two domains (represented by the two domain controllers), servers, and workstations in a Windows NT Server network. The interconnection between the Ethernet backbone of each domain, shown as a lightning bolt in Figure 17.4, can be twisted-pair (10BASE-T, 100BASE-T, or gigabyte Ethernet) wire; coaxial cable (10BASE-2); FDDI; or a T1, T3, FrameRelay, or ATM data line. Only two workstations per domain are shown in the illustration, but a single domain commonly supports 100 or more workstations and several servers. Users in one domain can share files that are stored on another domain's servers and run applications on other domains. Running applications from another domain over a WAN link, however, is uncommon because of the relatively slow speed of the WAN connections.

FIGURE 17.4

Two interconnected network domains.

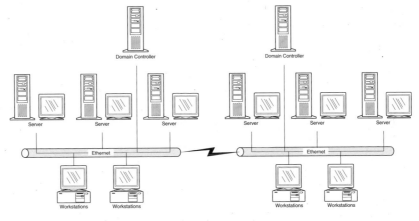

The advantage of assigning servers and workstations to domains is that a workstation user can gain access to any server in the domain with a single logon operation. Network administrators don't need to create new user accounts for each server in a domain, because each user account is validated by the domain controller, not by the individual server(s) in the domain. The domain controller maintains the user account records for each person who is authorized to use a workstation in the domain. Domains also provide a method of segmenting administrative responsibilities for the network. Domain controllers also can act as conventional file, application, and/or database servers.

> **NOTE**
>
> Windows NT Server carries the single-logon process one step farther by authenticating user accounts across trusting domains. If the domain responsible for the user's account data is trusted by the other domains to which the domain with the user account is connected, the user automatically has an account in each of the other domains. A full discussion of trust relationships between domains is beyond the scope of this book. The *Concepts and Planning Guide* that accompanies Windows NT Server provides a complete explanation of domain topology.

If you have more than one server in a Windows NT Server domain, every 5 minutes or so the primary domain controller (PDC) replicates the user-account data to other servers in the domain, called backup domain controllers (BDCs). To minimize replication overhead, only changes to the user-account records are reflected in the servers' user-account tables. Replicating user-account data provides a backup in case the domain controller fails. The domain administrator can promote any BDC to a PDC; promoting a server to PDC demotes the current domain controller to BDC status.

WORKING WITH NETWORK HARDWARE AND OPERATING PROTOCOLS

Windows NT Server supports various network adapter cards (also called *NICs*—network interface cards) and operating protocols. Both the Server and Workstation use the Open Systems Interconnection (OSI) Reference Model, which divides the flow of data in a connection between an application running under a computer operating system and the network hardware into the seven layers shown in Figure 17.5. The layered configuration results in the various protocols used to communicate between networked computers as a stack. Each layer in the workstation's stack communicates with the same layer in the server's stack.

The OSI Reference Model has been adopted by the United Nations International Standards Organization (ISO) and is accepted on a worldwide basis as the standard methodology for network software implementation. The sections that follow provide the details of Microsoft's implementation of the OSI Reference Model.

FIGURE 17.5
OSI Reference Model protocol stacks for a workstation and a server.

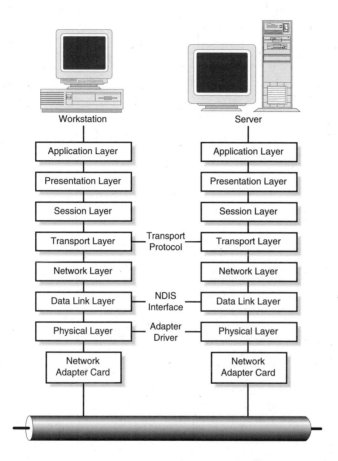

The Network Driver Interface Specification and Network Adapter Card Drivers

The protocol stack (also called protocol, transport protocol, or protocol driver) for Windows 3.11, 95, 98, and Windows NT includes the transport and network layers. The application, presentation, and session layers are attached to the operating system kernel (NTW and NTS) or the environment (Windows 95/98 and Windows 3.11). The data link layer of each product is based on Microsoft's Network Driver Interface Specification (NDIS) standard for Windows. When you install 32-bit Windows, you choose the NDIS driver supplied by Microsoft or the NIC vendor for the adapter card in your computer. The process of connecting the driver to the data link layer and the adapter card is called *binding*.

> **NOTE**
>
> Some network protocols include the transport, network, data link, and physical layer in a single monolithic protocol. The advantage of Microsoft's NDIS approach is that you can use more than one protocol with a single adapter card. In this case, the multiple protocols share the transport and network layers of the protocol stack. The computer first transmits data in the primary protocol and then in the other protocols (if multiple protocols are used). Windows automatically assigns a new number (LANA number) to the adapter card for each protocol in use. Novell's Open Datalink Interface (ODI) is similar in concept to NDIS and also enables multiple-protocol stacks, but is not widely used in Windows NT networking systems.

Network Protocol Stacks Included with Windows NT

Windows NT 4.0+ includes four primary protocol stacks: TCP/IP, IPX, NetBEUI, and DLC. Windows NT Server also includes a protocol stack for the AppleTalk networking system built into all Macintosh computers. The following list briefly describes the purpose and capabilities of each protocol supplied with NTS:

- *TCP/IP* is a routable protocol that was developed by ARPA (later DARPA—the U.S. Defense Advanced Research Projects Agency) for communication among government agencies and contractors (especially university research institutes) participating in defense-related research activities. The wide area network created by ARPA was first called ARPAnet and then the Internet. Admission to the Internet later was granted to corporations, to individuals able to afford a direct connection, and to Internet service providers who provide dial-up access to the Internet. When this book was written, almost all of the Internet host sites were commercial. The Internet is now the ultimate implementation of a wide area network and links many million computers around the world. TCP/IP is discussed in two sections that follow.

- *IPX* (internetwork packet exchange, more properly *IPX/SPX*) is the Novell protocol for NetWare networks. Thirty-two-bit Windows implements IPX through an NDIS-compliant data link layer called NWLink, which supports the STREAMS interface described in the next section. Novell is in the process of converting from its proprietary IPX (NetWare) to standards-based TCP/IP (intraNetWare).

- *NetBEUI* (NetBIOS extended user interface) is a protocol developed by IBM that has been used in both IBM and Microsoft products since the mid-1980s. (IBM LAN Server and Microsoft LAN Manager both derive from the original 3Com NOS that Microsoft licensed for incorporation in OS/2.) NetBEUI is a very fast protocol within a single LAN, but it is not a routable protocol. WANs require routable protocols, which include a hierarchical addressing method to specify the destination of data packets. Therefore, NetBEUI is best suited for use on a single LAN.

- *Services for Macintosh* includes the capability to share files and printers between PCs and Macs. NTS can act as the sole file server for all Macs connected to the network. NTS Services for Macintosh also enables you to create an AppleTalk "internet" that connects two or more separate AppleTalk networks. Services for Macintosh supports AppleTalk Phase 2, which supports routing and network protocols other than the AppleTalk protocol. (The current version of Services for Macintosh does not support AppleTalk Phase 1.) Macintosh clients can use only files stored on NTFS partitions.

- *DLC* (IBM data link control) protocol can be (but now seldom is) used to connect Windows NT clients to IBM mainframe computers. DLC also enables you to use printers that are connected directly to the network, rather than connected to a network server or to a Windows 9*x* workstation. (High-end Hewlett-Packard LaserJet printers support DLC.) Microsoft's SNA Server for Windows NT, part of Microsoft BackOffice 1.5, is a more satisfactory approach to IBM mainframe connectivity. Most directly networked printers now support TCP/IP printing.

Although Windows supports the TCP/IP protocol that was once primarily used by UNIX applications, there is no provision in NTS for connecting to Network File System (NFS) servers that enable UNIX and DOS/Windows applications to share a common set of files. NFS was developed by Sun Microsystems, Inc., in 1983 for use with Sun UNIX workstations. Sun offers PC-NFS, an add-in application for Windows 3.11 clients that provides NFS connectivity in Ethernet environments. Several firms offer NFS drivers for Windows NT.

TCP/IP in Windows 9*x* and Windows NT

TCP/IP has attained the status of the de facto protocol standard for wide area communication between local area networks. Most firms that have heterogeneous LANs (LANs that support a variety of workstation types or transport protocols) also use TCP/IP as their primary LAN transport protocol. Virtually all mainframes, minicomputers, RISC workstations, and PC operating systems support TCP/IP, at least over Ethernet cabling. Thus, if you are developing Visual Basic 6.0 database applications for organizations of any size, you probably need to deal with TCP/IP.

TCP/IP is a connection-oriented protocol that is made up of two protocols, TCP and IP. The IP protocol establishes a connection between two devices on a network, based on 4-byte (32-bit) addresses; inclusion of the IP address makes TCP/IP a routable protocol. The IP address is represented by the decimal values of each of the four bytes of the address, separated by periods, as in 115.27.88.33, which corresponds to &H731B5821& in Visual Basic hex notation. The IP address consists of the following two components:

- A system network ID that identifies groups of devices (hosts) that are located on the same network

- A system host ID that identifies a particular device, such as a workstation or a server, on the network with the specified network ID

A second 4-byte value, called the *subnet mask*, specifies which bytes of the IP address are to be interpreted as the network ID and which are host ID values. You create a subnet mask by creating a 32-bit binary value whose bits are set to 1 in positions corresponding to the network ID byte(s) and to 0 in positions representing the host ID byte(s). Thus a subnet mask with a value of 255.255.0.0 (&HFFFF0000&) applied to the IP address used in the preceding example specifies that the network ID is 115.27 and the host ID is 88.33.

> **NOTE**
>
> An address with a 2-byte network ID and a 2-byte host ID is called a class B network address. A 1-byte network ID and 3-byte host ID is a class A address. A 3-byte network ID and 1-byte host ID is a class C address. Using different address classes enables you to determine how many individual networks can be addressed. As you assign more bytes to network addresses, the number of devices allowed on each network decreases. All computers connected on a single network must use the same network ID and subnet mask.

After the connection is created between the two network devices specified by the IP address and subnet mask, TCP creates individual IP packets from the data to be transmitted. Each packet has a header that includes the following information:

- A port ID that identifies the application running on the transmitting device.

- A checksum that is used to verify that the packet was transmitted without error; if an error occurs, the packet is retransmitted.

- A sequence number that enables the receiving device to reassemble the packets into a stream of received data that is identical to the original transmitted data.

- Other control information related to the type of data and the transmitting application.

Windows NT provides the following three UNIX-related utility services that are associated with the TCP/IP network protocol:

- SNMP (Simple Network Management Protocol) reports the current status of a server or a workstation on a network. SNMP enables you to specify the communities and host(s) from which the server or workstation will accept requests for network status information and to send an authentication trap (request for identification) when an unspecified community or host makes a request from the server or workstation. Communities are called *user groups* in a TCP/IP network environment.

- Telnet provides character-based terminal emulation that enables you to operate TCP/IP hosts that support Telnet. You can start Telnet from the Services option of the Control Panel. Once Telnet services start, NT's Terminal applet launches with the Telnet port open.

- FTP file transfer enables you to send and receive files over TCP/IP networks with File Transfer Protocol (FTP) and Trivial File Transfer Protocol (TFTP). Both of these protocols use the Windows NT command line. Anonymous FTP, one mode of which enables you to use Anonymous as the username and password or anything else as the password, is the most common method of transferring text and binary files over the Internet.

> **NOTE**
>
> Microsoft's implementation of TCP/IP in Windows NT 4.0 does not, in itself, provide file-sharing services between PC clients and UNIX client/server network systems. TCP/IP originally was designed for communication and file transfer, rather than the sharing of files in a multiuser environment. Suppliers of UNIX-based RDBMSs license connectivity products to let DOS/Windows, DOS/WfWg, and NT act as RDBMS clients. You currently need an NFS server (described briefly in the preceding section) and an NFS add-on application to share other types of files, such as desktop database table files, with UNIX workstations.

Windows NT also offers various other TCP/IP command-line utilities, principally for testing network connections (Ping) and interacting with UNIX systems. A complete technical description of TCP/IP; UNIX utilities; and sharing files between computers running UNIX, DOS/Windows 3.11, and Windows NT is beyond the scope of this book. Many good books are devoted to the subject of UNIX networking. If you are developing a Visual Basic 6.0 database application that uses a UNIX-based RDBMS such as Oracle or Sybase, or needs to share database files with UNIX workstations, an investment in a good UNIX networking book is quickly repaid.

NetBIOS over TCP/IP, the Windows Socket API, and Remote Access

TCP/IP for Windows is implemented with both NetBIOS over TCP/IP (NBT) and the Windows Sockets API (WinSock 2.0). The two implementations share the same levels in the protocol stack. NBT provides naming services so that NetBIOS applications can locate NetBIOS workstations and servers on the TCP/IP network by a valid NetBIOS name, rather than by a numeric IP network ID. NetBIOS names are the computer names, such as OAKLEAF0, that you assign to PC servers and workstations; NetBIOS names derive from the original PC peer-to-peer networking application developed by IBM, PC-LAN, and must comply with DOS filenaming conventions. You use the LAN Manager hosts (LMHOSTS) file to associate NetBIOS names with

IP addresses. The format of the LMHOSTS file is identical to that used for the HOSTS file associated with implementations of TCP/IP for DOS, such as FTP Software's PC/TCP, which also includes NFS services. A typical entry in the LMHOSTS file appears as follows:

```
131.254.7.1     OAKLEAF0
```

When you specify a computer name or an IP address, the corresponding entry in LMHOSTS provides the required name resolution.

> **NOTE**
>
> You don't need LMHOSTS files if you take advantage of Windows NT 4.0+'s Domain Name Service (DNS) and/or Windows Internet Naming Service (WINS). The Windows NT 4.0 Server Resource Kit provides extensive coverage of DNS and WINS. The "Logging on to Servers and Joining Workgroups" section that follows briefly describes the use of WINS on the client side.

WinSock is modeled after the Berkeley Sockets included in the Berkeley Software Distribution (BSD) version 4.3 of UNIX developed by the University of California at Berkeley. In UNIX terminology, a *socket* is a bidirectional connector to an application. Two sockets, each identified by an address, participate in a two-way network conversation. If you intend to create a Visual Basic 4.0 application that needs to connect directly to another application with TCP/IP, using the Windows Sockets API is the most straightforward approach. Several third-party software publishers, such as NetManage, Inc., provide VBXs and OLE Controls that support WinSock.

Point to Point Protocol (PPP) and Serial Link Interface Protocol (SLIP) are the two most common forms of providing TCP/IP remote access services (RAS). You can use either PPP or SLIP to redirect TCP/IP transmission from the network adapter card to a serial port, enabling remote dial-up connection to a network with a server that implements SLIP. Windows NT supports PPP and SLIP, but Windows 9x supports only PPP, which has become far more popular than SLIP. PPP differs from the NetBIOS RAS provided by NTS: PPP enables you to run queries against RDBMS servers using the ODBC API, whereas NetBIOS-based RAS is designed only for file access operations.

Hubs, Switches, Bridges, Routers, and Gateways

The following four types of hardware devices are commonly employed in LANs and WANs and to connect to mainframe computers:

- Hubs are used to connect groups of computers to LANs that use topologies that are more complex than 10BASE-2 Ethernet's simple inline connections. For example, you need a hub to connect one or more computers to a network that uses unshielded twisted-pair

Networking Secure Multiuser Jet Databases

CHAPTER 17

645

17

NETWORKING
MULTIUSER JET
DATABASES

(UTP, 10BASE-T) cabling or to token-ring networks. 10BASE-T hubs are quite inexpensive, and the price of 100BASE-T hubs was declining rapidly in mid-1998.

- Switches replace hubs and provide substantially better performance for a group of network computers. Switches set up a private connection between the workstation and server (or a high-speed backbone connection to servers). As an example, a 32-port switch might provide 31 10BASE-T connections to workstations and a 100BASE-T connection to a workgroup server. Up to 10 workstations can communicate simultaneously at 10Mbps to the server, assuming the server has the horsepower to handle the 100Mpbs of traffic. Switches are substantially more expensive than hubs.

- Bridges provide connectivity between similar and dissimilar LANs. You can use a bridge, for example, to connect an Ethernet LAN to a token-ring LAN or an ATM network.

- Routers are used in WANs to direct network data packets to the appropriate transmission device. The most common use of routers is to partition a LAN into subnets for improved performance. If you have a T1 switch and a satellite link that serve remote computers, the router connects the LAN to the switch and link hardware. Smart routers maintain a list of addresses and handle the routing chores without requiring computers on the network to intervene. Routers also handle mixtures of 100BASE-T and 10BASE-T clients on a single LAN.

- Gateways provide connectivity between networks with different application layer protocols. Gateways commonly are used to interconnect PC LANs and mini- or mainframe computers. IBM provides a token-ring gateway for its AS/400 minicomputer and all of its current mainframe computers. Gateways often consist solely of software that you add to the mainframe's operating system or a specific application, such as an IBM DB2 server, and to the client application. In this case, the client connects to an IBM I/O controller. Information Builders, Inc.'s EDA/SQL combined with EDA/Link for Windows and EDA/Extender for Microsoft ODBC is an example of a gateway from Windows database front-end applications to a DB2 back end running under MVS on IBM mainframes.

Data Storage Redundancy and Backup Systems

Fault tolerance for the fixed disks of network servers is achieved by employing redundant array of inexpensive disks (RAID) technology. At the time this edition was written, the following five levels (strategies) for providing fault tolerance with RAID hardware were the most common:

- RAID level 1 (disk mirroring). RAID level 1 uses a disk mirror set to provide an exact duplicate of data on two fixed disk drives. Disk writes to one member of the mirror set are duplicated on the other member. If one disk of the mirror set fails, NTS automatically transfers disk operations to the remaining operable disk. The advantage of disk mirroring is that only two disk drives are required; other methods of providing fault tolerance require three or more disks. Only one mirror set disk drive can have a boot sector, so you need to boot from the Windows NT recovery disk that you created when you installed Windows NT if the disk with the boot sector fails.

- RAID level 2 writes blocks of data across multiple disks (a process called *disk striping*) and uses an error-correcting code to regenerate good data from the data blocks on a failed drive. RAID level 2 requires at least two data disks and usually more than one disk to store the error-correction data. RAID level 2 provides a faster read data rate than level 1, but it is no longer in common use because of its inefficient method of storing data.

- RAID level 3 is a disk-striping method similar to RAID level 2, but it offers better price-performance ratings because the size of the error-correcting code is smaller. (Only one disk drive is required to store the parity information for data on the other disk drives.) RAID level 3 often is used for applications such as client/server RDBMSs that use relatively few large files.

- RAID level 4 is the same as RAID level 3, except that the blocks of striped data are larger.

- RAID level 5 uses a technique called *striping with parity*. RAID level 5 uses the large-block striping method of RAID level 4, but it also stripes the parity data across all disks. Logic in the software and RAID disk controller ensure that the parity information for a data block and the data block itself never reside on the same disk drive. Read performance is better than with RAID level 1, but write performance is slower because of the time required to calculate and write the parity values.

NOTE

RAID level 0 (disk striping only) provides improved fixed disk read performance by sequentially placing blocks of data on multiple disks. RAID level 0 is not included in the preceding list because RAID level 0 disk striping by itself does not provide fault tolerance. Raid 0 is primarily of interest in applications, such as nonlinear digital video editing, that require sustained disk I/O read and write rates of 4MB/sec and higher.

Windows NT Server offers a no-cost software alternative to RAID systems implemented in hardware, but software RAID extracts a performance penalty. You can choose either RAID level 1 or RAID level 5 redundancy to keep the network operating despite the failure of a single disk drive. Unless you have a particular reason for choosing RAID level 1, RAID level 5 is currently the favored method of providing disk drive fault tolerance. If more than one disk drive at a time fails, you are out of luck because you cannot reconstruct the missing data with either RAID level 1 or level 2 strategies. Low-cost ($100/GB or less) fixed disk drives with an advertised mean time between failures (MTBF) of 1 million hours or more were available at the time this book was written, so multiple-drive failure is unlikely unless the server experiences a power surge that your power line conditioning system cannot take in stride.

> **CAUTION**
>
> If you believe advertised MTBF figures, the probability of two disk drives failing simultaneously because of mechanical or on-board electronic component malfunction is exceedingly small. On the other hand, the first disk drive installed in the OAKLEAF0 domain controller experienced an unexplained catastrophic failure within the first 96 hours of operation. The replacement drive failed after 5 days of 24-hour operation. (Neither of these drives were the Seagate Barracudas presently installed and operating satisfactorily for more than 2 years.) Mean time to failure (MTTF) is a more useful measure of the reliability of fixed disk drives, but manufacturers rarely report MTTF values. Fault-tolerance strategies are not a substitute for regular backups of server data.

Windows NT's backup utility supports a variety of SCSI tape drives, including drives that use the 4mm digital audio tape (DAT), 8mm (camcorder), and digital linear tape (DLT) formats. Many suppliers of backup tape drives that are not supported by the drivers included by Microsoft provide their own drivers for Windows NT 4.0+. The backup options in third-party backup utilities, such as Seagate Software's Backup Exec, are much more flexible than those found in the Windows NT 4.0 built-in utility.

> **NOTE**
>
> Hardware products that have been tested and found to perform satisfactorily with Windows NT 4.0+ and the hardware drivers that are included with the retail version of Windows NT 4.0 Server and Workstation are listed in the Hardware Compatibility List that accompanies both versions of Windows NT. Periodic additions to the list of tested hardware products appear in updated versions of the guide that are available for downloading from the Microsoft Web site at
> `http://www.microsoft.com/ntserver/showcase/hwcompatibility.asp`.

The Topology and Protocols Used for This Chapter's Examples

The examples in this chapter use Windows Networking as the peer-to-peer NOS, Windows NT 4.0 and 5.0 Server as the client/server NOS, and both Windows NT 4.0 and 5.0 Workstations and Windows 9x as client workstation environments. Windows NT Server is a superset of the

Workstation product; Server provides a number of features missing from the Workstation built-in peer-to-peer (workgroup) networking capability, which is limited to 10 connections per peer server. One of the additional features offered by Windows NT Server is trust relationships between domains (as briefly discussed in the preceding section). Other added features, such as fixed disk fault tolerance and replication, are discussed later in this chapter. SQL Server 6.5 and 7.0, used in the client/server examples of this book, runs as a service under Windows NT Server.

> **NOTE**
>
> Microsoft Windows NT 5.0 and SQL Server 7.0 were in the beta-testing stage when this book was written. Windows NT 5.0 and SQL Server (beta 3+) are open betas; Microsoft does not require nondisclosure agreements (NDAs) for open-beta programs.

To understand many of the examples shown in this and the next chapter, you need to know the configuration of the computers and the topology of the network used to create the examples. (Otherwise, you might not know why drives with letters such as G: and H: appear in the examples.) Most of the computers use Intel EtherExpress 16 Ethernet cards connected by thin Ethernet (10BASE-2) cabling. Here are the specifications and the configuration of the disk drives of the server and workstation computers, including their IP addresses, in the OAKLEAF domain:

- OAKLEAF0 (131.254.7.1), the primary domain controller for a six-computer network, runs Windows NT Server 4.0 on a 133MHz Pentium PC with 64M of RAM. OAKLEAF0 is the primary database server and runs both SQL Server 6.5 and 7.0 in switched mode. OAKLEAF0 also runs Internet Information Server 4.0, Proxy Server 2.0, Transaction Server 2.0, and a beta version of Microsoft OLAP Server (code-named *Plato*). OAK-LEAF0 uses an Adaptec AHA-2940UW SCSI adapter card to connect to a single Seagate ST15150W 4.3G Barracuda disk drive formatted with two New Technology File System (NFTS) partitions, a Tandberg 1G tape backup drive, and a SCSI CD-ROM drive.

> **NOTE**
>
> SQL Server 6.5 and 7.0 can coexist on a single server, but cannot run simultaneously. A Microsoft SQL Server - Switch (Common) choice of the Start, Programs menu enables you to select the version to run. Switching between servers is necessary for same-machine conversion of SQL Server 6.5 device (.dat) files to SQL Server 7.0 database (.mdf) and log (.ldf) files. Unlike prior iterations of SQL Server, the file structure of version 7.0 has changed dramatically. Switching between server versions on the same server permits comparing the performance of the two products without introducing hardware-related variables.

- OAKLEAF1 (131.254.7.2) is a 266MHz Pentium II PC server with 128MB of RAM dual-booting Windows 98 and Windows NT 4.0 Server with Service Pack 4. The desktop version of SQL Server 7.0 (often called Sphinx Lite during the beta program) runs under Windows 98 and the full version (Sphinx Heavy, as in the Air Traffic Control term for high gross weight aircraft, for example, United 386 Heavy) runs under Windows NT 5.0 Server. OAKLEAF1 has two 4.3GB Quantum Fireball ST Ultra-DMA IDE drives, one formatted with FAT32 and the other with NTFS, and a 12X CD-ROM drive. Two 4.3GB Seagate Barracuda 4XL Ultra-SCSI drives formatted with NTFS in a RAID 0 striped set are connected to an Adaptec AHA-8945 SCSI/IEEE-1394 adapter. OAKLEAF1 is used for Digital Video (DV) editing and testing beta software. All Visual Basic 6.0 examples in this book were written and tested on OAKLEAF1.

NOTE

Microsoft announced in late 1997 that the next version of Access will offer the single-user version of SQL Server 7.0 as an alternative to Jet.

- OAKLEAF2 (131.254.7.4) is a 200MHz Pentium MMX PC workstation with 32MB of RAM dual-booting Windows 95 and Windows NT 4.0 Workstation. The single-user version of SQL Server 7.0 runs under Windows 95 and Windows NT 4.0. OAKLEAF2 has two 4.3GB Quantum Fireball ST Ultra-DMA IDE drives, both formatted with FAT16, an Iomega Zip drive, and a 12X CD-ROM drive. OAKLEAF2 was used to write this edition; no beta software is allowed on this machine.

- OAKLEAF3 (131.254.7.3) is a 233MHz Pentium II server with 96MB of RAM dual-booting Windows 95 and Windows NT 4.0 Server, which serves as a BDC for the OAKLEAF domain. OAKLEAF3 has two 4.3GB Quantum Fireball ST IDE drives formatted with FAT16, an 8X CD-ROM drive, an Iomega Jaz drive and uses an Adaptec AHA-2940UW SCSI adapter card to connect to two Seagate ST15150W 4.3GB Barracuda disk drives in a RAID 1 configuration formatted with NTFS. OAKLEAF3 runs SQL Server 7.0 as a secondary database server, Exchange Server, SMS Server, Internet Information Server 4.0, and Transaction Server 2.0. When running Windows 95, OAKLEAF3 is used for video and audio capture, editing, special effects, and still-graphics production.

- OAKLEAF4 (131.254.7.5) is a 90MHz Pentium notebook computer with 32MB of RAM running Windows 95. OAKLEAF4 connects to the network occasionally to update files.

- OAKLEAF5 (131.254.7.6) is a 200MHz Pentium MMX PC workstation with 32MB of RAM running Windows 98 and the single-user version of SQL Server 7.0. OAKLEAF5 has a 4.3GB Quantum Fireball ST IDE drive formatted with FAT32, and a 12X CD-ROM drive. OAKLEAF5 is used for MIDI music composition and beta-testing software that's incompatible with the beta software installed on OAKLEAF2.

Figure 17.6 illustrates the OAKLEAF2 Windows 95 Explorer displaying server shares of root folders of OAKLEAF0 (C:\ and D:\), OAKLEAF1 (C:\), OAKLEAF3 (C:\), OAKLEAF4 (C:\), and OAKLEAF5 (C:\) as mapped (logical) drives G: through L:, respectively. Network Neighborhood also shows the network computers. OAKLEAF0 and OAKLEAF3 are the two OAKLEAF domain servers; the OAKLEAF1, OAKLEAF2, OAKLEAF4, and OAKLEAF5 machines use Windows peer-to-peer networking to share files as members of the Test workgroup. All workstations use Windows NT security for network logon.

FIGURE 17.6

Windows 95 Explorer displaying mapped drive-letter allocations of the OAKLEAF2 workstation.

At the time this edition was written, the combination of Windows NT Server and SQL Server, which are the primary components of the Microsoft BackOffice server suite, had the lowest entry cost of any product combination that implements a full-featured, networked client/server computing environment. (Depending on the number of users, the cost of Windows NT Server/SQL Server installation is likely to be less than 25 percent of the cost of a comparable UNIX-based client/server database system.) Windows NT Server is much easier to install, administer, and maintain than any other currently available client/server NOS for enterprisewide networks. SQL Server 6.5, and especially SQL Server 7.0, is equally easy to install and includes server administrative tools and utilities that run under Windows NT, Windows 95, and Windows for Workgroups 3.11 workstations. The ability to run Windows NT Server and SQL Server on RISC-based computers using DEC's Alpha chip sets provides an alternative to the use of PCs based on Intel Pentium, Pentium Pro, and Pentium II MPUs.

> **NOTE**
>
> Windows NT and SQL Server also offer scalability through SMP. *Scalability* means that you can add microprocessor (MPU) chips to a Windows NT server (or workstation) to achieve improved performance with multithreaded applications that take advantage of SMP. Windows NT 4.0+ Server and Workstation theoretically can divide processing chores among as many as 16 processors. Increasing the number of MPUs, however, does not always lead to improved server performance. The most common configurations are two and, to a lesser extent, four processors. Many server operations, such as file replication, import, and export, are I/O bound. You can streamline interrupt-driven I/O operations by purchasing servers that use the Intel I2O design
> (`http://www.intel.com/procs/servers/i2otech/index.htm`). Compared to adding more MPU chips, adding memory (beyond 256MB) to increase the size of the disk cache usually is more effective in increasing server throughput. Many SMP servers use 512MB or more of RAM to improve performance.

LOGGING ON TO SERVERS AND JOINING WORKGROUPS

When you log on to a Windows NT Server network from a Windows NT workstation, you specify the domain you want to join in the From text box of the dialog titled Logon to Windows NT. If you're using a Windows 95 or 98 workstation, you can join a workgroup and simultaneously log on to the domain when you launch Windows by following these steps:

1. Create an account for yourself in your Windows NT domain. You need to have an account in the domain and in the workgroup with the same username and password for simultaneous logon to work.

2. Launch Control Panel and double-click the Network icon to open the Network properties sheet.

3. Verify that you have at least one network operating system, NIC, and network protocol installed in the list box of the Network Configuration page. Figure 17.7 shows a configuration for OAKLEAF2 using the Microsoft Windows Network (NOS), a DialUp Adapter (modem), an Intel EtherExpress 16 NIC, and the TCP/IP protocol for the modem and NIC.

FIGURE 17.7

Configuration entries for use of the TCP/IP protocol with the Windows Network client included with Windows 95.

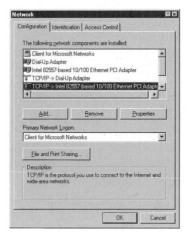

4. Click the icon titled Client for Microsoft Networks to select the NOS and then click the Properties button to display the General page of the Client for Microsoft Network Properties sheet.

5. Mark the Log on to Windows NT Domain check box, type the name of the domain in which your NTS account is located in the Windows NT Domain text box, and click the Logon and Restore Network Connections option button (see Figure 17.8). Click OK to close the Client for Microsoft Networks Properties sheet.

FIGURE 17.8

Entering the Windows NT Server domain name and selecting the Restore Network Connections option when logging on to the server.

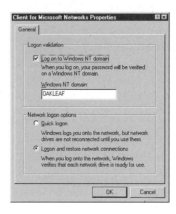

6. Click the Identification tab to display the Identification page of the Network dialog; then type the name of your computer in Computer Name text box, the workgroup you want to join in the Workgroup text box, and a description of your computer in the Computer Description text box, as shown in Figure 17.9.

FIGURE 17.9

Establishing your computer's name, the name of your workgroup, and the description of your computer.

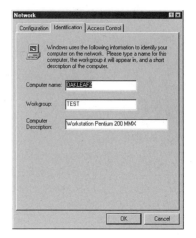

7. If you use TCP/IP as a network protocol, double-click the TCP/IP->*NIC Name* entry to display the TCP/IP Properties sheet. If your Windows NT Server(s) run Dynamic Host Configuration Protocol (DCHP), accept the default option Obtain an IP Address Automatically. Otherwise, select the Specify an IP Address option and type the IP Address and Subnet Mask values assigned to your workstation (see Figure 17.10).

   If your TCP/IP network uses WINS, click the WINS tab, select the Enable WINS Resolution option, and type the IP addresses of your Primary WINS Server and Secondary WINS Server, as shown in Figure 17.11. Click OK to close the TCP/IP Properties sheet.

FIGURE 17.10

Specifying an IP address and subnet mask for a Windows 95 workstation.

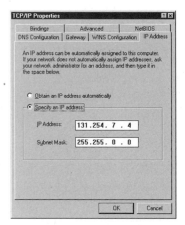

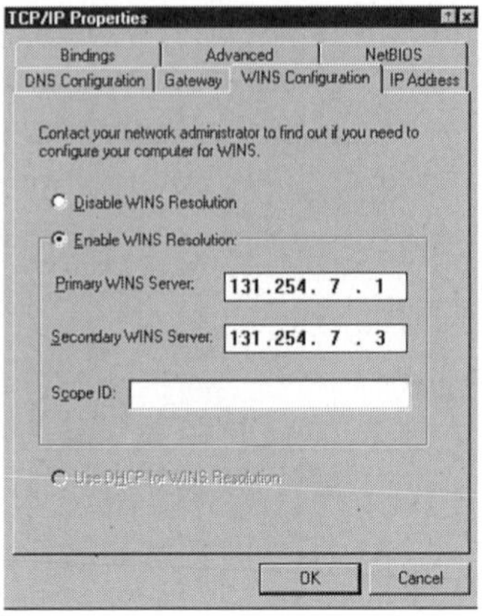

FIGURE 17.11

Setting the IP addresses of primary and secondary WINS servers.

NOTE

The preceding step assumes that a network administrator has assigned you a computer name, IP address (unless DHCP is used), subnet mask, and WINS server address(es). If you're setting up your own network, you must use the subnet mask value that you assigned to the server, the same subnet byte values, and unique byte value(s) for the IP address of network clients.

8. Click OK to close the Network properties sheet and save the new settings; Windows automatically builds a new driver information database. A message indicates that you must close and restart Windows 95 for the new settings to become effective.

TIP

Don't run more network protocols than you need. Unused protocols consume resources and can slow network operations. If you're using TCP/IP as your network protocol, remove the NetBEUI and IPX/SPX-compatible protocol bindings from your network devices. To remove a protocol binding in Windows 95 or 98, select the item from the list in the Network properties sheet's Configuration page and then click the Remove button. You must restart Windows to apply the change.

When you restart Windows 95, the Welcome to Windows 95 dialog appears with the default domain name—in this example, OAKLEAF. When you enter your username and password and then click the OK button, you are logged on to the domain you chose and become a member of the specified workgroup (Test). After you log on, you can map server shares (shared directories

on Windows NT Server) to drive letters by choosing <u>T</u>ools, <u>M</u>ap Network Drive from
Explorer's menu to display the Map Network Drive dialog. Open the Path drop-down list and
type the universal naming convention (UNC) path to the server share to map to the specified
drive letter (see Figure 17.12); then click OK to close the dialog.

FIGURE 17.12

*Using Explorer to
map a shared
server folder to a
workstation logical
drive.*

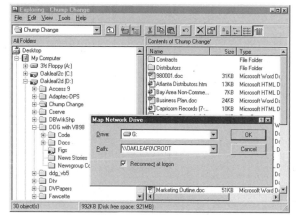

You don't need to map server shares to logical drives on workstations. Thirty-two–bit
Windows supports long filenames (LFNs) and UNC to point to servers (*ServerName*), shares
(*ServerName**ShareName*), and files *ServerName**ShareName*\[*Path*\]*FileName.ext*). As an
example, \\Oakleaf0\Croot\Ac303\Dsmkt.mdb specifies the Dsmkt.mdb database file in the
\Ac303 folder of the C: drive of OAKLEAF0—the equivalent of G:\Ac303\Dsmkt.mdb for a
mapped drive. The advantage to using UNC is that drive-letter mappings vary from computer to
computer, depending on the complement of physical drives installed and how the drives are
partitioned. Always use UNC to specify shared files in 32-bit applications to avoid the need for
application users to map server shares to specific drive letters.

> **NOTE**
>
> Sharing the root folders of server partitions is very uncommon in production
> networks. The usual approach is to provide each user with a shared home folder
> (full permissions) and then grant access to other shared folders on a need-to-
> know (read-only) or need-to-use (read-write) basis. The OAKLEAF domain is
> used primarily for testing and application development purposes, which often
> require full access to all server and workstation folders and files, including the
> root folders (OAKLEAF*n*\Croot, OAKLEAF*n*\Droot).

You can share folders of your computer with other members of your workgroup. Creating a workgroup and peer-sharing a multiuser database file is useful for limited-scale testing of applications. To share a folder, follow these steps:

1. Right-click the folder's icon in Windows Explorer; then choose Sharing from the pop-up menu to display the Sharing page of the folder's Properties sheet.

2. Click the Shared As option button and enter the alias for the share (up to 12 characters) in the Share Name text box. You can let anyone access the shared folder by clicking the Read-Only or Full (read-write) option button and leaving the Password text box empty.

   To restrict access, you can specify a single password for read-write access or two passwords to differentiate users with read-only from those with read-write access. Figure 17.13 illustrates the use of a single password for read-write access.

3. Click OK to close the folder Properties sheet. The new shared folder appears in Explorer's folder under the folder with the workgroup name (see Figure 17.14). Folders shared by other workgroup members also appear in the workgroup folder.

FIGURE 17.13

Sharing a folder in a peer-to-peer Windows 95 or 98 workgroup network.

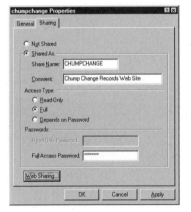

FIGURE 17.14

Server and workgroup shares shown in Network Neighborhood.

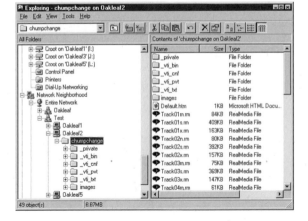

> **NOTE**
>
> The preceding example assumes that the Windows 95/98 default, Share-Level Access Control, is selected in the Access Control page of the Network properties sheet. If you're connected to a Windows NT domain, you can select User-Level Access Control, specify the domain name, and select who has access to your shared folders from a list of Windows NT groups and users.

MAINTAINING DATABASE SECURITY IN A NETWORK ENVIRONMENT

The security features of Jet .mdb files often are described as labyrinthine or even Byzantine. In reality, Jet's database security system is modeled on conventional network and RDBMS security methodology. Jet 3+ provides access to the Groups and Users collections of .mdw files, so you can manage individual User and Group accounts with a Visual Basic 6.0 application. You cannot, however, create a secure Jet 3+ .mdb file with Visual Basic 6.0; only Access 95 or 97 can create the required System.mdw *workgroup information file* to implement Jet security. If you don't want to use a System.mdw file, you can control access to database files by individual users or groups of users through the security features of the network.

> **NOTE**
>
> ADO 2.0 and the OLE DB data providers for Jet databases (Jolt and MSDASQL) don't support the Groups and Users collections whose members are defined in System.mdw, nor do they support the Containers and Documents collections stored in the .mdb file. You must use DAO 3.5*x* to manipulate these Access-specific database objects.

Most Visual Basic 6.0 applications can achieve results that are similar or equivalent to the applicable security features built into Access 97 and its predecessors if you implement a well-planned network security system. Even when you use Access, the first line of defense against unauthorized viewing or modification of database files is network security. The sections that follow describe how network security works in a Windows NT Server 4+ environment and how to design Visual Basic 6.0 database applications to take maximum advantage of network security. If you're an Access developer, much of the terminology in the sections devoted to network security will be familiar to you.

Network Authority, Permissions, and Accounts

Network operations are divided into the following two basic categories:

- Administration of the network, which includes adding and deleting user accounts; assigning accounts to particular groups of users; granting users the ability to read from, write to, copy, or delete specific files or a collection of files in a specific directory; and backing up server files. The administrator's authority determines what administrative activities he or she can perform. Windows NT defines *authority* as a combination of rights and abilities that are inherent in a user's group. Firms with large client/server networks usually employ one or more full-time network administrators to manage the LAN.

- Use of network resources, which encompasses file transfer and file sharing, access to database servers on the network, printing on network printers, using network modems to send faxes or to communicate with remote computers, and the like. A user's permissions determine which network resources he or she can use and how the resources can be used.

The basic element of network security in client/server networks is the user account. Administrators and users each must have a user account that enables logon to the network. The user account record, at the minimum, includes fields to hold the user's logon ID (username) and password, and to indicate the group(s) to which the user belongs. Regular network users must belong to at least one group, most commonly called Users, but there is no limit to the number of groups to which users can be assigned. Most NOSs create a unique, encrypted system ID (SID) to identify the user. A system ID prevents confusion between users who might accidentally use the same logon ID. Duplicate logon IDs easily can be intercepted and prevented on a LAN. However, a user on a WAN in San Francisco might unknowingly use the same logon ID as a WAN user in Sydney, Australia. Maintaining user accounts is one of the principal duties of network administrators.

Security Limitations of Workgroup Networks

There is little distinction between network administrators and users in workgroup environments. Workgroup networks are self-administered; any user can share files located in directories on his or her computer with other members of a workgroup. Workgroups do not maintain user accounts. Therefore, files in any directory that are shared by a user are, by default, up for grabs by anyone else who is connected to the network. The user sharing files can restrict other users from modifying the files by sharing the files in read-only mode and can require workgroup members to enter a password to access shared-directory files. The lack of security offered by conventional workgroup networking environments has limited their acceptance by IS departments of large firms. Using the Jet database security system with Visual Basic 6.0 applications (the subject of the next section) can overcome the security limitations of workgroup file sharing.

The peer-to-peer networking features of Windows NT Workstation provide an increased level of security compared to that offered by Windows 95/98. Windows NT requires you to log on with a user ID and password, whereas logon IDs and passwords are optional for Windows 95 and 98. If you have administrative authority, you can assign users of individual computers to groups and then grant group authority to share your directories. The normal practice is to create a user group with the same name as the workgroup. If you use the NTFS instead of the DOS FAT system, you can grant users permissions on a file-by-file basis. The FAT file system, required by dual-boot installations of Windows NT 4.0 and Windows 95/98 that need access to the same folders, restricts you to granting permissions to share entire folders. Using predefined groups and creating new groups, as well as granting directory and file permissions to members of groups, are covered later in this chapter.

Windows NT overcomes many of the objections of MIS managers to the lack of security within self-administered networks, but peer-to-peer networking remains a threat to the centralized authority (and in many organizations, the perceived status) of IS departments. The likelihood of a large number of corporate PC clients running Windows NT instead of Windows 95/98 (at least in the economic climate that prevailed at the time this edition was written) remains quite small because of the expense of upgrading PCs to meet the resource requirements of Windows NT.

Supplementing Workgroup Security with Jet's Security Features

One of the advantages of using Jet databases with Visual Basic 6.0 applications is that you can use the retail version of Access to implement database security with System.mda (Jet 2.5 and earlier) or System.mdw (Jet 3+) in addition to restricting access to the *FileName*.mdb file through network security. Jet uses the System.md? file to store group names, user IDs, passwords, and SIDs. When you add a new user to a Jet security group, you enter the user ID and a four-digit PIN (personal identification number). (The PIN number distinguishes among users with the same user ID.) Jet combines the user ID and PIN to create an encrypted binary SID value that Jet .mdb files use to identify each user who has permissions for files that exceed the scope of default permissions (also called implicit permissions) granted to that user's group(s).

CAUTION

System.md? is used in this chapter and elsewhere in this book to indicate either the Jet 2.5 and earlier System.mda system file or the Jet 3+ System.mdw workgroup information file. Jet 3+ links (attaches) both 16-bit SYSTEM.MDA and 32-bit System.mdw files. If you must support users of both 16-bit and 32-bit .mdb files, don't convert your Jet 2.x SYSTEM.MDA file to a Jet 3+ System.mdw file; Jet 2.x cannot link a 32-bit System.mdw file.

Using Jet database security features means that at least one individual should be appointed as a DBA to manage the user accounts in the System.md? file that is shared by members of one or more workgroups. You can use a single System.md? file, which all members of all workgroups share, or multiple System.md? files, each of which is located in the folder that contains the .mdb file(s) that the workgroup members share. Workgroup members must have read-write access to System.md? so that users can change their passwords periodically to enhance database security. Therefore, if you want to use network security to provide one group of users read-only permissions and to grant another group of users read-write permissions, you should use the single System.md? approach and place System.md? in a directory to which all members of all workgroups have read-write network permissions.

Jet enables you to grant read-only or read-write permissions to groups and individual users for tables in the database; however, members of the Users group, by default, have read-write and modify permissions on all database tables. You need to explicitly remove write (Administer, Modify Design, Update Data, Insert Data, and Delete Data) permissions for the Users group and then assign write permissions only to authorized users.

You can specify a name other than System.md? for the security database or locate System.md? in a folder other than the one that contains the associate .mdb file(s). For Access applications, this approach requires you to use the workgroup administration application supplied with Access or to manually edit the Registry. To change the name or location of *System*.md?, perform at least one of the following operations:

- For DAO 3+, add a `DBEngine.SystemDB` = `"d:\path\system.mdw"` or, preferably, `DBEngine.SystemDB` = `"\\servername\sharename\path\system.mdw"` statement prior to any other statement that refers to the `DBEngine` object.

▶ **See** "Specifying a Jet Workgroup File for Secure Databases," **p. 140**

- For ADO 2.0 with the native Access provider (Jolt), add `cnnName.Properties("Jet OLEDB:System database")` = `"\\ServerName\ShareName\System.mdw"` after setting up the connection. You must provide the username and password in the connection string.

- For ADO 2.0 with MSDASQL, using a DSN-less ODBC connection, add `systemdb=\\ServerName\ShareName\System.mdw;UID=UserName;PWD=Password` to the connection string.

- For ADO 2.0 with MSDASQL and a file, user, or system ODBC data source, select the Database option in the System Database frame of the ODBC Microsoft Access 97 Setup dialog, click the System Database button, and specify the location and name of the System.mdw file in the Select System Database dialog. Add `UID=UserName;PWD=Password` to the connection string.

See the end of this chapter for details of the methods you use, as the DBA, for Jet databases in Visual Basic 6.0 database applications. Jet database security is modeled on the security system of NTS, so describing network security prior to a full discussion of Jet database security methodology makes Jet's labyrinthine security features (a bit) more comprehensible.

Network Administrators, Operators, and Users

Windows NT Server 4+ has an xtraordinary number of predefined groups of administrators and users. Table 17.1 lists the predefined groups that are created when you install Windows NT Server 4.0, those groups predefined by Windows NT 4+ workstations, and groups of database users defined by Jet. The rows in Table 17.1 are ordered by descending level of authority-to-administer and permission-to-use domain resources. The Domain Admins and Domain Users groups are global groups; the remainder of the groups are local to a specific server computer. An N/A entry indicates that the group is not available in the particular environment.

TABLE 17.1 THE AUTHORITY AND PERMISSIONS OF PREDEFINED WINDOWS 4+ GROUPS

Windows NT Domains	*NT Workstations*	*Jet*
Administrators	Administrators	Admins (all versions)
Domain Admins	N/A	Admins (all versions)
Backup Operators	Backup Operators	N/A
Server Operators	N/A	N/A
Account Operators	N/A	N/A
Print Operators	N/A	N/A
Replicator	Replicators	N/A
N/A	Power Users	N/A
Everyone	Everyone	N/A
Users	Users	Users (all versions)
Domain Users	Users	Users (all versions)
(Guests)	Guests	Guests (1.*x* and 2.*x*)
(Domain Guests)	Guests	Guests (1.*x* and 2.*x*)

> **NOTE**
>
> Windows NT services added to your server create additional accounts, such as Cert Requestors and Cert Server Admins (Certificate Server), and MTS Trusted Impersonators (Microsoft Transaction Server.)

The following list provides a brief description of the basic categories of predefined groups for Windows NT Server, Workstation, and Jet databases.

- **Administrators.** A person with an administrator account on a domain controller is given domain administrator authority as a member of the Domain Admins group. The trust relationship between Windows NT domains also enables a domain administrator who has an account with the same authority in another domain administer that domain. This relationship means that a domain administrator in North America can administer a domain located in Europe or Asia. Members of the Domain Admins and Administrators groups have the rights and abilities to do anything within the domains and on the servers that are within the scope of their authority. When you install Windows NT Server, you are automatically granted domain administrator authority with the Administrator account. Similarly, an administrator of an NT workstation exercises full authority over that workstation. Members of the Jet Admins group in a particular System.md? file have *full permissions for all objects* that were created with the specific System.md? file in use. (The emphasis is added because this is a very important point that is discussed at the end of this chapter.) Admins members cannot revoke the permissions of the creator of an object in a Jet database.

- **Operators.** NTS administrators can delegate some of their responsibilities to members of the Backup, Server, Account, and Print Operators groups. The names assigned to Operators groups imply the scope of authority of members of these groups. There is no equivalent to Operators groups in Windows NT or Jet. The Replicators group is used only in conjunction with Windows NT file-replication services, not Jet 3.0's briefcase replication features.

- **Users.** This term encompasses any group that is not an administrative or operative group. "Everyone" is a special entity that refers to all users, but not Administrators or Operators. (Operators do not have user privileges.) Special entities also include SYSTEM, NETWORK, INTERACTIVE, and CREATOR OWNER. The CREATOR OWNER entity is equivalent to the Jet Creator (object owner) entity. People who simply use the network to get their work done usually are made members of the Users group. NT Workstation's Power Users group have limited administrative authority; this group primarily is designed for establishing and maintaining secure workgroups. Jet requires that anyone who opens a secure Jet database be a member of the Users group. (Being a member of the Admins group is not sufficient to open a secure Access database. Members of the Admins group, however, are the only people who can directly modify the System.md? file.)

- **Guests.** Guests are not permitted to do anything at a Windows NT Server computer, including log on to the server (thus the parentheses surrounding Windows NT Domain Guests in Table 17.1). Guests are allowed to log on to Windows NT workstations, but they cannot participate in any network activities. Access 1.*x* and 2.0 provide Guests with read-only permissions for database tables. The Guest user of the Guests group (neither of which you can delete) is used for transitory access to a Windows NT workstation or to Access 1.*x* database applications. The best approach with secure Jet 1.*x* and 2.*x* databases is to assign a password to the mandatory Guest account and then forget the password. Access 95 and 97 do not provide a default Guests group.

Chapter 2, "Network Security and Domain Planning," in the *Windows NT Server Networking Guide* (part of the *Windows NT Server 4.0 Resource Kit*), provides a complete description of the rights and abilities of each predefined group and special entity of Windows NT Server 4.0.

File Permissions Using NTFS Partitions

Windows NT Server folders that are located on fixed-disk partitions formatted as FAT (DOS) partitions can be shared on the network, but you cannot control network access to individual files or subfolders of a shared FAT directory. To control access to individual files, the files must be located in a folder of an NTFS partition. Most Windows NT Server installations now use NTFS exclusively for shared files.

> **NOTE**
>
> A common practice is to install Windows NT Server system files on a C:\ FAT partition and then create one or more NTFS partitions for file sharing and services such as SQL Server, Exchange Server, and Transaction Server. Putting system files on a FAT partition enables you to boot with a DOS diskette, in the event of a boot failure, and gain access to the system files.

After you add the NTFS logical drive (volume), you can create the folder structure for the files to be shared by the server. Files in folders and subfolders on NTFS drives can be assigned one or more of the permissions listed in Table 17.2 for individual users or groups of users.

TABLE 17.2 NTFS FILE AND SUBFOLDER PERMISSIONS

Permission	Abbreviation	Permission	Abbreviation
Read	R	Execute	X
Write	W	Change Permission	P
Delete	D	Take Ownership	O

17

NETWORKING MULTIUSER JET DATABASES

Table 17.3 lists the standard Windows NT permissions for shared NTFS folders. The Folder column lists the abbreviations of the permissions that apply to the folder itself, and the New Files column lists the abbreviations of the permission for files that are added to the shared folder after directory-level permissions are granted. Permissions you assign to file and subfolder shares apply to users who log on to the server itself, as well as to users of workstations. Only members of the Administrators and Operators groups are allowed to log on to the server with Windows NT Server's default security settings.

TABLE 17.3   STANDARD PERMISSIONS FOR SHARED DIRECTORIES AND THEIR FILES IN NTFS PARTITIONS

Permissions	Directory	New Files	Description
No Access	None	None	A user cannot obtain access to the directory or its subdirectories.
List	RX	N/S	A user can list the files and subdirectories, but not read the files.
Read	RX	RX	A user can read and execute files in the directory (basic read-only access).
Add	WX	N/S	A user can add and execute files but cannot read or change existing files.
Add & Read	RWX	RX	A user can read and execute files in the directory but cannot modify files.
Change	RWXD	RWXD	A user can read, write, and delete files in the directory.
Full Control	All	All	In addition to Change permissions, a user can set permissions for and take ownership of any file in the directory.

Table 17.4 lists the standard Windows NT permissions and the Jet 3.0 database file permissions applicable to Access `Table` and `QueryDef` objects that correspond to the Windows NT file permissions. Permissions that apply to Access forms, reports, macros, and modules are not applicable to Visual Basic 4.0 database applications.

TABLE 17.4 STANDARD PERMISSIONS FOR SHARED FILES IN NTFS PARTITIONS AND JET 3.0
DATABASE FILES

Permissions	Files	Description	Jet 3.0
No Access	None	A user cannot obtain access to the file.	No permissions.
Read	RX	A user can read or execute the file.	Read Definitions and Read Data.
Change	RWXD	A user can read, write, or delete the file.	Read Definitions, Read Data, Update Data, Insert Data, and Update Data.
Full Control	All	A user can read, write, delete, set permissions for, or take ownership of the file.	Full Permissions, but the ownership of objects in the file requires importing objects into a new .mdb file.

The Windows NT Explorer is similar to that of Windows 95 and 98, but the method of sharing folders and files differs. To share a Northwind folder from a Windows NT Server 4.0 FAT or NTFS partition, do the following:

1. Select the folder to share in Windows NT Explorer and then choose File, Sharing to open the Sharing page of the Northwind Properties sheet.

2. Select the Shared As option, accept or change the Share Name, and type a brief description in the Comment text box. Accept the Default Maximum Allowed option as the User Limit, unless you want to restrict the number of connections to the shared files (see Figure 17.15).

FIGURE 17.15

Specifying the share name for a folder shared by Windows NT 4.0.

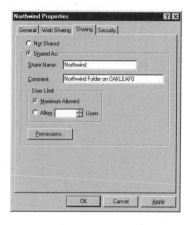

3. Click the Permissions button to open the Access Through Share Permissions dialog. The default permissions are Full Control for Everyone.

4. Select Everyone in the list and click Remove to empty the list.

5. Click Add to open the Add Users and Groups dialog. Select Domain Admins in the Names list and click Add to add Domain Admins to the Add Names list.

6. Select Full Control from the Type of Access list (see Figure 17.16). Click OK to add Domain Admins and close the dialog.

FIGURE 17.16

Adding Domain Admins with full control of the share.

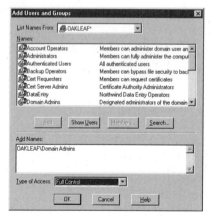

7. Assuming you have created a Windows NT group called DataEntry, repeat step 5 for the DataEntry group.

8. Select Change from the Type of Access list; click OK to add DataEntry and close the dialog. Your Access Through Share Permissions dialog appears as shown in Figure 17.17.

9. Click OK to close the Access Through Share Permissions dialog; then click OK again to close the Northwind Properties sheet. If your share name doesn't conform to the DOS 8.3 naming convention, click OK when you receive the warning message.

FIGURE 17.17

Adding Domain Admins with full control of the share.

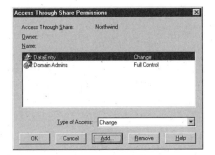

Like shared folders, the files within shared folders have Full permissions for Everyone, but in this case "Everyone" means those who have share permissions. To change permissions for a file or a group of files, in this case a System.mdw file, within a shared NTFS folder, follow these steps:

1. In Windows NT Explorer, select the file(s) whose permissions you want to change and choose File, Properties to open the System.mdw Properties sheet.

2. Click the Permissions button to open the File Permissions dialog.

3. Select Everyone and click Remove.

4. Click Add to open the Add Users and Groups dialog. Select Domain Admins in the Names list and click Add to add Domain Admins to the Add Names list.

5. Select Full Control from the Type of Access list and click OK to add Domain Admins and close the dialog.

6. Click Add again in the File Permissions dialog and select the group to which you want to give restricted file access, in this case read-only access to the DataEntry group.

7. Select Read (the default) from the Type of Access list and click OK to add DataEntry and close the dialog. Your File Permissions dialog appears as shown in Figure 17.18.

FIGURE 17.18

Restricting file permissions within a shared folder on an NTFS partition.

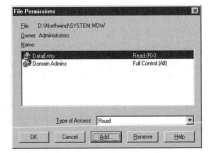

8. Click OK twice to close the File Permissions dialog and the System.mdw Properties sheet.

> **NOTE**
>
> If you created the share and added the files as a member of the Administrators local group (typically using the Administrator account), you are the owner of the share and the files. Ownership grants Full permissions. Technically, it's not necessary to add the Domain Admins group with Full permissions, but it's a normal practice to do so.

FATHOMING THE JET SECURITY SYSTEM

As mentioned earlier in the chapter, the Jet database security system has been called labyrinthine, Byzantine, and even Machiavellian. The security methodology of Jet is derived from a mixture of LAN Manager, SQL Server, and Windows NT security techniques. If you decide to implement Jet security in conjunction with Visual Basic 6.0 database applications or if your Visual Basic database applications share secure .mdb files with Access applications, you must have a fundamental understanding of how Jet implements security for `Table` and `QueryDef` objects. You don't need to worry about security issues for Access `Form`, `Report`, `Macro`, and `Module` objects, because Visual Basic doesn't recognize these objects. It's far easier to use Access to manage Jet security features than to do so programmatically with Visual Basic 6.0. The sections that follow assume that you possess a license for the retail version of Access 97.

> **WARNING**
>
> Before you use any of the security features of Access that are discussed in the following sections, make a backup copy of the System.md? file in use and back up any .mdb files whose permissions you plan to modify. If you have not made any changes to the default values in the System.md? file that was installed when you set up Access, make a copy of the System.md? file on a floppy disk and save it for future use as the base System.md? file for creating new applications.

Assigning User Accounts and Securing Jet Databases

When you first launch Access, you are assigned a default user ID of `Admin`, a member of Access's `Admins` and `Users` groups, with an empty (`""`) password. This combination of user ID and empty password prevents the Logon dialog from appearing when you launch Access. If the Logon dialog (see Figure 17.19) appears when you launch Access, you may have the beginning of a secure database system. (This statement assumes that unauthorized users do not know the valid user ID and password combinations contained in System.md?.)

FIGURE 17.19

The Access 97's Logon dialog.

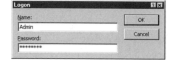

> **NOTE**
>
> Access 97 provides a simpler method of implementing database security by password protection. If you password protect a database, a dialog appears when you open the database requesting a password, which is common to all users. Password protection provides only a low level of security, and you cannot use password protection with Jet 3.5 replicated databases. You can, however, use the full security system described in this section for database replication.

To initiate database security with Access, you need to add a new user ID and assign the new user account membership in the Admins group. After you add the new member of the Admins group and take ownership of the objects in the database(s) you intend to secure, you can remove the default Admin user account from the Admins group (if other Access System.md? files do not depend on the presence of the Admin user) and take away all permissions from the Admin user. You also need to change the ownership of any existing database objects created by the Admin user that you want to make secure. Follow these steps to secure Access 97 so that only DBAs can launch Access:

1. Launch Access 97 and choose <u>T</u>ools, Securi<u>t</u>y, User and Group <u>A</u>ccounts to display the User and Group Accounts properties sheet. (Access 2.0 and earlier versions don't allow you to enter the security subsystem without opening a database.)

2. Click the Change Logon Password tab, press the Tab key to bypass the Old Password text box, and type a valid password (14 characters maximum) in the New Password and Verify text boxes (see Figure 17.20). Click the Apply button to set the password without closing the properties sheet. (The Admin user must be assigned a password to display the logon dialog upon launching Access.)

FIGURE 17.20

Adding a password for the default Admin user.

3. Click the Users tab and click the New button to display the New User/Group dialog.

4. Type the new Admins user ID in the Name text box and type a four-digit personal identification number in the Personal ID text box, as shown in Figure 17.21. (Access user IDs are not case sensitive.)

FIGURE 17.21

The User and Group Accounts property sheet and New User/Group dialog of the Access 97 security system.

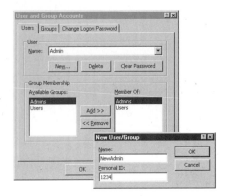

5. Click the OK button of the New User/Group dialog to close it. Access automatically makes the new user a member of the Users group.

6. Select Admins in the Available Groups list box and click the Add button to add the new user to the Admins group. The User and Group Accounts property sheet now appears as shown in Figure 17.22. (This step is critical. The new user must be a member of both the Admins and Users group.) Click the OK button to complete the record for the new user's account and close the properties sheet.

FIGURE 17.22

The User and Group Accounts properties sheet after adding NewAdmin as a member of Users and Admins groups.

7. Close and relaunch Access. If you followed the instruction in step 6, the Logon dialog appears. Enter your new user ID in the Name text box (see Figure 17.23) and click the OK button. (You have not yet assigned a password to the new user account.)

FIGURE 17.23

*The Logon dialog
for the NewAdmin
account.*

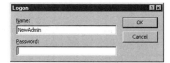

8. Repeat step 2 for your new account. The password you choose for your new Admins account should contain at least eight characters and should consist of a combination of letters and numbers. Using a combination of uppercase and lowercase letters provides even better password security.

9. Relaunch Access and enter your new user ID and the new password to verify that your new account is established correctly and that the new user is a member of the Admins group.

10. Select Admin from the Users list, select Admins in the Member Of list, and click the Remove button to remove Admin from the Admins group. (Access won't let you delete the Admin account.)

Securing Existing Database Files with the Access 97 User-Level Security Wizard

At this point, Access itself is secure, and any new Access databases you create also will be secure. Henceforth, your new user ID is the owner of any new database objects you create. However, all Access database objects you and others previously created with the Admin account (using the blank password) are not secure for the following reasons:

- The Admin user is the owner (the *Creator* in Access terminology) of all objects in every database you or others created using the Admin account, as well as the sample databases supplied with Access.

- No user, including an Admins user, has the authority to revoke the object owner's permissions. By default, the owner of an object has Full Permissions for the object.

- The SID of the default Admins user is created by combining the username and company name (if any) you entered when you installed Access and then encrypting the combination.

- Anyone can install a bootleg copy of Access that creates a System.mdw file with the same SID that you (and possibly others) used to create database objects until you (and others) logged on with new user IDs and passwords.

- The user with the bootleg copy of Access has Full Permissions for every database object in every unsecured database.

To secure database objects whose creation date precedes your securing Access, you need to take ownership of the database objects by importing the objects into a new database file. Traditionally, you change ownership of Jet database objects by importing the objects into a new database and then removing permissions for the Admin user. Access 97 includes a User-Level Security Wizard that handles the entire process for you. (If you are using an earlier version of Access, you might want to skip to the next section).

Follow these steps to assume ownership of objects in an existing Jet 3.5*x* database and encrypt the file for additional security:

1. Launch Access with your new user ID and password and open the database you want to secure.

2. Choose <u>T</u>ools, Securi<u>t</u>y, User-Level Security <u>W</u>izard to open the first Wizard dialog.

3. Mark the check boxes of the types of objects you want to secure (see Figure 17.24); then click OK to display the Destination Database dialog. Multiuser applications with split databases usually only include `TableDef` and `QueryDef` objects.

FIGURE 17.24

Selecting object types to secure with the Access 97 User-Level Security Wizard.

4. By default, the Wizard prefixes the existing filename with Secure. Enter a different filename, if you want, and click OK to create the new database.

5. Access exports the selected objects to the new database and sets permissions for each object. When the process is complete, the message shown in Figure 17.25 appears. Click OK to close the dialog.

FIGURE 17.25

This message confirms successful creation of a secure version of the original .mdb file.

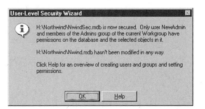

6. Close the original database and open the new, secure database; then choose <u>T</u>ools, Securi<u>t</u>y, User and Group <u>P</u>ermissions to open the User and Group Permissions properties

sheet. Click the Groups option button and select Users to verify that the Users group now has no permissions for any `Table` or `Query` object.

7. Mark the check boxes to add group permissions for the Users group. Typically, Users have read-write permissions for online transaction processing and read-only permissions for decision-support applications. Hold down the Shift key and click each object name to select all `TableDef` objects (see Figure 17.26) and then click the Apply button. Repeat this step for the `QueryDef` objects in the secure database. (Members of the Admins group have full permissions for all objects.)

17

NETWORKING MULTIUSER JET DATABASES

FIGURE 17.26

Adding read-write TableDef permissions for the Users group.

8. Click the Change Owner tab to verify that the objects in the secure database are owned by the new account you created, as shown in Figure 17.27.

FIGURE 17.27

Verifying ownership of database objects with the Change Owner page of the User and Group Permissions properties sheet.

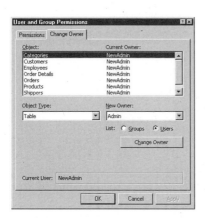

9. The Admin user is a member of the Users group and has all permissions granted to Users. You cannot remove the Admin user from the Users group. However, the Admin user account is password protected; if you don't reveal the Admin password, you need not be concerned about unauthorized use of the Admin account.

You now have a secure database in which you are the undisputed owner of all database objects. If Microsoft had made the Take Ownership (O) permission of Windows NT applicable to Jet database objects, the transfer of title would be a much simpler process. However, an additional benefit of the User-Level Security Wizard is that the Wizard encrypts the secure database so that the data in `TableDef` objects cannot be read with a binary file editing application.

Granting and Revoking Access Permissions for Groups and Users with Earlier Versions of Access

If your Visual Basic database application must run under Windows 3.11, you must use a 16-bit version of Access to implement security features. In this case, you create a new database (using your new account) and then import the objects into the new database to change ownership from the Admin account to the new user account. The names of permissions in the sections that follow, such as Modify Data, are for Access 1.*x* databases. Access 2.0 databases use the same permissions terminology (Read Data, Update Data, and so forth) described in the preceding section for Access 95.

By default, all versions of Access grant Full Permissions on all `TableDef` and `QueryDef` objects (as well as other Access database object types) to members of the Users group. Granting Full Permissions by default to the Users group has been the subject of many complaints from Access developers. These complaints led to the addition of the User-Level Security Wizard in Access 95. You probably don't want everyone who can open the database to have read-write access to all, or even to any, tables in the database. This statement is especially true of databases that are the source of data for decision-support applications. (One of the canons of database administration is this: I shall grant no one with a title other than data entry operator or data entry supervisor read-write permissions in my databases.)

Because all users except the Guest user of secure Access databases must be a member of the Users group, you need to revoke Modify Data privileges from the Users group and create a new group, DataEntry, which has both Read Data and Modify Data privileges. (Everyone with access to the database should be granted Read Definitions privileges.)

Revoking Permissions from the User Group

To revoke Modify Definitions and Modify Data permissions from the Users group for objects in Access 1.*x* databases, follow these steps:

1. Open the database whose permissions you want to modify; choose Permissions from the Security menu to open the Permissions dialog. The first `TableDef` object in the database is the default object.

2. Click the Groups option button of the List group to display groups instead of users in the Name combo box. Select Users from the Name combo box.

3. Click the Modify Definitions and Modify Data check boxes to clear the check marks.

4. Click the Assign button to make the revocation of Modify Definitions and Modify Data permissions permanent.

5. Choose the remaining objects in the database and repeat steps 3 and 4 to revoke the write permissions for each object.

6. When you've completed this tedious operation, click the Close button to return to Access's main window.

Members of the Users group no longer have default (implicit) permissions to modify the design of tables or queries or to update tables in this database. You can give Modify Data permission to specific members of the Users group by listing Users instead of Groups, selecting the user from the combo box, and ticking the Modify Data check box. Implicit permissions of users inherited from group membership do not appear in the check boxes when you display individual user permissions. (This condition is a peculiarity of the Access 1.*x* security system.)

> **NOTE**
>
> The process for revoking Group permissions is the same for Access 1.*x* and 2.0 except that the permission names are not the same.

Creating a New Access Group and Assigning Group Permissions

To create a new DataEntry group and set up the correct permissions for the new group, follow these steps:

1. Open one of the databases that you want to make available for updating by members of the DataEntry user group. Choose Groups from the Security menu to open the Groups dialog.

2. Click the New button of the Groups dialog to open the New User/Group dialog. Type the name of the new group (DataEntry) in the Name text box and type a personal identification number for the group in the Personal ID Number text box.

3. Click the OK button to close the New User/Group dialog and then click the OK button of the Groups dialog to close it.

4. Perform steps 2 through 6 of the preceding section with the following changes: Select the DataEntry group in step 2 and remove the check mark only in the Modify Definitions check box (step 3) so that members of the DataEntry group can update tables in the database.

PROGRAMMING JET SECURITY FEATURES WITH VISUAL BASIC 6.0 AND DAO 3.5

After you secure a Jet database, you must establish a pointer to the location of the System.md? file as described in the "Supplementing Workgroup Security with Jet's Security Features" section earlier in this chapter. If you're using DAO 3.5, your 32-bit **Sub** Main subprocedure or the Form_Open event handler of your first form must include one of the following lines prior to any code that refers to the database:

```
DBEngine.SystemDB = "d:\path\system.mdw"
DBEngine.SystemDB = "\\servername\sharename\path\system.mdw"
```

If you don't add this code (or the appropriate Registry or *AppName*.ini entry), the message shown in Figure 17.28 appears when you attempt to run your application that contains a reference to or a Data control based on a secure Jet database. If Jet can't open the designated System.md? file, the message shown in Figure 17.29 appears.

FIGURE 17.28

This message indicates a missing pointer to the System.md? workgroup file for a secure Jet database.

FIGURE 17.29

This message indicates an incorrect pointer to the System.md? workgroup file.

The first form must be a logon dialog that provides text boxes for entry of a user ID (account name) and password. You pass the value of the user ID and password to the DefaultUser and DefaultPassword properties of the DBEngine object with the following two lines of code, executed by the OK button of your logon dialog:

```
DBEngine.DefaultUser = txtUserID.Text
DBEngine.DefaultPassword = txtPassword.Text
```

The user ID and password applies to the default Workspace object, Workspaces(0). For test purposes, you can add the preceding lines immediately after the DBEngine.SystemDB = statement with literal strings substituted for the text box values. If you don't provide a user ID or password, or either the user ID or password is incorrect, you receive the message shown in Figure 17.30.

FIGURE 17.30

This message indicates a missing or incorrect user ID and/or password.

> **NOTE**
>
> An alternative to the `Default...]` approach is to use the `CreateWorkspace(str`*WSName*`, str`*UserID*`, str`*Password*`)` method of the `DBEngine` object and apply the `Append str`*WSName* method to the `Workspaces` collection. You then refer to the new `Workspace` object by a `Set ws`*Name* `= DBEngine.Workspaces(str`*WSName*`)` statement.

Exploring the `Users` and `Groups` Collections with DAO 3.5

After you open the System.md*?* file, you have access to the `Users` and `Groups` collections of the newly created `Workspace` object. You can use the Debug Window to enumerate the members of the `Users` collection by typing **? wsName.Users(*i*).Name**. Jet provides the names of the first three `User` objects (`admin`, `Creator`, and `Engine`) for both secure and unsecured databases; the first secure `User` is `Users(3)`, as illustrated by Figure 17.31. The first two members of the `Groups` collection are `Admin (0)` and `Users (1)`; the `Group` objects you add begin with index 2.

FIGURE 17.31

Iterating the `Users` collection of a secure database in the Debug Window.

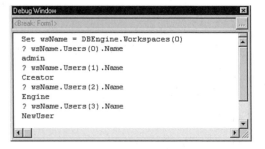

Each `Group` object has a `Users` collection, which enumerates the members of the `Group`, and each `User` object has a `Groups` collection, which enumerates the `Groups` to which each `User` belongs. Figure 17.32 illustrates in the Debug Window the relationship between `Groups(`*i*`).Users(`*j*`)` and `Users(`*i*`).Groups(`*j*`)`. You add and delete members of the `Groups` and `Users` collections by applying the `CreateUser`, `CreateGroup`, and `Delete` methods. Only members of the `Admins` group can manipulate the `Users` and `Groups` collections.

FIGURE 17.32

*Exploring relation-
ships between
Groups(i).User
s(j) and
Users(i).Group
s(j) in the Debug
Window.*

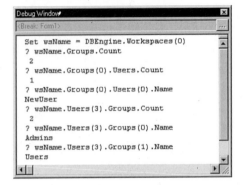

```
Debug Window
<Break: Form1>
  Set wsName = DBEngine.Workspaces(0)
  ? wsName.Groups.Count
   2
  ? wsName.Groups(0).Users.Count
   1
  ? wsName.Groups(0).Users(0).Name
  NewUser
  ? wsName.Users(3).Groups.Count
   2
  ? wsName.Users(3).Groups(0).Name
  Admins
  ? wsName.Users(3).Groups(1).Name
  Users
```

To add a new User object to the workgroup information file, you apply the
CreateUser(str*UserID*[, str*PID*[, str*Password*]]) method to the default Workspace object.
Next, you Append the newly created User object to the Users collection of the default
Workspace and then Append the User object to the Users collection of at least the Users group,
as the following example shows:

```
Dim wsName As Workspace
Dim usrNew As User

Set wsName = DBEngine.Workspaces(0)

'Create the new user with a PID and password
Set usrNew = wsName.CreateUser("new", "1234", "bogus")

'Append the new user to the Users collection
wsName.Users.Append usrNew

'Append the new user to the Users group
Set usrNew = wsName.CreateUser("new")        'Recreate usrNew
wsName.Groups(1).Users.Append usrNew

'Optionally, append the new user to the Admins group
Set usrNew = wsName.CreateUser("new")        'Recreate usrNew
wsName.Groups(0).Users.Append usrNew
```

NOTE

When you create a form to enable Admins members to add new users, your
cmdOK_Click event handler should include addition of each new user to the
Users group. You must recreate the User object each time you append the new
User object to the Users collection of a Group object.

It's easier to experiment with the addition of new users in the Debug Window. Figure 17.33 shows the code of the preceding example with intermediate tests for Group membership.

FIGURE 17.33

Adding a new user to the Users *and* Admins *groups in the Debug Window.*

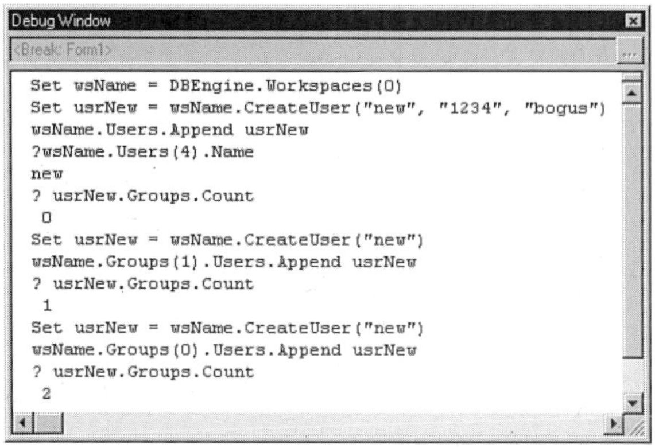

```
Debug Window                                              [x]
<Break: Form1>                                         ...
Set wsName = DBEngine.Workspaces(0)
Set usrNew = wsName.CreateUser("new", "1234", "bogus")
wsName.Users.Append usrNew
?wsName.Users(4).Name
new
? usrNew.Groups.Count
 0
Set usrNew = wsName.CreateUser("new")
wsName.Groups(1).Users.Append usrNew
? usrNew.Groups.Count
 1
Set usrNew = wsName.CreateUser("new")
wsName.Groups(0).Users.Append usrNew
? usrNew.Groups.Count
 2
```

Altering Permissions for Container and Document Objects

Permissions of Groups are inherited by members of Groups. Thus a new user added to the Users group will inherit permissions previously assigned in the System.md? file to the Users group. You grant or revoke explicit permissions using the Containers collection of the Database object and the Documents collection of the Container object. The Tables container includes both TableDef and QueryDef Document objects. Figure 17.34 illustrates experimentation with Container and Document objects for an open database in the Debug Window.

FIGURE 17.34

Experimenting with Database Container *and* Document *objects.*

```
Debug Window                                              [x]
<Break: Form1>                                         ...
Set wsName = DBEngine.Workspaces(0)
Set dbCurrent = wsName.Databases(0)
Set cntTables = dbCurrent.Containers("Tables")
? cntTables.Documents.Count
 32
? cntTables.Documents(0).Name
Categories
? cntTables.Documents(0).Permissions
 1048575
? cntTables.Documents(0).UserName
NewUser
cntTables.Documents(0).UserName = "new"
? cntTables.Documents(0).Permissions
 0
? cntTables.UserName
NewUser
? cntTables.Permissions
 1048575
```

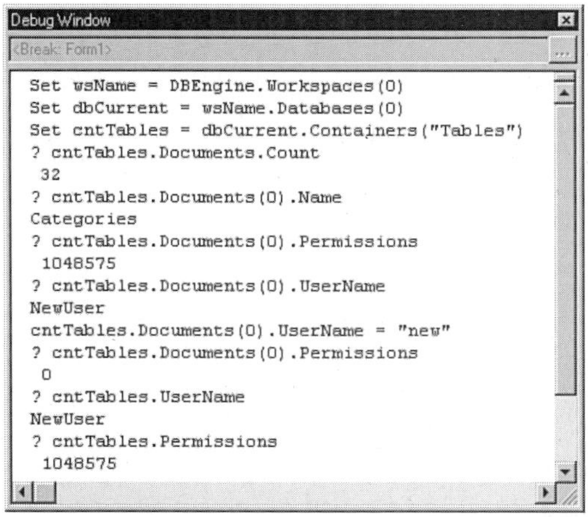

To gain access to the `Tables` container of an open database—the `TableDef` and `QueryDef` documents—and assign or revoke permissions to the Tables `Container` and each `Document` object, use the following code:

```
Dim wsCurrent As Workspace
Dim dbCurrent As Database
Dim cntTables As Container
Dim docTable As Document

Set wsCurrent = DBEngine.Workspaces(0)
Set dbCurrent = wsCurrent.Databases(0)

'Set the Container object variable
Set cntTables = dbCurrent.Containers("Tables")

'Establish the user ID and set Container permissions
cntTables.Inherit = True
cntTables.UserName = strUserID
cntTables.Permissions = intPermissionFlags

'Establish the user ID and set all Document permissions
For Each docTable In cntTables.Documents
    docTable.UserName = strUserID
    docTable.Permissions = intPermissionFlags
Next
```

Table 17.5 lists values and permissions (int*PermissionFlags*) for the intrinsic dbSec... constants defined by the Jet 3.5 DAO. As with other constant flags, you can combine various permissions with the bitwise **Or** operator.

TABLE 17.5 JET 3.5 INTRINSIC SECURITY CONSTANTS (FLAGS) FOR THE Permissions PROPERTY

Constant Name	Value	Object Permission(s)
dbSecCreate	1	Create new documents (Container object only)
dbSecDelete	65536	Delete the object
dbSecDeleteData	128	Delete records
dbSecFullAccess	1048575	Full access
dbSecInsertData	32	Append records
dbSecNoAccess	0	No access
dbSecReadDef	4	Read TableDef or QueryDef object properties, but not data
dbSecReadSec	131072	Read security-related properties
dbSecReplaceData	64	Update records
dbSecRetrieveData	20	Read data
dbSecWriteDef	65548	Modify or delete TableDef or QueryDef object

Constant Name	Value	Object Permission(s)
dbSecWriteOwner	524288	Change the `Owner` property value
dbSecWriteSec	262144	Alter permissions

OLE DB, ADO 2.0, AND JET SECURITY

▶ **See** "Specifying a Jet Workgroup File for Secure Databases," **p. 140**

As noted in Chapter 3, "Migrating from DAO to ADO," the native Microsoft Jet 3.51 OLE DB Provider and ADO 2.0 provide very limited support for secure Jet databases. You can specify the name and location of the *System*.md? file, as well as a user name and password, but ADO 2.0 doesn't provide access to the System.md? tables to add or delete users, or modify user's object permissions.

At the time this book was written, Microsoft had announced that Access 9.0 (a.k.a Access 2000) will support ADO, but the precise details of the upgrade to ADO 2.0 to implement Jet security were under NDA. Kevin Collins, Microsoft's Jet Program Manager, in early June 1998 gave a preview of Access 9.0's Jet 4.0 in his "Planning for New Features in Jet 4.0" presentation at Microsoft Tech*Ed 98. The most important elements of the presentation for multiuser Jet 4.0 databases are:

- Support for ANSI SQL `GRANT` and `REVOKE` permissions statements for `Container`, `User`, and `Group` objects.

- Row-level locking via cursors for improved concurrency with `INSERT`, `UPDATE`, and `DELETE` operations. (Row-level locking is provided for data pages only; index locks remain page-level).

- Automatic escalation from row- to page- to table-level locks, depending on the number of locks requests generated by the query.

- Support for SQL-92 {DELETE¦UPDATE} CASCADE [NULL] DDL syntax to enforce referential integrity.

- ADO support for replication, including replication to and from desktop and standard SQL Server 7.0 databases.

> **NOTE**
>
> SQL Server 7.0 beta 3 and later installs a beta version of the Microsoft Jet 4.0 OLE DB Provider to support replication operations between Jet 3.5x and SQL Server 7.0 databases. Unfortunately, the extensions to ADO required to let Visual Basic developers use the new features of Jet 4.0 aren't installed with the Provider.

17

NETWORKING
MULTIUSER JET
DATABASES

WORKING WITH CLIENT/SERVER DATABASES

IN THIS CHAPTER

This chapter introduces you to the management of client/server relational database management system (RDBMS) back ends and the modifications in the design of your Visual Basic 6.0 front ends to take maximum advantage of the client/server model. The RDBMS used for most of the examples in this chapter is a beta version Microsoft SQL Server 7.0 (code-named "Sphinx") running under Windows 9x or as a service of Windows NT Server 4.0 and 5.0 (also a beta version). SQL Server 7.0, which offers a variety of new features for enterprise computing, was scheduled for retail release in late 1998 and will replace version 6.5 in future releases of BackOffice. SQL Server 7.0 is backwardly compatible with Visual Basic front ends written for prior versions of SQL Server.

NOTE

This chapter's "Using the Access 97 Upsizing Wizard" section uses SQL Server 6.5. The Access 97 Upsizing Wizard fails with SQL Server 7.0 and requires SQL Server 6.5 or earlier. Future versions of Microsoft Access are likely to include an SQL Server 7.0-compatible Upsizing Wizard. To use SQL Server 6.5 with Visual Studio 6.0's Visual Data Tools (VDTs), you must first run the new version of Instcat.sql script that installs from the \OS\System folder of distribution CD-ROM 1 to your computer's \Windows\System or \WinNT\System32 folder. Open Instcat.sql in SQL Server 6.5's ISQL_w utility and execute the script against each SQL Server you want to use with the VDTs.

The Visual Basic examples near the end of this chapter use ADO 2.0 and the native OLE DB provider for SQL Server, SQLOLEDB. If you're using Oracle 7.3+, substitute MSDAORA, the Microsoft OLE DB Provider for Oracle. MSDAORA, the subject of the "Connecting to Oracle8 Database" section near the end of the chapter, offers features similar to SQLOLEDB. If you don't have a native OLE DB provider for your client/server RDBMS, you must use the Microsoft OLE DB Provider for ODBC Drivers, MSDASQL, and the appropriate 32-bit ODBC driver.

Designing Visual Basic 6.0 front ends for client/server databases follows the same methodology you use to design applications that manipulate tables of conventional desktop databases, as described in preceding chapters. One of the primary benefits of ADO is consistency of implementation across a wide range of data source types. If you have an RDBMS table structure that exactly duplicates the structure of the tables that compose your desktop database, you need only change the value of the `Provider` and `ConnectionString` properties of the `Connection` object to connect to the client/server RDBMS. If you've used proprietary SQL keywords, such as Jet's SQL's `PIVOT` and `TRANSFORM` verbs, you must rewrite your SQL-specific code to conform to the SQL dialect of the new RDBMS. In Jet terminology, all queries executed by ADO and native OLE DB providers are *passthrough queries*.

> **NOTE**
>
> Jet databases are capable of linking client/server tables using an ODBC data source to a Jet .mdb file. This configuration permits heterogeneous joins between client/server and local Jet tables. The native OLE DB provider for Jet, Microsoft.Jet.OLEDB.3.51 (Jolt), supports linked client/server tables. Connecting to linked client/server tables with ADO and Jolt is a very resource-intensive process; the client must load DAO 3.5, Jet, the ODBC driver manager, the ODBC driver, ADO, and Jolt to make the connection to the RDBMS. For best performance, avoid use of linked tables and minimize or eliminate heterogeneous joins. SQL Server 7.0 supports heterogeneous queries against back-end databases, including Jet databases.

The initial examples in this chapter use Microsoft Access 97 to export files to an SQL Server database. All versions of Access provide automated exporting of table structures and data to client/server RDBMS. If you intend to develop client/server front-end applications using local .mdb files for subsequent upsizing to a client/server RDBMS, Access is an indispensable tool for making the transition. Alternatively, you can use the Visual Database Tools (VDTs) to design an entire back-end database from scratch.

> **NOTE**
>
> Another alternative is to use the SQL Server 6.x or 7.0 Enterprise Manager to create new tables in a database. It's also possible to use VBA code and SQL CREATE TABLE statements to generate server table structures and INSERT INTO statements to export data to the tables. Creating tables with VBA code is a very tedious process and ordinarily is reserved for developers writing database-related wizards, such as the Access Upsizing Wizard.

USING MICROSOFT SQL SERVER

Microsoft's objective for its BackOffice software suite is to gain market share in the "enterprise computing" sector, which today remains dominated by mainframes, minicomputers, and high-end PC servers running UNIX. Microsoft has established an aggressive price structure for BackOffice and its components; the licensing cost for SQL Server is substantially less than competitive RDBMSs offering similar performance and features. Installation and administration of Windows NT 4+ and especially SQL Server 7.0 is far simpler than that of UNIX and UNIX-based RDBMSs. Therefore, many smaller firms, which traditionally have employed shared-file systems for multiuser database systems, are moving to client/server systems. The practical limit for shared-file desktop database systems is 20 to 50 simultaneous users, depending on the ratio of decision-support to online transaction-processing applications in use. Migration from shared-file to client/server systems has created a substantial demand for Visual Basic developers with client/server credentials. It's a reasonably sure bet that most new Visual Basic 6.0 client/server front ends will use Microsoft SQL Server as the back end. The sections that follow describe the most important features of SQL Server in general, plus the benefits and drawbacks of SQL Server 7.0.

Networking Features of SQL Server

You can connect to SQL Server via NetBEUI, IPX/SPX, TCP/IP, and various other network protocols. The current trend is toward TCP/IP as the favored protocol for client/server networking because of TCP/IP's support of heterogeneous networks, which are likely to include servers running NetWare, UNIX, and Windows NT. Use by the Internet also has contributed to the general acceptance of TCP/IP as the primary networking protocol for at least the last half of this decade. Microsoft calls TCP/IP its "strategic protocol for scalable Windows-based networking."

The networking features of SQL Server are designed for maximum user convenience; for example, you can set up SQL Server with integrated or mixed security so that users are automatically logged on to SQL Server when they log on to the Windows NT network. Automatic logon to the database server also is provided across remote servers in Windows NT domains that share a trust relationship. Successive versions of SQL Server have demonstrated substantial improvements in performance with increasing numbers of simultaneous users. The database objects of SQL Server 6.*x* are compatible with those of SQL Server 4.21a, so upgrading to newer versions has been a relatively painless process. SQL Server 7.0 uses a completely revamped database and log file system, so converting to version 7.0 is a major operation.

SQL Server uses one or more *Net-Libraries* to provide access by various networked clients. SQL Server simultaneously supports *named pipes* connections over TCP/IP, IPX/SPX, and NetBEUIand uses the TCP/IP sockets API for communication with Macintosh, UNIX, and DEC MVS clients. Windows 3.1+ clients use a 16-bit library (DBNMP3.DLL) to implement named pipes; Windows 95 and Windows NT use a 32-bit named pipes library (Dbnmpntw.dll) on the client side.

Connections, Threads, and Symmetrical Multiprocessing

A conversation between an application and SQL Server takes place through one or more connections established by the named pipes service or by one of the other Net-Libraries supported by SQL Server. A connection is similar in concept to that of the Windows Sockets for TCP/IP communication. Each open connection is dedicated to the client workstation that originated the connection and may persist for a period of time after the client is finished using the connection, a process called *connection caching*.

When you use ADO and either a native OLE DB provider (or MSDASQL and an ODBC driver) to connect to a server back end and create a `Recordset` object from a query, the operation usually requires at least two connections. (One connection obtains information about the query from the server, and the other passes the data to your application.) Updatable `Recordset` objects having less than 100 records and forward-only `Recordset` objects require only a single connection. If your query is based on a complex SQL statement that involves multiple `JOIN`s, involves many `GROUP BY`s, or creates the equivalent of a crosstab query, your application is likely to open three connections at once. Although ADO and OLE DB attempt to share connections when they can, many situations may require several simultaneous connections by your application.

NOTE

Each user connection to SQL Server 6.*x* requires about 18KB of server memory; on installation, 25 is the default maximum number of SQL Server 6.*x* connections (30 for version 7.0) and is likely to support about 10 simultaneous users. You must increase the maximum number of SQL Server 6.5 connections as workstations running SQL Server front ends are added to the network. SQL Server 7.0 automatically manages connections for you, but you can use the `sp_configure` stored procedure to manage connections manually.

Both Windows 9*x* and Windows NT are multithreaded operating systems. A *thread* is a single task that is executed by an application or the operating system. Multithreaded operating systems enable multiple tasks to appear to run simultaneously; the operating system determines the priority of the task and enables tasks with the highest priority to execute first and most often. Tasks with higher priorities can suspend processing of lower priority tasks; operating systems that enable task priorities to govern the flow of the execution of tasks are called *preemptive multitasking* applications. 32-bit applications must be coded explicitly to support multiple threads of execution. SQL Server is a multithreaded 32-bit application; Jet 3.5*x* supports up to three threads of execution, but you can increase the number of threads by the `Threads` setting in the `\HKEY_LOCAL_MACHINE\SOFTWARE\Jet\3.5\Engines\Jet3.5` Registry key.

Windows NT provides a thread for each connection to SQL Server from a worker pool of threads whose population is set by the `sp_configure` stored procedure. The default is 255 threads, with a maximum of 1,024. When a client workstation makes a request from SQL Server, one of the threads from the worker pool is assigned to the workstation's connection. When the request is fulfilled and the connection is terminated, the connection thread is returned to the pool. If a client workstation requests a thread and none are available in the pool, the first thread released by another connection is assigned to the request. When a fault occurs during execution of a thread, only the connection associated with the thread is affected. Thus a page fault on a single connection does not bring down the server.

18

WORKING WITH
CLIENT/SERVER
DATABASES

The advantages of a multithreaded operation are evident only when you add more than one microprocessor unit (MPU) to the server. Windows NT supports thread-level multiprocessing, usually called symmetrical multiprocessing (SMP), and is referred to as a scalable operating system. These terms mean that multiple processors that share the same memory region can execute any thread. SMP also is called *symmetrical load balancing*. If a thread is executing on a processor that is running near capacity, the thread can be transferred so that it executes on another processor. Windows NT 4.0, and thus SQL Server 6+, supports up to eight Intel processors.

> **NOTE**
>
> Microsoft claims SQL Server provides "100 percent scalability" for up to four processors; this claim implies that a four-processor server theoretically has four times the capacity of a single-processor server. Microsoft says four to eight processors provide "80 percent scalability." Many reviews in the computer press dispute these claims, and today's most common SMP server configurations for Intel CPUs use two or four processors. Intel considers four processors to be the "electrical limit" for a single bus. However, Data General Corporation in March 1998 established a transaction-processing record for Intel-based servers: 16,101 order-entry transactions per minute (tmpC, Transaction Processing Performance Council Benchmark C) with an eight-way, 200MHz Pentium Pro server running the Enterprise Editions of Windows NT 4.0 and SQL Server 6.5.

SQL Server 7.0 (Sphinx)

Paul Flessner, Microsoft's General Manager of SQL Server Development, said in January 1998: "SQL Server 7.0 is the largest non-1.0 release in the industry." There's no question that SQL Server 7.0, known as Sphinx during the beta-testing stage, is the most momentous upgrade in the history of the product. The extent of the product's rework helps explain the more than 1-year delay from its originally scheduled release date, the second quarter of 1997.

One of the most important features of SQL Server 7.0 for many Visual Basic database developers is its new Desktop version that runs under Windows 9x and Windows NT 4.0+ Workstation. You can develop and test client/server applications on a laptop or desktop PC that's not connected to Windows NT Server. Microsoft announced in late 1997 that Access 9.0 will include Desktop SQL Server 7.0 as an alternative to the Jet database engine. Microsoft also offers independent software vendors (ISVs) an embedded version to replace the venerable Btrieve database.

Following is a list of the most important advantages of SQL Server 7.0 over prior versions and many of its higher-priced competitors:

- UNIX-style, fixed-size device (.dat) files are replaced by conventional 32-bit operating system files for data and log segments. Data (.mdf) and log (.ldf) files expand and contract automatically; you don't need to periodically expand .dat files to accommodate data and log growth.

- Automatic memory management and database tuning eliminates the need for advanced DBA skills in single-user and small workgroup installations. The sp_configure system stored procedure lets you override SQL Server 7's autotune settings.

- Structural changes deliver improved performance. 8K pages and 64KB extents, increased from 2KB and 16KB, respectively, speed updates and file I/O operations. Dbcc (SQL Server's database consistency checker) runs remarkably faster than in prior versions. Live backup operations have a minimal (less than 5%) effect on concurrent database operations.

- OLE DB lets SQL Server's query engine deal with heterogeneous joins that include tables from any record source having an OLE DB provider. Distributed queries joining tables from multiple databases on individual servers also receive a performance boost.

- The Query Planner takes the least-cost approach to SELECT queries by optimizing JOIN operations depending on the WHERE clause constraint(s) and ORDER BY sorting. SELECT query optimization is especially important in data warehousing applications. Figures 18.1 and 18.2 use the new SQL Server Query Analyzer, which replaces ISQL_w, to show the difference in the query execution plan when adding an ORDER BY clause to a simple SELECT statement.

18

Figure 18.1

The query execution plan for a simple SELECT *query.*

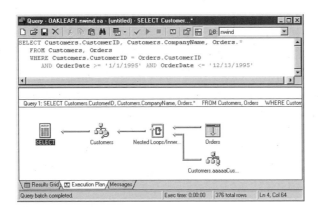

FIGURE 18.2

The execution plan for the query of Figure 18.1 with an ORDER BY clause added.

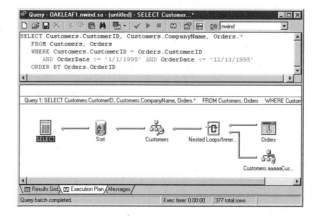

- INSERT and UPDATE locking are now supported at the row level. (SQL Server 6.0's row locking was limited to INSERTs.) Depending on the number of locks required, the planner escalates locking from the row level to the page or table level.

- Data Transformation Services (DTS) adds an OLE DB front end to bulk copy process (BCP), dramatically speeding up imports of a wide range of relational and other tabular data. You also can quickly export SQL Server data to other RDBMSs and common tabular file types, including Jet .mdb files.

- Enterprise, Standard, Desktop, and embedded versions of SQL Server 7.0 share the same source code base. All SQL Server 7.0 variants are compatible with one another and offer almost-identical sets of server tools.

- Twenty-some wizards aid users in performing routine operations such as creating new databases, adding tables and indexes, and importing/exporting data. SQL Server Enterprise Manager is a Microsoft Management Console (MMC) plug-in (see Figure 18.3), providing a consistent interface with Internet Information Server (IIS) 4.0, Microsoft Transaction Server (MTS) 2.0, and Windows NT 5.0 management tools. Experienced DBAs, however, will miss SQL Server 6.5 Enterprise Manager's more direct, menu-driven approach for many routine management chores.

FIGURE 18.3

SQL Server 7.0's Enterprise Manager, a snap-in for MMC, using Dynamic HTML (DHTML) to display database properties.

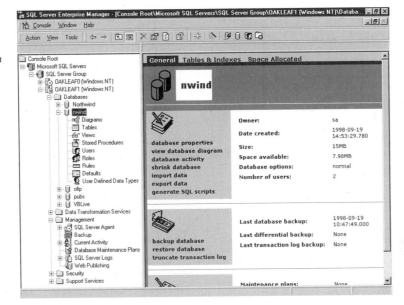

- Replication operations are streamlined by improved multisite update replication capabilities, less contention on replication tables, and optional replication of stored procedure execution. An Anonymous subscriber account lets large numbers of disconnected users update tables over the Internet.

- Switching between SQL Server 6.5 and 7.0 installed on a single server is simple and fast. Choose Start, Programs, Microsoft SQL Server - Switch (Common), Microsoft SQL Server to toggle the version and its corresponding tool set. The entire process takes less than 15 seconds.

NOTE

With the exception of Microsoft Query Analyzer, which works with both SQL Server 6.5 and 7.0, each version uses its own set of management tools. Version 6.*x*'s SQL Enterprise Manager uses the C-based Dblib (database library), whereas SQL Server 7.0 Enterprise Manager uses Automation (SQL-DMO, Data Management Objects) for management operations. SQL Server 7.0's implementation of SQL-DMO isn't backwardly compatible with prior SQL-DMO versions. You can register but not manage version 6.5 servers; attempting to manage a version 6.5 server opens the 6.5 version of Enterprise manager.

- Data warehousing is enhanced with support for terabyte databases, automatic load-dependent memory management, parallel I/O and read-ahead, merge and hash joins, hash aggregations, and multi-index optimization.

- Microsoft OLAP Server (code-named "Plato" in beta) enhances online analytical processing (OLAP) operations by creating Data Cubes. Data Warehousing and OLAP are the subjects of Chapter 28, "Analyzing Multidimensional Data with OLAP and MDX."

The downside of upgrading to SQL Server 7.0 is the need to re-create all database and log files from version 6.5 and earlier because of the change to the file format. Fortunately, Microsoft provides a Version Upgrade Wizard to automate the process. Microsoft claims that data transfers from version 6.*x* to 7.0 at a rate of 1G to 4G per hour, depending on hardware, database size, and complexity. These rates are achieved only when the old and new files are on the same server, an upgrade process called *pipelining*. Dumping SQL Server 6.*x* databases to backup tape and restoring to version 7.0, called *offlining*, is a much slower process.

UPSIZING NWIND.MDB TO SQL SERVER 6.5 WITH THE ACCESS 97 WIZARD

The quickest and most effective method of moving a Jet database to SQL Server is to use the Access 97 Upsizing Wizard. The Upsizing Wizard creates the SQL Server database for you, copies the tables, adds indexes, and adds triggers to maintain referential integrity constraints you specify in Access's Relationships window. (The Wizard also offers a declarative referential integrity choice that uses SQL constructs in place of triggers.) The alternatives, exporting the tables of the .mdb file from Access or using SQL Server 7.0's DTS to import the tables, require you to manually create indexes and write your own triggers in Transact-SQL, SQL Server's dialect of ANSI SQL-92.

> **NOTE**
>
> As mentioned earlier in the chapter, the Access 97 Upsizing Wizard doesn't work with SQL Server 7.0. If you have both SQL Server 6.*x* and 7.0, you can upsize to SQL Server 6.*x* and then use the Version Upgrade Wizard to convert the database to SQL Server 7.0. If you don't have SQL Server 6.5, you must export or import the tables to SQL Server 7.0. Access 9.0 undoubtedly will include an Upsizing Wizard that's fully compatible with SQL Server 7.0.

Preparing for Upsizing

The Access 97 Upsizing Wizard (Wzcs97.mda), part of the Access 97 Upsizing Tools, isn't included with Microsoft Office 97 Professional Edition. Before proceeding, you must download the wizard (about 2MB) from `http://www.microsoft.com/AccessDev/ProdInfo/AUT97dat.htm` or install the Upsizing Tools from the MSDN CD-ROM.

Visual Basic 6.0's Nwind.mdb includes queries, forms, reports, and other Access objects that aren't accessible to Visual Basic programmers using ADO 2.0. The wizard alters table names and queries to accommodate links to the SQL Server tables. To avoid changes to Visual Basic 6.0's Nwind.mdb or Access 97's Northwind.mdb, use Access 97's Database Splitter add-in to create a tables-only database.

The following steps create a tables-only version of Nwind.mdb from Access 97's Northwind.mdb:

1. Launch Access 97, don't open a database, and choose <u>T</u>ools, <u>D</u>atabase Utilities, <u>C</u>ompact Database to open the Database to Compact From dialog. Select Northwind.mdb in the \Program Files\Microsoft Office\Office\Samples folder and click Compact.

2. In the Compact Database Into dialog, change the file name from db1.mdb to Northback.mdb and then click Save to perform the compaction.

3. Open Northback.mdb choose <u>T</u>ools, Add-<u>I</u>ns, <u>D</u>atabase Splitter to start the Database Splitter Wizard's first dialog.

4. Click Split Database to open the Create Back-end Database dialog.

5. Change the name of the back-end database, which contains the tables, from Northback_be.mdb to Nwind.mdb (see Figure 18.4) and then click Split.

18

FIGURE 18.4

Specifying the name of the back-end (tables) database for the database-splitting operation.

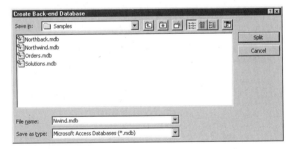

6. Click OK when the `Database sucessfully split` message appears.

7. Delete the Northback.mdb database to save disk space.

8. Open Nwind.mdb and verify that the database contains all the tables and that the Relationships window shows the appropriate relationships between the tables.

Using the Access 97 Upsizing Wizard

Unlike most of the examples in this book, which use the native OLE DB data provider for SQL Server, the Upsizing Wizard uses ODBC to make the connection to SQL Server. Access 97 doesn't directly support ADO, which was introduced after the release of Office 97.

Follow these steps to create an SQL Server 6.5 nwind database in the master.dat or another device from Nwind.mdb with the Access 97 Upsizing Wizard:

1. Choose Tools, Add-Ins, Upsize to SQL Server to start the Upsizing Wizard. In the first dialog, select the Create New Database option and click Next.

2. In the Select Data Source dialog, click the Machine Data Source tab; then click the New button to open the Create New Data Source dialog.

3. Select the System Data Source option and click Next to select the driver. Select SQL Server in the list (see Figure 18.5), click Next to confirm your selection, and then click Finish to start the ODBC Data Source Wizard.

FIGURE 18.5

Specifying the SQL Server ODBC driver in the Create New Data Source dialog.

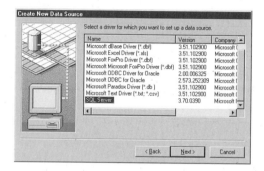

NOTE

ODBC 3.*x* offers three types of Data Sources (called DSN for Data Source Name). System DSNs are available to all users of a computer and are stored in the HKEY_CURRENT_MACHINE Registry hive. User DSNs are available only to a specific logged-on user and are held in HKEY_CURRENT_USER. File DSNs store their settings in *Name*.dsn files, which may be shared from a file server.

4. Type the name of your data source (DSN), in this case Nwind0, a brief description of the data source (including the server name), and select the network name of the server from the drop-down list (see Figure 18.6). Click Next.

NOTE

If the drop-down list is empty, type the server's name in the combo box.

FIGURE 18.6

Specifying the
ODBC data source
name (DSN) and
server name.

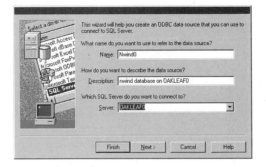

5. If you're using SQL Server integrated or mixed security, you can select the With Windows NT Authentication[el] option; otherwise select With SQL Server Authentication... and type your login ID and password (see Figure 18.7). Click next to continue.

This book uses unsecured SQL Server databases with the default sa (system administrator) login ID and no password in most cases.

FIGURE 18.7

Specifying the SQL
Server authentica-
tion method for the
data source.

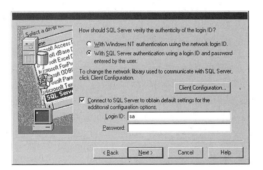

6. You must log on to the master database to create new devices and databases. Marking the check box displays a list of the database on the server. Accept the default master database, accept the remaining default options (see Figure 18.8), and click Next.

FIGURE 18.8

Selecting the mas-
ter database for
new device and
database opera-
tions.

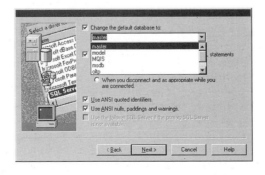

7. Accept the defaults (Perform Translation for Character Data and don't Use Regional Settings or Log Operations) in the last of the ODBC Data Source dialogs and click Finish to display a summary of your data source properties (see Figure 18.9).

FIGURE 18.9

The properties of the Nwind0 data source.

8. Click Test Data Source to attempt a connection to the server. The Test Results text box reports success or failure of the operation. Click OK twice to return to the Machine Data Source page of the Select Data Source dialog, which displays your new DSN (see Figure 18.10). Click OK to continue with the Upsizing Wizard.

FIGURE 18.10

The new ODBC DSN added as a System data source.

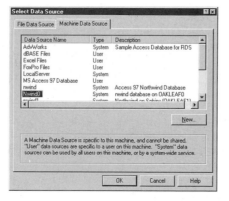

9. Type your Login ID and Password, if necessary, in the SQL Server Login dialog and click OK to open the Upsizing Wizard's device dialog with the default (Master.dat) database and log devices and sizes (50MB).

10. If you're working on a production server, it's not wise to add working databases to Master.dat. In the Database Device list, select <Create New Device> and type **ddg_data** in the Device Name text box of the New Device dialog; then click OK.

> **NOTE**
>
> It's a tradition among DBAs to use all lowercase for names of SQL Server devices and databases. SQL Server 4.21a, by default, used case-sensitive object names (Nwind <> nwind). SQL Server 6.*x* and 7.0 defaults during installation to object names that are not case sensitive.

11. Repeat the preceding step for the (transaction) Log Device, specifying ddg_log as the Device Name.

12. Set the size of both devices to 5MB (see Figure 18.11) and click Next.

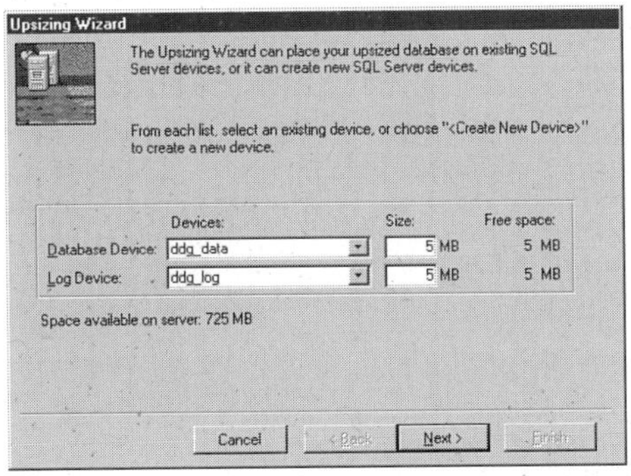

FIGURE 18.11

Specifying the names and sizes of the database and log devices.

13. Change the name of the database from NwindSQL to **nwind**, change the size reservations for the database (5MB) and log (5MB), respectively (see Figure 18.12), and click Next.

> **NOTE**
>
> It's especially important to set the initial transaction log size to 5MB. If you leave the size at the default 1MB, upsizing fails due to lack of Syslog space.

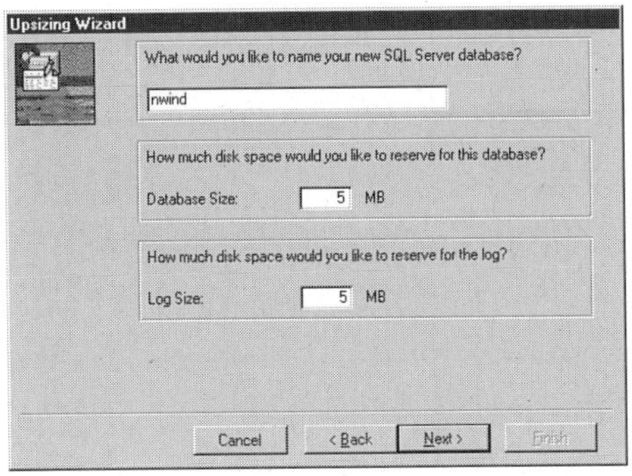

FIGURE 18.12

Setting the initial size of the database and transaction log.

14. Click the >> button to move all table items from the Available Tables list to the Export to SQL Server list and then click Next.

15. Accept the Wizard's table export defaults (see Figure 18.13). The defaults take maximum advantage of the Wizard's prowess by adding indexes, validation rules, default values, and table relationships to the database. Click Next.

FIGURE 18.13

Accepting the Upsizing Wizard's default table attributes, options, and database modifications.

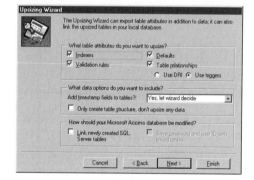

16. Clear the Create Upsizing Report check box (unless you want to view or print the report) and click Finish. The wizard provides a progress indicator for the upsizing process (see Figure 18.14).

FIGURE 18.14

The progress report for the upsizing process.

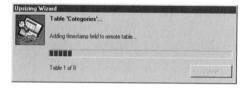

17. Click OK when the Upsizing Complete message appears.

Verifying Your Upsized SQL Server 6.5 Database

SQL Server 6.5 Enterprise Manager is the basic tool for creating, modifying, and deleting (dropping) indexes, constraints, tables, databases, and devices. This section assumes that you've installed the SQL Server 6.5 client tools on a workstation connected to a remote server. The examples use the OAKLEAF2 client running Windows 95 and the OAKLEAF0 server, which can run SQL Server 6.5 or 7.0.

To verify that the Upsizing Wizard created the tables, indexes, and referential integrity triggers, do the following:

1. Choose Start, Programs, Microsoft SQL Server 6.5 Utilities, SQL Enterprise Manager to launch the application.

2. If you haven't previously registered a server, the Register Server dialog appears. Type the server name in the combo box and select the authentication option. If you select Standard Security, type your SQL Server Login ID and Password, if applicable, in the text boxes (see Figure 18.15).

FIGURE 18.15

Registering a server as a member of the SQL 6.5 group.

3. Click Register to register the server and close the dialog. Expand in the Server manager window the entry for your server; then progressively expand the Databases, nwind, Objects, and Tables items.

4. Double-click the Orders table to display the Manage Tables window for the Orders table (see Figure 18.16). The Upsizing Wizard specified the OrderID field as the primary key and assigned SQL Server's Identity field attribute, the equivalent of Jet's Increment (autonumber or counter) attribute.

FIGURE 18.16

Inspecting the field properties of the upsized Orders table.

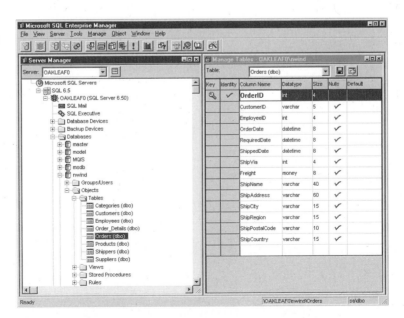

18

WORKING WITH CLIENT/SERVER DATABASES

5. Choose <u>M</u>anage, <u>T</u>riggers to open the Manage Triggers window for the Orders table, which displays the Transact-SQL code for the Orders_DTrig (DELETE) trigger (see Figure 18.17). The Orders_DTrig trigger enforces the cascade deletions option of the relation between the Orders and OrderDetails table originally specified in the Relations window of the Nwind.mdb database.

FIGURE 18.17

The Transact-SQL code for the Orders_DTrig trigger that implements cascading deletions.

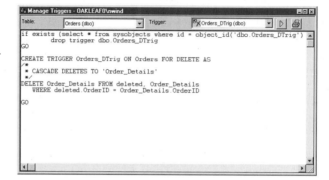

6. Select Orders_ITrig (INSERT) and Orders_UTrig (UPDATE) from the Triggers list to inspect the trigger code. These two triggers prevent adding or updating records of the OrderDetails table without an OrderID value corresponding to a valid OrderID value in the Orders table

7. Close the Manage Triggers window.

Running a Test Query with ISQL_w

ISQL_w is the Windows version of the ISQL command-line tool for executing queries against SQL Server databases. Follow these steps to execute a simple SELECT query against the nwind database:

1. Choose Tools, SQL Query Tool to open the ISQL_w window from Enterprise Manager. Alternatively, you can open ISQL_w from the Microsoft SQL Server 6.5 Utilities menu.

2. With nwind selected in the DB window, type a simple SELECT query with at least one join in the query page of the window (see Figure 18.18).

FIGURE 18.18

A test SELECT query against the nwind database.

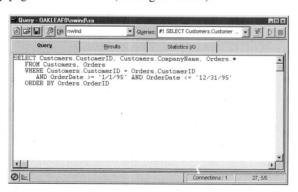

3. Click the Execute Query button (green triangle) to execute your query and then click the Results tab to display the query result set (see Figure 18.19).

FIGURE 18.19

Part of the query result set from the SELECT *query of Figure 18.18.*

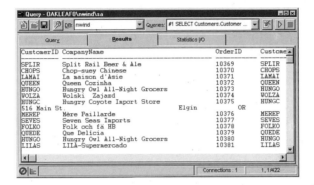

> **NOTE**
>
> The occasional address that appears in the first column of the Results page is caused by the inclusion of carriage-return/line-feed (vbCrLf) pairs in the ShipAddress field of the Orders table.

4. Close the Query window and close SQL Enterprise Manager.

Importing Jet Tables to SQL Server 7.0

If you don't have Microsoft Access and SQL Server 6.5, SQL Server 7.0's DTS is the best approach to importing tables from your Jet database. The DTS import operation doesn't affect the Nwind.mdb file used in the example, so you don't need to work from a split or backup copy.

> **NOTE**
>
> SQL Server 7.0 includes a Northwind sample database that's similar to Visual Basic 6.0's Nwind.mdb. The sections that follow create an nwind database that's identical to Nwind.mdb, with the exception of the name of the Order Details table. Although SQL Server 7.0 permits spaces in table names, nwind's Order Details is renamed to Order_Details, in conformance with ANSI standards, which don't support spaces in database object names. The succeeding client/server chapters use the nwind, not the Northwind, database.

Creating a New nwind Database

The first step in the import process is to create a new nwind database. This is a much simpler process in version 7.0 because of the elimination of device files and automatic resizing of database and log files.

To create the SQL Server 7.0 nwind databas, do the following:

1. Choose Start, Programs, Microsoft SQL Server 7.0 , SQL Server Enterprise Manager to launch MMC with the SQL Server Enterprise Manager snap-in active.

2. If you haven't registered a server, the Registered SQL Server Properties sheet appears. Alternatively, you can open the sheet by selecting the SQL Server item in the left (scope) pane and choosing Action, Register SQL Server. If you've already registered the server, skip to step 6.

3. If you're working at the server or are running the Desktop version of SQL Server 7.0, select (local) from the Server list. Otherwise, type in the name of the server.

4. Select the authentication option. If you're running the Desktop version under Windows 9x, as in this example, the Use Windows NT Authentication option is disabled.

5. Accept the rest of the defaults (see Figure 18.20) and click OK to register the server.

FIGURE 18.20

Registering the Desktop version of SQL Server running under Windows 9x.

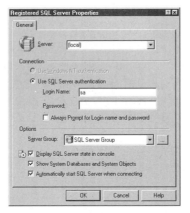

NOTE

Windows NT authentication isn't available when you run the Desktop version of SQL Server 7.0 under Windows 9x, because Windows 9x doesn't incorporate Windows NT's security system.

6. Expand in the scope pane the entries for your server (OAKLEAF2 in this example) and Databases (see Figure 18.21). The Northwind and pubs databases are installed by SQL Server 7.0 setup.

FIGURE 18.21

The expanded view of a registered Desktop version of SQL Server.

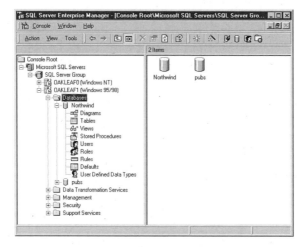

7. Right-click Databases and choose New <u>D</u>atabase from the pop-up menu to open the Database Properties sheet.

8. With the General page selected, type **nwind** in the Name text box; the filename becomes nwind_Data(.mdf) with a default size of 1MB. Accept the remaining default values (see Figure 18.22).

FIGURE 18.22

Specifying the properties of the new nwind database.

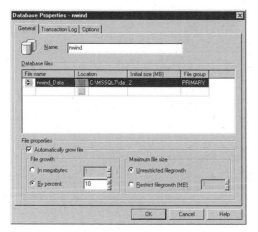

18

WORKING WITH CLIENT/SERVER DATABASES

NOTE

You can specify the increments by which the data file grows and the maximum additional disk space that can be allocated to the file. For most databases, the default values of 10% growth increment and no limit on the database size are satisfactory.

9. Click the Transaction Log tab. SQL Server automatically creates an nwind_Log(.ldf) transaction log file with a 1MB default size.

10. Click the Options tab and mark the ANSI NULL Default, Select Into/Bulk Copy, and Truncate Log on Checkpoint options (see Figure 18.23). The latter two options prevent the creation of large log files during the import process.

FIGURE 18.23

Setting options for the nwind database.

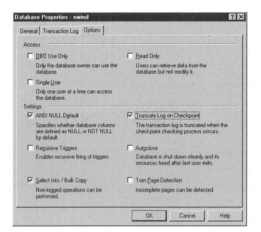

NOTE

To maintain the transaction log needed to restore the database from the last backup operation, clear the Select Into/Bulk Copy and Truncate Log on Checkpoint check boxes after you load and back up the initial data.

11. Click OK to create the new database and close the dialog. Creating the new database takes 5 to 15 seconds, depending on your PC hardware.

12. Select and expand the nwind item in the scope pane. The right pane displays a DHTML view of nwind database properties (see Figure 18.24).

FIGURE 18.24

Properties of the new nwind database.

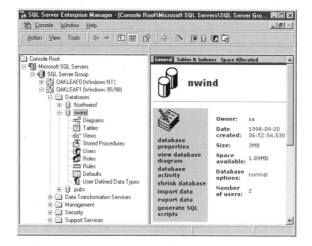

Using the Data Transformation Service to Import Tables

SQL Server 7.0 has a wizard to automate almost all multistep tasks.

1. With the nwind database selected, click the Run a Wizard button (with the magic wand) to open the Select Wizard dialog. Alternatively, choose Help, <u>W</u>izards. Select the DTS Import Wizard from the list (see Figure 18.25), click OK to open the first wizard dialog, and click Next.

FIGURE 18.25

Selecting the DTS Import Wizard.

2. In the Choose a Data Source dialog, select Microsoft Access from the Source list and then click the File builder button (with ellipsis) to open the Open dialog. Navigate to the folder with Nwind.mdb and double-click Nwind.mdb to select the file and close the Open dialog. Use of the default Admin User Name for unsecured Access databases is optional

18

(see Figure 18.26). The Advanced button lets you specify the values of provider-specific properties, such as `Jet OLEDB:System Database` for secure Jet databases. Click Next.

FIGURE **18.26**

Specifying Nwind.mdb as the data source for the DTS copy operation.

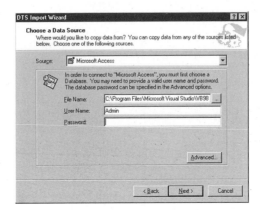

NOTE

The Source list includes all sources of data for which an ODBC driver or OLE DB data provider is installed on the PC running SQL Server Enterprise Manager. Thus you can import data from a wide variety of files, including Excel worksheets, dBASE, FoxPro, and Paradox tables, and even fixed-width and delimited text files. The DTS import process has capabilities similar to those of Access 97.

3. In the Choose a Destination dialog, accept the defaults for the local server, and click Next.

4. In the Specify Table Copy or Query dialog, accept the default Copy Table(s) from Source Database, and click Next.

5. In the Select Source Tables dialog, click the Select All button, clear the check box for tables you added to Nwind.mdb, then change the name of dbo.[Order Details] to dbo.[Order_Details] (see Figure 18.27).

FIGURE 18.27

Selecting the Nwind.mdb tables to import into the nwind database.

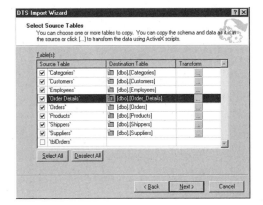

6. Click the Transform builder button of the Categories table to open the Column Mappings and Transformations dialog. The Columns mapping page displays the proposed SQL Server field data types mapped from each field of the Categories table (see Figure 18.28). You can change the data type of any field by clicking its Type cell to open a list of available data types.

FIGURE 18.28

Column data type mappings from Nwind.mdb to standard SQL Server 7.0 data types.

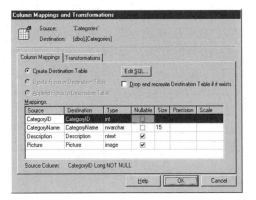

7. Click the Transformations tab and temporarily select the Transform information as it is copied to the destination option. You can write your own custom transformation scripts in VBScript or JavaScript (ECMAScript). Custom transformation scripts most commonly are used in data warehousing applications. Figure 18.29 shows the default transformation script for the Categories table.

FIGURE **18.29**

The standard VBScript transformation function for the Categories table.

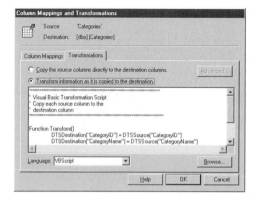

8. Click Cancel to return to the Select Source Tables page and click Next.

9. In the Save and Schedule Package dialog, accept the Run Immediately default, and then click Next.

10. The Completing the DTS Import Wizard dialog displays a summary of the pending import operation (see Figure 18.30).

FIGURE **18.30**

A summary of the pending Data Transformation Service operation.

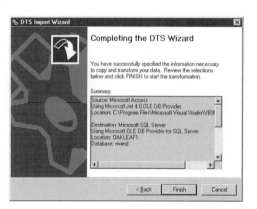

11. Click Finish to open the Transferring Data progress dialog and start the transformation. Click OK when the DTS Wizard message box appears to indicate the process is complete. The Transferring Data dialog appears as shown in Figure 18.31. Click Done to close the wizard dialog and return to SQL Server Enterprise Manager.

FIGURE 18.31
The DTS checklist at completion of the import process.

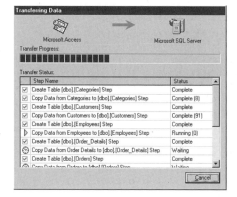

12. Double-click the Tables item in the scope pane to display a list of the data tables you imported in the right pane (see Figure 18.32).

FIGURE 18.32
SQL Server Enterprise Manager displaying the data and system tables of the nwind database.

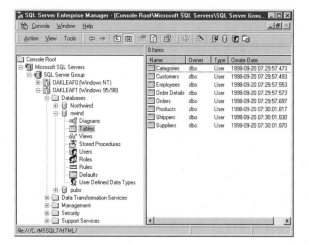

Testing the nwind Database with the SQL Server Query Analyzer

SQL Server Query Analyzer, the replacement for SQL Server 6.5's ISQL_w query tool, includes a variety of new features, such as color-coding Transact-SQL reserved words, displaying query result sets in a sizable grid, and providing the graphical query execution plan (show-plan) window described earlier in this chapter. Query Analyzer lets you run a quick test of your imported tables to verify that their behavior conforms to their Jet counterparts.

To run a simple SELECT query against the nwind database in SQL Server Query Analyzer, do the following:

1. With the nwind database selected in Enterprise Manager's scope pane, choose Tools, SQL Server Query Analyzer to open the application. Alternatively, choose Start, Programs, Microsoft SQL Server 7.0, SQL Server Query Analyzer.

2. Select the nwind database, if necessary, from the Database list.

3. Type a valid SELECT query in the empty pane. The SELECT query for this example, which includes a join, a constraint, and a sorting operation, is

```
SELECT Customers.CustomerID, Customers.CompanyName, Orders.*
   FROM Customers, Orders
   WHERE Customers.CustomerID = Orders.CustomerID
      AND OrderDate >= '1/1/95' AND OrderDate <= '12/31/95'
   ORDER BY Orders.OrderID
```

4. Click the Execute Query into Grid button (with the grid symbol) or choose Query, Execute with Grid to run your query. The query result set appears in a new pane as shown in Figure 18.33.

FIGURE 18.33

SQL Server Query Analyzer display-ing the result set for a simple SELECT query in a sizable grid.

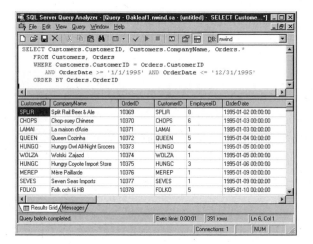

5. Click the Display Execution Plan button or choose Query, Display Execution Plan to display the execution plan for the query (refer to Figure 18.2).

6. If you want to save the SQL statement of the query for future reuse, choose File, Save and assign a filename, such as NwindSorted.sql.

Modifying Imported SQL Server 7.0 Tables

Importing tables to SQL Server 7.0 doesn't provide the benefits of using the Access Upsizing Wizard, such as automatic creation of identity fields and triggers or SQL DRI statements to maintain referential integrity. Until Microsoft releases Access 9.0 and Upsizing Tools compatible with SQL Server 7.0, you must alter the table properties and add indexes and relationships with SQL Server Enterprise Manager.

> **NOTE**
>
> SQL ALTER TABLE and CREATE INDEX Data Modification Language (DML) statements are an option for modifying existing tables and adding indexes, but using SQL Enterprise Manager is a much simpler and faster process.

Altering Table Properties

Most of the fields of the tables you import from Nwind.mdb allow NULL values in all but primary key fields. To maintain referential integrity, as well as to adhere to business rules, foreign key fields shouldn't permit NULL values. Several of the Jet tables, such as Orders and Categories, use Jet AutoNumber (Increment) fields as primary keys. As noted earlier in the chapter, the SQL Server equivalent of the Jet autoincrement field is the int data type with the identity attribute specified.

Follow these steps to modify the Order and Order Details tables to conform to the original Jet design:

1. In SQL Server Enterprise Manager, double-click in the scope pane the Tables item of the nwind database; then right-click the Orders table and choose <u>D</u>esign Table from the context menu.

   The Design Table grid lets you change the data type, allow or disallow NULL column values, and specify an identity column, together with the identity column's Seed (starting value) and Increment value. You also can specify that a column should contain a globally unique identifier (GUID).

2. Clear the Allow Nulls check box for the CustomerID, EmployeeID, OrderDate, and ShipVia columns. The CustomerID, EmployeeID, and ShipVia values are foreign keys and are required upon order entry. OrderDate also is a required value.

3. Mark the OrderID column's Identity check box, replace the Identity Seed column's default 1 with **10248** (the first OrderID value in the Orders table used in this example), and accept the Identity Increment value of 1 (see Figure 18.34).

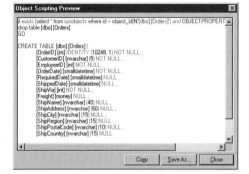

4. Click Save to execute the changes. After a brief delay, the Save Change Script dialog appears with the Transact-SQL statement to effect the changes (see Figure 18.35).

> **NOTE**
>
> ALTER TABLE statements can't be used to add identity attributes to tables with existing data. Instead, you must append data from the existing table to a temporary table (Tmp_Orders) with the identity column attribute. After the INSERT process completes, you replace the original table (Orders) with Tmp_Orders.

5. Click Save if you want to retain the SQL statement for further analysis in an automatically named file (DbDgm1.sql, for this example). Listing 18.1 is the complete SQL statement for the preceding operation.

6. Close the Design Table window to return to the main Enterprise Manager window; then right-click the Order_Details table and choose Design Table from the pop-up menu.

7. Clear the Allow Nulls check box for the OrderID column, click the Save button, and then close the Design Table window.

LISTING 18.1   TRANSACTIONS FOR RE-CREATING THE ORDERS TABLE WITH AN IDENTITY KEY AND COLUMNS SPECIFIED AS NOT NULLABLE

```
BEGIN TRANSACTION
    SET QUOTED_IDENTIFIER ON
    GO
    SET TRANSACTION ISOLATION LEVEL SERIALIZABLE
    GO
COMMIT
BEGIN TRANSACTION
    CREATE TABLE dbo.Tmp_Orders(
        OrderID int NOT NULL IDENTITY (10248, 1),
        CustomerID varchar(5) NOT NULL,
        EmployeeID int NOT NULL,
        OrderDate datetime NOT NULL,
        RequiredDate datetime NULL,
        ShippedDate datetime NULL,
        ShipVia int NOT NULL,
        Freight money NULL,
        ShipName varchar(40) NULL,
        ShipAddress varchar(60) NULL,
        ShipCity varchar(15) NULL,
        ShipRegion varchar(15) NULL,
        ShipPostalCode varchar(10) NULL,
        ShipCountry varchar(15) NULL)
    ON [default]
    GO
    SET IDENTITY_INSERT dbo.Tmp_Orders ON
    GO
    IF EXISTS(SELECT * FROM dbo.Orders)
        EXEC('INSERT INTO dbo.Tmp_Orders(OrderID, CustomerID, EmployeeID,
            OrderDate, RequiredDate, ShippedDate, ShipVia, Freight,
            ShipName, ShipAddress, ShipCity, ShipRegion, ShipPostalCode,
            ShipCountry)
                SELECT OrderID, CustomerID, EmployeeID, OrderDate,
                    RequiredDate, ShippedDate, ShipVia, Freight, ShipName,
                    ShipAddress, ShipCity, ShipRegion, ShipPostalCode,
                    ShipCountry
                    FROM dbo.Orders TABLOCKX')
    GO
    SET IDENTITY_INSERT dbo.Tmp_Orders OFF
    GO
    DROP TABLE dbo.Orders
    GO
    EXECUTE sp_rename 'dbo.Tmp_Orders', 'Orders'
    GO
COMMIT
```

18

WORKING WITH
CLIENT/SERVER
DATABASES

> **NOTE**
>
> Using identity columns to automatically generate successive primary key values guarantees uniqueness but adds complexity to order entry and similar applications requiring INSERT operations on related tables. You must add the record with the identity column and then query for its value to use as the foreign key of the related records. This process leads to multiple server round-trips for a single transaction.

Adding Indexes to Tables

Indexes improve performance for tables with large numbers of records, especially for complex joins. It's a common SQL Server practice to add a clustered index on the primary key field of a table; clustered indexes arrange the physical order of the records in the order of the primary key field. For tables with records that are added in the sequence of the primary key field, such as Orders (OrderID), or in the approximate sequence of the primary key field, as is the case for Order Details (OrderID, ProductID), a clustered index is less important.

The Orders table of Access 97's Northwind.mdb has indexes on the OrderID (PrimaryKey), CustomerID, EmployeeID, OrderDate, ShippedDate, and ShipPostalCode fields. Indexes on the foreign key fields, CustomerID and EmployeeID, improve join and lookup performance; indexes on the OrderDate, ShippedDate, and ShipPostalCode fields improve only lookup performance. Similarly, the Order Details table has a composite index on OrderID and ProductID (PrimaryKey) plus individual indexes on OrderID and ProductID to aid join and lookup performance.

Adding Indexes with the Create Index Wizard

To add foreign key indexes on the CustomerID and EmployeeID fields and a lookup index on the OrderDate field of the Orders table, do the following:

1. With the nwind database selected in SQL Server Enterprise Manager, click the Run a Wizard button, select Create Index Wizard from the Database node of the Select Wizard dialog's list, and click OK.

2. Click Next to bypass the first wizard dialog; select nwind, if necessary, and Orders from the Database name and Table name lists, respectively, of the Select a Database and Table dialog. Click Next.

3. Indexes created during the import or upsizing process appear in Current Index Information dialog. Click Next.

4. In the Select Columns dialog, mark the Include in Index check box for the CustomerID column (see Figure 18.36).

FIGURE 18.36

Specifying an index on the CustomerID column of the Orders table.

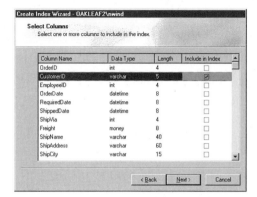

5. Accept the defaults, not clustered or unique, in the Specify Index options dialog and click Next.

6. In the Completing the Create Index Wizard dialog, change the Index name from Orders_Index_1 to **Orders_Index_CustomerID** (see Figure 18.37) and click Finish to create the index.

FIGURE 18.37

Naming the index on the CustomerID column.

7. Click OK when `The index was successfully created` message appears to close the wizard dialog and return to SQL Server Enterprise Manager.

8. Repeat steps 1 through 7, substituting EmployeeID for CustomerID in step 4 and **Orders_Index_EmployeeID** for Orders_Index_CustomerID in step 6.

9. Repeat steps 1 through 7, substituting OrderDate for CustomerID in step 4 and **Orders_Index_OrderDate** for Orders_Index_CustomerID in step 6.

> **NOTE**
>
> If an existing index on the OrderID column doesn't appear in preceding step 3, run the wizard again and create a clustered, unique index on the Order ID column. Name this index Orders_Index_PrimaryKey.

Adding indexes on the CustomerID and OrderDate fields changes the query execution plan for the SELECT query in the "Testing the nwind Database with the SQL Server Query Analyzer" section earlier in the chapter. If you rerun the query in showplan mode, additional icons for the index (Index Seek), Bookmark Lookups, and a Delay appear in the Plan pane. SQL Server 7.0's query optimizer uses both of these indexes to speed execution. Choosing the proper set of indexes is especially important for tables, such as those in data warehouses, with a very large number of rows.

Adding a Unique Composite Index to the Order_Details Table

Adding indexes in the properties sheet for a table is faster than using the Create Index Wizard, especially when adding more than one index to a table. A composite index consists of an index on a sequential combination of two or more fields of a table. The Jet Order Details table uses a unique composite index to assure that only one record per product is added as a line item for a particular order.

> **NOTE**
>
> Depending on how you imported the Order_Details table, a composite clustered index may already exist. If the index exists, you can delete it and perform all of the following steps. Alternatively, you can skip the composite index operation (steps 4 through 7) and add only the ProductID index. You replace the composite index with a primary key constraint in the "Specifying Primary Keys and Relationships in Database Diagrams" section that follows.

To add the composite index and an index on the ProductID field, follow these steps:

1. Click in the scope pane the Tables item of the nwind database, if necessary, to display the list of tables in the right pane.

2. Right-click the Order_Details table item and choose <u>D</u>esign Table from the context menu to open the Design Tables window.

3. Click the Properties button to open the table properties sheet and click the Index/Keys tab.

4. Click the New button and select OrderID from the drop-down list in the first row of the Column Name list.

5. Select ProductID from the drop-down list in the second row of the Column Name list to create the composite index.

6. Change the Index name from the default, IX_Order Details to **Order_Details_Index_PrimaryKey**.

7. Mark the Create UNIQUE check box, select the Index option, mark the Create as CLUSTERED check box, and select the Data Already Sorted option (see Figure 18.38). The data is imported in sorted order because of the composite key of the Jet Order Details table.

FIGURE 18.38

Creating a composite index on the OrderID and ProductID fields of the Order Details table.

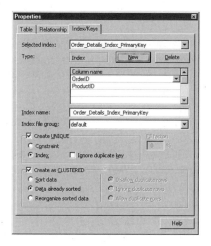

8. Click the New button and select ProductID from the drop-down list in the first row of the Column Name list.

9. Change the Index name from the default, IX_Order Details to **Order_Details_Index_ProductID**. Accept the defaults (not UNIQUE or CLUSTERED) to permit duplicate ProductID values.

10. Close the Properties sheet and close the Design Table window. Click Yes when the Do you want to save changes to table 'Order Details' message appears.

11. Click Yes if you want to save to an .sql file the query that creates the indexes.

Listing 18.2 illustrates the Transact-SQL CREATE...INDEX statements generated by the preceding steps.

18

WORKING WITH
CLIENT/SERVER
DATABASES

> **NOTE**
>
> Another advantage of using the Design Table procedure to add indexes is that you can review (and save, if desired) the Transact-SQL statements that modify the tables.

LISTING 18.2   TRANSACTIONS FOR CREATING A COMPOSITE AND A SINGLE-FIELD INDEX ON THE ORDER DETAILS TABLE

```
BEGIN TRANSACTION
    SET QUOTED_IDENTIFIER ON
    GO
    SET TRANSACTION ISOLATION LEVEL SERIALIZABLE
    GO
COMMIT
BEGIN TRANSACTION
    CREATE UNIQUE CLUSTERED INDEX Order_Details_Index_PrimaryKey
        ON dbo.[Order Details] (OrderID, ProductID)
        WITH SORTED_DATA
        ON [default]
    GO
    CREATE NONCLUSTERED INDEX Order_Details_Index_ProductID
        ON dbo.[Order Details] (ProductID)
        ON [default]
    GO
COMMIT
```

SPECIFYING PRIMARY KEYS AND RELATIONSHIPS IN DATABASE DIAGRAMS

▶ See "Categories of SQL Statements," p. 251

You can enforce uniqueness for a single-field or composite primary key with a no-duplicates index, as described in the preceding section, but use of SQL Server's primary key constraint is the favored approach. You specify primary key field(s) and their relationship(s) to foreign key fields in an SQL Server database diagram. Creating a database diagram requires the VDTs (often called the da Vinci tools), which were introduced with the Enterprise Edition of Visual Basic 5.0 and Visual Studio 97. The VDTs for the Enterprise Editions of Visual Studio 6.0 and Visual Basic 6.0 have been upgraded to use OLE DB and ADO to connect to SQL Server, Oracle, and Jet databases.

NOTE

If you use the SQL Server 7.0 Version Upgrade Wizard to upgrade an SQL Server 6.*x* database that was created with the Access 97 Upsizing Wizard, a database diagram named CustomersOrdersOrder_Details already exists. You can safely delete this diagram and create a new one. Alternatively, you can add only the Products table to the diagram.

To use the Create Diagram Wizard to create a database diagram and thenset primary keys for the nwind database, do the following:

1. In SQL Server Enterprise Manager's scope pane, click the nwind database item to display its properties in the right pane, and click the Database Diagram heading.

2. Click Yes when the Default Database Diagram message box appears to open the first Create Diagram Wizard dialog, and click Next to display the Select Tables to be Added dialog.

3. Click the Add button repeatedly to add all of the tables to the Tables to Add list, then click Next.

4. Accept the default option in the Select Layout Option dialog, and click Next.

5. In the Completing the Create Diagram Wizard, click Finish to add the tables to the new diagram.

6. Right-click the right pane and choose Zoom, 25% to make the field lists visible.

7. Position Customers, Orders, Order_Details, and Products left-to-right in the first row of field lists. Position Employees under Customers, Shippers and Categories under Order_Details, and Suppliers under Products.

8. Click the field selection button for the CustomerID field of the Customers table to select the field; then click the Primary Key button (with the key symbol) of the toolbar to set the primary key of the Customers table. When you set the primary key, a key symbol appears in the field selection button.

18

WORKING WITH CLIENT/SERVER DATABASES

NOTE

You can't create a primary key on a field that allows nulls. If you receive a warning message that the field is nullable, right-click the field list title bar and select Column Properties from the pop-up menu to expand the field list. Clear the Allow Nulls check box for the primary key field, then right-click and choose Column Names.

9. Repeat step 6 for the Orders table (select the OrderID field), Products (ProductID), Shippers (ShipperID), Categories (CategoryID), Suppliers (SupplierID), and Employees (EmployeeID).

10. Click the field selection button for the OrderID field of the Order Details table; then press Ctrl and click the field selection button for the ProductID field. With both fields selected, click the Set Primary Key button to create the composite primary key of the Order_Details table (see Figure 18.39).

FIGURE 18.39

Specifying primary keys for the Customers, Orders, Order Details, Shippers, Categories, and Employees tables (100% zoom).

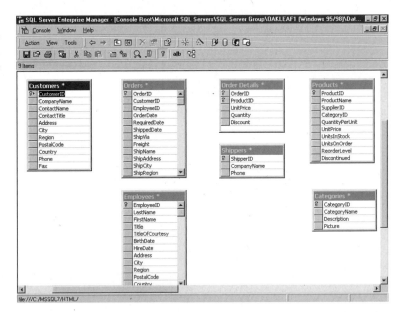

To add relationships between the tables to the database diagram, follow these steps:

1. Drag the CustomerID field selection button of the Customers table to the CustomerID field selection button of the Orders table. The Create Relationship dialog opens with a proposed relationship name (FK_*DependentTable_BaseTable*) and primary key table and field names (see Figure 18.40). FK is an abbreviation for foreign key.

   Options for testing the relationship on creation of the relationship and during INSERT and UPDATE operations are provided. Enabling the relationship for replication assures that related table updates are processed during replication operations.

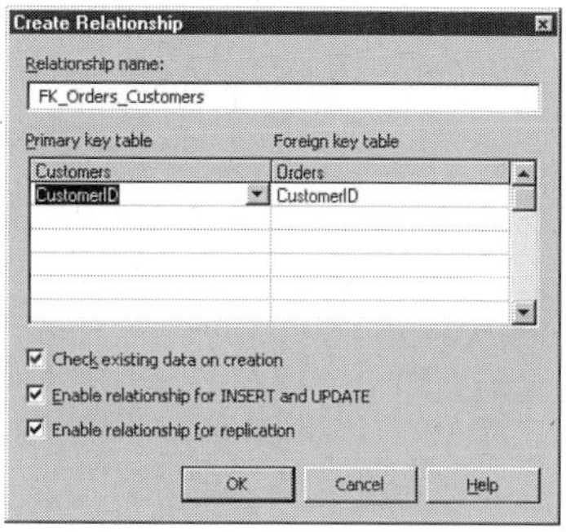

FIGURE 18.40

The default name, tables, fields, and options for a one-to-many relationship between the Customers and Orders tables.

2. Click OK to accept the default values and add the FK_Orders_Customers relationship to the database diagram.

3. Drag the OrderID field of the Orders table to the OrderID field of the Order Details table and click OK in the Create Relationship dialog to add the FK_Order Details_Orders relationship.

4. Drag the ProductID field of the Products table to the ProductID field of the Order Details table and click OK in the Create Relationship dialog to add the FK_Order Details_Products relationship.

5. Repeat step 4 for the remaining relationships. Note that ShipVia of the Orders table is the foreign key field for the ShipperID primary key of the Shippers table.

6. Align the relationship symbols and field lists as illustrated in Figure 18.41.

FIGURE 18.41

The New Diagram window depicting primary keys and relationships between primary and foreign keys of tables.

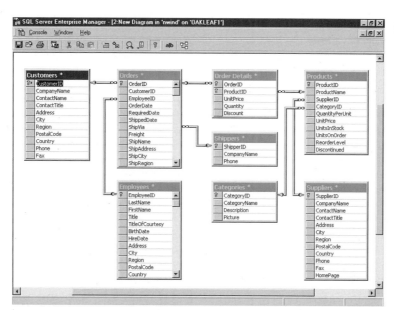

18

WORKING WITH
CLIENT/SERVER
DATABASES

7. Click the Save button to open the Save As dialog, type a name for the diagram such as **nwind_diag**, and click OK to create the Transact-SQL statements for the changes to the nwind database.

8. When the Save dialog appears, click Yes to save the new database diagram in the nwind database.

   The Save dialog includes a Save Text File button. The text file includes only the contents of the Save dialog's text box, which lists the table names to be modified.

9. Close the New Diagram window. If asked again for a diagram name, type **nwind_diag** and click OK.

NOTE

Changes to tables don't occur until you close the database diagram window.

---

10. If the Save Incomplete dialog appears, save the text of the message for troubleshooting and click OK.

11. Click Yes in the Save Change Script dialog to save a copy of the Transact-SQL query that adds the primary keys to the nwind tables.

The Database Diagram tool, by default, adds nonclustered indexes to the tables. Nonclustered indexes are adequate for the Orders, Order Details, and Products tables because records for these tables are added in the sequence of the primary key. The CustomerID field is alphabetic (based on the CompanyName field), so records added to the table aren't in primary key sequence.

You can improve performance of queries that join the Customers table by changing the index to clustered with the following procedure:

1. Select Database Diagrams for the nwind database in the scope pane. Then right-click the nwind_diag icon in the right pane and choose Design Diagram from the context menu to open the Edit Diagram 'nwind_diag' window.

2. Right-click the title bar of the Customers field list and choose Properties from the context menu to open the Properties sheet for the table.

3. Click the Index/Keys tab to display the properties for the PK_Customers key.

4. Mark the Create as CLUSTERED check box (see Figure 18.42). Close the Properties sheet.

   When you change a primary key index to a clustered index, all option buttons are disabled.

5. Close the Edit Diagram window to make the changes to the nwind database.

FIGURE 18.42

Changing the primary key index to a clustered index.

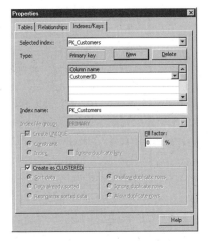

Connecting to Client/Server Tables with the Data Environment

One of Microsoft's design objectives for OLE DB and ADO was to eliminate differences in procedures and code when connecting to a variety of data sources. For Access developers, changing from Jet to ODBCDirect involves a substantial amount of alteration to VBA code. Similarly, Visual Basic developers migrating from Jet passthrough queries to RDO 2.0 must rework almost all data-related code in the project. Using OLE DB and ADO 2.0 doesn't eliminate all code changes when moving from Jet or other shared-file databases to client/server RDBMSs. The first step in migration is to alter the value of the ConnectionString property and other Connection object property values to suit the OLE DB data provider for the client/server data source.

NOTE

The following sections describe how to connect to an SQL Server 6.x or 7.0 data source with Microsoft's native and ODBC OLE DB data providers. SQL Server is used for the examples in this book because most Visual Basic developers of client/server database front ends have access to SQL Server. Creating connections with other native OLE DB providers, such as the Microsoft OLE DB Provider for Oracle, MSDAORA, is quite similar to that for SQL Server.

USING THE NATIVE SQL SERVER PROVIDER

The Microsoft OLE DB Provider for SQL Server, SQLOLEDB, is the native data provider for SQL Server versions 6.x and 7.0. Native OLE DB data providers offer significant performance advantages over the only ADO alternative for client/server RDBMSs—the Microsoft OLE

DB Provider for ODBC (MSDASQL) and a 32-bit ODBC driver for the RDBMS. The most convenient method for creating a connection to a client/server RDBMS is to use a DataEnvironment object's Create New Data Link Wizard.

Follow these steps to create a Connection object for the nwind database created earlier in the chapter:

1. Open a new DataProject with the default DataEnvironment1 and DataReport1 objects. Rename DataEnvironment1 to **envNwindSQL**.

2. Right-click Connection1 and choose Properties to open the Data Link Properties sheet to the Provider page. The OLE DB Provider(s) list displays the providers installed on your PC.

3. Select the Microsoft OLE DB Provider for SQL Server (see Figure 18.43), and click Next to display the second Wizard dialog.

FIGURE 18.43

Selecting the OLE DB data provider for the connection.

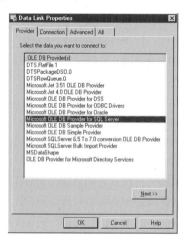

4. Type the server name in the location text box—**OAKLEAF0** for this example. Use (Local) if you're running SQL Server on the same PC as Visual Basic 6.0. Type your SQL Server login ID and password, if applicable. Type the database name, **nwind**, in the Data Source text box (see Figure 18.44).

FIGURE 18.44

Specifying the server, login ID, and database name for the connection.

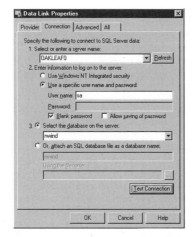

5. Click the Test Connection button to verify that `Connection1` works. Click OK when the Test Connection Succeeded message appears.

6. Click the All tab to display a summary of the properties of Connection1 (see Figure 18.45), then click OK to close the Data Link Properties sheet.

   You can change property values by selecting a property name and clicking Edit Value to open an input box.

FIGURE 18.45

Displaying a summary of the properties of the Connection *object.*

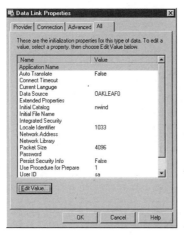

7. In the DataEnvironment window, rename `Connection1` to `cnnServerName`, `cnnOAKLEAF0` for this example.

To see the actual value of the `ConnectionString` property, close the envNwindSQL designer window, run and break the project, and press Ctrl+G to open the Debug window. Type **?** **envNwindSQL.cnnOAKLEAF0.ConnectionString** to return the property value. Following is the value returned from the preceding example:

```
Provider=SQLOLEDB.1;Persist Security Info=False;User ID=sa;
Initial Catalog=nwind;Data Source=OAKLEAF0;Connect Timeout=15
```

Using the ODBC Provider with SQL Server

If the RDBMS to which you need to connect doesn't yet have a native OLE DB data provider, you must use MSDASQL and the appropriate 32-bit ODBC provider until a native provider becomes available. The example of this section uses SQL Server 7.0 as the data source. As noted earlier in the chapter, creating a connection to another client/server RDBMS with the ODBC data provider follows a similar course.

> **NOTE**
>
> International Software Group, Inc. (ISG) offers third-party OLE DB providers for various client/server RDBMSs and mainframe databases, including nonrelational types. ISG's Navigator product is an OLE DB service provider that lets you write SQL statements to specify heterogeneous joins between supported databases. ISG's Web site is at http://www.isgsoft.com.

To create a connection with the SQL Server ODBC driver, do the following:

1. Click the New Connection button of the DataEnvironment window to add a new Connection1, then open the Provider page of the Data Link Properties sheet for Connection1.

2. Accept the default Microsoft OLE DB Provider for ODBC, click Next to open the Connection page, and click the Build button to open the Select Data Source dialog.

3. Select the Machine Data Source option unless you have a specific reason for creating a File Data Source; then click New to open the first Create New Data Source dialog.

4. Select the System Data Source option and click Next.

5. Select SQL Server from the list of drivers, click Next, and click Finish to open the first Create a New Data Source to SQL Server dialog.

6. Type the name of the data source, **nwind**, a brief description of the data source, and the server name (see Figure 18.46). If you're running the Desktop version of SQL Server 7.0, accept the default (local) value in the Server combo box. Click Next to open the authentication dialog.

FIGURE 18.46

Specifying the name, description, and location of the ODBC data source.

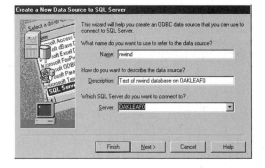

7. If you installed SQL Server under Windows NT with Integrated or Mixed Security, you can accept the default With Windows NT Authentication… option. Otherwise, select the With SQL Server Authentication… option, mark the Connect to SQL Server… check box, and type your login ID and password (see Figure 18.47). Click Next to log onto SQL Server and open the database selection dialog.

FIGURE 18.47

Setting the authentication option and specifying your login ID and password.

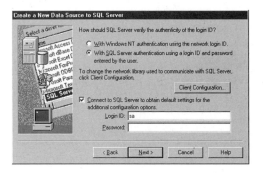

8. Mark the Change the Default Database To check box, select nwind from the drop-down list, and accept the default ANSI SQL settings for quoted identifiers and for nulls, paddings, and warnings (see Figure 18.48). Click Next to open the final dialog.

FIGURE 18.48

Setting the database plus ANSI quoted identifiers, nulls, paddings, and warnings.

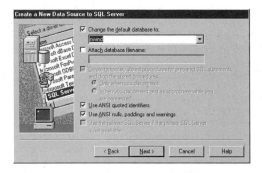

18

WORKING WITH
CLIENT/SERVER
DATABASES

9. Accept the defaults for miscellaneous ODBC data source property values; then click Finish to display the ODBC Microsoft SQL Server Setup dialog, which summarizes the properties set in the preceding steps (see Figure 18.49).

FIGURE 18.49

A summary of the properties of the newly created ODBC data source.

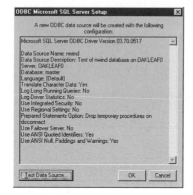

10. Click the Test Data Source button to check the connection to the nwind database (see Figure 18.50). Click OK to return to the Data Link Properties sheet, and rename Connection1 to **cnnODBC**.

FIGURE 18.50

A Test Report for a successful SQL Server 7.0 connection with the Microsoft OLE DB Provider for ODBC.

An alternative to creating a System, User, or File data source is to select the Use Connection String option and type a DSN-less connection string into the text box. This DSN-less connection string is the equivalent to that created in the following procedure:

```
provider=MSDASQL;driver={SQL Server};server=OAKLEAF0;
uid=sa;pwd=;database=nwind
```

NOTE

Client PCs must have ADO 2+ and ODBC 3+ installed to use ODBC data sources with MSDASQL. DSN-less connections eliminate the need to create ODBC data sources for each client PC that runs your client/server front end. The only disadvantage of DSN-less connections is that you must redistribute your application if you change the location (server name) of the database.

Specify a File Data Source (.dsn) file on a server share that's accessible to all clients if you want to make your front end independent of the server location. Like a Data Link (.mdl) file, you need only edit the shared copy of the file to change the server or database name.

TIP

Don't use File DSNs with middle-tier components, especially components running under Microsoft Transaction Server 2.0. Using File DSNs with middle-tier components causes a major performance hit.

CONNECTING TO ORACLE8 DATABASES

Creating a new Connection object using the Microsoft OLE DB Provider for Oracle is similar to specifying a Connection for SQL Server. To establish a Connection to the Oracle8 DEMO database, do the following:

1. Create a new Connection1, if necessary, open its Data Link Properties sheet, select the Microsoft ODBC Driver for Oracle, and click Next.

2. In the Connection page, type the name of the Oracle server (OAKLEAF1 for this example), the user name (DEMO), and password (DEMO). Mark the Allow Saving of Password checkbox to eliminate the need to log in each time you open the connection.

3. Click the Test Connection button to make a connection to Oracle8.

4. Add a new Command1 to Connection1, select Synonym as the Database Object, and select ALL_ALL_TABLES as the Object Name to test the Microsoft Oracle Provider.

5. Click OK to return to the DataEvironment window, then expand the Command1 node to display the fields of the synonym.

You can substitute an Oracle8 database for the SQL Server 7.0 example databases created in this chapter, but you can't use the Access 97 Upsizing Wizard with Oracle databases. Oracle's dialect of SQL differs significantly from that of SQL Server's Transact-SQL.

USING VISUAL DATA TOOLS WITH VISUAL BASIC 6.0

The Enterprise Edition of Visual Basic includes the VDTs used by SQL Server 7.0's SQL Server Enterprise Manager. Once you've created one or more DataEnvironment connections, choose <u>V</u>iew, Data <u>V</u>iew Window to open the Data View window needed to launch the VDTs. The Data View window displays each `Connection` object of the current DataEnvironment object (see Figure 18.51). The behavior of the Data View window is similar to that of SQL Server Enterprise Manager's scope pane, but expansion of database objects occurs in a dual ListView tree. Database Diagrams, Tables, Views, and Stored Procedures objects appear in the Data View window for both SQL Server 6.5+ and Oracle 7.3+ databases. Oracle databases add Synonyms and Functions as object types.

FIGURE 18.51

The Data View window expanded to display database diagrams and tables of the upsized nwind database from a Data Link.

The two main branches of the Data View window are as follows:

- *Data Links* are a collection of `Connections` whose properties are stored in the `HKEY_CURRENT_USER\Software\VB and VBA Program Settings\Microsoft Visual Basic AddIns\VBDataViewWindow` entry of the Registry. Data Links are user-specific and appear in the Data View window, regardless of whether your project includes a `DataEnvironment` object. To create a new Data Link, right-click the Data Links node, and choose <u>A</u>dd a New Data Link to open the Data Link Properties sheet.

- *DataEnvironment Connections* is a collection of one or more DataEnvironment instances of the current project.

> **NOTE**
>
> To include system tables in the expanded Data View window, right-click the connection object and choose Show System Objects from the context menu. You can restrict the display of objects by owner by choosing Filter by Owner and typing the login ID of the owner (dbo is the default for the examples in this chapter).

Running the Database Diagram Tool from Visual Basic

The only differences between the Database Diagram tool of Visual Basic and that of SQL Server Enterprise Manager are the following methods for launching the tool and dragging tables to its window:

- To open an existing database diagram, expand the Database Diagrams and double-click the diagram you want to view or edit.

- To create a new database diagram and add tables, primary keys, and relationships to the database, right-click the Database Diagrams item and choose New Diagram from the context menu.

- To add existing tables to the diagram, drag the table object from the Data View window to the Database Design window.

All other operations in the Database Diagram window are identical to those described in the "Specifying Primary Keys and Relationships in Database Diagrams" section earlier in the chapter.

Creating SQL Server VIEWs

An SQL Server VIEW is the equivalent of a simple Jet SELECT QueryDef object. VIEWs provide a layer of isolation between users and the underlying tables. Many DBAs provide user access to SQL Server data only through VIEWs that are customized to deliver specific sets of columns of tables to particular groups of users. The primary limitation of a VIEW is that you can't include an ORDER BY clause in the SQL statement that creates the view.

To create a new SQL Server View, do the following:

1. Right-click the Views item of the cnn*ServerName* connection (cnnOAKLEAF0 for this example) in the Data View window and choose New View from the context menu to open an empty New View window.

2. Drag the Customers, Orders, Order_Details, and Products tables from the Data View window to the top pane of the New View window.

3. If relationships between the tables are missing, drag the primary key field name of the base table to the corresponding foreign key field name of the related table.

Relationships are indicated by join lines connecting two tables. Right-click and choose Properties from the pop-up menu to open a Properties sheet in which you can specify a LEFT, RIGHT, or FULL OUTER JOIN. The symbol on the join line changes if you specify an outer join.

4. Specify the fields to be included in the view by dragging field names to the Columns cells of the second pane. Include the OrderDate field of the Orders table in your query. As you add fields to the second pane, the View tool adds to the SQL SELECT statement in the third pane.

5. Add a criterion on the OrderDate field by typing >=1/1/95 AND <=12/31/95 in the Criteria cell. The View tool adds the required single quotes and spaces (>= '1/1/95' AND <= '12/31/95') for you. The formatted SQL statement that returns the result set is

```
SELECT Customers.CustomerID, Customers.CompanyName,
    Orders.OrderID, Orders.OrderDate,
    Order_Details.ProductID, Order_Details.Quantity,
    Products.ProductName
FROM Order_Details INNER JOIN
    Orders ON
    Order_Details.OrderID = Orders.OrderID INNER JOIN
    Products ON
    Order_Details.ProductID = Products.ProductID INNER JOIN
    Customers ON
    Orders.CustomerID = Customers.CustomerID
WHERE (Orders.OrderDate >= '1/1/95' AND
    Orders.OrderDate <= '12/31/95')
```

6. Right-click in any of the panes and choose Run from the pop-up menu to execute your query. The query result set appears in the bottom pane (see Figure 18.52).

FIGURE 18.52

Testing the SELECT statement prior to saving a new VIEW to SQL Server.

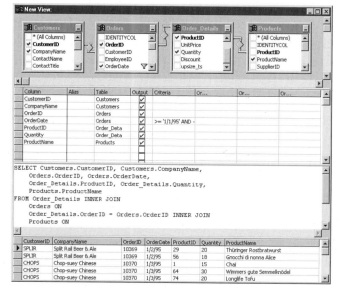

7. Close the New View window and click Yes when asked whether you want to save your VIEW. Type a name for the view, **VW_1995_Customer_Orders** for this example, in the Save As dialog; then click OK to save the VIEW in the nwind database.

8. Expand the Views item in the Data View window to display the entries for the new VIEW and its tables (see Figure 18.53).

FIGURE 18.53

The VW_1995_Customer_Orders VIEW added to the nwind database.

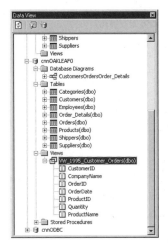

9. Right-click the VW_1995_Customer_Orders item and choose Open from the pop-up menu to display the rows of the VIEW in the Run View window (see Figure 18.54).

FIGURE 18.54

The last few records of the VW_1995_Customer_Orders VIEW displayed in the VDT Run View window.

CustomerID	CompanyName	OrderID	OrderDate	ProductID	Quantity	ProductName
MAISD	Maison Dewey	10529	6/7/95	55	14	Pâté chinois
MAISD	Maison Dewey	10529	6/7/95	68	20	Scottish Longbreads
MAISD	Maison Dewey	10529	6/7/95	69	10	Gudbrandsdalsost
PICCO	Piccolo und mehr	10530	6/8/95	17	40	Alice Mutton
PICCO	Piccolo und mehr	10530	6/8/95	43	25	Ipoh Coffee
PICCO	Piccolo und mehr	10530	6/8/95	61	20	Sirop d'érable
PICCO	Piccolo und mehr	10530	6/8/95	76	50	Lakkalikööri
OCEAN	Océano Atlántico Ltda.	10531	6/8/95	59	2	Raclette Courdavault
EASTC	Eastern Connection	10532	6/9/95	30	15	Nord-Ost Matjeshering
EASTC	Eastern Connection	10532	6/9/95	66	24	Louisiana Hot Spiced Okra
FOLKO	Folk och fä HB	10533	6/12/95	4	50	Chef Anton's Cajun Seasoning
FOLKO	Folk och fä HB	10533	6/12/95	72	25	Mozzarella di Giovanni
FOLKO	Folk och fä HB	10533	6/12/95	73	24	Röd Kaviar
LEHMS	Lehmanns Marktstand	10534	6/12/95	30	10	Nord-Ost Matjeshering
LEHMS	Lehmanns Marktstand	10534	6/12/95	40	10	Boston Crab Meat
LEHMS	Lehmanns Marktstand	10534	6/12/95	54	10	Tourtière
ANTON	Antonio Moreno Taquería	10535	6/13/95	11	50	Queso Cabrales
ANTON	Antonio Moreno Taquería	10535	6/13/95	40	10	Boston Crab Meat
ANTON	Antonio Moreno Taquería	10535	6/13/95	57	5	Ravioli Angelo
ANTON	Antonio Moreno Taquería	10535	6/13/95	59	15	Raclette Courdavault
LEHMS	Lehmanns Marktstand	10536	6/14/95	12	15	Queso Manchego La Pastora
LEHMS	Lehmanns Marktstand	10536	6/14/95	31	20	Gorgonzola Telino
LEHMS	Lehmanns Marktstand	10536	6/14/95	33	30	Geitost

You can determine whether the VIEW is updatable by navigating to the last row of the Run Table window. If the last row has an asterisk (*) symbol in the record selection button, the VIEW is updatable, at least in theory. If you include joins in the query, you can't update values in columns whose values are derived from primary key fields of base tables. You can, however,

18

WORKING WITH CLIENT/SERVER DATABASES

update other base table and related table values. For example, you can update values in the CompanyName and Quantity columns in the Run View window of Figure 18.60. It is not a good database programming practice to allow updates to tables from VIEWs with joins because of the lack of safeguards against modification to base tables.

> **NOTE**
>
> You can display the rows of any table in the Tables list of the Data View window by right-clicking and choosing Open.

WORKING WITH CLIENT/SERVER CONNECTIONS IN VBA CODE

OLE DB and ADO are designed to minimize the data source-related differences in programming code, as noted earlier in this chapter. Thus examples in prior chapters that connect to Jet databases require only minor modifications to accommodate client/server data sources.

The primary code changes involve modifications to the value of the ConnectionString property to specify the provider, database name, server name. Specifying values for the Mode (defaults to adModeUnknown) and CursorLocation (defaults to adUseServer) properties is optional. You must also change any Jet SQL-specific code to conform to ANSI SQL, such as replacing the # date delimiter with a single quote ('). Listing 18.3 illustrates changes to the code behind the ADOFind.vbp project of Chapter 3, "Migrating from DAO to ADO," to connect to the SQL Server nwind database with the native OLE DB or the ODBC provider. Modified code is prefaced with 'Change: comments.

LISTING 18.3 MODIFIED CODE TO CONVERT CHAPTER 3'S ADOFIND.VBP PROJECT FROM A LOCAL JET DATABASE TO THE CLIENT/SERVER NWIND DATABASE USING EITHER THE SQLOLEDB OR MSDASQL DATA PROVIDER

```
Private Sub Form_Load()
   'Open the connection
   'Change: Use native OLE DB provider for SQL Server
   strConnect = "Provider=SQLOLEDB;User ID=sa;" & _
      "Data Source=OAKLEAF;Initial Catalog = nwind"
   'Change: Alternatively, use DSN-less ODBC data source for SQL Server
   'strConnect = "provider=MSDASQL;driver={SQL Server};server=OAKLEAF1;" & _
                "uid=sa;pwd=;database=nwind"
   With cnnOrders
      'Change: Add property value settings
      .Mode = adReadWrite
      .CursorLocation = adUseClient
      .Open strConnect
   End With
```

```
    'Load the combo list
    strSQL = "SELECT DISTINCT CustomerID FROM Orders ORDER BY CustomerID"
    Set rstOrders = cnnOrders.Execute(strSQL)
    Do Until rstOrders.EOF
        cboCustomerID.AddItem rstOrders.Fields(0).Value
        rstOrders.MoveNext
    Loop
    cboCustomerID.ListIndex = 0
    rstOrders.Close
End Sub

Private Sub Form_Activate()
    'Populate the DataGrid
    'Change: Replace # with ' in date constraint
    strSQL = "SELECT * FROM Orders WHERE OrderDate BETWEEN '1/1/95' AND '12/31/95'"
    rstOrders.Open strSQL, cnnOrders, adOpenKeyset, adLockOptimistic, adCmdText
    Set adcOrders.Recordset = rstOrders
End Sub
```

PROCESSING TRANSACTIONS AND BULK OPERATIONS

IN THIS CHAPTER

Transaction-processing (TP) applications are classified in this book as database processes that update data on an all-or-nothing basis. If any element of the update process fails for any reason, updates made prior to the failure are undone and the database tables are restored to their state immediately prior to attempted execution of the transaction. Most TP applications update two or more database tables. A *distributed transaction* involves simultaneous or just-in-time updates to tables in multiple databases, which often are located on different servers connected by a wide-area network (WAN).

Online transaction processing (OLTP) is a category of TP in which individual updates occur on a real-time basis. Examples of OLTP are withdrawals or deposits at automatic teller machines (ATMs), airline or hotel reservation systems, and telephone order entry applications. The next chapter, "Porting Access OLTP Applications to Visual Basic 6.0," describes in detail a typical OLTP application for order entry.

An alternative to OLTP is batch processing, in which updates to database tables are accumulated as rows of temporary tables. A separate database application processes the data in the temporary tables. The second application deletes the temporary tables when the batch update process is complete. Batch processing often is used in accounting applications, such as submitting daily collections of credit card vouchers to a bank. Traditional batch processing involves two applications—one to add the records to the temporary tables and another to send the accumulated records to the destination. The nature of the batch determines whether to apply the all-or-nothing constraint. Transactions are required for double-entry accounting so that debits and credits balance, but credit-card processing systems can accommodate a batch in which processing of some records fails while that of other records succeeds.

> **NOTE**
>
> In this book, the lowercase word *update*, when applied to making changes to the tables of a database, includes INSERT, UPDATE, or DELETE operations or any combination of these operations.

This chapter deals primarily with OLTP with Jet and SQL Server databases, although most of the techniques you learn here also are applicable to batch-processing methods. Some OLTP applications, such as order entry with multiple-line items, use a combination of batch and online TP methods. You add the line items to a local temporary table and then add the completed order information to multiple tables in a single transaction.

▶ **See** "Disconnected Recordsets," **p. 111**

Remote Data Objects (RDO) 1.0 introduced *bulk operations* on disconnected rdoResultset objects, RDO's equivalent of DAO and ADO Recordsets. Bulk operations differ from traditional batch methods by operating on a partial image of the back-end tables stored on the client as a connectionless `Recordset`. ADO 2.x supports RDO 2.0's bulk operations on disconnected `Recordsets`, which permit sending only changes to the database. Bulk operations differ from transactions because bulk operations don't have an inherent all-or-nothing restriction. Disconnected `Recordsets` created with batch optimistic cursors and the `UpdateBatch` method of the `Recordset` object are covered near the end of this chapter.

DEFINING TRANSACTIONS AND THE ACID TEST

In everyday English, a transaction implies a business deal, such as trading cash for a new CD player or for a tank car of toluene diisocyanate. The dictionary defines *to transact* as "to drive through" or "to complete." Database transactions can involve changes to or additions of one or more records in a single table or, more commonly, in several tables. Collectively, the changes are called a *unit of work*. When more than one record or table is involved in a transaction, all the records must be updated either simultaneously or as close to simultaneously as possible. The database is said to be in an "inconsistent state" until the records of each table involved in the transaction have been updated successfully.

If hardware or software errors occur, if a domain or referential integrity violation is detected, or if the application is unable to alter or add a record because of locks placed on one or more of the records involved by others in a multiuser environment, the updates to all tables must be canceled. Any changes made to tables before the transaction operation terminates must be undone. An example is an automatic teller transaction—your bank credits its cash account and debits your checking account whenever you make a cash withdrawal at an ATM terminal. Obviously, your bank does not want a one-sided transaction to occur wherein you receive the cash but your account is not debited. Canceling or undoing a transaction is called *rolling back the transaction*.

`UPDATE`, `INSERT`, and `DELETE` operations on database tables must be atomic, consistent, isolated, and durable. The initial letters of these requirements (acid) have come to be formalized as the *ACID test* of TP. Following is the generally accepted description of the four ACID test requirements:

- *Atomicity* requires all updates of a specific transaction to be committed (made durable) or all updates to be aborted and rolled back to values existing immediately prior to execution.

- *Consistency* requires that all operations result in data entities that preserve consistency constraints on the tables participating in the update.

- *Isolation* requires that a transaction's intermediate (uncommitted work) results not be visible to other concurrent transactions operating on the same tables. Isolation is the subject of the "Serializability and Transaction Isolation Levels" section later in this chapter.

- *Durability* means that committed updates to managed resources (such as a database record) survive failures, including communication failures, process failures, and server system failures.

> **NOTE**
>
> The term *acid test* originated in inorganic chemistry as a means of identifying noble (precious) metals. Noble metals, such as gold, platinum, and iridium are unaffected by immersion in strong acids, such as sulfuric, hydrochloric, or nitric acid, at room temperature. Aqua Regia (a 3:1 mixture of hydrochloric acid and nitric acid) dissolves gold and attacks platinum. Even hot Aqua Regia doesn't attack rhodium and ruthenium.

Transactions against Jet databases meet the ACID test, with the exception of one criterion of the durability requirement. Jet doesn't offer transaction logging in a separate file for disaster recovery in the event of server hardware failure. Mainstream client/server RDBMSs, such as Microsoft SQL Server, maintain a transaction log to enable restoration of the database from the last backup. In the event of a server media failure, which is more common than other server hardware failures, you restore the database backup and then apply the transaction log to the database. Obviously, the transaction log must be stored on physical disk(s) other than those used for database storage.

> **NOTE**
>
> You can protect against server media failure by using a Redundant Array of Inexpensive Disks (RAID) subsystem for database and log storage. Fail-over clustering, which involves two independent servers (each with its own application disk drives) sharing a single external RAID subsystem, protects against other types of server failure. The Enterprise Editions of Windows NT 4.0+ and SQL Server 6.5+ support fail-over clustering with Microsoft-qualified hardware.

Explicit and Implicit Transactions

▶ See "ANSI SQL Reserved Words and Jet SQL Keywords," **p. 281**

SQL-92 defines two transaction verbs: COMMIT [WORK] and ROLLBACK [WORK]. These two verbs determine the outcome of a transaction. There is no reserved word in SQL-92 to define the beginning of a transaction. RDBMSs that let you determine the outcome of a series of update instructions with COMMIT or ROLLBACK without specifying the start of a transaction support *implicit* transactions. Jet and some client/server RDBMSs offer *implicit* transactions; Jet's capability to cancel (roll back) updates is limited in most cases to a single row in one or more tables. Following are three examples of RDBMSs that differ in their method of handling transactions:

- By default, Microsoft SQL Server requires an explicit BEGIN TRAN[SACTION] statement to start a transaction and an explicit COMMIT TRANS[ACTION] or ROLLBACK

`TRANS[ACTION]` statement to execute (make durable) or terminate (abort) the transaction. Without the `BEGIN TRAN` statement, SQL Server executes (makes durable) each update statement immediately. This chapter uses explicit transactions in all cases.

- IBM's DB2 databases implicitly start a transaction and require a `COMMIT [WORK]` or `ROLLBACK [WORK]` statement to execute or terminate the transaction. SQL Server also accepts the `COMMIT [WORK]` or `ROLLBACK [WORK]` verbs.

- SQL Server, IBM's AS/400, and, to a limited extent, Jet databases support both implicit and explicit transactions. To enable SQL Server's implicit transactions, send a `SET IMPLICIT_TRANSACTIONS {ON¦OFF}` statement on the current connection. Implicit transactions are then accepted over the current connection only. You must terminate SQL Server transactions with a `COMMIT [TRAN¦WORK]` or `ROLLBACK [TRAN¦WORK]` statement. If the client drops the connection, SQL Server automatically rolls back all of the client's open transactions.

> **NOTE**
>
> It's more straightforward and readable to preface transactions with a `BEGIN TRAN` statement or call the `BeginTrans` method, so all examples in this chapter use explicit transactions. Transact-SQL lets you add a transaction name as an argument of `BEGIN TRAN` to identify a particular transaction. `COMMIT TRAN` and `ROLLBACK TRAN` accept transaction names; `COMMIT [WORK]` and `ROLLBACK [WORK]` don't.

Serializability and Transaction Isolation Levels

Transactions are *serializable* if the result of executing two or more transactions simultaneously is identical to the result of running the transactions in sequence. The sequence in which the transactions execute isn't important; what's important is that the simultaneous transactions don't interfere with one another. As an example, a Northwind Traders road warrior is in the process of entering a customer order for 15 cases of product 12 (Queso Manchego La Pastora). At the same time, the customer calls the home office and changes the order to 10 cases of product 11 (Queso Cabrales). Depending on who commits his or her transaction first, the Quantity and ProductID values of the Order Details record must be 15 and 12, or 10 and 11, respectively. If at any time the record contains 15 and 11, or 10 and 12, the transaction isn't serializable.

Serialization is achieved by locking table records or pages, which prevents more than one transaction from simultaneously reading or updating the same row. If the RDBMS uses page locking, locking a single row might lock a large number of rows. For example, Jet and SQL Server 6.x and earlier use 2K page locks. The size of an Order Details record is about 24 bytes, so a page locks 83 records. With an average of four line items per order, a page lock is likely to prevent simultaneous serializable updating of the last 20 or so orders entered. Serialized transactions provide total isolation of transactions at the cost of reduced concurrency. Reducing concurrency reduces performance in OLTP operations with many simultaneous users because each front-end application must wait for locks to be released before processing its transaction.

> **TIP**
>
> SQL Server 6.5 offers optional row locking for INSERT operations. SQL Server 7.0 provides automatic row locking for both INSERT and UPDATE operations unless you specify otherwise. To minimize concurrency problems, make sure to use row locking for databases involved in production OLTP.

If you can't accept the lack of OLTP performance brought on by the concurrency problems of serializable transactions, you must settle for one or more of the following undesirable occurrences:

- A *dirty read* is defined as reading data that has not yet been committed. An example is the home office clerk seeing the salesperson's attempted update to the Order Details table before it is rolled back because of the clerk's record lock. The formal term for a dirty read is an *uncommitted dependency problem.*

- A *nonrepeatable read* (*inconsistent analysis problem*) is defined as an operation in which reading the record twice results in different data. An example is a third person accessing the Order Details table, first seeing 15 cases of product 12, then seeing 10 cases of product 11 on the second access.

- A *phantom* (*lost update problem*) is a row that meets a search criterion, does not appear on the first read, but appears on successive reads. A phantom read would occur if a third person attempted to total the number of orders for product 12 while the two simultaneous transactions were in process.

▶ See "Connection Properties," p. 69

Transaction isolation levels determine which of the preceding occurrences are allowed when processing transactions. Table 19.1 lists the four transaction isolation levels defined by SQL-92 and their corresponding ADODB.*Connection*.IsolationLevel property values in descending order of isolation and ascending order of execution speed. The default isolation level for SQL Server is READ COMMITTED and for ADODB.*Connection*.IsolationLevel is adXactReadCommitted.

TABLE 19.1 SQL-92 AND ADODB.Connection OBJECT TRANSACTION ISOLATION LEVELS

SQL-92 Transaction ISOLATION LEVEL	Connection *Object* IsolationLevel *Property Value*	*Dirty Reads*	*Non repeat- able Reads*	*Phantoms*
SERIALIZABLE	adXactSerializable	No	No	No
REPEATABLE READ	adXactRepeatableRead	No	No	Yes
READ COMMITTED	adXactReadCommitted	No	Yes	Yes
READ UNCOMMITTED	adXactReadUncommitted	Yes	Yes	Yes

> **NOTE**
>
> The transaction isolation level doesn't affect a transaction's ability to see the uncommitted changes it makes to the underlying tables.

The SQL-92 syntax for specifying the transaction isolation level is

```
SET TRANSACTION
   {READ ONLY¦READ WRITE},
   ISOLATION LEVEL
      {SERIALIZABLE¦REPEATABLE READ¦READ COMMITTED¦READ UNCOMMITTED}
```

SQL Server doesn't support the READ ONLY or READ WRITE reserved words, so the Transact-SQL syntax is

```
SET TRANSACTION ISOLATION LEVEL
   {SERIALIZABLE¦REPEATABLE READ¦READ COMMITTED¦READ UNCOMMITTED}
```

Some OLE DB data providers don't support transactions, and those that support transactions might have limited or no ability to specify the isolation level. If you specify an unsupported isolation level, the data provider escalates to the next higher level if supported. Otherwise, ADODB.*Connection*.IsolationLevel returns adXactUnknown.

Understanding the Role of Transaction Monitors

Transaction monitors (TMs, often called transaction processors or managers) are a class of TP applications that were originally designed to manage very large numbers of simultaneous transactions against mainframe database-management systems. TMs are more robust and handle more simultaneous transactions than standalone client/server RDBMSs. IBM's Customer Information Control System (CICS) TM application is undoubtedly the most widely used mainframe TM in North America. Many third-party TMs—all of which require rather high licensing fees—are available for UNIX, NetWare, and Windows NT Server. TMs commonly are used for transactions that span more than one database, the subject of the "Distributing Transactions Across Multiple Databases" section later in the chapter.

Microsoft Transaction Server (MTS) 2.0 is a combination transaction monitor/processor and object request broker (ORB) for Windows 9x and Windows NT. MTS works with SQL Server's Distributed Transaction Coordinator (DTC) service to coordinate transactions across multiple databases and servers. MTS offers many benefits, not the least of which is its low licensing cost; MTS 2.0 is included with the free Option Pack for Windows NT Server 4 and will be a component of Windows NT Server 5.0. Although MTS runs only on Windows platforms, usually Windows NT Server 4+, MTS can connect to UNIX and mainframe RDBMSs through X/Open DTP XA-compliant UNIX transaction monitors, such as Encina, TopEnd, and Tuxedo. X/Open SNA Server 4+ enables MTS connections to IBM's CICS and Information Management System (IMS) with Microsoft's COM Transaction Integrator (COMTI).

> **NOTE**
>
> X/Open Company Ltd is an industry standards association for information systems that, together with the Open Software Foundation (OSF), constitutes the umbrella Open Group, which is headquartered in Cambridge, Massachusetts. In 1996 the Open Group's Active Group became officially responsible for managing the evolution of Microsoft's ActiveX technologies, including COM, DCOM, and Automation. Nothing of substance has emerged from the Open Group since its creation.

In its role as an ORB, MTS aids in creating and managing the middle tier of three-tier client/server applications. In a typical three-tier application, the client front end provides user services, the UI, and the minimum amount of code necessary to move user input to the middle tier. The middle tier, business services, implements business rules (data validation and the like) and processes transactions. Chapter 26, "Taking Advantage of Microsoft Transaction Server 2.0," describes in detail the architecture of three-tier client/server applications and the role of MTS as TM and ORB middleware.

You create middle-tier components for MTS as 32-bit Visual Basic DLLs, as described in Chapter 27, "Creating and Deploying MTS Components." You also can write middle-tier components in C++ and Java. The data services tier is the back-end database; ADO/OLE DB is the preferred connection between MTS middle-tier components and RDBMSs regardless of the language you use to create the components.

PROCESSING TRANSACTIONS WITH ADO 2.X AND VBA CODE

▶ **See** "Connection Methods," **p. 75**

ADO 2.x provides the `BeginTrans`, `CommitTrans`, and `RollbackTrans` methods of the `Connection` object to maintain database consistency in TP applications. These three instructions actually are methods that apply to a locally cached buffer that contains the pending update(s) to the database tables. Another buffer, the transaction log, stores a copy of the data contained in the affected rows of the tables before the updates occur. These instructions, in conjunction with the underlying database engine, ensure that all updates to database tables proceed to completion and that the database returns to a consistent state when the transaction completes or when the updates are rolled back.

> **NOTE**
>
> As noted in Chapter 2, "Understanding OLE DB and Universal Data Access," transaction isolation in DAO is provided by using the `CreateWorkspace` method to run transactions within individual `Workspace` objects. Similarly, RDO uses individual `rdoEnvironment` objects for transaction isolation. ADO doesn't provide `Workspaces` or `rdoEnvironments` collections, so transactions must be specified on individual top-level `Connection` objects. SQL Server is an example of a client/server RDBMS that requires a separate connection for each concurrent transaction. Another change from DAO and RDO is that ADO's `RollbackTrans` method replaces the `Rollback` method.

Structure of the Transaction Instructions

The general structure of ADO 2.x TP commands, expressed in metacode, is as follows:

```
{Sub|Function} Name()
   ...
   On Error GoTo RollbackLabel
   Connection.BeginTrans
      Do While Condition
        [Recordset.AddNew]
        [Field update code...]
         Recordset.{Update|Delete}
      Loop
   Connection.CommitTrans
   Exit {Sub|Function}
```

```
RollbackLabel:
   Connection.RollbackTrans
   [MsgBox Error$, vbCritical, strTitle]
   Exit {Sub¦Function}
End {Sub¦Function}
```

The following is the metacode for an alternative structure that incorporates error processing within a loop structure to allow for a retry in the event of an error, such as a lock on an updated record:

```
{Sub¦Function} Name()
   ...
   Connection.BeginTrans
      Do While Condition
         [Recordset.AddNew]
         [Field update code...]
         Recordset.{Update¦Delete}
         Connection.CommitTrans
         If Error Then
            Connection.RollbackTrans
            'Message box with option to try again or abort
            If Abort Then
               Exit Do
            Else
               Error = 0
            End If
         Else
            Exit Do
         End If
      Loop
End {Sub¦Function}
```

The `BeginTrans` and `CommitTrans` methods of the `Connection` object always are used in pairs. Code within the `BeginTrans...CommitTrans` structure ordinarily is indented to identify the elements that constitute the transaction. You can nest transactions applied to Jet databases up to five levels deep. When you nest transactions, you need to write code that commits or rolls back each set of transactions, beginning with the innermost nested transaction.

When the `BeginTrans` statement is executed, the following operations occur:

1. ADO instructs the database engine to open a temporary update buffer and, for Jet databases, a temporary transaction log. (Client/server RDBMSs have persistent transaction logs.) Both the update buffer and the Jet transaction log are virtual tables that are stored in memory; client/server RDBMSs use transaction log files, such as SQL Server 7.0's *DBName*_Log.ldf. If you have insufficient available RAM to store a temporary Jet transaction log, it's written to C:\Temp or the location you specify in your `Temp=` environmental variable.

2. All records for transactions that occur prior to the execution of the `CommitTrans` statement are stored in the update buffer.

3. When the `CommitTrans` statement is reached, the database engine commences the execution of the transactions stored in the update buffer.

4. Prior to replacing or deleting records, the record that is to be updated or deleted is saved in the transaction log.

5. The database engine then attempts to update, delete, or add new records to the table. If no errors occur, the changes are made permanent in the tables and the temporary transaction log is cleared.

6. If an error is generated during the transaction process, the update buffer is cleared, program execution jumps to your error-handling routine, and the `RollbackTrans` instruction is executed.

7. The `RollbackTrans` instruction replaces records that were updated or deleted with records from the transaction log file. Any records added to tables during with the `AddNew` method are deleted.

8. When the `RollbackTrans` operation is completed, Jet's temporary transaction log file is cleared. Client/server RDBMSs retain the transaction log for use in data recovery operations; the transaction log is truncated after a full database backup.

One of the advantages of using Jet's TP instructions is that bulk updates to tables occur faster than when you apply the `Update` or `Delete` methods to a single record. Each time you apply the `Update` or `Delete` methods singly, Jet adds, modifies, or deletes parts of the physical table file and then flushes all disk write buffers in the process. When you use the TP instructions, all the operations are conducted in buffers (in memory), with a single write-buffer flush operation at the end of the process.

> **NOTE**
>
> Jet 2.*x* gained at least a 3:1 improvement in bulk update performance by the use of TP transactions. Jet 3.*x* uses implicit transactions for updates by applying the equivalent of the `BeginTrans...CommitTrans` methods "under the covers." Tests of very large bulk updates with Jet 3.*x*, such as the starting date change to the 19,000-record table of the VBPG.vbp project of Chapter 14, "Scheduling and Device Control with Jet and VBA," indicate that using explicit transactions with Jet 3.5*x* delivers gives about a 10% performance gain.

19

PROCESSING TRANSACTIONS AND BULK OPERATIONS

Multitable Transaction Code for Jet Databases

Listing 19.1 illustrates VBA code that adds an order with a variable number of line items to the Orders and Order Details tables of Nwind.mdb, using the native OLE DB provider for Jet, Microsoft.Jet.OLEDB.3.51 (Jolt). The line items are added to a temporary local table prior to execution of the transaction. Because referential integrity is enforced between the Orders and Order Details tables, the order must be entered first, followed by the line items. This example uses the traditional Visual Basic database programming style, rst*Name*.AddNew...rst*Name*.Update, to add records to Recordset objects within a transaction.

LISTING 19.1   A JET ORDER ENTRY TRANSACTION WITH VBA Recordset CODE

```
Private Sub AddNewOrder()
    'Purpose: Add a new order to the Orders and Order Details tables
    'Note:    cnnData, rstOrders, and rstOrderDetails are declared
    '         and opened in the FormActivate event handler

    Dim rstLineItems As New ADODB.Recordset
    Dim lngOrderID As Long

    'Obtain a tentative order ID
    strSQL = "SELECT MAX(OrderID) AS LastOrder FROM Orders;"
    rstLineItems.Open strSQL, cnnData, adOpenForwardOnly
    lngOrderID = rstLineItems(0) + 1
    rstLineItems.Close

    'Populate the Recordsets
    strSQL = "SELECT * FROM Orders WHERE CustomerID = 'ZZZZZ'"
    rstOrders.Open strSQL, cnnData, adOpenKeyset
    strSQL = "SELECT * FROM tblOrderDetails" 'Local table
    rstLineItems.Open strSQL, cnnData, adOpenStatic

    'Add order and detail items as a transaction
    On Error GoTo RollbackOrder
    cnnData.BeginTrans
        'Add the order to the Orders table
        With rstOrders
            .AddNew
            !OrderID = lngOrderID
            !CustomerID = txtCustomerID
            !EmployeeID = intEmployeeID
            !OrderDate = txtOrderDate
            !RequiredDate = txtRequiredDate
            !ShipVia = intShipVia
            !ShipName = txtShipName
            !ShipAddress = txtShipAddress
            !ShipCity = txtShipCity
            !ShipRegion = txtShipRegion
            !ShipPostalCode = txtShipPostalCode
```

```
            !ShipCountry = txtShipCountry
            'Following fields are not updated for a new order
            '!ShippedDate = txtShippedDate
            '!Freight = txtFreight
            .Update
        End With
        'Add the line item(s) to the Order Details table
        rstLineItems.MoveFirst
        Do Until rstLineItems.EOF
            With rstOrderDetails
                .AddNew
                !OrderID = lngOrderID
                !ProductID = rsLineItems!ProductID
                !Quantity = rsLineItems!Quantity
                !UnitPrice = rsLineItems!UnitPrice
                !Discount = rsLineItems!Discount
                .Update
            End With
            rstLineItems.MoveNext
        Loop
    cnnOrders.CommitTrans
    Set rstLineItems = Nothing
Exit Sub

RollbackOrder:
    MsgBox Error$, 48, "Unable to Add Order " & lngOrderID & "."
    cnnData.RollbackTrans
    Set rstLineItems = Nothing
    Exit Sub

End Sub
```

NOTE

The DAO.Recordset object offers an dbAppendOnly option for the OpenRecordset method when you specify dbOpenDynaset as the value of the Type argument. Append-only Recordsets improve performance by not returning records or keys when opened. ADO 2.x doesn't offer an equivalent append-only option. To maximize performance with ADO, add a WHERE criterion that doesn't return rows to the SQL statement that creates the Recordset, such as the WHERE CustomerID = 'ZZZZZ' clause in the preceding listing, and specify a keyset-type cursor.

Some desktop databases, such as Paradox, don't support transactions, either when linked to a Jet database or opened directly with an ODBC driver and the MSDASQL data provider. Regardless of whether you can roll back changes you make to tables, using the BeginTrans...CommitTrans structure for bulk changes to tables almost always improves the performance of your application. However, there is substantial risk inherent in using

BeginTrans...CommitTrans when you can't roll back changes. If your transaction fails, you have no means of determining at what point the failure occurred.

> **NOTE**
>
> DAO.Database and DAO.Recordset objects have a Transactions property. If Transactions returns **True** for a DAO.Database object, the RDBMS supports transactions; all Jet databases return **True**. If you create a DAO.Recordset with field(s) from a linked table, such as a Paradox table, that doesn't support transactions, Transactions returns **False** for the DAO.Recordset object. Unfortunately, ADO 2.0 Connection and Recordset objects don't have a Transactions (or equivalent) property that you can test to determine whether the RDBMS or Recordset supports transactions.

Using Jet SQL Within a Transaction

In all but exceptional cases, Jet SQL INSERT INTO statements execute slightly faster than the preceding Recordset manipulation code. Another benefit of using SQL for transactions is ease of upsizing to client/server RDBMSs. You need only make minor changes to the code that generates the Jet SQL statement to accommodate the SQL dialect of the back-end RDBMS.

The code example of Listing 19.2 uses Jet SQL to add a new order and its line items to the Nwind.mdb Orders and Order Details tables. Each INSERT INTO operation, which Jet requires to be executed individually, adds rows to the locally cached transaction Recordset. Executing the cnnData.CommitTrans statement adds the rows of the local Recordset to the underlying tables. If the table update operation encounters page locks, the Jet database engine raises an error and the error handler applies the RollbackTrans method.

> **NOTE**
>
> Transaction execution time is critical for production OLTP operations that add new records to tables of databases that employ page locking. When many order entry persons simultaneously are adding orders to the end of a table, the probability of encountering a page lock is inversely proportional to the speed of transaction execution.

LISTING 19.2 EXECUTING AN ORDER ENTRY TRANSACTION WITH JET SQL

```
Private Sub AddNewOrder()
    'Purpose: Add a new order to the Jet Orders and Order Details tables
    'Note:    cnnData and rstOrders are declared and opened previously
```

```
Dim rstLineItems As New ADODB.Recordset
Dim lngOrderID As Long

On Error GoTo RollbackOrder

'Obtain the tentative order ID
strSQL = "SELECT MAX(OrderID) AS LastOrder FROM Orders;"
If rstOrders.State = adStateOpen Then
    rstOrders.Close
End If
rstOrders.Open strSQL, cnnData, adOpenForwardOnly
lngOrderID = rstOrders(0) + 1

'Create the line items Recordset
strSQL = "SELECT * FROM tblOrder_Details"  'Local table
rstLineItems.Open strSQL, cnnData, adOpenStatic

cnnData.BeginTrans
    'INSERT the order information
    strSQL = "INSERT INTO Orders VALUES(" & _
    txtOrderID & ", '" & _
    txtCustomerID & "', " & _
    intEmployeeID & ", '" & _
    txtOrderDate & "', '" & _
    txtRequiredDate & "', NULL, " & _
    intShipVia & ", NULL, '" & _
    txtShipName & "', '" & _
    txtShipAddress & "', '" & _
    txtShipCity & "', '" & _
    txtShipRegion & "', '" & _
    txtShipPostal_Code & "', '" & _
    txtShipCountry & "');"
    cnnData.Execute(strSQL)

    'INSERT the line item information for each record
    rsLineItems.MoveFirst
    Do Until rsLineItems.EOF
        strSQL = "INSERT INTO [Order Details] VALUES(" & _
        lngOrderID & ", " & _
        With rsLineItems
            !ProductID & ", " & _
            !UnitPrice & ", " & _
            !Quantity & ", " & _
            !Discount & ")"
            .MoveNext
            If .EOF Then
                strSQL = strSQL & ";"
            End If
        End With
        cnnData.Execute(strSQL)
    Loop
```

continues

LISTING 19.2   EXECUTING AN ORDER ENTRY TRANSACTION WITH JET SQL

```
    cnnData.CommitTrans
    Set rstLineItems = Nothing

RollbackOrder:
    'Roll back the Jet transaction
    MsgBox Error$, 48, "Unable to Add Order " & lngOrderID & "."
    cnnData.RollbackTrans
    Set rstLineItems = Nothing
    Exit Sub

End Sub
```

> **NOTE**
>
> The VBA code of Listing 19.2 and following Listing 19.3 are condensed versions of the AddNewOrder subprocedure of the ADO_OLTP.vbp application described in the next chapter.

Following are the four Jet SQL statements created by the code of Listing 19.2 for adding one order with three line items to Nwind.mdb:

```
INSERT INTO Orders
    VALUES(11093, 'KOENE', 1,
        '5/15/1998', '6/1/1998', NULL, 3, NULL,
        'K^niglich Essen',
        'Maubelstr. 90',
        'Brandenburg', '', '14776',
        'Germany';)

INSERT INTO Order_Details
    VALUES(11093, 24, 4.5, 24, 0);

INSERT INTO Order_Details
    VALUES(11093, 36, 19, 36, 0);

INSERT INTO Order_Details
    VALUES(11093, 42, 9.8, 12, 0);
```

The preceding SQL statements use VALUES lists without a preceding fields list. When you eliminate the optional fields list, you must supply a value for each field—thus the presence of the two NULL values (for the ShippedDate and Freight fields) in the first INSERT INTO statement. Eliminating the fields list shortens the length of the SQL statement by 25% or more, depending on the number of line items entered. The length of SQL statements is not a significant factor in the speed of execution of a Jet transaction, because the SQL statement is executed on the client to create the temporary Recordset. Eliminating the fields list, however, improves the overall execution time of client/server transactions by reducing the number of characters in the SQL statement sent over the network.

Executing the Order Entry Transaction with Transact-SQL

The general rule of thumb among Access and Visual Basic developers is that multiuser Jet databases can accommodate up to 20 or 30 simultaneous OLTP clients. Database applications that are critical to an organization's operations ordinarily run on client/server RDBMSs, which are much more robust than Jet .mdbs. Client/server RDBMSs offer a substantial increase in the number of simultaneous OLTP connections, online database backup, and transaction logs to restore a failed database to the consistent state immediately before the failure occurred.

> **NOTE**
>
> The Jet-based DAO requires the use of ODBC passthrough queries to execute SQL statements directly on the back-end RDBMS. ODBCDirect and RDO, which bypass DAO but use ODBC, rely on the server to process all queries. ADO passes SQL directly to the OLE DB data provider or to an intermediate query engine configured as an OLE DB service provider, bypassing ODBC. SQL Server 7.0's query engine is an almost-independent OLE DB service provider; the SQL Server 6.5 and earlier query engine is fully integrated with the data engine.

Listing 19.3 illustrates the modifications required to the VBA code of Listing 19.2 to accommodate Microsoft SQL Server Transact-SQL syntax. The changes consist of the following elements:

- SQL Server handles TP entirely on the server. You identify an explicit transaction with the BEGIN TRANS and COMMIT TRANS statements. You don't need a ROLLBACK TRANS statement for a simple transaction; SQL Server automatically rolls back the transaction when execution encounters a record lock or other problem.

- Transact-SQL doesn't require the INTO preposition after INSERT statements; omitting INTO saves a few characters in transmission of the statement to the server.

- You can include as many INSERT statements in a multiple-table transaction as necessary to complete the transaction and then execute the statement with a single Connection.Execute method call. Jet requires separate execution of each INSERT INTO statement.

19

PROCESSING TRANSACTIONS AND BULK OPERATIONS

LISTING 19.3   EXECUTING A TRANSACTION ON AN SQL SERVER 6+ DATABASE

```
Private Sub AddNewOrder()
    'Purpose: Add a new order to the SQL Server tables
    'Note:    cnnData and rstOrders are declared and opened in the
    '         FormActivate event handler
```

LISTING 19.3 CONTINUED

```
Dim rstLineItems As New ADODB.Recordset
Dim lngOrderID As Long

On Error GoTo RollbackOrder

'Obtain the tentative order ID (works with all connections)
strSQL = "SELECT MAX(OrderID) LastOrder FROM Orders"
If rstOrders.State = adStateOpen Then
    rstOrders.Close
End If
rstOrders.Open strSQL, cnnData, adOpenForwardOnly
lngOrder_ID = rstOrders(0) + 1

'Create the line items Recordset
strSQL = "SELECT * FROM tblOrder_Details"  'Local table
rstLineItems.Open strSQL, cnnData, adOpenStatic

'INSERT the order information
strSQL = "BEGIN TRAN INSERT Orders VALUES("
txtOrderID & ", '" & _
txtCustomerID & "', " & _
intEmployeeID & ", '" & _
txtOrderDate & "', '" & _
txtRequiredDate & "', NULL, " & _
intShipVia & ", NULL, '" & _
txtShipName & "', '" & _
txtShipAddress & "', '" & _
txtShipCity & "', '" & _
txtShipRegion & "', '" & _
txtShipPostal_Code & "', '" & _
txtShipCountry & "')"

'INSERT the line item information for each record
rsLineItems.MoveFirst
Do Until rsLineItems.EOF
    strSQL = strSQL & " INSERT Order_Details VALUES(" & _
    lngOrderID & ", " & _
    With rsLineItems
        !ProductID & ", " & _
        !UnitPrice & ", " & _
        !Quantity & ", " & _
        !Discount & ")"
        .MoveNext
        If .EOF Then
            strSQL = strSQL & " COMMIT TRAN"
        End If
    End With
Loop
```

```
    'Execute the SQL statement
    cnnData.Execute (strSQL)
    Exit Sub

RollbackOrder:
    'Roll back the Transact-SQL transaction
    MsgBox Error$, 48, "Unable to Add Order " & lngOrderID & "."
    Exit Sub

End Sub
```

Following is the Transact-SQL statement generated by the code of Listing 19.3 for a new order with three line items:

```
BEGIN TRAN
    INSERT Orders
        VALUES(11093, 'KOENE', 1,
        '5/15/1998', '6/1/1998', NULL, 3, NULL,
        'K^niglich Essen',
        'Maubelstr. 90',
        'Brandenburg', '', '14776',
        'Germany')
    INSERT Order_Details
        VALUES(11093, 24, 4.5, 24, 0)
    INSERT Order_Details
        VALUES(11093, 36, 19, 36, 0)
    INSERT Order_Details
        VALUES(11093, 42, 9.8, 12, 0)
COMMIT TRAN
```

▶ **See** "Upsizing Nwind.mdb to SQL Server 6.5 with the Access 97 Wizard," **p. 692**
and "Importing Jet Tables to SQL Server 7.0," **p. 701**

> **NOTE**
>
> You can't run the preceding transaction on a database upsized to SQL Server by the Access 97 Upsizing Wizard. The Upsizing Wizard adds an identity attribute to the OrderID field of the Orders table. You receive an error message, An explicit value for the identity column in table 'Orders' can only be specified when a column list is used and IDENTITY_INSERT is ON, when executing the query. You can, however, execute the transaction against tables generated by SQL Enterprise Manager's Data Transformation Services (DTS) Import Wizard, which imports only the basic table structures and data.

There is a momentary delay between execution of the SELECT MAX(OrderID) statement and execution of the transaction based on the incremented OrderID value. With a high-performance network and a fast client PC, the delay is a hundred milliseconds, at most. If a longer delay occurs, and another user inserts an order during the delay, attempts to execute the transaction will fail because OrderID is the primary key field of the Orders table. This failure mode is acceptable because the first transaction rolls back.

> **NOTE**
>
> Record (rather than page) locking is especially beneficial in sequential INSERT operations because newly added records can't be locked by other users. You also can use a lower-than-standard isolation level for INSERT-only operations. You can enhance transaction speed by specifying adXactReadUncommitted isolation, but you risk failure to maintain strictly sequential order numbering as a result of rolled-back transactions having created phantom values in the OrderID field. Strict sequential order is more important for invoice generation, which must be auditable, than for order entry.

An alternative approach to reduce the potential delay is to declare a server-side variable and obtain the new OrderID value at the server. An added benefit is that you save a round-trip to the server if you don't need to know the value of the new OrderID. The Transact-SQL statement to use a server-side variable for the new OrderID value is

```
DECLARE @OrderID int
SELECT @OrderID = MAX(OrderID) FROM Orders
SELECT @OrderID = @OrderID + 1

BEGIN TRAN
   INSERT Orders
      VALUES(@OrderID, 'KOENE', 1,
      '5/15/1998', '6/1/1998', NULL, 3, NULL,
      'K^niglich Essen',
      'Maubelstr. 90',
      'Brandenburg', '', '14776',
      'Germany')
   INSERT Order_Details
      VALUES(@OrderID, 24, 4.5, 24, 0)
   INSERT Order_Details
      VALUES(@OrderID, 36, 19, 36, 0)
   INSERT Order_Details
      VALUES(@OrderID, 42, 9.8, 12, 0)
COMMIT TRAN
```

▶ See "Connection Methods," **p. 75**

Figure 19.1 shows a test of the preceding Transact-SQL statement in SQL Query Analyzer. Update queries return the number of rows affected to the Results pane and, optionally, to the lng*RecordsAffected* argument of the Connection object's Execute method. After executing the transaction, click the Display Execution Plan button to see a graphical showplan diagram. The Plan window shows the DECLARE and SELECT statements and the four INSERT operations in a separate diagram.

FIGURE 19.1

Executing a complete transaction statement with SQL Query Analyzer.

A third approach, which assures a unique order number, is to add the identity attribute to the OrderID field, which automatically increments the OrderID value for each INSERT. This method, however, isn't suited to a multitable transaction, because you must add the record to the Orders table, query for the new OrderID, and then assign the new OrderID value to the INSERT statements for the Order_Details table. SQL Server doesn't offer a method for dependably returning the value of an incremented identity field to a local variable for use in adding dependent records, because the new OrderID value isn't known until the transaction commits.

> **NOTE**
>
> SQL Server's @@IDENTITY global variable returns the last value of an identity column for the current connection, not the value of the identity column about to be inserted by a transaction on the connection. It's unsafe to use the value @@IDENTITY + 1 for foreign keys, because other users might add records before the transaction commits.

19

PROCESSING
TRANSACTIONS AND
BULK OPERATIONS

DISTRIBUTING TRANSACTIONS ACROSS MULTIPLE DATABASES

It's not uncommon to have multiple databases participate in transactions. As an example, an Accounts database might contain the main customers table, plus additional tables for accounts receivable, credit, and other customer-related information. The Sales database might include sales order, salesperson, commission, and customer contact data. Production databases are likely to harbor available (uncommitted) inventory, work-in-process, purchasing, and related manufacturing data. In such a scenario, the order entry application must query tables in each database and then update at least the sales order and available inventory tables in the Sales and Production databases, respectively. Sales-oriented transactions must roll back if updates to the available inventory table fail or if the amount of the order exceeds the customer's current credit line. The capability to rollback updates across more than one database is the primary feature of distributed transactions.

Figure 19.2 illustrates a distributed transaction for the credit-card sale of books or audio CDs to be shipped from local inventory or, if out of stock, from a book distributor's fulfillment center. The order originates on the seller's Internet site and is entered into an Orders database by Internet Information Server (IIS) 4.0. The steps within the transaction are as follows:

1. Verify the customer's credit card information and place a hold the amount of the order.

2. Determine whether the item(s) ordered are in local inventory and reserve those in stock.

3. Determine whether out-of-stock items are available from the distributor; if so, place an order for direct delivery to the customer. Optionally, order all items from the distributor to save shipping costs.

4. Instruct the warehouse to ship the in-stock items. If the distributor ships the entire order, release the hold on the items in local stock.

5. Process the credit card debit.

FIGURE 19.2

A distributed transaction for sale of books from an Internet e-commerce site.

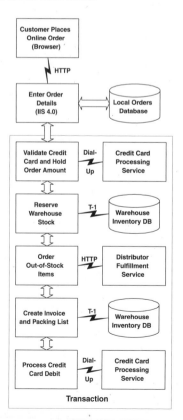

If any step within the transaction fails, all elements of the transaction must be rolled back. The update to the Orders database isn't included in the transaction because it's desirable to retain the order information to advise the customer of the transaction's outcome. Assuming that all WAN (dialup, T-1, and HTTP) connections are intact, it's possible to complete the entire transaction, without human intervention, in less than a minute.

Two-Phase Commit and the Distributed Transaction Coordinator

Two-phase commit is the traditional method of assuring consistency of tables in multiple databases on the same or different servers. Using the analogy of a contract, the first phase (preparation) consists of parties to the transaction reading and agreeing to the contract's terms and provisions. The second phase is signing the contract. If all parties sign, the contract takes effect; if any party refuses to sign, the contract is void.

SQL Server 6+ uses the Microsoft Distributed Transaction Coordinator (DTC) to manage distributed transactions. DTC uses the OLE Transactions (OLE Tx) model to define resource managers and transaction managers, both of which are installed on participating servers during the SQL Server setup process. In this chapter, resources are limited to SQL Servers. The active transaction manager is that for the server that initiates the distributed transaction with the Transact-SQL BEGIN DISTRIBUTED TRANS[ACTION] statement. Other participants in a Transact-SQL distributed transaction must have a predefined stored procedure to execute their components of the transaction. Transact-SQL stored procedures are the subject of Chapter 21, "Using Transact-SQL Stored Procedures."

> **Note**
>
> Launch SQL Server Books Online and search for "Jim Gray" (with the quotes) to read a detailed description of the architecture and implementation of distributed transactions.

Following is a sample interactive Transact-SQL statement for a distributed transaction that updates the authors table of the pubs database on two servers, OAKLEAF0 and OAKLEAF3 for this example:

```
USE pubs
GO
BEGIN DISTRIBUTED TRANSACTION
    UPDATE authors
        SET au_lname = 'McDonald' WHERE au_id = '409-56-7008'
    EXECUTE oakleaf3.pubs.dbo.changeauth_lname '409-56-7008','McDonald'
COMMIT TRAN
GO
```

19

Processing Transactions and Bulk Operations

The preceding code executes on OAKLEAF0's SQL Server; `changeauth_lname` is the name of the stored procedure on OAKLEAF3's SQL Server. The stored procedure executes the following statement by a remote procedure call (RPC), where `@au_id` and `@au_lname` are input parameters:

```
UPDATE authors
   SET au_lname = @au_lname WHERE au_id = @au_id
```

When the `BEGIN DISTRIBUTED TRAN` statement executes, the following steps occur:

1. The front-end application (for example, SQL Query Analyzer) on OAKLEAF1 calls OAKLEAF0's transaction manager, which creates a transaction object for the connection.

2. OAKLEAF0's SQL Server resource enlists in the transaction with its local transaction manager.

3. Executing the stored procedure enlists OAKLEAF3's SQL Server resource in the transaction.

4. Upon execution of the `COMMIT TRAN` statement, OAKLEAF0's SQL Server automatically calls DTC's `ITrasaction::Commit` method.

5. DTC requests OAKLEAF0 and OAKLEAF3 to confirm whether each is prepared to commit the transaction. At this point, the outcome of the transaction is said to be "in doubt."

6. If OAKLEAF0 and OAKLEAF3 return **True**, DTC issues the commit instruction to both servers; however, the outcome of the transaction is still in doubt. If either server returns **False**, the transaction is aborted (rolled back) at this point.

7. If both OAKLEAF0 and OAKLEAF3 commit successfully, the transaction completes on both servers. If not, the transaction rolls back on both servers.

The MS DTC Admin Console, installed during SQL Server setup, lets you check the status of current and past distributed transactions and force the commit or rollback of transactions that remain in doubt for extended periods.

NOTE

As mentioned near the beginning of this chapter, DTC provides the underpinnings for MTS. You can use MTS components, rather than stored procedures, to execute distributed transactions on multiple servers. Chapters 26 and 27 extend the preceding description of DTC to include Visual Basic 6.0 components running within MTS's process to update multiple databases and preserve transactional consistency.

DTC also is capable of interacting with UNIX transaction managers that conform to the X/Open DTP TX standard for APIs that involve initiating, committing, and rolling back transactions and the DTC, X/Open DTP XA APIs for communicating between resource managers and transaction managers. DTC includes an XA Mapper layer to convert from the C APIs of DTP XA to DTC's OLE Tx `ITransaction` interfaces. Figure 19.3 compares the architecture of OLE Tx-only and hybrid UNIX/OLE Tx using X/Open XA/TX APIs.

FIGURE 19.3

A comparison of OLE Tx-only (left) and hybrid X/Open DTP XA/TX and OLE Tx transaction management.

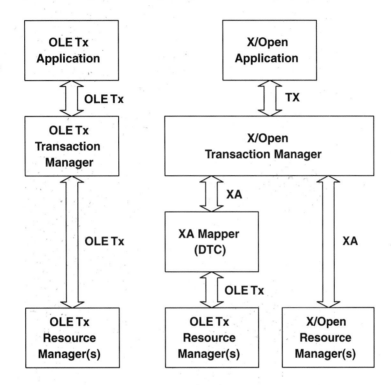

Replication

Large, decentralized organizations have multiple RDBMS servers, some of which may be separated by distances that exceed the capabilities of LANs. Distributed transactions running two-phase commit across a WAN take substantially longer to complete than those on a 10Mbps or 100Mbps LAN. If you don't need the tight transactional consistency of real-time distributed transactions, SQL Server replication is likely to be a more efficient approach than two-phase commit.

SQL Server 7.0 replication is based on version 6.0's *publish and subscribe* model. Servers are Publishers, Subscribers, and/or Distributors. Push and pull subscriptions are offered to articles and publications. Following are basic definitions of replication terms:

- *Articles* are specific groups of data to be replicated, such as a group of specific rows and/or columns. You specify the rows and columns with horizontal and vertical filters, respectively.

- *Publications* are collections of related articles replicated as a group.

- *Publishers* are servers that offer data for replication to other servers. Publishers identify the publications to be replicated, log updates made after the last subscriber synchronization, and maintain a database of all publications.

- *Subscribers* are servers for storing database replicas and receiving updates to replicas. SQL Server 7.0 also lets Subscribers update data.

- *Distributors* hold the distribution database that routes publications from Publishers to Subscribers.

- *Push subscriptions* cause Publishers to replicate without a specific request by Subscribers. Push operations can occur immediately upon updates to articles or on a time-scheduled basis.

- *Pull subscriptions* require Subscribers to request publication updates. Requests can be on demand for mobile users, who often are disconnected from the network, or scheduled for desktop users at periods of low server activity. Pull subscriptions are used when you have a large number of Subscribers, such as anonymous Internet subscribers.

You set up replication on SQL Server 7.0 servers with SQL Server Enterprise Manager's Configure Publishing and Distribution Wizard. To open the wizard, select a server to configure in the scope pane and then choose Tools, Replication, Configure Publishing and Distribution. Figure 19.4 shows the third dialog of the wizard running on the OAKLEAF1 client setting up OAKLEAF0 as the Distributor. When you click Finish, the wizard performs the sequence of operations shown in Figure 19.5.

FIGURE 19.4

Setting up a server (OAKLEAF0) as a replication Distributor from a client PC (OAK-LEAF1).

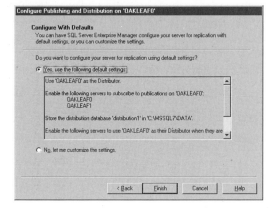

FIGURE 19.5

Steps in the process of establishing OAK-LEAF0 as the Distributor and Publisher and enabling OAK-LEAF0 and OAK-LEAF1 as Subscribers.

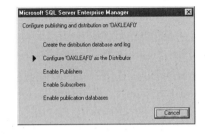

After you set up a Distributor/Publisher server, choose Tools, Replication, Publish and Push Subscription or Pull Subscription to create new publications or subscriptions.

SQL Server offers the following three types of replication:

- *Snapshot replication* delivers a complete image of the schema and data of a publication to the Distributor. Snapshots are the starting point of a publication for new Subscribers.

- *Transactional replication* pushes publications to Subscribers after each UPDATE, INSERT, or DELETE operation on any article of the publication. Transactional replication offers loose transactional consistency because changes propagate to Subscribers connected by a LAN or WAN in 5 to 10 seconds. Disconnected Subscribers get their updates when they reconnect to the network.

- *Merge replication* applies publication changes to a snapshot of the publication on Subscribers' computers. Merge replication, which is similar to Access 7.0's incremental replication feature, also lets Subscribers send changes back to the Publisher. Merge replication, which doesn't guarantee transactional consistency, is especially designed for mobile users who connect only periodically to the LAN or WAN. Each row of the base table(s) of the publication is identified by a globally unique ID (GUID).

One of Microsoft's primary objectives in creating the single-user version of SQL Server 7.0 is to enable merge replication for laptop PCs that is more robust than that afforded by Access's briefcase replication for Jet databases.

NOTE

For a more complete discussion of replication, launch SQL Server 7.0 Books Online, expand the Distributed Data and Replication item, and double-click the Major Components of SQL Server 7.0 Replication item.

Messaging and Transactions

Microsoft Message Queue Server (MSMQ, originally code-named "Falcon") is an optional component for Windows NT Server 4.0 and is included with Windows NT 4+ Enterprise Edition. Like MTS 2.0, MSMQ 1.0 is included in the Windows NT 4.0 Option Pack. MSMQ enables asynchronous execution of transactions over unreliable networks, such as the dialup, T-1, and HTTP connections shown earlier in Figure 19.2. MSMQ lets applications communicate by sending and receiving messages that can contain data in any format compatible with both the sending and receiving systems. In a transaction environment, request messages contain the equivalent of an update Recordset. The messages are placed into a queue for each destination. As the destination application processes the messages, return messages to the originating application indicate the success or failure of the operation.

MSMQ is interoperable with mainframe transaction monitors and messaging systems, such as IBM's CICS and MQSeries, via a third-party layer available from Level 8 Systems. MSMQ has an Automation wrapper, so it acts as an ActiveX component and can be programmed with Visual Basic, VBScript, or ECMAScript (JScript).

> **NOTE**
>
> MTS is most commonly used to integrate message queuing in transactional systems because of the complexity of the messaging process. MTS provides granular control of the individual steps involved in complex transactions. For an overview of MSMQ and its integration with MTS, go to
> http://www.microsoft.com/ntserverenterprise/guide/msmq.asp.

WORKING WITH BULK UPDATES AND DISCONNECTED RECORDSETS

Bulk updates are similar to transactions but don't guarantee transactional consistency unless you wrap the bulk update within a BeginTrans...CommitTrans method pair. The advantage of bulk updates is that you can determine exactly what caused update(s) to fail and take specific action to resolve concurrency or other problems. When a conventional transaction fails, you receive a "no can do" error message from the server, but you don't get the information you need to handle the particular problem that caused the rollback. Bulk updates provide the detailed error information and related data necessary to determine the outcome of the operation.

NOTE

Error handling for ADO bulk operations has changed. RDO 1.0 and 2.0 generate an error only if *all* updates in a bulk operation fail. ADO 2.*x* generates an error if *any* update fails. The new behavior is critical to resolving problems with individual rows in a bulk operation.

▶ See "Recordset Methods," **p. 106**

Enabling Bulk Updates

To enable bulk updates, you open a Recordset with the adLockBatchOptimistic LockEdits option and substitute UpdateBatch for the Update method, as in the following code fragment:

```
Dim rstBatch As New ADODB.Recordset
With rstBatch
    .ActiveConnection = cnnBatch
    .CursorType = adStatic
    .LockEdits = adLockBatchOptimistic
    .Open "SELECT * FROM Table WHERE Criteria", Options:=adCmdText

    'Code to update rows of rstBatch

    .UpdateBatch
End With
```

Disconnecting Recordsets

▶ See "Disconnected Recordsets," **p. 75**

Disconnected Recordsets are an optional feature of bulk update operations. The advantage of a disconnected Recordset is that you can close the Recordset's connection to the server while editing the Recordset, then reopen the existing connection (or open a new connection) and send the changes to the database. To disconnect the Recordset, you set the ActiveConnection property to **Nothing** and then set it to the existing or a new connection before calling the UpdateBatch method, as in this fragment:

```
Dim rstBulk As New ADODB.Recordset
With rstBulk
    .ActiveConnection = cnnBulk
    .CursorType = adStatic
    .LockEdits = adLockBatchOptimistic
    .Open "SELECT * FROM Table WHERE Criteria", Options:=adCmdText
    Set .ActiveConnection = Nothing

    'Code to update rows of rstBulk
```

19

PROCESSING
TRANSACTIONS AND
BULK OPERATIONS

```
    Set .ActiveConnection = cnnBulk
    .UpdateBatch
End With
```

Testing Bulk Updates with Bound Controls

Browse-mode editing with bound controls, such as DataGrid or DataRepeater controls, isn't well suited to client/server systems. Each cell update requires a round-trip to the server, and concurrency issues with heavily trafficked tables slows the editing process. ADO lets you share Connection objects, minimizing the number of active connections to the server, but conventional bound controls require a continuous connection to the server. Thus most client/server developers avoid the use of ADODC-DataGrid controls and similar combinations, such as the Data-DBGrid pair of Visual Basic 3.0, 4.0, and 5.0.

▶ **See** "Recordset Properties," **p. 97**

Batch optimistic Recordsets let you perform multiple browse-mode edits and then send the updates in a single server round-trip. This capability makes browse editing practical in client/server environments. Browse editing is useful in applications that must deal with groups of related records, such as line items of an order or invoice. If the edit operation occurs over a long time period, you can disconnect the Recordset and then reconnect prior to calling the UpdateBatch method. To minimize traffic to the server, set the MarshallOptions property on an open Recordset to adMarshallModifiedOnly; MarshallOptions is one of the few property values you can set on an open Recordset.

▶ **See** "Upsizing Nwind.mdb to SQL Server 6.5 with the Access 97 Wizard," **p. 692** and "Importing Jet Tables to SQL Server 7.0," **p. 701**

The ADO_Bulk.vbp project in the C:\Ddg_vb6\Chaptr19 folder of the accompanying CD-ROM is an interactive application for demonstrating ADO bulk operations. ADO_Bulk uses the NW_Data.mdb database (with the name of the Order Details table changed to Order_Details) or the SQL Server nwind database created in the preceding chapter. Run ADO_Bulk.vbp to display the single form of ADO_Bulk. Figure 19.6 shows frmData displaying a deliberately induced error in the upsized nwind database.

FIGURE 19.6

ADO_Bulk.vbp's form with two data grid controls bound to two hidden ADO Data controls.

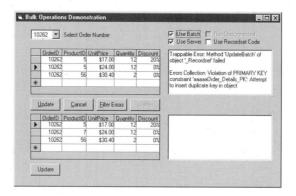

The DataCombo, dcbOrders, is bound to the cmmOrders command of the envData1 DataEnvironment and fills with a set of order numbers from the Orders table. The two DataGrids, dtgData1 (top) and dtgData2 (bottom), are bound to two hidden ADOData controls, adcData1 and adcData2, respectively. Changing the order number fills both grids with corresponding Order_Details records. By default, both grids are connected via the Jet native OLE DB provider (Jolt). You change the operating mode of adcData1/adcData2 by marking the following check boxes:

- *Use Batch* (chkUseBatch1) sets adcData1 and Recordset code to batch optimistic locking. The default mode is conventional optimistic locking.

- *Use Server* (chkUseServer1) sets the ConnectionString property of adcData1 and cnnData1 to SQLOLEDB, the native OLE DB provider for SQL Server. Search for OAKLEAF0 behind frmData and change the Location to point to your server, plus the User ID and Password if you aren't using integrated security or the default sa login ID.

- *Use Recordset Code* (chkUseRst1) creates a Recordset (rstData1) from cnnData1 and then replaces adcData1's Recordset with rstData1. Recordset code enables the use of a disconnected Recordset with bound controls.

- *Run Disconnected* (chkDisconnect1) sets the ActiveConnection property of the Recordset to **Nothing** and then sets the property back to cnnData1 prior to calling the UpdateBatch method. Run Disconnected is enabled by marking both the Use Batch and Recordset Code check boxes.

The adcData2/dtgData2 combination uses conventional optimistic locking to display the status of records for the current order in the Order_Details table before and after you make changes in the upper DataGrid. You must click the Update button to apply the Refresh method to adcData2 to see the changes. Listing 19.4 contains the essential setup and event-handling code for ADO_Bulk.vbp.

Listing 19.4   Sub Main Code to Specify the Location of NW_Data.mdb and Handle the Essential Events of the ADO_Bulk.vbp Project

```
Option Explicit
Sub Main()
   'Changes to properties of DataEnvironment objects
   'must be made before opening the form that uses them
   Dim strJolt As String
   'Following makes the data environment location-independent
   strJolt = "Provider=Microsoft.Jet.OLEDB.3.51;Data Source=" & _
      App.Path & "\NW_Data.mdb"
   envData.Connections("cnnData1").ConnectionString = strJolt
   frmData.Show
End Sub
```

19

Processing Transactions and Bulk Operations

continues

LISTING 19.4   CONTINUED

```vb
'Code behind frmData
Option Explicit
Private cnnData1 As New ADODB.Connection
Private rstData1 As New ADODB.Recordset
Private strSQL As String
Private blnUseRst1 As Boolean
Private blnUseServer1 As Boolean
Private blnUseBatch1 As Boolean
Private blnRunDisc1 As Boolean
Private strJolt As String          'Default Jolt provider
Private strSQLOLEDB As String      'SQL Server provider

Private Sub Form_Activate()
    'Set the two connection strings
    strJolt = "Provider=Microsoft.Jet.OLEDB.3.51;Data Source=" & _
        App.Path & "\NW_Data.mdb"
    strSQLOLEDB = "Provider=SQLOLEDB;User ID=sa;" & _
        "Location=OAKLEAF0;Data Source=nwind"

    txtErrors1.Text = ""
    txtErrors2.Text = ""
    strSQL = "Select * FROM Order_Details WHERE OrderID = " & _
        dcbOrders.Text & " ORDER BY ProductID"
    Me.MousePointer = vbHourglass
    DoEvents  'Improves form painting
    If blnUseRst1 Then
        'Open the Connection and Recordset
        Call cnnData1_Open
        DoEvents
        Call rstData1_Open
    Else
        'Set up the ADODC
        Call adcData1_SetSource
    End If
    DoEvents
    'Set up the ADODC
    Call adcData2_SetSource
    DoEvents
    Me.MousePointer = vbDefault
End Sub

Private Sub adcData1_SetSource()
    'Set up the upper ADODC
    With adcData1
        If blnUseServer1 Then
            .ConnectionString = strSQLOLEDB
        Else
            .ConnectionString = strJolt
        End If
```

```
            .RecordSource = strSQL
            If blnUseBatch1 Then
                .CursorType = adOpenStatic
                .LockType = adLockBatchOptimistic
            Else
                .CursorType = adOpenDynamic
                .LockType = adLockOptimistic
            End If
            .Refresh
            If .Recordset.RecordCount > 4 Then
                'Make room for the scrollbar
                dtgData1.Width = 4185 + 220
            Else
                dtgData1.Width = 4185
            End If
            dtgData1.Refresh
        End With
    End Sub

    Private Sub adcData2_SetSource()
        'Set up the lower ADODC
        With adcData2
            If blnUseServer1 Then
                .ConnectionString = strSQLOLEDB
            Else
                .ConnectionString = strJolt
            End If
            .RecordSource = strSQL
            .CursorType = adOpenDynamic
            .LockType = adLockOptimistic
            .Refresh
            If .Recordset.RecordCount > 4 Then
                dtgData2.Width = 4185 + 220
            Else
                dtgData2.Width = 4185
            End If
            dtgData2.Refresh
        End With
    End Sub

    Private Sub cnnData1_Open()
        'Open a new cnnData1
        With cnnData1
            If .State = adStateOpen Then
                .Close
            End If
            .CursorLocation = adUseClient
            .Mode = adModeReadWrite
            If blnUseServer1 Then
                .ConnectionString = strSQLOLEDB
```

continues

LISTING 19.4 CONTINUED

```
        Else
            .ConnectionString = strJolt
        End If
        .Open
    End With
End Sub

Private Sub rstData1_Open()
    'Create the Recordset
    With rstData1
        If .State = adStateOpen Then
            .Close
        End If
        .ActiveConnection = cnnData1
        If blnUseBatch1 Then
            .CursorType = adOpenStatic
            .LockType = adLockBatchOptimistic
        Else
            .CursorType = adOpenDynamic
            .LockType = adLockOptimistic
        End If
        .Open strSQL, Options:=adCmdText
        'Only send changes to the server (must be set on an open Connection)
        .MarshalOptions = adMarshalModifiedOnly
    End With
    With adcData1
        Set .Recordset = rstData1
        .Refresh
        If .Recordset.RecordCount > 4 Then
            'Make room for the scrollbar
            dtgData1.Width = 4185 + 220
        Else
            dtgData1.Width = 4185
        End If
    End With
    If blnUseBatch1 And blnRunDisc1 Then
        'Disconnect the Recordset
        Set rstData1.ActiveConnection = Nothing
        cnnData1.Close
    End If
    dtgData1.Refresh
End Sub

Private Sub dcbOrders_Click(intArea As Integer)
    'Update the two ADODCs and DataGrids for a new OrderID value
    If intArea = dbcAreaList Then
        'Display the OrderDetails items for the selected order
        strSQL = "Select * FROM Order_Details WHERE OrderID = " & _
            dcbOrders.Text & " ORDER BY ProductID"
```

```
        Me.MousePointer = vbHourglass
        If blnUseRst1 Then
            Call rstData1_Open
        Else
            Call adcData1_SetSource
        End If
        Call adcData2_SetSource
        Me.MousePointer = vbDefault
    End If
End Sub

'*********************
'Update and Cancel event handlers

Private Sub cmdUpdate1_Click()
    'Update the tables in conventional or batch optimistic mode
    Dim blnErrors As Boolean
    On Error Resume Next

    blnErrors = False
    cmdUpdate1.Enabled = False
    Me.MousePointer = vbHourglass
    txtErrors1.Text = ""
    If blnUseRst1 Then
        If blnUseBatch1 Then
            Set rstData1 = adcData1.Recordset
            If blnRunDisc1 Then
                Call cnnData1_Open
                Set rstData1.ActiveConnection = cnnData1
            End If
            rstData1.UpdateBatch
        End If
    Else
        If blnUseBatch1 Then
            adcData1.Recordset.UpdateBatch
        End If
    End If
    If Err Then
        blnErrors = True
        'Display the errors
        txtErrors1.Text = ""
        txtErrors1.Text = "Trappable Error: " & Err.Description _
            & vbCrLf & vbCrLf
        Err = 0
    End If
    If Not blnUseRst1 Then
        'A connection is required to test for errors
        Set cnnData1 = adcData1.Recordset.ActiveConnection
    End If
```

continues

19

**PROCESSING
TRANSACTIONS AND
BULK OPERATIONS**

LISTING 19.4 CONTINUED

```
    If cnnData1.Errors.Count Then
        blnErrors = True
        Dim errData1 As Error
        With cnnData1
            For Each errData1 In .Errors
                txtErrors1.Text = txtErrors1.Text & "Errors Collection: " _
                    & errData1.Description & vbCrLf
            Next errData1
        End With
        cnnData1.Errors.Clear
    End If
    If blnErrors Then
        If blnUseBatch1 Then
            cmdFilter1.Enabled = True
        End If
    Else
        cmdFilter1.Enabled = False
        adcData1.Refresh
    End If
    Me.MousePointer = vbDefault
    cmdUpdate1.Enabled = True
End Sub

Private Sub cmdUpdate2_Click()
    'Update the lower DataGrid in optimistic mode
    On Error Resume Next
    cmdUpdate2.Enabled = False
    Me.MousePointer = vbHourglass
    txtErrors2.Text = ""
    If Err Then
        'Display the error(s)
        txtErrors2.Text = "Error: " & Err.Desctiption & vbCrLf
        Err = 0
    Else
        adcData2.Refresh
    End If
    Me.MousePointer = vbDefault
    cmdUpdate2.Enabled = True
    On Error GoTo 0
End Sub

Private Sub dtgData1_AfterColEdit(ByVal ColIndex As Integer)
    cmdCancel1.Enabled = True
End Sub

Private Sub cmdCancel1_Click()
    On Error Resume Next
    If blnUseBatch1 Then
        adcData1.Recordset.CancelBatch
```

```
      Else
          adcData1.Recordset.CancelUpdate
      End If
      On Error GoTo 0
End Sub


'********************
'Filter event handlers

Private Sub cmdFilter1_Click()
      'Filter to display only the updates that fail
      adcData1.Recordset.Filter = adFilterConflictingRecords
      adcData1.Refresh
      dtgData1.Refresh
      cmdFilter1.Enabled = False
      cmdUnfilter1.Enabled = True
End Sub

Private Sub cmdUnfilter1_Click()
      'Remove the conflicting records filter
      adcData1.Recordset.Filter = adFilterNone
      adcData1.Refresh
      dtgData1.Refresh
      cmdFilter1.Enabled = True
      cmdUnfilter1.Enabled = False
End Sub
```

The following steps serve as a guide to experimenting with batch optimistic updating with ADO_Bulk:

1. Launch ADO_Bulk.vbp and select an order with two or three Order_Details records.

2. In the default mode, change the Quantity of an item or two in the upper DataGrid.

3. Verify that the Quantity changes propagate to the database by clicking the lower DataGrid's Update button.

4. Mark the Use Batch check box and change the Quantity value of two or more rows in the upper DataGrid.

5. Click the lower DataGrid's Update button to verify that no changes have occurred to the underlying table.

6. Click the upper DataGrid's Update button to call the BatchUpdate method.

7. Verify the changes in the lower DataGrid.

8. In the upper DataGrid, change one of the ProductID values so that two rows have identical ProductIDs, creating a primary key violation on the Order_Details table. Change each of the Quantity values.

9. Click the Update button of the upper DataGrid to generate the error (refer to Figure 19.6).

10. Click the lower Update button to verify that table records without conflicts change Quantity values.

11. Click the Filter button to display the single row with the conflict and correct the ProductID conflict.

12. Click the Unfilter button to remove the filter from the Recordset.

13. Click the upper Update button to make the final change.

14. Click the lower Update button to verify that all records are updated.

> **NOTE**
>
> ADO_Bulk isn't representative of a production application, because ADO_Bulk doesn't incorporate validation logic to assure conformance to business rules. As an example, you can edit OrderID and UnitPrice values, both of which are supplied by base tables (Orders and Products).

▶ See "Recordset Properties," p. 97

In production applications, conflict resolution for bulk updates ordinarily is handled by code. Apply the `adFilterConflictingRecords` filter and then traverse the conflicting records of the `Recordset`, using the `Status` property flags of `RecordStatusEnum` to determine the cause of the conflict. The need for user intervention to resolve conflicts depends on the nature of the problem; many conflict-resolution issues, such as attempts to update a deleted record, can be handled by applying the appropriate rules in VBA code.

PORTING ACCESS OLTP APPLICATIONS TO VISUAL BASIC 6.0

IN THIS CHAPTER

Microsoft Access is an extraordinarily powerful database development platform. Microsoft has licensed tens of millions of copies of Access 2.0, 95, and 97 as members of three successive Office Professional editions. Access has all but annihilated its direct, third-party competition: IBM-Lotus's Approach, Borland International's dBASE, and Corel Systems's (formerly Borland's) Paradox, just as Microsoft Excel has done in Lotus 1-2-3 and Corel's (also formerly Borland's) QuattroPro. Microsoft's Visual FoxPro continues to appeal to heavyweight xBase programmers, but the legions of FoxPro developers are growing thinner as a result of the popularity of Access, Visual Basic, and, increasingly, various flavors of Java.

Database developers have a variety of reasons for porting existing 16-bit and 32-bit Access applications to Visual Basic 6.0. Many organizations have standardized on Visual Basic as their sole or primary Windows application development platform. Visual Basic has been perceived by many as offering better performance than Access, primarily as a result of the lethargic Access 95, the first 32-bit Access version. Access 2.0 and Access 97, however, execute database code at about the same speed as Visual Basic 6.0 does. Visual Basic offers more UI flexibility than Access's MDI design, but creating a basic OLTP application in Access is a faster, and thus less costly, approach. The primary objective of this chapter is to point out the differences between Access 97+ and Visual Basic 6.0 control objects and coding techniques, not to denigrate Access.

> **NOTE**
>
> Investing in application upgrades is a controversial subject. The conservative approach, "if it works, don't fix it," clearly was applicable to decisions to upgrade applications from Access 2.0 to 95. The 32-bit Access 95 version of the OLTP front end described in this chapter ran about 50% slower than its 16-bit predecessor and consumed almost twice the system resources. Access OLTP applications gain the most benefit by conversion to Visual Basic and ADO for reasons explained in this chapter.

DESIGNING FRONT ENDS FOR HEADS-DOWN DATA ENTRY

High-performance OLTP applications used for applications such as airline and hotel reservation systems involve heads-down data entry. The term *heads down* usually means that the operator's sole responsibility during an 8-hour shift is entering or updating data at the maximum feasible rate. The source of the data may be paper forms or the operator may be equipped with a headset to take telephone orders. Heads-down data entry is a grueling task, thus the data input application must be designed to minimize operator fatigue, which is the primary cause of data entry errors. The application also must be designed to minimize risk of repetitive stress injury (RSI), such as carpal tunnel syndrome.

Use the following guidelines, called the "Ten Commandments of OLTP Front Ends," when designing applications for heads-down data entry:

1. Don't require the data entry operator to use a pointing device. Many of the best operators come from the mainframe or DOS environment where keyboard-only operations are the rule. Requiring the operator to remove a hand from the keyboard to use a mouse or track-ball slows data entry speed and contributes to operator fatigue. Provide accelerator key designations in text box and other control label captions to aid keyboard navigation.

2. Use a single form for data display and data entry where possible. Opening and closing forms distracts the data entry operator and slows performance, even with Visual Basic 6.0's improved form-loading time. Most OLTP applications are designed for a single purpose, such as reviewing and entering customer orders, where multiple forms aren't required. Display only the controls that are applicable to the operator's current activity. Design for 640×480 resolution, which is the most common display mode on the low-end PCs often assigned to data entry operators, unless 800×600 is the standard resolution for all data entry operations.

3. Minimize the use of message boxes and modal dialogs. Message boxes and dialogs are distracting. Open message boxes only for severe errors that you can't intercept and highlight by VBA code.

4. Avoid gratuitous decoration on forms. Colorful backgrounds, company logos, and multiple type faces lead to data entry operator fatigue and eyestrain. It's more than likely that the operator knows for whom he or she works. Stick with simple black type on a light gray background, with white backgrounds for active text boxes, list boxes, and grids. Turn labels red to highlight data entry errors.

5. Use a single sans serif typeface and a 10-point or larger font. Although 17-inch video display units are becoming common, many organizations still use 14-inch or 15-inch monitors for data entry. Visual Basic's standard 8-point MS Sans Serif font is difficult for many operators to read, especially on smaller monitors. Use the bold attribute to make labels stand out on the gray background.

6. Minimize the use of grids. Replace read-only grids with list boxes, which are easier for operators to navigate. If you need to format list box columns, use a Flex Grid control to emulate Access's multicolumn list box.

7. Don't use bound controls for data entry. Unbound controls and VBA code offer more flexibility and, especially in client/server front ends, deliver better performance. If you need a bound DataGrid control for multiline editing, link the DataGrid to a local table and then send the new or updated data in the local table to the server.

8. Use ADO, not DAO, to optimize client/server performance. Many Access applications link client/server tables to a local Jet .mdb to minimize programming chores. Using ADO eliminates the overhead of Jet's query parser and sends SQL statements to the server

RDBMS in its native SQL dialect. Most RDBMSs support ANSI SQL-92 standards for queries. You must write more code than is needed for linked server tables to take advantage of SQL passthrough, but you gain a significant performance benefit.

9. Replace edit operations on Recordset objects with SQL statements. SQL INSERT, UPDATE, and DELETE statements executed by Command objects against client/server tables almost always are more efficient than the equivalent AddNew, Delete, and Update methods applied to Recordset objects. Where feasible, pass parameters to stored procedures or parameterized Jet queries rather than sending a long SQL query string to the server.

10. Avoid the temptation to use Web-based client/server front ends for high-performance OLTP applications. HTTP is designed for delivering information to browsers, not for high-speed submission of data to RDBMSs. The HTTP protocol carries substantial overhead, and writing Active Server Pages (ASP) for a complex database front end is a major undertaking. Compared to vanilla HTTP, OLE DB and Remote Data Services (RDS) offer better performance but still can't compete in execution speed with a well-designed Visual Basic 6.0 (or Access) front end. RDS and lightweight ADOR.Recordset objects are the subjects of Chapter 24, "Working with Remote Data Services."

The OLTP front end described in this chapter, with a few minor exceptions, conforms to the Ten Commandments of OLTP Front Ends. Using stored procedures to deliver customer and order information is one of the subjects of the next chapter, "Using Transact-SQL Stored Procedures."

FOLLOWING THE OLTP PROJECT'S UPGRADE PATH

The Ado2oltp.vbp project that's the primary subject of this chapter began life in 1995 as an Access 2.0 OLTP demonstration application written for Microsoft's Tech*Ed 95 symposium in New Orleans. The overall goal was to prove that Access 2.0, running under Windows 3.11, was a viable front end for production client/server applications; MSA_OLTP.MDB was designed to use Jet 2.0 or an SQL Server 4.21 database created by the original Access Upsizing Wizard. Microsoft's specific objectives were to take full advantage of Access's native control set and ODBC passthrough techniques to achieve very high-speed customer/order searches and fast online order data entry.

> **NOTE**
>
> You can download the original 16-bit Tech*Ed 95 version, which uses data from the 16-bit NWIND.MDB sample database, from
> http://premium.microsoft.com/msdn/library/conf/f4f/f50/d52/sa060.htm.
> It's also available on the Microsoft Developer Network Library CD-ROM as

Client-Server Development Using Microsoft Access. You need the retail version of Access 2.0 to run this version. A commercial Access 2.0 client/server application, National Semiconductor Corp.'s ASK (Access to Sales and marKeting data) application, which ran against an IBM DB/2 database on a Hitachi mainframe, accompanied the demonstration of MSA_OLTP at Tech*Ed 95.

The original MSA_OLTP application was upgraded to Access 95, then to Access 97 (see Figure 20.1), and was later ported to Visual Basic 5.0. The objectives for the Visual Basic 5.0 port were to compare the data entry efficiency of data-bound Visual Basic and Access controls and hopefully to gain a performance boost from Visual Basic 5.0's native code compiler. About 90% of the Access 97 VBA code ran under Visual Basic 5.0 without modification. The availability of International Software Group's ISGData control, which is compatible with Visual Basic 5.0's data-bound controls, made it practical to upgrade the Visual Basic 5.0 application from DAO to ADO.

FIGURE 20.1

The Access 97 version of the OLTP application in 640x480 display mode.

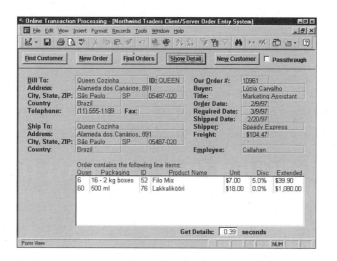

The Access 97 version of the OLTP application, Msa8oltp.mdb and its local database, Msa8data.mdb, is included in the \Ddg_vb6\Chaptr20 folder of the accompanying CD-ROM. You must have the retail version of Access 97 or later to run Msa8oltp.mdb. If you install this application in a folder other than the default C:\Ddg_vb6\Chaptr20, use the Linked Table Manager add-in to change to the folder containing Msa8data.mdb. Msa8data.mdb is an upgraded version of the data tables from the original Access 2.0 NWIND.MDB database, which is not compatible with the Jet 3.5 NW_Data.mdb database used in the preceding chapter.

▶ **See** "Upsizing Nwind.mdb to SQL Server 6.5 with the Access 97 Wizard," **p. 692** and "Importing Jet Tables to SQL Server 7.0," **p. 701**

To use the SQL Passthrough option, upsize Msa8data.mdb to an OLTP database on SQL Server 6.*x* or export the tables to SQL Server 7.0. Then create an ODBC System DSN named OLTP for the OLTP database. If you use a secure login ID for SQL Server, you must change the values of the strUserID and strPassword constants in the modOrderEntry module.

> **NOTE**
>
> If you want to test the conformance of Msa8oltp.mdb to the Ten Commandments of OLTP Front Ends, skip to the "Running the Vb5oltp Project" section later in the chapter for instructions on how to review existing orders and enter new orders. The operational features of the three versions of the OLTP project discussed in this chapter are identical.

There are no significant changes to data entry operations in any of the front ends discussed in this chapter. All versions of the OLTP application include text boxes to display the execution time of each database operation to 1/100 of a second. This feature lets you compare relative performance of the Access and Visual Basic 6.0 versions, as well as to contrast performance with a local Jet database or an SQL Server back end. To eliminate the effect of network traffic on comparative performance, move the Jet database to the same machine that runs SQL Server. Use Access's Linked Table Manager add-in and modify the Visual Basic 6.0 code to point to the new data location.

STEPPING THROUGH THE FIRST PHASE OF THE MIGRATION PROCESS

The Msa8oltp.mdb application database consists of one form (frmOrderEntry) and one subform (sbfOrder_Details), plus a module (modOrderEntry) that contains only Public variable and constant definitions that are shared between the form and subform. The frmOrderEntry form includes many overlapping controls that are repositioned and hidden during the form-loading process. Figure 20.2 shows some of the hidden and repositioned controls in Access 97 form design view. All the controls on frmOrderEntry are unbound and are populated from DAO.Recordsets; sbfOrder_Details is bound to a local tblOrder_details table.

FIGURE 20.2

*Hidden and reposi-
tioned controls on
the main Access 97
form in design
view.*

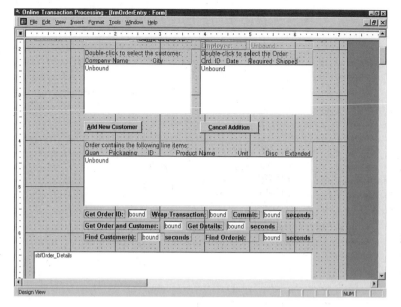

FIGURE 20.2

*Hidden and reposi-
tioned controls on
the main Access 97
form in design
view.*

Single-form applications are relatively rare in Access, and most Access applications make extensive use of bound controls. Thus the recommendations in the sections that follow aren't specific to Msa8oltp.mdb, but apply to any Access application you intend to convert to Visual Basic 6.0.

Preparing Your Access Application

The first step in the Access-to-Visual Basic conversion process is to modify your Access application .mdb as follows:

1. If your .mdb is a single-user product that contains both application and data objects, use the Database Splitter add-in to move the tables to a separate .mdb. This step doesn't apply to mainstream OLTP applications that use client/server RDBMSs or mid-range OLTP front ends that connect to shared .mdb files.

2. Convert the application .mdb to the latest version, Access 97 when this edition was written; compile all of the code; and test each feature. You may need to make a few manual alterations to the upgraded version. This step conforms the Access VBA code as closely as possible to VBA 6.0. Don't upgrade the data .mdb or workgroup (System.mda or System.mdw) file if you intend to continue to use the existing Access application.

3. If the application contains Access macros, run the Macro to VBA Converter (Tools, Macro, Convert Form's Macros to Visual Basic) for each form. Although much of the converted macro code won't run unmodified in Visual Basic 6.0, the conversion process creates the required program structure.

20

4. Change the name of objects that don't conform to Visual Basic object-naming standards. This step usually involves eliminating spaces or other illegal punctuation, shortening names, and applying the Leszynski Naming Conventions to object names.

TIP

Black Moshannon Software's Speed Ferret for Access can save many hours of searching for and replacing object names. Further information on Speed Ferret is available at `http://www.moshannon.com/speedferret.html`.

---

5. Run the Database Documenter (Tools, Analyze, Documenter) to create a printed list of all forms and reports and of the controls on forms and reports. Referring to a printed list of form names, control names, properties, and values usually is handier than using Alt+Tab to move from Access to Visual Basic design mode to confirm these values.

TIP

FMS, Inc.'s, Total Access Analyzer provides much more extensive and customizable documentation than Access 97's built-in Database Documenter. FMS's Web site is at `http://www.fmsinc.com/`.

Creating Required Visual Basic Objects

In the long run, Microsoft might achieve its goal of making forms, reports, and control objects interchangeable between Office applications, Visual Basic, and other Microsoft development environments. As John Maynard Keynes, the knighted English economist, observed, "In the long run, we are all dead." In the short run, you must manually recreate Access form, report, and control objects in Visual Basic. When this book was written, the only commercial form-conversion utility was limited to Access 95 and Visual Basic 4.0.

NOTE

OLTP applications, the primary subject of this chapter, ordinarily don't include reports. If your Access application includes reports, you can recreate the reports from scratch with Visual Basic 6.0's new Report Designer or use VideoSoft's VSREPORTS ActiveX control to import each report design and print the report from within your Visual Basic application. For more information of VSREPORTS, go to `http://www.videosoft.com/`. A product review of VSREPORTS is at `http://www.vbxtras.com/techzine/febvideosoft.asp`.

Access 97 and earlier versions depend entirely on DAO and Jet or ODBCDirect for data binding and Recordset manipulation. If the Access application contains a substantial amount of VBA code (Msa8oltp.mdb runs about 2,000 lines), it's usually more efficient to use conventional (version 5.0 and earlier) Visual Basic bound controls, such as the DBGrid, in the first conversion pass and then migrate from DAO to ADO. This approach minimizes the code changes required to get the application running in Visual Basic 6.0.

> **NOTE**
>
> The project files (Vb5oltp.vbp, Vb5oltp.mdb, OrderEnt.frm, and OrderEnt.bas) for the port of Msa8oltp.mdb to Visual Basic 5.0 are included in the \Ddg_vb5\Chaptr20 folder of the accompanying CD-ROM. The Vb5oltp application uses Msa8data.mdb as the Jet data source and DAO for all database operations; thus you can run Vb5oltp.vbp under Visual Basic 5.0 or 6.0. Like Msa8oltp.mdb, to use the SQL Passthrough feature you must create an ODBC System DSN named OLTP that points to the upsized OLTP database. Vb5oltp.vbp can't substitute ODBCDirect for Jet because of the need for a local Jet table that binds to the DBGrid for line-item data entry. The ODBCDirect code of Vb5oltp.vbp is for illustrative purposes only.

The following steps are a basic guide to the DAO-based migration process:

1. Duplicate your Access forms as Visual Basic forms, adding the Visual Basic equivalents of Access controls, such as text, list, and combo boxes, with names identical to their Access counterparts. Add the controls in their tab order on the Access form.

2. Visual Basic doesn't offer Access labels attached to controls, so add labels for controls. Name the labels lblControlName unless you assigned appropriate label names in Access. Use the same accelerator key character as the Access form. Labels with accelerator keys shift the focus to the adjacent text box.

3. If your Access front end uses bound controls, add a Data control and the corresponding (version 5.0) data-bound controls. Naming the Data control adcName, not dtcName, avoids the need to change the property values of bound controls when you upgrade from DAO to ADO. Substitute the read-only MSFlexGrid 6.0 control for Access's multicolumn bound list boxes. Visual Basic doesn't offer multicolumn combo boxes, but several third-party suppliers provide an Access-equivalent combo box as an ActiveX control.

> **NOTE**
>
> You must add a substantial amount of code to format MSFlexGrid controls so they emulate Access's multicolumn list boxes. The FormSetup subprocedure of Vb5oltp.vbp illustrates the formatting code for the three MSFlexGrid controls, grdCustomers, grdOrders, and grdOrderDetails. An alternative to the MSFlexGrid or MSHFlexGrid is a multi-column ListView control.

4. Visual Basic doesn't have a direct equivalent of a subform. For the first conversion step, substitute a DBGrid control bound to another Data control for an Access continuous or data sheet–style subform. If you need continuous subform features, change to a DataRepeater control and write a custom ActiveX control to emulate the subform. Don't change to Visual Basic's subform equivalent until after the ADO conversion step.

5. Check the tab order of the controls to verify that they conform to tab sequence of the Access form. Visual Basic doesn't offer Access's automated Tab Order dialog, so you must manually modify the TabOrder property value of any out-of-sequence control. The Taborder.vbp project in the \Program Files\...\Samples\VB6\Taborder folder eases the process of modifying the tab order of complex forms.

6. If you attach shared Jet tables or tables from a client/server RDBMS to your application .mdb file, continue to use the attached tables during the first (DAO) conversion step.

7. If your Access project references one or more libraries and the library contains forms, you also must duplicate the library form(s). Depending on the nature of the library's UI component(s) and code, consider subsequently converting the library into a Visual Basic User Control or a compiled ActiveX control.

Figure 20.3 illustrates the Visual Basic version of frmDataEntry in the first (DAO) conversion step represented by Vb5oltp.vbp. All three Data controls are hidden. Code in the FormSetup subprocedure, called by the Form_Load event, resizes, repositions, and hides the two MSFlexGrid and the DBGrid controls. Controls that aren't needed at startup are either hidden or disabled by FormSetup code.

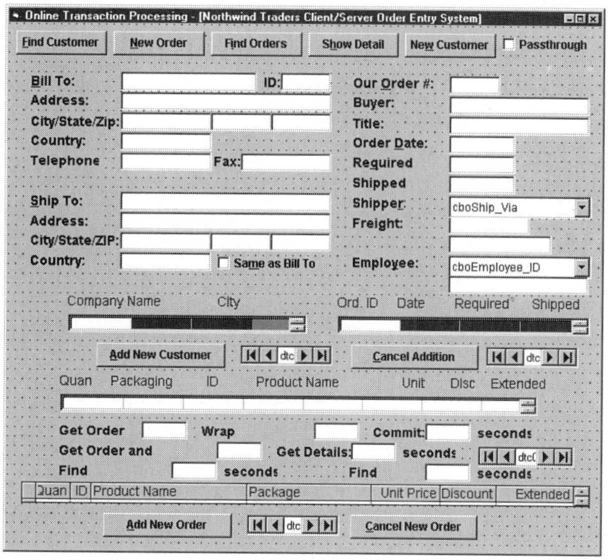

FIGURE 20.3

*The Visual Basic
5.0/6.0 version of
the Access 97
order entry form in
design view.*

> **NOTE**
>
> Access 97 Graph objects, which use Microsoft Office's Graph8.exe, an out-of-process Automation server, differ greatly from the Visual Basic charts you create with the MSChrt20.ocx ActiveX control. You must add a substantial amount of code to your Visual Basic project to emulate an Access graph. Chapter 11, "Graphing Summary Data from Crosstab Queries," covers programming techniques for the MSChart control.

Importing and Debugging the DAO Code

The number of lines of Access VBA code you must alter depends, to a large degree, on the version of Access used when writing the original application. The more recent the front end's vintage, the fewer the changes. Following is a basic guide to converting the Access flavor of VBA to VBA 6.0:

1. If the Access project (including required libraries) has one or more modules, add corresponding Visual Basic module files. Copy the Access VBA module code to the clipboard and paste it into module files.

2. Open each Access form and paste the class module code behind the corresponding Visual Basic form.

3. Search for the `CurrentDB()` function and replace **Set** `dbName` = `CurrentDB()` with **Set** `dbName` = `DBEngine.Workspaces(0).OpenDatabase("d:\path\filename.mdb")`. The remaining statements that use the `dbName` `Database` object are likely to require few, if any, changes.

4. Search for other Access instructions that Visual Basic doesn't support, such as `DoCmd`, the domain aggregate functions, and `DDE...` instructions and functions. Workarounds for unsupported instructions are the subject of the two sections that follow.

5. Comment or delete the unnecessary, unsupported instructions. If you comment the code (a better practice), precede the commented-out code with `'Rev:` or something similar.

6. Replace the necessary macro actions and other unsupported Access VBA code with the appropriate Visual Basic code.

7. Change Access VBA functions that don't return values to subprocedures. The Access `RunCode` macro action and event processing using `=FunctionName` syntax require such functions.

8. Attempt to compile and run the code to find other, less obvious incompatibilities between the Access and Visual Basic flavors of VBA. Make changes to the code as required for successful compilation.

9. Test the application thoroughly to verify that all features behave identically to the original Access version.

When the DAO version of the Access application runs correctly, you can improve performance by changing data-bound combo boxes or lists that contain static data to conventional native controls and use code to populate them from forward-only `Recordsets`. The `LoadComboBoxes` subprocedure of Vb5oltp.vbp illustrates such code with Jet and ODBCDirect `Recordsets`.

Replacing Access *DoCmd* Statements

The Access VBA `DoCmd` statement executes macro actions in Access VBA code. When you convert Access macros to code, you're likely to create a substantial number of `DoCmd` statements. Only macro actions can manipulate Access application objects such as forms and reports, and perform operations on the `Recordsets` to which forms and reports are bound. Therefore, you're likely to encounter a substantial number of `DoCmd` objects in Access VBA code that you must convert to Visual Basic code. In most cases, the code you substitute for `DoCmd{ ¦.}ActionName Arguments...` statements is identical to the code you write to substitute for the `ActionName` macro action. (Access 1.x and 2.0 use a space to separate `DoCmd` from `ActionName`; Access 95+ uses a period separator because `ActionName` now is defined as a method of the `DoCmd` object.) Tables 20.1, 20.2, and 20.3 supply Visual Basic code counterparts for Access macro actions executed by `DoCmd` statements in all versions of Access.

TABLE 20.1 VISUAL BASIC COUNTERPARTS OF ACCESS FORM AND CONTROL ACTIONS

Access Action	*Purpose*	*VBA Substitute*
Close (form or report)	Closes a form or report object	Unload or Hide methods for report custom control for reports
GoToControl	Sets the focus to a control on a form	ctrlName.SetFocus method
Maximize, Minimize, Restore	Sets the window style of a form	frmName.WindowState property
MoveSize	Determines the size and position of a form	Left, Top, Width, and Height properties of forms
OpenForm	Opens and displays a form	frmName.Show method
OpenReport	Opens a report for print preview or printing	Report control
Print	Prints the active object (forms only)	[frmName].PrintForm method for forms (except MDI forms)
RepaintObject	Redraws the selected object	objName.Refresh method
Requery	Updates a specified control method	dtcName.Requery (Data control only)
SetValue	Sets the value of a property (macros only)	Sets the value of the property with code

TABLE 20.2 VISUAL BASIC DAO COUNTERPARTS OF ACCESS DATABASE OBJECT MANIPULATION ACTIONS

Access Action	*Purpose*	*VBA Substitute*
Close (Table or QueryDef object)	Closes a database object	Close method

continues

TABLE 20.2   CONTINUED

Access Action	*Purpose*	*VBA Substitute*
FindNext	Finds the next record meeting specified criteria	FindNext method
FindRecord	Finds the first record meeting specified criteria	FindFirst method
GoToRecord	Goes to the record specified by an argument value (previous, next, first, last, record number, new record)	Move... methods (except record number) and AddNew method (new record only)
OpenQuery	Opens a QueryDef object in datasheet, design or print preview views, or executes an action query	dbName.OpenQueryDef(strQueryName) method and additional code
OpenTable	Opens a specified Table object in datasheet, design, or print preview views	dbName.OpenTable(strTableName) method and additional code

NOTE

The workaround code in the VBA Substitute column of Table 20.2 applies primarily to DAO, not ADO, objects. For example, ADODB.Recordset objects have a Find method, but not FindFirst or FindNext. You can execute QueryDef objects as stored procedure equivalents with ADODB.Command objects, but persistent QueryDefs should be replaced by equivalent SQL statements executed by Command objects or serving as the Source property of Recordsets.

TABLE 20.3 ACCESS MACRO ACTIONS THAT HAVE EXACT VISUAL BASIC COUNTERPARTS

Access Action	Purpose	VBA Substitute
Hourglass	Turns the mouse pointer to the hourglass shape	`Screen.MousePointer` property
MsgBox	Displays a message box with an optional title	`MsgBox` instruction or `MsgBox()` function
Quit	Exits the Access application	`End` statement
RunApp	Runs another Windows application	`Shell()` function
SendKeys	Sends keystrokes to the application with the focus	`SendKeys` instruction
Beep	Sounds the standard Windows message beep	`Beep` instruction

DoCmd statements that employ Access global symbolic constants to represent the values of arguments are quicker and easier to convert than those statements that use integer arguments. Using symbolic constants instead of integer values for arguments makes the objective of the DoCmd statement readily understandable. If the DoCmd statements use integers to represent argument values, you need to refer to the Access Language Reference to make the integer values meaningful.

> **NOTE**
>
> Msa8oltp.mdb has relatively few DoCmd statements because the application uses a single form specified in the Display Form text box of the Startup menu. The frmOrderEntry form isn't bound to a table or query, so DoCmd statements aren't required to manipulate the underlying Recordset. Most DoCmd statements in Msa8oltp.mdb are DoCmd.Hourglass {**True**¦**False**}, which you change to **Me**.MousePointer = {vbHourglass¦vbDefault}.

Handling Other Access Keywords That Are Missing from or That Differ in Visual Basic 6.0

A few Access VBA reserved words and keywords are not duplicated exactly in Visual Basic 6.0. Domain aggregate functions are examples of Access-only keywords that Visual Basic 6.0 lacks. Domain aggregate functions return values that represent the count, average, and a number of other characteristics of a specified domain (a set of records). To duplicate a domain aggregate function in Visual Basic, you need to create a Recordset object that corresponds to the domain and then perform a record-by-record arithmetic operation or search on the Recordset object. You can speed the operation by specifying a forward-only Recordset. The exception to the described procedure is the DCount() function that you replace with the RecordCount property of the Recordset object. (Make sure to apply the MoveLast method before returning the RecordCount property to obtain a valid result.)

Visual Basic also does not support the SysCmd function. SysCmd primarily is used to return status information for Access objects, such as whether forms and reports are open in design or run mode, and the Access application itself, such as whether the application is operating under the retail or runtime version of Access. (The runtime and retail versions of Access 95+ use the same executable file, Msaccess.exe; an entry in the Registry determines whether Msaccess.exe operates in runtime mode.) The preceding uses of SysCmd aren't applicable to Visual Basic applications, so in most cases you can delete the SysCmd statements with no ill effect. SysCmd also is used to create a programmable progress indicator in the status bar; you can emulate the progress indicator with a ProgressBar control, which is one of the Win32 common controls.

Access VBA DDE... instructions and functions differ greatly from the Link... methods you apply in Visual Basic. Microsoft didn't include in Visual Basic 6.0 DDEInitiate, DDEExcecute, and other DDE.... instructions and functions that are employed by the Office dialects of VBA. All the DDE methods of Visual Basic are bound to form or control objects, whereas DDE methods in other VBA dialects obtain values from or return values to variables. DDE is obsolete technology that's been replaced by (OLE) Automation, so make the transition to Automation when migrating your Access project to Visual Basic. Visual Basic 6.0's Link... methods are for backward compatibility only and might disappear in future versions of Visual Basic.

The Access VBA Eval function, which returns a **Variant** string or numeric value from a **String** expression, also is missing in VBA 6.0. You can substitute Visual Basic 6.0's CallByName function, which executes an object method or returns an object property value, if your code uses Eval with an object variable.

Running the Vb5oltp or Ado2oltp Project

Vb5oltp.vbp and Ado2oltp.vbp don't have an accompanying help file, so the following instructions and figures provide a walk-through of the operation of the Vb5oltp project. The instructions apply to the original Access project (Msa8oltp) plus the Visual Basic DAO (Vb5oltp) and ADO (Ado2oltp) ports. To review customer orders, add a new order for a customer, and add a new customer record, follow these steps:

1. Launch the application, type **q** in the Bill To text box, and press Enter to list all customers whose company name begins with *q*. The City field appears in the MSFlexGrid control to resolve companies having the same name in different locations, such as chain stores. The time in seconds to retrieve and populate the list box appears in the Find text box.

2. Press the down arrow key to select Queen Cozinha and press Enter to display a list of Queen Cozinha's orders in descending date sequence in the second MSFlexGrid control (see Figure 20.4). The disabled text boxes display information from the Customers table.

FIGURE 20.4

Selecting customer data and displaying open and shipped orders for the customer.

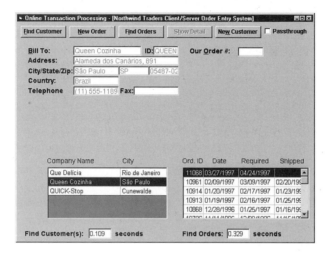

3. Press the down arrow key to select an existing order and press Enter to display the line items of the order from the Order_Details table in the third MSFlexGrid control. This operation also makes disabled text boxes containing information from the Orders table visible (see Figure 20.5). Freight charges appear only for shipped orders.

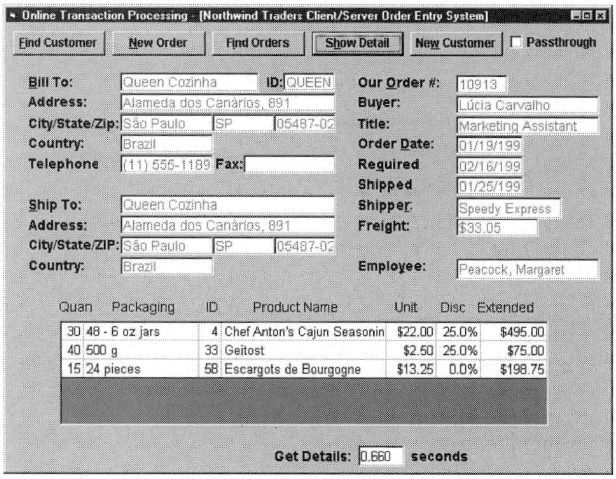

FIGURE 20.5

Displaying order data, including line items for a selected order.

4. Press Alt+N to enter a new order for the customer. The Ship To and Required Date text boxes are cleared and enabled, and combo lists replace the Shipper and Employee ID text boxes.

5. Press Alt+M to enter the Bill To address as the Ship To address, type the Required Date, and then press Tab to move to the Shipper combo list.

6. Press the down arrow key to select a ShipVia value, press Tab again, and use the down arrow key to set the EmployeeID value.

> **NOTE**
>
> If you omit any of the preceding required entries for a new order, attempting to add the order results in a highlighted (red) label and the focus moves to the control with the missing value.

7. Press Tab to move to the Quan(tity) column of the tentative append record for the first line item. Type a quantity and press Tab or the right arrow key to move to the Product ID column.

8. Type a valid Product ID value (1 through 77) and press Tab or the right arrow key. Moving to the Product ID column performs a lookup operation against the Products table and fills in the Product Name, Package, Unit Price, and Extended (amount) columns (see Figure 20.6).

FIGURE 20.6

Adding a new order and line items to the Orders and Order_Details tables.

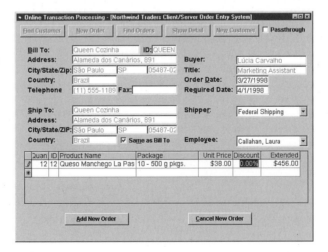

9. Type the decimal equivalent of the discount, if any, in the Discount column; press Tab or the right arrow to apply the discount to the calculated Extended column.

10. Press Tab or right arrow again and type a quantity to add an additional line item and then repeat steps 8 and 9. Repeat the process for as many line items as you want to add.

11. Press Alt+A to add the new order to the Orders and Order_Details tables. The times to obtain the new incremental OrderID value, add the items to the temporary tblOrder_Details table, and commit the transaction appear in the text boxes at the bottom of the form. The completed order and its line items appear as illustrated by Figure 20.7.

FIGURE 20.7

Confirmation of addition of the new order and line items.

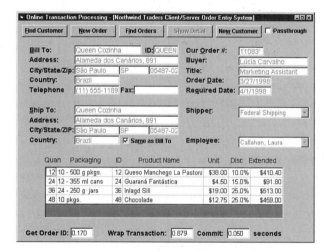

12. Press Alt+F to return to the customer entry mode.

13. To display an existing order from an order number, tab to the Our Order # text box and enter a valid order number, equal to or less than the number assigned to your new order in step 11.

14. To add a new customer, press Alt+W and type the Bill To name. In this version, you can't use an apostrophe (') in a CompanyName value. Press the tab key to automatically assign a unique five-character CustomerID value. If the CustomerID value exists, the program progressively replaces characters from right to left with X until it generates a nonduplicate key value.

15. Complete all the fields for the Customers table record (see Figure 20.8); then press Alt+A to add the new customer record and press Enter when the confirming message box appears.

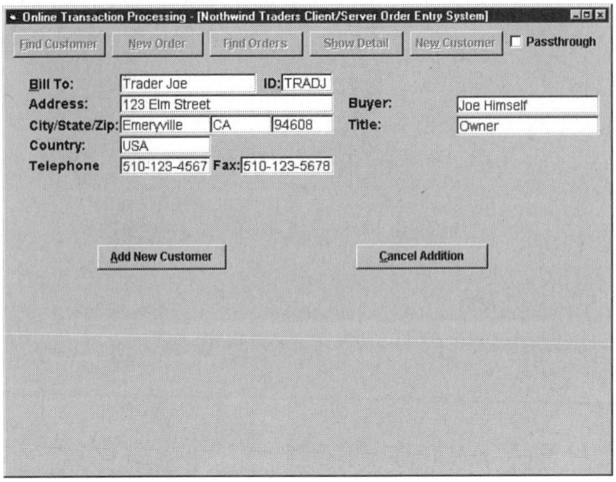

FIGURE 20.8

Adding a new record to the Customers table.

The single-form design, customer record retrieval, order review, new order entry, and new customer addition procedures comply with the Ten Commands of OLTP Front Ends outlined at the beginning of this chapter.

NOTE

If you've created the SQL Server OLTP database and the required OLTP DSN, mark the Passthrough checkbox to create a connection to SQL Server 6+ and compare the speed of ODBCDirect with a client/server RDBMS to operations against a local Jet table. Such comparisons aren't a valid measure of relative database performance because of network delays. As mentioned earlier in the chapter, to make an accurate speed comparison, you must move the Msa8data.mdb file to the server hosting SQL Server to obtain valid comparative timing data.

MAKING THE TRANSITION FROM DAO TO ADO

When you've made the conversion from Access to Visual Basic 6.0 with DAO 3.5 and verified that your project correctly emulates the original Access application, the final step is to replace DAO-based controls and code with ADO-compliant counterparts.

1. Save your DAO-based forms and modules with new names. For this chapter's example, Vb5oltp.frm and Vb5oltp.bas are saved as Ado2oltp.frm and Ado2oltp.bas, respectively. The project has only one form, so the Public constants and variables of Ado2oltp.bas are copied to the Declarations section of Ado2oltp.frm and changed to Private constants and variables.

2. Open a new DataProject and add the forms and modules to the project. The DataProject adds the required references to ADO 2.0 and the basic set of ADO data-bound controls to the toolbox. The ADO version of the project is Ado2oltp.vbp.

A `DataEnvironment` object is required to support the Report Designer and to bind MSFlexGrid, MSHFlexGrid, DataGrid, DataCombo, DataList, and other data-bound controls directly to `Recordsets` created by `Command` objects. The Designer file for this project is Ado2oltp.dsr, and the name of the `DataEnvironment` object is envOLTP.

If your project doesn't include reports, remove the `DataReport1` object from the Designers list. You can dispense with the `DataEnvironment` object if you intend to bind data-related controls to ADO Data (ADODC) controls and use code to create your `Connection` and `Recordset` objects. Don't remove the Designer file, however, until you complete the conversion.

3. Replace each Data control with a `DataEnvironment` `Command` object or an ADODC control. Use `Command` objects unless you need the navigation features of ADODC controls. If you change the name of the ADODC control or substitute a `Command` object, change the `DataSource` (and for `Command` objects, the `DataMember`) property value(s) of the bound control accordingly. Ado2oltp.frm doesn't need an ADODC control.

4. Replace DBGrid control(s) that update data with DataGrid control(s); substitute MSFlexGrid controls for read-only DBGrids. Vb5oltp.frm's dbgOrderDetails becomes dtgOrderDetails in Ado2oltp.frm. The `DataSource` for dtgOrderDetails is envOLTP, and the `DataMember` is envOLTP's `Jolt` command, which automatically creates a `Recordset` named rsJolt.

TIP

Right-click each DBGrid control and choose Retrieve Fields from the pop-up menu to initialize the column bindings. If you use code to set the corresponding ADODC's `ConnectionString` property value or assign a code-created `Recordset` to the `ADODC.Recordset` property, use the ADODC's `ConnectionString` builder to make a temporary connection to the data source to enable the Retrieve Fields operation.

---

5. Replace data-bound combo boxes and list boxes with DataCombo and DataList controls, respectively, unless you previously wrote code to populate conventional combo and list boxes. Ado2oltp.frm populates the cboShipVia and cboEmployeeID combo lists from temporary forward-only Recordsets.

6. Right-click each MSFlexGrid and DBGrid control and choose Properties from the pop-up menu to display the properties sheet for the control. Format the controls as necessary to correspond as closely as possible to the appearance of the original Access list box control and, if used, datasheet-style subform(s).

7. Search for and replace all DAO.DBEngine, DAO.Workspace, DAO.Database and other DAO declarations and references in code with the appropriate ADODB.Connection, ADODB.Command, and ADODB.Recordset declarations and instructions. Use Chapter 3, "Migrating from DAO to ADO," as your guide to the necessary code changes. Upgrading Vb5oltp.vbp to Ado2oltp.vbp required changes to about 5% of the code (approximately 100 of 2,000 lines).

8. Remove all unnecessary references and ActiveX controls in your project. The inability to remove a reference to DAO 3.5x or to a replaced control indicates that you haven't completed the ADO upgrade process.

9. Take advantage of persistent Recordset objects to eliminate the need for local tables and, for client/server applications, the resource consumption of Jet on the client.

When the project runs and all operating modes behave as expected, turn your attention to tuning the VBA code to gain the full performance benefits of ADO.

▶ See "Preparing for Upsizing," **p. 692**
and "Altering Table Properties," **p. 711**

NOTE

The Orders table of the NW_Data.mdb database used by Ado2oltp.vbp has a structure different from Msa8oltp.mdb. NW_Data.mdb's Order Details table is renamed Order_Details, and the AllowZeroLength property value is set to **True** for fields in the Orders and Customers table that aren't required. There is no valid reason to disallow zero-length strings in optional fields.

Similarly, the nwind database used with the SQL Server connections of Ado2oltp.frm differs from the OLTP database used with Msa8oltp.mdb and Vb5oltp.vbp. If you created an SQL Server 6.x nwind database with the Access Upsizing Wizard, verify that you followed the instructions to change the OrderID data type of the Orders table from AutoNumber to Number (Long Integer). Similarly, verify that you removed the identity attribute added to the OrderID field of the Orders table. An identity attribute on the OrderID field causes an error when you attempt to add a new order to the nwind database.

REVIEWING THE CODE OF THE ADO2OLTP PROJECT

The Ado2oltp project is intended to demonstrate ADO coding techniques, as well as to compare the performance between native OLE DB data providers and the MSDASQL provider for ODBC with Jet and SQL Server tables. Figure 20.9 shows Ado2oltp.frm with the data source

Connection options—Jet - Native (Jolt); Jet - ODBC (MSDASQL, DSN-less); SQL (Server) - Native (SQLOLEDB); and SQL (Server) - ODBC (MSDASQL, DSN-less)—at the upper-right corner of the form.

FIGURE 20.9

Ado2oltp.frm in add new order mode showing data source Connection *options.*

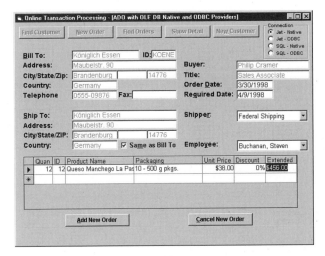

In addition to the Connection options, three constants defined in the Declarations section of Ado2oltp.form let you choose the Connection methods for the Recordset that underlies dtgOrderDetails, the DataGrid control for adding line items. The three constants are as follows:

- blnUseODBC substitutes MSDASQL for the default Jolt OLE DB provider for the connection to the tblOrder_Details table of Ado2oltp.mdb that stores line items prior to executing the order addition transaction.

- blnUseADODC substitutes the adcOrderDetails control for the default envOLTP.{cnnJolt.Jolt¦cnnODBC.ODBC} Connection and Command objects. The value of blnUseODBC determines which Command is used as the DataMember property value of dtgOrderDetails.

▶ **See** "Saving and Opening File-Type Recordsets," **p. 144**

- blnUseFile substitutes a persistent Recordset file, LineItem.rst, for tblOrder_Details. Using a persistent Recordset lets you dispense with the local database, Ado2oltp.mdb.

Listing 20.1 shows the VBA code that determines the type of connection to the NW_Data.mdb or nwind database. You can change the connection type at any point in Ado2oltp except when entering data for a new order or new customer. DSN-less ODBC connections eliminate the need to create ODBC data sources on clients. When using the nwind SQL Server database, the Orders table is tested for an identity attribute on the OrderID field and the OrderDetails table is checked for a timestamp field added by the Access 97 Upsizing Wizard.

LISTING 20.1 THE OPTCONNECT_CLICK EVENT HANDLER FOR CHANGING THE CONNECTION TO NW_DATA.MDB OR THE NWIND SQL SERVER DATABASE

```
Private Sub optConnect_Click(intIndex As Integer)
    'Don't change modes while entering a new order
    If blnNewOrder Or blnNewCustomer Then
        MsgBox "Can't change connection at this time.", _
            vbExclamation, "New Entry Pending"
        Exit Sub
    End If

    Dim strCnn As String

    On Error GoTo ConnectTypeError
    Me.MousePointer = vbHourglass

    'Create a new Connection for each change
    Set cnnData = Nothing
    Set cnnData = New ADODB.Connection
    Select Case intIndex
        Case 0
            'Jet with Jolt (the default)
            cnnData.Provider = "Microsoft.JET.OLEDB.3.51"
            cnnData.Open App.Path & "\NW_Data.mdb", "Admin"
            blnSQLServer = False
            blnANSI = False
        Case 1
            'Jet via DSN-less ODBC
            cnnData.Provider = "MSDASQL"
            strCnn = "driver={Microsoft Access Driver (*.mdb)};dbq=" & _
                App.Path & "\NW_Data.mdb;uid=Admin;pwd="
            cnnData.Open strCnn
            blnSQLServer = False
            blnANSI = True
        Case 2
            'SQL Server with native provider
            cnnData.Provider = "SQLOLEDB"
            strCnn = "Location=" & strServer & ";User ID=" & strUserID & _
                ";Password=" & strPassword & ";Data Source=nwind"
            cnnData.Open strCnn
            blnSQLServer = True
            blnANSI = True
        Case 3
            'SQL Server via DSN-less ODBC
            cnnData.Provider = "MSDASQL"
            strCnn = "driver={SQL Server};server=" & strServer & _
                ";uid=" & strUserID & ";pwd=" & strPassword & _
                ";database=nwind"
            cnnData.Open strCnn
            blnANSI = True
            blnSQLServer = True
    End Select
```

```
    If blnSQLServer Then
        'Create a temporary Recordset
        Dim rstTemp As New ADODB.Recordset
        With rstTemp
            'Check for an identity attribute of OrderID field
            .ActiveConnection = cnnData
            'Don't return any records, just the structure
            .Source = "SELECT OrderID FROM Orders WHERE OrderID = 0"
            .Open
            If .Fields(0).Attributes < 24 Or _
                    .Fields(0).Attributes > 256 Then
                'OrderID with identity returns 16; should return 16 + 256
                'OrderID without identity returns 24
                MsgBox "OrderID field of Orders table appears to" & _
                    "have an identity column.", vbOKOnly, _
                    "Potential Problem with the 'nwind' Database"
            End If
            .Close

            'Check for a timestamp field in Order_Details
            .ActiveConnection = cnnData
            'Don't return any records, just the structure
            .Source = "SELECT * FROM Order_Details WHERE OrderID = 0"
            .Open
            If .Fields.Count > 5 Then
                blnHasTimestamp = True
            Else
                blnHasTimestamp = False
            End If
        End With
        Set rstTemp = Nothing
    End If

    'Repopulate the two combo boxes
    Call LoadComboBoxes
    Me.MousePointer = vbDefault

    'Start from the beginning
    Call ClearForm
    Exit Sub

ConnectTypeError:
    Me.MousePointer = vbDefault
    MsgBox Error, 48, "Set Connection Type Error"
    Exit Sub
End Sub
```

Figure 20.10 is a diagram of the flow of execution of Ado2oltp.frm's primary activities: finding a company (FindCompany), listing orders from a selected company (FindOrders), showing line items of a selected order (ShowDetail), and adding a new order (cmdNewOrder_Click and

cmdAddNewOrder_Click) or customer (cmdNewCustomer_Click and
cmdAddNewCustomer_Click). The procedures listed to the right of the main subprocedure boxes,
with the exception of LoadComboBoxes, perform housekeeping chores. About 30% of the code
of Ado2oltp.frm is devoted to clearing, hiding, showing, locking, and unlocking operations, collectively called *housekeeping*. Housekeeping code requires little, if any, change when porting
applications from Access to Visual Basic 6.0.

FIGURE 20.10

*Execution flow for
the Ado2oltp.frm's
primary order
retrieval and entry
functions.*

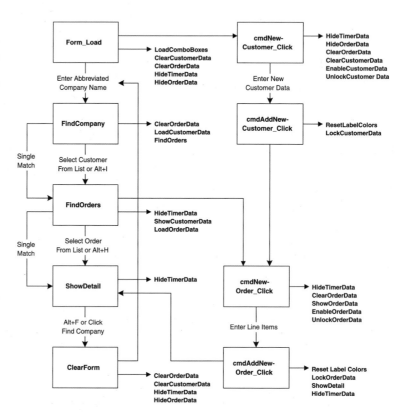

The FindCompany subprocedure, whose code appears in Listing 20.2, does double duty. Most
commonly, FindCompany displays a list of company names corresponding to one or more characters entered in the txtCompanyName text box. If only one company name matches the entry,
the Bill To text boxes display the company information; otherwise, you select the company you
want in the grdCustomers MSFlexGrid control. In either case, a list of orders for the company
appears. When adding a new customer, FindCompany creates a unique CustomerID value based
on the value of txtCompanyName.

LISTING 20.2 CODE FOR THE FindCompany SUBPROCEDURE, THE FIRST STEP IN DISPLAYING
EXISTING ORDERS OR ADDING A NEW ORDER

```vb
Private Sub FindCompany()
    'Purpose: Find company from text box entry

    If Len(txtCompanyName.Text) = 0 Then
        Exit Sub
    End If

    'Test for illegal SQL characters ('"%*?) in company name
    For intCtr = 1 To Len(txtCompanyName.Text)
        If InStr("'""%*?", Mid(txtCompanyName.Text, intCtr, 1)) Then
            strMsg = "You can't use the characters " _ &
                "', "", %, *, or ? in a search."
            MsgBox strMsg, 64, "Illegal Character in Name"
            txtCompanyName.Text = ""
            txtCompanyName.SetFocus
            Exit Sub
        End If
    Next intCtr

    Dim strChar As String
    Dim sngTimer1 As Single   'Local variable required in this case

    On Error GoTo FindCompanyError

    If blnNewCustomer Then
        'Check length
        If Len(txtCompanyName.Text) < 5 Then
            strMsg = "Customer name must be five characters or longer."
            MsgBox strMsg, 64, "Illegal Customer Name"
            txtCompanyName.Text = ""
            Exit Sub
        End If

        'Create a new customer ID (five alpha characters)
        txtCustomerID = UCase(Left(txtCompanyName.Text, 4))
        If InStr(txtCompanyName.Text, " ") > 0 Then
            txtCustomerID.Text = txtCustomerID.Text & _
                UCase(Mid(txtCompanyName.Text, _
                InStr(txtCompanyName.Text, " ") + 1, 1))
        Else
            txtCustomerID.Text = txtCustomerID.Text & _
                UCase(Mid(txtCompanyName.Text, 5, 1))
        End If

        'Replace spaces and illegal characters with X
        For intCtr = 2 To 5
            strChar = Mid(txtCustomerID.Text, intCtr, 1)
            If Asc(strChar) < 65 Or Asc(strChar) > 90 Then
```

continues

LISTING 20.2 CONTINUED

```
         If intCtr < 5 Then
            txtCustomerID.Text = Left(txtCustomerID.Text, _
               intCtr - 1) _
               + "X" + Mid(txtCustomerID.Text, intCtr + 1)
         Else
            txtCustomerID.Text = Left(txtCustomerID.Text, _
               intCtr - 1) + "X"
         End If
      End If
   Next intCtr

   'Test for duplicate company ID
   For intCtr = 5 To 2 Step -1
      strSQL = "SELECT CustomerID FROM Customers WHERE " & _
         CustomerID = ' & txtCustomerID.Text & "'"
      If rstCustKey.State = adStateOpen Then
         rstCustKey.Close
      End If
      rstCustKey.Open strSQL, cnnData, adOpenStatic
      If rstCustKey.RecordCount = 0 Then
         'Key is unique
         rstCustKey.Close
         Exit For
      End If

      'Attempt to create a non-duplicate key with Xs
      If intCtr = 5 Then
         txtCustomerID.Text = Left(txtCustomerID.Text, 4) + "X"
      Else
         txtCustomerID.Text = Left(txtCustomerID.Text, intCtr - 1) _
            + "X" + Right(txtCustomerID.Text, 5 - intCtr)
      End If
   Next intCtr
   Exit Sub
End If

Dim strSearch As String
strMsg = "No customers found beginning with " & _
   UCase(txtCompanyName) & _
   ". Re-enter customer name or click the New Customer button."

Me.MousePointer = vbHourglass

sngTimer1 = Timer
If blnANSI Then
   strSearch = "CompanyName LIKE '" & txtCompanyName & "%'"
Else
   strSearch = "CompanyName LIKE '" & txtCompanyName & "*'"
End If
```

```
strSQL = "SELECT CustomerID, CompanyName, City FROM Customers " & _
    "WHERE " & strSearch
If rstCustomers.State = adStateOpen Then
    rstCustomers.Close
End If
'RecordCount is needed, otherwise forward-only would be OK
rstCustomers.Open strSQL, cnnData, adOpenStatic
If rstCustomers.RecordCount = 0 Then
    grdCustomers.Visible = False
    lblCustomers.Visible = False
    MsgBox strMsg, 48, "Order Entry"
Else
    rstCustomers.MoveLast
    If rstCustomers.RecordCount = 1 Then
        strSQL = "SELECT * FROM Customers WHERE " & strSearch
        rstCustomers.Close
        rstCustomers.Open strSQL, cnnData, adOpenStatic
        grdCustomers.Visible = False
        lblCustomers.Visible = False
        Call ClearOrderData
        Call LoadCustomerData
        cmdFindOrders.Enabled = True
        cmdNewOrder.Enabled = True
        cmdFindOrders.SetFocus
        Call FindCustomerOrders
    Else
        'Load the customer selection FlexGrid
        With grdCustomers
            .Rows = rstCustomers.RecordCount
            rstCustomers.MoveFirst
            For intRow = 0 To .Rows - 1
                .Row = intRow
                For intCol = 0 To 2
                    .Col = intCol
                    If Not IsNull(rstCustomers(intCol).Value) Then
                        .Text = rstCustomers(intCol).Value
                    End If
                Next intCol
                rstCustomers.MoveNext
            Next intRow
            .Visible = True
            .Row = 0
            .Col = 0
            .ColSel = 2
            .SetFocus
        End With
        lblCustomers.Visible = True
    End If
End If
txtFindCustomer.Text = Format(Timer - sngTimer1, "#0.000")
txtFindCustomer.Visible = True
```

continues

LISTING 20.2 CONTINUED

```
    lblFindCustomer.Visible = True
    lblCustSeconds.Visible = True

    Me.MousePointer = vbDefault
    Exit Sub

FindCompanyError:
    Me.MousePointer = vbDefault
    MsgBox Error, 48, "Find Company Error"
    Exit Sub
End Sub
```

The FindOrders subprocedure displays order(s) placed by the selected company (see Listing 20.3). The FindCompany subprocedure and clicking Find Orders (or pressing Alt+I) calls FindOrders. The FindOrders code is similar to that of FindCompany; a single order for a company automatically displays the Ship To and other order-related information and displays Order_Details records. If the company has placed more than one order, you select the order from the grdOrders list. The code is updated to conform to Year 2000 (Y2K) standards.

LISTING 20.3 CODE TO FIND ONE OR MORE ORDERS FOR A SELECTED COMPANY AND DISPLAY ORDER-RELATED DATA

```
Private Sub FindOrders()
    'Purpose: Find orders for customer

    On Error GoTo FindOrdersError

    Dim strSearch As String
    Dim sngTimer1 As Single

    sngTimer1 = Timer
    'Timer box housekeeping
    Call HideTimerData
    txtFindCustomer.Visible = True
    lblFindCustomer.Visible = True
    lblCustSeconds.Visible = True

    grdOrderDetails.Visible = False
    lblOrderDetails.Visible = False
    cmdShowDetail.Enabled = False

    Me.MousePointer = vbHourglass

    'Syntax for all providers is the same
    strSearch = "CustomerID = '" & txtCustomerID & "'"
    strMsg = "No orders found for '" & txtCompanyName & "'."
    strSQL = "SELECT * FROM Orders WHERE " & strSearch
```

```
If rstOrders.State = adStateOpen Then
    rstOrders.Close
End If
rstOrders.Open strSQL, cnnData, adOpenStatic
rstOrders.MoveLast
If rstOrders.RecordCount = 0 Then
    Me.MousePointer = vbDefault
    MsgBox strMsg, 48, "Order Entry"
Else
    rstOrders.MoveLast
    If rstOrders.RecordCount = 1 Then
        Call LoadOrderData
        cmdShowDetail.Enabled = True
        cmdShowDetail.SetFocus
        Call ShowDetailList
    Else
        strSQL = "SELECT OrderID, OrderID, OrderDate, " & _
            "RequiredDate, ShippedDate " & _
            "FROM Orders WHERE " & strSearch & _
            " ORDER BY OrderID DESC"
        If rstSelect.State = adStateOpen Then
            rstSelect.Close
        End If
        'Load the customer selection FlexGrid
        rstSelect.Open strSQL, cnnData, adOpenStatic
        rstSelect.MoveFirst
        With grdOrders
            .Rows = rstSelect.RecordCount
            For intRow = 0 To .Rows - 1
                .Row = intRow
                For intCol = 0 To 4
                    .Col = intCol
                    If IsNull(rstSelect(intCol).Value) Then
                        'Required to prevent prior values from appearing
                        'in rows with null values
                        .Text = ""
                    Else
                        If intCol > 1 Then
                            'Year 2000 fix
                            .Text = Format(rstSelect(intCol).Value, _
                                "mm/dd/yyyy")
                        Else
                            .Text = rstSelect(intCol).Value
                        End If
                    End If
                Next intCol
                rstSelect.MoveNext
            Next intRow
            .Visible = True
            .Col = 0
            .Row = 0
```

20

**PORTING ACCESS
OLTP APPS TO
VB 6**

continues

LISTING 20.3 CONTINUED

```
            .ColSel = 4
            .SetFocus
        End With
        lblOrders.Visible = True
        'Debug.Print strSQL
    End If
End If
sngTimer1 = Timer - sngTimer1
If rstOrders.RecordCount > 1 Then
    txtFindOrders.Visible = True
    lblFindOrders.Visible = True
    lblOrdersSeconds.Visible = True
    txtFindOrders.Text = Format(sngTimer1, "#0.000")
Else
    txtGetDetails.Text = Format(sngTimer1, "#0.000")
End If
Me.MousePointer = vbDefault
Exit Sub

FindOrdersError:
    Me.MousePointer = vbDefault
    MsgBox Error, 48, "Find Customer Orders Error"
    Exit Sub
End Sub
```

The `ShowDetail` subprocedure is called by `FindOrders` or `cmdAddNewOrder_Click` (after the new order transaction completes). `ShowDetail` displays the order's line items based on many-to-one relationships between Order_Details, Orders (OrderID), and Products (ProductID). The Products table supplies the ProductName and QuantityPerUnit (package) data for the `grdOrderDetails` MSFlexGrid control. The Extended column is calculated by multiplying Quantity by UnitPrice. Listing 20.4 shows the VBA code for `ShowDetail`.

LISTING 20.4 THE `ShowDetail` SUBPROCEDURE, WHICH DISPLAYS A LIST OF LINE ITEMS CREATED FROM JOINS BETWEEN THE ORDERDETAILS, ORDERS, AND PRODUCTS TABLES

```
Private Sub ShowDetail()
    'Purpose: Get information for and display order details list box

    On Error GoTo ShowDetailError

    Dim strTemp As String
    Dim intCtr As Integer
    Dim sngExtended As Single

    If Not txtGetOrder.Visible Then
        Call HideTimerData
    End If
```

```
grdCustomers.Visible = False
lblCustomers.Visible = False
grdOrders.Visible = False
lblOrders.Visible = False
sngTimer = Timer
'Use SQL-89 WHERE syntax for joins
'SQL Server database created with Access 97 Upsizing Wizard
'[Order Details] table renamed to Order_Details in NW_Data.mdb
strSQL = "SELECT Order_Details.Quantity, " & _
    "Products.QuantityPerUnit, " & _
    "Order_Details.ProductID, Products.ProductName, " & _
    "Order_Details.UnitPrice, Order_Details.Discount " & _
    "FROM Order_Details, Products " & _
    "WHERE Order_Details.ProductID = Products.ProductID " & _
    "AND Order_Details.OrderID = " & txtOrderID
'Debug.Print strSQL
If rstSelect.State = adStateOpen Then
    rstSelect.Close
End If
'Must open other than forward-only to obtain record count
rstSelect.Open strSQL, cnnData, adOpenStatic
rstSelect.MoveLast
If rstSelect.RecordCount > 6 Then
    grdOrderDetails.Width = 7920
Else
    grdOrderDetails.Width = 7692
End If
rstSelect.MoveFirst
'ColAlignment must be applied after loading grid
'Format the columns (can't use VBA functions in ADODB.Recordsets)
With grdOrderDetails
    .Rows = rstSelect.RecordCount
    .Cols = 7
    .ColAlignment(4) = flexAlignRightCenter
    .ColAlignment(5) = flexAlignRightCenter
    .ColAlignment(6) = flexAlignRightCenter
    For intRow = 0 To .Rows - 1
        .Row = intRow
        For intCol = 0 To 5
            .Col = intCol
            If Not IsNull(rstSelect(intCol).Value) Then
                .Text = rstSelect(intCol).Value
            End If
        Next intCol
        'Format the $ and % columns, calculate extended amount
        .Col = 0
            sngExtended = CSng(.Text)
        .Col = 4
        sngExtended = sngExtended * CSng(.Text)
        If .Row = 0 Then
            .Text = Format(.Text, "$0.00")
```

continues

LISTING 20.4   CONTINUED

```
         Else
             .Text = Format(.Text, "0.00")
         End If
         .Col = 5
         sngExtended = (1 - CSng(.Text)) * sngExtended
         .Text = Format(.Text, "0.0%")
         .Col = 6
         If .Row = 0 Then
             .Text = Format(sngExtended, "$0.00")
         Else
             .Text = Format(sngExtended, "0.00")
         End If
         rstSelect.MoveNext
      Next intRow
      .Visible = True
   End With
   lblOrderDetails.Visible = True
   lblGetDetails.Visible = True
   txtGetDetails.Visible = True
   lblGetSeconds.Visible = True
   txtGetDetails.Enabled = True
   txtGetDetails.Text = Format$(Timer - sngTimer, "#0.000")
   'Debug.Print strSQL
   Exit Sub

ShowDetailError:
   MsgBox Error, 48, "Show Detail List Error"
   Exit Sub
End Sub
```

The `cmdNewOrder_Click` event handler sets up `frmOrderEntry` to add a new order for the selected customer (see Listing 20.5). The values of the `blnUseADODC`, `blnUseFile`, and `blnUseODBC` constants determine the source of the `Recordset` for the `dtgOrderDetails` DataGrid control. After setting the `Recordset` source, records from the prior order stored in tblOrder_Details or the saved `Recordset` are deleted. All MSFlexGrid controls are hidden, and the DataGrid opens with a single tentative append record for entry of the first line item.

LISTING 20.5   CODE TO SET UP THE DTGORDERDETAILS DATAGRID CONTROL FOR NEW ORDER LINE ITEM ENTRY

```
Private Sub cmdNewOrder_Click()
   'Purpose: Set up for for new order entry

   On Error GoTo NewOrderError

   Call HideTimerData
```

```
If blnUseADODC Then
    If blnUseFile Then
        'Use the saved recordset
        Dim rstTemp As New ADODB.Recordset
        rstTemp.Open App.Path & "\LineItem.rst", , _
            adOpenStatic, adLockOptimistic, adCmdFile

        With adcOrderDetails
            '.ConnectionString = ""
            Set .Recordset = rstTemp
            '.Recordset.Open App.Path & "\LineItem.rst", , _
                adOpenStatic, adLockOptimistic, adCmdFile
            .Refresh
        End With
        Set rstTemp = Nothing
    End If

    'Clear the recordset
    With adcOrderDetails.Recordset
        If .RecordCount Then
            Do Until .EOF
                .Delete
                .MoveNext
            Loop
        End If
    End With
    adcOrderDetails.Refresh
Else
    'Eliminate the existing records
    If blnUseODBC Then
        envOLTP.cnnODBC.Execute ("DELETE * FROM tblOrder_Details")
        envOLTP.rsODBC.Requery
    Else
        envOLTP.cnnJolt.Execute ("DELETE * FROM tblOrder_Details")
        envOLTP.rsJolt.Requery
    End If
End If
dtgOrderDetails.Refresh

'Mucho Housekeeping
grdCustomers.Visible = False
lblCustomers.Visible = False
grdOrders.Visible = False
lblOrders.Visible = False
grdOrderDetails.Visible = False
lblOrderDetails.Visible = False
dtgOrderDetails.Visible = True
cmdAddNewOrder.Visible = True
cmdCancelNewOrder.Visible = True
dtgOrderDetails.SetFocus
```

continues

LISTING 20.5 CONTINUED

```
cmdFindCust.Enabled = False
cmdNewOrder.Enabled = False
cmdFindOrders.Enabled = False
cmdShowDetail.Enabled = False
cmdNewCustomer.Enabled = False
Call ClearOrderData
Call ShowOrderData
Call EnableOrderData
Call UnlockOrderData
lblOrderID.Visible = False
txtOrderID.Visible = False
lblShippedDate.Visible = False
txtShippedDate.Visible = False
lblFreight.Visible = False
txtFreight.Visible = False
txtEmployeeID.Visible = False
txtShipVia.Visible = False
cboEmployeeID.Visible = True
cboShipVia.Visible = True
cboEmployeeID.Enabled = True
cboShipVia.Enabled = True
chkUseBillTo.Visible = True
chkUseBillTo.Value = False
txtOrderID.Enabled = False
txtShippedDate.Enabled = False
txtFreight.Enabled = False
'Today's date is the default
txtOrderDate.Text = Format$(Date, "m/d/yyyy")
'The remaining defaults are to speed testing, not for production
'10 days is the default RequiredDate
txtRequiredDate.Text = Format(Date + 10, "m/d/yyyy")
'Default is the BillTo address
chkUseBillTo.Value = 1
'Default is Federal Shipping
cboShipVia.ListIndex = 0
'Default is Steve Buchanan
cboEmployeeID.ListIndex = 0
blnNewOrder = True
Exit Sub

NewOrderError:
  MsgBox Error, 48, "New Order Setup Error"
  Exit Sub
End Sub
```

▶ See "Using Jet SQL Within a Transaction," **p. 750**

and "Executing the Order Entry Transaction with Transact-SQL," **p. 753**

The `cmdAddNewOrder_Click` event handler creates the Jet SQL or Transact-SQL statement that adds the new Order record and its associated Order_Details record(s) to the tables as a transaction (see Listing 20.6). Prior to processing the transaction, the code tests for missing or incorrect entries. Turning the label color red draws the operator's attention to the erroneous entry. As noted in Chapter 19, "Processing Transactions and Bulk Operations," using VALUES lists greatly reduces the number of bytes sent to the server by eliminating field names from the transaction statement. With VALUES lists, NULL values must be supplied for fields not updated by the transaction, including any timestamp fields used by SQL Server to resolve concurrency issues. When the transaction completes, a call to the `ShowDetail` subprocedure replaces the DataGrid with the MSFlexGrid to display the line items, confirming that the transaction completed.

LISTING 20.6 CODE TO TEST FOR COMPLETE DATA ENTRY AND EXECUTE THE TRANSACTION THAT ADDS THE NEW ORDER TO THE DATABASE

```
Private Sub cmdAddNewOrder_Click()
    'Purpose: Add a new order to the Orders and Order_Details tables

    Dim lngOrderID As Long
    Dim sngStart As Single
    Dim sngGetID As Single
    Dim sngWrap As Single
    Dim sngCommit As Single
    Dim intCtr As Integer
    Dim intEmployeeID As Integer
    Dim intShipVia As Integer
    Const RED_TEXT = 255 'Red in RGB color values

    'On Error GoTo AddOrderError

    'Test the text box entries
    Call ResetLabelColors
    If Len(txtShipName) = 0 Then
        lblShipName.ForeColor = RED_TEXT
        txtShipName.SetFocus
        Exit Sub
    End If
    If Len(txtShipAddress) = 0 Then
        lblShipAddress.ForeColor = RED_TEXT
        txtShipAddress.SetFocus
        Exit Sub
    End If
    If Len(txtShipCity) = 0 Then
        lblShipCity.ForeColor = RED_TEXT
        txtShipCity.SetFocus
        Exit Sub
    End If
```

continues

LISTING 20.6   CONTINUED

```
If Len(txtShipCountry) = 0 Then
    lblShipCountry.ForeColor = RED_TEXT
    txtShipCountry.SetFocus
    Exit Sub
End If
If CVDate(txtOrderDate) < Date Then
    lblOrderDate.ForeColor = RED_TEXT
    txtOrderDate.SetFocus
    Exit Sub
End If
If txtRequiredDate = "" Then
    lblRequiredDate.ForeColor = RED_TEXT
    txtRequiredDate.SetFocus
    Exit Sub
End If
If CVDate(txtRequiredDate) <= CVDate(txtOrderDate) Then
    lblRequiredDate.ForeColor = RED_TEXT
    txtRequiredDate.SetFocus
    Exit Sub
End If
If cboShipVia.ListIndex = -1 Then
    lblShipVia.ForeColor = RED_TEXT
    cboShipVia.SetFocus
    Exit Sub
Else
    intShipVia = cboShipVia.ItemData(cboShipVia.ListIndex)
End If
If cboEmployeeID.ListIndex = -1 Then
    lblEmployeeID.ForeColor = RED_TEXT
    cboEmployeeID.SetFocus
    Exit Sub
Else
    intEmployeeID = cboEmployeeID.ItemData(cboEmployeeID.ListIndex)
End If

If blnUseADODC Then
    'Make sure the last line item takes
    With adcOrderDetails
        .Recordset.Update
        Set rstLineItems = .Recordset
    End With
Else
    If blnUseODBC Then
        Set rstLineItems = envOLTP.rsODBC
    Else
        Set rstLineItems = envOLTP.rsJolt
    End If
End If
```

```
If rstLineItems.RecordCount = 0 Then
   strMsg = "No line items have been added. Please add an item " & _
      "or cancel this order."
   Beep
   MsgBox strMsg, 48, "New Order Entry Error"
   Exit Sub
Else
   'Test for missing field values
   With rstLineItems
      .MoveFirst
      Do Until .EOF
         'Don't test OrderID field
         For intCtr = 1 To .Fields.Count - 1
            If IsNull(.Fields(intCtr)) Then
               MsgBox "Missing entry in " & _
                  rstLineItems.Fields(intCtr).Name & " field."
               Exit Sub
            End If
         Next intCtr
         .MoveNext
      Loop
   End With
End If

cmdAddNewOrder.Enabled = False
cmdCancelNewOrder.Enabled = False
Me.MousePointer = vbHourglass
sngStart = Timer

'Obtain the tentative order ID (works with all connections)
If blnSQLServer Then
   strSQL = "SELECT MAX(OrderID) LastOrder FROM Orders"
Else
   'Note that MSDASQL-Jet requires a trailing semi-colon
   strSQL = "SELECT MAX(OrderID) AS LastOrder FROM Orders;"
End If
With rstOrders
   If .State = adStateOpen Then
      .Close
   End If
   .Open strSQL, cnnData, adOpenForwardOnly
   lngOrderID = .Fields(0).Value + 1
End With
txtOrderID.Enabled = True
txtOrderID.Text = lngOrderID
sngGetID = Timer - sngStart
sngStart = Timer

'INSERT the order information
If blnSQLServer Then
```

continues

LISTING 20.6 CONTINUED

```
    On Error GoTo SQLServerError
    'Valid for Transact-SQL only
    strSQL = "BEGIN TRAN INSERT Orders "
Else
    On Error GoTo RollbackOrder
    'Jet SQL syntax
    cnnData.BeginTrans
    strSQL = "INSERT INTO Orders "
End If
strSQL = strSQL & "VALUES(" & _
txtOrderID & ", '" & _
txtCustomerID & "', " & _
intEmployeeID & ", '" & _
txtOrderDate & "', '" & _
txtRequiredDate & "', NULL, " & _
intShipVia & ", NULL, '" & _
txtShipName & "', '" & _
txtShipAddress & "', '" & _
txtShipCity & "', '" & _
txtShipRegion & "', '" & _
txtShipPostalCode & "', '" & _
txtShipCountry & "')"
'ShippedDate and Freight (NULL above) aren't applicable to orders

'INSERT the line item information for each record
rstLineItems.MoveFirst
Do Until rstLineItems.EOF
    If blnSQLServer Then
        'Use Transact-SQL syntax for the transaction
        strSQL = strSQL & " INSERT Order_Details "
    Else
        'Split into two queries with Jet SQL syntax
        strSQL = strSQL & ";"
        'Debug.Print strSQL
        cnnData.Execute (strSQL)
        strSQL = "INSERT INTO Order_Details "
    End If
    strSQL = strSQL & "VALUES(" & _
    lngOrderID & ", " & _
    rstLineItems(1) & ", " & _
    rstLineItems(4) & ", " & _
    rstLineItems(0) & ", " & _
    rstLineItems(5)
    'Value (NULL) must be supplied for a timestamp field
    If blnSQLServer And blnHasTimestamp Then
        strSQL = strSQL & ", NULL) "
    Else
        strSQL = strSQL & ") "
    End If
```

```
    rstLineItems.MoveNext
    If rstLineItems.EOF Then
       If blnSQLServer Then
          'Finish the transaction (Transact-SQL)
          strSQL = strSQL & " COMMIT TRAN"
       Else
          'Semi-colon for Jet
          strSQL = strSQL & ";"
       End If
    End If
Loop
sngWrap = Timer - sngStart
sngStart = Timer

'Execute the SQL statement
cnnData.Execute (strSQL)
If Not blnSQLServer Then
    'Commit the Jolt transaction
    cnnData.CommitTrans
End If
sngCommit = Timer - sngStart
'Debug.Print strSQL

lblOrderID.Visible = True
txtOrderID.Visible = True

On Error GoTo AddOrderError

'Prevent further editing
Call LockOrderData

'Form and button housekeeping
dtgOrderDetails.Visible = False
cmdAddNewOrder.Visible = False
cmdCancelNewOrder.Visible = False
cmdAddNewOrder.Enabled = True
cmdCancelNewOrder.Enabled = True
cmdFindCust.Enabled = True
cmdNewOrder.Enabled = True
cmdFindOrders.Enabled = True
cmdNewCustomer.Enabled = True

'Display the order details in the listbox
Call cmdShowDetail_Click

'Display the transaction times
Call HideTimerData
txtGetID.Text = Format(sngGetID, "#0.000")
txtWrap.Text = Format(sngWrap, "#0.000")
txtCommit.Text = Format(sngCommit, "#0.000")
```

continues

20

PORTING ACCESS OLTP APPS TO VB 6

LISTING 20.6 CONTINUED

```
    Call ShowTimerData
    Me.MousePointer = vbDefault
    blnNewOrder = False
    Exit Sub

SQLServerError:
    'SQL Server automatically rolls back a single failed transaction
    Me.MousePointer = vbDefault
    MsgBox Error, 48, "Unable to Add Order " & lngOrderID & " to server."
    cmdAddNewOrder.Enabled = True
    cmdCancelNewOrder.Enabled = True
    Exit Sub

RollbackOrder:
    'Roll back the Jet transaction
    Me.MousePointer = vbDefault
    MsgBox Error, 48, "Unable to Add Order " & lngOrderID & " to NW_Data."
    cnnData.Rollback
    cmdAddNewOrder.Enabled = True
    cmdCancelNewOrder.Enabled = True
    Exit Sub

AddOrderError:
    Me.MousePointer = vbDefault
    MsgBox Error$, 48, "Add New Order Error"
    cmdAddNewOrder.Enabled = True
    cmdCancelNewOrder.Enabled = True
    Exit Sub
End Sub
```

> **NOTE**
>
> It's not necessary to use a loop structure to repeat the transaction in case of a network problem, server error, or concurrency problem caused by a page lock. (SQL Server's INSERT row-locking feature eliminates concurrency issues with additions to tables.) All the data for the transaction is saved locally, so the operator can repeatedly click Add New Order or press Alt+A until the transaction succeeds.

The preceding six listings show only a few of the 2,000+ lines of code in Ado2oltp.frm. The chosen subprocedures and event handlers demonstrate ADO coding techniques for a variety of data sources and OLE DB data providers. A production version of the Ado2oltp project with a single data source and OLE DB provider requires about 1,500 lines.

USING TRANSACT-SQL STORED PROCEDURES

IN THIS CHAPTER

A *stored procedure* is a precompiled set of SQL statements saved within a specified database. SQL-92 doesn't specify a standard syntax for creating and executing stored procedures, so you must use the RDBMS's dialect of SQL for these purposes. Oracle, for example, implements stored procedures with the PL/SQL cartridge. SQL3, the successor to SQL-92 presently in the development stage, is likely to include standardized stored procedure syntax. This chapter uses SQL Server 7.0 and Transact-SQL for all examples. There are few substantive differences in stored-procedure syntax or execution in SQL Server 6.*x*.

▶ **See** "SQL Server 7.0 (Sphinx)," **p. 688**

NOTE

SQL Server 7.0 adds ALTER TABLE, ALTER VIEW, ALTER PROCEDURE, and ALTER TRIGGER reserved words, but none of these new Transact-SQL statements are used in the examples of this chapter. The primary new features of SQL Server are simpler administration, improved performance, and greater scalability.

Stored procedures accept replaceable input parameter values (also called argument values) that let you set WHERE clause criteria values for SELECT, INSERT, UPDATE, and DELETE queries. The vast majority of stored procedures have one or more parameters. Stored procedures also provide return values, which often are used to indicate success or failure of execution, and output parameters to return multiple values after execution.

All recent versions of Visual Basic and Access let you execute stored procedures with input parameters. The Remote Data Object (RDO) 1.0 was Microsoft's first offering that accommodated return values, output parameters, and less-common input/output (bidirectional) parameters. RDO 2.0, included in the Enterprise Versions of Visual Basic 5+, provided a performance boost for row-returning stored procedures. Access 97's ODBCDirect offers an alternative to the use of DAO and Jet with a lightweight Automation wrapper over RDO 2.0. Both RDO and ODBCDirect, however, require you to write arcane ODBC escape syntax for stored procedures with return values and output parameters.

Visual Basic 6.0 and ADO 2.0 offer a considerable improvement over RDO/ODBCDirect's stored procedure execution syntax and parameter handling. The code examples in this chapter, based on the Ado2oltp.vbp project of the preceding chapter, take advantage of many of these new or improved features. As an example, stored procedures return forward-only Recordsets with valid RecordCount values, whereas conventional forward-only Recordsets created from SQL statements return only **True** (one or more rows) or **False** (no rows).

TRIGGERs and VIEWs are special types of stored procedures. TRIGGERs execute in tandem with INSERT, UPDATE, and DELETE operations and most commonly are used to maintain the database's

Using Transact-SQL Stored Procedures

CHAPTER 21

819

21

USING TRANSACT-
SQL STORED
PROCEDURES

referential integrity. VIEWs are predefined SELECT queries that usually return a subset of the fields of the table(s) in the FROM clause..

> **NOTE**
>
> The Visual DataTools (da Vinci) treat row-returning Jet QueryDef objects (SELECT queries) as Views, but don't show action queries as Stored Procedures. QueryDefs are similar to SQL Server stored procedures, but aren't compiled; Jet stores a relatively simple execution plan for SELECT QueryDefs. SQL Server 7.0's cost-based query optimizer is far more sophisticated than that of Jet 3.5*x*.

GAINING A PERFORMANCE BOOST WITH STORED PROCEDURES

Stored procedures offer the following performance advantages compared with sending individual SQL statements to the server:

- You execute the stored procedure by name, which minimizes network traffic by reducing the number of bytes sent to the server. Comma-separated parameter values follow the name, much like the VALUES list of an INSERT or UPDATE query. Unlike VALUES lists, you can omit values of parameters that have defined default values, such as NULL.

- You can take full advantage of Transact-SQL's flow-control instructions, such as IF...ELSE... and CASE...WHEN...ELSE...END, as well as predefined server variables, which include the very useful @@rowcount to return the number of rows affected by the latest operation. You also can use the @@identity variable to return the last value of a field having the identity attribute.

> **NOTE**
>
> The version of the @@rowcount variable in SQL Server 7.0 differs from that of version 6.5 and earlier. COMMIT and IF statements preceding the use of the variable don't affect the 7.0 version. Such non-row-returning or row-effecting statements set the 6.5 version to zero.

- Precompiling the SQL statement eliminates the SQL parsing and compilation step for each execution of the stored procedure. Depending on the complexity of the query, skipping these two steps significantly improves overall execution speed.

- The first time you execute the stored procedure, SQL Server generates and stores an execution plan for the query. Unless you specify otherwise, the stored execution plan remains in effect for all subsequent stored procedure calls.

- SQL Server 7.0 caches stored procedures in RAM. Unless displaced by other cached data, the cached stored procedure remains available for execution by all database users. In previous versions, each user required a separate copy of the stored procedure in RAM.

NOTE

Another benefit of stored procedures, not performance related, is database schema independence for front ends. If you make changes to the names or structures of back-end databases, add fields, or change field names or data types, you change only the stored procedure's SQL statement. Changing the stored procedure eliminates the need to change client-side code, recompile, and redistribute the client application.

You can grant user permissions for stored procedures, but not the underlying tables, forcing all data access to occur via stored procedures. Restricting data access to stored procedures greatly improves the overall security of the database.

Figure 21.1 compares the execution path of an SQL statement sent to the server versus that of a parameterized stored procedure. Substituting parameter values is very much faster than validating object names, optimizing the execution plan, and compiling the statement.

FIGURE 21.1

SQL Server execution paths for a conventional SQL statement and a parameterized stored procedure.

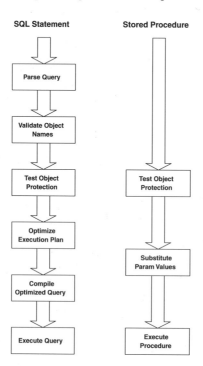

Using Transact-SQL Stored Procedures

CHAPTER 21

821

21

USING TRANSACT-
SQL STORED
PROCEDURES

NOTE

RDO 2.0 and ADO 2.*x* create temporary stored procedures, called prepared statements, that remain in the server cache. Temporary stored procedures offer some of the advantages of permanent stored procedures, such as precompilation, when you change only parameter values. Multiple users can share a single copy of a temporary stored procedure. To use temporary stored procedures, add ;Use Procedure For Prepare=1 to the OLE DB ConnectionString value. With ADO 2.0 Connection and Command objects created in the Data Environment, you can force recompilation of temporary stored procedures on each execution by marking the Prepare Before Execution check box of the Advanced page of the Connection property sheet. For production applications, conventional stored procedures are the better approach.

UNDERSTANDING STORED PROCEDURE SYNTAX

The generic Transact-SQL syntax for creating a new stored procedure is

```
CREATE PROC[EDURE] proc_name [;group_number]
    [@param1name data_type [VARYING ][= default_value ][OUTPUT]]
    [, @param2name data_type [VARYING ][= default_value ][OUTPUT]]
    [,... ]
    [WITH {RECOMPILE|ENCRYPTION|RECOMPILE, ENCRYPTION}][ FOR REPLICATION][sr]

AS sql_statement
```

Following is a description of each element of the CREATE PROC[EDURE] statement:

- *proc_name* is the name of the procedure. System stored procedures, which are located in the master database, commonly use the sp_ prefix. SQL Server 7.0's predefined database stored procedures carry a dt_ prefix. The examples of this chapter use the ddg_ and ado_ prefixes.

- *group_number* is an optional integer value, prefixed by a semicolon, that lets you assign the same name to members of a group of sequentially numbered procedures. A single DROP PROCEDURE *proc_name* statement removes the entire group.

- @param1name, @param2name, ... are named parameters. SQL Server accepts a comma-separated list of up to 1,024 parameters. Transact-SQL uses the preceding ampersand (@) to identify a parameter variable. Parameter values must be of a valid SQL Server data type; you can't use an object name (such as the name of a table or field) as a parameter value.

- *data_type* is the name of a valid SQL Server data type, such as int, varchar(*n*), datetime, text, or image, which usually corresponds to the data type of the field for which the value is supplied, either as a WHERE clause criterion or as a field value replacement in INSERT or UPDATE queries.

- VARYING is an optional qualifier that indicates that an OUTPUT parameter value is created by SQL Server. The most common use of VARYING ... OUTPUT is passing a cursor to another stored procedure. You can't pass a scrollable cursor to your Visual Basic application with a stored procedure, so VARYING isn't used in this chapter.

- = *default_value* is an optional value to be substituted when the calling application doesn't supply a value for the parameter.

- WITH RECOMPILE optionally specifies that SQL Server is to reoptimize and recompile the SQL statement prior to execution. This step negates the performance advantage of the stored procedure but sometimes is useful when major changes to parameter values occur.

- WITH ENCRYPTION optionally encrypts the text of the stored procedure maintained in the syscomments table.

- FOR REPLICATION optionally specifies that the stored procedure will be executed only by a replication operation. You can't use the WITH RECOMPILE and FOR REPLICATION options together.

- *sql_statement* is a complete Transact-SQL statement that you can execute directly, plus the RETURN reserved word, server-side (@@*name*) variables, and other stored-procedure-only elements.

If you attempt to edit a stored procedure and save the edited version in the same SQL Server 6.5 and earlier database, you receive an error message. Thus it's traditional to precede CREATE PROC[EDURE] statements with the following block statement:

```
IF EXISTS (SELECT name FROM sysobjects
     WHERE name = 'proc_name' AND type = 'P')
   DROP PROCEDURE proc_name
GO
```

or the more common SQL Server 6.5 and earlier version:

```
IF EXISTS (SELECT * FROM sysobjects
   WHERE id = object_id('dbo.proc_name')
     AND sysstat & 0xf = 4)
   DROP PROCEDURE dbo.proc_name
GO
```

SQL Server 7.0 supports the ALTER PROC[EDURE] statement, so you change CREATE to ALTER to resave an edited procedure without the IF EXISTS... block. SQL Server 6.x syntax is used in the examples of this chapter for version independence.

The simplest parameterized stored procedures return one or more rows that meet a criterion supplied as an input parameter. The following procedure returns rows based on a ShipCountry criterion from the Orders table of an SQL Server nwind database upsized from Nwind.mdb:

```
USE nwind
```

```
IF EXISTS (SELECT name FROM sysobjects
      WHERE name = 'ddg_OrdersByCountry' AND type = 'P')
   DROP PROCEDURE ddg_OrdersByCountry
GO
USE nwind
GO
CREATE PROC ddg_OrdersByCountry
   @ShipCountry varchar(15) = 'USA'
AS SELECT * FROM Orders WHERE ShipCountry = @shipCountry
```

The USE nwind elements aren't necessary if you execute the query from a connection to the nwind database. Figure 21.2 illustrates creating the ddg_OrdersByCountry procedure from SQL Server Query Analyzer.

FIGURE 21.2

Creating with SQL Server Query Analyzer a new ddg_OrdersBy-Country stored procedure.

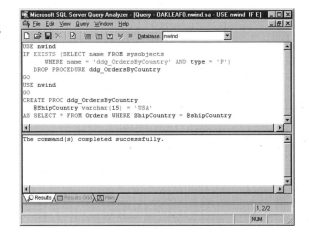

NOTE

Technically, you don't need the IF EXISTS...GO block in your code unless you use ISQL_w. If you omit the IF EXISTS...GO block, ISQL_w returns a Procedure 'proc_name' group number 1 already exists in the database. Choose another procedure name error message and won't let you update the Transact-SQL code. With SQL Server 7.0, in SQL Server Enterprise Manager's and the Visual Data Tools' Stored Procedure window, you receive a message asking whether you want to overwrite the existing procedure if the procedure exists in the database. When you overwrite the procedure, the substitution of ALTER PROC[EDURE] for CREATE PROC[EDURE] is automatic.

To execute a stored procedure interactively, you use the reserved word EXEC[UTE] followed by the procedure name and a comma-separated list of input parameter values, where applicable. Figure 21.3 shows part of the result set returned by EXEC ddg_OrdersByCountry, which uses the default value, USA. Figure 21.4 shows the result set returned when supplying 'Germany' to @ShipCountry.

FIGURE 21.3

Part of the query result set returned by the ddg_OrdersBy-Country *procedure using the default value for the* @ShipCountry *parameter.*

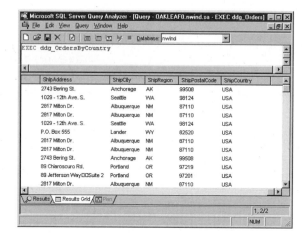

FIGURE 21.4

Part of the query result set returned by the ddg_OrdersBy-Country *procedure with* 'Germany' *supplied as the* @ShipCountry *parameter value.*

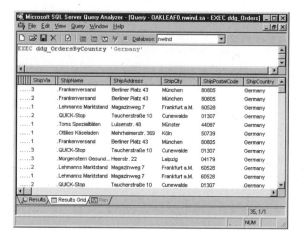

REPLACING SQL STATEMENTS WITH STORED PROCEDURES

Row-returning stored procedures deliver forward-only (nonupdatable) Recordsets because stored procedures can't pass a server-side scrollable cursor to the OLE DB or ODBC APIs. Forward-only Recordsets use what Microsoft calls a *firehose cursor*. Thus record-returning

Using Transact-SQL Stored Procedures

CHAPTER 21

825

21

USING TRANSACT-
SQL STORED
PROCEDURES

stored procedures are limited to supplying information to your client/server front end; INSERT, UPDATE, or DELETE queries or stored procedures alter the server data.

▶ **See** "Upsizing Nwind.mdb to SQL Server 6.5 with the Access 97 Wizard," **p. 692** and "Importing Jet Tables to SQL Server 7.0," **p. 701**

> **NOTE**
>
> The Ado2proc.vbp project in the \Ddg_vb6\Chaptr21 folder of the accompanying CD-ROM lets you compare execution time differences between conventional SQL statements and stored procedures. You must upsize the Nwind.mdb database to an SQL Server 6.*x* nwind database or import its tables to an SQL Server 6.*x* or 7.0 nwind database prior to running Ado2proc.vbp. Create the stored procedures in the nwind database before marking the Stored Procs check box on the form. Change the strServer, strUserID, and strPassword constant values in the Declarations section of Ado2proc.frm to suit your SQL Server installation. The "Replacing SQL Statements with Stored Procedures" section, later in the chapter, describes how to execute stored procedure scripts (.sql files).

Deciding on a Stored Procedure Naming Convention

Before you begin replacing SQL statements with stored procedure calls, decide on a consistent naming convention for the procedures. The objective is to make the purpose of the stored procedure discernible from its name while minimizing the overall length of name. The following stored procedure naming convention is used in this and later chapters:

1. Start with a two- to four-character prefix followed by an underscore to identify the database or application(s) that use the application. This chapter's examples use ado_ as the prefix, but nw_ or nwind_ also is suitable. The ado_ prefix is chosen here because the procedures are called by the Ado2proc project.

2. Append the name of the table involved in the procedure. To minimize the length of the stored procedure name, use unambiguous abbreviations, such as Custs for Customers and OrdDtls for Order_Details.

3. Append a code for the purpose of the stored procedure, such as Data when returning all fields of a single row or List when returning only a few fields to populate combo or list boxes. Examples are ado_CustsData and ado_OrdersList. Use Upd, Ins, or Del to specify UPDATE, INSERT, or DELETE operations, respectively, as in ado_OrdersUpd or ado_CustsIns.

4. If the procedure requires a WHERE clause constraint, append an underscore and the field name(s) of the constraint. If the constraint is the primary key field, such as OrderID for the Orders table, use _ID; otherwise identify the field, as in ado_OrdersList_CustID.

5. If the procedure involves SQL aggregate functions, such as MIN, MAX, or COUNT, append an underscore, the field (abbreviation), and the function name, as in ado_Orders_IDMax.

> **NOTE**
>
> Historically, stored procedure names are all lowercase with underscore separators to aid readability, as in ado_orders_list_cust_id. The current trend is to use mixed-case naming for readability and underscores only to separate name elements.

Converting Ado2oltp.frm's SELECT Statements to Procedures

▶ **See** "Reviewing the Code of the Ado2oltp Project," **p. 796**

The Ado2oltp.vbp application described in the preceding chapter has many SQL SELECT statements that are amenable to conversion to stored procedures.

- SELECT EmployeeID, FirstName, LastName FROM Employees ORDER BY LastName (ado_EmpsList) and SELECT ShipperID, CompanyName FROM Shippers ORDER BY CompanyName (ado_ShipsList) in the LoadComboBoxes subprocedure. These two statements are executed only during the Form_Load event and return forward-only Recordsets. Converting to a stored procedure isn't likely to improve performance significantly.

- SELECT CustomerID FROM Customers WHERE CustomerID = 'txtCustomerID.Text' (ado_CustsIDTest_ID), SELECT CustomerID, CompanyName, City FROM Customers WHERE CompanyName LIKE 'txtCompanyName%' (ado_CustsList_Name), and SELECT * FROM Customers WHERE CompanyName LIKE 'txtCompanyName%' (ado_CustsData_Name) in the FindCompany subprocedure. The first query tests for uniqueness of the CustomerID value for a new customer. The remaining two queries populate the grdCustomers MSFlexGrid and the Bill To text boxes.

- SELECT * FROM Customers WHERE CustomerID = 'grdCustomers.Text' (ado_CustsData_ID) in the grdCustomers_DblClick subprocedure populates the Bill To text boxes.

- SELECT * FROM Orders WHERE CustomerID = 'txtCustomerID' (ado_OrdersData_CustID) and SELECT OrderID, OrderID, OrderDate, RequiredDate, ShippedDate FROM Orders WHERE CustomerID = 'txtCustomerID' ORDER BY OrderID DESC (ado_OrdersList_CustID) in the FindOrders subprocedure. The first query populates the Ship To and other order-related text boxes; the second populates the grdOrders MSFlexGrid.

Using Transact-SQL Stored Procedures

CHAPTER 21

827

21

USING TRANSACT-
SQL STORED
PROCEDURES

- SELECT Order_Details.Quantity, Products.QuantityPerUnit, Order_Details.ProductID, Products.ProductName, Order_Details.UnitPrice, Order_Details.Discount FROM Order_Details, Products WHERE Order_Details.ProductID = Products.ProductID AND Order_Details.OrderID = txtOrderID (ado_OrdDtlsList_OrdID) in the ShowDetails subprocedure populates the grdOrderDetails MSFlexGrid.

- SELECT * FROM Orders WHERE OrderID = txtOrderID (ado_OrdersData_ID) and SELECT * FROM Customers WHERE CustomerID = 'rstOrders!CustomerID' (ado_CustsData_ID) in the FindOrderByNumber subprocedure. The first query populates the order-related text boxes; the second query is identical to the query of the grdCustomers_DblClick subprocedure.

- SELECT ProductID, ProductName, QuantityPerUnit, UnitPrice FROM Products WHERE ProductID = dtgOrderDetails.Text (ado_ProdsData_ID) in the FindProductName subprocedure retrieves product information based on entry of a ProductID value.

- SELECT ProductID, ProductName, QuantityPerUnit, UnitPrice FROM Products WHERE ProductName LIKE 'dtgOrderDetails.Text%' (ado_ProdsList_Name) in the FindProductID subprocedure retrieves product information based on a partial text match. If SQL Server is set to case-insensitive matching (the default), you can dispense with the UPPER and UCase functions.

> **NOTE**
>
> The SELECT statements of the preceding list are pseudocode SQL versions derived from the VBA code in Ado2oltp.frm.

Stored procedures that return multiple records to grids, such as ado_CustsList_Name, ado_OrdersList_CustID, and ado_OrdDtlsList_OrdID include an optional RETURN @@rowcount at the end of the SQL statement to provide the equivalent of the RecordCount value for testing or setting Rows property value of the grid. The RETURN @@rowcount statement isn't required for ADO 2.0+; as mentioned at the beginning of this chapter, RecordCount property values are valid for Recordsets returned by stored procedures. RETURN @@rowcount statements are included for backward compatibility with applications that use RDO.

Creating the Stored Procedures

Writing stored procedures based on existing VBA code for SQL statements is relatively easy when you follow these steps:

1. Add a temporary **Debug.Print** *strSQL* **&** vbCrLf statement immediately preceding each *Recordset*.Open statement that uses *strSQL*.

2. Clear the Immediate window.

3. Run the application, exercising all of its features.

4. Open the Immediate window to display the SQL statements (see Figure 21.5).

FIGURE 21.5

SQL statements in the Immediate window generated by `Debug.Print strSQL & vbCrLf` *statements in the VBA code.*

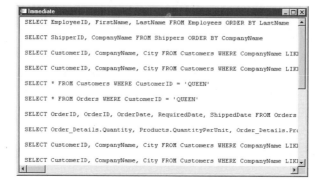

5. Optionally, copy the SQL statements to Notepad and save the text file.

   If you have a large number of SQL statements in the Immediate window, many of which are duplicates, copy the statements to Excel and sort the rows to ease removal of duplicates.

6. Launch SQL Server 7.0's Query Analyzer or version 6.5's ISQL_w. Set the database to nwind for this example.

7. Copy each SQL statement into the upper pane of a New query window and format the statement to improve readability. Execute the query to verify its syntax (see Figure 21.6).

FIGURE 21.6

Nine of the 13 SQL SELECT *statements of the preceding section copied into SQL Server Query Analyzer.*

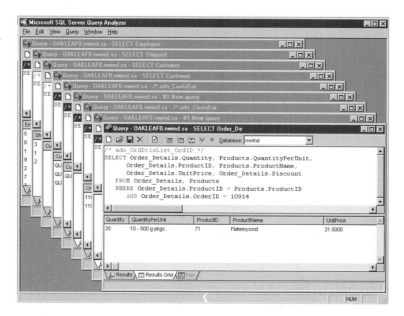

Using Transact-SQL Stored Procedures

CHAPTER 21

829

21

USING TRANSACT-
SQL STORED
PROCEDURES

> **TIP**
>
> Adding a comment with the name of the stored procedure as you copy SQL statements into ISQL_w or SQL Server Query Analyzer windows makes it easier to keep track of the current query. Transact-SQL uses C-style comments, which are delimited by /* ... */ pairs

8. Add the standard IF EXISTS ... AS block before the SQL statement if you're using SQL Server 6.5 or earlier, specify the procedure name, and define the parameter(s) of the stored procedure (see Figure 21.7).

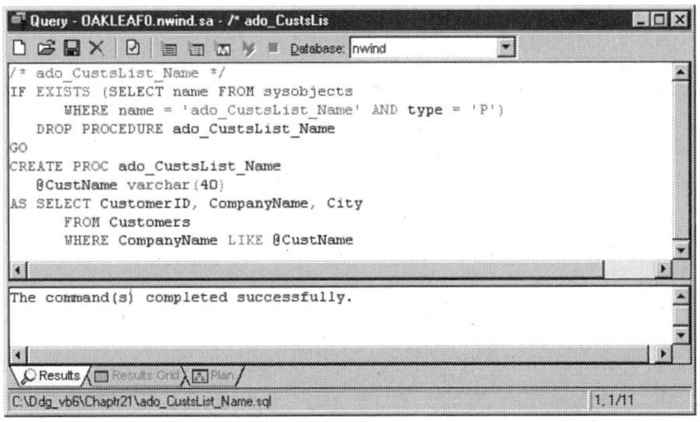

FIGURE 21.7

Nine of the 12 SQL SELECT *statements of the preceding section copied into SQL Server Query Analyzer.*

> **TIP**
>
> You can save a substantial amount of time by creating a generic block, pasting it into all your query windows, and then replacing the elements shown in italic below the procedure name and parameter declarations.
>
> ```
> IF EXISTS (SELECT name FROM sysobjects
>       WHERE name = 'ado_' AND type = 'P')
>    DROP PROCEDURE ado_
> GO
> CREATE PROC ado_
>    @var varchar(??)[ = 'default']
> AS
> ```
>
> Copying the procedure name from the comment at the beginning of the procedure and pasting it in the three *ado_* locations above saves time and avoids potential naming errors.

9. Add RETURN @@rowcount to the end of any query capable of returning more than one row if you want to make your stored procedure compatible with RDO.

10. Execute the stored procedure to check your SQL statements (see Figure 21.8).

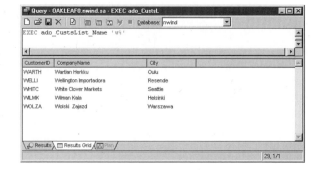

FIGURE 21.8

Testing the
`ado_CustsList_`
`Name` *stored proce-dure code.*

11. Save the query to a *ProcName*.sql file in your project development folder for future refer-ence and to guard against losing your work in case of a crash.

12. Repeat steps 8 through 11 for each SQL statement you copied.

13. Launch SQL Server Enterprise Manager, connect to the server, expand the database item in the scope pane (nwind for this example), and then double-click Stored Procedures to verify that the procedures you added are in the correct database (see Figure 21.9).

FIGURE 21.9

Verifying the pres-ence of newly added stored pro-cedures with SQL Server Enterprise Manager.

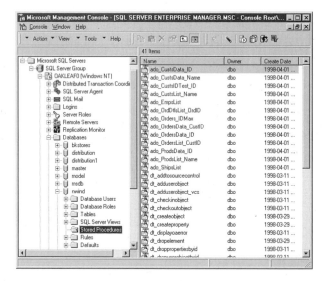

14. Close the Query windows of SQL Server Query Analyzer or ISQL_w.

Using Transact-SQL Stored Procedures

CHAPTER 21

831

21

USING TRANSACT-
SQL STORED
PROCEDURES

> **NOTE**
>
> The 13 SELECT stored procedure query (.sql) files for the nwind database are included in the \Ddg_vb6\Chaptr21 folder of the accompanying CD-ROM. After you've created a few of the stored procedures required to run Ado2proc.vbp, you can save time by opening the ado_*QueryName*.sql file and executing the query to create the ado_*QueryName* stored procedure. You must add all SELECT stored procedures, plus the two INSERT procedures described in the sections that follow, to use the Stored Proc option of ado2proc.vbp.

Using SQL Server Enterprise Manager to Author Stored Procedures

SQL Server 7.0's Enterprise Manager includes a New Stored Procedure feature that's a "lite" alternative to SQL Server Query Analyzer. Follow these steps to check out the Stored Procedure Properties sheet:

1. Launch SQL Server Enterprise Manager and expand the scope pane to display the object classes in the nwind database.

2. Right-click the Stored Procedures class and choose New Stored Procedure from the pop-up menu to open the Stored Procedure Properties - New Stored Procedure dialog. The dialog's text box provides a default CREATE PROCEDURE <PROCEDURE NAME> AS skeleton statement.

3. Type your stored procedure statement in the text box (see Figure 21.10). Like Query Analyzer, Transact-SQL reserved words are color-coded blue.

FIGURE 21.10

Writing a stored procedure in SQL Server Enterprise Manager's New Stored Procedure dialog.

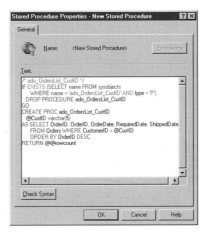

4. Click the Check Syntax button to have SQL Server's query parser test your stored procedure without executing it. Click OK to close the `Syntax check successful` message box.

5. Click OK to close the dialog and save your stored procedure with the name specified in the `CREATE PROCEDURE` statement.

6. Right-click the procedure in the list of procedures in the right pane and choose Properties from the pop-up menu to open the Store Procedure Properties - *ProcedureName* dialog. SQL Server removes the `IF EXISTS ... GO` block, which isn't necessary when you use SQL Server Enterprise Manager to edit stored procedures.

7. Click Permissions to display the Permissions page of the Object Properties sheet. By default, the stored procedure has undefined permissions identified by cleared check boxes. You can set explicit execute permissions for SQL Server groups, roles, and users by clicking the appropriate check boxes (see Figure 21.11). The dbo always has full permissions on objects, so marking the dbo execute check box has no effect.

FIGURE 21.11

Setting explicit permissions to execute a stored procedure.

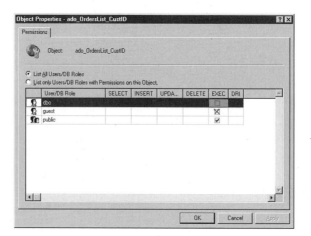

8. Click OK to close the Object Properties sheet. Click OK again to close the Stored Procedures dialog.

It's unlikely that you would use SQL Server Enterprise Manager to write new stored procedures, but the Permissions feature is useful for implementing security on stored procedure execution.

Working with Visual Data Tools and Stored Procedures

The third alternative for creating stored procedures is to use Visual Studio 6.0 Enterprice Edition's Visual Data Tools (VDTs, also called da Vinci), which requires a DataEnvironment connection to the nwind database. To use the VDTs with stored procedures, do the following:

1. Launch the Ado2proc.vbp project and open the ADO2PROC - envOLTP DataEnvironment window.

2. Add a new `Connection`, `cnnNwind`, with the Use Connection String option, specifying SQLOLEDB as the data provider and nwind as the data source.

3. Choose <u>V</u>iew, Data <u>V</u>iew Window and expand the new `cnnNwind Connection` object.

4. Expand the Stored Procedures item to display the existing stored procedures in the nwind database (see Figure 21.12, left).

5. Expand one of the procedures, `ado_CustsData_ID` for this example, to display a list of fields, parameters, and the return value if present (see Figure 21.12, right).

FIGURE 21.12

The Data View window displaying a list of stored procedures (left) and fields, parameters, and the return value (right).

6. Right-click the `@CustID` parameter and choose Properties from the pop-up menu to display the mini-properties sheet for the parameter (see Figure 12.13). Click OK to close the sheet.

FIGURE 21.13

Properties of the `@CustID` parameter of the `ado_CustsData_ID` procedure.

7. Right-click the Stored Procedures item and choose <u>N</u>ew Stored Procedure from the pop-up menu to open the New Stored Procedure dialog, which appears with a skeleton `CREATE PROCEDURE` statement.

8. Remove all but the `CREATE PROCEDURE` statement and write your stored procedure. Alternatively, you can import a .txt or .sql script file with existing stored procedure code (see Figure 21.14). If you import the code, the first noncommented statement must be `CREATE PROCEDURE`, not `CREATE PROC` or `IF EXISTS`.

FIGURE 21.14

Writing a stored procedure in the New Stored Procedures dialog of the VDTs.

9. Click the Save to Database button to create or overwrite the existing stored procedure.

10. If you have the T-SQL Debugger running, click the Debug button (with the arrow symbol) to test your procedure. The T-SQL Debugger is the subject of the "Debugging Stored Procedures with the T-SQL Debugger" section later in the chapter.

Like SQL Server Enterprise Manager's New Stored Procedure feature, the VDTs alternative ranks a poor second or third to writing stored procedures from scratch in Query Analyzer or ISQL_w.

Testing the SELECT Procedures

With SQL Server Query Analyzer and ISQL_w, you can test your stored procedures interactively before rewriting your VBA code to execute them. To test the procedures you created in the preceding steps, do the following:

1. Launch SQL Server Query Analyzer or ISQL_w. SQL Server 7.0's Query Analyzer is used for this example.

2. Log on to your server and then select the database (nwind for this example.)

3. Type **EXEC ado_CustsList_Name 'w%'** in the upper pane and click the Execute Query button to list all customers whose company name begins with *W* (refer to Figure 20.8). Single quotes surround character (char, varchar, text) and datetime parameter values.

4. Type **EXEC ado_OrdersList_CustID 'WELLI'** and click Execute Query to return a list of all orders for Wellington Importers in reverse date sequence.

5. Type **EXEC ado_OrdersData_ID 10935** and click Execute Query to deliver a single row of order data. Numeric (int, bigint, smallint, money, decimal, and the like) parameters don't use single quotes.

6. Type **EXEC ado_OrdDtlsList_OrdID 10935** and click Execute Query into Grid to list the Order_Details records for order 10935 (see Figure 20.15).

Using Transact-SQL Stored Procedures

CHAPTER 21

835

21

USING TRANSACT-
SQL STORED
PROCEDURES

FIGURE 21.15

Executing a stored procedure with an int *parameter.*

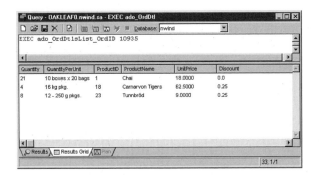

7. Test the remaining nine stored procedures to verify that they execute correctly.

NOTE

You can view the query execution plan for any of your stored procedures by clicking the Display Execution Plan button. The Execute icon represents your EXEC statement. The diagram below shows the execution path of the stored procedure's SELECT statement. The more elements in the SELECT statement's execution path, the greater the performance benefit of a stored procedure.

Replacing INSERT, UPDATE, and Transaction Code with Stored Procedures

Single-table INSERT and UPDATE operations are well suited to execution through stored procedures, although you seldom gain the performance benefits of converting complex, multitable SELECT statements to stored procedures. As an example, a typical SQL statement to add a new customer to the Customers table of the nwind database is

```
INSERT Customers VALUES('ALFKI', 'Alfreds Futterkiste',
    'Maria Anders', 'Sales Representative', 'Obere Str. 57',
    'Berlin', '', '12209', 'Germany', '030-0074321', '030-0076545')
```

The corresponding stored procedure call is

```
EXEC ado_CustsData_Ins 'ALFKI', 'Alfreds Futterkiste',
    'Maria Anders', 'Sales Representative', 'Obere Str. 57',
    'Berlin', '', '12209', 'Germany', '030-0074321', '030-0076545'
```

which represents only one less character transmitted to the server. For consistency, however, it's a good practice to use stored procedures throughout an application. The SQL code for the ado_CustsData_Ins stored procedure is as follows

```
CREATE PROC ado_CustsData_Ins
    @CustID varchar(5),
```

```
   @CompName varchar(40),
   @ContName varchar(30) = NULL,
   @ContTitle varchar(30) = NULL,
   @Addr varchar(60),
   @City varchar(15),
   @Region varchar(15) = NULL,
   @ZIP varchar(10) = NULL,
   @Country varchar(15) = 'USA',
   @Phone varchar(24),
   @Fax varchar(24) = NULL
AS INSERT Customers VALUES(@CustID, @CompName, @ContName, @ContTitle,
   @Addr, @City, @Region, @ZIP, @Country, @Phone, @Fax)
RETURN @@rowcount
```

Testing stored procedures that have many parameters is straightforward, laborious, and necessary. Don't forget to remove the spurious test records from a production database.

Transaction processing examples commonly involve trivial, single-record operations on two tables. One of the marketing favorites for claims that low-cost hardware and software can deliver millions of transactions per day is the "ATM emulator." One table has AccountNumber, DebitAmount, and TranTime fields, representing the withdrawal from the ATM. The other table has AccountNumber, CreditAmount, and TranTime fields, representing the withdrawal from a bank account. The simulated stored procedure for such a transaction is

```
CREATE PROC atm_bogus
   @AcctNum bigint,
   @DebitAmt money,
   @TranTime datetime
   DECLARE @CreditAmt money
   SELECT @CreditAmt = - @DebitAmt
BEGIN TRAN
   INSERT atm_table VALUES(@AcctNum, @DebitAmt, @TranTime)
   INSERT bank_table VALUES(@AcctNum, @CreditAmt, @TranTime)
COMMIT TRAN
```

NOTE

You use DECLARE *@varname vartype* to define the name and data type of a local Transact-SQL variable and SELECT *@varname = expression* to assign a value to the variable.

Real-world OLTP operations seldom, if ever, involve transactions as simple as the preceding ATM emulator.

▶ **See** "Reviewing the Code of the Ado2oltp Project," **p. 796**

Using Transact-SQL Stored Procedures

CHAPTER 21

837

21

USING TRANSACT-
SQL STORED
PROCEDURES

Use of stored procedures is problematic in OLTP applications that add an unknown and theoretically unlimited number of records (line items) dependent on a single added record (an order or invoice). Adding a new order and its line items in the preceding chapter's Ado2oltp project is an example in which a stored procedure precludes addition of an order with multiple line items in a single transaction.

The cmdAddNewOrder_Click event handler of Ado2oltp.frm requires two round-trips to the server: The first obtains the last OrderID value, and the second executes the entire transaction. A stored procedure lets you combine obtaining the OrderID value, incrementing it by one, and adding the data for the Orders record. A transaction on the Orders table requires at least one line item, so you can include addition of the first line item in the procedure. If the order contains only one line item, the order entry process completes with a single server round-trip. Another benefit of the stored procedure is minimizing the time between obtaining the last OrderID value and adding the new Orders record.

Following is the SQL code for the ado_NewOrder_Ins stored procedure:

```
IF EXISTS (SELECT name FROM sysobjects
      WHERE name = 'ado_NewOrder_Ins' AND type = 'P')
   DROP PROCEDURE ado_NewOrder_Ins
GO
CREATE PROC ado_NewOrder_Ins
   /* Orders table */
   @CustID varchar(5),
   @EmpID int,
   @OrdDate datetime,
   @ReqDate datetime,
   @ShipVia int,
   @ShipName varchar(40),
   @ShipAddr varchar(60),
   @ShipCity varchar(15),
   @ShipReg varchar(15) = NULL,
   @ShipZIP varchar(10) = NULL,
   @ShipCtry varchar(15),
   /* Order_Details table */
   @ProdID int,
   @Price money,
   @Quan int,
   @Disc real
AS
   /* OrderID varible */
   DECLARE @OrderID int
BEGIN TRAN
   SELECT @OrderID = MAX(OrderID) FROM Orders
   SELECT @OrderID = @OrderID + 1
   /* NULL for ShippedDate and Freight on new order entry */
   INSERT Orders VALUES(@OrderID, @CustID, @EmpID, @OrdDate,
      @ReqDate, NULL, @ShipVia, NULL, @ShipName, @ShipAddr,
```

```
        @ShipCity, @ShipReg, @ShipZIP, @ShipCtry)
    /* Field list used to eliminate timestamp dependency */
    INSERT Order_Details(OrderID, ProductID, UnitPrice, Quantity, Discount)
        VALUES(@OrderID, @ProdID, @Price, @Quan, @Disc)
COMMIT TRAN

/* You can use @@rowcount > 0 instead of @@error with SQL Server 7.0 */
IF @@error = 0
    RETURN @OrderID
ELSE
    RETURN 0
```

> **NOTE**
>
> You can easily modify the preceding Transact-SQL code to accommodate an
> identity column. You can't, however, include the single Order_Details table
> INSERT within the transaction, because the INSERT to the Orders table must
> complete before you can obtain the autoincremented OrderID value from the
> @@identity value. In this case, there's no benefit to adding the BEGIN TRAN and
> COMMIT TRAN statements, because a single-row operation on one table com-
> pletes or fails atomically.

The instruction to execute the procedure is considerably shorter than that of an equivalent SQL statement sent to the server, even without taking into consideration the DECLARE and SELECT statements required to obtain and increment the OrderID value within the transaction. BEGIN TRANS, INSERT *TableName* VALUES, and COMMIT TRANS statements and values for internally generated variables and NULL values aren't required. A typical EXEC statement to test the stored procedure is

```
DECLARE @retval int
EXEC @retval = ado_NewOrder_Ins 'KOENE', 1, '5/15/1998', '6/1/1998', 3,
    'Kˆniglich Essen', 'Maubelstr. 90', 'Brandenburg', '', '14776',
    'Germany', 24, 4.5, 24, 0
SELECT @retval
```

The first time you execute the stored procedure, there's a brief delay while SQL Server creates and saves the execution plan (showplan) and then caches the procedure in server RAM. Figure 21.16 shows SQL Server Query Analyzer's Execution Plan window displaying the sequence of events in the execution of ado_NewOrder_Ins. The elements of the display have been compressed to fit within the figure's window.

Using Transact-SQL Stored Procedures

CHAPTER 21

839

21

USING TRANSACT-
SQL STORED
PROCEDURES

FIGURE 21.16

SQL Server 7.0's execution plan for the `ado_NewOrder_Ins` *stored procedure.*

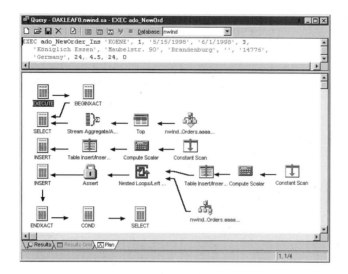

It's possible to add the remaining line items, if any, with multiple executions of a stored procedure, but you pay a server round-trip penalty for doing so. The RETURN statement provides the newly added OrderID value for use by a single successive SQL statement to add the second and higher line items, such as

```
INSERT Order_Details VALUES(12345, 42, 9.8, 12, 0[, NULL])
INSERT Order_Details VALUES(12345, 25, 6.75, 24, .1[, NULL])
INSERT Order_Details VALUES(12345, 36, 5.5, 9, 0[, NULL])
```

The trailing NULL value is required only if the Order_Details table includes a timestamp field.

TIP

If you're using SQL Server 6.5, you might encounter an error when executing the preceding INSERT statements including timestamp NULL values from code. In this case, you must omit the trailing NULL value and supply a field list, as in the following example:

```
INSERT Order_Details(OrderID, ProductID, UnitPrice, Quantity, Discount)
   VALUES(12345, 42, 9.8, 12, 0)
INSERT Order_Details(OrderID, ProductID, UnitPrice, Quantity, Discount)
   VALUES(12345, 25, 6.75, 24, .1)
INSERT Order_Details (OrderID, ProductID, UnitPrice, Quantity, Discount)
   VALUES(12345, 36, 5.5, 9, 0)
```

Addition of field lists greatly increases the number of characters sent to the server. Unless you must use a timestamp to resolve concurrency issues for UPDATEs, don't use timestamp fields with SQL Server 6.5 and ADO.

Until SQL Server stored procedure parameters accept **Variant** arrays, which would permit multiple line item addition with a single stored procedure call, sending grouped SQL INSERT statements to the server is the more efficient approach.

▶ See "Converting a Monolithic Client to Use MTS Components," **p. 1013**

> **NOTE**
>
> You can use Microsoft Transaction Server (MTS) to aggregate stored procedure transactions and individual INSERT operations within a single transaction context. You marshal **Variant** arrays to MTS with DCOM and then let MTS execute the stored procedure and multiple-INSERT SQL statement. MTS is the subject of Chapter 26, "Taking Advantage of Microsoft Transaction Server 2.0," and Chapter 27, "Creating and Deploying MTS Components."

CALLING STORED PROCEDURES IN VBA CODE

▶ See "The ADODB.Connection Object," **p. 69**
and "The ADODB.Command Object," **p. 85**

The general syntax for calling stored procedures from Visual Basic 6.0 ADO code for row-returning Recordsets from Connection and Command objects is

```
Set rstName = cnnName.Execute("ProcName", [lngRecordsAffected], _
    adCmdStoredProc)

Set cmmName.ActiveConnection = cnnName
cmmName.CommandText = "ProcName"
Set rstName = cmmName.Execute([lngRecordsAffected], [avarParameters], _
    adCmdStoredProc)
```

The preceding alternatives clearly show that executing stored procedures from a Connection object is the simplest approach. You use Command objects only when you want to receive return values or pass output parameters. (The following section describes the simplest method of passing input parameters.) Parameters are contained in a **Variant** array that the OLE DB data provider translates to the syntax required by the RDBMS. If you create your own **Variant** array of parameters with an **Array** statement, which is not a recommended practice, output parameters don't return correct values.

Using Transact-SQL Stored Procedures

CHAPTER 21

841

21

USING TRANSACT-
SQL STORED
PROCEDURES

> **NOTE**
>
> Calling the `Execute` method substitutes for the interactive `EXEC[UTE]` command when executing stored procedures from code. The `adCmdStoredProc` value of the Options argument is shown as required, although it technically is optional. Specifying the type of the `Command` argument of the `Connection` object or the type of the `CommandText` property of the `Command` object usually results in a small performance boost.

As an example, Ado2proc.frm's `LoadComboBoxes` subprocedure uses the following code to create the `rstEmployees` and `rstShippers` `Recordsets`:

```
Set rstEmployees = cnnData.Execute("ado_EmpsList", lngCount, adCmdStoredProc)

Set rstShippers = cnnData.Execute("ado_ShipsList", lngCount, adCmdStoredProc)
```

The `lngCount` (`RecordsAffected`) argument is a buffer that returns **True** if the `Recordset` has one or more rows or **False** if no rows return. In this respect, the value of `lngCount` is equivalent to the `RecordCount` property of a conventional forward-only `Recordset`.

For non-row-returning stored procedures, the `Connection` and `Command` syntax is

```
cnnName.Execute "ProcName"[, lngRecordsAffected[, _
    adCmdStoredProc]]

Set cmmName.ActiveConnection = cnnName
cmmName.CommandText = "ProcName"
cmmName.Execute [lngRecordsAffected[, avarParameters[, _
    AdCmdStoredProc]]]
```

The following sections describe the three methods of executing parameterized stored procedures with VBA code.

Executing Procedures with Input Parameters Only

If your stored procedure has only input parameters (or if a `RETURN` statement is included, but its value isn't needed), you can pass the parameter value(s) in the `Execute` method call of the `Connection` object. Following is the generic execution syntax for input-only parameterized stored procedures:

```
[Set rstName = ]cnnName.Execute{(¦ }"ProcName(values_list)", _
    lngRecordsAffected, adCmdStoredProc{)¦ }
```

> **NOTE**
>
> In the version of ADO 2.0 used to write this book, parenthesis must enclose the values list. An error results if you omit the parenthesis. Use of parenthesis to set off argument lists is common in most programming languages, but Transact-SQL uses a space after the stored procedure name to indicate the start of a parameters list. Execution of input-only parameterized stored procedures with DAO, ODBCDirect, and RDO requires Transact-SQL syntax, not parenthesis.

As an example, you can pass the single parameter to the `ado_CustsList_Name` procedure with the following code:

```
Set rstCustomers = cnnData.Execute("ado_CustsList_Name('" & _
   txtCompanyName & "%'")) ', lngCount, adCmdStoredProc)
```

Parameters you pass by this method must enclose **String** values, including dates, with single quotes ('). DECLARE statements of the stored procedure cast the parameter data types.

This syntax is the simplest of the three execution methods and involves minimal changes to existing code that sends VALUES lists to the server.

> **TIP**
>
> Save time by using `cnnName.Execute("ProcName(strCallProc")` when converting SQL INSERT `TableName` VALUES(...) statements to stored procedures. Copy the list elements, including the parenthesis, to the clipboard and then paste the list to a `strCallProc = "(...)"`

> **NOTE**
>
> When using ADO 2.0, MSDASQL.1, and ODBC 3.60, the preceding example of passing input parameters is the only method that executes without returning an ODBC error message.

Using a `DataEnvironment.Command` Object with Parameters

▶ See "Parameters Collection," p. 87

Microsoft designed the DataEnvironment's Command object to minimize the code necessary to assign values to input parameters and obtain return or output parameter values. You create an individual Command object for each parameterized stored procedure in your application and then pass the required parameter value to each input member of the Command object's Parameters collection. After execution, the procedure passes its return value to the RETURN_VALUE parameter.

Creating `Command` Objects Required for the Ado2proc Project

The Ado2proc.dsr Designer file of the Ado2proc.vbp project contains all Command objects required by Ado2proc.frm. Thus you don't need to execute the following steps, which are included to demonstrate how to create parameterized Command objects. Creating the Command objects for the stored procedures in the nwind database involves the following steps:

1. Opening the envOLTP DataEnvironment and adding a Connection object to the nwind database the SQLOLEDB provider. The new Connection is named cnnNwind.

2. Adding a new Command object using the cnnNwind Connection and named for the stored procedure without the ado_ prefix. For example, the Command name for the ado_CustsData_ID procedure is cmmCustsData_ID.

3. Accepting the default Database Object, Stored Procedure, and opening the Object Name list to retrieve the stored procedure names from the nwind database (see Figure 21.17).

FIGURE 21.17

Selecting the stored procedure for a new Command object.

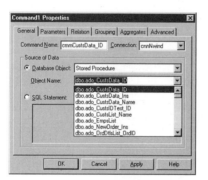

4. Selecting the stored procedure for the Command and clicking the Parameters tab to retrieve the names of parameters of the selected stored procedure in the Parameters page. If the procedure has a return value, it appears as the first item, RETURN_VALUE, in the Parameters list. Click the input parameter to display its properties (see Figure 21.18).

FIGURE 21.18

Properties of the CustID *parameter of the* cmmCustsData_ID *procedure.*

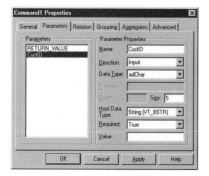

> **NOTE**
>
> Unless you have a valid reason for doing so, don't change any properties of the `Parameter` object except the `Value` property. You can assign in design mode an optional default value for the parameter; you assign in run mode the `Parameter.Value` property value with code.

5. Clicking the Advanced tab to display settings for additional `Command` properties. If the procedure returns records, marking the Recordset Returning check box (see Figure 21.19) is necessary.

FIGURE 21.19

Advanced properties for a stored procedure with a single parameter and a return value.

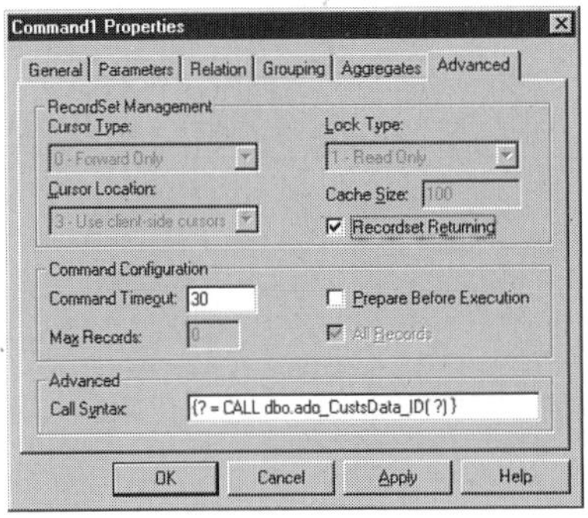

> **NOTE**
>
> The ODBC escape syntax for executing the stored procedure appears in the Call Syntax text box. The Call Syntax value is identical to that used by the RDO and ODBCDirect to execute stored procedures via ODBC. When you add parameters to a `Command` object, ADO automatically alters the `CommandText` property to use the `{ [? = ]call proc_name[(param1[, param2[, paramN]])] }` escape syntax.

6. Repeating steps 2 through 5 for each stored procedure in the nwind database, with the exception of `ado_EmpsList` and `ado_ShipsList`, which don't have parameters and are executed directly from the `cnnNwind` connection. The `cmmOrders_IDMax` procedure is omitted because this procedure isn't required when using the `ado_NewOrder_Ins` procedure.

After completing the preceding steps for each active stored procedure used in Ado2proc.frm, the 12 active `Commands` appear in the `envOLTP` DataEnvironment as illustrated by Figure 21.20.

Using Transact-SQL Stored Procedures

CHAPTER 21

845

21

USING TRANSACT-
SQL STORED
PROCEDURES

21

USING TRANSACT-
SQL STORED
PROCEDURES

FIGURE 21.20

The Commands *required by the code in* Ado2proc.frm.

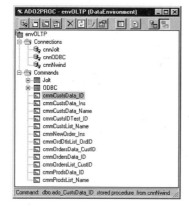

Modifying Project Code to Use DataEnvironment.Command Objects

The code to execute stored parameterized procedures with DataEnvironment.Command objects almost always is simpler than sending SQL statements to the server. The general VBA syntax for supplying parameter values, receiving a return value, and executing the procedure with a Command object is

```
With envOLTP.Commands("cmmName")
    .Parameters(1).Value = typValueFirst
    ...
    .Parameters(n).Value = typValueLast
    [Set rstSelect = ].Execute
    typReturnValue = .Parameters(0)
End With
```

The ADODB type library doesn't include Connections and Commands collections; the DERuntimeObjects library for the DataEnvironment object supplies these two collections. Like other collections, you must supply the name or the ordinal value to access a member of the Commands collection to set property values; specifying the ordinal value is faster. The RETURN_VALUE, if present, is Parameters(0); input and output parameters are numbered in the sequence of their definition in the stored procedure's CREATE PROC statement. The "Adapting the Ado2oltp Application to Stored Procedures" section in this chapter includes several samples of replacing of SQL statements with calls to parameterized stored procedures.

TIP

If you open a connection to the server with code and use Command objects based on a DataEnvironment.Connection object, you create two connections to

continues

the RDBMS. If your VBA code opens a connection (*cnnName*) to the RDBMS independently of the DataEnvironment's `Connection` object (cnn*DataEnv*), replace
the *cnnName* setup code and the `Open` method with

```
With envName.Connections("cnnDataEnv")
   If .State = adStateClosed Then
      .Open
   End If
End With
Set cnnName = envName.Connections("cnnDataEnv")
```

This code causes *cnnName* to point to the DataEnvironment's `Connection` and
uses only one server connection for all operations.

NOTE

You can't use the preceding method for return value or output parameters with
the versions of ADO 2.0, MSDASQL.1, and ODBC 3.60 used to write this book.
This method works only with SQLOLEDB as the data provider. The ODBC-related
problem is likely to be corrected in future versions of ADO.

Programming the Parameters Collection

▶ See "Parameters Collection," **p. 87**

An alternative to using the DataEnvironment is to declare `ADODB.Command` objects and set their
properties, including appending members of the `Parameters` collection with VBA code.
Creating parameters manually is a far more code-intensive approach and is included in this
chapter primarily for completeness. Testing with the Ado2proc.vbp project indicates that substituting `Commands` and `Parameters` created with VBA code doesn't result in measurable performance improvement. The only benefit appears to be a slight reduction in resource consumption
by not including the DERuntimeObjects in your project.

Following is the generalized syntax for creating and appending *N* multiple `Parameter` objects to
a `Command` object, cmm*Name*:

```
Declare prmName1 As ADODB.Parameter
...
Declare prmNameN As ADODB.Parameter
...
Set prmName1 = cmmName.CreateParameter [strName[, lngType[, _
   lngDirection[, lngSize[, varValue]]]]]
cmmName.Parameters.Append prmName1
...
```

Using Transact-SQL Stored Procedures

CHAPTER 21

847

21

USING TRANSACT-
SQL STORED
PROCEDURES

```
Set prmNameN = cmmName.CreateParameter [strName[, lngType[, _
    lngDirection[, lngSize[, varValue]]]]]
cmmName.Parameters.Append prmNameN
```

If you don't set the optional argument values of `CreateParameter`, you must set the corresponding property values prior to executing the parameterized `Command`, as shown in the following example with a return value and an input parameter:

```
With cmmCustomers
    .CommandText = "ado_CustsList_Name"
    .Parameters(0).Direction = adParamReturnValue
    .Parameters(0).Type = adInteger
    .Parameters(0).Size = 0
    .Parameters(1).Direction = adParamInput
    .Parameters(1).Type = adChar
    .Parameters(1).Size = 40
    .Parameters(1).Value = txtCompanyName.Text & "%"
    Set rstCustomers = .Execute
    lngCount = .Parameters(0).Value
End With
```

Executing the `Command` object changes the value of the `CommandText` property from the name of the stored procedure to the ODBC escape syntax used by RDO, regardless of whether you use the SQLOLEDB or MSDASQL data provider. In the preceding example, the `CommandText` value changes from ado_CustsList_Name to { ? = call ado_CustsList_Name(?) } prior to `Command` execution. The ? characters are placeholders for parameters; ? = specifies a return value, and (?) represents an input or output parameter. Multiple input or output parameters use comma-separated ? characters.

> **CAUTION**
>
> Make sure to set the `CursorLocation` property of your `Connection` object to `adUseClient` when using return value parameters. `DataEnvironment.Connection` objects default to a client-side cursor, but the `ADODB.Connections` you create with code default to `adUseServer`. Server-side cursors don't supply a return value until you close the `Recordset`, which makes the `RETURN_VALUE` parameter useless for its most common purpose[md]determining the row count of the forward-only `Recordset`.

Declaring `Parameters` and coding `CreateParameter` and `Append` methods becomes especially laborious for `INSERT` procedures, which commonly have many parameters. As an example, the ado_NewOrder_Ins procedure has 15 input parameters, plus a return value, which requires 48 lines of code to create the `Parameters` collection, plus an additional 15 lines in the execution code to set `Parameter(n).Value`.

> **NOTE**
>
> Like the `DataEnvironment.Command` object, you can't use the preceding method for return value or output parameters with the versions of ADO 2.0, MSDASQL.1, and ODBC 3.60 used to write this book. This method works only with SQLOLEDB as the data provider. The ODBC-related problem is likely to be corrected in future releases of ADO.

ADAPTING THE ADO2OLTP APPLICATION TO STORED PROCEDURES

▶ **See** "Running the Vb5oltp or Ado2oltp Project," **p. 790**

Ado2proc.vbp lets you compare the execution speed of conventional SQL statements versus corresponding Transact-SQL stored procedures, as well as the execution speed of SQLOLEDB (the default) and MSDASQL with the SQL Server ODBC driver. Chapter 20, "Porting Access OLTP Applications to Visual Basic 6.0," provides the instructions on how to search for customers and orders and to enter new orders with this application.

The code behind the Ado2proc.vbp project's single Ado2proc.frm involves major modifications to the Ado2oltp.frm code. Ado2proc.vbp is client/server only, so code to access the Ado2data.mdb local Jet database is removed. **Public** variables declared in Ado2oltp.bas are moved to **Private** variables in Ado2proc.frm. The majority of the added code relates to substituting stored procedures for internally generated SQL statements. Housekeeping code is removed from the listings in the sections that follow.

> **NOTE**
>
> A file-type `Recordset` (LineItem.rst) replaces the `Recordset` created over the tblOrder_Details table of Ado2oltp.mdb, so Ado2proc.vbp doesn't need to load Jolt and Jet 3.51. Using a file-type `Recordset` saves more than 1MB of resource consumption. The hidden `adcOrderDetails` ADODC control is removed and the file-type `Recordset` is assigned directly to the DataGrid control by setting the DataGrid's `DataMember` property to an empty string and setting the `DataSource` property to the `Recordset`.

The Declarations section of Ado2proc.frm defines two constants, `blnCodeParams` and `blnUseDataEnv`, to determine parameter creation and connection methodology. Setting `blnCodeParams` to **True** results in creating the `Parameters` collection and setting `Parameter` property values with code, rather than employing `envOLTP`.*Command* objects. Setting

Using Transact-SQL Stored Procedures

CHAPTER 21

849

21

USING TRANSACT-
SQL STORED
PROCEDURES

blnUseDataEnv to **True** opens the cnnData Connection from the envOLTP.cnnNwind connection, rather than with code, executing all Commands over a single server connection.

> **NOTE**
>
> When you select the SQL - ODBC option and mark the Stored Proc check box in the Connection frame of the form, all stored procedures execute with conventional cnnData.Execute statements having parameter list arguments. The versions of ADO 2.0 and MSDASQL used to write this edition won't execute stored procedures with return values or output parameters. Thus you can't add new orders with MSDASQL-executed stored procedures. This problem is likely to be corrected in future versions of ADO and/or MSDASQL.

Opening Connections

Activating the form or changing the connection from the default SQL - Native to SQL - ODBC (or vice versa) executes the optConnect_Click subprocedure of Listing 21.1. In addition to testing for an identity attribute of the OrderID field of the Orders table and the presence of a timestamp field in the Order_Details table, the subprocedure checks the version of SQL Server in use. The version test is necessary because the two SQL Server versions differ in their handling of NULL values passed to timestamp fields. If blnUseDataEnv is **True** (the default), a connection created with code shares the Data Environment Connection.

LISTING 21.1   SETTING UP Connections WITH SQLOLEDB OR MSDASQL

```
Private Sub optConnect_Click(intIndex As Integer)
    'Don't change modes while entering a new order
    If blnNewOrder Or blnNewCustomer Then
        MsgBox "Can't change connection at this time.", vbExclamation, _
            "New Entry Pending"
        Exit Sub
    End If

    Dim strCnn As String

    On Error GoTo ConnectTypeError
    Me.MousePointer = vbHourglass

    'Create a new Connection for each change
    Set cnnData = Nothing
    Set cnnData = New ADODB.Connection
    Select Case intIndex
        Case 0
            'SQL Server with native provider
            strCnn = "Location=" & strServer & ";User ID=" & strUserID & _
```

continues

LISTING 21.1   CONTINUES

```
                    ";Password=" & strPassword & ";Data Source=nwind"
            If blnUseDataEnv Then
                'Use the DataEnvironment's connection
                With envOLTP.Connections("cnnNwind")
                    If .State = adStateOpen Then
                        .Close
                    End If
                    '.Provider = "SQLOLEDB" 'Can't set provider property
                    strCnn = "Provider=SQLOLEDB;" & strCnn
                    .ConnectionString = strCnn
                    .Open
                End With
                Set cnnData = envOLTP.Connections("cnnNwind")
            Else
                cnnData.Provider = "SQLOLEDB"
                cnnData.CursorLocation = adUseClient
                cnnData.Open strCnn
            End If
            blnMSDASQL = False
        Case 1
            'SQL Server via DSN-less ODBC
            strCnn = "driver={SQL Server};server=" & strServer & _
                ";uid=" & strUserID & ";pwd=" & strPassword & ";database=nwind"
            If blnUseDataEnv Then
                'Use the DataEnvironment's connection
                With envOLTP.Connections("cnnNwind")
                    If .State = adStateOpen Then
                        .Close
                    End If
                    strCnn = "Provider=MSDASQL;" & strCnn
                    .ConnectionString = strCnn
                    .Open
                End With
                Set cnnData = envOLTP.Connections("cnnNwind")
            Else
                cnnData.Provider = "MSDASQL"
                cnnData.CursorLocation = adUseClient
                cnnData.Open strCnn
            End If
            blnMSDASQL = True
    End Select

    'Create a temporary Recordset
    Dim rstTemp As New ADODB.Recordset
    With rstTemp
        'Check for an identity attribute of OrderID field
        .ActiveConnection = cnnData
```

Using Transact-SQL Stored Procedures

CHAPTER 21

851

21

USING TRANSACT-
SQL STORED
PROCEDURES

```
        'Don't return any records, just the structure
        .Source = "SELECT OrderID FROM Orders WHERE OrderID = 0"
        .Open
        If .Fields(0).Attributes < 24 Or .Fields(0).Attributes > 256 Then
            'OrderID with identity returns 16, but should return 16 + 256
            'OrderID without identity returns 24
            MsgBox "OrderID field of Orders table appears to have " & _
                "an identity column.", vbOKOnly, _
                "Potential Problem with the 'nwind' Database"
        End If
        .Close
        'Check for a timestamp field in Order_Details
        .ActiveConnection = cnnData
        'Don't return any records, just the structure
        .Source = "SELECT * FROM Order_Details WHERE OrderID = 0"
        .Open
        If .Fields.Count > 5 Then
            blnHasTimestamp = True
        Else
            blnHasTimestamp = False
        End If
        .Close
        'Check the SQL Server version number
        .ActiveConnection = cnnData
        .Source = "SELECT @@version"
        .Open
        If InStr(.Fields(0).Value, "6.") Then
            blnSQLS7 = False
        Else
            blnSQLS7 = True
        End If
    End With
    Set rstTemp = Nothing

    'Repopulate the two combo boxes
    Call LoadComboBoxes
    Me.MousePointer = vbDefault
    'Start from the beginning
    Call ClearForm
    Exit Sub

ConnectTypeError:
    Me.MousePointer = vbDefault
    MsgBox Error, 48, "Set Connection Type Error"
    Exit Sub
End Sub
```

> **NOTE**
>
> You can't change the `Provider` property value of a `DataEnvironment.Connection` object. You must specify the provider as part of the `ConnectionString` property value.

Setting Up Stored Procedure Parameters

If `blnCodeParams` is **True** (the default), the `chkStoredProc_Click` event handler creates and appends `Parameter` objects to the `Parameters` collections of the `cmmCustomers`, `cmmOrders`, `cmmProducts`, and `cmmNewOrd` commands. The first three commands execute procedures that return `Recordsets`, so you can omit adding their `Parameters` collections if you use parameter list syntax to supply parameter values. The following section, "Using Alternative Stored Procedure Execution Methods," illustrates the use of the parameter list syntax. The `cmmNewOrd` command requires a complete `Parameters` collection, because the return value is the new OrderID value required for adding more than one line item to the new order. Setting `blnCodeParams` to **False** uses the `Parameters` collection of the `envOLTP.Command` object.

LISTING 21.2 CREATING AND APPENDING Parameters TO Command OBJECTS WITH CODE

```
Private Sub chkStoredProc_Click()
   Me.MousePointer = vbHourglass
   If chkStoredProc.Value Then
      blnStoredProc = True
      If blnCodeParams Then
         'Create the Customers command (multi-purpose)
         Set cmmCustomers = Nothing
         Set cmmCustomers = New ADODB.Command
         With cmmCustomers
            .ActiveConnection = cnnData
            .CommandType = adCmdStoredProc
            Set prmCustRetVal = .CreateParameter("RETURN_VALUE", _
               adInteger, adParamReturnValue, 0, 0)
            Set prmCustomers = .CreateParameter("CustsParam", _
               adChar, adParamInput, 5, "ABCDE")
            .Parameters.Append prmCustRetVal
            .Parameters.Append prmCustomers
         End With

         'Create the Orders command (multi-purpose)
         Set cmmOrders = Nothing
         Set cmmOrders = New ADODB.Command
         With cmmOrders
            .ActiveConnection = cnnData
            .CommandType = adCmdStoredProc
```

```
   Set prmOrdRetVal = .CreateParameter("RETURN_VALUE", _
      adInteger, adParamReturnValue, 0, 0)
   Set prmOrders = .CreateParameter("OrdsParam", _
      adChar, adParamInput, 5, "ABCDE")
   .Parameters.Append prmOrdRetVal
   .Parameters.Append prmOrders
End With


'Create the Products command (multi-purpose)
Set cmmProducts = Nothing
Set cmmProducts = New ADODB.Command
With cmmProducts
   .ActiveConnection = cnnData
   .CommandType = adCmdStoredProc
   Set prmProdRetVal = .CreateParameter("RETURN_VALUE", _
      adInteger, adParamReturnValue, 0, 0)
   Set prmProduct = .CreateParameter("Product", _
      adInteger, adParamInput, 0, 0)
   .Parameters.Append prmProdRetVal
   .Parameters.Append prmProduct
End With


'Create the NewOrder command (single-purpose; created here for speed)
Set cmmNewOrd = Nothing
Set cmmNewOrd = New ADODB.Command
With cmmNewOrd
   .ActiveConnection = cnnData
   .CommandType = adCmdStoredProc
   .CommandText = "ado_NewOrder_Ins"
   Set prmNewOrdRV = .CreateParameter("RETURN_VALUE", _
      adInteger, adParamReturnValue, 0, 0)
   'Parameters for Orders table
   Set prmCustID = .CreateParameter("Param1", _
      adChar, adParamInput, 5)
   Set prmEmpID = .CreateParameter("Param2", _
      adInteger, adParamInput, 0)
   Set prmOrdDate = .CreateParameter("Param3", _
      adDate, adParamInput, 0)
   Set prmReqDate = .CreateParameter("Param4", _
      adDate, adParamInput, 0)
   Set prmShipVia = .CreateParameter("Param5", _
      adInteger, adParamInput, 0)
   Set prmSName = .CreateParameter("Param6", _
      adChar, adParamInput, 40)
   Set prmSAddr = .CreateParameter("Param7", _
      adChar, adParamInput, 60)
   Set prmSCity = .CreateParameter("Param8", _
      adChar, adParamInput, 15)
   Set prmSReg = .CreateParameter("Param9", _
      adChar, adParamInput, 15)
```

continues

LISTING 21.2   CONTINUED

```
        Set prmSZIP = .CreateParameter("Param10", _
            adChar, adParamInput, 10)
        Set prmSCtry = .CreateParameter("Param11", _
            adChar, adParamInput, 15)
        'Parameters for Order_Details table
        Set prmProdID = .CreateParameter("Param12", _
            adInteger, adParamInput, 0)
        Set prmPrice = .CreateParameter("Param13", _
            adCurrency, adParamInput, 0)
        Set prmQuan = .CreateParameter("Param14", _
            adInteger, adParamInput, 0)
        Set prmDisc = .CreateParameter("Param15", _
            adSingle, adParamInput, 0)
        'Append all parameters
        .Parameters.Append prmNewOrdRV
        .Parameters.Append prmCustID
        .Parameters.Append prmEmpID
        .Parameters.Append prmOrdDate
        .Parameters.Append prmReqDate
        .Parameters.Append prmShipVia
        .Parameters.Append prmSName
        .Parameters.Append prmSAddr
        .Parameters.Append prmSCity
        .Parameters.Append prmSReg
        .Parameters.Append prmSZIP
        .Parameters.Append prmSCtry
        .Parameters.Append prmProdID
        .Parameters.Append prmPrice
        .Parameters.Append prmQuan
        .Parameters.Append prmDisc
      End With
    End If
  Else
    blnStoredProc = False
  End If
  'Repopulate the two combo boxes
  Call LoadComboBoxes
  cmdFindCust.Enabled = True
  cmdNewCustomer.Enabled = True
  Me.MousePointer = vbDefault
  'Start from the beginning
  Call ClearForm
End Sub
```

Using Alternative Stored Procedure Execution Methods

The FindOrders subprocedure of Listing 21.3 uses the following three methods to execute the adoOrdersList_CustID procedure:

- Conventional stored procedure calling syntax with parenthetical parameter lists in conjunction with a `Connection` object (SQL - ODBC option and Stored Proc check box marked and `blnCodeParams` set to **True**)

- Parameterized, reusable `Command` object with parameter `Type`, `Size`, and `Value` properties set by code (SQL - Native option and Stored Proc check box marked and `blnCodeParams` set to **True**)

- Parameterized, single-purpose `DataEnvironment.Command` object with `Value` the only property value set by code (SQL - Native option and Stored Proc check box marked and `blnCodeParams` set to **False**)

Of the three preceding methods, the first requires the minimum investment in writing and maintaining code and is satisfactory for executing any stored procedure that doesn't require output parameters or return values. The second and third methods appear in the `FindOrders` subprocedure as examples.

LISTING 21.3   THREE METHODS OF EXECUTING THE `ado_OrdersList_CustID` PROCEDURE

```
Private Sub FindOrders()
    'Purpose: Find orders for customer

    On Error GoTo FindOrdersError

    Dim strSearch As String

'... (Housekeeping code removed)

    Me.MousePointer = vbHourglass

    strMsg = "No orders found for '" & txtCompanyName.Text & "'."
    'The following code is changed to reduce server traffic
    If blnStoredProc Then
        If blnMSDASQL Then
            strCallProc = "ado_OrdersList_CustID('" & txtCustomerID.Text & "')"
            Set rstOrders = cnnData.Execute(strCallProc, lngCount, _
                adCmdStoredProc)
            lngCount = rstOrders.RecordCount
        Else
            If blnCodeParams Then
                With cmmOrders
                    .CommandText = "ado_OrdersList_CustID"
                    .Parameters(1).Type = adChar
                    .Parameters(1).Size = 5
                    .Parameters(1).Value = txtCustomerID.Text
                    Set rstOrders = .Execute
                    lngCount = rstOrders.RecordCount
                End With
```

continues

LISTING 21.3   CONTINUED

```
        Else
            With envOLTP.Commands("cmmOrdersList_CustID")
                .Parameters(1).Value = txtCustomerID.Text
                Set rstOrders = .Execute
                lngCount = .Parameters(0).Value
            End With
        End If
    End If
Else
    strSQL = "SELECT OrderID, OrderID, OrderDate, " & _
        "RequiredDate, ShippedDate " & _
        "FROM Orders WHERE CustomerID = '" & txtCustomerID.Text & _
        "' ORDER BY OrderID DESC"
    With rstOrders
        If .State = adStateOpen Then
            .Close
        End If
        .Open strSQL, cnnData, adOpenStatic
        If .RecordCount Then
            .MoveLast
            lngCount = rstOrders.RecordCount
            .MoveFirst
        End If
    End With
End If
If lngCount = 0 Then
    Me.MousePointer = vbDefault
    MsgBox strMsg, 48, "Order Entry"
Else
    If lngCount = 1 Then
        Call GetOrderData(False)
    Else
        With grdOrders
            .Rows = lngCount
            For intRow = 0 To .Rows - 1
                .Row = intRow
                For intCol = 0 To 4
                    .Col = intCol
                    If IsNull(rstOrders(intCol).Value) Then
                        'Required to prevent prior values from appearing
                        'in rows with null values (new in MSFlexGrid 6.0)
                        .Text = ""
                    Else
                        If intCol > 1 Then
                            'Year 2000 fix
                            .Text = Format(rstOrders(intCol).Value, "mm/dd/yyyy")
                        Else
                            .Text = rstOrders(intCol).Value
                        End If
```

```
            End If
          Next intCol
          rstOrders.MoveNext
        Next intRow
        .Visible = True
        .Col = 0
        .Row = 0
        .ColSel = 4
        .SetFocus
      End With
      lblOrders.Visible = True
    End If
  End If

  '... (Housekeeping code removed)

  Me.MousePointer = vbDefault
  Exit Sub

FindOrdersError:
  Me.MousePointer = vbDefault
  MsgBox Error, 48, "Find Customer Orders Error"
  Exit Sub
End Sub
```

Substituting a Locally Saved `Recordset` Object for a Jet Table

Prior versions of the OLTP application (Vb5oltp.vbp and Ado2oltp.vbp) use a hidden data control bound to the tblOrder_Details table of a local Jet 3.5x database; a bound DBGrid or DataGrid, respectively, manages the addition of line items to the Order_Details table. You can bind Visual Basic 6.0 DataGrid controls directly to `Recordset`s, so an ADODC control isn't needed. The `cmdNewOrder_Click` event handler of Listing 21.4 illustrates opening the `rstLineItems` `Recordset` over the LineItem.rst `Recordset` file and then assigning `rstLineItems` as the `DataSource` property of `dtgOrderDetails`.

LISTING 21.4 ASSIGNING A FILE-TYPE `Recordset` TO THE `DataSource` PROPERTY OF A DATAGRID

```
Private Sub cmdNewOrder_Click()
  'Purpose: Prepare for new order entry

  'Problem: MSDASQL tries to execute the command with EXEC and fails.
  If blnMSDASQL And blnStoredProc Then
    strMsg = "This version of ADO and MSDASQL is unable to process " & _
        "return values or output parameters with stored procedures. " & _
        "Choose SQL - Native in the Connection frame to test order addition."
```

continues

LISTING 21.4   CONTINUED

```
        MsgBox strMsg, vbOKOnly + vbCritical, "Unable To Add Order"
        Exit Sub
    End If

    On Error GoTo NewOrderError

    Set rstLineItems = New ADODB.Recordset
    With rstLineItems
        'Open the Recordset from the local saved copy
        .Open App.Path & "\LineItem.rst", , adOpenStatic, _
            adLockOptimistic, adCmdFile
        'Remove existing records
        If .RecordCount Then
            .MoveFirst
            Do Until .EOF
                .Delete
                .MoveNext
            Loop
        End If
    End With
    With dtgOrderDetails
        'DataMember must be empty when setting the DataSource directly
        .DataMember = ""
        Set .DataSource = rstLineItems
        .Refresh
    End With
    dtgOrderDetails.Refresh

    '... (Housekeeping code removed)

    blnNewOrder = True
    Exit Sub

NewOrderError:
    MsgBox Error, 48, "New Order Setup Error"
    Exit Sub
End Sub
```

> **TIP**
>
> You can speed the design of DataGrid controls bound directly to Recordsets by creating a temporary DataEnvironment.Command object and retrieving the fields from the underlying data source. After you format and test the DataGrid, delete the temporary Command object and set the DataSource and DataMember property values to an empty string (" "). Be particularly sure to set the DataMember property value of DataGrid controls to an empty string when you assign Recordsets as DataSources; failure to do so results in a runtime error.

Using Transact-SQL Stored Procedures

CHAPTER 21

859

21

USING TRANSACT-
SQL STORED
PROCEDURES

Passing Command Objects to Subprocedures

Passing pointers to ADO components as arguments of subprocedure or function calls lets you take advantage of common code for setting parameter values. The cmdAddNewOrder_Click event handler of Listing 21.5 calls the NewOrdParams subprocedure shown in Listing 21.6. For parameters created with code (blnCodeParams = **True**), NewOrdParams sets the cmmNewOrd parameter values; otherwise, NewOrdParams sets the parameter values of the appropriate member of the DataEnvironment.Commands collection (cmmNewOrder_Ins).

LISTING 21.5 CALLING A SUBPROCEDURE TO SET PARAMETER VALUES

```
Private Sub cmdAddNewOrder_Click()
    'Purpose: Add a new order to the Orders and Order Details tables

    Dim lngOrderID As Long
    Dim intCtr As Integer
    Dim lngEmployeeID As Long
    Dim lngShipVia As Long
    Const RED_TEXT = 255 'Red in RGB color values

    On Error GoTo AddOrderError

    '... (Housekeeping and validation code removed)

    rstLineItems.MoveFirst

    cmdAddNewOrder.Enabled = False
    cmdCancelNewOrder.Enabled = False
    Me.MousePointer = vbHourglass

    If blnStoredProc Then
        If blnCodeParams Then
            With cmmNewOrd
                Call NewOrdParams(cmmNewOrd, lngEmployeeID, lngShipVia)
                .Execute
                lngOrderID = .Parameters(0).Value
            End With
        Else
            With envOLTP.Commands("cmmNewOrder_Ins")
                Call NewOrdParams(envOLTP.Commands("cmmNewOrder_Ins"), _
                    lngEmployeeID, lngShipVia)
                .Execute
                lngOrderID = .Parameters(0).Value
            End With
        End If
        If lngOrderID > 0 Then
            txtOrderID.Text = lngOrderID
            With rstLineItems
```

continues

LISTING 21.5 CONTINUES

```
                .MoveNext
            If Not .EOF Then
                'Add the remaining line items
                strSQL = ""
                Call AddLineItems(lngOrderID)
                cnnData.Execute strSQL, lngCount, adCmdText
                If lngCount = .RecordCount Then
                    'All is OK
                Else
                    'Couldn't add the records
                End If
            Else
                'Only one line item, so finished
            End If
        End With
    Else
        'Error condition
        MsgBox "Order not added by ado_NewOrder_Ins", vbOKOnly, _
            "Stored Procedure Failure"
        Exit Sub
    End If
Else
    'Obtain the tentative order ID
    strSQL = "SELECT MAX(OrderID) LastOrder FROM Orders"
    With rstOrders
        If .State = adStateOpen Then
            .Close
        End If
        .Open strSQL, cnnData, adOpenForwardOnly
        lngOrderID = .Fields(0).Value + 1
    End With
    txtOrderID.Enabled = True
    txtOrderID.Text = lngOrderID

    'INSERT the order information
    On Error GoTo SQLServerError
    'Valid for Transact-SQL only
    strSQL = "BEGIN TRAN INSERT Orders "
    strSQL = strSQL & "VALUES(" & _
    txtOrderID.Text & ", '" & _
    txtCustomerID.Text & "', " & _
    lngEmployeeID & ", '" & _
    txtOrderDate.Text & "', '" & _
    txtRequiredDate.Text & "', NULL, " & _
    lngShipVia & ", NULL, '" & _
    txtShipName.Text & "', '" & _
    txtShipAddress.Text & "', '" & _
    txtShipCity.Text & "', '" & _
    txtShipRegion.Text & "', '" & _
    txtShipPostalCode.Text & "', '" & _
```

Using Transact-SQL Stored Procedures

CHAPTER 21

861

21

USING TRANSACT-
SQL STORED
PROCEDURES

```
        txtShipCountry.Text & "')"
        'ShippedDate and Freight (NULL above) aren't applicable to orders
        'Now add the line items
        Call AddLineItems(lngOrderID)
        'Execute the SQL statement
        'Problem: Works with SQL Server 7.0, fails with 6.5
        'cnnData.Execute strSQL

        With cmmTrans
            .ActiveConnection = cnnData
            .CommandType = adCmdText
            .CommandText = strSQL
            .Execute
        End With
    End If


    '... (Housekeeping code removed)


    'Display the order details in the listbox
    Call cmdShowDetail_Click

    Me.MousePointer = vbDefault
    blnNewOrder = False
    Exit Sub

SQLServerError:
    'SQL Server automatically rolls back a single failed transaction
    Me.MousePointer = vbDefault
    MsgBox Error, 48, "Unable to Add Order " & lngOrderID & " with MSDASQL"
    cmdAddNewOrder.Enabled = True
    cmdCancelNewOrder.Enabled = True
    Exit Sub

AddOrderError:
    Me.MousePointer = vbDefault
    MsgBox Error, 48, "Add New Order Error"
    cmdAddNewOrder.Enabled = True
    cmdCancelNewOrder.Enabled = True
    Exit Sub
End Sub
```

LISTING 21.6 CODE TO SET MULTIPLE INPUT PARAMETER VALUES FOR AN INSERT OPERATION

```
Private Sub NewOrdParams(cmmTemp As ADODB.Command, _
                         lngEmployeeID As Long, _
                         lngShipVia As Long)

    'An example of passing a Command object as a parameter
    With cmmTemp
        .Parameters(1).Value = txtCustomerID.Text
```

continues

LISTING 21.6 CONTINUED

```
    .Parameters(2).Value = lngEmployeeID
    .Parameters(3).Value = CDate(txtOrderDate.Text)
    .Parameters(4).Value = CDate(txtRequiredDate.Text)
    .Parameters(5).Value = lngShipVia
    .Parameters(6).Value = txtShipName.Text
    .Parameters(7).Value = txtShipAddress.Text
    .Parameters(8).Value = txtShipCity.Text
    If Len(txtShipRegion) > 0 Then
        .Parameters(9).Value = txtShipRegion.Text
    Else
        .Parameters(9).Value = Null
    End If
    .Parameters(10).Value = txtShipPostalCode.Text
    .Parameters(11).Value = txtShipCountry.Text
    .Parameters(12).Value = rstLineItems(1).Value
    .Parameters(13).Value = rstLineItems(4).Value
    .Parameters(14).Value = rstLineItems(0).Value
    .Parameters(15).Value = rstLineItems(5).Value
  End With
End Sub
```

> **TIP**
>
> Send NULLs, not empty strings, to stored procedure parameters that obtain values from text boxes. Your stored procedure can supply default values, if desired, for information not supplied by the client application.

Adding Field Lists to Accommodate `Timestamp` Fields

To minimize server round-trips, the Ado2proc.vbp project doesn't use a stored procedure to add multiple line items to an order. Thus the SQL statement's VALUES list must accommodate tables, such as Order_Details, that have timestamp fields to resolve concurrency issues. SQL Server 7.0 lets ADO 2.0 send NULL values to timestamp fields; version 6.5 doesn't. Thus users of version 6.5 must add a field list to the VALUES statement to prevent the need to send values for every field of the table. Code in the optConnect_Click event handler (refer to Listing 21.1) detects whether SQL Server 6.*x* serves as the back end. If so, blnSQLS7 is set to **False**, and code in the AddLineItems subprocedure (see Listing 21.7) adds the field list and omits the trailing timestamp NULL value.

LISTING 21.7 ADDING A FIELD LIST TO AVOID ERRORS WHEN SENDING NULL VALUES TO SQL SERVER 6.5 Timestamp FIELDS

```
Private Sub AddLineItems(lngOrderID As Long)
  'INSERT the line item information for each record
  With rstLineItems
```

Using Transact-SQL Stored Procedures

CHAPTER 21

863

21

USING TRANSACT-
SQL STORED
PROCEDURES

```
  Do Until .EOF
      strSQL = strSQL & " INSERT Order_Details"
      If blnHasTimestamp And Not blnSQLS7 Then
          strSQL = strSQL & "(OrderID, ProductID, " & _
              "UnitPrice, Quantity, Discount)"
      End If
      strSQL = strSQL & " VALUES(" & _
      lngOrderID & ", " & _
      rstLineItems(1).Value & ", " & _
      rstLineItems(4).Value & ", " & _
      rstLineItems(0).Value & ", " & _
      rstLineItems(5).Value
      'Value must be supplied for a timestamp field, if present
      If blnHasTimestamp And blnSQLS7 Then
          strSQL = strSQL & ", NULL) "
      Else
          strSQL = strSQL & ") "
      End If
      .MoveNext
      If .EOF And Not blnStoredProc Then
          'Finish the transaction (Transact-SQL)
          strSQL = strSQL & " COMMIT TRAN"
      End If
  Loop
  End With
End Sub
```

TROUBLESHOOTING STORED PROCEDURES WITH THE T-SQL DEBUGGER

You can solve most problems with stored procedures by executing them in SQL Server 6.*x*'s ISQL_w or version 7.0's SQL Server Query Analyzer. Both of these applications return error messages with reasonably complete explanations for execution failure. If your stored procedure is very complex or you experience unexpected problems when executing the stored procedure from code, you might need Visual Studio 6.0 Enterprise Edition's T-SQL Debugger to troubleshoot the source of the problem.

T-SQL Debugger works only with Microsoft SQL Server 6.5 with Service Pack 1 or higher or SQL Server 7.0 and does not differ markedly from the T-SQL Debugger of Visual Basic 5.0. The primary changes to the Visual Studio 6.0 version is support for ADO through the Data Environment Designer, in addition to handling RDO stored procedure calls via the User Connection Designer. The Debugger uses a combination of RDO 2.0, ODBC, SQL Server Data Management Objects (SQL-DMO), and DCOM or Automation Manager to enable interactive debugging of stored procedures.

> **NOTE**
>
> You can use T-SQL Debugger to execute batch SQL scripts, but ISQL_w and, especially, SQL Server Query Analyzer offer a much better approach to interactive SQL batch execution. T-SQL Debugger uses SQL-DMO, so execution time is considerably slower than with ISQL_w or Query Analyzer.

Setting Up and Testing T-SQL Debugger

Before running T-SQL Debugger from Visual Basic 6.0, perform the following setup and initial test operations:

1. Open Windows NT 4+ Control Panel's Services tool to verify that SQL Server runs from a domain account with Administrator privileges, not the System Account. Select MSSQLServer in the Service list and click Startup to open the Service dialog. If SQL Server is running on the System Account, select the This Account option, select the Administrators account to use, type the password and password confirmation, and then click OK to close the Service dialog and Close to exit the Services tool.

2. Install and register the server-side components for SQL Server 6.5 SP3 or later and Automation Manager for Windows NT, if you haven't already done so. Run Setup.exe from the Visual Studio 6.0 or Visual Basic 6.0 distribution CD-ROM, skip through the Setup Wizard dialogs to Server Setups dialog, select Launch BackOffice Installation Wizard and click Install.

   Insert the Visual Studio 6.0 distribution CD-ROM 2, and click OK. In the first dialog of the BackOffice Server Setup 4.0, select Custom and click Next. Click Next to bypass the Disk Space Requirements dialog. In the BackOffice Programs and Their Components dialog, select SQL Server Debugging, MS Data Access Components, and Visual InterDev Server. Click Next until installation commences. You must reboot the server to finish the installation.

3. To set up DCOM on your Windows NT 4.0 server for SQL Server debugging, run Dcomcnfg.exe (in your \Winnt\System32 folder) to open the Distributed COM Configuration Properties sheet. Click the Default Security tab, and then click Edit Default in the Default Access Permissions frame to open the Registry Value Permissions dialog. If security isn't an issue, give Everyone access permissions; otherwise, add individual accounts for developers who need to debug stored procedures. Stop and restart SQL Server after making changes to access permissions.

4. If your client runs Windows 95, make sure you have the latest version of DCOM for Windows 95 installed and operating. When this book was written, DCOM version 1.1 was current and available for download from http://www.microsoft.com/cominfo/dcom95/default.htm. Execute Dcomcnfg.exe from your \Windows\System folder, click the Default Properties tab, and make sure the Enable

Using Transact-SQL Stored Procedures

CHAPTER 21

865

21

USING TRANSACT-
SQL STORED
PROCEDURES

Distributed COM on This Computer check box is marked. The Default Authentication Level must be set to Connect and the Default Impersonation Level to Impersonate.

> **NOTE**
>
> Windows 98 and Windows NT 4.0 Workstation install DCOM during the Setup process with the default settings described in the preceding step.

5. Add the T-SQL Debugger to Visual Basic by choosing <u>A</u>dd-Ins, <u>A</u>dd-In Manager to open the Add-In Manager dialog, double-click the VB T-SQL Debugger in the Available Add-Ins list, and click OK to close the dialog and add the T-SQL Debugger as an Add-Ins menu choice. Click OK to close the message box that confirms the addition.

> **TIP**
>
> Don't specify the Load on Startup option for the T-SQL Debugger. Running the Debugger when you don't need it consumes substantial client resources and might greatly slow execution of stored procedures on the server.

6. Choose <u>A</u>dd-Ins, T-SQL Debugger to open the Visual Basic Batch T-SQL Debugger properties sheet.

7. In the Settings page, open the DSN list and select an ODBC DSN for an SQL Server database that includes stored procedures, such as this chapter's nwind or the pubs sample database. A fully qualified DSN completes settings for the SQL Server, Database, UID, and Password combo boxes. You can create a new System DSN by clicking Register DSN.

8. Accept the default Lock Type value (`rdConcurReadOnly`) and set the Result Set value to `rdOpenForwardOnly` to improve performance. Accept the default Options value (`rdExecDirect`), as illustrated by Figure 21.21.

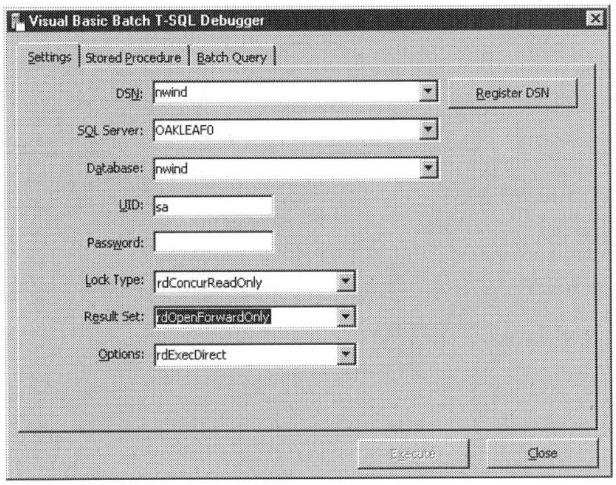

FIGURE 21.21
Setting up the T-SQL Debugger to use the nwind database.

8. Click the Stored Procedures tab, open the Procedure Name list and select a row-returning stored procedure, such as nwind's `ado_CustLists_Name` procedure. Type an appropriate parameter value, such as **w%**, in the Value text box. The value you type appears in the parameters list of the CALL statement in the Query text box (see Figure 21.22).

FIGURE 21.22

Selecting a stored procedure to execute and providing parameter value(s).

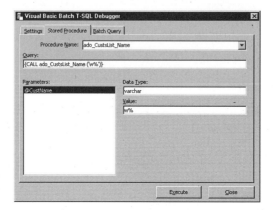

9. Click Execute to open the T-SQL Debugger window. After a few seconds, the procedure's `CREATE PROC` statement appears in the upper pane. Click the Go button or press F5 to execute the procedure; the execution statement and query result set appear in the lower pane. Figure 21.23 illustrates the result set for the procedure and parameter value of the preceding step.

FIGURE 21.23

Executing a stored procedure from the T-SQL Debugger window.

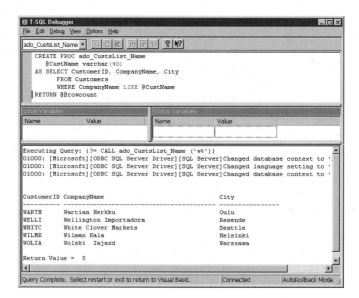

> **NOTE**
>
> The return value parameter placeholder (?=) doesn't appear in the CALL state-
> ment of the Stored Procedures page of the Visual Basic Batch T-SQL Debugger
> properties sheet. It appears correctly in the T-SQL Debugger window as { ?=
> CALL *ProcName* (*paramlist*) }.

10. Close the T-SQL Debugger window to return to the Visual Basic Batch T-SQL Debugger
    properties sheet; then click Close to return to Visual Basic.

Debugging Stored Procedures in Design Mode

To execute and step through stored procedures from the Data View window, do the following:

1. Open the Data View window of a project having stored procedures executed by
   *DataEnvironment.*Command objects, such as Ado2proc.vbp.

2. In the DataEnvironment window, open the *ConnectionName* properties sheet, cnnNwind
   for this example. Set the Connection property values to point to the server with T-SQL
   debugging enabled, and specify the database (nwind).

> **NOTE**
>
> Code in the optConnect_Click event handler of frmOrderEntry sets the
> cnnNwind Connection property values. For debugging via the Data View win-
> dow, you must set design-time properties for the Connection.

3. Right-click the Command object for the stored procedure, ado_OrdersData_ID for this
   example, and choose De*bug* to open the Parameters dialog.

4. Type an appropriate parameter value in the Value text box (see Figure 21.24) and click OK.

FIGURE 21.24

*Providing a para-
meter value to a
stored procedure
when debugging in
design mode.*

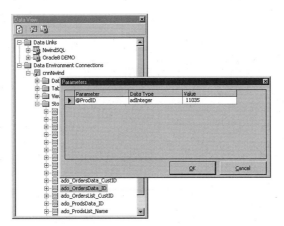

5. Press F5 or click the Go button to execute the stored procedure in the T-SQL Debugger window (see Figure 21.25).

FIGURE 21.25

Providing a parameter value to a stored procedure when debugging in design mode.

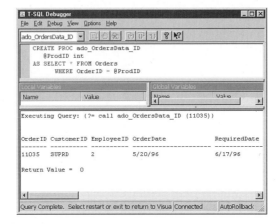

Debugging in Run Mode

To debug T-SQL stored procedures in run mode, do the following:

1. In the Visual Basic menu choose Tools, T-SQL Debugging Options to open the T-SQL Debugging Options . . . dialog.

2. Verify that both check boxes are marked, and alter the maximum number of query rows to return and timeout value (in milliseconds), if desired (see Figure 21.26).

FIGURE 21.26

Setting T-SQL Debugging Options for run mode.

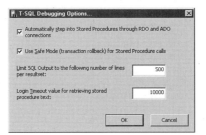

3. Set a breakpoint in your code on a line that executes a stored procedure from a *DataEnvironment.*Command object.

4. Run the application to the breakpoint, then press F8 to execute the line and start the T-SQL Debugger.

5. Click Step or Go in the T-SQL Debugger window's toolbar to proceed with stored procedure execution.

NOTE

Visual Basic 6.0's T-SQL Debugger exhibits inconsistent behavior with the Beta 3 version of SQL Server 7.0 used to write this book, but generally behaves as expected with SQL Server 6.5 SP3 or higher. It's likely that T-SQL Debugger's problems with SQL Server 7.0 will be resolved when Microsoft releases the commercial version.

DATABASES, INTRANETS, AND THE INTERNET

PART
VI

IN THIS PART

INTEGRATING DATABASES WITH INTRANETS AND THE INTERNET

IN THIS CHAPTER

The phenomenal growth of the Internet and expansion of corporate intranets throughout the world has resulted in an epidemic of browser mania. Conventional client database front ends, including a large percentage of existing Visual Basic database projects, are giving way to browser-based applications. The incentive to adopt a Web browser as a universal GUI is ubiquity; virtually everyone with a PC has at least some inkling of browser-based document display and navigation. Thus information technology managers expect to reduce user training costs and give computer-illiterate top executives direct access to information from individual databases, data marts, and large-scale data warehouses.

Another goal of browser-based database front ends is to move their execution to a combination of Web and application servers, eliminating (or at least minimizing) the need to distribute new and updated data access executables to desktop and laptop clients. Browser-based applications and, potentially, operating systems are the foundation of the lightweight Network Computer (NC) client championed by Oracle's Larry Ellison. Despite the lack of commercial success of the NC to date, lightweight client PCs with a browser as the primary GUI are useful for routine database lookup operations and light-duty data entry. HTML is a relatively inefficient method for transferring data over a network, so Web-based applications are ill suited for high-performance, heads-down data entry applications.

Browser-based applications have the potential to threaten the desktop hegemony of Windows, because all PC operating systems offer Web browsers. Thus, Microsoft has taken a middle-of-the-road approach with Web page generation on the server using Active Server Pages (ASP), complex GUI components delivered to and stored on the client as ActiveX controls or documents, and Dynamic HTML (DHTML) for client-side page manipulation and state maintenance. Microsoft also promotes Microsoft Transaction Server (MTS) 2.0 as the "Web glue" for the components that form the middle tier of three-tier Internet and intranet applications.

This chapter begins with an explanation of Microsoft's "Digital Nervous System" concept and Windows Distributed interNet Applications Architecture, both of which are Internet- and data-centric technologies. Next comes an overview of the new Internet and intranet features of Visual Basic 6.0 and their significance to database developers. The chapter concludes with simple sample projects for two of these new features—WebClasses and DHTML applications. The remaining chapters of the "Databases, Intranets, and the Internet" part cover ActiveX Documents, Remote Data Service, and creating commercial Internet applications with Visual Basic 6.0.

> **NOTE**
>
> This chapter assumes familiarity with HTML semantics, simple Web page author-
> ing, and Microsoft-specific technologies, such as ASP. You need Internet
> Explorer (IE) 4+ (installed by Visual Studio 6.0) and Internet Information Server
> (IIS) 4+ running under Windows NT Server 4+ with Service Pack 3+ or the
> Personal Web Server (PWS) running under Windows 9x to run the sample appli-
> cations of this chapter. You can install IIS 4.0 and PWS from Microsoft's free
> Windows NT Option Pack CD-ROM. The Option Pack also installs MTS 2.0 and,
> optionally, Microsoft Message Queue Server (MSMQ) 1.0.

CUTTING THROUGH THE HYPE FOR MICROSOFT'S DIGITAL NERVOUS SYSTEM

Bill Gates introduced Microsoft's vision of a Digital Nervous System (DNS) at the first annual Microsoft CEO Summit Conference held in Seattle on May 8, 1997. Subsequently, Microsoft has run full-page (and even multipage) advertisements in major business publications in an attempt to articulate what was then a very vague concept. The idea behind DNS was that remaining competitive in the "digital age" requires firms to adopt a new information technolo-gy mindset. By the second CEO Summit in May 1998, the Digital Nervous System concept had evolved to the following six tenets:

- *PC computing architecture* (running Windows NT Workstation and Server)
- *All information in digital form* (stored in Microsoft SQL Server, located with Microsoft Index Server, or both)
- *Universal email* (handled by Microsoft Exchange Server)
- *Ubiquitous connectivity* (via intranets and Internet sites running Microsoft Internet Information Server)
- *Common end-user productivity tools* (specifically Microsoft Office, Internet Explorer, and add-ons such as Microsoft NetShow)
- *Integrated business-specific applications* (created with Visual Studio 6.0, having ActiveX components running under Microsoft Transaction Server, and with summarized data sup-plied by Microsoft Decision Support Services)

The last of the preceding items holds the greatest significance for Visual Basic database devel-opers. Regardless of Microsoft's considerable oversimplification of what's needed for organi-zations to remain competitive in 2000 and beyond, Microsoft's multi-million-dollar advertising campaign for DNS in *Fortune*, *Business Week*, *Forbes*, and other business journals has a continuing, substantial impact on top management. Understanding the buzzwords and what's behind them is now as important to developers as the ability to write professional-quality VBA code.

> **NOTE**
>
> Only the initial italicized phrases in the preceding and following lists are direct quotations from Microsoft's DNS Web site and white papers.

The purported benefits of implementing a Digital Nervous System are the ability of an organization to:

- *Act faster* by making information immediately available to those who need it
- *React to anything* by allowing affected decision makers and their subordinates to collaborate, regardless of location and time zone
- *Make informed decisions* by providing access to summarized and detailed data
- *Get closer to customers* with extranets that allow selective external access to private intranet data via a secure network connection
- *Focus on business, not technology,* by using only Microsoft's integrated software solutions to gain the preceding benefits

The last member of the preceding list may appear cynical on first reading, but Microsoft's primary objective in promoting the benefits of DNS is to improve Microsoft's competitive position. If Visual Basic developers and their clients improve *their* competitive position, so much the better.

> **NOTE**
>
> Microsoft's DNS site appeared to be missing a few strands of deoxyribonucleic acid (DNA) in late August 1998. Every link on the More Information - Bill Gates Describes the Digital Nervous System page (`http://www.microsoft.com/dns/moreinfo/default.asp`) returned `HTTP Error 404 - Not Found` messages.

▶ **See** "Organizing a Chart-Based Decision-Support Application," **p. 412** and "Delivering Information to the Client," **p. 1056**

Bill Gates used his satellite broadcast to the September 2, 1998, Microsoft Developer Days (DevDays) gatherings, during which Microsoft formally announced Visual Studio 6.0, to expand on the relationship between DNS and Visual Studio 6.0 components. On the topic of "make informed decisions," Gates said, "Our vision is that the knowledge workers should be empowered to see the information, to dive in, get down at the detail level, to use things like rich graphs and PivotTable views, to understand what's going on inside the business." Databases provide the source for "rich graphs and PivotTable views." Databases are central to DNS's "All information in digital form" mandate.

GETTING A GRIP ON WINDOWS DISTRIBUTED INTERNET APPLICATIONS ARCHITECTURE

Windows Distributed interNet Applications Architecture (DNA, not WDNAA) is Microsoft's implementation layer for the Digital Nervous System. Microsoft defines Windows DNA as follows:

> "Windows DNA applications use a standard set of Windows-based services that address the requirements of all tiers of modern distributed applications: user interface and navigation, business processes, and storage.

> "The heart of Windows DNA is the integration of Web and client/server application development models through a common object model. Windows DNA uses a common set of services such as components, Dynamic HTML, Web browser and server, scripting, transactions, message queuing, security, directory, database and data access, systems management, and user interface. These services are exposed in a unified way at all tiers for applications to use.

> "In addition, because Windows DNA fully embraces an open approach to Web computing, it builds on the many important standards Efforts approved by bodies such as the World Wide Web Consortium (W3C) and the Internet Engineering Task Force (IETF)."

NOTE

The preceding quotation is from Microsoft's September 1997 Windows DNA white paper, "Integrating Web and Client/Server Computing," available at `http://www.microsoft.com/dna/overview/dnawp.asp`.

Windows DNA is a synonym for "COM everywhere." The Common Object Model (COM) or Distributed COM (DCOM) is the "unified way" to interconnect the components of Windows DNA. ADO is Microsoft's preferred implementation of "database and data access," and you can expect that all future Microsoft intranet- and Internet-related products will depend on COM-based OLE DB and ADO, to the exclusion of ODBC, DAO, RDO, and other traditional database connectivity technologies.

> **NOTE**
>
> Dynamic HTML is an interim technology that ultimately will be replaced by Extensible Markup Language (XML), probably in the first few years of the next millenium. XML, like HTML, is derived from the Standardized General Markup Language (SGML), an international standard used for publishing complex, formatted documents, such as aircraft operating manuals. The XML object model lets Web page authors and database developers define custom tags to represent any entity, such as data returned by a query, as *structured data*. Thus XML permits virtually all Web content for a site to be retrieved from databases. XML is a radical departure from the well-defined syntax of HTML and requires a completely new set of development tools. IE 4.0 includes limited support for XML; IE 5.0 provides much more comprehensive support of the forthcoming W3C XML standard. Microsoft intended to XML-enabled `ADODB.Recordset` objects by providing an `adPersistXML` option for the `Recordset.Save` method, but removed this feature prior to release of ADO 2.0. The Microsoft Site Builder's XML section (`http://www.microsoft.com/workshop/xml/default.asp`) offers a series of white papers describing Microsoft's implementation of XML.

EXAMINING THE NEW INTERNET-RELATED FEATURES OF VISUAL BASIC 6.0

Visual Basic 5.0 introduced several new Internet- and intranet-related features to Visual Basic developers. ActiveX Documents (formerly OLEDocs) made Visual Basic forms viewable in IE 3+, letting programmers easily develop browser-enabled database front ends. Many of the other Visual Basic 5.0 Internet features provided relatively low-level TCP/IP services, such as the Winsock control for TCP and UDP communication, and the Internet Transfer control for file transfer via FTP or HTTP. Visual Basic 5.0 also introduced apartment-model multithreading for ActiveX DLLs running under multithreaded applications, such as IE 3+ and IIS.

In conformance with Microsoft's newly clarified DNS and Windows DNA strategies, Visual Basic 6.0 offers a variety of features designed for Internet- and intranet-based projects. The following sections describe the new features in the context of DNS and Windows DNA.

Remote Data Service for Database Access

 Remote Data Service (RDS) 2.0, formerly known as the Advanced Data Connector (ADC), is a "lightweight" version of ADO designed specifically for but not limited to three-tier applications using MTS 2.0. RDS delivers a disconnected (stateless) `ADOR.Recordset` object from the Web server via HTTP to an ActiveX-compliant browser, presently limited to IIS 3+.

`ADOR.Recordset` objects can serve as data providers to data-bound ActiveX controls contained in the browser's Document object. The user can update the data at his or her leisure and then return the data to the server to update the underlying tables.

▶ **See** "Working with Bulk Updates and Disconnected `Recordsets`," **p. 764** (Ch19)

`ADOR.Recordset` objects behave similarly to disconnected `ADODB.Recordset` objects having the `LockType` property set to `adLockBatchOptimistic`. Unlike `ADODB.Recordsets`, you can manipulate `ADODB.Recordset` objects with ActiveX scripting languages within the IE environment. A client-side `RDS.DataControl` object emulates an invisible ADODC to serve as the `DataSource` for ADO-compliant ActiveX controls, such as the DataGrid or DataCombo, and IE 4+'s Dynamic HTML. `RDS.DataControl` employs the `RDS.DataSpace` object to create a proxy that handles communication with the server-side `RDS.DataFactory` object that, in turn, connects to the OLE DB data provider. You can substitute a custom MTS 2.0 component for the default `RDS.DataFactory` object. Figure 22.1 shows Object Browser listing a few of the properties and methods of the `ADOR.Recordset` object, which you must add to your Data Project by specifying a reference to the Microsoft ActiveX Data Objects Recordset 2.0 Library (Msador15.dll).

22

INTEGRATING
DATABASES

FIGURE 22.1
Object Browser displaying methods and properties of the `ADOR.Recordset` object.

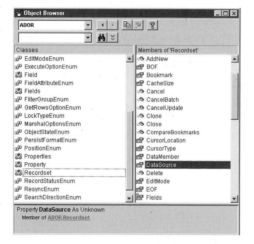

Chapter 24, "Working with Remote Data Service," provides examples of the use of RDS 2.0 with IE 4.01 and IIS 4.0. Microsoft's "Remote Data Service in MDAC 2.0" white paper at `http://msdn.microsoft.com/developer/news/feature/datajul98/remdata.htm` explains the architecture of RDS.

NOTE

RDS 2.0 is now considered an intranet-only feature because it's limited to deployment with IE 3+ browsers and requires the full set of ADO 2.0 support components on the client. (Earlier versions of RDS had a much lighter-weight set of ADOR support DLLs).

WebClasses for Internet Information Server 4.0 Applications

A *WebClass* is a special type of Visual Basic 6.0 project that lets you create IIS-hosted Internet Services API (ISAPI) applications to run within an ASP. You create an .asp file with your favorite HTML editor (even Visual Notepad) or take an existing ASP; then add VBA code in a WebClass DLL to respond to events such as clicking a Submit button. Alternatively, you can write a WebClass that generates all the HTML for the page, but it isn't likely that many Visual Basic programmers would want to design complex pages with `Response.Write` `<HTML>...Response.Write</HTML>` statements. An .asp file can host only one WebClass, but a WebClass can contain multiple modules called *WebItems*. Each WebClass project creates a virtual directory on your Web server, which must be either IIS 4.0 or the current version of PWS. Figure 22.2 shows the WebClass Designer (Wbcls1.dsr) for Visual Basic 6.0's wcDemo.vbp sample project in the ...\Samples\Vb98\Wcdemo folder.

FIGURE 22.2

The WebClass Designer for the wcDemo.vbp sample application.

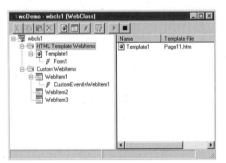

WebClass DLLs run on the server and generate browser-independent HTML in .htm or .asp files; thus WebClasses are suited for both intranet and Internet applications. The "Creating a Simple Data-Enabled WebClass Project" section later in the chapter explains how to write and deploy elementary WebClass projects.

> **NOTE**
>
> Six printed pages of release notes for WebClasses are available in the Readmevb.htm file, which is located in your \Program Files\Microsoft Visual Studio folder. Be sure to read all the WebClass topics before attempting to run Microsoft's Wcdemo.vbp sample project. As an example, you must change all instances of **Me** in wbcls1 to `WebClass` before compiling Wcdemo.vbp to Wcdemo.dll.

Dynamic HTML Applications

Dynamic HTML (DHTML) is a client-side feature of IE 4+ that lets you move operations on Web pages from the server to the client. DHTML challenges the trend toward running applications from the server, as discussed in the introduction to this chapter, by running a substantial amount of scripting code on the client. The primary advantage of DHTML is that you don't need to reload the page from the server each time you want to change a property of a page element. DHTML pages also can hold application state locally between DHTML page requests; unlike conventional HTML pages, you don't need to temporarily store client state on the Web server. Microsoft promotes DHTML as the preferred approach to delivering data to the browser.

DHTML combines the three following elements:

- *Cascading Style Sheets* (CSS), a W3C standard for formatting text and other objects and precisely positioning objects on a Web page.

- *Scripting language(s)*, such as ECMAScript (formerly JavaScript) or VBScript, to respond to browser- and user-generated events on the page.

- *Document Object Model (DOM)*, which defines collections of paragraphs, images, and other objects on the page that can be manipulated by the scripting language. IE 4.0 and Netscape Navigator 4.0 have different DOMs, so Visual Basic 6.0 DHTML applications currently are suited only for intranets having IE 4.01 installed on all connected clients.

Figure 22.3 shows the DHTML Page Designer for the Event Bubbling page of the Dhshowme.vbp sample project in the ...\Samples\Vb98\Dhshowme folder. The Page Designer consists of a tree view of members of the page's DOM in the left pane and the rendered page view of the selected object in the right pane. The modDHTML module of Dhshowme.vbp contains PutProperty and GetProperty subprocedures to persist the state of the page as a **String** variable in a cookie.

FIGURE 22.3

The DHTML Page Designer for the Dhshowme.vbp sample application's Event Bubbling page.

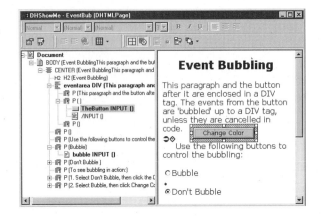

NOTE

You can find release notes for the DHTML Page Designer in the Readmevb.htm file (which also contains release notes for WebClasses). Be sure to read the Page Designer topics before attempting to use the DHTML Page Designer.

Cab File Distribution with the Package and Deployment Wizard

 The new Package and Deployment Wizard, which replaces Visual Basic 5.0's Setup Wizard, automates the packaging of entire projects, ActiveX controls, and ActiveX documents for Web-based deployment. Figure 22.4 shows the Package and Deployment Wizard's Web Publishing Site dialog in which you specify the destination URL (in this case the root Web of the \OAK-LEAF1 server) and the publishing protocol (HTTP Post).

FIGURE 22.4

The Web Publishing Site dialog of Visual Basic 6.0's Package and Deployment Wizard.

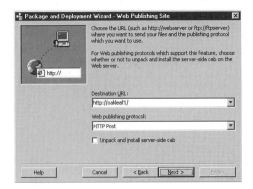

> **NOTE**
>
> You must have previously installed Posting Acceptor 2.0 for IIS 4.0 from the BackOffice Setup program and verify that you have write permissions for the location in which you want to install the package with the HTTP Post publishing protocol. As you do for the other new Visual Basic 6.0 Internet features, make sure to view the Package and Deployment Wizard topics in Readmevb.htm before using the Wizard.

Download Support for ActiveX Documents with Internet Explorer 4+

▶ See "Packaging ActiveX Document Objects," p. 912

The Package and Deployment Wizard automatically adds to the *Project*.vbd file the ActiveX document version and the location of the server from which to download the ActiveX document's *Project*.cab file. These additions to the .vbd file eliminate the need for a separate download page and manual coding of the location and name of the ActiveX document for clients using IE 4+; to support IE 3.0 you must continue to provide the download page and the standard VBScript code that specifies the *Project*.cab and *Project*.vbd files for the document.

> **NOTE**
>
> Contrary to the information in the Manually Deploying ActiveX Documents online help topic, there is no CodeBase Fixup Utility or Readme.txt file in the Tools folder.

Microsoft Transaction Server 2.0 Support

▶ See "Designing Efficient MTS Components," p. 1005

Visual Basic 6.0's added support for Microsoft Transaction Server (MTS) 2.0 isn't specific to Internet and intranet applications, but MTS plays an important role in three-tier Windows DNA. The MS Transaction Server add-in automates refreshing of MTS components, and the new `MTSTransactionMode` property of class modules lets you specify how the transaction processor feature of MTS treats the packaged component. Chapter 26, "Taking Advantage of Microsoft Transaction Server 2.0," and Chapter 27, "Creating and Deploying MTS Components," provide detailed coverage of MTS 2.0.

CREATING A SIMPLE DATA-ENABLED WEBCLASS PROJECT

The sample WebClass project mentioned in the "WebClasses for Internet Information Server 4.0 Applications" section earlier in the chapter writes HTML to demonstrate the dynamic creation of very simple Web page text. Visual Basic database developers usually need to display and update information in someone else's complex Web pages. WebClasses let you leverage your investment in gaining Visual Basic database programming expertise, eliminating the need to learn additional scripting languages, such as ECMAScript or VBScript.

> **NOTE**
>
> The wcPrdList.vbp project in the \Ddg_vb6\Chaptr22 folder of the accompanying CD-ROM is a complete WebClass project that you can compile and run without performing the sometimes-tedious work described in the sections that follow. You won't gain the experience and satisfaction from writing your first WebClass project if you simply run the project and examine the code.

The following subsection demonstrates how to design a simple tabular Web page optimized for displaying field values of a query against the Products, Categories, and Suppliers tables of Nwind.mdb. The remaining subsections lead you through the steps required to write the WebClass code to display in IE 4.01 the first record of the query.

Creating the WebClass Template with FrontPage 98

WebClasses can output HTML from a Visual Basic **String** variable, but writing HTML in a text editor for even a simple page from scratch is a daunting project, except for experienced (or masochistic) page designers who prefer Visual Notepad to WSIWYG authoring applications. Microsoft FrontPage 98, included with Visual Studio 6.0, lets you create a simple template page with minimal effort.

To create a template page with a table to accommodate display of the first record of the product list query result set, do the following:

1. Launch FrontPage Explorer and add a new folder named **WebClasses** to your Web root (http://*servername*/WebClasses).

2. Use FrontPage editor to create a new page named **Products** in the WebClasses folder. Specify **Northwind Product List** as the title of the page.

3. Add a text title at the top of the page; then add a table with three columns and 12 rows.

> **NOTE**
>
> The FrontPage Server extensions for IIS 4.0 or PWS are required to use FrontPage Explorer and Editor. Setup installs the appropriate version of the FrontPage Server extensions unless you specify otherwise during installation. You must manually install the FrontPage 98 client executables from the \Frontpage folder of Visual Studio 6.0 CD-ROM 2. If you don't want to install FrontPage, you can skip this section and use in the next section the OrigProd.htm file in the \Ddg_vb6\Chaptr22 folder of the accompanying CD-ROM. Fp98prod.htm is the HTML code generated by the FrontPage 98 Editor in this section.

4. In the left column of the table, type a set of captions for the fields of the product list. In the right column, type the field names corresponding to the captions. Table 22.1 lists the captions and field names for the table.

5. Optionally, add a background color to the form and set the minimum width property of the table to about 75%. Adjust the width of the columns approximately as shown in Figure 22.5

FIGURE 22.5

The design of the Products.htm WebClass template in FrontPage Editor.

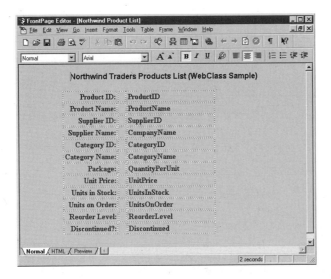

6. Close FrontPage Editor and save changes to Product.htm; then close FrontPage Explorer.

TABLE 22.1 CAPTIONS AND FIELD NAMES FOR THE PRODUCTS LIST TABLE

Table Caption (Left)	Field Name (Right)
Product ID:	ProductID
Product Name:	ProductName
Supplier ID:	SupplierID
Supplier Name:	CompanyName
Category ID:	CategoryID
Category Name:	CategoryName
Package:	QuantityPerUnit
Unit Price:	UnitPrice
Units in Stock:	UnitsInStock
Units on Order:	UnitsOnOrder
Reorder Level:	ReorderLevel
Discontinued?:	Discontinued

Creating the WebClass Project and Adding a `DataEnvironment` Object

Visual Basic 6.0's IIS Application template to create WebClass projects doesn't assume the project requires a database connection. Thus, you must either add ADO code or a `DataEnvironment` object to the `WebClass` object to generate the `ADODB.Recordset` that populates the table. Opening a new IIS Project adds to the project the Microsoft WebClass Library v. 1.0 (Mswcrun.dll) reference.

To start a new WebClass project with `DataEnvironment Connection` and `Command` objects for the product list, follow these steps:

1. Launch a new Visual Basic 6.0 IIS Application. Project Explorer opens Project1 with a `WebClass1` designer.

2. Right-click the Project Explorer window and select Add, Data Environment Designer to the project, which opens the Data Link Properties sheet. Adding a `DataEnvironment` object automatically adds the required data-related references to your project.

3. In the Provider page, select the Microsoft Jet 3.51 OLE DB Provider and click Next to select the Connection page.

4. Click the Browse button and select the Nwind.mdb sample database. Test the connection and then click OK to create `Connection1`.

5. Rename Connection1 to **cnnNwind** and add a new command named **ProductList**, select SQL Statement, and click the SQL Builder button to open the Query Designer.

6. Open the Data View window, if necessary, and expand the Tables node to display the tables in Nwind.mdb.

7. Drag the Categories, Products, and Suppliers tables from the Data View window to the top pane of the Design: ProductList window.

8. In the Products table field list, mark the ProductID, ProductName, and CategoryID fields to add them in sequence to the fields list of the central pane.

9. In the Categories table field list, mark the CategoryName field.

10. In the Products table field list, mark SupplierID, and in the Suppliers table field list mark CompanyName.

11. In the Products table field list, mark the QuantityPerUnit, UnitPrice, UnitsInStock, UnitsOnOrder, ReorderLevel, and Discontinued fields. The Query Designer window appears as shown in Figure 22.6.

FIGURE 22.6

Creating the SELECT query to provide the fields corresponding to the rows of the Products.htm template.

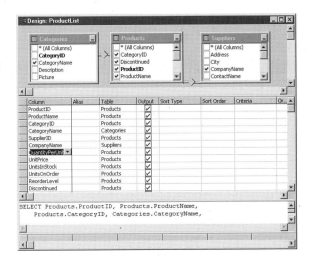

12. Right-click the Query Designer window and choose Run to test the query; then close the window. Click Yes to save the changes.

13. Rename DataEnvironment1 to **envProds** and Project1 to **prjProds**, accepting the remaining default project property values.

14. Right-click WebClass1, choose Properties, and change the Name property value of WebClass1 to **wcProds**. Change the NameInURL property value to **ProductList**.

15. Choose a folder other than \Ddg_vb6\Chaptr22 and save envProds as **envProds.dsr**, wcProds as **wcProds.dsr**, and prjProds as **wcPrdLst.vbp**.

The complete SQL statement for the `ProductList Command` object is

```
SELECT Products.ProductID, Products.ProductName,
      Products.CategoryID, Categories.CategoryName,
      Products.SupplierID, Suppliers.CompanyName,
      Products.QuantityPerUnit, Products.UnitPrice,
      Products.UnitsInStock, Products.UnitsOnOrder,
      Products.ReorderLevel, Products.Discontinued
  FROM Categories, Products, Suppliers
  WHERE Categories.CategoryID = Products.CategoryID
    AND Products.SupplierID = Suppliers.SupplierID
```

Adding Products.htm as the Template HTML WebItem

When you add an HTML page as a template, the WebClass designer parses the HTML code and identifies each tag pair, such as `<td>...</td>` for table data. The tag pairs and the contents between the tags appear in the right pane of the WebClass Designer when you select the template.

To add Products.htm to the project as a Template HTML WebItem and add the two lines of code that display the template, do the following:

1. Open the `wcProds` designer from Project Explorer, right-click the HTML Template WebItems node, and choose Add <u>H</u>TML Template to open the dialog of the same name.

2. Navigate to the location of Products.htm created in FrontPage, select the file, and click Open to add Products.htm as `Template1`.

> **NOTE**
>
> If you use the Fp98prod.htm file in \Ddg_vb6\Chaptr22, the designer creates a Fp98prod1.htm copy for the template. Using a copy retains the original version of the template, presumably for historical purposes.

3. Select `Template1` to display a list of its HTML tags in the right pane of the `wcProds` designer (see Figure 22.7).

FIGURE 22.7

The wcProds *designer displaying the HTML tags in* Template1 *(Products.htm).*

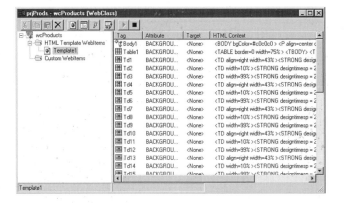

4. Rename Template1 to **tplProds** and double-click the tplProds item to open the code-editing window for the template.

5. Replace the nine lines of default code in the WebClass_Start event handler with the following single line:

```
Set NextItem = tplProds
```

NOTE

The preceding line is necessary only if you have more than one template and need to specify the startup template. It's a good programming practice, however, to add this line to all WebClass projects.

6. Add the following line to the tplProds_Respond event handler:

```
tplProds.WriteTemplate
```

The *Template*_Respond event fires when the browser opens. The preceding line sends the HTML content of the template to the browser.

7. Press Ctrl+F5 to compile and run the project. Click OK when the Debugging page of the Project properties sheet appears. Click OK when the input box suggests prjProds as the virtual root for the project.

8. IE 4.01 opens and displays tplProds as ProductList.asp in the /localhost/prjProds virtual root (see Figure 22.8). Close IE 4.01 and return to design mode.

FIGURE 22.8

The prjProds displaying tplProds in IE 4.0.

Displaying the Data from the First Record of the ProductList Query

When the WebClass object sends the HTML code to the browser, the ProcessTag event fires for each *replacement tag* encountered. You identify an HTML element for replacement by surrounding the text to replace by a WebClass tag pair. A WebClass tag consists of a tag prefix, WC@ by default, and a tag name, enclosed between angle brackets. The following is an example of a WebClass tag pair:

```
<WC@ProductID>ProductID</WC@ProductID>
```

> **NOTE**
>
> You can change the WebClass tag identifier from the default WC@ to another code, such as WC: by selecting the template in the WebClass Designer, opening its Properties window, and changing the value of the TagPrefix property. WC: is used as the TagPrefix in the following example.

1. Right-click tplProds and choose Edit HTML Template to open tplProds in Notepad.

2. Replace each instance of the field name in the template with **<WC:*FieldName*>*FieldName*</WC:*FieldName*>** (see Figure 22.9). Listing 22.1 shows the complete HTML code for the template.

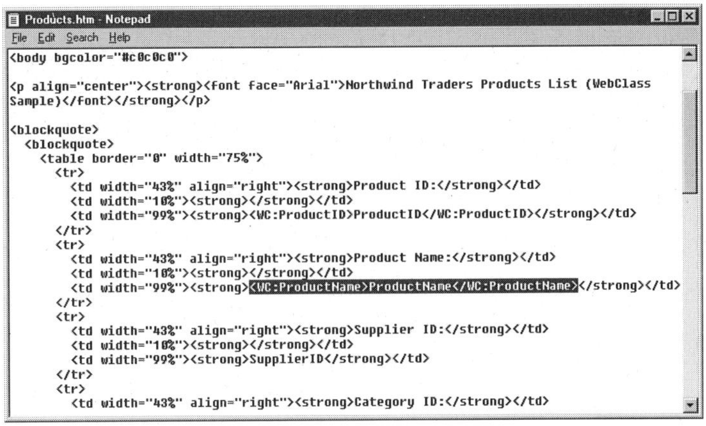

FIGURE 22.9

Adding WebClass tag pairs to the field name text of the template's table.

```
Products.htm - Notepad
File  Edit  Search  Help
<body bgcolor="#c0c0c0">

<p align="center"><strong><font face="Arial">Northwind Traders Products List (WebClass
Sample)</font></strong></p>

<blockquote>
  <blockquote>
    <table border="0" width="75%">
      <tr>
        <td width="43%" align="right"><strong>Product ID:</strong></td>
        <td width="10%"><strong></strong></td>
        <td width="99%"><strong><WC:ProductID>ProductID</WC:ProductID></strong></td>
      </tr>
      <tr>
        <td width="43%" align="right"><strong>Product Name:</strong></td>
        <td width="10%"><strong></strong></td>
        <td width="99%"><strong><WC:ProductName>ProductName</WC:ProductName></strong></td>
      </tr>
      <tr>
        <td width="43%" align="right"><strong>Supplier ID:</strong></td>
        <td width="10%"><strong></strong></td>
        <td width="99%"><strong>SupplierID</strong></td>
      </tr>
      <tr>
        <td width="43%" align="right"><strong>Category ID:</strong></td>
```

22

INTEGRATING
DATABASES

TIP

Periodically check to make sure the tag pairs you entered don't have typo-graphic errors. Add a **Debug.Print** *TagName*, *TagContents* line to the tplProds_ProcessTag event handler. Save Products.htm in Notepad; then com-pile and run the project. Inspect the *WC:FieldName FieldName* result in the Immediate window to make sure all your tags work.

---

3. In the WebClass_Start event handler, add an envProds.ProductList line above the **Set** NextItem = tplProds line.

   You must execute the ProductList Command to open the cnnNwind Connection prior to executing HTML replacement operations. Failure to include this line in WebClass_Start results in a Runtime error '3704': The operation requested by the application is not allowed if the object is closed error. An Application-defined or object-defined error line appears in IE 4.01.

NOTE

If you write ADO code to open the Connection and Command objects, instead of using DataEnvironment Connection and Command objects, put the ADO code in the WebClass_Start event handler.

4. In the `tplProds_ProcessTag` event handler, add the following line:

```
TagContents = envProds.rsProductList.Fields(TagContents).Value
```

This line substitutes the value of the specified field of the first record of `rsProductList` for the tagged field name.

5. Press Ctrl+F5 to compile and run the WebClass project. IE 4.01 displays the field values of the first record in the right column of the table (see Figure 22.10).

FIGURE 22.10

The result of the ProcessTag event handler replacing field names with corresponding field values.

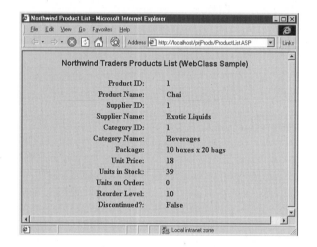

LISTING 22.1 THE HTML CODE CREATED IN THE FRONTPAGE EDITOR WITH WEBCLASS REPLACEMENT TAGS ADDED

```html
<html>

<head>
<meta http-equiv="Content-Type" content="text/html; charset=iso-8859-1">
<title>Northwind Product List</title>
</head>

<body bgcolor="#c0c0c0">

<p align="center"><strong><font face="Arial">Northwind Traders
Products List (WebClass Sample)</font></strong></p>

<blockquote>
  <blockquote>
    <table border="0" width="75%">
      <tr>
        <td width="43%" align="right"><strong>Product ID:</strong></td>
        <td width="10%"><strong></strong></td>
        <td width="99%"><strong>
```

```
      <WC:ProductID>ProductID</WC:ProductID></strong></td>
</tr>
<tr>
  <td width="43%" align="right"><strong>Product Name:</strong></td>
  <td width="10%"><strong></strong></td>
  <td width="99%"><strong>
    <WC:ProductName>ProductName</WC:ProductName></strong></td>
</tr>
<tr>
  <td width="43%" align="right"><strong>Supplier ID:</strong></td>
  <td width="10%"><strong></strong></td>
  <td width="99%"><strong>
    <WC:SupplierID>SupplierID</WC:SupplierID></strong></td>
</tr>
<tr>
  <td width="43%" align="right"><strong>Supplier Name:</strong></td>
  <td width="10%"><strong></strong></td>
  <td width="99%"><strong>
    <WC:CompanyName>CompanyName</WC:CompanyName></strong></td>
</tr>
<tr>
  <td width="43%" align="right"><strong>Category ID:</strong></td>
  <td width="10%"><strong></strong></td>
  <td width="99%"><strong>
    <WC:CategoryID>CategoryID</WC:CategoryID></strong></td>
</tr>
<tr>
  <td width="43%" align="right"><strong>Category Name:</strong></td>
  <td width="10%"><strong></strong></td>
  <td width="99%"><strong>
    <WC:CategoryName>CategoryName</WC:CategoryName></strong></td>
</tr>
<tr>
  <td width="43%" align="right"><strong>Package:</strong></td>
  <td width="10%"><strong></strong></td>
  <td width="99%"><strong>
    <WC:QuantityPerUnit>QuantityPerUnit</WC:QuantityPerUnit>
    </strong></td>
</tr>
<tr>
  <td width="43%" align="right"><strong>Unit Price:</strong></td>
  <td width="10%"><strong></strong></td>
  <td width="99%"><strong>
    <WC:UnitPrice>UnitPrice</WC:UnitPrice></strong></td>
</tr>
<tr>
  <td width="43%" align="right"><strong>Units in Stock:</strong></td>
  <td width="10%"><strong></strong></td>
  <td width="99%"><strong>
    <WC:UnitsInStock>UnitsInStock</WC:UnitsInStock></strong></td>
</tr>
```

continues

LISTING 22.1 CONTINUED

```html
      <tr>
        <td width="43%" align="right"><strong>Units on Order:</strong></td>
        <td width="10%"><strong></strong></td>
        <td width="99%"><strong>
           <WC:UnitsOnOrder>UnitsOnOrder</WC:UnitsOnOrder></strong></td>
      </tr>
      <tr>
        <td width="43%" align="right"><strong>Reorder Level:</strong></td>
        <td width="10%"><strong></strong></td>
        <td width="99%"><strong>
           <WC:ReorderLevel>ReorderLevel</WC:ReorderLevel></strong></td>
      </tr>
      <tr>
        <td width="43%" align="right"><strong>Discontinued?:</strong></td>
        <td width="10%"><strong></strong></td>
        <td width="99%"><strong>
           <WC:Discontinued>Discontinued</WC:Discontinued></strong></td>
      </tr>
     </table>
   </blockquote>
 </blockquote>
 </body>
 </html>
```

A relatively simple modification to the code of the `tplProds_ProcessTag` event handler formats the UnitPrice field for currency and the Discontinued field for a Yes/No response. Listing 22.2 shows the VBA code for the final version of the `wcProducts WebClass`. Chapter 25, "Developing Data-Enabled Internet Applications," offers a more sophisticated version of the wcPrdLst.vbp project with `Recordset` navigation and other user-generated event handling. Chapter 25 also shows you how to compile and deploy the project to your Web site.

LISTING 22.2 VBA CODE FOR THE wcProducts WebClass WITH FORMATTING CODE IN THE tplProds_ProcessTag EVENT HANDLER

```vba
Option Explicit
Option Compare Text

Private Sub WebClass_Start()
   'IMPORTANT: You must start the DataEnvironment first
   envProds.ProductList
   'Specify the opening template (optional for a single template)
   Set NextItem = tplProds
End Sub

Private Sub tplProds_ProcessTag(ByVal strTagName As String, strTagContents As String,
SendTags As Boolean)
```

```
    'Replace the field name with the field value
    With envProds.rsProductList.Fields(strTagContents)
        If.Type = adCurrency Then
            'Format the value as currency
            strTagContents = Format(.Value, "$#,##0.00")
        ElseIf .Type = adBoolean Then
            'Translate True/False to Yes/No
            If.Value Then
                strTagContents = "Yes"
            Else
                strTagContents = "No"
            End If
        Else
            strTagContents =.Value
        End If
    End With
End Sub

Private Sub tplProds_Respond()
    'Send the modified HTML to the browser
    tplProds.WriteTemplate
End Sub
```

22

INTEGRATING
DATABASES

> **NOTE**
>
> The wcProducts WebClass delivers a result similar to the HTX/IDL
> (template/query) combinations of the sample database applications originally
> provided with IIS 1.0 and still added to the \InetPub\wwwroot\samples\dbsamp
> and \InetPub\scripts\samples folder when you install IIS 4.0.

STARTING A SIMPLE DHTML PROJECT

DHTML projects offer dynamic text addition and replacement features similar to WebClasses, but DHTML pages execute the contained VBA code within IE 4.01 running on the client rather than in an ISAPI process running on the server. The example DHTML project (dhPrdLst.vbp) you create in the following sections emulates the data presentation of the preceding WebClass project. Data is provided to the DHTML page from a local database, so dhPrdLst.vbp isn't representative of a production DHTML project. The purpose of dhPrdLst.vbp is to provide a comparison of programming techniques for and the performance of simple WebClass and DHTML pages.

> **NOTE**
>
> One of the drawbacks of DHTML pages is the need to gain some familiarity with Microsoft's version of the DHTML DOM. The DOM is exceedingly complex and has a myriad of objects, and the relationships between the objects are by no means obvious. An explanation of the DHTML DOM is beyond the scope of this book. Sams' *Teach Yourself Internet Programming with Visual Basic in 21 Days* (ISBN 0-672-31459-2) covers DHTML DOM basics for Visual Basic programmers.

Opening a New DHTML Project and Adding a DHTML Page

Starting a DHTML project is similar to starting a WebClass project, but the DHTML Designer also offers a DHTML Editor in which to design pages. The DHTML Editor also includes its own toolbox with lightweight HTML versions of common Visual Basic native controls, such as command buttons (Button), text boxes (TextField), check boxes (Checkbox), combo boxes (Select), and list boxes (List).

To open a new DHTML Project, add an existing Data Environment Designer, and add an existing HTML file to create a DHTML page, do the following:

1. Make a copy in your project folder of the original version of the Products.htm file you created with FrontPage. Alternatively, make a copy of OrigProd.htm from the \Ddg_vb6\Chaptr22 folder of the accompanying CD-ROM.

> **NOTE**
>
> Using an existing HTML file eliminates the process of recreating the page in the DHTML Designer. The version of the DHTML Designer included with Visual Studio 6.0 has many peculiarities, some of which are documented in the Readmevb.htm file.

2. Open a new DHTML Project. Project Explorer opens with a default module (modDHTML) and default DHTML Designer (DHTMLPage1). Remove DHTMLPage1 without saving changes.

> **NOTE**
>
> Opening a new DHTML Project adds to the project the Microsoft DHTML Runtime Library (Mshtmpgr.dll) reference, which includes the DHTMLPAGELIB and MSHTML libraries.

3. Right-click DHTMLProject; choose Add, Add File; and add the envProds.dsr Data Environment Designer to the project.

4. Right-click DHTMLProject again and choose Add, DHTML Page to open the DHTMLPage1 Properties sheet. Select the Save HTML in an External File option button and click the Open button. In the open dialog, select the copy of the file you created in step 1 (dhtmProd.htm for this example) and click OK to create a new DHTMLPage1 with the FrontPage 98 source.

   Choosing Save HTML in an External File, rather than the Save HTML with Project option, lets you use an external text editor (usually Visual Notepad) to modify the source code.

5. The DHTML Editor doesn't recognize the Times Roman bold font attributes of the table, so select all the text in the table and then select Times New Roman in the Fonts list.

6. Change WebClass in the page title to **DHTML**. The page in the DHTML Editor appears as illustrated by Figure 22.11.

FIGURE 22.11
The HTML code for the Product List generated by FrontPage 98 in the DHTML Editor.

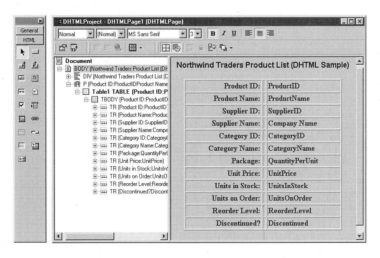

7. Press Ctrl+F5 to compile and run the DHTMLPage1 component. Click OK when the Debugging page of the Project Properties sheet appears with the Start Component option selected. DHTMLPage1 appears in IE 4.01 as shown in Figure 22.12.

FIGURE 22.12

*IE 4.01 displaying
the initial version
of* DHTMLPage1
(dhtmProd.htm).

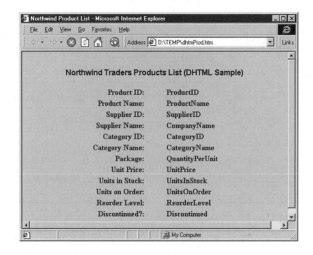

8. Save your project, naming DHTMLPage1 as **dhProds1.dsr**, modDHTML as **dhProds1.bas**, and the project as **dhPrdLst.vbp**.

Displaying Data from the rsProductList Recordset

The DHTML Designer parses the HTML of the page to create an object model hierarchy based on the DHTML DOM. The object model appears as a tree view in the Designer's left pane. Each of the elements of the page (Document), such as a table (TABLE) and its cells (TD), can be exposed for programming by VBA code. You assign an identification (Id) property to objects whose properties you want to change or events you want to trap.

To display the field values of the first record of the rsProductList Recordset in the right column of the page's table, do the following:

1. Expand each of the 12 table row (TR) nodes in the left pane to display the three table data (TD) elements representing the cells of the row.

2. Select the third TD element of the first TR node, which corresponds to the right column of the table, and open the properties page for the element.

3. Type **idProductID** as the value of the (Id) property. You must assign a unique Id value to each element that you want to expose properties and events for programming.

4. Repeat steps 2 and 3 for each of the remaining 11 rows, typing **id***FieldName* as the (Id) property value (see Figure 22.13).

FIGURE 22.13

Adding Id *property values to the table data element for the values in the third column of the table.*

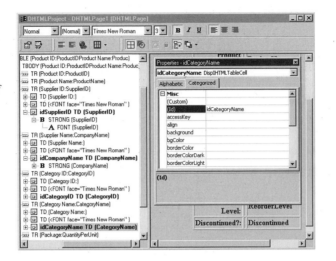

5. Select the TABLE element, open the Properties window, and assign **idProdList** as its Id property value.

6. In Project Explorer, select DHTMLPage1, open its Properties window, and change the Id property value to **dhProductList**.

7. Open the code-editing window for dhProductList and add **Option** Explicit at the top of the Declarations section. Microsoft's developers forgot to include the standard requirement for predeclaring variables.

8. Add to the DHTMLPage_Load event handler the code shown in Listing 22.3. Code in DHTMLPage_Load assures that the cnnNwind Connection opens and the ProductList Command executes before calling the ReplaceTableData subprocedure.

NOTE

The DHTMLPage_Load event handler executes after the first element of the page (the title) loads when using the default asynchronous loading (AsyncLoad = **True**) option.

---

9. Add the ReplaceTableData subprocedure with the code shown is Listing 22.3. The objCell object of the MSHTML.IHTMLTableCell type is a surrogate for the individual table cells identified in preceding steps 2 and 3. Using a surrogate object simplifies the data replacement code.

NOTE

You can determine the MSHTML object type of a DHTML Document subobject by opening its Properties window and noting the object type that appears after the object Id value in the object list. For example, the object type of idProductID appears as DispIHTMLTableCell; drop the Disp prefix to obtain the corresponding MSHTML object type.

The code replaces the innerHTML, rather than the innerText, property value, because you must provide a ... tag pair to apply the bold attribute to the cell text. If you use innerText, the replacement text has standard weight.

---

10. Press Ctrl+F5 to compile and run the DHTML project. The DHTML page appears as shown in Figure 22.14.

LISTING 22.3   VBA CODE FOR THE DHPRDLST.DSR DHTML DESIGNER WITH HTML TEXT REPLACEMENT AND FORMATTING CODE

```
Option Explicit 'Add manually

Private Sub DHTMLPage_Load()
    'Triggers when the first element is loaded (AsyncLoad = True)
    'Make sure the DataEnvironment starts
    envProds.ProductList
    'Replace the data
    Call ReplaceTableData
End Sub

Private Sub ReplaceTableData()
    Dim intRow As Integer
    Dim objCell As MSHTML.IHTMLTableCell
    Dim strHTML As String

    With envProds.rsProductList
        For intRow = 1 To .Fields.Count
            Select Case intRow
                Case 1
                    Set objCell = idProductID
                Case 2
                    Set objCell = idProductName
```

```
        Case 3
            Set objCell = idSupplierID
        Case 4
            Set objCell = idCompanyName
        Case 5
            Set objCell = idCategoryID
        Case 6
            Set objCell = idCategoryName
        Case 7
            Set objCell = idQuantityPerUnit
        Case 8
            Set objCell = idUnitPrice
        Case 9
            Set objCell = idUnitsInStock
        Case 10
            Set objCell = idUnitsOnOrder
        Case 11
            Set objCell = idReorderLevel
        Case 12
            Set objCell = idDiscontinued
    End Select

    'Construct the replacement HTML string
    'Set font bold
    strHTML = "<strong>"
    If .Fields(intRow - 1).Type = adCurrency Then
        'Format for currency
        strHTML = strHTML & Format(.Fields(intRow - 1).Value, "$#,##0.00")
    ElseIf .Fields(intRow - 1).Type = adBoolean Then
        'Format for Yes/No
        If .Fields(intRow - 1).Value Then
            strHTML = strHTML & "Yes"
        Else
            strHTML = strHTML & "No"
        End If
    Else
        'No formatting required
        strHTML = strHTML & .Fields(intRow - 1).Value
    End If
    'Reset the bold attribute
    strHTML = strHTML & "</strong>"
    objCell.innerHTML = strHTML
    Next intRow
    End With
End Sub
```

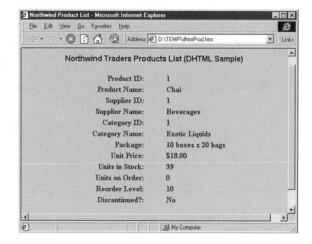

Loading the DHTML page into IE 4.01 takes substantially longer than loading the identical WebClass page. On the 266MHz Pentium II PC with 128MB of RAM used to write this book, loading and displaying the dhProductList DHTML page takes about 4 seconds. The wcProductList page requires about 2.5 seconds to load and display. Both tests were run with Windows NT 4.0 Server (SP4) and IIS 4.0 with an ATI All-in-Wonder graphics card having 4MB of RAM set to 256-color depth.

Adding Recordset Navigation Buttons to dhProductList

The DHTML Editor makes it easy to add a set of Recordset navigation buttons to the form. Follow these steps:

1. Position the DHTML cursor below the table and add a couple of empty of lines.

2. In the DHTML Designer, drag a Button control from the toolbox to a location a line or two under the table. Open its Properties window and change its Id and name to **btNext**, and its value (caption) to **Next**.

> **NOTE**
>
> If you don't add an empty line or two and drag the button to an empty line, the button might end up in the last cell of the table. A button in the last table cell doesn't appear when you run the project.

3. Double-click the button to open the code-editing window with the `btNext_onclick` event handler active. Add the following two lines to the event handler:

```
envProds.rsProductList.MoveNext
Call ReplaceTableData
```

4. If you want to complete the navigation button set, add First, Previous, and Last buttons, with the usual *Recordset*.EOF protection code to prevent EOF or BOF errors when calling the MoveNext or MovePrevious methods, respectively.

Alternatively, you can add buttons and other standard HTML controls in a conventional HTML editor and then add Id property values in the DHTML Editor to make them programmable.

Neither of the projects described in this chapter are candidates for Web graphic arts awards, other than "Worst of the Web." The objective of this chapter and the remaining chapters in this part is to demonstrate Internet and intranet database techniques, not Web page design.

USING ACTIVEX DOCUMENT OBJECTS WITH INTRANETS

IN THIS CHAPTER

Visual Basic 5.0 added ActiveX Documents as a simplified method of porting Visual Basic applications to intranets. ActiveX Documents began life as persistent (file based) OLE Document (OLEDoc) objects that you could insert into OLE container applications, such as Word, Excel, or Microsoft Binder. OLEDocs, like Microsoft Binder, aroused very little interest among developers. ActiveX Documents, however, offered the ability to easily intranet enable simple Visual Basic database projects without dramatic changes to their structure or code. Thus the primary container for ActiveX Documents became Microsoft Internet Explorer (IE) 3+.

It doesn't take a major effort to adapt to ActiveX Document's approach to project design. Visual Basic forms become user documents, which closely resemble user controls. Binder and other OLE containers handle modeless user documents, but IE throws an error if you attempt to load a modeless form. ActiveX Documents don't have a `Form_Load` event, so setup code that you normally execute in the `Form_Load` event handler moves the `UserDocument_Initialize` event handler. You must use a global flag to prevent code in `UserDocument_Initialize` from executing every time the user reopens the form when returning from another page. You use `PropertyBags` to preserve state between instances of the document. You also must change `ADODB.Connection` properties for networked Jet databases from mapped drive letters to UNC format because users seldom adhere to a uniform set of network drive mappings.

> **NOTE**
>
> ActiveX Documents, like Visual Basic forms, can contain ActiveX controls and all native controls except the OLE Container control. You can't embed OLE objects, such as Word documents or Excel spreadsheets, in ActiveX Documents.

Most commercial ActiveX Document projects begin life as conventional Visual Basic projects. Fortunately, Microsoft provides the ActiveX Migration Wizard to automate many of the required alterations. Thus, the ActiveX Document examples of this relatively brief chapter are derived from projects developed in prior chapters. The chapter also explains how to compile and deploy ActiveX documents on an intranet server.

CONVERTING THE ADO2OLTP.VBP PROJECT TO AN ACTIVEX DOCUMENT

Heads-down OLTP applications aren't primary candidates for conversion to ActiveX Documents running on an intranet, but the ADO2OLTP.vbp project of Chapter 20, "Porting Access OLTP Applications to Visual Basic 6.0," is a single-form application that demonstrates the code changes you must make to accommodate a browser container and provide universal access to the application over a conventional LAN or WAN, not the Internet. The ADO2OLTP.vbp project includes timers so you can compare its performance as an ActiveX Document with the original version.

> **NOTE**
>
> It's unlikely that an important activity, such as customer order entry, would be conducted over the Internet without establishing a Virtual Private Network (VPN) and taking other security precautions to avoid unauthorized interception of order information, which might included credit card information, or hacking of the orders database. Setting up secure data entry systems for Internet connectivity, such as e-commerce sites, is beyond the scope of this book. Most e-commerce applications provide a complete database infrastructure for Internet storefronts.

Starting with the ActiveX Document Migration Wizard

Visual Basic 6.0's ActiveX Document Migration Wizard is surprisingly effective in handling the basic chore of converting a convention Visual Basic form to a `UserDocument` object. Do the following to convert Ado2oltp.frm to Ado2oltp.dob:

1. Copy all files from the \Ddg_vb6\Chaptr20 folder of the accompanying CD-ROM to a project folder other than \Ddg_vb6\Chaptr23; then open the ADO2OLTP.vbp project from the new location.

2. Choose <u>A</u>dd-Ins, <u>A</u>dd-In Manager to open the Add-In Manager's dialog. Double-click the VB 6 ActiveX Doc Migration Wizard item in the Available Add-Ins list to load the Wizard and then close the dialog.

3. Launch the Active X Document Migration Wizard (henceforth Wizard) and click Next to bypass the Introduction dialog.

4. In the Form Selection dialog, select frmOrderEntry (see Figure 23.1) and click Next.

FIGURE 23.1

Selecting the form(s) to convert to user document(s).

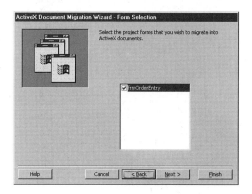

5. In the Options dialog, mark the Comment Out Invalid Code and Remove Original Forms After Conversion check boxes and select the Convert to an ActiveX DLL option (see Figure 23.2). Click Next.

FIGURE 23.2

Specifying form conversion options.

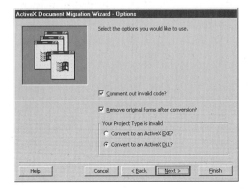

6. Accept the default entries in the Finished! dialog, click Finish, and click OK when the ActiveX Document(s) Created message box appears.

7. Save the report created by the Wizard, if you want, and then open frmOrderEntry, saved by default as frmOrderEntry.dob. Your form appears in the Visual Basic IDE's container, as illustrated by Figure 23.3.

FIGURE 23.3

The `frmOrderEntry` *UserDocument object in design mode.*

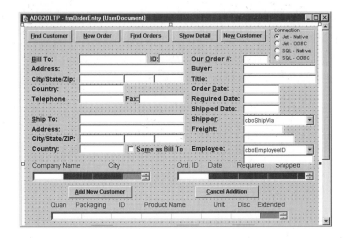

8. Press Ctrl+F5 in an attempt to compile and run the user document. The first error you encounter is a failure of the Wizard to change `With Me` to `With UserDocument` in the `Form_Load` event handler. Make the correction and try again.

> **NOTE**
>
> The Wizard converts all valid **Me** self-references to UserDocument; as the
> wcDemo.vbp WebClass example in the preceding chaper demonstrates, **Me**
> doesn't work in Internet-enabled objects.
>
> When the Wizard encounters a Form_Load event handler, she adds a
> UserDocument_Initialize event handler that calls Form_Load.

9. When the Debugging page of the Project Properties sheet appears, click OK to accept
    frmOrderEntry as the Start Component.

10. You encounter a run mode error stating: 'Width' property can't be set at run
    time. Neither can the Height property, so click Debug and delete the entire **With...End
    With** structure.

11. Deleting or commenting the **With** structure requires resetting the project, so press
    Ctrl+F5 to try again. Voilà! This time the UserDocument appears in IE 4.01 and operates
    exactly as it did as a conventional project (see Figure 23.4).

FIGURE 23.4

The frmOrderEntry
UserDocument *run-
ning in Internet
Explorer 4.01.*

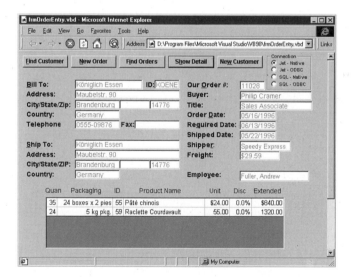

> **NOTE**
>
> If you've associated .vbd files with an application other than IE, you must
> change the association to Microsoft Internet Explorer when debugging ActiveX
> Documents for use on intranets.

12. If you've set up the nwind SQL Server 6.5+ database, as described in Chapter 20, test the other modes of operation, such as SQL - Native and SQL - ODBC. There is no significant performance difference between the ActiveX Document version and original ADO2OLTP.vbp application.

13. Close IE, return to design mode, change the name of frmOrderEntry to **axdOrderEntry**, save frmOrderEntry.dob as **Ado2oltp.dob**, and then save the project.

> **NOTE**
>
> Changing the name of frmOrderEntry to axdOrderEntry doesn't cause problems because all references to frmOrderEntry are cast as Me in the original code; the Wizard changed all valid instances of Me to UserDocument.

14. The Ado2oltp.vbp project file has detritus from its origins in \Ddg_vb6\Chaptr20, so open a new ActiveX DLL project and remove UserDocument1 from Project Explorer.

15. Right-click Project1; choose Add, Add File; and add Ado2oltp.dob to the new Project1.

16. Add the Microsoft ActiveX Data Objects 2.0 Library reference to the project; then verify that the project compiles and runs as before.

17. Save the project, saving Project1.vbp as **Oltp_axd.vbp**. Delete Ado2oltp.vbp.

18. Ado2oltp.mdb isn't required because axdOrderEntry stores newly added order line items in a persistent Recordset file (LineItem.rst), so delete Ado2oltp.mdb.

Coding Changes for Networked Databases and Compiling the ActiveX DLL

The Ado2oltp.dob user document contains ADODB.Connection code that expects NW_data.mdb to be located in the application's current folder. NW_data.mdb must be deployed to a server share for use by intranet clients. Thus you must change the value of the ConnectionString property to point to the new location of NW_data.mdb.

> **NOTE**
>
> If you're moving from a test to a production client/server database, you must also change the ConnectionString property to specify the proper Location= and DefaultCatalog= values.

You compile ActiveX Documents designed for IE 3+ containers as ActiveX DLLs, not as .exe files. ActiveX DLLs run in the same process space as IE and can take advantage of IE 3+'s multithreading capabilities.

To alter the code of Ado2oltp.dob to support the new NW_data.mdb location and compile the project to Oltp_axd.dll, do the following:

1. Create a public share, if necessary, on your test server (//OAKLEAF0/Nwind is the share for this example).

2. Copy NW_data.mdb from your development client to the public share and then delete the local copy of NW_data.mdb.

> **NOTE**
>
> If your Jet database is secure, you must also make the workgroup file (usually System.mdw) available to users of the database. Chapter 17, "Networking Secure Multiuser Jet Databases," describes how to share Jet workgroup files.

3. Change the `App.Path & "\NW_Data.mdb"` element of all `ConnectionString` property values to `"\\`*ServerName*`\`*ShareName*`\NW_Data.mdb"` ("`\\OAKLEAF0\Nwind\NW_Data.mdb`" in the code example).

> **NOTE**
>
> If you're using the sample application from \Ddg_vb6\Chaptr23, search and replace `\\OAKLEAF0\Nwind` with your share name.

4. Run the application to verify proper operation with the Jet - Native and Jet - ODBC options.

5. Save the project and then compile Oltp_axd.dll.

> **NOTE**
>
> You can shorten the preceding process by using the sample files in the \Ddg_vb6\Chaptr23 folder of the accompanying CD-ROM. However, following the preceding steps and performing the operations yourself should take 5 minutes or less.

23

USING ACTIVEX DOCUMENT OBJECTS

PACKAGING ACTIVEX DOCUMENT OBJECTS

ActiveX DLLs run from IE require an Internet package for distribution of the necessary support files. The Package and Deployment Wizard automates the creation of the required .cab (cabinet) files that contain compressed copies of dependency (support) files.

To package Oltp_axd.vbd for distribution, do the following:

1. Add the Package and Deployment Wizard (Wizard from now on) Add-In, if necessary, and then open the Wizard with the Oltp_axd.vbp project open in design mode. The fully qualified path and project file appears in the Active Project text box.

2. Click Package to open the Package Type dialog. Select Internet Package to create a downloadable .cab file (see Figure 23.5).

FIGURE 23.5

Selecting the type of installation package.

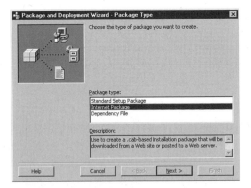

3. Click Next to open the Package dialog. The default location for the files is the Package subfolder of your project folder (see Figure 23.6).

FIGURE 23.6

Specifying the location of the package files.

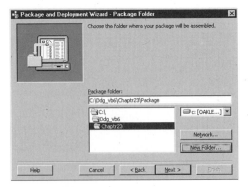

4. Click Next; then click OK when the message box asks whether you want to create the folder or to open the Included Files dialog. The Files list specifies all the ActiveX controls and dependency DLLs for the project. Click Add and select LineItem.rst to include in the package (see Figure 23.7).

Technically, you don't need to include LineItem.rst because code to create it is included in axdOrderEntry, but including all dependency files in the package is a good programming practice.

FIGURE 23.7

The file list for the .cab file including the manually added LineItem.rst file.

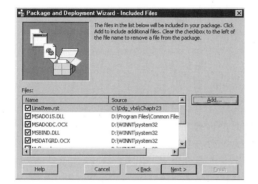

5. Click Next to open the File Source dialog. Microsoft assumes that everyone has at least a full-time T-1 (if not a T-3 or OC-3) connection to the Internet, so the Wizard defaults to downloading support dependency files from www.microsoft.com. Select each file that defaults to the Microsoft Web site and select the Include in This Cab option (see Figure 23.8).

FIGURE 23.8

Adding runtime .cab files to the package.

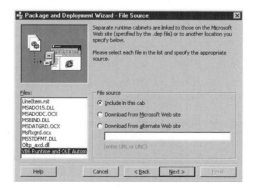

23

USING ACTIVEX
DOCUMENT
OBJECTS

> **NOTE**
>
> The Wizard doesn't offer suggestions for users who can't install the ActiveX document on their PCs because they encounter a Not Found or Server Too Busy error at the Microsoft Web site.
>
> When you supply dependency files in the .cab file, the Wizard copies all distribution support files to the ...\Package\Support folder.

6. Click Next to open the Safety Settings dialog. The axdOrderEntry DocumentObject has a known (and presumably virus free) source, so change the Safe for Scripting and Safe for Initialization settings from No to Yes.

7. Click Next to open the Finished! dialog and accept the default Internet Package 1 package name or substitute a package name of your choice.

8. Click Finish to create the Oltp_axd.cab file, which takes several seconds to complete. Close the Packaging Report dialog to return to the Wizard's first dialog.

> **NOTE**
>
> The Oltp_axd.cab file with all the dependency files is about 1.7MB, which is not an excessive size for application installation on a LAN or even a WAN.

Deploying from Internet Information Server 4.0

The final step in the process is to deploy Oltp_axd.vbd and Oltp_axd.cab to IIS 4.0 for distribution to clients. As it does with the packaging process, the Package and Deployment Wizard automates the entire deployment process. You must have installed Posting Acceptor 2.0 for IIS 4.0 during the IIS 4.0 setup process to use the HTTP Post protocol with the Packaging and Deployment Wizard.

> **NOTE**
>
> As with the WebClass and DHTML applications described in the preceding chapter, there are many Package and Deployment Wizard caveats in the Readmevb.htm file. Be sure to read the Package and Deployment Wizard topics in this file before attempting to set up deployment from IIS 4.0.

To deploy Oltp_axd.vbp and Oltp_axd.cab to IIS 4.0, do the following:

1. Click the Deploy button to open the Wizard's Package to Deploy dialog. Accept the package name entered in step 7 of the preceding section.

2. Click Next to open the Deployment Method dialog and select Web Publishing.

3. Click Next to open the Items to Deploy dialog. Accept the default items, which include the .vbd and .cab files, plus an HTML file for installation (see Figure 23.9).

FIGURE 23.9

Specifying the files to deploy to the Internet server.

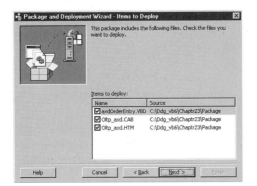

4. Click Next to open the Additional Items to Deploy dialog. You don't need any more items, so click Next to open the Web Publishing Site dialog.

5. Type the URL of the Web server that serves as the distribution site, accept HTTP Post as the Publishing Protocol, and mark the Unpack and Install Server-side Cab check box(see Figure 29.10). The other publishing option is FTP transfer.

FIGURE 23.10

Specifying the location of the installation files on an Internet server.

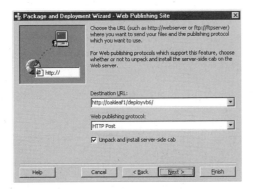

6. Click Next to open the Finished! dialog. Accept the default or change the deployment script name, as desired. Click Finish to copy the files to the folder for the selected location and expand the .cab file.

23

USING ACTIVEX
DOCUMENT
OBJECTS

> **NOTE**
>
> You must have write permissions for the Web server location in which you install the .cab file.

The Oltp_axd.htm file installed in the specified folder by the Wizard is required only for .cab file download by clients running IE 3.0. You must remove the second set of HTML comment lines to adapt Oltp_axd.htm for IE 3.0 clients (see Listing 23.1).

LISTING 23.1   HTLM CODE FOR THE OLTP_AXD.HTM FILE INSTALLED BY THE PACKAGING AND DEPLOYMENT WIZARD

```
<HTML>
<HEAD>
<TITLE>Oltp_axd.CAB</TITLE>
</HEAD>
<BODY>

<a href=axdOrderEntry.VBD>axdOrderEntry.VBD</a>
<!--*********** Comment Begin **********
    Internet Explorer Version 3.x HTML
    =====================================
    The following HTML code has been commented
    out and provided for ActiveX User Documents
    download support in IE 3.x only.  This
    HTML script may not work properly in later
    versions of Internet Explorer.

    Additional information about downloading
    ActiveX User Documents in IE 3.x can be
    found in Microsoft's online support on the
    internet at http://support.microsoft.com.
    *********** Comment End    ********** -->

<!--*********** Comment Begin **********
<HTML>
<OBJECT ID="axdOrderEntry"
CLASSID="CLSID:01C90C4F-45AF-11D2-8F97-0080C867751E"
CODEBASE="Oltp_axd.CAB#version=1,0,0,0">
</OBJECT>

<SCRIPT LANGUAGE="VBScript">
Sub Window_OnLoad
    Document.Open
    Document.Write "<FRAMESET>"
    Document.Write "<FRAME SRC=""axdOrderEntry.VBD"">"
```

```
      Document.Write "</FRAMESET>"
      Document.Close
End Sub
</SCRIPT>
</HTML>
      *********** Comment End    ********** -->

</BODY>
</HTML>
```

You can delete Oltp_axd.htm if all of the client PCs running the ActiveX Document have
IE 4+ installed. In this case, clicking the Oltp_axd.htm hyperlink simply opens
Oltp_axd.vbd. When IE 4+ clients access Oltp_axd.vbd for the first time, the .cab file automat-
ically expands and installs the support files. All clients can run Oltp_axd.vbd as IE's default
URL or add it to IE's Favorites list for easy access.

DEALING WITH THE ARCHITECTURAL ISSUES OF MULTI-FORM PROJECTS

Most of the examples in this book use a single-form design; single-form projects are ideally
suited to deployment as ActiveX Documents on intranets. As demonstrated at the beginning of
this chapter, the ActiveX Document Migration Wizard quickly converts typical single-form
projects to run with converted UserDocument and makes most of the code changes for you.
Only a few code changes result in a usable ActiveX Document port.

Complex projects with multiple forms, typical of production Visual Basic 6.0 database applications, usually involve multiple forms. Applications with multiple modeless forms require navigation by URL. The `UserDocument.Hyperlink.NavigateTo` method handles the navigation
process for multiple modeless forms. The ActXDoc.vbp sample project in the \Program
Files\Microsoft Visual Studio\MSDN98\98VS\1033\Samples\VB98\ActXDoc folder offers an
example of URL navigation between two modeless forms, `FirstDoc` and `SecndDoc`.

If all forms (except the main form) are modal, you needn't change the basic architecture of the
application; presumably all modal forms (dialogs) open from the main form. In this case, convert only the main form to a `UserDocument`, leaving all of the other forms as conventional
Visual Basic 6.0 forms (Forms3 version 2.01). The TV Program Guide application
(Vb6pg.vbp) of Chapter 14, "Scheduling and Device Control with Jet and VBA," is a useful
example of a multiform application in which all the subsidiary forms (except the splash screen)
are modal. The sections that follow describe the issues involved in adapting a complex database application to an ActiveX Document.

Performing the Initial Form Conversion

Using the ActiveX Document Migration Wizard to convert a complex project follows the course described for Ado2oltp.vbp in the early sections of this chapter. To start the migration, do the following:

1. Copy all of the files, except Vb6pg.exe, from the \Ddg_vb6\Chaptr14 folder of the accompanying CD-ROM to a new folder (other than \Ddg_vb6\Chaptr23).

2. Open Vb6pg.vbp; then open frmGuide in the code editor and delete or comment out the frmSplash.Show and **DoEvents** lines at the beginning of the Form_Load event handler. Search for all instances of frmNewGuide in frmGuide and delete or comment out the code. The frmSplash and frmNewGuide forms are modeless.

3. Launch the ActiveX Document Migration Wizard and click Next to open the Form Select dialog. Select only frmGuide to convert to an ActiveX Document and click Next.

4. In the Options dialog, mark the Comment Out Invalid Code and Remove Original Forms After Conversion check boxes, select the Convert to an ActiveX DLL option, and click Next.

5. In the Finshed! dialog, click Finish. Click OK to close The Wizard found some invalid code... message box, click Close to close the Report dialog, and then click OK when the final message appears.

6. In the Vb6ProgGuide Project Properties sheet, click the Debugging tab and select the Start Component option. If you don't select this option, the docGuide UserDocument won't initialize when you run the project.

7. Press Ctrl+F5 to compile and run the project. After a second or two, you encounter compile errors.

Fixing the Code

The Wizard fixes some, but not all, of the code to accommodate the limitations of UserDocuments. The following steps take you to the point where you can run (but not compile) the project:

1. To provide access to public procedures behind Guide, you must declare in a module a **Public** object variable of the docGuide type. Add the following line to the Declarations section of modGlobals:

   Public gdocGuide **As** docGuide

2. Change the name of frmGuide to **docGuide**.

3. Search and replace with **docGuide** all instances of frmGuide in the Current Project.

4. To point `gdocGuide` to the current instance of `docGuide`, add the following line after the Wizard-added call to `Form_Load` in the `UserDocument_Initialize` event handler:

   Set `gdocGuide` = **Me**

5. The Wizard changes `Form_Activate` to `UserDocument_Activate`, but the `UserDocument_Activate` event doesn't fire during the document loading process. Thus you must rename `UserDocument_Activate` back to `Form_Activate` and add the following line after **Set** `gdocGuide` = **Me**:

   Call `Form_Activate`

6. `UserDocuments` don't expose controls with conventional *frmName*.*ctlName* statements. Thus you must move the `PGRecordset` and `ShowToRecord` **Public** subprocedures from the `modPublicProcs` module to `docGuide`. Cut and paste the two subprocedures to the end of the code in `docGuide`.

7. Select the `PGRecordset` and `ShowToRecord` subprocedures and replace `gdocGuide` with **UserDocument** in the Selected Text only.

8. The `SetFocus` method isn't allowed, so search and comment out all lines in `docGuide` containing `SetFocus`.

9. At this point, the project will run, but not compile. Press F5 to run the project. After a few seconds to create the 19,000-line `ADODB.Recordset`, `docGuide` appears in IE 4.01 (see Figure 23.11).

10. Change the project name to **ActiveXDocTVProgGuide** and save the project as **Pg6axd.vbd**.

23

USING ACTIVEX
DOCUMENT
OBJECTS

FIGURE 23.11

The TV Program Guide displayed in IE 4.01.

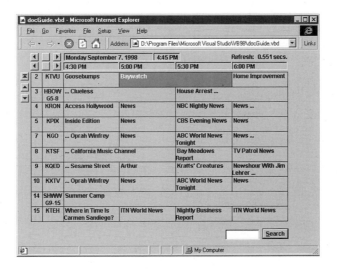

> **NOTE**
>
> The menus of docGuide don't appear in the UserDocument container during design mode. When docGuide runs in IE 4.01, however, docGuide negotiates its menus with IE. The docGuide menus add the second File, plus the Setup, View, and Help choices. File, Exit doesn't work, because the **End** reserved word isn't permitted in a UserDocument.

Cleaning Up the Remaining Code

You might be satisfied with simply getting the TV Program Guide to run in IE 4.01, but it's a good programming practice to make sure that your projects compile without errors. To correct the remaining nonconforming code that prevents compiling and throws errors when returning to design mode, do the following:

1. Other forms, such as frmSatellite, call the PGRecordset subprocedure, so search for **Call** PGRecordset and replace each instance (except in docGuide) with **Call gdocGuide.PGRecordset**.

2. You can't directly access controls on the UserDocument from other forms, so press Ctrl+F5 to attempt compilation. Temporarily comment out code in this category that results in compile errors. The most common culprits are changes to docGuide's label captions and menu commands.

3. After you can successfully compile the project, save it.

4. The UserDocument_Initialize event also fires when shutting down the form, so wrap all three lines of active code in this event handler within an **If** gdocGuide **Is Nothing Then...End If** structure. This addition causes the Form_Load and Form_Activate event handlers to execute only when necessary.

5. Run the project and test the menu commands; then double-click an episode to open the Record Selected Episodes dialog (see Figure 23.12). Verify that the VCR Setup and the Print or Clear buttons operate correctly.

> **NOTE**
>
> You can't set the Alignment property of the column header and the columnar data independently. Thus you can't emulate exactly the formatting of Access 97 datasheets, which center column headers regardless of the formatting of the data in the column.

FIGURE 23.12

Testing the modal frmRecord *form in the* docGuide *UserDocument.*

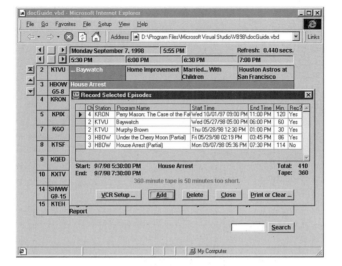

You can access controls on the UserDocument from other forms by declaring a global **Public** variable, such as glbl*Name* **As** Label, and then adding **Set** glbl*Name* = UserDocument.lbl*Name* statements in the Form_Load event handler. Similarly, add **Public** gmnu*Name* **As** Menu and glbl*Name* = UserDocument.lbl*Name* statements for each menu whose attributes you want to change from another form.

NOTE

An operating version of the Pg6axd.vbp project is available in the \Ddg_vb6\Chaptr23\Pg6axd folder of the accompanying CD-ROM.

Working with Remote Data Services

24

IN THIS APPENDIX

Microsoft Remote Data Service (RDS) began life as the Advance Data Connector (ADC) 1.0. The objective of ADC was to provide a means of marshalling via HTTP "live data" in the form of disconnected, lightweight ADOR.Recordset objects from Internet servers to data-bound ActiveX controls hosted in IE 3.0 browsers. ADC marshaled user changes to the Recordset back to the database tables. ADC 1.0, like ADO 1.0, generated a substantial amount of interest on the part of database developers, but not production deployment.

With the introduction of version 1.1 in late September 1997, Microsoft changed the ADC terminology to RDS and provided an updated version of the Microsoft ActiveX Data Objects Recordset Library (ADOR). Subsequently, Microsoft released version 1.5 of ADOR, which is included with Internet Information Server (IIS) 4.0 and is installed during the setup process from the Windows NT 4.0 Option Pack. Version 1.1 and 1.5 had their own set of support DLLs and didn't require installation of the full ADO 1.x support package on the client.

RDS version 2.0 requires the full set of ADO 2.0 support DLLs on the client and server, plus the Microsoft ActiveX Data Objects 2.0 Recordset Library, Msador15.dll. The library filename carries the 1.5 version number for backward compatibility. Installing Visual Studio 6.0 automatically updates RDS 1.5 client software to RDS 2.0; you must run the BackOffice server installation to update the IIS 4.0 RDS 1.5 server components to RDS 2.0.

> **NOTE**
>
> Microsoft continues to distribute RDS 1.1 for support of Internet Explorer (IE) 3.02 and 16-bit clients. RDS 1.1 doesn't support ADO data binding. RDS 2.0 requires IE 4+, so RDS applications currently are limited to use on intranets and communication over the Internet with users having IE 4+ installed.

This chapter introduces you to RDS architecture; provides tables of RDS Automation component properties, methods, and, where applicable, events; and shows you how to implement a conventional HTML Web page with an embedded RDS.DataControl acting as a data provider to DataGrid and DataCombo controls contained in the page.

UNDERSTANDING RDS ARCHITECTURE

Microsoft's mantra for 1999 and beyond is "simplicity." Bill Gates said in his September 2, 1998, Microsoft Developer Days broadcast:

> "Simplicity is another big initiative for us. It's one that has really risen to the top of the list....So underneath, it will be complicated, but what the user has to look at doesn't have to be complicated. A lot of work to do there."

RDS isn't simple for the developer; it has a complicated object model and requires many support DLLs on both the client and server. The sections that follow describe how RDS projects differ from conventional HTML-based Web database techniques and the object model of RDS.

> **NOTE**
>
> Kamaljit Bath's 19-page July 1998 white paper, "Remote Data Service in ADO 2.0" provides a detailed explanation of RDS architecture. You can read or download the white paper in Word 97 format at `http://msdn.microsoft.com/developer/news/feature/datajul98/remdata.htm`.

Conventional Versus RDS Database Operations

Delivering data to and updating data using conventional Web techniques follows this course:

1. The user navigates to a URL of a conventional HTML page with a POST form method that calls a script or an Active Server Page (ASP) containing a script to execute a particular query.

2. The user types an SQL WHERE clause criterion into an INPUT text box to specify the set of records to display.

3. The user clicks the SUBMIT button, and the browser sends the data request via HTTP to the server.

4. The server executes the script, creates a Recordset, and returns via HTTP the Recordset data to the user as a new page in the form of an HTML table.

5. Updating tables requires the user to type data into INPUT boxes and then click the SUBMIT button to execute an INSERT or UPDATE query on the server.

The most accessible example of conventional database query techniques are the Internet Database Connector (IDC) samples included with all versions of IIS. IDC scripts provide the ODBC data source name, user name, password, the template filename, and an SQL statement with one or more named replaceable parameters. An HTML template (.htx) file defines the format of the table that's returned to the user. IDC is a simple, straightforward approach to creating database applications for the Web; IDC was the forerunner of ASP. Like ASP, all IDC work is done on the server, and all pages generated are browser-independent HTML. Edits to multiple records usually require one round-trip to the server for each record changed.

RDS lets you move more of the processing load to the client and UPDATE or INSERT multiple records of a Recordset in a single server round-trip. RDS makes browse mode editing of large Recordsets practical in intranet applications. Following is the typical scenario for RDS database operations:

1. The user navigates to the URL of an ASP or Dynamic HTML (DHTML) page containing an embedded RDS.DataControl and visible data-bound controls.

2. The server returns the HTML or DHTML page, which usually includes a text box to enter a WHERE clause criterion.

3. The user types the criterion and clicks a button to create the SQL statement to populate the data-bound control.

4. The RDS.DataControl sends the SQL statement and Connection data to the server via HTTP or DCOM, depending on the client's type of connection to the server. If the user is permitted to update tables, the request specifies batch-optimistic locking.

5. The server marshals via HTTP or DCOM the resulting ADOR.Recordset to the client by value, not by reference. The ADOR.Recordset is disconnected because HTTP is a stateless protocol and doesn't permit a continuing connection to the server. In the RDS environment, DCOM communication emulates HTTP and doesn't maintain state.

6. The client-side cursor engine receives the marshaled WHERE ADOR.Recordset and connects to the RDS.DataControl, which populates the data-bound controls, such as a DataGrid, with a static cursor. For read-only operation, you can bind a DHTML table to the RDS.DataControl.

> **NOTE**
>
> You can specify asynchronous fetch operations for large ADOR.Recordsets by setting the ExecuteOptions and FetchOptions properties of the RDS.DataControl.

7. The user makes multiple changes to the DataGrid, adds a few new records, and clicks an Update button to execute the UpdateBatch method of the ADOR.Recordset.

> **NOTE**
>
> Unlike batch-optimistic updates to conventional ADODB.Recordset objects, batch updating an ADOR.Recordset is an all-or-nothing operation. RDS 2.0 doesn't support update conflict resolution; Microsoft states that this feature will be included in a future version of RDS. If the batch update fails, the RDS.DataControl fires an onerror event.

8. The RDS.DataControl marshals only the altered and added records to the server, assuming that the adMarshalModifiedOnly option is specified for the ADOR.Recordset.

> **NOTE**
>
> In its default configuration within a browser environment, RDS permits communication only with data sources that reside on the server supplying the HTML page. In a configuration where you specify the server name in the URL (http://oakleaf1 for the examples of this chapter), the data source (pubs and other SQL Server 7.0 database in this chapter) must reside on the OAKLEAF1 server.

The advantages of RDS become most evident when working with relatively large query result sets, such as hierarchical Recordsets created with SHAPE statements or online analytical processing (OLAP) result sets returned by Microsoft Decision Support Services. Unfortunately, RDS 2.0 doesn't support parameterized hierarchical Recordsets; like conflict resolution, Microsoft promises this feature for a future version of RDS.

> **NOTE**
>
> The current version of the DHTML Page Designer doesn't support the Hierarchical FlexGrid control or the Microsoft Chart control. Other controls incompatible with the released version of the Visual Basic 6.0 DHTML Page Designer are listed in the Page Designer: Control Issues topic of the Readmevb.htm release notes.

Most database developers discourage browse mode editing of production tables, but browse mode editing remains the most practical approach to adding or altering line items in order entry and invoicing applications. If you *must* use a browser-based application for online order entry, RDS probably is the best choice.

RDS 2.0 Automation Components

RDS 2.0's working set consists of the following four Automation objects:

- ADOR.Recordset objects from the Microsoft ActiveX Data Objects 2.0 Recordset Library (ADOR, Msador15.dll) have an almost complete subset of the properties and methods of the ADO.Recordset object, but no events. You can program ADOR.Recordset objects with Visual Basic, VC++, VBScript, or ECMAScript.

- RDS.DataControl objects from the Microsoft Remote Data Services 2.0 Library (RDS, Msadco.dll) request ADOR.Recordsets from the server and bind ADO-enabled ActiveX controls on an HTML page to ADOR.Recordsets. The ADOR.Recordset binds to the invisible RDS.DataControl's SourceRecordset property and acts as an embedded data

24

WORKING WITH REMOTE DATA SERVICES

provider to controls on the page. The properties, methods, and events of the
RDS.DataControl, have little in common with the ADO Data control (ADODC).

> **NOTE**
>
> There appears to be controversy within Microsoft whether RDS is singular
> (Remote Data Service as in the Bath white paper) or multiple (Remote Data
> Services as in the type library names).

- RDS.DataSpace objects, also from the RDS library, instantiate a generic proxy for server-based Automation objects, such as components in Microsoft Transaction Server 2.0 packages. The default Automation object for two-tier applications is the RDSServer.DataFactory object. You don't need to consider the RDS.DataSpace object unless you're calling an MTS 2.0 custom business object.

- RDSServer.DataFactory objects from the Microsoft Remote Data Service Server 2.0 Library (RDSServer, Msadco.dll) provides a Recordset request connection between IIS and an OLE DB data provider via ADO 2.0. Version 2.0 of the DataFactory object offers a Customization Handler feature that lets you replace the default handler (MSDFMAP.Handler) with a custom handler to intercept client-side SQL statements and change the SQL string. In a three-tier MTS 2.0 application, MTS-hosted component(s) replace the DataFactory object.

> **NOTE**
>
> The Customization Handler feature is beyond the scope of this book. For more
> information, read "Using the Customization Handler Feature in RDS 2.0" paper
> at http://www.microsoft.com/data/ado/rds/custhand.htm.

> **TIP**
>
> You can quickly review the properties and methods of the preceding four
> Automation components by opening a new Standard EXE project, adding refer-
> ences to the type libraries of the three DLLs, and opening the component's type
> library in Object Browser.

Figure 24.1 illustrates the relationship between the preceding four Automation objects. In addition to the four Automation components, the following low-level objects, which aren't directly accessible to Visual Basic programmers, provide support services for RDS:

FIGURE 24.1

The architecture of Microsoft Remote Data Service 2.0.

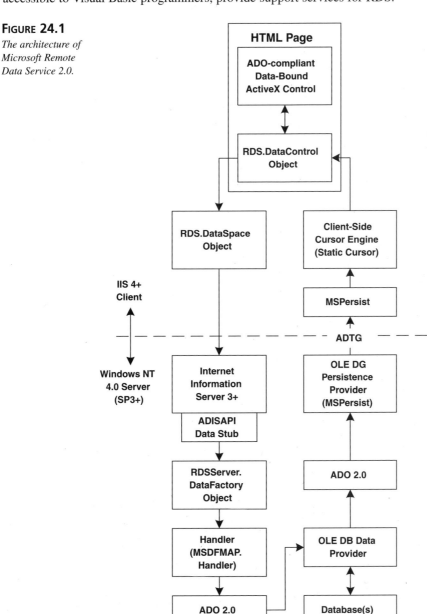

- *Client Cursor Engine* (CE) is a client-side OLE DB service provider that provides a subset of the ADO 2.0 cursor engine's services for Recordset objects. CE cursors are static only; they support Bookmarks, but the Bookmarks are valid only for client-side cursor positioning. The CE Bookmark values don't correspond to a Bookmark for the same record on the server.

▶ See "Recordset Properties," **p. 97**

- *OLE DB Persistence* (MSPersist) providers on the server side save (persist) a Recordset as a binary stream (IStream interface) in HTTP or DCOM format, depending on the protocol in use. The client-side CE uses MSPersist to marshal ADOR.Recordsets by value across the client-server process boundary using the Advanced Data Tablegram (ADTG) Multipurpose Internet Mail Extensions (MIME) format.

NOTE

The Save method persists ADODB.Recordsets as files in ADTG format (*Recordset*.PersistFormat = adPersistADTG) and the Open method of the ADODB.Command object (lng*Options* = adCmdFile) with the MSPersist provider. According to the Bath white paper, future versions of RDS will support persisting ADOR.Recordsets in Extensible Markup Language (XML) format.

- *ADISAPI* is an IIS data stub that instantiates RDSServer.DataFactory or MTS 2.0 components. ADISAPI includes a parser for the MIME elements that make up the data request from RDS.DataSpace objects.

EXPLORING THE METHODS, PROPERTIES, AND EVENTS OF RDS COMPONENTS

▶ See "The ADODB.Recordset Object," **p. 97**

The following three sections describe the properties, methods, and events of the RDS.DataControl object; the properties and methods of the RDS.DataSpace object, and the methods of the RDSServer.DataFactory object. Properties and methods of the ADOR.Recordset object aren't included in this chapter, because they are essentially identical to the properties and methods of the ADODB.Recordset object described in Chapter 2, "Understanding OLE DB and Universal Data Access." Unlike the ADODB.Recordset, the ADOR.Recordset object doesn't fire events.

RDS.DataControl Object

The `RDS.DataControl` and its bound `ADOR.Recordset` are the only two objects that you need to program for conventional two-tier Visual Basic 6.0 WebClass and DHTML applications.

Table 24.1 lists the properties of the `RDS.DataControl` object, which are accessible in design mode and through VBA code in IIS Application and DHTML Application projects. Unless otherwise noted in the Purpose column of the table, all properties are read-write in run mode.

TABLE 24.1 PROPERTIES OF THE RDS.DataControl OBJECT

Property	Description
Connect	A **String** that specifies the OLE DB data provider and the database (with SQLOLEDB) or the system data source name (with MSDASQL)
ExecuteOptions	A flag that specifies synchronous (adcExecSync, the default) or asynchronous (adcExecAsync) execution
FetchOptions	A flag the specifies the type of asynchronous delivery of the ADOR.Recordset (adcFetchAsync, adcFetchBackground, or adcFetchUpFront)
FilterColumn	A **String** the specifies the name of the field on which to apply a filter
FilterCriterion	A **String** consisting of one of the following operators for the FilterValue: <, <=, =, >=, >, or <>
FilterValue	A **String** that represents the text or numerical value of the filter, such as 123 or 'Garcia Lorca'
InternetTimeout	A **Long** value that sets the time (in milliseconds) within which the server must be respond to a request
ReadyState	A flag that returns (read-only) the progress of execution of a request (adcReadyStateComplete, adcReadyStateInteractive, or adReadyStateLoaded)
Recordset	Returns (read-only) a pointer to the {ADOR¦ADODB}.Recordset bound to the control
Server	A **String** that specifies the name of the server and the communications protocol (*ServerName* for DCOM, http://*servername* for HTTP)
SortColumn	A **String** that specifies the name of the field on which to sort the Recordset
SortDirection	A **Boolean** value that determines ASC (**False**, the default) or DESC (**True**) sort direction
SourceRecordset	Binds (write-only) an independently created {ADOR¦ADODB}.Recordset to the control
SQL	A **String** that specifies the SELECT query string to return the Recordset

The properties and methods of the RDS.DataControl are, for the most part, a subset of properties of the ADODC and its underlying ADODB.Recordset adapted for embedding in an HTML or DHTML Web page. Table 24.2 lists the methods of the RDS.DataControl object.

TABLE 24.2 PROPERTIES OF THE RDS.DataControl OBJECT

Method	Description
Cancel	Terminates a currently executing asynchronous operation (same as Cancel for ADODB.Recordset objects)
CancelUpdate	Clears all changes made to the bound Recordset and restores the Recordset to its condition immediately after the last Refresh method call (same as CancelUpdate for ADODB.Recordset objects)
CreateRecordset	Creates an empty, disconnected Recordset that you can populate on the client, but not return to the server
Refresh	Requeries the specified OLE DB data source and refreshes the Recordset (same as Requery for ADODB.Recordset objects)
Reset	Executes filter and sort operations specified by the respective current values of the FilterColumn, FilterCriterion, and FilterValue and the SortColumn and SortDirection properties
SubmitChanges	Sends changes to the Recordset as a batch to the OLE DB data provider (equivalent to the UpdateBatch method of ADODB.Recordsets).

Object Browser displays two RDS.DataControl events—onerror and onreadystatechange— that don't appear in the code editor for an early-bind instance of the RDS.DataControl object with a Private rdcName **As New** RDS.DataControl statement. These events are accessible only if you create a late-bound instance of the object, using the VBA `CreateObject` function or the HTML `<object ...>` tag.

THE `RDS.DataSpace` OBJECT

You need to program the `RDS.DataSpace` object only if your page connects to a custom business object that provides the connection to the database. Table 24.3 describes the one property and one method of the `RDS.DataSpace` object.

TABLE 24.3   THE PROPERTY AND METHOD OF THE `RDS.DataSpace` OBJECT

Name	Description
`InternetTimeout` (property)	A **Long** value that sets the time (in milliseconds) within which the business object must be respond to a request (read/write)
`CreateObject` (method)	Creates a proxy for the business object based on its Programmatic ID (ProgID) and returns a pointer to the proxy.

THE `RDSServer.DataFactory` OBJECT

The `RDSServer.DataFactory` object is the default business object called by the `RDS.DataSpace` object and has the six methods listed in Table 24.4. Three of the methods are identical to those of the client-side `RDS.DataControl` object, which the `RDSServer.DataFactory` emulates on the server side.

TABLE 24.4   METHODS OF THE `RDSServer.DataFactory` OBJECT

Method	Description
`ConvertToString`	Converts a `Recordset` to a MIME string in ADTG format for transmission via HTTP
`CreateRecordset`	Creates an empty, disconnected `Recordset`
`Query`	Creates a `Recordset` from a valid SQL statement supplied as an argument value
`Refresh`	Requeries the specified OLE DB data source and refreshes the `Recordset` (same as `Requery` for `ADODB.Recordset` objects)
`Reset`	Executes filter and sort operations specified by the respective current values of the `FilterColumn`, `FilterCriterion`, and `FilterValue` and the `SortColumn` and `SortDirection` properties
`SubmitChanges`	Sends changes to the `Recordset` as a batch to the OLE DB data provider (equivalent to the `UpdateBatch` method of `ADODB.Recordsets`)

24

WORKING WITH
REMOTE DATA
SERVICES

CODING FOR IMPLICIT AND EXPLICIT REMOTING

The `RDS.DataControl` automates the creation of an `ADOR.Recordset`, a process Microsoft calls "implicit remoting." Alternatively, you can create an `ADODB.Connection` for an `ADODB.Recordset` or `ADOR.Recordset` and bind the `Recordset` to an `RDS.DataContol`, a process called "explicit remoting." The two sections that follow describe the differences in VBA coding for implicit and explicit remoting.

Implicit Remoting with the `RDS.DataControl`

The `RDS.DataControl` minimizes the code to create a disconnected `ADOR.Recordset`. The following VBA code creates an instance of the `RDS.DataControl` object within a `DHTMLPage` object from a query against the authors table of SQL Server's pubs database:

```
Option Explicit
Private rdcAuthors As New RDS.DataControl

Private Sub DHTMLPage_Load()
    'Connect using the RDS.DataControl
    With rdcAuthors
        .Connect = "Provider=MSDASQL;DSN=pubs"
        .Server = "http://oakleaf1"
        .SQL = "Select * FROM Authors"
        .Refresh
    End With
End Sub
```

Alternatively, you can create an instance of the `RDS.DataControl` object with the following HTML `<OBJECT ...></OBJECT>` statement:

```
<OBJECT
    CLASSID="clsid:BD96C556-65A3-11D0-983A-00C04FC29E33"
    ID="rdcAuthors">
    <PARAM NAME="Connect" VALUE="Provider=SQLOLEDB;Database=pubs">
    <PARAM NAME="Server" VALUE="http://oakleaf1">
    <PARAM NAME="SQL" VALUE="SELECT * from authors">
</OBJECT>
```

To activate the `RDS.DataControl` object instance in an HTML page, you must call the `rdcAuthors.Refresh` method from a script. You also can set all property values except that of the `Server` property with script statements.

Explicit Remoting with ADO 2.0 Objects and the RDS.DataControl

Microsoft includes an OLE DB service provider, MS Remote, that lets you pass disconnected ADODB.Recordset objects over an HTTP connection. This approach permits the use of conventional ADO 2.0 code or the Data Environment Designer to create the ADODB.Connection and ADODB.Command objects that RDS omits. If you specify MS Remote as the data provider, you must include the Remote Server=http://*servername* and the appropriate Remote Provider=*ProviderName*;DataSource=*Name* strings as the argument of the cnn*Name*.Open method or as the value of the cnn*Name*.ConnectionString property.

The following code creates an ADOR.Recordset object and binds it to the RDS.DataControl by pointing its SourceRecordset property to the Recordset:

```
Option Explicit
Private rdcAuthors As New RDS.DataControl
Private rsdAuthors As New ADOR.Recordset
Private cnnPubs As New ADODB.Connection

Private Sub DHTMLPage_Load()
    With cnnPubs
        .Mode = adModeReadWrite
        .CursorLocation = adUseClient
        .Provider = "MS Remote"
        .Open "Remote Server=http://oakleaf1;Remote Provider=MSDASQL;DSN=pubs"
    End With
    With rsdAuthors
        Set .ActiveConnection = cnnPubs
        .Source = "Select * FROM Authors"
        .CursorType = adOpenStatic
        .LockType = adLockBatchOptimistic
        .Open
        'Only send changes, if any
        .MarshalOptions = adMarshalModifiedOnly
        'Disconnect the Recordset
        Set .ActiveConnection = Nothing
    End With
    cnnPubs.Close
    'Bind the ADOR.Recordset to the RDS.DataControl
    Set rdcAuthors.SourceRecordset = rsdAuthors
End Sub
```

NOTE

You can substitute an `ADODB.Recordset` for the `ADOR.Recordset` in the preceding Declarations section, but there is little advantage to doing so. `ADODB.Recordset` events aren't accessible within a Web page, and there appears to be a slight performance penalty for opening the "heavyweight" `ADODB.Recordset`.

PROGRAMMING RDS WITH VBA IN THE DHTML PAGE DESIGNER

A DHTML Project is the best approach for Visual Basic database programmers to become acquainted with the intricacies of RDS programming for Web pages. The primary objective of the DHTML Page Designer is to let programmers steeped in VBA use the familiar Visual Basic IDE, debugging features, and richer programming language to create data-driven Web pages. The RdsDhtml.vbp project, described in sections that follow, duplicates on a Web page a simple Visual Basic data display and editing form that uses RDS to retrieve and update data from SQL Server's pubs database. The RdsDhtml.vbp project also compares the VBA code required to bind `ADOR.Recordsets` to the `RDS.DataControl` with implicit and explicit remoting.

NOTE

This DHTML example uses the SQL Server 6.5+ pubs database. If you don't have SQL Server, you can use the Jet 3.5 pubs.mdb table from the \Ddg_vb6\Chaptr24 folder of the accompanying CD-ROM.

Setting Up IIS 4.0 and SQL Server 6.5+ for the DHTML Application

The RdsDhtml.vbp project connects to SQL Server 6.5+'s pubs sample database through IIS 4.0. Following are the requirements to provide SQL Server database connectivity to DHTML Projects and IIS Applications:

1. Your Internet test server must have a Windows NT 4.0 Internet Guest Account, IUSR_*servername* (IUSR_OAKLEAF1 for this example). If this account does not exist on your computer, create it with User Manager for Domains (see Figure 24.2). Make sure to mark the User Cannot Change Password and Password Never Expires check boxes; clear the other two enabled check boxes.

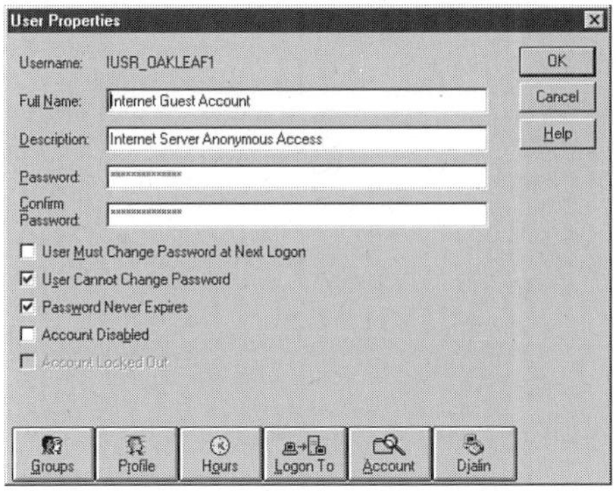

FIGURE 24.2

The Properties sheet for the Internet Guest User account.

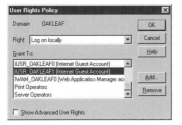

2. To run Visual Basic Internet applications on the test server, the IUSR_*servername* account must have Log on Locally permission, in addition to default User group permissions. To add this permission in User Manager, choose Policies, User Rights to open the User Rights Policy dialog. Select Log on Locally in the Rights list and then scroll through the Accounts list to determine whether IUSR_*servername* is present (see Figure 24.3). If not, click the Add button to open the Add Users and Groups dialog, select IUSR_*servername*, add the account to the Add Names list, and then click OK twice to return to User Manager.

FIGURE 24.3

Log on Locally permission granted to the Internet Guest Account.

3. Launch Internet Service Manager for IIS 4.0, right-click the Default Web Site node, and choose Properties to open the Default Web Site Properties sheet. Click the Directory Security tab, click Edit in the Anonymous Access and Authentication Control frame to open the Authentication Methods dialog, and then click Edit to open the Anonymous User account dialog. Mark the Enable Password Synchronization check box (see Figure 24.4) and exit Internet Service Manager.

24

WORKING WITH
REMOTE DATA
SERVICES

FIGURE 24.4

Verifying the IUSR_servername account name and enabling password synchronization between Windows NT 4.0 and IIS 4.0.

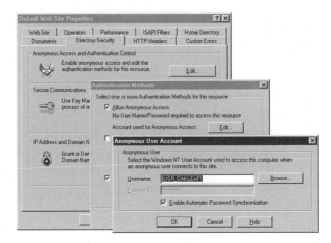

4. Depending on your security settings for SQL Server, you might need to add the IUSR_*servername* account to SQL Server. If you receive a permissions-related error from SQL Server when running the RdsDhtml.vbp application, you must add the IUSR_*servername* account. Launch Enterprise Manager, open the node for your server, right-click Log-Ins, and choose New Login to open the SQL Server Login Properties - New Login sheet. Add ISUR_servername with Windows NT Authentication and select pubs or another noncritical database as the default database (see Figure 24.5). Click the Server Roles tab and assign a Server Role if you want the account to have permissions in addition to the default permissions for users.

FIGURE 24.5

Adding the IUSR_servername account to SQL Server 7.0.

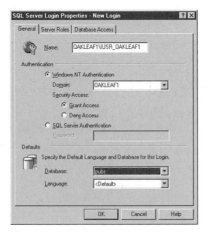

> **NOTE**
>
> As noted in the "Conventional Versus RDS Database Operations" section earlier in the chapter, SQL Server must be located on the same machine as IIS 4.0.
>
> Using the Database sample pages installed by IIS 4.0 setup to check SQL Server connectivity doesn't test the IUSR_*servername* account. The Database samples use the Web SQL System DSN that specifies the SQL Server sa login and an empty password.

5. Create an ODBC system data source (System DSN) named pubs for the local server (see Figure 24.6). Click Next and verify selection of the With Windows NT Authentication Using the Network Login ID option. Click Next and mark the Change the Default Database To check box and select pubs in the list. Click Next, accept the default values, and click Finish to display a summary of the ODBC System DSN properties. Click Test to connect to SQL Server and check the System DSN.

FIGURE 24.6

Adding the pubs ODBC System DSN for the sample DHTML Project.

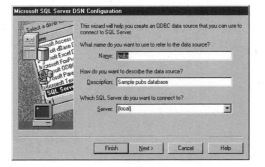

> **NOTE**
>
> You can use either the SQLOLEDB native OLE DB provider or the default MSDASQL ODBC data provider plus the ODBC System DSN in the sample application. The ODBC System DSN is included in the preparatory steps in case security problems arise when using SQLOLEDB.

24

Designing the DHTMLPage

The DHTML page comprises title text; a five-column, two-row table; five INPUT (TextField) boxes; a row of four Recordset navigation buttons; and a second row of two buttons to submit Recordset changes and to requery the database for verification of the changes. Figure 24.7 shows the page in the DHTML Page Designer. Like the Web page examples of previous chapters, DHTMLPage1 isn't a candidate for a graphics award. DHTMLPage1 is intended to emulate the simple Visual Basic 6.0 data display and entry form examples in the early chapters of this book.

FIGURE 24.7

DHTMLPage1 of the RdsDhtml.vbp project in the DHTML Page Designer.

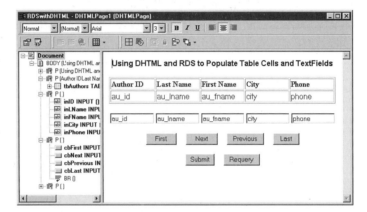

> **NOTE**
>
> The form and VBA code for the RdsDhtml.vbp project is included in the \Ddg_vb6\Chaptr24 folder of the accompanying CD-ROM. Many of the property values of this project are specific to the OAKLEAF1 computer on which the code was written and the project compiled. It's simpler to create the following sample application than to alter the existing code.

To create the sample page, do the following:

1. Open a new DHTML application and display the DHTML Page Designer.

2. Click the Properties button of the DHTML Page Designer toolbar to display the General page, select the Save HTML in an External File option, click New to open the Create HTML File dialog, and navigate to your project folder. Type **RdsDhtml.htm** as the name of the new HTML file. Click Save and then click OK to return to the DHTML Page Designer.

3. Save the project in your project folder, naming the designer **RdsDhtml.dsr**, the module **RdsDhtml.bas**, and the project **RdsDhtml.vbp**.

4. Type the title line, click the Center button, press Return, click the Center button again, and add a centered table to the page. Add four more columns to the table.

5. Type **Author ID**, **Last Name**, **First Name**, **City**, and **Phone** in the columns of the first row of the table. Type the corresponding field names of the authors table of pubs— **au_id**, **au_lname**, **au_fname**, **city**, and **phone**—in the second row.

6. Place the cursor in the au_id cell, click the Properties button to open the Properties window and assign **tdID** as the Id property of the cell.

7. Repeat step 6 for the remaining four cells of the row, assigning **tdLName**, **tdFName**, **tdCity**, and **tdPhone** as the Id property values.

8. In the left pane of the designer, select the TABLE node, open the Properties window, and assign **tdAuthors** as the Id.

9. Press Return below the table, click the Center button, add a TextField control (INPUT element), and add five spaces to separate it from the next button. In the Property window for the TextField, change the Id property to **inID** and the name and value properties to **au_id**.

TIP

If you're familiar with editing HTML, open the HTML text editor, copy and paste the first INPUT element to create the remaining INPUT fields, and edit the HTML to provide the proper id, name, and value for each INPUT element. It's faster to edit the HTML code than to drag INPUT elements from the Toolbox and set property values in the Properties window.

---

10. Repeat step 9 for the remaining four fields, assigning **inLName**, **inFName**, **inCity**, and **inPhone** as the Id values and **au_lname**, **au_fname**, **city**, and **phone** as the name and value properties.

11. Press Return to add a new line, click Center, and add a Button control (INPUT element of type button), plus five spaces to separate it from the next button. In the Properties window, assign **cbFirst** as the Id and name property values, and **First** as the value (caption).

12. Repeat step 11 for the remaining three buttons, **cbNext** (**Next**), **cbPrevious** (**Previous**), and **cbLast** (**Last**).

13. Repeat step 11 to add **Submit** (**cbSubmit**) and **Requery** (**cbRequery**) buttons below the navigation buttons. Set the disabled property of the Submit button to **True**.

14. Add references to the Microsoft Remote Data Services 2.0 Library (Msadcf.dll), the Microsoft ActiveX Data Objects Recordset 2.0 Library (Msador15.dll), and the Microsoft ActiveX Data Objects 2.0 Library (Msado15.dll) to the project.

NOTE

Msado15.dll is required only for demonstrating explicit remoting. If you don't want to add the extra code required to create ADODB.Connection objects, you can dispense with the reference to the Microsoft ActiveX Data Objects 2.0 Library.

15. Run the project to check your work so far (see Figure 24.8) and then save the project.

FIGURE 24.8

DHTMLPage1 of the RdsDhtml.vbp project running in IE 4.01.

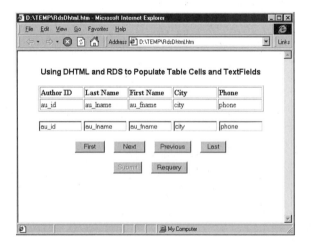

Adding Code to Populate the Page Elements

Double-click one of the buttons and add the code of Listing 24.1 to the Declarations section, the DHTMLPage_Load event handler, and the General section. If you don't want to test explicit remoting, you can omit the code in the **Else...End If** structure of the DHTMLPage_Load event handler. Other event handlers, added later in this section, call the PopulateElements subprocedure to refresh the data in the table cells and TextField controls.

LISTING 24.1 VISUAL BASIC 6.0 CODE TO POPULATE TABLE CELLS AND TEXTFIELD CONTROLS WITH THE FIRST RECORD FROM THE AUTHORS TABLE OF THE PUBS DATABASE

```
Option Explicit
Private rdcAuthors As New RDS.DataControl
Private rsdAuthors As New ADODB.Recordset
Private cnnPubs As New ADODB.Connection
Private blnUseRDSDataControl As Boolean

Private Sub DHTMLPage_Load()
    blnUseRDSDataControl = True
    If blnUseRDSDataControl Then
        'Implicit remoting
        cbRequery.disabled = False
        'Connect using the RDS.AuthorsControl
        With rdcAuthors
            '.Connect = "Provider=SQLOLEDB;Initial Catalog=pubs"
            .Connect = "Provider=MSDASQL;DSN=pubs"
            .Server = "http://oakleaf1"
            .SQL = "Select * FROM Authors"
            .ExecuteOptions = adcExecSync
            .FetchOptions = adcFetchBackground
            .Refresh
            'Create a test Recordset
            Set rsdAuthors = .Recordset
        End With
    Else
        'Explicit remoting
        cbRequery.disabled = True
        'Connect using conventional ADODB code with explicit remoting
        With cnnPubs
            .Mode = adModeReadWrite
            .CursorLocation = adUseClient
            .Provider = "MS Remote"
            '.Open "Remote Server=http://oakleaf1;" & _
            '    Remote Provider=SQLOLEDB;Database=pubs"
            .Open "Remote Server=http://oakleaf1;" & _
                "Remote Provider=MSDASQL;DSN=pubs"
        End With
```

continues

24

WORKING WITH
REMOTE DATA
SERVICES

Listing 24.1 Continued

```
      With rsdAuthors
          Set .ActiveConnection = cnnPubs
          .Source = "Select * FROM Authors"
          .CursorType = adOpenStatic
          .LockType = adLockBatchOptimistic
          .Open
          'Only send changes, if any
          .MarshalOptions = adMarshalModifiedOnly
          'Disconnect the Recordset
          Set .ActiveConnection = Nothing
      End With
      cnnPubs.Close
      'Bind the ADOR.Recordset to the RDS.DataControl
      Set rdcAuthors.SourceRecordset = rsdAuthors
   End If
   Call PopulateElements
End Sub

Private Sub PopulateElements()
   With rdcAuthors.Recordset
      tdID.innerText = .Fields("au_id").Value
      tdLName.innerText = .Fields("au_lname").Value
      tdFName.innerText = .Fields("au_fname").Value
      tdCity.innerText = .Fields("city").Value
      tdPhone.innerText = .Fields("phone").Value
      inID.Value = .Fields("au_id").Value
      inLName.Value = .Fields("au_lname").Value
      inFName.Value = .Fields("au_fname").Value
      inCity.Value = .Fields("city").Value
      inPhone.Value = .Fields("phone").Value
   End With
End Sub
```

At this point, press Ctrl+F5 to compile and run the project. IE 4.01 opens and, after a second or two, field values of the first record of pubs' authors table appear in the table cells and TextField controls (see Figure 24.9).

FIGURE 24.9

Table cells and TextField controls displaying field values of the first record of the query.

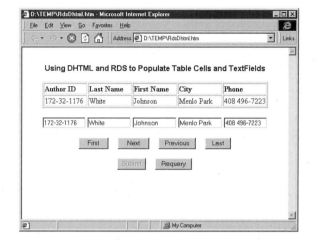

Adding ADOR.Recordset Navigation Code

Add the event-handling code of Listing 24.2 to navigate the ADOR.Recordset. Unlike Visual Basic, DHTML event handlers are functions that return a **Boolean** value to control *event bubbling*, a Microsoft term meaning that untrapped events "bubble up" to the next higher element in the Document object hierarchy.

LISTING 24.2 CODE TO NAVIGATE THE ADOR.Recordset

```
Private Function cbFirst_onclick() As Boolean
    rdcAuthors.Recordset.MoveFirst
    Call PopulateElements
End Function

Private Function cbNext_onclick() As Boolean
    With rdcAuthors.Recordset
        'MoveNext requires different treatment than MovePrevious
        .MoveNext
        If .EOF Then
            Beep
            .MoveLast
        End If
    End With
    Call PopulateElements
End Function

Private Function cbPrevious_onclick() As Boolean
    With rdcAuthors.Recordset
        If .BOF Then
            .MoveFirst
            Beep
```

continues

LISTING 24.2 CONTINUED

```
        Else
            .MovePrevious
        End If
    End With
End Function

Private Function cbLast_onclick() As Boolean
    rdcAuthors.Recordset.MoveLast
    Call PopulateElements
End Function
```

> **NOTE**
>
> The RDS.DataControl doesn't have BOFAction and EOFAction properties, so code to trap BOF and EOF errors differs in the cbPrevious_onclick and cbNext_onclick event handlers, respectively.

Compile and run the project; then check the action of the record navigation buttons. Record navigation occurs on the client and doesn't require round trips to the server to retrieve individual records.

Enabling ADOR.Recordset Editing with TextField Controls

The code of Listing 24.3 passes the changed value of a TextField to the appropriate field of the current record. The onchange event fires when the user edits a field value and then shifts the focus to another control. You must include the *inName*_onchange = **True** statement to prevent recursive execution of the event handler as a result of event bubbling. Setting the return value of the event-handling function to **True** "swallows the event." The Submit button is enabled only after a change to at least one field value.

LISTING 24.3 EVENT-HANDLING CODE FOR UPDATES TO THE TEXTFIELD CONTROLS

```
Private Function inLName_onchange() As Boolean
    With rdcAuthors.Recordset
        .Fields("au_lname").Value = inLName.Value
        .Update
    End With
    'Swallow the click
    inLName_onchange = True
    cbSubmit.disabled = False
End Function
```

```
Private Function inFName_onchange() As Boolean
    With rdcAuthors.Recordset
        .Fields("au_fname").Value = inFName.Value
        .Update
    End With
    inFName_onchange = True
    cbSubmit.disabled = False
End Function

Private Function inCity_onchange() As Boolean
    With rdcAuthors.Recordset
        .Fields("city").Value = inCity.Value
        .Update
    End With
    inCity_onchange = True
    cbSubmit.disabled = False
End Function

Private Function inPhone_onchange() As Boolean
    With rdcAuthors.Recordset
        .Fields("phone").Value = inPhone.Value
        .Update
    End With
    inPhone_onchange = True
    cbSubmit.disabled = False
End Function
```

> **NOTE**
>
> An `inID_onchange` event handler isn't included, because the au_id field is the primary key of the table. To prevent users from altering primary key values, set the `disabled` property of the primary key TextField to `True`.

Submitting the Changes and Verifying the Result

In implicit remoting mode, the code of Listing 24.4 simply calls the `SubmitChanges` method of the `RDS.DataControl` to send accumulated `ADOR.Recordset` changes to the server. Explicit remoting requires a substantial amount of code to accomplish the same objective, because you must reestablish the connection and synchronize the contents of the `ADOR.Recordset` with the altered `RDS.DataControl.Recordset`.

LISTING 24.4   EVENT-HANDLING CODE TO SUBMIT CHANGES AND REQUERY THE PUBS TABLE

```
Private Function cbSubmit_onclick() As Boolean
    'Send the changes to pubs
    If blnUseRDSDataControl Then
        rdcAuthors.SubmitChanges
    Else
        'Reconnect to the data source
        cnnPubs.Open
        With rsdAuthors
            .ActiveConnection = cnnPubs
            'Clone the DataControl
            Set rsdAuthors = rdcAuthors.Recordset
            .UpdateBatch
        End With
        cnnPubs.Close
    End If
    cbSubmit.disabled = True
End Function

Private Function cbRequery_onclick() As Boolean
    'Verify that the change(s) took place
    rdcAuthors.Refresh
    Call PopulateElements
End Function
```

After adding the code and compiling your project, make a change to one or more fields of the first record; then click Submit, followed by Requery, to refresh the RDS.DataControl with new authors table values. To verify that explicit remoting changes propagate to the underlying table, end and restart the project. You can verify that batch operations propagate by making changes to several records.

NOTE

The preceding example doesn't take advantage of the data-binding features of DHTML in the release version of Visual Basic 6.0's DHTML Page Designer. You can bind ActiveX controls to RDS.DataControls with HTML code and a script (VBScript or ECMAScript). Binding an ActiveX control to early- or late-bound RDS.DataControl in the DHTML Page Editor, however, appears to fail. Further, many current ActiveX controls aren't compatible with DHTML Pages, as noted in the "PageDesigner: Control Issues" topic of the Visual Basic 6.0 Readme file. These issues probably will be resolved by a Visual Studio 6.0 update. Visual Studio 6.0 Service Pack 1, released in late October 1998, does not address DHTML issues. Service Pack 1 fixes compatibility and other problems with Mfc42.dll, Mscvrt.dll, Msvbvm60.dll. Search at http://www.microsoft.com the "Support & the Knowledgebase" category with the term "DHTML Page Designer" or "kbPageDesigner" for up to date information on the resolution of data binding issues.

DEVELOPING DATA-ENABLED INTERNET APPLICATIONS

IN THIS CHAPTER

Most of the browser-based database applications described in the preceding three chapters require client PCs running Internet Explorer (IE) 4+. Such applications are suited for LAN- or WAN-based intranets and mobile employees who have a secure Internet connection to the organization's Web site. Commercial Web sites, however, must accommodate recent versions of IE and Netscape Navigator/Communicator. Both of these browsers were at version 4+ when this book was written, with version 5.0 in development. In 1999 commercial Web sites must support at least versions 3.*x*, 4.*x*, and 5.0 of IE and Navigator.

▶ **See** "WebClasses for Internet Information Server 4.0 Applications," p. ??? (Ch23)

Visual Basic 6.0 IIS Applications (WebClasses), introduced in Chapter 22, "Integrating Databases with Intranets and the Internet," and Active Server Pages (ASP) let Visual Basic 6.0 developers generate dynamic, data-enabled Web sites with VBA 6.0 code. WebClasses, compiled ActiveX DLLs, reside on the server and run within an Internet Information Server (IIS) 4.0 process. The combination of WebClasses and ASP generates "vanilla" HTML that's compatible with virtually all browsers in widespread use today. WebClasses clearly are the most important of the new Internet technologies of Visual Basic 6.0.

NOTE

If you're new to WebClasses, go to `http://msdn.microsoft.com/vbasic/downloads/samples.asp` and download the WebClass Example: Building the Support Application, a data-enabled sample with an accompanying "twelve step" paper (Wctutor.exe), and WebClass Example: Key Concepts [in] Building an IIS Application, an update to the Wcdemo.vbp application included with Visual Basic 6.0 (Wcdemo.exe). You must register your copy of Visual Studio 6.0 or Visual Basic 6.0 before downloading these samples.

This chapter analyzes and modifies a commercial data-enabled WebClass application created by Microsoft for its Visual Basic Web site. The VBLive application, accessible at `http://msdn.microsoft.com/vbasic/downloads/vblive.asp`, is the framework for downloading Visual Basic 6.0 sample applications. The first and only application available for downloading as of mid-September 1998 was the VBLive application itself. The Microsoft copyright license for the VBLive code lets you "… use, modify, reproduce, and distribute [VBLive] in any way you find useful."

NOTE

You can download the original VBLive application as a 421KB self-extracting executable (VBLive.exe) from the VBLive site. You don't need to register your product, but you do need to register yourself to download VBLive.exe. The modified version of VBLive (VBLiveLib.vbp) is located in the \Ddg_vb6\Chaptr25\VbLive folder of the accompanying CD-ROM. The examples of this chapter describe modifications to the original VBLive files that adapt the project to control access to a specific set of Web pages on a commercial Internet site.

SETTING UP TO RUN VBLIVE

You must have Visual Basic 6.0, SQL Server 6.5+, and IIS 4.0 set up and running under Windows NT 4.0 with Service Pack 3+ on your development server to run the VBLive application. The instructions that follow use SQL Server 7.0, but the installation process for SQL Server 6.5 is quite similar.

To install the modified VBLive application, do the following:

1. Create a new project folder and copy all the files in the \Ddg_vb6\Chaptr25\VBLive folder and subfolders on the accompanying CD-ROM to the project folder.

▶ **See** "Verifying Your Upsized SQL Server 6.5 Database," **p. 698**

2. Launch SQL Server Enterprise Manager, expand the node for your local server (OAKLEAF1 in the examples), right-click Databases, and choose New Database to open the Database Properties sheet.

3. Type **VBLive** in the Name text box of the General page.

4. Click the Options page and mark the Truncate Log on Checkpoint checkbox; then click OK to create the new database.

> **NOTE**
>
> If you're using SQL Server 6.5, Microsoft recommends that you create a new 5MB device or use an existing device with 5MB of free space for the VBLive database.

▶ **See** "Testing the nwind Database with the SQL Server Query Analyzer," **p. 709**

5. Click Tools, choose SQL Server Query Analyzer, and log on to your local server.

6. Choose File, Open and open the CCRScript.sql script from your *Project*\Data folder.

7. Select VBLive in the Database list; then right-click the query pane and choose Execute Query to run the query.

> ### CAUTION
>
> Make sure to change the Database entry from master to VBLive before running CCRScript.sql. If you accidentally run the script in the master database, you won't be able to gain access to its contents through Enterprise Manager. You can, however, alter the contents in the Data View window.

> ### NOTE
>
> CCRScript.sql is a modified version of the original VBLive.sql script that creates the tables of the database, establishes declarative referential integrity (DRI) between the tables, adds indexes, creates stored procedures, and then adds a set of records to the Samples table. The script also adds an InternetLogin account for the database. VBLive.sql has one sample record that lets you download VBLive.exe; CCRScript.sql has eight records that describe and point to individual pages on a Web site. The modified script also removes the IDENTITY attribute from the SampleID field of the Samples table to simplify the SQL INSERT INTO statements that add new records.

8. Double-click the VBLive.udl Data Link file to open the Data Link Properties sheet.

9. Type your local server name in the top text box (see Figure 25.1) and select VBLive in the database list. Click Test to check the SQLOLEDB connection and click OK to save the Data Link file.

FIGURE 25.1

Specifying the properties of the VBLiveLib virtual root.

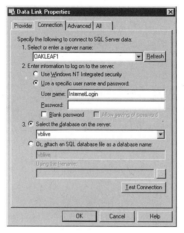

10. Open the VBLiveLib.vbp project and press Ctrl+F5 to compile and run the project.

11. The first time you run the project, a dialog opens requesting that you specify an IIS virtual root for the project. Click OK to accept the default VBLiveLib virtual root. IE 4.01 opens with the Log In page for the site (see Figure 25.2).

FIGURE 25.2

The opening Log In page of the modified VBLive project.

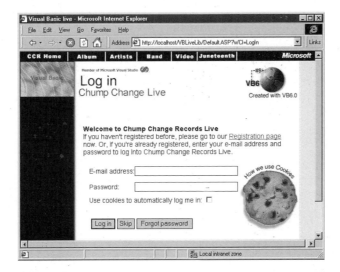

12. Launch Internet Service Manager, expand the Default Web Site node, right-click VBLiveLib, and choose Properties to open the VBLiveLib Properties sheet.

13. Clear the Directory Browsing Allowed check box in the Virtual Directory page to prevent users from gaining direct access to files in the …\VBLive folder.

14. Click the Documents tab, click the Add button and add **Default.asp**, the starting page of VBLive, to the default documents list. Remove Default.htm from the list; then click OK to make the changes.

> **NOTE**
>
> The last two steps in the preceding list aren't necessary until you compile VBLiveLib.vbp to an ActiveX DLL and test the live site. The steps are included in this section because they're elements of the complete setup process.

TOURING THE VBLIVE APPLICATION

The VBLive WebClass generates the HTML content for the site from HTML templates located in the …\VBLive\AppTemplates and …\VBLive\SampleTemplates folders and graphics in the

…\VBLive\AppGraphics and …\VBLive\AppGraphics folders. Modifications to the template HTML and graphics reflect the change from a Visual Basic–oriented site to that for an independent record label, Chump Change Records.

Figure 25.3 is a partial flow diagram of the modified VBLive IIS Project. Only the modified templates appear in the diagram; the modified templates represent the core of the project. Templates for peripheral activities, such as ForgotPassword.htm and PasswordSent.htm, aren't included in the diagram.

Figure 25.3

Flow diagram for the VBLive project showing modified templates for core activities.

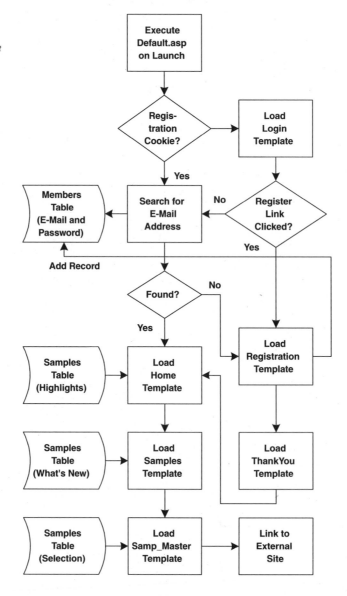

NOTE

The Log In page appears if you don't have a registration cookie created during a prior registration. The Members table of the VBLive database stores membership information in the MemberID (IDENTITY column), Password, EMail, Name, NotifyUpdates, and VBVersionID fields.

The following steps navigate the modified elements of the VBLive IIS Project:

1. Compile and run VBLiveLib.vbp to display the Log In page (generated by the LogIn.htm template) if you didn't do so in the preceding section.

2. Click the Registration link to open the Registration page (generated by Registration.htm).

3. Complete the Registration form (see Figure 25.4) and click Submit to open the Thank You page (Thankyou.htm).

FIGURE 25.4

The completed Registration page.

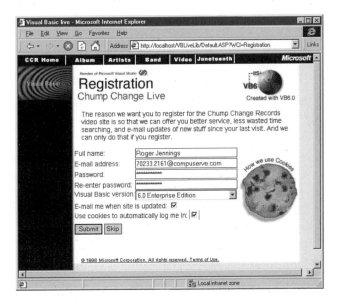

4. Click the Enter Chump Change Live link to open the Welcome to Chump Change Records Live page (Home.htm). The Highlights section of the page contains a list created from the eight records added to the Samples table (see Figure 25.5).

FIGURE 25.5

The modified home page of the site showing three of the records in the Samples table.

> **NOTE**
>
> The Samples table supplies the heading (Title field), name of the linked download page (ArticleTemplate), and descriptive text (Description).

5. Click the View Pages and Videos That Are New to You link to open the Samples page (Samples.htm). This is your first visit to the site, so all eight pages are new.

> **NOTE**
>
> The VisitID, MemberID, and SampleID fields of the SamplesVisited table store the history of your prior visit.

6. Click the first highlighted link to open the Destinations page (Samp_Master.htm). The link points to a specific page of the Chump Change site. The body text of the Destinations page is identical for all links (see Figure 25.6).

FIGURE 25.6

One of the Destinations pages with text added from the VBLive database.

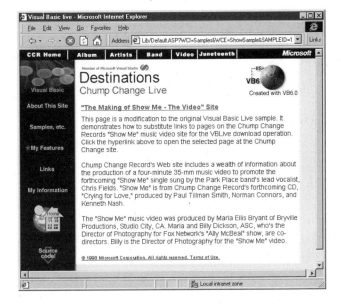

NOTE

The DownloadURL field of the Samples table stores the URL for the link to the Chump Change site. A substantial change to the VBA code is needed to substitute the `http://www.chumpchange.com/...` page URL for the download operation of the original version.

You can substitute an individual template for the generic Samp_Master.htm template by changing the value of the ArticleTemplate field to point to a destination-specific template.

---

7. With a live Internet connection, click the "The Making of Show Me - The Video" Site link to open the `http://www.chumpchange.com/parkplace/video/musicvideo.htm` page (see Figure 25.7). Return to VBLive.

NOTE

FrontPage 98 was used to create the Chump Change Records Web site, which has a variety of music-oriented content. Many of the site's pages are very graphics intensive; for best viewing of the site, use 800x600 resolution, 24-bit or higher color depth, and a 56kbps or faster connection. Most of the streaming audio and video content of the site requires Microsoft's NetShow 3.0 viewer. Audio clips from the album are in RealAudio 5.0 format.

25

DEVELOPING INTERNET APPLICATIONS

FIGURE 25.7

The page of the Chump Change Records site corresponding to the Destinations page of Figure 25.6.

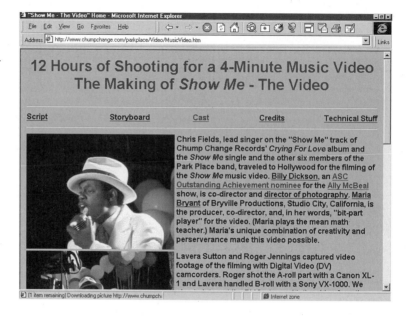

Figure 25.8 shows the Data View window displaying the tables of the VBLive database (left) and the stored procedures (right) created by CCRScript.sql. All database access is via stored procedures to enhance security and improve performance. You can alter existing records in Data View's Run Table window, but you can't add new records to the tables because of the execute-only security settings.

FIGURE 25.8

The Data View window displaying the tables and fields (left) and stored procedures (right) of the VBLive database.

UNDERSTANDING THE ARCHITECTURE OF VBLIVE

VBLive has only a single page, Default.asp, which consists of a set of ASP directives to open an instance of the `WebClassRuntime` library's `WebClassManager` class and the `VBLive` class created by the VBLive WebClass Designer or VBLiveLib.dll (compiled from VBLiveLib.vbp). Following is the entire content of Default.asp:

```
<%
Server.ScriptTimeout=600
Response.Buffer=True
Response.Expires=0

If (VarType(Application("~WC~WebClassManager")) = 0) Then
    Application.Lock
    If (VarType(Application("~WC~WebClassManager")) = 0) Then
Set Application("~WC~WebClassManager") = _
    Server.CreateObject("WebClassRuntime.WebClassManager")
    End If
    Application.UnLock
End If

Application("~WC~WebClassManager").ProcessNoStateWebClass "VBLiveLib.VBLive", _
    Server, _
    Application, _
    Session, _
    Request, _
    Response
%>
```

> **NOTE**
>
> Each time you compile VBLiveLib.vbp to VBLiveLib.dll, the WebClass Designer replaces the content of Default.asp unless you specify otherwise.

Figure 25.9 shows the WebClass Designer displaying the Custom WebItems of VBLive.dsr. Each custom WebItem corresponds to an HTML template; MSToolbar WebItem appears on every page. Clicks on links or buttons fire the events that appear in Figure 25.9.

VBA Code Conventions and Locations

VBLiveLib.vbp is an interesting example of the use of production-class C coding conventions in a relatively simple Visual Basic database project. The VBA coding style differs dramatically from that used in this book. As an example, the VBLive developer makes use of structures (VBA user-defined types or UDTs) for form responses and tokens (**Public Const**ants) for **String** variables. The Microsoft developer also has prepared the application for localization by adding a resource file.

FIGURE 25.9

VBLiveLib.dsr's Custom WebItems displayed by the WebClass Designer.

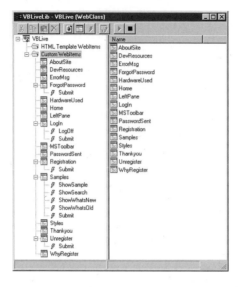

The following four files contain VBLiveLib.vbp's VBA code:

- *VBLiveDefs.bas* adds the GetPrivateProfileString Win32 API function prototype, **Public Const**ants (tokens) for virtually every **String** used in the project, several enumerations, and a variety of UDTs.

- *VBLiveData.bas* declares **Public** and **Private Const**ants for field names, ConnectionStrings, stored procedures, and Parameters. A **Public Function** GetConnection returns an ADODB.Connection object to serve as the ActiveConnection of stored procedure Commands. GetConnection was a **Private Function** in the original VBLive version. VBLiveData.bas also includes subprocedures and functions that operate on the Members and Samples tables.

- *VBLiveFuncs.bas* contains several utility functions, the most important of which is GetResData. GetResData returns localized resource strings from the VBLive.res file.

- *VBLive.dsr* contains all the VBA code that interacts directly with the Custom WebItems defined in the VBLive WebClass Designer.

To support the designer, ASP, and database objects, the project includes references to the Microsoft WebClass Library 1.0 (Mswcrun.dll), Microsoft Active Server Pages Object Library v1.0 (Asp.tlb), and Microsoft ActiveX Data Objects 2.0 Library (Msado15.dll).

TIP

The code of VBLive.dsr makes extensive use of classes of the Active Server Pages Object Library. If you're not familiar with the ASP object model, review in

Object Browser the properties and methods of the Request and Response classes
of the ASPTypeLibrary.

WebClass Code Execution Tracing

Understanding the flow of VBA code written by another developer challenges many Visual
Basic users. This is especially the case if you don't have a flow diagram for the code. The C
coding style of the VBLive WebClass further detracts from easy comprehension of program
flow. The most effective method of gaining a basic understanding of VBLive's execution path
is to set a breakpoint at the beginning of the application and single-step or procedure-step
through code execution.

The following execution trace assumes that you previously have logged on to VBLive and
completed the registration process:

1. Set a breakpoint on the **Set** Webclass.NextItem = Home statement of the
   WebClass_Start event handler; then run the project.

> **TIP**
>
> If you set the breakpoint and execution doesn't halt as expected, reboot your
> machine. Many Visual Basic 6.0 users have reported that WebClass debugging
> fails after compiling or recompiling an IIS Application.

2. Press F8 to single-step through the execution process. The preceding statement results in
   a call to the Home_Respond event hander, which calls the WriteHTMLUsingStructure subprocedure to write the opening page. The next section, "Generating HTML from
   Structures," describes the code of WriteHTMLUsingStructure.

3. Press Ctrl+Shift+F8 to step out of the subprocedure and move to the Home_ProcessTag
   subprocedure, which calls the IsMemberLoggedOn function. IsMemberLoggedOn calls the
   GetMemberID function to obtain and return the MemberID value by calling the
   WebClass.Session.Value("MemberID") method.

4. Continue to single-step through repeated execution of Home_ProcessTag, which next
   calls the GetMemberNameWithID function in the VBLiveData module.
   GetMemberNameWithID establishes an ADODB.Connection to the VBLive database by calling the GetConnection function and then executes the sp_MemberNameWhereMemberID
   stored procedure with the MemberID parameter value to return the MemberName value
   from the Members table.

25

DEVELOPING
INTERNET
APPLICATIONS

5. Continue single-stepping through repeated executions of `Home_ProcessTag` until the `GetResData` function executes with `HighlightResult` resource name (`sResName` value). `GetResData` returns the following HTML snippet (structure resource) from VBLive.res:

```
<!--Start highlight record -->
<TR><TD>
   <IMG SRC="appgraphics/spacer.gif"
   WIDTH=1
   HEIGHT=10
   BORDER=0>
</TD></TR>
<TR><TD>
   <A HREF="<@WRITEFIELD>"
   CLASS="highlight"><@WRITEFIELD></A>
</TD></TR>
<TR><TD>
   <@WRITEFIELD>
</TD></TR>
<!--End highlight record -->
```

The preceding HTML code is the template for each of the eight Highlights topics.

> **NOTE**
>
> The VBLive.res file is the subject of the "Localizing Content with a Resource File" section later in the chapter.

6. Single-step until reaching `GetSampleHighlightRecords`, which calls `GetHighlightSamples` to execute the `sp_SamplesWhereHighlight` stored procedure. The code converts the first row of the resulting `ADODB.Recordset` into the first member of the `sRecords` array:

```
<!--Start highlight record -->
<TR><TD>
   <IMG SRC="appgraphics/spacer.gif"
   WIDTH=1
   HEIGHT=10
   BORDER=0>
</TD></TR>
<TR><TD>
   <A HREF="Default.ASP?WCI=Samples&WCE=ShowSample&SAMPLEID=1"
   CLASS="highlight">"The Making of Show Me - The Video" Site</A>
</TD></TR>
<TR><TD>
   This is the home page for Chump Change Records' new music video
   for the "Show Me" single. "Show Me" is from the forthcoming album
   "Crying for Love."
</TD></TR>
<!--End highlight record -->
```

7. Set a breakpoint at the GetSampleHighlightRecords = **Join**(sRecords, vbCrLf) statement and then press F5 and F8. Listing 25.1 is the return value of GetSampleHighlightRecords pasted from the Immediate window and reformatted. The new **Join** string function concatenates all the records of the array with vbCrLf as the record separator.

8. Press F5 to continue execution to end of the Home_Respond event handler and then compare the HTML code of Listing 25.1 with the home page displayed by IE 4.01 (refer to Figure 25.5

Listing 25.1 HTML CODE FOR GENERATING THE HIGHLIGHTS TOPIC OF THE HOME PAGE OF VBLIVE BY THE WriteHTMLUsingStructure

```
<!--Start highlight record -->
<TR><TD>
   <IMG SRC="appgraphics/spacer.gif"
   WIDTH=1
   HEIGHT=10
   BORDER=0>
</TD></TR>
<TR><TD>
   <A HREF="Default.ASP?WCI=Samples&WCE=ShowSample&SAMPLEID=1"
   CLASS="highlight">"The Making of Show Me - The Video" Site</A>
</TD></TR>
<TR><TD>
This is the home page for Chump Change Records' new music video for
the "Show Me" single. "Show Me" is from the forthcoming album
"Crying for Love."
</TD></TR>
<!--End highlight record -->

<!--Start highlight record -->
<TR><TD>
   <IMG SRC="appgraphics/spacer.gif"
   WIDTH=1
   HEIGHT=10
   BORDER=0></TD>
</TR>
<TR><TD>
   <A HREF="Default.ASP?WCI=Samples&WCE=ShowSample&SAMPLEID=2"
   CLASS="highlight">"Show Me" Original Shooting Script</A>
</TD></TR>
<TR><TD>
This is the original shooting script by Gerard Brown for the
Chump Change Records "Show Me" music video.
</TD></TR>
<!--End highlight record -->
```

continues

25

DEVELOPING INTERNET APPLICATIONS

Listing 25.1   CONTINUED

```
<!--Start highlight record -->
<TR><TD>
   <IMG SRC="appgraphics/spacer.gif"
   WIDTH=1
   HEIGHT=10
   BORDER=0></TD>
</TR>
<TR><TD>
   <A HREF="Default.ASP?WCI=Samples&WCE=ShowSample&SAMPLEID=3"
   CLASS="highlight">"Show Me" Original Storyboard</A></TD>
</TR>
<TR><TD>
   This is the original storyboard by Stuart Rosen for the
   Chump Change Records "Show Me" music video.
</TD></TR>
<!--End highlight record -->

<!--Start highlight record -->
<TR><TD>
   <IMG SRC="appgraphics/spacer.gif"
   WIDTH=1
   HEIGHT=10
   BORDER=0>
</TD></TR>
<TR><TD>
   <A HREF="Default.ASP?WCI=Samples&WCE=ShowSample&SAMPLEID=4"
   CLASS="highlight">"Show Me" Cast</A>
</TD></TR>
<TR><TD>
   These are the folks who appeared in the Chump Change Records
   "Show Me" music video.
</TD></TR>
<!--End highlight record -->

<!--Start highlight record -->
<TR><TD>
   <IMG SRC="appgraphics/spacer.gif"
   WIDTH=1
   HEIGHT=10
   BORDER=0>
</TD></TR>
<TR><TD>
   <A HREF="Default.ASP?WCI=Samples&WCE=ShowSample&SAMPLEID=5"
   CLASS="highlight">"Show Me" Credits</A>
</TD></TR>
<TR><TD>
   This is the complete list of all of the film and video professionals
   responsible for the production of the "Show Me" music video.
</TD></TR>
```

```
<!--End highlight record -->

<!--Start highlight record -->
<TR><TD>
   <IMG SRC="appgraphics/spacer.gif"
   WIDTH=1
   HEIGHT=10
   BORDER=0></TD>
</TR>
<TR><TD>
   <A HREF="Default.ASP?WCI=Samples&WCE=ShowSample&SAMPLEID=6"
   CLASS="highlight">Billy Dickson at Work</A>
</TD></TR>
<TR><TD>
   Billy Dickson, ASC, is the Co-director and Director of Photography
   for the "Show Me" video. His day job is Director of Photography
   for the "Ally McBeal" show on the Fox Network. "Ally McBeal" gained
   10 nominations for 1998 "Emmy" awards.
</TD></TR>
<!--End highlight record -->

<!--Start highlight record -->
<TR><TD>
   <IMG SRC="appgraphics/spacer.gif"
   WIDTH=1
   HEIGHT=10
   BORDER=0>
</TD></TR>
<TR><TD>
   <A HREF="Default.ASP?WCI=Samples&WCE=ShowSample&SAMPLEID=7"
   CLASS="highlight">Maria Bryant Ellis at Work</A>
</TD></TR>
<TR><TD>
   Maria Bryant Ellis is the Producer and Co-director of the "Show Me"
   video. In her spare time, Maria works at Panavision Hollywood.
</TD></TR>
<!--End highlight record -->

<!--Start highlight record -->
<TR><TD>
   <IMG SRC="appgraphics/spacer.gif"
   WIDTH=1
   HEIGHT=10
   BORDER=0>
</TD></TR>
<TR><TD>
   <A HREF="Default.ASP?WCI=Samples&WCE=ShowSample&SAMPLEID=8"
        CLASS="highlight">"Show Me" Video Technical Stuff</A>
</TD></TR>
<TR><TD>
```

continues

Listing 25.1 CONTINUED

```
This page describes the production and postproduction process,
and includes technical articles on the Digital Video (DV) format
and the editing process for "The Making of Show Me - The Video."
</TD></TR>
<!--End highlight record -->
```

GENERATING HTML FROM STRUCTURE RESOURCES

The WriteHTMLUsingStructure subprocedure generates HTML content from a body template file concatenated with an expansion of a structure resource. The structure resource, obtained from VBLive.res, acts as a localized template having replaceable content.

Following is an explanation of the arguments of WriteHTMLUsingStructure, based on the developer's comments preceding the function code:

- oBodyItem is an object reference to the WebItem that replaces the body token of the structure resource. In step 2 of the preceding section, oBodyItem.Name returns Home.

- sBodyTemplate is the relative path and name (URL) of the template file for the body of the page, AppTemplates\Home.htm.

- sHeadImageUrl is the URL of the image that appears at the top of the left pane of the page, AppGraphics/Head_home.jpg.

- bIncludeNavButtons is a **Boolean** argument to specify whether the left pane includes the standard set of site navigation buttons. bIncludeNavButtons is **True** for IE 4+ or Navigator 4+ and **False** otherwise.

- bUseTemplate is an **Optional Boolean** argument to specify whether an additional template file is used. In the preceding section, bUseTemplate always is **False**.

- sSampleTitle is an **Optional String** argument specifying the name of a subheading for the template. The value of sSampleTitle isn't used unless bUseTemplate is **True**.

 Listing 25.2 shows the code for the WriteHTMLUsingStructure subprocedure. The sStructPieces = **Split**(GetResData(sResourceName, RES_HTML_TYPE), WRITETEMPLATE_DELIMITER) statement uses the new **Split** function (the inverse of the **Join** function discussed in the preceding section) to create an array from a string having elements separated by a specified delimiter, <@WRITETEMPLATE> for this example.

Listing 25.2 CODE TO GENERATE LOCALIZABLE HTML FROM A STRUCTURE RESOURCE

```
Private Sub WriteHTMLUsingStructure(oBodyItem As WebItem, _
        sBodyTemplate As String, _
        sHeadImageUrl As String, _
        bIncludeNavButtons As Boolean, _
        Optional bUseTemplate As Boolean = False, _
```

```
        Optional sSampleTitle As String = "")

Dim sStructPieces() As String
Dim bIsIE4 As Boolean
Dim sResourceName As String

On Error GoTo ErrorHandler
bIsIE4 = IsBrowserIE4
'Cache the head image URL for use in LeftPane_ProcessTag
msHeadImageUrl = sHeadImageUrl

'Get the page structure from the resource and split it into sections
'Choose the structure to use according to the browser
If bIsIE4 Then
    sResourceName = RES_STRUCTURE
ElseIf IsBrowserNetscape4 Then
    sResourceName = RES_STRUCTURE_NETSCAPE
Else
    sResourceName = RES_STRUCTURE_LOTECH
End If

'Between each section, write the contents of a WebItem
sStructPieces = Split(GetResData(sResourceName, RES_HTML_TYPE), _
    WRITETEMPLATE_DELIMITER)

'Validate the array before continuing
If UBound(sStructPieces) < 5 Then
    'Write an error message because there was not enough
    'divisions in the resource
    Response.Write Replace(LoadResString(resNotEnoughTemplateTokens), _
        NAME_TOKEN, WRITETEMPLATE_DELIMITER)
Else
    With Response
        .Write sStructPieces(0)
        'Write the styles template
        Styles.WriteTemplate TPLT_STYLES
        .Write sStructPieces(1)
        If bIncludeNavButtons And bIsIE4 Then
            'Write Popup Menus template
            'Use the LeftPane item to process the popup menu template
            LeftPane.WriteTemplate TPLT_POPUPMENUS
        End If
        .Write sStructPieces(2)

        'Rev by RJ 9/15/98: MS Toolbar template revised for CCR site
        MSToolbar.WriteTemplate TPLT_MSTOOLBAR
        .Write sStructPieces(3)
        If bIncludeNavButtons Then
            If bIsIE4 Then
                'Write Left Pane template
                LeftPane.WriteTemplate TPLT_LEFTPANE
```

continues

Listing 25.2 CONTINUED

```
            Else
                'Write low tech left pane
                LeftPane.WriteTemplate TPLT_LEFTPANE_LOWTECH
            End If
        Else
            'Write the blank left pane template
            LeftPane.WriteTemplate TPLT_LEFTPANE_NONAV
        End If
        .Write sStructPieces(4)

        'Write Body Pane template
        If bUseTemplate Then
            WriteArticleUsingTemplate sBodyTemplate, sSampleTitle
        Else
            oBodyItem.WriteTemplate sBodyTemplate
        End If
        .Write sStructPieces(5)
    End With
    End If
    Exit Sub

ErrorHandler:
    'Write the error message as an HTML comment for debugging purposes
    Response.Write HTML_COMMENT_BEGIN & Err.Description & HTML_COMMENT_END
    Resume Next
End Sub
```

GENERATING HTML DIRECTLY FROM TEMPLATE FILES

The `WriteArticleUsingTemplate` subprocedure generates the individual Destination pages that provide links to the Chump Change Records site (refer to Figure 25.6). Unfortunately, the VBLive developer didn't include the DownloadURL field value in the array returned by `GetSampleRecords`. The DownloadURL value is required for the URL of the specific page at www.chumpchange.com. The alternative to rewriting (and retesting) a substantial amount of existing code is to revert to conventional VBA style, connect to the database, and execute the existing stored procedure (`sp_SampleSearch`) to deliver the matching single-row `Recordset`.

> **NOTE**
>
> The code added to the `WriteArticleUsingTemplate` subprocedure is classified as a "hack" because its structure doesn't follow the conventions established by the originating developer.

Listing 25.3 shows the modified code of `WriteArticleUsingTemplate` to substitute an `<A HREF>...</A>` link for the title of the page. In all cases, the value of `sTemplate` is the SampleTemplates\Samp_Master.htm file. The value of `sTitle` depends on the selection in the Highlights section of the `Home WebItem`. If you click the first link, the value of `sTitle` is `"The Making of Show Me - The Video"` Site.

Listing 25.3 CODE TO GENERATE LOCALIZABLE HTML FROM A STRUCTURE RESOURCE

```
Private Sub WriteArticleUsingTemplate(sTemplate As String, sTitle As String)
    Dim sStructPieces() As String

    '*****Rev by RJ 9/16/98: Obtain DownloadURL value for link
    Dim cnnVBLive As New ADODB.Connection
    Dim cmmSample As New ADODB.Command
    Dim rstSample As New ADODB.Recordset
    Dim strCCR_URL As String

    Set cnnVBLive = GetConnection
    'Find the record with the search stored procedure using sTitle
    If sTemplate = "SampleTemplates\Samp_Master.htm" Then
        With cmmSample
            Set .ActiveConnection = cnnVBLive
            .CommandType = adCmdStoredProc
            'Undocumented parameter syntax
            .CommandText = "sp_SamplesSearch('" & sTitle & "', 0)"
            Set rstSample = .Execute
        End With
        With rstSample
            If .RecordCount Then
                strCCR_URL = .Fields("DownloadURL")
            End If
        End With
    End If
    '*****End Revision

    'Get the article template from the resource and
    'split it into sections.
    sStructPieces = Split(GetResData(RES_ARTICLETEMPLATE, _
        RES_HTML_TYPE), WRITETEMPLATE_DELIMITER)
    'Validate the array before continueing
    If UBound(sStructPieces) < 2 Then
        'Write an error message because there was not enough
        'divisions in the resource
        Response.Write Replace(LoadResString(resNotEnoughTemplateTokens), _
            NAME_TOKEN, WRITETEMPLATE_DELIMITER)
    Else
        With Response
            .Write sStructPieces(0)
```

continues

25

Listing 25.3   CONTINUED

```
                '*****Rev by RJ 9/16/98: Add the DownloadURL to the link
                If Len(strCCR_URL) Then
                    'Change sTitle text to a Chump Change URL
                    .Write "<A HREF=" & Chr(34) & strCCR_URL & _
                        Chr(34) & ">" & sTitle & "</a>"
                Else
                    .Write sTitle
                End If
                .Write sStructPieces(1)
                Samples.WriteTemplate sTemplate
                .Write sStructPieces(2)
            End With
        End If
End Sub
```

LOCALIZING CONTENT WITH A RESOURCE FILE

The VBLive.res resource file included with the example project has only a U.S. English string table and doesn't specify custom resources for other languages. To load the VB 6 Resource Editor add-in and view the contents of VBLive.res, do the following:

1. Choose Add-Ins, Add-In Manager to open the Add-In Manager dialog.

2. Double-click the VB 6 Resource Editor item to load the editor; then click OK.

3. Choose Tools, Resource Editor to open the Resource Editor with VBLive.res active (see Figure 25.10).

FIGURE 25.10

The Resource Editor displaying the resources of VBLive.res.

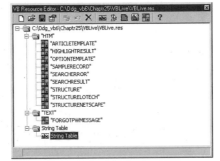

NOTE

A Visual Basic 6.0 project can have only one resource file, so there's no need to specify the file to open.

4. Double-click the String Table item to open the Edit String Tables dialog (see Figure 25.11) with messages in U.S. English.

FIGURE 25.11

The U.S. English messages displayed in the Edit String Tables dialog.

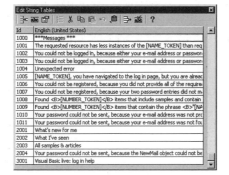

Id	English (United States)
1000	***Messages ***
1001	The requested resource has less instances of the [NAME_TOKEN] than req
1002	You could not be logged in, because either your e-mail address or passwor
1003	You could not be logged in, because either your e-mail address or passwor
1004	Unexpected error
1005	[NAME_TOKEN], you have navigated to the log in page, but you are alread
1006	You could not be registered, because you did not provide all of the require
1007	You could not be registered, because your two password entries did not m
1008	Found <B>[NUMBER_TOKEN]</B> items that include samples and contain
1009	Found <B>[NUMBER_TOKEN]</B> items that contain the phrase <B>"[NA
1010	Your password could not be sent, because your e-mail address was not pr
1011	Your password could not be sent, because your e-mail address was not fou
2001	What's new for me
2002	What I've seen
2003	All samples & articles
2004	Your password could not be sent, because the NewMail object could not be
3001	Visual Basic live: log in help

> **NOTE**
>
> The Resource Editor lets you create multiple String Tables and Custom Resources in any of the languages supported by Windows. For more information on the use of resource files with Visual Basic 6.0, open the Working with Resource Files topic in online help.

Compiling and Deploying the VBLiveLib Project

The compiled VBLive.dll isn't included on the accompanying CD-ROM. To compile, deploy, and test the VBLiveLib project on your test server, do the following:

1. Return to design mode and choose File, Make VBLive.dll.

2. If you've previously compiled VBLive.dll, click Yes when asked whether you want to replace the file. The compiler completes its work.

> **NOTE**
>
> If you've previously compiled VBLive.dll and receive a VBLive.dll Is in Use message, you probably need to reboot your computer. Stopping the WWW Publishing Service doesn't release the lock on VBLive.dll.

3. Click Yes when asked if you want to overwrite Default.asp. Unless you change the programmatic ID (ProgID) of VBLiveLib, the contents of the new version of Default.asp are identical to the file it replaces. The operation renames the replaced file to Default.bk0.

25

DEVELOPING INTERNET APPLICATIONS

4. In the browser of a networked client, navigate to `http://servername/vblivelib` to test the compiled version.

You can use the Package and Deployment Wizard to install VBLive on a remote Web server.

ENTERPRISE-LEVEL DEVELOPMENT TECHNIQUES

PART

VII

IN THIS PART

TAKING ADVANTAGE OF MICROSOFT TRANSACTION SERVER 2.0

IN THIS CHAPTER

Microsoft Transaction Server (MTS) 2.0 is middleware for creating scalable, *n*-tier client/server applications. *Middleware* is loosely defined as software that provides interapplication communication, conversion, and/or translation services. Transaction processors (TPs), one of the subjects of Chapter 19, "Processing Transactions and Bulk Operations," and object request brokers (ORBs) are examples of software classified as middleware. ORBs supply the methods objects use to locate and instantiate other objects across a network. MTS combines the features of a TP and ORB in a single service that runs under Windows NT Server 4.0+ and depends on Distributed COM (DCOM) for communication. MTS's ORB features and DCOM replace Remote Automation, covered briefly in Chapter 15, "Writing Local Automation Components and ActiveX DLLs." MTS provides a surrogate server process in which to run ActiveX DLLs, which substitute for Automation components, plus a host of other features to make deploying n-tier applications a relatively straightforward process.

> **NOTE**
>
> The two chapters of this book devoted to MTS 2.0 comprise a basic description of the capabilities of and programming techniques for MTS. *Roger Jennings' Database Workshop: Microsoft Transaction Server 2.0* by Steven Gray and Rick Lievano (SAMS Publishing, ISBN 0-672-31130-5) provides thorough coverage of all MTS 2.0 features and component programming methodology.

POSITIONING MTS IN THE MIDDLEWARE MARKET

MTS, which runs only on Windows platforms, competes with cross-platform ORBs and transaction management systems supplied by Visigenic (acquired by Borland International, now Imprise) and Iona Technologies. Visigenic and Iona offerings, which have been licensed primarily by UNIX-oriented RDBMS and development tool vendors, use the Common Object Request Broker Architecture (CORBA) standard promoted by the Object Management Group (OMG). OMG's Object Transaction Service (OTS) runs on top of CORBA to provide distributed transaction management services. CORBA claims to be a platform-independent "open system." In reality, CORBA is closely tied to the UNIX world and more loosely connected to Java. Several third parties provide CORBA-DCOM bridges to accommodate Windows, but DCOM and MTS currently appear to have garnered the lion's share of the ORB/TP market. MTS enjoys the benefit of low cost; it's a free add-on to Windows NT Server 4.0.

MTS depends on the Distributed Transaction Coordinator (DTC) introduced by SQL Server 6.0 to interoperate with UNIX and mainframe transaction managers. DTC includes an XA Mapper to provide interoperability with X/Open Distributed Transaction Processing Group (X/Open DTP) XA-compliant UNIX transaction monitors, such as Encina, TopEnd, and Tuxedo. Following are brief descriptions of X/Open DTP terminology:

Taking Advantage of Microsoft Transaction Server 2.0

CHAPTER 26

977

26

TAKING
ADVANTAGE OF
MTS 2.0

- *X/Open Company Ltd* is an industry standards association for information systems that, together with the Open Software Foundation (OSF), makes up the umbrella Open Group, which is headquartered in Cambridge, Massachusetts. The X/Open DTP is responsible for establishing distributed transaction standards.

- *X/Open DTP TX* (TX) is the X/Open standard for APIs that involve initiating, committing, and rolling back transactions. X/Open DTP does not support aborting transactions from within a resource manager; OLE Transactions allows a resource manager to abort its transaction, causing the transaction manager to roll back the entire transaction.

- *X/Open DTP XA* (XA) is the X/Open standard API for communicating between resource managers (RMs) and transaction managers (TMs). Encina, TopEnd, and Tuxedo are X/Open-compliant TPMs; DTC's XA mapper lets X/Open TPMs communicate with OLE Transactions RMs.

The COM Transaction Integrator (COMTI, called "Cedar" during development) provides a layer between MTS and Microsoft SNA Server 4.0 that lets you map Automation object methods to mainframe transaction processor invocations or message sequences and map object properties to LU 6.2 message fields for IBM's Customer Information Control System (CICS) and Information Management System (IMS). Figure 26.1 illustrates the basic elements of MTS and how MTS connects to mainframe and UNIX TPs, and databases that support OLE Transactions (OLE Tx) through DTC. Currently, only SQL Server 6.5+ is OLE Tx compliant.

FIGURE 26.1

Connectivity of MTS 2.0 to mainframe and UNIX transaction processors, and OLE Tx-compliant RDBMSs (SQL Server 6.5 and 7.0).

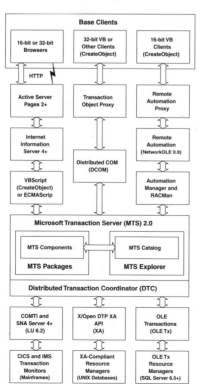

In addition to its ORB and TP features, MTS 2.0 provides the following additional functions:

- Resource pooling. MTS 2.0 provides pooling of threads and database connections. Pooling threads lets you write single-threaded components; MTS provides a thread pool for fast response by components to client requests. Pooling database connections reduces database server resource requirements and speeds database operations.

- Security. MTS offers both declarative and programmatic security. Declarative security lets you define groups of users that have access to specific components. Programmatic security lets your component code take action based on the role of the user. MTS user roles, which define users by category, are similar to SQL Server 7.0 roles.

- Administration. MTS Explorer, a Microsoft Management Console (MMC) 1.0 snap-in, is a user interface that lets you configure components, their properties, and locations. MTS Explorer also provides transaction monitoring and component diagnostic features.

- Client deployment. MTS includes a client configuration utility that lets you create a simple client setup program for MTS packages. A *package* is a group of related components that run in a single process. You run the client setup program on each workstation to add the MTS proxy stub for the package in the workstation's Registry.

NOTE

Microsoft announced the forthcoming release of MTS 3.0 at Tech*Ed 98, held the first week of June 1998 in New Orleans. MTS 3.0 will use Microsoft's COM+ technology to add load-balancing services and an attribute-based object programming model. COM+ features object activation by *interceptors*, which monitor MTS components and determine the services they require. COM+ uses the publish and subscribe approach, similar to that of SQL Server 7.0 replication, that lets multiple subscribing objects intercept event messages from publishers and process the events in different ways. The final version of MTS 3.0 is expected to be included in an Option Pack for Windows NT Server 5.0.

UNDERSTANDING THE ROLE OF MTS IN *N*-TIER CLIENT/SERVER ARCHITECTURE

▶ See "Defining the Role of Automation Components," **p. 573**

Chapter 15 defines three-tier architecture as a means of separating user services (GUI front ends, called *base clients* by MTS) from data services (SQL databases) by an intervening business services layer. Business services implement various validation and other operations on data passed by relatively lightweight front ends to underlying RDBMSs. Another role played by the business services layer is to isolate the base client application's code from the data access methodology and underlying schema of the database(s). User- and business-service code doesn't need updating when you migrate from DAO to RDO to ADO. Schema isolation eliminates the need to update every client application when database, table, or field names change or database structures undergo alteration.

> **NOTE**
>
> You can write middle-tier components for MTS in any programming language that supports COM, and you can create Windows DLLs or their equivalent, such as Visual C++, Visual Basic, Visual J++, Borland's Delphi, and COM-enabled COBOL. Some developers (and book authors) promote Java as the language of choice for writing middle-tier components that run under MTS. Using current Java implementations for authoring components is more difficult and time-consuming than writing MTS-compliant ActiveX DLLs, especially for developers already skilled in Visual Basic. This chapter and the next, "Creating and Deploying MTS Components," assumes the use of Visual Basic 6.0 for writing components and ADO 2.0 with native OLE DB 2.0 data providers for data access.

Three-Tier versus *N*-Tier Structures

In three-tier applications, the business services layer connects to the data services' RDBMs. Four-tier applications often abstract database connectivity into a separate layer, often called data access services. Figure 26.2 illustrates the differences in data flow between the three- and four-tier approach. Other business services components can connect to a common data access services component, and complex (coarse-grained) business services can be broken into individual (fine-grained) components, each of which performs a specific function. Dividing complex service components into single-function components commonly is called *increasing granularity*. Business rules implemented as Automation components are coarse-grained by necessity; each instance of an Automation component consumes about 600K of RAM. MTS runs multiple ActiveX DLLs within a single process, which dramatically reduces memory resource requirements. Thus MTS makes feasible fine-grained, multi-tiered architecture.

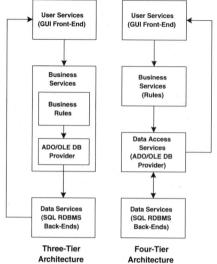

FIGURE 26.2

Data flow in three-and four-tier client/server architectures.

▶ **See** "Gaining a Performance Boost with Stored Procedures," **p. 819**

NOTE

Stored procedures executed by client front ends offer an alternative method of gaining database schema independence, but not data access method independence. Stored procedures, however, offer similar performance benefits to conventional two-tier and *n*-tier architectures.

Intertier Communication and Statefulness

The majority of today's three-tier client/server systems process database content modifications as INSERT, UPDATE, or DELETE operations where traditional business rules, such as data validation, apply. Thus it's a common practice to execute row-returning stored procedures or queries directly against the RDBMS, bypassing the middle tier. In four- or higher-tier structures, the data access service layer handles both row-returning and update operations. Communication between layers usually is in the form of **Variant** arrays of parameter values or the content of Recordset objects passed as method arguments, not property values.

The primary benefits of passing data to and from components as method arguments are

- Minimizing server round trips. Passing each property value to a component requires a server round-trip. An extreme example is adding a new order with the Ado2proc.vbp

Taking Advantage of Microsoft Transaction Server 2.0

CHAPTER 26

981

26

TAKING
ADVANTAGE OF
MTS 2.0

project described in Chapter 21, "Using Transact-SQL Stored Procedures." Adding a new order with a single line item requires 16 server round-trips if you pass parameters as property values.

- Minimizing resource consumption. Passing multiple property values requires the component to store the values until receiving a method call to execute a particular operation with the values received. The component must maintain its state for a specified timeout period or until explicitly shut down by the user because network traffic or other problems might delay the method call. Such components are called *stateful* objects.

- Providing compatibility with MTS. MTS doesn't support stateful components; data must be passed to MTS components as method arguments. The method call either succeeds or fails; unlike stateful objects, there is no indeterminate waiting period for the method call from the client or other component. The *stateless* components used by MTS deliver optimal performance.

> **NOTE**
>
> MTS provides a mechanism, called the Shared Property Manager (SPM), for preserving state information between successive method calls without resorting to `Public` variables or stateful components.

MTS components residing on the same machine communicate via in-process COM; clients communicate with servers with out-of-process DCOM. DCOM also is the communication method when your middle-tier components reside on a server other than the RDBMS server(s). The ability to distribute components over multiple servers contributes to the scalability of MTS *n*-tier applications.

> **NOTE**
>
> MTS 2.0 doesn't support local object pooling, recycling, or load sharing of heavily used objects between multiple servers. These capabilities are required to create components that support thousands of simultaneous users. MTS 2.0 has a dummy `CanBePooled` property for forward compatibility with MTS 3.0, which will provide all three features. MTS 2.0's just-in-time activation and thread pooling minimize the performance hit when instantiating a component, and connection pooling provides a group of shared database connections for use by all components.

Transactions in N-Tier Applications

Transaction processing isn't obligatory for MTS-hosted components; MTS justifies its presence solely as an ORB. MTS provides the following four levels of transaction support:

- Requires a transaction. The component always executes in a transactional context. A new transaction is started if the creator of the component hasn't already established the transaction context.

- Requires a new transaction. A new transaction is started regardless of whether the creator of the component has already started a transaction. Success or failure of the new transaction doesn't affect the outcome of the creator's transaction if any.

- Supports transactions. Execute the component under the creator's transaction context if the creator has started a transaction. Otherwise, the object runs without a transaction context.

- Does not support transactions. Disregard all MTS transaction support features.

> **NOTE**
>
> The creator of the component is an MTS component that instantiates and maintains a reference to the component.

 You can set the level of transaction support for a component with MTS Explorer; the most common level is Requires a transaction. You also can take advantage of a new property of Visual Basic 6.0 Classes, `MTSTransactionMode`. Table 26.1 lists the values of the `MTSTransactionMode` property and thecorresponding MTS transaction levels.

TABLE 26.1   VALUES OF THE `ClassName.MTSTransactionMode` PROPERTY AND CORRESPONDING MTS TRANSACTION LEVELS.

Value	*MTSTransactionMode*	*MTS Transaction Level*
0	NotAnMTSObject	None (isn't an MTS component)
1	NoTransactions	Does not support transactions
2	RequiresTransactions	Requires a transaction
3	UsesTransactions	Supports transactions
4	RequiresNewTransaction	Requires a new transaction

MTS's TP features aren't required for transactions that execute with a single SQL batch statement or stored procedure. Transact-SQL's BEGIN TRAN ... COMMIT TRAN structures deliver optimum performance for such transactions. Thus you can choose Does Not Support Transactions for components that rely on the RDBMS to complete a transaction in a single operation.

If your application requires more than one SQL batch statement or stored procedure execution to complete a transaction, MTS provides the TP solution with its `ObjectContext` object, an Automation wrapper for MTS's `IObjectContext` interface. `SetAbort` and `SetComplete` are the two primary methods of `ObjectContext`; both objects employ the DTC to manage the two-phase commit process required for multiple-transaction management, even on a single server. If all the individual transactional operations succeed, invoke `SetComplete` to commit the database changes. If any modification fails, invoke `SetAbort` to roll back the changes. Figure 26.3 illustrates skeleton base client and MTS component code for calling `SetComplete` or `SetAbort`.

FIGURE 26.3

Simplified base client and transaction code to execute a transaction under MTS control.

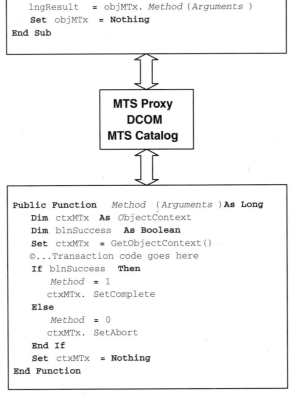

Base Client

```
Private Sub   UseMTS
    Dim  objMTS  As  Name.Class
    Set  objMTS  = CreateObject  ("Name.Class ")
    lngResult    = objMTx. Method (Arguments )
    Set  objMTx  = Nothing
End Sub
```

**MTS Proxy
DCOM
MTS Catalog**

```
Public Function   Method  (Arguments )As Long
    Dim ctxMTx  As  ObjectContext
    Dim blnSuccess   As Boolean
    Set ctxMTx  = GetObjectContext()
    ©...Transaction code goes here
    If blnSuccess   Then
       Method  = 1
       ctxMTx.  SetComplete
    Else
       Method  = 0
       ctxMTx.  SetAbort
    End If
    Set ctxMTx  = Nothing
End Function
```

MTS *Method* of *Name.Class*

▶ See "Replacing INSERT, UPDATE, and Transaction Code with Stored Procedures," **p. 835** and "Passing Command Objects to Subprocedures," **p. 859**

The cmdAddNewOrder_Click event handler of the Ado2proc.frm described in Chapter 21 includes an example of a two-part transaction. The ado_NewOrder_Ins stored procedure is capable of obtaining a new order number, adding a record to the Orders table, and adding one line item to the Order_Details table in a single transaction. If the order has more than one line item, you must run another stored procedure for each additional line item or execute a batch SQL statement to add all additional line items in a single round-trip to the server. It's unlikely, but possible, that INSERT operations for additional line items might fail, resulting in an incomplete order. With MTS you pass the parameter values for the Order record as a single-dimensional **Variant** array and parameters for as many Order_Details records as required as a two-dimensional **Variant** array. If adding any Order_Details record fails, you call SetAbort to roll back both the Orders and Order_Details INSERTs; otherwise you call SetComplete to commit the two transactions. The AddNewOrder method of the MTS Orders component, described in Chapter 27, illustrates how to encapsulate multiple transactions in a single method call.

SETTING UP MTS 2.0 UNDER WINDOWS NT SERVER 4.0

MTS 2.0 is included in the Windows NT 4.0 Option Pack, available from Microsoft resellers on CD-ROM or for free download from http://backoffice.microsoft.com/downtrial/ optionpack.asp. The downloadable Option Pack also includes Internet Information Server 4.0, Microsoft Message Queue Server 1.0, Internet Connection Services for Microsoft RAS, and the Personal Web Server for Windows 9x and Windows NT Workstation 4.0. The CD-ROM version also includes Certificate Server, Index Server, and Site Server Express. Installing the Option Pack on Windows NT 4.0 requires Service Pack 3 or greater. Service Pack 3+ installs Internet Explorer 4.01+, which is needed to provide support for Microsoft Management Console (MMC) and to install the Java Virtual Machine. The default folder for MTS is C:\Program Files\MTS.

> **NOTE**
>
> Install SQL Server 6.5 prior to installing MTS 2.0 because MTS depends on components (primarily DTC) installed by SQL Server. If you're setting up a new system, shut down and restart Windows NT Server 4.0 after installing SQL Server and before installing MTS 2.0 from the Option Pack. Failure to reboot is likely to cause problems with MTS 2.0 installation.

Adding the MTS Administrator Account

After installing the selected Option Pack components, Setup adds a Windows NT 4.0 Option Pack submenu to the Start, Programs menu, which includes a Microsoft Transaction Menu

Choice. Before using MTS 2.0, take the following steps to add the MTS Administrator user to the local server and add the Log on as a Service right:

1. Launch User Manager for Domains and choose <u>U</u>ser, New <u>L</u>ocal Group to open the New Local Group dialog.

2. Type **MTS Administrators** in the Group Name text box and a brief description of the group in the Description text box (see Figure 26.4). Remove the default member of the new group. Click OK to close the dialog and add the new group.

FIGURE 26.4

Adding the MTS Administrators local group.

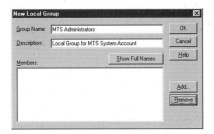

3. Choose <u>U</u>ser, New <u>U</u>ser to open the New User dialog.

4. Type **MTS Administrator** as the Username, add a Full Name entry, provide a Description for the new user, and complete the Password and Confirm Password entries.

5. Clear the User Must Change Password at Next Logon check box and mark the Password Never Expires check box (see Figure 26.5).

FIGURE 26.5

Setting properties of the MTS Administrator local account.

6. Click Account to open the Account Information dialog, verify that the Account Never Expires option is set, and click OK to close the dialog.

7. Click Groups to open the Group Memberships dialog.

8. Choose Administrators from the Not a Member of list, and click Add. All new users are added to the Domain Users group.

9. Choose Domain Admins from the Not a Member of list, and click Add.

10. Choose MTS Administrators from the Not a Member of list, and click Add (see Figure 26.6).

FIGURE 26.6

Adding the MTS Administrator account to the local Administrators and MTS Administrators groups.

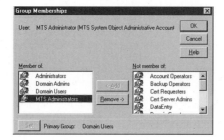

11. Click OK to close the Groups Memberships dialog, Add to add the MTS Administrator user, and Close to close the New User dialog.

12. Choose Policies, User Rights to open the User Policy Rights dialog.

13. Mark the Show Advanced User Rights check box and select Log on as a Service from the Right list (see Figure 26.7).

FIGURE 26.7

Selecting the Log on as a service advanced user right.

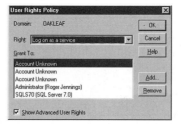

14. Click Show Users, select the MTS Administrator account, and click Add to assign the right to the account in the Add Names list (see Figure 26.8).

FIGURE 26.8

Adding the Log on as a Service right to the MTS Administrator account.

15. Click OK to close the Add Users and Groups dialog, verify that MTS Administrator appears in the Grant To list, click OK to close the User Policy Rights dialog, and close User Manager for Domains.

If you install MTS 2.0 on other servers in the domain, you can use the MTS Administrator account you create with the preceding steps.

> **NOTE**
>
> The preceding steps are an expansion of the instructions in the "Late-Breaking Information and Known Limitations" section of the Microsoft Transaction Server Readme file. Clicking the help (?) button of the toolbar displays Microsoft Transaction Server Help, which includes the Readme file.

Setting the Identity of the MTS System Package

By default, the MTS System package, whose components are required by other packages you install, runs under the local Administrator account. To verify installation of MTS 2.0 and change the identity under which the MTS System package runs, do the following:

1. Choose Start, Programs, Windows NT 4.0 Option Pack, Microsoft Transaction Server, Transaction Server Explorer to start MMC 1.0 with the MTS 2.0 snap-in.

2. Expand the scope (left) pane's tree view to display the Packages Installed list (see Figure 26.9).

FIGURE 26.9

MTS packages installed by the Option Pack Setup program.

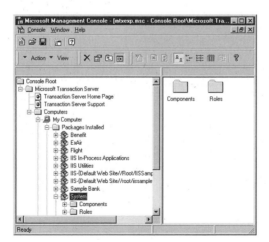

3. Right-click the System package item and choose Properties to open the System Properties sheet.

4. Click the Identity tab; then click the Browse button to open the Set Package Identity dialog.

5. Select MTS Administrator from the domain list and click Add to place MTS Administrator in the Add Names text box (see Figure 26.10). Click OK to close the Set Package Identity dialog.

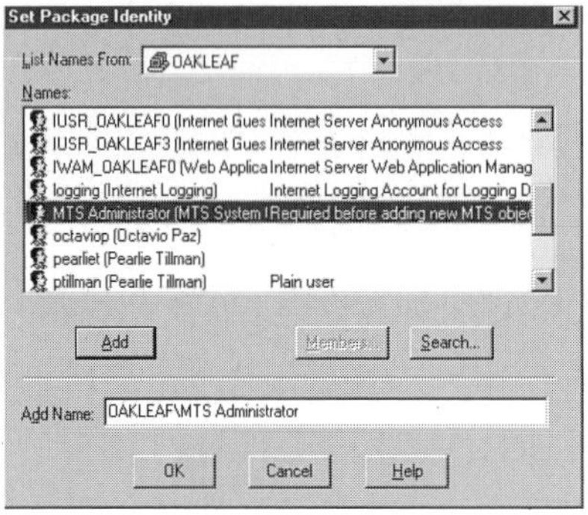

FIGURE 26.10

Changing the identity of the System package from Administrator to MTS Administrator.

6. Type the MTS Administrators password and a confirming copy in the text boxes (see Figure 26.11); then click OK to close the System Properties sheet.

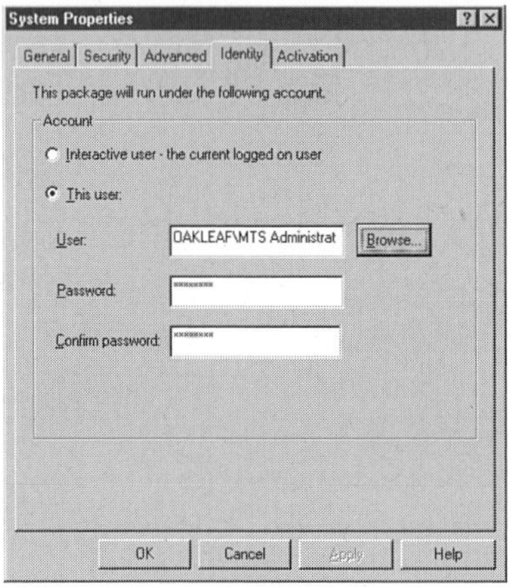

FIGURE 26.11

Completing the System package identity change.

Taking Advantage of Microsoft Transaction Server 2.0

CHAPTER 26

989

26

TAKING
ADVANTAGE OF
MTS 2.0

7. Right-click the My Computer item in the scope pane and choose S̲hut Down Server Processes to require the System package to start up with the new identity.

> **NOTE**
>
> The "Late-Breaking Information and Known Limitations" section of the Readme file instructs you to Shut down the System package so that it will be restarted with the new identity. All packages except the System package have a S̲hut Down choice on their context menu. To shut down the System package, you must shut down all server processes on the selected computer.

> **TIP**
>
> Make access to MTS Explorer faster by creating a desktop shortcut to C:\Program Files\Mts\Mtxexp.msc, the MMC snap-in for MTS Explorer.

Testing the MTS Installation Locally

Setup installs several MTS packages for sample applications, which appear as Packages Installed items in the scope pane, and adds two Visual Basic 5.0 base client applications, Bank Client and Tic-Tac-Toe Client, to the Microsoft Transaction Server menu. Bank Client is more interesting for local testing of your MTS installation, because Bank Client lets you compare performance of simple middle-tier components written in Visual Basic, Visual C++, and Visual J++. Figure 26.12 shows the Components list for the Sample Bank package; components without the .VC and .VJ extensions are Visual Basic 5.0 ActiveX DLLs.

FIGURE 26.12

MTS Explorer's list of components in the Sample Bank package.

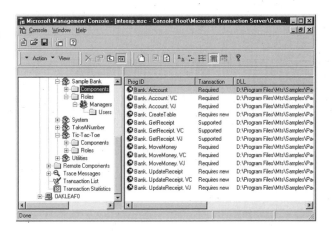

> **NOTE**
>
> Setup normally installs the MTS 2.0 test samples and documentation by default. If you're missing the two MTS clients and the sample packages, open Control Panel's Add/Remove Programs tool, select Windows NT 4.0 Option Pack to restart the Setup program, select Transaction Server, and mark all the Transaction Server components for installation.

To test your MTS 2.0 installation with the Bank Client, do the following:

1. Verify that the DTC service is running by right-clicking My Computer to open the context menu; DTC is running if the Stop MS DTC choice appears. If not, choose Start MS DTC to start the service.

2. Verify that SQL Server 6.5+ is running with SQL Service Manager. The Sample Bank components expect to connect to the pubs database of a local SQL Server installation via ODBC. All testing in this chapter is done with SQL Server 7.0.

3. If you're running SQL Server on another computer, are using integrated security, or have a login ID other than sa with an empty password, you must change the MTSSamples file DSN accordingly.

4. Close all programs except MTS Explorer if the computer on which you're running MTS and SQL Server has less than 64MB of RAM. You can run MTS and SQL Server under Windows NT Server 4.0 with 32MB of RAM, but performance, especially during startup, is likely to be less than stellar.

5. Choose Start, Programs, Windows NT 4.0 Option Pack, Transaction Server, Bank Client to open the Sample Bank - Visual Basic form.

6. Double-click Sample Bank's Components item, click MTS Explorer's Status View and Show/Hide Scope toolbar buttons, and arrange the window to minimally overlap the Sample Bank form. Status view lists the components and provides Objects, Activated, and In Call counters for each component.

7. Type **2** in the Transfer to Account text box and select the Transfer and Move Money options to perform the most complex operation offered by the Sample Bank application. Visual Basic 5.0 components are selected by default.

8. Click the Submit button to process the transaction. If your MTS installation is operational, a receipt in the Result text box displays the credit and debit operations and the new account balance information. The `Bank.Account`, `Bank.GetReceipt`, `Bank.MoveMoney`, and `Bank.UpdateReceipt` component balls spin during activation of the components and the corresponding Objects, Activated, and In Call counters change from 0 to 1 to 0 (see Figure 26.13).

FIGURE 26.13

*The Sample Bank
Client form and
MTS Explorer's
Status View dis-
playing activity
counters for
Sample Bank com-
ponents.*

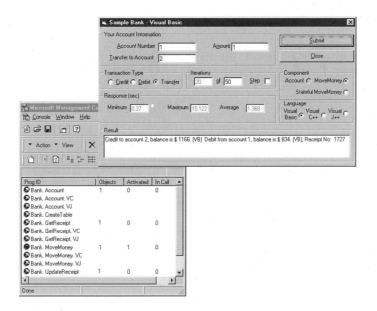

NOTE

The first execution of Bank Client takes substantially longer than successive executions. The first transaction opens a connection to SQL Server and creates the
sample tables in the pubs database. Starting the MTS servers also consumes a
substantial amount of system resources.

---

9. Type **50** in the Iterations text box and make sure the Step check box is clear. Click
   Submit to run the Move Money operations 50 times.

10. Select the Visual C++ or Visual J++ options to compare the performance with Visual
    Basic components. You must repeat the 50 iterations at least twice to obtain representative
    minimum values. Average and maximum values include time to start the servers and
    make database connections.

NOTE

Tests performed on OAKLEAF1 (32MB RAM) and OAKLEAF0 (128MB RAM) indicate that Visual J++ components using the Java Virtual Machine of Internet
Explorer 4.01 run about 30% to 40% slower than the Visual C++ or Visual Basic
components. Visual C++ components run about 3% to 5% faster than Visual
Basic components.

11. Click MTS Explorer's Show/Hide Scope button and double-click the Transaction Statistics item in the scope pane. Submit the 50 iterations again and watch the statistics bars as the transactions execute (see Figure 26.14). The transaction statistics accumulate timing data for all components of all packages installed on the selected server.

FIGURE 26.14.

MTS Explorer's Transaction Statistics pane.

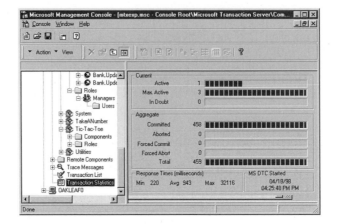

Setting Properties of the Sample Bank Package and Components

Default properties of the Sample Bank package and its components are designed for local, interactive execution under Windows NT Server 4.0. To set up Sample Bank for use by remote clients, follow these steps:

1. Right-click the Sample Bank package and choose Properties from the context menu to open the Sample Bank Properties sheet. The General page lets you add a description of the package and specifies the packages Package ID, a standard Win32 GUID.

2. Click the Identity tab, mark the This User option, click Browse, and select MTS Administrator in the Set Package Identity dialog. Click OK to close the dialog and put MTS Administrator in the User text box (see Figure 26.15). The default Interactive User requires a login to Windows NT Server; MTS Administrator runs MTS as a service on Windows NT startup.

FIGURE 26.15

The Identity page of the Sample Bank Properties sheet after changing identity.

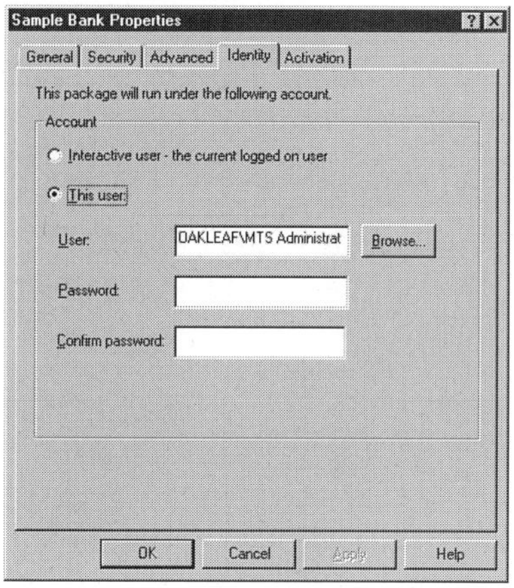

> **NOTE**
>
> You don't need to make entries in the Password and Confirm Password text boxes; MTS can't confirm passwords in this context because of Windows NT security.

3. Click the Security tab and, if Windows 9x clients must access MTS, select Connect in the Authentication Level for Calls list (see Figure 26.16). Connect checks the identity of the client only when the first connection is made to the package. Temporarily clear the Enable Authorization Checking check box until tests with remote clients succeed.

FIGURE 26.16

The Security page of the Sample Bank Properties sheet with Connect authentication specified, but authorization checking disabled for testing.

4. Click the Advanced tab and type **30** in the Shut Down After Being Idle text box (see Figure 26.17). This minimizes the number of startups of the server when testing with remote clients.

FIGURE 26.17

The Advanced page of the Sample Bank Properties sheet with the idle before shutdown period extended from 3 to 30 minutes.

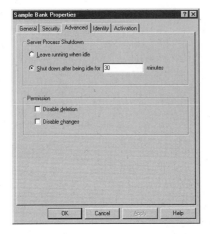

5. Click OK to close the Properties sheet and make the changes to the Sample Bank package properties.

NOTE

The Activation page offers the choice of running the package as a server process or in the process of the creator of the package. All packages installed except the utilities package run as an individual server process.

SETTING UP AND RUNNING THE BANK CLIENT ON A REMOTE COMPUTER

Versions of MTS prior to 2.0 required a convoluted installation process to enable client PCs to connect to MTS packages with DCOM. MTS 2.0 greatly simplifies the process by creating a custom executable file for client installation that performs the following functions:

1. Creates a temporary directory on the client into which to extract the required type libraries and custom proxy-stub DLLs.

2. Moves the type library (typlib) and DCOM proxy stub for the MTS package to the \Program Files\Remote Applications*GUID* folder. The GUID is the Package ID mentioned in step 1 of the preceding section.

3. Adds entries for the typlib and proxy stub in the client's Registry.

4. Adds an entry to Control Panel's Add/Remove Programs tool so users can delete obsolete package files and Registry entries.

To create a BankPack.exe file that clients can use to enable a connection to the Sample Bank package, do the following:

1. Right-click the Sample Bank package and choose Export from the context menu to open the Export Package dialog.

2. Click browse to open the Export Package to File dialog, navigate to the ...\MTS\Packages folder (for this example), type **BankPack.pak** as the name of the package file, and click Save to close the dialog and return to the Export Package dialog (see Figure 26.18).

FIGURE 26.18

Exporting a package to a file on the local computer.

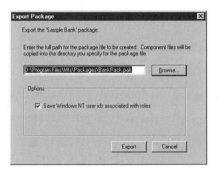

3. Click OK to close the Package was successfully exported message box. Exporting the file creates a Clients subfolder of the Packages folder that contains the executable file, BankPack.exe, required by the client to register the Sample Bank proxy stub to enable client access via DCOM.

TIP

You can include the client executable with your Visual Basic 6.0 Setup program and execute it after installation of required front-end files on the client.

To set up and run the Bank Client on a remote Windows 9x computer, follow these steps:

1. Run Dcomcnfg.exe from the \Windows\System folder and click the Default Properties tab to verify that DCOM is enabled. Mark the Enable Distributed COM on this computer check box, set the Default Authentication Level to Connect, and set the Default Impersonation Level to Impersonate (see Figure 26.19).

   Windows 98 includes DCOM and Internet Explorer 4+ installs DCOM, including Dcomcnfg.exe, on computers running Windows 95.

FIGURE 26.19

Setting Windows 9x client DCOM properties with Dcomconfg.exe.

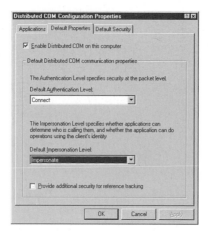

2. Copy the Bank Client executable, Vbbank.exe, from the ...\MTS folder to a \Program Files\MTS Test folder on the client PC.

3. Run BankPack.exe from the server share to install the required files and Registry entries on the client PC. You can verify proper execution of BankPack.exe by opening Control Panel's Add/Remove Program Tools and searching for Remote Application entries (see Figure 26.20).

FIGURE 26.20

The entry created by running BankPack.exe in the Add/Remove Programs Control Panel tool.

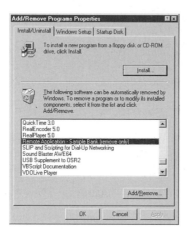

4. Run Vbbank.exe and submit a single Transfer with Move Money and Visual Basic to test the Sample Bank package over a DCOM network connection.

5. Specify 50 iterations and compare the minimum execution time with that for local operation. Minimum execution time is only slightly slower than local execution on a network with light traffic (see Figure 26.21 and refer to Figure 26.13).

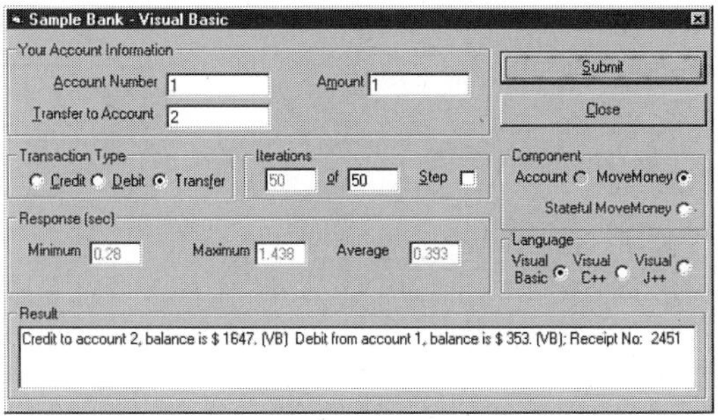

FIGURE 26.21

Minimum, average, and maximum execution times for Visual Basic components from a Windows 9x Sample Bank client.

6. In MTS Explorer, right-click the Sample Bank package, select Properties, and click the Security tab of the Sample Bank Properties sheet.

7. Mark the Enable Authorization Checking check box to apply security to the package and then click OK to save the change.

8. Close and restart the Sample Bank client; then run a transaction to verify that the client properly implements Connect level authentication.

> **NOTE**
>
> Installation on PCs running Windows NT Workstation 4.0 is identical to the preceding procedure. Although Windows NT offers more DCOM security options than Windows 9x offers, use Connect level authentication on all machines if some clients run Windows 9x. Connect authentication is adequate for all but highly confidential information processed by the package.

INSTALLING MTS 2.0 ON WORKSTATIONS

You don't need to install MTS 2.0 on client PCs that connect to MTS 2.0 servers. The client executable created in the preceding section takes care of client-related setup operations. If you want to administer MTS 2.0 on remote servers, rather than working in the server closet, you must install a copy of MTS 2.0 on the administrative workstation.

The Windows NT 4.0 Option Pack installs the appropriate components for all current Win32 operating systems. For workstations, the Option Pack lets you selectively install the following components:

- Microsoft Personal Web Server 4.0, including FrontPage 98 Server Extensions. Installation of this component is optional.

- Microsoft Transaction Server 2.0 with Core Documentation by default, but you can add Development Files with the Custom installation option. Microsoft Transaction Explorer is a standalone application (Mtxexp.exe) in the Windows 9*x* version.

- Microsoft Data Access Components (MDAC) 1.5, which (unfortunately) you can't disable when choosing Upgrade Plus. Fortunately, MDAC 1.5 doesn't overwrite the MDAC 2.0 (ADO 2.0 and OLE DB 2.0) files you installed with Visual Basic or Visual Studio 6.0.

- Internet Explorer 4.01 (optional). A later version is included with Visual Studio 6.0.

- Internet Connection Services for Microsoft Remote Access Services for setting up Virtual Private Networks (VPNs) and improved dial-up connections (optional).

- Microsoft Message Queue Server (MSMQ) Client (optional).

> **NOTE**
>
> If you're installing MTS 2.0 on a Windows 95 client, be sure to download and install version 1.2 or later of DCOM for Windows 95 from `http://www.microsoft.com/com/` before running the Option Pack Setup program. Version 1.2 now checks version numbers to prevent overwriting newer with older versions and supports all Visual Basic 6.0 data types.

To install MTS 2.0 on a Win32 workstation, do the following:

1. Run Setup.exe from the Option Pack CD-ROM's root folder if AutoPlay doesn't start the setup program. Alternatively, you can install the Option Pack components from CD-ROM 2 of the Visual Studio 6.0 distribution CD-ROMs.

2. Setup first installs Winsock 2.0 on Windows 95 computers that don't have Winsock 2.0. You must reboot the computer to complete the Winsock 2.0 installation.

3. If you have a version of Personal Web Server (PWS) earlier than 4.0 installed, Setup removes the FTP server, which is no longer supported by PWS.

4. Choose Custom installation and select the components you want to install.

5. Reboot the computer at the end of the installation process.

6. Choose Start, Programs, Microsoft Personal Web Server, Microsoft Transaction Server, Transaction Explorer to launch the program. If you selected Development Files in the preceding step, the Bank and Tic-Tac-Toe clients also appear in the Microsoft Transaction Server submenu.

7. To connect to other MTS installations, right-click the Computers item in the scope pane and choose New, Computer to open the Add Computer dialog.

8. Type the server name in the text box or click browse to open the Select Computer dialog to display available servers. When you close the dialog(s), the new server is added to the Computers list (see Figure 26.22).

9. Repeat steps 7 and 8 for each MTS installation you want to administer from the workstation.

FIGURE 26.22
MTS installations on OAKLEAF0 and OAKLEAF1 servers appearing in OAKLEAF2's MTS Explorer for Windows 95.

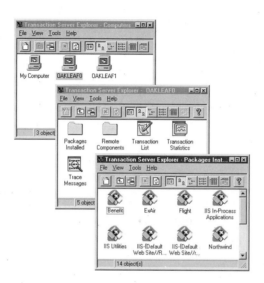

Workstations can be used to develop and deploy middle-tier MTS packages, but Windows NT Server 4+ should be used to host all MTS components for production applications.

CREATING AND DEPLOYING MTS COMPONENTS

IN THIS CHAPTER

"Componentize your applications" is the mantra of object-oriented software seminars and trade shows. Object reusability, like enterprise reengineering, has led many organizations down the primrose path of major programming investments that ultimately deliver little or no demonstrable return. Objects intended to embody organizationwide business rules often turn out to be single-use components suited only to a particular application. Designing a truly reusable business object that other developers are willing to employ in their applications is not a trivial project. Classes developed as client-side in-process servers seldom are properly designed for server-side execution. As an example, most textbook examples of Visual Basic business objects are stateful, but MTS requires stateless components to optimize performance and scalability.

Relatively few Visual Basic database front-end projects begin with a *tabula rasa* (blank slate). The more common client/server development scenarios involve existing databases and what are perceived to be underperforming front ends. The source of performance problems might be the design or tuning of the underlying database, inadequate server hardware resources, network congestion, a combination of these defects, or other bottlenecks wholly independent of the existing front end. Database users and their supervisors, however, instinctively blame the front-end application for almost all performance problems. Don't expect a sluggish monolithic client application to gain performance points by extracting middle-tier code to run within MTS on an already-overloaded server against a poorly designed or badly tuned database.

> **NOTE**
>
> MTS doesn't improve the performance of a well-designed monolithic front end that executes stored procedures. As this chapter demonstrates, using an object-oriented component design extracts a significant performance penalty, especially for row-returning procedures, regardless of whether the objects run in the client's process or in an MTS 2.0 process on the server.

This chapter begins by describing the best application candidates for conversion to MTS and the code framework for MTS components to maximize performance. The chapter concludes with an example of converting an existing monolithic client front end to use MTS for database connectivity and transaction processing.

DEFINING MTS COMPONENT CANDIDATES

Virtually all MTS packages connect to one or more relational databases, most commonly Microsoft SQL Server 6.5+. Although MTS 2.0 is a general purpose Object Request Broker (ORB), as well as a transaction manager (TM), one of its primary features is the ability to pool database connections for users of a single package. MTS also is designed to provide object pooling, but this feature isn't implemented in MTS 2.0. The following sections describe the three primary types of data-related applications or application elements that are suited for use as MTS base clients.

> **NOTE**
>
> ODBC 3+ supports database connection pooling for users of the same DSN and identity. ODBC 3+ connection pooling is implemented by Mtxdm.dll, one of the MTS DLLs. Native data providers that conform to the OLE DB 2.0 specification, such as the Microsoft OLE DB Provider for SQL Server (SQLOLEDB), also support ODBC-like connection pooling. Instances of MTS objects share the identity you assign when creating their package; thus all users who instantiate an MTS object within a particular package share the pooled connections.

Transaction-Oriented Components

MTS supports multiple, distributed, and nested transactions with the `SetComplete` and `SetAbort` methods of the `ObjectContext` object. Thus you should consider MTS as a transaction manager for any application that modifies data, especially operations that require multiple server round-trips to complete a transaction.

▶ See "Replacing INSERT, UPDATE, and Transaction Code with Stored Procedures," **p. 835**

> **NOTE**
>
> Ado2proc.vbp's `cmdAddNewOrder` event handler, which requires two round-trips to the server to add an order with two or more line items to the Nwind database, is a logical candidate for conversion to an MTS method. You pass the Order table data and multiple Order_Details records in a single method call; MTS maintains transactional consistency across the two database operations with the `ObjectContext` object. If both operations succeed, you call the `SetComplete` method. If either operation fails, the error handler calls `SetAbort` to roll back any modifications to tables made prior to the failure.

Even relatively trivial transaction applications, such as the Windows NT 4.0 Option Pack's Bank application, described in the preceding chapter, require fairly complex code to properly implement simple transactions. You must design, program, install, and secure MTS packages and then alter the client code to instantiate the packaged components. Despite the additional effort, moving transaction code from the client to an MTS component usually pays scalability dividends.

MTS transactional packages are most effective in situations where the time required to complete a transaction isn't readily predictable, such as when validating credit card purchases. In this case, the Shared Property Manager (SPM) maintains the state of a particular transaction until all elements of the transaction complete successfully or a failure occurs in any element. Using SPM to maintain state is far more efficient than executing multiple methods of stateful components.

Resource Isolation Components

Microsoft promotes MTS as "Web Glue" to connect Active Server Pages (ASP) and other intranet or Internet components to databases. The theory of Web Glue is to employ MTS to isolate the data services layer from the Web server, thereby improving data security. In addition, Web Glue involves implementing business rules, such as data validation, in an MTS component instead of a client-side script. You can write MTS components in Visual Basic, Visual J++, or Visual C++, each of which offers a much richer programming environment than today's lightweight scripting languages. Internet applications require ECMAScript (aka JavaScript or JScript) for cross-browser compatibility; VBScript is useful only in intranet scenarios where Internet Explorer is the sole browser.

The effectiveness of MTS 2+ as Web Glue remains to be determined. Isolating and securing confidential information in databases usually is better accomplished by views, stored procedures, and conventional database security features than by Web Glue. Using MTS components to validate data entry requires at least one round-trip to the server to resolve a data entry error. Server round-trips are especially costly in Internet/intranet scenarios. If the data validation process is complex, involving access to lookup tables or complex logic, the Web application is likely to warrant an MTS data validation object in conjunction with one or more transaction components.

Decision-Support Components

▶ **See** "Converting Ado2oltp.frm's SELECT Statements to Procedures," **p. 826**

It's difficult to beat the performance of Transact-SQL stored procedures running SELECT statements that return relatively few rows. For example, the single-row-returning stored procedures of the Ado2proc.vbp sample application in Chapter 21, "Using Transact-SQL Stored Procedures," execute in 50 milliseconds or less on a lightly loaded 10BaseT network. As mentioned at the beginning of the chapter, partitioning monolithic front-end applications into classes that call row-returning stored procedures results in a major-scale performance hit, often slowing execution by a factor of five. Marshalling COM arguments to in-process servers extracts a similar speed penalty; passing Recordsets and argument values out-of-process via DCOM is an even slower operation.

▶ **See** "Setting Properties of the Sample Bank Package and Components," **p. 992**

TIP

Restarting an MTS component that has timed out takes 5 to 15 seconds on a lightly loaded server. If your component server has sufficient hardware resources, such as multiple CPUs and 128MB or more of RAM, consider setting the Server Process Shutdown option for packages requiring faster initial response times to Leave Running When Idle.

Consider moving decision-support functions to MTS now only if architectural consistency—pooling all database connections through MTS packages—is your primary objective. Future versions of MTS that support object pooling are likely to improve execution time for row-returning operations. Routing Recordsets through an MTS layer, however, undoubtedly will remain slower than direct execution of stored procedures by the client.

> **NOTE**
>
> Microsoft announced in mid-1998 that MTS 3.0 will be released after Windows NT 5.0. When this edition was written, Microsoft had not provided an official estimate for the release date of either product.

DESIGNING EFFICIENT MTS COMPONENTS

Proper component design is the key to gaining all potential benefits of MTS. The following rules apply to classes intended for use as MTS components and clients calling these components:

1. You must add a reference to the Microsoft Transaction Server Type Library to compile MTS components that include MTS objects, such as ObjectContext.

2. You must add a reference to Microsoft ActiveX Data Objects 2.0 Library to projects that use ADO.

3. A copy of the Visual Basic 6.0 virtual machine (runtime library), Msvbvm60.dll, must reside in the \Winnt\Systems32 folder of the server hosting the MTS components. Both Msvbvm60.dll and the component must have appropriate Registry entries.

4. The Microsoft Distributed Transaction Coordinator (DTC) must be running on the component server and any workstation(s) that run MTS Explorer or client applications.

5. Use code to open ADODB.Connection, Command, and Recordset objects. Don't attempt to use Connection, Command, or Recordset objects created with the Data Environment Designer.

6. Class modules must be compiled as MultiUse (creatable) ActiveX DLLs for unattended execution.

7. MTS permits the use of single-threaded components, but Microsoft recommends specifying apartment-threaded DLLs. Future versions of MTS are expected to support apartment-threaded components. The examples in this chapter are compiled as apartment-threaded DLLs.

8. You must create MTS components on the client with **Set** obj*Name* = **CreateObject**(*ClassName.ObjectName*). **Dim** obj*Name* **As New** *ClassName.ObjectName* doesn't work for MTS components, even with a client-side reference to *ClassName.ObjectName* created by the client installation executable.

Following is a set of general guidelines for optimizing classes to serve as members of MTS packages:

- Use ADO 2+ and native OLE DB 2.0 data providers, if available, for all database operations. Use MSDASQL and ODBC 3+ drivers only if your RDBMS vendor doesn't supply a qualified OLE DB 2+ data provider that supports connection pooling or your RDBMS is running on a UNIX box.

- Create objects in the client as late as possible and release components with **Set** *objName* = **Nothing** as soon as possible. Open client DCOM references to MTS objects consume resources.

- Pass method arguments **ByVal**, not **ByRef**, whenever possible. Marshalling references, especially to large objects, creates a substantial performance hit.

- Pass multiple method arguments as **Variant** arrays, rather than as long lists of individual argument values. Always use arrays to pass data for single-record INSERT or UPDATE operations. For multiple-record inserts, passing two-dimensional (row, column) **Variant** arrays or Recordsets results in approximately equal performance.

- Don't write stateful components. If you must retain state information, use SPM to store the equivalent of **Public** variables. Specify class-level variables and constants for ADODB objects and connection strings used by multiple methods.

- Enable transactions for all components to take advantage of just-in-time component activation for reuse. Use *objContext*.SetComplete or *objContext*.SetAbort to release the component for reuse by your application or other clients. Visual Basic 6.0 lets you specify the value of the MTSTransactionMode property of the class. To utilize the ContextObject object, you must select property values other than 0 (NotAnMTSObject) or 1 (NoTransactions). Alternatively, you can set the transaction mode of the component with MTS Explorer.

> **NOTE**
>
> The MTSTransactionMODE property appears in the class module Properties sheet after you add a reference to the Microsoft Transaction Server Type Library to your project.

- Replace distributed transactions that involve stored procedure calls to other databases with MTS transactions. MTS provides much greater programming flexibility for DTC than T-SQL stored procedures do.

- Put all classes for which you want to pool database connections into a single package. Connection pooling occurs at the package level.

- Add `ObjectControl` for all components by adding **Implements** `ObjectControl` at the top of the Declarations section of each class module. `ObjectControl` provides `Activate` and `Deactivate` event handlers that you employ to create and release the `ObjectContext` object, respectively. Release open `Connection`, `Command`, and `Recordset` objects in the `Deactivate` event handler.

- Pass read-only, forward-only ("1firehose cursor") `Recordsets` as method arguments or return values. Passing live cursors to clients through MTS 2.0 is problematic, at best. Minimize the number of returned rows and specify only the columns you need for your application.

- Use `INSERT`, `UPDATE`, and `DELETE` stored procedures to modify tables. If your client *must* edit `Recordsets`, use disconnected `Recordsets` with batch-optimistic locking and try to implement conflict resolution within your MTS component.

- Include an `ObjectControl_CanBePooled` event handler for each class, setting `ObjectControl_CanBePooled` to **True**. MTS 2.0 doesn't support object pooling, but it's probable that MTS 3.0 will pool objects. (MTS 2.0 pools threads, which is an approximation of full object pooling.)

- Take advantage of MTS's declarative and programmatic security. Establishing security at the package, component, and method levels lets you specify the user groups that have access to individual classes and methods. The `IsCallerInRole` method of the `ObjectContext` object provides security at the method level.

- Use stored procedures for all database access and update operations. Very few Microsoft and third-party examples of MTS components code use (or even mention) stored procedures. You gain similar performance benefits from execution of stored procedures by MTS objects as you do by calling stored procedures directly from client front ends.

To the maximum extent practical, consistent with minimizing structural changes to this book's standard client/server frontsend application, the code examples of this chapter follow the preceding guidelines.

> **NOTE**
>
> Microsoft recommends keeping your MTS components "close to the data source." This recommendation, which relates primarily to architecture not component design, implies running MTS on the same server as the RDBMS. The problem with this approach is competition for server resources (primarily threads) between the RDBMS and MTS. For maximum scalability, use individual multiprocessor servers for the RDBMS(s) connected by high-speed switched network media, such as 100BaseT or Gigabit Ethernet. Add processors and RAM to the MTS server as the load increases. If you haven't implemented high-speed switching for server interconnects, consider multihoming the RDBMS and MTS servers, adding 100BaseT network cards and a hub to create a direct 100Mbps connection.

The `ObjectContext` Object

An *MTS object* is an instance of a component (class) within an MTS package. Each MTS object associates an implicit `ObjectContext` object for the thread on which the object executes. This object has intrinsic properties that specify the identity of the base client that instantiates the object and the object's transactional requirements specified by the `MTSTransactionMode` property value or from the component properties sheet.

After adding a project reference to Mtxas.dll, Object Browser displays the properties and methods of MTS classes (see Figure 27.1). Help topics in Mts20.hlp are available for most (but not all) MTS properties and methods.

FIGURE 27.1

Object Browser displaying the methods and properties of the `ObjectContext` *object.*

You create a reference to the `ObjectContext` object with the `GetObjectContext` function, as in the following example:

```
Dim objCtxt As ObjectContext
Set objCtxt = GetObjectContext
```

After you create a reference to the `ObjectContext` object, you can invoke its methods in your component code. Table 27.1 lists the methods of the `ObjectContext` object and their usage. The `Count`, `IsInTransaction`, `Item`, and `IsSecurityEnabled` methods emulate properties.

TABLE 27.1 METHODS OF THE `ObjectContext` OBJECT

Method	Description
Count	`objCtxt.Count` returns the number of properties of `objCtxt`.
CreateInstance	`objCtxt.CreateInstance(strProgID)` creates an instance of another MTS component within the package having the specified Programmatic ID (*Class.Object*). If transactions are enabled, the created object runs in the context of the caller's transaction.

Method	Description
DisableCommit	obj*Ctxt*.DisableCommit prevents a transaction from committing until calling EnableCommit (stateful objects only).
EnableCommit	obj*Ctxt*.EnableCommit indicates that the transaction state of the object is consistent and ready to commit (stateful objects only).
IsCallerInRole	obj*Ctxt*.IsCallerInRole(str*Role*) returns **True** if the identity of the call is a member of the specified role.
IsInTransaction	obj*Ctxt*.IsInTransaction returns **True** if the context has an active transaction.
IsSecurityEnabled	obj*Ctxt*.IsSecurityEnabled returns **True** unless the object is running in the client's process.
Item	obj*Ctxt*.Item(str*Name*) returns the value of the named property.
Security	obj*Ctxt*.Security returns a reference to the SecurityProperty object.
SetAbort	obj*Ctxt*.SetAbort specifies that the object's work is complete and associated transactions, if any, must be rolled back.
SetComplete	obj*Ctxt*.SetComplete specifies that the object's work is complete and associated transactions, if any, are to be committed.

Mtxas.dll, the primary MTS library, provides the set (not an Enum) of error constants listed in Table 27.2. You can return the values of these error constants to the client (with Err.Raise statements) to aid in troubleshooting. The client must have a reference to Mtxas.dll to use the constant names.

TABLE 27.2 ObjectContext OBJECT NAMED ERROR CONSTANTS

Constant Name	Value	Description
mtxErrCtxAborted	**&H**8004E002	The transaction's object aborted.
mtxErrCtxAborting	**&H**8004E003	The transaction's object is in the process of aborting.
mtxErrCtxNoContext	**&H**8004E004	The ObjectContext isn't available.
mtxErrCtxNotRegistered	**&H**8004E005	The object isn't registered properly.
mtxErrCtxActivityTimeout	**&H**8004E006	The object's activity timed out prior to completion.
mtxErrCtxOldReference	**&H**8004E007	The object has become invalid.
mtxErrCtxRoleNotFound	**&H**8004E00C	The specified role isn't in the catalog.
mtxErrCtxNoSecurity	**&H**8004E00D	Security isn't enabled.

The Shared Property Manager

SPM lets you maintain component state without writing stateful components. Using SPM requires you to add a component project reference to the Shared Property Manager Type Library (Mtxspm.dll) to gain access to the `SharedPropertyGroupManager` (SPGM) object. SPGM lets you define a collection of `SharedPropertyGroup` objects, each of which contains a collection of `SharedProperty` objects.

```
Dim objSPGM As SharedPropertyGroupManager
Dim objSPG As SharedPropertyGroup
Dim objSPName As SharedProperty

Dim blnExists As Boolean
Dim lngValue As Long

Set objSPGM = CreateObject("Mtxspm.SharedPropertyGroupManager")
Set objSPG = objSPGM.CreatePropertyGroup("Group", LockSetGet, Process, blnExists)
Set objSPName = objSPG.CreateProperty("Name", blnExists)

'Set the value to something
objSPName.Value = 150
```

LockSetGet and Process are **Long** constant values provided by the LockModes and Release Modes enumerations, respectively, of SPMAfter you create SharedPropertyGroup and SharedProperty objects, you can reference the shared property value with an *intValue* = objSPG.objSPName.Value statement.

> **NOTE**
>
> Properties should share only within a single package created with a single DLL. Shared properties must run within the same server process to allow access to the property values by successive instances of the component.

The `SecurityProperty` Object of `ObjectContext`

The `SecurityProperty` object lets you determine the user names associated with the creation of objects and execution of methods when using programmatic security. You create a reference to the `SecurityProperty` object with the following code:

```
If objCtxt.IsSecurityEnabled Then
    Dim objSecProp As SecurityProperty
    Set objSecProp = objCtxt.Security
    'Apply SecurityProperty methods
End If
```

The `SecurityProperty` methods, listed in Table 27.3, are useful for auditing purposes in a programmatic security environment.

TABLE 27.3   METHODS OF THE `SecurityProperty` OBJECT

Method	Description
GetDirectCallerName	`objSecProp.GetDirectCallerName` returns the user name associated with the external process that called the currently executing method.
GetDirectCreatorName	`objSecProp.GetDirectCreatorName` returns the user name associated with the external process that directly created the current object.
GetOriginalCallerName	`objSecProp.GetOriginalCallerName` returns the user name from the base client that initiated the call sequence from which the current method was called.
GetOriginalCreatorName	`objSecProp.GetOriginalCreatorName` returns the user name from the base client that initiated the call sequence from which the current method was called.

The `ObjectControl` Object

Next to `ObjectContext`, `ObjectControl` is MTS's most important element. The `ObjectControl` object offers the three methods, described in Table 27.4, which are implemented as events. You must add an **Implements** `ObjectControl` statement immediately after **Option** `Explicit` to add the event-handler stubs to your class module.

TABLE 27.4   METHODS OF THE `ObjectControl` OBJECT

Method	Usage
Activate	**Private Sub** `ObjectControl_Activate()` is the event handler for object startup in which you create a reference to the `ObjectContext` object.
CanBePooled	**Private Function** `ObjectControl_CanBePooled()` **As Boolean** is the event handler in which you activate object pooling when MTS supports this feature. You can set `ObjectControl_CanBePooled` to **True** for forward compatibility because MTS 2.0 ignores the return value.
Deactivate	**Private Sub** `ObjectControl_Deactivate()` is where you release all references, including `ObjectContext` and open ADODB objects.

An MTS Component Template

Much of the MTS-specific code for classes is common to all classes, so an MTS component template can save you a substantial amount of time when writing your classes. Listing 27.1 illustrates a template with code that's common to almost all MTS data-related classes and that implements the majority of the elements of the preceding guideline list. The template doesn't include SPM code, because shared properties are uncommon in conventional MTS components. As a rule, it's more usual to persist state in database tables; dedicated object-oriented programmers consider RDBMSs simply as containers to persist the state of their objects.

LISTING 27.1   TEMPLATE CODE TO SPEED WRITING OF MTS CLASSES

```
Option Explicit

'Provide activate/deactivate, plus object pooling when available
Implements ObjectControl

'Provide just-in-time activation
Private objCtxt As ObjectContext

Private cnnData As New ADODB.Connection
Private cmmData As New ADODB.Command
Private strCnn As String

Private Const strServer = "OAKLEAF0"
Private Const strDatabase = "nwind"
Private Const strUserID = "sa"
Private Const strPassword = ""

Public Function Template (ByVal Argument1 As DataType, _
                          ByVal Argument2 As DataType, _
                          ByVal Argument3 As DataType) As Long

    On Error GoTo TemplateErr

    'Connect to an SQL Server data source
    strCnn = "Location=" & strServer & ";User ID=" & strUserID & _
        ";Password=" & strPassword & ";Data Source=" & strDatabase
    cnnData.Provider = "SQLOLEDB"
    cnnData.CursorLocation = adUseClient
    cnnData.Open strCnn

    'Data manipulation code goes here

Exit Function
```

```
TemplateErr:
    objCtxt.SetAbort
    Err.Raise Err.Number, "Class.Object", Err.Description
    Exit Function
End Function

Private Sub ObjectControl_Activate()
    'Get the object context on class activation
    Set objCtxt = GetObjectContext
End Sub

Private Function ObjectControl_CanBePooled() As Boolean
    'Pooling isn't available, but set True for uplevel compatibility
    ObjectControl_CanBePooled = True
End Function

Private Sub ObjectControl_Deactivate()
    'Release the ADODB and Context objects
    Set cmmData = Nothing
    Set cnnData = Nothing
    Set objCtxt = Nothing
End Sub
```

> **NOTE**
>
> MTS components are stateless, so each method invocation must establish a connection to the RDBMS. Thus it's important to close the database connection during object deactivation so pooled connections can be recycled for use by other methods.

CONVERTING A MONOLITHIC CLIENT TO USE MTS COMPONENTS

The introduction to this chapter observed that relatively few MTS applications originate from scratch; most involve existing databases and front ends. Upgrading an existing production application to MTS is the best approach for determining whether MTS is an aid or a detriment to current application performance and ultimate scalability. Developers new to MTS are better served by converting an existing front end to MTS than by writing new code to implement trivial classes, such as MTS's example Bank application. Thus the example in this chapter starts with the Ado2proc.vbp project from Chapter 21 in a four-step process that results in a new version of Ado2proc.vbp, named Ado2mts3.vbp, which calls components in the Northwind package running on a remote MTS server.

> **NOTE**
>
> The sample code for the sections that follow is located in the \Ddg_vb6\Chaptr27\Step1, ...\Step2, and ...\Step3 folders of the accompanying CD-ROM. The first three Step subfolders include all the code required for the step. The fourth step, which moves the package to MTS running on a remote server, uses the same client code and component DLL as the third step.

▶ **See** "Creating the Stored Procedures," **p. 827**

It's easier to test MTS components on the development machine running Visual Basic 6.0 than on a remote server, so the examples that follow are created and executed under Windows NT 4.0 SP 4 on OAKLEAF1, the workstation used to create the majority of the examples of this book. Ado2proc.vbp executes its stored procedures against a remote server (OAKLEAF0), but you can run the client code and MTS package on the same machine that hosts SQL Server 6.5+. Before running the examples of this chapter, you must create the ado_* stored procedures in the SQL Server nwind database.

Figure 27.2 shows Ado2mts1.frm after the control modifications required to compare performance with the following connection options:

- *SProc - All* causes direct client execution of all stored procedures using the SQLOLEDB driver, identical to the operation of Chapter 21's Ado2proc.frm with the SQL - Native option and the Stored Procs check box marked. The SProc - All option provides the baseline timing data for performance comparisons. The values of blnMTSXact and blnMTSAll are set **False** in the optConnect event handler.

- *MTS - Xact* redirects AddNewCustomer and AddNewOrder operations to call the AddCust method of the Customer component and the AddOrder method of the Order component, respectively. Subprocedures that require Recordset objects call the stored procedures directly (blnMTSXact is set **True** and blnMTSAll is set **False**.)

- *MTS - All* redirects all stored procedure calls to methods of the OrderData, Order, and Customer components (blnMTSXact and blnMTSAll are set **True**). All form-level ADODB objects are set to **Nothing**.

Step 1: Moving Data Access Operations to Classes

Debugging MTS 2.0 components with Visual Studio isn't a simple process, so the better approach is to make incremental changes to the client code that are easy to test and debug if necessary. It's also easier to partition database-related code into class modules that are part of the client project.

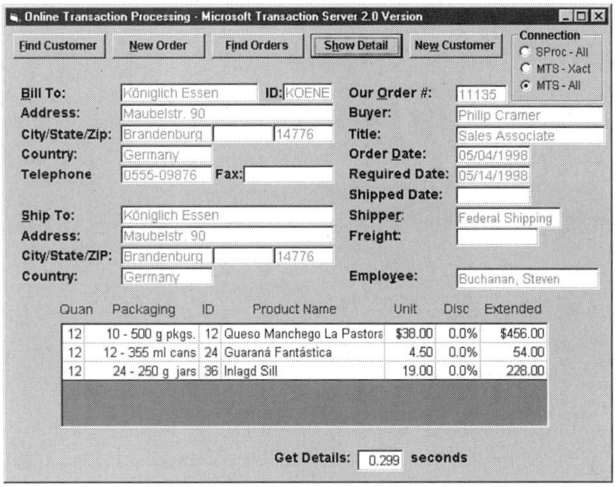

FIGURE 27.2

The common form design for the three versions of the example MTS client.

The first step in migration to MTS involves the following operations:

1. Eliminate superfluous client code. Ado2proc.frm includes code to generate SQL statements, which can be removed because all database calls originate from MTS components. Ado2mts1.frm retains code to make stored procedure calls directly to SQL Server 6.5+ in order to provide a baseline for execution time comparisons. A production front end doesn't need to make performance comparisons, but retaining the ability to make direct stored procedure calls is useful as a workaround if the client can't connect to the MTS server.

2. Determine component granularity. Row-returning stored procedures cross several database tables; transaction-related operations operate on one (Customers) or two (Orders and Order_Details) tables. The initial Ado2mts1.vbp implementation uses three classes: `OrderData`, `Customer`, and `Order`. The `OrderData` component eliminates the need to make calls to instantiate `Customer` and `Order` objects to retrieve order information. MTS's declarative security is an additional reason for implementing `OrderData` as a separate component. Many categories of users (Roles) can share order information, but only data entry operators and their supervisors should be allowed to add or modify customer and order information.

3. Move data access code to the class modules. Defining methods for the initial object implementation is simple; each object has only one **Public Function**—GetData for `OrderData` and AddObject for `Customer` and `Order`. Other related applications expect to be able to call `EditObject` and `DeleteObject`, but Ado2mts1.frm only reads and adds objects. In most cases, you can cut and paste the data access code from the client form to the class module.

4. Specify the method arguments. Ado2proc.frm treats all stored procedures as individual objects, but procedure calls that share common elements can be executed by a single

method. Adding a new customer or order requires passing a **Variant** array of Customer or Order information; adding an order with more than one line item requires an additional **Variant** array of Order_Details.

5. Substitute method calls for stored procedure calls. As an example, if your OrderData component's method is defined by the following:

```
Public Function GetOrderData(ByVal strProcName As String, _
                             ByVal varParam As Variant, _
                             ByRef rstData As ADODB.Recordset) As Long
```

call the GetOrderData method with the following client-side code:

```
Dim objData As New OrderData
If objData Is Nothing Then
    'Error occurred
Else
    If objData.GetOrderData("ado_EmpsList", Null, rstEmployees) Then
        'OK, so close the object if it's not reused
        Set objData = Nothing
    Else
        'Error occurred
    End If
End If
```

6. Add appropriate error handling procedures to your client code if the client is to be used in a production environment.

7. Test the execution of your component; then repeat steps 3 through 5 for each occurrence of a database-related method call.

Moving `Recordset`-Based Procedures to a Class

It's much easier to debug your components within a single project that includes your client form(s) and class modules than as components of a separate DLL. Listing 27.2 shows the code of the `GetCustomerData` subprocedure of Ado2mts1.frm that, when `blnMTSAll` is **True**, calls the `GetOrderData` method of the newly created `OrderData` class module of Listing 27.3 to return a single-row `Recordset` with values from the Customers table.

LISTING 27.2   THE GetCustomerData SUBPROCEDURE OF ADO2MTS1.FRM

```
Private Sub GetCustomerData(blnFromGrid As Boolean)
    'Purpose:   Load customer data from list

    'On Error GoTo ListCustsError

    grdOrders.Visible = False
    lblOrders.Visible = False

    If blnMTSAll Then
        Dim objData As New OrderData
        If objData Is Nothing Then
            'Error
        Else
            If blnFromGrid Then
                lngCount = objData.GetOrderData("ado_CustsData_ID", _
                    grdCustomers.Text, rstCustomers)
            Else
                lngCount = objData.GetOrderData("ado_CustsData_Name", _
                    txtCompanyName.Text & "%", rstCustomers)
            End If
        End If
    Else
        With cmmCustomers
            If blnFromGrid Then
                .CommandText = "ado_CustsData_ID"
                .Parameters(1).Size = 5
                .Parameters(1).Value = grdCustomers.Text
            Else
                .CommandText = "ado_CustsData_Name"
                .Parameters(1).Size = 40
                .Parameters(1).Value = txtCompanyName.Text & "%"
            End If
            Set rstCustomers = .Execute
            lngCount = rstCustomers.RecordCount
        End With
    End If
```

continues

LISTING 27.2   CONTINUED

```
    If lngCount = 0 Then
        MsgBox "Customer entry not found.", 48, "Order Entry Error"
    Else
        Call LoadCustomerData
        DoEvents
        cmdFindOrders.Enabled = True
        cmdFindOrders.SetFocus
        cmdNewOrder.Enabled = True
        Call FindOrders
    End If
    Exit Sub

ListCustsError:
    MsgBox Error, 48, "List Customers Error"
    Exit Sub
End Sub
```

LISTING 27.3   THE OrderData CLASS OF ADO2MTS1.VBP THAT RETURNS Recordset OBJECTS AS ARGUMENTS OF METHOD CALLS

```
Option Explicit

Private Const strServer = "OAKLEAF0"
Private Const strDatabase = "nwind"
Private Const strUserID = "sa"
Private Const strPassword = ""

Public Function GetOrderData(ByVal strProcName As String, _
                             ByVal varParam As Variant, _
                             ByRef rstData As ADODB.Recordset) As Long
    'General purpose method to return Recordsets
    'from parameterized queries

    Dim cnnData As New ADODB.Connection
    Dim cmmGetData As New ADODB.Command
    Dim prmRetVal As ADODB.Parameter
    Dim prmParam As ADODB.Parameter
    Dim lngParam As Long
    Dim strParam As String
    Dim strCnn As String
    Dim lngCount As Long

    On Error GoTo GetOrderDataErr

    'Connect to SQL Server with native provider and stored procedures
    strCnn = "Location=" & strServer & ";User ID=" & strUserID & _
        ";Password=" & strPassword & ";Data Source=" & strDatabase
    cnnData.Provider = "SQLOLEDB"
    cnnData.CursorLocation = adUseClient
    cnnData.Open strCnn
```

```
If IsNull(varParam) Then
    'Execute against the Connection object
    Set rstData = cnnData.Execute(strProcName, lngCount, adCmdStoredProc)
    GetOrderData = lngCount
Else
    'Create and execute the GetData command (multi-purpose for parameters)
    With cmmGetData
        .ActiveConnection = cnnData
        .CommandType = adCmdStoredProc
        .CommandText = strProcName
        Set prmRetVal = .CreateParameter("RETURN_VALUE", adInteger, _
            adParamReturnValue, 0, 0)
        .Parameters.Append prmRetVal
        If VarType(varParam) = vbString Then
            strParam = CStr(varParam)
            Set prmParam = .CreateParameter("Param", adChar, _
                adParamInput, Len(strParam), "")
            .Parameters.Append prmParam
            .Parameters("Param").Value = strParam
        Else
            lngParam = CLng(varParam)
            Set prmParam = .CreateParameter("Param", adInteger, _
                adParamInput, , 0)
            .Parameters.Append prmParam
            .Parameters("Param").Value = lngParam
        End If
        Set rstData = cmmGetData.Execute
        If prmRetVal Then
            GetOrderData = prmRetVal.Value
        Else
            GetOrderData = rstData.RecordCount
        End If
    End With
End If
Exit Function

GetOrderDataErr:
    Err.Raise Err.Number, "OrderData.GetOrderData", Err.Description
    Exit Function
End Function
```

Moving Transactional Procedures to a Class

Migrating transactional procedures to a class usually is a more complex process than moving Recordset-related operations. As mentioned earlier in the chapter, **Variant** arrays are the most expeditious method of passing values for INSERT and UPDATE operations as method arguments, especially when multiple records are involved in a single transaction. Ado2mts1.frm's cmdAddNewOrder_Click event handler, shown without housekeeping code in Listing 27.4, creates a 15-member **Variant** array, avarOrder, that contains the values to be added to the Orders table and the first line item to be inserted into the Order_Details table. A two-dimensional (row, column) **Variant** array, avarItems, supplies Order_Details values for two or more line items per order. The blnHasTimeStamp and blnSQLS7 arguments are needed for SQL Server version and Order_Details table compatibility; production code would not include these arguments.

NOTE

You can simplify the creation of **Variant** arrays from Recordsets by applying the GetRows method of an ADODB.Recordset object to return automatically a two-dimensional (column, row) **Variant** array. The rstLineItems Recordset has a column sequence different from that of the Order_Details table, so GetRows isn't readily usable in this case. It's a good application design practice to use GetRows whenever possible.

LISTING 27.4 THE cmdAddNewOrder_Click EVENT HANDLER OF ADO2MTS1.FRM

```
Private Sub cmdAddNewOrder_Click()
    'Purpose: Add a new order to the Orders and Order Details tables

    Dim lngOrderID As Long
    Dim sngStart As Single
    Dim sngGetID As Single
    Dim sngWrap As Single
    Dim sngCommit As Single
    Dim intCtr As Integer
    Dim lngEmployeeID As Long
    Dim lngShipVia As Long

    'Data validation and housekeeping code is omitted for clarity

    If blnMTSAll Or blnMTSXact Then
        'Create the Variant arrays to pass data to the Order.AddOrder method
        Dim avarOrder(15) As Variant
        Dim avarItems As Variant
        ReDim avarItems(0, 0)
        avarOrder(1) = txtCustomerID.Text
        avarOrder(2) = lngEmployeeID
        avarOrder(3) = CDate(txtOrderDate.Text)
        avarOrder(4) = CDate(txtRequiredDate.Text)
        avarOrder(5) = lngShipVia
        avarOrder(6) = txtShipName.Text
        avarOrder(7) = txtShipAddress.Text
        avarOrder(8) = txtShipCity.Text
        If Len(txtShipRegion) > 0 Then
            avarOrder(9) = txtShipRegion.Text
        Else
            avarOrder(9) = Null
```

```
    End If
    avarOrder(10) = txtShipPostalCode.Text
    avarOrder(11) = txtShipCountry.Text

    'Note: Can't readily use GetRows here because of column sequence
    avarOrder(12) = rstLineItems(1)
    avarOrder(13) = rstLineItems(4)
    avarOrder(14) = rstLineItems(0)
    avarOrder(15) = rstLineItems(5)

    If rstLineItems.RecordCount > 1 Then
        'Add additional line items
        ReDim avarItems(rstLineItems.RecordCount - 1, 4)
        With rstLineItems
            .MoveNext
            'Add the remaining line items to the array
            intCtr = 0
            Do Until .EOF
                avarItems(intCtr, 0) = rstLineItems(1)
                avarItems(intCtr, 1) = rstLineItems(4)
                avarItems(intCtr, 2) = rstLineItems(0)
                avarItems(intCtr, 3) = rstLineItems(5)
                intCtr = intCtr + 1
                .MoveNext
            Loop
        End With
    End If
    sngWrap = Timer - sngStart
    sngStart = Timer
    Dim objOrder As New Order
    If objOrder Is Nothing Then
        'Error
    Else
        lngOrderID = objOrder.AddOrder(avarOrder, avarItems, _
            blnHasTimestamp, blnSQLS7)
    End If
Else
    Call NewOrdParams(cmmNewOrd, lngEmployeeID, lngShipVia)
    With cmmNewOrd
        .Execute
        lngOrderID = .Parameters(0).Value
    End With
    sngWrap = Timer - sngStart
    sngStart = Timer
    If lngOrderID > 0 Then
        txtOrderID.Text = lngOrderID
        With rstLineItems
            .MoveNext
            If Not .EOF Then
                'Add the remaining line items
                strSQL = ""
```

continues

LISTING 27.4   CONTINUED

```
                Call AddLineItems(lngOrderID)
                cnnData.Execute strSQL, lngCount, adCmdText
                If lngCount = .RecordCount Then
                    'All is OK
                Else
                    'Couldn't add the records
                End If
            Else
                'Only one line item, so finished
            End If
        End With
    End If
End If
txtOrderID.Text = lngOrderID

'Get the commit time or time to add the additional line items
sngCommit = Timer - sngStart

'Display the order details in the listbox
Call cmdShowDetail_Click

'Display the transaction times
Call HideTimerData
txtGetID.Text = Format(sngGetID, "#0.000")
txtWrap.Text = Format(sngWrap, "#0.000")
txtCommit.Text = Format(sngCommit, "#0.000")
Call ShowTimerData
Me.MousePointer = vbDefault
blnNewOrder = False
End Sub
```

The AddOrder method of the Order class (Listing 27.5) handles parameter creation and value assignment for the order and line item(s) transaction. The code assigns values extracted from the avarOrder and avarItem arrays to the appropriate Parameter objects. Most of the AddOrder method code is cut and pasted from the client's original cmdAddNewOrder_Click event handler. The GetOrder, EditOrder, and DelOrder method stubs are included to provide binary class compatibility when adding the code for these currently unimplemented methods.

LISTING 27.5   THE AddOrder METHOD OF THE Order CLASS

```
Option Explicit

Private Const strServer = "OAKLEAF0"
Private Const strDatabase = "nwind"
Private Const strUserID = "sa"
Private Const strPassword = ""
```

```vb
Public Function AddOrder(ByVal avarOrder As Variant, _
                         ByVal avarItems As Variant, _
                         ByVal blnHasTimestamp As Boolean, _
                         ByVal blnSQLS7 As Boolean) As Long
    Dim cnnOrder As New ADODB.Connection
    Dim cmmOrder As New ADODB.Command
    Dim prmNewOrdRV As ADODB.Parameter
    Dim prmCustID As ADODB.Parameter
    Dim prmEmpID As ADODB.Parameter
    Dim prmOrdDate As ADODB.Parameter
    Dim prmReqDate As ADODB.Parameter
    Dim prmShipVia As ADODB.Parameter
    Dim prmSName As ADODB.Parameter
    Dim prmSAddr As ADODB.Parameter
    Dim prmSCity As ADODB.Parameter
    Dim prmSReg As ADODB.Parameter
    Dim prmSZIP As ADODB.Parameter
    Dim prmSCtry As ADODB.Parameter

    'Order_Details parameters for new order
    Dim prmProdID As ADODB.Parameter
    Dim prmPrice As ADODB.Parameter
    Dim prmQuan As ADODB.Parameter
    Dim prmDisc As ADODB.Parameter

    Dim strCnn As String
    Dim lngOrderID As Long
    Dim lngCount As Long
    Dim intCtr As Integer
    Dim strSQL As String

    On Error GoTo AddOrderErr

    'Connect to SQL Server with native provider and stored procedures
    strCnn = "Location=" & strServer & ";User ID=" & strUserID & _
        ";Password=" & strPassword & ";Data Source=" & strDatabase
    With cnnOrder
        .Provider = "SQLOLEDB"
        .CursorLocation = adUseClient
        .Open strCnn
    End With

    With cmmOrder
        .ActiveConnection = cnnOrder
        .CommandType = adCmdStoredProc
        .CommandText = "ado_NewOrder_Ins"
        Set prmNewOrdRV = .CreateParameter("RETURN_VALUE", _
            adInteger, adParamReturnValue, 0, 0)
        'Parameters for Orders table
        Set prmCustID = .CreateParameter("Param1", adChar, adParamInput, 5)
        Set prmEmpID = .CreateParameter("Param2", adInteger, adParamInput, 0)
```

continues

LISTING 27.5   CONTINUED

```
Set prmOrdDate = .CreateParameter("Param3", adDate, adParamInput, 0)
Set prmReqDate = .CreateParameter("Param4", adDate, adParamInput, 0)
Set prmShipVia = .CreateParameter("Param5", adInteger, adParamInput, 0)
Set prmSName = .CreateParameter("Param6", adChar, adParamInput, 40)
Set prmSAddr = .CreateParameter("Param7", adChar, adParamInput, 60)
Set prmSCity = .CreateParameter("Param8", adChar, adParamInput, 15)
Set prmSReg = .CreateParameter("Param9", adChar, adParamInput, 15)
Set prmSZIP = .CreateParameter("Param10", adChar, adParamInput, 10)
Set prmSCtry = .CreateParameter("Param11", adChar, adParamInput, 15)
'Parameters for Order_Details table
Set prmProdID = .CreateParameter("Param12", adInteger, adParamInput, 0)
Set prmPrice = .CreateParameter("Param13", adCurrency, adParamInput, 0)
Set prmQuan = .CreateParameter("Param14", adInteger, adParamInput, 0)
Set prmDisc = .CreateParameter("Param15", adSingle, adParamInput, 0)
'Append all parameters
.Parameters.Append prmNewOrdRV
.Parameters.Append prmCustID
.Parameters.Append prmEmpID
.Parameters.Append prmOrdDate
.Parameters.Append prmReqDate
.Parameters.Append prmShipVia
.Parameters.Append prmSName
.Parameters.Append prmSAddr
.Parameters.Append prmSCity
.Parameters.Append prmSReg
.Parameters.Append prmSZIP
.Parameters.Append prmSCtry
.Parameters.Append prmProdID
.Parameters.Append prmPrice
.Parameters.Append prmQuan
.Parameters.Append prmDisc
For intCtr = 1 To .Parameters.Count - 1
    .Parameters(intCtr).Value = avarOrder(intCtr)
Next intCtr
.Execute
lngOrderID = .Parameters("RETURN_VALUE").Value
If lngOrderID > 10000 Then
    If UBound(avarItems, 1) Then
        strSQL = ""
        For intCtr = 0 To UBound(avarItems, 1) - 1
            strSQL = strSQL & " INSERT Order_Details"
            If blnHasTimestamp And Not blnSQLS7 Then
                strSQL = strSQL & "(OrderID, ProductID, " & _
                    "UnitPrice, Quantity, Discount)"
            End If
            strSQL = strSQL & " VALUES(" & _
            lngOrderID & ", " & _
            avarItems(intCtr, 0) & ", " & _
```

```
                avarItems(intCtr, 1) & ", " & _
                avarItems(intCtr, 2) & ", " & _
                avarItems(intCtr, 3)
                'Value must be supplied for a timestamp field, if present
                If blnHasTimestamp And blnSQLS7 Then
                    strSQL = strSQL & ", NULL) "
                Else
                    strSQL = strSQL & ") "
                End If
            Next intCtr
            cnnOrder.Execute strSQL, lngCount, adCmdText
            If lngCount <> UBound(avarItems, 1) Then
                'Error
            End If
        End If


        'Return the newly assigned Order ID
        AddOrder = lngOrderID
    Else
        AddOrder = 0
    End If
  End With
  Exit Function

AddOrderErr:
  Err.Raise Err.Number, "Order.AddOrder", Err.Description
  Exit Function
End Function

Public Function GetOrder(ByRef avarOrder As Variant, _
                         ByRef avarItems As Variant) As Long
   Err.Raise 50001, "Order.GetOrder", "Not Implemented"
End Function

Public Function EditOrder(ByRef avarOrder As Variant, _
                          ByRef avarItems As Variant) As Long
   Err.Raise 50001, "Order.EditOrder", "Not Implemented"
End Function

Public Function DelOrder(ByVal lngOrderID As Long) As Long
   Err.Raise 50001, "Order.DelOrder", "Not Implemented"
End Function
```

The AddCust method of the Customer class is simpler than AddOrder because AddCust requires only a single **Variant** array of values to populate the fields of the Customers table.

Comparing the Performance of Direct and Indirect Execution

▶ **See** "Running the Vb5oltp or Ado2oltp Project," **p. 790**

Indirect execution of stored procedures by methods of class objects extracts a significant performance toll. Compare the execution speed of direct execution (SProc - All option) of stored procedures from the client against calls to GetData and AddOrder (MTS - Xact option). When testing, disregard the first two results to eliminate the effect of SQL Server stored procedure and table caching operations. Table 27.5 compares the direct and indirect execution times (average of five calls each) for the OAKLEAF1 client executing a set of stored procedures against the OAKLEAF0 server in both direct and indirect execution.

TABLE 27.5 AVERAGE EXECUTION TIMES (SECONDS) FOR ORDER ENTRY OPERATIONS WITH ADO2MTS1.VBP

Operation	Direct	Indirect
Find Customer(s)	0.027	0.168
Find Orders	0.059	0.180
Get Details	0.090	0.301
Get Customer from Order ID	0.129	0.672
Get Details from Order ID	0.051	0.262
Add New Order (total time for three items)	0.190	0.292

NOTE

There is no significant difference in the comparative execution times for the interpreted and compiled versions of Ado2mts1.vbp. The values listed in Table 27.5 are for interpreted execution from the design environment. Your results are likely to differ from those of Table 27.5, depending on RAM, processor speed, network congestion, and other conditions.

Step 2: Creating and Testing the Nwind ActiveX DLL

After you test and debug your class modules within the project, the next step is to compile the classes as an ActiveX DLL and alter the client code to use the **CreateObject** method, required by MTS, to instantiate the in-process components with COM. No changes to component code are required in this step.

The following steps create Nwind.vbp (the class modules) project and Nwind.dll:

1. Open a new ActiveX DLL project, Nwind.vbp; delete the default Class1 module; and add copies of the Customer.cls, Order.cls, and OrderData.cls modules to the project in a new folder (...\Step2 for this example).

2. Add a reference to the Microsoft ActiveX Data Objects 2.0 Library.

3. Choose Project, Nwind Properties to open the General page of the Nwind - Project Properties sheet. Accept the default ActiveX DLL project type, type **Nwind** in the Project Name text box, and type a brief description in the Project Description text box.

4. Mark the Unattended Execution check box and select Apartment Threaded from the Threading Model list (see Figure 27.3).

FIGURE 27.3

Setting the properties of the Nwind.dll component.

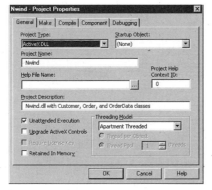

5. Click the Component tab and accept the default Project Compatibility option in the Version Compatibility pane; then click OK to close the Properties sheet.

    When you recompile the project without changing the method and argument definitions, it's a standard practice to choose the Binary Compatibility option to avoid the need to re-reference the Nwind.dll in client applications. In this case, the client uses the programmatic ID to late-bind the components with **Set** *objName* = **CreateObject**(ProgID).

6. Choose File, Make Nwind.dll; navigate to the new folder (...\Step2 for this example); and click OK to compile the project.

To convert Ado2mts1.vbp to Ado2mts2.vbp, do the following:

1. Copy Ado2mts1.frm the new folder (...\Step2) and change its filename to Ado2mts2.frm.

2. Copy LineItem.rst to the new folder.

3. Create a new Standard EXE project named Ado2mts2.vbp, remove Form1, and add Ado2mts2.frm.

4. Add a reference to the Microsoft ActiveX Data Objects 2.0 Library.

5. Change each instance of the New reserved word used to instantiate the Nwind.dll classes to use **CreateObject** for MTS's late binding, as in the following example:

```
'Dim objData As New OrderData
Dim objData As Object
Set objData = CreateObject("Nwind.OrderData")
```

6. Save Ado2mts2.vbp and test execution of the client with Nwind.dll.

> **NOTE**
>
> Ado2mts2.vbp doesn't require a reference to Nwind.dll, because all calls to the methods of Nwind.dll create late-bound objects.

As Table 27.6 illustrates, the execution times for order entry operations with the Ado2mts2.vbp client don't vary significantly from those of Ado2mts2.vbp (refer to Table 27.5). Compiling the components to a DLL doesn't result in a perceptible improvement in execution speed, nor does compiling Ado2mts2.vbp.

TABLE 27.6   AVERAGE EXECUTION TIMES (SECONDS) FOR ORDER ENTRY OPERATIONS WITH ADO2MTS2.VBP

Operation	*Direct*	*Nwind.dll*
Find Customer(s)	0.029	0.129
Find Orders	0.057	0.160
Get Details	0.088	0.129
Get Customer from Order ID	0.131	0.309
Get Details from Order ID	0.055	0.141
Add New Order (total time for three items)	0.192	0.329

Step 3: Creating, Installing, and Testing the Northwind Package

Step 3 makes the transition from a conventional client/server application to a local MTS package. The client-side code Ado2mts2.frm needs only minor alterations to accommodate a change of object names. The primary changes are additions of code to the class modules to accommodate MTS 2+. After compiling the modified class project (NwindMTS.dll), you install it as a package in the local copy of MTS 2.0 and then test package execution. The \Ddg_vb6\Chaptr27\Step3 folder of the accompanying CD-ROM contains sample files for this step.

Optimizing the NwindMTS Classes for MTS

The final code-related step in the MTS migration process is to add the MTS optimization code from the standard MTS component template (refer to Listing 27.1) to each component. Follow these steps to create a copy of Ado2mts2.vbp and a new version of Nwind.dll in a new folder, . . .\Step3 for this example:

1. Repeat the steps in the preceding section, but change the name of Ado2mts2.frm to Ado2mts3.frm, name the new client project Ado2mts3.vbp, and name the new component project NwindMTS.vbp. Don't compile NwindMTS.vbp at this point.

2. Add the MTS template code to the beginning and end of each class module (see Listings 27.6 and 27.7 as examples).

3. Change ADODB.Connection and ADODB.Command object declarations from procedure level (**Dim**) to class level (**Private**).

4. Add a reference to the Microsoft Transaction Server Type Library to the project.

5. Open the Properties window for each class and set the value of the Instancing property value to 5 - Multiuse. Set the value of the MTSTransactionMode property to 4 - RequiresNewTransaction for the Customer and Order class and to 3 - UsesTransactions for the OrderData class.

6. Choose <u>R</u>un, Start with <u>F</u>ull Compile to verify that your project has all needed references; then return to design mode.

7. Compile the NwindMTS.vbp project to create NwindMTS.dll in the project folder.

LISTING 27.6 THE OrderData COMPONENT WITH MTS OPTIMIZATION CODE ADDED

```
Option Explicit

'Provide activate/deactivate, plus object pooling when available
Implements ObjectControl

'Provide for just-in-time activation
Private objCtxt As ObjectContext

Private cnnData As New ADODB.Connection
Private cmmGetData As New ADODB.Command

Private Const strServer = "OAKLEAF0"
Private Const strDatabase = "nwind"
Private Const strUserID = "sa"
Private Const strPassword = ""


Public Function GetOrderData(ByVal strProcName As String, _
                             ByVal varParam As Variant, _
                             ByRef rstData As ADODB.Recordset) As Long
    'General purpose method to return Recordsets
    'from parameterized and non-parameterized queries
```

continues

LISTING 27.6   CONTINUED

```
Dim prmRetVal As ADODB.Parameter
Dim prmParam As ADODB.Parameter
Dim lngParam As Long
Dim strParam As String
Dim strCnn As String
Dim lngCount As Long


On Error GoTo GetOrderDataErr

'Connect to SQL Server with native provider and stored procedures
strCnn = "Location=" & strServer & ";User ID=" & strUserID & _
    ";Password=" & strPassword & ";Data Source=" & strDatabase
cnnData.Provider = "SQLOLEDB"
cnnData.CursorLocation = adUseClient
cnnData.Open strCnn


If IsNull(varParam) Then
    'Execute against the Connection object
    Set rstData = cnnData.Execute(strProcName, lngCount, adCmdStoredProc)
    GetOrderData = lngCount
Else
    'Create and execute the GetData command (multi-purpose for all Recordsets)
    With cmmGetData
        .ActiveConnection = cnnData
        .CommandType = adCmdStoredProc
        .CommandText = strProcName
      Set prmRetVal = .CreateParameter("RETURN_VALUE", adInteger, adParamReturnValue, 0, 0)
        .Parameters.Append prmRetVal
        If VarType(varParam) = vbString Then
            strParam = CStr(varParam)
            Set prmParam = .CreateParameter("Param", adChar, _
                adParamInput, Len(strParam), "")
            .Parameters.Append prmParam
            .Parameters("Param").Value = strParam
        Else
            lngParam = CLng(varParam)
            Set prmParam = .CreateParameter("Param", adInteger, _
                adParamInput, , 0)
            .Parameters.Append prmParam
            .Parameters("Param").Value = lngParam
        End If
        Set rstData = cmmGetData.Execute
        If prmRetVal Then
            GetOrderData = prmRetVal.Value
        Else
            GetOrderData = rstData.RecordCount
        End If
        objCtxt.SetComplete
```

```
      End With
   End If
   Exit Function

GetOrderDataErr:
   objCtxt.SetAbort
   Err.Raise Err.Number, "OrderData.GetOrderData", Err.Description
   Exit Function
End Function


Private Sub ObjectControl_Activate()
   'Get the object context on class activation
   Set objCtxt = GetObjectContext
End Sub


Private Function ObjectControl_CanBePooled() As Boolean
   'Pooling isn't available, but set True for uplevel compatibility
   ObjectControl_CanBePooled = True
End Function


Private Sub ObjectControl_Deactivate()
   'Release the ADODB and Context objects
   Set cmmGetData = Nothing
   Set cnnData = Nothing
   Set objCtxt = Nothing
End Sub
```

LISTING 27.7 THE Customer COMPONENT WITH MTS OPTIMIZATION CODE ADDED

```
Option Explicit

Implements ObjectControl

Private objCtxt As ObjectContext
Private cnnCust As New ADODB.Connection
Private cmmCust As New ADODB.Command

Private Const strServer = "OAKLEAF0"
Private Const strDatabase = "nwind"
Private Const strUserID = "sa"
Private Const strPassword = ""

Public Function AddCust(ByVal avarCustData As Variant) As Long
   'ADO Objects
   Dim prmNewCustRV As ADODB.Parameter
   Dim prmCustID As ADODB.Parameter
   Dim prmName As ADODB.Parameter
   Dim prmCont As ADODB.Parameter
   Dim prmTitle As ADODB.Parameter
   Dim prmAddr As ADODB.Parameter
```

continues

LISTING 27.7   CONTINUED

```
Dim prmCity As ADODB.Parameter
Dim prmReg As ADODB.Parameter
Dim prmZIP As ADODB.Parameter
Dim prmCtry As ADODB.Parameter
Dim prmPhone As ADODB.Parameter
Dim prmFax As ADODB.Parameter

Dim strCnn As String
Dim lngCount As Long
Dim intCtr As Integer

On Error GoTo AddCustErr

'Connect to SQL Server with native provider and stored procedures
strCnn = "Location=" & strServer & ";User ID=" & strUserID & _
    ";Password=" & strPassword & ";Data Source=" & strDatabase
With cnnCust
    .Provider = "SQLOLEDB"
    .CursorLocation = adUseClient
    .Open strCnn
End With

'Create the Command and add the parameters
With cmmCust
    .ActiveConnection = cnnCust
    .CommandType = adCmdStoredProc
    .CommandText = "ado_CustsData_Ins"
    Set prmNewCustRV = .CreateParameter("Param0", adInteger, _
        adParamReturnValue, 0)
    Set prmCustID = .CreateParameter("Param1", adChar, adParamInput, 5)
    Set prmName = .CreateParameter("Param2", adChar, adParamInput, 40)
    Set prmCont = .CreateParameter("Param3", adChar, adParamInput, 30)
    Set prmTitle = .CreateParameter("Param4", adChar, adParamInput, 30)
    Set prmAddr = .CreateParameter("Param5", adChar, adParamInput, 60)
    Set prmCity = .CreateParameter("Param6", adChar, adParamInput, 15)
    Set prmReg = .CreateParameter("Param7", adChar, adParamInput, 15)
    Set prmZIP = .CreateParameter("Param8", adChar, adParamInput, 10)
    Set prmCtry = .CreateParameter("Param9", adChar, adParamInput, 15)
    Set prmPhone = .CreateParameter("Param10", adChar, adParamInput, 15)
    Set prmFax = .CreateParameter("Param11", adChar, adParamInput, 15)
    .Parameters.Append prmNewCustRV
    .Parameters.Append prmCustID
    .Parameters.Append prmName
    .Parameters.Append prmCont
    .Parameters.Append prmTitle
    .Parameters.Append prmAddr
```

```
                .Parameters.Append prmCity
                .Parameters.Append prmReg
                .Parameters.Append prmZIP
                .Parameters.Append prmCtry
                .Parameters.Append prmPhone
                .Parameters.Append prmFax
                For intCtr = 1 To .Parameters.Count - 1
                    .Parameters(intCtr).Value = avarCustData(intCtr)
                Next intCtr
                .Execute lngCount
            End With
            AddCust = lngCount
            objCtxt.SetComplete
            Exit Function


AddCustErr:
            objCtxt.SetAbort
            Err.Raise Err.Number, "Customer.AddCust", Err.Description
            Exit Function
End Function


Public Function GetCust(ByRef avarCustData As Variant) As Long
            Err.Raise 50001, "Customer.GetCust", "Not Implemented"
End Function


Public Function EditCust(ByVal avarCustData As Variant) As Long
            Err.Raise 50001, "Customer.EditCust", "Not Implemented"
End Function


Public Function DelCust(ByVal strCustID As String) As Long
            Err.Raise 50001, "Customer.DelCust", "Not Implemented"
End Function


Private Sub ObjectControl_Activate()
            'Get the object context on class activation
            Set objCtxt = GetObjectContext
End Sub


Private Function ObjectControl_CanBePooled() As Boolean
            'Pooling isn't available, but set True for uplevel compatibility
            ObjectControl_CanBePooled = True
End Function


Private Sub ObjectControl_Deactivate()
            Set cmmCust = Nothing
            Set cnnCust = Nothing
            Set objCtxt = Nothing
End Sub
```

> **NOTE**
>
> If you use the sample code in the ...\Step3, rather than making the modifications described in the preceding steps, you must compile NwindMTS.vbp to NwindMTS.dll prior to installing the DLL in the Northwind package.

Installing the Northwind Package

To install NwindMTS.dll as the Northwind MTS package on the local machine, do the following:

1. Launch MTS Explorer and navigate to My Computer\Packages Installed.

2. Choose Action, New, Package to open the first Package Wizard dialog (see Figure 27.4).

FIGURE 27.4

The first dialog of the MTS Package Wizard.

3. Click Create an empty package to open the second Wizard dialog.

4. Type **Northwind** in the Enter a name for the new package text box and click Next to open the Set Package Identity dialog.

▶ See "Adding the MTS Administrator Account," p. 984

5. For operation on the local computer, you can choose the Interactive User option for package identity. It's a good practice, however, to specify the MTS Administrator account, which has Log on as a service rights (see Figure 27.5). This account is required when you run the package on a remote server, because the Interactive User account is likely not to be active.

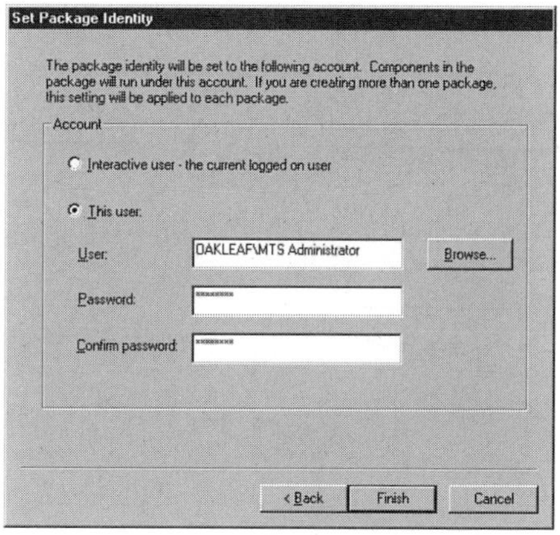

FIGURE 27.5

*Specifying the
identity of the new
package.*

6. Click Finish to close the Set Package Identity dialog and create the empty Northwind
   package.

7. Expand MTS Explorer's Northwind Package entry and click the Components item to
   open an empty right pane.

8. Launch Windows NT Explorer and navigate to the folder containing NwindMTS.dll.

9. Resize Windows NT Explorer and MTS Explorer so that both windows fit your desktop.

10. Drag the NwindMTS.dll icon to the empty right pane of MTS Explorer. After a few sec-
    onds of disk activity, the three components of NwindMTS.dll appear in the right pane
    (see Figure 27.6).

FIGURE 27.6

*Adding the
NwindMTS com-
ponents to the
Northwind pack-
age.*

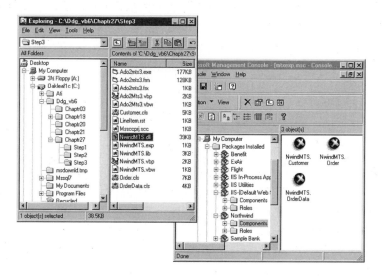

11. Right-click the Northwind package and choose Properties to open the Northwind Properties sheet.

12. Click the Security tab and choose Connect from the Authentication Level for Calls list. Connect authentication gives Windows 9x clients access to the components.

13. Click the Advanced tab and type **30** in the Shutdown after being idle text box; then click OK to close the Northwind Properties sheet.

Modifying and Testing the Client Code

To modify the client code to accommodate the MTS object name change and test your MTS installation, do the following:

1. Find and replace all instances of `Nwind.ClassName` with `NwindMTS.ClassName` in Ado2mts3.frm.

2. Save the project and, optionally, compile the project to Ado2mts3.exe.

3. Run Ado2mts3 and choose the MTS - All option. Expect an initial delay of 5 to 15 seconds for MTS to instantiate the Northwind package components, make the connection to SQL Server, and populate the `cboEmployees` and `cboShippers` combo boxes.

4. Compare the performance of the components running under MTS 2.0 with direct execution of stored procedures from the client.

See "Adding the MTS Administrator Account," **p. 984**

> **TIP**
>
> If you receive a `Permission Denied` message when MTS attempts to instantiate the Northwind package, your MTS Administrator account doesn't have necessary rights on the local machine. Temporarily change the `Identity` property of the package to Interactive User or your login account (with Domain Admins group membership) to determine whether the MTS Administrator account has a problem.

Table 27.7 compares the average execution time of common order entry operations with direct execution of stored procedures and execution by the components of the Northwind MTS package on the local computer. With the exception of transactions (Add New Order), execution of MTS-hosted components are significantly slower than indirect execution with conventional Visual Basic classes (refer to Tables 27.5 and 27.6).

TABLE 27.7 AVERAGE EXECUTION TIMES (SECONDS) FOR ORDER ENTRY OPERATIONS WITH ADO2MTS3.VBP

Operation	Direct	MTS 2.0
Find Customer(s)	0.031	0.281
Find Orders	0.056	0.352
Get Details	0.088	0.332
Get Customer from Order ID	0.131	0.523
Get Details from Order ID	0.055	0.284
Add New Order (total time for three items)	0.192	0.309

Step 4: Moving the MTS Components to the Production Server

After testing local execution of the components, the final step is to move the Northwind package to the MTS production server for execution by remote clients. The following procedure describes the process of setting up the Northwind Package on MTS 2.0 running on the OAKLEAF0 production server, which also runs SQL Server 6.5 and 7.0. OAKLEAF0 has the required Msvbvm60.dll runtime library as a result of installing Visual Basic 6.0. OAKLEAF1 dual-boots Windows 98 and Windows NT 4.0, so the remote client executable, Northwind.exe, can be installed safely under Windows 98.

> **CAUTION**
>
> Don't run the Northwind.exe remote client installation executable in the development environment you use to write and/or compile ActiveX DLLs for production use. As mentioned in Chapter 26, "Taking Advantage of Microsoft Transaction Server 2.0," running remote client installation executables redirects in the Registry the location of the Microsoft Transaction Server Type Library (Mtxas.dll) from \Winnt\System32\Mts to the \Program Files\Remote Applications\{*GUID*} folder with *GUID* created as a random value. If you delete the Remote Application - *PackageName* client, the Registry entry for the MTS typelib is not restored to \Winnt\System32\Mts\Mtxas.dll, and Microsoft Transaction Server Type Library no longer appears in the project's References list. You must manually edit the Registry value for the ...\win32 entry to repoint the typelib to \Winnt\System32\Mts\Mtxas.dll.

27

CREATING AND
DEPLOYING MTS
COMPONENTS

Follow these steps to move the Northwind package to the production server:

1. Right-click the Northwind package in MTS Explorer and choose Export to open the Export Package dialog.

2. Click Browse and navigate to the \Ddg_vb6\Chaptr27\Step3 folder.

3. Type **Northwind.pak** as the filename, click Save, and then click Export to close the dialog and create the package file.

4. Launch MTS Explorer on the component server and navigate to My Computer\Packages Installed.

5. Right-click Packages Installed and choose New Package to launch the Package Wizard.

6. Click Install Pre-built Packages to open the Select Package Files dialog.

7. Click Add to open the Install from Package File dialog.

8. Navigate to the ...\Step3 folder, select Northwind.pak, and click Open to select the file and return to the Select Package Files dialog. *ServerName**ShareName*\Ddg_vb6\Chaptr27/Step3\Northwind.pak appears in the Package Files to Install list (see Figure 27.7).

FIGURE 27.7

Specifying the package file to add to MTS running on the component server.

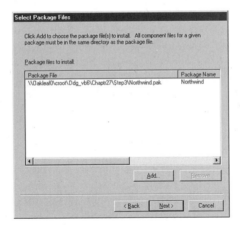

9. Click Next to open the Set Package Identity dialog and assign the account under which to run the package. (Interactive User is adequate for testing if you don't have an MTS Administrator account.)

10. Click Next to open the Installation Options dialog and accept the default location for the package, C:\Program Files\Mts\Packages.

11. Click finish to terminate the Package Wizard and install the Northwind package.

12. Verify in MTS Explorer that the Northwind package and its components are installed.

13. Export the Northwind package to a server copy of Northwind.pak in C:\Program Files\ Mts\Packages to create the Northwind.exe client installation executable in C:\Program Files\Mts\Packages\Clients.

14. From a Windows 9x or Windows NT Workstation 4+ client machine with Visual Basic 6.0 installed, launch Windows Explorer and navigate to \\ServerName\ShareName\\ Program Files\Mts\Packages\Clients.

15. Execute Northwind.exe on the client.

16. Launch Visual Basic 6.0 and run Ado2mts3.vbp. If the component server's monitor is visible from the client workstation, you can watch the component balls spin in MTS Explorer's window as you run the tests.

The performance of Ado2mts3.vbp with the Northwind package on a remote component server is almost identical to that for the local server version. Marshalling DCOM method calls to MTS has only slightly more overhead than the combination of COM method calls to a local copy of MTS and execution of stored procedures over a network connection.

ADDING SECURITY TO YOUR PACKAGES AND COMPONENTS

MTS provides declarative and programmatic security through MTS package Roles, which are quite similar in concept to SQL Server 7.0 Server Roles. You add individual user accounts or Windows NT groups as users to specific roles. After creating a set of Roles for a package, you add the Roles to the Role Membership for each component. Declarative security with Role Membership is available at the component and interface levels. You must test the return value of the IsCallerInRole("Role Name") method to institute programmatic security at the method level.

The following steps add MTS Administrators, Order Entry Operators, and Authenticated Users Roles to the Northwind package at the component level:

1. Launch MTS Explorer and expand the entry for the Northwind package.

2. Right-click Roles and choose New, Role to open the New Role dialog.

3. Type the name of the role, in this case **MTS Administrators**, in the text box; click OK to close the dialog and add the Role.

4. Expand the new Role entry, right-click Users, and choose New, User to open the Add Users and Groups to Role dialog.

5. Select Domain Admins and click Add to specify members of the Domain Admins group as MTS Administrators (see Figure 27.8).

FIGURE 27.8

Adding a Windows NT user group to the users of a Role.

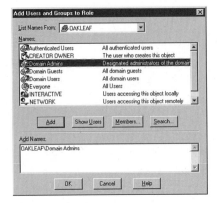

> **NOTE**
>
> You can add as many groups or individual users as you want to the Role by repeatedly selecting the user or group and clicking Add.

6. Click OK to close the dialog and add the group(s) or user(s) to the role.

7. Repeat steps 2 through 6 to add Order Entry Operators and Authenticated Users Roles with appropriate users or user groups (see Figure 27.9).

FIGURE 27.9

Three Roles with member groups added to the Northwind package.

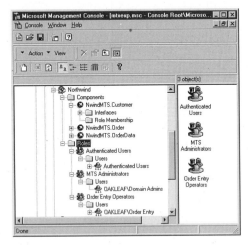

8. Expand the `NwindMTS.Customers` component, right-click Role Membership, and select New, Role to open the Select Roles dialog.

9. Select MTS Administrators and Order Entry Operators from the list (see Figure 27.10). Click OK to close the dialog and add the members.

FIGURE 27.10

Adding two Roles to the Role Membership of the NwindMTS.Custo mers *component.*

10. Repeat steps 8 and 9 for the NwindMTS.Orders and NwindMTS.OrderData components. Add Authenticated Users to the NwindMTS.OrderData component. The expanded Components entries appear as shown in Figure 27.11.

FIGURE 27.11

Role Membership of the three components of the Northwind package.

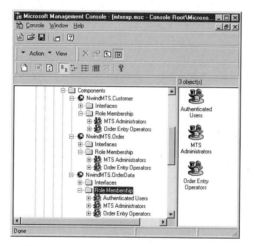

The preceding steps establish declarative security at the component level. Authenticated Users (anyone with a Domain User account) can obtain data from the Customers, Orders, and Order_Details tables through the NwindMTS.OrderData component. Only MTS Administrators and Order Entry Operators can update these tables.

ANALYZING MULTIDIMENSIONAL DATA WITH OLAP AND MDX

IN THIS CHAPTER

Data warehouses and their smaller sibling, data marts, introduce a new database lexicon and an alternative approach to analyzing data. Traditional relational database structures comprise a two-dimensional set of columns and rows, analogous to a spreadsheet. Conventional aggregation techniques, typified by Jet crosstab queries, enable managers to review summary data. Front ends for data analysis usually provide multiple combo lists to choose attributes (tables and WHERE clause constraints), such as products, employees, regions, and time periods, and to create a crosstab representation in a gridlike control, an Excel pivot table, or a graph. Drill-down techniques, typified by expanding a column of a Hierarchical FlexGrid control, provide access to two or more levels of two-dimensional detail.

The primary objective of data warehouses and marts is to provide a central source of decision-support information, available to all who need it, that lends itself to *unstructured analysis* by users. Unstructured analysis lets users, not database developers and administrators determine views of the data. One of the benefits of letting the user specify his or her own view of data is the ability to perform heuristic analysis. *Heuristic analysis* begins with an ad hoc question, the answer to which intuitively leads to another question, and so on. Online analytic processing (OLAP) almost universally involves interactively querying of data in a heuristic function. Developers and database administrators are very unlikely to be able to predefine queries that satisfy all requirements of all users, because the path of an analysis often evolves by serendipitous observation of interesting relationships between successive views of data.

OLAP introduces the concept of data analysis based on multidimensional data modeling (MDM) of a business process (from a data mart) or the operations of an entire enterprise (from a data warehouse). MDM revolves around numerical aggregations, such as dollar or unit sales, margin percentages, gross and net profits, and the like, the values of which represent the intersection of dimensions, such as product and time period. Unlike the two-dimensional crosstab or pivot table, MDM implies three or more data dimensions. Data models with five or six dimensions are common; the maximum number of dimensions usually is limited by the data store or the OLAP toolset you choose but is likely to be 64 or more.

▶ **See** "SQL Server 7.0 (Sphinx)," p. **688**

Creating data warehouses and marts, which involves the collection, cleansing, and storing of information in a central location, is beyond the scope of this book. Microsoft SQL Server 7.0 includes a Data Transformation Service (DTS) for relational and other tabular data that automates much of the drudgery of creating the data store for a warehouse or mart. Microsoft OLAP Server, code-named "Plato" and in the beta-testing stage when this edition was written, is an OLAP data store that runs on Windows NT Server 4+. OLAP Server is included with SQL Server 7.0 but can be used with any client/server RDBMS having an OLE DB data provider or, by using the MSDASQL provider, an ODBC 3+ driver. This chapter deals primarily with MDM concepts, the Microsoft ADO MD automation wrapper over the OLE DB for OLAP API

(Tensor), Multidimensional Expressions (MDX), and Visual Basic 6.0 front ends to a sample persistent data cube created by Microsoft OLAP Server.

> **NOTE**
>
> You need a license for Microsoft OLAP Server to create your own data cubes, but OLAP Server isn't required to manipulate persistent data cubes (*.cub files.) You must install the Microsoft Data Access 2.0 SDK (MSDASDK) to obtain the MSOLAP (OLE DB for OLAP) data provider, the Bobsvid.cub file, and the Visual Basic 5.0 Mdxsampl.vbp application for experimenting with MDXs. The MDAC 2.0 SDK is available on the MSDN CD-ROMs and can be downloaded from `http://www.microsoft.com/data/mdac2.htm`.

UNDERSTANDING MEASURES AND DIMENSIONS

Measures are numerical values, such as unit and dollar sales, advertising and promotion expenditures, and populations. Measures often are called *metrics* or *facts*. The sources of internal measures commonly are OLTP databases for order entry and invoice processing. In this case, a line items table provides the values to aggregate, often called *rolling up the data*. External measures, such as market research information, is called *syndicated data*. Syndicated data is available by subscription from a variety of market research firms and governmental agencies. Aggregated measures (roll-ups), regardless of the source, are stored in *fact tables* of data warehouses/marts or OLAP servers. If a relational database holds the facts table, an OLAP engine provides access to the measures.

Dimensions categorize measures; the most common dimension is a range of dates, usually called a (time) period. The next most popular dimensions are product classifications and geopolitical boundaries, which (with period) form the classic data cubes illustrated by Figure 28.1. Data cubes are not true cubes, because the sides of the cube are not necessarily of the same "length," that is, number of dimensions. A better term is data *hypercube*; a hypercube is an abstract mathematical object having three or more flat-sided dimensions with each dimension perpendicular to all other dimensions. Unless you're a mathematician, four- or more-sided hypercubes are difficult to visualize. This book uses the term *data cube* for general representations of multidimensional data and *PivotTable* when referring to Microsoft's desktop multidimensional service component.

> **NOTE**
>
> In a hypercube, each dimension belongs only to a single cube; thus hypercubes are said to "own" their dimensions. *Multicube* is an alternative multidimensional model in which dimensions are independent of cubes. Multicube dimensions are specified in the OLAP catalog or schema, and dimensions or subsets of dimensions may be shared by multiple cubes.

Dimensions, for the most part, are hierarchical; the time dimension hierarchy is year, quarter, month, and, for many businesses, week. Large retailers commonly analyze sales on a daily basis. For the recording industry, the product dimension hierarchy might be category, genre, artist, album, and media. A typical U.S. geopolitical dimension comprises country, region, state, Metropolitan Statistical Area (MSA), city, and ZIP code. Moving downward in the hierarchy of one or more dimensions, as in conventional decision-support applications, is called a *drill-down* operation.

FIGURE 28.1

Three-dimensional data cubes for sales of a record company.

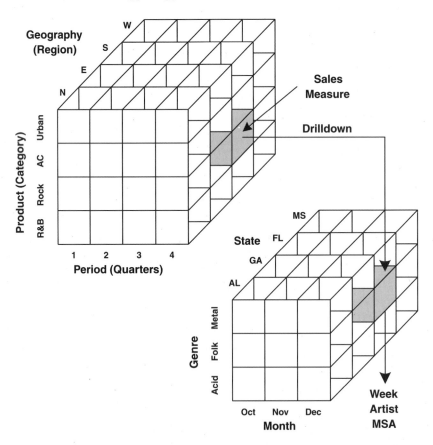

Exploring the Differences Between OLTP and Star Schema

The design of OLTP databases focuses on expediting data entry and executing individual transactions quickly. OLTP schema are characterized by a linear relationship of one-to-many relationships between tables, together with cyclic (circular) relationships, as illustrated by Figure 28.2. Cyclic relationships exist between the Customers, Orders, Invoices, OrderItems, and InvoiceItems tables. Queries to obtain total sales to a particular customer (or class of customers) of albums by a particular artist are join intensive. Cyclic joins result in the possibility of multiple paths to obtain the sales data for a customer: Customers to Orders to OrderItems to InvoiceItems or Customers to Invoices to InvoiceItems to OrderItems. Join-intensive queries are needed to load the OLAP server's fact table, but aren't at all suited to ad hoc querying by analysts or managers.

OLAP schema are designed to make the underlying data structure more comprehensible to users and to simplify the query process. The star schema has a central facts table with dimension tables at the points of the star. The single facts table's composite primary key requires a foreign key field corresponding to the primary key field of each dimension table. The dimensions tables are hierarchical and thus highly denormalized. (Five tables are needed to normalize year, quarter, month, and week dimensions.) Star schema offer the advantages of simplicity, easily defined hierarchies, and simple queries and metadata. *Metadata* is defined as "data about data" and is stored in a proprietary OLAP catalog or a central repository database. The star schema assumes that the database is static; that is, updates from source tables can require read-locking the entire fact table. Figure 28.3 illustrates a star schema for analysis of a record company's sales.

Facts tables for classic star schema include aggregations at all levels of the dimension hierarchy. Thus dimension tables for star schema must include a level (or equivalent) field to prevent adding aggregations to one another when processing the OLAP equivalent of SELECT SUM(*FieldName*) ... queries. If the user forgets to include the level value in a query, the query returns an inflated result set.

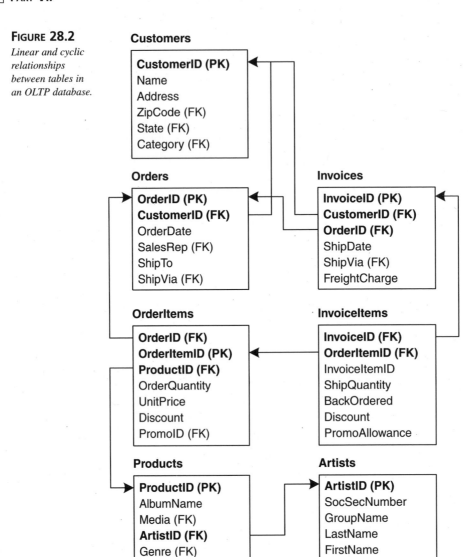

FIGURE 28.2

Linear and cyclic relationships between tables in an OLTP database.

FIGURE 28.3

A simple (classic) star schema for sales analysis.

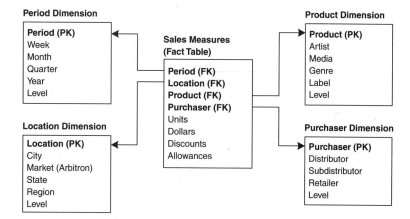

> **NOTE**
>
> Specifying a fixed set of levels when defining the dimension tables results in a schema that's cast in concrete. Alternative schema, such as "fact constellation" and "snowflake," use separate fact tables for the lowest level of the hierarchy (called *base* data) and for each progressively higher aggregation. The fact constellation schema eliminates the need for fixed-level IDs in the dimension tables. The snowflake schema, which also dispenses with dimension levels, uses multiple, relational tables for each dimension. Relational tables improve response times for queries against dimension tables with a very large number of records. This chapter deals only with data cubes with star schema.

Reducing Fact Table Storage Requirements

The number of levels in the hierarchies determines the *granularity* of the dimensions. Increasing granularity dramatically increases the number of potential rows in the fact table. As an example, assume that a record company sells 1,000 albums of 200 artists in six genres on four labels. Weekly, monthly, quarterly, and yearly sales data is reported for 200 markets in 50 states making up five regions. The potential number of combinations (facts table rows) for a single year is $(1,000 + 200 + 6 + 4) * (52 + 12 + 4 + 1) * (200 + 50 + 5) = 1,210 * 69 * 255 = 21,289,950$. Assuming that an album has a 3-year life and that the sales fact table contains measures for actual unit and dollar sales, plus budgeted unit sales, the number of fact table rows grows to 63,869,850 and the total number of fact table cells is 191,609,550. Assuming an average of six bytes per cell, the size of the fact table is about 1.15GB, disregarding the size of key fields and indexes.

> **NOTE**
>
> The size of key fields is a major concern when designing fact tables with a substantial number of dimensions. Conventional period key values, such as 1998, 1998Q1, 1998M01, and 1998W01, combined with long product IDs and geophysical codes result in fact tables in which the space occupied by primary keys far exceeds that for the measures. As noted in the preceding section, dimension tables are denormalized, so it's feasible to substitute sequential numbers for conventional key values. Using `int` (4-byte) key values requires a total of 16 bytes for a fact table with four dimensions, plus 18 bytes for the measures. Thus the actual size of the of the fact table of the preceding example is about 2GB.

A fact table of 2GB is well within the capability of department-level OLAP servers, but you can save a substantial amount of disk space by storing values only for the lower members of the hierarchy in the fact table and dynamically aggregating these values to create higher-level measures on-the-fly. As an example, if only the lowest (most granular) values are stored in the fact table, the number of rows becomes 1000 * 52 * 200 = 10,400,000, about half the size of the preceding example. The trade-offs between fact table size and performance is one the subjects of the "Categorizing OLAP Servers and Engines" section later in the chapter.

Taking Advantage of Sparse Matrixes

If you increase the granularity of the dimensions, size increases dramatically. Moving to daily sales tracking for 1,000 cities results in a theoretical fact table with 659,050,700 rows and a size of about 20G. In reality, only some products will have sales in a given city on a particular day. Thus many cells of a highly granular fact table contain zero or null values. Relational databases require cells for all possible values. Efficient OLAP servers employ *dynamic sparse matrixes* to eliminate the need to store zero or null values. The first widespread use of sparse matrixes occurred in spreadsheet software, eliminating the need to save empty cells in files. Use of sparse matrixes is especially important for chain retailers that track sales on a daily basis. The chain may stock tens of thousands of items in thousands of stores, but sell only 10% or 20% of these items in a particular store on a given date. In this case, using sparse matrix techniques results in base data fact tables that are dramatically smaller than conventional relational tables. Sparse matrixes offer little benefit to fact tables that contain only broadly based aggregations.

DEFINING MEASURES AND DIMENSIONS AT THE DEPARTMENT LEVEL

Fact table measures determine the hierarchy of dimensions. The marketing and accounting departments supply order, invoice, and expense data, so you can define the dimension hierarchy in accordance with the firm's reporting conventions. Much of the information stored in a warehouse or mart, however, is syndicated data obtained from third-party market research firms and government agencies. Internal and syndicated data are stored in *fact table families*, which ideally have an identical hierarchy for shared dimensions.

You're likely to have little control over the format of syndicated data, such as whether the information is provided weekly, monthly, or quarterly. Further, the geopolitical dimensions are likely to vary from those defined internally. Thus marketing departments, for instance, need dimension hierarchies and fact table fields that differ from those used by the accounting and production departments. Specialized departmental requirements are one of the major reasons for adopting data marts, rather than enterprise-level data warehouses.

As an example, the U.S. marketing department of a large record company is likely to promote hundreds of CD albums, cassette tapes, plus CD and vinyl singles simultaneously. Production costs for an album can range from less than $100,000 to well over $1,000,000, as can advertising and promotion expenditures. Making informed marketing decisions in the recording industry requires in-house and several sources of syndicated (subscription) or other exogenous data. Following are some of the more important measures and their dimensions for a record company:

- *Products* categorized by album/single, media, label (category), genre, artist, and release date. Measures are selling price, cost, and budgeted unit sales. Cost is determined, at least initially, by adding manufacturing cost and fixed costs divided by budgeted sales.

- *Sales* by product, geographical location, class of customer, and time period. Some labels have their own distribution organization; others use national or regional distributors. Measures are unit sales, selling price, discounts, and allowances. If there is a significant delay between the receipt of orders and the invoicing of shipments, an orders from distributors dimension is warranted. A few days is a significant delay in the record industry.

- *Purchases from retailers* by product, location, class, and time period. The basic information (called *sell-through*) is provided by SoundScan, a service that supplies weekly online reports of individual album purchases from retailers and music-oriented Web sites. Measures are unit sales.

- *Returns* by region, type, and time period. Most albums are sold on a consignment basis, which allows retailers to return unsold copies to the distributor and then to the manufacturer for credit. Over time, unit sales minus returns should track SoundScan data. Measures are unit returns and credited amount.

- *Airplay* by market (region), genre (radio station format), and time period. This information from about 1,000 radio stations is provided daily to subscribers' computers by Airplay Monitor, also known as BDS. BDSgenres are R&B, Country, Modern Rock, Mainstream Rock, Adult Contemporary (AC), Top 40/Adult, Spanish, Triple-A, and Top 40. Measures are times played, "daypart" (time of day), and audience demographics. Arbitron and AccuTrack provide radio listener demographics (market ratings).

- *Music video airplay* by album, programmer, and time period. Programmers are cable/satellite channels, such as MTV, CMT, BET, BET on Jazz, VH1, and The Box. Measures are times played, daypart, and Nielsen market ratings (number of households and viewer market share).

- *Advertising costs* by album, artist, publication, and time period. Space advertising in national music-industry publications such as *Billboard* and *College Music Journal* (*CMJ*) usually is directed to a particular product, for example, a single or album, but sometimes promotes an individual artist's concert tour or a label.

- *Promotion costs* by album, artist, genre, location, type, and time period. Promotion primarily involves convincing music directors of radio stations, radio programming packagers, and music video channels to give the album (or its music video) airplay. Measures are the promotion expenditures.

- *Concert tours* by artist, location, and date. The metric is audience size.

From these dimensions and measures, marketers can determine the answers to questions, such as: "How effective was my 150 percent increase of promotion expenditures in the San Francisco radio market on the sales of Chump Change Records' 'Crying for Love' single and album?" or "What's the relationship between airplay and sales of all albums by the Park Place band?" OLTP front ends that display a time-based graph from fact table families, such as that shown in Figure 28.4, provide the starting point for numerical analysis.

Figure 28.4 shows weekly summary data for four fact tables; another useful view of the data is cumulative values. Only the promotion expense data is generated internally; weekly airplay data comes from BDS, and SoundScan provides the weekly sales (sell-through) information. The common reporting interval in the recording industry is a week. The geopolitical dimensions of the promotion expenditure, BDS, and SoundScan data must correspond to make the analysis meaningful. In many cases, syndicated data must be manipulated to conform to a common dimension hierarchy by a set of business rules. Microsoft's DTS implements business rules through its support of scripting languages, such as VBScript and ECMAScript.

CATEGORIZING OLAP SERVERS AND ENGINES

Conventional SQL queries aren't well suited for adding sets of numbers in accordance with business rules and displaying results in a crosstab format with built-in drill-down capability. SQL is even less suitable for ranking, tiling (histograms), moving averages, or percentages such as market share. Multidimensional query languages and data extraction techniques vary with the type of OLAP database and reporting tool.

FIGURE 28.4

Graphical analysis of four fact tables showing the effect of added promotion on airplay and single/album sales.

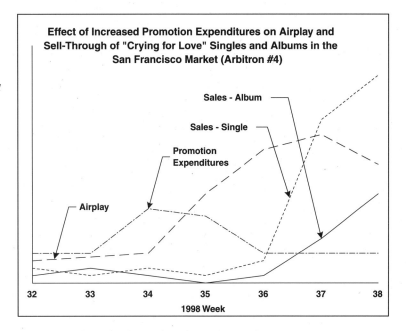

Following are the three generally accepted variations on the OLAP theme:

- *Multidimensional OLAP* (MOLAP) stores fact table base data and aggregations on the OLAP server. The best-known MOLAP database vendors, Applix (TM1), Arbor Software (Essbase), Gentia Software (GQL), Oracle (Express), and Seagate Software (Holos), sell proprietary multidimensional databases. MOLAP's query languages are optimized for analysis applications and best performance in terms of response time for complex queries. MOLAP is especially effective for financial modeling.

- *Relational OLAP* (ROLAP) takes the fact table base data from the original OLTP relational tables or a data warehouse and uses a separate set of relational tables to store and reference aggregated data. An OLAP engine is the intermediary between the data and the client. Information Advantage (AXSYS), MicroStrategy (DSS), and Platinum Technology (Prodea Beacon) are major ROLAP vendors. Red Brick Systems's well-known Red Brick Warehouse is a relational database designed and optimized specifically for MDM; Red Brick's RISQL extensions to SQL provide OLAP features. ROLAP is well suited to market analysis and determining the effectiveness of sales promotions.

- *Hybrid OLAP* (HOLAP, also called DOLAP, database OLAP) takes the fact table base data from the relational OLTP tables or a data warehouse but stores aggregations in a multidimensional format. HOLAP combines the best features of MOLAP and ROLAP, no industrywide consensus on the exact definition of HOLAP exists.

Microsoft claims that OLAP Server is suited for use in MOLAP, ROLAP, and HOLAP configurations, but most users are likely to opt for ROLAP or HOLAP implementation. ROLAP and HOLAP systems are capable of operating directly from the OLTP tables, but doing so is likely to cause a substantial OLTP performance hit. Thus a data warehouse server stores a current copy of base data, such as order or invoice line items. A primary incentive for storing base data in separate tables is that critical information, such as order date or invoice date (for the period dimension) and ship-to location (for the geopolitical dimension), can be added to line item records in the data transformation step.

Figure 28.5 illustrates the flow of information from an SQL Server 7.0 OLTP database through DTS to a data warehouse/mart server, which stores the base data and, if ROLAP is implemented, the aggregations. OLAP Server creates a multidimensional (MD) cache, also called a *virtual cube*, which implements selective preaggregation and sparse matrix methodology. The OLE DB for OLAP API, based on the OLE DB 2.0 specification, provides client access to OLAP Server's MD cache or to persistent data cubes provided by the PivotTable Service. ActiveX Data Objects/Multidimensional (ADO MD) is an automation wrapper for OLE DB for OLAP. You use ADO MD with MDX to create `Cellsets`, the ADO MD version of `Recordsets`.

OLAP Server includes an Aggregation Wizard to automate the selective preaggregation process. *Preaggregation* means storing persistent aggregations in the database, rather than generating the aggregations on-the-fly when creating the MD cube. According to Microsoft, 20% of the possible preaggregations provide 80% of the performance gain. The Wizard analyzes level counts for each dimension and parent-child ratios for each level of the dimension to find which aggregations have the most dependent aggregations. Figure 28.6 illustrates the typical relationship between performance gain and increased database size, starting with 4GB of base data in the fact table.

NOTE

OLAP Server has a limit of 65,535 virtual cubes per database; each virtual cube can have up to 32 "real" cubes. The dimension limit is 65,535 per database, with a maximum of 64 per cube, with up to 64 levels (63 plus the All level). The maximum number of measures is 128 per cube. It's unlikely that real-world OLAP operations would be hampered by any of these limits.

Microsoft OLAP Server appears to provide 60% to 80% of the capabilities of high-end MOLAP products, such as Essbase, but at far lower licensing and maintenance costs. It's a reasonably safe bet that OLAP Server can handle the departmental needs of large firms, as well as the entire organizational requirements of small- and medium-size enterprises. Like SQL Server 7.0, Microsoft designed OLAP Server to fulfil the requirements of about 90% of today's market (measured by unit sales).

FIGURE 28.5

Information flow in an ROLAP implementation that uses SQL Server 7.0 to store base data and aggregations for OLAP Server.

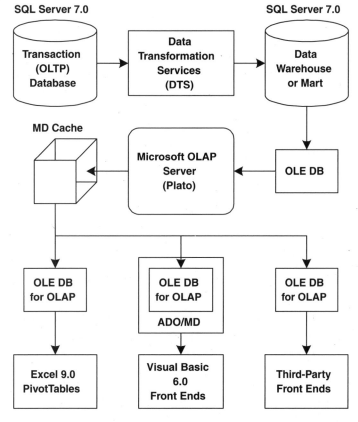

FIGURE 28.6

The typical pattern of performance improvement versus increasing database size with more preaggregation.

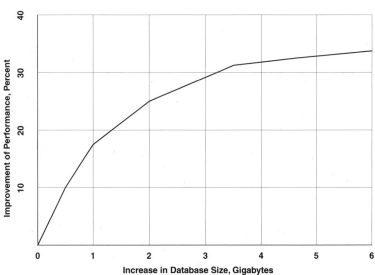

NOTE

OLAP Server 1.0 stores its metadata, such as dimension definitions, in a proprietary repository database. You can export the content of the OLAP Server
repository to Microsoft Repository 2.0, which ships with SQL Server 7.0 and
Visual Studio 6.0. Microsoft says that future versions of OLAP Server will integrate fully with Microsoft Repository.

DELIVERING INFORMATION TO THE CLIENT

The objective of installing an OLAP server or engine is to display data warehouse/mart information in client applications in a format suited to queries generated by users. The basic display
for numerical values is a browsing application that creates an expanded version of the two-
dimensional crosstab format of Jet crosstab queries or Excel PivotTables. Figure 28.7 illustrates
a simple crosstab view created by OLAP Manager's Cube Browser from the Bobs Video Store
cube. OLAP Manager, like SQL Server Enterprise Manager, is a snap-in for Microsoft
Management Console (MMC).

FIGURE 28.7

*Cube Browser dis-
playing an expand-
ed crosstab view of
a video rentals
cube with stacked
columns for cus-
tomer age range
and gender dimen-
sions.*

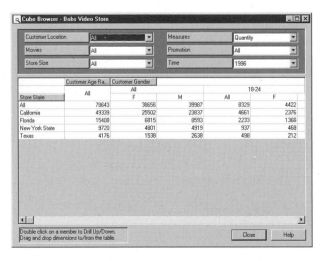

OLAP Server creates the Bobs Video Store cube from a Jet database, Bobsvid.mdb. Figure
28.7 shows the relationships between the five tables of Bobsvid.mdb. Figure 28.8 shows the
first few of the approximately 175,000 records in the Sales_Facts table that supplies the values for the Measures dimension (Price, Quantity, and Total_Amount). Bobsvid.mdb has a
structure typical of data mart databases. Excluding the Promotion table, Bobsvid.mdb has a
simple star schema.

FIGURE 28.8

The schema of the source tables for Bobsvid.cub shown in Access 97's Relationships window.

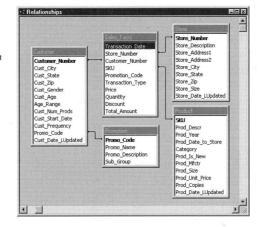

FIGURE 28.9

The first 28 of the 174,595 records of Bobsvid.mdb's Sales_Facts table.

Transaction_Date	Store_Number	Customer_Number	SKU	Promotion_Code	Transaction_Type	Price
12/8/94	2	544	3	1	VISA	$3.00
12/9/94	1	133	3	1	VISA	$3.00
12/18/94	2	266	3	1	VISA	$3.00
12/29/94	4	9	3	2	VISA	$3.00
1/18/95	2	94	3	3	VISA	$3.00
1/21/95	2	396	3	1	VISA	$3.00
2/23/95	1	764	3	1	VISA	$3.00
3/4/95	1	36	3	3	VISA	$3.00
4/9/95	2	17	3	2	VISA	$3.00
4/25/95	1	79	3	2	VISA	$3.00
4/29/95	2	722	3	1	VISA	$3.00
5/2/95	2	995	3	1	VISA	$3.00
5/13/95	2	83	3	2	VISA	$3.00
5/14/95	2	435	3	1	VISA	$3.00
5/19/95	2	40	3	3	VISA	$3.00
6/18/95	1	162	3	1	VISA	$3.00
7/2/95	2	883	3	1	VISA	$3.00
7/27/95	3	69	3	2	VISA	$3.00
8/23/95	1	373	3	1	VISA	$3.00
8/30/95	1	898	3	1	VISA	$3.00
10/1/95	2	490	3	1	VISA	$3.00
10/15/95	1	164	3	1	VISA	$3.00
10/19/95	1	452	3	1	VISA	$3.00

Record: |◄ ◄ | 1 | ► ►| ►*| of 174595

28

ANALYZING MULTIDIMENSIONAL DATA WITH OLAP

By default, the Cube Browser crosstab displays unit rentals (Quantity) of video tapes by Store State (Store_State), Customer Age Range (Age_Range), and Customer Gender (Cust_Gender) dimensions. You select the level of the dimensions, including Measures, from the six list view combo boxes in the top pane of Cube Browser's window. OLAP Server treats Measures as another dimension, despite the lack of a hierarchical structure within Measures, which has Price, Quantity, and Total Amount levels. Double-clicking the Store State button expands the grid to include the next lower level of the Store Location dimension. Double-clicking Store City adds the lowest-level Store Description column (see Figure 28.10).

Figure 28.10

Drilling down on the Store Location dimension.

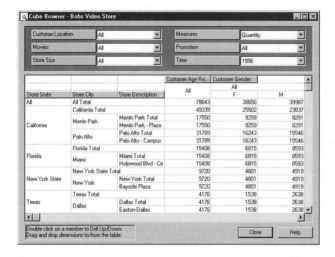

OLE DB for OLAP and Simple MDX Syntax

Behind the scenes, OLAP Manager's Cube Browser passes MDXs to the MSOLAP data provider (Msolap.dll), named Microsoft OLE DB Provider for DSS in the Registry. MSOLAP returns a `Dataset` object, which abstracts a multidimensional query result set. The OLE DB for OLAP API specification defines the MDX syntax, which consists of a very large set of extensions to ANSI SQL-92. The full MDX syntax appears in Appendix B, "Multidimensional Expressions (MDX) Grammar," of the OLE DB for OLAP Programmer's Guide. The Programmer's Guide is included with the MDAC 2.0 SDK documentation and is available for downloading from **http://www.microsoft.com/data/mdac2.htm**.

The syntax for the basic structure of an MDX statement is

```
SELECT axis_specification [, axis_specification ...]
   FROM cube_specification
      [WHERE slicer_specification]
```

The preceding SQL-92 syntax is deceptively simple. Following is a basic description of the *specification* elements:

- Dimensions included in the *axis_specification* retrieve data for multiple members, such as Store Location, Customer Age Range, and Customer Gender (refer to Figures 28.9 and 28.10). The Customer Gender dimension is *nested* within the Customer Age Range dimension. Nesting establishes the stacked crosstab structure of the grid.

- The *cube_specification* is the name of the data cube, Bobs Video Store.

- Dimensions included in the *slicer_specification* retrieve data for a single member, such as 1996 for the Time dimension and Quantity for the Measures dimension. The term *slicer* derives from "slicing and dicing" the data, the process of decreasing the number of columns or rows in the grid.

The MDX statement to return the Dataset displayed in preceding Figure 28.10 is

```
SELECT [Store Location].MEMBERS ON ROWS,
        NEST([Customer Age Range].MEMBERS,
            [Customer Gender].MEMBERS) ON COLUMNS
    FROM [Bobs Video Store]
        WHERE (Measures.Quantity, Time.Year.[1996])
```

> **NOTE**
>
> Like database object names, square brackets must surround dimension and dimension member names that contain spaces or other SQL-illegal characters, such as numeric values.

Following is an explanation of each element of the preceding MDX statements:

- [Store Location].MEMBERS ON ROWS specifies that all levels (members) of the Store Location dimension appear in rows. The members are Store State, Store City, and Store Description.

- NEST([Customer Age Range].MEMBERS, [Customer Gender].MEMBERS) ON COLUMNS stacks the Customer Age Range (18-24, 25-36, ...) columns over the Customer Gender (All, F, and M) columns.

- FROM [Bobs Video Store] specifies the Bobs Video Store cube contained by Bobsvid.cub.

- WHERE (Measures.Quantity, Time.Year.[1996]) is the slicer specification, which specifies the particular measure. Parentheses surround the slicer tuple.

If the Quantity measure and the value 1996 of the WHERE clause's *slicer_specification* are unique among all dimensions, the following MDX statement returns the same Dataset:

```
SELECT [Store Location].MEMBERS ON AXIS(1),
        NEST([Customer Age Range].MEMBERS,
            [Customer Gender].MEMBERS) ON AXIS(0)
    FROM [Bobs Video Store]
        WHERE (Quantity, [1996])
```

MDX grammar includes an extraordinary number of reserved words that extend SQL-92. The basic MDX statements used in the examples of this chapter are quite powerful, especially as you add nesting levels to both axes. A full exposition of MDX grammar requires a book in itself and is beyond the scope of this edition.

The MDX Sample Applications

OLAP Server and the MDAC 2.0 SDK include a Visual Basic 5.0 sample application, MDX Sample, that includes a collection of 19 prewritten queries stored in an MDXQuery.mdx file.

MDX Sample lets you edit existing and write new queries. Figure 28.11 shows the result of executing the first MDX statement of the preceding section against OLAP Server.

FIGURE 28.11

OLAP Server's MDX Sample application displaying the `Cellset` *of Figure 28.10.*

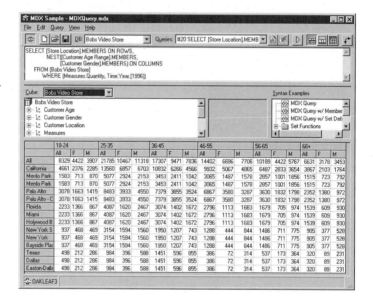

Both versions of MDX Sample obtain source data from Bobsvid.mdb and use ADO MD to provide the `ADOMD.Catalog` and `ADOMD.Cellset` objects for manipulation and display by Visual Basic code. Following are the primary differences between the two versions:

- OLAP Server's executable-only (Mdxsampl.exe) version uses a ROLAP cube created by OLAP Server. MSDASQL connects OLAP Server to Bobsvid.mdb with the Bobs Video Store ODBC data source. When logging on, type or accept the computer name of the OLAP Server, accept the MSOLAP provider, and type your user ID for the OLAP Server. MDXQuery.mdx opens as the default query file. The ROLAP cube has dimensions for multiple stores in three states.

- MDAC 2.0 SDK's version (Mdxsampl.vbp) connects to a persistent MOLAP cube (Bobsvid.cub) created by the PivotTable service. Mdxsampl.vbp runs in Visual Basic 5.0 or 6.0. Except for Figure 28.11, the examples of this chapter use the MOLAP cube. When logging on, type the fully qualified path to Bobsvid.cub (usually **C:\Msdasdk\Samples\Oledb\Olap\Data\Bobsvid.cub**) in the Database Name text box and accept MSOLAP as the provider. You must open MDXQuery.mdx to run the sample queries. The MOLAP cube has Store Location dimensions for only a single store (Menlo Park).

> **NOTE**
>
> The Microsoft PivotTable service is an in-process, client-side component that creates data cube (.cub) files from OLAP Server or relational data sources. A client cube is a local, persistent equivalent of OLAP Server objects and is stored in a structured (compound document) file. A .cub file can contain one or more independent MOLAP, ROLAP, and HOLAP data cubes.

The code for the MSFlexGrid control supports only a hierarchical fixed-row or fixed-column format on a single axis. Clicking the Pivot button at the extreme right of the toolbar inverts the axes (see Figure 28.12).

FIGURE 28.12

Pivoting the axes of Figure 28.11's `Cellset`.

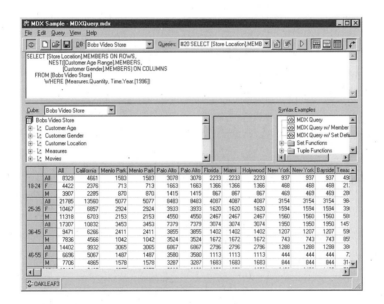

EXPLORING ADO MD OBJECTS

The Microsoft ActiveX Data Objects (Multidimensional) 1.0 Library (Msadomd.dll) is the Automation wrapper for OLE DB for OLAP. You can explore ADOMD objects, methods, and properties with Object Browser after adding a reference to Msadomd.dll to your Visual Basic project. The relationships between objects aren't evident in Object Browser, so Figure 28.13 provides a diagram of the hierarchical, collection-oriented ADOMD object model. Provider-specific Properties collections aren't included in the diagram.

FIGURE 28.13
The ADOMD *collection and object hierarchy.*

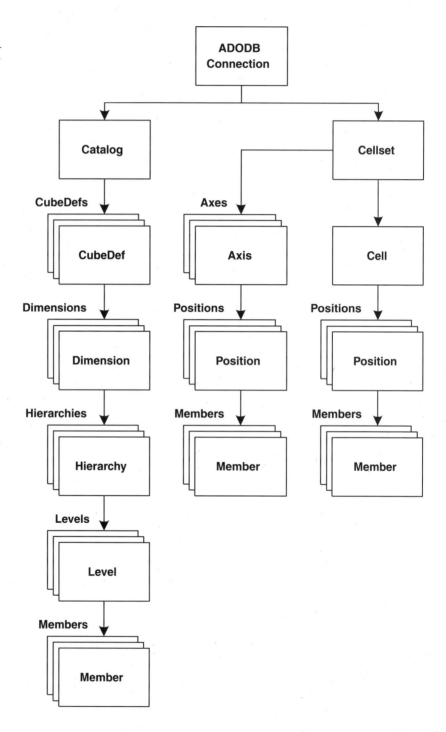

All ADOMD.*Collection*s have a default Item property, a Count property, and a Refresh method. ADOMD objects are designed for decision support, so ADOMD.*Collection*s are read-only, and most of the property values of their members are read-only.

ADOMD.Catalog Objects

The Catalog object provides access to metadata in OLAP Server's repository via an ADODB.Connection object. The Connection object is the only ADODB object used by ADO MD; you must include a reference to the Microsoft ActiveX Data Objects 2.0 and Microsoft ActiveX Data Objects (Multidimensional) 1.0 libraries in your project. The Catalog object has two properties, ActiveConnection and Name, and one collection, CubeDefs.

The VBA code to create a Catalog object from the Bobsvid.cub cube is as follows:

```
Dim cnnOLAP As New ADODB.Connection
Dim catOLAP As New ADOMD.Catalog

With cnnOLAP
    .Provider = "MSOLAP"
    .ConnectionString = "Location=d:\path\Bobsvid.cub"
    .Open
End With

Set catOLAP.ActiveConnection = cnnOLAP
```

Use the following code to connect to the Bobs Video Store cube on OLAP Server:

```
Dim cnnOLAP As New ADODB.Connection
Dim catOLAP As New ADOMD.Catalog

With cnnOLAP
    .Provider = "MSOLAP"
    .ConnectionString = "Data Source=Bobs Video Store;User ID=login;Password = password"
    .Open
End With

Set catOLAP.ActiveConnection = cnnOLAP
```

Properties of Objects in the Catalog Hierarchy

Catalog subobjects have relatively few properties and no methods. Table 28.1 lists the properties of the five Catalog subobjects.

TABLE 28.1 PROPERTIES OF Catalog SUBOBJECTS

CubeDef	Dimension	Hierarchy	Level	Member
Description	Description	Description	Description	Description
Name	Name	Name	Name	Name

continues

28

ANALYZING MULTIDIMENSIONAL DATA WITH OLAP

TABLE 28.1 CONTINUED

CubeDef	Dimension	Hierarchy	Level	Member
	UniqueName	UniqueName	UniqueName	UniqueName
			Caption	Caption
			Depth	LevelDepth
				LevelName
				Type
				Parent
				Children
				ChildCount

Most of the property names are self-describing; following is a list of those that aren't:

- UniqueName identifies a specific object when the name of the object isn't unique within a cube.
- Caption returns a string used for row or column headers.
- LevelDepth is the distance of the Level from the root of the Hierarchy.
- LevelName returns a string formatted as [*DimensionName*].[*LevelName*].
- Type is an enumeration (MemberTypeEnum) that identifies the Member category. Table 28.2 lists the allowable values of the Type property.
- Parent supplies a pointer to the Member's Level object.
- ChildCount is nonzero if there are Members in a lower level of the hierarchy.
- Children collection is populated if ChildCount is nonzero and provides a pointer.

TABLE 28.2 ALLOWABLE VALUES OF A Member's Type PROPERTY

MemberTypeEnum	Value	Description
adMemberRegular	1	An instance of a predefined business-related entity, such as a particular range of customer ages (default).
adMemberMeasures	2	A cell value.
adMemberFormula	4	A calculated value.
adMemberAll	8	The (All) Member of the Levels collection. Every Level of a Hierarchy has an (All) member.
adMemberUnknown	16	The type of the Member can't be determined.

Each object in the `Catalog` hierarchy supplies the collection of the next lower member of the `Hierarchy` and a `Properties` collection with a set of provider-specific properties. Table 28.3 lists the members of the `Properties` collections supplied by OLAP Server for each `Catalog` subobject. You use members of the `Properties` collection to return the many values that aren't available directly from the properties of the object.

TABLE 28.3 MEMBERS OF THE `Properties` COLLECTIONS OF `Catalog` SUBOBJECTS

CubeDef	*Dimension*	*Hierarchy*	*Level*	*Member*
CatalogName	CatalogName	CatalogName	CatalogName	CatalogName
SchemaName	SchemaName	SchemaName	SchemaName	SchemaName
CubeName	CubeName	CubeName	CubeName	CubeName
CubeType	DimensionName	Dimension UniqueName	Dimension UniqueName	Dimension UniqueName
CubeGUID	Dimension UniqueName	HierarchyName	Hierarchy UniqueName	Hierarchy UniqueName
CreatedOn	DimensionGUID	Hierarchy UniqueName	LevelName	LevelUnique Name
LastSchemaUpdate	DimensionCaption	HierarchyGUID	LevelUniqueName	LevelNumber
SchemaUpdatedBy	DimensionOrdinal	Hierarchy Caption	LevelGUID	Member Ordinal
DataUpdatedBy	DimensionType	DimensionType	LevelCaption	MemberName
Description	Dimension Cardinality	Hierarchy Cardinality	LevelNumber	Member UniqueName
	Default Hierarchy	Default Member	Level Cardinality	MemberType
	Description	AllMember	LevelType	MemberGUID
		Description	Description	MemberCaption
				Children Cardinality
				ParentLevel
				ParentUnique Name
				ParentCount
				Description

Use of `Catalog` Objects

Access to the `Catalog` object is necessary to populate combo or list boxes for each dimension. Users choose the `Dimension` hierarchy `Level`(s) to create the MDX statement that returns data. Listing 28.1 illustrates the code required to generate in the Immediate window a hierarchically formatted list of the names of members of the `Dimensions`, `Levels`, and `Members` collections of the Bobs Video Store cube of the Bobsvid.cub file. The `Name` and `Description` property values of the `Hierarchy` object are empty by default. The number of members of the `Members` collection printed is limited to prevent overflow of the Immediate window.

LISTING 28.1   CODE TO PRINT TO THE IMMEDIATE WINDOW THE NAMES OF MEMBERS OF THE Dimensions, Levels, AND Members COLLECTIONS OF THE BOBS VIDEO STORE CUBE

```
Private cnnOLAP As New ADODB.Connection

Private Sub Form_Load()
    'Print dimensions to the Immediate window
    Dim catOLAP As New ADOMD.Catalog
    Dim cbfOLAP As ADOMD.CubeDef
    Dim dimOLAP As ADOMD.Dimension
    Dim hrcOLAP As ADOMD.Hierarchy
    Dim lvlOLAP As ADOMD.Level
    Dim memOLAP As ADOMD.Member

    Dim strCube As String
    Dim intCtr As Integer

    'Open the Connection to the Catalog
    strCube = "C:\Msdasdk\Samples\Oledb\Olap\Data\Bobsvid.cub"
    With cnnOLAP
        .Provider = "MSOLAP"
        .ConnectionString = "Location=" & strCube & _
            ";User ID=Administrator"
        .Open
    End With
    Set catOLAP.ActiveConnection = cnnOLAP

    'Specify the cube name
    Set cbfOLAP = catOLAP.CubeDefs("Bobs Video Store")

    'Iterate through Dimensions, Hierarchies, Levels, and Members
    For Each dimOLAP In cbfOLAP.Dimensions
        Debug.Print dimOLAP.Name
        For Each hrcOLAP In dimOLAP.Hierarchies
            'Hierarchy returns empty Name and Description values
            For Each lvlOLAP In hrcOLAP.Levels
                Debug.Print "    " & lvlOLAP.Name
                    intCtr = 0
                    For Each memOLAP In lvlOLAP.Members
```

```
              Debug.Print "        " & memOLAP.Name
              intCtr = intCtr + 1
              If intCtr > 9 Then
                  Debug.Print "        ..."
                  Exit For
              End If
          Next memOLAP
      Next lvlOLAP
    Next hrcOLAP
  Next dimOLAP
  End
End Sub
```

Table 28.4 lists the contents of the Immediate window generated by the event handler of Listing 28.1 in newspaper-style (snaking) columns. A maximum of four Members appear for each Level to conserve space by changing the **If intCtr > 9 Then** line to **If intCtr > 3 Then**. The names of a few Members are truncated. Some Member values, such as those for Quarter and Month, print out of sequence with **For Each ... Next** iteration. To assure the proper ordering of collection members, iterate the collection with **For lngVar = 0 To** Collection.Count - 1 **... Next** lngVar and use lngVar to specify the index of the member.

The ADOMD.vbp project in the \Ddg_vb6\Chaptr28 folder of the accompanying CD-ROM uses a slightly modified version of the code of Listing 28.1 to display the contents of the Bobs Video Store Catalog in a text box when you click Catalog (see Figure 28.14). Iterating Levels with a large number of Members results in a significant delay in execution when the **For Each** statement retrieves every Member.

FIGURE 28.14
The ADOMD.vbp project displaying part of the Catalog *for the Bobs Video Store* CubeDef.

ADOMD.Cellset **Objects**

The Cellset object is the root of the object hierarchy for accessing and displaying quantitative (Measures) values. Like ADODB.Recordset objects, the Cellset object requires a Source property statement string to define the result set. Following is an example for opening a Cellset object:

```
Dim cnnOLAP As New ADODB.Connection
Dim cstOLAP As New ADOMD.Cellset
```

TABLE 28.4 Dimension, Level, AND Member NAMES PRINTED TO THE IMMEDIATE WINDOW BY THE EVENT HANDLER OF LISTING 28.1

Customer Age	Measures	All
(All)	MeasuresLevel	Store State
All	Price	California
Customer Age Range	Quantity	Store City
18-24	Total Amount	Menlo Park
25-35	Movies	Store
Description		
36-45	(All)	Menlo Park
46-55	All	Store Size
...	Product Category	(All)
Customer Gender	Action/Adventure	All
(All)	Children	Store Size
All	Classic	large
Customer Gender	Comedy	Time
F	...	(All)
M	Product Description	All
Customer Location	3 Ninjas	Year
(All)	A Bridge Too Far	1994
All	A Bullet for ...	1995
Customer State	A Challenge ...	1996
California	...	Quarter
Customer City	Promotion	Quarter 4
Atherton	(All)	Quarter 1
East Palo Alto	All	Quarter 2
Menlo Park	Promo Description	Quarter 3
Mountain View	Frequent Renter	...
...	Regular customer	Month
Customer Number	Promo Sub Group	December
121	control group	November
125	test particip...	February
129	none	January
141	Store Location	...
...	(All)	

```
With cnnOLAP
   .Provider = "MSOLAP"
   .ConnectionString = "Location=d:\path\Bobsvid.cub"
   .Open
End With

With cstOLAP
   Set .ActiveConnection = cnnOLAP
   .Source = strMDXStatement
   .Open
End With
```

Properties of Objects in the `Cellset` Hierarchy

The `Cellset` object's `Source` property value, an MDX statement, transforms `Dimension`, `Hierarchy`, and `Level` objects to `Axis` and `Position` objects upon opening the `Cellset`. `Axis.Position.Member` objects have a one-to-one correspondence with `Catalog Member` objects. Following are brief descriptions of `Cellset` subobjects:

- `Axis` objects define the number of dimensions for data presentation; usually two (Axes(0), x, columns, and Axes(1), y, rows) for grids and two or three (Axes(2), z, depth) for graphs. `Axis.Position.Member` objects provide captions for grids and graphs. `Axis` objects have read-only `Name` and `DimensionCount` properties and no methods. `DimensionCount` returns the number of `Dimensions` on an `Axis`, which is a useful way to specify the number of fixed columns and rows (headers) of a grid.

- `Position` objects represent the distance in coordinate units of a `Level` from intersection of the `Axes`. `Position` objects have a `Members` collection, but no methods or properties.

- `Cell` objects deliver quantitative values of `Measures`, usually specified by a pair of zero-based numerical coordinate arguments corresponding to `Positions` index values (`Cellset (x, y).Value`). You also can retrieve a `Cell` value with Member.Name arguments (`Cellset("18-24", "Menlo Park").Value`). `Cell.Position.Member` objects provide a reverse route to information about a particular `Cell`. `Cell` objects have read-only `Value` (numeric) and `FormattedValue` (**String**) properties and no methods. `Cell` objects have a `Properties` collection with the members listed in Table 28.5.

TABLE 28.5 MEMBERS OF THE `Properties` COLLECTION OF THE `Cell` OBJECT

Property Name	Description
BackColor	BackColor for cell display
ForeColor	ForeColor for cell display
FormatString	Value formatted as a string (FormattedValue)
FontName	FontName used to display the cell value
FontSize	FontSize used to display the cell value
FontFlags	Flags specifying other font attributes (bold, italic, and the like)

> **NOTE**
>
> The `Cellset` object has a `FilterAxis` property that returns a pointer to an `Axis` object that supplies a definition of the filter (slicer) for the `Axis`. The slicer `Axis` doesn't appear in the `Axes` collection.

Lists from `Cellset` Subobjects

Understanding the relationship of `Cellset.Axis.Position.Member.Caption` to `Cellset.Cell.Value` is best gained by writing code to create a formatted list of values displayed in the Immediate window or a text box (see Listing 28.2).

LISTING 28.2   CODE TO DISPLAY IN A TEXT BOX A SET OF DESCRIPTIVE HEADERS AND `Cell` VALUES FROM AN MDX STATEMENT

```
Private Sub cmdCellset_Click()
    'Execute an MDX and display result set in row format
    Dim cstOLAP As New ADOMD.Cellset
    Dim lngCol As Long
    Dim lngRow As Long
    Dim lngMem As Long
    Dim strMDX As String
    Dim strCaption As String
    Dim strLevel As String

    Me.MousePointer = vbHourglass
    strMDX = "SELECT [Store Location].MEMBERS ON AXIS(1), " & _
                "NEST([Customer Age Range].MEMBERS, " & _
                    "[Customer Gender].MEMBERS) ON AXIS(0) " & _
                "FROM [Bobs Video Store] " & _
                    "WHERE (Quantity, [1996])"
    With cstOLAP
        'Use the existing Connection
        Set .ActiveConnection = cnnOLAP
        .Source = strMDX
        .Open

        'Write a descriptive header
        txtOLAP.Text = "Videotape Rental Quantity for 1996 by "
        'Add the row Dimension name
        strLevel = .Axes(1).Positions(0).Members(0).LevelName
        strLevel = Mid(strLevel, 2, InStr(strLevel, "]") - 2)
        txtOLAP.Text = txtOLAP.Text & strLevel & ":" & vbCrLf
        'Add the row Level names
        For lngRow = 0 To .Axes(1).Positions.Count - 1
            strLevel = .Axes(1).Positions(lngRow).Members(0).LevelName
            strLevel = Mid(strLevel, InStr(strLevel, ".[") + 2)
```

```
            strLevel = Left(strLevel, Len(strLevel) - 1)
            txtOLAP.Text = txtOLAP.Text & vbTab & strLevel & vbCrLf
        Next lngRow
        txtOLAP.Text = txtOLAP.Text & vbCrLf

        'Iterate the Cellset
        For lngCol = 0 To .Axes(0).Positions.Count - 1
            'By columns (X-axis)
            For lngMem = 0 To .Axes(0).Positions(lngCol).Members.Count - 1
                'Get the column headers
                strCaption = .Axes(0).Positions(lngCol).Members(lngMem).Caption
                strLevel = .Axes(0).Positions(lngCol).Members(lngMem).LevelName
                strLevel = Mid(strLevel, InStr(strLevel, ".[") + 2)
                strLevel = Left(strLevel, Len(strLevel) - 1)
                If strLevel = "(All)" Then
                    'Use the Dimension name, not the Level name
                    strLevel = .Axes(0).Positions(lngCol).Members(lngMem).LevelName
                    strLevel = Mid(strLevel, 2, InStr(strLevel, "]") - 2)
                End If
                strLevel = strLevel & ": "
                'Add the Level name
                txtOLAP.Text = txtOLAP.Text & strLevel & strCaption
                If lngMem = .Axes(0).Positions(lngCol).Members.Count - 1 Then
                    'Last member needs a new line
                    txtOLAP.Text = txtOLAP.Text & vbCrLf
                Else
                    txtOLAP.Text = txtOLAP.Text & vbTab
                End If
            Next lngMem
            For lngRow = 0 To .Axes(1).Positions.Count - 1
                'By rows; get the row Level header
                txtOLAP.Text = txtOLAP.Text & _
                    .Axes(1).Positions(lngRow).Members(0).Caption & vbTab
                If .Axes(1).Positions(lngRow).Members(0).Caption _
                    <> "Menlo Park" Then
                    'Line up the measures (version specific)
                    txtOLAP.Text = txtOLAP.Text & vbTab
                End If
                'Add the measure value
                txtOLAP.Text = txtOLAP.Text & cstOLAP(lngCol, lngRow).Value _
                    & vbCrLf
                DoEvents
            Next lngRow
        Next lngCol
    End With
    Me.MousePointer = vbDefault
End Sub
```

Figure 28.15 shows the first few lines of text generated by the cmdCellset_Click event handler of Listing 28.2.

FIGURE 28.15

The list produced by the cmdCellset_Click *event handler of the ADOMD.vbp project.*

Grids to Display Cellset Subobjects

The basic column, row iteration to populate a grid with Measures values uses the following pseudocode:

```
For intColumn = 0 To Cellset.Axes(0).Positions.Count - 1
    For intRow = 0 To Cellset.Axes(1).Positions.Count - 1
        Grid.Column = intColumn + intFixedColumns
        Grid.Row = intRow + intFixedRows
        Grid.Value = Cellset(intColumn, intRow).FormattedValue
    Next intRow
Next intColumn
```

Adding fixed rows and columns to display Level names and Member captions adds substantial complexity to the code. Listing 28.3 shows the code, derived from Listing 18.2, required to populate an MSFlexGrid control. The slightly modified MDX statement displays unit videotape rentals for 1996 by Product Category, Customer Age Range, and Customer Gender. To display a grid with many more rows, change the MDX statement's [Product Category] Axis specification element to [Product Description].

LISTING 28.3   CODE TO PRESENT THE CONTENTS OF A Cellset IN AN MSFLEXGRID CONTROL

```
Private Sub cmdCellset_Click()
    'Execute an MDX and display the result set in a FlexGrid
    Dim cstOLAP As New ADOMD.Cellset
    Dim intCol As Integer
    Dim intRow As Integer
    Dim intMem As Integer
    Dim strMDX As String
    Dim strCaption As String
    Dim strLevel As String

    Me.MousePointer = vbHourglass
    strMDX = "SELECT [Product Category].MEMBERS ON AXIS(1), " & _
                "NEST([Customer Age Range].MEMBERS, " & _
                    "[Customer Gender].MEMBERS) ON AXIS(0) " & _
                "FROM [Bobs Video Store] " & _
```

```
                    "WHERE (Quantity, [1996])"
With cstOLAP
   'Use the existing Connection
   Set .ActiveConnection = cnnOLAP
   .Source = strMDX
   .Open

   'Set the grid dimensions and fixed rows
   With grdOLAP
      .Cols = cstOLAP.Axes(0).Positions.Count
      .Rows = cstOLAP.Axes(1).Positions.Count
      'Provide for header rows and column(s)
      .FixedCols = cstOLAP.Axes(1).DimensionCount
      .FixedRows = cstOLAP.Axes(0).DimensionCount
      .Cols = .Cols + .FixedCols
      .Rows = .Rows + .FixedRows
      'Let header rows merge
      For intRow = 0 To .FixedRows - 1
         .MergeRow(intRow) = True
      Next intRow
      'But not data rows
      For intRow = .FixedRows To .Rows - 1
         .MergeRow(intRow) = False
      Next intRow
      For intRow = 0 To cstOLAP.Axes(1).Positions.Count - 1
         'Get the row caption
         .Col = 0
         .Row = intRow + .FixedRows
         .Text = cstOLAP.Axes(1).Positions(intRow).Members(0).Caption
      Next intRow
   End With
   DoEvents

   'Iterate the Cellset
   For intCol = 0 To .Axes(0).Positions.Count - 1
      For intMem = 0 To .Axes(0).Positions(intCol).Members.Count - 1
         'Get the column headers
         strCaption = .Axes(0).Positions(intCol).Members(intMem).Caption
         If intCol = 0 Then
            strLevel = .Axes(0).Positions(intCol).Members(intMem).LevelName
            strLevel = Mid(strLevel, InStr(strLevel, ".[") + 2)
            strLevel = Left(strLevel, Len(strLevel) - 1)
            If strLevel = "(All)" Then
               'Use the Dimension name, not the Level name
               strLevel = _
                  .Axes(0).Positions(intCol).Members(intMem).LevelName
               strLevel = Mid(strLevel, 2, InStr(strLevel, "]") - 2)
            End If
            With grdOLAP
               'Add the Level identifier
               .ColWidth(intCol) = 2000
               .Col = 0
```

```
            .Row = intMem
            .Text = strLevel & ":"
        End With
    Else
        grdOLAP.ColWidth(intCol) = 500
    End If
    With grdOLAP
        'Add the column captions
        .Col = intCol + .FixedCols
        .Row = intMem
        .Text = strCaption
        .CellAlignment = flexAlignCenterCenter
    End With
Next intMem
'By columns (X-axis)
For intRow = 0 To .Axes(1).Positions.Count - 1
    'Add the measure value
    With grdOLAP
        .Col = intCol + .FixedCols
        .Row = intRow + .FixedRows
        'FlexGrid doesn't like Null values from sparse matrices
        If IsNull(cstOLAP(intCol, intRow).Value) Then
            .Text = 0
        Else
            .Text = cstOLAP(intCol, intRow).Value
        End If
    End With
    DoEvents
    Next intRow
    Next intCol
    End With
    Me.MousePointer = vbDefault
End Sub
```

The code of Listing 28.3 is included in the frmOLAP form of the OLAPGrid.vbp project in the \Ddg_vb6\Chaptr28 folder of the accompanying CD-ROM. Figure 28.16 shows the grdOLAP MSFlexGrid populated by the code of Listing 28.3.

FIGURE 28.16

An MSFlexGrid control populated from a Cellset created from the Bobs Video Store cube.

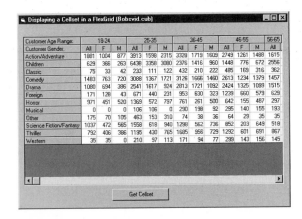

APPENDIX

Glossary

accelerator key   A key combination that provides access to a menu choice, macro, or other function of the application in lieu of a mouse click, usually by combining Alt+*key*. An accelerator key is identified on menus by an underlined character. It is sometimes (incorrectly) called a *shortcut key*, but shortcut keys usually consist of Ctrl+*key* combinations.

Access Control List (ACL)   Part of Windows NT's security description that controls access to a Windows NT object, such as a file. An object's owner can change access control entries in the list to grant or revoke permissions (access rights) for the object.

Access Developer's Toolkit   See *ADT* and *ODE*.

Access SQL   Former name of Jet SQL, a dialect of ANSI SQL. See *Jet SQL*.

access token   A Windows NT object that identifies a logged-on (authenticated) user. The access token contains the user's security ID (SID), the groups to which the user belongs, and other security information. See *SID*.

activation   An OLE 2+ term meaning to place an object in a running state, which includes binding the object, or to invoke a method of the object. See also *binding*.

active   In Windows, the currently running application or the window to which user input is directed; the window with the focus. See also *focus*.

Active Server Pages   See *ASP*.

ActiveX   A Microsoft trademark for a collection of technologies based on the Common Object Model (COM) and Distributed Common Object Model (DCOM). See *COM* and *DCOM*.

ActiveX components   A replacement term for OLE Automation miniservers and in-process servers, also called *Automation servers*. See *Automation*.

ActiveX controls   Insertable objects supplied in the form of OCX files that, in addition to offering a collection of properties and methods, also fire events. ActiveX controls are light-weight versions of earlier OLE Controls that also use the .ocx file extension.

ActiveX Data Objects   See *ADO*.

ActiveX documents   Files that can be inserted into the Microsoft Binder, such as files created by Microsoft Excel 7+ and Word 7+, as well as displayed in their native format in Internet Explorer 3+. ActiveX documents originally were called *Document Objects* or *DocObjects*.

ActiveX scripting   Microsoft's script-language hosting technology for Visual Basic, Scripting Edition (VBScript), ECMAScript (JavaScript or JScript), and Perl.

ActiveX server framework   ActiveX scripting for creating server-side Internet and intranet applications. Unlike ActiveX scripting, the ActiveX Server Framework allows file and other low-level operations.

ADC   An acronym for *Advanced Data Control*, the predecessor to Remote Data Service. See *RDS*.

add-in   Wizards and other programming aids that help Visual Basic programmers create and deploy applications. You use Visual Basic's Add-In Manager to install Microsoft and third-party add-ins. See also *builder*.

address   The numerical value, usually in hexadecimal format, of a particular location in your computer's random-access memory (RAM).

ADO   An acronym for *ActiveX Data Objects,* which are similar in concept to the Data Access Object (DAO) and Remote Data Object (RDO). ADO uses Microsoft's new OLE Database (OLE DB) technology to access data from various data sources, including text files and main-frame databases. ADO 2.0 is the preferred database connectivity method for Visual Basic 6.0. See *OLE DB*.

ADO MD   An acronym for *ADO Multidimensional (Expressions)*, the Automation library that provides access to `CubeDef` and `Cellset` objects created with the PivotTable Service or Microsoft SQL Server OLAP Services (formerly Microsoft Decision Support Services, MSDSS). See *Cellset, CubeDef, MDX, OLAP*, and *PivotTable Service*.

ADODB   An acronym and object library name for *ADO 2.0*. `ADODB` is used as an object prefix to specify the source of ADO data object, as in `ADODB.Recordset`.

ADODC   An acronym for the *ADO Data control*, which replaces the intrinsic Data control of Visual Basic 5.0 and earlier, and the Remote Data Control (RDC) of the Visual Basic 4.0 and 5.0 Enterprise Editions. See *ADO*.

ADT An acronym for the *Access Developer's Toolkit* for Access 2.0 and Access 95 that allowed distribution of files needed to run (but not design) Access 2.0 and Access 95 applications. For Access 97, the ADT is replaced by the Office 97 Developer's Edition (ODE), which provides the same features as the Access 95 ADT, plus developer products for other Office applications. See *ODE*.

ADTG An acronym for *Advanced Data TableGram,* a Microsoft-proprietary MIME format used by RDS to marshal Recordsets between client and server via the HTTP protocol. See *HTTP*, *MIME*, and *RDS*.

Advanced Data TableGram See *ADTG*.

aggregate functions The ANSI SQL functions AVG(), SUM(), MIN(), MAX(), and COUNT(), and Access SQL functions StDev(), Var(), First(), and Last(). Aggregate functions calculate summary values from a group of values in a specified column and are usually associated with GROUP BY and HAVING clauses. See also *domain aggregate functions*.

aggregate object An OLE 2.0 term that refers to an object class containing one or more member objects of another class.

alias A temporary name assigned to a table in a self-join, to a column of a query, or to rename a table, implemented by the AS reserved word in ANSI SQL. You can use AS to rename any field or table with Jet SQL; SQL Server's Transact-SQL substitutes a space for AS. **Alias** is also an embedded keyword option for the VBA **Declare** statement. The **Alias** keyword is used to register prototypes of DLL functions so that the function can be called from programs by another name. Aliasing the ANSI versions of 32-bit Windows API functions to function names without the A suffix is common when converting Visual Basic 4.0 and earlier applications to Visual Basic 6.0, which uses Unicode strings.

ANSI An acronym for the *American National Standards Institute*. ANSI in the Windows context refers to the ANSI character set that Microsoft decided to use for Windows (rather than the IBM PC character set that includes special characters such as those used for line drawing, called the *OEM character set*). The most common character set is *American Standard Code for Information Interchange* (ASCII), which for English alphabetic and numeric characters is the same as ANSI. Windows 9x and Windows NT include ANSI (suffix A) and Unicode (suffix W) versions of Windows API functions. See *ASCII* and *Unicode*.

API An acronym for *Application Program Interface*. Generically, a method by which a program can obtain access to or modify the operating system. In 32-bit Windows, the 1,000 or so functions provided by Windows 9x and Windows NT DLLs that allow applications to open and close windows, read the keyboard, interpret mouse movements, and so on. Programmers call these functions *hooks* to Windows. VBA provides access to these functions with the Declare statement. See also *DLL*.

application   The software product that results from the creation of a program, often used as a synonym for the programming (source) code that creates it. Microsoft Word and Microsoft Excel are called *mainstream Windows productivity applications* in this book. Applications are distinguished by the environment for which they are designed (such as Windows, DOS, Macintosh, and UNIX) and their purpose. Windows applications carry the DOS executable file extension, .exe. This book uses application and project interchangeably.

argument   A piece of data supplied to a function that the function acts on or uses to perform its task. Arguments are enclosed in parentheses. Multiple arguments, if any, are separated from each other by commas. Arguments passed to procedures usually are called *parameters*.

array   An ordered sequence of values (elements) stored within a single named variable, accessed by referring to the variable name with the number of the element (index or subscript) in parentheses, as in `strValue = strArray(3)`. VBA arrays may have more than one dimension, in which case access to the value includes indexes for each dimension, as in `strValue = strArray(3,3)`.

ASCII   An acronym for the *American Standard Code for Information Interchange*. A set of standard numerical values for printable, control, and special characters used by PCs and most other computers. Other commonly used codes for character sets are ANSI (used by Windows 3.1+), Unicode (used by Windows 9x and Windows NT), and EBCDIC (Extended Binary-Coded Decimal Interchange Code, used by IBM for mainframe computers). See *Unicode*.

ASP   An acronym for *Active Server Pages,* Microsoft's server-side technology for dynamically creating standard HTML (Internet) Web pages. Conventional ASP uses VBScript or ECMAScript to manipulate ASP objects. Visual Basic WebClasses let you substitute VBA 6.0 for scripting languages. See *ECMAScript* and *WebClasses*.

assign   To give a value to a named variable.

asynchronous   A process that can occur at any time, regardless of the status of the operating system or running applications.

attached table   A table that's not stored in the currently open Jet database (native or base table), but that you can manipulate as though the table were a native table. In Jet 3+ terminology, an attached table is a linked table. See *linked table*.

authentication   The process of verifying a user's login ID and password.

Automation   An ActiveX and OLE 2+ term that refers to a means of manipulating another application's objects.

Automation client   An ActiveX- or OLE 2-compliant Windows application with an application programming (macro) language, such as VBA, that can reference and manipulate objects exposed by (OLE) Automation servers.

Automation server   Technically, any COM- or OLE 2-compliant Windows application that supports Automation operations by exposing a set of objects for manipulation by Automation client applications. This book restricts the term *Automation server* to applications that aren't ActiveX full servers but expose application objects. The members of Office 97 are examples of full automation servers.

AutoNumber   A Jet 3+ replacement for the Counter field data type of Jet 2.0, Access 1.x, and Access 2.0. AutoNumber fields may be of the Increment or Random type. Fields of the Increment AutoNumber field data type usually are used to create primary keys in cases where a unique primary key can't be created from data in the table.

background   In multitasking computer operations, the application or procedure that's not visible onscreen and that doesn't receive user-generated input. In Windows, a minimized application that doesn't have the focus is in the background.

base date   A date used as a reference from which other date values are calculated. In the case of VBA and SQL Server, the base date is January 1, 1900.

base tables   The permanent tables from which a query is created. A synonym for underlying tables. Each base table in a database is identified by a name unique to the database. Jet also uses the term *base table* to refer to a table in the current database in contrast to a linked (attached) table. See *linked table*.

batch   A group of statements processed as an entity. Execution of DOS batch files, such as AUTOEXEC.BAT, and SQL statements are examples of batch processes.

batch update   A process in which multiple update operations on a `Recordset` are conducted on a locally cached copy of the `Recordset`. When all updates are completed, calling the `UpdateBatch` method attempts to make permanent (persist) all changes to the underlying tables in a single operation.

BDC   An abbreviation for *backup domain controller*, a Windows NT server that provides an alternative source of authentication for network users. Account and group information from a primary domain controller (PDC) is replicated periodically to each BDC in the domain. See *PDC*.

binary file   A file whose content doesn't consist of lines of text. Executable (.exe), dynamic link library (.dll), and most database files are stored in binary format.

binary string   A string consisting of binary, not text, data that contains bytes outside the range of ANSI or ASCII values for printable characters. Access 97 requires that you store binary strings as arrays of the Byte data type to avoid problems with Unicode/ANSI conversion.

binding   The process of connecting one object to another through interfaces. In Visual Basic 6.0, local object binding is accomplished by COM interfaces and remote object binding by DCOM interfaces. See *COM*, *DCOM*, and *data binding*.

bitwise   A process that evaluates each bit of a combination, such as a byte or word, rather than processes the combination as a single element. Logical operations and masks use bitwise procedures.

blitting   The process of using the `BitBlt()` function of the Windows Gdi32.exe file to modify a bitmap by using bit block transfer.

Boolean   A type of arithmetic in which all digits are bits—that is, the numbers may have only two states: on (true or 1) or off (false or 0). Widely used in set theory and computer programming, Boolean, named after the mathematician George Boole, also is used to describe a VBA data type that may have only two states: true or false. In VBA, true is represented by `&HFF` (all bits of an 8-bit byte set to 1) and false by `&H0` (all bits set to 0). **`Boolean`** is a VBA data type.

bound   See *binding*.

break   To cause an interruption in program operation. Ctrl+C, the standard DOS break key combination, seldom halts operation of a Windows application. Esc is more commonly used in Windows to cause an operation to terminate before completion.

breakpoint   A designated statement that causes program execution to halt after executing the statement preceding it. To toggle breakpoints on or off, choose or press F9 on the line of code before which you want execution to halt.

Briefcase replication   A feature of Jet 3+ running under Windows 9*x* or Windows NT 4.0 that permits the creation of Jet replication sets stored in Briefcase folders, which can be updated by mobile users. Subsequently, the Briefcase replicates are used to update the design-master replica to synchronize the design-master replica with the contents of the Briefcase replicas. ADO 2.0 doesn't support Jet replication. See *design-master replica*.

buffer   An area in memory of a designated size (number of bytes or characters) reserved, typically, to hold a portion of a file or the value of a variable. When string variables are passed as arguments of DLL functions, you must create a buffer of sufficient size to hold the returned string. This is accomplished by creating a fixed-length string variable of the necessary size, using the `String` function, before calling the DLL function.

builder   A component that provides assistance in defining new objects, writing SQL statements, or creating expressions. Buttons with an ellipsis symbol commonly open builders.

built-in functions   Functions that are included in a computer language and don't need to be created by the programmer as user-defined functions.

business rules   A set of rules for entering data in a database that are specific to an enterprise's method of conducting its operations. Business rules are in addition to rules for maintaining the domain and referential integrity of tables in a database. Business rules most commonly are implemented in a three-tier client/server database environment. See *three tier*.

cache   A block of memory reserved for temporary storage. Caches usually store data from disk files in memory to speed access to the data. By default, Windows 9x and NT cache all disk read and write operations.

caption   The title that appears in a window's title bar. Visual Basic calls the text of a label, check box, frame, and command or option button control object the Caption *property*.

caret   The term used by Windows to indicate the cursor used when editing a text field, usually shaped as an I-beam. The caret, also called the *insertion point*, can be positioned independently of the mouse pointer.

Cartesian product   Named for RenÈ Descartes, a French mathematician. Used in JOIN operations to describe all possible combinations of rows and columns from each table in a database. The number of rows in a Cartesian product is equal to the number of rows in table 1 times that in table 2 times that in table 3, and so on. Cartesian rows that don't satisfy the JOIN condition are disregarded.

cascading deletion   A trigger that deletes data from one table based on a deletion from another table to maintain referential integrity. Declarative referential integrity (DRI) is another means of implementing cascading deletions. Triggers or DRI usually are used to delete detail data (such as invoice items) when the master record (invoice) is deleted. Jet 2+ provides cascading deletion as an optional component of its referential integrity features. See *referential integrity*.

case sensitivity   A term used to define whether an interpreter, compiler, or database manager treats lowercase and uppercase letters as the same character. Most are not case sensitive. C is an exception; it is case sensitive, and all its keywords are lowercase. Many interpreters, including VBA, reformat keywords to its standard—a combination of uppercase and lowercase letters. VBA doesn't distinguish between uppercase and lowercase letters used as names for variables.

CDFS   The 32-bit CD-ROM file system shared by Windows NT and Windows 9x.

Cellset   The multidimensional equivalent of an ADO Recordset. See *ADO MD*, *CubeDef*, *OLAP*, and *PivotTable Service*.

channel   In Windows, ordinarily refers to a unique task ID assigned to a dynamic data exchange (DDE) conversation. Channel IDs are Long integers under Windows 9x and Windows NT. Also used to identify an I/O port in mini- and mainframe computers.

child   In Windows, usually a shortened form of *MDI child window*. Also used in computer programming in general to describe an object that's related to but lower in hierarchical level than a parent object.

chunk   A part of a RIFF or standard MIDI file that's assigned to a particular function and may be treated as a single element by an application. VBA uses the term *chunk* to refer to a part of any file that you read or write with the `GetChunk` and `AppendChunk` methods. See *RIFF*.

class identifier   See *CLSID*.

clause   The portion of an SQL statement beginning with a keyword that names a basic operation to be performed.

client   The device or application that receives data from or manipulates a server device or application. The data may be in the form of a file received from a network file server, an object from an ActiveX component or Automation server, or values from a DDE server assigned to client variables. See *Automation client*.

client tier   A logical entity that represents a networked computer where a Visual Basic application interacts with a client/server database or a browser displays a Web page from a remote data source. See also *middle tier* and *data source tier*.

CLSID   An identification tag that's associated with an Automation object created by a specific server. CLSID values appear in the Registry and must be unique for each ActiveX component or Automation server and each type of object that the server can create. See *Registry*.

clustered index   An index in which the physical record order and index order of a table are the same.

clustering   A server architecture that emulates multiprocessing by interconnecting two or more individual computers to share the application processing load. Microsoft's clustering technology for Windows NT Server 4.0 Enterprise edition provides failover clustering of two computers. A number of third parties offer proprietary clustering hardware and software for Windows NT Server 4.0.

code   Short for *source code*, the text you enter in your program to create an application. Code consists of instructions and their parameters, functions and their arguments, objects and their events, properties and methods, constants, variable declarations and assignments, and expressions and comments.

code template   Self-contained groups of modules and resources that perform a group of standard functions and that may be incorporated within other applications requiring these functions, usually with little or no modification.

coercion   The process of forcing a change from one data type to another, such as **Integer** to **String**.

collection   A group of objects of the same class that are contained within another object. Collections are named as the plural of their object class—for example, the Parameters collection is a group of `Parameter` objects contained in a `Command` object.

COM   An acronym for *Component Object Model*, the name of Microsoft's design strategy to implement ActiveX and OLE 2+. Distributed COM (DCOM) allows networked and cross-platform implementation of ActiveX and Automation. See *DCOM*.

COM+   Microsoft's answer to a future competitive threat from Enterprise JavaBeans. Microsoft's goals for COM+ include absorbing MTS, making COM components easier to deploy and manage, improving system performance, and increasing server scalability from hundreds to thousands of clients. COM+ adds event services, load balancing, asynchronous queuing services with MSMQ, and an in-memory database for the MTS catalog. See *COM*, *DCOM*, *MSMQ*, and *MTS*.

command   A synonym for *instruction*, specifies an action to be taken by the computer.

comment   Explanatory material within source code not designed to be interpreted or compiled into the final application. In VBA, comments are usually preceded by an apostrophe (') but can also be created by preceding them with the Rem keyword.

common dialog   A standardized dialog, provided by Windows 9x and Windows NT, that may be created by a Windows API function call to functions contained in Cmdlg32.dll and its successors. Common dialogs include File Open, File Save, Print and Printer Setup, ColorPalette, Font, and Search and Replace.

Common User Access   See *CUA*.

comparison operators   See *operator*.

compile   To create an executable or object (machine language) file from source (readable) code. In Visual Basic, *compile* means to create pseudocode (tokenized code) or native code from the VBA source code you write in the code-editing window.

Component Object Model   See *COM*.

composite key or index   A key or index based on the values in two or more columns. See also *index* and *key or key field*.

composite menu   A menu that includes menu choices from an Automation server application that uses in-place (in-situ) activation (editing). Creating a composite menu is also called *grafting a menu*. ActiveX documents graft their menus to those of Internet Explorer 3+.

composite moniker   The location within a container document or object where the compound document is located.

compound   In computer programming, a set of instructions or statements that requires more than one keyword or group of related keywords to complete. `Select Case...Case...End Select` is an example of a compound statement in VBA.

compound document   A document that contains OLE objects created by an application other than the application that originally created or is managing the document. OLE 2+ (not ActiveX) creates compound documents.

concatenation   Combining two expressions, usually strings, to form a longer expression. The concatenation operator is **&** in SQL and VBA, although VBA also permits the **+** symbol to be used to concatenate strings.

concurrency   The condition when more than one user has access to a specific set of records or files at the same time. Also used to describe the capability of a database management system to handle simultaneous queries against a single set of tables.

container   An object or application that can create or manipulate compound documents or host ActiveX controls.

context switching   The process of saving an executing thread or process and transferring control to another thread or process. Windows NT 4.0's context switching—one of the major bottlenecks in COM operations—is substantially faster than in Window NT 3.x.

control array   In Visual Basic, the term given to multiple controls on a single form with the same `Name` property. (Access doesn't support control arrays.) Individual controls (elements) of a control array are designated by their index, starting with zero, up to one less than the number of controls with the same name.

conversation   In DDE operations, the collection of Windows messages that are passed between two applications—the client and server—during an interprocess communication.

CORBA   An acronym for *Common Object Request Broker Architecture,* the primary competitor to Microsoft's COM- and DCOM-based technologies. See *COM* and *DCOM.*

correlated subquery   A subquery that can't be independently evaluated. Subqueries depend on an outer query for their result. See also *subquery* and *nested query.*

counter   A special field data type of Access 1.x and 2.0, and Jet 2.0 tables that numbers each new record consecutively; called an *AutoNumber field* in Jet 3+. See *AutoNumber.*

CUA   An abbreviation for *Common User Access,* an element of IBM's Systems Application Architecture (SAA) specification, which establishes a set of standards for user interaction with menus, dialogs, and other user-interactive portions of an application. The CUA was first implemented in Windows and OS/2 and has been an integral part of these GUIs since their inception.

CubeDef   An ADO MD object that provides the metadata for multidimensional data, such as that provided by Microsoft SQL Server OLAP or PivotTable Services. See *ADO MD, Cellset, OLAP,* and *PivotTable Service.*

current database   The database opened in Access by choosing Open Database from the File menu (or the equivalent) that contains the objects of an Access application. There is no equivalent of current database in Visual Basic.

current record   The record in a `Recordset` object whose values you modify. The current record supplies values of the current record's data cells to control objects that are bound to the table's fields. The current record is specified by a record pointer.

current statement   The statement or instruction being executed at a particular instance in time. In debugging or stepwise operation of interpreted development environments such as Visual Basic, the current statement is the next statement that the interpreter will execute when program operation resumes.

custom control   The former name for a control object not native to the application. Visual Basic 3.0 and Visual C++ 3.0 used 16-bit Visual Basic Extension custom controls (VBXs). Visual Basic 4.0 supported 16-bit VBXs and OCXs, plus 32-bit OCXs. Visual Basic 6.0 supports only 32-bit OCXs. See *ActiveX controls* and *OLE Control.*

data access object   The original container for all database objects in Visual Basic 4.0 and 5.0 Professional Editions, often abbreviated *DAO*. The top member of the Jet data access object hierarchy is the `DBEngine` object, which contains `Workspace`, `User`, and `Group` objects in collections. Database objects are contained in `Workspace` objects. ADO 2.0 replaces DAO 3.51 in Visual Basic 6.0, although DAO 3.51 and earlier are supported for backward compatibility. See also *ADO.*

data binding   Connecting two or more data-related objects, usually a data consumer to a data provider, to pass a `Recordset` or other data object between objects. Visual Basic 6.0 has the capability to bind a variety of OLE DB data providers to OLE DB data consumers via ADO. See *data consumer* and *data provider.*

data consumer   An OLE DB term for an object that presents and/or manipulates data. All new Visual Basic 6.0 data-bound controls are OLE DB data consumers.

data definition   The process of describing databases and database objects such as tables, indexes, views, procedures, rules, default values, triggers, and other characteristics. SQL's Data Definition Language (DDL) defines the components of SQL-compliant databases.

data dictionary   The result of the data definition process. Also used to describe a set of database system tables that contain the data definitions of database objects, often called *metadata.*

data element   The value contained in a data cell, also called a *data item* or simply an *element.* A piece of data that describes a single property of a data entity, such as a person's first name, last name, Social Security number, age, sex, or hair color. In this case, the person is the data entity.

data entity   A distinguishable set of objects that is the subject of a data table and usually has at least one unique data element. A data entity might be a person (unique Social Security number), an invoice (unique invoice number), or a vehicle (unique vehicle ID number, because license plates aren't necessarily unique across state lines).

Data Environment Designer   See *DED*.

data integrity   The maintenance of rules that prevent inadvertent or intentional modifications to the content of a database that would be deleterious to its accuracy or reliability. See *domain integrity* and *referential integrity*.

data provider   An OLE DB term for an object that connects to a database or other source of persistent data and supplies data to a data consumer. The SQLOLEDB OLE DB data provider for SQL Server is an example of a native OLE DB provider. MSDASQL, the OLE DB data provider for ODBC, is a nonnative (indirect) data provider.

Data Report Designer   Supplies a subset of the reporting capabilities of Microsoft Access, replacing the Crystal Reports add-in. Creating a new Data Project automatically adds a Data Report instance (`DataReport1`), which you should remove if your project doesn't require printed reports.

data shaping   The process of creating a hierarchical `Recordset` object using SHAPE syntax. See *hierarchical Recordset* and *SHAPE statements*.

data sharing   The feature that allows more than one user to access information stored in a database from the same or a different application.

data source   A database or other form of persistent (file) data storage. *Data source* commonly is used to describe an ODBC data source name (DSN). In Visual Basic 6.0, a data source is a named OLE DB data provider or service provider.

data-source tier   A logical entity that represents a server running a client/server RDBMS, such as SQL Server, also called the *data services*. See also *client tier, middle tier,* and *three tier*.

data type   The description of how the computer is to interpret a particular item of data. Data types are generally divided into two families: strings that usually have text or readable content, and numeric data. The types of numeric data supported vary with the compiler or interpreter used. Most programming languages support a user-defined record or structure data type that can contain multiple data types within it. Field data types, which define the data types of database tables, are distinguished from Access table data types in this book.

Data View window   The Data View window lets you explore the structure of databases and tables to which you have established a DED `Connection` object. The Data View window is the gateway to the Enterprise Edition's Visual Database Tools (VDTs). See *DED* and *VDT*.

database   A set of related data tables and other database objects, such as a data dictionary, that are organized as a group.

database administrator   The individual(s) responsible for the administrative functions of client/server databases. The database administrator (DBA) has privileges (permissions) for all commands that may be executed by the RDBMS and is ordinarily responsible for maintaining system security, including access by users to the RDBMS itself and performing backup and restoration functions.

database device   A file in which databases and related information, such as transaction logs, are stored. Database devices usually have physical names (such as a filename) and a logical name (the parameter of the USE statement). In SQL Server 6.5 and earlier, database devices use the .dat file extension. SQL Server 7.0 dispenses with database devices and stores databases and logs in conventional operating system files.

database object   A component of a database. Database objects include tables, views, indexes, stored procedures, columns, rules, triggers, database diagrams, and defaults.

database owner   The user who originally created a database. The database owner has control over all the objects in the database but may delegate control to other users. Access calls the database owner the *creator*. The database owner is identified by the prefix dbo in SQL Server.

date function   A function that provides date and time information or manipulates date and time values.

DCOM   An acronym for *Distributed Common Object Model*. Allows communication and manipulation of objects over a network connection. Windows NT 4.0 is the first Microsoft operating system to support DCOM (formerly called NetworkOLE). See *COM*.

DDE   An acronym for *dynamic data exchange*. DDE is a method used by Windows and OS/2 to transfer data between different applications. Automation implemented by ActiveX components provides a more robust method for communication between applications or components of applications.

deadlock   A condition that occurs when two users with a lock on one data item attempt to lock the other's data item. Most RDBMSs detect this condition, prevent its occurrence, and advise both users of the potential deadlock situation.

debug   The act of removing errors in the source code for an application.

declaration   A statement that creates a user-defined data type, names a variable, creates a symbolic constant, or registers the prototypes of functions incorporated within dynamic link libraries.

declaration section   A section of a VBA module reserved for statements containing declarations.

declare   In text and not as a keyword, to create a user-defined data holder for a variable or constant. As a VBA keyword, to register a function contained in a dynamic link library in the Declarations section of a module.

DED   An acronym for *Data Environment Designer,* an upgrade to Visual Basic 5.0 Enterprise Edition's User Connection designer for RDO. DED minimizes the amount of code required to establish connections to databases through OLE DB data providers and to return Recordset objects bound to ADO-compliant data-bound controls. See *ADO.*

default   A value assigned or an option chosen when no value is specified by the user or assigned by a program statement.

default database   The logical name of the database assigned to a user when he logs in to the database application.

demand lock   Precludes more shared locks from being set on a data resource. Successive requests for shared locks must wait for the demand lock to be cleared.

dependent   A condition in which master data in a table (such as invoices) is associated with detail data in a subsidiary table (invoice items). In this case, invoice items are dependent on invoices.

design mode   One of two modes of operation of the Visual Basic integrated development environment (IDE), also called *design time.* Design mode lets you create and modify objects and write VBA code. The other mode is run mode, also called *runtime* (when the application is executing).

design-master replica   The member of a Jet replica set that allows changes in the design of objects, such as tables. The design-master replica usually (but not necessarily) is the .mdb file that is updated by Briefcase replicas of the ile. See *Briefcase replication.*

destination document   A term used by OLE 1.0 to refer to a compound document.

detail data   Data in a subsidiary table that depends on data in a master table to have meaning or intrinsic value. If a user deletes the master invoice records, the subsidiary table's detail data for items included in the invoice lose their reference in the database—they become *orphan data.*

detail table   A table that depends on a master table. Detail tables usually have a many-to-one relationship with the master table. See also *detail data.*

device   A computer system component that can send or receive data, such as a keyboard, display, printer, disk drive, or modem. Windows uses device drivers to connect applications to devices. SQL Server 6.5 and earlier uses devices (.dat files) for database storage.

device context　A record (struct) containing a complete definition of all variables required to fully describe a window containing a graphic object. These include the dimensions of the graphic area (viewport), drawing tools in use (pen, brush), fonts, colors, drawing mode, and so on. Windows provides a handle (hDC) for each device context.

DHCP　An acronym for *Dynamic Host Configuration Protocol*, an Internet standard protocol that allows IP addresses to be pooled and assigned as needed to clients. Windows NT 4.0 includes DHCP Manager, a graphical DHCP configuration tool. See *IP* and *IP address*.

DHTML　An acronym for *Dynamic HTML,* a proprietary flavor of HTML that permits client-side scripting to modify the appearance and/or content of a Web page without requiring repeated round trips to the Web server. Microsoft and Netscape implement DHTML differently, so DHTML is suitable only for intranets.

DHTML pages　A new feature of Visual Basic 6.0 that lets you design Dynamic HTML pages with VBA code instead of VBScript or ECMAScript. The code behind DHTML pages executes on the client, not the server.

dialog　A pop-up modal child window, also called a *dialog box*, that requests information from the user. Dialogs include message boxes, input boxes, and user-defined dialogs for applications, such as choosing files to open.

DIB　An acronym for *Device-Independent Bitmap*, a Windows-specific bitmap format designed to display graphic information. DIB files take the extension .dib and use a format similar to .bmp.

difference　In data tables, data elements that are contained in one table but not in another.

directory list　An element of a file-selection dialog that selectively lists the subfolders of the designated folder of a specified logical drive.

disk mirroring　Creating on two or more physical disk drives exact duplicates of a disk volume to make files accessible in case of failure of one drive of the mirror set. See *RAID*.

disk striping　Distributing the data for a single logical disk volume across two or more physical disk drives. Simple disk striping (RAID 0) provides faster I/O operation. Disk striping with parity (RAID 5) provides faster I/O and protection from failure of a physical disk in a stripe set. See *RAID*.

distributed database　A database, usually of the client/server type, that's located on more than one database server, often at widely separated locations. Synchronization of data contained in distributed databases is most commonly accomplished by the two-phase commit or replication methods. See *replication* and *two-phase commit*.

Distributed Transaction Controller   See *DTC*.

DLL   An acronym for *dynamic link library*, a file containing a collection of Windows functions designed to perform a specific class of operations. Most DLLs carry the .dll extension, but some Windows DLLs, such as Gdi32.exe, use the .exe extension. Functions within DLLs are called (*invoked*) by applications, as necessary, to perform the desired operation.

docfile   The file format for creating persistent OLE objects, now called ActiveX documents. Docfiles usually have the extension .ole. Fully OLE 2-compliant applications create docfiles with specific extensions, such as .doc (Word) and .xls (Excel). Access 95 and 97 .mdb files also are OLE 2 docfiles. OLE 2.1 requires that docfiles include file property values derived from the File menu's Properties command. See also *ActiveX documents*.

document   A programming object that contains information originating with the user of the application rather than being created by the application itself. Document data usually is stored in disk files. Access tables, forms, and reports are documents, as are Excel or Lotus 1-2-3 worksheets. In Windows 9x and Windows NT 4.0, a document is a file with an association to an application that can display or manipulate the file.

domain   A group of workstations and servers that share a common security account manager (SAM) database and let a user log on to any resource in the domain with a single user ID and password. In Access, a *domain* is a set of records defined by a table or query. See also *BDC* and *PDC*.

domain aggregate functions   A set of functions, identical to the SQL aggregate functions, that you can apply to a specified domain, rather than to one or more Table objects. Access supports domain aggregate functions; DAO, ADO, and thus Visual Basic, do not. See also *aggregate functions*.

domain integrity   The process of assuring that values added to fields of a table comply with a set of rules for reasonableness and other constraints. For example, domain integrity is violated if you enter a ship date value that's earlier than an order date. In Jet, domain integrity is maintained by field-level and table-level validation rules. See *business rules*.

DTC   An acronym for *Microsoft's Distributed Transaction Coordinator,* a feature of SQL Server required to support distributed transactions and Microsoft Transaction Server. See *distributed database* and *MTS*.

dynamic data exchange   See *DDE*.

dynamic link library   See *DLL*.

dynaset   A set of rows and columns in your computer's memory that represent the values in an attached table, a table with a filter applied, or a query result set. You can update the values of the fields of the underlying table(s) by changing the values of the data cells of an updatable dynaset object. In Jet 2+, Dynaset is a type of `Recordset` object. See also *Recordset*.

ECMAScript   The official name for Netscape's JavaScript, now that standardization of JavaScript is under the aegis of the European Computer Manufacturers Association (ECMA).

embedded object   A source document stored as an OLE object in a compound or container document.

empty   A condition of a VBA variable that has been declared but hasn't been assigned a value. Empty is not the same as the `Null` value, nor is it equal to the empty or zero-length string (`""`).

enabled   The ability of a control object to respond to user actions such as a mouse click, expressed as the `True` or `False` value of the `Enabled` property of the control.

environment   A combination of the computer hardware, operating system, and user interface. A complete statement of an environment follows: a 166MHz Pentium computer with a VGA display and two-button mouse, using the Windows 9*x* operating system.

environmental variable   A DOS term for variables that are declared by `PATH` and `SET` statements, usually made in an AUTOEXEC.BAT file and stored in a reserved memory location by DOS. In Windows 9x and Windows NT, required environmental variables are stored in the Registry, although Windows 9x accepts environmental variables in the AUTOEXEC.BAT file for backward compatibility with 16-bit Windows applications. The environmental variables may be used by applications to adjust their operation for compatibility with user-specific hardware elements or folder structures.

equi-join   A `JOIN` in which the values in the columns being joined are compared for equality and all columns in both tables are displayed. An equi-join causes two identical columns (both joined columns) to appear in the result.

error trapping   A procedure by which errors generated during the execution of an application are rerouted to a designated group of code lines (called an *error handler*) that performs a predefined operation, such as ignoring the error. If errors aren't trapped in VBA, the standard modal message dialog with the text message for the error that occurred appears.

event   The occurrence of an action taken by the user and recognized by one of the objects event properties, such as VBA's `Click` and `DblClick` event handlers for most controls. Events are usually related to mouse movements and keyboard actions; however, events also can be generated by code with the `Timer` control object and during manipulation of database objects.

event driven   The property of an operating system or environment, such as Windows, that implies the existence of an idle loop. When an event occurs, the idle loop is exited and event-handler code, specific to the event, is executed. After the event handler completes its operation, execution returns to the idle loop, awaiting the next event.

exclusive lock   A lock that prevents others from locking data items until the exclusive lock is cleared. Exclusive locks are placed on data items by update operations, such as SQL's INSERT, UPDATE, and DELETE. In Jet and SQL Server 6.5, page locking is used. SQL Server 6.5 provides row locking for INSERT operations, and SQL Server 7.0 provides both INSERT and UPDATE row locking.

executable   Code, usually in the form of a disk file, that can be run by the operating system in use to perform a particular set of functions. Executable files in Windows carry the extension .exe and may obtain assistance from dynamic link libraries (DLLs) in performing their tasks. You compile conventional Visual Basic projects to .exe files.

exponent   The second element of a number expressed in scientific notation, the power of 10 by which the first element, the *mantissa*, is multiplied to obtain the actual number. For +1.23E3, the exponent is 3, so you multiply 1.23 by 1,000 (10 to the third power) to obtain the result 1,230.

expression   A combination of variable names, values, functions, and operators that return a result, usually assigned to a variable name. Result = 1 + 1 is an expression that returns 2 to the variable named Result. DiffVar = LargeVar-SmallVar returns the difference between the two variables to DiffVar. Functions may be used in expressions, and the expression may return the value determined by the function to the same variable as that of the argument. strVar = Mid$(strVar, 2, 3) replaces the value of strVar with three of its characters, starting at the second character.

facts table   The table of a multidimensional database, also called a *measures table*, that stores numeric data (metrics). The facts table is related to dimension tables. See *ADO MD*, *metrics*, *PivotTable Service*, *star schema*, and *snowflake schema*.

failover   A fault-tolerant clustering architecture in which two servers share a common set of fault-tolerant fixed disk drives. In the event of failure of one of the servers, the other transparently assumes all server processing operations. See *clustering* and *fault tolerance*.

FAT   An acronym for *file allocation table*, the disk file system used by MS-DOS, Windows 9x, and (optionally) Windows NT. Windows NT is compatible with the 16-bit FAT system but not the optional 32-bit FAT (FAT32) for Windows 9x that Microsoft announced in mid-1996. See *HPFS* and *NTFS*.

fault tolerance   A computer system's capability to maintain operability, despite failure of a major hardware component such as a power supply, microprocessor, or fixed-disk drive. Fault tolerance requires redundant hardware and modifications to the operating system. Windows NT Server includes fault tolerance for a failed disk drive by disk mirroring (RAID 1) or disk striping with parity (RAID 5). Clustering provides fault tolerance for individual computers. See *clustering* and *RAID*.

fiber   A lightweight thread, introduced in Windows NT 4.0, that makes it easier for developers to optimize scheduling within multithreaded applications. See *thread*.

field   Synonym for a column that contains attribute values. Also, a single item of information in a record or row.

fifth normal form   The rule for relational databases requiring that a table that has been divided into multiple tables must be capable of being reconstructed to its exact original structure by one or more JOIN statements.

file   The logical equivalent of a table. In dBASE, for instance, each table is a single .dbf file.

file moniker   The storage location of the well-formed path to a persistent OLE 2+ object.

first normal form   The rule for relational databases that dictates that tables must be flat. Flat tables can contain only one data value set per row. Members of the data value set, called *data cells*, are contained in one column of the row and must have only one value.

flag   A variable, usually `Boolean` (`True`/`False`), that's used to determine the status of a particular condition within an application. The term *set* is often used to indicate turning a flag from `False` to `True`, and *reset* for the reverse.

flow control   In general usage, conditional expressions that control the execution sequence of instructions or statements in the source code of an application. `If...Then...End If` is a flow-control statement.

focus   The currently selected application, or one of its windows, to which all user-generated input (keyboard and mouse operations) is directed. The object with the focus is said to be the *active object*. The title bar of a window with the focus is colored blue for the default Windows color scheme.

font   A typeface in a single size, usually expressed in points, of a single style or having a common set of attributes. Font often is misused to indicate a typeface family or style.

foreground   In multitasking operations, the application or procedure that's visible onscreen and to which user-generated input is directed. In Windows, the application that has the focus is in the foreground.

foreign key   A column or combination of columns whose value must match a primary key in another table when joined with it. Foreign keys need not be unique for each record or row. See also *primary key*.

form   A Visual Basic `Form` object contains the control objects that appear on its surface and the code associated with the events, methods, and properties applicable to the form and its control objects.

form level   Variables that are declared in the Declarations section of a Visual Basic form. These variables are said to have *form-level scope* and aren't visible to procedures outside the `Form` object in which the variables are declared, unless declared with the **Public** reserved word.

fourth normal form   The rule for relational databases that requires that only related data entities be included in a single table and that tables may not contain data related to more than one data entity when many-to-one relationships exist among the entities.

frame   In Windows, a rectangle, usually with a single-pixel-wide border, that encloses a group of objects, usually of the dialog class. When referring to SMPTE timing with MIDI files, a frame is one image of a motion picture film (1/24 seconds) or one complete occurrence of a television image (approximately 1/30 seconds in NTSC, 1/25 seconds in PAL).

front end   When used with database management systems, an application, a window, or a set of windows by which the user may access and view database records, as well as add to or edit them.

full server   An OLE 2-compliant executable application that can provide embeddable or linked documents for insertion into OLE 2+ container documents. Excel 95, Word 95, Project 4.1, and WordPad are examples of OLE 2.1 full-server applications. Access 97 is not a full server because you can't embed or link an Access .mdb file in an OLE 2.1 container application.

function   A subprogram called from within an expression in which a value is computed and returned to the program that called it through its name. Functions are classified as internal to the application language when their names are keywords. You can create your own user-defined functions in VBA by adding code between **Function** *FunctionName*...**End Function** statements.

global   Pertaining to the program as a whole. Global variables and constants are accessible to, and global variables may be modified by, code at the form, module, and procedure level. VBA uses the reserved word **Public** to create or refer to global variables.

global module A code module (container) in which all global variables and constants are declared and in which the prototypes of any external functions contained in DLLs are declared. Use of a global module in Visual Basic applications is common, but is not required if you don't need to share access to variables, procedures, and functions from multiple forms.

group In reports, one or more records that are collected into a single category, usually for the purpose of totaling. Database security systems use the term *group* to identify a collection of database users with common permissions. See also *permissions*.

HAL An acronym for *hardware abstraction layer*, a Windows NT DLL that links specific computer hardware implementations with the Windows NT kernel. Windows NT 4.0 includes HALs for 80x86, Alpha, MIPS, and PowerPC hardware platforms.

handle An unsigned Long integer assigned by Windows 9x and Windows NT to uniquely identify an instance (occurrence) of a module (application, hModule), task (hTask), window (hWnd), or device context (hDC) of a graphic object. Handles in 32-bit Windows applications, including applications for Windows 9x and Windows NT, are 32-bit unsigned long integers (dw or double words). Also used to identify the sizing elements of control objects in design mode. See also *sizing handle*.

header file A file type used by C and C++ programs to assign data types and names to variables and to declare prototypes of the functions used in the application. C header files usually carry the extension .h.

hierarchical menu A menu with multiple levels, consisting of a main menu bar that leads to one or more levels of submenus from which choices of actions are made. Almost all Windows applications use hierarchical menu structures.

hierarchical Recordset A Recordset that contains detail records in the form of a **Variant** array. Hierarchical Recordsets are more efficient than conventional Recordsets for displaying one-to-many query result sets, because cells of the one side aren't repeated. Only Visual Basic 6.0's new Hierarchical FlexGrid control is capable of displaying hierarchical Recordsets.

host Any computer on a network running an Internet Protocol (IP). See *IP* and *IP address*.

hotlink A DDE (dynamic data exchange) operation in which a change in the source of the DDE data (the server) is immediately reflected in the object of the destination application (the client) that has requested it.

HPFS An acronym for the *High-Performance File System* used by OS/2 and (optionally) Windows NT 3.x. Windows NT 4.0 doesn't support HPFS but can connect via a network to files on HPFS volumes of Windows NT 3.x PCs.

HTML   An abbreviation for *Hypertext Markup Language,* a variant of SGML (Standardized General Markup Language), a page-description language for creating files that can be formatted and displayed by World Wide Web browsers.

HTTP   An abbreviation for *Hypertext Transport Protocol,* the transport protocol used by the World Wide Web and private intranets.

identifier   A synonym for *name* or *symbol,* usually applied to variable and constant names.

idle   In Windows, the condition or state in which Windows and the application have processed all pending messages in the queue from user- or hardware-initiated events and are waiting for the next event to occur. The idle state is entered in VBA when the interpreter reaches the End Sub statement of the outermost nesting level of procedures for a form or control object.

Immediate window   A non-modal dialog in which you may enter VBA expressions and view results without writing code in a code-editing window. You also can direct information to be displayed in the Immediate window with the Debug object. The appearance of the Immediate and Debug windows varies slightly between VBA-enabled applications.

immediate window   Visual Basic's equivalent of the Debug window of other VBA-enabled applications. See *Debug window.*

index   For arrays, the position of the particular element with respect to others, usually beginning with 0 as the first element. When used with database files or tables, *index* refers to a lookup table, usually in the form of a file or component of a file, that relates the value of a field in the indexed file to its record or page number and location in the page (if pages are used).

infinite loop   A Do While...Loop, For...Next, or similar program flow-control structure in which the condition to exit the loop and continue with succeeding statements is never fulfilled. In For...Next loops, infinite looping occurs when the loop counter is set to a value less than that assigned to the To embedded keyword within the structure.

initialize   In programming, setting all variables to their default values and resetting the point of execution to the first executable line of code. Initialization is accomplished automatically in VBA when you start an application.

inner query   Synonym for *subquery.* See *subquery.*

in-place activation   The ability to activate an object (launch another application) and have the container application take on the capabilities of the other application. The primary feature of in-place activation (also called *in-situ activation*) is that the other application's menu choices merge with or replace the container application's menu choices in the active window.

in-process   A term applied to Automation servers, also called *ActiveX DLLs*, that operate within the same process space (memory allocation) of the Automation client. In-process servers commonly are called *InProc servers*. See *out-of-process*.

insertion point   The position of the cursor within a block of text. When the cursor is in a text field, it is called the *caret* in Windows.

instance   The temporary existence of a loaded application or one or more of its windows.

instantiate   The process of creating an instance of an object in memory.

integer   A whole number. In most programming languages, an integer is a data type that occupies two bytes (16 bits). Integers may have signs (as in the VBA Integer data type), taking on values from $-32,768$ to $+32,767$, or be unsigned. In the latter case, integers can represent numbers up to $65,535$.

interface   A connection between two dissimilar COM objects or Automation clients and servers. Another common phrase is *user interface*, meaning the "connection" between the display/keyboard combination and users. Adapter cards constitute the interface between the PC data bus and peripheral devices such as displays, modems, CD-ROMs, and the like. Drivers act as a software interface between Windows and the adapter cards. A *bridge* is an interface between two dissimilar networks. Use of *interface* as a verb is jargon.

intersection   The group of data elements included in both tables that participate in a JOIN operation.

intranet   A private network that uses Internet protocols and common Internet applications (such as Web browsers) to emulate the public Internet. Intranets on LANs and high-speed WANs provide increased privacy and improved performance compared with today's Internet.

invocation path   The route through which an object or routine is invoked. If the routine is deeply nested, the path may be quite circuitous.

invoke   To cause execution of a block of code, particularly a procedure or subprocedure. Also indicates application of a method to an object.

IP   An abbreviation for *Internet Protocol*, the basic network transmission protocol of the Internet.

IP address   The 32-bit hexadecimal address of a host, gateway, or router on an IP network. For convenience, IP addresses are specified as the decimal value of the four address bytes, separated by periods, as in 124.33.15.1. Addresses are classified as types A, B, and C, depending on the subnet mask applied. See *subnet mask*.

IPX/SPX   Abbreviation for *Internetwork Packet Exchange/Sequenced Packet Exchange*, the transport protocol of Novell NetWare, supported by Windows NT's NWLink service.

item   The name given to each of the elements contained in a list or the list component of a combo box.

JDBC   An acronym for *Java Database Connector,* despite Sun Microsystems' insistence that JDBC "doesn't stand for anything." JDBC is Java's purportedly platform-agnostic version of ODBC, which it closely resembles.

Jet   Microsoft's name for the database engine native to Access and Visual Basic. The name *Jet* came from the acronym for *Joint Engine Technology,* the predecessor of Jet 3.5 used by Access and Visual Basic 5.0.

Jet SQL   The dialect of ANSI SQL used by the Data Access Object and by all versions of Microsoft Access. For the most part, Access SQL complies with ANSI SQL-92. Jet SQL offers additional features, such as the capability to include user-defined functions within queries.

join   A basic operation, initiated by the SQL JOIN statement, that links the rows or records of two or more tables by one or more columns in each table.

jump   In programming, execution of code in a sequence that's not the same as the sequence in which the code appears in the source code. In most cases, a jump skips over a number of lines of code, the result of evaluation of a conditional expression. In some cases, a jump causes another subroutine to be executed.

key or key field   A field that identifies a record by its value. Tables are usually indexed on key fields. For a field to be a key field, each data item in the field must possess a unique value. See also *primary key* and *foreign key*.

key value   A value of a key field included in an index.

keyword   A word that has specific meaning to the interpreter or compiler in use and causes predefined events to occur when encountered in source code. Keywords vary from reserved words because you can use keywords as variable, procedure, or function names. Using keywords for this purpose, however, isn't a good programming practice. You can't use a reserved word as a variable or constant name.

label   In VBA programming, a name given to a target line in the source code at which execution results on the prior execution of a GoTo *LabelName* instruction. A label also is a Visual Basic control object that displays, but can't update, text values.

LAN   An acronym for *local area network*, a system comprising multiple computers that are physically interconnected through network adapter cards and cabling. LANs allow one computer to share specified resources, such as disk drives, printers, and modems, with other computers on the LAN.

launch   To start a Windows application.

leaf level   The lowest level of an index. Indexes derive the names of their elements from the objects found on trees, such as trunks, limbs, and leaves.

library   A collection of functions, compiled as a group and accessible to applications by calling the function name and any required arguments. DLLs are one type of library; those used by compilers to provide built-in functions are another type.

library database   An Access database that's automatically attached to Access when you launch it. Access library databases usually have the extension .mda; encrypted libraries use the extension .mde. Attachment of library databases to Access is controlled by Registry entries. Visual Basic doesn't have an equivalent of Access libraries.

linked object   A source document in a compound document that's included by reference to a file containing the object's data, rather than the source document be embedded in the compound document.

linked table   A table that's not stored in the currently open Access database (native or base table), but which you can manipulate as though it were a native table. Linked tables were called *attached tables* in Access 1.x and 2.0 and in Jet 2.0.

livelock   A request for an exclusive lock on a data item that's repeatedly denied because of shared locks imposed by other users.

local   The scope of a variable declared within a procedure, rather than at the form, module, or global level. Local variables are visible (defined) only within the procedure in which they were declared. VBA uses the prefix `Private` to define functions, subprocedures, and variable of local scope.

local area network   See *LAN.*

lock   A restriction of access to a table, portion of a table, or data item imposed to maintain data integrity of a database. Locks may be *shared*, in which case more than one user can access the locked element(s), or *exclusive*, where the user with the exclusive lock prevents other users from creating simultaneous shared or exclusive locks on the element(s). Access uses *page locks* (2K of the .mdb file), which may lock several adjacent records. Some RDBMSs provide *row locks* that lock only a single record. SQL Server 6.5 uses row locking for `INSERT` operations and page locking for `UPDATE` and `DELETE` operations.

logical   A synonym for Boolean, a data type that may have true or false values only. Logical is also used to define a class of operators whose result is only `True` or `False`. VBA includes a `Boolean` data type.

loop   A compound program flow-control structure that causes statements contained between the instructions that designate the beginning and end of the structure to be repeatedly executed until a given condition is satisfied. When the condition is satisfied, program execution continues at the source code line after the loop termination statement.

LRPC   An acronym for *lightweight remote procedure call* used for OLE 2+ and some ActiveX operations between OLE clients and OLE full servers on a single computer. LRPC requires that both applications involved in the procedure call be resident on the same computer. See *remote procedure call (RPC)*.

machine language   Program code in the form of instructions that have meaning to and can be acted on by the computer hardware and operating system. Object files compiled from source code are in machine language, as are executable files that consist of object files linked with library files.

mantissa   The first element of a number expressed in scientific notation that's multiplied by the power of 10 given in the exponent to obtain the actual number. For +1.23E3, the exponent is 3, so you multiply the mantissa, 1.23, by 1,000 (10 to the third power) to obtain the result: 1,230.

MAPI   An acronym for the Windows *Messaging API* created by Microsoft for use with Microsoft Mail, which implements Simple MAPI. Microsoft Exchange Server implements MAPI 1+ (also called *Extended MAPI*).

marshal   To package and send interface method parameters across thread or process boundaries. In database applications, marshaling is most commonly applied to moving Recordsets between a server and a client.

master database   A database that controls user access to other databases, usually in a client/server system.

master table   A table containing data on which detail data in another table depends. Master tables have a primary key that's matched to a foreign key in a detail table and often have a one-to-many relationship with detail tables. Master tables sometimes are called *base tables*.

MDI server   An OLE 2+ server that supports multiple compound documents within a single running instance of the application.

MDX   An acronym for *Multidimensional Expressions,* an SQL-like language for creating and manipulating multidimensional data (cubes) created by Microsoft SQL Server OLAP Services. See *ADO MD, Cellset, CubeDef, OLAP*, and *PivotTable Service*.

memo   A Jet field data type that can store text with a length of up to about 64,000 bytes. (The length of the Text field data type is limited to 255 bytes.)

metadata   Data that describes the structure, organization, and/or location of data. Metadata commonly is called "data about data."

metafile   A type of graphics file, used by Windows and other applications, that stores the objects displayed in the form of mathematical descriptions of lines and surfaces. Windows metafiles, which use the extension .wmf, are a special form of metafiles. Windows 9x and Windows NT 4.0 also support enhanced metafiles (.emf).

method   One characteristic of an object and a classification of keywords in VBA. Methods are the procedures that apply to an Access object. Methods that apply to a class of objects are inherited by other objects of the same class and may be modified to suit the requirements of the object by a characteristic of an object.

metrics   Numeric data, also called *measures*, contained within a facts table of a multidimensional database. See *facts table*.

Microsoft Transaction Server   See *MTS*.

middle tier   A logical entity that connects a data-source tier to a client tier and implements business rules or performs other data-related services. See also *business rule*, *client tier*, *data-source tier*, and *three tier*.

MIME   An acronym for *Multipurpose Internet Mail Extensions,* an Internet standard that lets binary data be published and read on the Internet or intranets. The header of a file containing binary data exposes the MIME type of the data. Recordsets transported by RDS use a special MIME data type called the Advanced Data TableGram protocol (ADTG).

miniserver   An applet with OLE server capabilities and having an .exe file extension that you can't run as a standalone application.

mirroring   See *disk mirroring*.

MISF   An abbreviation for *Microsoft Internet Security Framework*, a set of high-level security services that rely on CryptoAPI 2.0 functions to provide certificate- and password-based authentication. MISF also incorporates secure channel communication by using Secure Sockets Layer (SSL) 2.0 and 3.0, plus Personal Communications Technology (PCT), Secure Electronic Transactions (SET) for credit-card purchases, and the Microsoft Certificate Server for issuing authentication certificates.

mission critical   A clichÈ used in software and hardware advertising to describe the need to use the promoted product if you wants to create a reliable database system.

modal   A dialog that must be closed before users can take further action within the application.

modeless   A window or dialog that users can close or minimize without taking any other action; the opposite of *modal*.

module   A block of code, consisting of one or more procedures, for which the source code is stored in a single location (a `Form` or `Module` object in Access). In a compiled language, a code module is compiled to a single object file.

module level   Variables and constants that are declared in the Declarations section of a module. These variables have module-level scope and are visible (defined) to all procedures contained within the module, unless declared `Public`, in which case the variables are visible to all procedures.

moniker   A handle to the source of a compound document object.

MSMQ   An acronym for *Microsoft Message Queue Server,* a middle-tier component (similar to Microsoft Transaction Server) that uses messaging techniques to permit execution of transactions over unreliable network connections. See *middle tier*.

MTS   An acronym for *Microsoft Transaction Server,* a component-based transaction monitor (TM) and object request broker (ORB) for developing, deploying, and managing the middle tier of component-based applications. MTS 2.0 provides a runtime infrastructure for deploying and managing Visual Basic in-process ActiveX DLLs. MTS 2.0 is part of the Windows NT 4.0 Option Pack, which is included with Visual Basic 6.0. See also *middle tier*, *ORB*, *three tier*, and *TPM*.

Multidimensional Expressions   See *MDX*.

multiprocessing   The ability of a computer with two or more CPUs to allocate tasks (threads) to a specific CPU. Symmetrical multitasking (SMP), implemented in Windows NT, distributes tasks among CPUs by means of a load-sharing methodology. Applications must be multithreaded to take advantage of SMP.

multitasking   The capability of a computer with a single CPU to simulate the processing of more than one task at a time. Multitasking is effective when one or more of the applications spends most of its time in an idle state waiting for a user-initiated event, such as a keystroke or mouse click.

multithreaded   An application that contains more than one thread of execution; a task or set of tasks that executes semi-independently of other task(s). The Jet 3.51 database engine is multithreaded (three threads); VBA is capable of creating multithreaded DLLs. See *thread*.

multiuser   Concurrent use of a single computer by more than one user, usually through the use of remote terminals. UNIX is inherently a multiuser operating system. Jet uses the term *multiuser* to refer to database applications that share a common .mdb file on a network file server.

named pipes A method of interprocess communication, originally developed for OS/2, that provides a secure channel for network communication.

natural join An SQL JOIN operation in which the values of the columns engaged in the join are compared, with all columns of each table in the join that don't duplicate other columns being included in the result. Same as an equi-join except that the joined columns aren't duplicated in the result. See *equi-join*.

NBF An abbreviation for *NetBEUI Frame*, the transport packet structure used by NetBEUI.

nested An expression applied to procedures that call other procedures within an application. The called procedures are said to be *nested* within the calling procedure. When many calls to subprocedures and sub-subprocedures are made, the last one in the sequence is said to be *deeply nested.*

nested object An OLE 2+ compound document incorporated in another OLE 2+ compound document. You can nest OLE 2+ documents as deeply as you like. OLE 1.0 doesn't supported nested objects.

nested query AN SQL SELECT statement that contains subqueries. See *subquery*.

NetBEUI An abbreviation for *NetBIOS Extended User Interface*, the transport protocol of Microsoft Networking. NetBEUI isn't a routable network, so its popularity is declining compared with TCP/IP.

NetBIOS An abbreviation for *Network Basic Input/Output System*, the original network API for MS-DOS and the foundation for NetBEUI.

newline pair A combination of a carriage return, the Enter key (CR or Chr(13)), and line feed (LF or Chr(10)) used to terminate a line of text onscreen or within a text file. Other characters or combinations may be substituted for the CR/LF pair to indicate the type of newline character (soft, hard, deletable, and so on). The VBA newline constant is VbCrLf.

NFS An acronym for *Network File Server*, a file format and set of drivers, created by Sun Microsystems Incorporated, that allows DOS/Windows and UNIX applications to share a single server disk drive running under UNIX.

nonclustered index An index that stores key values and pointers to data based on these values. In this case, the leaf level points to data pages rather than to the data itself, as is the case for a clustered index. Equivalent to SET INDEX TO *field_name* in xBase.

normal forms A set of five rules, the first three originally defined by Dr. E. F. Cobb, that are used to design relational databases. Five normal forms are generally accepted in the creation of relational databases. See *first normal form, second normal form, third normal form, fourth normal form*, and *fifth normal form.*

normalization   Creation of a database according to the five generally accepted rules of normal forms. See also *normal forms*.

not-equal join   A JOIN statement that specifies that the columns engaged in the join don't equal one another. In Access, you must specify a not-equal join by using the SQL WHERE `field1 <> field2` clause.

NT   An acronym for *New Technology* used by Windows NT.

NTFS   An acronym for *New Technology File System*, Windows NT's replacement for the DOS file allocation table (FAT) and OS/2's high-performance file system (HPFS). NTFS offers many advantages over other file systems, including improved security and the ability to reconstruct files in the event of hardware failures. Windows 3.1+ and Windows 9x can access files stored on NTFS volumes via a network connection but can't open NTFS files directly.

null   A variable of no value or of unknown value. The default values—**0** for numeric variables and an empty string (**""**) for string variables—aren't the same as the **Null** value. The NULL value in SQL statements specifies a data cell with no value assigned to the cell.

object   In programming, elements that combine data (properties) and behavior (methods) in a single container of code called an *object*. Objects inherit their properties and methods from the classes above them in the hierarchy and can modify the properties and methods to suit their own purposes. The code container may be part of the language itself, or you can define your own objects in source code.

object code   Code in machine-readable form that your computer's CPU and operating system can execute. Object code is usually linked with libraries to create an executable file.

object library   A file with the extension .olb that contains information on the objects, properties, and methods exposed by an .exe or .dll file of the same filename that supports Automation. See also *type library*.

object permissions   Permissions granted by the database administrator for others to view and modify the values of database objects, including data in tables.

object request broker   See *ORB*.

ODBC   An acronym for the Microsoft *Open Database Connectivity API*, a set of functions that provide access to client/server RDBMSs, desktop database files, text files, and Excel worksheet files through ODBC drivers. ODBC most commonly is used to connect to client/server databases, such as Microsoft SQL Server, Sybase, Informix, and Oracle. Microsoft intends for OLE DB to replace ODBC, and it's unlikely that Microsoft will provide significant enhancements for ODBC.

ODBCDirect   A feature of the Jet 3.5+ database engine that lets you use ODBC to access client/server databases without needing to load all of Jet 3.5. ODBCDirect conserves client resources if you need to connect only to SQL Server or another client/server RDBMS. ADO 2.0 provides features equivalent to ODBCDirect.

ODE   An acronym for *Office 97 Developer Edition,* the replacement for the Access 2.0 and 95 Access Developer's Toolkit (ADT). The ODE includes a royalty-free license to distribute Msaccess.exe for runtime use, the runtime support DLL for VBA 5.0 (Vbrun500.dll), the run-time version of Microsoft Graph 8.0 (Graph8.exe and Graph8rt.srg), additional ActiveX controls, and other distributable components of Access 97. The ODE also includes the Setup Wizard you use to create images of the distribution disks for your application. Other developer-oriented features of the ODE are three printed manuals, the Replication Manager, and the Microsoft Help Compiler.

offset   The number of bytes from a reference point, usually the beginning of a file, to the particular byte of interest. The first byte in a file, when an offset is used to specify location, is always 0.

OLAP   An acronym for *online analytical processing,* a technology that operates on nonrelational, multidimensional databases (data cubes). Microsoft SQL Server OLAP Services, a component of SQL Server 7.0, enables the creation, manipulation, and distribution of multidimensional data. See *ADO MD*, *PivotTable Service*, and *star schema.*

OLE Automation   An extension of OLE 2+ that provides the framework (interfaces) for applications and libraries to expose programmable objects that can be manipulated by client applications. Applications that expose programmable objects are called Automation servers or ActiveX components. See *automation* and *programmable object.*

OLE Control   An in-process OLE Automation server with the extension .ocx that exposes a single object, plus the properties, methods, and events of the object. OLE Controls have been superceded by 32-bit ActiveX controls. *See ActiveX controls.*

OLE DB   A new Microsoft framework for providing a uniform interface to data from various sources, including text files and mainframe databases. OLE DB is intended to replace ODBC as a means of database access but includes an ODBC provider that takes the place of the ODBC driver manager. ADO is an Automation wrapper for OLE DB. See also *ADO* and *ODBC.*

OLE DLL   A synonym for an in-process OLE Automation server implemented as a Windows DLL. See *in-process.*

online analytical processing   See *OLAP.*

operand   One variable or constant on which an operator acts. In 1 + 2 = 3, 1 and 2 are operands, + and = are the operators. See *operator.*

operator   A keyword or reserved symbol that, in its unary form, acts on a single variable, or otherwise acts on two variables, to give a result. Operators may be of the conventional mathematics type such as + (add), – (subtract), / (divide), and * (multiply), as well as logical, such as **And** or **Not**. The unary minus (–), when applied to a single variable in a statement such as intVar = -intVar, inverts the sign of intVar from – to + or from + to –.

optimistic locking   A method of locking a record or page of a table that makes the assumption that the probability of other users locking the same record or page is low. With optimistic locking, the record or page is locked only when the data is updated, not during the editing process (LockType property set to adLockOptimistic).

ORB   An acronym for *object request broker,* a server-based application that provides a means for client applications to locate and instantiate middle-tier objects in three-tier applications. See *middle tier*, *MTS*, and *three tier.*

outer join   An SQL JOIN operation in which all rows of the joined tables are returned, whether or not a match is made between columns. SQL database managers that don't support the OUTER JOIN reserved words use the *= (LEFT JOIN) operator to specify that all the rows in the preceding table return, and =* (RIGHT JOIN) to return all the rows in the succeeding table.

outer query   A synonym for the primary query in a statement that includes a subquery. See also *subquery.*

out-of-process   An (OLE) Automation server in the form of an executable (.exe) file that operates in its own process space (memory allocation) and uses LRPCs (lightweight remote procedure calls) to communicate with the Automation client. The term *OutOfProc* often is used as shorthand for *out-of-process.*

page   In tables of client/server RDBMSs, such as Microsoft SQL Server and Access databases, a 2K block that contains records of tables. Client/server and Access databases lock pages, whereas DOS desktop databases usually lock individual records. Page-locking is required by most RDBMSs when variable-length records are used in tables.

parameter   The equivalent of an argument, but associated with the procedure that receives the value of an argument from the calling function. The terms *parameter* and *argument*, however, are often used interchangeably. An ADO Parameter object provides or returns a value to or from a query or a stored procedure.

parse   The process of determining whether a particular expression is contained within another expression. Parsing breaks program statements into keywords, operators, operands, arguments, and parameters for subsequent processing of each by the computer. Parsing string variables involves searching for the occurrence of a particular character or set of characters in the string and then taking a specified set of actions when found or not found.

PDC   An acronym for *primary domain controller*, the Windows NT server in a domain that's responsible for maintaining user and group accounts for a domain. Primary and backup domain controllers authenticate domain users during the logon process. See *BDC*.

permissions   Authority given by the system administrator, database administrator, or database owner to perform operations on a network or on data objects in a database.

persistent (graphics)   A Windows graphic image that survives movement, resizing, or over-writing of the window in which it appears. Persistent images are stored in global memory blocks and aren't released until the window containing them is destroyed.

persistent (objects)   An object that's stored in the form of a file or an element of a file, rather than only in memory. Jet `Table` and `QueryDef` objects are persistent because they're stored in .mdb files. `Recordset` objects, on the other hand, usually are stored in memory. Such objects are called *temporal* or *impersistent objects*. ADO 2.0 lets you persist `Recordset` objects as files.

pessimistic locking   A method of locking a record or page of a table that makes the assumption that the probability of other users locking the same record or page is high. With pessimistic locking, the record or page is locked during the editing and updating process (`LockType` property set to `adLockPessimistic`).

PivotTable Service   A Microsoft-trademarked desktop OLAP implementation that used ADO MD to operate on persistent (file based) multidimensional data cubes created by a subset of Microsoft SQL Server OLAP Services. See *ADO MD*, *Cellset*, *CubeDef*, and *OLAP*.

point   In typography, the unit of measurement of the vertical dimension of a font, about 1/72 of an inch. The point is also a unit of measurement in Windows, where it represents exactly 1/72 of a logical inch, or 20 twips. Unless otherwise specified, all distance measurements in VBA are in twips.

pointer   A data type that comprises a number representing a memory location. *Near pointers* are constrained to the 64K default local data segment. *Far pointers* can access any location in the computer's memory. Pointers are used extensively in C-language applications to access elements of arrays, strings, structures, and the like. VBA has only one pointer data type—to a zero-terminated string when the **ByVal...As String** keywords are applied to a VBA string passed to an external function contained in a dynamic link library.

poke   In DDE terminology, the transmission of an unrequested data item to a DDE server by the DDE client. In BASIC language terminology, placing a byte of data in a specific memory location. VBA doesn't support the BASIC POKE keyword and uses the DDEPoke method for DDE operations.

PPP   An acronym for *Point-to-Point Protocol*, the most common Internet protocol for connection to TCP/IP networks via conventional and ISDN modems.

PPTP   An acronym for *Point-to-Point Tunneling Protocol*, a Microsoft-sponsored protocol included with Windows NT 4.0 that uses encryption to assure privacy of communication over the Internet. See *VPN*.

precedence   The sequence of execution of operators in statements that contain more than one operator.

primary key   The column or columns whose individual or combined values (in the case of a composite primary key) uniquely identify a row in a table.

primary verb   The default verb for activating an OLE 2+ object. Edit is the default verb for most OLE objects, except multimedia objects, whose default verb is usually Play.

print zone   The area of a sheet of paper on which a printer can create an image. For most laser printers and standard dot-matrix printers, this area is 8 inches wide. The vertical dimension is unlimited for dot-matrix printers and usually is 13.5 inches for a laser printer with legal-size paper capabilities.

printer object   A VBA object representing the printer chosen as the default by the Control Panel Printers tool's Set Default choice.

procedure   A self-contained collection of source code statements, executable as an entity. All VBA procedures begin with the reserved word **Sub** or **Function** (which may be preceded by the **Public**, **Private**, or **Static** reserved words) and terminate with **End Sub** or **End Function**.

program   All code required to create an application, consisting basically of declarations, statements, and—in Windows—resource definition and help files.

programmable object   An object exposed by an Automation server with a set of properties and methods applicable to the object. The application programming language of an Automation client application can manipulate the exposed object.

projection   A projection identifies the desired subset of the columns contained in a table. You create a projection with a query that defines the fields of the table you want to display but without criteria that limit the records that are displayed.

property   One of two principal characteristics of objects (the other is methods). Properties define the manifestation of the object—for example, its appearance. Properties may be defined for an object or for the class of objects to which the particular object belongs, in which case they are said to be *inherited*.

protocol   A description of the method by which networked computers communicate. Windows NT and Windows 9x allow the simultaneous use of multiple network protocols, including TCP/IP, NetBEUI, and IPX/SPX.

protocol stack   Network protocol software that implements a specific protocol, such as TCP/IP.

proxy   An object that supplies parameter marshaling and communication methods required by a client to instantiate an Automation component running in another execution environment, such as on a server. The proxy is located on the client PC and communicates with a corresponding stub on the server. See *three tier*.

pseudo-object   Objects contained within other OLE 2+ objects, such as the cells of a spreadsheet object.

qualification   A search condition that data values must meet to be included in the result of the search.

qualified   To precede the name of a database object with the name of the database and the object's owner, or to precede the name of a file with its drive designator and the path to the directory in which the file is stored. The terms *well-qualified path* and *well-formed path* to a file appear often in documentation.

query   A request to retrieve data from a database with the SQL SELECT instruction or to manipulate data in the database, called an *action query* by Access.

QueryDef   A persistent Jet object that stores the Jet SQL statements that define a query. QueryDef objects are optimized, when applicable, by the Jet database engine's query optimizer and stored in a special optimized format.

RAID   An acronym for *redundant array of inexpensive disks*, a method of connecting multiple disk drives to a single controller card to achieve faster data throughput, data storage redundancy for fault tolerance, or both. See *disk mirroring*, *disk striping*, and *fault tolerance*.

RDBMS   An abbreviation for *relational database management system*. An RDBMS is an application that can create, organize, and edit databases; display data through user-selected views; and print formatted reports. Most RDBMSs include at least a macro or macro language, and most provide a system programming language. Access, dBASE, Paradox, and FoxPro are desktop RDBMSs.

RDS   An acronym for *Remote Data Service,* a purportedly lightweight version of ADO 2.0 that provides transport for Recordset objects via DCOM or HTTP over intranets.

record   A synonym for a user-defined data type, called a *structure* in C and C++. Also used in database applications to define a single element of a relational database file that contains each field defined for the file. Records don't need to contain data to exist, but Jet doesn't append a record without a value in at least one field. A record is the logical equivalent of the row of a table.

Recordset   A temporary local image of a table or a query result set stored in the PC's memory or virtual memory. Recordset objects are the primary means for manipulating data with VBA.

redirector   Software that intercepts requests for remotely provided services, such as files in server shares, and sends the request to the appropriate computer on the network.

reference   In VBA, the incorporation of pointers to specific sets of programmable objects exposed by Automation servers and manipulated by VBA code in the Automation client. You create a VBA reference to a set of objects exposed by an Automation component in the References dialog that's accessible by choosing References from the Tools menu when a module is the active Access object. After you declare a reference to the set of objects, the VBA interpreter checks the syntax of your code against the syntax specified for the referenced object. You also can use predefined intrinsic constants for the referenced objects in your VBA code.

referential integrity   Rules governing the relationships between primary keys and foreign keys of tables within a relational database that determine data consistency. Referential integrity requires that the values of every foreign key in every table be matched by the value of a primary key in another table. Access 2+ includes features for maintaining referential integrity, such as cascading updates and cascading deletions.

refresh   To redisplay records in Access's datasheet views or in a form or report so as to reflect changes others in a multiuser environment have made to the records.

Registry   A database that contains information required for the operation of Windows 9x and Windows NT, plus applications installed under Windows 9x and Windows NT. The Windows Registry takes the place of Windows 3.1+'s REG.DAT, WIN.INI, and SYSTEM.INI files, plus *PROFILE*.INI files installed by Windows 3.1 applications. The Registry also includes user information, such as user IDs, encrypted passwords, and permissions. Windows 9x and Windows NT include Regedit.exe for editing the Registry. ActiveX Components and OLE 2+ servers add entries to the Registry to specify the location of their .exe files. Automation servers add Registry entries for each object they expose. The Windows NT and Windows 9x Registries vary in structure and thus are incompatible.

relation   Synonym for a table or a data table in an RDBMS.

relational database   See *RDBMS*.

relational operators   Operators such as >, <, <>, and = that compare the values of two operands and return `True` or `False` depending on the values compared. They are sometimes called *comparative operators*.

Remote Automation Object   An out-of-process Automation server, usually called an *RAO*, that resides on a server and is accessible to RAO-compliant applications that connect to the server with DCOM. Most RAOs now are hosted within Microsoft Transaction Server. See also *DCOM and MTS*.

Remote Data Object (RDO)   A substitute for the Jet 3.5+ Data Access Object that provides a more direct connection to the ODBC API. Jet 3.5 offers ODBCDirect as an alternative to RDO. ADO 2.0 provides features equivalent to Visual Basic 5.0 Enterprise Edition's RDO 2.0. See also *ODBCDirect*.

Remote Data Service   See *RDS*.

remote procedure call (RPC)   An interprocess communication method that allows an application to run specific parts of the application on more than one computer in a distributed computing environment. Visual Basic 6.0 can create Remote Automation Objects (RAOs) that use RPCs for communication over a network.

replication   The process of duplicating database objects (usually tables) in more than one location, including a method of periodically rationalizing (synchronizing) updates to the objects. Unlike Jet 3.0, version 3.5 supports partial replication. Database replication is an alternative to the two-phase commit process. Microsoft SQL Server 6.5+ supports replication of databases across multiple Windows NT servers. See *Briefcase replication* and *two-phase commit*.

reserved word   A word that comprises the vocabulary of a programming language and that's reserved for specific use by the programming language. You can't assign a reserved word as the name of a constant, variable, function, or subprocedure. Although the terms *reserved word* and *keyword* often are used interchangeably, they don't describe an identical set of words. VBA reserved words are set in **bold monospace** type in this book. See *keyword*.

restriction   A query statement that defines a subset of the rows of a table based on the value of one or more of its columns.

RGB   A method of specifying colors by using numbers to specify the individual intensities of its red, green, and blue components, the colors created by the three "guns" of the cathode-ray tube (CRT) of a color display.

rollback   In transaction processing, the cancellation of a proposed transaction that modifies one or more tables and undoes changes, if any, made by the transaction before a COMMIT or COMMIT TRANSACTION SQL statement.

routine   A synonym for *procedure*.

row   A set of related columns that describes a specific data entity. A synonym for *record*.

row aggregation functions   See *aggregate functions*.

rowset   An OLE DB term for a set of rows returned by a fetch with a block cursor. ADO creates Recordsets from rowsets.

rule   A specification that determines the data type and data value that can be entered in a column of a table. Rules are classified as validation rules and business rules. See *business rules*.

run mode   The mode when Visual Basic is executing your project using its built-in VBA interpreter. Run mode is called *runtime* by Microsoft; however, the term *runtime* normally is used in conjunction with errors that occur when running the executable version of an application.

running state   The state of an OLE 2+ object in which the application that created the object is launched and has control of the object.

SAM   An acronym for *Security Accounts Manager*, a Windows NT subsystem that maintains a database of user account names and passwords for authentication.

scalable   The property of a multiprocessing computer that defines the extent to which the addition of more processors increases aggregate computing capability. Windows NT 4.0 Server is generally considered to be scalable to four Intel processors. Microsoft claims that Windows NT 4.0 Enterprise Edition is scalable to substantially more processors.

scope   In programming, the extent of visibility (definition) of a variable. VBA has global (**Public**, visible to all objects and procedures in the application), form/report (visible to all objects and procedures within a single form or report), module (visible to all procedures in a single module file), and local (**Private**, visible only within the procedure in which declared) scope. The scope of a variable depends on where it's declared. See also *form level*, *global*, *local*, and *module level*.

screen object   A VBA object and object class defined as the entire usable area of the video display unit. All visible form and control objects are members of subclasses of the **Screen** object.

second normal form   The rule for relational databases requiring that columns that aren't key fields each be related to the key field—that is, a row may not contain values in data cells that don't pertain to the value of the key field. In an invoice item table, for instance, the columns of each row must pertain solely to the value of the invoice number key field.

seek   To locate a specific byte, record, or chunk within a disk file. The `Seek` method of Access VBA can be used only with DAO `Recordset` objects of the `Table` type and requires that the table be indexed. ADO doesn't have a `Seek` method.

select list   The list of column names, separated by commas, that specify the columns to be included in the result of a `SELECT` statement.

selection   In Windows, one or more objects that have been chosen by clicking the object or otherwise assigning the focus to the object. When used with text, it means the highlighted text that appears in a text box or window. See also *restriction*.

self-join   An SQL `JOIN` operation used to compare values within the columns of one table. Self-joins join a table with itself, requiring that the table be assigned two different names, one of which must be an alias.

separator   A reserved symbol used to distinguish one item from another, as exemplified by the use of the exclamation point (`!`, bang character) in Access to separate the name of an object class from a specific object of the class, and an object contained within a specified object. The period separator (`.`, dot) separates the names of objects and their methods or properties.

sequential access file   A file in which one record follows another in the sequence applicable to the application. Text files, for the most part, are sequential.

service provider   An OLE DB term for an object that is both a data consumer and a data provider to another data consumer. OLE DB service providers include query engines and other intermediaries, such as the Remote Provider for enabling ADO 2.0 data sources to use Remote Data Service. See *RDS*.

session   In DAO, an instance of the Jet 3.5+ database engine for a single user represented by the `Workspace` object. You can establish multiple sessions that become members of the `Workspaces` collection. With ADO, a `Connection` object represents a session. In RDBMS terminology, the period between the time that a user opens a connection to a database and the time that the connection to the database is closed.

SHAPE statements   An SQL-like language for defining parent-child relationships within hierarchical `Recordsets`. See *hierarchical Recordsets*.

shared application memory   Memory that's allocated between processes involved in an LRPC call. See also *LRPC*.

shared lock   A lock created by read-only operations that doesn't allow the user who creates the shared lock to modify the data. Other users can place shared locks on data so they can read it, but none can apply an exclusive lock on the data while any shared locks are in effect.

shortcut key   A Ctrl+*key* combination that provides access to a menu choice, macro, or other function of the application in lieu of selection with the mouse. See *accelerator key*.

SID   An acronym for *security ID*, a numeric value that identifies a logged-on user who has been authenticated by Windows NT or a user group.

single-stepping   A debugging process by which the source code is executed one line at a time to allow you to inspect the value of variables, find infinite loops, or remove other types of bugs.

sizing handles   The small black rectangles on the perimeter of control objects that appear on the surface of the form or report in design mode when the object is selected. You drag the handles of the rectangles to shrink or enlarge the size of control objects.

SMB   An acronym for *Server Message Block*, a networking protocol used by NetBEUI to implement Microsoft Networking.

snowflake schema   An alternative to the star schema for multidimensional data. Snowflake schema store dimension definitions in a set of hierarchical tables, rather than in the star schema's individual tables. See *ADO MD*, *facts table*, *PivotTable Service*, and *star schema*.

source code   The readable form of code that you create in a high-level language. Source code is converted to machine-language object code by a compiler or interpreter.

source document   A term used by OLE 1.0 to refer to a compound object in a container document.

SQL   An acronym, pronounced as *sequel* or *seekel*, for *Structured Query Language*, a language developed by IBM Corporation for processing data contained in mainframe computer databases. (*Sequel* is the name of a language, similar to SQL, developed by IBM but no longer in use.) SQL has now been institutionalized by the creation of an ANSI standard for the language.

SQL aggregate functions   See *aggregate functions*.

star schema   The most common schema (database design) for multidimensional data. Multiple base tables storing dimension definitions form the points of a star. The body of the star is the dependent facts table. See *ADO MD*, *facts table*, *PivotTable Service*, and *snowflake schema*.

statement   A syntactically acceptable (to the interpreter or compiler of the chosen language) combination of instructions or keywords and symbols, constants, and variables that must appear on a single line or use the line-continuation pair (a space followed by an underscore) to use multiple lines.

static   When referring to a variable, a variable that retains its last value until another is assigned, even though the procedure in which it is defined has completed execution. All global variables are static. Variables declared as **Static** are similar to global variables, but their visibility is limited to their declared scope. The term is also used to distinguish between statically linked (conventional) executable files and those that use DLLs.

stored procedure   A set of SQL statements (and with those RDBMSs that support them, flow-control statements) that are stored under a procedure name so that the statements can be executed as a group by the database server. Some RDBMSs, such as Microsoft SQL Server, precompile stored procedures so that they execute more rapidly.

string   A data type used to contain textual material, such as alphabetic characters and punctuation symbols. Numbers can be included in or constitute the value of string variables but can't be manipulated by mathematical operators.

stripe set   See *disk striping* and *fault tolerance.*

structure   Two or more keywords used together to create an instruction, which is usually conditional in nature. In C and C++ programming, a user-defined data type. See also *compound.*

Structured Query Language   See *SQL.*

stub   Shortened form of *proxy stub.* See *proxy.*

stub   A procedure or user-defined function that, in VBA, consists only of **Sub** *SubName* . . . **End Sub** or **Function** *FnName* . . . **End Function** lines with no intervening code. Access automatically creates stubs for subprocedures for event-handling code stored in Form and Report objects. Stubs block out the procedures required by the application that can be called by the main program. The intervening code statements are filled in during the programming process.

subform   A form contained within another form. Access supports subforms, but Visual Basic doesn't.

subnet mask   A local bit mask (set of flags) that specifies which bits of the IP address specify a particular IP network or a host within a subnetwork. An IP address of 128.66.12.1 with a subnet mask of 255.255.255.0 specifies host 1 on subnet 128.66.12.0. The subnet mask determines the maximum number of hosts on a subnetwork.

subprocedure A procedure called by a procedure other than the main procedure (WinMain in Windows). In Access, all procedures except functions are subprocedures because Msaccess.exe contains the WinMain function.

subquery An SQL SELECT statement that's included (nested) within another SELECT, INSERT, UPDATE, or DELETE statement, or nested within another subquery.

subreport A report contained within another report.

syntax The rules governing the expression of a language. As with English, Spanish, Esperanto, or Swahili, each programming language has its own syntax. Some languages allow much more latitude (irregular forms) in their syntax. VBA has a relatively rigid syntax, whereas C provides more flexibility at the expense of complexity.

system administrator The individual(s) responsible for the administrative functions for all applications on a LAN or users of a UNIX cluster or network, usually including supervision of all databases on servers attached to the LAN. If the system administrator's (SA) responsibility is limited to databases, the term *database administrator* (DBA) is ordinarily assigned.

system colors The 20 standard colors used by Windows for elements of its predefined objects such as backgrounds, scroll bars, borders, and title bars. You can change the system colors from the defaults through Control Panel's Color and Desktop tools.

system databases Databases that control access to databases on a server or across a LAN. Microsoft SQL Server 6.5 has three system databases: the master database, which controls user databases; tempdb, which holds temporary tables; and model, which is used as the skeleton to create new user databases. SQL Server 7.0 doesn't have a model database. Any database that's not a user database is a system database.

system function Functions that return data about the database rather than from the content of the database.

system object An object defined by Visual Basic rather than by the user. Examples of system objects are the Screen and Debug objects.

system table A data dictionary table that maintains information on users of the database manager and each database under the control by the system. Jet system tables carry the prefix MSys.

T-1 The most common moderate-speed telecommunication connection between LANs to create a WAN. Dedicated T-1 lines provide 1.544Mbps of bandwidth. T-1 lines also are the most common method of connecting servers to the Internet.

tab order The order in which the focus is assigned to multiple control objects within a form or dialog with successive pressing of the Tab key.

table   A database object consisting of a group of rows (records) divided into columns (fields) that contain data or Null values. A table is treated as a database device or object.

TCP/IP   An acronym for *Transport Control Protocol/Internet Protocol*, the networking protocol of the Internet, UNIX networks, and the preferred protocol for Windows NT networks. TCP/IP is a routable network that supports subnetworks. See *IP*.

TDI   An acronym for *Transport Driver Interface*, used by Windows NT to implement multiple network protocols by using various network interface cards.

text box   A Windows object designed to receive printable characters typed from the keyboard. Access provides two basic types: single line and multiline. Pressing Enter terminates entries in single-line text boxes. Multiline text boxes accept more than one line of text, either by a self-contained word-wrap feature (if a horizontal scroll bar is not present) or by pressing Ctrl+Enter.

text file   A disk file containing characters with values ordinarily ranging from `Chr(1)` through `Chr(127)` in which lines of text are separated from one another with newline pairs (`Chr(13)` & `Chr(10)`).

theta join   AN SQL `JOIN` operation that uses comparison or relational operators in the `JOIN` statement. See also *operator*.

third normal form   The rule for relational databases that imposes the requirement that a column that's not a key column can't depend on another column that's not a key column. The third normal form is generally considered the most important because it's the first in the series that isn't intuitive.

thread   A part of a process, such as an executing application, that can run as an object or an entity.

three tier   The architecture of a database application, usually involving a client/server RDBSM, where the front-end application is separated from the back-end RDBMS by a middle-tier application. In Visual Basic applications, the middle tier usually is implemented as an Automation component, which implements the database connection, enforces business rules, and handles transfer of data to and from databases of the RDBMS. See *business rules* and *process server*.

timestamp   The date and time data attributes applied to a disk file when created or edited. SQL Server and the ODBC API support the timestamp field, which resolves concurrency issues when updating tables.

timer   A native Visual Basic control object that's invisible in run mode and used to trigger a `Timer` event at preselected intervals.

title bar   The heading area of a window, usually blue, in which the title of the window appears, usually in bright white (reverse).

TM   An acronym for *transaction monitor,* an application that manages database transactions, usually between more than one database, to assure data consistency during INSERT and UPDATE operations. See also *MTS.*

toggle   A property of an object, such as a check box, that alternates its state when repeatedly clicked or activated by a shortcut key combination.

topic   In DDE conversations, the name of the file or other identifying title of a collection of data. When used with help files, the name of the subject matter of a single help screen display.

transaction   A group of processing steps that are treated as a single activity to perform a desired result. A transaction might entail all the steps necessary to modify the values in or add records to each table involved when a new invoice is created. RDBMSs that can process transactions usually include the capability to cancel the transaction by a rollback instruction or to cause it to become a permanent part of the tables with the COMMIT or COMMIT TRANSACTION statement. See *rollback.*

Transaction Monitor   A synonym for transaction manager. See *TM.*

TRANSACT-SQL   A superset of ANSI SQL used by Microsoft SQL Server. TRANSACT-SQL includes flow-control instructions and the capability to define and use stored procedures that include conditional execution and looping.

trigger   A stored procedure that occurs when a user executes an instruction that may affect the referential integrity of a database. Triggers usually occur before the execution of INSERT, DELETE, or UPDATE statements so that the effect of the statement on referential integrity can be examined by a stored procedure before execution. See also *stored procedure.*

trust   In Windows NT domain terminology, a relationship between domain controllers in which users who are members of the trusted domain can access services on another trusting domain without the need to log on to the trusting domain.

twip   The smallest unit of measurement in Windows and the default unit of measurement of VBA. The twip is 1/20 of a point, or 1/1440 of a logical inch.

two-phase commit   A process applicable to updates to multiple (distributed) databases that prevents a transaction from completing until all the distributed databases acknowledge that the transaction can be completed. The replication process has supplanted two-phase commit in most of today's distributed client/server RDBMSs. See *replication.*

type   See *data type.*

type library   A file with the extension .tlb that provides information about the types of objects exposed by an ActiveX component or Automation server. See *object library*.

unary   See *operator*.

UNC   An acronym for *Uniform Naming Convention*, the method of identifying the location of files on a remote server. UNC names begin with \\. Windows 9x and Windows NT support UNC; 32-bit Windows applications must support UNC to qualify for application of Microsoft's "Designed for Windows 9x" logo. All Microsoft Office 95 applications support UNC.

Unicode   A replacement for the 7- or 8-bit ASCII and ANSI representations of characters with a 16-bit model that allows a wider variety of characters to be used. Windows 9x and Windows NT support Unicode. Access 95 automatically converts Unicode to ANSI and vice versa.

uniform data transfer (UDT)   The interprocess communication (IPC) method used by OLE 2+. OLE 1.0 uses DDE for IPC.

unique index   An index in which no two key fields or combinations of key fields on which the index is created may have the same value.

Universal Data Access   Microsoft's all-encompassing database strategy based on COM, DCOM, OLE DB, ADO, MTS, Internet Information Server, ASP, and other proprietary Windows technologies. See *ADO, ASP, COM, DCOM, MTS*, and *OLE DB*.

UNIX   Registered trademark of Novell Incorporated (formerly of AT&T) for its multiuser operating system, now administered by the Open Systems Foundation (OSF). Extensions and modifications of UNIX include DEC Ultrix, SCO UNIX, IBM AIX, and similar products.

update   A permanent change to data values in one or more data tables. An update occurs when the INSERT, DELETE, UPDATE, or TRUNCATE TABLE SQL commands are executed.

user-defined   A data type, also called a *record*, that's specified in your VBA source code by a `Type...End Type` declaration statement in the Declarations section of a module. The elements of the user-defined record type can be any data type valid for the language and may include other user-defined types.

user-defined transaction   A group of instructions combined under a single name and executed as a block when the name is invoked in a statement executed by the user.

validation   The process of determining whether an update to a value in a table's data cell is within a preestablished range or is a member of a set of allowable values. Validation rules establish the range or set of allowable values. Access 2+ supports validation rules at the field and table levels.

variable   The name given to a symbol that represents or substitutes for a number (numeric), letter, or combination of letters (string).

VBA   An acronym for *Visual Basic for Applications*, the official name of which is "Visual Basic, Applications Edition." VBA is Microsoft's common application programming (macro) language for members of Microsoft Office and Visual Basic. Each application has its own "flavor" of VBA as a result of automatically created references to the application's object hierarchy in VBA code.

VDT   An acronym for *Visual Data Tools,* which consists of the Query Designer and Database Designer. VDT (commonly called the *da Vinci* toolset) lets you create views, modify data structures, and add tables to SQL Server and Oracle databases. Visual Basic 6.0 VDTs are a substantial improvement over those in version 5.0.

view   The method by which the data is presented for review by users, usually onscreen. Views can be created from subsets of columns from one or more tables by implementing the SQL CREATE VIEW instruction.

Visual Basic for Applications   See *VBA.*

Visual Data Tools   See *VDT.*

VM   Abbreviation for *virtual memory*, a method of mapping a combination of RAM and images of RAM stored in a paging file to provide an address space larger than that available from the RAM installed in the computer.

VM manager   The Windows NT executive service that loads memory images stored in a paging file on demand, as well as saving memory images in the paging file when no longer needed by a thread.

VPN   An abbreviation for *Virtual Private Network*, a means of establishing secure communication channels on the Internet with various forms of encryption. See *PPTP.*

WAN   An acronym for *wide area network*, a system for connecting multiple computers in different geographical locations through the use of the switched telephone network or leased data lines, by optical or other long-distance cabling, or by infrared, radio, or satellite links.

WAVE file   A file containing waveform audio data, usually with a .wav extension.

Waveform audio   A data type standard of the Windows Multimedia Extensions that defines how digitally sampled sounds are stored in files and processed by Windows API functions calls.

WDM   An acronym for *Windows Driver Model*, a 32-bit architecture for creating device drivers that run under Windows NT and Windows 9*x*.

WebClass A new Automation component for Visual Basic 6.0 that permits the use of server-side VBA to generate dynamic Web pages with conventional HTML. Projects using `WebClasses` are called IIS Applications and are suitable for use with intranets and the Internet.

wild card A character that substitutes for and allows a match by any character or set of characters in its place. The DOS ? and * wild cards are similarly used in Windows applications.

Win32 An API for creating 32-bit applications that run under Windows 9x and Windows NT. Applications written to the Win32 API are purported to provide substantially improved performance when run under Windows 9x and Windows NT.

Winsock An abbreviation for *Windows Sockets*, a networking API for implementing Windows applications that use TCP/IP, such as FTP and Telnet.

workstation A client computer on a LAN or WAN that's used to run applications and is connected to a server from which it obtains data shared with other computers. It's possible, but not common, for some network servers to be used as both a server and a workstation (Windows NT permits this). The term is also used to describe a high-priced PC that uses a proprietary microprocessor and proprietary architecture to create what some call an *open system.*

WOSA An acronym for the *Windows Open Services Architecture* that's the foundation for such APIs as ODBC, MAPI, and TAPI. Microsoft also develops special vertical-market WOSA APIs for the banking, financial, and other industries.

WOW An acronym for *Windows on Win32*, a subsystem of Windows NT that allows 16-bit Windows applications to run in protected memory spaces called *virtual DOS machines (VDMs).*

xBase Any language interpreter or compiler or a database manager built on the dBASE III+ model and incorporating all dBASE III+ commands and functions. Microsoft's FoxPro and Computer Associates' Clipper are xBase dialects.

XML An abbreviation for *Extensible Markup Language,* a derivative of SGML (Standardized General Markup Language), that permits definition of custom markup tags. XML is especially useful for displaying and manipulating data when using the Internet HTTP protocol.

Yes/No field A field of a table whose allowable values are Yes (True) or No (False). Yes/No fields were called *logical* or *Boolean fields* by Access 95.

INDEX

I

IADO Data Control (bond controls), 172
Icursor (OLD DB), 129
ICursor interface
  ADO-specific ActiveX controls, 129
  third-party ActiveX controls, 129
IDC (Internet Database Connector), 925
identifiers, quoted
  SHAPE statements, 40
  SQL statements, 40
identity attributes (tables), 712
identity key, 713
IF EXISTS AS block, 829
IIS (DHTML application setup), 936
Image control, 399-409
images
  displaying, 399-409
  saving, 399-409
impersistent StdDataFormat objects, 625
implementation specific functions, 261
implicit remoting (RDS.DataControl object), 934
implicit transactions (SQL Server), 741
implicit trasactions, 740-741
importing
  DAO code, 785-790
  nwind database creation, 702-704
  SQL Server 7 (DTS), 701
  SQL statements from Access, 342, 345
  tables
    altering properties, 711-714
    Data Transformation Service, 705-706, 709
    modifying imported tables, 710-722

IN operator (SQL), 256
IN predicate
  arguments (values), 296
  column headers, 295-296
in-process Automation components, 576-577
in-process components, 576-577
inconsistent analysis problem, 742
increasing granularity, 979
independent entities (storage), 233
indexes
  balanced B-tree, 236
  composite, 718
  clustered, 236
  data pages, 234-235
  field values, 234
  fields, selecting, 236-238
  nonclustered, 722
  records, 234-235
  single-field, 718
  tables, 714-718
indexing tables, 233-238
indirect execution of stored procedures, 1026
information systems (IS), 333
initialization files (ODBC), 317-323
  Odbc.ini, 320-321
  Odbcinst.ini, 318-320
INNER JOIN clause, nesting, 291
INNER JOIN statements, nested, 294
inner joins, 266, 268
  WHERE clause, 295
inner queries, 274
input parameters in stored prcedures, executing, 818, 841-842
INSERT operation (multiple input parameter values), 861-862
INSERT statement, 739-740
  Recordset objects, 778
  row locking, 690
  stored procedures, replacing with, 835-839

  updates, 738
  WHERE clause, 818
INSERT statement (SQL), executing, 140
INSERT statements (multiple-table transactions), 753
INSERT( ) function, 314
inserting rows, 145-146
installation
  MTS
    Bank Client, 990-991
    test samples, 990
    testing locally, 989-992
    workstations, 997-999
  Northwind package, 1028-1036
  ODBC data sources, 309
  SQL Server (MTS), 984
  VBLive, 951-953
instantiation
  DAO objects, 57
  objects (ORBs), 976
instructions (transactions), 745-747
interactive SQL, 249
interactive SQL (ANSI), 249
interactively executing stored procedures, 824
interapplication communication, 976
interceptors, 978
interfaces, 52-57
  API, 52
  application usability, 349-355
  call-level (CLI), 309
  DAO, 52
  decision-support front ends (design), 348-356
  IRowset, 193
  ISAM databases, 52
  MDI (multiple document interface (decision-support application), 423-425
  ODBC, 52
  OLE DB, 56-57
internal consistency in decision-support front ends, 353
International Software Group, Inc. (ISG), 129, 726

Other Related Titles

**Visual Basic 6
Unleashed**
Rob Thayer
ISBN: 0-672-31309-X
$39.99 US/$57.95 CAN

**Visual Basic
Client/Server How-To**
Noel Jerke
ISBN: 1-57169-154-5
$49.99 US/$71.95 CAN

**Dan Appleman's
Developing COM/ActiveX
Components with Visual
Basic in 21 Days**
Dan Appleman
ISBN: 1-56276-576-0
$49.99 US/$71.95 CAN

**Visual Basic Database
How-To**
Eric Winemiller
ISBN: 1-57169-152-9
$39.99 US/$56.95 CAN

**The Waite Group's Visual
Basic Source Code
Library**
Brian Shea
ISBN: 0-672-31387-1
$34.99 US/$50.95 CAN

**The Waite Group's Visual
Basic 6 SuperBible**
David Jung
ISBN: 0-672-31413-4
$49.99 US/$71.95 CAN

**Doing Objects in Visual
Basic 6**
Deborah Kurata
ISBN: 1-56276-577-9
$49.99 US/$71.95 CAN

**Sams Teach Yourself
Internet Programming
with Visual Basic 6 in 21
Days**
Peter Aitken
ISBN: 0-672-31459-2
$29.99 US/$42.95 CAN

**Sams Teach Yourself
Object-Oriented
Programming with
Visual Basic in 21 Days**
John Conley
ISBN: 0-672-31299-9
$39.99 US/$57.95 CAN

SAMS

www.samspublishing.com

WHAT'S ON THE CD-ROM

WHAT'S ON THE CD ROM

The companion CD-ROM contains all of the author's source code and sample from the book, as well as many third-party software products.

WINDOWS 95/98/NT INSTALLATION INSTRUCTIONS

1. Insert the CD-ROM into your CD-ROM drive.
2. From the Windows 95 desktop, double-click on the My Computer icon.
3. Double-click on the icon representing your CD-ROM drive.
4. Double-click on the icon titled SETUP.EXE to run the installation program.
5. The installation program creates a program group with the book's name as the group name. This group contains icons to browse the CD-ROM.

> **NOTE**
>
> If Windows 95 is installed on your computer and you have the AutoPlay feature enabled, the SETUP.EXE program starts automatically when you insert the CD into your CD-ROM drive.

FREE ISSUE!

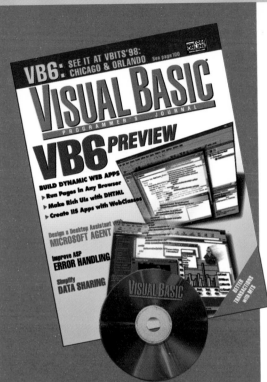

The Ultimate Add-on Tool for Microsoft Visual Basic

As part of your purchase, you are eligible to receive a free issue of *Visual Basic Programmer's Journal*, the leading magazine for Visual Basic programmers.

There's a lot to know about Visual Basic and its improved development tools. And *VBPJ* is the only magazine devoted to giving you the timely information you need with articles on subjects like:

- When—and how—to use the latest data access technologies
- How DHTML and the Web affect the way you develop and deploy apps
- Which new Visual Basic features save time—and which to avoid
- Creating reusable code with Visual Basic classes

But don't let the development information stop with your free issue. When you subscribe to *VBPJ*, we'll also send you a **FREE** CD-ROM – with three issues of *VBPJ* in electronically readable format, plus all the source code & sample apps from each issue.

Filled with hands-on articles and indispensable tips, tricks and utilities, *Visual Basic Programmer's Journal* will save your hours of programming time. And, *VBPJ* is the only magazine devoted to making VB programmers more productive.

A single tip can more than pay for a year's subscription.

Send for your free issue today.

MY GUARANTEE

If at any time I do not agree that *Visual Basic Programmer's Journal* is the best, most useful source of information on Visual Basic, I can cancel my subscription and receive a full refund.

❑ **YES!** Please rush me the next issue of *Visual Basic Programmer's Journal* to examine without obligation. If I like it, I'll pay the low rate of $22.95,* for a full year—eleven additional issues plus the annual *Buyers Guide* and *Enterprise* issue, (for a total of fourteen). Also, with my paid subscription, I'll receive a **FREE** gift—three issues (with sample apps and code) of *VBPJ* on CD-ROM! If I choose not to subscribe, I'll simply write cancel on my bill and owe nothing. The free issue is mine to keep with your compliments.

Name: _____

Company: _____

Address: _____

_____

City: _____ State: _____ Zip: _____

* Basic annual subscription rate is $34.97. Your subscription is for 12 monthly issues plus two bonus issues. Canada/Mexico residents please add $18/year for surface delivery. All other countries please add $44/year for air mail delivery. Canadian GST included. Send in this card or fax your order to 415.853.0230. Microsoft and Visual Basic are registered trademarks and ActiveX is a trademark of Microsoft Corporation.

8036

FREE ISSUE!

Find out for yourself what *Visual Basic Programmer's Journal* can do for you.

Visual Basic is the most productive Windows development environment. Get the most out of it by learning from the experts that write for ***Visual Basic Programmer's Journal.***

Check out select articles online at http://www.devx.com